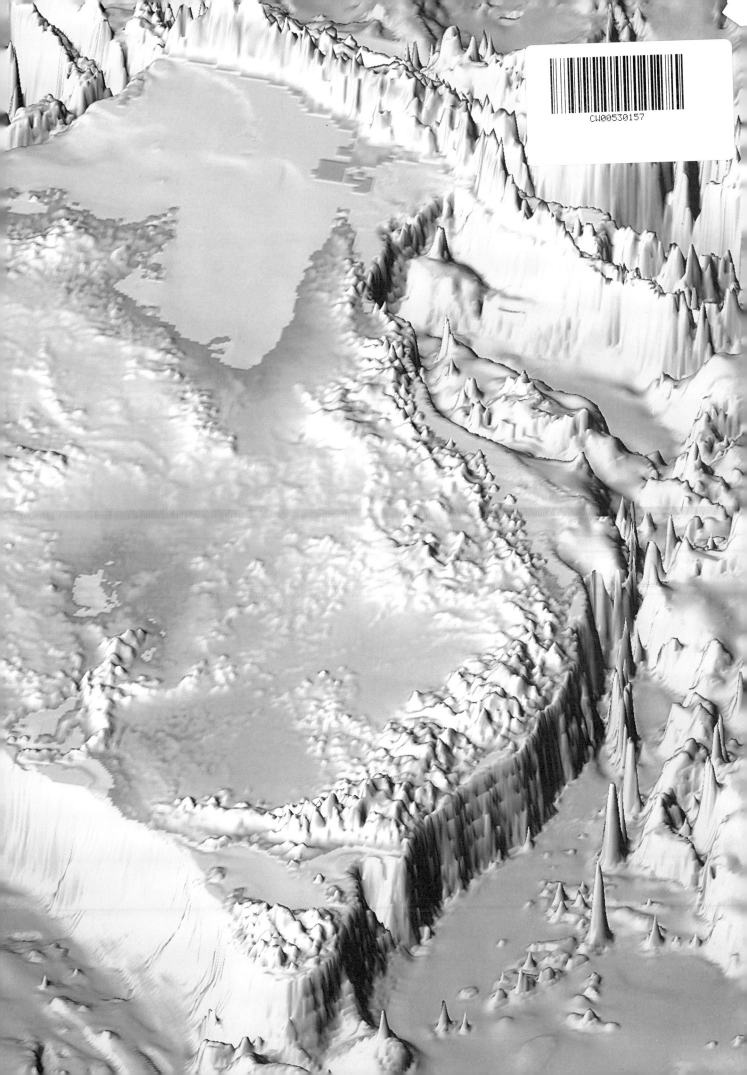

AUSTRALIA

THE ESSENTIAL TOURING ATLAS

SECOND EDITION

Published in Australia by Gregory's Publishing Company
(A division of Universal Publishers Pty Ltd)
ABN 83 000 087 132

The Publisher would be pleased to receive additional or updated material, or suggestions for future editions. Please address these to the Publishing Manager at Universal Publishers Pty Ltd.
If you would like to use any of the maps in this book please contact the CMS Manager at Universal Publishers Pty Ltd.

Marketed and distributed by Universal Publishers Pty Ltd
New South Wales: 1 Waterloo Road, Macquarie Park 2113
Ph: (02) 9857 3700 Fax: (02) 9888 9850

Queensland: 1 Manning Street, South Brisbane 4101
Ph: (07) 3844 1051 Fax: (07) 3844 4637

South Australia: Freecall: 1800 021 987

Victoria: 585 Burwood Road, Hawthorn 3122
Ph: (03) 9818 4455 Fax: (03) 9818 6123

Western Australia: 38a Walters Drive, Osborne Park 6017
Ph: (08) 9244 2488 Fax: (08) 9244 2554

International distribution
Ph: (61) 2 9857 3700 Fax: (61) 2 9888 9850

ISBN: 0 7319 1752-9

1st edition published 2002
2nd edition published 2005

Research, writing, editing, indexing, photographic research, DTP project management and cartography by the staff of Universal Publishers Pty Ltd

Cover Design: PlanBook Travel

Internal Design: D'Zign

Front and Back End Papers: Map Illustrations

Printed by: Sirivatana Interprint Public Co. Ltd

All cover photographs are from Australian Scenics

Front cover:
Main photograph (also book spine and title page):
Fitzroy River at Geikie Gorge, Western Australia
From left to right:
Toorongo River near Noojee, Gippsland, Victoria
The Nut at Stanley in northern Tasmania
The Pinnacles at Nambung National Park,
   Western Australia
Misty sunrise over snow gums at Mt Buller,
   Alpine National Park, Victoria

Back cover:
From left to right:
Patterned sand on the beach at St Helens Point,
   Tasmania
Sunset on the River Murray near Loxton,
   South Australia
Palm Creek in Finke Gorge National Park,
   Northern Territory
Kangaroo Island's Remarkable Rocks, Flinders Chase
   National Park, South Australia

Disclaimer
The publisher disclaims any responsibility to any person for loss or damage suffered from any use of this guide for any purpose. While considerable care has been taken by the publisher in researching and compiling this atlas, the publisher accepts no responsibility for errors or omissions. No person should rely upon this atlas for the purpose of making any business, investment or real estate decision.
The representation of any maps of any road or track is not necessarily evidence of public right of way. Third parties who have provided information to the publisher concerning the roads and other matters did not warrant to the publisher that the information was complete, accurate or current or that any of the proposals of any body will eventuate and, accordingly, the publisher provides no such warranty.

The tropical paradise look of Kewarra Beach, north of Cairns, Queensland

CONTENTS

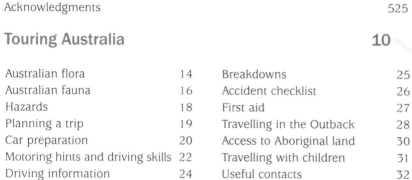

New South Wales   34

Australian Capital Territory   124

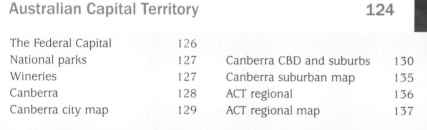

Victoria   138

Queensland 216

South Australia 288

Western Australia 350

Northern Territory 408

Tasmania 444

Map Symbols

City

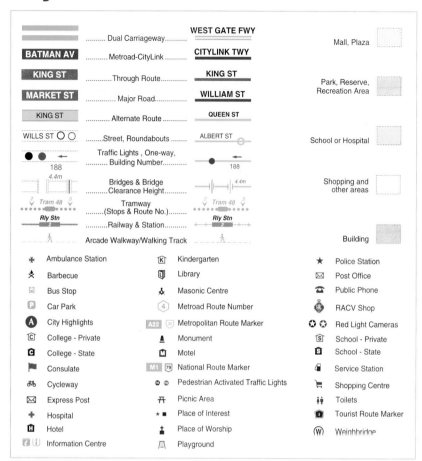

	.... Dual Carriageway	WEST GATE FWY
BATMAN AV	.... Metroad-CityLink	CITYLINK TWY
KING ST	.... Through Route	KING ST
MARKET ST	.... Major Road	WILLIAM ST
KING ST	.... Alternate Route	QUEEN ST
WILLS ST ○ ○	.... Street, Roundabouts	ALBERT ST
● ■ ← 188	Traffic Lights, One-way, ... Building Number	← 188
4.4m	Bridges & Bridge .... Clearance Height	4.4m
Tram 48	Tramway .... (Stops & Route No.)	Tram 48
Rly Stn	.... Railway & Station	Rly Stn
	Arcade Walkway/Walking Track	

	Mall, Plaza
	Park, Reserve, Recreation Area
	School or Hospital
	Shopping and other areas
	Building

✳	Ambulance Station	Ⓚ	Kindergarten	★	Police Station
⚒	Barbecue	📖	Library	✉	Post Office
🚌	Bus Stop	⚘	Masonic Centre	☎	Public Phone
Ⓟ	Car Park	④	Metroad Route Number		RACV Shop
Ⓐ	City Highlights	A22	Metropolitan Route Marker	◐ ◑	Red Light Cameras
Ⓒ	College - Private	▲	Monument	Ⓢ	School - Private
Ⓖ	College - State	▥	Motel	Ⓢ	School - State
▶	Consulate	M1 79	National Route Marker		Service Station
⊛	Cycleway	⦿ ⦿	Pedestrian Activated Traffic Lights	🛒	Shopping Centre
✉	Express Post	⋔	Picnic Area	♀♂	Toilets
✚	Hospital	★ ■	Place of Interest		Tourist Route Marker
Ⓗ	Hotel	♁	Place of Worship	Ⓦ	Weighbridge
ℹ ℹ	Information Centre	⚏	Playground		

Suburban

	Dual Carriageway, Proposed	✚	Hospital
	CityLink (Melbourne)	ⵊ	Lighthouse
①	Metroad (Sydney & Brisbane) & No.	☀ ☀	Lookout
	Through Route, Proposed	⋔	Picnic area
	Main Road	★	Point of Interest
	Alternate Route		RACV Depot
	Suburban Street		RACV Shop
	Railway and Station	🛒	Shopping Centre
☍ ⊛ ☍	Walking, Cycle Track, Horse Trail	ℹ ℹ	Tourist Information
	Car, Passenger Ferry	⚲	Winery
M1 ① 60	National, State Highway Marker		National Park
30	Road Distance from GPO		State Forest
+ Burkes 630	Elevation, in metres		Reserve, Recreation Area
✈	Boat Launching Ramp		Restricted Area
▲	Camping Ground		Government Utility
⛺	Caravan Park		Institution
⛳	Golf Course		Marine Park
▲	Historic Marker		

Sand-dune patterns and spinifex, Innamincka Regional Reserve, South Australia

Sydney icons—the Opera House and Harbour Bridge New South Wales

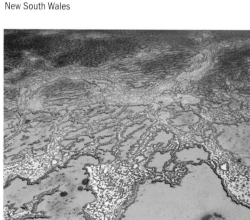

Aerial view of Hardy Reef, Great Barrier Reef, Queensland

KEY TO ATLAS

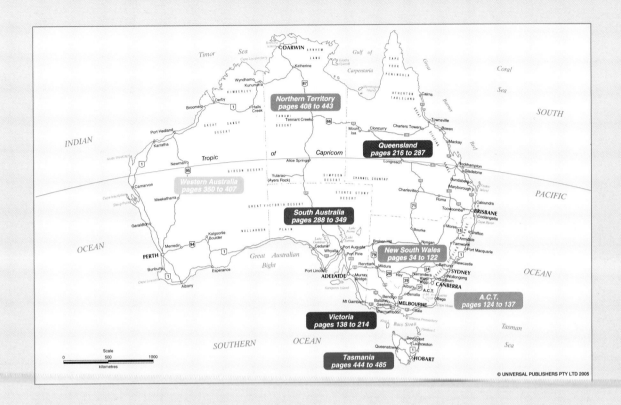

State and Regional

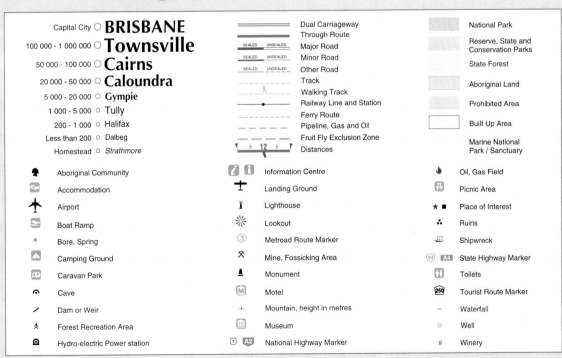

Capital City ○ **BRISBANE**		Dual Carriageway		National Park
100 000 - 1 000 000 ○ **Townsville**		Through Route		
50 000 - 100 000 ○ **Cairns**	SEALED UNSEALED	Major Road		Reserve, State and Conservation Parks
20 000 - 50 000 ○ **Caloundra**	SEALED UNSEALED	Minor Road		State Forest
5 000 - 20 000 ○ Gympie	SEALED UNSEALED	Other Road		
1 000 - 5 000 ○ Tully		Track		Aboriginal Land
200 - 1 000 ○ Halifax		Walking Track		
Less than 200 ○ Dalbeg		Railway Line and Station		Prohibited Area
Homestead □ *Strathmore*		Ferry Route		Built Up Area

Aboriginal Community
Accommodation
Airport
Boat Ramp
Bore, Spring
Camping Ground
Caravan Park
Cave
Dam or Weir
Forest Recreation Area
Hydro-electric Power station

Information Centre
Landing Ground
Lighthouse
Lookout
Metroad Route Marker
Mine, Fossicking Area
Monument
Motel
Mountain, height in metres
Museum
National Highway Marker

Pipeline, Gas and Oil
Fruit Fly Exclusion Zone
Distances

Oil, Gas Field
Picnic Area
Place of Interest
Ruins
Shipwreck
State Highway Marker
Toilets
Tourist Route Marker
Waterfall
Well
Winery

Marine National Park / Sanctuary

INTERCITY DISTANCE CHART

Approximate Distance	Adelaide SA	Albany WA	Albury NSW	Alice Springs NT	Ayers Rock/Yulara NT	Bairnsdale VIC	Ballarat VIC	Bathurst NSW	Bega NSW	Bendigo VIC	Bordertown SA	Bourke NSW	Brisbane QLD	Broken Hill NSW	Broome WA	Bunbury WA	Cairns QLD	Canberra ACT	Carnarvon WA	Ceduna SA	Charleville QLD	Coober Pedy SA	Darwin NT	Dubbo NSW	Esperance WA
Adelaide SA		2642	932	1526	1570	1006	611	1183	1329	770	267	1129	2054	514	4242	2855	2964	1153	3556	769	1583	837	3018	1175	216
Albany WA	2642		3424	3558	3602	3648	3253	3664	3810	3251	2909	3366	4291	2751	2582	361	5201	3634	1292	1873	3820	2869	4375	3503	47
Albury NSW	932	3424		2458	2502	310	372	443	426	297	665	847	1375	866	4905	3637	2650	346	4338	1551	918	1619	3662	531	295
Alice Springs NT	1526	3558	2458		442	2532	2137	2548	2694	2135	1793	2250	3004	1635	2735	3771	2293	2518	4128	1685	2332	689	1492	2387	308
Ayers Rock/Yulara NT	1570	3602	2502	442		2574	2181	2592	2738	2179	1837	2294	3219	1679	3177	3815	2735	2562	4516	1729	2748	733	1934	2431	312
Bairnsdale VIC	1006	3648	310	2532	2574		395	724	326	432	739	1157	1691	1120	5215	3861	2960	450	4562	1775	1611	1843	3972	841	31?
Ballarat VIC	611	3253	372	2137	2181	395		815	721	121	344	995	1655	753	5436	3466	2830	718	4167	1380	1449	1448	3629	882	277
Bathurst NSW	1183	3664	443	2548	2592	724	815		468	740	1093	574	1004	958	5015	3877	2325	274	4578	1791	1028	1859	3772	206	319
Bega NSW	1329	3810	426	2694	2738	326	721	468		758	1065	965	1373	1292	5406	4023	2723	222	4724	1937	1419	2005	4163	604	333
Bendigo VIC	770	3251	297	2135	2179	432	121	740	758		368	874	1534	697	4851	3464	2795	643	4165	1378	1328	1446	3627	761	277
Bordertown SA	267	2909	665	1793	1837	739	344	1093	1065	368		1242	1929	781	4509	3122	3160	1011	3823	1036	1779	1104	3285	1085	243
Bourke NSW	1129	3366	847	2250	2294	1157	995	574	965	874	1242		924	615	4441	3579	1835	743	4280	1493	454	1561	3198	368	289
Brisbane QLD	2054	4291	1375	3004	3219	1691	1655	1004	1373	1534	1929	924		1540	4659	4504	1701	1223	5205	2418	754	2486	3416	844	381
Broken Hill NSW	514	2751	866	1635	1679	1120	753	958	1292	697	781	615	1540		4351	2964	2450	1080	3665	878	1069	946	3127	752	227
Broome WA	4242	2582	4905	2735	3177	5215	5436	5015	5406	4851	4509	4441	4659	4351		2416	3948	5184	1461	3569	3987	3405	1861	4809	294
Bunbury WA	2855	361	3637	3771	3815	3861	3466	3877	4023	3464	3122	3579	4504	2964	2416		5414	3847	1069	2086	4033	3082	4183	3716	68
Cairns QLD	2964	5201	2650	2293	2735	2960	2830	2325	2723	2795	3160	1835	1701	2450	3948	5414		2435	5429	3328	1381	2982	2705	2119	472
Canberra ACT	1153	3634	346	2518	2562	450	718	274	222	643	1011	743	1223	1080	5184	3847	2435		4548	1761	1197	1829	3941	382	316
Carnarvon WA	3556	1292	4338	4128	4516	4562	4167	4578	4724	4165	3823	4280	5205	3665	1461	1069	5429	4548		2787	4734	3783	3254	4417	160
Ceduna SA	769	1873	1551	1685	1729	1775	1380	1791	1937	1378	1036	1493	2418	878	3569	2086	3328	1761	2787		1947	996	3177	1630	139
Charleville QLD	1583	3820	918	2332	2748	1611	1449	1028	1419	1328	1779	454	754	1069	3987	4033	1381	1197	4734	1947		2015	2744	822	334
Coober Pedy SA	837	2869	1619	689	733	1843	1448	1859	2005	1446	1104	1561	2486	946	3405	3082	2982	1829	3783	996	2015		2181	1698	239
Darwin NT	3018	4375	3662	1492	1934	3972	3629	3772	4163	3627	3285	3198	3416	3127	1861	4183	2705	3941	3254	3177	2744	2181		3566	430
Dubbo NSW	1175	3503	531	2387	2431	841	882	206	604	761	1085	368	844	752	4809	3716	2119	382	4417	1630	822	1698	3566		302
Esperance WA	2168	474	2950	3084	3128	3174	2779	3190	3336	2777	2435	2892	3817	2277	2948	687	4727	3160	1600	1399	3346	2395	4307	3029	
Eucla WA	1256	1386	2038	2172	2216	2262	1867	2278	2424	1865	1523	1980	2905	1365	3082	1599	3815	2248	2300	487	2434	1483	3664	2117	91?
Geraldton WA	3083	819	3865	3999	4043	4089	3694	4105	4251	3692	3350	3807	4732	3192	1934	596	5642	4075	473	2314	4261	3310	3727	3944	131
Grafton NSW	1815	4079	1162	2963	3007	1334	1522	735	1034	1401	1725	813	339	1328	4901	4292	2048	884	4993	2206	997	2274	3658	640	360
Horsham VIC	424	3066	508	1950	1994	582	187	951	908	211	157	1085	1745	609	4666	3279	3006	854	3980	1193	1539	1261	3442	972	259
Kalgoorlie/Boulder WA	2153	799	2935	3069	3113	3159	2764	3175	3321	2762	2420	2877	3802	2262	2185	764	4712	3145	1161	1384	3331	2380	3978	3014	389
Katherine NT	2709	4066	3353	1183	1625	3663	3884	3463	3854	3318	2976	2889	3107	2818	1552	3874	2396	3632	2945	2868	2435	1872	309	3257	399
Kununurra WA	3202	3554	3865	1695	2137	4175	4396	3975	4366	3830	3488	3401	3619	3330	1040	3362	2908	4144	2433	3380	2947	2384	821	3769	348
Longreach QLD	2097	4334	1432	1818	2260	1671	1963	1542	1933	1842	2293	968	1186	1583	3473	4547	1053	1711	4954	2461	514	2507	2230	1336	386
Mackay QLD	2475	4712	2009	2396	2838	2319	2341	1684	2082	2220	2588	1346	980	1961	4051	4925	729	1860	5532	2839	892	2907	2808	1478	423
Meekatharra WA	2872	1116	3654	3788	3832	3837	3483	3894	4040	3481	3139	3596	4521	2981	1466	924	5344	3864	620	2103	4050	3099	3248	3733	110
Melbourne VIC	723	3365	314	2249	2293	283	112	759	609	149	456	989	1658	837	4965	3578	2933	660	4279	1492	1443	1560	3741	814	289
Mildura VIC	372	2849	571	1733	1777	821	454	811	957	398	411	877	1647	299	4449	3062	2749	781	3763	976	1368	1044	3225	803	237
Moree NSW	1548	3812	904	2696	2740	1214	1255	579	977	1134	1458	445	479	1061	4616	4025	1790	755	4726	1939	629	2007	3373	373	333
Mt Gambier SA	435	3077	677	1961	2005	695	305	1120	1026	426	183	1300	1960	870	4677	3290	3135	1023	3991	1204	1754	1272	3453	1187	260
Mount Isa QLD	2702	4734	2074	1176	1618	2313	2605	2184	2575	2484	2852	1610	1828	2225	2831	4947	1117	2353	4312	2861	1156	1865	1588	1978	427
Newcastle NSW	1509	3884	693	2768	2812	865	1065	326	570	990	1358	749	818	1133	5099	4097	2339	415	4798	2011	1121	2079	3856	381	341
Perth WA	2689	406	3471	3605	3649	3695	3300	3711	3857	3298	2956	3413	4338	2798	2234	182	5248	3681	903	1920	3867	2916	4017	3550	714
Port Augusta SA	305	2337	1087	1221	1265	1311	916	1327	1473	914	572	1029	1954	414	3937	2550	2864	1297	3251	464	1483	532	2713	1166	186
Port Hedland WA	3744	1988	4526	3349	3791	4750	4355	4766	4912	4353	4011	4468	5205	3853	614	1812	4543	4736	867	2975	4533	3971	2407	4605	198
Port Lincoln SA	642	2277	1424	1558	1602	1648	1253	1664	1810	1251	909	1366	2291	751	3973	2490	3201	1634	3191	404	1820	869	3050	1503	180
Renmark SA	247	2724	696	1608	1652	940	573	1714	1082	517	279	1039	1772	424	4324	2937	2874	906	3638	857	1493	919	3100	928	225
Rockhampton QLD	2268	4505	1676	3389	3433	1986	2027	1351	1749	1906	2230	1139	647	1754	4154	4718	1062	1527	5419	2632	780	2700	2911	1145	403
Sydney NSW	1384	3865	562	2749	2793	734	934	201	418	859	1227	775	957	1159	5216	4078	2400	284	4779	1992	1229	2060	3973	407	339
Tamworth NSW	1510	3774	866	2658	2702	1129	1217	430	813	1096	1420	584	574	1023	4879	3987	2062	704	4688	1901	901	1969	3636	335	330
Tennant Creek NT	2040	4072	2736	514	956	2975	2651	2846	3237	2649	2307	2272	2490	2149	2221	4285	1779	3015	3614	2199	1818	1203	978	2640	359
Toowoomba QLD	1894	4158	1250	3042	3086	1560	1601	925	1314	1480	1786	791	125	1407	4534	4371	1702	1205	5072	2285	629	2353	3291	719	368
Townsville QLD	2617	4854	2303	2067	2509	2613	2483	1978	2420	2362	2813	1488	1376	2103	3722	5067	347	2088	5203	2981	1034	3049	2479	1772	438
Wagga Wagga NSW	936	3417	125	2301	2345	435	497	318	393	422	790	722	1250	863	5017	3630	2525	244	4331	1544	1176	1612	3793	406	294
Warrnambool VIC	617	3259	544	2143	2187	513	171	986	839	292	365	1162	1826	850	4859	3472	3001	889	4173	1386	1621	922	3635	1053	278
West Wyalong NSW	919	3400	278	2284	2328	588	626	264	501	505	829	572	1100	846	5000	3613	2375	271	4314	1527	1026	1595	3776	256	292

Gregory's Australia

Intercity distance chart (right-hand portion). Row labels (city names) are cut off at the left margin; only the trailing digits of the adjacent cut-off column are visible and are shown in the first column below. Diagonal (same city) cells are blank.

	Geraldton WA	Grafton NSW	Horsham VIC	Kalgoorlie/Boulder WA	Katherine NT	Kununurra WA	Longreach QLD	Mackay QLD	Meekatharra WA	Melbourne VIC	Mildura VIC	Moree NSW	Mt Gambier SA	Mount Isa QLD	Newcastle NSW	Perth WA	Port Augusta SA	Port Hedland WA	Port Lincoln SA	Renmark SA	Rockhampton QLD	Sydney NSW	Tamworth NSW	Tennant Creek NT	Toowoomba QLD	Townsville QLD	Wagga Wagga NSW	Warrnambool VIC	West Wyalong NSW
56	3083	1815	424	2153	2709	3202	2097	2475	2872	723	372	1548	435	2702	1509	2689	305	3744	642	247	2268	1384	1510	2040	1894	2617	936	617	919
86	819	4079	3066	799	4066	3554	4334	4712	1116	3365	2849	3812	3077	4734	3884	406	2337	1988	2277	2724	4505	3865	3774	4072	4158	4854	3417	3259	3400
88	3865	1162	508	2935	3353	3865	1432	2009	3654	314	571	904	677	2074	693	3471	1087	4526	1424	696	1676	562	866	2736	1250	2303	125	544	278
72	3999	2963	1950	3069	1183	1695	1818	2396	3788	2249	1733	2696	1961	1176	2768	3605	1221	3349	1558	1608	3389	2749	2658	514	3042	2067	2301	2143	2284
16	4043	3007	1994	3113	1625	2137	2260	2838	3832	2293	1777	2740	2005	1618	2812	3649	1265	3791	1602	1652	3433	2793	2702	956	3086	2509	2345	2187	2328
62	4089	1334	582	3159	3663	4175	1671	2319	3837	283	821	1214	695	2313	865	3695	1311	4750	1648	940	1986	734	1129	2975	1560	2613	435	513	588
67	3694	1522	187	2764	3884	4396	1963	2341	3483	112	454	1255	305	2605	1065	3300	916	4355	1253	573	2027	934	1217	2651	1601	2483	497	171	626
78	4105	735	951	3175	3463	3975	1542	1684	3894	759	811	579	1120	2184	326	3711	1327	4766	1664	1714	1351	201	430	2846	925	1978	318	986	264
24	4251	1034	908	3321	3854	4366	1933	2082	4040	609	957	977	1026	2575	570	3857	1473	4912	1810	1082	1749	418	813	3237	1314	2420	393	839	501
65	3692	1401	211	2762	3318	3830	1842	2220	3481	149	398	1134	426	2484	990	3298	914	4353	1251	517	1906	859	1096	2649	1480	2362	422	292	505
23	3350	1725	157	2420	2976	3488	2293	2588	3139	456	411	1458	183	2852	1358	2956	572	4011	909	279	2230	1227	1420	2307	1786	2813	790	365	829
80	3807	813	1085	2877	2889	3401	968	1346	3596	989	877	445	1300	1610	749	3413	1029	4468	1366	1039	1139	775	584	2272	791	1488	722	1162	572
05	4732	339	1745	3802	3107	3619	1186	980	4521	1658	1647	479	1960	1828	818	4338	1954	5205	2291	1772	647	957	574	2490	125	1376	1250	1826	1100
65	3192	1328	609	2262	2818	3330	1583	1961	2981	837	299	1061	870	2225	1133	2798	414	3853	751	424	1754	1159	1023	2149	1407	2103	863	850	846
82	1934	4901	4666	2185	1552	1040	3473	4051	1466	4965	4449	4616	4677	2831	5099	2234	3937	614	3973	4324	4154	5216	4879	2221	4534	3722	5017	4859	5000
99	596	4292	3279	764	3874	3362	4547	4925	924	3578	3062	4025	3290	4947	4097	182	2550	1812	2490	2937	4718	4078	3987	4285	4371	5067	3630	3472	3613
15	5642	2048	3006	4712	2396	2908	1053	729	5344	2933	2749	1790	3135	1117	2339	5248	2864	4543	3201	2874	1062	2400	2062	1779	1702	347	2525	3001	2375
48	4075	884	854	3145	3632	4144	1711	1860	3864	660	781	755	1023	2353	415	3681	1297	4736	1634	906	1527	284	704	3015	1205	2088	244	889	271
00	473	4993	3980	1161	2945	2433	4954	5532	620	4279	3763	4726	3991	4312	4798	903	3251	867	3191	3638	5419	4779	4688	3614	5072	5203	4331	4173	4314
87	2314	2206	1193	1384	2868	3380	2461	2839	2103	1492	976	1939	1204	2861	2011	1920	464	2975	404	857	2632	1992	1901	2199	2285	2981	1544	1386	1527
34	4261	997	1539	3331	2439	2941	514	832	1060	1119	1960	600	1160	1188	1121	3007	1403	4600	1009	1103	790	1229	901	1818	629	1034	1176	1621	1026
83	3310	2274	1261	2380	1872	2384	2507	2907	3099	1560	1044	2007	1272	1865	2079	2916	532	3971	869	919	2700	2060	1969	1203	2353	3049	1612	922	1595
64	3727	3658	3442	3978	309	821	2230	2808	3248	3741	3225	3373	3453	1588	3856	4017	2713	2407	3050	3100	2911	3973	3636	978	3291	2479	3793	3635	3776
17	3944	640	972	3014	3257	3769	1336	1478	3733	814	803	373	1187	1978	381	3550	1166	4605	1503	928	1145	407	335	2640	719	1772	406	1053	256
12	1319	3605	2592	389	3998	3486	3860	4238	1108	2891	2375	3338	2603	4279	3410	714	1863	1980	1803	2250	4031	3391	3300	3598	3684	4380	2943	2785	2926
	1827	2693	1680	897	3355	3867	2948	3326	1616	1979	1463	2426	1691	3348	2498	1433	951	2488	891	1388	3119	2686	2731	2468	2031	1873	2014	3700	3841
27		4520	3507	988	3418	2906	4775	5153	540	3806	3290	4253	3518	4697	4325	430	2778	1340	2718	3165	4946	4306	4215	4087	4599	5295	3858	3700	3841
693	4520		1612	3590	3349	3861	1428	1319	4309	1476	1443	368	1827	2070	479	4126	1742	5447	2079	1568	986	618	305	2732	367	1701	1046	1693	890
580	3507	1612		2577	3133	3645	2053	2431	3296	299	310	1345	261	2695	1201	3113	729	4168	1066	429	2117	1070	1307	2464	1691	2573	633	241	580
97	988	3590	2577		3669	3157	3845	4223	719	2876	2360	3323	2588	4264	3395	594	1848	1591	1788	2235	4016	3376	3285	3583	3669	4365	2928	2770	2911
355	3418	3349	3133	3669		512	1921	2499	2948	3432	2916	3064	3144	1279	3547	3708	2404	2098	2741	2791	2602	3664	3327	669	2982	2170	3484	3326	3467
867	2906	3861	3645	3157	512		2433	3011	2436	3944	3428	3576	3656	1791	4059	3196	2916	1586	3253	3303	3114	4176	3839	1181	3494	2682	3996	3838	3979
948	4775	1428	2053	3845	1921	2433		793	4564	1957	1845	1143	2268	642	1626	4381	1997	4068	2334	2007	681	1743	1406	1304	1061	706	1690	2134	1540
326	5153	1319	2431	4223	2499	3011	793		4942	2175	2223	1105	2624	1220	1764	4759	2375	4646	2712	2385	333	1715	1377	1882	973	382	1884	2512	1734
616	540	4309	3296	719	2948	2436	4564	4942		3595	3079	4042	3307	4227	4114	758	2567	872	2507	2954	4735	4095	4004	3617	4288	5094	3647	3489	3630
979	3806	1476	299	2876	3432	3944	1957	2175	3595		538	1187	412	2599	1007	3412	1028	4467	1365	657	1959	876	1180	2763	1533	2477	439	230	558
463	3290	1443	310	2360	2916	3428	1845	2223	3079	538		1176	571	2524	1137	2896	512	3951	849	125	1948	1012	1138	2247	1522	2365	564	551	547
426	4253	368	1345	3323	3064	3576	1143	1105	4042	1187	1176		1560	1785	492	3859	1475	4914	1812	1301	772	610	272	2447	346	1443	779	1426	795
691	3518	1827	261	2588	3144	3656	2268	2624	3307	412	571	1560		2910	1370	3124	740	4179	1077	462	2332	1239	1522	2475	1906	2788	802	182	795
348	4697	2070	2695	4264	1279	1791	642	1220	4227	2599	2524	1785	2910		2268	4781	2397	3426	2734	2649	1323	2385	2048	662	1703	891	2332	2776	2182
498	4325	479	1201	3395	3547	4059	1626	1764	4114	1007	1137	492	1370	2268		3931	1884	4986	1884	1262	1264	152	277	2930	778	1992	591	1236	590
433	430	4126	1201	594	3708	3196	4381	4759	758	3412	2896	3859	3124	4781	3931		2384	1630	2324	2771	4552	3912	3821	4119	4205	4901	3464	3306	3447
051	2778	1742	729	1848	2404	2916	1997	2375	2567	1028	512	1475	740	2397	1547	2384		3439	337	387	2168	1528	1437	1735	1821	2517	1080	922	1063
488	1340	5447	4168	1591	2098	1586	4068	4646	872	4467	3951	4914	4179	3426	4986	1630	3439		3776	3826	5607	4967	4876	2767	5080	4317	4519	4361	4502
391	2718	2079	1066	1788	2741	3253	2334	2712	2507	1365	849	1812	1077	2734	1884	2324	337	3776		724	2505	1865	1774	2072	2158	2854	1417	1259	1400
388	3165	1568	429	2235	2791	3303	2007	2385	2954	657	125	1301	462	2649	1262	2771	387	3826	724		2073	1137	1263	2122	1647	2527	689	676	672
119	4946	986	2117	4016	2602	3114	681	333	4735	1959	1948	772	2332	1323	1264	4552	2168	5607	2505	2073		1382	1044	1985	640	715	1554	2198	1401
479	4306	618	1070	3376	3664	4176	1743	1715	4095	876	1012	610	1239	2385	152	3912	1528	4967	1865	1137	1382		395	3263	896	2053	470	1105	465
388	4215	305	1307	3285	3327	3839	1406	1377	4004	1180	1138	272	1522	2048	277	3821	1437	4876	1774	1263	1044	395		2710	501	1715	741	1388	591
686	4087	2732	2464	3583	669	1181	1304	1882	3617	2763	2247	2447	2475	662	2930	4119	1735	2767	2072	2122	1985	3263	2710		2365	1553	2815	2657	2798
772	4599	367	1691	3669	2982	3494	1061	973	4288	1533	1522	346	1906	1703	778	4205	1821	5080	2158	1647	640	896	501	2365		1355	1125	1772	975
468	5295	1701	2573	4365	2170	2682	706	382	5094	2477	2365	1443	2788	891	1992	4901	2517	4317	2854	2527	715	2053	1715	1553	1355		2178	2654	2028
031	3858	1046	633	2928	3484	3996	1690	1884	3647	439	564	779	802	2332	591	3464	1080	4519	1417	689	1554	470	741	2815	1125	2178		668	153
873	3700	1693	241	2770	3326	3838	2134	2512	3489	230	551	1426	182	2776	1236	3306	922	4361	1259	676	2198	1105	1388	2657	1772	2654	668		661
014	3841	896	580	2911	3467	3979	1540	1734	3630	558	547	629	795	2182	590	3447	1063	4502	1400	672	1401	465	591	2798	975	2028	153	661	

TOURING AUSTRALIA

Australia: The Land Down Under

- Area: 7 692 300 km^2
- World's smallest continent and largest island
- World's lowest and flattest continent; average elevation is only 330m; Lake Eyre is 15m below sea level
- World records: Uluru (largest monolith); Great Barrier Reef (longest coral reef); Nullarbor Plain (largest flat bedrock surface); Simpson Desert (largest sand ridge desert); and Mount Augustus (largest exposed rocky outcrop)
- Sixth largest country in the world after the Russian Federation, Canada, China, USA and Brazil
- Fifth longest coastline in the world with the world's largest Exclusive Economic Marine Zone when offshore territories are included
- The Great Dividing Range is the fourth longest mountain range in the world
- About 39% of Australia lies within the tropical zone and 61% in the temperate zone
- Australia extends across 40° of longitude and almost 33° of latitude
- World's oldest fossilised life forms microbes (about 3.5 billion years old) have been found in Western Australia

Geography: The Island Continent

The oldest minerals discovered in Australia (zircon crystals), thought to be around 4.4 billion years old, are also the world's most ancient. Australia is the world's sixth largest country, the largest island, and the world's smallest continent. Covering approximately 7 700 000km^2 of the earth's Southern Hemisphere, Australia is the only continent occupied by one nation alone, albeit multicultural. It is often difficult for visitors, as well as many Australians, to grasp just how huge the country is. Australia is approximately the same size as the European continent, excluding the former USSR, and around 2% smaller than the mainland area of the United States of America.

This very old and enormous area forms the earth's flattest and, apart from Antarctica, driest continent. In the east, a narrow, fertile coastal plain meets the **Great Dividing Range** which itself stretches almost the entire length of the country, from north Queensland to Victoria.

Red desert earth of Uluru-Kata Tjuta National Park, Central Australia

The highest peak in Australia, **Mount Kosciuszko**, rises only 2228m above sea-level in the south of the Great Dividing Range. Relative to international standards, Mount Kosciuszko is but a foothill upon this seemingly endless plateau. West of the range, grassy plains supporting sheep and cattle gradually give way to the hot, dry Outback for which Australia is famous. The red dirt and central deserts of the continent stretch almost the entire way to the coastline of Western Australia. There are more than 700 national parks occupying around 450 000km^2 of the island continent and 16 unique sites have been declared World Heritage Areas.

The Australian environment is so diverse, ranging from the tropical rainforests and coral reefs of the north-east, to the harsh and inhospitable deserts and huge but mainly dry, salt lakes, (occasionally filled by inland flowing rivers in

Snow-laden tree near Mount Kosciuszko, Great Dividing Range

flood) in the central west. The **Darling River** is the longest in Australia, stretching 2736km from southern Queensland to the junction of the **Murray River** in the south of New South Wales.

Australia's 59 000km coastline (including islands) is washed by three oceans—the **Indian** in the west, the **Pacific** in the east, and the spectacular cliff-carving **Southern Ocean** in the south. Four seas lap Australia's shores—the **Timor** and **Arafura** seas on the northern shores, the **Coral Sea** surrounding the north-east coastline and the **Tasman Sea** bordering the south-east of the continent. There are more than 11 000 beaches around the mainland coastline.

Climate

Australia's climate is as diverse and varied as its environment, due to the continent's size, location and the dominance of low plateaus and plains. It is the driest continent in the world (excluding Antarctica) with an average annual rainfall of 465mm. The seasons are the reverse of those in the Northern Hemisphere. The months of December and January are mid-summer months—it is always a hot

Christmas in Australia; and, depending on the area, the months of July and August bring wintry conditions, almost always perfect for skiing in the **Australian Alps**.

In the northern parts of Western Australia, Queensland and the Northern Territory, the weather is tropical and often conditions are monsoonal, depending on the season. Here, above the Tropic of Capricorn, there are really only two seasons: the Wet and the Dry. The Wet, November–April, is characterised by rainfall and hot, humid conditions. The Dry season, May–October, is often still hot, although in the desert areas and around Alice Springs in Central Australia, temperatures at night can be quite cold.

South of the Tropic of Capricorn, the climate becomes more temperate. Generally the seasons in Australia are not as defined as those in the Northern Hemisphere, except in highland regions. Any season is a good time to visit Australia, depending of course on the places and activities you plan. It is possible to dive on the reefs off the northern coasts, even in winter, and a day later ski in the southern **Snowy Mountains**.

Statue of Capt James Cook in Hyde Park, Sydney

History

Before European settlement in 1788, the entire continent of Australia was inhabited by different **Aboriginal societies**. It is thought the Aborigines first crossed to the continent from Asia more than 60 000 years ago, when the sea level was much lower than it is today. Aboriginal histories and stories were not written down in the conventional sense; they were painted on bark, rocks, inside caves and sculpted on the ground and on trees, spoken and sung.

For a long time it was thought that **Capt James Cook** was the first European to discover Australia, in 1770. However, it is now known that **Macassan** sailors visited the northern shores of Australia long before that date, and that the Dutchman, **Willem Jansz**, landed here in 1601. The first Englishman to land was **William Dampier**, a pirate/buccaneer who went ashore in 1688, somewhere near the town in Western Australia that is named after him. Dampier recorded nothing good about the land or its inhabitants.

Lady Elliot Island sits like a jewel in the Coral Sea, at the southern end of the Great Barrier Reef, Queensland

Goldrush architecture in Sturt St, Ballarat, Victoria

Cook, however, gave a more favourable report of the eastern coastline in 1770, and this was remembered when the harsh criminal laws in Britain resulted in overcrowded prisons.

A penal colony was created in 1788, when 11 tall ships of the **First Fleet** sailed into Botany Bay, in what is now New South Wales. The fleet brought only enough food to last two years, so until farms could be established, the threat of starvation loomed. By 1790, the **Second Fleet** had landed and a year later the arrival of the **Third Fleet** increased the population to 4000.

For the first 20 years the spread of settlement was slow. **Sydney** was established and there were small colonies at **Norfolk Island** and **Hobart**. Any expansion inland from Sydney was restricted until the formidable barrier of the **Blue Mountains** was crossed in 1813. Following this, a wave of exploration occurred. Explorers such as **Charles Sturt**, **Ludwig Leichhardt** and **Burke** and **Wills** have been noted in history for making journeys across often rugged and inhospitable terrain to open the way for European settlement.

When gold was discovered near **Ballarat** and then **Bendigo** in 1851, in what is now Victoria, miners from all over the world made their way to Australia. The **Goldrushes** of the 1850s and 1860s increased the population and opened up large areas of the country. Wealth from the mines helped to build inland towns, and when the rushes were over, many of the miners settled where they had found their fortunes and turned to farming, grazing and other pursuits.

Government

It was not until 1 January 1901 that the **Commonwealth of Australia** came into being. Rivalry between the cities of **Sydney** and **Melbourne** meant that neither would agree to the other having primacy—a new capital had to be created.

Today, the government of Australia sits in the nation's purpose-built capital, **Canberra**, in the **Australian Capital Territory**. The land on which the city is located was acquired in 1911 by the Commonwealth Government. In 1927 Parliament House, now known as **Old Parliament House**, was completed, and used for the following 60 years. The new **Parliament House** was opened in 1988 and is the current seat of the **Federal Government**.

Australia's democratic political system is a complex three-tiered structure of federal, state and local levels. The federal and state governments are modelled on the **British Westminster system** with elected parliamentary representatives. In the Federal Government there are two houses of parliament—the House of Representatives and the Senate. The **Prime Minister** is the national leader. Each of the states and territories has a **Premier** or **Chief Minister**, who is the leader of the party in power. Local regions are led by an elected mayor and council.

Australia's Parliament House, Canberra, with the forecourt mosaic designed by an Aboriginal artist

Aboriginal women in Arnhem Land, Northern Territory

People

There are no accurate estimations of the **Aboriginal** population before European settlement. In 1788, there may have been more than 600 000 Aborigines living in Australia, but by 1830 only around 100 000 remained. The population was considerably reduced due to the introduction of diseases like measles and smallpox and dispossession of land. There was an ongoing decline in the Aboriginal population itself, and a continuing mistreatment of their communities following European settlement.

It is only in more recent years that there has been an acknowledgment of injustices, and an attempt at reconciliation, although many would argue that there is still a deficiency of understanding. The Sydney 2000 Olympic Games portrayed to the world a young nation in the first stages of unification, in the throes of compromise, understanding and acceptance.

In the years before WWII, the majority of the population was of English, Scottish and Irish descent; a mix of descendants of the convicts and free settlers. A variety of nationalities made up a minority of the population originally as refugees or as prospectors during the goldrushes of the 19th century. After WWII, a strong drive for immigration brought in more people from Britain and thousands of refugees from Italy, Greece, Yugoslavia, Germany and other parts of war-torn Europe. Since then, and especially after the Vietnam War in the 1960s and 1970s immigration from many countries has continued to play an integral, sometimes controversial part in the development of the Australian nation.

Today, Australia can truly be considered a diverse and **multicultural society**. It has also become one of the world's most urbanised countries, with more than 90% of the population living in the cities, which are located along the coast. Australia's population has recently reached 20 million.

Economy

Australia has a prosperous Western-style capitalist economy. A land rich in natural resources, Australia is a major exporter of **minerals, metals, fossil fuels,** and **agricultural products**—despite around two-thirds of Australia being arid or semi-arid. Primary products account for more than 60% of exports.

Australia leads the world in **wool** production, and is a significant contributor to the world supplies of **cotton, wheat, dairy products, meat, sugar, fruit, fisheries products** and **timber**.

While the Australian government is encouraging an increase in the export of manufactured goods, severe competition from international markets means that these exports currently account for approximately 14% of total GDP.

The **service industry** is now the largest, and fastest growing, segment of the economy. It includes property, finance, construction, trade, communication, education, tourism and business services. **Tourism** is currently the fastest growing sector of the Australian service industry.

The Australian **wine industry** is a relatively recent addition to the international export trade. Known for their good quality and distinctive flavour, Australian wines are increasingly popular and seem set for a prosperous future.

Migrant dancers outside Sydney Opera House

AUSTRALIAN FLORA

Red flowering gum, *Eucalyptus ptychocarpa x ficifolia*

Floral Emblems

❧ **Commonwealth of Australia**
   Golden Wattle, *Acacia pycnantha*

❧ **Australian Capital Territory**
   Royal Bluebell,
   Wahlenbergia gloriosa

❧ **New South Wales**
   Waratah,
   Telopea speciosissima

❧ **Northern Territory**
   Sturt's Desert Rose,
   Gossypium sturtianum

❧ **Queensland**
   Cooktown Orchid,
   Dendrobium bigibbum

❧ **South Australia**
   Sturt's Desert Pea,
   Clianthus formosus

❧ **Tasmania**
   Tasmanian Blue Gum,
   Eucalyptus globulus

❧ **Victoria**
   Pink Heath, *Epacris impressa*

❧ **Western Australia**
   Red and Green Kangaroo Paw,
   Anigozanthos manglesii

For thousands of years before European settlement, the Aboriginal people lived on the Australian continent in harmony with the native flora and fauna. Regular burning of plants was a practice of various Aboriginal tribes, and earned them the name **'firestick farmers'**. This practice is now thought to be at least partly responsible for the evolution of Australia's fire-resistant and regenerative native flora.

Australia is home to an exceptionally diverse group of flora. Regions range from tropical and subtropical rainforests and desert environments to sub-alpine areas. These, combined with the latitudinal spread of the country and the resulting variable climates, create a continent rich in diversity. With two of the most unique floristic provinces in the world, Australia provides scientists with vital records of plant evolution and heritage. In the south-west of Western Australia, the wildflowers dominate, while in the north-east of the continent the 'green dinosaurs' (cycads and king ferns), inhabit some of the oldest rainforests in the world.

In 1788, the arrival of the First Fleet introduced various exotic plants and domestic animals that altered the natural botanical balance of the country forever. However, most of the native plants that existed then can still be found today. More than 85% of the continent's species of plants, trees and wildflowers are uniquely Australian.

Eucalypts

The eucalypt, more commonly known as the **gum tree**, is perhaps the most dominant plant of the Australian landscape. There are close to 600 species of eucalypts found across the continent, thriving in environments ranging from coastal forests and woodlands, to the arid inland, and the mountainous sub-alpine terrain.

Eucalypts at Lake Brewster, New South Wales

WATTLE

Australia's floral emblem is the **Golden Wattle**, *Acacia pycnantha*, which produces a profusion of rounded flowerheads in spring. Of the 1200 species of *Acacia*, Australia is home to 900, which are scattered throughout the continent. The green and gold of the wattles have become an internationally recognised representation of Australia and its flora.

It is thought that wattles have been growing in Australia for eons. Africa and South America are home to the majority of the other 300 species. These often short-lived plants have adapted over time to drought, poor soil and bushfire conditions, making them the perfect Australian symbol.

Wattles range in size from low ground mats and shrubs to tall forest trees. Many wattles are cultivated for their attractive yellow

The green-and-gold of *Acacia pycnantha*, Australia's floral emblem

blossom, but others are used for timber, for example, blackwood, used for furniture making. Aborigines used wattle wood for tools and weapons, and the seeds and gum for food. Wattles are also valuable to native fauna. Possums like to nibble on the flowers, and the nectar and seeds are food for birds such as cockatoos and galahs. Wattle seed is also popular 'bush tucker' food today.

The term 'gum tree' is derived from particular eucalyptus trees that leak a sticky, gum-like substance from the trunk. Although this is not a general characteristic of all eucalypts, 'gum tree' has become a generic term. Names have also been given to certain groups of trees because of their appearance or growth habits. Some examples include ash, blackbutt, bloodwood, box, ghost, ironbark, ribbon, scribbly, snow and stringybark.

Wildflowers

Australia has a colourful and distinct array of wildflowers. There are 92 species of **banksias** ranging from small shrubs to trees. These plants were named after **Sir Joseph Banks**, botanist and noted naturalist on Capt James Cook's *Endeavour* voyage of discovery in 1770.

Sturt's desert pea, which is the floral emblem of South Australia, was named after **Charles Sturt**, who explored the Simpson and Sturt's Stony deserts in 1844–46. The state flower of New South Wales, the **waratah**, is an unusual and beautiful flower that has been a favourite of artists for years. The **kangaroo paw**, Western Australia's state flower, is noted for its velvety appearance and claw-like structure, hence its name. Other distinctly Australian flowers include **boronias**, **bottlebrushes**, **Christmas bushes**, **everlasting daisies** and **grevilleas**.

Both Western Australia and South Australia are famous for their beautiful array of wildflowers, and there are festivals all around the country, at different times of the year, in celebration of local unique flowering plants.

Waratah, *Telopea speciosissima*

AUSTRALIAN FAUNA

Australia's geographic isolation for millions of years is believed to be the main reason for the existence of so many species of fauna found nowhere else in the world. The unique wildlife crosses all animal families, from marsupials and reptiles, to fish and birds. Perhaps the best way to see the variety of wildlife is by visiting the many sanctuaries and zoos found across the continent.

Short-beaked echidna, *Tachyglossus aculeatus*

Fauna Emblems

◈ **Commonwealth of Australia**
Red Kangaroo, *Macropus rufus,* and Emu, *Dromaius novaehollandiae*

◈ **Australian Capital Territory**
Gang Gang Cockatoo, *Callocephalon fimbriatum*

◈ **New South Wales**
Platypus, *Ornithorhynchus anatinus*

◈ **Northern Territory**
Red Kangaroo, *Macropus rufus*

◈ **Queensland**
Koala, *Phascolarctos cinereus*

◈ **South Australia**
Southern Hairy-nosed Wombat, *Lasiorhinus latifrons*

◈ **Tasmania**
Tasmanian Devil, *Sarcophilus harrisii*

◈ **Victoria**
Leadbeater's Possum, *Gymnobelideus leadbeateri*

◈ **Western Australia**
Numbat, *Myrmecobius fasciatus*

Marsupials

Marsupials are defined as a group of mammals where the female has a pouch to carry her young. A large proportion (almost 50% or 141 species) of the mammals of Australia are marsupials and Australia has 52% of the world's marsupials.

The largest of them, the **kangaroo** (macropod), has become a wildlife symbol of the nation. It flies around the world on the tail of the national airline, Qantas, and it is depicted on the Australian Coat of Arms. There are 40 species of kangaroos bounding across the continent, varying in size from 30cm to 2m; they are well adapted to the hot and dry regions of Australia.

The **koala**, best known as a cute and cuddly 'bear', has a somewhat patchier distribution than the kangaroo. Koalas are found only on the eastern side of the continent, feeding off about 35 of the 600 species of eucalyptus trees found in Australia. Koalas are now a protected species. The easiest way to see them is in the national parks, koala parks or zoos.

There are three species of **wombat** in Australia. The **common wombat** is found in woodlands and sclerophyll forests throughout the eastern part of the continent. The **southern hairy-nosed wombat** is found in isolated areas of the Nullarbor Plain, and in parts of South Australia. The rarest—the **northern hairy-nosed wombat**—is found in an isolated area of central Queensland. This wombat is nearly extinct—numbers are estimated at between 40 to 70 animals, making it one of the most endangered animals in the country.

There are many varieties of **possums** in Australia, but the most numerous is the **common brushtail possum**, which resides in the bush and suburbs over much of Australia.

Monotremes

Monotremes are relatively primitive animals. They are warm-blooded egg-layers who feed their young milk. Australia is home to two of the world's three monotremes.

These two unique Australian residents are the **echidna** and the **platypus**. The echidna, known commonly as the spiny anteater, can be found all over the continent. The platypus is a more confined resident than its spiky relation, and is found in the streams and rivers of eastern Australia. It is an unusual animal, with a soft, leathery, duck-like bill and clawed, webbed feet. In the past platypus were hunted by the fur industry but they are now fully protected.

Red kangaroo, *Macropus rufus*—symbol of Australia

DANGEROUS CREATURES

Australia is renowned for its array of dangerous creatures. However, the threat to visitors of encountering danger or harm is unlikely if common sense prevails.

Snakes

Australia has more poisonous snakes than any other country in the world, although few species will attack unless threatened. By far the most dangerous is the **inland taipan**—the most venomous terrestrial snake known. Its venom is 100 times more deadly than that of the infamous king cobra. Other varieties of snake are found throughout Australia—the more common are **brown snakes** found in the eastern half of the country. The **tiger snake**, **death adder** and **red-bellied black snake** all have potent venom and are capable of serious harm if you are bitten.

Spiders

There are 2000 spider species in Australia; two in particular are known to be deadly. The world's most poisonous spider, the **Sydney funnel-web** has caused 15 deaths in the last 60 years—antivenom is now available. The male is six times more venomous than his larger female counterpart. Interestingly, this is in contrast to the **redback spider**, the male of which is completely harmless. The female, however, caused 13 deaths prior to the development of the antivenom in 1956.

Marine creatures

Australia's most beautiful coral reefs and northern beaches are home to another group of dangerous creatures. Perhaps the most feared is the **box jellyfish**, or sea wasp. Encountered in the northern waters from October to May, it can kill a human in four minutes. Also found in northern waters, the highly venomous **stonefish** lurks in rockpools. Another creature—the tiny and misleadingly beautiful **blue-ringed octopus**—is found in rockpools off the east coast. The painless bite that has been known to cause death has no known antitoxin.

Found in the temperate and tropical waters around Australia, the **great white shark** can grow to 7m in length. Although it is aggressive when provoked, fatal shark attacks are relatively rare in Australia. It is thought that sharks commonly mistake swimmers and surfers for their food source—seals.

Saltwater crocodiles inhabit fresh and saltwater in the northern parts of the country and are internationally feared creatures. The 'saltie' can grow up to 6m long, and is the world's largest living reptile. Saltwater crocodiles are now a protected species in the wild and are farmed commercially for their meat and skin.

Saltwater crocodile, *Crocodylus porosus*

The Dingo

Another symbol of Australia is the 'native dog', the dingo, which is found all over the country except in Tasmania. However, dingos are not considered native, as they were introduced from Asia some 3500–4000 years ago.

Reptiles

Australian reptiles include saltwater and freshwater crocodiles, sea and freshwater turtles, 172 snake species and more than 520 lizard species. They range from the common gecko, to the more exotic-looking **frilled lizard** and **thorny devil**. Other lizard types include **goannas** that can grow to 2m in length.

Birds

Australia has more than 770 bird species, of which 300 are unique to this country. Alongside the red kangaroo on the Coat of Arms is the large flightless **emu** which is found throughout Australia.

Australia's native birds are renowned for their variety, colourful plumage and interesting (and noisy) calls. The **kookaburra** is noted for its famous laugh-like call. Colourful **parrots** and **cockatoos**—the most common of which are the **galahs**—are famous for their wing-flapping and crest raising. The **rainbow lorikeet** can be found in abundant numbers in eastern Australia. **Budgerigars** are found over most of inland Australia. The **wedge-tailed eagle** is the largest bird of prey.

Hazards

Bushfires

Bushfires are a common Australian environmental hazard. In a continent as dry as Australia, fire, and the damage it can cause to life, property and wildlife, is a continual threat.

Fires can be inadvertent or malicious—the result of human carelessness or arson. Common causes of fire are lightning, discarded cigarette butts, broken glass on dry leaves, firecrackers, and smouldering BBQs left unattended. Experienced firefighters may conduct backburning in fire-prone areas, to reduce the fuel available to wildfires in the hotter months, but even these deliberate small fires can get out of control.

Hundreds of lives have been lost in bushfires in Australia, and several billion dollars worth of property has been destroyed. Major fire disasters such as those in Victoria (1983), New South Wales (1994 and 2001–2002) and South Australia (2005) demonstrated the brutal nature of bushfires fuelled by high temperatures, dry undergrowth and pushed by the wind.

Cyclones

Cyclones are large tropical storms accompanied by gale-force winds and heavy rain. They originate as low-pressure systems out to sea and often bring tidal surges, which result in low-level areas being flooded by the sea. Heavy rain can also cause rivers and creek banks to burst, creating further flooding. In the northern coastal zones of Australia, cyclones are a potential hazard in the summer months.

Flash Floods

These can occur without warning after periods of heavy rain in many regions of Australia. As a safety precaution, it is inadvisable to camp in dry river beds or near the banks of creeks or rivers.

Solar Radiation

The Australian sun is a well-known health hazard and Australia has the highest rate of skin cancer in the world. Skin cancer is caused by the ultraviolet (UV) light in the sun's beams. These UV rays operate not only in bright sunlight but even when days are overcast. It is imperative to use an effective sunscreen, wear a hat and protective clothing whenever you are outdoors.

Reptiles

Saltwater crocodiles are common in northern Australia and extreme caution should be exercised around both salt and fresh water locations. Freshwater crocodiles are far less dangerous, but have been known to bite humans. Australia has many species of venomous snakes, but very few will attack unless they feel threatened (*see* p.17).

Sharks

Several species of shark, considered dangerous to man, are commonly found around the Australian coastline and in river estuaries. To minimise the risk, avoid swimming in murky water, swimming at dusk or later, and wherever possible seek out beaches that are patrolled by lifeguards. *See* p.17 for further information on marine creatures.

Small creatures

Only a few of Australia's estimated 2000 species of spider are considered dangerous (*see* p.17). Centipedes and scorpions can deliver a painful sting. Paralysis ticks, found in coastal bushland in eastern Australia, are best removed with tweezers or by a medical practitioner. Blood-sucking leeches are prevalent in moist forests of eastern Australia (including Tasmania) and, like ticks, can be difficult to remove. Many species of wasps, bees, ants and flies can bite or sting, but are usually dangerous only to those with allergies. The persistent bushflies of Australia's Outback are a nuisance as they seek moisture from human sweat; midges and beach sandflies often bite. Mosquitoes are rarely carriers of malaria in Australia, but in certain areas may transmit diseases such as dengue fever and Ross River virus.

Poisonous plants

Aboriginal peoples have used Australian wild plants for food and medicinal purposes with skill and knowledge honed over thousands of years. Without such expert knowledge, such plants, which may contain toxins, should be treated with caution.

Cyclone Tracy

The most ferocious cyclone ever to hit modern Australia arrived on Christmas Day 1974. For six hours, winds of around 250km/hr tore the city of Darwin apart. Cyclone Tracy destroyed almost 90% of the city and killed 50 people in the process. Building laws have since been passed in the Northern Territory to regulate the minimum safety standards for all new buildings—if a cyclone happened again, the modern city is better placed to withstand the onslaught.

PLANNING A TRIP

Before any road trip, either short or long, it is important to be prepared. The following are a few tips to ensure a comfortable, safe, enjoyable and memorable trip.

Passes and permits

Passes and permits are necessary for travelling through certain parts of Outback Australia and should be organised well before you begin the journey. For information on permits to travel in Aboriginal land, see the section on *Access to Aboriginal Land* on p.30.

If travelling into the desert parks of northern South Australia, you will need to obtain a **Desert Parks Pass**. It is issued by the Department for Heritage and Environment and replaces the usual daily camping permit required for entering the parks. Passes include detailed maps as well as information on first aid and survival skills. For information on the splendidly varied national parks of Australia, refer to the specific state/territory national parks sections of this book.

What to take

As a good deal of your holiday may be spent driving in the car, make sure you take lots of comfortable, loose-fitting clothing. Even if travelling in summer, take at least one set of warm clothing because nights can still get cool in many inland parts of the continent. Soft luggage bags are ideal for packing, as they can be squashed into small, tight spaces.

Essential items that you should not forget when travelling in Australia include plenty of water, hats, walking shoes and good socks, sunscreen, sunglasses, insect repellent and a camera. It is also a good idea to have tissues, snacks and maps in the car within easy reach. Remember to take important documents with you, such as your driver's licence, vehicle registration, the details of your insurance policy, emergency contacts and medical prescriptions. It is also worthwhile making a note of any allergies you are aware of and your blood type.

Things to check before you leave

Vehicle and trailer/caravan

It is essential that your car is well maintained and just needs some minor fluid level checks before the trip. Keep in mind that a two or three day trip with a light load is a lot less taxing on the car than weeks of extensive touring fully laden. If you are going to be towing a trailer, the car will be working much harder than normal, so car preparation needs to be even more thorough. See the section on *Car Preparation* (pp.20–21) for a suggested list of things to check if you are undertaking a big trip.

Home and contents

- Secure your home (all windows and doors) and belongings carefully.
- Cancel any regular deliveries— milk/newspaper.
- Organise someone to collect your mail and keep an eye on the house.
- Leave a light on in the house, or arrange a time switch to turn lights on and off regularly.
- Organise pet care.
- Organise someone to water the garden and mow the lawn.
- Leave contact details and a spare set of house keys with someone you trust.

Road sign at Travellers Village, South Australia–Western Australia border

Personal preparation

If you are going on a long trip it is most important that enjoyment and lack of stress are high priorities. If you don't know how to do the things listed below and they could be part of your trip, practise in a quiet location with a friend before you go, so that they will not be an issue when travelling.

- Changing a tyre—both the car and trailer.
- Basic car maintenance—courses are run by Evening Colleges and Motoring Organisations.
- Reversing a trailer into a tight spot.
- Using a GPS (Global Positioning System).

Fuel storage tips

- Carry extra fuel in metal jerry cans. Plastic containers might crack and break.
- Store extra fuel on the back of the 4-wheel drive or in a trailer.
- Do not pack fuel on the roof racks or inside the vehicle in case of fire or fumes.

CAR PREPARATION

Many of Australia's roads are now sealed or well-graded, so driving conditions are suitable for most cars. However, if venturing off the bitumen and into the rough is more your style, perhaps hiring or buying a 4-wheel drive is worth investigating. If you are planning to tow a caravan or trailer, it's best to stay on sealed roads, regardless of whether you are travelling in a 4-wheel drive or not.

Before You Leave Home ...

Make sure that your car has been checked by a qualified mechanic and that he/she knows that you are going on a long trip. If you are towing a caravan or trailer, get that serviced as well—particularly the tyres, wheel bearings, suspension, brakes, coupling and lights.

Before and during the trip you need to check:
- There is anti-freeze coolant in the radiator
- Lubricant levels—engine, transmission etc
- Heater and demister work properly
- The battery and mountings
- Tyre condition and pressure (remember the spare!)
- Wheel balance and alignment

Pre-trip inspection by a qualified mechanic

- Wheel bearings
- Condition of windscreen wipers—blades and reservoir
- Brake system
- Exhaust system
- Cooling system—radiator, hoses and thermostat
- Engine drive belt
- Automatic transmission
- Air conditioning
- Lights, including high/low beam
- Filters—air, oil and fuel
- Suspension

Packing the car

Try not to overload your car or 4-wheel drive, as extra loads can cause suspension problems. It is a good idea to have heavy duty suspension fitted if you think you may need to carry unusual loads. Pack the heaviest items inside the car, in the boot or in the trailer. The weight of heavy items on the roof could easily throw the car off balance. When packing lighter items on a roof rack, make the load lower at the front and higher at the back. This reduces wind resistance when travelling.

Spare Keys

Spare keys are important. Most cars are now equipped with engine immobilisers and these rely on getting a coded electronic signal from the ignition key or remote unit. This is why it is so important to carry a spare key/remote unit with you on a trip. Without a spare, the car may have to be towed a long distance to an authorized dealer or you may have to wait until the spare keys can be sent from home.

Servicing the air filter

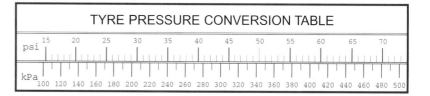

TYRE PRESSURE CONVERSION TABLE												
psi	15	20	25	30	35	40	45	50	55	60	65	70
kPa	100 120	140 160	180 200	220 240	260 280	300 320	340 360	380 400	420 440	460 480 500		

If carrying tools and equipment inside the car, make sure they are tightly secured. It is sensible to install a cargo barrier for this purpose. Emergency equipment, such as a fire extinguisher, should be easily accessible. Keep close at hand the things you may want or need during the journey.

Extras to take

It is always sensible to carry a spare set of car keys, a jack and tools wherever you go. The Tools and Spare Parts lists below are suggested for more remote areas and if packed carefully would take up very little room in the car. The lists are just a guide and may have to be adapted for different makes and models. Most cars use metric fasteners but it pays to check.

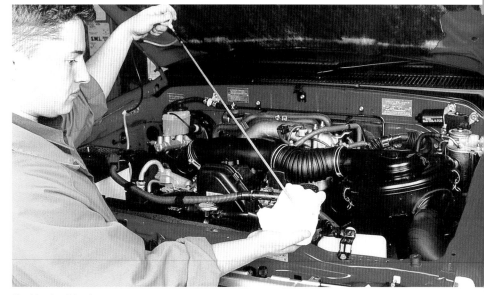
Checking the oil level

Tools and Equipment
- Set of ring/open end spanners
- Set of socket spanners
- Assorted screwdrivers
- Assorted pliers—combination, long nose and multi-grip

- Vise grips
- 30 cm and 15 cm adjustable spanners (shifters)
- Cold chisel and scraper
- Medium ballpein hammer
- Assorted files
- Feeler gauges
- Hacksaw/blade
- Epoxy fuel tank repair kit
- Radiator sealant
- Loctite Blue Max or equivalent gasket maker
- Rolls of cloth (Gaffer) and electrical tape
- Pump or siphon
- Hand drill and bits
- Plastic sheets (tarp) and blanket
- Collapsible water container
- Aerosol puncture repair
- Tyre pump—12 volt
- Puncture repair kit
- Tyre-pressure gauge
- Four-way wheel brace
- Jack with plywood base 30 cm × 30 cm × 3 cm for sand or mud
- Jumper leads—surge protected for late model vehicles
- Small spade and axe
- Snatchum strap or quality tow rope
- Heavy duty torch, spare globe and batteries
- Pocket knife
- WD40 or equivalent

- Fire extinguisher(s)
- Rags and some hand cleaner
- Folding red warning triangle

Spare Parts
- Radiator and heater hoses—with clamps
- Engine drive belt(s)
- Length of fuel hose—with clamps
- Length of 4mm wire and assorted connectors
- Assorted globes and fuses
- Distributor cap and rotor— if applicable
- High tension leads
- Spark plugs
- Set of points and condenser— if applicable
- Spare fuel, oil and air filters
- Engine and transmission oil
- Assorted nuts, bolts, washers and split pins

Spare Tyre

At least one spare wheel with air pressure slightly above normal should be carried at all times. In remote areas or if the car has a space-saver spare, consider taking an extra spare wheel if space permits.

On the road near Dubbo, New South Wales

Motoring Hints

Fuel economy

Fuel consumption is affected by both the condition of the car and the roads it will be travelling on. Here are some ways to help conserve petrol.

- Try to avoid delays such as peak-hour traffic or scheduled bridge closures.
- Try to distribute weight of passengers and baggage evenly.
- Drive as smoothly as possible.
- Ensure the tyres are properly inflated and that wheel alignment and balance are correct.
- Service and tune the vehicle regularly following the manufacturer's recommendations. The air cleaner, spark plugs and, on older cars, ignition timing are especially important.
- Avoid long periods of idling. When held up in traffic, switch the engine off if it is safe to do so.
- Make sure you fully release the handbrake when driving.
- Avoid driving at high speeds.
- Only use air-conditioning when absolutely necessary.

Measuring fuel consumption

When covering long distances on remote roads, you need to keep a check on your car's fuel consumption. Here is a basic formula for working out fuel consumption.

Total Litres	÷	$\dfrac{\text{Total km}}{100}$	=	Litres per 100km
60 Litres	÷	$\dfrac{300\text{km}}{100}$	=	20 Litres per 100km

Driving in northern Australia

There are two distinct seasons in the north, the Wet (November–April) and the Dry (May–October). Generally, the Dry season consists of comfortable daytime temperatures of around 25°C and cool nights. It is the safest and best time of year to explore northern Australia by car. During the Wet season, it is quite common for roads to become impassable due to heavy monsoonal rainfall. Refer to *Travelling in the Outback* (pp.28–29) for other driving skills not covered here.

Night driving

Avoid long overnight drives. Road accidents are three times more likely to occur at night because depth perception, colour recognition and peripheral vision are compromised in the dark. Be aware that the risk of encountering kangaroos and wallabies on some roads is increased at night because it is cooler and they often feed on the grass at the edge of the road. Stock wandering onto roads is also a major hazard especially in unfenced parts of the country. If you do have to drive at night, here are some tips so that you can avoid problems.

- Prepare your car for night driving by specifically checking and cleaning the headlights, tail-lights, indicators and all windows, inside and out.
- Ensure your headlights are on when you are driving! Remember,

Driving on an icy road, Ben Lomond National Park, Tasmania

being seen by other drivers is just as important as you seeing them.

- Always dim high-beam lights for oncoming cars and those in front of you as a safety measure and as a courtesy.
- If someone fails to do this for you, avoid the glare by watching the left edge of the road and using it as a guide.

Driving in alpine regions

Driving in alpine regions can be difficult, and, in the winter and snow season, dangerous. Here are some tips for driving in snowy and icy conditions.

- Don't put the handbrake on when parking unless necessary. Leave vehicle in reverse.
- Use brakes as little as possible to avoid skidding.
- Control speed—on downhill sections, use low gear instead of brakes.
- Use higher gears when going up hills to avoid over-revving and slipping.
- When changing down gears, do so smoothly with engine speed the same as wheel speed.
- Always put lights on low beam and chains on tyres when travelling while it is snowing.

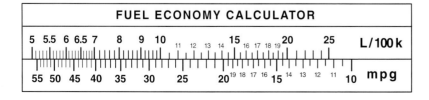

FUEL ECONOMY CALCULATOR

| 5 | 5.5 | 6 | 6.5 | 7 | 8 | 9 | 10 | 11 12 13 14 | 15 16 17 18 19 | 20 | 25 | **L/100k** |

| 55 | 50 | 45 | 40 | 35 | 30 | 25 | 20 19 18 17 16 | 15 14 13 12 11 | 10 | **mpg** |

AND DRIVING SKILLS

Driving in fog
- If there is near zero visibility, then pull off the road and wait for fog to lift.
- Always put headlights on, and if you feel the need, hazard lights as well.
- Try to avoid crossing roads or highways when visibility is reduced.
- Drive slowly and cautiously.

Driving in wet weather
- Always have properly inflated tyres with good tread.
- Slow down, especially when taking curves.
- Try to avoid the large puddles, which can cause aquaplaning.
- Steer and brake lightly.
- If you go into a skid, decelerate slowly and try to control the steering. Also try to remain calm!
- Try to drive in the tyre tracks left by other cars.

Beating fatigue
It is a well-known fact that driving in a fatigued state is highly danger-ous, and can be fatal. Fatigue happens more often on long drives and at night, but it can be felt at any time. Here are some tips to help combat driver fatigue.
- Have at least eight hours of sleep the night before any trip.
- Start a long road trip in the morning when you are fresh.
- Try not to drive alone, take turns driving and keep talking to your fellow traveller.
- Keep the temperature cool or the windows open.
- Take frequent breaks—rest at least every two hours.
- When you stop, get out and walk around. Exercise combats fatigue.
- Have light meals and snacks (avoid eating heavy meals).

- Drink lots of water.
- Wear comfortable clothes and drive sitting upright with shoulders back.
- Wear sunglasses to fight glare.
- Don't use cruise control (stay involved in the driving).
- Keep the windscreen clean.
- Never drink and drive. It's illegal, stupid, and even one drink can induce fatigue.
- If you feel tired, even just a little, Stop and Rest, even if it means having a 20 minute snooze, or checking into a motel for the night. Arriving a day later is better than not arriving at all.

Survival hints
If you get stuck in the 'middle of nowhere', here are some tips for staying safe.
- Try not to panic—think of a course of action that will see you helped or rescued.
- Stay with your vehicle—it provides shelter, increasing chances of survival. If a search for you is underway, spotting a car is easier than a person.
- Conserve food and water—always carry enough food and water to keep you supplied for a few days (four litres of water per person per day).
- Stay in the shade—keep clothes on to protect against exposure.
- Prepare adequate signals—if in a remote area light a smoky fire to attract attention. Remember to be careful—you don't want to start a bushfire.

Surviving a bushfire
If you get caught in a bushfire, it is important that you don't keep driving through the dense smoke. Also note that there is little risk of the petrol tank exploding in a

bushfire. Here are some guidelines for your safety.
- Pull to the side of the road away from the leading edge of the fire and stop.
- Switch on the headlights.
- Stay in the car.
- Wind up windows and close the air vents.
- Crouch in the car and shelter your body.
- Stay there until the fire passes.

Surviving a flash flood
If your car is caught in a flash flood, remember that your life is more important than the car or its contents.
- Get out of the car and onto higher ground as quickly as possible.
- Swim or float with the current, not against it, if you cannot keep your footing.
- Look for an overhanging limb or embankment to help you reach the safety of higher ground.
- After the flood has passed, you may be able to retrieve your car and dry it out. It is unlikely to have travelled far.

Negotiating a developing flash flood, Northern Territory

DRIVING INFORMATION

Here are some useful tips on driving in Australia.

Travelling with pets

If you want to go on a driving holiday and take the family pet along, it is advisable to plan where you are going to stay before you leave. This is to ensure your pet will be welcomed wherever you go. Even if you plan on camping, check that the site you're choosing does not have restrictions on animals. Most national parks restrict domestic animals from entering.

Driving Licence

- Tourists can drive in Australia if they have a valid licence from their home country for the same class of vehicle.
- Drivers must always carry their licence with them.
- Tourists cannot drive on an international permit alone. It must always be accompanied by a valid overseas licence.

Motoring in the Charters Towers district, Queensland

Quarantine and fruit fly

The Australian countryside is relatively free of disease. There are, however, places where it will be necessary to dispose of certain foods and materials before entering another region. State border regulations require that plant materials, sugarcane, banana plants and fruit are not carried from one state to another. If you plan to travel across the country, be sure to note the relevant quarantine laws for each state—particularly on fruit flies: spreading the pest is a chargeable offence.

Defensive driving

If you are planning a long trip, it might be wise to enrol in a defensive driving course, or at least read up on some driving skills. Defensive driving means that you are not only taking responsibility for yourself, your passengers and your actions, but you are also able to watch out for other motorists and minimise or avoid potentially dangerous situations. The keys to survival are awareness, anticipation and confidence in your defensive driving skills. Here are a few pointers to get you started.

- Be alert and do not assume that everyone else will drive perfectly on the road.
- Do not start the engine without being 100% sure that all passengers have their seat belts on and pets and luggage are secured.
- Do not be extreme by driving too fast, or too slow. Follow the speed limits and enjoy the drive.
- Only overtake other vehicles when it is completely safe to do so. Don't take unnecessary risks.
- Never cut in too quickly when overtaking another vehicle. Allow

Fuel

- A variety of fuels are sold at petrol stations across Australia.
- They are sold by the litre and prices are usually higher in country or remote areas.
- You can find petrol stations everywhere. Many are open 24 hours daily—except in more remote or Outback areas.

at least four–five car lengths before you signal and pull in front of the other vehicle.

- Always indicate your change of direction allowing plenty of time for other drivers to see you.
- If you have to pull over on the side of the road for any reason, allow a safe distance from the road and make sure you are clearly visible.
- Most importantly, have courtesy and respect for all other motorists, as well as the road rules.
- Always be 100% aware of what's going on around you.

Driving Laws

- Drive on the left hand side of the road.
- Maximum speed in some suburban areas and in most cities and towns is now 50km/hr.
- Country roads and highways have a limit of between 100 and 110km/hr, unless otherwise stated.
- It is illegal to drink and drive.
- It is illegal to not wear a seatbelt (all passengers).
- It is illegal to speed.
- Driving offences carry heavy fines and sometimes a jail sentence. Police patrol the highways in both marked and unmarked cars, and they carry out regular speed radar checks as well as conduct random breath tests.

BREAKDOWNS

Distances between towns in country Australia can be vast. If you are on a driving holiday around Australia, it is possible that your car will break down or get a flat tyre at some time during the journey. Here are some tips for how to deal with a breakdown.

General tips

- Your first concern should always be your personal safety and the safety of your passengers.
- If possible, try to get your car to a safe place, out of the way of passing traffic, before getting out to examine any damage to the vehicle.
- If the vehicle is undriveable, stay inside it and call for help. If you do not have a phone and you have to get out to flag down help, take care where you position yourself in relation to passing traffic.
- Put the hazard lights on to alert other motorists that there is a problem.

Breakdown on the Gunbarrel Highway, Western Australia

Tips for breakdowns on highways/freeways/motorways

- At the first sign of car trouble, take your foot off the accelerator very gently.
- Do not apply the brakes suddenly or with great force.
- Use indicators as you move to the side of the road. Always alert other motorists to your movements.
- Once you are off the road, make your car as visible as possible. Turn on the hazard lights.
- Call for help on a mobile or emergency phone. If not possible, take care when trying to attract the help of a passing motorist.
- Always stand clear of the passing traffic.
- If you think you can walk to a source of help, lock your car, take valuables and take great care.

Help in the event of breakdowns

Wherever you are in Australia, you can call this emergency number for assistance—**13 11 11**

- Never attempt to cross a multi-lane highway, freeway or motorway without extreme caution.

Dealing with a flat tyre

- At the first sign of trouble, hold the steering wheel firmly.
- Slowly decelerate.
- Signal all movement intentions to fellow motorists as you move off the road.
- Move your car off the road if you can—to avoid collisions and traffic hold ups.
- Brake very lightly until you come to a stop.
- Change the tyre if you feel you are a safe distance from the road and have the appropriate tools.
- If you are unable to do so, or your position is precarious, signal for help.
- After you have changed a tyre, and are in a centre where there is a qualified mechanic, get the car checked to ensure no other damage has been caused to the wheel or car.
- Get the damaged tyre fixed as soon as possible.

Calling for assistance on a two-way radio

Accident Checklist

If you are involved in a road accident and not injured, it is worthwhile recording the facts while still at the scene. You will need a record of the accident if you are reporting it to the police, filling in your insurance claim, or taking any other action to cover your repair costs.
Here is a checklist:

Details of accident
- Date, time and location of accident.
- Was the road wet or dry?
- Width of road.
- Was your car on the correct side of road?
- Estimated speed of both cars at time of impact.
- If accident occurred after sunset, was the site well lit?
- What lights were on, in cars involved?
- Sketch of accident scene.
- Names, addresses and phone numbers of witnesses (this information can be very useful in case of dispute).

Other car(s)
- Driver's name, licence number, address and phone number.
- Owner's name and address (if different from driver).
- Make, model and registration number.
- Extent of damage.
- Was car already damaged before this accident?
- Name of insurance company, policy number and type.
- Did other driver admit liability? Record exact words.

Injured persons
- Names and addresses of injured persons.
- Degree of injuries.

Damage to property
- Details of damage to property other than cars.
- Name and address of owner of damaged property.

Towing
- Name of tow-truck service.
- Destination of towed car.

Summoning help
Dial 000 to summon emergency help from Ambulance, Police or Fire Brigade. Instruct a bystander or passing motorist to contact the necessary emergency services, giving:
- The location—district, suburb etc.
- The name of the street and the nearest cross-street (suburban).
- The distance from a town or major landmark (country) in kilometres north, south, east or west.
- The nature of the accident—two cars, a pedestrian, a motor cycle etc.
- The number of people injured or trapped.
- Suspected nature of the injuries.
- Special hazards—electricity cables, fuel spilled, fire, railway crossing or any others.
- The time of the accident.
- Ensure that the message is understood and repeated by the person receiving it.

Police involvement
Police must be called to an accident if anyone is hurt or killed, if either of the drivers involved appear to be affected by alcohol or drugs or if a driver leaves the scene without exchanging details.
If the police are called, record the names of attending officers and their police station.
If the police are not called, the accident should be reported to the nearest local police station within 24 hours.

Checking the vehicle after an accident
Where the vehicle has been involved in only a minor accident it may be quite possible to drive the vehicle. Use the following checks to determine the vehicle's roadworthiness. If any doubt exists do not take the risk, have the vehicle towed.
- Check the radiator and cooling system for damage or leaks. DO NOT remove the radiator cap if the engine is hot.
- Ensure there is clearance between the fan and the radiator.
- Inspect all wheels and tyres for damage.
- Turn the steering from lock to lock ensuring that there is adequate clearance between the mudguards and the tyres. At the same time check for suspension and steering damage.
- Check the fluid level in the brake master cylinder. If the fluid level is low, investigate the cause.
- Depress the brake pedal and hold it under pressure. The brake pedal must be hard and should not fall away.
- Check the engine oil for correct level on the dipstick.
- Check the battery for correct electrolyte level and the security of clamps and terminals.
- Ensure that no electrical wiring is caught between damaged components.
- Check lights and wipers for damage and correct operation.
- Ensure that the bonnet closes securely and will not open unexpectedly while travelling.

FIRST AID

It is a good idea to keep a first-aid kit in your car. You can buy commercially prepared first-aid kits from chemists and camping equipment shops. Alternatively, you can make up your own kit in a clean, waterproof container.

Recommended contents of a first-aid kit
- Absorbent gauze
- Alcohol swabs
- Antihistamine (for bee stings)
- Antiseptic cream and swabs
- Aspirin or paracetamol
- Clinical thermometer
- Conforming bandages
- Cotton wool
- Crepe bandages
- Current first aid manual
- Eye bath
- Latex gloves
- Pen torch
- Safety pins
- Saline eyewash
- Scissors
- Sterile dressings
- Sticking plaster and assorted adhesive dressings
- Tongue depressor
- Travel-sickness tablets
- Triangular bandages
- Tweezers

First aid

Snake and spider bites
Try to identify the snake or spider—at no further threat to safety.
- Wrap the area bitten with an elastic bandage or use a strip of cloth if you don't have a bandage. This should slow the flow of venom in the bloodstream and, most importantly, keep the venom localised.
- Do not apply a tourniquet. This can cause gangrene if it stops the flow of blood completely.

- Don't loosen the bandage once it is applied.
- Get the victim to a hospital so that antivenom can be administered.

Bleeding
Wipe away blood and/or remove clothing to find source of bleeding. Apply direct pressure to the source with a bandage, piece of material or your hand.
- If possible, elevate the affected area (site of bleeding).
- Apply a tourniquet, firm and not too tight, only if you can't stop the bleeding any other way.

Shock
A person is in shock if he or she exhibits some of these symptoms: is cold and clammy to the touch, has a fast but weak pulse, is breathing shallowly, has a thirst, is anxious and restless, and feels nauseous.
- First, cover the person to keep him or her warm.
- Raise the legs so that blood flows to the heart.
- Protect from external elements—wind, cold, rain.
- Moisten the person's lips.
- Do NOT give him/her alcohol.

Heat stroke
Suffering heat stroke is common in Outback areas after long exposure to sun and heat. Symptoms include feeling hot and flushed, a rapid pulse rate, dizziness, fatigue, irrational behaviour and cessation of sweating.
- Seek a cool and shady place and move the heat-stroke victim out of the sun.
- Apply ice packs or cold water to the skin.
- Ensure the head, neck and chest are cooled.

- Ensure the person drinks plenty of fluids.
- Ensure the person gets sufficient rest.

Confidently managing a first-aid emergency
When travelling in Australia, with its vast distances, unpredictable and sometimes harsh climate, help may not be close at hand. Knowing what to do in the case of an emergency could save a life.

Before heading out on your next trip, it makes good sense to do a certified first-aid course, such as those run by St John Ambulance Australia. A fully stocked first-aid kit and copy of a St John authorised first-aid manual, or remote area first-aid books, could also be life-savers. First aid gives you the confidence to effectively deal with an emergency until medical attention arrives. Two guides that are especially recommended are the *Remote Area First Aid Field Guide* and *Emergency First Aid*, both available from St John Ambulance Australia. Call 1300 360 455 for information on St John first-aid training, kits and publications.

General assistance after an accident
Injuries should only be treated by competent first aiders. Where possible:
- Keep the casualty comfortable by careful handling, support and reassurance.
- Gently support the injured parts and avoid overhandling.
- Pay particular attention to an unconscious casualty who has an airway problem, breathing difficulty or serious bleeding.
- Hand over immediately when qualified help arrives.

TRAVELLING IN THE

The Australian Outback is vast, and very different from the coastal cities and developed towns. Some of Australia's most spectacular scenery can be found in remote and isolated areas of the Outback. A multitude of shades of red earth contrast with the clear blue of the sky and a horizon that seems to go on forever. With its stark desert landscapes, the Outback is both a beautiful and formidable place. The roads in the Outback are generally unsealed, and there are often no people or pit stops for hundreds of kilometres. If you are considering driving in the Outback independently of a tour, there are some points you should note.

You can employ special driving techniques for avoiding problems on unsealed roads.

- Most Outback roads are unfenced. This means that any wildlife and livestock around can suddenly appear. It is quite common for kangaroos to bound in front of a car. If this happens, try not to panic or brake dangerously. Often a roo will cause less damage to you and your family than a rolled car will. Emus have been known to pace cars (run alongside them), and then dart out in front of the car when they get tired of the race!
- When overtaking, beware of soft or loose verges. The dust caused by the vehicle in front can mask turns, dips et cetera, so make absolutely sure that you can see properly.
- Driving directly into the harsh sun can make visibility almost impossible. If you are travelling in a westerly direction, try to arrive at your destination by 4pm. If travelling in an easterly direction, do not start your journey until the sun has risen well above the horizon.

A typical Outback dirt road, South Australia

- Drive carefully and at a safe speed on dirt roads, as dust can mean reduced visibility of potholes and oncoming traffic.
- Avoid driving at night, as the ability to see livestock or wildlife crossing the road is hindered.
- Bulldust can be encountered on many Outback roads. It's a fine dust with the consistency of talcum powder that settles on the road, masking severe potholes or corrugations. Bulldust can also quickly clog the car's air cleaner and can permeate every component and cavity of the car, causing wear and deterioration. Drive with caution through bulldust and, if following another vehicle, always drop right back to allow the dust cloud to clear so that the effect is minimised.
- Road trains are multi-trailer trucks that require special caution. The size of the rig means that the driver cannot brake or turn in a hurry and there is a huge amount of momentum. If one is coming towards you on a dirt road, pull

Road train on an Outback gravel road, Northern Territory

OUTBACK

well off to the side and wait until it has passed. Overtaking is often best avoided, especially on dirt roads. It's better to have a rest break than tangle with one of these monsters. If you absolutely must overtake, make sure you get your vehicle in a position where the road-train driver can see you in the mirrors, then wait for a signal from the driver that it is safe to proceed.

- Driving through mud is difficult. To avoid getting bogged, use speed and power. Put the car into low, second or third gear and maintain a steady pace through the muddy terrain.
- On sand, keep the 4-wheel drive in a straight line—if you have to make a turn, do it by turning the wheel quickly, then back to the original position. Try to stick to existing tyre tracks. When driving down a dune, avoid braking, but don't go too fast, or too slow so that the wheels stop turning. If you get stuck in sand, lower the tyre pressure, use floor mats to

Driving near Red Lily Lagoon, Oenpelli, Arnhem Land, Northern Territory

give support and traction, dig out excess sand in front of the tyres to help get moving again.

- When attempting to cross a creek, check the underlying surface, depth and flow of the water by first wading across. A 4-wheel drive should be able to manage water about 60cm deep, but be careful of soft, sandy bottoms and strong currents. Drive slowly into the centre of the crossing, keep the wheels straight and do not change gear midstream. Remember to keep the engine running even if you have to stop the car midstream. Covering the radiator grille with a tarp and removing the fan belt might be advisable on some vehicles.
- Before setting out, know the conditions and distances of your journey, and leave the details of your trip with a family member or friend. If you know you are going to be driving through an isolated area, always notify the local authority of your intended destination and arrival time. This way they can help find you, if you become lost or break down.

- The featureless land of the Outback can make it difficult to know which direction you are travelling in. Always carry a compass—an orienteering compass is reliable, easy to use and inexpensive—and a topographical map. Make sure that the scale on the map is accurate and sufficient detail is given.
- If your vehicle has broken down, do not abandon it unless you are absolutely sure of where you are going and that you can get there safely. If it becomes necessary for others to search for you, remember it is easier to find a car than a person on foot. If you do decide to walk for help, always leave a note with details of who you are and where you are heading. Remember to take plenty of water and suitable clothing, matches or lighter and a torch, which can be used for signalling, if necessary.
- Cover the risk of getting stranded or lost in a remote area by carrying enough food and plenty of water to keep you supplied for a few days—allow at least four litres of water per person per day.

Fording a creek, Cape Tribulation, Queensland

ACCESS TO
ABORIGINAL LAND

If you are planning to visit or travel through Aboriginal land, you must obtain a special permit. There are several types of permits, which vary considerably between different land councils in different states. A transit permit will allow you to drive through Aboriginal land but you may not stop or leave the designated road. An entry permit will allow you to enter a certain area for a specific reason and period of time. Public roads that cross Aboriginal land are generally exempt from permit requirements, with the exemption applicable only to the immediate road corridor.

Applying for a Permit

Permit applications are available on land council websites or at the offices listed below, and may be made by email, fax or in person. To avoid disappointment, please allow enough time for your application to be processed. Generally speaking, an application can be issued within ten working days. However, in peak tourist seasons and in the event of an extended stay or deviation off the main road, it may take up to four weeks for a permit to be issued.

There is no charge for a transit permit, but there may be a levy or fee charged by the Aboriginal community for extended stays. For more detailed information about the permits, conditions, rules and safety regulations, it is essential that you contact one of the following offices well in advance of your intended travel.

Western Australia
Department of Indigenous Affairs
Level 1, 197 St George's Tce
Perth, WA 6850
P.O. Box 7770, Cloisters Sq,
Perth, WA 6850
Ph: (08) 9235 8000
Fax: (08) 9235 8093
www.dia.wa.gov.au

Northern Territory
Central Land Council
(for Alice Springs and Tennant Creek regions)
31–33 Stuart Hwy North
Alice Springs, NT 0871
P.O. Box 3321
Alice Springs, NT 0871
Ph: (08) 8951 6211, 8951 6320
Fax: (08) 8953 4345
www.clc.org.au
(permit applications are closed between 12noon and 2pm)
Northern Land Council
(for Darwin, Jabiru, Katherine and Nhulunbuy regions)
9 Rowling St,
Casuarina, NT 0810
P.O. Box 42921

Aboriginal traditional land owner, Arnhem Land, Northern Territory

Casuarina, NT 0811
Ph: (08) 8920 5100
Fax: (08) 8945 2633
www.nlc.org.au
Tiwi Land Council
(for Bathurst and Melville Islands)
Unit 5, 3 Bishop St
Stuart Park, NT 0820
Ph: (08) 8981 4898
Fax: (08) 8981 4282

South Australia
Maralinga Tjarutja Lands
PO Box 435
Ceduna, SA 5690
Ph: (08) 8625 2946
Fax: (08) 8625 3076

Queensland
Queensland Aboriginal Co-ordinating Council
P.O. Box 6512,
Cairns Mail Centre
Cairns, Qld 4870
Ph: (07) 4044 2999
Fax: (07) 4031 2534

Aboriginal land sign at Cahill's Crossing, East Alligator River, Northern Territory

TRAVELLING WITH CHILDREN

A long drive and travelling with children does not have to be a difficult or uncomfortable experience. Here are some tips for making long car trips more enjoyable for your children—and you!

- First, prepare the children's first-aid kit with basic ointments, creams, over-the-counter medications and importantly, any individual medications for personal conditions: for example, asthma sprays.
- Make sure you schedule enough time during the trip to make frequent stops. Try to have a 15 minute stop every two hours. Use parks, rest stops and picnic areas to let children run around and play.
- When you stop for lunch, try having a picnic outside rather than sitting in a restaurant, even if it means buying takeaway food to eat outside. You will all be much happier.
- Pack separate bags for your children and place them on top of other luggage, as this minimises inconvenience.
- If they are old enough, give them a map of the route and a highlighter, and let them follow the road. They will be much more interested in the journey and it will occupy some of their time.
- Entertain your younger children with stories—made up or true. Tell them yourself or get some audiobooks—the tapes can provide hours of fun and concentration.
- Play a variety of interactive games like 'I spy' and 'Guess what I am',

that everyone can play. Variety is the antidote to boredom.

- Try to schedule your departure for early in the morning. Children will be more likely to sleep for a couple of hours at the start of the trip and wake up for a breakfast stop.
- Try to make children as comfortable as possible. Use car shades and sunglasses to stop the heat and glare. Take pillows to prop up their heads, and blankets for warmth and comfort.
- If your children are old enough, swap seats with them if they are bored or fighting with each other. Give everyone a turn in the front seat on really long trips.
- Make sure you have plenty of dry and salty snacks, and enough water for each person.
- Always pack tissues, face cleaners, a towel and a change of clothes.
- Try to dress your children in layers so they can be comfortable whatever the temperature is.

Avoiding travel sickness

Motion or travel sickness occurs because of a conflict between what the eyes and ears are taking in. The inner ear senses the car as moving, while the eyes (if they are focused inside) do not. Therefore, the brain gets confused, and nausea results. If your children complain of feeling 'yucky' or 'sick', there are a few different things you can do.

- Suggest they look outside the car. You can do this by playing 'I spy...' or, if possible, reposition the seats so they can see out.
- Limit reading and hand-held games.
- Give them some fresh air—open the window.
- Avoid any strong smelling food, and especially smoke from cigarettes or cigars.
- Feed them dry biscuits—this often settles the stomach.
- Remember to drive smoothly.
- Stop for rests frequently.
- Inquire about over-the-counter medication and remedies from your chemist or doctor before you leave. There are also some very good herbal remedies available, which can be taken prior to setting off on your journey.

Family group on the beach at Currumbin, on Queensland's Gold Coast

USEFUL CONTACTS

NEW SOUTH WALES
Tourism New South Wales
Sydney Visitor Centre
106 George St
The Rocks, NSW 2000
Ph: (02) 9240 8788
NSW Visitor Information Line,
Ph: 132 077
www.visitnsw.com.au

National Parks Centre
102 George St, The Rocks
Sydney, NSW 2000
Ph: (02) 9253 4600, 1300 361 967
www.nationalparks.nsw.gov.au

ACT
**Canberra and Region
Visitors Centre**
330 Northbourne Ave
Dickson, ACT 2602
Ph: (02) 6205 0044
www.visitcanberra.com.au

Environment ACT
Level 2, Macarthur House
12 Wattle St, Lyneham, ACT 2602
Ph: (02) 6207 9777
www.environment.act.gov.au

4-wheel drive at Mount Hay, Blue Mountains, New South Wales

Camel sign, Central Australia

VICTORIA
Melbourne Visitor Centre
Federation Square
cnr Swanston St and Flinders St
Melbourne, VIC 3000
Ph: (03) 9658 9658
Victorian Visitor Information Line,
Ph: 132 842
www.visitvictoria.com

Parks Victoria
Level 10, 535 Bourke St, Melbourne,
VIC 3000
Ph: 131 963
www.parkweb.vic.gov.au

QUEENSLAND
Queensland Travel Centre
Tourism Queensland House
30 Makerston St
Brisbane, QLD 4000
Ph: 138 833
www.queenslandtravel.com

**Brisbane Visitor
Information Centre**
Queen St Mall
Brisbane, QLD 4000
Ph: (07) 3006 6290
www.ourbrisbane.com.au

Queensland Parks and
Wildlife Service
160 Ann St
Brisbane, QLD 4000
Ph: (07) 3227 8185
www.epa.qld.gov.au

SOUTH AUSTRALIA
South Australian Travel Centre
18 King William St
Adelaide, SA 5000
Ph: 1300 655 276
www.southaustralia.com

Department for Environment
and Heritage
GPO Box 1047
Adelaide, SA 5001
Ph: (08) 8124 4700
Desert Parks Hotline
Ph: 1800 816 078
www.environment.sa.gov.au

WESTERN AUSTRALIA
Western Australian Visitor Centre
Forrest Place
cnr Wellington St
Perth, WA 6000
Ph: (08) 9483 1111, 1300 361 351
www.westernaustralia.com

Conservation and Land Management (CALM)
17 Dick Perry Ave, Western Precinct, Kensington, WA 6151
Ph: (08) 9334 0333
www.naturebase.net

NORTHERN TERRITORY
Tourism Top End
Cnr Mitchell St and Knuckey St, Darwin, NT 0800
Ph: (08) 8936 2499, 1300 138 886
www.tourismtopend.com.au

Central Australian Visitor Information Centre
60 Gregory Tce,
Alice Springs, NT 0870
Ph: (08) 8952 5800, 1800 645 199
www.centralaustraliantourism.com

Conservation and Natural Resources
Goyder Centre, 25 Chung Wah Tce
Palmerston, NT 0831
Ph: (08) 8999 4582

TASMANIA
Tasmanian Travel and Information Centre
20 Davey St, Hobart, TAS 7000
Ph: (03) 6230 8233, 1800 990 440
www.discovertasmania.com.au

Parks and Wildlife Service
PO Box 1751, Hobart, TAS 7001
Ph: 1300 135 513
www.parks.tas.gov.au

Please note that the contact address and phone number for local tourist information centres are shown at the end of each featured city or town in the A to Z sections of this book. Contacts for Aboriginal Land Councils are shown on p.30.

MOTORING ORGANISATIONS
NSW
NRMA (National Roads and Motorists Association)
388 George St, Sydney, NSW 2000
Ph: 132 132
www.nrma.com.au

ACT
NRMA (National Roads and Motorists Association)
92 Northbourne Ave
Canberra, ACT 2601
Ph: 132 132
www.nrma.com.au

Victoria
RACV (Royal Automobile Club of Victoria)
360 Bourke St, Melbourne, VIC 3000
Ph: 131 955
www.racv.com.au

Queensland
RACQ (Royal Automobile Club of Queensland)
2649 Logan Rd
Eight Mile Plains, QLD 4113
Ph: (07) 3361 2444, 131 905
www.racq.com.au

Crocodile warning sign in Kakadu National Park

South Australia
RAA (Royal Automobile Association)
101 Richmond Rd
Mile End, SA 5031
Ph: (08) 8202 4600
www.raa.net

Northern Territory
AANT (Automobile Association of the Northern Territory)
AANT Building
79-81 Smith St
Darwin, NT 0800
Ph: (08) 8981 3837
www.aant.com.au

Western Australia
RACWA (Royal Automobile Club of Western Australia)
228 Adelaide Tce, Perth, WA 6000
Ph: (08) 9421 4444
www.rac.com.au

Tasmania
RACT (The Royal Automobile Club of Tasmania Ltd)
Cnr Patrick St and Murray St
Hobart, TAS 7000
Ph: (03) 6232 6300
www.ract.com.au

Road Service Nationwide
Ph: 13 11 11

EMERGENCIES
Nationwide, Ph: 000

Travellers at Mary Cairncross Park, Queensland, overlooking the Glass House Mountains

NEW SOUTH

From the Snowy Mountains to the beaches of the state, New South Wales certainly has something for everyone. Spend a few days skiing; explore the magnificent gorges and waterfalls of the Blue Mountains by foot; take a tour of the Hunter Valley, home to some of the best wineries in Australia; discover hidden rainforests; fish in some of the country's most secluded spots; sail or cruise the bays of Sydney Harbour; watch whales and dolphins off the coast, visit the country's oldest townships; or perhaps just let a saltwater wave wash you ashore on one of the state's golden beaches.

The oldest state in Australia, New South Wales is a prime example of the diversity of the continent's land-scape and climate. Located in the south-east of the country, New South Wales is seven times the size of Great Britain and the same size as California. It boasts the largest population of any state or territory in Australia with around 6.5 million people. The climate varies from subtropical temperatures in the north and along parts of the coast, to the dry, desert-like conditions of the far west, and to the snowfalls of the Southern Alps.

New South Wales: The Premier State

- Population: 6 500 000
- Total area: 801 400km^2
- % of Australia: 10.42%
- Floral emblem: Waratah
- Fauna emblem: Platypus

WALES

Main ATTRACTIONS

◈ Blue Mountains

The spectacular World Heritage-listed blue-grey gorges and mountainous walking paths are home to some of the state's most amazing rock formations, native flora and fauna, and quaint townships.

◈ Central Coast

With around 1000ha of coastal hinterland, this area is more than just a playground of beaches, holiday retreats and waterways. Horse trails, walking tracks and cycle paths make the region easily accessible for the whole family.

◈ Hunter Valley

The Hunter is home to some of the country's most respected vineyards. In the Lower and Upper valley regions there are more than 130 wineries, ranging from small, family owned businesses, to larger companies with outstanding tourist facilities.

◈ Port Stephens

The magical beaches and waterways of this area make it an ideal recreational destination. Watersports, whale- and dolphin-watching, fishing are popular activities.

◈ Snowy Mountains

Encompassing the state's largest national park, Kosciuszko, this alpine region boasts world-class ski resorts. Not only known for the powdery winter ski fields, the Snowy Mountain region has walking, camping, fishing and sightseeing opportunities to be enjoyed all year round.

◈ Southern Highlands

Not far from Sydney, the Southern Highlands is a paradise for garden, art, craft and antique lovers. Picturesque towns and local national parks make it the perfect destination for a daytrip or weekend away.

Throughout New South Wales, there are many reminders of a rich historical and cultural heritage. Aboriginal middens, rock art and 60 000 year-old artefacts at Lake Mungo, are amongst the lasting legacy of the first Australians.

European settlement, despite its relatively shorter history, has had a profound impact on the land. The relics of gold-mining towns, heritage-listed buildings and the present-day built environment are testament to the tremendous changes that have taken place since Capt Arthur Phillip raised the British flag at Sydney Cove in 1788.

The capital—Sydney—also has the largest population of any city in the country and is the business and financial capital of Australia. Since the 2000 Olympic Games, Sydney has cemented its reputation as a city with a uniquely welcoming and cosmopolitan atmosphere.

Photo above: The Three Sisters, Blue Mountains

THE PREMIER STATE

In 1770, Capt James Cook named the eastern half of the continent New South Wales. When the First Fleet arrived in 1788, they landed at **Botany Bay**, but found it an unsuitable spot for settlement. Once Capt Arthur Phillip and his crew discovered the outstanding harbour further north with its reliable supply of fresh water, the convict colony was established at Sydney Cove. The oldest buildings in the country still stand in **The Rocks** today.

The goldrushes of the 1850s transformed the fledgling colony, increased population, stimulated industries and hastened the granting of responsible government in 1856. Today, mining and manufacturing are still major sectors of the state's economy with **Sydney**, **Newcastle** and **Wollongong-Port Kembla** being the largest industrial centres in Australia. Coal was first discovered in the Newcastle area in the 1790s, and today, New South Wales still produces two-thirds of

Australia's coal from rich deposits in the **Hunter** and **Illawarra** regions. Silver, lead and zinc continue to be mined, particularly in **Broken Hill**—a major mineral provider since 1883.

Wheat, wool, beef, dairy and cotton farms contribute hugely to national and international markets. One-third of Australia's sheep are bred in New South Wales, carrying on the tradition established by Elizabeth and John Macarthur, who developed the merino breed. Along the northern coast of New South Wales, bananas and sugarcane are cultivated. Rice is an important crop in the **Murrumbidgee Irrigation Area**. Forestry resources are also important, especially in the north-east and south-east of the state. With most of the population living within 50km of the coast, fisheries are well developed.

New South Wales can be divided into four geographic regions. The coastal strip, where Sydney is

The Archway Cave at Abercrombie Caves, south of Bathurst

located, is blessed with sunny beaches, some of which are well-known surfing destinations. Most of the towns in the state are located near the coast. Further inland, the rugged mountains and plateaus of the **Great Dividing Range** display some of the most diverse landforms the state has to offer. The **Blue Mountains**, officially uncharted by Europeans until 1813, the **Snowy Mountains**, and the **New England Plateau** are all well-known tourist destinations in this region. The grassy western slopes, ideal for sheep and cattle grazing and wheat and cotton growing, expand further inland giving way to the western plains that stretch over the remaining two-thirds of the state. Settlement in this region is sparse and drought is frequent, making extensive grazing of sheep and cattle the predominant activity.

Tall Ships in Port Jackson (Sydney Harbour), on Australia Day

TOURISM REGION HIGHLIGHTS

New South Wales is Australia in microcosm, from the rugged beauty of the Outback to the alpine splendour of the Snowy Mountains, the lush subtropical rainforests of the north and south and the sparkling beaches of the coast.

A Sydney (pp.42–49)
Bondi Beach; Darling Harbour; Parramatta; Richmond and Windsor; Royal Botanic Gardens; Royal NP; Sydney Harbour; Sydney Harbour Bridge; Sydney Opera House; Sydney Tower; Taronga Zoo; The Rocks

B Blue Mountains (pp.79–81)
Blue Mountains NP; Everglades Gardens; Hartley Historic Site; Jenolan Caves; Kanangra Walls; Katoomba; Mount Tomah Botanic Garden; Mount Wilson; Norman Lindsay Gallery; Three Sisters; Zig Zag Railway

C Capital Country
Berrima; Bradman Museum, Bowral; Braidwood; Bundanoon; Bungonia Gorge; Burrinjuck Dam; Canberra; Goulburn; Wombeyan Caves; Young

D Central Coast (pp.70–71)
Australian Reptile Park; Bouddi NP; Brisbane Water NP; Tuggerah Lakes

E Explorer Country
Abercrombie Caves; Age of Fishes Museum, Canowindra; Bathurst; Carcoar; Cowra Japanese Garden; Gulgong; Hill End and Sofala; Lake Burrendong; Mudgee Vineyards; Orange; Parkes Radio Telescope; Siding Spring Observatory; Warrumbungle NP; Wellington Caves; Western Plains Zoo, Dubbo

F Hunter (pp.58–59 and 90–91)
Barrington Tops NP; Lake Macquarie; Lower Hunter Wineries; Maitland and Morpeth; Newcastle; Port Stephens; Upper Hunter Wineries

G Illawarra (pp.106–107)
Fitzroy Falls; Jamberoo; Kiama Blowhole; Minnamurra Rainforest; Shellharbour; Wollongong

H The Living Outback
Broken Hill; Kinchega NP; Menindee Lakes; Mungo NP; Silverton; Sturt NP; White Cliffs Opal Mines

I Lord Howe Island

J The Murray
Albury; Corowa; Deniliquin; Ettamogah Pub; Holbrook; Jindera Pioneer Museum; Lake Hume; Lake Mulwala; Murray River; Tocumwal

K New England/North West
Armidale; Bald Rock NP; Ebor Falls; Inverell Pioneer Village; Lightning Ridge; Moree Hot Mineral Baths; Mount Kaputar NP; Oxley Rivers NP; Tamworth; Tenterfield

L North Coast NSW
Bellingen; Coffs Harbour; Dorrigo NP; Ellenborough Falls; Great Lakes; Kempsey and Macleay Valley; Myall Lakes; Nambucca Heads; Port Macquarie; Seal Rocks; Taree and Manning Valley; Timbertown; Trial Bay Gaol

M Northern Rivers
Ballina; Border Ranges NP; Byron Bay; Evans Head; Lismore; Mount Warning NP; Nightcap NP; Nimbin; Thursday Plantation; Tropical Fruit World; Tweed Heads

N Riverina
Cootamundra; Griffith Wineries; Gundagai; Khancoban; Narrandera; Shear Outback, Hay; Tumut; Wagga Wagga; Willandra NP

O Snowy Mountains (pp.76–77)
Kosciuszko NP; Lake Jindabyne; Snowy Mountains Scheme; Thredbo/Blue Cow Mountain/Perisher Valley Ski Resorts; Yarrangobilly Caves

P South Coast
Australian Museum of Flight, Nowra; Batemans Bay; Bermagui; Central Tilba; Jervis Bay; Kangaroo Valley; Killer Whale Museum, Eden; Merimbula; Montague Island; Murramarang NP; Narooma

Rainforest, Mount Warning National Park

NATIONAL PARKS

New South Wales embraces some of the most varied landscapes in Australia. There are more than 600 national parks and other protected areas in the state. They range in environments from coastal hinterland, to dry bush, lush waterways and dense forests.

facts

◈ No. of parks/reserves: more than 600
◈ Total area: 59 572km^2
◈ % of state: 7.44%
◈ World Heritage Areas: Central Eastern Australian Rainforest Reserves, Greater Blue Mountains Region, Lord Howe Island Group, Willandra Lakes Region

Walls of China in Mungo National Park, far western New South Wales

A Ben Boyd NP (Map 122, D6)

In the south-east of the state, Ben Boyd NP is separated by the town of **Eden** and **Twofold Bay**. This 103km^2 park is a haven of historic whaling sites, clear-water inlets and coastal forests. The coastline is well-known for its rock formations, flowering heaths, the banksia forest and specifically, the **Quoraburagen Pinnacles**. Visitors are welcome to camp, fish, BBQ, swim, dive and picnic.

B Blue Mountains NP
(Map 81, H2)

With the highest number of visitors of any national park in New South Wales, the World Heritage-listed Blue Mountains NP is a feast of lookouts, bushwalks, wildflowers and wildlife. Only 105km west of Sydney, the park has some of the most spectacular rock formations and gorges in the state. Within the 2482km^2 of bushland, **The Three Sisters** and the **Grose Valley** are popular spots. There are plenty of walking tracks, and camping, picnic and BBQ facilities. Well worth a visit are the cable cars at **Scenic World**, and the towns of **Katoomba**, **Leura** and **Blackheath** with look-outs for keen photographers. For the adventurous there is abseiling, rockclimbing and canyoning.

C Kosciuszko NP
(Map 77, C1)

The largest in the state, Kosciuszko NP, 6744km^2 in area, is home to the continent's highest mountain peak, the New South Wales snowfields and the **Snowy River**. The park expands from the Victorian border across to the **Brindabella Range** west of Canberra. Visit from June to September for skiing, and anytime during spring/summer for bush-walking, camping, horseriding, swimming, BBQs, picnicking and trout fishing. A major attraction is the **hydro-electric scheme** (est.1949) that has reshaped the mountains and added to the electricity generating capacity of eastern Australia.

D Mungo NP (Map 116, E5)

In outback New South Wales, Mungo NP, 278km^2, and Sturt NP, 3106km^2, can reach over 50°C in summer. Therefore, they are best explored in the cooler months. Both national parks are of historic significance, and remote, semi-arid

New South Wales

desert environments with 4-wheel drive access. **Lake Mungo**, now dry, is an archaeologist's dream, with bones, middens and artefacts dating back to the earliest human existence in Australia. The bones of the well-known Mungo Woman have been recently redated to 60 000 years old.

E Myall Lakes NP
(Map 95, D1)
The 442km^2 of Myall Lakes NP contains the largest coastal lake system in New South Wales and is a great spot for waterbird watching and watersports like sailing, wind-surfing, canoeing and waterskiing. Camping, BBQ, picnic and boat hire facilities are available.

F Sturt NP
(Map 111, C2)
Sturt NP, 3106km^2, is referred to as **'the Living Outback'** and is home to red kangaroos, emus, goannas, bearded dragons and wedge-tailed eagles. The park has camping, BBQ, picnic and lookout facilities, with extensive walk and drive touring routes.

G Sydney Harbour NP
(Map 47, K6)
Set on perhaps the most beautiful harbour in Australia, Sydney Harbour NP is a landscape of natural bush-land, sandy beaches and sandstone cliffs. With the city as a backdrop,

Blue-faced honeyeater, *Entomyzon cyanotis*, feeding on nectar

the park is divided into a number of sections around the harbour. There is easy access to most parts via public transport. Attractions include Middle Head, North Head, South Head and The Gap, Manly Scenic Walkway, Nielson Park, the Quarantine Station, the harbour islands and Fort Denison.

H Warrumbungle NP
(Map 118, D1)
The most popular national park of central New South Wales is Warrumbungle. Best visited in spring and autumn, the 232km^2 park boasts great walking tracks, rugged scenery and 4-wheel drive access. It lies on ancient volcanoes, which makes rockclimbing popular, although you need a permit to do so. BBQ, camping, picnic and lookout facilities make it a favourite destination for families.

I Wollemi NP (Map 119, F4)
The largest wilderness area in New South Wales, World Heritage-listed Wollemi NP is a rugged 4930km^2 landscape of canyons, undisturbed forests, plateaus and escarpments. Perhaps its most recent claim to fame was the 1994 discovery of the Wollemi pine (*Wollemia nobilis*), 'the living fossil', which is only known to exist in the wild in this park at a secret location. Canoeing, bushwalking, camping, canyoning, 4-wheel driving and swimming are all popular activities.

> ## National Park Information
> **National Parks Centre**
> 102 George St,
> The Rocks,
> Sydney, NSW 2000
> Ph: (02) 9253 4600, 1300 361 967
> www.nationalparks.nsw.gov.au

WINERIES

The first vines to be planted in Australia were from cuttings that arrived with Capt Arthur Phillip on the First Fleet of 1788. They were planted at **Farm Cove** in Sydney, but due to poor, sandy soil conditions they did not thrive.

Subsequently, vineyards sprang up in other areas around Sydney and the first commercial wine was produced at **Camden Park** in 1807. **Gregory Blaxland**, of the famous pioneering family, also made commercial wine from his vineyard at **Brush Farm**. Much of the credit for the establishment of an Australian wine industry goes to **James Busby**. Busby arrived in Sydney in 1824 and decided to try to change the drinking habits of colonial New South Wales. He established his vineyard at **Kirkton** in the **Hunter Valley** in 1825. Another New South Wales wine industry pioneer was **George Wyndham**, whose **Branxton** vineyard in the Hunter Valley, established in 1828, is the oldest continuously operating winery in Australia.

The New South Wales wine industry has grown to a point where there are now over 300 wineries, large and small, spread around the state. Today, New South Wales produces high quality wines and is firmly placed on the international wine map.

A Cowra
(p.64)

From modest beginnings in 1973, vine plantings in this area now total 2000ha, with over 30 vineyards between **Woodstock**, Cowra and **Canowindra**. Cowra chardonnays have won many awards, with verdelho, cabernet sauvignon, merlot and shiraz also gaining widespread recognition.

B Hastings River
(p.98)

There are several wineries in the subtropical region around **Port Macquarie**, pioneered in the 1980s by the Cassegrain family. The main wines produced are pinot noir, chardonnay, merlot, semillon, verdelho, and chambourcin, a French red varietal which is perfect with Mediterranean dishes.

C Hawkesbury/Nepean
(maps 46 and 48)

Several small wineries are to be found near Sydney, close to the Hawkesbury/Nepean river system. Locations include **Ebenezer** near Windsor, **Luddenham** and the **Camden** district where it all began. **Gledswood** at Catherine Field is situated on a historic property that produced wines in early colonial times. Classic grape varieties such as chardonnay, semillon, merlot and cabernet sauvignon are grown in the region.

D Lower Hunter Valley
(pp.58–59)

Although wine production began here in 1832, it was not until the 1960s that the industry started to flourish. By 2005 there were more than 5000ha of vines and over 115 wineries with cellar doors open to the public. The region, centred around **Pokolbin**, near Cessnock, on the slopes of the Broken Back Range, produces around 5% of Australia's wine. Famous names such as **McWilliams**, **Lindemans**, **Wyndham**, **Tyrrells** and **McGuigan** have been joined by dozens of boutique winemakers. Despite 'unsuitable' soils and climate, Hunter wines are rich and full-flavoured, with the capacity to develop in the bottle over many years, and internationally acclaimed. Wines of note include chardonnay, verdelho, traminer, merlot, riesling, shiraz (hermitage) and the exceptional Hunter semillon.

Tyrrells winemaker taking wine samples from barrels for tasting

Vineyard in the Upper Hunter Valley

E Mudgee (p.88)

Like the Barossa Valley in South Australia, Mudgee's wine industry was inaugurated by German immigrants in the mid-19th century. Mudgee grapes are in high demand due to their rich flavours, especially the spectacularly flavoured shiraz and cabernet sauvignon. A Mudgee winery provided the first cuttings for Australia's famous chardonnays in the 1960s.

F Orange (p.95)

Wine grapevines were first planted here in 1983, and there are already about 50 vineyards in the area (including **Mount Panorama** at

nearby Bathurst). At 860m above sea level, these are the highest vineyards in New South Wales, Nutrient-rich volcanic soils, mild summers and cold winter nights assist in producing quality wine with intense flavour and colour.

G Riverina (pp.72 and 83)

The area around **Griffith** and **Leeton** in the **Murrumbidgee Irrigation Area** is the largest winemaking region in New South Wales and one of the largest in Australia. **J J McWilliam** planted the first vines here in 1912. Today, 100 000 tonnes of grapes are produced by 500 growers in an average year. Dry semillon wine is produced in the Riverina as well as shiraz, chardonnay, cabernet sauvignon, merlot and verdelho. The delicious dessert wine 'Riverina Gold' has won international recognition.

H Shoalhaven
(pp.53 and 96–97)

There are several wineries in the triangle formed by **Shoalhaven Heads**, **Berry** and **Bomaderry**,

including one at the historic **Coolangatta Village**. Verdelho and chambourcin have made their mark here, with Australia's first gold medallist for the latter emanating from this area.

I Tumbarumba (map 77)

The newest wine-producing region of New South Wales lies in the foothills of the **Snowy Mountains**. Contemporary viticulture methods are used to produce fine cool-climate wines, mainly pinot noir, chardonnay and sauvignon blanc, with smaller quantities of pinot meunier, cabernet sauvignon and merlot.

J Upper Hunter Valley
(pp.90–91)

The wineries scattered around **Denman** and **Muswellbrook** are generally smaller than those of the Lower Hunter with the notable exception of **Arrowfield** and **Rosemount**. Rosemount's rieslings and traminers first brought wide acclaim to the area in the 1970s. More recently, its chardonnays have won worldwide accolades. Other wine varieties include semillon, verdelho, chambourcin, pinot noir, shiraz and cabernet sauvignon.

K Young (Hilltops) (p.109)

The vineyards around Young thrive on deep fertile soils. A local wheat and sheep farmer pioneered the first winery in 1969 and the success of his 1974 cabernet sauvignon encouraged others to plant vines. Riesling, sauvignon blanc and shiraz are also popular.

The **Pericoota region** (L on map at left) around Moama, and the **New England region** (M on map), between Tenterfield, Inverell and Quirindi, are emerging new wine areas. Canberra District wineries are covered on p.127.

SYDNEY

A harbour ferry passes Sydney Opera House

main attractions

◈ Chinatown
The Dixon St area features many restaurants and authentic Chinese stores. Kam Fook, the biggest Chinese restaurant in the Southern Hemisphere is here.

◈ Darling Harbour
This is a waterside plaza with parks, shops, restaurants, nightclubs and museums.

◈ Macquarie St
This is an elegant street lined with many historic sandstone buildings such as Government House, the State Library of NSW, Parliament House and The Mint.

◈ Queen Victoria Building
The QVB is a beautifully restored heritage building next door to Sydney Town Hall.

◈ Royal Botanic Gardens
Covering 30ha, these lovely gardens display a variety of rare and exotic plant life.

◈ Sydney Harbour Bridge
The world's widest single span arch bridge links the city to the North Shore.

◈ Sydney Opera House
This has been regarded as one of the architectural wonders of the modern world since it opened in 1973.

◈ The Rocks
This historic area now has galleries, shops, restaurants and Sydney's oldest pubs and buildings. There is a tourist market of handicrafts on weekends.

Australia's most vibrant city, Sydney, is a flourishing cosmopolitan cultural and financial centre. Although Sydney is not Australia's capital, it is the nation's oldest and largest city, occupying 3700km^2 of the country. Sydney's urban sprawl is an immense natural playground bordered by the **Pacific Ocean** in the east, the **Blue Mountains** in the west and stunning national parks in both the north and south. With its temperate climate, it is possible to make the most of Sydney's striking surroundings in any season.

The major gateway to Australia, Sydney is undoubtedly a leading tourist destination in its own right. Featuring many prime tourist attractions, sightseeing in and around the city is easy. The CBD itself is a manageable size, with many people preferring to see the attractions on foot. Alternatively, the bright red **Sydney Explorer** bus takes in almost all of the major tourist attractions on its 20km route. No one should visit Sydney without taking a ferry ride or cruise on magnificent **Sydney Harbour**. Cruises and regular harbour ferries all depart from **Circular Quay**.

ℹ Visitor information
Sydney Visitor Centre
106 George St, The Rocks, NSW 2000
Ph: (02) 9240 8788
NSW Visitor Information Line Ph: 132 077
www.sydneyvisitorcentre.com

facts
- ◈ Population: 4 086 000
- ◈ Date founded: 1788
- ◈ Tallest building: Sydney Tower, 305m
- ◈ Average temperature:
  22.5°C (January), 13°C (June)

Places of Interest
Art Gallery of NSW (A) D3
Australian Museum (B) C4
Cadman's Cottage (C) C2
Chinatown (D) B4
Chinese Garden (E) B4
Circular Quay (F) C2
Customs House (G) C2
Darling Harbour (H) B4
Hyde Park (I) C4
Martin Place (J) C3
Museum of Contemporary Art (K) C2
Museum of Sydney (L) C3
National Maritime Museum (M) B3
Powerhouse Museum (N) B4
Queen Victoria Building (O) C4
Royal Botanic Gardens (P) D3
Star City Casino (Q) A3
State Library of NSW (R) C3
Sydney Aquarium (S) B3
Sydney Harbour Bridge (T) C1
Sydney Observatory (U) B2
Sydney Opera House (V) D2
Sydney Tower (W) C3
Sydney Town Hall (X) B4
The Rocks (Y) C2
Victoria Barracks (Z) E5

Sydney's famous Harbour Bridge at sunrise

Scale 1:15 000

0   500 Metres

PORT

JACKSON

Goat Island
Sydney Harbour National Park Island

Mort Bay

BALMAIN EAST

Simmons Pt

Millers Pt

MILLERS POINT

DAWES POINT

Walsh Bay

THE ROCKS

North Sydney

McMahons Point

McMahons Pt

Blues Point Res

Blues Pt

Milsons Point

SYDNEY HARBOUR BRIDGE

Kirribilli Point

Fort Denison

Benelong Point

Sydney Opera House

Mrs Macquaries Point

Mrs Macquaries Chair

Garden Island

ADI Naval Dockyard

Captain Cook Graving Dock

Darling Harbour

Darling Island

PYRMONT

Star City

Pyrmont Bay

National Maritime Museum

Fish Market

Fish Markets

Convention Centre

SYDNEY

Circular Quay

Customs House

Museum of Contemporary Art

Cadman's Cottage

Observatory

Sydney Observatory

GROSVENOR

Wynyard

Martin Place

State Library of NSW

Parliament House

Royal Botanic Gardens

Farm Cove

Woolloomooloo Bay

The Art Gallery of N.S.W.

The Domain

POTTS POINT

ELIZABETH BAY

Elizabeth Bay

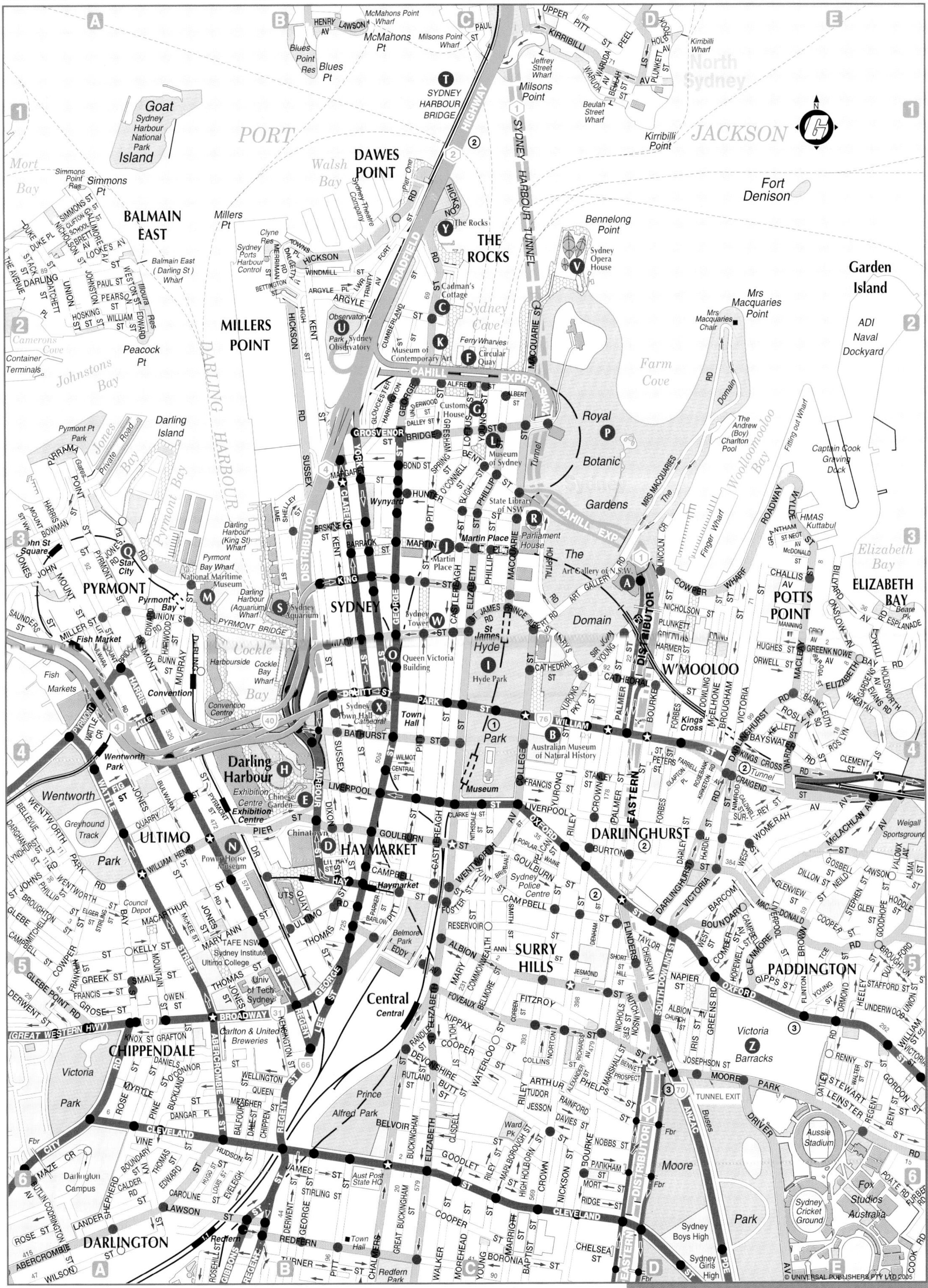

W'MOOLOO

HMAS Kuttabul

Sydney Tower

Queen Victoria Building

Hyde Park

St James

Town Hall

Sydney Town Hall Cathedral

DARLING HARBOUR

Exhibition Centre

Chinese Garden

Chinatown

HAYMARKET

Power House Museum

UTS

ULTIMO

Greyhound Track

Wentworth Park

Victoria Park

CHIPPENDALE

Carlton & United Breweries

DARLINGTON

Darlington Campus

Central

Belmore Park

Prince Alfred Park

SURRY HILLS

Australian Museum of Natural History

Kings Cross

DARLINGHURST

PADDINGTON

Victoria Barracks

Moore Park

Aussie Stadium

Sydney Cricket Ground

Fox Studios Australia

Sydney Boys High

Sydney Girls High

Redfern

EASTERN DISTRIBUTOR

CAHILL EXPRESSWAY

SYDNEY HARBOUR TUNNEL

BRADFIELD HIGHWAY

CLEVELAND ST

OXFORD ST

WILLIAM ST

GEORGE ST

GREAT WESTERN HWY

BROADWAY

CBD & SUBURBS

Sydney's CBD stretches from **Sydney Cove**, in the north, to **Central Railway Station** in the south. The best way to explore the city is on foot and by public transport. Try to avoid taking a car into the city—not only is there a lot of traffic, but parking is scarce and what is available in the city's car parks is expensive.

Walking tour of the CBD

Arrive at **Circular Quay** via ferry, train or bus. Begin with a wander through **The Rocks**, perhaps stopping to browse in the shops and markets. On the way, take a look at **Cadman's Cottage**—built in 1816. The **Museum of Contemporary Art** is a nice place to observe Australia's modern art and perhaps there's even time for a coffee on the terrace that overlooks the Quay. Wander around to **Sydney Opera House**, on the way taking a look at **Government House**, which sits at the opening to the **Royal Botanic Gardens**. Walking up Young St, past **Customs House** you will reach the **Museum of Sydney**. Inside, an interactive presentation brings Sydney's colonial heritage

Late afternoon view of Sydney Tower and CBD

to life. From here, venture along **Macquarie St**, past the **State Library**, **Parliament House**, **Sydney Hospital**, the **Mint** and **Hyde Park Barracks**. Once you reach **Hyde Park**, wander through to the **ANZAC War Memorial**, or perhaps visit the **Australian Museum** on William St. It is one of the top five natural history museums in the world, and is Australia's oldest. Take a detour to **Stanley St**, where some of the city's best cuisine is to be found, or walk back along College St, to see **St Mary's Cathedral**, which was finally resurrected after the 1865 fire that burnt it to the ground. The twin spires were completed in 2000. Walk through the **Domain** to the **Art Gallery of NSW**, to view some of the finest works of art in the country, including historic, contemporary and photographic works, as well as major overseas exhibitions.

For those who love to shop, don't miss getting a train to the **Queen Victoria Building**, or wander back down towards the Quay to find **Pitt Street Mall** and the **Strand Arcade**. Perhaps visit the tallest building in the city, **Sydney Tower**, for a superb panoramic view.

On the **Darling Harbour** side of the city (which can be reached by ferry, monorail or bus), take a stroll through **Chinatown**, and on the way, stop for an authentic Yum Cha experience. Worth a look on this side of town are the **Powerhouse Museum**, **Imax Theatre** and the **Chinese Garden**. Darling Harbour is also home to the **Sydney Aquarium**, **National Maritime Museum** and **Star City Casino**, as well as the variety of shops and the restaurants, clubs and bars of **Cockle Bay**.

Take a look at the well-regarded **Sydney Fish Markets** in Ultimo. Be tempted by some of the fresh produce available, and find a spot in the sun to enjoy your seafood experience.

For movie- and theatre-goers, there is an abundance of **cinemas** along George St, and **theatres** dotted throughout the city, all of which have a rich tradition of outstanding theatrical productions.

To the north

The beachside suburb of **Manly** is easily accessible by bus or ferry, and is a well-regarded surfing and tourist destination. Both the **Food and Wine Festival** (late May to early June) and **Jazz Festival** (October) draw huge crowds every year—locals and visitors alike.

Another beachside suburb, **Palm Beach**, is a holiday playground for many Sydneysiders. Beaches lie on both sides of the northernmost point of the peninsula, bordering a golf course and recreation reserve.

Closer to the city, **Taronga Zoo** sits nestled in Bradley's Head, Mosman and enjoys amazing harbour and city views. It is regarded as one of the world's finest zoos.

In a more secluded part of the northern suburbs, **Berowra Waters** is known for its quiet waterfront setting. There are four restaurants and two marinas to enjoy, or a picnickers' paradise on the western bank next to a handy boat ramp.

To the south

The south of Sydney boasts the famous **Bondi Beach**. Wander the promenade with its restaurants and cafes, or perhaps join the Christmas and New Year's Eve celebrations.

FESTIVALS AND EVENTS

The city of Sydney is known for its party atmosphere so there is never a shortage of annual festivals and events. The **Sydney Festival** is held in January, soon after locals and visitors have feasted on the spectacular **New Year's Eve Harbour Bridge fireworks display**. The following few weeks are filled with free street theatre, concerts, exhibitions and events. In late February, the **Gay and Lesbian Mardi Gras** takes over the heart of the city with a world famous parade and all-night parties in celebration of gay pride. Soon after, on April 25, the **ANZAC Day March** walks down the same streets in memory of our war heroes. The **City to Surf** is the most popular public sporting event in the city. Held in August, the 14km run starts from Hyde Park and finishes at Bondi Beach.

New Year's Eve fireworks display on Sydney Harbour Bridge

A most amazing sight is that of **Waverley Cemetery**, which is situated on a promontory of Sydney's south-east coastline and dominated by tall, white marble headstones.

Closer to the city centre is the bustling and colourful district of **Kings Cross**. Nestled together with the strip shows and sex shops are some of the city's best restaurants and night spots.

A visit to **Vaucluse** to see some of Sydney's most exclusive residences and the gothic mansion, **Vaucluse House**, could end with a lunchtime stop at **Watsons Bay**. This prime harbour position boasts the famous **Doyles Wharf Restaurant** and impressive scenic walks to **South Head**. Alternatively, picnic in shady **Nielsen Park**.

The **University of Sydney** in Camperdown is one of the most striking universities in Australia. Modelled on Cambridge and Oxford, Sydney Uni has a heritage worth discovering on one of the guided tours on offer.

To the north-west

This region is dominated by the mighty **Hawkesbury/Nepean** river system, which winds its way through recreational parks, picnic spots and holiday retreats.

The City of **Parramatta** contains 24 historic buildings as well as several memorials in and around **Parramatta Regional Park**.

While travelling the Great Western Hwy towards Penrith and the Blue Mountains, **Featherdale Wildlife Park** will be top of the children's list

of places to visit, with lots of friendly native animals to meet.

To the south-west

This is **Macarthur Country**, named after the early pioneers John and Elizabeth Macarthur who bred merino sheep and provided the foundation for Australia's wool industry. Today, it is a relatively urbanised region but has successfully preserved a few rural pockets and parts of its colonial heritage.

The historic centre of **Camden** boasts three reserves, which are perfect for picnicking, as well as many heritage-listed buildings.

Mount Annan Botanic Garden is the largest in Australia and will eventually include most of the country's 25 000 known plant species organised in themes.

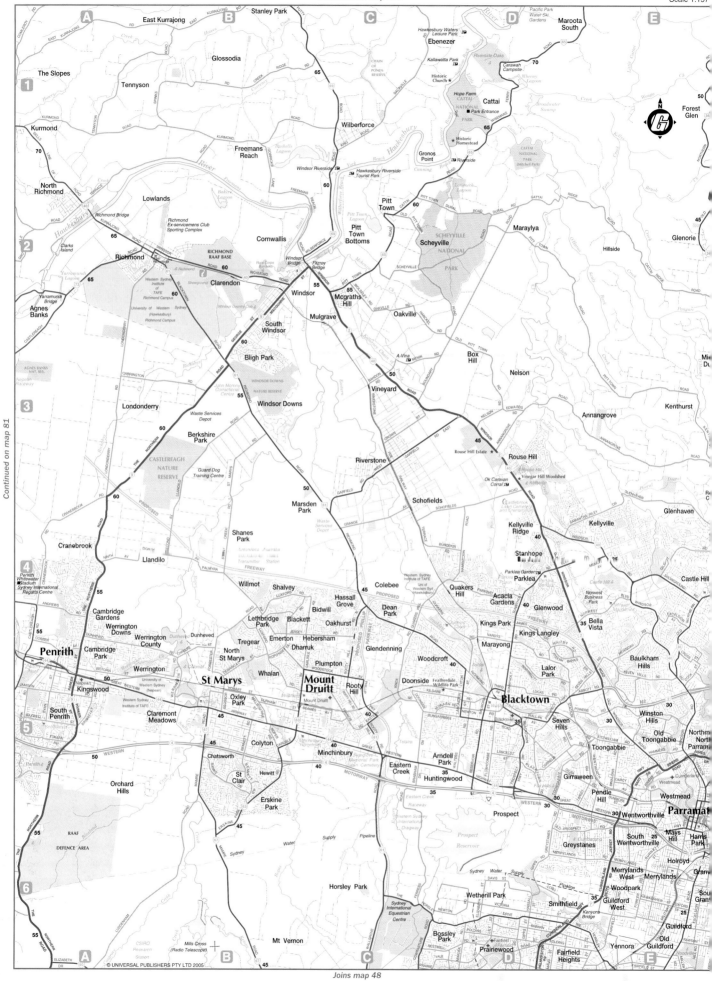

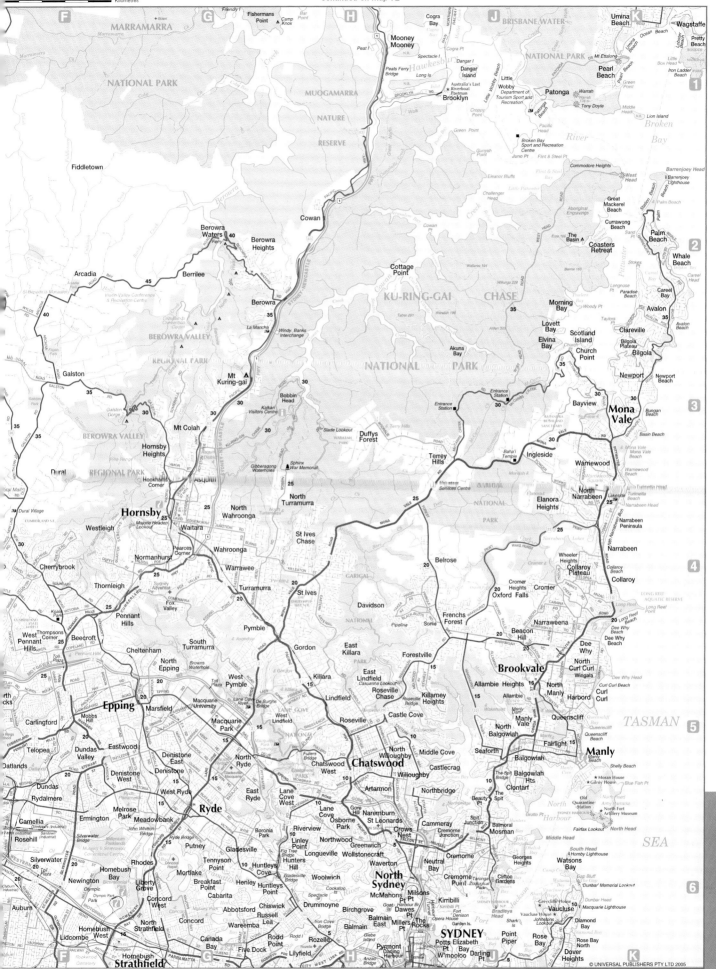

© UNIVERSAL PUBLISHERS PTY LTD 2005

Scale 1:157 1

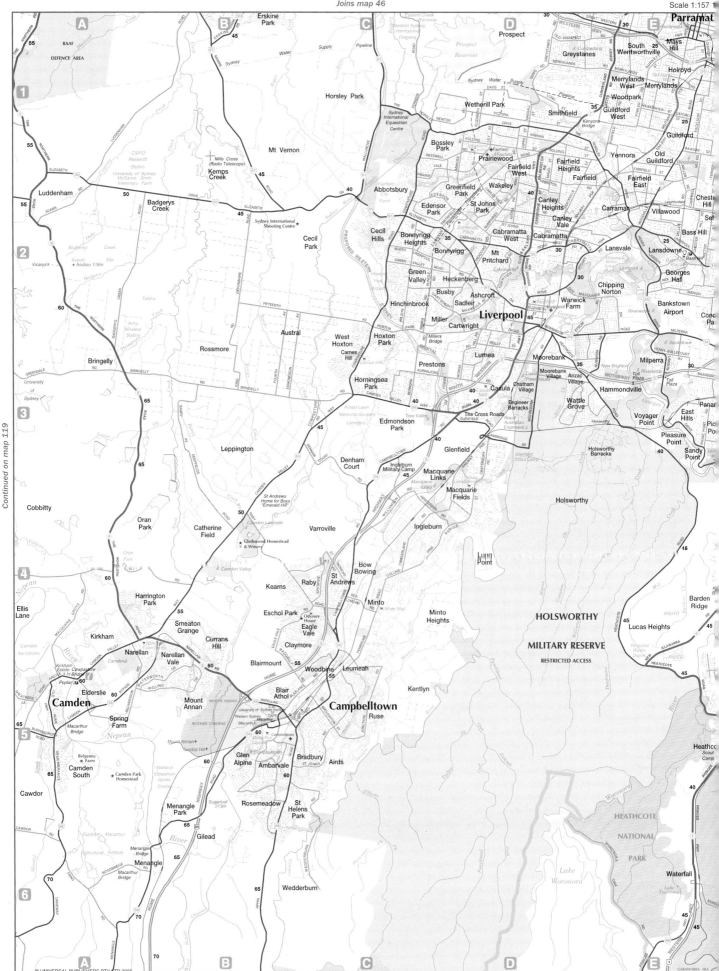

Continued on map 119

Continued on map 107

48 Gregory's Australia

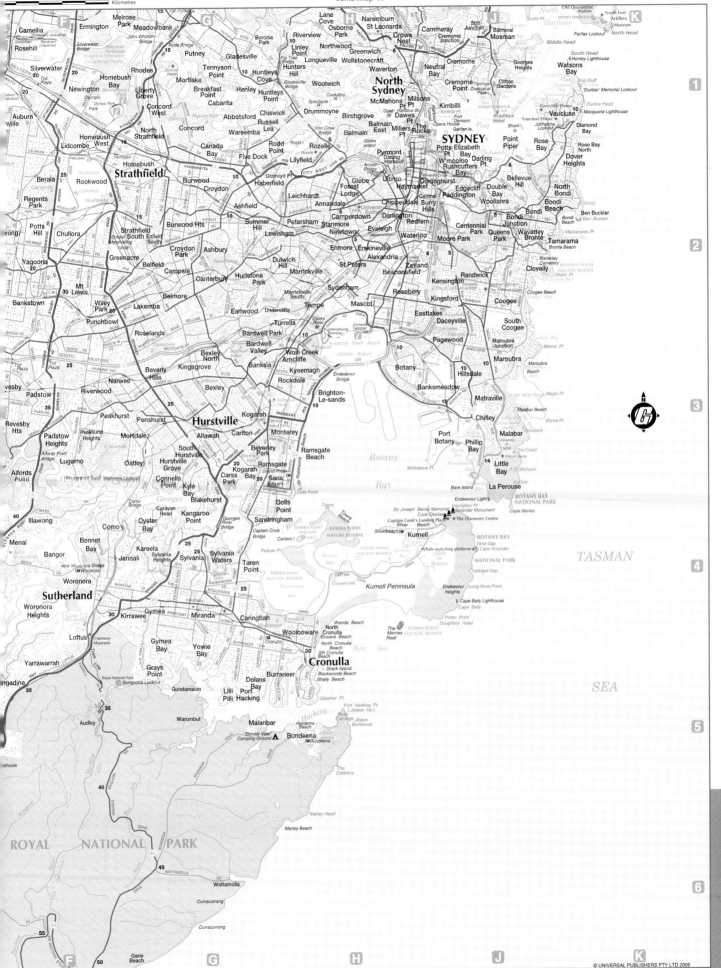

Continued on map 107

■ Albury   POP 41 500

Map 121, J4

Sometimes known as only Albury, the real city is a conjoining of two, Albury-Wodonga, and lies 575km south-west of Sydney on the **Murray River**. Albury lies within New South Wales, while Wodonga, is on the Victorian side. The region was

The original Ettamogah Pub, north of Albury

discovered by Hume and Hovell during their 1824 exploration, and Albury grew as an important paddlesteamer port in the heyday of the river trade. Today, the city serves a region rich in crops, cattle, wine and outstanding scenery. It is also a convenient stopover for those driving on the Hume Hwy between Sydney and Melbourne.

MAIN ATTRACTIONS: Points of interest include the many buildings dating from the late 1800s, such as the Turks Head Inn, which now houses **Albury Regional Museum**. **Albury Botanic Gardens** were established on Bungambrawatha Creek over 100 years ago. The **Regional Art Centre** features the locally made *Aurora Australis* tapestry, paintings, ceramics and photographs.

NEARBY ATTRACTIONS: **Ettamogah Sanctuary**, north of Albury, is the place to view native wildlife. Further on at **Table Top** is the eccentric **Ettamogah Pub**, a living replica of Ken Maynard's cartoon, published

in *Australia Post* in 1959. Opposite is **Table Top Winery**, which is open for tastings and sales. For those interested in military matters, **Bandiana Military Camp** covers a considerable area on the south-east outskirts of Wodonga. A hangar-type building houses the **RAA Ordnance Corps Museum**, which displays tanks, armoured vehicles, uniforms, weapons and other para-phernalia. In the warmer months, the paddlesteamer **PS *Cumberoona*** cruises the Murray River.

VISITOR INFORMATION: Gateway Complex, Lincoln Causeway, Wodonga, Ph: 1300 796 222

■ Armidale   POP 21 350

Map 115, F5

Nestled in the **New England Ranges**, 567km north of Sydney, is the main city of the Tablelands, Armidale. The city is renowned for its churches and as a seat of learning. The **University of New England** is located here as well as a TAFE college and some long-established private schools.

MAIN ATTRACTIONS: The **Heritage Tour** is a good way to see Armidale. The bus leaves the visitors centre at 10am weekdays, and 10.30am weekends and holidays for a two hour guided tour exploring the city's history and heritage—the cost is a gold coin donation. The **Heritage Walk** is also worthwhile. Leaflets are available from the visitor centre and the walk includes 34 points of interest. Armidale's parks and gardens are especially attractive during spring and autumn. **Apex Memorial Lookout** in **Drummond Park** provides a view of the whole city. There are many museums to visit, including the modern **Regional Art Museum** in Kentucky St. Exhibits include the collections of Howard Hinton, Chandler Coventry as well as works by other Australian artists. **Armidale and New England Folk Museum** is housed in the old School of Arts and Mechanics Institute (1863) and depicts the life and history of the city. Several rooms are furnished in period-style. The museum is located on the corner of Faulkner St and Rusden St and is open daily.

NEARBY ATTRACTIONS: The old gold-mining town **Hillgrove** is located 27km to the east. Hillgrove was once home to 3000 residents. The two mines here produced over $1.6 million worth of gold. **Hillgrove Rural Life and Industry Museum** is open Friday to Monday and holidays. Approximately 6km south is **Saumarez Homestead**, a house museum developed by the National Trust. The museum reflects the history of the New England pastoral properties. Surrounded by gardens and views of pastureland, the property is open daily from September to the June long weekend. Arrange to view inside the house with the information centre. Within a one hour drive of

Point Lookout, New England National Park

the city are three national parks: **New England**, **Cathedral Rock** and **Oxley Wild Rivers**. Oxley Wild Rivers NP contains **Dangars Gorge**, 23km south of Armidale and is well worth visiting. **Wollomombi Falls**, 40km east on Waterfall Way, is the second highest waterfall in Australia, with a drop of 220m.

VISITOR INFORMATION: 82 Marsh St, Ph: (02) 6772 4655 or 1800 627 736

▦ Ballina   POP 16 520
Map 84, D3

Ballina lies inside the breakwaters of the **Richmond River**. The area is the traditional home of the Bundjalung Aboriginal people. Capt Henry Rous named the Richmond River in 1828. Cedar-cutters were the first settlers in the area and the town was gazetted in 1856. Sugar and dairy farms were established in the 1860s and continue as major local industries, along with fishing and boat building. The tourism boom of the 1960s saw the town develop into a major attraction centred on its idyllic beaches, the river and attractive hinterland.

Ballina also has very good markets, cafes and restaurants.

MAIN ATTRACTIONS: The **Big Prawn Complex** on the Pacific Hwy is an instantly recognisable land-mark and a sign of the town's busy fishing industry. It has an **Opal and Gem Museum** as well as arts and crafts and fresh seafood. Other attractions in Ballina include the **Naval and Maritime Museum** in Regatta Ave and **Kerry Saxby Cycleway and Walkway**. River cruises, whale- and dolphin-watching cruises and parasailing are also popular as well as water-based recreational activities like fishing, surfing and swimming.

NEARBY ATTRACTIONS: On the Pacific Hwy, just north of Ballina are the **Bicentennial Gardens** and **Thursday Plantation Tea Tree Centre** —a working tea-tree plantation. **Macadamia Castle** at Knockrow and **Summerland House with No Steps**, located at **Alstonville**, west of Ballina, are popular family attractions.

VISITOR INFORMATION: Cnr River St and La Balsa Plaza, Ph: (02) 6686 3484

Batemans Bay   POP 10 200

Map 122, D3

Located at the mouth of the **Clyde River**, Batemans Bay is a fishing town and holiday destination—only 152km from **Canberra**, so it attracts many visitors from the capital. The town is also a service centre for the surrounding hinterland, which produces timber, dairy products and vegetables.

MAIN ATTRACTIONS: The beaches, rivers and lakes are prime attractions. Lunchtime river cruises, fishing charters and houseboat hire are all available. Boat ramps give boat owners easy access to the Clyde River or the ocean. The **Old Court House Museum** displays local history through collections of photographs and memorabilia. **Birdland Animal Park** offers a variety of Australian wildlife and a rainforest trail.

NEARBY ATTRACTIONS: South of Batemans Bay is the old gold-mining region of Mogo. **Old Mogo Town** is a re-creation of a 19th-century gold town and is open daily. Visitors can see a blacksmith's shop and forge, an ore-crushing plant, tavern and Cobb & Co freight station. In the same area is **Mogo Zoo**. Open daily, the zoo specialises in Australian native animals and wild cats, successfully breeding snow leopards. **Eurobodalla Regional Botanic Gardens** are located approximately 7km south of Batemans Bay at **Deep Creek Dam**. The gardens are open Wednesdays, Sundays and school holidays and offer visitors the chance to enjoy the native flora. There are several national parks close to Batemans Bay. **Budawang NP** in the hinterland is part of the eastern scarp of the **Southern Highlands**. It is rugged, remote and has no facilities. **Murramarang NP**, extending along the coast 20km to the north, is a more popular recreation area offering sandy beaches, surfing, rock and beach fishing, and beach-loving kangaroos!

VISITOR INFORMATION: Cnr Princes Hwy and Beach Rd, Ph: (02) 4472 6900

Bathurst   POP 26 950

Map 118, E4

Australia's oldest inland settlement, Bathurst is a thriving rural area with education being the city's largest industry. The main campus of **Charles Sturt University**, two TAFE campuses, four private and two public high schools are all located here. It is also well-known for its car-racing circuit, Mount Panorama. The **Bathurst 1000 V8 Race** is held in October and the **Bathurst 24 Hour Race** in November.

MAIN ATTRACTIONS: Ben Chifley, Prime Minister of Australia from 1945 to 1949, was born in Bathurst. Located at 10 Busby St, the **Chifley Home** is open to the public Saturday to Monday. Also worthwhile visiting is **Miss Traill's House and Garden**—a house museum recording 100 years of family life. Miss Ida Traill bequeathed her colonial Georgian house to the National Trust. Historic **Abercrombie House** can be visited most Sundays (closed July to September). The **National Motor Racing Museum**, located at Murray's Corner, is where you can experience the excitement of past motor racing, with displays, videos, photographs and memorabilia. Visitors can arrange to drive the famous international **Mount Panorama Motor Racing Circuit**. There are many parks in Bathurst. **Machattie Park** was developed in the late 19th century and visitors can enjoy the bandstand, fountain, fern house and duck ponds. **Macquarie River Bicentennial Park** is a popular site for picnics. It offers covered tables, BBQs, children's play areas, lovely gardens and the **Heritage Wall**.

NEARBY ATTRACTIONS: **Bathurst Goldfields**, a reconstruction of the historic gold-mining area, are located south-west of the city centre. The former goldfield, **Hill End**, still has many original buildings and has inspired paintings by John Olsen and Brett Whiteley. It is about 86km north-west of Bathurst. **Abercrombie Caves**, 72km to the south of Bathurst, has camping areas and features the largest natural limestone bridge in the Southern Hemisphere.

VISITOR INFORMATION:
Kendall Ave, Ph: (02) 6332 1444

Eastern grey kangaroo, *Macropus giganteus*, and joey at Pebbly Beach, Murramarang National Park, north of Batemans Bay

Coastline at Tathra, near Bega, showing the historic 1860s wharf

▪ Bega POP 4400

Map 122, D5

This picturesque town is located in prime dairy country, 431km south of Sydney, near the junction of the Princes Hwy and Snowy Mountains Hwy linking with Sydney, Canberra and Melbourne.

MAIN ATTRACTIONS: Lookouts around Bega include the **Dr George**, 8km to the north-east, and **Bega Valley**, 2km north, offering views of the **Bega River** winding around the town. **Bega Co-operative Cheese Factory** is open daily. Here visitors can watch the cheese-making process and sample the products. A Heritage Centre displays early cheese-making equipment and there is also a cafe and art gallery. **Grevillea Estate Winery** is 5km west of Bega, on Buckajo Rd. Open for tastings, the winery also has a restaurant. Leaflets describing Bega's **historic walk** are available from the information centre. Stops include the **Court House** (1881) and **Bega Family Museum**. The museum, a building that was once the Bega Family Hotel, displays pioneer memorabilia and local crafts. The museum is located on the corner of Bega St and Auckland St.

NEARBY ATTRACTIONS: In summer it is worthwhile visiting **Mumbulla Falls** with its many rockpools. The falls are located in the hills 15km north-east of the town. **Tathra** is the closest beach to Bega. At one end of the beach is the mouth of the **Bega River**. The original **1860s wharf** still stands and the old cargo shed houses an interesting maritime and history museum.

VISITOR INFORMATION: 91 Gipps St, Ph: (02) 6492 2045

▪ Berrima POP 880

Map 107, A2

This historic village is located 14km south of Mittagong on the old Hume Hwy. Still preserved as a village of the 1850s, Berrima offers the visitor many attractions.

MAIN ATTRACTIONS: A self-guided **walking tour** around Berrima is recommended. Leaflets describing the walk are available from the Court House. Buildings of interest include **Berrima Court House**, built in 1838. This Court House held the first trial by jury in New South Wales and now houses the information centre, which is open daily. Displays include a sentencing session of a 19th-century trial and a video history of the town and district. **Berrima Gaol**, built in 1839, is across the road and is now a medium security facility and rehabilitation centre. **Berrima and District Historical Society Museum** displays local memorabilia and items of historic interest. Now a member of the worldwide Booktown organisation, the **Petty Jury Bookshop**, located in the Court House complex, specialises in Australian history and copies of antique maps. It is open daily. **Berkelouw's Antiquarian Book Barn** is located on the Old Hume Hwy and stocks over 200,000 rare and second-hand books. **Holy Trinity** and **St Francis Xavier** churches are worthwhile visiting.

VISITOR INFORMATION: Berrima Court House, Cnr Wilshire St and Argyle St, Ph: (02) 4877 1505

▪ Berry POP 1600

Map 97, C1

Known as **'The Town of Trees'**, Berry is a picturesque town with beautiful deciduous trees, planted at the turn of the 19th century, lining its streets. Located on the Princes Hwy, 16km north of Nowra, Berry is popular as a weekend getaway and offers many B&B's, guesthouses and motels.

MAIN ATTRACTIONS: There are plenty of activities available in Berry: walking, horseriding, cycling and six local wineries open for tastings and sales. Many of Berry's heritage buildings have been renovated and now house cafes, antique shops, nurseries, and art and craft galleries.

NEARBY ATTRACTIONS: Alexander Berry, the district's first and most prominent settler, constructed **Coolangatta Estate**, a private village in 1822. It has been beautifully restored and is now a resort open to the public. The old Coolangatta schoolhouse has become **Coolangatta Craft Centre**, featuring wood and folk art, hand-blown glass and pottery. It is open Wednesday to Monday and daily during school holidays.

VISITOR INFORMATION: Cnr Princes Hwy and Pleasant Way, Nowra, Ph: (02) 4421 0778

■ Blayney   POP 2680
Map 118, E5

This mid-19th century gold-mining town is a centre for the surrounding farming and grazing region of the picturesque **Belubula River Valley**. The goldrush of the 1850s and 60s sparked development in the district and gold is still mined at **Cadia Gold Mine**. The opening of another mine is planned for the future.

MAIN ATTRACTIONS: Many items associated with the development of Blayney are displayed at the **Viv Kable Museum** in the **Blayney Library**, Adelaide St. Here you can also carry out family and local history research. The town has a number of art and craft outlets. There are two parks with picnic facilities: **Heritage Park** in Adelaide St and **Carrington Park** in Osman St. **Church Hill Lookout**, accessed through the industrial estate north of Blayney, gives a panoramic view of the surrounding Belubula Valley.

NEARBY ATTRACTIONS: Blayney is a good base for exploring the district's historic settlements. **Carcoar**, 13km south-west, is in a pleasant valley setting. In 1863, it was the scene of the first recorded daylight bank robbery in New South Wales. The third oldest town west of the Blue Mountains, Carcoar has remained relatively untouched since the 19th century. Some of the historic

Children in the grounds of Stoke's Stable Museum, Carcoar, near Blayney

buildings now house antique shops and tea-rooms. **Carcoar Dam** is a popular recreation area with camping facilities. From Carcoar Dam there are excellent views of the **Blayney Wind Farm**.
Millthorpe is a National Trust-classified village, 11km north-west, with bluestone churches and workers' cottages. Millthorpe's **Golden Memories Museum** displays more than 5000 items illustrating how people lived in the late 1800s.

VISITOR INFORMATION: 97 Adelaide St, Ph: (02) 6368 3534

■ Bourke   POP 2780
Map 113, F4

This far western **Darling River** town is the gateway to the real Outback and the main centre for an extensive pastoral district that produces more wool than anywhere else in New South Wales. In 1897, the construction of a lock and weir on the Darling River meant that

paddlesteamers were able to go further up the river and eventually, in 1964, there was sufficient water for irrigation, allowing crops such as citrus, grapes, lucerne and sorghum to be grown. In recent years cotton farming has become one of the main industries in the area.

MAIN ATTRACTIONS: Bourke has many historic buildings and places to see. **The Back O'Bourke Mud Map Tours** booklet is available from the information centre and is an essential guide. There is also a Back O'Bourke three hour minibus tour of the town. In season, there are tours of cotton farms. The paddle-vessel **PV *Jandra*** is available for cruises on the Darling River. More details on these tours are available from the information centre. There is an **historic wharf** at the end of Sturt St. The **Old Railway Station** in Anson St has displays of Aboriginal artefacts and a selection of literature on local history. The **Back O'Bourke Exhibition Centre** on

Kidman Way has state-of-the-art displays on local history and farming. The famous eye surgeon Fred Hollows' grave and memorial is in the cemetery.

NEARBY ATTRACTIONS: There is a wildlife sanctuary and Aboriginal rock art painted by the Ngemba tribe at **Gunderbooka**, 74km south. **Mount Oxley** is the highest landmark in the area, 34km north-east.

VISITOR INFORMATION: Old Railway Station, Anson St, Ph: (02) 6872 1222

■ Bowral   POP 10 320

Map 107, B2

A popular town in the **Southern Highlands**, Bowral is well known for its country resorts, B&B's, and excellent cafes and restaurants. A highlight of the year is **Tulip Time**, an annual spring celebration with thousands of tulips and spring flowers blooming in both public and private gardens—some open to the public. The deciduous trees planted along the roadside highlight the change of the seasons and are another attraction for visitors.

MAIN ATTRACTIONS: The **Bradman Museum** in St Jude St is a must-see for cricket fans. The museum highlights Sir Donald Bradman's achievements, displays cricket memorabilia, and documents the origins of the game and its growth in Australia, the history of the Ashes and the Bradman era. The museum is open daily. There is a self-guided walk, which takes in a number of sites around Bowral associated with Sir Donald. Called the **Bradman Walk**, it begins at the museum. Many buildings and houses built in the late 19th century have been beautifully preserved. Buildings of interest include the **Court House, Municipal Chambers, St Jude's Church and Rectory. Merrigang, Wingecarribee** and **Bendooley streets** are particularly attractive streetscapes.

NEARBY ATTRACTIONS: Over the town **Mount Gibraltar** rises 863m above sea level. Picnic facilities are located on top of the mountain and there are views from several lookouts. Native flora and fauna can also be seen from the tracks in **Gibbergunyah Reserve**, accessed off Boronia St.

VISITOR INFORMATION: 62–70 Main St (Old Hume Hwy), Mittagong, Ph: (02) 4871 2888

■ Broken Hill   POP 20 980

Map 116, B2

This city is located 1158km west of Sydney and operates on South Australian time. Broken Hill remains one of the world's great mining centres, despite its downsizing in recent years.

MAIN ATTRACTIONS: Broken Hill attracted many well-known Australian artists (the 'Brushmen of the Bush') during the 1970s. Showrooms and art galleries are now a feature of the city. **Pro Hart's Gallery** at 108 Wyman St displays his own work and his private collection. **City Art Gallery**, on the corner of Blende St and Chloride St, features European and Aboriginal art, and works by local artists. *The Big Picture* at **Silver City Mint and Art Centre** is the world's largest acrylic painting on canvas, measuring 12m by 100m.

NEARBY ATTRACTIONS: **Living Desert Reserve**, 6km from the city on Nine Mile Rd, displays the **Living Desert Sculptures**—12 works of art by international artists dedicated to renowned eye surgeon, Fred Hollows. **Delprats Underground Mine Tours** are located near the **Line of Lode Miners' Memorial. Day Dream Mine** on the Silverton road, 33km north-west, is a pioneers' mine, discovered in 1881, that offers underground tours. **Silverton**, known as 'Hollywood of the Outback', is popular with tourists. It is a virtual ghost town and was used as the setting for movies like *Mad Max*.

VISITOR INFORMATION: Cnr Blondo St and Bromide St, Ph: (08) 8087 6077

Palace Hotel, one of many historic buildings in Broken Hill

MYALL LAKES

Myall Lakes is a system of shallow waterways stretching along the coast of the Tasman Sea, 236km north of Sydney. The tranquillity of this area is conserved in a very popular national park with numerous camping retreats.

Myall Lakes NP contains the largest coastal lake system in New South Wales and is an important waterbird habitat. Walk through rainforest, hire a houseboat or take a 4-wheel drive along the beach. With an area of 442km^2, this popular park, which also extends to the west of the **Pacific Hwy,** has something to offer everyone.

The western edges of the lakes can be accessed via numerous roads and trails leading from the Pacific Hwy. Access in the east is possible from **Mungo Brush Rd,** via **Hawks Nest,** or the ferry at **Bombah Point** (map p.95).

Canoeing on the Myall Lakes

Part of the Great Lakes district, the Myall Lakes, which cover more than 100km^2, are ideal for water-sports and boating. Boats can be hired from **Myall Shores** and from **Tea Gardens** and houseboats from **Bulahdelah**.

i **Visitor information**

Bulahdelah Information Centre
Cnr Pacific Hwy and Crawford St
Bulahdelah, NSW 2423
Ph: (02) 4997 4981

■ Brunswick Heads   POP 1855
Map 84, D1

Located at the mouth of the **Brunswick River,** approximately 20km north of **Byron Bay,** is the commercial fishing town of Brunswick Heads. With its surf beaches stretching for many kilometres, particularly good fishing and boating and its warm climate, Brunswick Heads is a very popular holiday town.

NEARBY ATTRACTIONS: **Cape Byron,** to the south, is the easternmost point of Australia. **Ocean Shores** lies north of the Brunswick River and offers excellent coastal views from **Lions Lookout.** The hinterland is also very attractive and visitors can take advantage of the scenic drives and rainforest walks at **Minyon Falls** and **Nightcap NP**. **Tyagarah**

Nature Reserve is also worthwhile visiting and can be accessed by road and footbridge across the south arm of the Brunswick River.
VISITOR INFORMATION: 80 Jonson St, Byron Bay, Ph: (02) 6680 8558

■ Bulahdelah   POP 1150
Map 95, C1

Lying approximately halfway between Newcastle and Taree is the township of Bulahdelah. State forests and **Myall Lakes NP** are in close proximity, so those who enjoy bushwalking, horseriding, bird-watching, boating, canoeing, sailing, fishing and swimming will find the town a convenient base.
MAIN ATTRACTIONS: **Bulahdelah Mountain** is known locally as **Alum Mountain** because of its huge deposits of the substance used in

medicine, dyeing and many other technical processes. **Bulahdelah Mountain Park,** approximately 1km down Meade St, offers picnic and BBQ facilities. There are also many accessible walking trails in the rainforest leading to picnic areas with good views over Bulahdelah and the **Myall Valley** and to the ocean beyond.

NEARBY ATTRACTIONS: There are over 500km of forest roads throughout the state forests and national parks in the district. Maps and leaflets are available from the information centre. **Wang Wauk Forest Drive** passes through some of the largest stands of flooded gum trees in New South Wales and leads to a flooded gum (*Eucalyptus grandis*) known as **The Grandis**—the tallest tree in New South Wales. Access to this

tree is via the Old Pacific Hwy, to the north of Bulahdelah, then right into Stoney Creek Rd. **O'Sullivans Gap Flora Reserve** is also located in the Wang Wauk Forest, offering bushwalking and picnic facilities.
VISITOR INFORMATION: Cnr Pacific Hwy and Crawford St, Ph: (02) 4997 4981

■ Byron Bay   POP 6135
Map 84, D1
One of Australia's most fashionable and popular holiday destinations, Byron Bay is renowned for its balmy climate and excellent surfing beaches—it is also a popular area for scuba diving. A whaling town in the 1950s, Byron Bay is now full of galleries, boutiques, cafes and 'new age' shops, reflecting the holiday atmosphere and alternative lifestyle of the town. It is such a popular tourist destination, in summer the locals are frequently outnumbered by the tourists.
MAIN ATTRACTIONS. **Cape Byron**, a rocky promontory 107m high, is the most easterly point in Australia. **Cape Byron Lighthouse** beams its light over 40km out to sea. A walking trail leads past the lighthouse to the tip of the Cape and the amazing coastal views. In July, humpback whales can be seen as they migrate up the coast and then seen again in September, **Whale Festival** time, when they make their return journey. Exclusive **Wategos Beach** is wholly north-facing and therefore very popular with surfers.
NEARBY ATTRACTIONS: **Bangalow**, south-west of Byron Bay, is an interesting little village offering antique, craft and coffee shops.
VISITOR INFORMATION: 80 Jonson St, Ph: (02) 6680 8558

■ Canowindra   POP 1660
Map 118, D5
Hot-air balloons floating silently overhead have earned this **Central West** town the title '**Balloon Capital of Australia**'. Canowindra lies in

a natural basin on the **Belubula River**, 335km west of Sydney. The weather is almost always calm and conditions are usually ideal for balloon flights over the countryside.
MAIN ATTRACTIONS: There are two local balloon flight operators and many people travel to Canowindra for this experience alone. An interesting time to visit is during **Marti's Balloon Fiesta**, a special four-day annual event, held in April, attracting thousands of visitors. **Gaskill St**, Canowindra's main street, follows the route of an old bullock track. It is lined with early commercial buildings and is classified by the National Trust as a Heritage Conservation Area. There are many antique shops, a local memorabilia museum and a gallery offering quality crafts. One of the great fossil sites in Australia was

discovered between Canowindra and **Gooloogong** in 1955. Approximately 3500 fossils, dating to 360 million years, have been recovered, many of them complete. Seven new species have been discovered, with more expected. The collection is displayed at the **Age of Fishes Museum**, in Gaskill St, open daily and most holidays.
NEARBY ATTRACTIONS: Canowindra lies in Cabonne Shire, a rich agricultural district famous for the abundance and quality of its fresh produce. Many shops provide the opportunity to sample all kinds of locally grown food. Bushwalking, historic sites and highly regarded wineries can be experienced in the surrounding areas.
VISITOR INFORMATION: Age of Fishes Museum, Gaskill St, Ph: (02) 6344 1008

Cape Byron Lighthouse, at the most easterly point in Australia

A scenic two hour (180km) drive from Sydney, the Lower Hunter is one of Australia's premier wine-producing regions. The first vines were planted as far back as 1832 and medals for Hunter wines were won as early as 1882. Today, there are over 115 wineries, large and boutique, and many restaurants. Although only around 5% of Australia's wine comes from here, the Hunter is home to some of the most respected wineries, including **Draytons**, **Lindemans**, **McGuigan**, **Tyrrells** and **Tulloch**.

While the region is bursting with natural beauty, seams of high quality coal are found throughout the valley. Coal mining has been a pillar of the local economy, although the current focus is on wine tourism. **Maitland** is a main centre for the region and has a rich heritage, being one of colonial Australia's most important towns.

There is much to see and do in this region and while many may initially come to sample the fruits of the vine, it will not be just the wine that encourages their return.

main attractions

◈ **Hunter Valley Gardens**

25ha of spectacular display gardens next to a wine-theme village.

◈ **Koolang Observatory**

Nestled in bushland near Bucketty, this observatory offers viewings of the night sky.

◈ **Morpeth**

One of the most unspoilt heritage towns in New South Wales, the entire village of Morpeth has been classified by the National Trust.

◈ **Pokolbin**

Home to many wineries, both large and boutique, Pokolbin features the Hunter Valley Wine Society headquarters, a good starting point for a tour of the vineyards.

◈ **Richmond Vale Railway and Mining Museum**

This museum brings the era of steam locomotives to life.

◈ **Rusa Park Zoo**

See the only albino kangaroos in captivity, the white euros, at Rusa Park Zoo.

◈ **Wollombi**

This quaint country village includes the Endeavour Museum, cafes and antiques.

Church of The Immaculate Conception (1897), Morpeth

i Visitor information

Hunter Valley Wine Country Visitor Information Centre
455 Wine Country Dr, Pokolbin, NSW 2325
Ph: (02) 4990 4477
www.winecountry.com.au

Hunter Valley Harvest Festival

This is a perfect opportunity to experience wine-country culture and tradition at its best. After harvesting the crop (February to March), leading wineries toast their crop with banquets, lunches and dinners as well as more traditional activities like barrel tastings.

A wagon ride through the vines of the Lower Hunter Valley

New South Wales

0 _____ 3 Kilometres

Continued on map 119

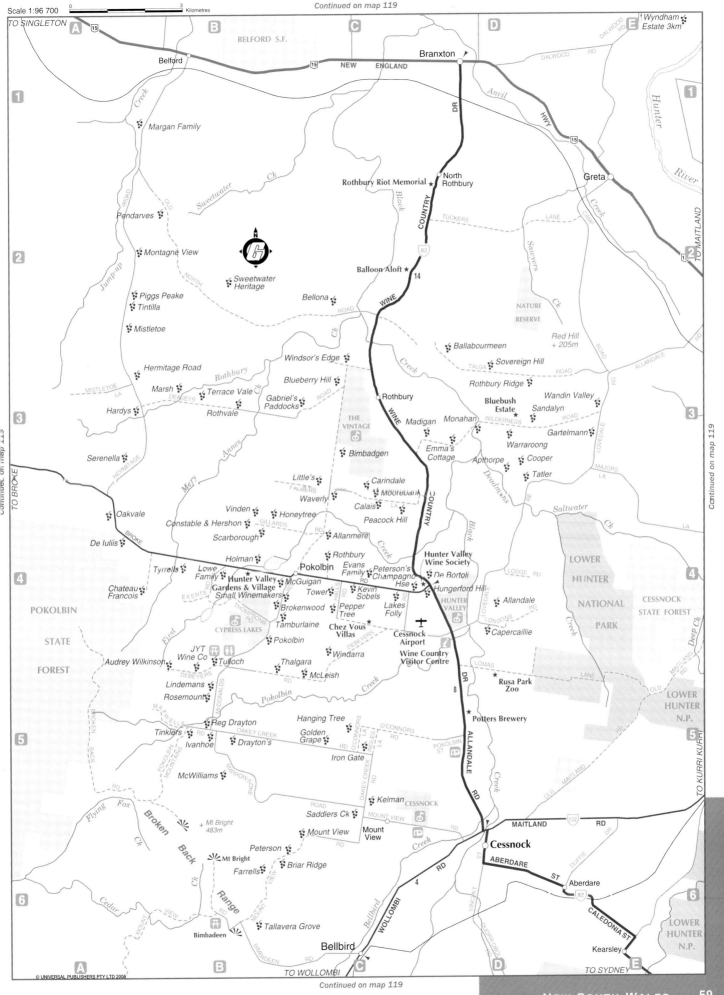

TO SINGLETON

BELFORD S.F.

Belford

NEW   ENGLAND

Branxton

Margan Family

Rothbury Riot Memorial ★ North Rothbury

Pendarves

Montagne View

Balloon Aloft ★ 14

Piggs Peake

Tintilla

Bellona

Sweetwater Heritage

Mistletoe

Ballabourmeen

NATURE RESERVE

Red Hill + 205m

Hermitage Road

Windsor's Edge

Sovereign Hill

Rothbury Ridge

Wandin Valley

Marsh

Blueberry Hill

Terrace Vale

Gabriel's Paddocks

Rothbury

Bluebush Estate

Sandalyn

Hardys

Rothvale

THE VINTAGE

Madigan

Monahan

Gartelmann

Serenella

Bimbadgen

Emma's Cottage

Warraroong

Apthorpe

Cooper

Little's

Carindale

Tatler

Vinden

Waverly

Moorebank

Calais

Oakvale

Honeytree

Peacock Hill

Constable & Hershon

Scarborough

Allanmere

De Iuliis

Holman

Rothbury

Hunter Valley Wine Society

LOWER HUNTER NATIONAL PARK

CESSNOCK STATE FOREST

Tyrrells

Lowe Family

Evans Family

Peterson's Champagne Hse

De Bortoli

Hungerford Hill

Pokolbin

McGuigan

Hunter Valley Gardens & Village

Small Winemakers

Tower

Kevin Sobels

Allandale

Chateau Francois

Brokenwood

Pepper Tree

Lakes Folly

HUNTER VALLEY

Capercaillie

POKOLBIN

Tamburlaine

Cypress Lakes

Pokolbin

Chez Vous Villas

Cessnock Airport

STATE

JYT Wine Co

Tulloch

Thalgara

Windarra

Wine Country Visitor Centre

FOREST

Audrey Wilkinson

McLeish

LOWER HUNTER N.P.

Lindemans

Rosemount

Pokolbin

Rusa Park Zoo

Reg Drayton

Hanging Tree

Potters Brewery

Tinklers

Golden Grape

Ivanhoe

Drayton's

Iron Gate

McWilliams

Kelman

CESSNOCK

Saddlers Ck

MAITLAND   RD

Mt Bright 483m

Mount View

Cessnock

Broken

Peterson

Mount View

ABERDARE

Mt Bright

Farrells

Briar Ridge

Aberdare

Range

Tallavera Grove

LOWER HUNTER N.P.

Bimbadeen

Bellbird

Kearsley

TO WOLLOMBI

TO SYDNEY

TO BROKE

Greta

TO MAITLAND

Hunter River

Wyndham Estate 3km

TO KURRI KURRI

Continued on map 119

The historic village of Wollombi, south-west of Cessnock

Casino   POP 9995

Map 115, H2

Casino is located on the **Richmond River** 733km north of Sydney. The town has about 20 parks attracting a variety of wildlife. While the surrounding land is rich in timber, Casino is primarily a beef-cattle town with a meatworks and tannery.

MAIN ATTRACTIONS: There are many historical buildings to be seen in Casino. The **public school**, built in 1861, and the **Court House** (in 1882) are located in Walker St. **Casino Historical Museum**, also in Walker St, exhibits mementos of pioneering days and a collection of early photographs. The museum is open Wednesdays and Sundays. You may be able to see wild platypus at **Platypus Pool**, downstream from Irving Bridge. **Jabiru Geneebeinga Wetlands**, next to the golf course in **North Casino**, has an abundance of birdlife, including black swans,

ducks, egrets and jabiru. On Sundays and public holidays, a **miniature railway** operates through the wetlands area.

NEARBY ATTRACTIONS: Visitors can fossick for gold, labradorite, and smoky and clear quartz. Fishing for a variety of freshwater species is popular along the Richmond River.

VISITOR INFORMATION: 86 Centre St, Ph: (02) 6662 3566

Cessnock   POP 14 880

Map 59, D6

Once a major coal-mining centre, this **Hunter Valley** city now attracts tourists who are visiting the wineries of the **Pokolbin** area just a short distance away.

MAIN ATTRACTIONS: Excellent food and wine are available throughout the region. There are also many antique shops, craft outlets and galleries worthwhile visiting. For thrill seekers there are skydiving flights and hot-air balloon flights available.

NEARBY ATTRACTIONS: The historic village of **Wollombi**, south-west of Cessnock, has many old sandstone buildings. The **Endeavour Museum** occupies the old Police Station and is generally open weekends. **Broke** is another historic village. Here, there is an interesting pioneer cemetery and several buildings dating back to the 1840s. South of Cessnock are the **Watagan Mountains**, where the walking tracks lead to views and attractive picnic and BBQ areas. There are over 115 wineries in the Lower Hunter area and these can be explored either by driving to the vineyards, or organising coach, chauffeur-driven, bicycle, horse-drawn or 4-wheel drive tours.

VISITOR INFORMATINO: 455 Wine Country Dr, Pokolbin, Ph: (02) 4990 4477

Cobar   POP 4525

Map 117, J1

Cobar is known for the mineral wealth—copper, zinc, lead and silver—extracted from its mines. The Great Cobar mine closed in 1919 but the opening up of new mining ventures in more recent times has seen Cobar become prosperous once again. Wool is also a local industry. The town is 723km north-west of Sydney and is a popular rest stop on the way to **Broken Hill**.

MAIN ATTRACTIONS: Brochures on self-guided **heritage walks** are available from the information centre. There are also heritage tours by bus. The **Great Western Hotel** in Marshall St has the longest iron-lace verandah in New South Wales. There is a **water recreation area** accessed off Knight Dr, where visitors can enjoy swimming, picnics, waterskiing and birdwatching in a relaxing setting.

NEARBY ATTRACTIONS: **Mount Drysdale**, a ghost mining town 30km north on the Kidman Way, was once home to 6000 people. Stone foundations are all that is left of the town.

Mount Grenfell Historic Site has Aboriginal cave paintings and is located 40km west of Cobar on the Barrier Hwy.

VISITOR INFORMATION: Great Cobar Heritage Centre, Barrier Hwy, Ph: (02) 6836 2448

Coffs Harbour   POP 25 850

Map 62, D3

A very attractive holiday destination, Coffs Harbour is in an area of contrasts: beaches, high mountains, dense rainforest and banana plantations.

MAIN ATTRACTIONS: Long stretches of sand and surf have been drawing visitors to Coffs Harbour for decades. **Park**, **Jetty** and **Boambee beaches** edge the city, and to the north some hideaway beaches include **Moonee**, **Emerald** and **Sandy**. The **Big Banana** theme park is perhaps the most popular tourist attraction. Hard to miss with its huge concrete banana on the Pacific Hwy, it is open daily. There are plantation tours, hydroponics exhibitions, a toboggan run, banana barn, food, souvenirs and a lookout; something for the whole family to enjoy. The **Pet Porpoise Pool** has performing dolphins and sea-lions,

with daily shows. There is also a native fauna sanctuary and a reef tank. **Muttonbird Island Nature Reserve** is an excellent spot to see whales and muttonbirds in season.

NEARBY ATTRACTIONS: **Coffs Harbour Zoo**, located 10 minutes drive to the north, allows visitors to hand-feed kangaroos and waterbirds, see a koala presentation, visit the animal nursery and walk through a rain-forest aviary. **Bruxner Park Flora Reserve**, 9km north-west of Coffs Harbour has a walking track through a mass of vines, ferns and orchids. The **Vincent Tree** (flooded gum) is a major attraction, and from **Sealy Lookout** there are panoramic views of the city, coastline and hills. **Dorrigo NP** is in the hinterland ranges and there are many rainforest walks, with a diversity of flora and fauna. **George's Goldmine** is located near **Coramba**, 40km north-west of Coffs Harbour and offers a guided tour into a tunnel mine and demonstrations of a working stamper battery. There are also picnic areas and food is available.

VISITOR INFORMATION: Cnr Pacific Hwy and McLean St, Ph: (02) 6652 1522

Condobolin   POP 3110

Map 118, A4

Located on the **Lachlan River**, Condobolin is near the geographic centre of New South Wales. It is the service centre for the surrounding pastoral district that produces wheat, wool, lambs, fruit and cotton.

MAIN ATTRACTIONS: The **Community Crafts Centre** in Denison St is located in what was the old bar of the Commercial Hotel. **Memorial Park**, beside the river bridge, is a shady picnic area.

NEARBY ATTRACTIONS: A monument marking the burial place of an Aborigine, believed to have been a Lachlan chief, stands beside the road 40km west of Condobolin. In the area are other **Aboriginal sites**, waterholes and grooved rocks. **Gum Bend Lake** is a small recreation area for swimming, sailing, wind-surfing and limited-power boating. Located 4km west, it was created by diverting water from the Lachlan River. **Lake Cargolligo**, 89km to the west, is one of the largest inland lake systems in New South Wales, with three linked lakes suitable for boating and birdwatching.

VISITOR INFORMATION: 18 William St, Ph: (02) 6895 3301

Cooma   POP 7160

Map 122, C4

Being the gateway to the **Snowy Mountains** resorts and **Kosciuszko NP**, and located at the junction of two highways linking **Canberra**, the coast and the mountains, Cooma is a busy tourist centre. The town is also the administrative centre for the **Snowy Mountains Hydro-Electric Scheme**.

MAIN ATTRACTIONS: **Centennial Park** is particularly worthwhile visiting. There is the **International Avenue of Flags** in honour of the people from 27 nations who worked on the Snowy River Scheme in the 1950s; a statue of Banjo Paterson's *Man From Snowy River*; and the

A bottlenose dolphin, *Tursiops truncatus*, at play at the Pet Porpoise Pool, Coffs Harbour

Scale 1:360 000

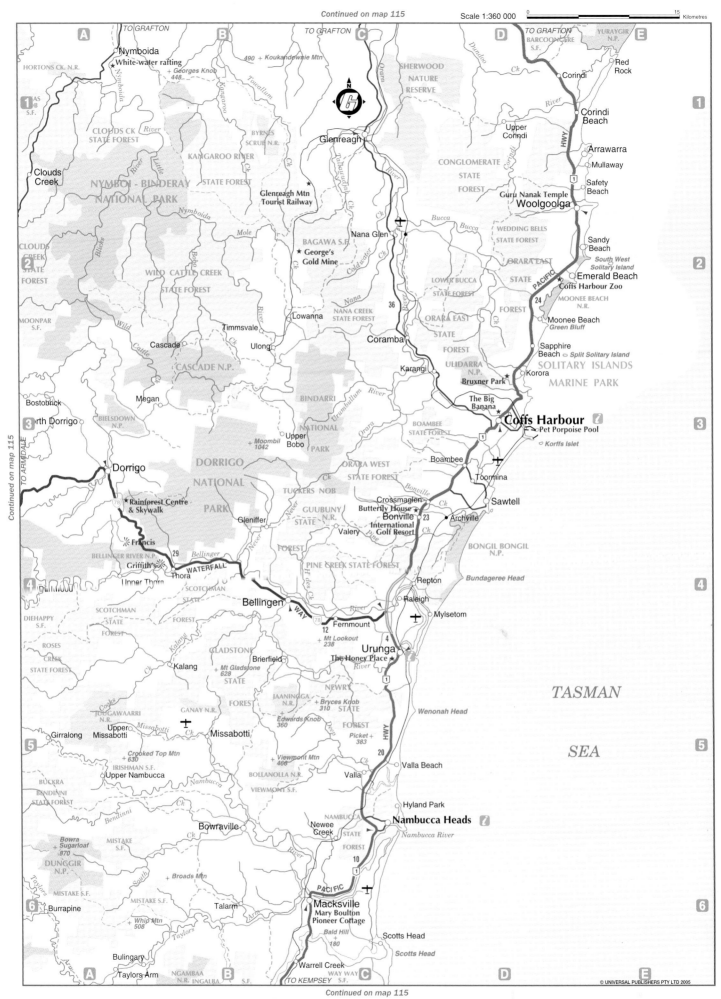

Continued on map 115

© UNIVERSAL PUBLISHERS PTY LTD 2005

Monaro Time Walk, a series of 40 mosaic murals depicting the history of the region. **Nannygoat Hill** is a reserve in the centre of Cooma with a 360° view of the Monaro district and the Snowy Mountains. **Mount Gladstone** also offers a panoramic view. Cooma's oldest street, Lambie St, has many buildings classified by the National Trust. These can be seen on the self-guided **Lambie Town Walk**—a 5km walk beginning at the visitors centre. Cooma's original Anglican Church, **Christ Church**, built in 1845, can be seen in Church Rd. **Cooma Monaro Tourist Railway** runs railmotor excursions to Bunyan and Chakola from Cooma Station on weekends and some weekdays.

NEARBY ATTRACTIONS: **Kosciuszko NP** incorporates much of the New South Wales section of the **Great Dividing Range**, west of Cooma, and contains Australia's highest point, **Mount Kosciuszko**, rising to 2228m. The park is a popular winter destination for skiers and a summer destination for bushwalkers and campers.

VISITOR INFORMATION: 119 Sharp St, Ph: (02) 6450 1742 or 1800 636 525

■ Coonabarabran   POP 3020
Map 114, B6

Coonabarabran is an agricultural town located 550km north-west of Sydney. The town started developing after an inn was built beside a crossing on the **Castlereagh River**. From the mid 1850s until the turn of the century, flour mills were important to the local economy. Today, timber and sheep are the other main agricultural activities.

MAIN ATTRACTIONS: At Coonabarabran Information Centre, visitors can see the full skeleton of a **diprotodon**—the largest known marsupial ever to have lived. The fossilised bones were found in the area and are believed to be approximately 35 000 years old. **Crystal Kingdom**, on the Oxley Hwy, displays minerals from Australia and overseas and is open daily.

NEARBY ATTRACTIONS: 35km west of Coonabarabran is **Warrumbungle NP**. The rock formations are the result of volcanic activity 13 million years ago. Warrumbungle NP Visitors Centre has walking trail maps and camping information and is open daily. North of Coonabarabran lies an area of wild forest and scrubland known as the **Pilliga Scrub**. Displays of wildflowers are common here between August and December and there is a series of small caves in the sandstone ridges and outcrops. **Pilliga Pottery and Bush Cafe**, located in the scrub, specialises in terracotta pots and ornamental figurines. Coonabarabran is known as the '**Astronomy Capital of Australia**', with the area being home to **Siding Spring Observatory**, which has the largest optical telescope in Australia. At **Skywatch Night and Day Observatory**, visitors can view the stars and play Astro Mini Golf

VISITOR INFORMATION: Newell Hwy, Ph: (02) 6842 1441 or 1800 242 881

■ Cootamundra   POP 5880
Map 122, A2

This crop-growing and grazing district 94km north-east of **Wagga Wagga**, was the birthplace of Sir Donald Bradman. Cootamundra is famous for the wattle that bears its name, and a special time to visit Cootamundra is **Wattle Time**, July and August, to see the vivid colour displayed throughout the town.

MAIN ATTRACTIONS: The information centre has brochures describing walking tours around Cootamundra. These include the **Two-Foot Tour**, a one to two hour walking tour of the town's main sites; and the **Captain's Walk**, which includes a walk through **Jubilee Park** to see the busts of 11 famous cricketers. **Bradman's Birthplace** is a stop on the Two-Foot Tour—it was the nursing home where Sir Donald

Bushwalkers on Crater Bluff, Warrumbungle National Park, west of Coonabarabran

was born. It is now a museum furnished in period-style and with displays of Bradman cricketing memorabilia. Located at 89 Admas St, it is open weekends and public holidays. The focal point of the CBD is **Bicentennial Post Office Plaza**, which incorporates the historic Post Office building and clocktower. The grand old Railway Station has been refurbished and is also a busy Countrylink rail and coach connection.

NEARBY ATTRACTIONS: For picnics and walks to get panoramic views, visitors shouldn't miss **Pioneer Park** which is a natural reserve on the southern outskirts of town. Around **Harden**, 37km north-east of Cootamundra, there are wineries offering tastings and sales.

VISITOR INFORMATION: Railway Station Complex, Hovell St, Ph: (02) 6942 4212

▦ Corowa   POP 5170

Map 121, J4

A rich wheat-growing district surrounds the New South Wales town of Corowa, located on the northern bank of the **Murray River**. The town was the birthplace of Australia's Federation. On the other side of the river is the Victorian town of **Wahgunyah**, joined to Corowa by the **John Foord Bridge**.

MAIN ATTRACTIONS: Watersports are popular, including boating, waterskiing and fishing. Heritage buildings with iron-lace balconies, built in the heyday of the river trade, line Corowa's **Sanger St** and give the town its character. The historic **Court House** has an important place in Australian history. It was here during the 1893 Federation Conference Meeting that the decision was made to draw up a constitution for the new nation. **Corowa Federation Museum** focuses on the full history of the Federation movement and also displays a collection of farming implements and machinery from

A section of the beautifully-landscaped Japanese Garden at Cowra

the early part of the 20th century. A collection of works by the Australian artist **Tom Roberts** is housed here, along with sketches by Aboriginal artist **Tommy McRae**.

NEARBY ATTRACTIONS: The wineries of the **Rutherglen** district are within a 15km radius of Corowa. Several wineries have restaurants attached. **All Saints Estate** is one of the most historic wineries in the district, located across the Murray River 5km south-east at Wahgunyah.

VISITOR INFORMATION: 88 Sanger St, Ph: (02) 6033 3221 or 1800 814 054

▦ Cowra   POP 8700

Map 118, D5

Located on the **Lachlan River**, 311km west of Sydney, Cowra is a busy country town. Part of a thriving farming district, much of the New South Wales asparagus crop, tomatoes and corn are processed at the local cannery. Cowra is also well-known for its **wineries**. A number of vineyards are open for wine tasting and cellar door sales.

MAIN ATTRACTIONS: Every September Cowra celebrates the **Cherry**

Blossom Festival. Flowering cherry trees line Sakura Ave, a walkway linking the Japanese Garden to the POW camp and on to the Japanese Cemetery. The largest prisoner-of-war breakout of modern military history occurred on August 5 1944, in Cowra. The remains of the prison camp and the site of the breakout are open to the public, as are the **Japanese** and **Australian War Cemeteries**. The beautifully landscaped **Japanese Garden and Cultural Centre** was donated by the Japanese Government and is renowned as one of the biggest and best Japanese gardens in the world. The Cultural Centre displays Japanese art and pottery, a traditional open-air Tea House, cabana restaurant and bonsai house. The garden is open daily. There are many parks with picnic and BBQ facilities to enjoy, both alongside the Lachlan River and around the town.

NEARBY ATTRACTIONS: **Conimbla NP** is a small park in two sections, located west of Cowra. Spring is the best time to visit and see the wildflowers, which are seen on two walks. Both walks commence from a car park adjacent to Barryrennie Rd.

VISITOR INFORMATION: Olympic Park, Mid Western Hwy, Ph: (02) 6342 4333

Crescent Head   POP 1180
Map 115, H6

This small **North Coast** resort town lies 19km south-east of Kempsey. National parks protect the coastline, both to the north and south. To the south, sandy beaches stretch all the way to **Port Macquarie**. The beaches of Crescent Head are excellent for surfing, swimming and fishing.

MAIN ATTRACTIONS: Facilities in the town include a country club with a six-hole waterfront golf course. **Killick Beach** is renowned as a board-riding and bodysurfing beach, whereas **Killick Creek** is sheltered and ideal for young children.

NEARBY ATTRACTIONS: **Hat Head NP** is full of birdlife, with the wetlands and lagoons providing breeding grounds for several species of waterbirds. Inland, the dry, open forest provides ideal nesting conditions for falcons and hawks. The national park also comprises a coastal strip of high dunes. The park is popular for fishing, swimming, bushwalking, camping and picnicking. Many visitors walk to **Korogoro Point** to spot whales (in season). An unsealed (mostly 4-wheel drive) road links Crescent Head with Port Macquarie and gives access to beautiful lonely beaches and rustic camping sites.

VISITOR INFORMATION: Pacific Hwy, South Kempsey, Ph: (02) 6563 1555

Crookwell   POP 2020
Map 122, C1

Situated high in the **Great Dividing Range**, 230km south-west of Sydney, Crookwell is the centre of some of Australia's best agricultural and pastoral land. It is also the birthplace of the Australian potato industry (1828). High quality fine wool, lambs, beef, apples and pears are also produced and there is an abundance of trout streams, stunning gardens and a wind farm.

MAIN ATTRACTIONS: The unusual Christmas shop **Santa's Hideaway** is open from April to December. **Linder's Sock Factory**, in the main street, is a great place to visit with socks at factory-direct prices.

NEARBY ATTRACTIONS: There are many historic villages in the area, which were once associated with gold and bushranging. These villages, all north of Crookwell, include **Roslyn**, **Tuena**, **Peelwood**, **Laggan**, **Bigga** and **Binda**. **Wombeyan Caves** is located 60km north-east and there are five caves open to the public, including a cave for self-guided tours. **Sheck Webster Lookout** at **Snowy Mount**, 42km north-west on the Bigga Rd, offers a scenic view of the surrounding countryside. For experienced walkers, the climb up **Decca Hill** (at **Grabine Lakeside State Park**, 65km north-west) provides views of **Wyangala Dam** and the surrounding countryside.

VISITOR INFORMATION : 106 Goulburn St, Ph: (02) 4832 1988

Deniliquin   POP 7825
Map 121, G3

Situated on the **Edward River**, this southern **Riverina** town is surrounded by extensively irrigated farmland producing wheat, canola, barley, sheep, pigs and cattle. Wool and rice are the region's main products, with the rice processed at **Deniliquin Mill**, the largest rice mill in the Southern Hemisphere.

MAIN ATTRACTIONS: The **Island Sanctuary**, opposite the town hall in End St, has free-roaming kangaroos and other wildlife in the heart of Deniliquin. A brochure about a self-guided **historical and nature walk** is available at the information centre. On the Hay Road north of town is **Pioneer Tourist Park**. The park incorporates a garden centre; craft gallery; and a display of restored antique steam

Aerial view of Hat Head National Park, near Crescent Head

engines, petrol pumps and pioneer pumping equipment from the Snowy Mountains Scheme, Deniliquin and South Australia.

NEARBY ATTRACTIONS: The **Conargo Pub**, located 25km north-east, has a gallery of photographs showing the history of merino wool in the area. There is also a winery close by.

VISITOR INFORMATION: Peppin Heritage Centre, George St, Ph: (03) 5898 3120

Dorrigo   POP 1015

Map 62, A3

This **North Coast** timber town lies 40km west of Coffs Harbour. Dorrigo is a relaxed and friendly town set amidst majestic scenery.

MAIN ATTRACTIONS: Local artists display their work at the **Art Place**, an art gallery in Cudgery St. The **Art of the Country**, a craft gallery, is next door. **Dorrigo and Guy Fawkes Historical Museum** is run by the local historical society. Located in Myrtle St, it is open Wednesday, Friday, Saturday, Sunday and all school holidays. **Griffith's Lookout** is probably the district's best view—looking over the mountains, out to sea and as far as **Kempsey** and **Armidale**. To reach it, turn off

at the Waterfall Way, near Dorrigo Lookout Motor Inn.

NEARBY ATTRACTIONS: **Dangar Falls** on the Bielsdown River are 2km to the north. **Dorrigo NP** is a World Heritage-listed rainforest park located a few kilometres south-east. At the **Rainforest Centre** visitors will find a shop, exhibition and cafe. Don't miss the **Skywalk**, a tree-top canopy walk and lookout platform hanging over the edge of the escarpment. There are several other national parks nearby including **New England**, **Bellinger River**, **Guy Fawkes River** and **Cathedral Rock**.

VISITOR INFORMATION: Hickory St, Ph: (02) 6657 2486

Dubbo   POP 30 990

Map 118, D2

Known as the **'Hub of the West'**, the rural city of Dubbo is a busy road, rail and air junction on the **Macquarie River**. The city is located about halfway between Melbourne and Brisbane and just over 400km from Sydney. The surrounding areas support pigs, sheep, cattle stud farms and produce wheat, fodder, cotton, wool, fruit and vegetables.

MAIN ATTRACTIONS: **Old Dubbo Gaol** is a major attraction in the heart of the city. Open daily, this sandstone gaol was built around 1871 and operated until 1966 when it was turned into a museum. **Dubbo Regional Art Gallery** has a permanent collection of works based on the theme 'Animals in Art', and presents regular touring exhibitions. Located at the corner of Macquarie St and Talbragar St, the gallery is open daily.

NEARBY ATTRACTIONS: There are several major attractions on the southern outskirts of Dubbo. **Western Plains Zoo** is perhaps the best-known attraction. There are more than 800 exotic and native animals in open exhibits. You can walk, cycle or drive around the 6km of sealed roads and walking trails. The National Trust property **Dundullimal** is in the same area as the zoo. Guided audio tours describe the timber-slab farmhouse (1840), one of the earliest surviving squatter's homesteads in the country. The homestead is open daily. **Dubbo Military Museum** (Dubbo Big M) on the Newell Hwy is open daily. There is a good display of WWII memorabilia, and a Jurassic Supermaze hands-on science exhibit. **Dubbo Observatory** has state-of-the-art computerised telescopes (bookings are essential due to weather conditions). **Miniland Dubbo** is a dinosaur-themed fun park for children, open Friday to Sunday and school holidays. There are also several local **wineries**.

VISITOR INFORMATION: Cnr Macquarie St and Erskine St, Ph: (02) 6884 1422

Dungog   POP 2185

Map 119, H3

First settled in the 1820s, Dungog is 225km from Sydney. This rural township is the service centre for surrounding logging, dairying, beef cattle and deer-farming industries.

Bengal tiger—one of many exotic animals at Western Plains Zoo, Dubbo

Dungog is also on the main southern route into **Barrington Tops NP**. This World Heritage-listed park offers a diversity of landscapes, including subtropical rainforests with refreshing clear-water rivers on a mountainous plateau. At approximately 1000m are spectacular **Antarctic beech forests**. There are many walking tracks to beautiful waterfalls and lookouts. Camping is permitted at a number of designated camping areas.

NEARBY ATTRACTIONS: **Chichester Dam** and **Chichester State Forest** lie 23km north of Dungog. The dam, opened in 1985, has picnic areas and walking trails. **Telegherry Forest Park**, located 30km north, offers walking trails along the **Telegherry River** with picnic, swimming and camping spots. One of the first European settlements in Australia, **Clarence Town** historical village is 24km south of Dungog.

VISITOR INFORMATION: Cnr Dowling St and Brown St, Ph: (02) 4992 2212

▨ Eden   POP 3150

Map 122, D6

Approximately 50km from the Victorian border, the fishing port of Eden is the southern gateway to the **South Coast**. A deepwater port and tourist centre with many attractions, Eden has a long history founded on the whaling industry, which flourished from 1818 until the 1930s.

MAIN ATTRACTIONS: Eden lies on the northern shore of **Twofold Bay**. **Eden Killer Whale Museum**, in Imlay St, features a skeleton of 'Tom the killer whale', which assisted early whalers. Whale-watching (southern right, minke, humpback and killer), between September and November is very popular; there are two viewing platforms along **Aslings Beach**.

NEARBY ATTRACTIONS: **Ben Boyd NP** is in two sections, covering the rocky coastline either side of Twofold Bay. The park offers scenic views, bushwalking, fishing, swimming and

wreck diving. **The Pinnacles** is an arresting red and white earth formation within the park. **Boyd's Tower**—a private lighthouse built with sandstone shipped from Sydney—is a highlight of the southern section of the park. **Davidson Whaling Station Historic Site**, 30km south on **Kiah Inlet**, is another local attraction.

VISITOR INFORMATION: The Roundabout, Princes Hwy, Ph: (02) 6496 1953

▨ Forbes   POP 7470

Map 118, C4

The centre of a prosperous farming district, located on the **Lachlan River**, Forbes is a town of historic buildings, parks and gardens. This former gold-mining town is located near where bushranger **Ben Hall** was shot by police in 1865.

MAIN ATTRACTIONS: **Forbes Historical Museum** in Cross St (open daily) was once a music hall. A large exhibit is devoted to the bushranging days of Ben Hall. **Forbes cemetery**, located in Bogan Gate Rd, has the graves of Ben Hall, Kate Foster (Ned Kelly's sister), and Rebecca Shields (Capt Cook's niece). Also worthwhile is a self-guided walk of the town's historic buildings, most of which are in **Court St** and **Lachlan St**. An historic buildings walk leaflet is available from the information centre in Union St.

NEARBY ATTRACTIONS: **Gum Swamp Wildlife Sanctuary** is 4km west of Forbes on the Newell Hwy. Here it is possible to view 60 to 70 species of birds within a few hours.

VISITOR INFORMATION: Railway Arts and Craft Centre, Union St, Ph: (02) 6852 4155

▨ Forster   POP 12 250

Map 119, K3

The twin towns of **Forster** and **Tuncurry** lie at the entrance to **Wallis Lake**, on either side of the **Wallamba River**. Part of the **Great Lakes** holiday region, Forster has long been popular for family

Coloured sands of The Pinnacles, Ben Boyd National Park, north of Eden

holidays, as it is a comfortable four hour drive from Sydney and is renowned for its clean, clear beaches, pristine waterways and fresh seafood. Oysters are a local specialty

MAIN ATTRACTIONS: Beach, estuary, lake and river fishing attract large numbers of visitors, especially in the winter months. Local tourist brochures offer tips on where to catch bream, flathead, whiting and tailor. Alternatively, you can enjoy fresh seafood at many of the local restaurants. The **Bicentennial Walk** links **Forster Main Beach** with **One Mile Beach**. An overall view of Forster-Tuncurry can be seen during this walk, from the **Scenic Platform** at **Bennetts Head**. **The Curtis Collection**—a museum exhibiting vintage to rare modern cars, horse-drawn vehicles, Cyclops toys and gramophones—is located in Angel Close, off Macintosh St. The **Great Lakes Historical Museum,** with fascinating local exhibits, is in Capel St, across the Wallamba River bridge in Tuncurry.

NEARBY ATTRACTIONS: **Booti Booti NP** covers the coastal strip between Forster to the north and **Pacific Palms** to the south. Many walking tracks lead to magnificent coastal views. Picnic areas are located around **Wallis Lake** where visitors can enjoy the many different watersports. At **Tiona**, 15km south, the open-air **Green Cathedral** is a consecrated church on the shores of Wallis Lake. Cabbage palms form the roof of the church and logs the seats, while the lake is a backdrop to the stone altar.

VISITOR INFORMATION: Little St, Ph: (02) 6554 8799

■ Gilgandra   POP 2822
Map 118, D2

This town is the centre of one of the best wheat-growing and wool-producing areas in New South Wales. Also produced are other cereal, oil seed and legume crops, lambs and cattle. Aquaculture is in the early stages of expansion. Located by the **Castlereagh River**, Gilgandra is 435km north-west of Sydney.

MAIN ATTRACTIONS: Before 1966, when the town water supply was connected, Gilgandra was famous for its many windmills, used for pumping water to residents' homes. Most were removed when town water was connected, but as a reminder, some of the old windmills now form an **Avenue of Windmills** from **Coo-ee March Memorial Park** along to the riverbank picnic area. The **Coo-Ee Heritage Centre** in the park houses the visitors centre, and four display areas, including a special collection dedicated to the **Coo-ee March** (1915) from Gilgandra to Sydney. The aim was to recruit men along the route willing to fight in WW1. **Orana Cactus World**

has a large collection of cacti, which has taken local grower Lester Meyers more than 40 years to accumulate. It is open most weekends or by appointment. The privately operated **Gilgandra Observatory** is a big attraction. Visitors are able to safely view sunspots and the stars through the 31cm-diameter telescope.

NEARBY ATTRACTIONS: Wildflowers and shrubs, including rare and ancient plants, grow in **Gilgandra Native Flora Reserve**. It is most spectacular during the spring-flowering period (August–October). To the north, **Warrumbungle NP**, with its volcanic pipes, is an ideal place for bushwalkers, birdwatchers and nature lovers.

VISITOR INFORMATION:

Coo-ee March Memorial Park, Newell Hwy, Ph: (02) 6847 2045

■ Glen Innes   POP 6105
Map 115, F3

The historic town of Glen Innes is perched high in the **New England Range** and surrounded by rich, rolling countryside. In the past it was often the scene of bushranger activity. The surrounding area produces wool, sheep, beef, honey, timber and yields sapphires, tin and other minerals.

MAIN ATTRACTIONS: Glen Innes is also known for its beautiful parklands, restored heritage buildings, and as the home of the **Australian Standing Stones**. A **walking tour** brochure is available from the information centre. On the corner of Mackenzie St and New England Hwy is the **Cooramah Aboriginal Cultural Centre**. Visitors can see Aboriginal arts and crafts, historic artefacts and there is a restaurant with bush tucker. **Land of the Beardies History House** also houses quality pioneering and cultural displays.

NEARBY ATTRACTIONS: Fossicking for gemstones has attracted many visitors to the district.

One of Gilgandra's colourful windmills

The information centre has details of what to look for, where to find gemstones in public fossicking areas and the equipment required. Popular places include **Emmaville**, 39km north and **Torrington**, 66km north. Fishing for trout, perch and cod is popular and at **Deepwater**, 40km north of Glen Innes on the New England Hwy, fishing safaris can be booked. World Heritage-listed **Washpool NP** and **Gibraltar Range NP** are located 75km east and are mostly areas of rainforest wilderness.

VISITOR INFORAMTION: 152 Church St, Ph: (02) 6732 2397

▦ Gloucester   POP 2682

Map 119, J2

This town lies in the sheltered valley of the **Gloucester River** and is surrounded by agricultural land ideal for beef and dairying. The main access road is the Bucketts Way, named after the unusual chain of hills known as **The Bucketts** that forms a backdrop to the town.

MAIN ATTRACTIONS: **Billabong Native Garden** in Denison St has a diverse range of flora and is an ideal spot for picnics and BBQs. Maps describing the town's **historic walk** are available from the information centre. Insights into local history can be found in the **Folk Museum**. Housed in the old Council Chambers in Church St, the museum is open Tuesdays, Thursdays and Saturdays.

NEARBY ATTRACTIONS: Gloucester is often considered the '**Base Camp of the Barringtons**', making this World Heritage-listed national park worthwhile exploring from the town. The rivers and streams in the area provide some of the best canoeing in New South Wales. In the fresh-water streams fish, including trout and perch, abound. There are scenic drives and walks in the surrounding countryside and scattered throughout are picnic and camping spots, and a number of old

Ferns in temperate rainforest, Barrington Tops National Park, near Gloucester

timber and gold-mining settlements. In the 1870s, gold was discovered at nearby **Copeland** and the workings of the old **Mountain Maid Gold Mine** can be seen. There is a walking track from the car park and visiting times for the mine are normally Wednesday to Sunday and school holidays.

VISITOR INFORMATION: 27 Denison St, Ph: (02) 6558 1408

▦ Gosford   POP 25 700

Map 71, B4

This Central Coast regional centre for commerce and industry is a popular tourist destination. It has also become a commuter suburb for the Sydney region.

MAIN ATTRACTIONS: Gosford offers easy access to the sheltered waters of **Brisbane Water**, **Broken Bay** and the **Hawkesbury River**, all presenting fishing and boating opportunities. Coastal beaches including **Pearl Beach** south of Woy Woy, and those stretching north from **MacMasters** to **Terrigal** are a major attraction.

NEARBY ATTRACTIONS: Covering a huge area south-west of Gosford, **Brisbane Water NP** offers opportunities for picnicking, fishing, bushwalking and photography. Many of the bushwalking tracks lead to lookouts with wonderful coastal views. The spring wildflowers are stunning. Also worth a visit is the **Bulgandry Aboriginal Engraving** site near **Kariong**. This collection of rock engravings is one of the best in the Sydney area. The renowned **Australian Reptile Park** is located at **Somersby**, 15km west of Gosford. Nearby **Somersby Falls** is an ideal place for a picnic.

VISITOR INFORMATION: 200 Mann St, Ph: 1300 130 708

▦ Goulburn   POP 21 300

Map 122, D2

Claimed as Australia's first inland city, Goulburn is the major centre of the **Southern Tablelands**. The surrounding country is famous for wool production and there are several well-known studs in the area. Goulburn has five big wool

THE CENTRAL COAST

Close proximity to **Sydney** and easy accessibility via fast freeways has ensured the Central Coast's development as a prime holiday destination. Characterised by large, calm saltwater lagoons, connected to the ocean via a number of small waterways, with an array of excellent beaches on the coastline, this area is a haven for watersports. Swimming, fishing and surfing opportunities abound, charter cruises and hire boats are available on all major bodies of water, and it is also possible to rent a houseboat on **Lake Macquarie**, the region's largest lake.

Much of the Central Coast is covered by national parks, where bushwalking, camping and picnicking are popular pastimes. **Gosford** is the hub of the Central Coast, while a number of smaller townships such as **Patonga** and **Umina** offer seaside retreats.

main attractions

- Australian Reptile Park
- Australian Rainforest Sanctuary, Ourimbah
- Brisbane Water National Park
- Bouddi National Park
- Bulgandry Aboriginal Engraving site
- Calga Springs Sanctuary
- Glenworth Valley horseriding
- Terrigal
- The Entrance
- The Fragrant Garden, Erina
- Watagans National Park

 Visitor information

Central Coast Tourism
200 Mann St, Gosford, NSW 2250
Rotary Park, Terrigal Dr, Terrigal, NSW 2260
Marine Pde, The Entrance, NSW 2261
Tollfree: 1300 130 708
www.visitcentralcoast.com.au

Bouddi National Park, Central Coast

The Big Merino, Goulburn

stores and one of the largest live-stock markets in New South Wales.
MAIN ATTRACTIONS: **Goulburn Regional Art Gallery**, in the Civic Centre, exhibits a wide range of arts and crafts. The gallery is open every day except Sunday and most public holidays. **Belmore Park**, across the road from the information centre, is an attractive picnic area with gardens, large trees and a band rotunda. The **Big Merino** is a landmark that's hard to miss on the southern outskirts of Goulbourne. It includes a wool exhibit, merino gift shop, licensed restaurant, tavern and service station. Other points of interest include the **Old Goulburn Brewery** complex. Situated on Bungonia Rd, it now operates as a hotel and function centre. Heritage buildings include

Australia's oldest brewery, a steam-powered flour mill, a cooperage, a tobacco curing kiln, mews and workers' cottages. The complex is open daily from 11am and tours are available on Sundays.
NEARBY ATTRACTIONS: **Pelican Sheep Station** is located 10km from Goulburn on the **Braidwood Rd**. For visitors there are tours of the property and a souvenir shop.
VISITOR INFORMATION: 201 Sloane St, Ph: (02) 4823 4492

■ **Grafton**   POP 17 400
Map 115, H3
The **Clarence River** almost encircles the city of Grafton, the commercial and cultural centre of the **Clarence Valley**. Beef cattle, timber and tourism are the mainstays of the district, while

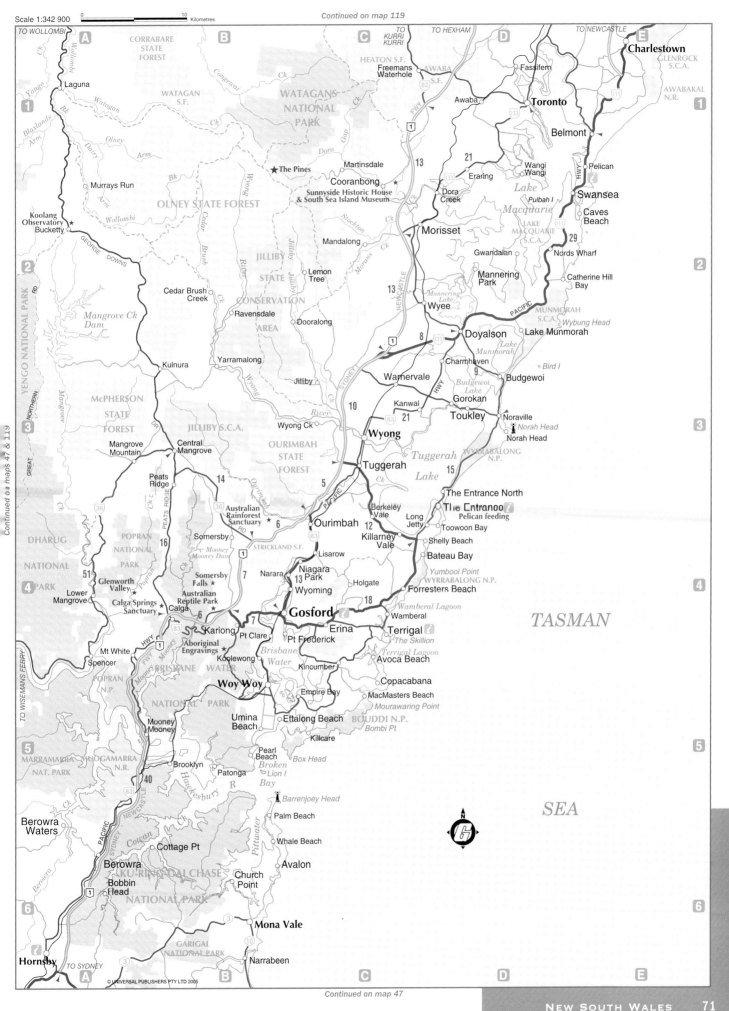

TO WOLLOMBI

CORRABARE
STATE
FOREST

WATAGAN S.F.

WATAGANS
NATIONAL
PARK

TO KURRI KURRI

TO HEXHAM

TO NEWCASTLE

Charlestown
GLENROCK
S.C.A.

HEATON S.F.
Freemans
Waterhole

Fassifern

AWABAKAL
N.R.

Laguna

Awaba

Toronto

Belmont

Murrays Run

The Pines

Martinsdale

Cooranbong

Sunnyside Historic House
& South Sea Island Museum

Eraring

Wangi
Wangi

Pelican

Lake
Macquarie

Swansea

Caves
Beach

OLNEY STATE FOREST

Dora
Creek

Pulbah I

Koolang
Observatory
Bucketty

Morisset

LAKE
MACQUARIE
S.C.A.

Nords Wharf

Mangrove Ck
Dam

Cedar Brush
Creek

Ravensdale

Lemon
Tree

Mandalong

Gwandalan

Mannering
Park

Catherine Hill
Bay

YENGO NATIONAL PARK

JILLIBY
STATE
CONSERVATION
AREA

Dooralong

Wyee

MUNMORAH
S.C.A.

Wybung Head

Kulnura

Yarramalong

Doyalson

Lake Munmorah

McPHERSON
STATE
FOREST

Jilliby

Warnervale

Charmhaven

Budgewoi

Budgewoi
Lake

Budgewoi

Mangrove
Mountain

Central
Mangrove

JILLIBY S.C.A.

Wyong Ck

Kanwal

Gorokan

Toukley

Bird I

Noraville

Norah Head

Wyong

Norah Head

Peats
Ridge

OURIMBAH
STATE
FOREST

Tuggerah

Tuggerah
Lake

WYRRABALONG
N.P.

DHARUG

Australian
Rainforest
Sanctuary

Somersby

Ourimbah

The Entrance North

The Entrance
Pelican feeding

NATIONAL

POPRAN
NATIONAL
PARK

Mooney
Mooney Dam

STRICKLAND S.F.

Lisarow

Berkeley
Vale

Killarney
Vale

Long
Jetty

Toowoon Bay

Shelly Beach

Bateau Bay

PARK

Glenworth
Valley

Somersby
Falls

Australian
Reptile Park

Narara

Niagara
Park

Wyoming

Holgate

Yumbool Point
WYRRABALONG N.P.

Lower
Mangrove

Calga Springs
Sanctuary

Calga

Gosford

Forresters Beach

Wamberal Lagoon

Wamberal

TASMAN

Kariong

Aboriginal
Engravings

Pt Clare

Erina

Pt Frederick

Terrigal

The Skillion

Mt White
Spencer

BRISBANE
WATER

Koolewong

Brisbane
Water

Kincumber

Terrigal Lagoon

Avoca Beach

NATIONAL PARK

Mooney
Mooney

Woy Woy

Empire Bay

Copacabana

MacMasters Beach

Mourawaring Point

MARRAMARRA
NAT. PARK

MOOGAMRRA
N.R.

Brooklyn

Umina
Beach

Ettalong Beach

Killcare

BOUDDI N.P.

Bombi Pt

Patonga

Pearl
Beach

Box Head

Broken

Lion I

Bay

SEA

Berowra
Waters

Cottage Pt

Barrenjoey Head

Palm Beach

Berowra

Bobbin
Head

KU-RING-GAI CHASE

Whale Beach

NATIONAL PARK

Avalon

Church
Point

Hornsby

TO SYDNEY

GARIGAL
NATIONAL PARK

Mona Vale

Narrabeen

© UNIVERSAL PUBLISHERS PTY LTD 2005

Gibraltar Range National Park, near Grafton

crops grown include maize, lucerne and sugarcane.

MAIN ATTRACTIONS: Known as the 'Jacaranda City', Grafton is famous for its many attractive parks and gardens and the broad streets lined with jacaranda trees. The **Jacaranda Festival** is held in October/November when the trees bloom, and attracts thousands of visitors. The parks remain worthwhile visiting at any time of the year, particularly **Market Square** in Prince St; **Memorial Park and Boulevard** at the river end of Prince St; and **See Park Arboretum** in Pound St.

NEARBY ATTRACTIONS: Grafton is centrally located for scenic drives to the fishing town of **Maclean**, on the Clarence River; **Glen Innes**, in the New England Ranges; and **Iluka**, **Yamba**, **Wooli** and **Coffs Harbour** on the coast. The historic river port village of **Ulmarra** is just 13km north-east and four major national parks—**Yuraygir** and **Bundjalung** on the coast and **Gibraltar Range** and **Washpool** in the ranges—make a worthwhile daytrip. The **Nymboida River** located 30km south-west offers white-water rafting trips and visitors can also hire canoes.

VISITOR INFORMATION: Cnr Pacific Hwy and Spring St, South Grafton, Ph: (02) 6642 4677

Grenfell POP 1504

Map 118, C5

Grenfell is a charming little town situated at the foot of the **Weddin Mountains**, and 377km west of Sydney. The town's streets feature many buildings relatively unaltered since the 1880s. Grenfell was the birthplace of the noted poet Henry Lawson.

MAIN ATTRACTIONS: The **Henry Lawson Obelisk** marks the site where Lawson was born in 1867. His father was a miner from Mudgee who brought his family to Grenfell to prospect for gold. **Grenfell Historical Museum** holds some unique cricket photographs as the Stan McCabe family have lived in the town for some time. The museum is located in Camp St and is open weekends, or by appointment. The most interesting place to picnic is at **O'Brien's Lookout** on the Cowra Rd. This is the place where gold was first discovered and there are walking tracks past the old workings and machinery. **Grenfell Endemic Garden** displays local plants; and the **Town Drive** takes in everything that is of interest in town. A leaflet is available from Grenfell's information centre.

NEARBY ATTRACTIONS: **Weddin Mountains NP** covers a range of hills 19km south-west of Grenfell. This large, natural area provides sanctuary from the surrounding agricultural land for many indigenous plants and animals. **Ben Hall's Cave**, the park's most popular attraction, was used by Hall, Johnnie Gilbert, Frank Gardiner and other members of the bushranger gang as a shelter and a place to hide their spoils. There are walking trails and two lookouts in the park.

VISITOR INFORMATION: Main St, Ph: (02) 6343 1612

Griffith POP 15 950

Map 117, J6

Designed by Walter Burley Griffin, Griffith is the largest centre in the rich agricultural **Murrumbidgee Irrigation Area**. Famous for its citrus crops, Griffith is also one of the most important wine and vegetable production areas in the country. More than 70% of New South Wales' wines are produced in this region.

MAIN ATTRACTIONS: **La Festa** is a music, food and wine festival held every Easter to celebrate Griffith's multicultural heritage. **Griffith Regional Art Gallery** is housed in the old Soldiers Memorial Hall, a 1930s Art Deco building. The gallery has a growing collection of Australian-designed jewellery displayed in one gallery, while touring exhibitions from all over Australia are in another. The gallery is located in Banna Ave, and is open Tuesday to Saturday.

NEARBY ATTRACTIONS: **Cocoparra NP** is 30km north-east of Griffith and can be reached via the Whitton Stock Route, the route taken by Cobb & Co coaches in early days. The spring wildflowers are spectacular and wildlife is abundant. Good views of the surrounding countryside can be seen from the summits of **Mount Caley** and **Mount Brogden**. Many of the wineries in the area are open for tastings and sales.

VISITOR INFORMATION: Cnr Banna Ave and Jondaryan Ave, Ph: (02) 6962 4145 or 1800 681 141

Gundagai POP 2064

Map 122, A2

The centre of prosperous wool and meat-producing country on the **Murrumbidgee River**, 398km south-west of Sydney, Gundagai is one of the best known country towns in Australia. Gold discoveries

Statues of Dad and Dave, north of Gundagai

in the 19th century attracted thousands of prospectors, as well as the notorious bushrangers Ben Hall and Captain Moonlite, to the district. Poems and songs, such as Jack O'Hagen's *Along the Road to Gundagai* have helped this town become part of Australian folklore.

MAIN ATTRACTIONS: **Rusconi's Marble Masterpiece** is on show at the visitor information centre. It is a unique miniature cathedral containing 20 948 pieces of Australian marble. Each piece was hand-cut and polished and it took 28 years to build. After the *Dog on the Tuckerbox*, the Rusconi sculpture is the town's number two attraction with over 50 000 people visiting every year. The **Gabriel Gallery** displays a collection of photographs, letters and possessions of **Henry Lawson**. It is located in Sheridan St. Also here is the National Trust-classified **Court House**, built in 1859. Trials held here include that of bushranger Captain Moonlite. For panoramic views of the area, visit **Mount Parnassus Lookout** in Hanley St, and **Rotary Lookout** in Luke St.

NEARBY ATTRACTIONS: Local sculptor Frank Rusconi created the *Dog on the Tuckerbox* memorial, which is 9km from Gundagai. It was built as a monument to pioneer teamsters and their dogs. Nearby are the copper statues of **Dad and Dave**, popular characters from the writings of Steele Rudd.

VISITOR INFORMATION: 249 Sheridan St, Ph: (02) 6944 0250 or 6944 0251

Gunnedah POP 8320

Map 114, D5

Surrounded by rich agricultural land, this modern country town lies on gentle sloping terrain on the southern side of the **Namoi River**. The livestock industry is important to the town: **Gunnedah Saleyard** handles the largest cattle sales in New South Wales.

MAIN ATTRACTIONS: The Gunnedah district has one of the largest and healthiest koala populations west of the **Great Dividing Range**. They can be seen in the trees around town. Standing in **Anzac Park** is a life-sized equestrian statue commemorating Gunnedah's link with the poet Dorothea Mackellar. Gunnedah Visitor Information Centre contains the **Dorothea Mackellar Wing**: a collection of memorabilia associated with her family. In front of the State Office Block in Abbott St stands a memorial to **Cumbo Gunnerah**, a legendary Aboriginal warrior of the Gunn-e-dar people, who died in the late 1700s and was immortalised in Ion Idriess' book, *The Red Chief*. In **Brock's Court**, opposite the Town Hall, stands Gunnedah's **Miners Memorial Statue** built (and dedicated in 2000) in remembrance of the 20 miners who have lost their lives in mining accidents since 1911. 125% life-size, the statue depicts a miner erecting a prop, with a symbolic broken shaft at his feet.

NEARBY ATTRACTIONS: **Lake Keepit**, approximately 34km east of town, offers watersports including boating, sailing, swimming, waterskiing and fishing. On the way to the village of **Mullaley**, approximately 40km south-west, visitors will pass the 150° east meridian marking Eastern Standard Time.

VISITOR INFORMATION: Anzac Park, South St, Ph: (02) 6740 2230

Hawks Nest POP 1175

Map 95, C2

This small town is a coastal resort on the northern shores of **Port Stephens**. Popular as a quiet getaway, Hawks Nest is isolated from the bustle of **Nelson Bay**. Swimming, boating and fishing and many other watersports are available.

MAIN ATTRACTIONS: There are many picnic and BBQ facilities in the area, including several riverfront reserves from **Tea Gardens** around to **Winda Woppa**. Both **Jimmys** and **Bennetts beaches** have picnic tables and **Lions Park** has headland and harbour views. **Koala Zone**, off Kingfisher Ave, gives visitors the opportunity to see a colony of koalas in their natural habitat.

NEARBY ATTRACTIONS: Dolphin-watching cruises on Port Stephens are available, as are cruises up the river to **Myall Lakes NP**. This national park is a favourite destination with both campers and boaties. There are four lakes, spectacular headlands, as well as long expanses of beaches and sand dunes. Watersports are popular on the lakes and canoes and powerboats can be hired at **Myall Shores** (Bombah Point). At **Bulahdelah** houseboats can be hired.

VISITOR INFORMATION: Myall St, Tea Gardens, Ph: (02) 4997 0111

◼ Hay   POP 2900

Map 121, F1

Almost surrounded by the **Murrumbidgee River**, Hay lies in the middle of flat saltbush plains, 720km south-west of Sydney. The

Bristol Point at Jervis Bay, near Huskisson

plains support merino flocks producing medium-fine wools. Although wool is the main industry of the Hay district, there are also beef cattle, and irrigation allows fruit and vegetable growing. Many world-famous sheep studs are located here, including **Mungadal**, **Uardry** and **Cedar Grove**.

MAIN ATTRACTIONS: **Shear Outback (Australian Shearers' Hall of Fame)**, on the corner of Cobb Hwy and Sturt Hwy, is a superb living museum showcasing shearing life in the Outback. **Hay Gaol Museum**, built in 1878, has been a penal institute, maternity hospital, asylum, POW camp and a security institute for girls. The building is now a local history museum in Church St. Behind the restored Railway Station is the **POW Internment Camp Interpretive Centre**, which documents WWII internment of over 3000 prisoners-of-war in Hay.

NEARBY ATTRACTIONS: The Murrumbidgee River offers many excellent fishing spots and is popular in summer for waterskiing, canoeing and swimming. There are several river beaches close to town offering swimming and picnicking. Over 62 species of birds have been identified at **Hay Wetlands**, located off the Old Thelangerin Rd north-west of town. Springtime is a lovely time to visit with many waterbirds, including swans and ducks, nesting and breeding.

VISITOR INFORMATION: 407 Moppett St, Ph: (02) 6993 4045

◼ Huskisson   POP 3360

Map 97, C4

A flourishing little tourist and fishing town lying in the curve of **Jervis Bay**, Huskisson is the main shopping and accommodation centre in the district. Around 24km south-east of Nowra, Huskisson is a popular destination for families as it offers easy access to the clear waters of the bay and all facilities. Popular

watersports include swimming, sailing, windsurfing, scuba diving and fishing.

MAIN ATTRACTIONS: Many visitors spend time on the beaches that line the shore of Jervis Bay. Regular dolphin-watching cruises leave from **Huskisson Wharf**. Anglers can hire boats or fish from the beach, rocks or riverbank. Those interested in the history of boat-building should visit the **Lady Denman Heritage Complex** in Dent St. The *Lady Denman*, a Sydney Harbour ferry built at Huskisson and launched in 1911, is the centrepiece of the **Lady Denman Museum** within the complex. **Laddie Timbery's Aboriginal Art and Craft Centre** is also located in the complex. Local Koori artists make artworks on site. The award-winning complex also features a stand of spotted gum trees, freshwater and saltwater wetlands, the **Wirreecoo Walking Trail**, mangrove boardwalk and fish feeding in the harbour.

NEARBY ATTRACTIONS: **Jervis Bay NP** is located both north and south of Huskisson and there are walking tracks to explore. The **Botanic Gardens**, located in **Booderee NP**, showcases the unique plants of the area. The park is south of Huskisson. **Barry's Bush Tucker Tours** offers guided walks while explaining the Aboriginal history of the area.

VISITOR INFORMATION: Cnr Princes Hwy and Pleasant Way, Nowra, Ph: (02) 4421 0778

◼ Iluka   POP 1865

Map 115, J3

This small fishing and resort town lies 20km off the Pacific Hwy at the mouth of the **Clarence River**. A regular passenger ferry service links Iluka, on the north shore, to the larger resort of **Yamba** on the south side of the river mouth. Both towns have their own commercial fishing fleets and attract keen anglers for the beach, rock, estuary and deep-sea fishing opportunities.

Fishing boat at dawn, Iluka

Main Attractions: The Iluka–Yamba passenger ferry offers river cruises to **Harwood Island** on Wednesdays and Fridays. There are also BBQ cruises on Wednesday evenings. Immediately behind the town is the World Heritage-listed **Iluka Nature Reserve** containing a remnant of what was once an extensive coastal rainforest. The seaward end of the park emerges at **Iluka Bluff** picnic area, where a short walk reveals a wonderful view of Iluka township and the Clarence River estuary.
Nearby Attractions: The **Clarence Valley** has many sites significant to the Bundjalung Aboriginal people and 13 of these sites are covered on the **Lower Clarence Aboriginal Site Tourist Drive**. Brochures are available from the information centres at **Grafton** and **Maclean**. **Bundjalung NP** stretches north to **Evans Head** with 38km of unspoilt beaches perfect for surfing and fishing.
Wombah Coffee Plantation, the world's southernmost coffee plantation, is located 4km from the Pacific Hwy on the Iluka Rd. It is open weekends and holidays. Tour guides explain the growing and processing of coffee.
Visitor Information: Ferry Park, Pacific Hwy, Maclean, Ph: (02) 6645 4121

Inverell   POP 9540
Map 114, E3
Known as the **Sapphire City**, Inverell is a major supplier of these lovely gems. This **New England** town is set on the **Macintyre River** and is the centre of a diverse rural district in the north of the state.
Main Attractions: Inverell's **Pioneer Village** contains an impressive collection of historic buildings relocated from the surrounding district. The museum realistically displays local history from 1840–1930. Original buildings include Paddy's Pub (1847), Grove Homestead (1840), Nullamanna Village Church (1901), Slaughter House Creek Bridge, a school, village hall, railway station and much more. The museum is open Tuesday to Sunday and Monday by appointment. **Town Walk** and **Town and Country Drive** leaflets are available from the information centre in Campbell St.
Nearby Attractions: **DeJon Sapphire Centre** is located 19km east on Glen Innes Rd. **Green Valley Farm**, 36km south-east, is home to the interesting **Smith's Mining and Natural History Museum**.
Visitor Information: Campbell St, Ph: (02) 6728 8161

Jindabyne   POP 4255
Map 77, C5
The gateway to the alpine ski resorts, Jindabyne lies on the shores of man-made **Lake Jindabyne**. The original township was beside the **Snowy River**. In 1962, in creating **Lake Jindabyne**, the site of the old township was flooded to form a water storage area as part of the **Snowy Mountains Hydro-Electric Scheme**.
Main Attractions: While being a good base for visiting the **ski resorts**, Jindabyne also attracts visitors during summer. Activities at this time of year include bushwalking, trout fishing, sailing, sailboarding, waterskiing, canoeing and swimming. There is also a walkway and cycleway around part of Lake Jindabyne's foreshore.
Nearby Attractions: **Kosciuszko NP** occupies most of the Snowy Mountains region; in fact it is the largest national park in New South Wales. The park has much to offer year-round, including horseriding, mountain-biking, trout fishing, canoeing and white-water rafting. At 2228m above sea level in the Snowy Mountains, **Mount Kosciuszko** is Australia's highest point. An accessible walking trail crosses the flattened top of the mountain providing stunning panoramic views.
Visitor Information: Kosciuszko Rd, Ph: (02) 6450 5600

SNOWY MOUNTAINS

Part of the New South Wales section of the **Great Dividing Range**, the Snowy Mountains arc approximately 160km long and 80km wide. Much of the rugged terrain is 900m or more above sea level, with the mountainous ridge rising to 2228m at **Mount Kosciuszko**, the highest point in Australia. Although the Snowy Mountains are situated in New South Wales, they are close to the **Australian Capital Territory** and their southern boundary extends to the Victorian border.

Kosciuszko NP occupies most of the Snowy Mountains region and at 6744km^2 is the largest national park in New South Wales.

Despite the mountain range's name, the Snowy Mountains lie below the line of permanent snow, so heavy snowfall will only be seen from June to October. During the winter months skiers, both local and international, flock to the many ski resorts in the mountains.

Summer also has much to offer visitors. Lower prices and fewer people make the area a perfect destination for a bushwalking, trout-fishing or mountain-biking holiday. The wildflowers and abundance of birdlife are particularly impressive during these months.

Snowfield resorts

Thredbo is a popular ski resort town, sandwiched in a small valley between Thredbo River and the Alpine Way. **Charlotte Pass**, **Perisher Valley**, **Smiggin Holes**, **Blue Cow Mountain** and **Mt Selwyn** lie within Kosciuszko NP's borders. All offer great skiing and visitors can travel between some of the resorts in winter on the **Skitube**.

 Visitor information

Snowy Region Visitor Information Centre
National Parks and Wildlife Service (NPWS)
Kosciuszko Rd, Jindabyne, NSW 2627
Ph: (02) 6450 5600
www.nationalparks.nsw.gov.au

Skiing at Thredbo

Khancoban Dam in autumn, Snowy Mountains

main attractions

◈ **Jindabyne**

This town on the shores of Lake Jindabyne is the gateway to the alpine ski resorts.

◈ **Kosciuszko National Park**

Two-wheel drive vehicles must carry snow chains between the June long weekend and the October long weekend.

◈ **Mt Kosciuszko**

A walking trail crosses the flattened top, providing breathtaking views.

◈ **Yarrangobilly Caves**

This limestone cave system consists of about 60 caves, only three of which are generally open to the public. Walking trails offer panoramic views of Yarrangobilly Gorge and there is a very popular thermal pool.

New South Wales

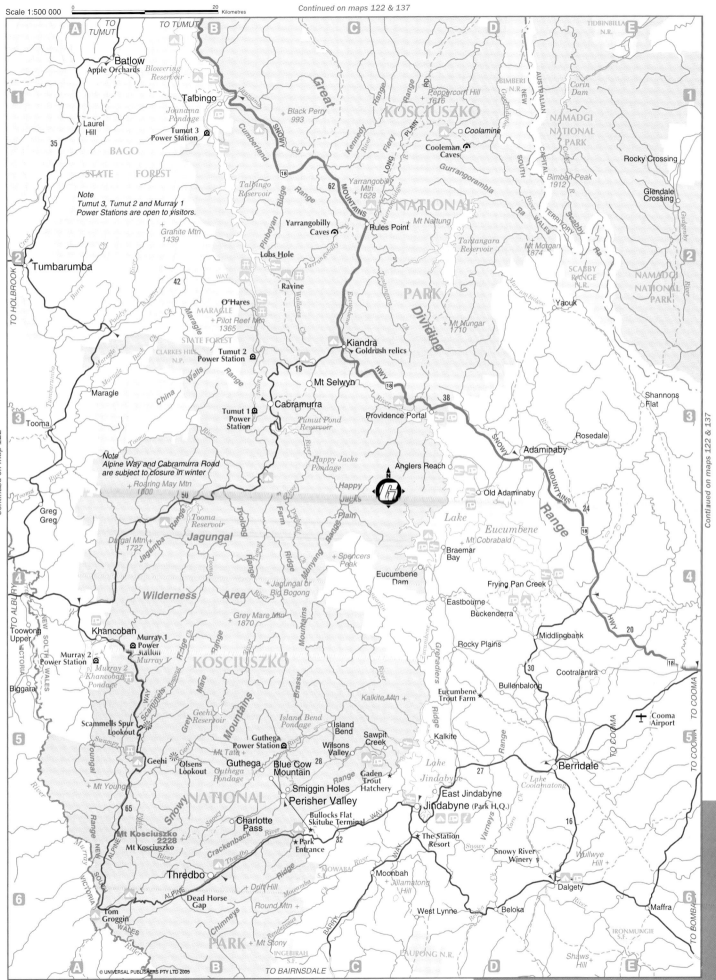

Continued on maps 122 & 137

Note
Tumut 3, Tumut 2 and Murray 1
Power Stations are open to visitors.

Note
Alpine Way and Cabramurra Road
are subject to closure in winter

Continued on map 122
Continued on map 122 & 137
Continued on map 122

© UNIVERSAL PUBLISHERS PTY LTD 2005

Katoomba Falls in Blue Mountains National Park

Junee POP 3685
Map 122, A2

An agricultural and grazing town, Junee is also an important rail centre for southern New South Wales. The railway track runs through the middle of the CBD and the station, built in 1883, is an impressive Renaissance-style building.

MAIN ATTRACTIONS: Railway memorabilia and the district's pioneering history are preserved in the **Historical Museum** in the old Broadway Hotel. **Junee Roundhouse Museum** incorporates the largest operational roundhouse in Australia. It features

a 32m turntable, the original workshop, heritage transport displays, memorabilia and a large model train layout. Guided tours and light refreshments are available. Visitors are welcome at the **Junee Licorice and Chocolate Factory** in Lord St and **Monte Cristo Homestead and Museum**, which is open daily. **Memorial Park**, located beside the railway crossing, is an attractive spot for a picnic. **Endeavour Park**, on the Olympic Way, has an interesting hedge maze and a pond.

VISITOR INFORMATION: Tarcutta St, Wagga Wagga, Ph: (02) 6926 9621

Katoomba POP 11 800
Map 80, E4

The major centre of the World Heritage-listed **Blue Mountains** west of Sydney, Katoomba has been a famous resort for lovers of the mountains since the end of the 19th century. It remains as popular today, with a variety of accommodation including charming guesthouses and beautifully restored hotels.

MAIN ATTRACTIONS: **The Three Sisters** are Katoomba's most famous natural attraction. This impressive rock formation is best seen from **Echo Point**, high above the **Jamison Valley**. An information centre is located at Echo Point. The **Scenic Railway**, located in Violet St, off Cliff Drive, is a heart-stopping ride for tourists. The **Scenic Skyway** and **Sceniscender** cable cars are also located at the **Scenic World** complex. For a step back in time, the **Paragon Cafe**, in Katoomba St, is the place to stop for morning or afternoon tea. Classified by the National Trust for its original Art Deco interiors, it is remembered by many generations for its delicious handmade chocolates. **The Edge** cinema, located on the Great Western Hwy, shows a spectacular movie of the Blue Mountains on a six-storey-high screen.

NEARBY ATTRACTIONS: **Jenolan Caves**, 75km south-west of Katoomba, offers a spectacular system of limestone caves, underground rivers and limestone formations. The partially restored silver-mining ghost town of **Yerranderie** is worth a visit. It is located 200km south via **Oberon** — the drive itself is an adventure over a 73km dirt road!

VISITOR INFORMATION: Echo Point, Katoomba; or Great Western Hwy, Glenbrook, Ph: 1300 653 408

Kempsey POP 8645
Map 115, H6

The largest urban centre in the rural **Macleay Valley**, Kempsey is divided by the Pacific Hwy and the **Macleay River**. The town attracts business and tourists, and is growing as a retirement centre. Kempsey is also the home of Australia's famous **Akubra hats**, although the factory is not open to the public.

MAIN ATTRACTIONS: Kempsey's most interesting historic buildings are located mainly in **Kemp**, **Elbow** and **Sea streets**. Many of these 19th-century buildings are listed on the town's **heritage trail**. **South Kempsey Park** is the location of **Kempsey Cultural Centre**. Here visitors will find the information centre and **Macleay River Historical Museum**, which is open daily. The museum displays feature an early settler's cottage and the local history of Aboriginal groups from the Macleay Valley. **Wigay Aboriginal Food and Cultural Park** in Dangar St, Kempsey, offers cultural tours and bush tucker experiences.

NEARBY ATTRACTIONS: One of Kempsey's main attractions is its proximity to the coastal resorts of **South West Rocks**, **Crescent Head**, **Hat Head**, **Stuarts Point** and **Grassy Head**, all offering unspoilt coastal scenery and clean beaches.

VISITOR INFORMATION: Pacific Hwy, South Kempsey, Ph: (02) 6563 1555

The Blue Mountains were named due to the blue haze that can be seen from Sydney—created by light interacting with the vapour emanating from millions of eucalypt trees. This rugged region features dramatic cliffs, rock formations, waterfalls and caves. Once seen as a barrier to the infant colony's expansion westwards, the Blue Mountains is now a popular holiday or weekend destination due to its proximity to Sydney.

This spectacular wilderness area—now World Heritage-listed—can be enjoyed year round. Seasonal changes here are more marked than in Sydney, and temperatures can plummet very quickly, especially in winter, so it is wise to always be prepared for cold weather. This climate makes the Blue Mountains an ideal location for **Yulefest**, a mid-winter 'Christmas' festival, held annually throughout the mountains between June and August. A number of villages are to be found in the Blue Mountains, offering excellent restaurants, cafes, pubs, gardens, galleries, antique stores and other shops to entertain less energetic visitors.

main attractions

◈ **Blue Mountains National Park**

This very popular park offers sandstone cliffs, canyons, lookouts and many walks.

◈ **Echo Point Lookout**

The lookout provides breathtaking views of the Jamison Valley and The Three Sisters.

◈ **Hydro Majestic**

Built last century on a cliff edge, this hotel at Medlow Bath remains a popular retreat.

◈ **Jenolan Caves**

Limestone caverns lie underground, with icy rivers and impressive limestone formations.

◈ **Leura**

A picturesque town classified by the National Trust.

◈ **Norman Lindsay Gallery and Museum**

Formerly the home of the controversial artist, cartoonist and writer, it is now a gallery of Lindsay's works.

◈ **Scenic World**

Popular rides here are the Scenic Railway, Scenic Skyway and Sceniscender.

◈ **Zig Zag Railway**

This railway was named in 1886, after a series of zig zags were constructed in the track enabling coal trains to descend into the valley near Lithgow.

Eastern water dragon, *Physignathus lesueurii*, at Glenbrook Gorge

World Heritage Area

The area was listed in 2000 as Australia's 14th World Heritage Area for its unique landforms, geological history, flora and fauna and its cultural significance to the Daruk and Gundungura Aboriginal people. Older than America's Grand Canyon, the area is home to living fossils like the Wollemi pine. Bushwalking, rockclimbing, canyoning, abseiling, mountain biking and 4-wheel driving are all possible.

ℹ Visitor information

Echo Point Visitor Information Centre
Echo Point Rd, Echo Point,
Katoomba, NSW 2780

Glenbrook Visitor Information Centre
Great Western Hwy, Glenbrook, NSW 2773
Tollfree: 1300 653 408

Blue Mountains National Park
NPWS Heritage Centre
Govetts Leap Rd, Blackheath, NSW 2785
Ph: (02) 4787 8877

Autumn garden *Nooroo* in Mount Wilson, Blue Mountains

LIDSDALE
STATE
FOREST

Rydal

Eagle View
Escape

Lake Lyell

Mt Walker
+1188m

Farmers

Creek

Zig Zag
Railway

Bottom Points
Top Points

Clarence
House

Newnes
Junction

Bowenfels

Vale of Clwydd

Clarence

CHIFLEY

19

Lithgow

Bowen Inn

Old
Bowenfels

Blue Mountains
SpaRadise ★

Hassans Walls

Bell

Magpie
Hollow

Lyell Dam

Lake Lyell

Blackmans Ck

Comet Inn

HOLLOW

RD

Cheetham
Flats

MAGPIE

Spirit of
the Lake

Coxs

Whites

Bowens

Ck

11

GREAT

Lett

River

Collits' Inn
(1823)

CAUSEWAY

Hartley
Vale

DARLING

10

BELLS

Grose

Creek

Jerrys
Meadows

Annes Ck

Beehive Mnt
+1189

Hartley Historic Site

Glenroy Crossing

WESTERN

Mt York
1061m

Butlers

Bardens

Kerosene

Creek

Little Hartley

11

Rosedale (1839) ★

Victoria
Pass

Mitchells
Ridge

32

Mt Victoria

Mary

Anns

Jocks

ROAD

Ck

Yorkeys

Creek

Grants

Moyne

Creek

Coxs & Ferris Cave

Locked Gate

Mt Boyce

HIGHWAY

Hat Hill

24

Lowther

JENOLAN

CAVES

Ryans Ck

Creek

Coxs

4WD

Kanimbla
800m +

Blackheath

Valley

Barbers

Centennial Glen Stables
Potters

Mt Blackheath

HAT HILL RD

NP
Heritage

Off Flats

HAMPTON

STATE

Jenolan Half-way

Hampton

Ganbenang

Ganbenang

Kanimbla

Creek

Schoolhouse

Logan Brae Orchards ★

Shipley

EVANS LOOKOUT

17

Gre015
Lake
Medlow

FOREST

War Trail

Wicketty

RD

RD

Millionth Acre

Long

Swamp

Table Mountain
+1107m

Sour Flat

Hargraves

Medlow Bath

Mercure Grand
Hydro Majestic

Greentrees

Chalet

Megalong Valley

Valley

RD

Cascade

Bindo

+1364m

DUCKMALOI

National

Gum Valley Ck

Bossy

JENOLAN CAVES

JENOLAN

STATE

FOREST

Cullenbenong

Creek

River

Chaplowe

Werriberri Trail Rides
& Lodge

Megalong Australian
Heritage Centre

Megalong

VALLEY

Pulpit Hill

Back Creek

Katoomba

Cahills
Scenic World

Echo Pt

Jenolan

Black Range

20

Bicentennial

McKeons

Beefsteak Ck

Black

Six Foot Track

Range

Cox's River
Camping Ground

Bowtells
Swing Bridge

Alum Creek
Camping Ground

Euroka
Homestead

Old Ford Reserve

Megalong

MEGALONG

Cyclorama Point

Ruined Castle ★

Jamiso

Castle Cliff
987m

The Th
Siste

Kedumba

Jenolan

6ft Track

Biddys

Diable

Creek

Bees Nest Ck

Alum Creek

River

Galong

McGees

Euroka

Green Gully

Narrow Neck
1072m +

Jenolan Caves Cottages

JENOLAN
KARST
CONSERVATION
RESERVE

Jenolan Caves

Caves House

Gatehouse

KANANGRA - BOYD

NATIONAL PARK

Coxs

River

R

Breakfast

Creek

Little Cedar Creek

Cedar

5
Kilometres

F
BLUE MOUNTAINS
(World Heritage Area)
NATIONAL PARK

G River

H

Mt Irvine

J (World Heritage Area) K
WOLLEMI NATIONAL PARK

1

Pheasants Cave
Du Faurs Rocks
Mt Wilson
MT IRVINE
RD

Wynnes Rocks
8
10

Bilpin Springs
Locked Gate
4WD
Locked Gate
Bilpin
Apple Orchards
BELLS 13
LINE OF
Madisons
Glenhuntly
Glenrose
Cut Rock Cottage
Grass Karting
Little Creek Island
Bellbird Hill

9 LINE
Warawaralong
BELLS
Chapel Hill
Berambing
Waratah Picnic Area
The Gorge Walking Track

Kurrajong Heights
Fernbrook Garden & Botanical Gallery
Opal Museum

Langi Dorn
ROAD

Mount Tomah Botanic Garden
Tomah Mountain Lodge
Mt Tomah 999m
Mt Bell 996m
Mt Charles 933m

2
24
ROAD

Barralow Picnic Ground

Loxley

Gumnut Cottage
Bowen Mountain
Enniskillen Orchard
Grose Vale

The Devils Wilderness
(World Heritage Area)
BLUE MOUNTAINS

Mt Banks 1062m
ces Pass
ramoko Hd
King Georges
Explorers Range
Grose Gorge

Mount Hay Range
NATIONAL
Grose

Faulconbridge Point
Vale
Grose Head South
River
4WD
3

Perrys Lookdown
Grose
Blue Gum Forest
Acacia Flat
Pulpit Rock
Lockley Pylon
Mt Hay 944m
Locked Gate

PARK

Faulconbridge Ridge

Locked Gate
Locked Gate

Hawkesbury Heights
22
Locked Gate
Hawkesbury Panorama

Evans
Point Pilcher
Flat Top 929m
Flat Top Brook
Wirralie Bronk
Wentworth Ridge
Lawson Ridge
Linden Ridge

4WD
4WD

Locked Gate

Norman Lindsay Gallery
WESTGROSE
RD
Springwood
Hawkesbury ROAD
YELLOMUNDEE REGIONAL PARK
Yellow Rock
Winmalee
4

toomba field

Minnehaha Falls

Lake Woodford
Locked Gate
Locked Gate

GREAT
Faulconbridge
WESTERN
Springwood
Locomotive Depot
Heritage Museum & Steam Tramway
Valley Heights

Yellow Rock

Leura
Wentworth Falls
Dantes Glen
Bungaree
Lawson
Bullaburra
Hazelbrook
Araluen
Selwood Science & Puzzles
30
Kings Cave
Bulls Camp
Linden

Glenbrook

Warrimoo
16

Emu Heights
Blaxland

FALLS RD
32

MURPHYS
Sublime Point
Woodford Academy
Locked Gate
Woodford
Braeside

THE

Martins
Bunyan

HIGHWAY
32

Leonay

Glenbrook
Lapstone

Red Hands Cave
Tunnel View
Portal

TABLELAND

KINGS

Ingar Picnic Ground
Murphys Glen Picnic Ground

OAKS

Mt Solitary
Valley

QUEEN VICTORIA
TABLELAND RD

Notts Ridge
ANDERSONS
Glen Erskine

FIRE TRAIL

FIRE

Campfire
Euroka
The Oaks Picnic Area

Euroka
The Rock

Waterfall

Reedy

Spring

Massif Ridge

FIRE TRAIL
Locked Gate

BLUE MOUNTAINS
NATIONAL PARK
Erskine Creek

Lincoln

Breakfast
Nepean River

MULGOA

ROAD

5

6

F G H J K

© UNIVERSAL PUBLISHERS PTY LTD 2005

Mulgoa

Continued on map 46

Kiama   POP 12 250
Map 107, C3

The centre of a rich dairying district, famous for its Illawarra shorthorn breed of cattle, Kiama is also a popular resort town. Located on the Princes Hwy, 119km south of Sydney, Kiama has a relaxed, country atmosphere as well as offering visitors excellent beaches, rockpools, good fishing and a scenic rural hinterland.

MAIN ATTRACTIONS: The famous **Kiama Blowhole** is a fascinating yet unpredictable attraction. In calm weather it is fairly unimpressive,

Kiama Blowhole

but when the seas are rough and running from the south-east, trapped water is forced to a height of up to 60m, creating a loud noise and spectacular sight. The Blowhole is floodlit until 9pm. **Kiama Family History (Genealogical) Centre** and **The Terrace** (art and craft shops) are historic buildings that are worthwhile visiting. A variety of fish can be caught around the town's rocky shoreline and there are plenty of fishing charters available.

NEARBY ATTRACTIONS: Brochures are available from the information centre about several scenic drives both along the coast and in the hinterland area. **Saddleback Mountain** can be reached by following the Jamberoo Rd from Kiama. The summit is 600m above sea level and views extend 240km along the coast and over farming land. The wonderful **Minnamurra Rainforest** and **Rainforest Centre** is close by in **Budderoo NP** which is also home to **Minnamurra Falls**.

VISITOR INFORMATION: Blowhole Point Rd, Ph: (02) 4232 3322

Kurri Kurri   POP 5575
Map 119, H4

Kurri Kurri is the centre of an agricultural and industrial region. Located midway between **Cessnock** and **Maitland**, Kurri Kurri was once an important coal-mining town. The surrounding area is devoted to dairying and orchards and Kurri Kurri is a thriving little town despite the decline of coal mining.

MAIN ATTRACTIONS: **Kurri Regional Museum** is housed in the old timber Pokolbin Schoolhouse, located in the grounds of Kurri Kurri High School. The museum displays a collection of memorabilia covering daily life and work in the coalfields region and is open Sunday, Wednesday and public holidays, or by appointment.

NEARBY ATTRACTIONS: **Buchanan Gallery**, east of Kurri Kurri in **Buchanan**, specialises in ceramics,

paintings, outdoor pots and restored colonial furniture displayed in an old schoolhouse. Picnic facilities are available. Only a 20 minute drive from town are the wineries of the **Lovedale** region, including **Wandin Valley Estate**, **Sandalyn Estate** and **Capercaillie Wine Co**.

VISITOR INFORMATION: Hunter Valley Wine Country Visitor Centre, 455 Wine Country Dr, Pokolbin, Ph: (02) 4990 4477

Kyogle   POP 2875
Map 115, H2

Located on **Summerland Way**, at the foot of **Fairymount**, is the township of Kyogle. Known as the '**Gateway to the Rainforests**', Kyogle overlooks the **Richmond Valley** and the scenery of the tall **McPherson**, **Tweed** and **Richmond mountain ranges** to the north, east and west.

MAIN ATTRACTIONS: The **Rainforest Botanic Gardens** are located alongside **Fawcetts Creek**. Existing rainforest was enhanced and developed to create the gardens, which are well worth visiting. **Captain Cook Memorial Lookout** is off Mount St.

NEARBY ATTRACTIONS: The **Border Ranges World Heritage Area** lies 30km north and offers excellent views, waterfalls, deep gorges, clear creeks and steep escarpments. Highlights of the park's eastern section are **The Pinnacle** rock formation and the view from **Blackbutts Lookout**.

VISITOR INFORMATION: Kyogle Council, 1Stratheden St, Ph: (02) 6632 1611

Lake Macquarie   POP 85 000
Map 71, D2

The largest permanent saltwater lake in Australia, Lake Macquarie is an extensive coastal lagoon with 174km of foreshore. The lake is located in the northern section of the coastal strip separating **The Central Coast** and **Newcastle**. A popular holiday resort, Lake

Reflections at Belmont Yacht Club, Lake Macquarie

Macquarie attracts thousands of visitors for the good fishing, sailing, swimming and year-round watersports.

MAIN ATTRACTIONS: Ocean beaches stretch for 20km from **Munmorah State Conservation Area** in the south to **Glenrock** in the north. All kinds of boats are available for hire—from outboard 'tinnies' to luxurious yachts and houseboats. With a boat, it is worthwhile visiting **Pulbah Island**, a wildlife sanctuary home to many native birds and animals.

NEARBY ATTRACTIONS: Munmorah SCA offers 12km of rugged coastline and on its western side, a frontage to **Lake Munmorah**. Activities include surfing, sailing, fishing, picnicking and bushwalking. **Glenrock Lagoon** is a major feature of **Glenrock State Conservation Area**. The area is renowned for its attractive waterfalls, rockpools, beaches and striking headlands. To the west of Lake Macquarie lies **Watagans NP**. At the foot of the Watagans is the historic village of **Cooranbong**, which was settled in the late 19th century by members of the Seventh Day Adventist Church. **Sunnyside Historic House**, open Saturday to Wednesday, was originally the home of Ellen White, a pioneer of the church. In the grounds of Sunnyside Historic House is the fascinating **South Sea Island Museum**.

VISITOR INFORMATION: 72 Pacific Hwy, Blacksmiths, Ph: (02) 4972 1172

■ Leeton   POP 6905
Map 121, J1

The administrative centre of the **Murrumbidgee Irrigation Area**, Leeton is located 30km off the Newell Hwy. The first rice mill opened here in 1951 and Leeton is now the headquarters for Australia's rice industry, which exports rice to many Asian countries, including Japan.

MAIN ATTRACTIONS: **Leeton SunRice Centre** at **Leeton Mill** is open to the public and gives morning and afternoon presentations on weekdays. Much of Leeton's architecture dates from the Art Deco Period: buildings of note include the **Roxy Theatre**, **McCaughey Mansion** (now a high school) and the **Hydro Motor Inn**. **Mountford Park**, near Leeton's town centre, is a relaxing spot for a picnic.

NEARBY ATTRACTIONS: **Toorak Wines** and **Lillypilly Estate**, local wineries, are open for tastings and sales Monday to Saturday. Approximately 23km west is the historic village of **Whitton**. Worthwhile visiting is the **Courthouse and Historical Museum** which is open on weekends and Tuesdays, or by appointment. **Fivebough Swamp**, on the northern outskirts of town, is a popular spot for birdwatchers. The sanctuary is an important feeding and breeding ground for over 149 species of migratory waterbirds.

VISITOR INFORMATION: 10 Yanco Ave, Ph. (02) 6953 6481

■ Lennox Head   POP 5815
Map 84, D3

Located 11km north of **Ballina**, Lennox Head is a small holiday town. Lying at the southern end of **Seven Mile Beach**, the town is renowned as a good surfing spot, but there are also calm areas for snorkelling and swimming.

NEARBY ATTRACTIONS: A good coastal road links Lennox Head to Ballina and also to **Byron Bay**, 20km north. **Lake Ainsworth** is a unique tea-tree freshwater lake only 50m from the ocean. This popular lake is ideal for swimming and watersports. South of Lennox Head is **Pat Moreton Lookout**, which can be reached either via road or through the foreshore reserve. Between May and October, migrating whales can frequently be seen offshore.

VISITOR INFORMATION: Cnr River St and La Balsa Plaza, Ballina, Ph: (02) 6686 3484

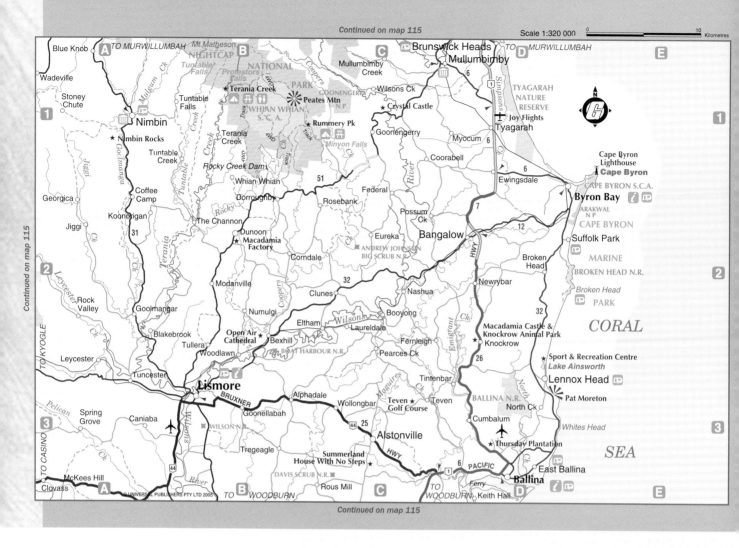

Continued on map 115

Lismore POP 28 400

Map 84, B3

A bustling commercial centre and university city, Lismore is located on the Bruxner Hwy, beside the **Wilsons River**, 760km north of Sydney. Lismore is in the heart of the **'Rainbow Region'** of northern New South Wales—referring not only to the district's many rainbows, but also to its reputation for attracting creative and alternative-lifestyle people.

MAIN ATTRACTIONS: The Lismore district is recognised as having some of the most unusual arts and crafts in the nation. **Lismore Regional Art Gallery** is located in Molesworth St and houses a permanent collection and regular local exhibitions. **Richmond River Historical Society Museum** is open from Monday to Friday, weekends and other times by appointment. Good picnic spots can be found at **Wade Park**, **Heritage Park** and **Lismore Lake**. Lismore's **Koala Hospital** cares for sick and injured koalas and a rehabilitation area is open daily. **Rotary Rainforest Reserve** is a 6ha area with a boardwalk. There is a **rainforest display** at Lismore Visitor Centre.

NEARBY ATTRACTIONS: The alternative lifestyle village of **Nimbin** is 31km to the north. Koalas can be seen in the wild at **Tucki Tucki Koala Reserve**, 15km south on Woodburn Rd. **Christmas All Year Round** offers macadamia nuts and other produce 11km east at **Alphadale**.

VISITOR INFORMATION: Cnr Ballina St and Molesworth St, Ph: (02) 6622 0122 or 1300 369 795

Totem Forest in Lismore's Heritage Park

New South Wales

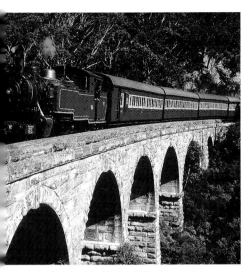
Viaduct on the Zig Zag Railway, near Lithgow

Lithgow POP 11 450
Map 80, C1

Located on the fringes of the **Blue Mountains**, Lithgow is a coal-mining town, with its coal-mining history dating back to 1841.

MAIN ATTRACTIONS: The most popular attractions in Lithgow are **Blast Furnace Park, Eskbank House, State Mine Heritage Park and Railway** and the **Lithgow Small Arms Museum**.

NEARBY ATTRACTIONS: **Mount Piper Energy Expo** is open daily and uses interactive exhibits to explain what electricity is and how it is made and distributed. There are daily tours and picnic and BBQ facilities are available. The **Zig Zag Railway** was built in 1869 to conquer the problem of transporting coal over the Blue Mountains. Considered one of the world's engineering marvels, the rail line crosses three huge sandstone viaducts and drops 150m into the **Lithgow Valley**. A section of the line has been restored and is now a major tourist attraction. Steam or diesel trains run daily. One of the most popular of the district's walks, the **Glow-Worm Tunnel Walk**, is accessed via 34km of dirt road. The walk follows the route of the railway that took shale from the mines at **Newnes** from

1906 until the 1930s. Lithgow is a good base for campers and bushwalkers wanting to explore **Wollemi NP**, the second largest national park in New South Wales. Both **Lake Lyell** and **Lake Wallace** are excellent spots for picnics, sailing and fishing, with powered boats and water-skiing permitted on Lake Lyell.

VISITOR INFORMATION: Cnr Cooerwull Rd and Great Western Hwy, Ph: (02) 6353 1859

Macksville POP 2715
Map 62, C6

This **Nambucca River** town, 10km upstream from Nambucca Heads, is a pleasant stop on your journey along the Pacific Hwy. Fishing and oyster farming are the main industries in Macksville. Crops grown in the surrounding district include bananas (the most southerly region where bananas are commercially grown) and other tropical fruit, as well as macadamia nuts and vegetables.

MAIN ATTRACTIONS: **Mary Boulton Pioneer Cottage** is a reminder of the settlement's early days. Stables on the property display tools, saddlery, harness and horse-drawn vehicles. The cottage is in River St and is open on Wednesday and Saturday afternoons. Riverbank parks on either side of the Pacific Hwy bridge offer picnic tables. Boat launching ramps are also located here. **Macksville Wharf**, a heritage project, was opened in 2001. The river provides ideal conditions for watersports and bottlenose dolphins are often seen swimming and playing in these waters.

NEARBY ATTRACTIONS: The **Cosmopolitan Pub**, made famous in Slim Dusty's song *A Pub with no Beer* is located at **Taylors Arm**, about 30km west. In the same area, **Bakers Creek Station** has horseriding, canoeing, BBQ and picnic areas and a public restaurant. Just off the Taylors Arm Rd at Congarinni, **Valley of the Mist**

offers canoe tours and gourmet bush tucker. The old township of **Bowraville**, upstream on the Nambucca River, has the **Joseph and Eliza Newman Folk Museum** and the **Frank Partridge VC Military Museum**. **Yarahappini Mountain Lookout**, 10km south, offers excellent views and a rainforest. **Scotts Head**, 18km south-east, is a scenic coastal town with great surfing conditions.

VISITOR INFORMATION: Cnr Pacific Hwy and Riverside Dr, Nambucca Heads, Ph: (02) 6568 6954

Maclean POP 3235
Map 115, H3

A fishing centre on the **Clarence River**, Maclean is also the southern gateway to Australia's sugarcane region, stretching north to Mossman in Queensland. Known as the **'Scottish Town in Australia'**, Maclean celebrates the birthplace of many of its settlers with an annual **Highland Gathering** at Easter.

MAIN ATTRACTIONS: The **Bicentennial Museum**, in Wharf St, is open on Wednesday, Friday and Saturday. One building has displays reflecting the history and development of the district. The other, a stone cottage built in 1886, is furnished to reflect life at that time. Panoramic views of the town, coast, bushland and canefields can be seen from **Maclean Lookout**, 2km east at the top of Wharf St. Festivals include the **International Tartan Day**, held in July. The Clarence Coast Visitors Centre also incorporates a restaurant, and art and craft gallery.

NEARBY ATTRACTIONS: **Brooms Head**, edged by **Yuraygir NP**, is a small coastal village south-east of Maclean. The sandy beach with its grassy verges and shady pines is delightful. Much activity centres on the Clarence River with fishing, sailing and waterskiing being popular.

VISITOR INFORMATION: Ferry Park, Pacific Hwy, Ph: (02) 6645 4121

Walka Water Works, Maitland

■ Maitland   POP 53 400

Map 119, H3

Located on the **Hunter River**, 35km upstream from the port of Newcastle, is the city of Maitland. Today, Maitland is the third largest provincial centre in New South Wales. This city began as two towns: **West Maitland** and **East Maitland**, and was not combined until 1944. East Maitland holds the most historic interest as it was a planned town, built above flood level, with spacious streets and fine public buildings. The area today still reflects the prosperity of the era in the mid 1800s when it served as the regional centre of the **Hunter Valley**.

MAIN ATTRACTIONS: Many of East Maitland's buildings were erected at a time when it was felt the new town could rival Sydney in size and power. Self-guided walks enable visitors to appreciate Maitland's architectural heritage. **Grossmann House** is used as a museum. **Maitland Regional Gallery** in High St is situated in a Federation Gothic building. **Maitland Gaol** was built in 1844 and was modelled on London's Pentonville prison. Located in John St, East Maitland, it has a number

of unique features, including an elaborate stairway system and tours are available. Antiques are popular in Maitland and there are many shops in Melbourne St and High St. Maitland has some of the best sport and recreation facilities in the Hunter region, including many licensed clubs.

NEARBY ATTRACTIONS: The historic river port of **Morpeth**, 5km north-east, has been classified by the National Trust. The village retains its 19th-century atmosphere, and is definitely worth visiting. **Walka Water Works Reserve**, located 1.5km north of Maitland, is the most intact water-works complex remaining in New South Wales. BBQs, a children's playground and a walking trail make it an interesting recreational area for the entire family.

VISITOR INFORMATION: Cnr High St and New England Hwy, Ph: (02) 4931 2800

■ Manilla   POP 2097

Map 114, D5

This small town is on the north-west slopes of the **Great Dividing Range**. A commercial centre, Manilla services the surrounding district of mixed farming, wheat, wool and cattle. The town is enhanced by a number of parks and is almost encircled by the **Namoi River**. The huge cartoon of a Murray cod outside the information centre announces Manilla is also a fishing destination.

MAIN ATTRACTIONS: Manilla is well-known among gliding, paragliding and hang-gliding enthusiasts. **Mount Borah** is the local take-off spot for hang-gliders. **Memorial Park** in the town centre is a pleasant place to wander and watch the birds in the aviary. **Royce Cottage** is a National Trust-classified building housing a local history museum. Located in Manilla St, the museum is open Monday, Wednesday and Friday afternoons, or by appointment.

NEARBY ATTRACTIONS: **Warrabah NP** is located north-east of Manilla. It is a

small but attractive park on the Namoi River. Huge granite boulders, gorges and pools are the main features, and the park is popular for swimming, fishing, canoeing, birdwatching, camping, 4-wheel driving and bushwalking.

VISITOR INFORMATION: 79 Arthur St, Ph: (02) 6785 1113

■ Merimbula   POP 4870

Map 122, D5

At the northern entrance of **Merimbula Lake**, 25km north of Eden, lies the fishing and tourist town of Merimbula. Popular for fishing, prawning and surfing, it attracts many visitors. There are three surf beaches and sheltered lake beaches. Boats can be hired and reef- and game-fishing trips leave from Merimbula Lake. From late October to mid December, there are whale-watching excursions.

MAIN ATTRACTIONS: **Merimbula Aquarium** is housed in an historic wharf building on Lake St and is open daily. Arts and crafts are popular in the region and a number of outlets sell local works.

NEARBY ATTRACTIONS: **Magic Mountain Family Recreation Park** is located 5km north on **Sapphire Coast Drive** and is open daily in summer and school holidays. It features heated waterslides, mini golf, a toboggan run and a mini-grand prix. **Yellow Pinch Wildlife Park** is situated about 9km north-west on the Princes Hwy. There are two national parks close by—**Bournda** and **Ben Boyd**. Both are attractive coastal parks and offer many walking tracks, swimming and fishing spots. At **Pambula Beach**, 10km south of Merimbula, there is a walking track, lookout and beach horseriding. Early morning and late afternoon, if you are quiet and still, you may see kangaroos and wallabies on the foreshore.

VISITOR INFORMATION: Beach St, Ph: (02) 6497 4900

Although the Illawarra and Southern Highlands are located on Sydney's south-west fringes and border each other (*see* pp.106–107), the Southern Highlands have their own distinct character. The cooler climate and picturesque villages lead to comparisons with rural England. In summer it is possible to experience the four seasons in a single daytrip by touring the many attractions in this diverse region. The towns and villages offer antique stores, arts and crafts, rustic cafes, B&Bs and museums. **Berrima**, founded in 1831, has several buildings listed on the National Estate. Other historic towns worth visiting include **Bowral**, **Mittagong** and **Moss Vale**. There are also local national parks, caves at **Wombeyan** and the natural beauty of the **Kangaroo Valley**. The region's best known festival is **Bowral Tulip Time**, an annual

Tulips at Milton Park, Bowral Tulip Time

spring celebration with thousands of tulips and other flowers in bloom. It is held late September until the October long weekend. There are mass plantings in **Corbett Gardens** and a number of private gardens are open to the public.

ℹ️ Visitor information

Southern Highlands Visitor Information Centre
62–70 Main St, Mittagong, NSW 2575
Ph: (02) 4871 2888
Tollfree: 1300 657 559

▥ Mittagong   POP 6275

Map 107, B2

Nestled in the valley of the **Nattai River**, Mittagong is the northern gateway to the **Southern Highlands**. It is an attractive town as many of the houses and public buildings have been built from the beautiful local sandstone.

MAIN ATTRACTIONS: Mittagong is well-known for its art and craft shops. Embroiderers will want to visit historic **Victoria House**, which has the largest display of embroidery and needlework kits in Australia. Located on the old Hume Hwy, it is open daily. **Sturt Craft Centre** in Range Rd holds workshops for pottery, weaving, glass, textiles, wood and jewellery. Its gallery displays quality local crafts and is

also open daily. Mittagong is a good base for walks in the Southern Highlands. One of the best walks in New South Wales begins here—the seven day walk on the **Barallier Track** to **Katoomba** in the Blue Mountains.

NEARBY ATTRACTIONS: **Wombeyan Caves** are located 65km north-west of Mittagong. Renowned for their beauty and spectacular limestone formations, five caves are open to the public. Guided tours are run through four of the Wombeyan Caves and **Figtree Cave** is open daily for self-guided tours. Accommodation at the caves includes cottages, a caravan park, cabins and campsites.

VISITOR INFORMATION: 62–70 Main St (Old Hume Hwy), Ph: (02) 4871 2888

▥ Moree   POP 9280

Map 114, C3

This wheat and wool town in the north-west of New South Wales has a landscape dominated by huge wheat silos. Sunflowers, pecan nuts, olives and cotton are also grown in the area. Moree is a renowned spa area, with many visitors coming to ease their aches and pains in the famous artesian baths.

MAIN ATTRACTIONS: In 1895, the **Moree Spa Pool** was completed at **East Moree** and the town became a famous health resort. It was originally thought that the bore water tapped at Moree would be used for irrigation, but the heavy mineral content meant it was unsuitable. The spa complex offers two hot pools with temperatures of

Dolphin Beach at Moruya Head

41°C, an Olympic-size pool, toddlers' pool and junior pool. Rheumatism and arthritis sufferers claim the water provides pain relief. The town has the largest Aboriginal population outside the major cities of New South Wales. **Moree Plains Regional Gallery** houses a large number of artefacts and contemporary works with exhibitions changing every six weeks. **Moree Regional Library** has the largest collection of Aboriginal reference books and information within New South Wales. Moree library staff continually update and record Aboriginal family history and genealogy.

VISITOR INFORMATION: Cnr Newell Hwy and Gwydir Hwy, Ph: (02) 6757 3350

■ Moruya   POP 2605
Map 122, D4
On the Princes Hwy, 307km south of Sydney, this rural centre services the surrounding timber and cattle country and is the base for exploring many beautiful beaches and national parks.

MAIN ATTRACTIONS: There are many beautiful old buildings of much historical interest. **Moruya Museum** preserves regional history, including that of the gold period at **Mogo**. Located in Campbell St, the museum is open Wednesday, Friday and Saturday, more often in January and Easter holidays.

NEARBY ATTRACTIONS: **Deua NP**, inland from Moruya, is a rugged and interesting area. A belt of limestone running through the park has resulted in many caves. One of the park's major attractions is the **Big Hole**, a 96m chasm, which probably resulted from the collapse of a limestone cavern. Old goldmining villages, such as **Majors Creek**, can be accessed from the unsealed Araluen Rd. Also interesting is the **old granite quarry**, off North Head Dr on the north side of the river. Stone for the pillars and façade of the **Sydney GPO** building was taken from here in 1872 and the quarry was reopened in 1924 to supply granite for the **Sydney Harbour Bridge** pylons and the **Cenotaph** in Martin Place, Sydney. When the Depression hit in the 1930s, the quarry was again closed. There are splendid coastal lookouts and scenery, as well as fishing opportunities, at **Moruya Head** and **Eurobodalla NP**.

VISITOR INFORMATION: Cnr Princes Hwy and Beach Rd, Batemans Bay, Ph: (02) 4472 6900

■ Moss Vale   POP 6610
Map 107, A2
A **Southern Highlands** market and tourist town, Moss Vale has become a popular retreat for retirees and home of the **Southern Highlands Country Fair**. The area is very scenic with sheep, cattle, horses, alpacas and goats feeding on the surrounding lush pastures.

MAIN ATTRACTIONS: **Throsby Park Homestead** was built by convicts in 1834, for the nephew of the explorer Charles Throsby. The fine Georgian sandstone and cedar home is open for inspection by request. **Leighton Gardens**, in the centre of Moss Vale, is a perfect spot for a leisurely stroll. The landscaped gardens are lovely in autumn when the deciduous trees display their glorious colours.

NEARBY ATTRACTIONS: **Cecil Hoskins Nature Reserve** is located 3km north-east of Moss Vale and here visitors will see a variety of birdlife.

VISITOR INFORMATION: 62-70 Main St (Old Hume Hwy), Mittagong, Ph: (02) 4871 2888

■ Mudgee   POP 8620
Map 118, E3
Located 264km north-west of Sydney, on the **Cudgegong River**, is the picturesque country town of Mudgee. The scenic landscape has attracted many artists to the region.

MAIN ATTRACTIONS: Mudgee is at the centre of one of the premium wine-growing areas of Australia. The wine industry dates back to the 1850s. The region is credited with introducing the chardonnay grape to Australia. Many of the surrounding wineries, including **Poet's Corner** and **Huntington Estate**, are open to the public, offering tastings and cellar door sales. Other local produce includes fine wool, honey, livestock and gourmet foods. The profusion of flora in the region attracts bees and several honey-processing companies have taken advantage of this, with different kinds of honey produced at various times of the year by skilled beekeepers. **Mudgee Honey Haven**, on the corner of Gulgong Rd and Hargraves Rd offers tastings and sales. There are many National Trust buildings in Mudgee and all can be seen on a self-guided **historical town walk**. A brochure is available from the visitor centre.

NEARBY ATTRACTIONS: **Gulgong**, the town on the old $10 note is 28km north of Mudgee. Around 130 buildings are classified by the National Trust. The streets are narrow and there are many reminders of its goldrush glory days. The **Pioneers Museum** is in the heart of Gulgong and includes a recreated bedroom, blacksmith shop, kitchen and bakehouse. The museum at 73 Herbert Rd is open seven days a week. The **Henry Lawson Centre** is located at 147 Mayne St, Gulgong and is a memorial to Henry Lawson's life. **Windamere Dam**, 24km south-east is a popular fishing and watersports venue with camping facilities.

VISITOR INFORMATION: 84 Market St, Ph: (02) 6372 1020

Mullumbimby   POP 2995
Map 84, C1

The **North Coast** town of Mullumbimby is surrounded by sub-tropical countryside which supports dairying and cattle properties and produces a wide range of tropical fruits. The town has a well-deserved reputation as a centre for creativity and alternative lifestyles.

MAIN ATTRACTIONS: Mullumbimby's major annual event is the **Chincogan Fiesta**, held in September. The town's streets are closed for stalls and entertainment and the highlight is the **Chincogan Charge**, a foot race from the Post Office to the top of **Mt Chincogan** and back. **Brunswick Valley Historical Museum** preserves local history and memorabilia. Housed in the old timber Post Office (1907) in Stuart St, it is open on weekdays.

NEARBY ATTRACTIONS: 8km east of Mullumbimby is **Brunswick Heads**, renowned for good surfing and excellent fishing. Further south,

15km away, is **Byron Bay** with its many attractions. The **Crystal Castle** is a popular attraction selling crystals from around the world, offering massage and meditation and also including a showroom, gallery and cafe. Housed in a 1920s-style homestead situated on the side of a hill to the south-west, it is open daily. In the same direction are **Minyon Falls** and other attractions in **Nightcap NP/Whian Whian State Conservation Area**.

VISITOR INFORMATION: 80 Jonson St, Byron Bay, Ph: (02) 6680 8558

Murwillumbah   POP 7660
Map 115, J1

A picturesque town, Murwillumbah spreads across the western bank of the **Tweed River** and up into the hills of the **McPherson Ranges**. Formerly a red-cedar timber town, it is now a service town for the sugarcane and banana-growing district of the **Tweed Valley**.

MAIN ATTRACTION: **Tweed River Regional Art Gallery** presents frequent exhibitions and is open Wednesday to Sunday.

NEARBY ATTRACTIONS: **Tropical Fruit World**, is located about 15km north of Murwillumbah and is open daily. **Rainforest Secrets**, at Mooball, is dedicated to educating visitors about the Mt Warning volcanic region—one of Australia's richest biodiversities. There are sensory and bush food rainforest trails, native animals and a restaurant. During the harvest season from July to November, **Condong Sugar Mill** opens for the public to see sugarcane being processed. The mill opens between 9am and 3pm but closes in wet weather. **Crystal Creek Miniatures** is a miniature animal stud, located just outside Murwillumbah, toward Chillingham. Enjoy an informative and amusing tour of the stud and play with the miniature animals. The stud is open Wednesday to Monday.

Fishing on the Tweed River, Murwillumbah, with Mount Warning in the distance

Wineries are a well-known feature of the Upper Hunter. Vines were originally planted in the area in the 1860s, but winemaking went into a long decline and farming took over the fertile valleys. Although dairy farming is still very important, the wine industry has made a comeback. Famous wineries such as **Rosemount** and **Arrowfield** offer wine tastings and cellar door sales.

The upper reach of the Hunter Valley, surrounding the pretty town of **Scone**, is widely regarded as Australia's premier thoroughbred and horse-breeding district. There are more than 70 stud farms in this part of the Hunter, some offering personalised tours. In May each year, Scone hosts **Scone Horse Festival**, complete with rodeos— a must for equestrian types. Coal mining, vineyards and horse studs have brought prosperity to the Upper Hunter—the site of some of Australia's oldest towns.

main attractions

◈ Barrington Tops National Park
◈ Denman
◈ Lake Glenbawn
◈ Muswellbrook
◈ Scone
◈ Upper Hunter Wineries

𝑖 Visitor information

Muswellbrook Visitors Centre
87 Hill St,
Muswellbrook, NSW 2333
Ph: (02) 6541 4050
www.muswellbrook.org.au

Bushwalker, Barrington Tops National Park

Murwillumbah is the gateway to five World Heritage-listed national parks: **Mount Warning**, **Nightcap**, **Border Ranges**, **Lamington** and **Springbrook**. Information is available from the **NPWS World**

Denman Hotel

Heritage Rainforest Centre incorporated with the visitor information centre. In Mount Warning NP, a 4.4km walking track leads from **Breakfast Creek** to the summit for good all-round views.
VISITOR INFORMATION: Cnr Tweed Valley Way and Alma St, Ph: (02) 6672 1340 or 1800 674 414

■ Muswellbrook POP 10 560
Map 91, E1
Known primarily for its premium white wines, Muswellbrook is also a pastoral district with fodder crops, stud cattle, horses, sheep and dairy products. Open-cut coal mining is a major industry of this area.
MAIN ATTRACTIONS: **Muswellbrook Town Walk** includes significant historical buildings and other highlights. Brochures are available

from the information centre.
Muswellbrook Regional Art Centre displays an extensive collection of contemporary art, on the corner of Bridge St and William St. Also worth a visit is the **Upper Hunter Wine Centre** beside the visitor centre.
NEARBY ATTRACTIONS: Several wineries, including **Rosemount Estate**, **Arrowfield Wines**, **Cruickshank Callatoota**, **Yarraman Estate**, **Verona Cellars** and **James Estate**, welcome visitors for tastings and sales. Some wineries provide picnic and BBQ facilities and a couple have restaurants attached. The historic town of **Denman**, 24km south-west of Muswellbrook, has changed little since the 1930s and a heritage order preserves the character of the main street.
Wollemi NP, to the south-west, is

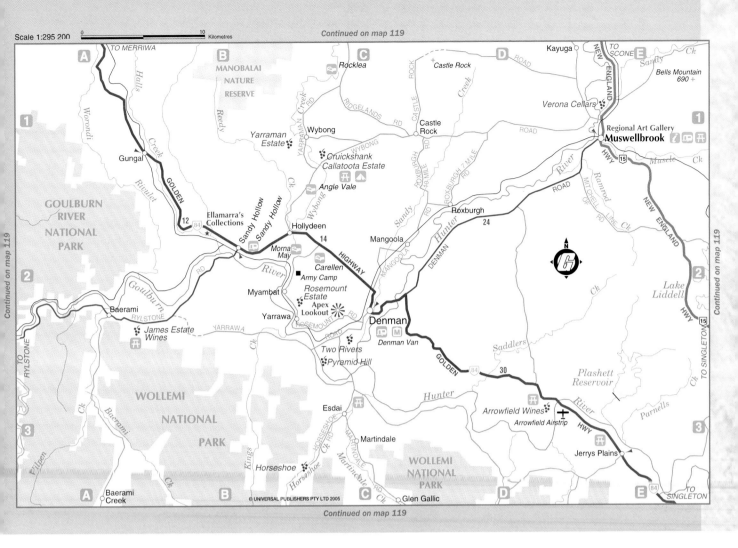

Continued on map 119

Scale 1:295 200

Continued on map 119

the second largest national park and the biggest wilderness area in New South Wales. **Lake Liddell** lies 14km south and is a water storage area with facilities for boating, waterskiing, camping and picnics.

VISITOR INFORMATION:

87 Hill St,
Ph: (02) 6541 4050

▓ Nambucca Heads POP 6255

Map 62, C5

A holiday resort, fishing and oyster-farming town, Nambucca Heads lies at the mouth of the **Nambucca River**. One of the prettiest town-ships on the **North Coast**, Nambucca Heads offers a relaxed lifestyle, a subtropical climate and safe, clean beaches. Fishing, boating and swimming are popular pastimes.

MAIN ATTRACTIONS: Stunning views of the surf, river, hills and long stretches of bush and sand dunes can be seen from four lookouts— **Rotary**, **Captain Cook**, **Pilot** and **Lions**. **Stuart Island Golf Course** is in the middle of the river and is the only island used exclusively as a golf course in Australia. A self-guided **historical walk** through the town is worthwhile exploring, including the river-foreshore walk past the sites of **Copenhagen Mill**, **Pioneer Well** and 19th-century shipyards. The **V Wall** is an outdoor graffiti gallery located on the northern breakwater. Here visitors are encouraged to paint a 'Postcard on Rock'. A 60m-long **mosaic mural sculpture**, depicting the journey of the Nambucca River, wraps around Nambucca Heads

Nambucca River estuary, Nambucca Heads

Police Station embankment in the centre of town.

NEARBY ATTRACTIONS: About 10km north of town is **Valla Beach**. Here the **Valla Smokehouse** makes delicious gourmet smoked products.

VISITOR INFORMATION: Cnr Pacific Hwy and Riverside Dr, Ph: (02) 6568 6954

Sawn Rocks, Mount Kaputar National Park, east of Narrabri

Narooma   POP 3390

Map 122, D4

A small town overlooking **Wagonga Inlet**, Narooma is 70km south of Batemans Bay. Timber, fishing and tourism are the main industries in Narooma. The surfing, family beaches, waterways and surrounding state forests make the town an appealing holiday destination.

MAIN ATTRACTIONS: Of the four main surfing beaches, Narooma's **Main Beach** and **Dalmeny Beach** are patrolled in season. The **Glasshouse Rocks** can be seen south of Main Beach. Below **Bar Rock Lookout** is **Australia Rock**, so-called because a hole in the shape of Australia has been weathered into it.

NEARBY ATTRACTIONS: The historic gold-mining town of **Central Tilba** is 17km south of Narooma. Founded in 1894, the little mountain village has been classified by the National Trust. Late 19th-century buildings now house craft workshops and the **Old Cheese Factory** gives tastings of the famous Tilba Club cheese. The waters around **Montague Island**, 8km from Narooma, are popular for anglers in search of

marlin. A flora and fauna reserve, the island is home to Australian fur seals and a variety of sea birds, including little penguins. Tours are run on the island by the National Parks and Wildlife Service and can be booked at the information centre. Diving schools also take people out to scuba dive with the seals off the island.

VISITOR INFORMATION: Princes Hwy, Ph: (02) 4476 2881

Narrabri   POP 6420

Map 114, C4

This town lies in the fertile **Namoi River Valley**, at the junction of **Narrabri Creek** and the Namoi River. Cotton is the major industry of Narrabri, although the rich, black soil of the valley supports a diversity of agricultural products, including wheat. Cotton, sunflower and a variety of other crops are processed at the **Cargill Oilseed Crushing Mill**, one of the largest of its type in the country.

MAIN ATTRACTIONS: During the cotton-picking season (April–July), guided tours help to explain the industry. Contact Narrabri Information

Centre for details. The majority of the town's historic buildings are found in **Maitland St**, the main street, others in **Dewhurst St** and **Bowen St**. The **Old Gaol** is now the local history museum and is open on Saturdays or by appointment. The **Australian Cotton Centre**, next to the information centre on Tibbereena St, has nine state-of-the-art interactive displays and is open daily. **Town Walk** and **Town Drive** leaflets are available from the information centre.

NEARBY ATTRACTIONS: The **CSIRO Australia Telescope National Facility** at Culgoora, is located 23km west of Narrabri. The visitor centre is open daily and offers hands-on experiences. **Mount Kaputar NP** is located 56km east of Narrabri. Ancient rock formations including **Sawn Rocks** and **Yullundunida Crater** are highlights. There are also scenic drives, bushwalks, campsites and cabins available.

VISITOR INFORMATION: Tibbereena St (Newell Hwy), Ph: (02) 6799 6760

Narrandera   POP 4685

Map 121, J2

Lying on the north bank of the **Murrumbidgee River**, Narrandera is surrounded by a district devoted to cereal crops, wool, fruit, lambs and cattle. It is the gateway to the **Murrumbidgee Irrigation Area** and is located 570km south-west of Sydney.

MAIN ATTRACTIONS: The **Royal Doulton ceramic fountain**, located in Victoria Square, is a memorial for those who served in WWI. The **Bundidgerry Walking Track**, which goes through the **Nature Reserve**, is the place to see koalas in the wild. **Lake Talbot** is a popular attraction for skiing, boating and fishing.

NEARBY ATTRACTIONS: **John Lake Centre** at the **Inland Fisheries Research Station** is open to the public on weekdays. Tours of the

New South Wales

centre feature live exhibits, displays and audio-visual presentations. The centre is located 5km south-east of Narrandera. **Lavender Aromatics**, 2km to the north, has fields of lavender in season and lavender products available daily.

VISITOR INFORMATION: Narrandera Park, Cadell St (Newell Hwy), Ph: (02) 6959 1766 or 1800 672 392

Narromine   POP 3550
Map 118, C3

A compact rural town on the southern bank of the **Macquarie River**, Narromine is located 40km west of Dubbo. The pastoral and wheat-growing country of the **Macquarie Valley** also produces cotton, citrus fruit, sorghum and vegetables (tomatoes and corn) as the area is so well irrigated.

MAIN ATTRACTIONS: The information centre has details of self-guided tours to local attractions. The **Blacksmith's Museum** is located off Burraway St.

NEARBY ATTRACTIONS: **Narromine Aerodrome** was visited by many famous pilots in its early days, including Charles Kingsford-Smith. Today it is home to the **Aviation Museum**. Garden lovers will want to

Queens Wharf and Tower, Newcastle

visit **Swane's Rose Nursery**, 5km north-west of town. There are old-fashioned and heritage roses as well as modern and miniature forms. The nursery has also produced a special rose for Narromine called 'Heart of Gold'. Also worthwhile visiting is the **Narromine Iris Farm**, which displays over 800 varieties of the plant. There is a picnic area. **The Lime Grove** is the largest lime orchard in Australia. **Gin Gin Weir** is an attractive beach and picnic area on the banks of the Macquarie River, 30km north-west of Narromine.

VISITOR INFORMATION: Edgerton Nursery, 42 Dandaloo St, Ph: (02) 6889 1187

Nelson Bay   POP 7975
Map 95, B3

Located on **Port Stephens**, 60km north-east of Newcastle on the **Mid-North Coast**, the resort town of Nelson Bay is the main commercial centre on the **Tomaree Peninsula**. Nelson Bay is a pretty town of gardens and galleries and home to the Port Stephens fishing fleet. Many visitors come for the oysters and other seafood.

MAIN ATTRACTIONS: Nelson Bay has dolphin- and whale-watching cruises and fishing charters. Cruises also visit **Broughton Island**, **Myall River** and **Lakes**. Game fishing is especially well-regarded in the area and there are several major competitions held throughout the year. The Heritage Trust-listed **Inner Lighthouse** at **Little Beach** has heritage displays and a maritime museum. It also has alfresco dining with great views. **Toboggan Hill Park** on Salamander Way has a 700m slope and also offers mini-golf, Krazy cars, canoe rides and indoor rockclimbing.

NEARBY ATTRACTIONS: The nearby townships of **Shoal Bay**, **Fingal Bay**, **Anna Bay**, **Salamander Bay** and **Soldiers Point** provide a wide range of accommodation and activities

year round. While most of the action is centred on Port Stephens waterways, there are many other activities available, including 4-wheel drive tours, golf courses, beach and bush horseriding. **Tomaree NP** is a good place to explore, with wonderful views from **Tomaree Headland Lookout**. The area is noted for its colonies of koalas. The **Native Flora Grand Walk** at **Fly Point** has 15 vantage points to enjoy the wildflowers and views. **Oakvale Farm and Fauna World** and **Port Stephens Winery** are a short drive away towards the Pacific Hwy.

VISITOR INFORMATION: Victoria Pde, Ph: 1800 808 900

Newcastle   POP 279 500
Map 119, H4

The second largest metropolitan area in New South Wales, Newcastle is an administrative, commercial, cultural and industrial centre for the **Hunter Region**. Located at the mouth of the **Hunter River**, Newcastle is one of the largest and busiest ports in the country. It is also a cosmopolitan tourist destination with a wide variety of restaurants, galleries, museums, beaches and parklands.

MAIN ATTRACTIONS: **The Town Walk**—brochure available from the information centre—features sites of heritage value to the city. This includes the **Convict Lumberyard**, which is the site of the old convict barracks; and **Fort Scratchley**, which now houses **Newcastle Maritime Museum**. **Newcastle Regional Museum**, housed in the former Castlemaine Brewery in Hunter St, includes permanent 'hands-on' science exhibits for children, **Supernova** and **Mininova**, as well as historical displays. **The Wetlands Centre** near Sandgate is well worth a visit. Newcastle has many excellent beaches that are great for surfing and family outings.

Described as **'Blue Water Paradise'**, Port Stephens is an expansive waterway two-and-a-half times the size of Sydney Harbour. It extends 24km inland from the sea and its sandy beaches, bays and sand dunes have proved a magnet to generations of holidaymakers. Capt James Cook, in May 1770, named the harbour in honour of Sir Phillip Stephens, Secretary of the Admiralty.

Pods of wild bottlenose dolphins are one of the region's most noted attractions. **Dolphin-spotting** and **whale-watching cruises** are very popular. A number of lookouts on **Tomaree Headland** offer excellent vantage points for sighting the migrating whales during winter and spring. Fishing is popular within the waterway and offshore for a wide variety of species. Port Stephens hosts the world's largest game-fishing competition each year and several other fishing competitions. Not surprisingly, it is renowned for the quality of its fresh seafood. Port Stephens is one of the biggest oyster-growing areas in Australia.

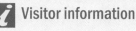

main attractions

- ◈ Dolphin- and whale-watching cruises
- ◈ Inner Lighthouse, Tearooms and Museum
- ◈ Stockton sand dunes
- ◈ Toboggan Hill Park
- ◈ Tomaree National Park

i Visitor information

Port Stephens Visitor Information Centre
Victoria Pde,
Nelson Bay, NSW 2315
Freecall: 1800 808 900
www.portstephens.org.au

Dolphin-spotting cruise, Port Stephens

NEARBY ATTRACTIONS: The wineries of the **Hunter Valley** are not far away. **Nelson Bay** is also nearby and visitors come here to join daily dolphin-watching cruises and whale-watching cruises in season. On the drive to Nelson Bay visitors will pass the **RAAF's Williamtown base**. **Fighter World**, a display centre for military fighter aircraft is located here and is open daily. **Stockton Beach**, in the same area, has the largest sand dune system in the Southern Hemisphere.
VISITOR INFORMATION: 361 Hunter St, Ph: (02) 4974 2999

■ Nowra   POP 18 765
Map 97, B2
The commercial and tourist centre for the **Shoalhaven Region**, Nowra is located about 80km south of Wollongong on the southern bank of the **Shoalhaven River**. An eight-span steel bridge links the city with **Bomaderry** on the other side of the river. Bomaderry is the terminus of the rail link to Sydney. Nowra's main industries are milk processing, pulp and paper milling, fishing and flour milling.
MAIN ATTRACTIONS: **Nowra Animal Park**, located on the western bank of the Shoalhaven River, has birds, and native and farm animals. Camping and BBQ facilities are available and visitors can enjoy light lunches or Devonshire teas at the riverside coffee lounge. Owned by the Historic Houses Trust, **Meroogal: Women's History Place**, built in 1885, contains the original contents collected by four generations of mostly women. It is open for guided tours. **Shoalhaven Historical Museum** is on the corner of Kinghorne St and Plunkett St.
NEARBY ATTRACTIONS: The **Australian Museum of Flight** at HMAS *Albatross* has an excellent collection of historic military aircraft, engines, uniforms and memorabilia. Located at the end of Albatross Rd, the museum is open daily. **Bundanon**, the former home and studio of artist Arthur Boyd, is accessed via Illaroo Rd to the west. There is an open day every Sunday.
VISITOR INFORMATION: Cnr Princes Hwy and Pleasant Way, Ph: (02) 4421 0778

■ Nyngan   POP 2250
Map 118, B1
Nyngan is the regional centre for surrounding wheat farms, sheep and cattle studs. The town is close to the geographical centre of New

Continued on map 119

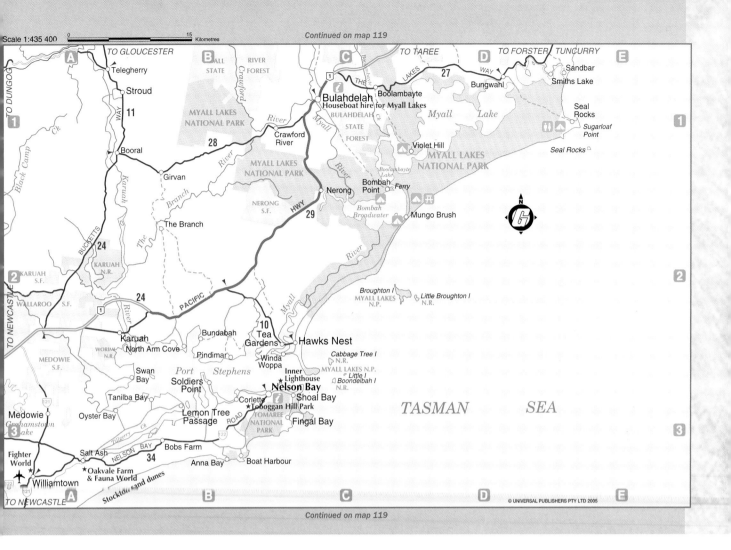

Scale 1:435 400   0   15   Kilometres

Continued on map 119

South Wales, 603km north-west of Sydney, beside the **Bogan River**.
MAIN ATTRACTIONS: Several public buildings, including the **Town Hall**, **Post Office** and **Court House** are testaments to the town's progressive phase in the 1880s and 1890s. They are all found on **Cobar St**, which runs parallel to the Mitchell Hwy. A tiled historic mural, located beside **Davidson Park**, records the history of the town and its pioneering families. Nyngan has an attractive 18-hole golf course and three licensed clubs. **Nyngan Museum** is in Pangee St and the **Shearing Shed Museum** is in Nymagee St. Both are usually open daily.
NEARBY ATTRACTIONS: Local landmarks include the grave of **Richard Cunningham**, a botanist with Sir Thomas Mitchell's exploration party.

The grave is on a station near **Tottenham**, 70km south-east of Nyngan. The **Macquarie Marshes** is an extensive wetland area on the **Murray-Darling system**, 62km north-east of Nyngan. A large part of this important bird and wildlife habitat is a wildlife sanctuary. Accommodation in the area includes a caravan park and campground, and bunk beds are available at **Willie's Retreat**.
VISITOR INFORMATION: Nyngan Video Parlour, 105 Pangee St, Ph: (02) 6832 1155

■ Orange   POP 31 935
Map 118, D4
The sixth largest city in New South Wales, Orange is surrounded by fertile farming land that produces an abundance of fruit, wheat, wine grapes, sheep, cattle and pigs. Not

actually known for citrus fruits, Orange does produce a good percentage of the State's apples. Cherry, pear and stone-fruit orchards also thrive in the red soil.
MAIN ATTRACTIONS: Wine tasting is a popular activity for those wanting to experience cool-climate wines. A brochure on wineries open to the public is available from the information centre in Byng St. The poet **Banjo Paterson** was born at Narrambla, near Orange in 1864. A memorial in **Banjo Paterson Park**, on the Ophir Rd, 5km north-east of Orange, marks his birthplace. Also worthwhile visiting are **Orange Botanic Gardens**, located off Kearneys Dr, in the north of the city. They were first planted in 1981. **Orange Regional Art Gallery**, in Byng St, houses a permanent art

(CONTINUED P.98)

Located approximately 163km south of Sydney the Shoalhaven-Jervis Bay region offers the best of rural and coastal scenery. Dairying on the rich rolling hills, fishing and tourism are the main industries, creating a peaceful ambience. The quaint rural villages, featuring teahouses, antique shops, galleries, cosy B&B cottages and old-fashioned pubs have lots of country charm.

From the massive coastal cliffs of the **Beecroft Peninsula** all the way round to **Governor Head** in **Booderee NP**, the sheltered waters of Jervis Bay (10km wide and 15km long) provide a wonderful ocean 'playground'.

Hyams Beach is reputed to have the whitest sand in the world. Home to several pods of dolphins, the clear waters of Jervis Bay are also well-known for diving and watersports. Not surprisingly, fishing is one of the region's key industries and a pleasant pastime for amateur anglers. The headlands are renowned as being one of the few spots in the world where it is possible to catch game fish like marlin and sailfish

from the shore. Dolphins, seals, little penguins and seasonally migrating whales frequent the area, and there are cruises on offer. **Jervis Bay NP** and **Booderee NP** preserve the unique landforms, flora and fauna of this area as well as important Aboriginal sites.

A Safe Haven

Abrahams Bosom Beach, near Currarong, was the site where the shipwrecked passengers of the SS *Merimbula* found safety. It is named after the Bosom of Abraham, described in the Old Testament of *The Bible*, where children found shelter and safety.

i Visitor information

Shoalhaven Visitors Centre
Princes Hwy, Nowra, NSW 2541
Ph: (02) 4421 0778 or 1800 024 261
www.shoalhaven.nsw.gov.au

Booderee National Park Visitors Centre
Jervis Bay Rd, Jervis Bay, NSW 2540
Ph: (02) 4443 0977

Coolangatta Estate winery

main attractions

◈ **Berry**
This pretty hamlet boasts many charming buildings classified by the National Trust.

◈ **Bundanon**
Visit famous painter Arthur Boyd's scenic property, now a gallery.

◈ **Coolangatta Historic Village**
This historic village was the first European South Coast settlement.

◈ **Jervis Bay**
This is a beautiful bay with a 50km shoreline of protected beaches.

◈ **Jervis Bay National Park**
The national park boasts pristine beaches.

◈ **Lady Denman Heritage Complex**
Once a ferry, *Lady Denman* is now housed within the maritime museum which is part of the complex at Huskisson.

◈ **Nowra Animal Park**
Native fauna is on show in a rainforest setting at Nowra Animal Park.

◈ **Nowra Historical Buildings**
St Andrews Church, the old Police Station and Meroogal House are all historical buildings in Nowra.

◈ **Seven Mile Beach National Park**
This national park has a long expanse of white, sandy beach flanked by sand dunes.

Slipway at Huskisson, Jervis Bay

New South Wales

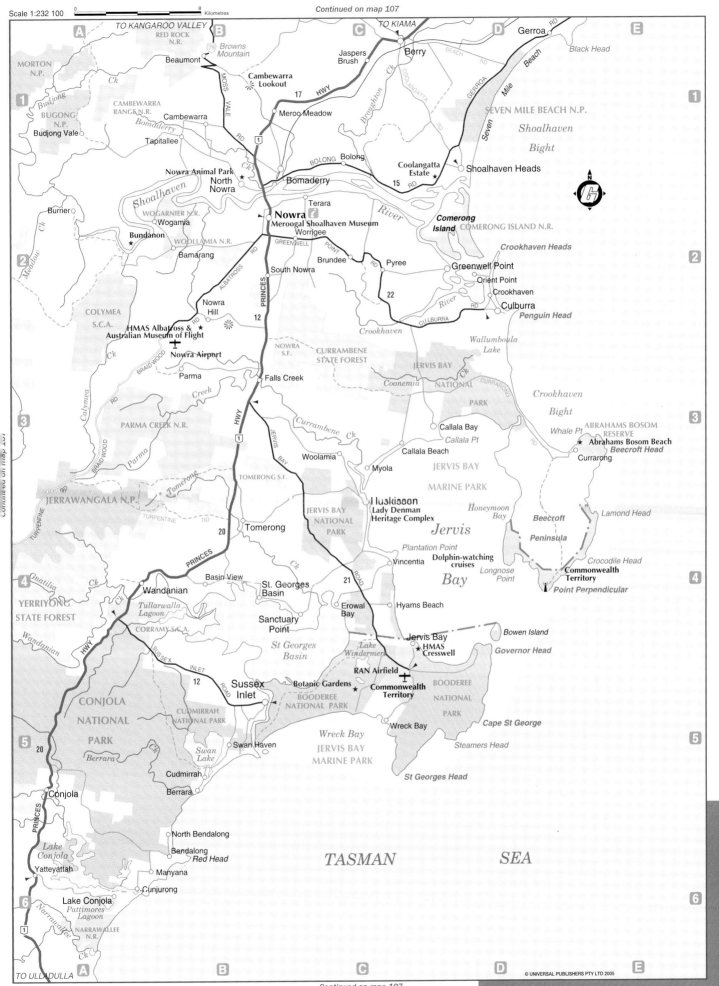

Continued on map 107

Scale 1:232 100

Kilometres

TO KANGAROO VALLEY

RED ROCK N.R.

(79) Browns Mountain

Beaumont

MORTON N.P.

Budjong Ck

BUGONG N.P.

Budjong Vale

CAMBEWARRA RANGE N.R.

Cambewarra

Bomaderry Ck

Tapitallee

Cambewarra Lookout

Meroo Meadow

Jaspers Brush

TO KIAMA

Berry

Gerroa

Black Head

Gerroa RD

SEVEN MILE BEACH N.P.

Seven Mile Beach

Shoalhaven Bight

Bolong

BOLONG

Bomaderry

Nowra Animal Park

North Nowra

Shoalhaven

WOGARNIER N.R.

Wogamia

Burrier

Bundanon

WOOLLAMIA N.R.

Bamarang

Terara

Nowra

Meroogal Shoalhaven Museum

Worrigee

GREENWELL

Brundee

Pyree

South Nowra

Coolangatta Estate

Shoalhaven Heads

Comerong Island

COMERONG ISLAND N.R.

Crookhaven Heads

Greenwell Point

Orient Point

Crookhaven

Culburra

Penguin Head

COLYMEA S.C.A.

Nowra Hill

HMAS Albatross & Australian Museum of Flight

Nowra Airport

Parma

BRAIDWOOD RD

Calymea Ck

PARMA CREEK N.R.

Parma

Falls Creek

NOWRA S.F.

CURRAMBENE STATE FOREST

Crookhaven

Currambene Ck

Wallumboula Lake

JERVIS BAY

Coonemia

NATIONAL

PARK

Crookhaven Bight

Whale Pt

ABRAHAMS BOSOM RESERVE

Abrahams Bosom Beach

Beecroft Head

Currarong

Woolamia

Callala Bay

Callala Pt

Callala Beach

Myola

JERVIS BAY

MARINE PARK

JERRAWANGALA N.P.

TURPENTINE RD

Tomerong

TOMERONG S.F.

JERVIS BAY NATIONAL PARK

Huskisson

Lady Denman Heritage Complex

Jervis

Honeymoon Bay

Lamond Head

Beecroft Peninsula

Crocodile Head

Commonwealth Territory

Point Perpendicular

Plantation Point

Dolphin-watching cruises

Vincentia

Bay

Longnose Point

Governor Head

Basin View

St. Georges Basin

Wandanian

YERRIYONG STATE FOREST

Tullarwalla Lagoon

CORRAMY S.C.A.

Sanctuary Point

Erowal Bay

Hyams Beach

Jervis Bay

HMAS Cresswell

Bowen Island

St Georges Basin

Lake Windermere

RAN Airfield

Commonwealth Territory

BOODEREE NATIONAL PARK

Cape St George

SUSSEX INLET RD

Sussex Inlet

Botanic Gardens

BOODEREE NATIONAL PARK

Wreck Bay

CONJOLA NATIONAL PARK

CUDMIRRAH NATIONAL PARK

Swan Haven

Swan Lake

Wreck Bay

JERVIS BAY MARINE PARK

Steamers Head

Berrara

Cudmirrah

Berrara

St Georges Head

North Bendalong

Bendalong

Red Head

TASMAN   SEA

Conjola

Lake Conjola

Yatteyattah

Manyana

Cunjurong

Lake Conjola

Pattimores Lagoon

NARRAWALLEE N.R.

Narrawallee Ck

TO ULLADULLA

Continued on map 107

© UNIVERSAL PUBLISHERS PTY LTD 2005

NEW SOUTH WALES   97

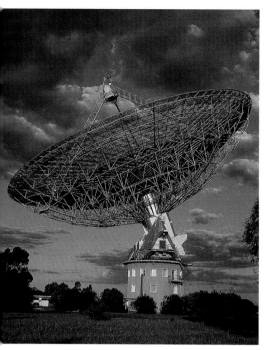

CSIRO Radio Telescope, north of Parkes

collection and also hosts touring exhibitions.

NEARBY ATTRACTIONS: **Borenore Caves Reserve** is located 17.5km west of Orange. A walking trail leads from **Arch Cave** and follows **Boree Creek** through to the more difficult **Tunnel** and **Verandah Caves**. Take a good torch to explore the caves. The reserve also has picnic facilities.
VISITOR INFORMATION: Byng St,
Ph: (02) 6393 8226

Parkes POP 10 100
Map 118, C4

This **Central Western** town is surrounded by productive agricultural and grazing land. Parkes is an important bulkhead and wheat storage facility strategically placed on the state's north/south road and east/west rail links.
MAIN ATTRACTIONS: Parkes' major bicentennial project involved the restoration of the former Bush-man's goldmine at **Bushman's Hill Reserve**, off the Newell Hwy. The main evidence of the mine's existence is an old chimney. Also in the reserve is an Aboriginal

walkway, and picnic and BBQ facilities. **Henry Parkes Historical Museum** is open daily and features pioneering and gold-mining items. The most impressive exhibit is Sir Henry Parkes' library, which contains some 1000 books. Panoramic views of the town, **Goobang Valley** and the **Bumberry Mountains** can be seen from the **Shrine of Remembrance** on Memorial Hill.
NEARBY ATTRACTIONS: Popularised in the movie, *The Dish*, and located 20km north off the Newell Hwy is the **CSIRO Radio Telescope**, one of the world's leading radio astronomy centres. The **Visitors Discovery Centre** has audio-visual and three-dimensional displays, BBQ facilities and a cafe. The 64m-wide dish was built in 1961. **Bumberry Dam**, 24km east off the Orange Rd, is a popular recreation area.
VISITOR INFORMATION: Kelly Reserve, Newell Hwy, Ph: (02) 6862 4365

Port Macquarie POP 37 700
Map 119, K1

Named after Governor Lachlan Macquarie, the town was established as a penal settlement in 1821. Present-day Port Macquarie is a fishing port and very popular tourist destination. Because of its pleasant year-round climate and lifestyle, it is attracting increasing numbers of families and retirees to settle in the area.
MAIN ATTRACTIONS: **Sea Acres Nature Reserve**, open daily, has a Rainforest Centre and rainforest boardwalk. The **Koala Hospital** at Roto House has daily koala feedings at 3pm. Popular **camel safaris** are available on **Lighthouse Beach**. The award-winning **Hastings Historical Museum,** on Clarence St, displays convict and pioneer relics in 15 different rooms. **St Thomas' Church** in Hay St was built by convicts in 1824 and is one of the oldest churches in Australia.

NEARBY ATTRACTIONS: Port Macquarie has an animal park close by, **Billabong Koala and Aussie Park**. Open daily, the park is located off the Oxley Hwy. **Cassegrain Winery**, on the Pacific Hwy, is open daily for tastings and sales, and offers picnic, BBQ and children's play areas. South of Port Macquarie, beside the **Camden Haven River**, are the townships of **North Haven**, **Laurieton** and **Dunbogan**; together they make up the holiday area of **Camden Haven**. The clean waterways, lakes, forests, national parks and unspoilt coastline make this a worthwhile place to stay.
VISITOR INFORMATION: Cnr Clarence St and Hay St, Ph: (02) 6581 8000 or 1300 303 155

Queanbeyan POP 29 780
Map 135, D4

Situated at the junction of the **Molonglo** and **Queanbeyan rivers**, 12km south-east of Canberra, Queanbeyan is the business centre for a wool-growing and mixed farming community.
MAIN ATTRACTIONS: **Queanbeyan and District Historical Museum** and **Queanbeyan Art Gallery** are interesting attractions. The sunken gardens of **Queanbeyan Park** and **Queen Elizabeth Park** beside the Queanbeyan River are ideal picnic spots. Good views can be had from the lookout in **Bicentennial Park**.
NEARBY ATTRACTIONS: Queanbeyan's location adjacent to the national capital, the snowfields, the scenic **South Coast** and historic towns make it an ideal base from which to explore. The major art and craft towns of **Bungendore** and **Braidwood**, both on Kings Hwy, have restored buildings, antique shops and lots of historic charm. The Australian Railway Historical Society runs diesel and steam trips on the **Michelago Tourist Railway** to Royalia and Bungendore. For fishing, bushwalking, birdwatching

and picnicking visit **Googong Foreshores**, 10km south, or **Molonglo Gorge**, 1km north. (refer also to Canberra section pp.124–137)

VISITOR INFORMATION: 1 Farrer Pl, Ph: (02) 6298 0241 or 1800 026 192

■ Sawtell   POP 13 740
Map 62, D3

A resort town with surfing beaches, quiet swimming spots, excellent fishing, boating and camping sites, Sawtell is 537km north of Sydney. **Coffs Harbour** and all its attractions are only 8km further north.

MAIN ATTRACTIONS: There are original buildings in Sawtell's main street reflecting the history of the area. The old **Sawtell Hotel** survives, as does the picture theatre which shows both classic and modern movies. **Boambee Creek Reserve** has picnic and BBQ facilities. The reserve behind **Sawtell Beach** is also a popular picnic area

NEARBY ATTRACTIONS: **Coffs Harbour Butterfly House and Maze** is home to hundreds of colourful Australian butterflies in a subtropical rainforest setting. There is also a maze, delightful gardens and a tearoom. Located on the Pacific Hwy at **Bonville**, the Butterfly House and Maze is open every day except Monday (every day during school holidays).

VISITOR INFORMATION: 71 First Ave, Ph: (02) 6658 3866

■ Scone   POP 4560
Map 119, G2

This **Upper Hunter Valley** town is the commercial centre for an area of beautiful country famous for its prosperous horse stud farms. Kentucky in the USA is the only horse-breeding region in the world larger than Scone Shire. The importance of horses to Scone is represented by Gabriel Sterk's statue *Mare & Foal* that stands in **Elizabeth Park**, at the northern end of town. The surrounding area

is also renowned for dairying and other primary products.

MAIN ATTRACTIONS: Visitors who are interested in working horses should try the **Australian Stock Horse Museum** located in Guernsey St. The museum is also the national headquarters for the Australian Stock Horse Society. The **Historical Society Museum** is housed in the original town gaol; there are still two old cells at the back of the building. The museum documents local history and opens Wednesdays and Sundays or by appointment.

NEARBY ATTRACTIONS: **Burning Mountain** is located on the New England Hwy, 20km north. Early settlers originally thought the mountain was a volcano after seeing smoke rising from it. The smoke is caused by a coal seam that has smouldered 30m underground for thousands of years.

VISITOR INFORMATION: Cnr Kelly St and Susan St, Ph: (02) 6545 1526

■ Singleton   POP 12 530
Map 119, H3

This **Hunter River** town is 77km north-west of Newcastle and historically has been the business centre for a rich dairying district. Beneath the farms are huge coal seams that have been mined since the beginning of the 19th century. More recently, open-cut mining,

supplying steaming and coking coals, has transformed the region.

MAIN ATTRACTIONS: **Rose Point Park**, beside the Hunter River, is the location of Singleton's **Bicentennial Sundial**. The sundial was a gift from a local mine and is reputed to be the largest of its kind in the world. There are many historical buildings in town. Some of the earliest are the **Post Office** and the **Court House**, both built in 1841. The latter is now occupied by the **Historical Museum**. **Sacred Spaces: The Sisters of Mercy Convent Chapel** in Queen St can be visited at weekends or by appointment.

NEARBY ATTRACTIONS: The vineyards of the **Lower and Upper Hunter** and **Broke region** are within easy reach of Singleton. (*see* pp. 58–59 and 90–91). Singleton is ideally located as a stepping-off point for exploration of the largest wilderness area in New South Wales, **Wollemi NP**. The area also boasts some beautiful scenery. **Lake St Clair** lies 33km north-east of Singleton and is a wonderful recreation area, ideal for waterskiing, sailing and fishing. The **Royal Australian Infantry Corps Museum** at Lone Pine Barracks, Singleton Army Camp, is open Wednesday to Sunday.

VISITOR INFORMATION: 39 George St, Ph: (02) 6571 5888 or 1800 449 888

Sawtell Beach

■ South West Rocks   POP 4120
Map 115, H5

The largest of the **Macleay Valley's** seaside towns, South West Rocks lies on the shores of **Trial Bay**, near the mouth of the **Macleay River**. Stunning scenery and beaches combine to make this a most relaxing resort town.

MAIN ATTRACTIONS: Fishing charter boats operate from **New Entrance**, and beach and estuary fishing are also popular. Scuba divers come to dive around **Fish Rock Cave**, about 2km south-east of **Smoky Cape Lighthouse**. Apart from the beaches and watersports, the main attraction is **Trial Bay Gaol**. The semi-ruined prison was built of local granite in 1886 by prisoners who had to build their own gaol while working on the breakwater. Abandoned in 1903, the gaol was used as an internment centre for 500 Germans during WWI. Surrounding the gaol is **Arakoon State Conservation Area**. Offering beaches, rainforest and coastal heathlands, there is much to explore, and advanced walkers can continue south along the coast as far as Smoky Cape Lighthouse in **Hat Head NP.**

VISITOR INFORMATION: Historic Boatmans Cottage, Horseshoe Bay, Ph Kempsey: (02) 6563 1555

■ Sussex Inlet   POP 3030
Map 97, B5

A very popular holiday destination for families, Sussex Inlet is located on the channel that connects **St Georges Basin** with the Pacific Ocean. Sussex Inlet has not escaped the trend of residential canal development, which has almost made it an island but fortunately has not spoilt the charm of this peaceful town.

MAIN ATTRACTIONS: Sussex Inlet is famous among anglers for its very good fishing; a fishing carnival is held here annually during the July school holidays. South of the town-

ship, the beaches at **Berrara** and **Cudmirrah** provide some great surfing. The local golf course is a drawcard for visiting golfers who don't mind sharing the fairways with kangaroos and other wildlife.

NEARBY ATTRACTIONS: Before the turn-off to Sussex Inlet, the Princes Hwy passes through **Wandandian**, a village steeped in the history of the region's early timber industry. There are two craft shops and an art gallery located here, and the **Riverside Plant and Herb Nursery**.

VISITOR INFORMATION: Cnr Princes Hwy and Pleasant Way, Nowra, Ph: (02) 4421 0778

■ Tamworth   POP 32 450
Map 114, E6

The commercial centre for the prosperous farming area of the **Peel Valley**, Tamworth is a progressive and growing city. There are fine restaurants, four licensed clubs, two major shopping centres and many specialty shops.

MAIN ATTRACTIONS: Renowned as the '**Country Music Capital of Australia**', Tamworth has hosted the **Golden Guitar Awards** for more than 30 years. Thousands of visitors arrive in Tamworth for the 10-day festival, which is held in January. There are hundreds of shows and much of the music is provided free-of-charge. **Bicentennial Park**, located alongside the **Peel River**, is a relaxing spot and a walk following the river's edge will reveal a war memorial, a distinctive fountain and busts of country music stars.

NEARBY ATTRACTIONS: **Nundle**, in the **Hills of Gold**, is an old gold-mining town with many original buildings to admire and craft shops to browse through. There are several scenic outlooks in the district. **Nundle Woollen Mill** is open daily. **Lake Keepit** is located 57km west of Tamworth and is the place for powerboats, waterskiing and fishing. There are also children's facilities and a caravan park.

VISITOR INFORMATION: Cnr Peel St and Murray St, Ph: (02) 6755 4300

Sailboats at Arakoon State Conservation Area, near South West Rocks

New South Wales

Indian Head at sunrise, Crowdy Bay National Park, north of Taree

■ Taree   POP 18 705

Map 119, K2

This town is the commercial and administrative centre for the prosperous dairying, grazing, timber, boat-building, fishing, oyster-farming and tourist district of the **Manning Valley**. Located at the southern end of the **North Coast**, 326km north of Sydney, Taree is rewarding for both sightseers and shoppers and is just a short detour off the Pacific Hwy.

MAIN ATTRACTIONS: With 150km of navigable waterways, the **Manning River** is a popular venue for cruising, rowing, sailing, water-skiing and fishing. In 1995, the river was the focus of worldwide media attention when a Brydes whale, 'Willy', stayed here for 100 days. **Queen Elizabeth Park**, edging the river, is an ideal spot for a picnic in the city centre. There is an interesting **art gallery** located on Macquarie St.

NEARBY ATTRACTIONS: Nearby beach resorts include **Old Bar Beach**, to the south, and **Crowdy Head** to the north. **Ellenborough Falls**, located 50km from Taree, is accessed on Tourist Drive 8. One of the highest-single drop waterfalls in the Southern Hemisphere, Ellenborough Falls plunges 200m into a rainforest gorge below. There are also walking trails with picnic areas clearly marked.

VISITOR INFORMATION: 21 Manning River Dr, Taree North, Ph: (02) 6592 5444 or 1800 182 733

■ Temora   POP 4150

Map 121, K1

The rail centre for the rich wheat and sheep belt of the **Riverina**, Temora is located 460km south-west of Sydney. The town is also recognised as a centre for harness racing and there are many trotting studs in the district. Races are held here regularly.

MAIN ATTRACTIONS: Temora has a range of sporting clubs and venues. For the adventurous, a skydiving company operates from the airport.

Temora Aviation Museum in Menzies St is open Wednesday to Sunday and organises flying on weekends. **Temora Rural Museum** in Junee Rd is open daily.

NEARBY ATTRACTIONS: **Lake Centenary**, 4km from Temora on the West Wyalong Rd, is a popular venue for picnics and watersports including boating, canoeing, sailing, swimming and fishing. **Ariah Park**, 34km west, is a village listed by the National Trust as a Conservation Area. Notable buildings include the **Lyons' Wool Store**, the hotel, and the **Westpac** and **National banks**.

VISITOR INFORMATION: 294-296 Hoskins St, Ph: (02) 6977 1511

■ Tenterfield   POP 3215

Map 115, G2

The northern gateway to the **New England** area, Tenterfield is the centre of a sheep- and cattle-grazing district. Autumn is a particularly beautiful time to visit as the banks of **Tenterfield Creek** are covered with the gold and red leaves of the deciduous trees.

MAIN ATTRACTIONS: The town can be investigated by taking the **Historic Walk**. A brochure for this tour is available at the information centre. Trains no longer run to Tenterfield Railway Station, and it is now the **Railway Museum**. Preserving railway memorabilia and history, the museum is open daily. The **Federation Museum** in Rouse St is also open daily. The historic **Saddlers Shop** (1860s), in High St, was made famous in Peter Allen's song, *Tenterfield Saddler*, commemorating his grandfather who was the saddler here for 50 years.

NEARBY ATTRACTIONS: There are several fascinating parks in the area, including **Boonoo Boonoo NP** and **Bald Rock NP**. The road to Bald Rock, the largest granite rock in Australia, is now fully sealed.

VISITOR INFORMATION: 157 Rouse St (New England Hwy), Ph: (02) 6736 1082

Terrigal   POP 9465
Map 71, C4

Only a few kilometres from Gosford, Terrigal is an attractive **Central Coast** holiday resort.
MAIN ATTRACTIONS: The beach, with its esplanade, boutiques, cafes and international-standard resort, is the main attraction. **Terrigal Beach** and beaches to the north and south attract surfers. Pedal boats, canoes and sailboards are available on the calm waters of **Terrigal Lagoon**. **The Skillion**, a headland, provides a good view over Terrigal. Deep-sea fishing, abseiling and rockclimbing are all available in the region for those feeling adventurous. Contact **Central Coast Charters** for deep-sea fishing; and for canyoning, abseiling, bushwalking, orienteering and rock-climbing contact **Central Coast Bushworks**.
NEARBY ATTRACTIONS: The good surfing beaches around Terrigal include **Wamberal Beach**, to the north; and **Avoca Beach**, 7.5km south. Half-way between Terrigal and Gosford is **Erina Fair**, the largest shopping centre on the Central Coast. Also at Erina is the **Fragrant Garden**, specialising in scented herbs and perfumed oils. **Matcham Valley** is a picturesque area just 8km from Terrigal Beach. Ken Duncan's **Australia Wide Gallery** is located here and well worth visiting. Ken Duncan is one of Australia's leading panoramic landscape photographers. There is a **waterslide** 6km north at **Forresters Beach**.
VISITOR INFORMATION: Rotary Park, Terrigal Dr, Ph: 1300 130 708

The Entrance   POP 5350
Map 71, D4

A commercial fishing centre and busy tourist resort, The Entrance is renowned for its fishing, surfing, swimming and picturesque scenery. Typical of many seaside resorts on the **Central Coast**, The Entrance is situated between the coast and the quiet waters of **Tuggerah Lake**.
MAIN ATTRACTIONS: Pelicans can be seen everywhere on Central Coast waterways and are now the tourist symbol of The Entrance. Hundreds of pelicans gather for the **Pelican Feeding** at 3.30pm daily, at **Memorial Park**, off Marine Pde.

Another local attraction is the **Shell Museum** at **Dunleith Caravan Park**, where local memorabilia and old photographs complement the extensive shell collection. All forms of watersports are available at The Entrance. There are boat ramps on each side of **The Entrance Bridge** and picnic facilities can be found in the recreation areas facing the lake.
NEARBY ATTRACTIONS: **Wyrrabalong NP** covers much of the spit of land between The Entrance North and **Toukley**. Another section of the national park is known locally as **Red Gum Forest**.
VISITOR INFORMATION: Marine Pde, Ph: 1300 130 708

Toukley   POP 4985
Map 71, D3

With lakes to the west, the Tasman Sea to the east and national parks both north and south, this **Central Coast** town is an ideal location for boaties, fishermen and nature lovers. Toukley faces the narrow strip of land that separates **Tuggerah** and **Budgewoi lakes**. Both lakes offer excellent fishing, swimming, safe boating and wind-surfing. Foreshore prawning is a popular summer activity.
NEARBY ATTRACTIONS: **Munmorah State Conservation Area** is north of Toukley. It edges **Lake Munmorah** and the Tasman Sea and encompasses several beaches. It is best visited in spring to see the wildflowers. There are two lookouts, both accessed by road. Close to town are many picnic areas: at **Canton Beach**, facing Tuggerah Lake; at **Osborne Park**, in Peel St; and in **Toukley Gardens**, facing Budgewoi Lake. **Edward Hargraves**, the first man to discover payable gold in Australia, built his all-cedar house in the 1860s. The house, in Elizabeth Dr, **Noraville**, still stands and can be seen from the road.
VISITOR INFORMATION: Wallarah Rd, Gorokan, Ph: 1300 130 708

Pelican feeding at Memorial Park, The Entrance

New South Wales

Tumut POP 6200

Map 122, A3

Located on the north-west slopes of the **Snowy Mountains**, Tumut is surrounded by forests and rich pastoral and agricultural land. The northern gateway to the Snowy Mountains, Tumut is the commercial centre for the district.

MAIN ATTRACTIONS: The town's history is reflected in its original buildings, including early homes; the Edmund Blacket-designed **All Saints Church** (1875); the stucco-brick **Court House** (1878); and the historic **racecourse grandstand** framed by poplars and English oaks. Fishing is popular given the well-stocked rivers, dams and streams. Other activities available include 4-wheel driving, canoeing, horseriding, abseiling, hang-gliding and scenic flights. There are many walking trails, including the famous **Hume and Hovell Walking Track**, tempting walkers into **Kosciuszko NP**. Huge inland lakes created by the **Snowy Mountains Hydro-Electric Scheme** provide areas for watersports and many kinds of boating.

NEARBY ATTRACTIONS: Just over 20km west of Tumut is the historic gold town of **Adelong**. Here, the attractive **Adelong Falls** and old gold workings near the stream are to be found. Further afield is another historic gold-mining site at **Kiandra**, 95km south of Tumut.

VISITOR INFORMATION: Cnr Snowy Mountains Hwy and Gocup (Gundagai) Rd, Ph: (02) 6947 7025

Tweed Heads POP 37 800

Map 115, J1

Sitting on the New South Wales border next to **Coolangatta** in Queensland, Tweed Heads and Coolangatta have been labelled the **'Twin Towns'** and form a family holiday resort destination at the southern end of the **Gold Coast** tourist strip. Quieter than the Gold Coast, Tweed Heads is an ideal holiday base, with accommodation to suit all budgets and easy access to beaches and the towns and villages of the hinterland. For a change of pace, the Gold Coast with its nightlife and themed attractions is only a few kilometres north.

MAIN ATTRACTIONS: Morning and afternoon tea, and lunch cruises, flat-bottomed boat cruises and cruises with special activities are all available on the **Tweed River**. Deep-sea fishing charters are also offered. **Minjungbal Aboriginal Cultural Centre** is beside **Boyds Bay Bridge**.

NEARBY ATTRACTIONS: Not far to the north of Coolangatta is **Currumbin Wildlife Sanctuary**, open daily. Here, at this famous wildlife park, visitors can hand-feed the native animals and brightly coloured lorikeets. Further south towards **Murwillumbah** there are major tourist attractions such as **Tropical Fruit World**. Open daily, there is a huge plantation and visitors can see, touch, taste and smell a variety of tropical fruits. Inland there are many small mountain villages to explore and three World Heritage-listed national parks; **Mount Warning**, **Nightcap** and **Border Ranges**.

VISITOR INFORMATION: Centro Tweed, Wharf St, Ph: (07) 5536 4244 or 1800 674 414

Ulladulla POP 9590

Map 107, B6

Known for its coastal waterways and excellent golf courses, Ulladulla and its twin town, **Mollymook**, form a pleasant South Coast holiday centre.

MAIN ATTRACTIONS: The annual **Blessing of the Fleet** in Ulladulla Harbour is one of a number of events held over the Easter weekend. **One Track For All** on the northern headland, is a fascinating trail with paintings and carvings illustrating Aboriginal and non-Aboriginal history of the area. White

Fruits from Tropical Fruit World, south of Tweed Heads

sandy beaches and clear water are the main attraction with surfers heading for Mollymook. Those looking for sheltered swimming spots should try the **Bogey Hole**, near the golf course, or **Narrawallee Inlet**.

NEARBY ATTRACTIONS: **Lake Conjola**, to the north, and **Burrill** and **Tabourie lakes** to the south, are good for swimming and fishing. Prawning is a popular activity in the shallow waters of all three lakes. **Pigeon House Mountain** is a distinctive landmark, located 26km inland, in the southern section of **Morton NP**. A 4-wheel drive vehicle is recommended. There are panoramic views from the summit, about a four hour return trip from the car park. **Coomie Nulunga Cultural Trail** is located at **Warden Head**. There is an iron lighthouse built on the headland and the walk features a totem man called Bunan and dream poles depicting local birds and animals.

VISITOR INFORMATION: Civic Centre, Princes Hwy, Ph: (02) 4455 1269

Wagga Wagga   POP 56 750
Map 121, K2

The largest inland city in New South Wales, Wagga Wagga is known as the **'Garden City of the South'**. It is a university city and the commercial centre of the **Riverina** district which is devoted to wheat, lambs, dairying and mixed farming. The city's growth as a regional centre was assured by its position on the banks of the **Murrumbidgee River**, almost halfway between Sydney and Melbourne, just off the Hume Hwy.

MAIN ATTRACTIONS: Attractions include **Charles Sturt University winery and cheese factory**, and the **RAAF Museum** at Forest Hill. **Wagga Wagga Art Gallery** houses the superb **National Art Glass Collection**. Public sculptures by notable local artists have been installed throughout the city centre. The **Botanic Gardens** includes a zoo, model trains, free-flight aviary and walking trails. The city hosts many events throughout the year covering jazz, horse racing, antiques, sports and gardens. Wagga Wagga has been home to sporting champions such as Mark Taylor, Tony Roche, Steve Elkington, Wayne Carey and Paul Kelly. A **Sporting Hall of Fame** is located in the **Museum of the Riverina** in Lord Baden Powell Dr.

NEARBY ATTRACTIONS: **Lockhart**, 64km to the west, has a 19th century streetscape and is known as **'The Verandah Town'**. There are **wineries** off the Sturt Hwy to the east of Wagga Wagga and the Olympic Way to the south.

VISITOR INFORMATION: Tarcutta St, Ph: (02) 6926 9621

Walgett   POP 1975
Map 113, K4

Near the junction of the **Namoi** and **Barwon rivers**, Walgett is the centre of a vast pastoral area that stretches to the Queensland border.

MAIN ATTRACTIONS: Fishing has been a

Tourist train at Timbertown, Wauchope

popular local activity since 1902, when three bridge workers camped on the river near Walgett caught a 115kg cod. Murray cod and golden perch are two of the many types of fish to be caught in the local rivers. Picnic and BBQ facilities are located in **Rotary Park** at the southern side of town. The river walk, linking the levee on the east bank of the river to the stock crossing, is a very pleasant 2km round trip.

NEARBY ATTRACTIONS: The opal-mining districts of **Lightning Ridge, Grawin, Glengarry** and **The Sheepyards** are within an hour's drive of Walgett. Lightning Ridge is the only place in the world where black opal is mined. Precious stones, including agate, jasper and topaz are also found in the surrounding area. Fossickers can venture out to the opal fields, but must remember that these fields are undeveloped and there are no facilities. **Narran Lake**, a bird and wildlife sanctuary, is located 96km west of Walgett near the opal fields.

VISITOR INFORMATION: 88 Fox St, Ph: (02) 6828 6139

Wauchope   POP 4770
Map 119, K1

A timber town at the centre of the prosperous **Hastings River** dairying and cattle-raising region, Wauchope is 19km west of **Port Macquarie**.

MAIN ATTRACTIONS: **Timbertown**, a working replica of a 19th-century village, is the main tourist attraction. Demonstrations of traditional skills, such as shingle-splitting and wood-turning, and a steam locomotive, steam sawmill and bullock team bring the village to life. Timbertown is open daily. The **Hastings River** provides a venue for swimming, boating, fishing, canoeing, jet-skiing and waterskiing.

NEARBY ATTRACTIONS: Picnic spots and well-maintained recreation areas can be found in the state forests that surround Wauchope. Port Macquarie's hinterland is worthwhile visiting. The area includes valleys, mountains, waterfalls, rivers, eucalypt forests, rainforests and a number of excellent national parks. Wildlife includes wedge-tailed eagles, parrots, koalas, wallabies and platypus in the waterholes.

VISITOR INFORMATION: Cnr Clarence St and Hay St, Port Macquarie, Ph: (02) 6581 8000 or 1300 303 155

Wellington   POP 4925
Map 118, D3

Wellington is located at the junction of the **Macquarie** and **Bell rivers**. This **Central West** town services the surrounding agricultural and pastoral district.

MAIN ATTRACTIONS: **Cameron Park** occupies one side of the main street of Wellington. The Bell River flows through the park past picnic areas, a sunken garden and interesting landscaping. Brochures on the **historic town walk** are available from the information centre and there is a cycleway that runs through the local streets and along the highway to **Wellington Caves**.

NEARBY ATTRACTIONS: Wellington Caves, 9km south of the town, have been a popular tourist destination for many years. In 1826, the **Cathedral Cave** was painted by the travelling artist Augustus Earle, and in 1830, fossilised bones were discovered in the caves. Guided tours operate daily to the Cathedral and **Gaden caves**, also the **Phosphate Mine**. The **Wellington-Osawana Japanese Gardens** are adjacent to the caves and holiday lodges and a caravan park form part of the complex. **Lake Burrendong**, to the south-east, is three-and-a-half times the surface area of Sydney Harbour. **Lake Burrendong State Park** is on the western foreshore of the lake. Activities include fishing, watersports and golf. Camping and caravanning is permitted, and there are cabins and a kiosk. **Lake Burrendong Arboretum and Botanic Garden** is close by.

VISITOR INFORMATION: Cameron Park, Nanima Cres, Ph: (02) 6845 1733 or 1800 621 614

West Wyalong   POP 3420

Map 118, B5

A former gold-mining town, West Wyalong is now the business centre of a vast wheat-growing area. Located at the junction of the Mid Western and Newell highways, 470km west of Sydney, the town is a convenient stopover for travellers.

MAIN ATTRACTIONS: There is a pleasant 3.5km walking track known as the **Green Corridor**, which leads from McCann Park to **Cooinda Bush Reserve**. Here, a simulated mine poppet head and a replica of the

Neeld Family's bark hut are located near the picnic area. Gold was discovered on the Neeld property in the late 1800s. **West Wyalong Cemetery**, 5km north-east, holds many graves dating back to the late 1800s, including the Neeld family vault. **Bland District Historical Museum** on the Newell Hwy displays a scale model of a working goldmine.

NEARBY ATTRACTIONS: The waters of **Barmedman Mineral Pool**, located 32km south-east, are reputed to have healing properties. **Lake Cowal**, 48km north-east, is a bird sanctuary and it is also possible to fish there.

VISITOR INFORMATION: CTC Building, 89-91 Main St, Ph: (02) 6972 3645

Wingham   POP 4665

Map 119, J2

A small rural town, Wingham services the rich dairying, timber and beef-cattle country of the **Manning Valley**. The town has been heritage-listed and is the oldest town along the **Manning River**, 13km upstream from Taree. A sawmill, an export abattoir, a horseshoe factory and a range of light engineering and service industries provide employment in the town.

MAIN ATTRACTIONS: **Manning Valley Historical Museum** is located in an attractive village square, surrounded by historical buildings and is worthwhile visiting. A self-guided

historical walk through the town is also recommended and brochures are available from the museum. Located adjacent to the Manning River, **Wingham Brush** is a subtropical floodplain rainforest. There are designated raised walkways where visitors can view giant Moreton Bay figs, which dominate the Brush, and see flying foxes, birds and native marsupials. A BBQ and picnic area is provided, and there is a boat-launching facility and a designated swimming area.

NEARBY ATTRACTIONS: For a scenic drive north through dairying and beef-cattle country, it is worthwhile visiting the high country of **Bulga Plateau** and the beautiful **Ellenborough Falls**. The falls are 40km north-west of Wingham and are signposted from the village of **Elands**. They plunge 200m—one of the longest single-drop falls in the Southern Hemisphere.

VISITOR INFORMATION: 21 Manning River Dr, Taree North, Ph: (02) 6592 5444 or 1800 182 733

Wollongong   POP 227 685

Map 107, C2

The third largest city in New South Wales, Wollongong is the administrative, commercial, cultural and industrial centre of the **Illawarra**. Steel and heavy industry were the initial growth areas for the city, although tourism and other

The common ringtail possum, *Pseudocheirus peregrinus*, may be seen in the Wingham Brush rainforest

THE ILLAWARRA

The Illawarra—the name is an adaptation of an Aboriginal word meaning 'between the high place and the sea'—has **Wollongong** as its centre and is flanked by the Tasman Sea shores and the **Illawarra Escarpment**. The area is ideal for watersports and outdoor activities such as surfing at **North Beach**, hang gliding at **Stanwell Park**, fishing at **Lake Illawarra** and swimming at any one of the 17 patrolled surf beaches. The spectacular shoreline is interrupted by rocky headlands, which provide panoramic views and sheltered beaches. There are also attractions away from the water, including **Minnamurra Falls** and the nearby **Minnamurra Rainforest Centre**, located in **Budderoo NP**, which has won many tourist awards and is definitely worthwhile visiting. **Nan Tien Temple**, the largest Buddhist temple in the Southern Hemisphere, attracts visitors from around the world. The unspoilt bushland and rural scenery of **Kangaroo Valley** is breathtakingly beautiful. Some of the very best waterfalls in Australia are to be found in the national parks and reserves of the Illawarra, such as the 80m-high **Fitzroy Falls**.

> ## *i* Visitor information
>
> **Wollongong Visitor Information Centre**
> 93 Crown St, Wollongong, NSW 2500
> Ph: (02) 4227 5545 or 1800 240 737
> www.tourismwollongong.com

> ## Best Kept Secret
> **Wollongong Harbour** is a major fishing port offering charters for game and offshore fishing as well as seasonal whale-watching.

Coastal view south from Stanwell Park towards Wollongong

industries have developed in recent times.

MAIN ATTRACTIONS: The **Historic Walk** explores the harbour area, which was a port for cargo and passenger vessels built in the 1860s. Today there are many seafood outlets, picnic areas and children's play facilities. **Illawarra Historical Society Museum** is housed in the city's first Post Office building at 11 Market St and is open Thursdays and weekends. The museum contains authentically furnished rooms, and outside there is a blacksmith's shop and stockman's hut. From the museum visitors can also pick up the historic walk. **Wollongong City Gallery**, on the corner of Kembla St and Burelli St, has a collection of Aboriginal, colonial and contemporary art by some of the best-known names in the Australian art world. The **Botanic Gardens** are in **Keiraville**, opposite the University of Wollongong.

NEARBY ATTRACTIONS: **Nan Tien Buddhist Temple** in **Berkeley** has beautifully landscaped gardens and views of the escarpment. Several sections, including a museum, meditation hall and other areas are open to the public daily, except Monday. **Lake Illawarra**, a large saltwater lagoon 5km south of Wollongong, and home to many waterbirds, is popular for fishing, prawning, sailing, waterskiing, canoeing and windsurfing. There are parks with play facilities spread along its shoreline, a cycle path and many walks along the shore.

VISITOR INFORMATION: **93 Crown St,** Ph: (02) 4227 5545 or 1800 240 737

Black swans, *Cygnus atratus*, are common on Lake Illawarra, south of Wollongong

New South Wales

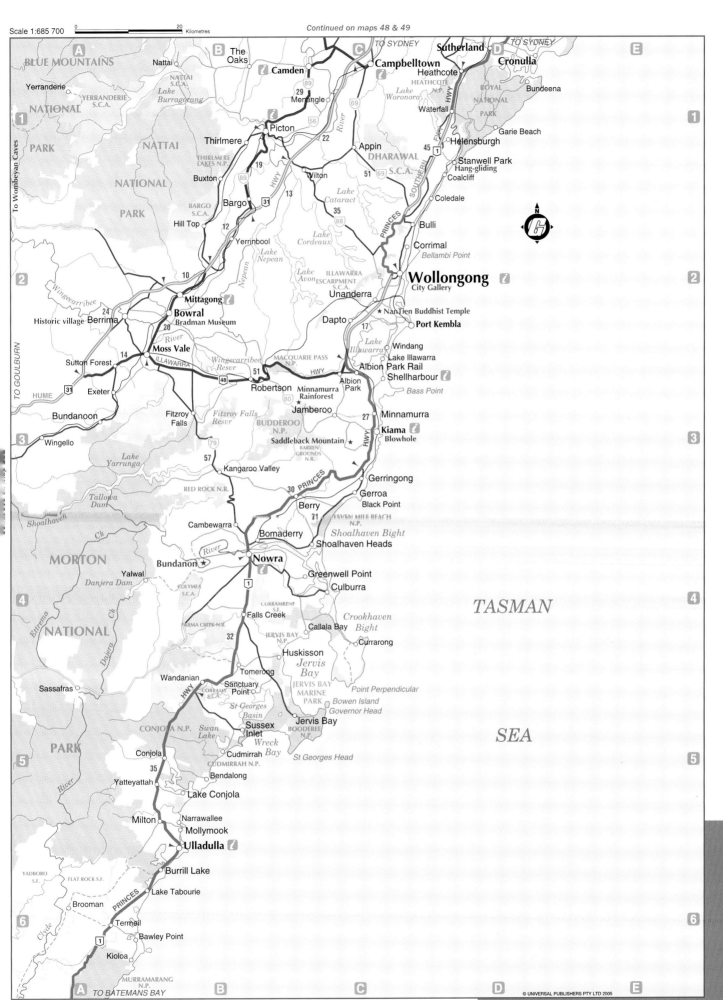

TASMAN

SEA

Continued on map 122

Bushwalker at Girrakool, Brisbane Water National Park

▣ Woolgoolga   POP 3795
Map 62, E2

Known to the locals as 'Woopi', Woolgoolga is a quiet **North Coast** town with lots of character and spectacular coastal views. It is the centre of a fertile rural district that grows bananas and vegetables.

MAIN ATTRACTIONS: Wide bays and sandy beaches line the coast and tourists come for the excellent surfing, swimming, snorkelling and scuba diving. Conditions are perfect for fishing and **Woolgoolga Beach** has a boat ramp used by anglers heading for the fishing grounds on the reefs off the beach and near the **Solitary Islands**. Here there is a marine reserve with a vast array of fish and magnificent dive sites. Other activities include horseriding, whale-watching, bushwalking, bowls and golf. Woolgoolga is home to the largest Punjabi Sikh community in Australia. Members of the community are always keen to give visitors an understanding of their religion and culture through tours of the **Guru Nanak Temple**, which sits at the entrance to the town. Shady picnic spots are located in the reserve on the edge of **Woolgoolga Lake**, a safe swimming spot north of town.

NEARBY ATTRACTIONS: **Mullaway**, **Arrawarra**, **Corindi** and **Red Rock** are quiet beaches located to the immediate north of Woolgoolga. **Coffs Harbour** and its many attractions is 25km south.

VISITOR INFORMATION: Boundary St, Ph: (02) 6654 8080

▣ Woy Woy   POP 11 050
Map 71, B5

A **Central Coast** town that is part of the **City of Gosford**, Woy Woy covers a peninsula on the western shores of **Brisbane Water**. Over recent years the town has become part of the spreading residential area for people who commute back and forth to Sydney to work.

MAIN ATTRACTIONS: Surrounded by **Woy Woy Inlet**, Brisbane Water and **Broken Bay**, Woy Woy is an ideal spot for boaties and fishermen. Nearby beaches include **Ettalong**, **Ocean Beach**, **Umina**, **Pearl Beach** and **Killcare**. Pelican feeding is popular and there are many waterfront picnic areas and picturesque lookouts. It is worthwhile visiting **Brisbane Water NP**. There are many walks with views of the waterways, and the park is renowned for its brightly coloured waratahs in autumn, and Christmas bells and Christmas bush in summer. Aboriginal rock carvings are also located in the park.

NEARBY ATTRACTIONS: **Bouddi NP** is worthwhile exploring and allows beachfront camping. **Ettalong Markets**, in Ocean View Rd, are the largest markets on the Central Coast. Every Saturday and Sunday there are over 150 stalls. The **Australian Reptile Park** is located within a 25 minute drive of Woy Woy. (*refer* Gosford, pp.69–71)

VISITOR INFORMATION: 18-22 The Boulevard, Ph: 1300 130 708

▣ Wyong   POP 6220
Map 71, C3

Formerly a centre for dairying, citrus-growing and timber-cutting, Wyong is now a commercial centre and commuter town on the northern **Central Coast**. The town is on the banks of the **Wyong River**, which flows into **Tuggerah Lake** a few kilometres east. Tuggerah Lake is linked to **Budgewoi** and **Munmorah lakes** and, with this chain of lakes being close to surf beaches, the area attracts many holiday-makers and permanent residents.

MAIN ATTRACTIONS: **Alison Homestead**, built in 1885, is a history museum with a family history resource and a good collection of local memorabilia. Located in Cape Rd, West Wyong, the museum is open at weekends. It incorporates displays concerning forest logging and the early services across the lakes.

NEARBY ATTRACTIONS: The surrounding hinterland and state forests are popular for bushwalking and camping. For those interested in gardens, **Burbank Nursery** features 20ha of azaleas and is located 3km south. The **Australian Rainforest Sanctuary** is at nearby **Ourimbah**. During the **Firefly Festival** (mid-November–mid-December) the Sanctuary remains open late on Friday and Saturday. Visitors should be there at dusk and bring a torch. Nearby **Watagans NP**, **Jilliby State Conservation Area** and **Olney State Forest** offer bushwalks, picnic areas, camping and lookouts.

VISITOR INFORMATION: Marine Pde, The Entrance, Ph: 1300 130 708

Yamba POP 5625

Map 115, J3

This **North Coast** holiday resort and fishing town is located on the south side of the **Clarence River**, 693km north of Sydney.

MAIN ATTRACTIONS: The beaches of Yamba, considered to have the warmest waters in New South Wales, are a major drawcard for visitors. The main beach is patrolled all summer and there is a rockpool, offering safe swimming year-round. Fishing is one of the most popular activities with anglers choosing from rock, beach, estuary and deep-sea fishing. Boats can be hired and there are estuary fishing charters. **Clarence River Ferries** operate a regular passenger service to **Iluka** where there are even more fishing spots. The local seafood shops and restaurants supply fish bought straight from the fishing boats based in the Clarence River. **Yamba Lighthouse** stands 41m above the sea and its automatic navigation light beams out as far as 17km. From here, the views are excellent and it is worthwhile visiting at dusk when the fishing fleet heads out into the Coral Sea.

NEARBY ATTRACTIONS: There are two coastal national parks in close proximity to Yamba—**Yuraygir** and **Bundjalung**. Both parks offer bushwalks and access to pristine beaches. The famous **Blue Pool** is at the northern tip of Yuraygir NP. South of Yamba is the small village of **Angourie**, one of the best surfing spots in Australia.

VISITOR INFORMATION: Ferry Park, Pacific Hwy, Maclean, Ph: (02) 6645 4121

Yass POP 4890

Map 122, C2

A country town on the **Yass River**, Yass is close to where the Barton Hwy to Canberra meets the Hume Hwy. An interesting and historic town, Yass is the service centre for the surrounding country which is famous for its merino sheep studs.

MAIN ATTRACTIONS: The area's history is represented by pioneer relics and historic photographs in the **Hamilton Hume Museum**. The museum is closed in winter and visitors should contact the visitor centre in Coronation Park for opening times.

NEARBY ATTRACTIONS: The explorer Hamilton Hume and his wife bought **Cooma Cottage** in 1839. The weatherboard house, with its return verandah and fine cedar woodwork is now a National Trust property to the east of Yass, open Thursday to Monday. Yass **town drive** includes a visit to the cemetery where Hamilton and Elizabeth Hume are buried. Some of Australia's best cool-climate wines are produced in the Yass region. Most of the wineries are found in the **Murrumbateman area** south of Yass and the majority welcome visitors for tastings and sales. **Lake Burrinjuck** and **Burrinjuck Waters State Park** are popular for watersports, picnics and cruises. **Careys Cave** in the **Wee Jasper Valley** is easily accessed and there are guided tours daily.

VISITOR INFORMATION: Coronation Park, Comur St, Ph: (02) 6226 2557

Young POP 6805

Map 118, C6

The '**Cherry Capital of Australia**', Young is the centre of a district that primarily produces cherries for the table, but also grows and processes plums and has a growing number of wineries. It was once one of the richest and most populated goldfields in New South Wales.

MAIN ATTRACTIONS: Many of Young's cherry orchards invite visitors to pick their own cherries and other fruit in season—containers are supplied. Some orchards have BBQ areas and other facilities. **Burrangong Art Gallery** has changing exhibitions; located next to the information centre, it is open daily. **Blackguard Gully**, at the end of Whiteman Ave, is a dedicated fossicking area where you can pan for gold. **J D's Jam Factory** processes fruit into jams and other products. There are factory and orchard tours, a gift shop and a restaurant with panoramic views. Located in Grenfell Rd, the factory is open daily.

NEARBY ATTRACTIONS: The **Chinese Tribute Garden**, 3km from Young, commemorates the contribution of the Chinese community to the settlement of Young in the 1860s. Wine produced in the **Hilltops Wine Region of Young**, **Harden** and **Boorowa** is available in local outlets and some of the wineries have tastings and cellar door sales.

VISITOR INFORMATION: 2 Short St, Ph: (02) 6382 3394 or 1800 628 233

A rocky coastline near Pebbly Beach in Yuraygir National Park, south of Yamba

KEY MAP

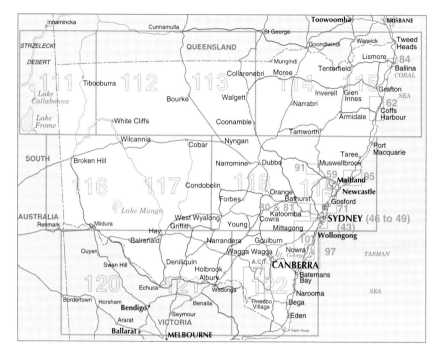

DISTANCE CHART

Approximate Distance	Albury	Bathurst	Bega	Bourke	Broken Hill	Canberra	Cooma	Dubbo	Goulburn	Grafton	Mildura VIC	Moree	Newcastle	Port Macquarie	Sydney	Tamworth	Tweed Heads	Wagga Wagga	West Wyalong	Wollongong
Albury		443	426	847	866	346	315	531	367	1162	571	904	693	935	562	866	1401	125	278	505
Bathurst	443		468	574	958	274	382	206	185	735	811	579	326	568	201	430	974	318	264	237
Bega	426	468		965	1292	222	111	604	283	1034	957	977	570	809	418	813	1275	393	501	336
Bourke	847	574	965		615	743	854	368	720	813	877	445	749	861	775	584	1052	722	572	811
Broken Hill	866	958	1292	615		1080	1181	752	1101	1328	299	1061	1133	1300	1159	1023	1567	863	846	1195
Canberra	346	274	222	743	1080		111	382	89	884	781	755	415	657	284	704	1123	244	271	227
Cooma	315	382	111	854	1181	111		493	197	992	882	866	523	765	392	815	1231	282	390	335
Dubbo	531	206	604	368	752	382	493		352	640	803	373	381	612	407	335	879	406	256	443
Goulburn	367	185	283	720	1101	89	197	352		795	802	725	326	568	195	569	1034	265	292	138
Grafton	1162	735	1034	813	1328	884	992	640	795		1443	368	479	249	618	305	239	1046	896	700
Mildura VIC	571	811	957	877	299	781	882	803	802	1443		1176	1137	1415	1012	1138	1682	564	547	940
Moree	904	579	977	445	1061	755	866	373	725	368	1176		492	498	610	272	568	779	629	692
Newcastle	693	326	570	749	1133	415	523	381	326	479	1137	492		252	152	277	718	591	590	234
Port Macquarie	935	568	809	861	1300	657	765	612	568	249	1415	498	252		391	277	488	833	868	473
Sydney	562	201	418	775	1159	284	392	407	195	618	1012	610	152	391		395	857	470	465	82
Tamworth	866	430	813	584	1023	704	815	335	569	305	1138	272	277	277	395		544	741	591	477
Tweed Heads	1401	974	1275	1052	1567	1123	1231	879	1034	239	1682	568	718	488	857	544		1299	1166	939
Wagga Wagga	125	318	393	722	863	244	282	406	265	1046	564	779	591	833	470	741	1299		153	403
West Wyalong	278	264	501	572	846	271	390	256	292	896	547	629	590	868	465	591	1166	153		430
Wollongong	505	237	336	811	1195	227	335	443	138	700	940	692	234	473	82	477	939	403	430	

All distances in this chart have been measured over highways and major roads, not necessarily by the shortest route.

Continued on maps 284 & 285

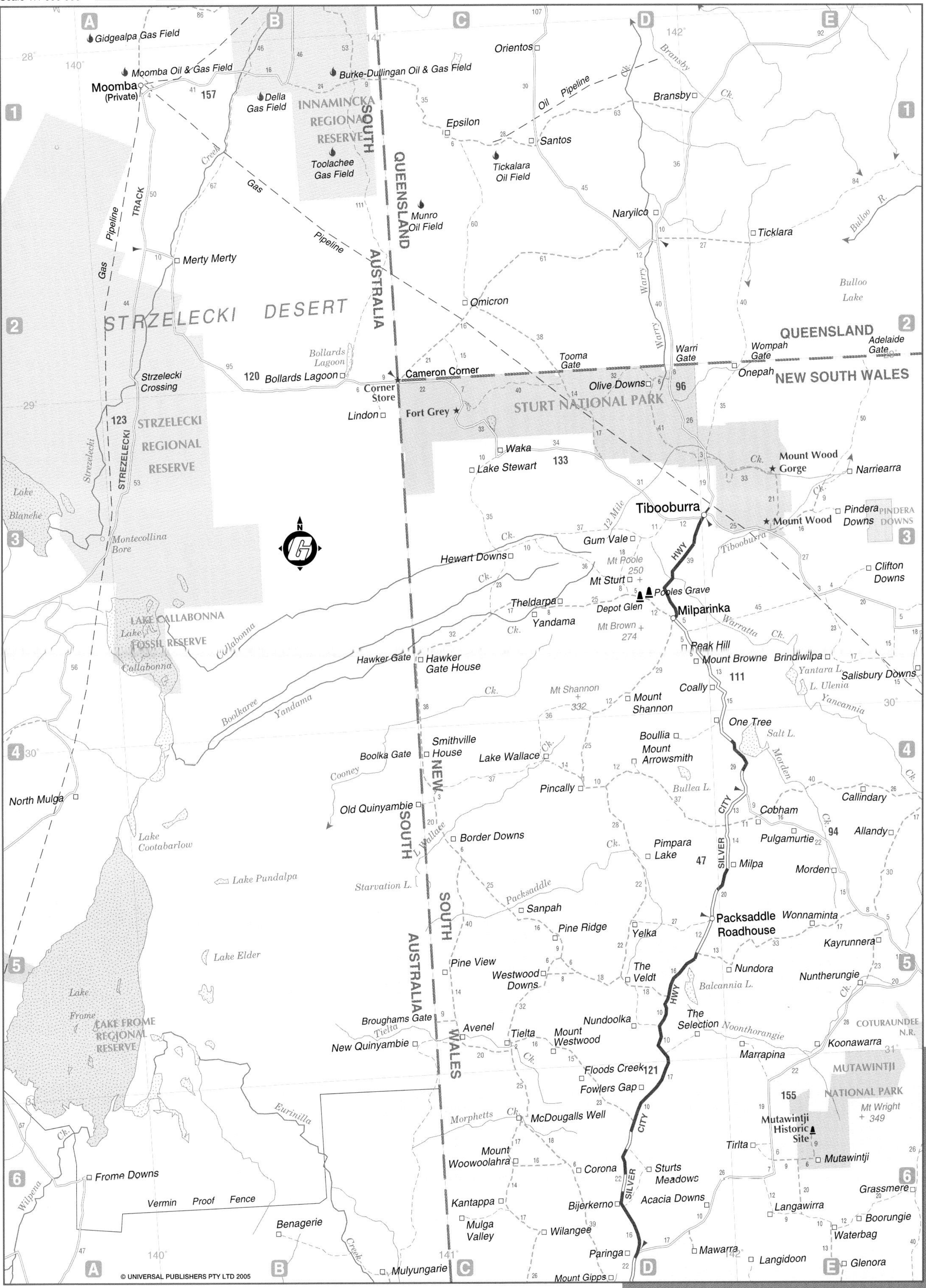

Kilometres

Gidgealpa Gas Field
Moomba Oil & Gas Field
Moomba (Private)
Della Gas Field
Burke-Dullingan Oil & Gas Field
INNAMINCKA REGIONAL RESERVE
157
Toolachee Gas Field
SOUTH AUSTRALIA
QUEENSLAND
Orientos
Bransby
Oil Pipeline
Epsilon
Santos
Tickalara Oil Field
Munro Oil Field
Naryilco
Ticklara
Bulloo R.
Merty Merty
STRZELECKI DESERT
Omicron
Bulloo Lake
QUEENSLAND
Bollards Lagoon
Strzelecki Crossing
120 Bollards Lagoon
Cameron Corner
Tooma Gate
Warri Gate
Wompah Gate
Adelaide Gate
Onepah
NEW SOUTH WALES
96
Corner Store
Lindon
Fort Grey
Olive Downs
STURT NATIONAL PARK
123 STRZELECKI REGIONAL RESERVE
Waka
133
Lake Stewart
Mount Wood Gorge
Narriearra
Lake Blanche
Montecollina Bore
Pindera Downs
PINDERA DOWNS
Tibooburra
Mount Wood
Hewart Downs
Gum Vale
12 Mile
HWY
Clifton Downs
LAKE CALLABONNA FOSSIL RESERVE
Lake Callabonna
Mt Poole 250
Mt Sturt
Pooles Grave
Milparinka
Theldarpa
Depot Glen
Yandama
Mt Brown 274
Warratta Ck.
Peak Hill
Mount Browne
Brindiwilpa
Hawker Gate
Hawker Gate House
Mt Shannon 332
Mount Shannon
Coally
111
Yantara L.
L. Ulenia
Salisbury Downs
Yancannia
North Mulga
Smithville House
Lake Wallace
Boulia
Mount Arrowsmith
One Tree
Salt L.
Boolka Gate
Pincally
Bullea L.
CITY
SILVER
Cobham
Callindary
Allandy
94
Lake Cootabarlow
Old Quinyambie
Border Downs
Pimpara Lake
Pulgamurtie
Morden
Lake Pundalpa
Packsaddle
Sanpah
Milpa
47
Starvation L.
Pine Ridge
Yelka
Packsaddle Roadhouse
Wonnaminta
Kayrunnera
Lake Elder
Pine View
Westwood Downs
The Veldt
Nundora
Balcannia L.
Nuntherungie
Lake Frome
LAKE FROME REGIONAL RESERVE
Broughams Gate
Avenel
Tielta
Nundoolka
Mount Westwood
The Selection
Noonthorangie
Marrapina
Koonawarra
COTURAUNDEE N.R.
New Quinyambie
MUTAWINTJI NATIONAL PARK
155
Mt Wright 349
Floods Creek
121
Fowlers Gap
Morphetts
McDougalls Well
Mutawintji Historic Site
Tirlta
Mutawintji
SILVER CITY
Mount Woowoolahra
Corona
Sturts Meadows
Langawirra
Grassmere
Frome Downs
Kantappa
Bijerkerno
Acacia Downs
Boorungie
Waterbag
Vermin Proof Fence
Mulga Valley
Wilangee
Paringa
Mawarra
Langidoon
Glenora
Benagerie
Mulyungarie
Mount Gipps

HWY
NEW SOUTH WALES
AUSTRALIA
SOUTH AUSTRALIA

Joins map 112

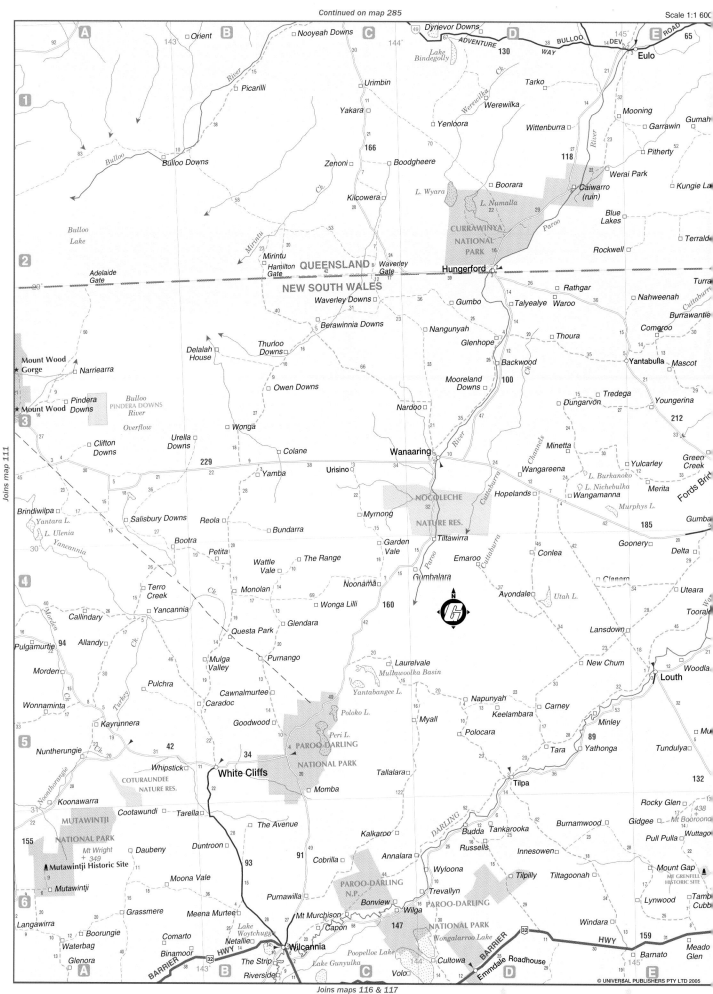

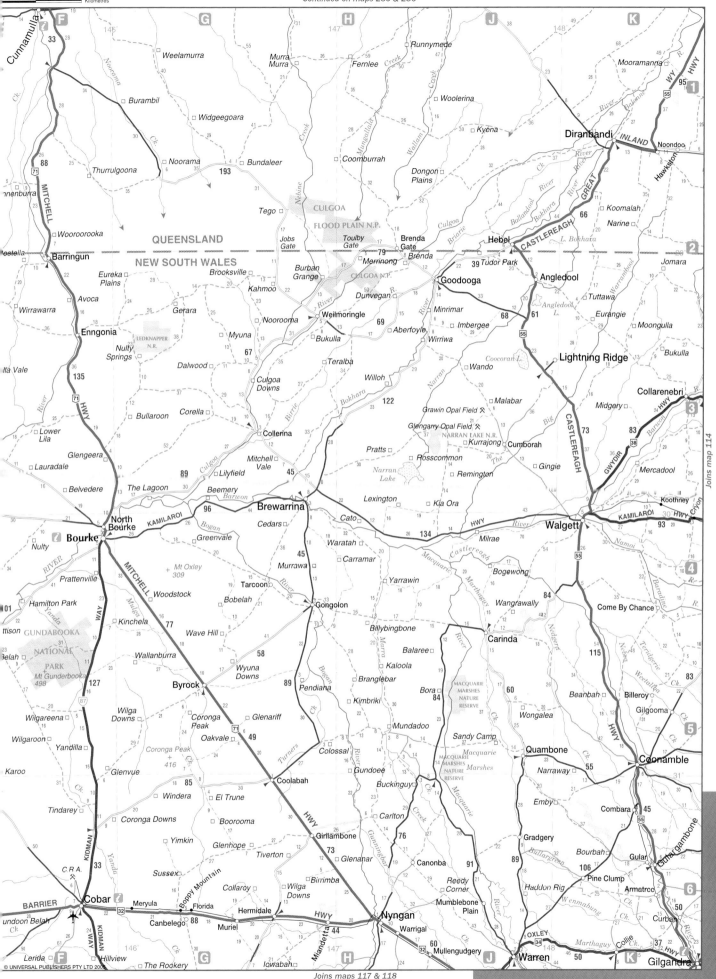

Scale 1:1 600

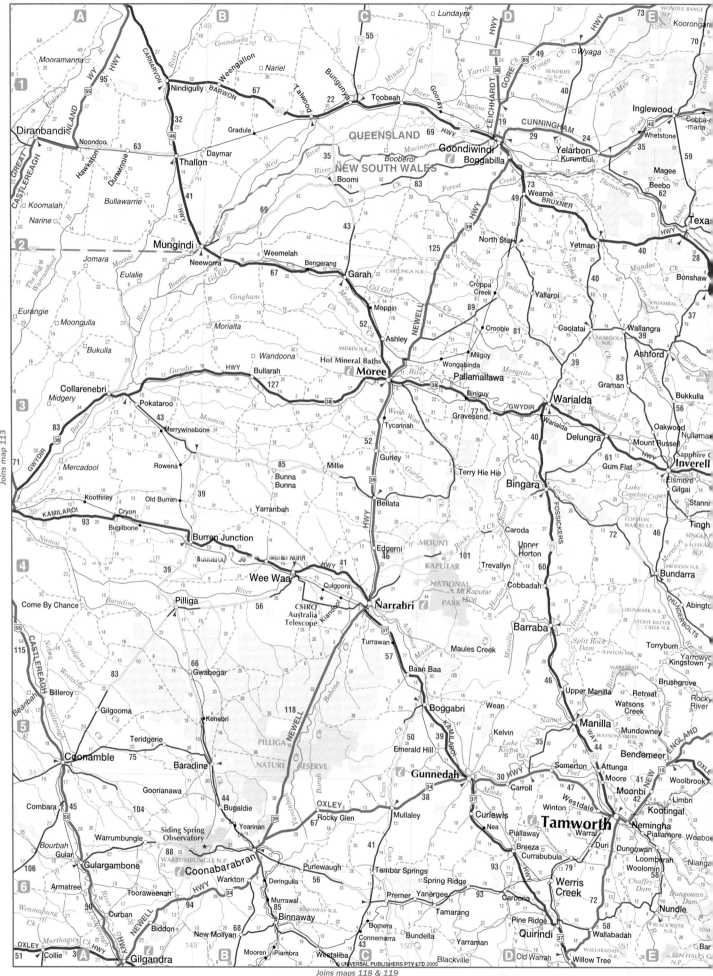

New South Wales

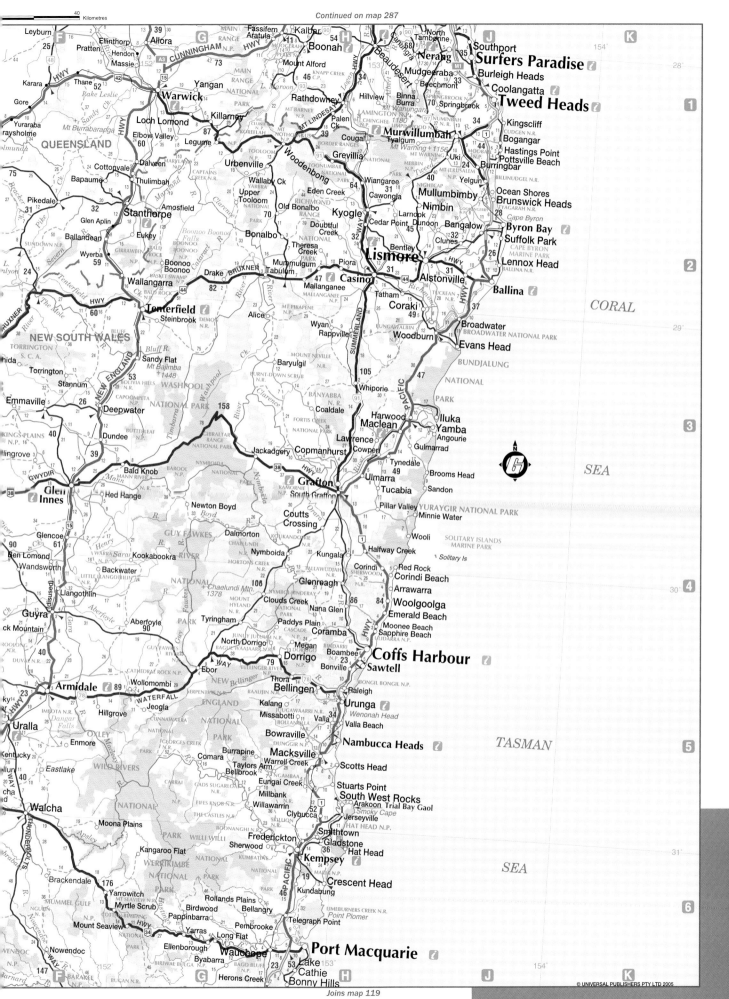

Kilometres
40

154°
28°

F
G
H
J
K

Leyburn
Ellinthorp
Pratten
Allora
39
30
Fassifern
Aratula
Kalbar
54
North
Tamborine
90
Southport
154°

Hendon
Massie
Boonah
11
Beaudesert
658
Nerang
735
Surfers Paradise

Karara
Thane
52
Yangan
Mount Alford
46
34
Mudgeeraba
33
Burleigh Heads
Beechmont

Gore
Warwick
Killarney
Rathdowney
Hillview
70
Springbrook
Coolangatta
Tweed Heads

Yuraraba
Loch Lomond
87
Palen Ck
Murwillumbah
34
Kingscliff
1

rraysholme
QUEENSLAND
Elbow Valley
60
Legume
Cougal
Tyalgum
Bogangar
Hastings Point

Cottonvale
Dalveen
Urbenville
Grevillia
Uki
24
Pottsville Beach
Burringbar

Bapaume
Thulimbah
Wallaby Ck
40
Yelgun

Stanthorpe
Amosfield
Upper
Tooloom
Eden Creek
Wiangaree
31
Mullumbimby
Ocean Shores
Brunswick Heads

Glen Aplin
Eukey
Old Bonalbo
Kyogle
Cawongla
Nimbin
Byron Bay

Ballandean
Wyerba
59
Boonoo
Boonoo
Bonalbo
Doubtful
Creek
Cedar Point
Dunoon
Larnook
Bangalow
Suffolk Park

Wallangarra
Theresa
Creek
Murrumulgum
Tabulum
Piora
Bentley
Clunes
Lennox Head
2

Tenterfield
Drake
BRUXNER
47
Casino
31
Lismore
Alstonville
Ballina

Steinbrook
Alice
Mallanganee
Tatham
Coraki
Broadwater
CORAL
29°

NEW SOUTH WALES
Wyan
Rappville
Woodburn
Evans Head

Torrington
Sandy Flat
Baryulgil
105
Whiporie
47
BUNDJALUNG

Stannum
Deepwater
158
Coaldale
Harwood
Maclean
Iluka
Yamba
3

Emmaville
Dundee
Jackadgery
Copmanhurst
Cowper
Gulmarrad

ingrove
Bald Knob
38
Grafton
South Grafton
Ulmarra
Tynedale
49
Brooms Head
SEA

Glen Innes
Red Range
Newton Boyd
Coutts
Crossing
Tucabia
Sandon

Glencoe
61
Dalmorton
Nymboida
Kungala
Halfway Creek
Wooli
SOLITARY ISLANDS
MARINE PARK

Ben Lomond
Backwater
106
Glenreagh
Corindi
Corindi Beach
Red Rock
30°
4

Wandsworth
Llangothlin
Clouds Creek
Nana Glen
86
84
Arrawarra
Woolgoolga
Emerald Beach

Guyra
Aberfoyle
90
Tyringham
Paddys Plain
Coramba
Moonee Beach
Sapphire Beach

Armidale
89
Wollomombi
North Dorrigo
Megan
Boambee
Coffs Harbour

Uralla
Hillgrove
Jeogla
Dorrigo
79
Ebor
Bonville
Sawtell

Kentucky
Enmore
Eastlake
Kalang
Thora
Bellingen
Raleigh
Urunga
TASMAN
5

Walcha
Comara
Burrapine
Missabotti
Valla
Valla Beach
Wenonah Head

Moona Plains
Taylors Arm
Bellbrook
Bowraville
Macksville
Scotts Head

Kangaroo Flat
Eungai Creek
Millbank
Warrell Creek
Scotts Head
Stuarts Point
South West Rocks
Trial Bay Gaol
31°

Brackendale
176
Willawarrin
Clybucca
Jerseyville
Smoky Cape

Yarrowitch
Myrtle Scrub
Rollands Plains
Fredrickton
Smithtown
Gladstone
Hat Head
SEA

Mount Seaview
Birdwood
Pappinbarra
Bellangry
Kempsey
Crescent Head
6

Nowendoc
Yarras
Long Flat
Pembrooke
Kundabung

Ellenborough
Byabarra
Wauchope
Telegraph Point
Port Macquarie

Herons Creek
Lake
Cathie
Bonny Hills

Joins map 119

© UNIVERSAL PUBLISHERS PTY LTD 2005

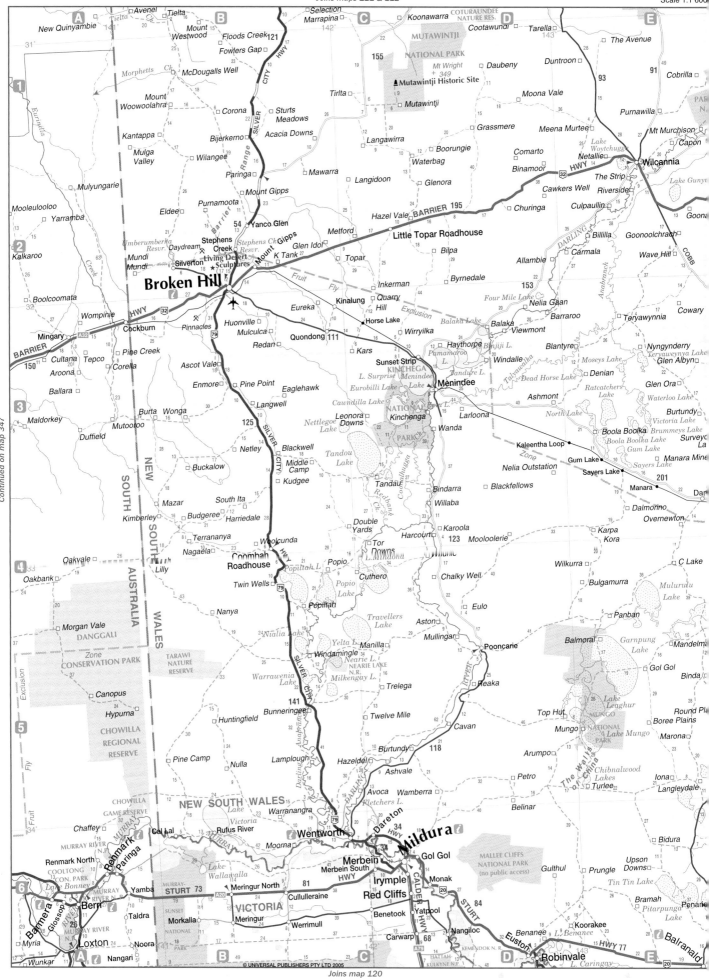

New South Wales

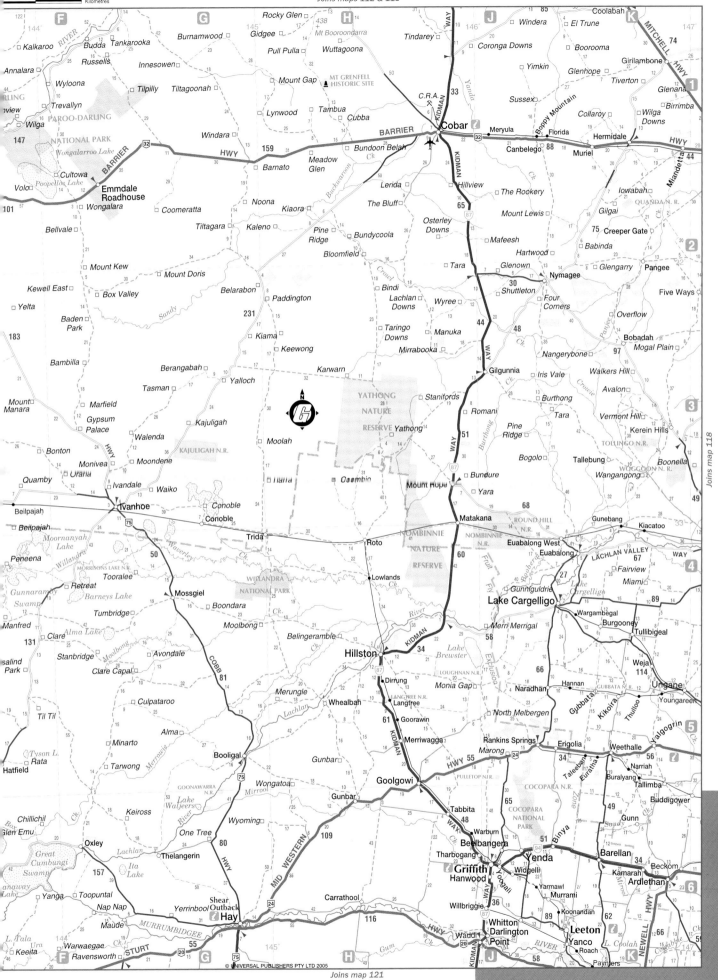

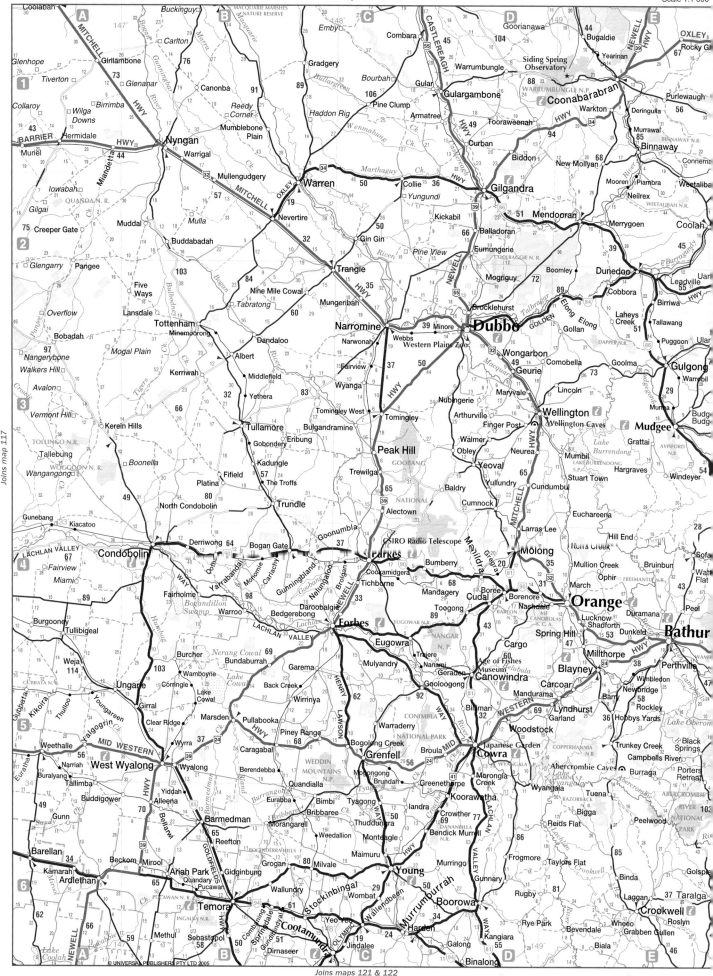

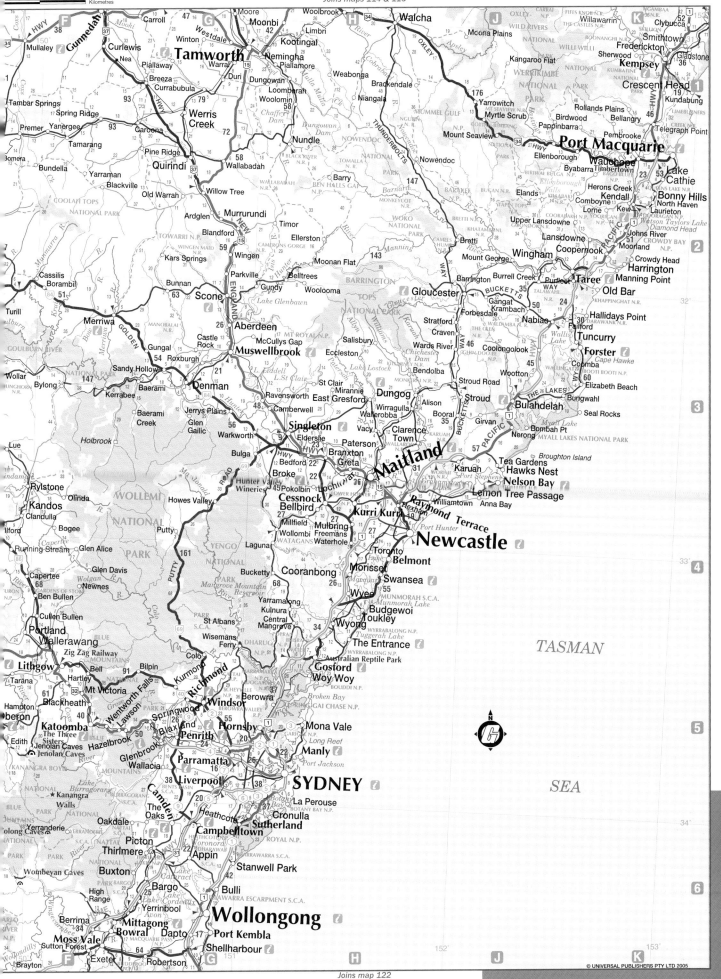

© UNIVERSAL PUBLISHERS PTY LTD 2005

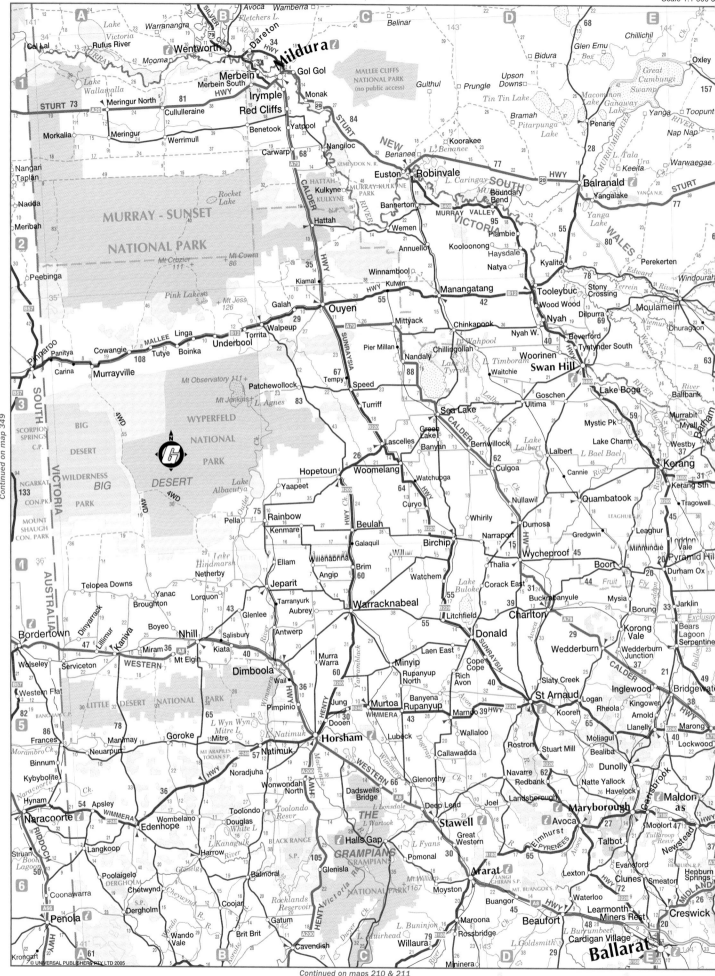

Continued on map 349

Continued on maps 210 & 211

New South Wales

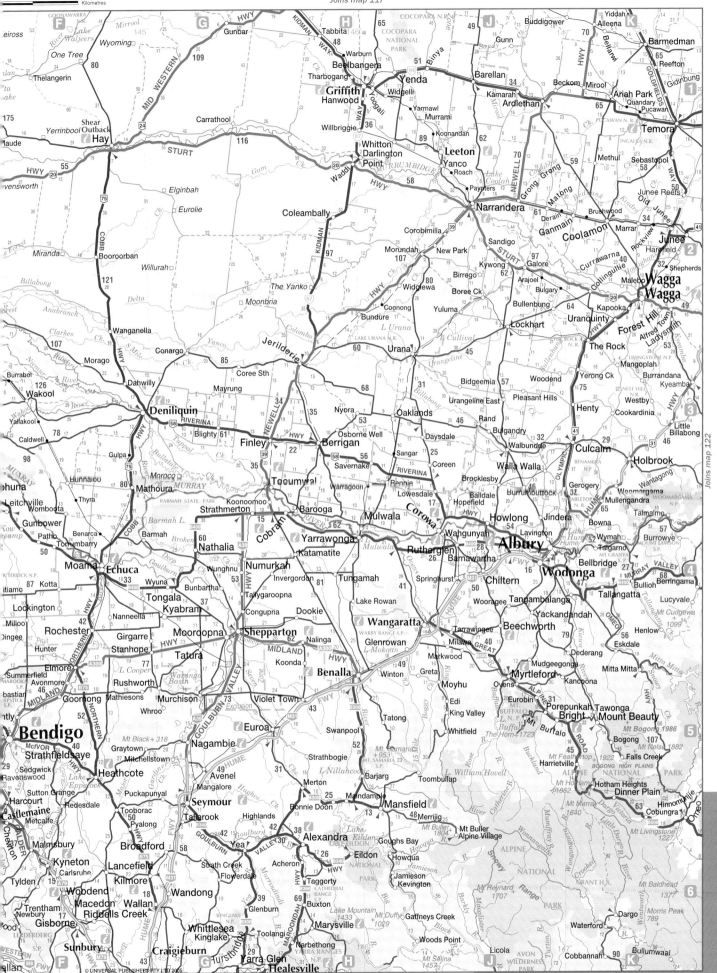

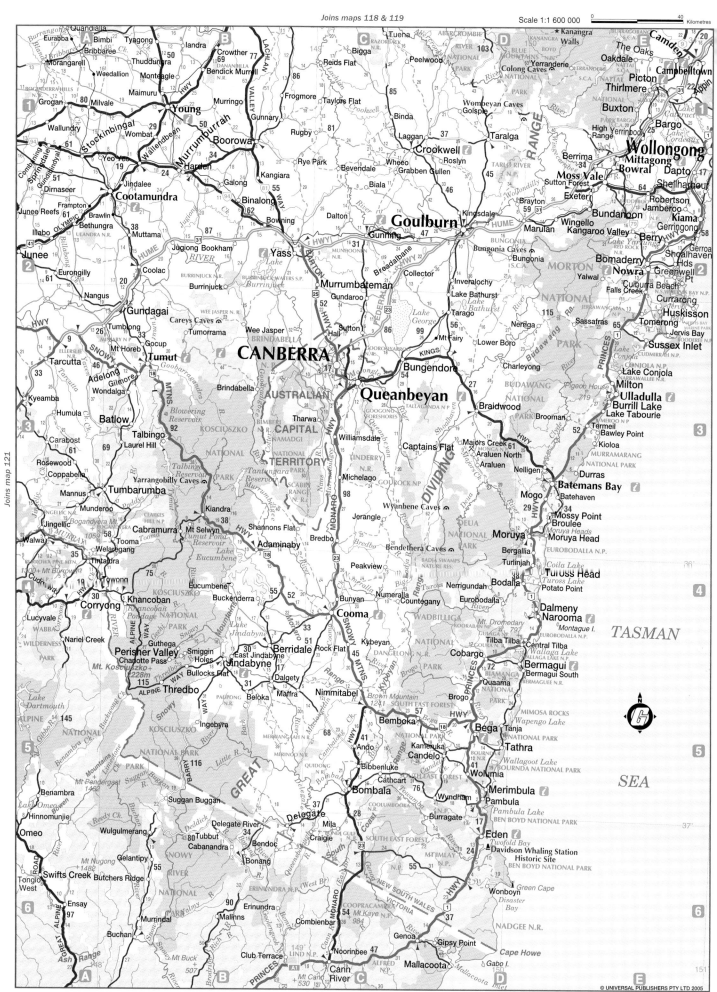

Continued on maps 213 & 214

© UNIVERSAL PUBLISHERS PTY LTD 2005

Sunset illuminates the Green Patch coastline in Booderee National Park, Jervis Bay, New South Wales

The Australian Capital Territory has more to offer than just an insight into the political workings of the country, although it does this well. It's a place where Australia's history comes face-to-face with architectural modernity. You can discover the scientific workings of the universe, pay your respects to the soldiers who fought and died in the wars, venture back in time to the dinosaurs, create your own

dollar coin or catch a close-up view of the fittest bodies on the continent. You can see artworks from all over the world, cycle around or sail on a large man-made lake, rise above it all in a hot-air balloon, visit Australia's only zooquarium, or stroll through the Australian National Botanic Gardens. The Australian Capital Territory has a diverse range of attractions and sights to suit every taste.

Located on perhaps some of the best sheep and cattle grazing land in Australia, the national capital is bordered by farmland, bushland, national parks and the Boboyan, Tidbinbilla and Booth ranges. It is completely surrounded by New

Australian Capital Territory: The Federal Capital

- Population: 356 000
- Total area: 2400km²
- % of Australia: 0.03%
- Floral emblem: Royal Bluebell
- Fauna emblem: Gang Gang Cockatoo

ℹ️ Visitor information

Canberra and Region Visitors Centre
330 Northbourne Ave,
Dickson, ACT 2602
Ph: (02) 6205 0044 or 1300 554 114
www.visitcanberra.com.au

Main ATTRACTIONS

◈ Australian War Memorial

The most visited building in Canberra and one of the most visited attractions in Australia, the War Memorial honours all Australians who fought and died for their country. It is the site for remembrance ceremonies and its museum contains historic information, artefacts and interactive displays. The volunteer guides are very passionate about the Memorial.

◈ Lake Burley Griffin

Lake Burley Griffin is the geographic centre of the city, named after the American architect who won the international competition to design Canberra. Many of the city's attractions and most beautiful picnic spots are located on the 35km shoreline of the lake.

◈ National Gallery of Australia

This gallery houses a fine collection of Australian and international art, and displays major travelling exhibitions. There is a sculpture garden and a restaurant. Guided and audio tours are highly recommended.

◈ National Museum of Australia

The museum uses three main themes—Land, Nation and People, to focus on what it means to be an Australian. Cutting-edge technology, including a huge three-dimensional map of Australia, and displays of rare and unique objects, help tell the stories and cultural histories of Australians. Visitors can see the heart of racing legend Phar Lap, the sword of Governor Macquarie and much more.

◈ Parliament House

Completed in 1988 (in time for Australia's Bicentennial celebrations) Parliament House is now the focal point of the city. This impressive modern building forms part of Capital Hill, with extensive cityscape views from the entry forecourt.

South Wales and was selected as the site of the national capital in 1909, eight years after Federation. Located inland, the creation of the Australian Capital Territory was a compromise to appease bitter interstate rivalry between New South Wales and Victoria.

The Australian Capital Territory encompasses only 0.03% of the entire continent, yet it is the political centre of the nation—rich with history and fine examples of modern architecture, art and culture. The capital city, Canberra, occupies around 15% of the Australian Capital Territory—a large percentage relative to the other capital cities of Australia. In addition to being Australia's only planned modern capital city, Canberra also has the distinction of being the only Australian capital city located inland.

Photo above: Parliament House, Canberra

THE FEDERAL CAPITAL

The Australian Capital Territory is home to **Canberra**, capital of Australia and seat of the Federal Government. It is situated 306km from Sydney and 655km from Melbourne. Before the original Parliament House was completed in 1927, Melbourne was the temporary home of government. **Old Parliament House** was used for 60 years until the new Parliament House was finished in 1988.

In 1913, construction began on the first public buildings and the rail link between Sydney and Canberra was completed in 1914. Canberra is renowned as one of the world's most planned cities—in 1911, an international competition for its design was won by American landscape architect **Walter Burley Griffin**. The **Molonglo River**, a tributary of the **Murrumbidgee River** that ran through the city, was dammed in 1964 to create the centrepiece of the city—**Lake Burley Griffin** in honour of the first city planner. Canberra has continued to evolve around the 35km shoreline of the lake.

The name Canberra is thought to have originated from that of the homestead of the first European settler in the area, Joshua Moore. In 1824, his property of 25km^2 was located by the Murrumbidgee River, and called 'Canberry'—the Aboriginal word for 'meeting place'.

The population of the Australian Capital Territory is very diverse. Although it is assumed that a large proportion of Canberra's workforce are politicians and bureaucrats, they in fact make up less than half of the working population. With 99.4% of the population living in the Canberra urban area, the Australian Capital Territory is different from the other Australian states and territories in that it has a virtual city-state status.

There is huge ethnic diversity within the Australian Capital Territory, the diplomatic community itself adding to the character of the capital. Two out of five people are either immigrants or children of immigrants, which is higher than the average ratio for all of Australia. Canberra is a favoured

Australian Institute of Sport

site for international and national conferences and delegations, and the pursuit of excellence in all aspects of research (**Australian National University**), science (**CSIRO**), sport (**Australian Institute of Sport**) and culture, greatly influences the character of the city and surrounds.

The Australian Capital Territory is increasingly becoming home to younger people. With two world-class universities (Australian National University and the **University of Canberra**) as well as campuses of the **University of New South Wales** (**Australian Defence Force Academy**) and the **Australian Catholic University**, young students comprise a significant percentage of the population.

National Multicultural Festival, held in Canberra in February

NATIONAL PARKS

Namadgi NP covers 45% of land in the ACT, but there are 28 smaller parks and recreation areas, inlcuding **Molonglo Gorge Recreation Reserve** and **Murrumbidgee River Corridor. Canberra Nature Park** is a series of mostly hilltop reserves throughout Canberra. It includes **Black Mountain** (812m), **Mount Ainslie** (842m) and **Mount Majura** (890m). The lookout at Mount Ainslie is renowned for its exclusive views of the city, day and night.

A Namadgi NP (Map 137, B4)

Namadgi NP lies to the south of the city and borders Kosciuszko NP and Bimberi Nature Reserve in New South Wales. It covers 45% of land in the ACT. Namadgi NP is the most northern alpine environment in Australia and offers amazing views, Aboriginal rock art, rare sub-alpine species of flora and fauna, walking tracks, camping, BBQ and picnic facilities. There are three campgrounds, each with toilets, picnic tables and fireplaces. Campervan facilities are available at Honeysuckle campground. Bush camping is allowed but fire permits are required; and a camping permit is needed for the Cotter catchment—part of Canberra's water supply.

Namadgi Visitor Centre, located on Naas Rd, offers exhibits and information about bushwalks, trails

Kangaroos in Canberra Nature Park

and paths for all adventure levels and ages. Ranger guided activities are regularly advertised. The most popular activities in Namadgi NP are bushwalking, picnicking and sightseeing.

facts

◈ Number of parks/reserves: 29
◈ Total area: 1272km^2
◈ % of territory: 53%

National Park Information

Environment ACT
Level 2, Macarthur House
12 Wattle St, Lyneham, ACT 2602
Ph: (02) 6207 9777 or (02) 6207 2900
(Namadgi National Park)
www.environment.act.gov.au

WINERIES

Vineyard at Lark Hill Winery, near Lake George

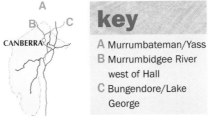

key

A Murrumbateman/Yass
B Murrumbidgee River west of Hall
C Bungendore/Lake George

The wine industry around Canberra is both young and old. There were wineries in the area in the 1860s, but production ceased around the turn of the 19th century. The modern pioneers of Canberra district wines were scientists Dr John Kirk and Dr Edgar Riek, who planted vines at **Murrumbateman** and **Lake George** in 1971.

There are about 20 wineries within an hour's drive of the Australian capital. Nearly all of these are in New South Wales, just outside the Australian Capital Territory border.

The Canberra region has a variety of soils, mild temperatures and ample sunshine for ripening grapes. In table wines, riesling, pinot noir and chardonnay excel, as does premium sparkling wine. Other grape varieties, which are made into a range of wine styles, include cabernet sauvignon, merlot, shiraz and sauvignon blanc. Visit the **Kamberra Wine Company** in the city for more information.

CANBERRA

National Library of Australia, seen from Commonwealth Park in springtime

main attractions

◈ National Capital Exhibition
The extraordinary story of Canberra, from its indigenous heritage to modern-day political capital, is told with interactive displays, laser models and audiovisual presentations.

◈ National Library of Australia
The vast collection of beautiful, rare and unusual Australian books, manuscripts, newspapers, maps and paintings is held in more than 200km of shelving.

◈ National Portrait Gallery
Housed in Old Parliament House, the beautifully renovated gallery features portraits of people who have helped shape the nation. The permanent collection includes artists such as Arthur Boyd, David Moore, Howard Arkley and Nora Heysen.

◈ Questacon — The National Science & Technology Centre
Discover the science behind the fun in this interactive centre where lightning strikes several times a day and visitors can experience the force of an earthquake.

◈ Royal Australian Mint
See the minting process in action, trace the history of Australia's coinage and make your own special $1 coin at the Mint.

◈ ScreenSound Australia
Explore Australia's radio, film, television and sound recordings from the late 1800s to the present at McCoy Circuit, Acton. Displays include memorabilia from 100 years of movie-making and original equipment from the early days.

Canberra is widely acclaimed as the best landscaped city in the world. Its geometrically circular street pattern, set around key urban planning elements, is complemented by millions of trees and shrubs, which give the city its ambience. Canberra is planned around Lake Burley Griffin and a 'parliamentary triangle' consisting of Parliament House, the High Court and other important public buildings. It extends more than 40km from the satellite towns of **Tuggeranong** in the south to **Gungahlin** in the north.

The best way to explore Canberra is by car, but make sure you have a good map. The city's attractions are quite spread out, although parking in Canberra is easy to find and inexpensive. If investigating by foot is appealing, then wander along King Edward Tce, or the Lake's shore and find the National Library, Questacon—The National Science and Technology Centre, Old Parliament House, High Court, Aboriginal Tent Embassy and the National Gallery of Australia—all within close proximity of each other. Visiting the city's other attractions will require you to travel via the city's wide, planned streets and many roundabouts.

ℹ Visitor information

Canberra and Region Visitors Centre
330 Northbourne Ave, Dickson ACT 2602
Ph: (02) 6205 0044 or 1300 554 114
www.visitcanberra.com.au

facts

- ◈ Population: 353 900
- ◈ Date founded: 1913—foundation stone laid and name 'Canberra' adopted
- ◈ Lake Burley Griffin: created in 1964 when the Molonglo River was dammed
- ◈ Tallest building: Telstra Tower, 195m
- ◈ Average temperature: 21°C (January), 6.5°C (June)

Places of Interest

Anzac Parade (A) E3
Australian National Botanic Gardens (B) A1
Australian National University (C) B2
Australian War Memorial (D) E2
Blundell's Cottage (E) E3
Canberra Theatre Centre (F) D2
Captain Cook Memorial Water Jet (G) C3
Casino Canberra (H) D2
City Hill Lookout (I) C2
Commonwealth Park (J) D3
Gorman House Arts Centre (K) D2
High Court of Australia (L) D4
National Capital Exhibition (M) D3
National Carillon (N) E4
National Gallery of Australia (O) D4
National Library of Australia (P) C4
National Museum of Australia (Q) C3
Old Parliament House and National Portrait Gallery (R) C4
Parliament House (S) C5
Prime Minister's Lodge (T) B5
Questacon — The National Science and Technology Centre (U) D4
ScreenSound Australia (V) C2

Questacon — The National Science and Technology Centre

Australian Capital Territory

Scale 1:25 000

0   750   Metres

Canberra Nature Park

Black Mountain Nature Reserve

Australian National Botanic Gardens

Australian National Botanic Gardens

Black Mountain Peninsula

West Lake

Springbank Island

Acton Peninsula

Spinnaker Island

National Museum of Australia

Lake Burley Griffin

Yarralumla Bay

Swimming Area

Canberra Rowing Club
ANU Sailing Club
YMCA Sailing Club

Stirling

Yarralumla Bay Oval

Yarralumla Neighbourhood Ent Oval
Tennis Club
Yarralumla Primary

DEAKIN

Deakin Oval

The Grange

Canberra Nature Park

Red Hill 720m

TURNER

BRADDON

North Oval

Australian National University

ACTON

ScreenSound Australia

City Hill Lookout

Canberra Theatre Centre

Casino National Convention Centre

Olympic Pool

Commonwealth Park

Stage 88

Nerang Pool

National Capital Exhibition

Canadian Flagpole

Captain Cook Memorial Water Jet

West Basin

Central Basin

Griffin

Ferry Terminal & Boat Hire

Archbishops Residence

National Library of Australia

Questacon

Reconciliation Place

National Rose Garden

High Court of Australia

National Gallery of Australia

PARKES

Parkes Place

Old Parliament House

CAPITAL HILL

Parliament House

Prime Minister's Lodge

FORREST

Forrest Primary

Forrest Tennis Club

Manuka Oval

Manuka Cinema

BARTON

Charles Sturt University Canberra Campus

Police College

Kingston Foreshore Info Cntr

Old Bus Depot Markets

Temp Rowing Shed

East Basin

KINGSTON

REID

Reid Park

Anzac Parade

Australian War Memorial

Blundell's Cottage

Kings Park

National Carillon

Aspen Island

RUSSELL

Russell

Canberra Institute of Technology

Gorman House Arts Centre

Campbell High

CSIRO Head Office

Ainslie Village

Merci College

CSIRO

Visitors Centre

Mosque

European Union
Netherlands
Germany
Greece
Japan
Thailand
Saudi Arabia
Nigeria
Korea
Norway
Spain

Church of England Girls Grammar

Collins Park

Canberra Nature Park

© UNIVERSAL PUBLISHERS PTY LTD 2005

Historic Attractions

Australian National University
Occupying 145ha of Canberra City, the ANU was the first Australian research-based university; it was inaugurated in 1946. By 1960 ANU had begun to award undergraduate degrees. Three Nobel Prizes have been won by ANU researchers, and the **ANU Library** holds around two million books. Wander the landscaped campus planted with native and exotic tree species, or perhaps drop into the **Drill Hall Gallery** and see some free exhibitions. Ph: (02) 6249 5111, or visit: www.anu.edu.au

Australian War Memorial
The Australian War Memorial—the most popular museum in the country—commemorates the sacrifices made by the men and women who served this country in war and in peacekeeping efforts. The memorial is internationally recognised for its exhibitions. The Hall of Memory, the Tomb of the Unknown Australian Soldier, the Pool of Reflection and the Roll of Honour are the focal points of the Memorial. **The ANZAC Hall**, completed in 2001, showcases a large technology collection. The redeveloped **World War II Gallery** and the Bradbury Aircraft Hall should not be missed.
Ph: (02) 6243 4211 or visit: www.awm.gov.au

Blundell's Cottage
For more than 40 years this cottage has been a genuine museum of life in the Canberra area before Federation. It was built in 1860 on the **Molonglo River**, and was originally part of the Campbell family's 'Duntroon' estate of 119km^2. Ph: (02) 6273 2667

Calthorpes' House
Built in 1927, Calthorpes' contains original furnishings, appliances and memorabilia, which reflect early life in Canberra. It is open for inspection every day, except Mondays and Fridays.
Ph: (02) 6295 1945

Hyatt Hotel Canberra
The Hyatt Hotel is one of Canberra's premier hotels. Opened in 1924, it was originally named 'Hotel Canberra'. Today it is a sympathetically restored showcase of original Art Deco architecture, surrounded by landscaped gardens.
Ph: (02) 6270 1234 or visit: www.hyatt.com

Lanyon
This historic station homestead is surrounded by gardens and out-buildings, with guided and audio tours available. **The Sidney Nolan Gallery** is also located here and features the artist's works and changing exhibitions of modern Australian art. Enjoy a picnic in the garden or a light meal in the cafe.
Ph: (02) 6237 5136

National Archives of Australia
A visit to the National Archives is an exploration into the past; a place that holds the memories of the nation. Take a look at the evolving exhibitions, peruse original files, photographs, posters, maps and paintings in the reading room, or perhaps enjoy a film or audio recording. Located just behind **Old Parliament House**, the secrets of the nation are just waiting to be discovered. Ph: (02) 6212 3600 or visit: www.naa.gov.au

National Dinosaur Museum
Located in **Gold Creek Village** off the Barton Hwy, the National Dinosaur Museum displays full-sized dinosaur replicas, information panels, fossils of plants and fish dating to 500 million

Re-creation of the Battle of Lone Pine (1915), Australian War Memorial

Australian Capital Territory

National Museum of Australia on Acton Peninsula, Lake Burley Griffin

years ago, and a discovery area where children can build a dinosaur and investigate the process of their extinction.
Ph: (02) 6230 2655 or visit: www.nationaldinosaurmuseum.com.au

National Museum of Australia

Opened in March 2001 for the Centenary of Federation celebrations, the National Museum of Australia is an architecturally striking configuration of structures. Located on the **Acton Peninsula** it showcases the history of the nation, and has an outdoor amphitheatre, an Aboriginal Gallery, and evolving exhibition halls.
Ph: (02) 6208 5000 or visit: www.nma.gov.au

Nature and Animal Attractions

Australian National Botanic Gardens

Located in **Acton** on the lower slopes of **Black Mountain**, the Australian National Botanic Gardens maintains and displays a diverse collection of native Australian flora. With a visitor centre, bookshop, cafe and free guided walks, the gardens offer a wonderful outdoor experience. Take a picnic and wander through the Rainforest Gully, Rock Garden, Eucalypt Lawn and Mallee Shrublands.
Ph: (02) 6250 9540 or visit: www.anbg.gov.au

Australian Reptile Centre Canberra

Discover the history and evolution of our reptiles, or examine live specimens close up. The Australian Reptile Centre, a fascinating place, is open 364 days a year and is an educational adventure for the whole family. Like the **Bird Walk Aviary,** it is located in **Gold Creek Village** off the Barton Hwy.
Ph: (02) 6253 8533 or visit: www.contact.com.au/reptile

Ginninderra Falls

The falls are located about a 20 minute drive from the city centre, situated in a bushland park on **Ginninderra Creek**. Picnic, BBQ, swim, hire a canoe, abseil or walk along scenic trails that range from 10 minutes to two hours.

National Zoo and Aquarium

Australia's only zoo and aquarium combined, the National Zoo and Aquarium is situated on 8ha only five minutes from the city centre at **Scrivener Dam**. See Australian and exotic animals, 34 endangered species, plus freshwater and marine exhibits. The natural enclosures are vast and there are educational guided tours available.
Ph: (02) 6287 8400 or visit: www.zooquarium.com.au

Cultural Attractions

Captain Cook Memorial Water Jet

Constructed by the Commonwealth Government in 1970, the Captain Cook Memorial Jet commemorates the bicentenary of James Cook's discovery of the east coast of Australia. Similar to the Jet d'Eau in Geneva, Switzerland, the water jet is located in **Lake Burley Griffin** and can be seen from most points along the lake.

Embassies

There are around 80 diplomatic missions in Canberra, creating a cultural diversity and contributing architectural masterpieces to the cityscape. Some of the embassies and high commissions are open to visitors, but most are just open for business. Still, it is worth driving through **Yarralumla** to look at the different architectural styles of the buildings.

High Court of Australia

The highest point in the Australian judicial system, the High Court was permanently transferred from Sydney to Canberra in May 1980. Located on the shores of **Lake Burley Griffin**, it is adjacent to the National Gallery of Australia. Opened by Her Majesty Queen Elizabeth II, it is 40m tall at its highest point. The Public Hall is an unusual venue for functions and exhibitions, and a small theatre together with display cases offers an understanding of the court's history and the workings of the judicial system. Ph: (02) 6270 6811 or visit: www.hcourt.gov.au

National Carillon

A gift from the British Government for the 50th Anniversary of the National Capital, the Carillon is situated on **Aspen Island**, Lake Burley Griffin. With 55 bronze bells, it is large by international standards. All styles of music are played by different carillonists throughout the year. Ph: (02) 6257 1068 or visit: www.nationalcapital.gov.au

National Gallery of Australia

The National Gallery of Australia is located on the shores of Lake Burley Griffin and contains one of the finest collections of art in the country. With travelling exhibitions, a children's gallery, sculpture garden, guided and audio tours, educational services, a cafe and two restaurants, Gallery Shop and free parking both above and underground, the National Gallery is worth a whole day's outing. Ph: (02) 6240 6502 or visit: www.nga.gov.au

National Library of Australia

Situated on the shore of Lake Burley Griffin, the National Library offers free entry and a range of reading rooms, lounges and changing exhibitions. There are facilities for people with a disability and the vision impaired. Ph: (02) 6262 1111 or visit: www.nla.gov.au

National Portrait Gallery

Located in **Old Parliament House**, the National Portrait Gallery is one of only four in the world. Portraits of the famous, from Captain Cook to sporting heroes, politicians, musicians, scientists, superstars and criminals adorn the walls of refurbished rooms in the building. There is an annexe at **Commonwealth Place** near Lake Burley Griffin. Open every day except Christmas, a small entry fee applies. Ph: (02) 6270 8210 or visit: www.portrait.gov.au

Royal Australian Mint

The Mint is a fully functional money factory located in **Deakin**. With an extensive coin collection and an informative hands-on experience, the Mint is a fascinating destination for all ages. Ph: (02) 6202 6999 or visit: www.ramint.gov.au

ScreenSound Australia

The National Screen and Sound Archive in McCoy Circuit is Australia's largest collection of recorded sound and moving images, with more than a million radio titles, thousands of newsreels and a remarkable 100 years of films. Ph: (02) 6248 2000 or visit: www.screensound.gov.au

18ft skiffs on Lake Burley Griffin

FLORIADE (AUSTRALIA'S CELEBRATION OF SPRING)

From mid September to mid October each year, a floral display that rivals all others in the country is held in **Commonwealth Park**. More than a million flowering bulbs and annuals bloom around the pools, streams, marsh gardens and sculptures of the park, which is located on the shores of Lake Burley Griffin. Private gardens are also opened and there are demonstrations and talks about flowers and gardening, as well as family entertainment. It is one of the major attractions of the city in spring and is accompanied by other events held throughout the capital. Visit: www.floriadeaustralia.com

Floriade Spring Festival, Commonwealth Park

Science and Technology Attractions

Australian Institute of Sport
The Australian Institute of Sport (AIS) is situated in **Bruce**. Visitors to the institute can take a tour with an elite Australian athlete; catch a glimpse of gymnasts and swimmers in training; test personal skills in the interactive sports exhibit, Sportex; see the latest exhibitions in sporting technology, equipment and clothing; have a bite to eat at the Time Out Cafe; or visit the AIS shop for souvenirs and gifts.
Ph: (02) 6214 1010 or visit: www.aisport.com.au

Canberra Space Dome and Observatory
Only a five minute drive from the city centre in **Dickson**, Canberra Space Dome is one of Australia's best public observatories. The domed theatre offers unique shows to educate children and adults alike, while the four research-grade telescopes provide the opportunity to view the night sky.
Ph: (02) 6248 5333 or visit: www.ctuc.asn.au/planetarium

CSIRO Discovery
This relatively new complex on the slopes of **Black Mountain** is 'an interactive showcase of Australian scientific innovation'. Exhibits explore CSIRO research in health, agriculture, manufacturing industries and the environment. Great for children and anyone with an interest in science, the Discovery Centre is a place of Australian achievements in scientific research.
Ph: (02) 6246 4646 or visit: www.discovery.csiro.au

Questacon—The National Science and Technology Centre
Known as the 'hands-on science and technology centre,' Questacon offers over 200 different displays and programmes. Officially opened in November 1988, it is the leading interactive science and technology centre in Australia, attracting over 300 000 visitors annually. Questacon certainly achieves its goal of 'making science fun and relevant for everyone'.
Ph: (02) 6270 2800 or visit: www.questacon.edu.au

Telstra Tower
Soaring 195m above the peak of **Black Mountain**, Telstra Tower boasts an amazing 360^0 view of the Australian Capital Territory. The tower is open day and night, so visitors can venture onto the viewing platforms or the viewing gallery at their convenience. There is an exhibition gallery, theatrette, licensed revolving restaurant, cafe and gift shop. Admission charges apply. Ph: 1800 806 718

Political Attractions

Parliament House
The central point of the city, the flagpole of Parliament House is 81m high, and the flag itself is 12m

by 6m. The landscaped gardens and lawns that surround this magnificent building are planted with native species, while the more formal gardens feature exotics. Free tickets are available to Question Time in the **House of Representatives**; tickets are not required for Question Time in the **Senate**. Ph: (02) 6277 5399 or visit: www.aph.gov.au

Old Parliament House

Originally in use from 1927 until 1988, Old Parliament House is open for viewing and visitors can see the chambers where former Prime Ministers—Menzies, Evatt, Casey, Whitlam and Hawke among them—performed. Now housing the **National Portrait Gallery**, Old Parliament House is situated directly in front of Parliament House. The lawn in front of the building is the site of the **Aboriginal Tent Embassy**, and has been the place of protests by conservationists, farmers and Vietnam War objectors. Ph: (02) 6270 8222 or visit: www.oph.gov.au

Cockington Green, Canberra

Canberra Balloon Fiesta, held near Old Parliament House in March

Other Attractions

Canberra City Sightseeing Bus

This red double-decker bus, complete with commentary in various languages, completes a circuit around the city every 80 minutes. You can stay on board for all the major sights or hop on and off as you please. Canberra and Region Visitors Centre has more details. Ph: (02) 6205 0044 or visit: www.visitcanberra.com.au

Cockington Green

Located in **Gold Creek Village**, this award-winning land of miniature buildings (one-twelfth scale) and gardens is open seven days a week. View the modellers' workshop, enjoy a steam train ride, have a coffee or light meal, picnic or BBQ, and possibly buy a souvenir to take home. With access and facilities for people with a disability, Cockington Green will provide opportunities to entertain the whole family.

Ph: (02) 6230 2273 or visit: www.cockington-green.com.au

Ferry Cruises on the Lake

For a relaxed view of the city's attractions, why not take a ferry around Lake Burley Griffin. For more information contact Canberra and District Visitors Centre. Ph: (02) 6205 0044

Harley Davidson and Hot-Air Balloon Tours

For the more adventurous, take a Harley Davidson motorcycle tour, or a hot-air balloon flight above the city, for a very different view of the sights. For more information contact Canberra and District Visitors Centre. Ph: (02) 6205 0044

Kamberra Wine Company

This unique urban winery, just north of the city centre, is a focal point for the Canberra Region wine industry and local vineyards. Ph: (02) 6262 2333

Australian Capital Territory

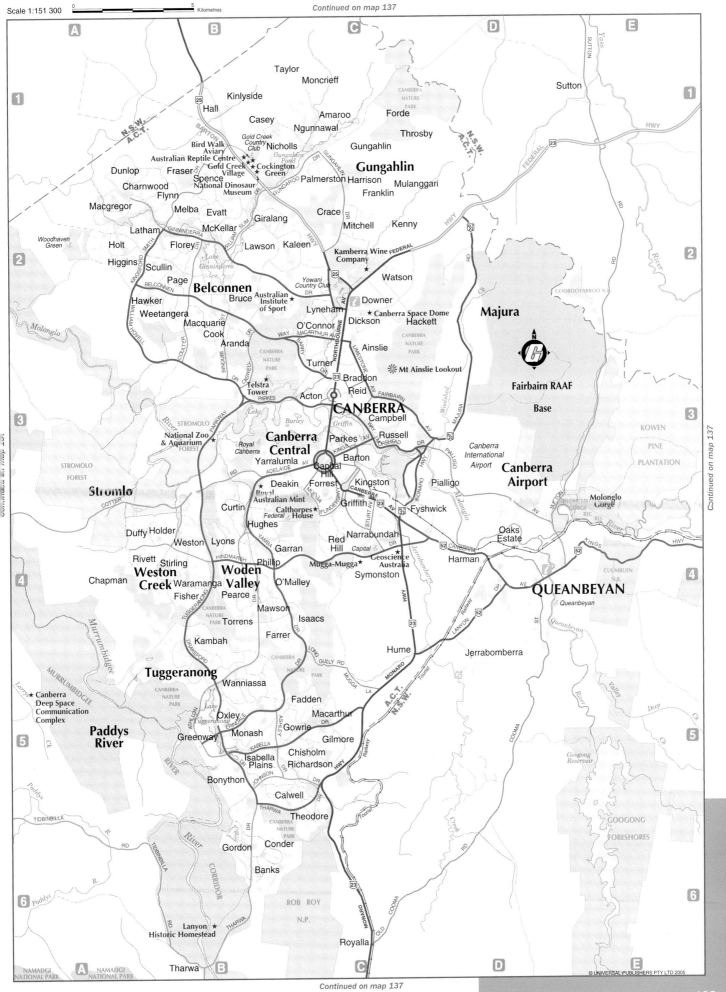

Kilometres

Sutton

Gungahlin

Taylor
Moncrieff
Kinlyside
Casey
Amaroo
Ngunnawal
Forde
Hall
Throsby
Gold Creek Country Club
Nicholls
Gungahlin
Bird Walk Aviary
Australian Reptile Centre
Gold Creek Village
Cockington Green
National Dinosaur Museum
Palmerston Harrison
Mulanggari
Dunlop
Fraser
Spence
Franklin
Charnwood
Flynn
Macgregor
Melba
Evatt
Giralang
Crace
Latham
McKellar
Lawson
Kaleen
Mitchell
Kenny
Holt
Florey
Higgins
Scullin
Page
Woodhaven Green
Bruce
Australian Institute of Sport
Kamberra Wine Company
Watson
Belconnen
Downer
Majura
Hawker
Weetangera
Macquarie
Cook
Aranda
O'Connor
Lyneham
Dickson
Canberra Space Dome
Hackett
Ainslie
Fairbairn RAAF
Turner
Base
Telstra Tower
Braddon
Reid
Mt Ainslie Lookout
Acton
Campbell
Russell
CANBERRA
National Zoo & Aquarium
Royal Canberra
Parkes
Canberra International Airport
Stromlo
Canberra Central
Yarralumla
Barton
Canberra Airport
Capital Hill
Kingston
Deakin
Forrest
Royal Australian Mint
Calthorpes House
Griffith
Fyshwick
Curtin
Federal House
Hughes
Narrabundah
Oaks Estate
Weston
Lyons
Garran
Red Hill
Geoscience Australia
Harman
Duffy Holder
Mugga-Mugga
QUEANBEYAN
Rivett
Stirling
Woden Valley
Phillip
O'Malley
Symonston
Chapman
Weston Creek
Waramanga
Pearce
Mawson
Fisher
Torrens
Isaacs
Jerrabomberra
Kambah
Farrer
Hume
Tuggeranong
Wanniassa
Fadden
Canberra Deep Space Communication Complex
Oxley
Macarthur
Gowrie
Paddys River
Greenway
Monash
Gilmore
Isabella Plains
Chisholm
Richardson
Bonython
Calwell
Theodore
Gordon
Conder
Banks
ROB ROY N.P.
Lanyon Historic Homestead
Royalla
Tharwa

Continued on map 137

© UNIVERSAL PUBLISHERS PTY LTD 2005

REGIONAL ATTRACTIONS

Although the majority of the tourist attractions are in and around the city centre, there are a few regional attractions worth investigating in the surrounding area. These are mainly reserves, parklands and recreational spots, which some believe are the hidden wonders of the Australian Capital Territory.

Canberra Deep Space Communications Complex

Located in the countryside south-west of Canberra, 5km from Tidbinbilla Nature Reserve, is the only NASA deep space tracking station in Australia. Within the grounds is the **Canberra Space Centre**, which showcases the history of space exploration and Australia's role in it. Tour the centre and see an Andy Thomas space suit, real space food, a piece of the moon obtained from *Apollo 11* astronauts and interactive exhibits and displays. Views from the centre take in the four large antennae used to communicate with spacecraft and for making radio investigations of space. One of them is 70m in diameter—the largest steerable antenna in the Southern Hemisphere. The centre has the Moonrock Cafe, picnic and BBQ facilities. Ph: (02) 6201 7880 or visit: www.cdscc.nasa.gov

Corin Forest

Known as the Australian Capital Territory's '**mountain playground**', Corin Forest lies at an altitude of 1200m. The region averages ten snowfalls a year, but with the resort's snowmaking facilities there is a snow cover available most of the winter. Corin Forest is a very accessible daytrip destination from the city on Tourist Drive 5 (around 45 minutes from Parliament House). It boasts an 800m bobsled run/alpine slide, a 110m water slide, a dual 350m flying fox, as well as tobogganing and snow play in winter, and a cafe. It is open weekends, public holidays and Australian Capital Territory school holidays. Ph: (02) 6235 7333 or visit: www.corin.com.au

Murrumbidgee River Corridor

The Murrumbidgee River Corridor runs from the mountains in the south through some of the most picturesque countryside that the Australian Capital Territory has to offer. Enjoy a picnic, walk along rocky gorges and planned trails, or have a splash in the cool waters of the river. The only place to camp along the Murrumbidgee is at **Cotter campground** where there are BBQs, toilet and hot shower facilities, but no power. Ph: (02) 6207 2425 or visit: www.environment.act.gov.au

Tidbinbilla Nature Reserve

This reserve is nestled in the slopes of the **Tidbinbilla Range** about 40 minutes drive from Canberra city off Tourist Route 5. Experience Australian wildlife in specially designed enclosures. Walk amongst the koalas, kangaroos, wallabies, emus and waterbirds or maybe catch a glimpse of the elusive platypus. Regular ranger-guided tours are available but bookings are essential. Tidbinbilla is open every day except Christmas Day. There are walking trails, BBQs, picnic areas, and a visitor centre. Ph: (02) 6205 1233 or visit: www.environment.act.gov.au

Gilbraltar Rocks, Tidbinbilla Nature Reserve

Scale 1:400 000

0   10 Kilometres

Continued on map 122

TO YASS
TO GUNNING   TO GOULBURN

A **B** **C** **D** **E**

1

Lake Jasper N.R.
Lake Burrinjuck
Wee Jasper

Oakey Ck

Wandana
Surveyor's Hill
Pankhurst
Brindabella Hills
Ginninderra Falls ★

Hall

Gungahlin
CANBERRA NATURE PARK

Sutton

Lake George

Hillbrook Purrorumba 886
Affleck
Bywong
Gidgee

Wombat Mountain Ra

BRINDABELLA NATIONAL PARK

NEW SOUTH WALES
AUSTRALIAN CAPITAL TERRITORY

Woodstock N.R.
Uriara Crossing

Belconnen
Australian Institute of Sport

Lambert
MILIMANI
Lark Hills

Wamboin

2

BONDO STATE FOREST

BRINDABELLA STATE CONS. AREA

Devils Peak
Corse Mtn 1421

Cotter Dam

Coppins Crossing
Black Mtn 813m

Mt Majura 888
Mt Ainslie 843
CANBERRA
CANBERRA NATURE PARK
Capital Hill

Majura Field
Fairbairn RAAF Base
Canberra International

KOWEN
PINE FOREST

Bungendore

TO BRAIDWOOD

Brindabella

National Zoo & Aquarium
Red Hill
Woden Valley

Weston Creek

Murrays Corner

Queanbeyan
CUUMBUIN N.R.
Burbong
HWY

3

BIMBERI N.R.

TIDBINBILLA

Flints Crossing
Canberra Deep Space Communication Complex ★

Kambah Pool
NATURE RESERVE

Tuggeranong

Gibraltar

Murrumbidgee

Michelago Tourist Railway Steam Train Excursions

Mt Jerrabomberra 781
Balcombe Hill 953

GOOGONG FORESHORES
Googong Reservoir

Mt Molonglo 1120

Hoskinstown

Mt Aggie 1496
Mt Franklin 1644
★ Franklin Chalet

Bendora Dam

TIDBINBILLA NATURE RESERVE

Booroomba
Woods Reserve
Lanyon

ROB ROY N.R.

Googong Hill 1019

YANUNUNBEYAN NATIONAL PARK

4

KOSCIUSZKO NATIONAL PARK

Brindabella
BIMBERI NATURE RESERVE
Mt Ginni 1775

Corin Dam

NAMADGI
Booroomba Rocks
Track
Former Space Tracking Station (Honeysuckle Campground)
Honeysuckle

Tharwa
Craft Centre
Namadgi Visitor Centre
GIGERLINE N.R.
Mt Tennent 1383

Nuyalla

Burra

Williamsdale

YANUNUNBEYAN STATE CONSERVATION AREA

TINDERRY NATURE RESERVE

Captains Flat

TO BRAIDWOOD

Mt Gingera 1857

Naas
Walking

Orroral Former Space Tracking Station

MONARO HWY

Michelago

Tinderry 1613

5

KOSCIUSZKO NATIONAL PARK

Mt Bimbem 1911
Alps
Australian
King Rock 1495
KOSCIUSZKO
Mt Murray 1845

Orroral Crossing Campground

Rocky Crossing

Glendale Crossing

Middle Ck
Mt Kelly

NATIONAL PARK

Ballinafad

GOUROCK NATIONAL PARK

Mt Tamanang 1476

Jingera

Tantangara reservoir
Morgan Peak 1875

SCABBY RANGE NATURE RESERVE
Gudgenby Hill 1740
Sams
Booth Ra

TINDERRY MOUNTAINS

BURNT SCHOOL N.R.

6

SNOWY MOUNTAINS HWY

Yaouk
YAOUK N.R.

Boboyan Range

Mt Clear Campground
Mt Clear 1603

Shanahans Mtn

Murrumbidgee

Clear Ra
Inga

STRIKE-A-LIGHT N.R.

Wallaby Hill 1310

Jerangle

Anembo

TO COOMA
Bredbo

© UNIVERSAL PUBLISHERS PTY LTD 2005

AUSTRALIAN CAPITAL TERRITORY   **137**

VICTORIA

Covering 227 600km^2 of the south-eastern corner of Australia, Victoria is a relatively compact state, the second smallest after Tasmania. The state's mostly temperate climate has four distinct seasons, each with its own attractions. As a result of its manageable size and efficient road system, travelling the state is easy and comfortable. Transport options are excellent: coaches, trains and planes carry visitors into and around the state, and for those who want to explore independently, touring by car is convenient. Most places can be reached within a day's drive of the capital city, Melbourne, and there is a huge array of natural, cultural and historic areas just waiting to be discovered.

Victoria packs a lot within its boundaries. The Murray River stretches along the border with New South Wales and is a delightful destination in itself. The southern coastline is spectacular and varied, taking in the Great Ocean Road to the west, Wilsons Promontory and the beautiful Gippsland Lakes area to the east. Victoria's magnificent

Victoria: The Garden State

- Population: 4 900 000
- Total area: 227 600km²
- % of Australia: 2.96%
- Floral emblem: Pink Heath
- Fauna emblem: Leadbeater's Possum

Main ATTRACTIONS

◈ The Dandenongs

Renowned for their green hills, lookouts and pretty townships, these ranges are only one hour's drive from Melbourne.

◈ Echuca

On the banks of the Murray River, Echuca is home to the largest collection of paddlesteamers in Australia.

◈ Gippsland Lakes

A boating and fishing paradise, this is the most extensive system of estuarine lagoons in Australia.

◈ The Goldfields

Ballarat, the Goldfields capital since the 1850s, has many ornate Victorian buildings and large parks.

◈ Grampians National Park

Over 400 hundred million years old, this national park is a spectacular landscape of rock formations, lakes and waterfalls.

◈ Great Ocean Road

Beginning at Torquay and winding 285km west along the coast to Warrnambool, this is truly one of the world's most spectacular coastal routes.

◈ Phillip Island

Mostly known for its Penguin Parade, Phillip Island attracts 50 000 visitors annually.

◈ Spa Country

A region of historic towns, Spa Country is said to have mineral water springs with a quality equal to anywhere in the world.

◈ Victorian Alps

Home to some of Australia's premier ski resorts, the southernmost part of the Great Dividing Range is protected by national parks.

Alpine region has much to explore and the Goldfields districts reveal an exciting episode in the state's history. Tranquil lakes, an exciting selection of national parks, cool forests and fertile countryside await the visitor, with accessible cities, towns and villages offering their hospitality.

Victoria caters well for the discerning traveller. Fresh produce is a specialty all over the state, with specific gourmet focal points like the Milawa Gourmet Region near Wangaratta and the Gourmet Deli Trail in West Gippsland. Wine-lovers can select from 14 winery regions and over 350 wineries, ranging from the Grampians in the south-west to Rutherglen in the north-east. Victorian vineyards are renowned for producing excellent vintages for the Australian and international market.

Photo above: The Twelve Apostles, Port Campbell National Park, Great Ocean Road

THE GARDEN STATE

The third British Colony to be established in Australia, Victoria was a collection of small, unauthorised settlements before 1834. In 1851, Victoria separated from New South Wales, so that it too did not end up becoming a penal settlement. When gold was discovered in **Ballarat** the same year, there was a rush of immigrants from all over the world, as well as from within the country, resulting in a explosion of Victoria's population within a year.

Cities such as **Melbourne** and **Bendigo** were originally built on wealth accumulated from the gold diggings. Interestingly, the land on which Melbourne is sited was 'bought' by John Batman in 1834 from its Aboriginal owners for 20 blankets, 30 knives, 12 red shirts, 4 flannel jackets and 50 handkerchiefs. It remained a small and slow-growing town until the discovery of gold, when it boomed and the population flourished.

Today, Victoria produces almost one-quarter of Australia's gross value of agricultural products. Together, the agriculture and food industry account for 31% of the state's export income. The main rural industries of the state are wheat, vegetables and wool. On a smaller scale, beef, dairy products, wine, dry vine fruits and timber are also important to its economy. Oil and gas fields in the **Bass Strait** produce more than 60% of the country's crude oil, and brown coal comes from the **Latrobe Valley** coalfields.

Like New South Wales, temperatures are moderate, though less predictable in some areas. The best times to tour this state are spring, late summer and autumn. The northern and western plains of Victoria are much hotter, drier and prone to drought.

Victoria can be broadly divided into five main regions. In the north

Daffodils in bloom at St Arnaud

east highlands, the peaks of the **Great Dividing Range** attract skiers in winter and bushwalkers and climbers in the summer. The southeast is punctuated with lakes, caves, forests, waterways and coastal scenery, while the central west is a preserved goldfields heartland of goldrush and spa towns. Western districts are characterised by open pastoral lands and the striking **Grampians NP**. The 285km stretch of the **Great Ocean Road** is a major attraction of this region, offering some of the most amazing coastal scenery in the world. The **Murray River region**, which forms the northern border of the state, boasts quaint old river ports, wineries and citrus groves.

The Murray River flows alongside Hattah-Kulkyne National Park in north-west Victoria

Victoria

TOURISM REGION HIGHLIGHTS

Victoria has a great deal to offer within its relatively small area. The southern coastline includes the world-famous Great Ocean Road and the Gippsland Lakes region. The High Country offers superb mountain scenery and the Goldfields recall a colourful past. A few hours drive from Melbourne—the sophisticated 'cultural capital' of Australia—reveals rolling farmlands, picturesque winery regions, temperate forests and the mighty Murray River.

A Melbourne (pp.146–153)
Albert Park; Crown Entertainment Complex; Federation Square; Fitzroy Gardens; *Polly Woodside* Maritime Museum; Melbourne Cricket Ground; Melbourne Museum; Melbourne trams; Melbourne Zoo; National Gallery of Victoria; Melbourne Aquarium; Queen Victoria Market; Royal Botanic Gardens; Southgate

B Goldfields (pp.158–159)
Ballarat; Bendigo; Castlemaine; Clunes; Maldon; Maryborough; Pyrenees Ranges; Sovereign Hill

C Goulburn Murray Waters
Alexandra; Euroa; Goulburn Valley; Lake Eildon; Nagambie Lakes; Nagambie Wineries; Shepparton; Strathbogie Ranges; Trawool Valley

D The Grampians (pp.194–195)
Ararat; Byaduk Caves; Grampians NP; Halls Gap; Hamilton; Little Desert NP; Mount Arapiles; Stawell

E Great Ocean Road (pp.199–201)
Apollo Bay; Cape Bridgewater; Lorne; Lower Glenelg NP; Melba Gully SP; Otway Fly; Otway NP; Port Campbell NP; Port Fairy; Portland; The Shipwreck Coast; Torquay; Tower Hill; Warrnambool

F Lakes and Wilderness
Bairnsdale; Buchan Caves; Croajingolong NP; Gippsland Lakes; Lakes Entrance; Mallacoota; Mitchell River NP; Omeo; Snowy River

G Legends Wine and High Country (pp.186–187)
Alpine NP; Beechworth; Benalla; Bright; Chiltern; Glenrowan; King Valley; Mansfield; Milawa Vineyards; Mount Beauty; Mount Buffalo NP; Mount Buller, Falls Creek, Mount Hotham and Dinner Plain Ski Resorts; Wangaratta; Yackandandah

H Macedon Ranges and Spa Country (pp.166–167)
Daylesford; Hanging Rock; Hepburn Springs; Macedon Ranges Wineries; Mount Macedon; Organ Pipes NP

I Melbourne's Bays and Peninsulas (pp.152–153)
Arthur's Seat; Bellarine Peninsula; Cape Schank; Frankston; Geelong; Hastings; Mornington Peninsula; Port Melbourne; Port Phillip; Portsea; Queenscliff; St Kilda; Sorrento; Victoria's Open Range Zoo; Werribee Park

J Mildura and Murray Outback
Murray River; Murray-Sunset NP; Ouyen; Wyperfeld NP

K The Murray
Albury-Wodonga; Corryong; Lake Hume; Mildura; Murray River; Port of Echuca; Rutherglen Wineries; Swan Hill; Yarrawonga

L Phillip Island and Gippsland Discovery (pp.164–165 & 178–179)
Churchill Island; Coal Creek, Korumburra; Gippsland Heritage Park, Moe; Gourmet Deli Region; Latrobe Valley; Mount Baw Baw; Ninety Mile Beach; Penguin Parade; Phillip Island; PowerWorks, Morwell; Sale; Strzelecki Ranges; Tarra-Bulga NP; Walhalla; Wilsons Promontory; Wonthaggi State Coal Mine

M Yarra Valley, Dandenongs and the Ranges (pp.170–171)
Dandenong Ranges; Healesville Sanctuary; Lake Mountain; Marysville; Mystic Mountains; *Puffing Billy* Railway; William Ricketts Sanctuary; Yarra Valley Wineries

Rocks at Shipwreck Beach, Croajingolong National Park

NATIONAL PARKS

Victoria's national parks protect a great variety of landscapes—from beaches, rainforests and snowy mountains to semi-arid areas. They offer a range of scenery, natural features and cultural heritage, as well as a variety of recreational activities. A few of Victoria's most popular and diverse national parks are listed here.

A Alpine NP

(Map 209, G5)

Stretching to the New South Wales border, the Alpine NP is the largest park in Victoria at 6605km^2 and protects most of the state's High Country. The park offers spectacular gorges, waterfalls, wild rivers, green valleys and extensive winter snowfields. It is the perfect destination for downhill and cross-country skiers in winter. At other times of the year the park offers swimming, walking, 4-wheel driving, cycling, horseriding, canoeing, and places of historical interest. Be prepared for sudden weather changes—snow can fall at any time, even in summer.

B Croajingolong NP

(Map 214, C5)

Located 450km east of Melbourne, Croajingolong NP is a pristine environment of eucalypt forests, rainforests, coastal heathlands, estuaries and sandy beaches. Created in 1979, the 875km^2 park is home to over 1000 species of native plants as well as more than 300 bird species. Enjoy short or long walks, camping, swimming, diving, sailing and sea kayaking and great 4-wheel driving opportunities.

C Grampians NP

(Map 195, B3)

In the central west of the state, the 1672km^2 Grampians NP has some of the state's most rugged and spectacular scenery. The Grampians are widely known for their spring-time display of wildflowers and their Aboriginal rock-art sites. Popular activities include walking, cycling, rockclimbing, nature studies and scenic driving. There are picnic and camping areas, toilet facilities and walking tracks. Visit **Brambuk the National Park and Cultural Centre** at **Halls Gap** for park information.

D Little Desert NP

(Map 206, B4)

North-west of the Grampians, Little Desert NP is a great choice for 4-wheel driving, camping and walking. Around 1320km^2, the park—a desert in name only—has many types of vegetation and abundant native fauna. Winter and spring are good times to visit the state's drier north-west parks as summer can be very hot. North of Little Desert NP, **Wyperfeld** and **Murray-Sunset national parks** protect extensive areas of mallee eucalypt vegetation, and **Hattah-Kulkyne NP** also has huge river red gum trees and lakes filled by the **Murray River**.

facts

❖ No. of parks/reserves: 196
❖ Total area: 41 000km²
❖ % of state: 17%

A trio of rainbow lorikeets, *Trichoglossus haematodus*

E Mornington Peninsula NP

(Map 152, C5)

Only 95km from Melbourne, Mornington Peninsula NP is a 40km sweep of ocean coastline and hinterland. With picnic areas, lookouts and other facilities, the park is a haven for swimmers, surfers, anglers and walkers. Walking tracks allow for both short easy strolls and more challenging hikes. The historic military fortifications at **Point Nepean**, which were out of bounds to the public for more than 100 years, are now one of the park's major attractions.

F Mount Buffalo NP

(Map 187, B2)

Mount Buffalo NP, established over 100 years ago, is 350km north-east of Melbourne and covers 310km^2. It's a year-round family attraction, with snowsports in winter and wildflowers and walking in summer. It is notable as one of Victoria's top hang gliding and rockclimbing spots, and offers wonderful views. Visitors can camp or stay in comfort at the historic Chalet or at Mt Buffalo Lodge. Facilities include picnic areas, BBQs, toilets and well-marked walking tracks.

G Port Campbell NP

(Map 200, D5)

Port Campbell NP, a narrow coastal strip along the **Great Ocean Road**, has some of Australia's most recognised features, including The Twelve Apostles—towering rock islands rising out of the surf. There are also cliffs, historic shipwreck sites and walking opportunities.

H Wilsons Promontory NP

(Map 179, C3)

Wilsons Promontory NP, the southernmost tip of mainland Australia, is one of Victoria's most beautiful and popular parks. The park protects some 500km^2 of eucalypt forest, rainforest, heathland, sandy

Tree ferns, Wilsons Promontory National Park

beaches, granite peaks, headlands and their resident wildlife. It is 200km south-east of Melbourne, about a three hour drive, and is surrounded by marine parks that protect underwater ecosystems and historic shipwrecks. Swimming, surfing, snorkelling and scuba diving are popular attractions and walking opportunities range from short one or two hour strolls to overnight hikes, which require permits. Camping, lodge and hut accommodation is available.

I Yarra Ranges NP

(Map 212, C2)

Established in 1995, Yarra Ranges NP, about 100km north-east of Melbourne, is home to some of Australia's tallest trees. Much of the park's 760km^2 are set aside for water catchment and not open to the public. Elsewhere there are scenic drives, walking tracks and picnic areas. In winter, there are opportunities for cross-country skiing or snow play at **Mount Donna Buang** and **Lake Mountain**. Approach the park via Warburton, Healesville or Marysville.

National Park Information

Parks Victoria
Level 10, 535 Bourke St
Melbourne, VIC 3000
Ph: 13 19 63
www.parkweb.vic.gov.au

WINERIES

William Ryrie planted Victoria's first vines in the **Yarra Valley** in 1838. Largely through the efforts of Swiss immigrants, further vineyards were established in **Geelong**, the Yarra Valley and suburban Melbourne. Large suburban vineyards were located at South Yarra, **Toorak** and **Brighton** and by 1890 Victoria was the largest producer of wine in the country.

The Victorian wine industry was, however, devastated before the turn of the century, first by an economic downturn, then by an outbreak of *phylloxera*, a tiny vine-eating aphid. Most vineyards had to be destroyed and their soils chemically sterilized.

The industry experienced a renaissance in the 1960s as table wines regained popularity. There are now over 350 wineries in Victoria, more than any other state. At least 200 of them welcome visitors to their cellar doors and about 100 of these are within an hour's drive from Melbourne.

Scotchmans Hill vineyard on the Mornington Peninsula

A Alpine Valleys, King Valley and Glenrowan

This fertile region of north-east Victoria showcases century-old wineries such as Brown Brothers of Milawa and Baileys of Glenrowan. Several King Valley wineries had a much later start when Italian tobacco farmers switched to grape-growing in the 1970s. The area is renowned for complex red wines of great longevity. Recent innovations include Italian varietals such as sangiovese, nebbiolo and barbera.

B Ballarat (pp.156, 158–159)

The wine history of this goldrush town began as recently as the 1970s. There are now about 10 wineries around the city offering mainly chardonnay and pinot noir. Yellowglen is one of Victoria's top-selling sparkling labels.

C Bendigo and Heathcote (pp.158–159, 173)

In 1893, this was the first Victorian region to be struck with the *phylloxera* problem. Nowadays it is prime red-wine country, producing superb shiraz and full-flavoured cabernet from small family-owned vineyards.

D Geelong (p.172)

Once the most significant wine region in Victoria, Geelong and the neighbouring **Bellarine Peninsula** still support a number of quality wineries. The region has a cool, maritime climate and an extended growing season producing cabernet sauvignon, shiraz and chardonnay.

E Gippsland

A number of small family wineries are spread across Gippsland from **Phillip Island** to **Lakes Entrance**. Some of the finest pinot noirs in Australia have come from these tiny vineyards, as well as classic varieties such as shiraz, cabernet sauvignon, chardonnay, riesling and sauvignon blanc.

F Goulburn Valley

The large region between **Seymour** and **Echuca** has a warm climate that is ideal for Rhone varietals. Marsanne, shiraz, viognier, grenache, roussanne, and mourvedre are all planted, as well as riesling, chardonnay, cabernet sauvignon, pinot noir and merlot. Tahbilk and Mitchelton are well-known historic wineries in this area, both south of Nagambie.

G Grampians (pp.155, 159)

Beneath the dramatic backdrop of the Grampian Mountains, wineries around **Ararat** produce fine shiraz, riesling, chardonnay, pinot noir and cabernet sauvignon. The Great Western district is synonymous with sparkling wine in Australia.

H Macedon Ranges
(pp.166-167)

The rolling hills around **Kyneton**, **Lancefield** and **Woodend** have major plantings of chardonnay and pinot noir, much of which are used for methode champenoise wines. Shiraz does especially well in the cool climate and granite soils.

I Mornington Peninsula
(pp.152-153)

Blessed with rich soil, a cool climate, adequate rainfall during the growing season and high summer humidity, the Peninsula supports about 55 wineries producing fine table wines. Predominant varieties are chardonnay and pinot noir, used in table and sparkling wines, as well as cabernet sauvignon, merlot, shiraz, riesling, sauvignon blanc, semillon and pinot gris.

J Murray Valley and Swan Hill

The Murray River region between **Mildura** and Swan Hill basks in a sunny Mediterranean climate. Huge quantities of grapes are produced for the bulk wine and dried fruit markets, whilst smaller wineries offer high quality varietals.

K Pyrenees

Winemakers of the Pyrenees Ranges around **Avoca** and **Redbank** are famous for their minty reds, notably shiraz and cabernet sauvignon, as well as chardonnay and sauvignon blanc. The French Remy Martin group have specialised first in brandy and later in sparkling wines in the Pyrenees region.

L Rutherglen (p.191)

The Rutherglen wineries were established in the 1850s by German winemakers from the Barossa Valley. The region is best known for its unique muscats, tokays and rich red wines, but flavoursome whites and lighter reds are gaining popularity.

M Sunbury

This is the closest wine region to Melbourne, with a 150-year-old pedigree. The area is best known for shiraz, especially the Craiglee Shiraz. Other varieties include chardonnay, semillon, cabernet sauvignon, cabernet franc and pinot noir.

N Yarra Valley

The historical home of the Victorian wine industry has suffered the boom-and-bust cycle of other areas. After 80 successful years, most Yarra Valley vineyards had ceased operating by 1920. The cause was not the *phylloxera* scourge, from which the region was spared, but a growing fashion for fortified rather than table wines. After a resurgence in the 1960s there are now over 45 wineries in the area around **Yarra Glen**, **Lilydale** and **Healesville**, and the Yarra Valley attracts wine enthusiasts from around the world. Chardonnay and pinot noir are the most acclaimed grape varieties for both still and sparkling wines.

Domaine Chandon Winery in the Yarra Valley

MELBOURNE

State Orchestra of Victoria, Victorian Arts Centre

main attractions

◈ **AFL (Australian Football League)**

During the winter months, Aussie Rules Football is a Victorian obsession.

◈ **Lygon Street**

Renowned as one of the city's best 'eat streets', Lygon St is full of all things Italian, as well as a multicultural feast of Japanese, Lebanese, African, Greek, Chinese, Vietnamese and French flavours.

◈ **Old Melbourne Gaol**

The old gaol now houses a museum with interesting exhibits.

◈ **Royal Botanic Gardens**

Within walking distance of the CBD, the gardens are home to over 10 000 different plant species.

◈ **Shopping in Melbourne**

Wander along Collins St, Bourke St and the streets running west off Swanston St, where most of the city's major stores, boutiques and designer label shops are to be found.

◈ **Southgate**

On the banks of the Yarra River, there is an overwhelming selection of cafes, restaurants, bars and boutiques. Crown Casino is nearby.

◈ **Yarra River Cruises**

The Yarra offers an array of cruises to enjoy year round.

The capital of the **'Garden State'**, Melbourne is located on **Port Phillip**, with the picturesque **Yarra River** meandering through it. By any standard, it is a sophisticated and vibrant city.

The grand-scale city architecture, wide streets, symmetrical grid design and formally landscaped parks and gardens are all legacies of the goldrushes in nearby Ballarat and Bendigo. Melbourne's trams give the city an old-world charm. Quiet and pollution free, they are an efficient and attractive means of transport, quickly carrying passengers up and down the main thoroughfares. The free **City Circle Tram** transports visitors in a loop that takes in major CBD sights.

Melbourne's changeable climate is renowned, with the more marked seasonal changes giving the city its European feel. Large-scale immigration from Europe also adds to this atmosphere and, along with more recent immigration from South-East Asia, contributes to the diverse mix of cultures, foods and people, which make Melbourne the cosmopolitan city that it is today.

ℹ️ Visitor information

Melbourne Visitor Centre
Federation Square
Cnr Swanston St and Flinders St
Melbourne, Vic 3000
Ph: (03) 9658 9658
www.thatsmelbourne.com.au

facts

◈ Population: 3 650 000
◈ Date founded: 1835
◈ Tallest building: Rialto Towers, 251m
◈ Average temperature:
20°C (January), 10.5°C (June)

Places of Interest

Albert Park Ⓐ D6
Australian Grand Prix Ⓑ D6
Chinatown Ⓒ D2
Crown Casino Ⓓ B4
Federation Square Ⓔ D3
Gold Treasury Museum Ⓕ E2
Immigration Museum Ⓖ C3
Melbourne Aquarium Ⓗ C4
Melbourne Central Shopping Centre Ⓘ C2
Melbourne Cricket Ground Ⓙ E3
Melbourne Museum Ⓚ D1
Melbourne Park Ⓛ E4
Melbourne Observation Deck Ⓜ C3
Myer Music Bowl Ⓝ D4
National Gallery of Victoria Ⓞ D4
Old Melbourne Gaol Ⓟ C2
Parliament House Ⓠ D2
Polly Woodside Maritime Museum Ⓡ B4
Queen Victoria Market Ⓢ B2
Royal Botanic Gardens Ⓣ E5
Royal Exhibition Building Ⓤ D1
Shrine of Remembrance Ⓥ D5
Southgate Ⓦ C4
State Library of Victoria Ⓧ C2
Victorian Arts Centre Ⓨ D4

Princes Bridge over the Yarra River, Melbourne, at sunrise

Victoria

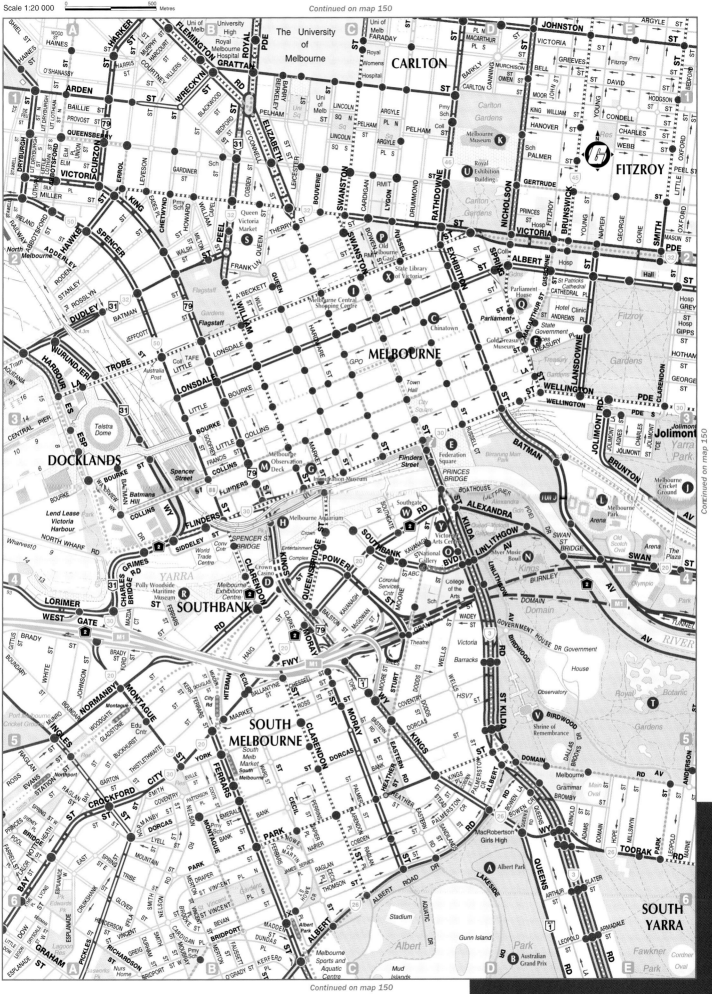

Continued on map 150

CARLTON

FITZROY

MELBOURNE

DOCKLANDS

SOUTHBANK

SOUTH MELBOURNE

SOUTH YARRA

Jolimont

Continued on map 150

Continued on map 150

CBD & SUBURBS

With so much to see and do in the centre of this vibrant city, it is best explored in specific sections. For those wanting to shop there is the **Central Retail District** which is the heartbeat of Melbourne's shopping trade. **Bourke St Mall** is a popular site for big-name department stores. Not too far away, **Melbourne Central** is a 20-storey tower with cafes, restaurants and shops. Worth investigating are the **Royal Arcade** and **Centre Way** for their specialty shops and historic significance. The **Block Arcade** is very exclusive, while **Howey Place** and **Australia on Collins** are less so, but also very popular.

Chinatown is found in and around **Little Bourke St**, where Chinese business, commerce and culture have been thriving since the goldrushes of the 1850s. A popular destination for fans of authentic Chinese cuisine, Chinatown is also home to the **Chinese Museum**, an excellent showcase of Chinese culture, history and immigration.

The **Greek precinct**, at the top end of **Lonsdale St**, is a metropolis of Greek food, culture and specialty stores. With alfresco dining, visitors are tempted to sit and sample the delicacies, or just soak up some afternoon sun and traditional Greek music.

Swanston St is largely a pedestrian mall, overtaken by pavement cafes and shops. Meander along the mall and down the surrounding streets and view some of Melbourne's most historic buildings, such as **St Paul's Cathedral**, **Flinders Street Station**, **Young and Jackson's Hotel** and **Melbourne Town Hall.**

Definitely worth visiting is **Queen Victoria Market**, which contains over 1000 stalls in the indoor/outdoor area, ranging from fresh produce, deli goods, coffee stands to clothing, leather goods and manchester.

Further uptown are **Parliament House** and the **Gold Treasury Museum**. Some of the city's oldest churches are to be found along these streets, as well as many of its great live theatres. North of the **Yarra River**, you'll find the innovative **Melbourne Aquarium** and the ultra-modern attractions of **Federation Square,** built over the railway lines.

South of the Yarra River, **Southgate** is the spot for arts and entertainment and the **Crown Entertainment Complex** includes a casino. Also in this precinct, the **Victorian Arts Centre**, with its famous spire, and the **Melbourne Concert Hall** are worth visiting. The refurbished **National Gallery of Victoria** is also situated here.

Part of the reason for Victoria's claim as the 'Garden State' is Melbourne's gracious parks, including **Flagstaff Gardens, Royal Botanic Gardens, Treasury Gardens** and **Parliament House Gardens**. Wander through these parks and discover manicured lawns and hedges, towering European trees and native Australian flora and landscapes. **Fitzroy Gardens** are home to historic **Captain Cook Cottage**.

To the north

The suburbs to the north of Melbourne are a multicultural delight, offering theatres, galleries and restaurants among the more bohemian bookshops, specialty stores and eateries. For more shopping, the streets of **Brunswick, Carlton, Collingwood, Fitzroy** and **Richmond** have an array of stores.

The **University of Melbourne** meant that **Carlton** was for a long time the place of student digs. Today, the dominant style is distinctly Italian, with restaurants, cafes, cinemas and shops lining the streets. Not far away is **Melbourne Cemetery**, a unique attraction with fascinating theme tours and even an Elvis Presley memorial.

The domed **Royal Exhibition Building**, constructed in 1880 for the World Fair, is located in the picturesque **Carlton Gardens**. It was World Heritage-listed in 2004 and now hosts exhibitions, concerts, balls and expositions. Right next door, the very modern **Melbourne Museum** is innovative and interactive.

Leafy sea-dragon, *Phycodurus eques*, at Melbourne Aquarium

THE MELBOURNE CUP

The most famous horse race in Australia, the Melbourne Cup is held at Flemington Racecourse and brings the entire country to a standstill for at least three minutes on the first Tuesday in November.

The Melbourne Cup has been a major sporting and social carnival since 1861. Past winners have included such legendary horses as Carbine and Phar Lap, but as a handicap race it has been won by colts and seven-year olds alike.

Almost everybody in Australia has a bet on the famous race. In Victoria the whole state takes an official holiday, as punters from around the country and overseas gather and raise their flutes of champagne to the horses, hats and fashions of the day.

Running of the Melbourne Cup at Flemington Racecourse

For lovers of nightlife, these northern suburbs offer creative nights out. Everything from cinema, comedy, dance, theatre, jazz and rock, to world music can be found in these streets.

To the west

To the west is **Footscray** where it is worth taking the 6am breakfast tour of the **Wholesale Fruit and Vegetable Market** and the **National Flower Centre,** or perhaps enjoying a cruise on the **Maribyrnong River**.

To the east

Visit the **Melbourne Cricket Ground (MCG)**, home to Australian cricket and Aussie Rules Football, with its seating capacity of 100 000. Why not book a ticket to a cricket match or AFL game to see what the fuss is all about. Pop into the **Australian Gallery of Sport and**

Olympic Museum to find out about the stadium and history of the Olympic Games.

A must-see is the **Museum of Modern Art** at Heidelberg, where support was offered in the 1940s and 1950s to Australian artists such as Arthur Boyd, Albert Tucker, John Perceval and Sidney Nolan. The permanent exhibition is always a worthwhile experience, and there are also travelling exhibitions. The museum also has a cafe, sculpture park and beautiful gardens.

To the south

The art, culture and history of Melbourne are not limited to the CBD. In the south, galleries and shopping abound, with the added delight of beaches and parks.

St Kilda, one of the best-known suburbs of outer Melbourne, is not only a beachside address, but also a

cosmopolitan centre for food (don't miss the delicious cakes in Acland St), boutiques, art, entertainment and history. Some places of interest include **St Kilda Pier**; the funfair attraction, **Luna Park**; the **Esplanade Hotel**; and the **National** and **Astor theatres**.

Luna Park funfair face, St Kilda

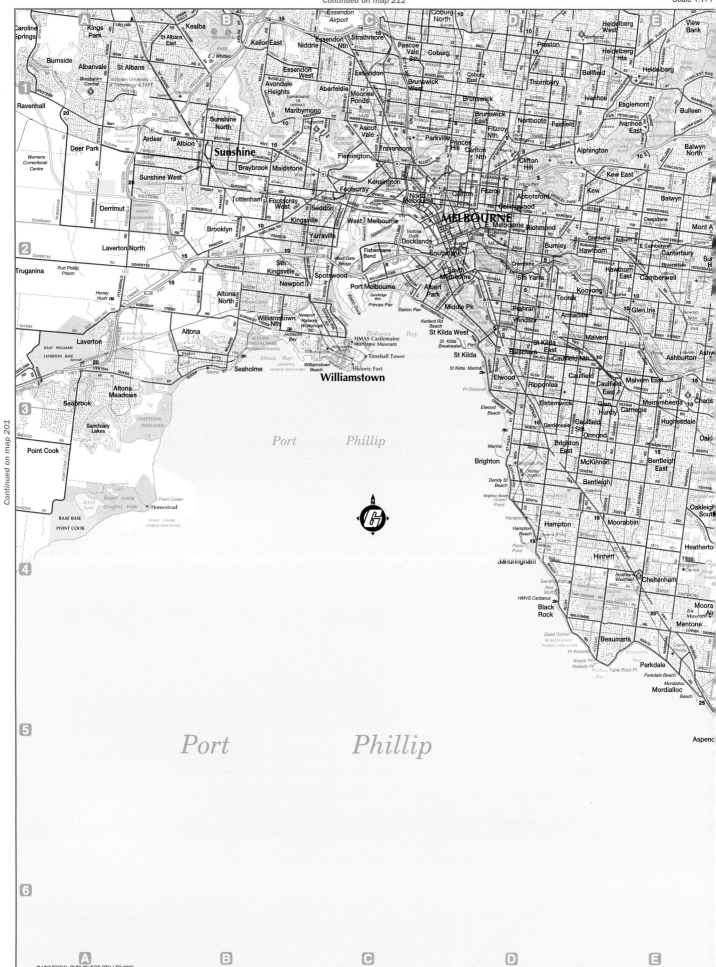

Victoria

© UNIVERSAL PUBLISHERS PTY LTD 2005

5
Kilometres

Continued on map 212

Lower Plenty
Templestowe
Doncaster East
Doncaster
Donvale
Schramms Cottage
Park Orchards
Warrandyte
Warrandyte South
Warranwood
Croydon Hills
Croydon North
Chirnside Park
Lilydale
Mount Evelyn
Mont De Lancey Home & Museum
Wandin North
Seville
Blackburn North
Box Hill North
Box Hill
Box Hill South
Blackburn
Blackburn South
Forest Hill
Nunawading
Mitcham
Ringwood North
Ringwood
Ringwood East
Croydon
Croydon Sth
Bayswater North
Kilsyth
Kilsyth South
Mooroolbark
Montrose
Kalorama
Mt Dandenong Arboretum
Mount Dandenong
Silvan
Wandin East
Tessellaar Silvan Yarra Tulip Farm
Vermont
Heathmont
Bayswater
The Basin
Olinda
Edward Henty Cottage
Sassafras
R.J. Hamer Forest Arboretum
Monbulk
Burwood East
Vermont South
Wantirna
Wantirna South
Boronia
Ferny Creek
Tremont
Sherbrooke
The Patch
Mount Waverley
Glen Waverley
Scoresby
Knoxfield
Ferntree Gully
Upper Ferntree Gully
Upwey
Tecoma
Kallista
Oakleigh East
Notting Hill
Wheelers Hill
Rowville
Belgrave
Belgrave Heights
Selby
Clematis
Menzies Creek
Avonsleigh
Emerald
Emerald Lake Pk
Clayton
Mulgrave
Lysterfield
Belgrave South
Springvale
Sandown Park
Noble Park
Dandenong North
Lysterfield South
Narre Warren East
Clayton South
Dingley Village
Springvale South
Braeside
Keysborough
Dandenong
Endeavour Hills
Narre Warren North
Harkaway
Dewhurst
Beaconsfield Upper
Aspendale Gardens
Dandenong South
Doveton
Eumemmerring
Hallam
Narre Warren
Berwick
Guys Hill
Bangholme
Lyndhurst
Hampton Park
Beaconsfield
Chelsea Heights
Chelsea
Patterson Lakes
Carrum
Carrum Downs
Skye
Narre Warren South
Cranbourne North
Clyde North
Officer
Officer South
Pakenham
Seaford
Cranbourne West
Cranbourne
Cranbourne East
Clyde

Continued on map 212

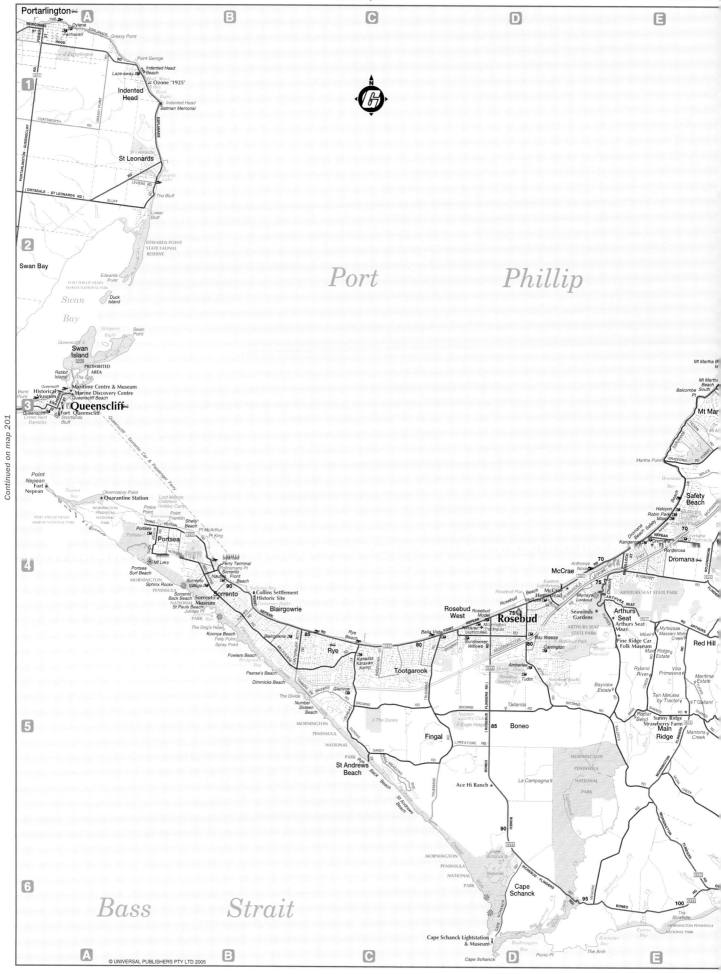

Portarlington

A | B | C | D | E

1

Indented Head

Point George

Indented Head Beach

Laze-away

Ozone '1925'

Half Moon Bay

Batman Memorial

St Leonards

The Bluff

Lower Bluff

2

Swan Bay

Edwards Point

EDWARDS POINT STATE FAUNAL RESERVE

Duck Island

PORT PHILLIP HEADS MARINE NATIONAL PARK

Port Phillip

Swan Bay

Stingaree Bight

Swan Point

Queenscliff

Swan Island

PROHIBITED AREA

Rabbit Island

The Spit

3

Burnt Point

Historical Museum

Maritime Centre & Museum

Marine Discovery Centre

Queenscliff Beach

Queenscliff

Fort

Queenscliff Crown Rest Barracks

Shortlands Bluff

Continued on map 201

Queenscliff Sorrento Car & Passenger Ferry

4

Point Nepean Fort Nepean

Nepean Bay

Quarantine Station

Observatory Point

MORNINGTON PENINSULA NATIONAL PARK

PORT PHILLIP HEADS MARINE NATIONAL PARK

Police Point

Point Franklin

Shelly Beach

Lord Mayors Childrens Holiday Camp

Pt McArthur

Pt King

Portsea

Mt Levy

Ferry Terminal

Policemans Pt

Nautilus

Sorrento Front Beach

Portsea Surf Beach

Sphinx Rocks

MORNINGTON PENINSULA

Sorrento Village

Sorrento

90

Sorrento

Museum

Sorrento Back Beach

NATIONAL

St Pauls Beach

PARK

Jubilee Pt

The Dog's Head

Koonya Beach

Pelly Point

Spray Point

Collins Settlement Historic Site

Camerons Bight

Blairgowrie

85

Rye Beach

Blairgowrie Jetty

Rye

80

Tootgarook

Fowlers Beach

Bridgewater Bay

Pearse's Beach

Dimmicks Beach

The Divide

Number Sixteen Beach

Glenvue

5

The Dunes

MORNINGTON PENINSULA NATIONAL

Fingal

St Andrews Beach

Back Beach

St Andrews Beach

Boneo

90

Ace Hi Ranch

La Campagna

6

Bass Strait

Cape Schanck

ROSEBUD FLINDERS

95

BONEO

MORNINGTON PENINSULA NATIONAL PARK

Cape Schanck Lightstation & Museum

Cape Schanck

Bushrangers Bay

Picnic Pt

The Arch

Mt Martha B

Mt Martha Beach South

Balcombe Pt

Mt Mar

Martha Point

Dromana Bay

Safety Beach

Halcyon

Robin Park

Miami

Dromana

70

Kangerong Beach

Safety Beach

McCrae

Anthonys Nose

70

Rosebud Pier

McCrae Beach

75

McCrae Homestead

Murrays Lookout

ARTHURS SEAT STATE PARK

Rosebud West

75

Rosebud Model

Rosebud

Seawinds Gardens

Arthurs Seat

Arthurs Seat Maze

Bella Vista

Sundowner Willows

80

Bay Breeze

Carrington

ARTHURS SEAT STATE PARK

Pine Ridge Car Folk Museum

Red Hill

Amberlee

Tudor

Rosebud South

Bayview Estate

Ten Minutes by Tractor

Myrtaceae

Masani Malt Creek

Villa Primavera

Maritime Estate

T'Gallant

Poplar Bend

Sunny Ridge Strawberry Farm

Main Ridge

Mantons Creek

Tallarida

85

Boneo

100

Dromana

Ponderosa

Dromana

Victoria

Kilometres 5

F G Frankston North

Keith Turbull Research Institute

H Cranbourne⁵⁰

Cranbourne East

J Clyde K

Frankston

McClelland Art Gallery

Junction Village

ROYAL BOTANIC GARDENS

Cranbourne South

Olivers Hill

Ballam Pk Homestead

Langwarrin

55

Mt Eliza
Mount Eliza

Devon Meadows

Point Davey

45

Morning Star

Frankston South

50

Mulberry Hill (National Trust)

Langwarrin South

Ranelagh Beach

Pearcedale

Cannons Creek

Blind Bight

Tooradin

60

Moondah Beach

Baxter

65

North Sunnyside Beach

Sunnyside Beach

mington

Warneet

50

TV World

60

Somerville

PEARCEDALE CONS. PK & MOONLIT SANCTUARY

Quail Island

Bembridge

55

Moorooduc

Western Port Harbour

Watsons Inlet

QUAIL ISLAND WILDLIFE RESERVE

YARINGA MARINE NATIONAL PARK

Chinaman Island

Mornington Gardens

Mornington Peninsula Regional Art Gallery

60

Tyabb

65

Scrub Point

The Briars Park

Moorooduc

Western Port Airfield

BHP Steel Western Port Works

3 FRENCH ISLAND MARINE NATIONAL PARK

Nedlands Lavender Farm

70

Tyabb Old Township

Hastings

FRENCH ISLAND NATIONAL PARK

65

Mt Mariha

Hodgins

Mt Wellington +98

60 Mornington

65

Tuerong

Harwood Box Stallion

Hastings

Long Island Point

Marina View

The Pinnacles +56

4 FRENCH ISLAND

Tanglewood Estate

Sandstone Island

Bayview Chicory Kiln

Bittern

75 75

Jacks Beach

Woolleys Beach Crib Point

BAYVIEW Park Office

Elgee Park

Kings Creek

Crib Point Terminal Shell - Mobil

Willow Creek

Balnarring

Balnarring

Crib Point

Stony Point

Tankerton

Merricks North

80

HMAS CERBERUS

Passenger Ferry

Red Hill Gallery

HMAS Cerberus

Tea Tree Point

Red Hill South

Coolart Historic Homestead

Somers

Merricks

Balnarring Beach

Somers Beach

South Beach

HMAS CERBERUS

Tortoise Head

5

Merricks Beach

Merricks Beach

Sandy Point

Elizabeth Island

Point Leo

Pack Point

Long Point

Shoreham

Point Leo Beach

90

Shoreham Beach

Cowes

Mussel Rocks

Erehwon Point

Red Rooks Point

Anchor Belle

Cowes Bayside

Kaloha Heritage Centre

Silverleaves

Observation Point

Bushy Pk

Seaview

Boomerang

Islander

Rhylston Park Historic Homestead

Cowes - Rhyll

Rhyll

McHaffie Point

Wimbledon Heights

Koala Conservation Centre

PHILLIP ISLAND

A Maze'n Things

Sunset Strip

PHILLIP ISLAND NATURE PARK

Swan Bay

Phillip Island Historic Homestead

Grants Monument

Ventnor

Summerlands

Smiths Beach

Sunderland Bay

CHURCHILL ISLAND MARINE NATIONAL PARK

Newhaven

F G H J K

Continued on map 165

VICTORIA 153

Alexandra   POP 2090
Map 208, C5

Rich pastoral land and trout streams surround this **Goulburn River** town, located about 110km north-east of Melbourne. Gold discoveries in the 1850s and 1860s brought an influx of miners to the area. This prosperous period led to the construction of important civic buildings, including the Law Courts, Shire Hall, Post Office and the

Houseboat on Lake Eildon, near Alexandra

National Trust-classified **ANZ Bank building**. Alexandra's economy relies on sawmilling—Gould's Timber Mill exports to Japan; there are also four trout farms in the area.
MAIN ATTRACTIONS: Alexandra's main tourist attraction is the **Timber and Tramway Museum** housed in the old Railway Station, Station St. On the second Sunday of each month, and on public and school holidays, the restored narrow-gauge engines are steamed up for tourist trips. Bookings are essential. On the second Saturday of each month, September to June, a **bush market** is held in Perkins St.
NEARBY ATTRACTIONS: **McKenzie Flora Reserve**, located off Mount Pleasant Rd, has signposted walking tracks and visitors have the opportunity of spotting rare local wildflowers. Excavations and sites of past gold-mining activity abound. Alexandra is the gateway to **Lake Eildon NP** on the shores of **Lake Eildon**. The park is a popular family recreation area with holiday units, two caravan

parks, camping areas, houseboats, boat-launching ramps and bushwalks. Trout fishing is popular in the Goulburn, **Acheron** and **Rubicon rivers**.
VISITOR INFORMATION: Rotary Park, Grant St, Ph: (03) 5772 1100 or 1800 652 298

Anglesea   POP 2125
Map 201, H4

A popular coastal resort, Anglesea lies on the **Great Ocean Road**, 110km south-west of Melbourne. Tourism is the main industry of this town, with fishing, swimming, surfing and walking popular activities.
MAIN ATTRACTIONS: Views of the town, coastline and ocean are provided from the lookout behind **Front Beach**, Anglesea's main surfing spot. **Heathland Cliff Walk** also offers scenic views; the walk begins at the carpark at the end of Purnell St. **Coogoorah Reserve**, located on the **Anglesea River**, offers waterways, islands, picnic areas, playground equipment and walking

tracks. The golf course attracts many visitors for a round of golf and unusual companions—resident kangaroos graze on its greens.

NEARBY ATTRACTIONS: **Angahook-Lorne State Park** is close by and **Aireys Inlet**, 11km south-west on the Great Ocean Road, offers many activities, including horseriding. Further south is the **Memorial Arch**, which commemorates the construction of the Great Ocean Road, itself a memorial to the Australian soldiers killed in WWI.

VISITOR INFORMATION: Surfworld Museum, Beach Rd, Torquay, Ph: (03) 5261 4219

Apollo Bay   POP 1360

Map 201, F5

Apollo Bay is set on the coast with excellent surfing and swimming beaches and the **Otway Ranges** as a backdrop. Located 183km south-west of Melbourne, it is a thriving tourist centre.

MAIN ATTRACTIONS: The local historical museum is housed in the **Old Cable Station**, where the original telephone cable between Tasmania and the mainland came ashore. Situated on the Great Ocean Road, it is open on weekend afternoons, and school and public holidays. **Bass Strait Shell Museum**, in Noel St, displays a collection of shells and old photographs of the shipwrecks which litter the coast. **Marriners Lookout** provides great views and is popular with hang-gliding enthusiasts.

NEARBY ATTRACTIONS: Guided or self-guided scenic drives, boat charters and walking or mountain biking tours are on offer; details are available from the information centre. Scenic flights are available at Marengo airstrip to the south. **Otway NP**, 13km south-west, provides bushwalking trails throughout the park to the coast. **Cape Otway Lightstation**, built in 1848, is located in the park. **Melba Gully State Park**, 50km west, has a glow-worm habitat and there is a

self-guided rainforest walk to explore.

VISITOR INFORMATION: 100 Great Ocean Rd, Ph: (03) 5237 6529

Ararat   POP 7050

Map 159, A2

Lying east of the **Grampian Ranges**, and 203km north-west of Melbourne, Ararat is surrounded by rich farmland noted for producing top merino wool. It is also a grape-growing region, which produces excellent wines. The town is an ideal base for exploring the **Mount Cole Forest Range** and **Grampians NP**. It is also the gateway to the **Pyrenees and Grampians Wine Trail**.

MAIN ATTRACTIONS: Details of the town's **Historic Walk** can be found at the tourist centre. Visitors can relax in the **Alexandra Gardens**, located in the centre of Ararat. Nearby is the old bluestone **J Ward Gaol**, which housed the criminally insane from 1887 to 1991. In 1993, the gaol opened to the public and guided tours are available. **Langi Morgala Museum** was previously a Cobb & Co coach-changing station and woolstore. It has an Aboriginal history collection, and displays trace the stories of Chinese miners and Indian hawkers in the district, open on weekends. **Gum San Chinese Heritage Centre** celebrates Ararat's gold-mining heritage.

NEARBY ATTRACTIONS: **Langi Ghiran State Park**, 14km east of Ararat, has rugged granite peaks and gentle sloping woodlands. It offers scenic walks and a picnic and camping area. Many of the **wineries** surrounding Ararat are open for tastings and cellar door sales. **Seppelt Great Western Winery**, located 17km north-west, was established in 1865 and specialises in dry red and sparkling wines. Its underground cellars are National Trust-classified.

VISITOR INFORMATION: 91 High St, Ph: (03) 5355 0281 or 1800 657 158

Ararat Town Hall

Bacchus Marsh   POP 12 115

Map 201, J1

This town is located between the **Werribee** and **Lerderderg rivers**, 49km west of Melbourne. Close enough to Melbourne to be a commuter town, Bacchus Marsh is surrounded by orchards and market gardens.

MAIN ATTRACTIONS: Many buildings, including the **Manor House** built by Capt William Henry Bacchus in 1846, are classified by the National Trust. Others include the sandstone **Court House**, built in 1858—and still used today; the **gaol**; and the **National Bank**. The avenue of English oaks, elms and plane trees called the **Avenue of Honour** was planted as a memorial to the citizens of Bacchus Marsh. An extension of Main St, it provides an impressive entrance to the town, and is claimed to include the best stand of elm trees in the world.

NEARBY ATTRACTIONS: **Lerderderg Gorge**, located 10km north, is a popular spot for swimming, picnics and bushwalking. **Brisbane Ranges NP**, with its many walking tracks and spring wildflowers, is 16km south-west. Wineries in the area include **St Anne's Vineyard**, 6km west on the Western Fwy. This winery has a bluestone cellar built from the remains of the old Ballarat Gaol.

VISITOR INFORMATION: 197 Main St, Ph: (03) 5366 7100

Bairnsdale POP 10 900
Map 177, C2

This **Gippsland** town lies on the **Mitchell River** flats at the tip of **Lake King**, 280km east of Melbourne. Bairnsdale and the surrounding district is promoted as the '**Victorian Riviera**' with winter temperatures up to 6°C warmer than Melbourne. Situated near the junction of the Princes Hwy and Great Alpine Rd, Bairnsdale is a perfect base for exploring the surrounding region.

MAIN ATTRACTIONS: **St Mary's Catholic Church** is famous for its magnificent wall and ceiling murals painted by Italian artist Francesco Floreani in the 1930s. The **Historical Museum** is located in the old St Andrew's College in Macarthur St. It is open on weekends. **MacLeod Morass**, visible from the museum, is a deep freshwater marsh and reserve with more than 130 species of wildlife. Access to the reserve boardwalk is from Bosworth Rd. The **Bataluk Cultural Trail**, extending through **East Gippsland** from **Sale** to the **Cann River**, stops at an Aboriginal keeping place in Bairnsdale. **Krowathunkoolong**, located at 37 Dalmahoy St, has displays tracing Aboriginal culture from the Dreamtime to the present. **Bairnsdale Clocks**, at 704 Princes Hwy, has one of the largest collections of clocks in the country and is certainly worth a visit.

NEARBY ATTRACTIONS: The information centre has details about self-guided scenic drives, walks and 4-wheel drive tours of the area. The picturesque town of **Metung**, 30km south-east, is a fishing village on the shores of Lake King. **Mitchell River NP** is 45km north-west and offers excellent bushwalking tracks and the cavern known as the **Den of Nargun**, a significant site on the Bataluk Cultural Trail.

VISITOR INFORMATION: 240 Main St, Ph: (03) 5152 3444 or 1800 637 060

Ballarat POP 73 000
Map 159, D3

Ballarat is the perfect place for a short break or longer stay; it is an easy 112km drive from Melbourne. Victoria's largest inland city and regional centre has retained many of its classic Victorian buildings erected from the wealth of the 1850s goldrush. Ballarat was the site of Australia's only civil uprising—in 1854, a group of miners led by Irishman Peter Lawlor refused to pay Government licence fees. The rebellion led to clashes with police and soldiers, resulting in the deaths of 22 diggers and three soldiers. The event is now known as the **Eureka Stockade**.

MAIN ATTRACTIONS: Historic buildings include **Her Majesty's Theatre** (1875) and **Craig's Royal Hotel**. The **Eureka Centre**, located within **Eureka Reserve** is a multi-million dollar interpretive centre. Many visitors come to **Sovereign Hill**, a superb re-creation of Ballarat's first ten years as an early gold town. This outdoor museum offers visitors the chance to purchase a licence, pan and wash for gold and shop in businesses just like those in the period 1851–1861. There are underground mine tours. The sound and light show, *Blood on the Southern Cross,* is a dramatic night-time re-creation of Eureka Stockade events. Adjoining Sovereign Hill, the **Gold Museum** houses a unique collection and exhibits of the history of goldmining in the area. Australia's oldest (1884) and largest provincial gallery, **Ballarat Fine Art Gallery**, in Lydiard St, has an impressive collection of Australian art; it also houses the original **Eureka Flag**. The **Australian Ex-Prisoner of War Memorial** is an outstanding new attraction in the beautiful **Ballarat Botanical Gardens**. A **Vintage Tramway** operates near **Lake Wendouree** on weekends and holidays. **Ballarat**

'Gold prospector' at Sovereign Hill, Ballarat

Wildlife Park, on the corner of York St and Fussell St, features native animals.

NEARBY ATTRACTIONS: **Kryal Castle**, 9km east, offers family entertainment, mediaeval jousting and re-enactments. The well-known **Yellowglen Winery**, located at **Smythesdale**, 24km south-west, is one of several local vineyards. **Ballarat Birdworld**, 13km south at **Buninyong**, has a raised walkway and dozens of colourful parrots.

VISITOR INFORMATION: 39 Sturt St, Ph: (03) 5320 5741 or 1800 446 633

Barwon Heads POP 2800
Map 201, K3

A popular fishing, boating and swimming holiday town, Barwon Heads is located on the estuary of the **Barwon River**, about 100km from Melbourne. A bridge links Barwon Heads with neighbouring **Ocean Grove**, 2km away on the eastern side of the river. There is a limestone covered lava bluff protecting the town from the sea and the treacherous conditions that wrecked at least a dozen ships in the 1800s. The town was featured in the ABC TV series *Sea Change*.

MAIN ATTRACTIONS: A cairn commemorating the *Earl of Charlemont*, wrecked in this area in 1853, is located on **Bluff Lookout**. The ship's anchor is mounted in a riverside park. **Thirteenth Beach**, located on the western edge of Barwon Heads, is ideal for surfing. Calmer waters for swimming can be found at the mouth of the Barwon River. The **Lobster Pot Interpretive Centre**, off Ewing Blyth Dr, is open at weekends. **Jirrahlinga Koala and Wildlife Sanctuary** is located in Taits Rd. Sick and wounded animals are nursed back to health at the hospital in the grounds. Visitors will find a variety of animals and birds as well as many koalas.

VISITOR INFORMATION: 55 Hesse St, Queenscliff, Ph: (03) 5258 4843

▨ Beechworth   POP 2953
Map 187, B1

Located in the foothills of the **Alpine region** and 270km north-east of Melbourne, this well-preserved 1850s goldfields town is famous for its fine honey-coloured granite buildings. Over 30 buildings are classified by the National Trust. Beechworth is also notable for its colourful autumn foliage.

MAIN ATTRACTIONS: **Beechworth Historic and Cultural Precinct** is a series of historically significant buildings from the goldrush era. There are interpretations on police life, the legal system and the history of the town's development. The recordings, heard in various buildings, are sometimes humorous, sometimes sad, but always instructive. They include messages from people such as Ellen Kelly and Elizabeth Scott and transport visitors to another time. **Burke Museum**, in Loch St, is named after ill-fated **Robert O'Hara Burke**, who at one time was officer-in-charge of police in the town. There are relics of the goldrush on display at the museum and a 'strand of time', a re-creation of Beechworth's shops as they were over 100 years ago. The **Court House** (1858), was the scene of many famous trials involving bushrangers such as Ned

Kelly and Harry Power. The **Carriage Museum** and **Light Horse Exhibition** are located in **Murray Breweries**, which produces gourmet cordials, such as chilli punch and raspberry vinegar; open seven days a week. Visitors can still fossick for gold and gems in the area. Maps, 'miner's rights' permits and walking tour leaflets are available through the information centre.

NEARBY ATTRACTIONS: **Beechworth Historic Park** surrounds the town and contains significant sites, including **Woolshed Falls**, **Beechworth Gorge** and the **Yedonbba** Aboriginal rock-art site. Nearby is **Mount Pilot Lookout**, offering panoramic views of the **Murray Valley**. The **Gorge Scenic Drive** starts north of Beechworth and passes through gold-fossicking areas.

VISITOR INFORMATION: 103 Ford St, Ph: (03) 5728 8065 or 1300 366 321

▨ Benalla   POP 8600
Map 208, D4

This city, 191km north-east of Melbourne, was war hero **Sir Edward 'Weary' Dunlop's** home during his early years. The local Court House was the venue for a number of trials involving bushranger Ned Kelly.

MAIN ATTRACTIONS: The **Gliding Club of Victoria** is located at Benalla Aerodrome. **Lake Benalla** is popular for swimming and sailing. The artificial lake was created by damming the **Broken River** in 1974. **Benalla Gardens**, located beside the lake, are worthwhile visiting for walks through the **rose garden** and along the lake's shores. The success of the rose garden, established in 1959, led to Benalla earning the title '**The Rose City on the Lake**'. **Benalla Art Gallery**, also located by the lake, houses the noted **Ledger Collection** of works by major Australian artists from colonial times to the 1960s. At the **Costume and Pioneer Museum—**

incorporating the information centre—are pioneer clothing and artefacts, including the cummerbund worn by Ned Kelly when he was captured at nearby Glenrowan.

NEARBY ATTRACTIONS: **Reef Hills State Park** offers 204km^2 of forest with a variety of native flora and fauna. It is 4km south of Benalla. For moviegoers, **Swanpool**, 23km south, shows classic films in a 1950s-style cinema. To the north-east, off the Hume Hwy, are **Lake Mokoan**, **Warby Range State Park**, **Winton Speedway**, several wineries and historic **Glenrowan**, central to the legend of Ned Kelly.

VISITOR INFORMATION: Costume and Pioneer Museum, 14 Mair St, Ph: (03) 5762 1749

▨ Bendigo   POP 68 500
Map 159, E1

This elegant, old city is located in the geographic centre of Victoria. Its character and streetscapes were created during the gold boom years of the 1850s to 1870s, when the local goldfield was one of the world's richest. Less than a two hour drive from Melbourne, Bendigo is a very popular tourist destination.

Historic Beechworth Post Office

THE GOLDFIELDS

Situated in **Central Victoria**, just over 100km north-west of Melbourne, the Goldfields region is filled with opportunities for those wanting to experience the heady days of the goldrush era.

In 1851, news of the discovery of gold spread like wildfire around the colonies of Victoria and New South Wales, and reached as far as China, England and the USA. A population explosion occurred—by October of that year, 8000 prospectors descended on the area; the number swelled to 30 000 a year later; and by 1856 a record 100 000 people were at the gold-fields. Tiny settlements became boom towns virtually overnight. Melbourne was almost deserted during 1851, after 20 000 of its 25 000 population left for the **Mount Alexander** diggings.

As prosperity spread to the trades, services and agricultural industries that supported the gold miners and developing mining companies, towns became thriving regional centres, bearing all the hallmarks of wealth.

The rich history of the Goldfields and Victorian architecture is evident everywhere and visitors can explore the area through activities such as prospecting, fossicking, camping and bushwalking.

The Goldrushes

The wealth from the gold diggings made Melbourne the largest city in Australia at that time. The status of the whole country was transformed. Australia changed from a colonial settlement with a dubious reputation to a respectable place for migration and investment.

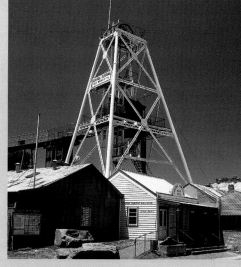

Central Deborah Gold Mine, Bendigo

i Visitor information

Ballarat Visitor Information Centre
39 Sturt St, Ballarat, Vic 3350
Ph: (03) 5320 5741 or 1800 446 633
www.ballarat.com

Bendigo Visitor Information Centre
51-67, Pall Mall, Bendigo, Vic 3550
Ph: (03) 5444 4445 or 1800 813 153
www.bendigotourism.com

main attractions

❖ **Ararat**
Ararat was officially founded in 1857, when a group of 700 Chinese discovered alluvial gold in the area.

❖ **Ballarat**
This is the site of Sovereign Hill and the Eureka Centre.

❖ **Ballarat Wildlife Park**
Meet emus, koalas, wallabies, wombats and other Australian animals.

❖ **Bendigo**
Built on its goldrush prosperity, Bendigo is still a thriving and influential city.

❖ **Buda Historic Home and Gardens**
Visit this colonial home in Castlemaine and see the best of 19th and 20th century landscaping.

❖ **Castlemaine**
Castlemaine is noted as much for its artistic endeavours as for its goldrush past. Castlemaine Art Gallery boasts a fine collection of Australian art.

❖ **Clunes**
This was Victoria's first gold town.

❖ **Golden Dragon Museum**
This Bendigo museum is a tribute to the Chinese gold miners.

Sovereign Hill, Ballarat's re-creation of an early goldrush town

Victoria

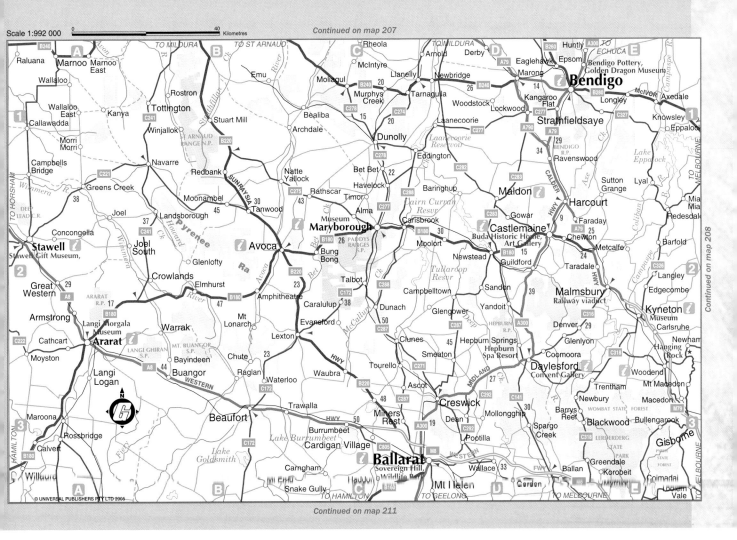

Continued on map 207

Scale 1:992 000

Continued on map 211

© UNIVERSAL PUBLISHERS PTY LTD 2005

MAIN ATTRACTIONS: A **Heritage Walk** along the main street, Pall Mall, passes grand buildings, including the Post Office and Law Courts, **Alexandra Fountain** (1881), **Beehive Store building** (1872) and **Shamrock Hotel** (1897). The **Poppet Head Lookout Tower** is located in **Rosalind Park** in the heart of Bendigo. An impressive collection of Australian and European art is displayed at the recently refurbished **Bendigo Art Gallery** in View St. The **Golden Dragon Museum**, located in the city centre, displays Chinese ceremonial regalia and two famous imperial dragons: Sun Loong and Loong. The **Chinese Joss House**, in north Bendigo, was built by Chinese miners and has been refurbished and classified by the National Trust.

Among Bendigo's most popular attractions are the **Central Deborah Goldmine** and the famous **Talking Tram Tours** that start there and visit a number of Bendigo's highlights.

NEARBY ATTRACTIONS: **Bendigo Pottery** established in 1858, is Australia's oldest operating pottery and a major attraction. The complex also features a pottery museum and the **Living Wings and Things** zoological exhibits. Wineries surrounding Bendigo are open for tastings and cellar door sales. The information centre has maps for self-guided **Goldfields tours**. **Bendigo Regional Park** and **Greater Bendigo NP** have designated picnic and camping areas amongst box-ironbark trees.

VISITOR INFORMATION: Pall Mall,
Ph: (03) 5444 4445
or 1800 813 153

Detail from Bendigo's Alexandra Fountain (1881)

Bright   POP 2130

Map 187, C2

Bright is a picturesque town situated on the **Ovens River**, 303km north-east of Melbourne. The town is conveniently located near the **Victorian Alps** and the ski fields at **Mount Hotham**, **Mount Buffalo** and **Falls Creek**. Industries important to the local economy include tourism, timber and agriculture. Bright was established after the discovery of alluvial gold in the area.

MAIN ATTRACTIONS: Bright is especially worthwhile visiting in autumn and spring due to the variety of deciduous trees planted throughout the town, including Japanese maples, Lombardy poplars, oaks, elms and dogwoods. Each year the town celebrates the seasons with **autumn and spring festivals**. There is also an annual autumn art exhibition attracting artists and buyers from around Australia. Worthwhile walks in Bright include the **Canyon Walk** along the **Ovens River**, where visitors can see the remains of gold workings. **Centenary Park** has a children's playground and a deep weir, popular for swimming in summer.

NEARBY ATTRACTIONS: The surrounding area is excellent for bushwalking, trout fishing, 4-wheel driving and cycling. Nearby **Alpine NP** is also ideal for bushwalkers, with many varied tracks. **Mount Buffalo NP**, also nearby, has a variety of landscapes. **Boyntons of Bright Winery** is located at **Porepunkah**, 6km north-west. The information centre has details of lavender, deer, emu and berry farms in the district that are open to visitors in season.

VISITOR INFORMATION: 119 Gavan St, Ph: (03) 5755 2275 or 1800 500 117

Buninyong   POP 1800

Map 211, H2

The small township of Buninyong is located 10km south of Ballarat. It was one of the first inland towns in Victoria and was the site of the district's first gold find at **Hiscocks Gully** in 1851. After the goldrush, Buninyong once again became an agricultural centre.

MAIN ATTRACTIONS: **Ballarat Birdworld** is a fascinating introduction to Australia's colourful birdlife. Several buildings are of historic interest. The **Crown Hotel** claims to hold the oldest continuous licence, dating from 1842, although the first hotel on the site burnt down in 1884. The Italianate Council Chambers and Court House were both built in 1882. Walks worthwhile taking include the **Town Walk**, starting at the junction of Warrenheip St and Learmouth St. This route passes through the **Botanic Gardens**, planted in the 1860s, where there are picnic facilities. Another walk follows **Buninyong Creek**.

NEARBY ATTRACTIONS: A scenic drive in the area includes **Mount Buninyong**, an extinct volcano which offers panoramic views of the surrounding countryside; **Lal Lal Falls**, dropping 34m; and one of Australia's most important industrial archaeological sites, the ruins of the **Lal Lal Blast Furnace**, which once supplied smelted wrought iron to Ballarat. There are boardwalks enabling visitors to explore the area.

VISITOR INFORMATION: 39 Sturt St, Ballarat, Ph: (03) 5320 5741 or 1800 446 633

Camperdown   POP 3160

Map 200, D3

Volcanic activity over 20 million years ago shaped the landscape of this **Western District** town. Surrounded by crater lakes and lying at the foot of the extinct volcano **Mount Leura**, Camperdown is in the centre of the world's third largest volcanic plain. The town has many elegant buildings and avenues of elms. In 1876, schoolchildren planted the avenue of elms that runs for 2km along **Manifold St**.

MAIN ATTRACTIONS: Camperdown has many statues, war memorials and monuments which commemorate the district's pioneers. The **town walk** takes in many of Camperdown's historic buildings, including the red-brick Court House (now the information centre), bluestone Post Office, Railway Station, commercial buildings and cottages. The **Historical Society Museum** at 241 Manifold St is open on Tuesday,

The Cathedral at sunrise, Mount Buffalo National Park, near Bright

Friday and Sunday afternoons. The road to the top of Mount Leura leads to a lookout with panoramic views of the surrounding volcanic plain.

NEARBY ATTRACTIONS: There are two crater lakes lying side-by-side 3km west of Camperdown. Of these, freshwater **Lake Bullen Merri** is popular for swimming and fishing. **Lake Corangamite** is Victoria's largest saltwater lake and is 13km east of Camperdown. **Lake Purrumbete**, located 15km south-east, is well stocked with Quinnat salmon for fishing, has picnic areas and a caravan park.

VISITOR INFORMATION: The Court House, Manifold St, Ph: (03) 5593 3390

Casterton   POP 1740
Map 210, C2

Located halfway between Melbourne and Adelaide, and 42km east of the South Australian border, this picturesque town is noted for its heritage streetscape and surrounding countryside of agricultural and grazing land, forests and rivers. **Glenelg River** runs beside **Island Park** and through the town.

MAIN ATTRACTIONS: Casterton's vibrant pioneering history can be seen in the many buildings dating back to the early days of European settlement. In the centre of town, a statue of a kelpie marks the district as the birthplace of this famous Australian working dog. The shopping centre offers an art gallery, bric-a-brac and craft shops. A walk or drive to **Mickle Lookout**, off Robertson St, provides excellent views of the town and surrounding countryside. In 1941, a large **Scout emblem**, 91.5m high, was carved into the hillside overlooking Casterton. The symbol is surrounded by strip lighting and serves as a beacon for the town.

NEARBY ATTRACTIONS: The kelpie was originally bred 32km north of Casterton at **Warrock Homestead**. Today, the homestead comprises 33

Castlemaine Art Gallery showcases many Australian artists

National Trust-classified buildings dating from the 1840s, including a woolshed, belfry, blacksmith's shop, homestead and cottage. Open daily, the homestead provides an insight into pastoral life 150 years ago. Within a short drive of Casterton are wildflowers and native forests with kangaroos and emus. **Bilstons Tree**, Australia's largest red gum—a mere sapling in 1200AD—stands near the road to Edenhope to the north. **Dergholm State Park**, 50km to the north-west, has giant green boulders.

VISITOR INFORMATION: Shiels Tce, Ph: (03) 5581 2070

Castlemaine   POP 6825
Map 159, D2

This is a prosperous industrial centre and a popular tourist destination, 120km north-west of Melbourne. Castlemaine lies at the foot of **Mount Alexander** at the inter-section of the Pyrenees Hwy and Midland Hwy and is surrounded by old goldfields. In the 1850s and 1860s, the area experienced a gold boom and the town grew rapidly.

Many of the town's fine Victorian buildings were built during these boom years.

MAIN ATTRACTIONS: **Buda Historic Home and Gardens** are open daily. **Castlemaine Market** is one of the most impressive buildings in the town. A produce market was held in the building until 1967 and it is now the town's information centre and a gold interpretive centre. Tours of **Old Castlemaine Gaol** are self-guided or by appointment. Accommodation is available for visitors wishing to 'spend a night in gaol'. **Castlemaine Botanical Gardens** is one of Victoria's oldest provincial public gardens. **Barkers Creek**, located north of the town centre, is an attractive spot for a picnic. Works by many well-known Australian artists hang in **Castlemaine Art Gallery and Historical Museum** in Lyttleton St.

NEARBY ATTRACTIONS: A guide to the gold digging sites in the area is available from the information centre. Close by are **Forest Creek Diggings** and **Herons Reef Gold Diggings**. At the **dingo farm** in

Hopetoun Falls, in the Otway Ranges to the south of Colac

Chewton, visitors can learn all about this Australian wild dog. Natural mineral springs are quite common in the area and the most easily accessible is **Vaughan Springs**, to the south.
VISITOR INFORMATION: Market Building, Mostyn St, Ph: (03) 5470 6200 or 1800 171 888

▧ Clunes   POP 1095
Map 159, C2
The site of Victoria's first registered strike of payable gold; Clunes is located 36km north of Ballarat. Extinct volcanoes surround the historic town, providing an interesting view.
MAIN ATTRACTIONS: The **Town Hall** and **Court House** give a sense of Clunes' influential past. Several buildings are classified by the National Trust. The **Bottle Museum**, located on Talbot Rd, boasts the largest collection of bottles on display in the Southern Hemisphere; it is also home to the information centre, doll and mining equipment displays. A **Creek Walk** takes visitors out to **Port Phillip Mine**, which crushed more than 1.3 million tonnes of quartz yielding 16 tonnes of gold.
NEARBY ATTRACTIONS: The historic town of **Talbot** is 18km north-west of Clunes and has fine old Victorian

buildings dating from the 1860s and 1870s.
VISITOR INFORMATION: 70 Bailey St (Talbot Rd), Ph: (03) 5345 3896

▧ Cobram   POP 4525
Map 208, C2
This **Murray River** town is located 250km north of Melbourne on the Murray Valley Hwy. Cobram was established in 1887 to service the railway from Melbourne. After WWII, the area became part of a large Soldier Settlement Scheme, which saw the growth of dairy farms and orchards—one of which was responsible for the development of the clingstone variety of peach.
MAIN ATTRACTIONS: With its wide sandy river beaches, Cobram is popular for swimming, watersports, picnicking and fishing, and for houseboats and paddlewheeler cruises. The town's monthly market is held in Punt Rd on the first Saturday of each month.
NEARBY ATTRACTIONS: Wineries in the area include **Strathkellar Wines**, 8km east; **Fyffefield Wines**, 15km east; **Heritage Farm Wines**, 5km west; and **Monichino Winery** at **Katunga**. The wineries are open for tastings and cellar door sales. **Koonoomoo**, 5km west, offers strawberry picking in season.

Australia's largest cacti gardens, **Cactus Country**, is located at **Strathmerton**, 16km west. **Daveile Gallery**, located in **Barooga**, houses a fine collection of antiques including some 400 Victorian oil lamps.
VISITOR INFORMATION: Cnr Station St and Punt Rd, Ph: (03) 5872 2132 or 1800 607 607

▧ Cohuna   POP 1980
Map 207, J2
Cohuna, 305km north-west of Melbourne, is located in the centre of a dairying district. The region is characterised by attractive landscapes created by the lagoons and waterways of the **Murray River**, including nearby **Gunbower Island**, which is encircled by the Murray River and **Gunbower Creek**.
MAIN ATTRACTIONS: **Cohuna Historical Museum** boasts some interesting exhibits. In late February or early March, the **Bridge to Bridge Swim** is held at Cohuna.
NEARBY ATTRACTIONS: A bridge connects Cohuna to **Gunbower Island State Forest**, which protects a river red gum and box habitat. Walking tracks and dirt roads penetrate the forest, which is home to emus, kangaroos, possums, gliders and a variety of birdlife. **Mathers Waterwheel Museum** is an interesting private museum on a farm west of Cohuna.
VISITOR INFORMATION: 15 Murray St, Barham, Ph: (03) 5453 3100 or 1800 621 882

▧ Colac   POP 10 270
Map 201, F4
Lying at the eastern edge of the world's third largest volcanic plain, Colac is located at the foothills of the **Otway Ranges**. The town is also the eastern gateway to the **Volcanic Discovery Trail** and is at the centre of some of Australia's richest farming areas.
MAIN ATTRACTIONS: Promoted as the **'Gateway to the Otways'**, Colac is also a good base for those exploring

south to the **Great Ocean Road**—it is an hour's drive to **The Twelve Apostles**—and north to **Ballarat**. Colac is located on the shores of **Lake Colac**: the largest freshwater lake in Victoria. The lake is popular for boating, waterskiing and fishing and there are many picnic spots situated around its shores. A nature walk leads from the information centre to **Colac Botanic Gardens**, on the foreshore at the northern end of Queen St. Here, there are picnic and BBQ facilities, and a children's playground.

NEARBY ATTRACTIONS: **Lake Corangamite**, located 17km west, is one of the district's many crater lakes. This very large lake has no outlet and is four times saltier than seawater. Boating is not allowed, as the lake is principally a wildlife habitat. **Red Rock Lookout**, 17km north-west, is located on twin volcanic peaks and offers a view of 30 volcanic lakes and craters. The scenic **Otway Ranges** are 30km south and definitely worthwhile visiting. The **Otway Fly** is a spectacular treetop walk near Beech Forest, about 45km to the south. It is 25m above the ground, with a lookout tower 45m above the ground. **Birregurra**, 20km east of Colac, has interesting old buildings.

VISITOR INFORMATION: Cnr Queen St and Murray St, Ph: (03) 5231 3730

▣ Coleraine   POP 1120

Map 210, C2

This historic township in a lovely **Western District** valley, is located 323km west of Melbourne. Settled in 1839, this is mainly a pastoral district producing fine wool and beef cattle.

MAIN ATTRACTIONS: The **Historical Society Museum** is housed in the old Court House and open by appointment only. The **Chocolate Factory**, in Whyte St, is open for tastings. Local arts and craft are displayed in Coleraine's historic **Railway Station**.

NEARBY ATTRACTIONS: A view of Coleraine and the surrounding countryside can be seen from the lookout in **Points Reserve Arboretum**, accessed off the Portland Rd. The reserve offers a picnic ground, shade house, walking tracks, children's playground and BBQs. The arboretum features the largest collection of eucalyptus species in Australia.

Konongwootong Reservoir, about 9km north on Harrow Rd, is a good recreation and fishing spot: catches include rainbow trout. Between Coleraine and **Hamilton** are **Nigretta Falls** and **Wannon Falls**, both on the **Wannon River**. These are popular recreation areas with walking trails. National Trust-classified historic homesteads in the area include **Glendinning Homestead and wildlife sanctuary**, located 49km to the north-east.

VISITOR INFORMATION: Old Railway Station, Pilleau St, Ph: (03) 5575 2733

▣ Corryong   POP 1220

Map 187, E1

Lying near the source of the **Murray River** beneath **Mount Mittamatite**, this town is the Victorian gateway to the **Snowy Mountains** and **Kosciuszko NP**.

MAIN ATTRACTIONS: **Jack Riley**, the man generally accepted as the main character in the *Man from Snowy River*, Banjo Paterson's epic poem, was buried at **Corryong Cemetery** in 1914. A granite headstone and snow gum logs mark his grave. There is also a **Man From Snowy River Museum**, which has both interior and exterior exhibits and an array of historical items from the area, including a ski collection dating from the 1870s.

NEARBY ATTRACTIONS: The mountain location and excellent trout streams draw many visitors to the area. Other activities include scenic drives, canoeing, white-water rafting, cycling and 4-wheel driving. Canoes can be hired at **Walwa** and **Tintaldra**. Information on local tours is available from the information centre. **Burrowa-Pine Mountain NP**, 27km west, offers scenic bushwalks. Kosciuszko NP is a short drive to the east.

VISITOR INFORMATION: 50 Hansen St, Ph: (02) 6076 2277

Mount Mittamatite, overlooking Corryong

PHILLIP ISLAND

Located in the calm waters of **Western Port** and a 1.5 hour drive from Melbourne, Phillip Island is accessed by a bridge from the mainland at **San Remo**. It is Victoria's premier destination for international visitors and boasts superior surfing and unspoilt beaches, an array of wildlife, including colonies of koalas, seals and the famed **little penguins**— the island's major drawcard.

Phillip Island also has some outstanding geological formations, including **The Pinnacles**, ancient columns of pink granite; the **Forrest Caves**, large sea-eroded caverns; and **Pyramid Rock**, a column of basalt in the shape of a pyramid.

Cowes is the administrative centre of the island and where the majority of the island's accommodation is to be found. The Australian leg of the 500cc world motorcycle championships is held at the **Phillip Island Grand Prix Circuit**, not far from Cowes, each October. The combined attractions of Phillip Island make it an ideal holiday location.

Watching the little penguins, *Eudyptula minor*, on parade at Summerland Beach

attractions

- ◈ Cape Woolamai walk
- ◈ Koala Conservation Reserve
- ◈ Penguin Parade, Summerland Beach

i Visitor information

Phillip Island Information Centre
Phillip Island Tourist Rd
Newhaven, Vic 3925
Ph: (03) 5956 7447 or
1300 366 422

Safe swimming beach at Cowes

■ Cowes POP 3500
Map 165, C1

Situated on the northern side of **Phillip Island**, Cowes is the main town on the island. The popular resort town is about 19km from the bridge linking the island to the mainland.

MAIN ATTRACTIONS: The Cowes foreshore is a popular BBQ and picnic area and there are safe beaches for children to swim. The town's jetty is popular for fishing. Every Sunday there are markets in Settlement Rd. Ferries and bay cruises leave from Cowes. A walk to the end of the jetty provides views to **French Island** to the east and **Stony Point** to the west.

NEARBY ATTRACTIONS: **Summerland Beach**, 11km south-west, is best known for its nightly **Penguin Parade**. The little penguins are the world's smallest and they nest on the island. These delightful birds can be seen from a specially constructed viewing area. Bookings are essential in peak season. The colonies of fur seals on **Seal Rocks**, 13km south-west, can be viewed from binoculars at Point Grant or a seal-watching cruise from Cowes. In Berrys Beach Rd, **Phillip Island Winery** is open daily for tastings and cellar door sales. At the **Koala Conservation Reserve**, visitors walk on elevated boardwalks for the best view of koalas in a natural habitat. **Churchill Island**, near Newhaven, has a nature reserve and an historic homestead.

VISITOR INFORMATION: Phillip Island Tourist Rd, Newhaven, Ph: (03) 5956 7447 or 1300 366 422

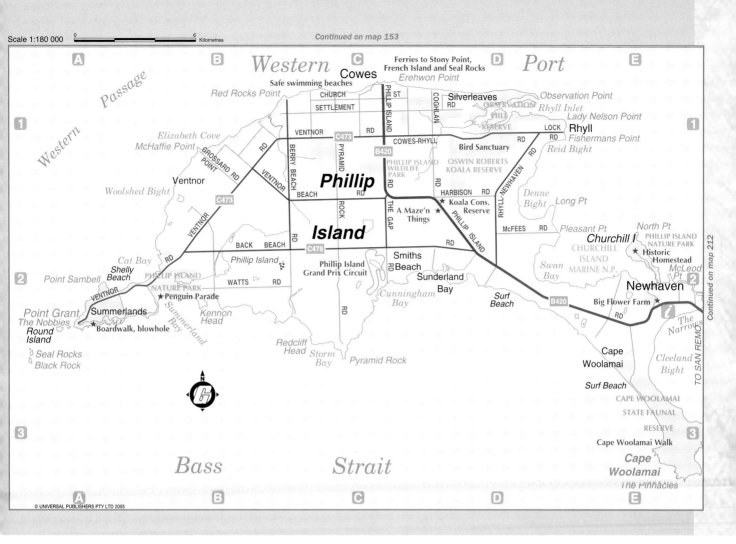

Continued on map 153

Scale 1:180 000

Kilometres

Western **Passage**

Western C **Port**

Ferries to Stony Point,
French Island and Seal Rocks
Erehwon Point

Cowes

Safe swimming beaches

Red Rocks Point

Silverleaves

Observation Point

Rhyll Inlet
Lady Nelson Point

CHURCH
SETTLEMENT

OBSERVATION
HILL
RESERVE

LOCK RD

Rhyll
Fishermans Point

VENTNOR RD

COWES-RHYLL

Bird Sanctuary

Reid Bight

Elizabeth Cove
McHaffie Point

GROSSARD POINT RD

BERRY BEACH

PYRAMID RD

PHILLIP ISLAND
WILDLIFE
PARK

OSWIN ROBERTS
KOALA RESERVE

Phillip

Ventnor

Woolshed Bight

C473

VENTNOR

BEACH

RD

HARBISON RD

RHYLL-NEWHAVEN RD

Denne
Bight

Long Pt

Island

BACK BEACH

ROCK RD

THE GAP

A Maze'n
Things

PHILLIP ISLAND

McFEES RD

Pleasant Pt

North Pt
PHILLIP ISLAND
NATURE PARK

Churchill I

CHURCHILL
ISLAND
MARINE N.P.

Historic
Homestead

McLeod
Pt

Cat Bay
Shelly
Beach

Point Sambell

PHILLIP ISLAND
NATURE PARK

VENTNOR

C478

Phillip Island

WATTS RD

Phillip Island
Grand Prix Circuit

Koala Cons.
Reserve

Smiths
Beach

Sunderland
Bay

Swan
Bay

Newhaven

Penguin Parade

Summerlands

Kennon
Head

Summerland Bay

RD

Cunningham
Bay

Surf
Beach

B420

Big Flower Farm

Point Grant
The Nobbies
Round
Island

Boardwalk, blowhole

Redcliff
Head

Storm
Bay

Pyramid Rock

RD

The
Narrows

Cape
Woolamai

Cleeland
Bight

Seal Rocks
Black Rock

N

Surf Beach

CAPE WOOLAMAI

STATE FAUNAL

RESERVE

Cape Woolamai Walk

Bass

Strait

Cape
Woolamai

The Pinnacles

© UNIVERSAL PUBLISHERS PTY LTD 2005

Creswick   POP 2450

Map 159, D3

This historic gold-mining town is
located 15km north of Ballarat,
and contains some fine historic
dwellings. Surrounded by pine
plantations, Creswick is ideally
positioned between the **Goldfields**
and **Spa Country**.

MAIN ATTRACTIONS: Creswick was the
birthplace of former Australian
Prime Minister **John Curtin** and
also home to the artistic **Lindsay**
family. Norman, the most famous
member, was born here in 1879.
Works by the Lindsays and
T G Moyle are exhibited in **Creswick**
Historical Museum, in the Town Hall
on Albert St. Walking tour notes, de-
tailing the town's historic buildings,
and a booklet on the **Buried Rivers**
of Gold Trail, are available.

NEARBY ATTRACTIONS: Visitors can try
gold panning in **Slatey Creek**, 4km
east of town. **Calembeen Park**, a
recreational area on the Midland
Hwy, offers a caravan park, picnic
area, BBQs, playground and a
natural lake, safe for swimming.
VISITOR INFORMATION: 98 Vincent St,
Daylesford, Ph: (03) 5321 6123

Daylesford   POP 3400

Map 167, A2

The **'Spa Centre of Australia'**
comprises the twin towns of
Daylesford and **Hepburn Springs**.
This is a popular destination for
short breaks and is located 115km
north-west of Melbourne. A
picturesque town, the surrounding
area has lakes, forests, relics from
the goldmining era and Australia's
largest concentration of natural

Boathouse, Lake Daylesford

MACEDON RANGES AND SPA COUNTRY

Boasting over 65 mineral springs concentrated within a relatively small area, this region is recognised as a premier boutique holiday destination due to the resurgence of belief in the healing properties of mineral water. Located a short distance from Melbourne, Spa Country is an ideal locale for 'taking the waters'. This is a European tradition dating to the 1840s, when the large Swiss-Italian community realised the healing potential of the waters surrounding them. Mineral water has been bottled here since 1850 and the towns of **Daylesford** and **Hepburn Springs** have been spa resorts in the European style since the 1880s. Alternative and natural therapies, including herbal baths and massages, are also offered in this region.

The Spa Country district also offers wineries and relics of the old goldfields. The surrounding rugged bushland has a number of local reserves such as **Lerderderg State Park** and **Hepburn Regional Park**. The **Macedon Ranges** are ideal for bushwalking, horseriding, fishing and picnicking. The **Tipperary Walking Track** links Hepburn Springs and Daylesford, passing through old gold-mining areas. Surrounded by lakes and regional parks, this lovely area offers a relaxing holiday destination with a diversity of attractions.

main attractions

- ❖ Convent Gallery, Daylesford
- ❖ Hanging Rock
- ❖ Hepburn Spa Resort
- ❖ Lake House Restaurant
- ❖ Lavandula Lavender Farm
- ❖ Macedon Ranges Wineries

 Visitor information

Daylesford Regional Visitor Information Centre
98 Vincent St, Daylesford, Vic 3460
Ph: (03) 5321 6123
www.visitdaylesford.com

Kyneton Visitor Information Centre
High St, Kyneton, Vic 3444
Ph: (03) 5422 6110

---

mineral springs. There are at least 65 mineral springs in the Daylesford and Hepburn Springs region. MAIN ATTRACTIONS: A mineral bathhouse is located at **Hepburn Spa Resort**, in the **Hepburn Mineral Springs Reserve**. Both public and private baths, flotation tanks and a sauna are offered. There are a number of practitioners in the district providing massage and natural therapies. **Convent Gallery** houses fine art, pottery, antiques and a superb collection of jewellery. The town's history is displayed in the **Historical Society Museum** housed in the old School of Mines, which was once used for smelting and refining gold and is easily identified by the tall brick chimney. Maps of the **Tipperary Walking Track**—part of the **Great Dividing Trail**—from Lake Daylesford to Hepburn Mineral Springs Reserve, are available from the information centre in Vincent St. **Wombat Hill Botanic Gardens** and **Lookout** are popular.
NEARBY ATTRACTIONS: **Lavandula Lavender Farm**, to the north, has a beautiful garden, farmyard animals, a restaurant and a variety of lavender-based products are offered for sale. There are other mineral springs in the surrounding area, including **Lyonville Spring**, 15km south-east of Daylesford. There are at least 14 **Macedon Ranges Wineries** with cellar doors and tastings. The extinct volcano **Mount Franklin** is located 13km north. 18km north-west, at **Yandoit**, are the remnants of stone homesteads from the district's Swiss-Italian pioneer families.

VISITOR INFORMATION: 98 Vincent St, Ph: (03) 5321 6123

▇ Donald   POP 1390
Map 207, F3
This town is situated on the **Richardson River**, 286km north-west of Melbourne. Wheat has long been the principal product of this part of the **Wimmera**, and grain silos still dominate the skyline.
MAIN ATTRACTIONS: Donald's history is preserved at the old **Banyenong Police Camp**, now an historic precinct located on the Sunraysia Hwy. The old police building was constructed by Johann Meyer in 1874. Tours of local industries include the **Pea Company**, **Kooka's Country Cookies**, **Fair Mark Shirt Factory**, **Australian Eatwell**, **Cloth Kidz** and **Snowy River**

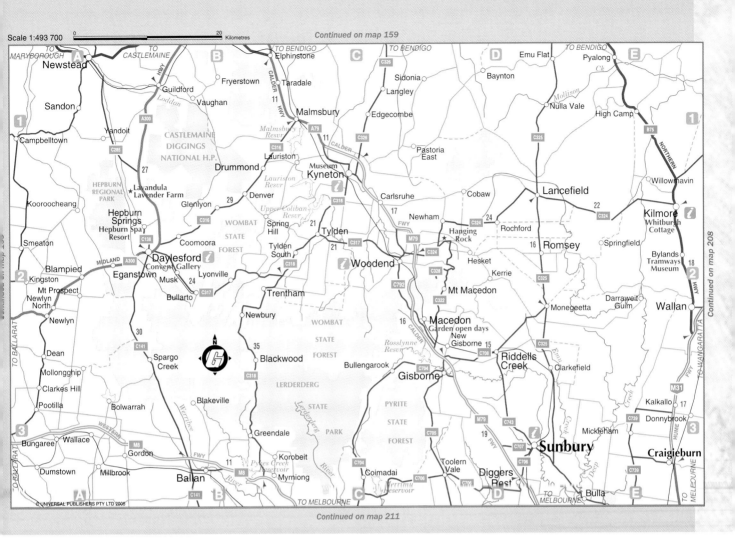

Continued on map 159

Scale 1:493 700

Continued on map 211

Leathergoods. The **Agricultural Museum**, on the corner of Borung Hwy and Mill St, has displays which include hand chaffcutters, shearing tables, a grubbing machine and a stump-jump plough. **Lions Train Park**, across the road, is the site of an old J524 class steam locomotive; BBQ facilities are provided. **Apex Wayside Park**, adjacent to the highway, has picnic and BBQ facilities. In Byrne St is **Bullocks Head Lookout**, so-called because a large growth on a box tree looks like a bullock's head. There is good fishing in the Richardson River.
NEARBY ATTRACTION: **Lake Buloke** is a wetlands area that attracts an array of wildlife, 10km north of Donald.
VISITOR INFORMATION: Buloke Shire Council, cnr Houston St and McCulloch St, Ph: (03) 5497 1300

Drouin   POP 5815

Map 212, D3

This **West Gippsland** town is located in an agricultural and dairying district. Drouin is 94km south-east of Melbourne.
MAIN ATTRACTIONS: **Drouin Nature Reserve** has 3km of walking tracks set in 14ha of natural bushland. In summer, the town is ablaze when the red-flowering gum trees (*Eucalyptus ficifolia*) are in full bloom. This beauty is celebrated with the **Ficifolia Festival** in February each year in Drouin.
NEARBY ATTRACTIONS: The region is renowned for the quality of its fresh produce. Many of the local producers of cheese, wine, fish, fruit, herbs and meat participate in the **Gourmet Deli Trail**, which also includes the regions around **Tarago**, **Neerim**

South, **Warragul** and **Yarragon**. Wineries, craft and antique shops complement the area. **Glen Cromie Park**, 8km north of Drouin, is an attractive flora and fauna reserve offering bushwalking, camping and picnic spots on the **Tarago River**.
VISITOR INFORMATION: 'The Old Church', Princes Hwy, Traralgon, Ph: 1800 621 409

Gourmet Deli Trail produce

Sorting fresh mussels at Portarlington Pier, north-east of Drysdale

Drysdale   POP 1740

Map 211, K3

The small township of Drysdale, 18km east of Geelong, services the surrounding farming community on the **Bellarine Peninsula**.

MAIN ATTRACTIONS: Drysdale's historic 19th century buildings include the **Old Court House Museum**, **Anglican Church** and **War Veterans Home**. The museum is open on Sundays, between January and April. **Bellarine Peninsula Railway** offers tourist rides between Drysdale and **Queenscliff** on Sundays and during school holidays.

NEARBY ATTRACTIONS: Neighbouring **Clifton Springs** was a spa resort in the 1880s, and featured a pier, baths and a kiosk for holiday-makers. Today, a modern sporting and public complex stands on the site of the original spa hotel. There are several wineries in the area, including **Scotchmans Hill Winery**, 8km north-east. The fishing and seaside resort of **Portarlington** is 8km north-east. Attractions at this resort include **Portarlington Mill** and the **Portarlington Miniature Train**.

VISITOR INFORMATION: 55 Hesse St, Queenscliff, Ph: (03) 5258 4843

Echuca   POP 10 940

Map 208, A2

Founded in 1863, Echuca is one of the state's oldest river towns. Echuca was originally a **Murray River** crossing point to and from its twin town **Moama** in New South Wales. An historic iron bridge still joins the two towns.

MAIN ATTRACTIONS: Echuca's interesting history, old paddlesteamers and picturesque setting have contributed to it becoming a thriving tourist destination. **Echuca Wharf**, built of red gum in 1865, was once five times its present size and is still a massive structure built on three levels to accommodate the rise and fall of the Murray River. There are also a number of paddlesteamers moored at the wharf, including the **Pevensey**, once used in a TV mini-series. The paddlesteamers are all available for cruises. A museum in the **Cargo Wharf Shed** houses dioramas portraying the life and activity of the port and runs a ten minute audiovisual presentation on Echuca's history. The **Bridge Hotel**, built by the ex-convict founder of Echuca, Henry Hopwood, has some rooms furnished in period-style; the most interesting is the squatter's suite. **Echuca Historical Society Museum** is located in the old Police Station and gaol (1867). Fun attractions for families include **Sharp's Magic Movie House and Penny Arcade**, **World in Wax**, **National Holden Museum** and **Oz Maze**. Echucha hosts several festivals, including the **Heritage Steam Festival** in October, and the **Riverboats Jazz and Wine Festival** in February.

NEARBY ATTRACTIONS: Just out of town, in the area registered as the **Perricoota Wine Region**, are several new wineries and a **Wine Trail** brochure is available. **Barmah State Forest**, with its ancient red gums, is located 39km north-east. Nearby, **Dharnya Aboriginal Interpretive Centre** has displays tracing the history and culture of the local Yorta Yorta people. **Barmah Lake** is ideal for fishing, canoeing, swimming or enjoying a wetlands cruise.

VISITOR INFORMATION: 2 Heygarth St, Ph: (03) 5480 7555 or 1800 804 446

Edenhope   POP 780

Map 206, B5

This small west **Wimmera** town is the administrative centre for sheep and cattle country that was first settled in 1845. Vast wetlands surround the town, which lies on the shores of **Lake Wallace**.

MAIN ATTRACTIONS: A cairn beside the lake commemorates the first Aboriginal cricket team to tour England (1868). The team was made up of players from the Edenhope and Harrow district and was coached on the shores of Lake Wallace; they also played in Melbourne and Sydney. Lake Wallace is 7m deep when full and is a habitat for many waterbirds. It is one of the best fly-fishing spots in the district with anglers targeting trout and redfin. There are two boardwalks on the walking and cycling track around the lake for viewing the birdlife. Lake Wallace is also a popular recreational area for swimmers, anglers and boating enthusiasts. The endangered red-tailed black cockatoo can be seen around the golf course at certain times of the year.

NEARBY ATTRACTIONS: **Baileys Rocks**, huge pink and green granite boulders, 30km south of Edenhope, is a significant local landmark and an impressive geological feature. It is a popular picnic area.

VISITOR INFORMATION: Old Court House, 96 Elizabeth St, Ph: (03) 5585 1509

Eildon POP 725

Map 208, D5

In a region that once thrived on timber and goldmining, Eildon, 130km north-east of Melbourne, was built in the 1950s to house employees of the **Lake Eildon Dam** project. Construction of the dam created **Lake Eildon**—officially opened in 1956—the largest artificial lake in Victoria and the main storage for the vast **Goulburn Irrigation System**. The lake is almost surrounded by **Lake Eildon NP**.

MAIN ATTRACTIONS: Eildon has become a popular destination for inland waterskiers, wakeboarders, anglers, sailing enthusiasts, canoeists and jet skiers. Over 800 houseboats are moored on the lake. Houseboats can be hired at **Eildon Boat Harbour** and 'picnic boats' at **Jerusalem Creek**. **Eildon Pondage** is stocked with rainbow and brown trout, with all-weather electric BBQs, bike and walking trails on the perimeter. There are a variety of self-guided walks, drives and horse-riding trails available from Eildon.

NEARBY ATTRACTIONS: Part of Lake Eildon is contained within Lake Eildon NP. Watersports, fishing, walking and camping are popular activities in the 300km² park, which

Puffing Billy steam train near Emerald

is home to a variety of birds, kangaroos, wombats, wallabies and deer. You can learn the art of fly-fishing at local **flyfishing centres** or catch your own trout at **Eildon Trout Farm**. **Freshwater Discovery Centre**, 6km south-west, breeds fingerling trout to stock the state's waterways; it is open to the public. Nearby, the creek drops downhill in a series of cascades known as **Snobs Creek Falls**.

VISITOR INFORMATION: Eildon Resource Centre, Main St, Ph: (03) 5774 2909

Emerald POP 6150

Map 171, D5

This picturesque township was the first European settlement in the **Dandenong Ranges**. It attracts many visitors.

MAIN ATTRACTIONS: **Emerald Lake Park** offers a footbridge over the lake, waterslides, children's wading pool, picnic tables, BBQs, tearooms and walking trails; pedal boats can be hired here. A major attraction, the *Puffing Billy* steam train runs between **Belgrave** and **Gembrook**. Emerald and the park are two of the train's stopping points. In April the **Great Train Race** is held, when runners race *Puffing Billy* from Belgrave to Emerald Lake Park. Emerald is home to the largest model railway in the Southern Hemisphere. **Emerald Lake Model Railway** has about 35 model trains, open Tuesday to Sunday, plus school and public holidays.

NEARBY ATTRACTIONS: The **Motorist Cafe and Museum** has heritage cars on display and is located in Main St, Gembrook, 14km east of Emerald. **Sherbrooke Equestrian Park**, 3km west, organises horseriding treks. **Puffing Billy Steam Museum** is at **Menzies Creek**, 4km north-west of Emerald, and is open weekends, Wednesdays and public holidays.

VISITOR INFORMATION: 1211 Burwood Hwy, Upper Ferntree Gully, Ph: (03) 9758 7522 or 1800 645 505

Euroa POP 2780

Map 208, C4

Euroa, 140km from Melbourne, is a pleasant town set against a backdrop of the **Strathbogie Ranges**. It is surrounded by one of the finest wool-producing regions in Victoria. Englishwoman Eliza Forlonge personally selected core breeding stock of Saxon merino sheep from war-torn northern Europe in the 1820s and early 1830s. One flock was sold to John Macarthur, others went to Tasmania and Western Australia. Eliza eventually came to Australia and settled first in Goulburn, then walked her flock to Victoria, settled close to where Euroa now stands and built **Seven Creeks Station**. Her impact on the Australian economy was and remains enormous. In 1878, bushranger Ned Kelly and his gang staged a daring robbery at Euroa, rounding up many hostages and stealing cash and gold worth nearly £2000.

MAIN ATTRACTIONS: A 19th-century inn houses the **Farmers Arms Museum**, displaying historic items from the district, including patchwork quilts dating back to 1896. One room is dedicated to Eliza Forlonge and there are two machinery sheds where equipment from the past is on display. The museum, located at 25 Kirkland Ave West, is open in school holidays or by appointment. Starting from the museum is a 2.7km **heritage trail**, which explores Euroa township. **Seven Creeks Park** offers picnic and BBQ facilities.

NEARBY ATTRACTIONS: A self-guided scenic drive leads visitors to **Gooram Falls**, 20km south-east, and around the Strathbogie Ranges. For a panoramic view of the **Victorian Alps** and surrounding country, visit **Mount Wombat lookout**, 25km south-east, via a scenic drive.

VISITOR INFORMATION: BP Service Station, 29 Tarcombe St, Ph: (03) 5795 3677

DANDENONG RANGES

Only an hour's drive from Melbourne, the beautiful Dandenong Ranges form a natural backdrop to Victoria's capital city, attracting hordes of city visitors annually to this green haven of hills and forests. Rising to an average elevation of 500–600m, the Dandenong Ranges peak at **Mount Dandenong**, 633m above sea level.

Colourful, inviting and cool, especially in summer, the Dandenongs are popular for daytrips, not only for their intrinsic beauty but also for the many beautiful gardens and great variety of European and native trees and shrubs. The Dandenongs are home to six of the **Great Gardens of Melbourne**. The rich volcanic soil and plentiful rain ensures that plants flourish here, and there are many nurseries and arboreta. The smattering of restaurants, art galleries, antique shops and tearooms in the many townships of the Dandenongs provide excellent detours from exploring the region's stunning scenery.

Sculpture at William Ricketts Sanctuary, Mount Dandenong

 Visitor information

Dandenong Ranges and Knox Visitor Information Centre
1211 Burwood Hwy
Upper Ferntree Gully, Vic 3156
Ph: (03) 9758 7522 or 1800 645 505
www.yarrarangestourism.com

Puffing Billy

This vintage steam train has run almost continuously since its debut in 1900. With its open carriages and restaurant car, it is one of Victoria's top attractions. On total fire ban days, diesel locomotives replace it. The 48km return journey between **Belgrave** and **Gembrook** and back again is beautiful and includes travelling over timber trestle bridges and through forests and tree ferns.

main attractions

❖ **Belgrave**
Home to the beloved vintage steam train *Puffing Billy*.

❖ **Dandenong Ranges National Park**
See the world's tallest flowering plant in the Dandenongs—the mountain ash tree.

❖ **Mount Dandenong Lookout**
This lookout offers a breathtaking vantage point for panoramic views over Melbourne, Port Phillip and Western Port.

❖ **Olinda**
An ideal time to visit Olinda is in spring, when the town is a riot of colour.

❖ **Sassafras**
Picturesque Sassafras offers charming stores and galleries.

❖ **William Ricketts Sanctuary**
This sanctuary is a testimony to the work of Ricketts, who spent much time with the Aboriginal people of Central Australia. The setting of fern gardens and rock waterfalls provide a natural gallery for his kiln-fired sculptures of Aboriginal people.

Tesselaar's Tulip Festival, Silvan

Victoria

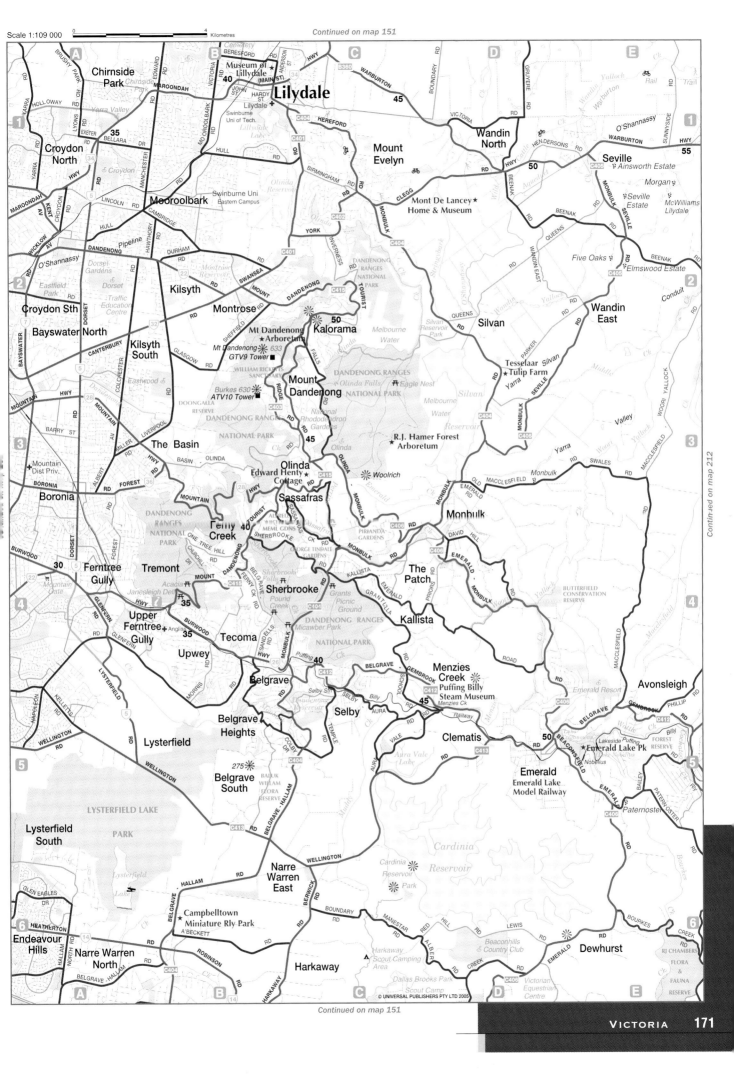

Museum of Lilydale
Lilydale
Swinburne Uni of Tech.

Chirnside Park

Croydon North

Mooroolbark

Croydon Sth

Bayswater North

Kilsyth

Kilsyth South

Montrose

Mt Dandenong ★ Arboretum
Mt Dandenong 633
GTV9 Tower

Kalorama

Mount Evelyn

Wandin North

Seville
Ainsworth Estate

Morgan

Seville Estate
McWilliams Lilydale

Elmswood Estate

Five Oaks

Wandin East

Silvan

Mont De Lancey ★ Home & Museum

Tesselaar Tulip Farm

Mount Dandenong

Burkes 630
ATV10 Tower

Doongalla Reserve

National Rhododendron Gardens

Olinda

Eagle Nest

R.J. Hamer Forest Arboretum

The Basin

Olinda

Edward Henty ★ Cottage

Sassafras

Woolrich

Monbulk

Boronia

Ferny Creek

Tremont

Sherbrooke

The Patch

Kallista

Ferntree Gully

Upper Ferntree Gully

Tecoma

Upwey

Belgrave

Menzies Creek
Puffing Billy Steam Museum
Menzies Ck

Avonsleigh

Clematis

Lysterfield

Belgrave Heights

Selby

Emerald
Emerald Lake Model Railway

★ Emerald Lake Pk

Belgrave South

Lysterfield South

Lysterfield Lake Park

Narre Warren East

Cardinia Reservoir

Cardinia Reservoir Park

Campbelltown Miniature Rly Park

Endeavour Hills

Narre Warren North

Harkaway

Dewhurst

Beaconhills Country Club

RJ Chambers Flora & Fauna Reserve

© UNIVERSAL PUBLISHERS PTY LTD 2005

◼ Geelong POP 130 000

Map 201, J3

The second largest provincial city in Victoria, Geelong is a deepwater port and industrial centre on the shores of **Corio Bay**. Much of Geelong's early wealth was created by wool exports and added to by thousands of gold-seekers passing through on their way to **Bendigo** and **Ballarat**; gold was exported through the port. Geelong is a well-planned city with many parks and open spaces.

MAIN ATTRACTIONS: The renowned botanist Ferdinand von Mueller laid out Geelong's fine **Botanic Gardens**, recently expanded and overlooking Corio Bay. A special feature is the historic first **Customs House**, prefabricated in Sydney and shipped to Geelong in 1838. **Eastern Beach** is in the same vicinity as the gardens. The 1930s beach facilities have been refurbished in recent years and the enclosed pool is a popular swimming area. **Waterfront Geelong** is an attractive leisure precinct with restaurants and attractions, plus 105 delightful hand-painted bollards illustrating

Volunteer Rifle Band, three of Jan Mitchell's hand-painted bollards around Corio Bay, Geelong

Geelong's colourful history. **The National Wool Museum** is one of many National Trust buildings in the city. There are displays in the bluestone museum telling the story of the Australian wool industry as well as re-created shearers' quarters. The **Ford Discovery Centre**, in Brougham St, reveals the story of Australian car manufacture. **Christ Church**, in Moorabool St, is the oldest Anglican church in Victoria still in use. **Geelong Art Gallery**, the largest regional gallery in Victoria, and the **Performing Arts Centre** are both located in Little Malop St.

NEARBY ATTRACTIONS: There are many **wineries** in the Geelong area offering tastings of cabernet sauvignon, shiraz and chardonnay. Details are available from the information centre. **You Yangs Regional Park**, a range of granite hills 20km north, offers picnic grounds and walking tracks. **Serendip Sanctuary**, close to the You Yangs, is 250ha of open grassy woodlands and wetlands. There are nature trails, bird hides and a visitors centre with displays of brolgas, bustards and pademelons. **Brisbane Ranges NP**, located 34km north, offers the state's richest wildflower habitat. The old gold town of **Steiglitz**, 10km north-west of **Anakie**, features a restored **Court House**.

VISITOR INFORMATION: National Wool Museum, cnr Moorabool St and Brougham St, Ph: (03) 5222 2900 or 1800 620 888

◼ Gisborne POP 4235

Map 167, D3

Jacksons Creek flows through the town of Gisborne, which lies in the foothills of **Mount Macedon**. Gisborne is a pretty little town, about 52km from Melbourne.

MAIN ATTRACTIONS: There are many art and craft shops in the town. **Jacksons Creek** and **Gisborne Botanic Garden** offer recreation

areas and picnic facilities. The local **Macedon Ranges Wineries** specialise in cool-climate wines and most are open for tastings and sales at various times.

NEARBY ATTRACTIONS: **Barringo Wildlife Reserve** is an area of natural bushland which protects native wildlife. There are also deer, pea-cocks and a lake well stocked with trout. The township of **Mount Macedon** is north of Gisborne. Here, in the late 1800s, wealthy residents of Melbourne built estates to escape the heat of summer. Locals and tourists continue to visit the old homes and grand European-style gardens, despite so many of them having been devastated in the 1983 Ash Wednesday bush fires. Springtime flower shows and open garden days in spring and autumn are highlights of the Macedon area.

VISITOR INFORMATION: High St, Woodend, Ph: (03) 5427 2033 or 1800 244 711

◼ Hamilton POP 9250

Map 210, D2

A major centre for **south-west Victoria**, Hamilton has been known for many years as the '**Wool Capital of the World**'. Around 294km from Melbourne, it is located on the largest volcanic plain in the Southern Hemisphere.

MAIN ATTRACTIONS: **Lake Hamilton** is located on the eastern side of town and is a focus for local recreation. A walking track follows the lake and ends at a small swimming beach. **Sir Reginald Ansett Transport Museum** is also beside the lake. The **Botanic Gardens**, in Thompson St, are ideal for picnics and relaxing. **Hamilton Pastoral Museum** is one of many historic buildings preserving the district's rural heritage. **Hamilton Art Gallery** has the impressive **Paul Sandby Collection**, which was donated by a local grazier. The **Big Woolbales Complex**, located in Coleraine Rd, displays woolshed memorabilia.

NEARBY ATTRACTIONS: Hamilton is a 20 minute drive from the foothills of **Grampians NP**. **Mt Baimbridge Lavender** (open September to January) and the rose gardens of **Cavendish** are also to the north. Features of **Mount Eccles NP**, 35km south, include three extinct volcanoes and there is a **Volcanic Interpretive Centre** at Penshurst, 32km south-east. Camping is permitted at Mount Eccles. **Wannon Falls** and **Nigretta Falls** can be accessed from Glenelg Hwy to the west.
VISITOR INFORMATION: Lonsdale St, Ph: (03) 5572 3746 or 1800 807 056

Healesville   POP 7145
Map 212, C2
This attractive town is a popular destination for Melbourne residents as it is just over an hour's drive north-east, through the renowned vineyard country of the **Yarra Valley**. The wineries are not the only attraction. Healesville is also the gateway to the **Great Dividing Range** with its huge mountain ash forests and waterfalls.
MAIN ATTRACTIONS: One end of the **Yarra Valley Tourist Railway** is located in Healesville. On Sundays and public holidays, motorised trolleys travel every 30 minutes through an historic 100m brick-lined tunnel.
NEARBY ATTRACTIONS: The renowned **Healesville Sanctuary** is located 4km south. Over 200 species of native birds, mammals and reptiles are displayed in their natural habitat. There are over **45 wineries** throughout the Yarra Valley, most open for cellar door sales and tastings. Some of the larger wineries have restaurants attached. Wine tours of the Yarra Valley are available. **Yarra Ranges NP** is east of Healesville and features mountain ash forest with an understorey of tree ferns. A rainforest gallery with an obser-

vation platform and walkway is provided on the slopes of **Mount Donna Buang**. Scenic drives include one through the forest over **Black Spur**. **Maroondah Reservoir** and the **Badger and Donnelly weirs** offer bushland walks as well as picnic and BBQ facilities.
VISITOR INFORMATION: Old Court House, Harker St, Ph: (03) 5962 2600

Heathcote   POP 1570
Map 208, A5
This town, 105km north of Melbourne, is located in picturesque countryside. Heathcote was a creation of the 19th century goldrush when the population reached 35 000. Today, its wide main streets with many historic buildings evoke feelings of the past.
MAIN ATTRACTIONS: **Pink Cliffs**, located in a reserve off Pink Cliffs Rd, are a local feature. The ever-changing pink shades of miniature gorges and pinnacles was created in the 1800s by mining activity. **Heathcote-Graytown NP**, at the edge of town, is ideal for bushwalking and birdwatching.
NEARBY ATTRACTIONS: There are walking tracks to **Devils Cave** and **Viewing Rock**, which provide panoramic views of Heathcote and the surrounding countryside. **Vineyards** in the surrounding area supply grapes to winemakers throughout Victoria. **Central Victorian Yabby Farm** is open for tours. **Lake Eppalock** is popular for fishing and boating.
VISITOR INFORMATION: Cnr High St and Barrack St, Ph: (03) 5433 3121

Heyfield   POP 1440
Map 213, F3
A prosperous timber-milling and tourist town, Heyfield is 195km east of Melbourne. It is located in the centre of a dairying district based around the **Thomson River** and **Glenmaggie Weir**.
MAIN ATTRACTIONS: Heyfield offers many recreational activities,

Yarra Valley vineyard in the Healesville area

including golf, fishing, yachting, power boating, bushwalking and trail bike riding. Local timber mills produce kiln-dried hardwood and several of them are open for inspection by appointment.
NEARBY ATTRACTIONS: Heyfield is ideally located as a departure point for tourist drives in the **Maffra** region. There are art and craft shops, markets, galleries and pottery studios. The scenic drive to **Licola** offers many natural attractions. There are several tracks and river crossings for 4-wheel driving. **Lake Glenmaggie**, 11km north, is popular for boating, swimming and fishing. Between June and September, cross-country skiing conditions can usually be found north of Licola, in the region of **Mount Tamboritha** and **Mount Skene**.
VISITOR INFORMATION: Commercial Rd, Ph: (03) 5148 3404

Horsham POP 13 210

Map 206, D4

Situated 300km north-west of Melbourne, Horsham is located in flat, open country and services a vast rural district producing cereals and livestock. Horsham is regarded as the capital of the **Wimmera** region and is a good base for travellers intent on exploring **The Grampians** and **Little Desert NP**.

MAIN ATTRACTIONS: **Horsham Regional Gallery**, located in an elegant 1930s Art Deco building, houses significant collections of Australian art and photography, and hosts a varied programme of exhibitions. The **Botanic Gardens** are laid out along the banks of the **Wimmera River**. A lemon-scented gum and a bunya pine stand sentinel at the entrance to the gardens, which were designed in the 1870s by William Guilfoyle, the curator of Melbourne's Royal Botanic Gardens. **Wimmera Ultra-Fine Wool Factory** is open for tours Monday to Friday.

Climber on Mount Arapiles, west of Horsham

NEARBY ATTRACTIONS: There are many daytrips visitors can make from Horsham. To the south are **Black Range State Park**, **Rocklands Reservoir** and The Grampians. To the west, **Mount Arapiles** attracts climbers from around the world. Little Desert NP protects many endangered native plants and animals. **Mt Zero Olives** and **Toscana Olives** are open for inspection near the northern section of **Grampians NP**. Fishing for trout and redfin is popular in **Taylors Lake**, 18km south-east.

VISITOR INFORMATION: 20 O'Callaghan Pde, Ph: (03) 5382 1832 or 1800 633 218

Inverloch POP 3750

Map 212, C4

This seaside town is situated on **Anderson Inlet**, 150km south-east of Melbourne. The many surfing beaches make Inverloch a popular destination for surfers and families.

MAIN ATTRACTIONS: Grouped together in the foreshore reserve are the **Environment Centre**, where **Inverloch Shell Museum** displays one of the best private collections of shells in Australia, and **Rainbow Park**, a colourful children's play area and picnic spot. Inverloch is located in **South Gippsland** and its coastline has many attractions. Mangroves grow here at their southern limit, and, when the tide is out, it is possible to walk over the sands of the inlet and see the mangroves fully exposed. There are many rockpools to explore. Fishing, birdwatching, sailing and wind-surfing are also popular activities.

NEARBY ATTRACTIONS: For watching waterbirds both **Townsend Bluff** and **Mahers Landing** are good spots. The scenic drive from Inverloch to **Cape Paterson** offers stunning coastal views and edges **Bunurong Marine NP**. There are **dinosaur fossils** between Inverloch and **Eagles Nest**, a remarkable rock formation to the south-west. The

Tarwin River, 20km south-east, provides good fishing opportunities.

VISITOR INFORMATION: 6 A'Beckett St, Ph: (03) 5671 2233 or 1300 762 433

Irymple POP 3515

Map 204, D2

In the heart of the **Sunraysia** district, 9km south of Mildura, Irymple is the centre of a citrus, dried fruit and winegrowing area.

MAIN ATTRACTIONS: Processing the region's crops into dried fruit is a major industry in Irymple. **Angas Park Dried Fruits**, in Koolong Ave, is the principal sales outlet. There are many wineries in the region, but only one vineyard in Irymple. **Salisbury Estate**, located in Campbell Ave, offers cellar door sales and tastings.

NEARBY ATTRACTIONS: Irymple offers easy access to many of the region's attractions, including the **Murray River** and **Mildura**.

VISITOR INFORMATION: Alfred Deakin Centre, 180-190 Deakin Ave, Mildura, Ph: (03) 5018 8380 or 1300 550 858

Kerang POP 3885

Map 207, H1

Located 280km north-west of Melbourne and around 30km from the **Murray River**, Kerang is the centre for a large rural area. Lakes, waterways and swamps surround the town. The waterways are breeding grounds for many waterbirds, including ibis—walking and flying pest controllers, especially valued for their appetite for locusts.

NEARBY ATTRACTIONS: More ibis breed in the rookeries around Kerang than anywhere else in the world. An estimated 200 000 white ibis, straw-necked ibis and the rare glossy ibis nest here each spring. There are major rookeries located at **Middle Lake** and **Third Lake** north-west of Kerang. A hide at **Middle Lake** allows easier viewing. The best time to see birds soaring gracefully over the lakes and waterways is early morning or evening. **Reedy Lake** offers a pleasant picnic area. Some of the larger lakes are available for watersports. **Lake Charm** and **Kangaroo Lake** are suitable for waterskiing and yatching. **Gunbower Island State Forest**, 25km east, is an important red gum habitat. **Murrabit**, 27km north, is a picturesque town near the Murray River. **Murrabit Markets** are held on the first Saturday of each month.

VISITOR INFORMATION: 15 Murray St, Barham, Ph: (03) 5453 3100 or 1800 621 882

▨ Kilmore   POP 3525

Map 167, E2

Kilmore was founded in 1841, making it Victoria's oldest inland town. Located 60km north of Melbourne, Kilmore is known for its historic buildings. Many of the fine old stone buildings have been refurbished and some are now antique and specialty shops.

MAIN ATTRACTIONS: **Whitburgh Cottage**, built in 1857, is now a museum providing an insight into the lifestyle of a typical 19th-century family. It is open by appointment only. An historic precinct, comprising the old **Post Office**, **Court House** and red-brick **Police Barracks**, dates back to the 1860s, and several main street shops and hotels date back to the 1850s. Kilmore is renowned for its horseracing events and hosts the **Kilmore Racing Cup** and **Kilmore Pacing Cup**, Australia's richest provincial harness racing event.

NEARBY ATTRACTIONS: **Victoria Tramway Museum** is located in **Bylands**, 7km south of Kilmore. The museum has an extensive display of cable cars and early electric trams, and offers tram rides. It is open on Sundays. On the **Mount Piper Walking Track**—a one hour return walk—visitors will see a variety of wildlife and wildflowers. **Strath Creek** and **Strath Creek Falls** are

Rural scene in the Strzelecki Ranges, north of Korumburra

also worthwhile exploring. From here visitors are urged to take the scenic drive through the **Valley of a Thousand Hills**.

VISITOR INFORMATION: 12 Sydney St, Ph: (03) 5781 1319

▨ Korumburra   POP 3040

Map 212, D4

Situated 118km south-east of Melbourne, Korumburra is surrounded by dairying country and is a regional cattle-sales centre. The **Bass Valley**, near Korumburra, is home to the rare and protected giant Gippsland earthworm, known as Karmai to the Aborigines. The worms can grow to an amazing 3m in length and 2.5cm in diameter.

MAIN ATTRACTIONS: **Coal Creek Heritage Village**, south of the town centre, is a re-creation of the coal-mining days of the 1890s. Features include the original Coal Creek Mine Tunnel, a bush tramway and authentic settlers' cottages. There is also a simulated mine explosion daily.

NEARBY ATTRACTIONS: The **South Gippsland Railway** operates train rides, which start from Korumburra or nearby **Leongatha**, and travel through the lower **Strzelecki**

Ranges to **Nyora**, stopping at **Loch**. This town, 14km north-west of Korumburra, has many antique, art and craft shops.

VISITOR INFORMATION: South Gippsland Hwy, Ph: (03) 5655 2233 or 1800 630 704

▨ Kyabram   POP 5740

Map 208, B3

A friendly tree-lined country town in the dairying and fruit-growing region of the western **Goulburn Valley**, Kyabram is 192km north of Melbourne.

MAIN ATTRACTIONS: **Kyabram Fauna Park** is an award-winning 55ha community reserve protecting wildlife, including free-roaming kangaroos and emus. Crocodiles are kept in a solar-heated reptile house. Wetlands support a variety of waterbirds, which can be observed from a raised hide. Also in the park are **Hazelmans Cottage**, a restored and refurnished settler's cottage, a cafe, kiosk, and picnic and BBQ facilities. **Eddis Park Arboretum** is lovely for picnics under 200-year-old grey box gums, and for pleasant walks.

VISITOR INFORMATION: Kyabram Fauna Park, 75 Lake Rd, Ph: (03) 5852 2883

Lying parallel to **Bass Strait** and separated from the ocean by **Ninety Mile Beach**, the Gippsland Lakes are Australia's largest system of inland waterways. Stretching from **Sale** in the west to **Lakes Entrance** in the east, this region is an extremely popular water playground. The area was once occupied by a clan of the Gunai/Kurnai Aboriginal people—evidence of their occupation can still be seen.

Five lakes cover around 400km²: **King**, **Coleman**, **Wellington**, **Reeve** and **Victoria**. These lakes parallel Ninety Mile Beach, providing a unique natural environment protected by **The Lakes NP** and **Gippsland Lakes Coastal Park**.

Promoted as the **'Victorian Riviera'**, temperatures here can be up to 6°C warmer than in Melbourne. Holiday villages around the Gippsland Lakes provide easy access to every imaginable form of water activity, including sailing, windsurfing and self-drive cruiser hire. Opportunities for fishing abound, making Gippsland Lakes a drawcard for lake, beach and offshore anglers seeking bream, flathead, whiting, skip jack, mullet, salmon and other species.

With the foothills of the High Country only a short drive away, visitors also have the chance to explore alpine mountains, forests and national parks and the many other attractions offered in this unique area.

Sailing on the Gippsland Lakes

 Visitor information

Lakes Entrance Visitor Information Centre
Cnr Marine Pde and Esplanade,
Lakes Entrance, Vic 3909
Ph: (03) 5155 1966 or 1800 637 060
www.lakesandwilderness.com.au

main attractions

- ❖ Bairnsdale
- ❖ Metung
- ❖ Ninety Mile Beach
- ❖ Paynesville
- ❖ The Lakes National Park

Bluestone railway viaduct at Malmsbury, north-west of Kyneton

▦ Kyneton POP 4115

Map 167, C1

Kyneton, 86km north of Melbourne, is an attractive historic town featuring 19th-century bluestone architecture. Small-scale manufacturing and farming boomed in the 1850s and 1860s in the rush to feed the thousands of miners who flocked to the district.
MAIN ATTRACTIONS: Historic **Piper St** offers many specialty stores selling antiques, furniture, crafts and gourmet food. **Kyneton Museum**, a bluestone building that was once the Bank of New South Wales, re-creates family life as it was in Victorian times. In the grounds are stables, a coach house and a drop-log cottage. The museum is open Friday to Sunday and selected public holidays. Other buildings of note include **Willis Steam Mill**, the **Court House** and several churches. **Kyneton Botanic Gardens**, in Clowes St, features a collection of rare and endangered trees, including a Chilean wine palm, blue atlas cedars and a golden English oak. The **Campaspe River** flows through the gardens and picnics on its banks are popular, as is the walking track from the gardens to the nearby racecourse.
NEARBY ATTRACTIONS: In recent years, the **Macedon wine region** has spread north-west to Kyneton and a number of wineries are within easy reach. **Malmsbury**, 10km north-west, has a number of historic bluestone buildings, including a bluestone railway viaduct.
VISITOR INFORMATION: High St,
Ph: (03) 5422 6110

Victoria

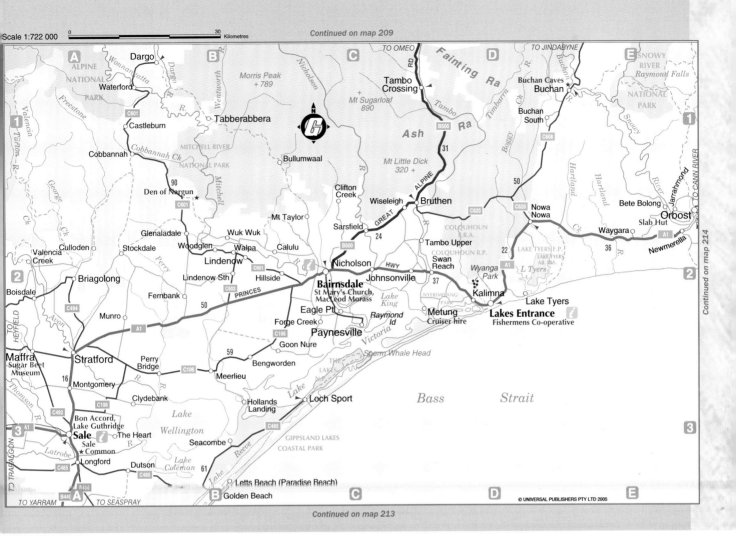

Scale 1:722 000   0   30 Kilometres

Continued on map 209

TO OMEO · TO JINDABYNE

A Dargo · **B** · **C** · **D** · **E**

ALPINE NATIONAL PARK
Waterford
Castleburn
Cobbannah
Den of Nargun
Tabberabbera
Morris Peak +789
Mt Sugarloaf 890
Bullumwaal
Clifton Creek
Wiseleigh · Bruthen
Sarsfield
Mt Taylor
Glenaladale
Wuk Wuk
Walpa
Calulu
Nicholson
Stockdale
Woodglen
Lindenow
Lindenow Sth
Hillside
Bairnsdale
St Mary's Church, MacLeod Morass
Johnsonville
Fernbank
Eagle Pt
Raymond Id
Metung
Lakes Entrance
Fishermens Co-operative
Forge Creek
Paynesville
Goon Nure
Briagolong
Munro
Bengworden
Perry Bridge
Meerlieu
Clydebank
Hollands Landing
Loch Sport
Seacombe
Lake Wellington
Maffra
Sugar Beet Museum
Stratford
Montgomery
Bon Accord, Lake Guthridge
Sale
The Heart
Sale Common
Longford
Dutson
Lake Coleman
Letts Beach (Paradise Beach)
Golden Beach
GIPPSLAND LAKES COASTAL PARK

Tambo Crossing
Mt Little Dick 320 +
Ash Ra
Fainting Ra
Buchan Caves · Buchan
Buchan South
Nowa Nowa
Bete Bolong
Slab Hut
Orbost
Waygara
Newmerella
SNOWY RIVER · Raymond Falls
NATIONAL PARK
Tambo Upper
Swan Reach
Wyanga Park
Kalimna
Lake Tyers
Lake King
Sperm Whale Head
Bass Strait

TO SEASPRAY · TO YARRAM

© UNIVERSAL PUBLISHERS PTY LTD 2005

Continued on map 214
Continued on map 213

Lakes Entrance   POP 5485

Map 177, D2

Situated on a permanent artificial opening to the **Gippsland Lakes** waterways, Lakes Entrance is a popular summer resort and active fishing port with a huge fleet, many of them engaged in deep-sea fishing. Lakes Entrance is located at the eastern end of the largest inland lakes system in Australia.

MAIN ATTRACTIONS: The greatest attractions of the area are the beaches and waterways. Famous **Ninety Mile Beach** (145km long) is a narrow stretch of sand, backed by extensive sand dunes, separating Bass Strait and the lakes. A footbridge over **Cunninghame Arm** connects the surf beach with the Esplanade. Ferry services and cruise boats offer a variety of ways to explore the lakes. Boats of all kinds can be hired for sightseeing, sailing or fishing expeditions. There are also a number of excellent launching places around the lake. The **Fishermens Co-operative** on **Bullock Island** offers freshly caught fish for sale. There is a **Seashell Museum** on The Esplanade.

NEARBY ATTRACTIONS: **Wyanga Park Winery** is 10km north and can be reached by boat. **Nyerimilang Heritage Park** is 10km west and the **East Gippsland Botanic Gardens**, also at Nyerimilang, offer pleasant walks in relaxing surroundings. **Lake Tyers Forest Park**, to the north-east, is an ideal spot for bush-walking, picnicking and camping.

VISITOR INFORMATION: Cnr Marine Pde and The Esplanade (Princes Hwy), Ph: (03) 5155 1966 or 1800 637 060

Canoeing on the Tambo River, west of Lakes Entrance

Once part of the ancient land bridge to Tasmania, Wilsons Promontory is the southernmost point of the Australian mainland. The area is protected by one of Victoria's oldest and most spectacular national parks, reserved in 1898. Its pristine beaches and coves framed by granite masses, rivers and creeks, and rugged mountain ranges, are preserved by their remoteness. However, the accommodation and camping grounds at **Tidal River** are lively during summer and school holidays.

Visitors have always been intrigued by the majestic coastline and botanical abundance of Wilsons Promontory. **'The Prom'** contains the largest coastal wilderness area in Victoria. It features over 700 flowering native plant species growing in diverse habitats. There are tall eucalypts, moist fern gullies, groves of brown and yellow stringy-barks, copses of banksias and tea-trees, salt marshes and stands of white mangrove.

In spring, see the abundant wildflowers or visit in autumn when temperatures are cool and ideal for walking. Conditions can be cold and bleak but sometimes fresh and bracing in winter. In summer it is extremely crowded.

The 500km^2 national park has more than 150km of walking tracks. Permits are required for overnight hiking and a ballot system is used for the holiday cabins.

Visitor information

Wilsons Promontory National Park Office and Visitors Centre
Tidal River, Vic 3960
Ph: (03) 5680 9500 or 1800 350 552
www.parkweb.vic.gov.au

Norman Bay, Wilsons Promontory National Park

■ Leongatha   POP 4225

Map 212, D4

Situated near the foothills of the **Strzelecki Ranges**, Leongatha is a service centre for the surrounding rural district. Dairying is a major industry here and the Murray Goulburn Cooperative Dairy is the largest in Australia.

MAIN ATTRACTIONS: The **Historic Society Museum** contains some interesting displays worthwhile investigating. **Leongatha Gallery** displays local arts and crafts and hosts changing exhibitions.

NEARBY ATTRACTIONS: Leongatha is a good base for exploring **Wilsons Promontory** and the seaside and fishing villages along the coast. The **South Gippsland Railway** operates train rides from Leongatha or nearby **Korumburra** to **Loch** and **Nyora**. The **Firelight Museum** displays a collection of antique lamps and firearms, some more than 400 years old. The **Grand Ridge Brewing Company**, located at **Mirboo North**, 26km north-east, offers views of the beer-brewing process and sales. **Moss Vale Park** with its avenue of redwoods, is 16km north-east, and offers good picnic and BBQ facilities. The **soundshell**, also located in the park, is the venue for a performance by the State Orchestra of Victoria each February.

VISITOR INFORMATION: South Gippsland Hwy, Korumburra, Ph: (03) 5655 2233 or 1800 630 704

South Gippsland picnic, near Leongatha

Scale 1:200 000

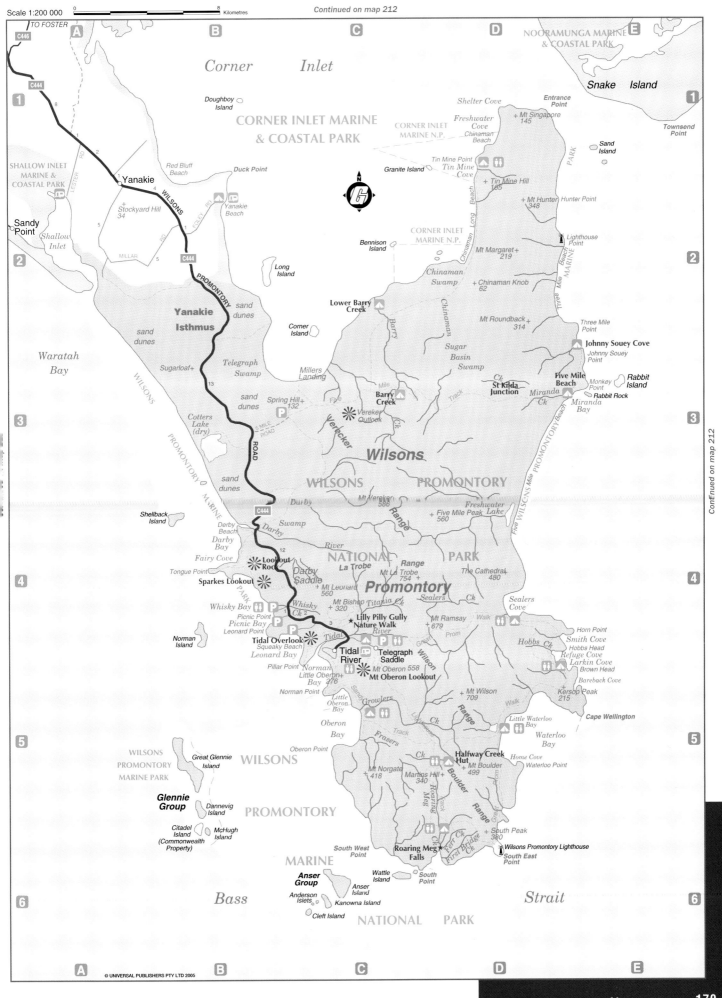

Continued on map 212

Lorne POP 1230

Map 201, H4

One of Victoria's most attractive coastal resorts, Lorne, 137km south-west of Melbourne, is located on the **Great Ocean Road** with the **Otway Ranges** as a backdrop. Despite the popularity of the town as a tourist destination, it has retained its charm and has many fine old buildings.

MAIN ATTRACTIONS: Swimming and surfing are the most popular activities here, as well as bush-walking in the Otway Ranges. **Teddys Lookout**, at the end of George St, offers panoramic views of the bay. There is a **Shipwreck Walk** along the beach for people interested in history and exercise. Fresh fish, caught by the local fleet, can be bought from **Lorne Fisheries** on the pier. For those more interested in the creative arts, visit **Qdos Arts** in Allenvale Rd.

NEARBY ATTRACTIONS: **Angahook-Lorne State Park**, west of the town, is a popular inland destination. There are many walking tracks and the park offers rivers, waterfalls, rapids, cliffs and an abundance of native flora. **Erskine Falls** is only 10km from Lorne by road. Scenic drives worthwhile taking include those to the Otway Ranges and along the

View over the Great Ocean Road from Teddys Lookout, Lorne

Great Ocean Road. At **Gentle Annie Berry Gardens**, 26km north-west, visitors are invited to pick-their-own berries in season (November–April).

VISITOR INFORMATION: 144 Mountjoy Pde, Ph: (03) 5289 1152

Maffra POP 4035

Map 177, A2

This town is located 228km east of Melbourne, and is surrounded by rich farming land. The 1890s saw the beginning of the sugar-beet industry in Maffra and the formation of the Maffra Sugar Beet Company. The company closed in 1946, and intensive dairying has since been the main industry on the irrigated land around Maffra.

MAIN ATTRACTIONS: The office building of the former sugar-beet factory has been moved to McMahon Dr, and is now the home of the **Maffra Sugar Beet Museum**, open Sunday afternoons. **Macalister Park** has excellent picnic facilities, BBQs and a playground. The **Pino Deriu Mineral and Gemstone Collection** is housed in the old Maffra Court House, built in 1888.

NEARBY ATTRACTIONS: **Macalister Research Farm** is a commercially run dairy farm used for testing and demonstrating improved farming practices. **Lake Glenmaggie**, 21km from Maffra, is popular for water-sports and there are many scenic drives in the area. Horse trail-riding tours of the surrounding country-side and 4-wheel drive tours into the High Country are available. The **Blue Pool** on **Freestone Creek**, 10km from **Briagolong**, has a natural swimming hole surrounded by bushland; camping is permitted.

VISITOR INFORMATION: 8 Foster St, Sale, Ph: (03) 5144 1108 or 1800 677 520

Maldon POP 1255

Map 159, D2

Established in 1853, this uniquely preserved gold town lies 16km north-west of **Castlemaine**, on the slopes of **Mount Tarrengower**. Maldon is 136km north-west of Melbourne and is a popular destination for daytrips. The town has managed to retain its 19th-century streetscapes. Preservation is so complete that in 1996, the National Trust declared it the **'First Notable Town in Australia'**.

MAIN ATTRACTIONS: Maldon is a particularly popular destination during the **Maldon Easter Fair** and **Maldon Folk Festival,** also in spring, when the wildflowers put on a magnificent display. Today, Maldon's buildings and the renovated shops sell craft, pottery and antiques. Lookouts on Mount Tarrengower and **Anzac Hill** offer panoramic views of the town and surrounding districts. Brochures on a self-guided **walking tour** of the town are available from the information centre. On Wednesdays, Sundays, public and school holidays, the **Victorian Goldfields Railway** operates steam train rides. In spring, the graves at the historic **Pioneer Cemetery** are covered with jonquils and various wildflowers.

NEARBY ATTRACTIONS: **Carman's Tunnel Goldmine**, 2km south-west, offers guided tours by candlelight on weekends and holidays. The reconstructed 1850s goldmining town, **Porcupine Township**, is located 3km north-east. **Cairn Curran Reservoir**, 10km south-west, provides picnic facilities and watersports and fishing are popular here.

VISITOR INFORMATION: 93 High St, Ph: (03) 5475 2569

Mallacoota POP 1035

Map 214, D4

A tranquil fishing and holiday town, Mallacoota is located at the mouth of **Mallacoota Inlet** in the far south-eastern corner of Victoria. The surrounding estuaries, bays, headlands and promontories are

Skiing at Mount Buller

especially scenic and many are protected by **Croajingolong NP**.
MAIN ATTRACTIONS: Swimming is popular along the foreshore reserve and there are several safe swimming areas. Good surfing spots are at **Bastion Point**, **Betka Beach** and **Tip Beach**.
NEARBY ATTRACTIONS: There are bush and beach walks within Croajingolong NP, which was declared a **World Biosphere Reserve** in 1977. This park has 100km of coastline, 320km of lake shoreline and many rivers and creeks to explore. There are many lake and river cruises available, as well as scenic drives and self-guided walks—brochures available from the Information Shed. Birdwatching is particularly popular along the walking track to **Genoa Peak** and at **Gipsy Point**. There are over 300 species to spot, including the glossy-black cockatoo and ground parrot. **Gabo Island Lightstation Reserve** is 11km east. It can be enjoyed as a daytrip by plane or boat, or visitors can arrange to stay in the Assistant Lightkeeper's residence on the island.
VISITOR INFORMATION: Information Shed, Main Wharf, Ph: (03) 5158 0800

Mansfield   POP 2675
Map 208, D5

The rural town of Mansfield lies in the foothills of the **Great Dividing Range**, 200km north-east of Melbourne. The area is renowned for its scenery. Summer visitors include bushwalkers, horseriders, anglers, watersports enthusiasts and those enjoying weekend getaways. Skiers descend on the area in winter. The region and some of its attractions have also been popular with film makers. The *Man from Snowy River*, *Cool Change* and *The Far Country* were all filmed here.
MAIN ATTRACTIONS: The town achieved notoriety when three policemen were ambushed at nearby **Stringybark Creek** and shot dead by the notorious Kelly gang in 1878. Their graves are in **Mansfield Cemetery** and a monument to their memory stands at the centre of the town's roundabout. Local tour operators offer various ways to see the countryside and mountain scenery, including horseriding safaris into the Victorian Alps, camel treks, 4-wheel drive tours and hot-air balloon flights.
NEARBY ATTRACTIONS: Mansfield is the gateway to skifields in **Mount Buller** and **Mount Stirling**. **Lake Eildon**, 15km south, is popular for fishing and all manner of watersports; houseboats are available for hire. The historic goldmining town of **Jamieson**, 37km south, is popular for gold fossicking and the **Jamieson River** is excellent for trout fishing. **Craig's Hut**, on Mount Stirling, is a replica of Jim Craig's hut in *The Man from Snowy River* movies. A half hour walk from the road gives access to the picnic area near the hut. However, there is no vehicle access in winter. **Powers Lookout** is 48km north-east.
VISITOR INFORMATION: Old Railway Station, Maroondah Hwy, Ph: (03) 5775 7000 or 1800 039 049

Maryborough   POP 7500
Map 159, C2

A former goldmining town, Maryborough is situated on the northern slopes of the **Great Dividing Range**, 160km north-west of Melbourne. Today, Maryborough is the centre of a farming district.
MAIN ATTRACTIONS: Legacies of gold boom times include many historic buildings, particularly the **McLandress Square** complex, which includes the Court House, Town Hall and Post Office. Maryborough's jewel in the crown is its famous **Railway Station**. An antique gallery and woodwork shop are located in the old station. Brochures on a self-guided **Historic Buildings Drive** are available from the information centre. **Worsley Cottage Complex and Museum**, located in Palmerston St, is open on Tuesdays, Thursdays and Sundays. The **Central Goldfields Art Gallery** is located in Neill St in Maryborough's old fire station.
NEARBY ATTRACTIONS: Brochures are available on scenic drives of the surrounding Goldfields area. **Honey's Bear Shed**, 4km west, has rare records, collectables and memorabilia, open weekends. The once vital **Aboriginal wells**, carved out of granite rock, hold 107 litres of water and can be seen 4km south of Maryborough.
VISITOR INFORMATION: Cnr Alma St and Nolan St, Ph: (03) 5460 4511 or 1800 356 511

Melton   POP 32 020
Map 212, A2

Melton is 35 minutes from Melbourne's city centre. Despite its size, easy access to the airport, ports, and national road and rail networks, it has maintained its country atmosphere. There are a number of top harness racing operators here and Melton is recognised as one of the nation's top thoroughbred breeding areas.

Hot-air balloon championships, Mildura

Main Attractions: **Warrensbrook Faire** is Melton's premier tourism precinct, featuring restaurants and wineries. **Melton Waves** leisure centre features Australia's first indoor wave pool, a rapid river, 25m pool, hydrotherapy pool and two outdoor pools. **Willows Historical Park and Homestead** is a museum of pioneer memorabilia in Reserve Rd. An ideal spot for picnics is **Hannah Watts Park**, beside **Toolern Creek**. Cycle paths and walking tracks follow the creek. A self-guided **heritage trail** passes the old town site, Melton Hotel, The Willows and Darlingsford. The walk takes about 1.5 hours to complete.
Nearby Attractions: Views across the town to the **You Yangs** and the **Macedon Ranges** are provided from **Mount Carberry Reserve** in Melton South.
Visitor Information: 323 High St, Ph: (03) 9746 7290

▨ Merbein   POP 1440
Map 204, D2
This area of citrus orchards, vine-yards and market gardens is located on the banks of the **Murray River**, 11km west of Mildura. Merbein was known as White Cliffs until 1909 when it was renamed.
Main Attractions: **Mildara Wines** is situated on the edge of the towering cliffs rising from the Murray River. The winery's reputation was initially built on its sherries and brandies, but has grown dramatically since being taken over by Fosters. The winery is open seven days a week for tastings and cellar door sales. Situated along the clifftop is the **Early Settlers Walk**, a short memorial walk in remembrance of the early settlers of the Merbein area. **Chaffey** and **Kenny parks** both have electric BBQs and children's playgrounds. Kenny Park is adjacent to a swimming pool open all week throughout the summer months.
Visitor Information: Alfred Deakin Centre, 180-190 Deakin Ave, Mildura, Ph: (03) 5018 8380 or 1300 550 858

▨ Mildura   POP 27 950
Map 204, D2
The **Murray River** city of Mildura is surrounded by irrigated land that produces grapes, citrus, olives, avocados and asparagus. Its river setting, sunny winters and plentiful accommodation make this city a popular holiday destination.
Main Attractions: Sandy beaches and swimming holes line the riverbanks. River cruises are available on the **PS Melbourne** Sundays to Thursdays and on the **PV Rothbury** Fridays and Saturdays. Every Thursday this boat offers a day cruise to **Trentham Winery**. Bookings can be made through the information centre. In 1915, a series of 13 locks, weirs and water storages were built along the river. **Lock 11** is in Mildura and visitors can see it in operation as vessels move from one level of water to another. A walkway links the lock to **Lock Island**, created when the canal was constructed and now an ideal spot for picnics. **Old Mildura Homestead** is located on a reserve on Cureton Ave, near the Murray River. There is a collection of pioneer-style buildings and a woolshed where displays illustrate the role of irrigation in the development of Mildura. **Rio Vista**, the original home of William Chaffey, the first mayor of Mildura, in Cureton Ave, is now a museum displaying colonial artefacts. The house is part of the **Mildura Arts Centre**, a complex with a theatre, museum and an art gallery with a collection of paintings and sculptures, surrounded by parkland. The **Alfred Deakin Centre** has interactive regional exhibits.
Nearby Attractions: The Sunraysia district can be explored on the 30km self-drive **Chaffey Heritage Trail** through Mildura and the surrounding areas. There are many wineries in the area, including the huge **Lindemans Karadoc Winery**, 20km south. **Woodsies Gem Shop**, 6km east at **Nichols Point**, has rock cutting and grinding displays daily. There is also a gift shop, garden maze and restaurant. **Murray-Sunset NP** and the smaller **Hattah-Kulkyne NP** lie south of Mildura. Birdlife is prolific in both parks, particularly in Hattah-Kulkyne when the Murray River floods the **Hattah Lakes** system, creating a bird haven and transforming the landscape with carpets of wildflowers.
Visitor Information: Alfred Deakin Centre, 180-190 Deakin Ave, Mildura, Ph: (03) 5018 8380 or 1300 550 858

Victoria

Moe POP 15 560

Map 212, E3

The gateway to the **Latrobe Valley** and alpine region, Moe, 134km south-east of Melbourne, is a major tourism centre in the region known as the **'Centre for Adventure'**.

MAIN ATTRACTIONS: Moe is home to **Gippsland Heritage Park**, a pioneer township with more than 35 buildings relocated from elsewhere in the Gippsland region. The park includes Bushy Park Homestead, the original home of Gippsland pioneer-explorer Angus McMillan; and an original Cobb & Co Coaching Inn from Pakenham East. Also part of the collection is a two-storey iron-frame house, prefabricated (1850s) in England and shipped to Australia; the packing box was then used in the construction of the interior of the house. There is also an excellent collection of horse-drawn vehicles from the 1850s to the 1900s. All buildings are furnished in period-style. **Edward Hunter Bush Reserve** is an area of natural bushland in the centre of Moe.

Holy Trinity Church of England, one of many relocated buildings at Gippsland Heritage Park, Moe

NEARBY ATTRACTIONS: **Lake Narracan**, 5km north, is popular for fishing and waterskiing. Moe is a good base for tours to the wonderful historic township of **Walhalla** with its narrow-gauge **Walhalla Goldfields Railway**. Also nearby is **Baw Baw Plateau** with its winter snowfields, and the **Thomson Dam**. There are easy or more difficult treks on offer in the Walhalla and **Mountain Rivers** district. Visitors can travel through **Willow Grove** to **Blue Rock Lake** for fishing and boating. A daytrip along Grand Ridge Rd, to the south, takes visitors through the lush, picturesque hills and rural scenery of Gippsland's **Strzelecki Ranges**.

VISITOR INFORMATION: 'The Old Church', Princes Hwy, Traralgon, Ph: 1800 621 409

Mornington POP 17 800

Map 153, F2

First settled in the 1840s, Mornington is now a growing residential area which retains its seaside village atmosphere. Its location makes it a good base for exploring the beautiful **Mornington Peninsula**.

MAIN ATTRACTIONS: Many historic buildings in town now house cafes and gift, book, antique and boating shops. **Mornington Peninsula Regional Art Gallery** houses a permanent collection of 1200 works and features many touring exhibitions. The collection includes works by Arthur Boyd, Brett Whiteley, Sidney Nolan and Russell Drysdale. The old **Post Office** on the corner of High St and the Esplanade, houses a local historical display. Unspoilt beaches around Mornington include **Mothers Beach**, where the town's fishing fleet, yacht club and boatshed are located, and **Fossil Beach**.

NEARBY ATTRACTIONS: There are many wineries on the Mornington Peninsula, including **Mount Eliza Estate**, **Morning Star Estate** and **Moorooduc Estate**. Many are open for tastings and cellar door sales. Festivals include the **Wine and Food Festival** in October and the **Winter Wine Weekend** in June. **Canadian Bay** beach, in nearby Mount Eliza, was made famous in the film *On the Beach*.

VISITOR INFORMATION: Point Nepean Rd, Dromana, Ph: (03) 5987 3078 or 1800 804 009

Morwell POP 13 830

Map 212, E3

A busy commercial centre in the heart of the famous coal-producing **Latrobe Valley**, Morwell is 150km south-east of Melbourne.

MAIN ATTRACTIONS: Tours of **Hazelwood**, **Yallourn** and **Loy Yang open-cut mines and power stations** can be organised at **PowerWorks Visitor Centre**. Visitors can inspect the operations, see the dredgers working the coalfaces and the coal being conveyed to the power stations, and see the inside of a power station. Group bookings of 20 or more people can request an evening tour that includes dinner. **Latrobe Regional Gallery** and **Morwell Centenary Rose Garden** are both located in Commercial Rd. The rose garden is renowned for being one of the most significant in rural Victoria.

NEARBY ATTRACTIONS: 5km south of Morwell is **Hazelwood Pondage**. Heated by the power station, the warm waters provide a year-round venue for watersports. **Morwell NP**, 12km south, offers walking trails through a high ridge of stringybark forest and through moist areas studded with tree ferns and cool gullies with clear mountain streams—this is one of the few remaining areas of remnant vege-tation in the **Strzelecki Ranges**.

VISITOR INFORMATION: 'The Old Church', Princes Hwy, Traralgon, Ph: 1800 621 409

Mount Beauty POP 1650

Map 187, C2

Situated at the foot of **Mount Bogong**, the highest peak in Victoria, Mount Beauty was built in the 1940s to house the workers on the Kiewa Hydro-Electric Scheme. Located 338km north-east of Melbourne, Mount Beauty is in one of Australia's best mountain-biking areas. It also attracts bushwalkers, especially in summer, and in winter it is a popular base for skiers.

MAIN ATTRACTIONS: The **Alpine Discovery Centre** has a 'walk through time' exhibition and historical information about the town. Close by is a large regulating pondage, created as part of the Hydro-Electric Scheme. It is now a popular recreation area for fishing and watersports. Visitors can borrow tape recorders and headsets from the information centre and listen to the history of the pondage, while they walk around it.

NEARBY ATTRACTIONS: In winter, Mount Beauty attracts skiers on their way to **Falls Creek**. Many ski hire businesses and affiliated enterprises service visitors and a coach service runs from the township to Falls Creek, allowing skiers to leave their cars below the slopes. The scenic road from Mount Beauty to Falls Creek and the **Bogong High Plains** is worthwhile exploring. The drive takes in **Clover Arboretum**, the village of **Bogong**, **Lake Guy** and Falls Creek. The Mount Beauty to **Bright** road passes **Sullivans Lookout**, offering panoramic views, before reaching **Tawonga Gap**, where there is a viewing platform looking over the **Kiewa Valley** and Mount Bogong.

VISITOR INFORMATION: Kiewa Valley Hwy, Ph: (03) 5754 1962 or 1800 033 079

Myrtleford POP 2715

Map 187, B2

Surrounded by the **Victorian Alps**, this town is located at the foot of **Mount Buffalo** and is the centre for a district that produces timber, hops, tobacco, grapes and many kinds of nuts. Myrtleford has some of the largest walnut groves in the Southern Hemisphere.

MAIN ATTRACTIONS: Interesting trees are a feature of Myrtleford. An ancient river red gum can be seen in Smith St. In **Lions Club Park**, in Myrtle St, Hans Knorr's sculptured **Phoenix Tree**, symbolising the cycle of life, is displayed. In Albert St, a 100-year-old linden tree from Germany stands beside an historic home. Attractive parks include **Cundy Park**, on O'Donnell Ave, ideal for picnics and BBQs; **Rotary Park**, on the highway at the junction of a number of streams that flow into Myrtleford; and **Jubilee Park**, offering walkways and gardens. Historic items from the district are displayed in the **Old School Museum**, on the corner of Elgin St and Albert St. It is open Thursday to Sunday.

NEARBY ATTRACTIONS: Myrtleford is a gateway to the great granite plateau of **Mount Buffalo NP**, a favourite destination for skiers in winter and walkers in summer. **Lake Buffalo**, 22km south, is ideal for boating, waterskiing, fishing and swimming.

VISITOR INFORMATION: Great Alpine Rd, Ph: (03) 5752 1044 or 1800 991 044

Nagambie POP 1410

Map 208, B4

Situated on the shores of **Lake Nagambie** in the **Goulburn Valley**, Nagambie is surrounded by land devoted to sheep, cattle, cereal, grapes and horses. The town hosts several annual, water-based events, including rowing, canoeing, speed boating and waterskiing on Lake Nagambie.

MAIN ATTRACTIONS: Constructed in 1887 through the establishment of **Goulburn Weir**, Lake Nagambie is a watery playground. **Nagambie**

Historical Museum, housed in the old Court House and shire hall, features period-furniture, horse-drawn vehicles and a collection of old coins. The **Nut House**, located at the visitor information centre, displays and sells different varieties of nuts grown in Australia. Nagambie offers regional skydiving, hot-air ballooning and gliding for the adventurous.

NEARBY ATTRACTIONS: There are many wineries within easy reach of Nagambie. Classified by the National Trust, **Tahbilk Winery**, located 6km south-west, is the oldest winery in Victoria and overlooks the **Goulburn River**. Points of interest at this charming winery include the unique architecture of the old buildings, an avenue of mulberry trees and old cellars. At **Mitchellstown**, 14km south-west, the award-winning **Mitchelton Winery** has a good restaurant, underground cellars, museum and art gallery. The information centre offers a self-drive tour map of local wineries. The Goulburn River is popular with trout and redfin anglers, and canoeists can hire boats here. **Goulburn River Cruises** offers daytrips on the *Major Mitchell* starting at Tahbilk Winery and finishing at Mitchelton Winery.

VISITOR INFORMATION: 145 High St, Ph: (03) 5794 2647 or 1800 444 647

Horseriding in the Goulburn Valley, in the Nagambie district

Nathalia   POP 1420

Map 208, B2

This small rural town located on the Murray Valley Hwy, 54km north-west of Shepparton, is surrounded by agricultural land that was settled in 1843. Wheat, barley and dairying are the main agricultural activities of the district.

MAIN ATTRACTIONS: Nathalia was settled on each side of **Broken Creek** in 1879. Blake St, the main street, was modelled on Sturt St, Ballarat. This attractive street has a central plantation leading down to Broken Creek where several old buildings can be seen, including the **Court House Hotel** and a row of 19th-century shop-fronts with verandahs. The **historical museum** displays memorabilia, old photographs, maps and books. It is housed in what was once the Mechanics Institute, built in 1887.

NEARBY ATTRACTIONS: The region's waterways—the **Goulburn** and **Murray rivers** and Broken Creek—provide good fishing and camping opportunities. **Barmah State Park**, the largest river red gum forest in Australia, is easily accessible and provides camping areas.

VISITOR INFORMATION: Nathalia Community Crafts (open weekends), Blake St, Ph: (03) 5866 3063

Nhill   POP 1990

Map 206, C3

Nhill, halfway between Melbourne and Adelaide, is a wheat and wool town in the **Wimmera** region. The town is surrounded by a number of national parks and wildlife areas and is within easy driving distance of **Lake Hindmarsh**, 45km north-east, and **Little Desert NP**.

MAIN ATTRACTIONS: The **Historical Museum**, located in McPherson St, is open only by appointment. A **Draught Horse Memorial** is located in Goldsworthy Park. Sculptured by Stanley Hammond, the memorial celebrates the Clydesdales that

hauled the agricultural machinery and wagons in the past. A single-bin **wheat silo**, claimed to be the largest in the Southern Hemisphere, is located in Davis Ave. There is a self-guided **historical walk** of the town and brochures are available from the information centre.

NEARBY ATTRACTIONS: A desert in name only, Little Desert NP, located 18km south, offers 600km of walking tracks. To avoid temperature extremes, the best time to visit the park is late winter to early summer—this is also the time when the wildflowers bloom. **Big Desert Wilderness Park** and **Wyperfeld NP**, to the north, are large wilderness areas with 4-wheel drive access.

VISITOR INFORMATION: Goldsworthy Park, Western Hwy, Ph: (03) 5391 3086

Numurkah   POP 3360

Map 208, C2

Numurkah is located 217km north of Melbourne, and a short distance from the attractions of the **Murray River**. The town serves irrigated farmlands supporting the dairy industry. A waterwheel, in the centre of a roundabout in Melville St, reminds passersby of the importance of irrigation to the region.

MAIN ATTRACTIONS: **Louis Hamon Rose Gardens** are located by **Broken Creek**, a tributary of the Murray River. The **historical museum** is housed in the old Bank of Victoria building, on the corner of Melville St and Knox St, and is open Sunday afternoons.

NEARBY ATTRACTIONS: **Monochino Wines**, located 11km north, offers tastings of award-winning red and white table wines, as well as dessert wines, port and muscat. **Strathmerton**, 26km north, is home to Australia's largest cactus farm, **Cactus Country**, open September to December during the flowering season. There are thousands of cacti growing in landscaped

gardens. **Ulupna Island Flora and Fauna Reserve**, near Strathmerton, has a large koala population; tours can be organised with **Red Gum Wildlife Tours**.

VISITOR INFORMATION: 99 Melville St, Ph: (03) 5862 3458

Ocean Grove   POP 9780

Map 201, K3

Situated at the mouth of the **Barwon River**, 96km south-west of Melbourne, this resort town is a popular fishing and surfing destination. On the other side of the Barwon River is **Barwon Heads**, another popular holiday spot offering safe swimming along the shores of the river. A bridge over the Barwon River links the two towns.

MAIN ATTRACTIONS: **Smiths Beach** is a fine surfing beach with a long stretch of sand, backed by a foreshore reserve. Located in town are facilities for fishing, yachting, waterskiing and scuba diving. The peninsula's last remaining stand of original bushland is protected in **Ocean Grove Nature Reserve**. Native flora and fauna can be seen

(CONTINUED P.187)

Point Lonsdale lighthouse, east of Ocean Grove

The Victorian Alps are the southern-most part of the **Great Dividing Range**. These dramatic yet rounded mountains are far less challenging for skiers than the extremely jagged peaks of their Northern Hemisphere counterparts, the European Alps.

Located south-east of **Wangaratta**, the Victorian Alps cover a vast and rugged terrain that is mostly protected by national parks. The various ski resorts of the High Country cater for different levels of skiers. **Mount Hotham, Falls Creek and Mount Buller** have ski runs for beginners, intermediate and advanced skiers, while **Mount Buffalo** caters for intermediate skiers and families. **Mount Baw Baw** is more suited to beginners. Around **Lake Mountain** there are some excellent cross-country runs.

The Victorian snow season usually starts in June and lasts until September, although in some years it has extended as late as November. Bushwalking, horse-riding, paragliding, hang-gliding and trout fishing are some of the many recreational activities that attract visitors during the warmer months. The **Great Alpine Road** offers a 307km mountain drive, commencing at Wangaratta.

White-water rafting, Victorian High Country

Visitor information

Bright Visitor Information Centre
119 Gavan St (Great Alpine Rd)
Bright, Vic 3741
Ph: (03) 5755 2275 or 1800 500 117

Wangaratta Visitor Information Centre
100-104 Murphy St,
Wangaratta, Vic 3677
Ph: (03) 5721 5711 or 1800 801 065

main attractions

⬆ Alpine National Park

This national park encompasses a large part of the Victorian Alps and is home to many of the region's ski resorts.

◈ Beechworth

Rich in history, this perfectly preserved Goldfields town is National Trust-classified.

◈ Bright

Bright is a picturesque town that began in the 1850s as a gold town. Today it is a centre for local timber, agriculture and tourism industries. It is especially popular in April during the Bright Autumn Festival.

◈ Falls Creek

Falls Creek has what are considered to be Victoria's best ski runs. Spectacular views of Falls Creek can be seen from Roper's Lookout. The walk to Mount Nelse traverses colourful slopes covered with Alpine wildflowers in summer.

◈ Mount Buffalo National Park

This stunning national park covers the huge plateau surrounding Mount Buffalo.

Horse riders, Howqua River, near Mansfield

Victoria

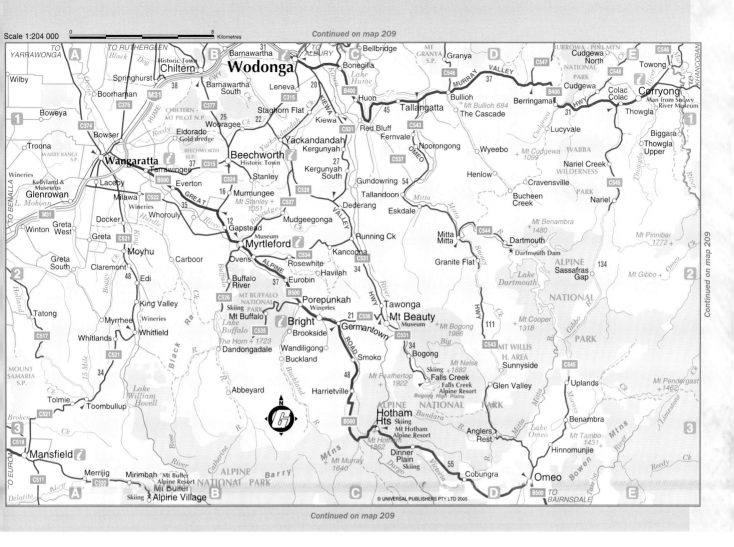

Continued on map 209

Scale 1:204 000

Continued on map 209

from two walking trails in the bushland reserve.

NEARBY ATTRACTIONS: **Jirrahlinga Koala and Wildlife Sanctuary** is in Taits Rd, Barwon Heads. **Wallington**, 8km north, is in the centre of the **Bellarine Peninsula**. **A Maze'N Things**, located here, features a giant wooden maze, mini golf, a puzzle centre, playground and BBQ areas. **Adventure Park**, also in Wallington, offers waterslides, pedal boats, aqua bikes, mountain bikes, golf, archery and go-karts.

VISITOR INFORMATION: 55 Hesse St, Queenscliff, Ph: (03) 5258 4843

■ Omeo POP 320

Map 187, D3

Located 401km north-east of Melbourne on the Great Alpine Rd, this mountain township is the southern gateway to the magnificent scenery of the **Victorian Alps**. Omeo is a cattle township and tourist centre servicing nearby **Alpine NP**. Omeo suffered earthquakes in 1885 and 1892, and was badly damaged in the 1939 Black Friday bushfires.

MAIN ATTRACTIONS: **Omeo Historical Park** is a precinct with a number of historic buildings, including the American Romanesque-style Court House (still in use), built in 1892 to dispense justice to what was reputed to be Australia's roughest goldfield. Positioned around the Court House are the log gaol, last used in the 1980s, stables, a blacksmith's shop, waterwheel and museum. For a magnificent collection of authentic cuckoo clocks, visit the **German Cuckoo**

Shop. An excellent view of Omeo is provided from **Mount Mesley**. Access is via a walking track leading up from **Livingston Creek** that runs through Omeo.

NEARBY ATTRACTIONS: The **Oriental Claims**, in the old goldfields to the west, offer interesting walks around **Ah Fong's Loop**. The district's streams are stocked with brown and rainbow trout, making angling a popular pastime. Omeo is an ideal base for bushwalkers attracted to the tracks in Alpine NP. White-water rafting is popular on the **Mitta Mitta River**. **McMillans Lookout**, on the road to **Benambra**, has 360° views of Omeo and the plains towards Benambra and the **Omeo Valley**.

VISITOR INFORMATION: German Cuckoo Clock Shop, Great Alpine Rd, Ph (03) 5159 1552

Orbost POP 2185

Map 177, E2

A farming and administrative town on the **Snowy River**, Orbost is 374km east of Melbourne and 14km from Marlow Inlet, where the river reaches the sea. Orbost is surrounded by stunning coastal and mountain scenery.

MAIN ATTRACTIONS: A **rainforest walk** can be accessed from **Forest Park**. Orbost's **Slab Hut** is a living museum. Originally built 40km away, it is now located in Forest Park. The hut's humble furnishings illustrate the spartan lifestyle of pioneers. More local memorabilia can be seen in the **historical museum** located in the Orbost Business Centre, Ruskin St. The museum is open on weekdays. **Netherbyre Gallery**, in Browning St, displays woodwork, local paintings and a gemstone collection.

NEARBY ATTRACTIONS: There are seven national parks within easy reach of Orbost. Walking tracks and forest drives explore scenic wilderness areas. **Raymond Creek Falls**, 42km north-west of Orbost, has a 40 minute return walk to the falls and a further one hour walk to the Snowy River. **Snowy River NP**, to the north, also offers a variety of walks. **Errinundra NP**, 54km north-east, has a rainforest boardwalk.

VISITOR INFORMATION: 152-156 Nicholson St, Ph: (03) 5154 2424

Ouyen POP 1255

Map 204, E5

This town, located 107km south of Mildura, began to grow in 1910, when the surrounding land was opened up for settlement and clearing for wheat, oats and sheep. Queues of trucks waiting to unload their grain at the silos are common here at harvest time.

MAIN ATTRACTIONS: Ouyen's pioneers cleared many thousands of stumps in their efforts to create farming land from the mallee scrub, which covers the region. A memorial to their labour is the largest mallee stump in Australia, beside the Calder Hwy on the southern side of town. The **Local History Resource Centre** is located in the old Court House in Oke St and comprises a significant collection of books, photographs, documents, maps, newspapers and cassettes.

NEARBY ATTRACTIONS: **Hattah-Kulkyne NP**, located 36km north, offers an extensive system of lakes and waterways that provide refuge for thousands of birds. Bushwalking and canoeing are popular activities here and the wildflower display is stunning in spring. **Murray-Sunset NP**, 60km west, contains unique **Pink Lakes**—under bright sunlight these shallow salt lakes glitter white, while overcast conditions produce a dull pink hue. Vegetation in this park includes native pine and mallee scrub. Birdlife is abundant and birdwatchers can spot emus, red-rumped parrots, mulga parrots and pink cockatoos.

VISITOR INFORMATION: 16 Oke St, Ph: (03) 5092 1000

Paynesville POP 2870

Map 177, C2

At the centre of the **Gippsland Lakes** system, surrounded by the waters of **Lake King** and **Lake Victoria**, Paynesville is the recreational boating capital of the lakes.

MAIN ATTRACTIONS: Local operators offer boats for hire or charters to explore the surrounding waterways, lagoons and islands. The **Church of St Peter-by-the-Lake** is located in Newlands Dr. Built in 1961, it has a seafaring theme, with a limestone brick spire designed to look like a lighthouse and a pulpit resembling the bow of a fishing boat. Lake Victoria can be seen through tall windows behind the church's altar.

NEARBY ATTRACTIONS: **Raymond Island**, on the other side of McMillan Strait, can be reached by car ferry from Paynesville. Popular with bush-walkers, the island is inhabited by native birds and animals, including koalas in their natural habitat. Those with a boat can access **Rotamah Island**, to the south, as well as **The Lakes NP** on **Sperm Whale Head**. The **Mitchell River Silt Jetties** are situated at Eagle Point. They stretch for about 8km towards the north-east shores of Lake King in the Gippsland Lakes. The silt jetties are second in size only to those on the Mississippi River in the Gulf of Mexico. They were formed by the deposition of large quantities of silt brought down the Mitchell River in floods over the last million years.

VISITOR INFORMATION: 240 Main St, Bairnsdale, Ph: (03) 5152 3444 or 1800 637 060

Junction of the Snowy River and Buchan River, north-west of Orbost

Petrified Forest, Cape Bridgewater, south-west of Portland

Port Fairy   POP 2630
Map 200, A4

This former whaling port is located at the estuary of the **Moyne River**. Port Fairy is a holiday resort bordered by both river and ocean and is home to a large fishing fleet. It is well-known for rock lobster, squid and abalone fishing. The town is also widely known for the **Port Fairy Folk Festival**.

MAIN ATTRACTIONS: One of Victoria's oldest towns, there are around 70 small stone cottages and bluestone buildings that are National Trust-classified. An **historic walk** leaflet is available from the information centre. There is a **history centre** in the old Court House, Gipps St. The old fort and signal station, **Battery Hill**, is located at the mouth of the Moyne River.

NEARBY ATTRACTIONS: Brochures are available on the **Mahogany Walk** to Warrnambool: a six to seven hour one-way walk with walkers able to return to Port Fairy by bus. A causeway links Port Fairy with **Griffiths Island**. Here, visitors can explore an area around the

lighthouse where there are muttonbird rookeries. **Mount Eccles NP** is 56km north-west. **Tower Hill State Game Reserve**, 14km east, is worthwhile exploring. There is an extinct volcano and crater lake with islands. A **Natural History Centre** and aboriginal cultural centre is within the reserve.

VISITOR INFORMATION: Bank St, Ph: (03) 5568 2682

Portland   POP 11 400
Map 210, C4

Located 366km west of Melbourne and 76km from the South Australian border, Portland is the only deepwater port between Melbourne and Adelaide. During the first half of the 19th century, Portland was a base for sealers and whalers. The modern fleet concentrates on fish, squid, crayfish and abalone. The major industry is a huge aluminium smelter, which is also open for tours (check times).

MAIN ATTRACTIONS: As Victoria's first permanent settlement (1834), Portland has many interesting old buildings, some of them still used for their original purpose. Most of them are included on a self-guided **historical walk**. The local **museum** is located in the old Town Hall. Nearby is the still-used bluestone Customs House, built in 1849. The information centre is located at **Portland Maritime Discovery Centre**. Displays include a 13m sperm whale skeleton and visitors can sit inside its rib cage. **Fawthrop Lagoon** is a unique wetland area within the city boundary. There are approximately 5km of walking tracks throughout the reserve. **Portland Botanic Gardens** (completed in 1857) feature stunning rose and dahlia gardens and a charming bluestone curator's cottage.

NEARBY ATTRACTIONS: **Cape Nelson State Park**, 11km south, features a National Trust-classified lighthouse. **Cape Bridgewater**, 21km south-

west, has blowholes and freshwater springs; a walking track leads to the **Petrified Forest**, the remains of a forest that was covered by a sand dune thousands of years ago. Nearby, the cape's colony of fur seals can be seen from a viewing platform or by taking a boat trip. The 250km **Great South West Walk** begins and ends in Portland. This loop walk can be undertaken in easy stages; it takes in a variety of landscapes and seascapes in a number of state, coastal and national parks through to **Discovery Bay** and **Cape Nelson**.

VISITOR INFORMATION: Maritime Discovery Centre, Lee Breakwater Rd, Ph: (03) 5523 2671 or 1800 035 567

Queenscliff   POP 3840
Map 152, A3

Surveyed in 1853, this seaside town has a noticeable 19th-century atmosphere generated by its old hotels, fishermen's cottages and public buildings. Queenscliff is located 107km south of Melbourne and 32km south-east of Geelong on the **Bellarine Peninsula**.

MAIN ATTRACTIONS: The **Historical Centre**, in Hesse St, displays items relating to Queenscliff's marine, military and tourist heydays. The **Maritime Museum** houses the last of the area's original lifeboats. The **Marine Discovery Centre** has living displays of marine life. Located on the Bellarine Hwy, west of Queenscliff, it is open during school holidays (at other times by arrangement). **Fort Queenscliff** is Australia's largest and best pre-served fortress; building began in the 1860s to protect investments from the threat—real or imagined—of foreign invasion. The most historic sections of the fort—the guardroom, cells, original lightkeeper's signal station, underground magazines and a military museum—are open for inspection. There are tours on

Vineyard at Lindemans Karadoc, to the east of Red Cliffs

weekends, public and school holidays (for weekday tours check at the information centre). Details of fishing charters, seal and dolphin-watching tours, and 'swimming with the dolphins and seals' can also be obtained at Queenscliff's information centre.

NEARBY ATTRACTIONS: The **Bellarine Peninsula Railway** originally linked Queenscliff and **Geelong**. Today the Geelong Steam Preservation Society displays its collection of vintage carriages and steam locomotives at the old station. The society also runs tourist trains along the 16km line to **Drysdale** on Sundays. Additional trips are run during school holidays. Queenscliff is linked to **Sorrento**, on the **Mornington Peninsula**, by vehicular and passenger ferries. The seaside holiday resort of **Point Lonsdale** is 6km south-west. Attractions here include **Point Lonsdale Lighthouse**, the **Rip View Lookout** and historic **Buckley's Cave** beneath the lighthouse.

VISITOR INFORMATION: 55 Hesse St, Ph: (03) 5258 4843

Red Cliffs   POP 2690
Map 204, D3

Located 559km north-west of Melbourne and 15km south of Mildura, Red Cliffs was first considered for fruit growing in the 1880s. After WWI, the government assisted soldier settlers to clear large tracts of land for irrigated agriculture: the biggest venture of its kind ever undertaken in Australia. A 45 tonne steam tractor, **Big Lizzie**, was built in Melbourne and was originally destined for Broken Hill. Instead, it cleared the mallee vegetation around Red Cliffs between 1917 and 1924.

MAIN ATTRACTIONS: Big Lizzie never made it to Broken Hill. The resting place of this huge piece of machinery is Barclay Square, opposite the Railway Station.

NEARBY ATTRACTIONS: **Cliff View Lookout**, 6km to the east, offers views of the 70m-high red cliffs from which the town gets its name. The Southern Hemisphere's largest winery, **Lindemans Karadoc**, is located 13km east. It is open for tastings and cellar door sales. There are also picnic and BBQ facilities. More wineries are located in the **Mildura region** to the north. On the tourist route drive, visitors will see **Carringbush Glass Gallery**, **Homwood Estate**, with its native wildflower farm, and artist **Alma Peterson's Gallery**.

VISITOR INFORMATION: Alfred Deakin Centre, 180-190 Deakin Ave, Mildura, Ph: (03) 5018 8380 or 1300 550 858

Robinvale   POP 2085
Map 205, F3

This small town is located 473km north-west of Melbourne and 83km south-east of Mildura. Robinvale is sited within a loop of the **Murray River** and is almost encircled by it. Fishing is popular by the river. The town's economy is based mainly on the production of wine grapes and dried fruits. The largest olive orchard and almond farms in Australia are also located here.

MAIN ATTRACTIONS: Most of the grapes used in making McWilliams cream sherry are grown locally and processed at **McWilliams Winery** in town. An original log cabin has become a tasting room, which is open weekdays. The information centre displays and sells locally made arts, crafts and produce. The **Machinery Museum** features steam engines and other farm machinery housed in a large split-log shed. It is open on Saturdays.

NEARBY ATTRACTIONS: **Robinvale Organic Wines**, located 5km east, has a variety of alcoholic and non-alcoholic wines, juices and fortified wines to taste and buy. The winery is open daily. **Robinvale-Euston Weir**, is 2km south of town. The **Lock 15 gardens** nearby are a good spot for a picnic. **Robinvale Estate Olive Grove**, near the Murray Valley Hwy to the south-east, is open daily. Daytrips can be made from Robinvale to **Hattah-Kulkyne NP**, where visitors can see the unique **Hattah Lakes** system with its prolific birdlife; the park has over 200 bird species.

VISITOR INFORMATION: Bromley Rd, Ph: (03) 5026 1388

Rochester   POP 2625
Map 207, K3

Located 180km north of Melbourne and 29km south of Echuca, Rochester is situated on the **Campaspe River**. The town is a service centre for surrounding dairy and small-crop farms. Rochester has the largest dairy factory in Australia.

MAIN ATTRACTIONS: There are many lakes and waterways in the region, making the town popular with fishing and watersports enthusiasts. Rochester was the birthplace of the renowned cyclist **Sir Hubert Opperman**, who achieved fame in the 1920s in the world of international cycling before becoming

a politician. A statue opposite the Railway Station commemorates his achievements and a museum of memorabilia donated by Sir Hubert is located in the Railway Station and opens by request. **Random House**, located on Bridge Rd, is a stately 19th-century home beside the Campaspe River. It was originally built as a station homestead but now offers accommodation, lunches and Devonshire teas. Tours of the house and 4ha gardens, which extend down to the river, are available. NEARBY ATTRACTIONS: The surrounding waterways yield redfin and carp. **Greens Lake** and **Lake Cooper**, located 14km south-east, are popular with anglers and swimmers.
VISITOR INFORMATION: Railway Station, Moore St, Ph: (03) 5484 2571

Rutherglen POP 1915
Map 208, E2
Located 265km north-east of Melbourne, Rutherglen is one of Victoria's leading wine producers. The first vines were planted in 1859 and Hamilton's Clydeside Cellars was established after the discovery of gold in 1861. Seppelts bought the property from the Hamiltons in 1916 and established Seppelts Clydeside Winery.
MAIN ATTRACTIONS: Rutherglen's main street has retained its historic streetscape with most buildings dating back to the late 1880s and early 1900s. The **Victoria Hotel**, **Post Office** and old **Court House** are classified historic buildings. The local **history museum** is located in the town's first government school, known as the **Common School** (1872), which is in the grounds of the local primary school. The museum is open on Sundays, October to June. Australia's largest wine festival, **Rutherglen Winery Walkabout** is held on the Queens Birthday long weekend in June.
NEARBY ATTRACTIONS: Rutherglen is known for its full-bodied red wines,

delicate whites, sherry, port and muscat. The region has more than 20 wineries, most within easy reach. Maps are available from the information centre. Cycling tours of the wineries are popular and bicycles can be hired from the information centre. The **Rutherglen Wine Show** is held in late September.
VISITOR INFORMATION: 57 Main St, Ph: (02) 6033 6300 or 1800 622 871

St Arnaud POP 2650
Map 207, G4
St Arnaud, 255km north-west of Melbourne, is an old goldmining town between Donald and Avoca. The National Trust has classified many of the town's historic buildings. Modern facilities have been introduced, fortunately without detracting from the old-world character and charm of the town.
MAIN ATTRACTIONS: The town's **Historic Precinct** includes the Court House, police lock-up, Crown Lands Office and the old Post Office. Napier St is a classified conservation area con-

taining elegant red-brick buildings, evidence of wealth created in the goldmining period. The **historical museum** opens by appointment and is located in the house of the town's former water overseer. **Josephine Coppers Gallery** displays fine arts and is housed in the Old Post Office in Napier St. Sporting facilities in **Lord Nelson Park** are located on the site of the famous **Lord Nelson Mine**. **Wilsons Hill Lookout** provides good district views of forests and hills; under Wilsons Hill are deep mine shafts running north and south.
NEARBY ATTRACTIONS: **Kara Kara Vineyard** is located 10km south and is open for tastings and cellar door sales. **Berrys Bridge Vineyard**, 11km south-east, is open weekends or by appointment. The **Avoca River**, 28km south-east, offers good fishing. Maps for a self-guided **scenic drive** of the surrounding region, including **St Arnaud Range NP**, are available from the information centre.
VISITOR INFORMATION: 4 Napier St, Ph: (03) 5495 1268 or 1800 014 455

Gardens at All Saints Estate Winery, Wahgunyah, near Rutherglen

St Leonards POP 1345

Map 152, A1

A coastal town on the **Bellarine Peninsula**, 110km south-west of Melbourne, St Leonards has long been a popular holiday destination for people from Melbourne. The town is twinned with **Indented Head**, another small holiday destination just 4km north.

MAIN ATTRACTIONS: St Leonards has many sheltered beaches ideal for swimming, boating and other watersports. **Harvey Park Foreshore** is a popular family recreation area overlooking **Port Phillip**.

NEARBY ATTRACTIONS: **Batman Park**, located at Indented Head, offers a picnic and BBQ area and a boat ramp. A stone cairn marks the place where John Batman's expedition landed in May 1835, before moving on to discover the site of Melbourne. Another memorial marks Matthew Flinders' landing in 1802. In the same area is the wreck of the paddlesteamer *Ozone* (1925). **Edwards Point State Fauna Reserve** is on a peninsula to the south. **Duck Island State Fauna Reserve** is a waterbird habitat and one of the few remaining homes for the rare orange-bellied parrot.

VISITOR INFORMATION: 55 Hesse St, Queenscliff, Ph: (03) 5258 4843

Sale POP 13 370

Map 177, A3

Sale originally developed as a result of its strategic location on the route to major gold diggings. It is located 209km south-east of Melbourne in the heart of **Gippsland**. The city is a gateway to an area of rich natural attractions, including the **High Country** and the **Gippsland Lakes**.

MAIN ATTRACTIONS: **Gippsland Regional Art Gallery** and **Sale Museum** are on the Princes Hwy. Of historic interest is **Bon Accord homestead**, built in the 1860s. Notable buildings include **St Pauls Cathedral and Rectory** (1885),

Bishops Court (1903) and the convent of **Notre Dame de Sion** (1892). The historic **Port of Sale** is currently undergoing extensive re-development. The **Botanic Gardens** are located on the shores of **Lake Guthridge**, which is connected by walkways to **Lake Guyatt**. In the same area is the **Ramahyuck Aboriginal Corporation**, selling local arts and crafts.

NEARBY ATTRACTIONS: **Sale Common State Game Refuge** is a protected wetland of mainly freshwater marsh. A 450m-long boardwalk provides views of permanent and migratory bird species' habitats. The **Bataluk Cultural Trail**, which begins at the Sale wetlands, contains 12 sites of significance to the Gippsland Aboriginal people. **Holey Plains State Park**, 14km south-west, has 530 species of native flora and fossils can be seen in a limestone quarry wall. Popular rivers for fishing include the **Avon**, **Thomson** and **La Trobe**.

VISITOR INFORMATION:
8 Foster St,
Ph: (03) 5144 1108

Seymour POP 6440

Map 208, B5

A **Goulburn River** town, Seymour is located 89km north of Melbourne. The town services a prosperous rural community and a huge military base 10km west at **Puckapunyal**.

MAIN ATTRACTIONS: There is a 4km scenic **walking trail** along the Goulburn River. The **Royal Hotel**, in Emily St, has been immortalised in Russell Drysdale's painting, *Moody's Pub*. The old **Log Gaol**, originally built in 1858 and re-erected behind the old Court House in Emily St, is one of the town's prominent historic buildings. **Seymour Railway Heritage Centre**, Railway Pl, displays restored steam engines and carriages; steam train tours are occasionally organised.

The sacred kingfisher, *Halcyon sancta*, may be seen at Sale Common State Game Refuge

The centre is open Tuesdays, Thursdays and weekends.

NEARBY ATTRACTIONS: Seymour is surrounded by fertile riverland supporting vineyards, including **Somerset Crossing Vineyard**, 2km north and **Hankin Estate**, 10km north. They are open for tastings and cellar door sales. At Puckapunyal the **Royal Australian Armoured Corps Tank Museum** displays one of the largest collections of tanks in the world. **Avenel Maze**, with a Ned Kelly theme, is a short drive to the north-east. At **Trawool**, 4-wheel drive tours into National Trust-classified **Tallarook State Forest** are available.

VISITOR INFORMATION: Old Court House, Emily St, Ph: (03) 5799 0233

Shepparton POP 35 800

Map 208, C3

Considered the capital of the **Goulburn Valley**, Shepparton is a thriving regional city, 180km north of Melbourne. Irrigated by the Goulburn Irrigation Scheme, Shepparton is known as the **'Food Business Hub of Australia'**.

MAIN ATTRACTIONS: **Campbells Soups** has a thriving sales outlet, open daily except Sundays. **Shepparton Art Gallery**, in Welsford St, has an

Victoria

outstanding ceramics reputation, housing 3000 works from the 19th century to the present day. In addition, it has works by notable artists, including Streeton, McCubbin and Perceval. The region's history is preserved in **Shepparton Historical Society Museum**, housed in Shepparton's first public hall. At **Victoria Park Lake**, the grassy banks invite visitors to picnic or enjoy a leisurely stroll along the foreshore. The **Shepparton Festival**, held in March, is a major event.

NEARBY ATTRACTIONS: The **Irrigation and Wartime Camps Museum** in **Tatura**, 13km south-west, houses one of the best collections of memorabilia from the prisoner-of-war camps that were once located in the area. The annual **Taste of Tatura**, a food and wine festival, is held in March. **Ardmona KidsTown** is popular with families, offering giant slides, a flying fox, miniature railway and much more; it is located between Shepparton and **Mooroopna**. In Mooroopna, **SPC Ardmona Factory Sales Outlet** is open daily, with a huge variety of canned products.

VISITOR INFORMATION: 534 Wyndham St, Ph: (03) 5831 4400 or 1800 808 839

Sorrento POP 1395

Map 152, B4

This town, located on a strip of land at the southern end of the **Mornington Peninsula**, has been a popular holiday destination since the 1890s. In those days, people came to Sorrento via paddlesteamer and steam tram. Sorrento has much to offer: surf and bayside beaches are easily accessible and there are upmarket shops and eateries along the main street.

MAIN ATTRACTIONS: Many of the shops are housed in historic limestone buildings. The peninsula's highest point, **Arthurs Seat**, can be seen from town. The Sorrento area was

the site of Victoria's first European settlement in 1803 (abandoned in 1804). **Collins Settlement Historic Site** on **Sullivan Bay** marks the place and there are four early settlers' graves located here. There are several self-guided walks around Sorrento, passing many fine examples of Victorian architecture. **Queenscliff–Sorrento Car and Passenger Ferry** departs from **Sorrento Pier**, on the front beach. Many other charter tours, including dolphin watching and seal watching also leave from here. **Sorrento Museum**, one of Victoria's top museums, displays memorabilia from pioneering days.

NEARBY ATTRACTIONS: Cruises to nearby **Pope's Eye Marine Reserve** are available. Here, there is a gannet rookery and snorkelling and diving opportunities. The seaside township of **Portsea** is 4km north-west. Swimming and fishing from the pier are popular here. **Mornington Peninsula NP** protects much of the dramatic and diverse coastal environment. Tours of the former **Quarantine Station** on **Point Nepean**, established in 1852 to protect the colony from diseases brought in on ships, are available on Sundays and public holidays. **Fort Nepean** has an extensive system of fortifications worthwhile touring.

VISITOR INFORMATION: Point Nepean Rd, Dromana, Ph: (03) 5987 3078 or 1800 804 009

Stawell POP 6275

Map 195, E2

A town with a rich history of gold-mining, Stawell is 129km north-west of Ballarat and still has Victoria's richest gold-producing mine. It is an ideal base for exploring the **Grampians region**, including the western vineyards. Stawell is renowned for the annual **Stawell Gift**, held at Easter, the richest professional footrace held in Australia.

MAIN ATTRACTIONS: The **Golden Trail Through Time** is a walking or driving cultural heritage trail that starts at the information centre. From the Pioneers Memorial on **Big Hill Lookout**, there are fine views over Stawell to the Grampians in one direction, and the wide flat **Wimmera** plain and the **Pyrenees** in the other. Other attractions include **Stawell Gift Hall of Fame Museum**, adjacent to Central Park and **Fraser Park**, which displays mining equipment.

NEARBY ATTRACTIONS: **Stawell Ironbark Forest** showcases spring wildflowers and rare orchids. The **Sisters Rocks**, 3km south-east, are huge granite boulders named after the Levi sisters whose mining family set up camp here. A rock shelter in the **Black Ranges**, 11km south, known as **Bunjil's Shelter**, is the most important Aboriginal art shelter in Victoria. A painting in the shelter depicts Bunjil, the All-Father and wise good spirit, and two dingos. There is also a good view of the Grampians from here. **Lake Bellfield**, 30km south-west, is popular for canoeing, kayaking and fishing.

VISITOR INFORMATION: 50-52 Western Hwy, Ph: (03) 5358 2314 or 1800 330 080

Surfers at Sorrento

This landscape of stark ridges and strangely shaped rocky outcrops rises spectacularly from western Victoria's plains and farmland. Known to Aboriginal people as Gariwerd, the area is renowned for its rock art and heritage. It has the largest proportion of rock-art sites in south-east Australia. Archaeologists have carbon-dated campfire charcoal in some rock shelters to approximately 22 000 years ago, although the earliest rock art suggests Aboriginal activity in the area may stretch back even further. For more information and tours, see the **Brambuk Cultural Centre** in Halls Gap.

The landscape is punctuated by four main ranges—**Mount Difficult Range** to the north, and the parallel ridges of **Victoria Range**, **Serra Range** and **Mount William Range** in the south. Protected by one of Victoria's largest national parks, the Grampians cover 1672km^2 of stunning scenery, including wildflowers, panoramic mountain views and intricate ecosystems.

Almost one-third of Victoria's indigenous flora, 35 species of native mammals, 200 bird species and 27 reptile species reside in this unique habitat. Activities include rockclimbing, abseiling, bushwalking and camping out in the rugged bushland.

Aboriginal Art Sites

Grampians National Park is an important area for the history of Aboriginal rock art. Rock paintings are believed to serve many functions, such as recording days or visits, retelling stories, communicating laws and teaching spiritual principles.

i Visitor information

Brambuk the National Park and Cultural Centre
Grampians Tourist Rd
Halls Gap, Vic 3381
Grampians NP, Ph: (03) 5356 4381
Brambuk Cultural Centre, Ph: (03) 5356 4452
www.parkweb.vic.gov.au

Halls Gap and Grampians Visitor Information Centre
Centenary Hall, Grampians Tourist Rd
Halls Gap, Vic 3381
Ph: (03) 5356 4616 or 1800 065 599

Lake Bellfield, Grampians National Park

main attractions

⌂ Aboriginal Art Tours

Run by the Brambuk Cultural Centre, these tours incorporate excursions to the region's main art shelters.

◈ Dunkeld

This town is a convenient southern departure point for touring the Grampians.

◈ Halls Gap Wildlife Park and Zoo

See a diverse range of animals, including monkeys, red deer and kangaroos. This 8ha park also has BBQs and a playground.

◈ MacKenzie Falls

This spectacular waterfall is a worthwhile destination during a visit to the Grampians.

◈ Mount William

A steep walk will bring you to the highest point of the Grampians for breathtaking 360° views of the ranges and open plains.

◈ The Balconies Lookout

An easy walk leaves from Reeds Lookout car park to spectacular rock formations and views across Grampians NP.

The Balconies Lookout, Grampians National Park

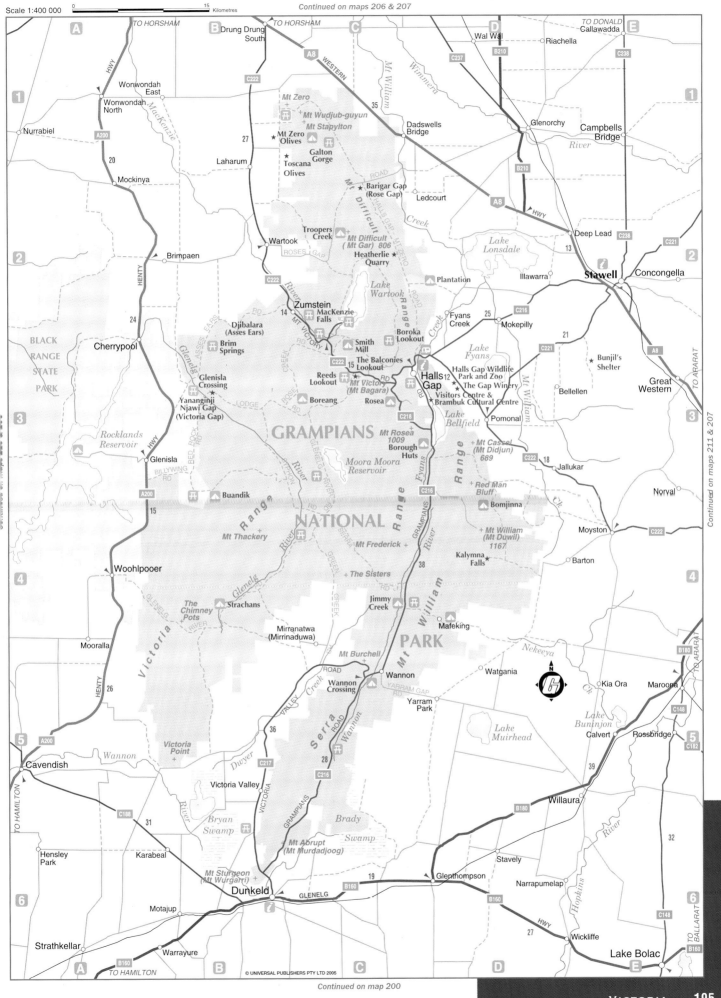

Scale 1:400 000

Continued on maps 211 & 207

© UNIVERSAL PUBLISHERS PTY LTD 2005

Swan Hill   POP 9750

Map 205, H5

Situated on the banks of the **Murray River** in the north of the state, Swan Hill is renowned for its pleasant climate. This major holiday destination is 335km north-west of Melbourne.

MAIN ATTRACTIONS: The river and surrounding waterways are popular for fishing and boating. Swan Hill's renowned **Pioneer Settlement** is an open-air living history museum. Set out as a Mallee township of the Riverland pioneers from the 1830s to the 1930s, its re-created streets include a replica 1860 coach house, post office, 1854 iron house, newspaper office and printery. It is also where traditional skills, such as printing, blacksmithing and woodturning are still practised. There are daily cruises offered on the paddleboat **PS Pyap**. **Swan Hill Regional Art Gallery** is close by.

NEARBY ATTRACTIONS: Historic **Tyntyndyer Homestead**, 17km north-west, is Australia's oldest brick-veneer home (1846) and is surrounded by colonial gardens. Furnished as a typical squatter's residence, it features Aboriginal artefacts found on the property. The homestead is open during public and school holidays or by appointment. There are six golf courses in the region, including the excellent **Murray Downs Golf Course**. Local wineries include **R.L. Buller**, **Andrew Peace** and **Best's St Andrews** at **Lake Boga**. A unique **Flying Boat Museum** is open daily near the lake. Luncheon cruises are available on the MV **Kookaburra** at **Murray Downs**.

VISITOR INFORMATION: 306 Campbell St. Ph: (03) 5032 3033 or 1800 625 373

100 year-old PS Pyap on the Murray River, Swan Hill

Terang   POP 1870

Map 200, D3

This **Western District** town, located 216km south-west of Melbourne, is a service centre for a farming district. Terang is noted for its horseracing facilities, early 20th-century architecture and wide tree-lined streets.

MAIN ATTRACTIONS: The National Trust has classified much of Terang, particularly the broad, oak-lined High St with its Gothic-style bluestone Presbyterian Church. The **District Historical Museum** houses some interesting memorabilia. The **Lions Walking Track** is 4.8km long and passes alongside dry **Lake Terang**.

NEARBY ATTRACTIONS: **Noorat**, 6km north of Terang, is the birthplace of Alan Marshall, author of the Australian classic novel, *I Can Jump Puddles*. The **Alan Marshall Walking Track** leads to the summit of an extinct volcano with excellent views extending to the **Grampians**. **Lake Keilambete**, 4km north-west, is said to have therapeutic properties, as it is 2.5 times saltier than the sea. Also worth visiting is the **Ralph Illidge Wildlife Sanctuary**, 17km south.

VISITOR INFORMATION: Court House, 22 High St, Ph: (03) 5592 1984

Torquay   POP 7950

Map 201, J4

This fast-growing, busy resort, 96km south-west of Melbourne, is renowned as the **'Surf Capital of Australia'**. **Jan Juc** and world-famous **Bells Beach** are the main surf beaches.

MAIN ATTRACTIONS: **Lions Park** has a children's playground, rotunda, picnic and BBQ areas. Natural parkland with walking tracks and a series of water features can be found in **Taylors Park**, also on the Esplanade. The aquatic **Sundial of Human Achievement** is on Fishermans Beach. Australia's only surfing museum, **Surfworld**, is located in **Surf City Plaza**. The interactive museum is dedicated to surfing and incorporates a Hall of Fame, memorabilia, photographs, historic boards, novel displays and working models.

NEARBY ATTRACTIONS: Torquay's location at the start of the **Great Ocean Road** makes it an ideal base from which to explore the spectacular coastline and hinterland. This stretch of coastline is recognised as having the best waves in Australia. Bells Beach is the venue for the international surf carnival **Rip Curl Pro Surfing Classic**, held each Easter. Jan Juc beach has a reputation for being a little wilder than Torquay. It is also the start of the 30km **Surf Coast Walk** to **Angahook-Lorne State Park**. This takes in the beach, clifftop tracks and coastal bushland. Tiger Moth joyflights are available at **Tiger Moth World** to the north-east.

VISITOR INFORMATION: Surfworld Museum, Beach Rd, Ph: (03) 5261 4219

Traralgon   POP 19 580

Map 212, E3

Once a supply depot for the goldfields to the north, Traralgon, 163km south-east of Melbourne, is now a principal regional centre for the **Latrobe Valley**.

MAIN ATTRACTIONS: National Trust-classified buildings in the town include the **Post Office** and **Court House**, both dating from 1887, and **Ryan's Hotel** with its iron lacework balconies. You can see artists from the **Traralgon and District Art Society** at work in the old railway building in Queens Rd.

NEARBY ATTRACTIONS: There are many **walking tours** and heritage drives in the district. The information centre has details. The **Festival of the Roses** is held in November at **Toongabbie**, a small town 19km north-east of Traralgon. Tours of the **Loy Yang** power station—one of the area's major employers—are available through **PowerWorks Visitor Centre** at Morwell.

VISITOR INFORMATION: 'The Old Church', Princes Hwy, Ph: 1800 621 409

▓ Wangaratta   POP 16 330
Map 187, A1

This commercial and agricultural city is located 234km north-east of Melbourne, at the junction of the **Ovens** and **King rivers**.

MAIN ATTRACTIONS: **Merriwa Park**, on the King River, is attractive with its sunken garden, mature river red gums, ferneries and ponds. **Sydney Beach**, on the Ovens River, is a pleasant picnic and swimming area. The **Exhibitions Gallery** is located in the old Presbyterian Church in Ovens St. Infamous bushranger Mad Dog Morgan's headless body is buried in the Tone Rd cemetery.

NEARBY ATTRACTIONS: Wangaratta is an ideal base for exploring Victoria's **High Country** including **Warby Range State Park, Mount Buffalo NP** and **Chiltern-Mount Pilot NP**. Glenrowan, to the south-west, has several attractions linked to the legend of Ned Kelly, including **Kellyworld Animated Theatre** and **Kate's Cottage and Museum**. There are also wineries, including famous **Baileys of Glenrowan**. **Eldorado**, 20km north-east, is an interesting

old gold town which has the largest gold dredge in the Southern Hemisphere. Gold fossicking is popular in nearby **Reids Creek**. There are many scenic roads leading to natural attractions, such as **Powers Lookout** and **Paradise Falls** in the **King Valley**. **Milawa Gourmet Region** offers wineries, hand-made cheeses, mustards, nuts and berry farms.

VISITOR INFORMATION: 100-104 Murphy St, Ph: (03) 5721 5711 or 1800 801 065

▓ Warracknabeal   POP 2495
Map 206, E3

Massive wheat silos mark Warracknabeal's status as the **'Cereal Capital of the Wimmera district'**. The town is 378km north-west of Melbourne.

MAIN ATTRACTIONS: The **Historical Centre**, in Scott St, displays pioneer memorabilia, including furniture, pictures and documents. Highlights are a pharmaceutical collection from Woolcott's Pharmacy. Warracknabeal's historic streets and buildings can be seen on the **Black Arrow Tour**, a 5km walk or drive described in a leaflet available from the historical centre or the information centre. There are 23 points of interest, including the town's six National Trust-classified buildings: **Christ Church**, the **Commercial Hotel, railway water tower, Court House, log lock-up** and **Warracknabeal Hotel**. **Wheatlands Machinery Museum** conveys the history of wheat farming in the district, with exhibits of farm machinery from the last 100 years.

VISITOR INFORMATION: 119 Scott St, Ph: (03) 5398 1632

▓ Warragul   POP 10 420
Map 212, D3

Warragul, 104km south-east of Melbourne, began as a construction camp for railway workers. It is now a dairying centre for the

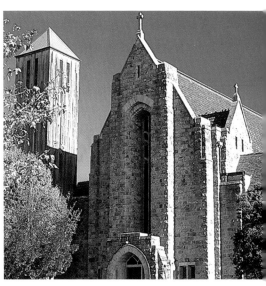
Cathedral Church of the Holy Trinity, Wangaratta

surrounding rich, green, rolling pastures of **West Gippsland**.

MAIN ATTRACTIONS: The region is renowned for the quality of its agricultural produce, supplying Melbourne with much of its milk. **Civic Park** offers a playground, picnic and BBQ facilities.

NEARBY ATTRACTIONS: The **Gourmet Deli Trail** is a gastronomic tour of the countryside and visitors can stop to taste and purchase fresh bread, cheeses, wine and fruits. Brochures are available from the information centre. **Mount Worth State Park** offers walking trails and picnic facilities and lookouts on the **McDonalds Track** provide views of the valley, the **Great Dividing Range** and **Western Port**. There are many scenic drives around the area. **Noojee Trestle Bridge** and **Tooronga Falls** are located near the road to **Mount Baw Baw**. **Darnum Musical Village**, 8km east, has a fine collection of antique player pianos, organs and other musical instruments. Visitors can play some of the instruments and see the workshop. **Yarragon**, 13km east, offers gourmet food, crafts and antiques.

VISITOR INFORMATION: 'The Old Church', Princes Hwy, Traralgon, Ph: 1800 621 409

■ Warrnambool   POP 29 500
Map 200, B4

Warrnambool was an important port until the 1920s, when silting virtually ended commercial shipping. The city's early prosperity is reflected in the sandstone buildings of Liebig, Timor and Fairy streets. Today, Warrnambool is a coastal resort and Victoria's fifth largest city. It is at the western end of the **Great Ocean Road**.

MAIN ATTRACTIONS: A major attraction in Warrnambool is **Flagstaff Hill Maritime Village**, an authentic replica of a typical 19th-century seaport. The village includes a group of lighthouse buildings, built in 1853 and still in use; and an old fort and cannons, built in 1887, to fend off a perceived threat of invasion by Russia. *Shipwrecked* is a superb sound and laser evening show, telling the tragic story of the *Loch Ard* shipwreck. The city's **Botanic Gardens** were laid out in 1872 and are worthwhile visiting. **Warrnambool Art Gallery**, on the corner of Liebig St and Timor St, displays a variety of works by 19th-

Proudfoots Boatshed on the Hopkins River, Warrnambool

and 20th-century European and Australian artists. **Lake Pertobe Adventure Playground** is a family venue, with pedal boats, islands, bicycles and walking tracks. **Lady Bay**, the main beach, offers a promenade edging the bay, recreation areas, safe swimming and surfing. **Whale watching** has become a popular pastime in Warrnambool. Between June and September each year, southern right whales return to breed in the sheltered waters off **Logans Beach**, and visitors can watch the whales from a viewing platform.

NEARBY ATTRACTIONS: **Tower Hill State Game Reserve** is located 14km west of Warrnambool. The reserve surrounds the peak and crater lake of an extinct volcano; wildlife includes kangaroos, koalas and emus. Scenic **Hopkins Falls** and **Allansford Cheese World** are to the east.

VISITOR INFORMATION: Flagstaff Hill, Merri St, Ph: (03) 5564 7837 or 1800 637 725

■ Wodonga   POP 27 700
Map 181, C1

Wodonga lies on the south bank of the **Murray River**, close to the historic towns of **Yackandandah**, **Beechworth** and **Chiltern**, and the wineries of **Rutherglen**. Wodonga, on the Victorian side of the river, is twinned with **Albury**, on the New South Wales side.

MAIN ATTRACTIONS: A number of attractions can be found on the Lincoln Causeway, the only road link between Wodonga and Albury. The **Gateway Complex** features art, craft, woodturning, pottery and jewellery. Also popular are the **Fitness Trail** and the **Wiradjuri Walkabout Aboriginal Heritage Trail**. **Harvey's Fish and Farm Park**, with mini-golf, mini-train rides and animals, is a perfect place for children. Visitors can also catch their own fish. On the third Sunday of each month, a miniature railway

runs in nearby **Diamond Park**. **Bandiana Army Museum** is at the southern end of Wodonga. The **National Museum of Australian Pottery** is a museum dedicated to 19th century Australian potters.

NEARBY ATTRACTIONS: There is much to do and see in the region, including winery tours, fishing, horse trail-riding and canoeing; the information centre has details. Areas worth touring include **Lake Hume** and north-east Victoria.

VISITOR INFORMATION: Gateway Complex, Lincoln Causeway, Ph: 1300 796 222

■ Wonthaggi   POP 6145
Map 212, C4

Originally a black-coal mining town, today this **South West Gippsland** town is a prosperous industrial and commercial centre. In an area characterised by rugged coastline, beaches and fishing activity, Wonthaggi is a good tourist base within easy reach of **Phillip Island** and **Wilsons Promontory**.

MAIN ATTRACTIONS: The **State Coal Mine Historical Reserve** has reopened **Eastern Area Mine** and offers underground-tours conducted by former coal miners. There is also a museum featuring mining activities. The historical reserve is open daily. Wonthaggi Historical Society displays local memorabilia in **Wonthaggi Railway Station**, open Saturdays.

NEARBY ATTRACTIONS: **Cape Paterson**, 9km south, is located in **Bunurong Marine NP**. The surf beach here is popular and there is a more sheltered beach for swimming. There are also excellent snorkelling and scuba-diving opportunities. From Cape Paterson to **Inverloch**, a scenic road winds 15km through **Bunurong Cliffs Coastal Reserve**. A coastal track offers walkers an alternative route.

VISITOR INFORMATION: Watt St, Ph: (03) 5671 2444

GREAT OCEAN ROAD

This legendary coastal route, starting at **Torquay** and extending 285km west via **Lorne, Apollo Bay** and **Port Campbell NP** to **Warrnambool**, is a journey along a stretch of spectacular coastline with seaside holiday towns, surf beaches, dramatic cliffs, expansive ocean views, rainforest and woodlands.

It was built between 1919 and 1932 as employment for returned servicemen and as a memorial to soldiers who died in WWI. The road was designed to be a tourist route of world repute along the wild seacoast. More than 100 (some believe as many as 700) ships have been sunk by reefs, foul weather and the treacherous waters of the **Southern Ocean**; the stretch to Peterborough is a stark reminder of the perils of this jagged coastline.

Historic seaside towns provide safe sandy beaches as well as surfing beaches. Whale watching, horseriding, bushwalking and mountain bike riding, are just some of the activities of this remarkable region.

The Twelve Apostles

Within **Port Campbell NP**, these majestic rock formations, seen from the Great Ocean Road, were once part of the mainland's limestone cliffs, demonstrating the power of the coastline's waves. Rising up to 65m from the ocean and stretching along the coastline, the offshore seastacks are an impressive sight. Other attractions of the national park include **London Bridge**, **The Grotto** and **Loch Ard Gorge**.

 Visitor information

Geelong and Great Ocean Road Visitor Information Centre
Stead Park, Princes Hwy
Corio, Vic 3214
Ph: (03) 5275 5797
www.greatoceanroad.org

Warrnambool Visitor Information Centre
Flagstaff Hill, Merri St
Warrnambool, Vic 3280
Ph: (03) 5564 7837 or 1800 637 725

Great Ocean Road

main attractions

◈ **Anglesea**

Anglesea is renowned for its large population of grey kangaroos inhabiting Anglesea Golf Course.

◈ **Cape Otway Lightstation**

Built in 1848, this is Australia's oldest standing lighthouse.

◈ **Little penguins**

To observe a colony of little penguins, cross at low tide to Middle Island from Thunder Point Coastal Reserve, Warrnambool.

◈ **Lorne**

Surrounded by densely forested bushland with plunging waterfalls, Lorne is a prime holiday location.

◈ **Port Campbell National Park**

This narrow strip of coastal park contains many spectacular rock formations, including The Twelve Apostles.

◈ **Torquay**

Torquay is the renowned centre of the surf culture on the Great Ocean Road.

◈ **Whale watching**

From June to September see southern right whales at Logans Beach, Warrnambool.

Bay of Islands, off the Great Ocean Road, near Peterborough

A · TO HALLS GAP · C188 · **i** · Dunkeld · 19 · **B** · Glenthompson · **C** · C148 · C182 · **D** · Streatham · **E** · C172 · TO BEAUFO · Skipton · GLENEL

TO HAMILTON · B160 · GLENGLG · HWY · 27 · Wickliffe · Lake Bolac · GLENELG · Westmere · 48 · B160 · Carranballac · HWY · C143

1 · Warrayure · C178 · Reedy · Ck · River · B160 · Lake Bolac · Nerrin Nerrin · Salt Lake · Bradvale

Lake Linlithgow · 28 · Grays · 37 · Ck · Lake Gellie · Pura Pura · 30 · Mingay · C172 · Mundy · Gully

HAMILTON · Muston · Hopkins · Chatsworth · Ck · Lake Eyang · Dundonnell · Lake Terrinallum · Mount Emu

Penshurst · HWY · Burchell · 43 · Woorndoo · Derrinallum · B140 · Lismore

2 · 24 · B140 · Caramut · Ck · Salt · C148 · 25 · Lake Toolorook · C140 · Lismore

C178 · Minhamite · Spring · HAMILTON · 33 · Hexham · B140 · Darlington · Lake Gnarpu

Minjah · C174 · River · Blind · B140 · HAMILTON · 24 · C165 · 38 · C164 · 56

Back · Moyne · Hawkesdale · Mortlake · B120 · Ck · 31 · Lake Bookar · C173 · Bookar · Kariah · Lake Corangamite

C176 · 58 · Ck · HWY · Stony · C156 · Glenormiston North · Lake Colongulac · C164

3 · Willatook · C176 · Woolsthorpe · Ellerslie · 50 · 23 · Glenormiston · Gnotuk · Lake Corangamite

Warrong · Merri · Winslow · The Sisters · Lake Keilambete · Noorat · 22 · Camperdown

Kirkstall · Drysdale · Framlingham · Terang · HWY · Weerite · A1 · Pomborneit North

4 · C183 · Grassmere · HOPKINS · Purnim · Hopkins · 35 · PRINCES · A1 · C156 · 23 · Bostocks Creek · 13 · C164 · Lake Purrumbete · Pomborneit

C178 · Koroit · Mailer Flat · B183 · C174 · Garvoc · Mount · Cobrico · River · 45 · Stoneyfor

C184 · Tower Hill State Game Reserve · B120 · Bushfield · Hopkins Falls · Cudgee · Dixie · Emu · Cobden · C149 · Pirron Yalloc

Rosebrook · Tower Hill · Illowa · Slagstaff Hill Maritime Village · Panmure · Taroon · Lake Elingamite · Miniature Railway · Swan Marsh

Port Fairy · Killarney · 29 · A1 · Whale-watching · Cudgee Creek Wildlife Park · Laang · C168 · 44 · Ecklin South · Purrumbete · C156 · Carpendeit · Irrewillipe

Mahogany Walk · Dennington · Warrnambool · 12 · Naringal · Ralph Illidge Sanctuary · Ayrford · C167 · 19 · Jancourt East · C163

Griffiths I · Allansford · C167 · Scotts Creek · Scotts · C163 · C156

Port Fairy Lighthouse · Cheese World · Mepunga West · Mepunga East · 31 · Curdies · C163 · 58 · Simpson

5 · B100 · 17 · Brucknell · Nirranda East · Timboon · Kennedys · Carlisle River

Nullawarre · C163 · Timboon Farmhouse · C156

Nirranda · Curdie Vale · Paaratte · 21 · Cooriemungle · Kennedys Creek · C156

GREAT · 36 · Curdies Inlet · Newfield · C164 · C166 · C161

Bay of Islands · B100 · Peterborough · OCEAN · Port Campbell · **i** · C156 · Lavers Hill

The Grotto · London Bridge (Broken) · The Arch · Loch Ard Gorge · Glenample Homestead · C156

PORT CAMPBELL N.P. · The Twelve Apostles · Princetown · 49 · B100 · Yuulong · MELBA GULLY S.P.

Gable Lookout · Wattle Hill · Johanna

TWELVE APOSTLES MARINE N.P. · Point Reginald

6

Bass

Victoria

20 Kilometres

TO BALLARAT
TO BALLARAT
TO BALLARAT

WESTERN

Melton

Pittong
Scarsdale
Buninyong
Fiskville
Bacchus Marsh
Melton

Linton
Newton
Napoleons
Scotsburn
Clarendon
Lal Lal
Lal Lal Reservoir
Rowsley
Rockbank

Italian Gully
Bungal
Mt Wallace
Exford

Enfield
Mt Doran
BRISBANE
RANGES
NAT. PK.
Tarneit

ENFIELD
S.P.
Berringa
Grenville
Morrisons
Balliang
Balliang East

Cape Clear
Dereel
Cargerie
Elaine
Durdidwarrah

Pitfield
Illabarook
Woodbourne
Staughton Vale

Wallinduc
Corindhap
Meredith
Anakie
YOU YANGS REGIONAL PARK
Werribee

Berrybank
Rokewood
Steiglitz
Anakie East
Little River
Werribee South

Werneth
Warrambine
Maude
Victoria's Open Range Zoo

Cressy
Shelford
Lethbridge
Lara Lake
Lara

Foxhow
Wingeel
Teesdale
Bannockburn
Corio
PRINCES

Lake Martin
Barpinba
Eurack
Inverleigh
Murgheboluc
Ford Discovery Centre, National Wool Museum, Waterfront Geelong
Geelong
Portarlington

Cundare
HAMILTON
Gnarwarre
Fyansford
Corio Bay
Clifton Springs
Indented Head

Dreeite
Beeac
Barwon Park
Ceres
Grovedale
Moolap
Drysdale
St Leonards
Murradoc

Lake Beeac
Warrion
Ondit
Winchelsea
Mount Moriac
Marshall
Leopold
Wineries Wallington
Swan Bay

Red Rock Lookout
Coragulac
Irrewarra
Armytage
Moriac
Mount Duneed
Lake Connewarre R.
Maritime Museum, Fort Queenscliff
Queenscliff

Cororooke
Warncoort
PRINCES
Paraparap
Breamlea
Ocean Grove
Point Lonsdale

Lake Colac
Colac
Botanic Gardens
Birregurra
Bambra
Tiger Moth World
Torquay
Surfworld Surfing Museum
Barwon Heads
Jirrahlinga Koala and Wildlife Sanctuary

Ellinminyt
Yeodene
Deans Marsh
Jan Juc
Bells Beach

Kawarren
Murroon
Benwerrin
GREAT OCEAN ROAD
Anglesea
Coogoorah Reserve
POINT ADDIS MARINE N.P.

Gellibrand
Barwon Downs
Erskine Falls
LORNE STATE PARK
Aireys Inlet
Split Point Lighthouse

Forrest
West Barwon Reservoir
Eastern View

Barramunga
Stevensons Falls
ANGAHOOK
Lorne
Point Grey

Beech Forest
Ferguson
Otway Fly
Beauchamp Falls
Tanybryn
Wye River

Wyelangta
Hopetoun Falls
Carisbrook Falls
Kennett River
Point Hawdor

Marriners Falls
Wongarra

Skenes Creek
Apollo Bay
Old Cable Station, Shell Museum

Maits Rest
OTWAY NATIONAL PARK

Cape Otway Lightstation
Point Franklin
Cape Otway

Strait

Port Phillip

Continued on maps 152 & 150

Bass Strait

VICTORIA 201

Woodend   POP 3015

Map 167, C2

This small township, 69km north-west of Melbourne, is surrounded by the **Macedon Ranges**. Woodend became a resort town after the goldrush and has retained its old-world atmosphere.

MAIN ATTRACTIONS: Woodend is characterised by quaint shops in the main street, old hotels, a bluestone Anglican Church and a stone bridge built in 1862, which spans **Five Mile Creek**. The clock tower was built as a WWI memorial.

NEARBY ATTRACTIONS: **Hanging Rock** is Woodend's most popular attraction. Located 6km north-east of town, this huge rock formation was made famous by Joan Lindsay's novel, *Picnic at Hanging Rock*, and then by the film of the same name. Visitors can discover the history, mystery and geology of the rock at the **Hanging Rock Discovery Centre**. Nearby **Hanging Rock Winery** produces a range of quality red, white and sparkling wines. It is open for tastings and cellar door sales. There are nearly 30 boutique wineries in the region. **Mount Macedon** is located 10km south-east and there is a huge memorial cross at its summit. The area is renowned for beautiful gardens and many are open to the public in spring and autumn. There are numerous scenic drives and bushwalks around Mount Macedon.

VISITOR INFORMATION: High St, Ph:(03) 5427 2033 or 1800 244 711

Yarram   POP 1825

Map 213, F4

A **South Gippsland** town on the **Tarra River**, Yarram is 225km south-east of Melbourne. Yarram offers easy access to the region's many coastal attractions as well as the rugged **Strzelecki Ranges**.

MAIN ATTRACTIONS: The historic **Regent Theatre**, built in 1930, has been restored and shows movies on weekends, some weekdays and during school holidays. It is located in Commercial Rd. **Yarram Golf Course** is very attractive with hundreds of ancient grass trees; it is also home to many kangaroos.

NEARBY ATTRACTIONS: **Tarra-Bulga NP**, north-west of Yarram, protects some of the best examples of cool temperate rainforest and tree-fern habitats in the Strzelecki Ranges. There are many native birds and animals to be seen in the park. A circular drive via **Hiawatha** passes **Minnie Ha Ha Falls**. To the south is **Port Albert**, an historic port with many fine old buildings. The **Maritime Museum** in Port Albert is open daily in summer, otherwise weekends only. **White Woman Waterhole** is of great beauty and is located in **Won Wron State Forest**, 10km north of Yarram.

VISITOR INFORMATION: Yarram Court House, cnr Commercial Rd and Rodgers St, Ph: (03) 5182 6553

Yarrawonga   POP 4025

Map 208, D2

Yarrawonga in Victoria and **Mulwala** in New South Wales are twin **Murray River** towns lying on the shores of **Lake Mulwala**. Both are popular holiday destinations.

MAIN ATTRACTIONS: **Lake Mulwala** is an ideal venue for watersports—on Anzac Day a large sailing regatta is held on the lake. The Yarrawonga foreshore is particularly attractive with abundant birdlife, willow trees, boat ramps, BBQs and picnic facilities. Trail rides through the forest and alongside the Murray River are available with **Billabong Trail Rides** during peak periods. The **Old Yarra Mine Shaft** displays a large collection of gems and fossils and is located at the information centre. The **MV Paradise Queen** and *Lady Murray* both offer lake cruises daily. Canoes and boats are available for hire, kayaks for hire and tours. Other Yarrawonga attractions include the **Pioneer Museum** and **Tudor House Clock Museum**.

NEARBY ATTRACTIONS: At **Linley Park Animal Farm**, in Corowa Rd, visitors can feed the baby animals in the nursery. **Fyffe Field Winery**, located 19km west of Yarrawonga on the Murray Valley Hwy, is open for tastings and sales.

VISITOR INFORMATION: Cnr Irvine Pde and Belmore St, Ph: (03) 5744 1989 or 1800 062 260

A boulder-filled stream in Tarra-Bulga National Park, north-west of Yarram

KEY MAP

Capital city CBD map
Melbourne p.147

Melbourne suburban maps
pp.150–153

Region maps
The Goldfields p.159
Phillip Island p.165
Spa Country p.167
The Dandenongs p.171
Gippsland Lakes p.177
Wilsons Promontory p.179
The High Country p.187
The Grampians p.195
Great Ocean Road pp.200–201

State maps
pp. 204–214

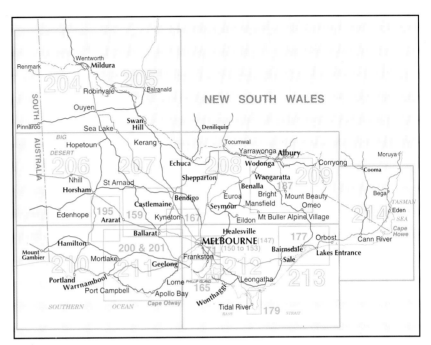

DISTANCE CHART

Approximate Distance	Albury NSW	Bairnsdale	Ballarat	Bega NSW	Bendigo	Bordertown SA	Cooma NSW	Geelong	Hamilton	Horsham	Melbourne	Mildura	Mount Gambier SA	Portland	Renmark SA	Shepparton	Swan Hill	Traralgon	Wangaratta	Warrnambool
Albury NSW		310	372	426	297	665	315	388	545	508	314	571	677	628	696	177	384	427	73	544
Bairnsdale	310		395	326	432	739	339	357	568	582	283	821	695	608	940	462	619	117	310	513
Ballarat	372	395		721	121	344	734	89	173	187	112	454	305	256	573	241	273	278	345	171
Bega NSW	426	326	721		758	1065	111	683	894	908	609	957	1026	934	1082	589	796	443	485	839
Bendigo	297	432	121	758		368	598	176	294	211	149	398	426	377	517	120	187	315	224	292
Bordertown SA	665	739	344	1065	368		966	433	259	157	456	411	183	281	279	488	396	622	592	365
Cooma NSW	315	339	734	111	598	966		696	907	921	622	1160	1039	947	1279	478	685	456	374	852
Geelong	388	357	89	683	176	433	696		238	276	74	543	338	251	662	253	362	240	315	156
Hamilton	545	568	173	894	294	259	907	238		129	285	439	132	83	558	414	368	451	526	112
Horsham	508	582	187	908	211	157	921	276	129		299	310	261	212	429	331	239	465	435	241
Melbourne	314	283	112	609	149	456	622	74	285	299		538	412	325	657	179	336	166	241	230
Mildura	571	821	454	957	398	411	1160	543	439	310	538		571	522	125	433	218	704	537	551
Mount Gambier SA	677	695	305	1026	426	183	1039	338	132	261	412	571		98	462	546	500	578	650	182
Portland	628	608	256	934	377	281	947	251	83	212	325	522	98		641	497	451	491	601	95
Renmark SA	696	940	573	1082	517	279	1279	662	558	429	657	125	462	641		558	343	657	662	676
Shepparton	177	462	241	589	120	488	478	253	414	331	179	433	546	497	558		215	345	104	412
Swan Hill	384	619	273	796	187	396	685	362	368	239	336	218	500	451	343	215		502	319	480
Traralgon	427	117	278	443	315	622	456	240	451	465	166	704	578	491	657	345	502		407	396
Wangaratta	73	310	345	485	224	592	374	315	526	435	241	537	650	601	662	104	319	407		471
Warrnambool	544	513	171	839	292	365	852	156	112	241	230	551	182	95	676	412	480	396	471	

All distances in this chart have been measured over highways and major roads, not necessarily by the shortest route.

Scale 1:975

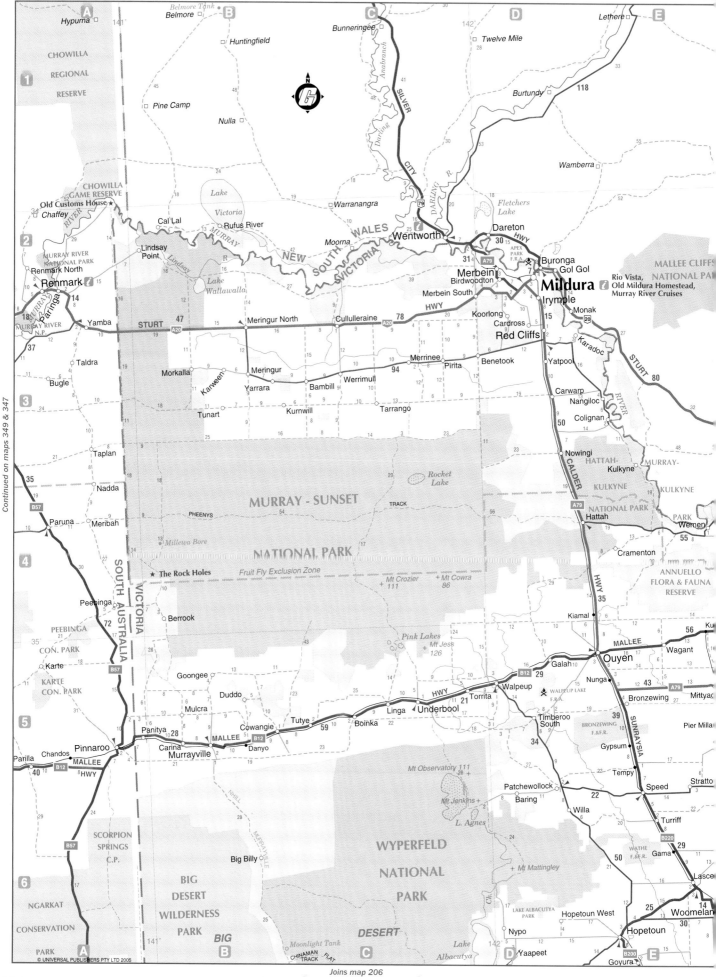

© UNIVERSAL PUBLISHERS PTY LTD 2005

30 Kilometres

F G H J K

Top Hut
Mungo
MUNGO
NATIONAL
PARK
Lake Leaghur
Lake Mungo
Boree Plains
Marona
Arumpo
Chibnalwood Lakes
The Walls of China
Turlee
Iona
Langleydale
Hatfield
Tarwong
Alma
GOONAWARRA N.R.
1

Bidura
Box
Oxley
One Tree
2
COBB HWY
Thelangerin

Prungle
Tin Tin Lake
Macommon Lake
Great Cumbungi Swamp
Ganaway Lake
Ita Lake
Lachlan River
Lake Waljeers

Penarie
Pitarpunga Lake
Nap Nap
Maude
Yerrinbool
RIVER

L. Benanee
L. Caringay
Robinvale
McWilliams Winery, Rural Life Museum
77
HWY
Balranald
Lake Tala
Ravensworth
STURT
HWY
3
55

20
Bannerton
MURRAY
VALLEY
Boundary Bend
75
MURRUMBIDGEE
Yangalake YANGA N.R.
Yanga Lake
20
STURT
20

7
45
Annuello
WANDOWN F. & F.R.
Yungera
Koorkab
Piamble
Kenley
55
Perekerten
62
Miranda
Booroorban
4
COBB

Kooloonong
Haysdale
Natya
Goodnight
Kyalite
80
The Forest

Winnambool
Bolton
Prooinga
78
Edward River
Windouran
Billabong
Anabranch
35

Kulwyne
Manangatang
41 HWY
B12
Piangil
Tooleybuc
Wood Wood
Stony Crossing
Yerreen
Wakool River
Moulamein
Forest
Clarkes
5

Cocamba
Chinkapook
Yarraby
Miralie
15
Koraleigh
Dilpurra 69
Niemur
Dhuragoon
107
Morago

24
Nyah
Nyah West
Vinifera
Speewa
Beverford
26
Tyntynder Central
Tyntynder South
Jimaringle
River

Chillingollah
Nowie Nth
Tyntynder Homestead
Woorinen
38
Burraboi

L. Wahpool
Lake Tyrrell
46
41
Waitchie
Swan Hill
Pioneer Settlement, Murray River Cruises
Tullakool
26
28
Wakool

Tyrrell Downs
L. Timboram
Gowanford
31
Fish Pt
MURRAY VALLEY
NEW
Ballbank
25
Yallakool
62

Long Plains
40
Ultima
Lake Boga
Banjeroop
Murrabit
Caldwell
56

Sea Lake
Boigbeat
Meatian
60
Goschen
Tresco
Kunat
Mystic Park
61
Myall
SOUTH
22
Thule
6

Banyan
34
Berriwillock
CALDER
A79
Lalbert Rd
Lake Charm
Capels Crossing
Westby
Culfearne
Koondrook
Barham
23
WALES
VICTORIA

56
Willangie
Watchupga
HWY
Culgoa
Kalpienung
Lalbert
Cokum
Bael Bael
Lake Bael Bael
Sandhill Lake
Cannie
Koroop
Gunbower Museum
Cohuna
Bunnaloo

Sutton Warne
Tittybong
58
Kerang
Gannawarra
Kerang Sth
144 HWY
48
Dingwall
K

VICTORIA

© UNIVERSAL PUBLISHERS PTY LTD 200?

VICTORIA **205**

F G H J K

Scale 1:97

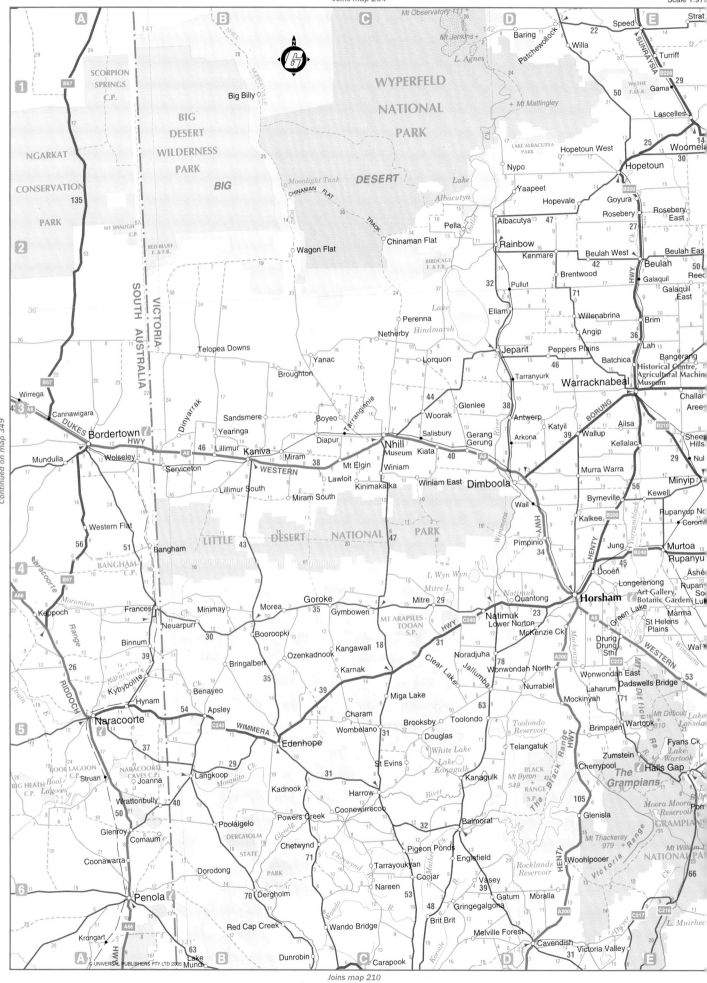

© UNIVERSAL PUBLISHERS PTY LTD 2005

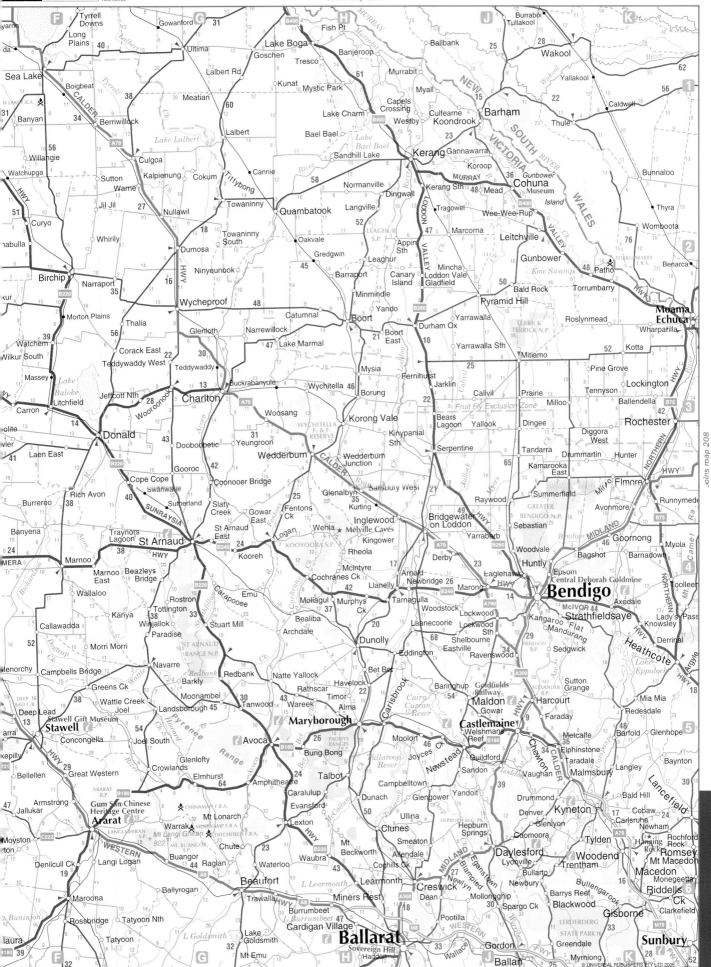

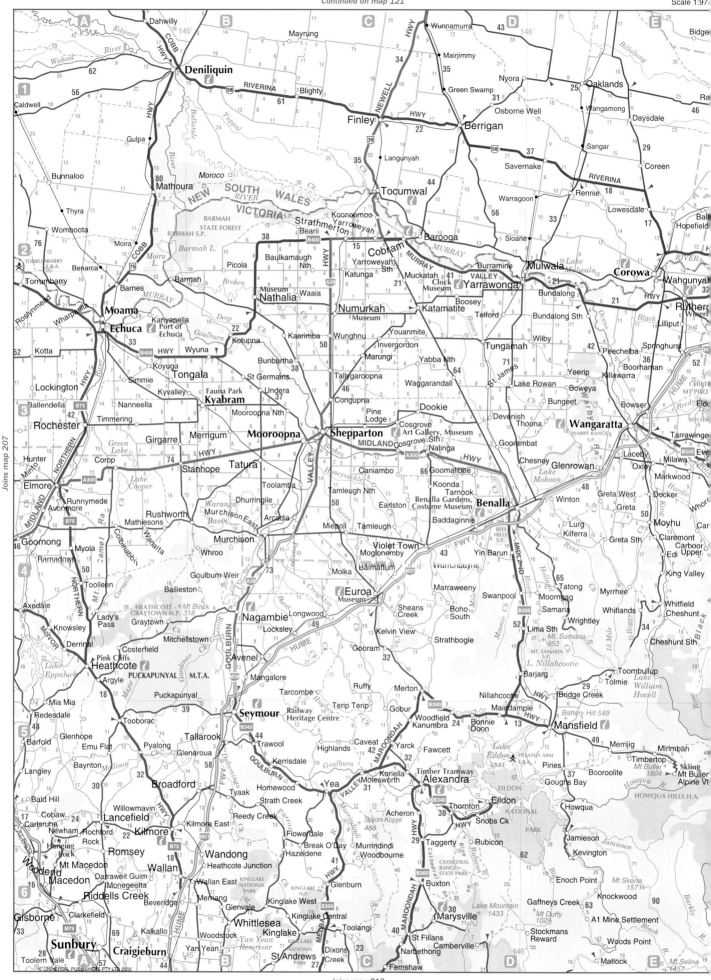

Gregory's Australia

© UNIVERSAL PUBLISHERS PTY LTD 2005

Bool Lagoon
Wrattonbully
Powers Creek
Kadnook
Harrow
Coonewirrecoo
BLACK RANGE S.P.
Glenisla
Moora Moora Resr
GRAMPIAN
Pom

Glenroy
Comaum
Poolaigelo
DERGHOLM STATE PARK
Chetwynd
Pigeon Ponds
Balmoral
Mt Thackeray 979
Mt William
NATIONAL PA

Coonawarra
Dorodong
Tarrayoukyan
Englefield
Woohlpooer
Victoria Range

Penola
Dergholm
Nareen
Coojar
Vasey
Gatum
Moralla
Rocklands Reservoir

RIDDOCH
Krongart
Red Cap Creek
Wando Bridge
Brit Brit
Gringegalgona
Melville Forest
Cavendish
Victoria Valley

Nangwarry
Lake Mundi
Dunrobin
Carapook
Coleraine
Karabeal
Glenthompson

Kalangadoo
Wepar
Lindsay
Casterton
Sandford
Paschendale
Wannon
Dunkeld

Tarpeena
Strathdownie
Henty
Merino
Tahara
Hamilton
Tarrington
Croxton East

Glencoe
Ardno
Digby
Grassdale
Branxholme
Yatchaw
Penshurst
Caramut

Tantanoola
Wandilo
Mil-Lel
Puralka
Hotspur
Byaduk North
MT NAPIER S.P.
Byaduk
Minhamite

Mount Gambier
Glenburnie
Dartmoor
Greenwald
Condah
Weerangourt
Macarthur

Kongorong
Caverton
Mumbannar
Drik Drik
Myamyn
Milltown
MT ECCLES N.P.
Hawkesdale

Blackfellows Cave
Bellum Bellum
Donovans
Nelson
Drumborg
Heywood
Homerton
Broadwater
Willatook

Allendale East
Port MacDonnell
Kentbruck
Mt Richmond
Tyrendarra
Bessiebelle
Orford
Warrong
Woolstho

LOWER GLENELG NATIONAL PARK
Gorae West
Gorae
Bolwarra
Narrawong
Tyrendarra East
Codrington
Kirkstall
Koroit

Cape Northumberland
DISCOVERY BAY COASTAL PARK
Cashmore
Trewalla
Portland
Maritime Discovery Centre
Yambuk
Tower Hill
Killarney
Bushfield

DISCOVERY BAY M.N.P.
Tarragal
Cape Bridgewater
Petrified Forest
Point Danger
Lady Julia
Percy Island
Port Fairy
Rosebrook
Dennington
Warrnambool
Whale Watching

SOUTHERN OCEAN

Victoria

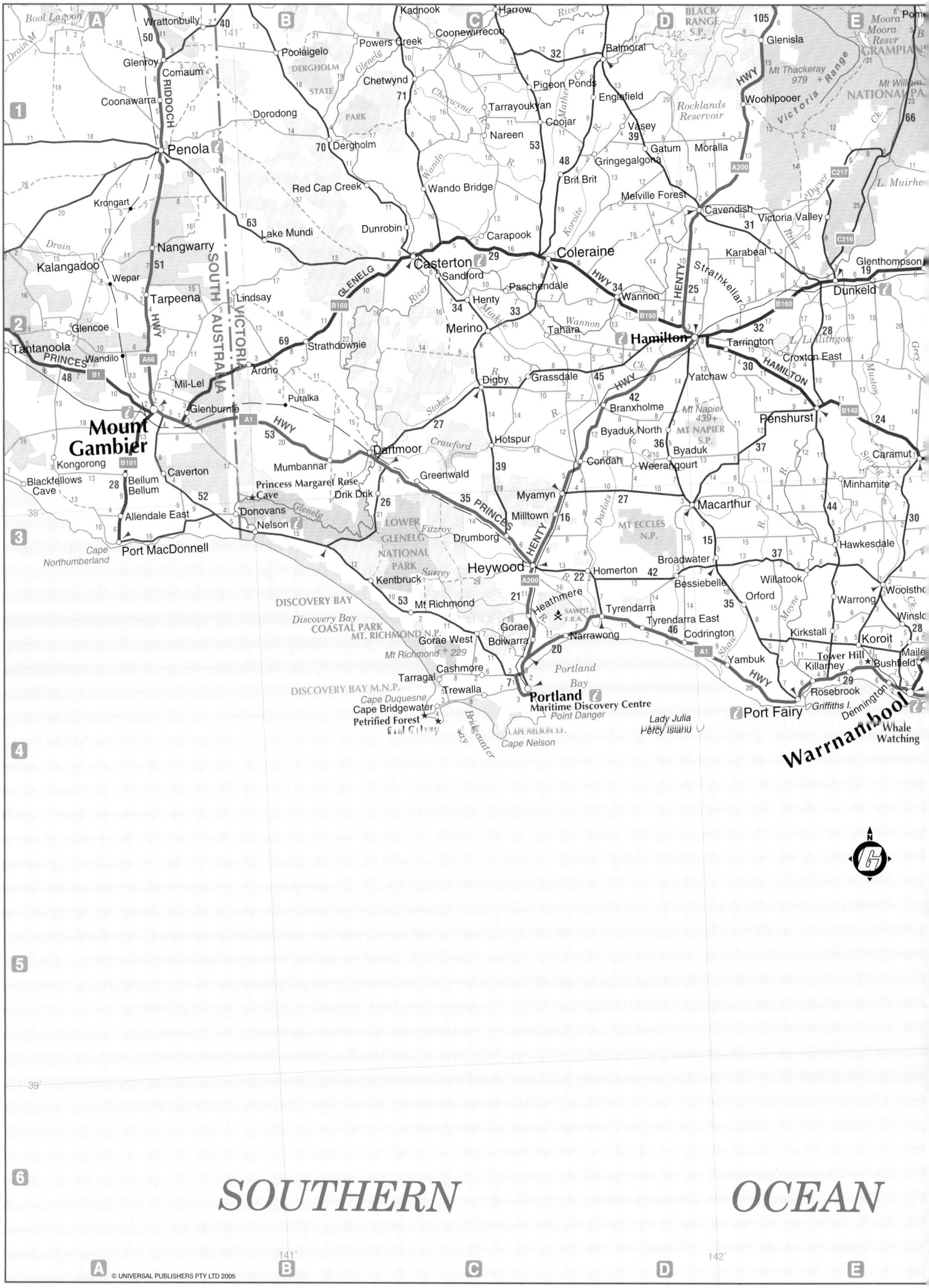

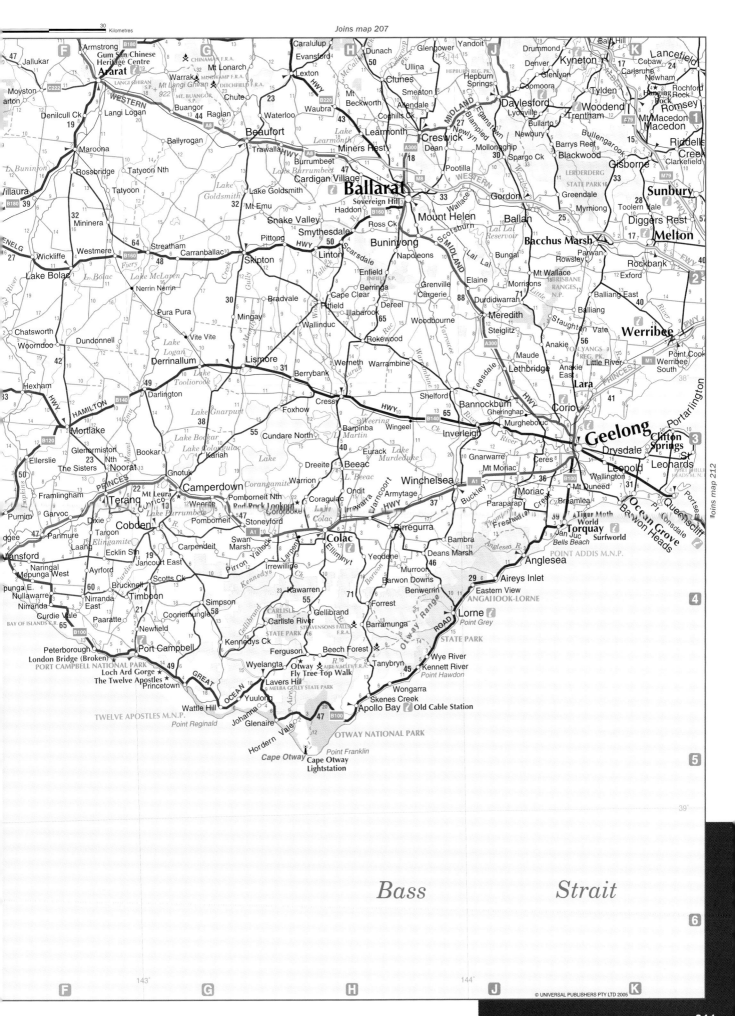

30 Kilometres

47 Jallukar
Moyston
arton
Denilcull Ck
19

F Armstrong
Gum San Chinese
Heritage Centre
Ararat
LANGI GHIRAN S.P.
Mt Langi Ghiran
922
Langi Logan
Buangor
Raglan
Ballyrogan

G CHINAMAN F.R.A.
Mt Lonarch
Warrak MIDSWAMP F.R.A.
DITCHFIELD F.R.A.
Mt BUANGOR S.P.
Chute
Waterloo
Waubra

H Caralulup
Evansford
Lexton
Mt Beckworth
Coghills Ck

Dunach
Clunes
Smeaton
Arendale

J Glengower Yandoit
Ullina
Hepburn
Springs
Newlyn
Egganstown
Brampled

Drummond
Denver Kyneton
Glenlyon
Coomoora
Daylesford
Lyonville
Bullarto
Trentham

K Ball Hill
Cobaw 24
Carlsruhe
Newham
Hanging Rock
Mt Macedon
Macedon
Romsey

Langi Logan
23
Beaufort
Trawalla
Burrumbeet
Lake Burrumbeet
Cardigan Village
Lake Goldsmith

44
Learmonth
Miners Rest
Creswick
Dean
Pootilla
Mollongghip
Spargo Ck

Learmonth
43
18
Ballarat
Sovereign Hill
Haddon
Ross Ck
33
Wallace
Gordon
Greendale

Mt Wallace
Newbury
Barrys Reef
Blackwood
Clarkefield
Gisborne
Riddells
Creek

Maroona
Rossbridge Tatyoon Nth
Tatyoon
Lake Goldsmith
Mt Emu
Snake Valley
Smythesdale

Mount Helen
Ballan
LERDERDERG
STATE PARK
Myrniong
Toolern Vale
Sunbury
Diggers Rest

Mininera
Westmere
Wickliffe
Streatham
Carranballac
Skipton
Pittong
HWY 50
Linton

Buninyong
Napoleons
Scotsburn
Lal Lal
Reservoir
Bungal
Morrisons
Mt Wallace
71
Durdidwarrah

Balliang
Balliang East
40
Rockbank
Exford
Melton

Lake Bolac
L. Bolac
Lake McLaren
Nerrin Nerrin
Bradvale
Pitfield
Illabarook
Cape Clear
Dereel

Enfield
INFIELD S.P.
Berringa
Grenville
Cargerie
88
Meredith
Steiglitz
Staughton Vale
Anakie

BRISBANE
RANGES N.P.
Anakie
East
Balliang
Werribee
Point Cook
Werribee
South

Chatsworth
Woorndoo
Pura Pura
Mingay
Vite Vite
Lake Logan
Dundonnell

Wallinduc
Rokewood
Werneth
Warrambine
Berrybank

Woodbourne
Maude
Lethbridge
Teesdale
YOU YANGS
REG. PK
Little River
Lara

42
Hexham
Derrinallum
Lake Tooliorook
Darlington
Lismore
31

Cress
Shelford
Bannockburn
Gheringhap
Inverleigh
Murgheboluc

Corio
41
Geelong
Drysdale
Clifton
Springs

Mortlake
Lake Gnarpurt
Foxhow
Cundare North
55
Barpinba
Wingeel
Weering

Eurack
Beeac
L. Beeac
Ondit
Winchelsea
Armytage
37

Gnarwarre
Mt Moriac
Ceres
Moriac
36
Mt Duneed
Wallington
31
Leopold
St
Leonards

Ellerslie
Glenormiston
Bookar
Kariah
Noorat
Gnotuk
Warrion
Dreeite

Paraparap
Buckley
Breamlea
Queenscliff
Ocean Grove
Barwon Heads
Portsea

Framlingham
Terang
Mt Leura
Camperdown
Pomborneit Nth
Coragulac

Tiger Moth
World
Bells Beach
Torquay
Jan Juc
Surfworld
POINT ADDIS M.N.P.

Purnim
Garvoc
Dixie
Taroon
Cobden
Weerite
Red Rock Lookout
Pomborneit
Stoneyford

Corangamite
Irrewarra
Lake
Colac
Birregurra
Bambra
Deans Marsh

Anglesea
ANGAHOOK-LORNE
STATE PARK

Wansford
Naringal
Mepunga West
Laang
Ayrford
Ecklin Sth
Jancourt East
Scotts Ck

Swan
Marsh
Yalloak
Irrewillipe
Colac
Elliminyt
Yeodene
Murroon
Barwon Downs
Benwerrin

29
Lorne
Point Grey
Eastern View
Aireys Inlet

punga E.
Nullawarre
Nirranda
Curdie Vale
65
Brucknell
Nirranda
East
Timboon
Simpson
Cooriemungle 58
Paaratte
Newfield

Kawarren
55
71
Forrest
Barramunga
Gellibrand
Carlisle River
CARLISLE
STATE PARK
STAVENSONS FALLS F.R.A.

Otway
Range
OTWAY
ROAD
STATE PARK
Wye River
Kennett River
Point Hawdon

BAY OF ISLANDS C.R.
B100
Peterborough
London Bridge (Broken)
PORT CAMPBELL NATIONAL PARK
Port Campbell
Loch Ard Gorge
The Twelve Apostles
Princetown

Kennedys Ck
Ferguson
Beech Forest
Wyelangta
AIRE VALLEY F.R.A.
Otway
Fly Tree Top Walk
Lavers Hill
MELBA GULLY STATE PARK

Tanybryn
45
Wongarra
Skenes Creek
Apollo Bay
Old Cable Station

TWELVE APOSTLES M.N.P.
Point Reginald
Yuulong
Wattle Hill
Johanna
Glenaire
Hordern Vale
Aire
47
B100

OTWAY NATIONAL PARK
Point Franklin
Cape Otway
Cape Otway
Lightstation

1
2
3
4
5
6

143°
144°

Bass   *Strait*

39°
38°

F **G** **H** **J** **K**

Joins map 212

Scale 1:975

Victoria

30
Kilometres

Bass Strait

Scale 1:975 000

0   30
Kilometres

TASMAN

SEA

Bass   *Strait*

⛽ Tuna Gas & Oil Field

🛢 Flounder Oil Field

Victoria

© UNIVERSAL PUBLISHERS PTY LTD 2005

A snow gum, *Eucalyptus pauciflora*, laden with winter snow in Victoria's Alpine National Park

QUEENSLAN

The second largest state in Australia, Queensland is big, covering some 1 727 200km², and incredibly varied, stretching as it does from the tropics to the temperate zone. From north to south its greatest distance is 2092km and from east to west 1448km.

Shadowing the coastline for about 2000km, the stunning Great Barrier Reef is one of the natural wonders of the world and perhaps the state's greatest asset. Even so,

the Reef is only one of the fabulous natural assets found throughout the state. Visitors to Queensland will also discover some of the world's most beautiful beaches, luxuriant tropical rainforests, paradisiacal islands, vast deserts, national parks and fascinating towns.

Evidence that Aboriginal people have lived in Queensland for many thousands of years can be seen in the traditional rock art found in such places as Carnarvon Gorge in

the Central Highlands and Quinkan Galleries, located in the Laura River valley on Cape York. There are opportunities for visitors to inspect significant sites with Aboriginal guides, learn about indigenous

Queensland:
The Sunshine State

- Population: 3 550 000
- Total area: 1 727 200km²
- % of Australia: 22.5%
- Floral emblem: Cooktown Orchid
- Fauna emblem: Koala

i **Visitor information**

Queensland Travel Centre
Tourism Queensland House
30 Makerston St,
Brisbane, Qld 4000
Ph: 138 833
www.queenslandtravel.com

Main ATTRACTIONS

◈ **Cairns**

Cairns is a point of departure for the huge region known as Tropical North Queensland, including the northern section of the Great Barrier Reef and its islands, the Wet Tropics Rainforest, Atherton Tableland and Cape York Peninsula.

◈ **Fraser Island**

A World Heritage-listed national park, Fraser Island is the world's largest sand island and a fascinating holiday destination.

◈ **Gold Coast**

The fun-filled Gold Coast offers a range of world-class theme parks and great surf beaches, backed by high-rise developments and shopping centres.

◈ **Great Barrier Reef**

The most extensive coral reef system in the world is a blue-water panorama of colourful marine life, including around 1500 species of fish, 4000 species of molluscs, 350 species of echinoderms and 400 species of coral. It attracts divers and snorkellers as well as holiday-makers in every kind of boat.

◈ **Sunshine Coast**

This is a region of unhurried and unspoiled beaches within easy driving distance of Brisbane. There are also some very popular national parks and major family-oriented attractions.

◈ **The Scenic Rim**

Also within a few hours drive from the state capital, this is a lush region of mountainous national parks bordered by the Gold Coast and New South Wales.

◈ **Whitsundays**

A group of 74 idyllic islands in the balmy waters of the Coral Sea.

lifestyles at cultural centres such as the Dreamtime Centre near Rockhampton or be entertained by the world-renowned Tjapukai Dance Theatre near Cairns.

Touring Queensland by car is easy, although a 4-wheel drive is required to reach some of the more remote Outback regions. The Bruce Hwy links Brisbane with Cairns and gives access to all coastal areas in between. A sealed road continues to Mossman, but dirt roads take over further north into the pristine wilderness of Cape York. A network of roads covers the vast Outback areas, with convenient links to many points on the Bruce Hwy. The enormous distances can also be covered by rail or air. Brisbane, Cairns and Coolangatta have international airports and there are regional airports at many of the larger towns and cities.

Photo above: Daydream Island, Whitsundays

THE SUNSHINE STATE

Seven times the size of Great Britain, twice the size of Texas and five times the size of Japan, Queensland occupies 22.5% of mainland Australia in the subtropical and tropical north-east of the continent. With beaches and islands among its key attractions, Queensland has 5207km of coastline, and from north to south its greatest distance is 2092km.

Known to Australians as the **'Sunshine State'**, weather conditions vary greatly between the coastal plain and the inland environment. In the north, the tropical conditions mean that the Wet season December to March is extremely hot and humid. Inland, days are usually hot and dry throughout the year, while the nights can get cold and frosty in winter. The majority of the coast is bathed in sunshine and warmth most of the year. **Brisbane**, the capital, boasts an average summer temperature of 25°C as well as dry winters. The state's attractions and climate make it the perfect holiday destination.

With over 1000 species of vertebrates, 86% of which are native to the region, Queensland is a wildlife-watcher's paradise. There are about 572 bird species in the state, while the rainforest vegetation, banksias, eucalypts, and the Mitchell-grass plains and spinifex of the south-west also await keen botanists.

Pastoralism has always been important to Queensland's economy. Agriculture, originally in the form of sugarcane farms, now includes cotton, fruits, peanuts, grains and vegetables. Queensland dominates the sugarcane industry, growing almost the country's entire export crop. Around 37% of Australian beef is farmed in Queensland.

The state accounts for around 23% of Australia's mining industry with coal featuring prominently,

Waterskiing at Brampton Island

followed by copper, lead, bauxite and zinc. There are mineral deposits all over the state, but perhaps the largest and most well-known are located in the mining town of **Mount Isa**.

Tourism, the other dominant industry in Queensland, is very important to the state's economy—a brief visit to the Sunshine State attests to this fact. There are around 4.5 million international visitors annually. They are attracted to the sunny coast, offshore islands, the underwater marine wonderland of the **Great Barrier Reef**, the rainforests, the Outback, Aboriginal rock art and, in the gulf country, unrivalled river and estuary fishing. Three international airports—Brisbane, Cairns and Coolangatta—provide gateways to Queensland's many attractions.

Zillie Falls, Atherton Tableland

Queensland

TOURISM REGION HIGHLIGHTS

Queensland is a state of extraordinary diversity. It has three of Australia's most treasured natural wonders—the 2000km-long **Great Barrier Reef**, **Fraser Island** and the ancient **Daintree** rainforest. All of these are World Heritage-listed. There are literally hundreds of tropical beaches, islands and national parks to explore and a vast Outback of rugged and austere beauty.

A Brisbane (pp.224–231)
Brisbane Forest Park; City Botanic Gardens; Ipswich; Lone Pine Koala Sanctuary; Moreton Bay; Moreton Island; Mount Coot-tha; Queen St Mall; Queensland Cultural Centre; Redcliffe; Roma Street Parkland; South Bank; Treasury Casino

B Bundaberg, Coral Isles and Country
Bundaberg Rum Distillery; Cania Gorge; Childers; Hinkler House; Lady Elliot Island; Lady Musgrave Island; Mon Repos Beach; Mystery Craters; Whale watching

C Capricorn (pp.266–267)
Dreamtime Cultural Centre; Gemfields; Great Barrier Reef; Great Keppel Island; Mount Morgan; Rockhampton; Yeppoon

D Fraser Coast South Burnett (pp.258–259)
Fraser Island; Hervey Bay; Kingaroy; Maryborough; Whale watching

Aboriginal hand-prints, Carnarvon National Park

E Gladstone
Agnes Water; Calliope River Historical Village; Gladstone Marina; Great Barrier Reef; Heron Island; Kroombit Tops; Seventeen Seventy

F Gold Coast (pp.246–247)
Currumbin Wildlife Sanctuary; Dreamworld; Jupiters Casino; Lamington NP; Movie World; Natural Arch; Sanctuary Cove; Sea World; Surfers Paradise

G Mackay
Brampton Island; Eungella NP; Finch Hatton Gorge; Great Barrier Reef; Hamilton Island; Lindeman Island; Sugar Mill tours

H Queensland's Outback
Barcaldine; Birdsville; Camooweal Caves; Hughenden Dinosaur Display Centre; Lark Quarry; Outback at Isa; Richmond Fossil Centre; Simpson Desert; Stockman's Hall of Fame

I South East Queensland Country
Bunya Mountains; Crows Nest Falls; Darling Downs; Granite Belt Wineries; Ipswich; Scenic Rim; Toowoomba; Warwick

J Sunshine Coast (pp.254–255)
Australia Zoo; Blackall Range; Caloundra; Glass House Mountains; Gympie; Noosa Heads; Noosa NP; Rainbow Beach; The Big Pineapple; The Ginger Factory; Teewah Coloured Sands; UnderWater World

K Townsville
Bedarra Island; Charters Towers; Dunk Island; Great Barrier Reef; Hinchinbrook Island; Magnetic Island; Museum of Tropical Queensland; Orpheus Island; Reef HQ; Wallaman Falls

L Tropical North Queensland (pp.238–239)
Atherton Tableland; Cairns; Cape Tribulation; Cape York; Chillagoe Caves; Cooktown; Crater Lakes; Daintree NP; Gulf Savannah; Green Island; Great Barrier Reef; Johnstone River Crocodile Farm; Kuranda; Kuranda Scenic Railway; Lawn Hill Gorge; Mission Beach; Mossman Gorge; Port Douglas; Riversleigh Fossil Fields; Skyrail Rainforest Cableway; Tjapukai Aboriginal Cultural Centre; Undara Lava Tubes; Waterfall Circuit; White-water rafting

M Western Downs
Carnarvon Gorge; Chinchilla Folk Museum; Goondiwindi; Miles; Roma

N Whitsundays (pp.262–263)
Airlie Beach; Conway NP; Daydream Island; Great Barrier Reef; Hamilton Island; Hayman Island; Lindeman Island; Proserpine; Whitehaven Beach; Whitsunday Passage

NATIONAL PARKS

Providing habitats for Queensland's diverse wildlife and plants and preserving some of the state's most unique scenery, the national parks of Queensland are distinctly beautiful samples of the state's natural landscapes and heritage. The national parks can be divided into six regions: the south-east, central coast, central highlands, western Queensland, north Queensland and far north Queensland. Interestingly, most of Queensland's national parks are also the state's major tourist attractions. Camping is possible in most of the national parks, but a small fee does apply.

facts

◈ No. of parks/reserves: 527

◈ Total area: 71 615km²

◈ % of state: 4.15%

◈ World Heritage Areas. Australian Fossil Mammal Site (Riversleigh), Central Eastern Rainforest Reserves, Great Barrier Reef, Fraser Island, and the Wet Tropics

A Boodjamulla (Lawn Hill) NP (Map 278, A5)

Located 350km north-west of Mount Isa, Boodjamulla NP borders the Northern Territory. Around 2820km², this national park is a haven for freshwater crocodiles, which are the 'friendlier' of the two varieties. It is best to visit the park in winter and early spring as access can be quite difficult, especially during the Wet season. The gravel and dirt roads are easier to navigate with 4-wheel drives. The rugged gorges, ancient creeks and wildlife make this park a wonderland for nature lovers and explorers. Take a stroll, a hike, a canoe or inflatable boat and adventure through one of Queensland's northernmost national parks.

B Brisbane Forest Park (Map 230, A2)

On the western outskirts of the state's capital, Brisbane Forest Park covers 285km² and is made up of four small parks, forests and reserves. The place for birdwatchers, bushwalkers and campers, the park's convenient location and optional ranger-guided activities are the main attractions for a quick, quiet escape from Brisbane. Visit year-round to picnic, BBQ, walk, and explore the lakes, creeks, rainforests and eucalypt forests. To camp, pre-arrange a permit with the park ranger.

C Cooloola (Great Sandy NP) (Map 255, C1)

Cooloola—part of Great Sandy NP—is located 200km north of Brisbane. Great to visit year-round, the national park offers the opportunities for water activities—canoeing, surf fishing, river fishing—as well as bushwalking, camping and 4-wheel driving. Common fishing catches include bream, whiting and flathead. The 560km² park has unique features such as the coloured sands of Teewah Beach and Rainbow Beach, rainforests that grow in sand and 'perched' lakes found high in sand dunes. Originally inhabited by the Kabi people, timber merchants arrived in the area in 1840, introducing diseases that devestated the Aboriginal people.

D Daintree NP (Map 239, A1)

Daintree NP (565km²) is situated about 80km north of Cairns, and the **Cape Tribulation** section is a further 25km north (170km²). The best time to visit the lush rainforest and rugged mountain ranges of the park is from April to October (to avoid the Wet season). Known for its unique and rare bird, animal and plant life, the national park is in parts quite inaccessible to the amateur hiker or walker. Permits for camping are necessary. Visitors need to be careful of saltwater crocodiles that are found in the creeks and rivers.

White-lipped tree frog, *Litoria infrafrenata*

Queensland

Diving in the Great Barrier Reef Marine Park

E Fraser Island (Great Sandy NP) (Map 259, D2)

Also part of Great Sandy NP, Fraser Island is administered as a separate park to Cooloola. Covering 1653km², the island is the largest sand island in the world and is listed as a World Heritage Area. Known for its variety of wildlife (over 230 bird species), Fraser Island is a popular destination with its amazing geographic heritage, coloured sands, perched dune lakes, desert-like sandblows, saltwater fishing, walking and hiking trails. Camping, cabin and resort accommodation is available. There are no formed roads on the island, so it is necessary to take a 4-wheel drive

Big Red Sand Dune, Simpson Desert National Park

for exploring. There are barges operating from four different points on the island and mainland, and it is possible to arrive via light plane. There are prearranged tours and daytrips available for those preferring a guided service.

F Great Barrier Reef Marine Park (Map 279, K2)

The world's largest World Heritage Area and the largest structure made by living organisms, the Great Barrier Reef consists of 2900 reefs and around 600 islands. Located on the outer edge of Australia's north-eastern continental shelf (once part of the Queensland coast), the Reef extends for 2000km from Bundaberg/Maryborough in the south to beyond Cape York in the tropical north. Coral is formed from the hard chalky skeletons of tiny marine polyps, which are invertebrate animals related to jellyfish and sea anemones. Given the right conditions, coral reefs are in a continual state of growth. The Reef attracts a multitude of brightly coloured fish and other sea creatures, as well as 215 species of birds, six species of turtles and the largest dugong population in the world. It offers some of the world's best diving and snorkelling sites.

The entire area is managed by the Great Barrier Reef Marine Park Authority which was established in 1975. Many of the Barrier Reef's islands are listed as separate national parks.

G Simpson Desert NP (Map 284, B1)

Bordered by South Australia and the Northern Territory, Simpson Desert NP is the largest national park in Queensland at 10 120km² and is a suitable destination for 4-wheel drives only. For those interested in remote desert camping, this national park should be top of the list. Red sand dunes carpeted with spinifex and broken intermittently by valleys spotted with wattles and scrub create a wonderful Australian scene. Inhabited mainly by small reptiles, birds and dingos, the national park is also home to beautiful salt lakes.

National Park Information

Environmental Protection Agency
Queensland Parks and Wildlife Service
PO Box 155,
Brisbane Albert St,
Qld 4002
Ph: (07) 3227 8185
www.epa.qld.gov.au

WINERIES

Queensland is generally regarded as a newcomer to the Australian wine industry, although wine grapes have been grown in the state since the 1860s. The oldest winery was established in the unlikely location of **Roma**, where **Samuel Bassett** planted vine cuttings from the Hunter Valley, New South Wales, in 1863. His **Romavilla** vineyard was a thriving business with several export markets and award-winning wines; it still exists today.

Vineyards were planted in other areas of south-east Queensland, however, it was not until the 1960s that the industry really burgeoned. **Ballandean Estate** was the first vineyard in the **Southern Downs**, which is now Queensland's most successful wine region. Experimentation with wine varieties, soils and microclimates has led to further successes in recent years. Continuing research is leading to new developments in coastal regions as far north as **Bundaberg** and **Gladstone**.

Queensland wines are light, crisp and fruity, and harmonise well with Queensland's fresh cuisine and the state's relaxed lifestyle.

Wine tasting at Cedar Creek Estate Vineyard and Winery, North Tamborine, Gold Coast Hinterland

A Brisbane and Gold Coast (pp.234–235)

Several wineries have recently been established within a short drive of Brisbane, both in the **Brisbane Valley** and on the **Scenic Rim** region in the **Gold Coast Hinterland**. Wines include semillon, chardonnay, shiraz, cabernet, merlot, chenin blanc and sauvignon blanc.

B South Burnett

Fertile soils and elevation well above sea level have contributed to the eminence of this new winery region around **Kingaroy** and **Murgon**. High quality table wines are produced and include merlot, shiraz, traminer and full-bodied chardonnays.

C Southern Downs

The success of the region around **Stanthorpe** has been helped by a combination of high altitude, cool climate and decomposed granite soils. The 30 or more Southern Downs wineries have earned a reputation for full-bodied reds and very crisp premium whites.

D Sunshine Coast and D'Aguilar Ranges (pp.254–255)

This is another fast-growing wine region on the rich volcanic soils of the **Blackall** and **D'Aguilar ranges**. The excellent views are matched by a range of classic table wines, including chardonnay, sauvignon blanc, cabernet and shiraz.

E Toowoomba (pp.270–271)

A number of boutique wineries are scattered around Toowoomba, a region enjoying a renaissance. A wide selection of red and white table wines is produced as well as fortified wines. Rimfire Winery won an award for Australia's best chardonnay in 1997.

F Western Downs

Queensland's oldest wine region is in the Western Downs and has long been known for liqueur muscats, ports and sweet dessert wines. Merlot, chardonnay, cabernet sauvignon, shiraz, crouchen, chenin blanc, riesling, semillon and ruby cabernet are also produced.

Queensland

ISLANDS

Islands are magnets for tourists and Queensland has a wealth of beautiful tropical and subtropical islands, which cater for most tastes. While accommodation ranges from budget to luxury resorts, many islands are uninhabited and invite exploration.

Sandy Islands

South Stradbroke Island lies just off the Gold Coast, while **North Stradbroke Island** is a short ferry ride from **Cleveland** in Brisbane. The **Moreton Bay islands**, made up of **Russell**, **Lamb**, **Macleay**, **Karragarra** and other islands, are known for watersports, sailing, swimming and fishing. **Moreton Island**, north-east of Brisbane, is renowned for its huge sandhills, lakes, dolphins and 4-wheel driving. **Fraser Island**, a World Heritage-listed national park with rainforests, perched lakes, great basalt headlands, salt pans and white-sand beaches is extremely popular. (*see* pp.258–259).

Great Barrier Reef Islands

Lady Elliot Island, north-east of **Bundaberg**, is an unspoiled coral cay known for its diving sites and birdlife. **Heron Island** is a true coral cay best known for diving, birdlife and turtles. **Green Island** has the only international five-star resort found on a coral cay; it is a short boat trip from **Cairns**. Just north of Green Island, **Michaelmas Reef** is a protected sanctuary for 27 000 migratory birds and nesting place for 14 bird species. The tiny **Low Isles** are a popular destination with their magnificent coral gardens and coconut-palm-fringed beaches.

Continental Islands

Great Keppel Island lies offshore from **Yeppoon**. Only eight of the 74 **Whitsunday Islands**, located between the Great Barrier Reef and **Airlie Beach**, are inhabited. Some of the most popular Whitsunday Islands include **Lindeman**, **Hayman**, **Brampton**, **Daydream**, **South Molle**, **Long** and **Hamilton**

Red-tailed frigate bird, *Phaethon rubricauda*

(*see* pp.262–263). **Magnetic Island** is **Townsville's** island playground—20 minutes by Cat Ferry from the city. **Hinchinbrook Island**, off **Cardwell**, is a huge national park with a resort that caters for up to 50 guests at a time. **Dunk Island** has a large resort and is known for horseriding, watersports and rainforest walks. Nearby **Bedarra** and **Orpheus islands** are secluded and relaxing. **Fitzroy Island** caters for a range of budgets and is close to Cairns. **Lizard Island**, north of Cooktown, is bordered by sandy beaches and coral; it is also home to a marine research station. At the top of **Cape York**, the **Torres Strait Islands** showcase the distinctive culture of the Torres Strait Islanders. The main tourist centre is on **Thursday Island**.

Hayman Island Resort, Whitsundays

BRISBANE

City Botanic Gardens, Brisbane

main attractions

◈ **City Botanic Gardens**

Formal gardens, bicycle tracks and duck ponds are some of the gardens' attractions.

◈ **Fortitude Valley and Chinatown**

The cosmopolitan area to the north of the CBD boasts a wide range of cafes and restaurants as well as clubs and a shopping mall.

◈ **Mount Coot-tha Lookout**

Superb panoramic views over the city, bay and hinterland can be enjoyed here. Nearby, Brisbane Botanic Gardens feature a scented garden and the Sir Thomas Brisbane Planetarium.

◈ **Queen St Mall**

With its blend of traditional and modern architecture, Queen St Mall brings to life the city's shopping centres.

◈ **Queensland Cultural Centre**

Located on Brisbane River's South Bank, the complex consists of the Queensland Museum, the Queensland Art Gallery, the State Library and the huge Performing Arts Complex.

◈ **South Bank**

This is a recreation area providing entertainment for all with gardens, waterways, a subtropical beach, riverside walkways, cafes, restaurants and BBQ facilities.

The northernmost of Australia's state capitals, subtropical Brisbane is an attractive city lying 14km inland on the banks of the **Brisbane River**. It enjoys warm summers and clear mild winters. Although for many years Brisbane was a capital with the atmosphere of a large country town, the 1984 Commonwealth Games and the 1988 World Expo helped to change that image. Visitors now find a modern and sophisticated city that is full of life and vitality.

Settled in 1825 by a detachment of 45 convicts and their guards, Brisbane was originally a penal settlement situated at **Redcliffe**, north of the city's current location. The move to Brisbane's current site beside the river was mainly due to a lack of fresh water, the failure of introduced crops and unrest among the local Aboriginal people. The riverside position has since played a pivotal role in the life of the city. Paddlewheelers, yachts, floating restaurants, ferries, cruise boats and bridges can be seen from many vantage points on the river's picturesque banks.

ℹ️ **Visitor information**

Brisbane Visitor Information Centre
Queen St Mall,
Brisbane, Qld 4000
Ph: (07) 3006 6290
www.ourbrisbane.com.au

facts

◈ Population: 1 655 000

◈ Date founded: 1825

◈ Tallest building: Riparian Plaza, 249m

◈ Average temperature: 25°C (January), 16°C (June)

Places of Interest

ANZAC Square Ⓐ D3
Brisbane City Hall and Tower Ⓑ C4
Brisbane Convention and
   Exhibition Centre Ⓒ B5
Brisbane Cricket Ground (The Gabba) Ⓓ E6
City Botanic Gardens Ⓔ D4
Conrad Treasury Casino Ⓕ C4
Customs House Ⓖ D3
Eagle St Pier and Riverside Markets Ⓗ D4
Kangaroo Point Ⓘ E3
Old Commissariat Store Ⓙ C4
Old Government House Ⓚ D5
Old Windmill Observatory Ⓛ C3
Parliament House Ⓜ D5
Queen St Mall Ⓝ C4
Queensland Art Gallery and Museum Ⓞ B4
Queensland Maritime Museum Ⓟ C5
Queensland Performing Arts Complex Ⓠ C4
Riverside Centre Ⓡ D3
Roma Street Parkland Ⓢ B3
South Bank Ⓣ C5
State Library of Queensland Ⓤ B4
Story Bridge Ⓥ E3
Victoria Barracks Ⓦ B3
Victoria Park Ⓧ C1

Brisbane CBD reflected in the Brisbane River

Queensland

Continued on map 230

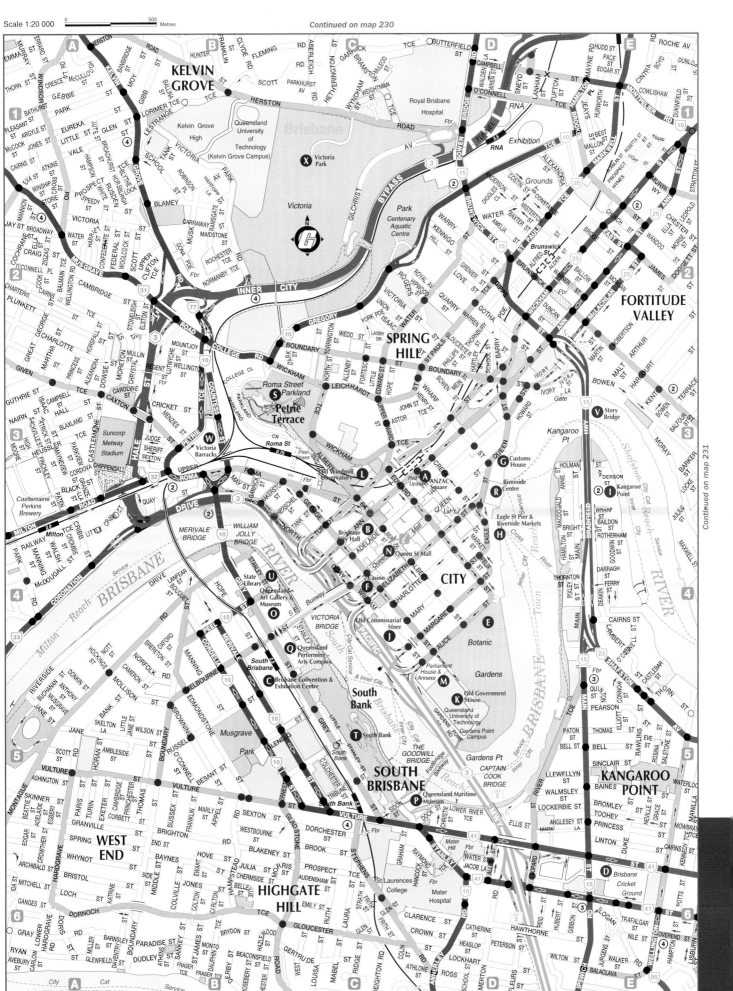

Continued on map 231

© UNIVERSAL PUBLISHERS PTY LTD 2005

CBD & SUBURBS

CBD ATTRACTIONS

Although more of Brisbane's population live outside the city compared to other capital cities, it is still vibrant and economically and culturally alive. With a lot to see and do, and an atmosphere of lazy sunny days, a good way to tour Brisbane is on the specific buses. The **City Sights Tour** takes in modern and historical sites around the CBD, while stopping at 19 strategic locations. The ticket is valid all day and gives unlimited access to river ferries and Brisbane Transport's commuter bus fleet. The **City Nights Tour** includes floodlit landmarks, the illuminated cliff faces of **Kangaroo Point**, and breathtaking night views over the city from **Mount Coot-tha Lookout**. For more details and timetables, contact Transinfo, ph: 13 1230.

For those who are more inclined to explore the city on foot, there is a **self-guided walk** through the CBD that begins at King George Square, along the way viewing **City Hall**, the **Shrine of Remembrance**, the three-storey **Palace Backpackers** hostel and **Parliament House**.

Other attractions to take in are **Customs House**, which is home to many cultural events, exhibitions and lectures. Not too far from here are **Eagle St Pier** and **Riverside Markets**—both popular for food and crafts and just strolling around. Paddlewheelers offer a variety of cruises on the **Brisbane River**; they depart from Eagle St Pier. The **Stamford Plaza Hotel** at the south end of the CBD has gardens and terraces worth wandering through, as well as bars and restaurants with views of the river and the **City Botanic Gardens**. Wandering to the south end of George St, **Parliament House**, constructed in 1868, is a beautiful French Renaissance-style building. Admission is free and includes a guided tour. **Queen St Mall**, located in the centre of the city, is brimming with retail shops, arcades and street performers. To view a neo-Gothic style cathedral, visit **St John's Anglican Cathedral**. Construction began in 1901 and continues to this day. **Conrad Treasury Casino** in George St contains over 100 gaming tables and 1000 poker machines with a variety of entertainment and a buzzing nightlife. **Roma Street Parkland** is the world's largest subtropical garden in a city centre, with a lake and a rainforest fern gully.

SUBURBAN ATTRACTIONS

The suburbs surrounding the Brisbane CBD can be divided into the **Inner Suburbs**, **Southside**, **Bayside**, **Northside** and **Westside**.

Inner Suburbs

Originally a place of farming, shipping, commerce and industry, the inner suburbs are now alive with a diversity of people and nightlife to rival any other city in Australia. **Fortitude Valley** is lined with indoor and outdoor eateries, shops and clubs. Also in the Valley is **Chinatown Mall**, a place of Chinese influence, with an array of clothes, shops, food and festivals. Visitors are attracted to this colourful area to sample authentic yum cha and Chinese culture.

For picnics and BBQs, visit **Kangaroo Point**, a magnificent outdoor reserve with abseiling and rockclimbing facilities, as well as great views from the clifftops. **New Farm**, once a prison farm, is now a leafy suburb brimming with grand

Chinese festival in Fortitude Valley

houses and old cottages. Well-known for its parks, restaurants, bookshops and art galleries, New Farm is worth a visit. Take the **Hail and Ride** bus service for a tour of the 15 galleries in the area. The **Powerhouse Centre for Live Arts** is close by.

For lovers of Australia's colonial heritage, visit **Newstead House**, situated on the eastern side of Fortitude Valley and open daily, except Saturday.

Southside

As one of the city's oldest suburbs, **South Brisbane** offers **South Bank**, 16ha of informal recreational gardens, as well as Brisbane's principal cultural precinct, with theatres, museums and an art gallery to explore.

Cricket lovers venture to **Woolloongabba**, the **Brisbane Cricket Ground** commonly known as **The Gabba**. You can sample the fresh fruit available at the **Brisbane Markets** in **Rocklea** or visit the famous rum distillery at **Beenleigh**. For a panoramic view of Brisbane city, try the **Mount Gravatt Lookout**, only 10km from the CBD.

Bayside

Situated on **Moreton Bay**, the bayside suburbs offer a relaxed ambience and water-based recreational activities. **Cleveland** has an historical precinct and is the departure point for ferries to **North Stradbroke Island**. **Manly** has a large marina and passenger ferry departures to **St Helena Island**. There is a mangrove boardwalk at **Wynnum** and a vehicular and passenger ferry links historic **Redcliffe** with the natural wonders of **Moreton Island**.

Pods of playful bottlenose dolphins are often seen riding the waves in Moreton Bay, and humpback whales sometimes venture into the bay during their winter

Beachfront at Tangalooma Wild Dolphin Resort, Moreton Island

migration (mid-June–October). **Fort Lytton**, at the mouth of the Brisbane River, played an important part in Queensland's defence for over 60 years. The 19th-century fort has a museum and guided tours are available on Sundays.

Northside

On the northside, the 'old money' suburbs of **Hamilton** and **Ascot** are 10km north-east of the CBD. Ascot is home to famous **Eagle Farm Racecourse**. **Boondall Wetlands** is a magnificent reserve about 15km from the CBD. A nature-based recreation area, the wetlands can be explored from a bikeway, walking trails or by canoe. Brisbane's **Alma Park Zoo** and **Lake Samsonvale** are attractions in the far northern suburbs. The lake has several picnic spots and designated areas for shoreside fishing.

Westside

Visit the famous **Lone Pine Koala Sanctuary** close to the Brisbane River at **Fig Tree Pocket** and the many attractions around **Mount Coot-tha**. **Brisbane Forest Park** stretches through the western suburbs, offering bushwalking, picnicking, camping, scenic drives, horseriding and cycling; a permit is required for camping. Lakes, mountains, eucalypt forest, lookouts, gullies, rainforest and waterfalls are all part of the park's natural environment. Park headquarters at **The Gap** has the **Walkabout Creek Wildlife Centre**, where platypus, turtles, lungfish, an aviary and nocturnal wildlife can be seen. Also worth visiting is **Brisbane General Cemetery**, established in 1871. An interesting place to wander around, it offers an insight into the history of Brisbane.

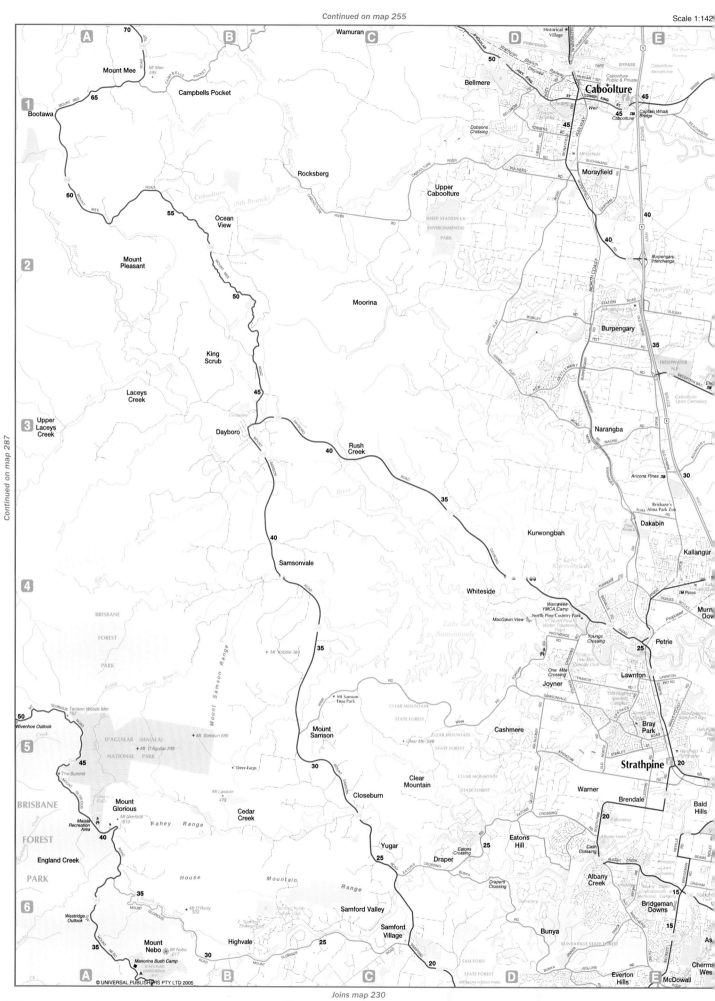

Continued on map 287

Gregory's Australia

Queensland

© UNIVERSAL PUBLISHERS PTY LTD 2005

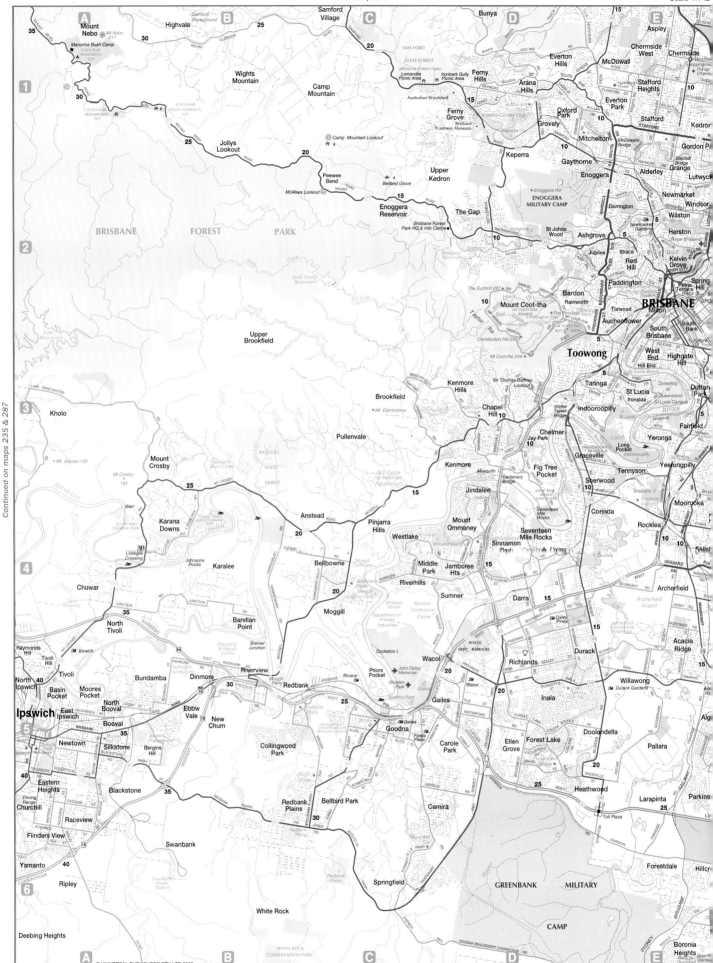

Continued on map 235

Continued on maps 235 & 287

Continued on maps 235 & 247

■ Atherton   POP 5860

Map 239, B5

Located at the heart of north Queensland's tropical **Atherton Tableland**, Atherton is an ideal base for exploring the region. The town is 91km south-west of Cairns and is surrounded by rainforests, pasture lands and tropical crops.

Horseriding on the Atherton Tableland

MAIN ATTRACTIONS: The **Old Post Office Gallery** displays and sells a variety of local art and craft works. The **Chinese Joss House**, next door, stands as a reminder of the once large Chinese population in Atherton. **Fascinating Facets and Crystal Caves** displays minerals, high quality gemstones and valuable rocks. This popular tourist spot is a combination museum, gallery and jewellery store. The basement area displays crystals and has been constructed to resemble a cave. **Halloran Hill Environmental Park** is a reminder of Atherton's volcanic past. The open eucalypt and rainforest walk winds up and around the slopes of an extinct volcano to a lookout at the summit.

NEARBY ATTRACTIONS: **Mount Hypipamee (The Crater) NP**, 26km south of Atherton, has a walking track leading to the stunning **Dinner Falls**. **Heberton** is an historic tin-mining town, 18km to the south-west.

VISITOR INFORMATION: Cnr Main St and Silo Rd, Ph: (07) 4091 4222

■ Ayr   POP 8700

Map 282, D1

This sugar, mango and melon town, north-west of the **Burdekin River** delta, is the main commercial centre of Burdekin Shire. Known as the **'Silver Link'**, the Burdekin Bridge connects Ayr with **Home Hill**. The **Burdekin River Irrigation Scheme** has enabled Ayr to become one of the largest horticultural areas in Australia. One result of this is that it has become a popular backpacker destination.

MAIN ATTRACTIONS: Ayr's most impressive building is the **Burdekin Theatre**, part of the **Burdekin Cultural Complex** in Queen St. The unusual award-winning design of the theatre and the 'Living Lagoon' sculpture in the theatre forecourt attracts many tourists. **Ayr Nature Display**, located in Wilmington St, exhibits an unusual collection of native fauna, butterflies, rocks and shells; a focal point at the centre is a colourful rock wall made from 9 400 pieces of Queensland rock.

NEARBY ATTRACTIONS: **Alva Beach**, 18km from Ayr, offers clean sand

The Boulders, adjacent to Wooroonooran National Park, west of Babinda

and calm waters, ideal for swimmers and fishing. Burdekin Shire attracts many native birds, including magpie geese, jabirus, pelicans, eagles, cockatoos and kingfishers. Spotting some of the area's 280 species is a favourite pastime. Fishing and crabbing in the Burdekin River and its estuaries are also popular. **Hutchings Lagoon**, 5km north-west, is a pleasant picnic spot, ideal for watersports.

VISITOR INFORMATION: Plantation Park, Bruce Hwy, Ph: (07) 4783 5988

▨ Babinda   POP 1230
Map 239, D5

This small sugar town, located 60km south of Cairns, lies in the shadow of **Mount Bartle Frere** in **Wooroonooran NP**. Babinda has an average annual rainfall of 4238mm and holds a long-standing record for the highest recorded annual rainfall in Australia.

NEARBY ATTRACTIONS: Wooroonooran NP boasts the two highest mountain peaks in Queensland: Mount Bartle Frere (1622 m) and **Mount Bellenden Ker** (1598m). Fit and experienced walkers can climb Mount Bartle Frere via a walking track, but Mount Bellenden Ker is

not accessible. There are many scenic walks through the rainforest and the spectacular **Josephine Falls** is worthwhile visiting. **The Boulders**, 6km west of Babinda, is a popular picnic and recreation spot. The area has bushwalking tracks along **Babinda Creek**, at the base of Mount Bartle Frere. There are waterfalls, mountain streams and swimming holes. Facilities include change rooms and BBQs together with a basic camping area. **Deeral**, 14km north, is a departure point for cruises of the **Mulgrave** and **Russell rivers**, and the **Frankland Islands**. Visitors can cruise along the rainforest rivers and see saltwater crocodiles and other wildlife.

VISITOR INFORMATION: Cnr Munro St and Bruce Hwy, Ph: (07) 4067 1008

▨ Barcaldine   POP 1595
Map 282, B5

Located in the heart of a vast wool-growing and cattle-raising district, the town is 106km east of Longreach. Barcaldine is known as the 'Garden City of the West'.

MAIN ATTRACTIONS: **Mad Mick's Funny Farm** offers tours of nine restored, refurnished settlers' buildings and old shearing sheds. Hand-reared wildlife includes kangaroos and emus. There are wool-shearing demonstrations and Billy tea and damper lunches are available. The farm is located on the corner of Pine St and Bauhinia St. **Barcaldine and District Folk Museum** houses a collection of memorabilia and is located on the corner of Gidyea St and Beech St. **The Tree of Knowledge** is a ghost gum which stands in Oak St. In 1891, political history was made when 400 striking shearers gathered beneath this tree for a series of meetings, out of which the Australian Labour Party was formed. The **Australian Workers' Heritage Centre** is located in Ash St. Centred around a billabong, there are heritage

buildings with displays of art and history, celebrating the achievements of working men and women. Barcaldine has several National Trust buildings, including the **Masonic Lodge** and **Anglican Church**.

VISITOR INFORMATION: Oak St, Ph: (07) 4651 1724

▨ Bargara   POP 3600
Map 259, A1

This popular resort is the site of the world's first artificially created surfing point-break. Located 13km east of Bundaberg, Bargara is the largest and closest of its seaside townships.

MAIN ATTRACTIONS: A temperate climate and year-round sunshine provide ample opportunities to swim, surf, snorkel, windsurf and sail at **Kelly's** and **Nielson Park beaches**. Bundaberg Surf Lifesaving Club patrols both beaches, but Kelly's is more attractive to families with small children due to its calm-water swimming area known as **Money's Creek**. Excellent diving and snorkelling is available just off **Bargara Beach**. Coral diving sites here are some of the closest to the Australian mainland.

NEARBY ATTRACTIONS: Panoramic views of the cane fields and ocean can be seen from **The Hummock**, an extinct volcano and the highest point in the district. A boardwalk travels through a patch of **Wongarra Scrub**—the last of the area's original vegetation—to the lookout. **Mon Repos Turtle Rookery**, Australia's best-known and most accessible sea turtle rookery, is a few kilometres north-west of town. Loggerhead, flatback, green and leatherback turtles come ashore after dark to lay their eggs. The nesting and hatching season occurs from November to March. Guided walks are conducted each night during this time.

VISITOR INFORMATION: 20 Baver St, Ph: (07) 4153 8888 or 1800 308 888

THE SCENIC RIM

Located south of Brisbane and on the border with New South Wales, the Scenic Rim's mountain rainforests form a barrier between the **Eastern Downs** and the coastal plains of the **Gold Coast**. A testament to nature's diversity, this lush expanse of sub-tropical rainforest hides national parks, the breathtaking **Lamington Plateau**, majestic waterfalls, remote river valleys and fertile farmlands, all with a backdrop of stunning mountain ranges. The national parks are part of the **Central Eastern Australian Rainforest Reserves World Heritage Area**. Cattle and dairy farms abound in the valleys and hills and there are quaint country towns with many galleries, shops and boutiques to explore.

A bushwalker's oasis, the Scenic Rim offers much to explore for daytrippers, campers and adventurers. The region combines well-trodden paths with more isolated tracks, so visitors have the choice of either joining or escaping the crowds. Three mountain groups dominate the landscape, providing the source for the numerous rivers and streams that keep this verdant region well-watered.

The resplendent male regent bowerbird, *Sericulus chrysocephalus*, is fairly common in the parks of the Scenic Rim

Tree Top Walkway

The highlight of a visit to **O'Reilly's Rainforest Guesthouse**, in **Lamington NP**, is an exhilarating walk 16m above the rainforest canopy and along nine suspension bridges spanning 160m. Anchoring one corner of the bridge is an ancient fig tree, where the adventurous can make the vertical climb to the crow's nest at the top of this forest giant. The reward is a magnificent view over the **Green Mountains**.

main attractions

◈ **Binna Burra**

Binna Burra is the north-east portion of Lamington NP. Binna Burra Lodge is a privately run resort in the middle of the rainforest.

◈ **Green Mountains**

This section of Lamington NP offers panoramic views of the park.

◈ **Lamington National Park**

This national park protects Australia's largest remaining subtropical rainforest.

◈ **O'Reilly's Rainforest Guesthouse**

A feature of visiting this guesthouse, which has been open since the 1920s, is the Tree Top Walkway.

◈ **Springbrook National Park**

This park showcases the Springbrook Plateau, Mount Cougal and Natural Bridge.

◈ **Tamborine Mountain**

The three villages of Tamborine Mountain feature galleries, cafes, gardens and sweeping views—some to the ocean.

 Visitor information

Beaudesert Community Arts and Information Centre
2-14 Enterprise Dr, Beaudesert, Qld 4285
Ph: (07) 5541 4495

Natural Bridge, Springbrook National Park

Queensland

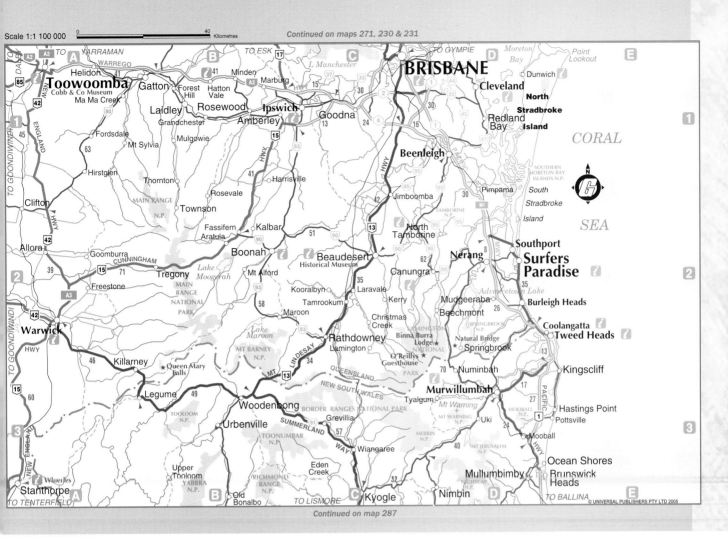

Continued on maps 271, 230 & 231

Continued on map 287

Beaudesert   POP 4460

Map 235, C2

Approximately an hour's drive from either **Brisbane** or the **Gold Coast**, Beaudesert is located in the middle of a region of rainforests, valleys and plains in the Gold Coast hinterland. A major rural centre, Beaudesert is known for its dairying, agriculture and beef cattle.

MAIN ATTRACTIONS: **Beaudesert Historical Museum** is located in Brisbane St and is open daily. Exhibits include the Pioneer Cottage, furnished in a style portraying early pioneering life, together with horse-drawn vehicles and farm implements.

NEARBY ATTRACTIONS: Beaudesert is an ideal base for exploring national parks, such as **Lamington**, **Mount Maroon** and **Mount Barney**. The Mount Barney area offers walking tracks and the **Logan River** and other streams provide great spots for swimming and carp fishing. A caravan and camping area is provided at the foot of Mount Barney, although campers must apply for a permit. **Tamborine Mountain** is a major tourist destination and comprises three small villages and several small national parks in an area of centuries-old rainforest.

VISITOR INFORMATION: Community Arts and Information Centre, 2-14 Enterprise Dr, Ph: (07) 5541 4495

Biloela   POP 5450

Map 283, G6

This rural town, in the centre of the **Callide Valley**, is located 647km north-west of Brisbane and is the largest town in Banana Shire, which has no bananas!

Rainforest walk in Lamington National Park, south of Beaudesert

MAIN ATTRACTIONS: **Greycliffe Homestead** (1840s) has been listed by the National Trust of Queensland and is filled with memorabilia of early days. It is open by appointment only. The **SILO**—an acronym for Simulated Interactive Learning Opportunities—is one of the most prominent features in Biloela and is located on Exhibition Ave. Displays focus on farming and mining technology and include electricity generation and alternative energy sources.

NEARBY ATTRACTIONS: **Callide Dam**, 5km north-east, is ideal for BBQs, boating, swimming and fishing. **Callide 'B' Power Station** is 15km east of Biloela. Free one hour guided tours of the station operate from the main gate, Tuesday to Friday afternoons. **Kroombit Tourist Park**, near **Kroombit Tops NP** to the east, offers farm activities, hiking, horseriding and accommodation ranging from bunkhouse to three-star. **Mount Scoria** lies 17km south. Its name comes from scoriaceous basalt, a type of volcanic rock.

VISITOR INFORMATION: 11 Exhibition St, Ph: (07) 4992 5400

Blackall   POP 1435

Map 282, B6

Located 106km south of Barcaldine and 969km north-west of Brisbane, Blackall, on the **Barcoo River**, is at the centre of sheep-farming country. It is also the site of the state's first artesian bore—drilled in 1815.

MAIN ATTRACTIONS: A replica of the original **'Black Stump'** for this area is located in Thistle St. Outside the **Universal Garden Centre and Gallery**, in Shamrock St, is the **Jackie Howe Memorial**. It commemorates this shearer's record set in 1892, when he blade-sheared 321 sheep in seven hours and 40 minutes. This astonishing record remained until 1950, but then it was only broken by the use of mechanical shears. There are Jackie Howe memorabilia at the Garden Centre.

NEARBY ATTRACTIONS: **Blackall Wool Scour** is considered the most complete relic of the wool-scouring industry in Australia. Located 4.2km north of Blackall, the steam-driven scour was built in 1907. Guided tours are offered daily. **Idalia NP** is 100km south-west of Blackall and covers 1440km^2. The park is best known as a home for the rare and endangered yellow-footed rock wallaby.

VISITOR INFORMATION: Shamrock St, Ph: (07) 4657 4637

Blackwater   POP 5935

Map 282, E5

This leading coal-mining centre of Queensland is located 190km west of Rockhampton. Coal from open-cut mines is transported to **Gladstone** for export and steaming coal provides fuel for the **Gladstone Power Station**. The discolouration of the town's waterholes, from the tannins released by the district's plentiful tea-trees, has given Blackwater its name.

MAIN ATTRACTION: The town park has a lovely **Japanese Garden** donated by Blackwater's sister town in Japan.

NEARBY ATTRACTIONS: **Blackdown Tableland NP**, 34km south-east of Blackwater, has deep gorges. **Carnarvon NP**, to the south-west, includes spectacular **Carnarvon Gorge**, clear-water creeks and waterfalls. There are fireplaces, lookouts, a camping area and scenic walking tracks throughout the park.

VISITOR INFORMATION: Clermont St, Emerald, Ph: (07) 4982 4142

Boonah   POP 2235

Map 235, B2

Surrounded by the hills of the **Great Dividing Range** known as the **Scenic Rim**, Boonah is located in the heart of the scenic Fassifern district, just over an hour's drive from Brisbane and one hour from the Gold Coast. Boonah is located in a picturesque area of Queensland and its rugged mountains, lakes and valleys attract many visitors. Bush-walking is popular given the many scenic walking tracks in the area.

MAIN ATTRACTIONS: The town's **art gallery** is located in **Boonah Cultural Centre** in High St, and features leadlight displays, local artworks and sculptures. The information centre has details on a broad range of activities, including gliding and ultralight flight tours.

NEARBY ATTRACTIONS: **Main Range NP**, 35km west, is part of the Scenic Rim and offers picturesque drives, bushwalking, trail riding and rockclimbing. **Cunninghams Gap Lookout** offers panoramic views. **Lake Moogerah** has picnic areas and is a popular venue for sailing, fishing and waterskiing. South of the lake lies **Moogerah Peaks NP**, which is made up of several small parks, rocky cliffs and volcanic peaks, including **Mount French**.

VISITOR INFORMATION: Bicentennial Park, Boonah–Fassifern Rd, Ph: (07) 5463 2233

Outback sunset near Blackall

Queensland

Bowen POP 9005

Map 282, E1

This holiday town on the coast halfway between Townsville and Mackay is called the **'Climate Capital of the North'**. Bowen is the oldest town in north Queensland first settled in 1861. Year-round warm weather and eight sandy beaches fringed by clear waters attract many visitors to Bowen.

MAIN ATTRACTIONS: The best-known beach is **Horseshoe Bay**, offering almost every kind of watersport. A highlight is scuba diving on the spectacular coral reef just offshore. There are many other secluded beaches close to town. Visitors can follow a number of signposted arrows on the **Golden Arrow Tour**. This scenic driving tour takes in many points of interest in Bowen. **Bowen Historical Museum** is one of the best country museums in Queensland. Located in Gordon St, it exhibits shells, minerals and Aboriginal artefacts. With 22 historic murals on the town walls and fishing, boating, snorkelling, diving and swimming, Bowen has much to offer visitors.

NEARBY ATTRACTIONS: The area surrounding Bowen is a birdwatcher's paradise with around 219 species to sight. Fossicking for gems (with a licence) is a popular activity, given the area's rich geology. Sapphires, amethysts, crystals, clear quartz, agate and jasper can be found in the area.

VISITOR INFORMATION: Bruce Hwy, Mount Gordon, Ph: (07) 4786 4222

Bundaberg POP 44 135

Map 259, A2

Surrounded by sugarcane fields, this city, which has many fine examples of Queensland architecture, is the southernmost centre for the **Great Barrier Reef**. Bundaberg, 368km north of Brisbane, is also an important centre for the rich **Burnett River** plains. The Burnett

Hinkler House, home of aviator Bert Hinkler, in Bundaberg's Botanical Gardens

River runs through the city and flows into the ocean 11km beyond Bundaberg.

MAIN ATTRACTIONS: **Alexandra Park and Zoo** is on the riverbank in Quay St; admission to the zoo is free. **Bundaberg Rum Distillery** is located next to Millaquin Sugar Mill. Tours of the plant show all aspects of the rum-making process. The distillery visitors centre, **Spring Mill House**, is a restored plantation house containing a museum, souvenir shop and tasting bar. **Schmeiders Cooperage and Craft Centre**, located near the distillery, offers an insight into local arts and crafts with glassblowing and wood-working demonstrations. The **Botanical Gardens**, in Mount Perry Rd, also contain **Hinkler House**, home of aviator Bert Hinkler and now a pioneer aviation museum; **Bundaberg Historical Museum**; and **Fairymead House Sugar Museum**, which showcases the story of the sugar industry. Close to the gardens is **Tropical Wines**, which offers free tastings of fruit wines.

NEARBY ATTRACTIONS: There are many coastal and hinterland self-drive tours to explore. **Mon Repos Conservation Park** is 15km north-east and contains the largest and most accessible mainland sea turtle rookery in Australia. Turtles nest

and hatch between November and March. **Lady Elliot Island** and **Lady Musgrave Island** are easily accessible from Bundaberg. The MV *Lady Musgrave* departs from Bundaberg Port Marina for Lady Musgrave Island, which boasts the largest lagoon of the Great Barrier Reef. A permit is required for camping on the island. Lady Elliot Island is a 25 minute scenic flight from **Bundaberg Airport**. The beautiful twin resorts of **Agnes Water** and **Seventeen Seventy** (so named for Captain Cook's first landfall in Queensland) are to the north-west.

VISITOR INFORMATION: 271 Bourbong St, Ph: (07) 4153 8888 or 1800 308 888

Cairns POP 92 280

Map 239, C3

Lying at the centre of a tropical paradise on the shores of **Trinity Bay**, Cairns has many natural attractions. It is a stepping-off point to so much, including the **Great Barrier Reef**, rainforests and scenic hinterland such as the **Cape York Peninsula**. Cairns is the premier holiday destination in northern Queensland. Its international airport is the sixth busiest in Australia, handling more than a million visitors each year.

(CONTINUED P.240)

Tropical North Queensland is bordered by the **Coral Sea islands** and the **Great Barrier Reef** to the east and the rainforest mountains that sweep down from the north-ernmost section of the **Great Dividing Range** to the west. Inland from the balmy, humid coast, the **Atherton Tableland** is elevated 600–900m above sea level. Known as the **'cool tropics'**, the weather is usually warm and sunny during the day, while nights are cool to cold.

The region offers waterfalls, lush **Wet Tropics World Heritage-listed rainforests**, idyllic palm-fringed tropical beaches and islands, the wonder of the Great Barrier Reef, extinct volcanoes and crater lakes—all waiting to be explored. Home to Queensland's most northerly city, eden-like Cairns, the region attracts millions of tourist dollars each year, taking pride of place as an international holiday destination. The townships of tropical North Queensland feature an eclectic combination of colonial tropical architecture, modern resorts and a laid-back lifestyle. Visitors can choose from an array of outdoor activities ranging from sunbathing to snorkelling.

Crater Lakes

Lake Barrine and **Lake Eacham** have formed in the craters of extinct volcanoes; volcanic activity ceased on the Tableland around 20 000 years ago. Lake Eacham was an early settlers' camp. Aborigines believed it to be haunted and steered clear of the vicinity, calling it 'No Man's Land of Devil Devils'. The lakes offer enchanting rainforest walks, accommodation, picnicking, swimming and cruises; they are also home to the unique rainbow fish. **Lake Euramo**, located nearby, is a third crater lake filled with swamp.

main attractions

◈ **Daintree National Park**

This wondrous park features ancient rainforest where activities include crocodile-spotting tours, forest walks and birdwatching. Cape Tribulation, where the rainforest meets the reef, is popular with visitors.

◈ **Great Barrier Reef**

One of the Seven Natural Wonders of the World, the reefs, coral cays and offshore islands are World Heritage-listed and accessed by cruise boats from Cairns and Port Douglas.

◈ **Kuranda**

This resort town's attractions include markets, the Australian Butterfly Sanctuary, Birdworld and a Scenic Railway.

◈ **Mossman Gorge**

This is a stunning river gorge filled with giant granite boulders and surrounded by rainforest. The Kuku Yalanji Aboriginal community conduct guided tours.

◈ **Port Douglas**

This is an upmarket tourist resort and the departure point for the Outer Reef and Low Isles.

◊ **Skyrail Rainforest Cableway**

The cable cars make their 7.5km journey from Smithfield near Cairns to Kuranda hovering above the treetops.

◈ **Tjapukai Aboriginal Cultural Park**

This park showcases the internationally acclaimed Tjapukai Aboriginal Dance Theatre. There is also a campsite, restaurant and history theatre.

◈ **Wooroonooran National Park**

Within this mountain wilderness park are Josephine Falls, Walshs Peak (The Pyramid) and Queensland's highest peaks, Mount Bartle Frere and Mount Bellenden Ker.

 Visitor information

Tourism Tropical North Queensland
Gateway Discovery Centre,
51 The Esplanade, Cairns, Qld 4870
Ph: (07) 4051 3588
www.tropicalaustralia.com.au

Diver with a Maori wrasse, *Cheilinus undulatus*, Great Barrier Reef

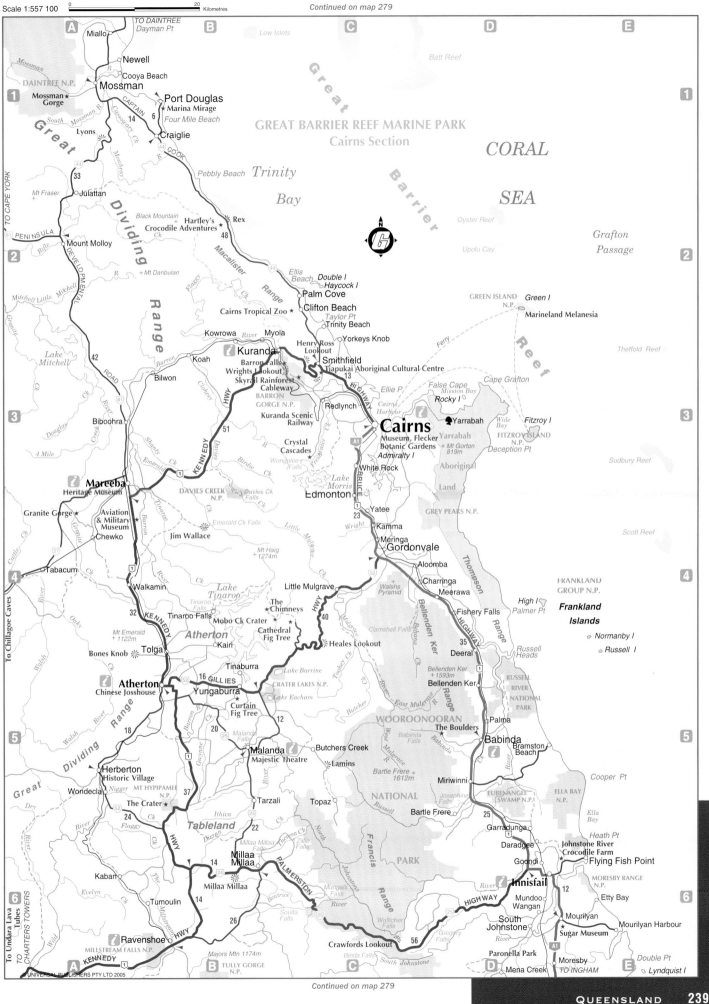

0 ___ 20 Kilometres

Continued on map 279

A **B** **C** **D** **E**

Miallo

TO DAINTREE
Dayman Pt

Low Islets

Newell

Cooya Beach

Mossman

DAINTREE N.P.

Mossman ★
Gorge

Batt Reef

1

Port Douglas

Marina Mirage
Four Mile Beach

14   6

Lyons

Craiglie

GREAT BARRIER REEF MARINE PARK

Cairns Section

CORAL

Mt Fraser

33

Julattan

Pebbly Beach

Trinity

Bay

SEA

Black Mountain

Hartley's ★
Crocodile Adventures

Rex

48

Mount Molloy

+ Mt Danbulan

Ellis
Beach

Double I

Haycock I

Palm Cove

Oyster Reef

Grafton

Passage

Upolu Cay

2

Cairns Tropical Zoo ★

Clifton Beach

Taylor Pt

Trinity Beach

GREEN ISLAND
N.P.

Green I

Marineland Melanesia

Lake
Mitchell

42

Kowrowa

Myola

Yorkeys Knob

Thetfold Reef

Koah

Kuranda

Henry Ross
Lookout

Smithfield

Tjapukai Aboriginal Cultural Centre

Ferry

Bilwon

Barron Falls ★
Wrights Lookout ★
Skyrail Rainforest ★
Cableway

13

Ellie P

False Cape
Mission Bay

Cape Grafton

3

Biboohra

BARRON
GORGE N.P.

Redlynch

Rocky I

Fitzroy I

Kuranda Scenic
Railway

Cairns
Harbour

Cairns

Yarrabah ★

FITZROY ISLAND
N.P.

Deception Pt

4 Mile

Crystal
Cascades

Museum, Flecker
Botanic Gardens

Admiralty I

Yarrabah

+ Mt Gorton
819m

Sudbury Reef

Mareeba

Heritage Museum

White Rock

Aboriginal

Granite Gorge ★

DAVIES CREEK
N.P.

Davies Ck
Falls

*Lake
Morris*

Edmonton

Land

Scott Reef

4

Aviation
& Military
Museum

Chewko

Emerald Ck Falls

Wright

23

Yatee

Kamma

GREY PEAKS N.P.

Tabacum

Jim Wallace

Mt Haig
+1274m

Meringa

Gordonvale

FRANKLAND
GROUP N.P.

Walkamin

*Lake
Tinaroo*

Little Mulgrave

Aloomba

Charringa

Walshs
Pyramid

Meerawa

High I
Palmer Pt

Frankland

Islands

32

Tinaroo Falls

The
Chimneys

Fishery Falls

Russell
Heads

Normanby I

Russell I

Atherton

Mobo Ck Crater

Cathedral
Fig Tree

40

Bellenden
Ker

35

Deeral

Mt Emerald
+1122m

Kairi

Heales Lookout

Clamshell Falls

RUSSELL

5

Bones Knob

Tolga

Tinaburra

Lake Barrine

Bellenden Ker
+1593m

Bellenden Ker

RUSSELL

RIVER

NATIONAL

PARK

16 GILLIES

CRATER LAKES N.P.

Palma

Atherton

Chinese Josshouse

Yungaburra

Lake Eacham

WOOROONOORAN

The Boulders

Babinda

Bramston
Beach

Curtain
Fig Tree

12

Butchers Creek

Babinda
Falls

18

20

Malanda
Falls

Malanda
Majestic Theatre

Lamins

Bartle Frere +
1612m

Miriwinni

Cooper Pt

Herberton
Historic Village

Wondecla

MT HYPIPAMEE
N.P.

37

Tarzali

Topaz

NATIONAL

Josephine
Falls

EUBENANGEE
[SWAMP N.P.]

ELLA BAY
N.P.

Ella
Bay

The Crater ★

25

PARK

Bartle Frere

25

Garradunga

Heath Pt

24

Tableland

22

Millaa Millaa
Falls

Zillie
Falls

Johnstone River
Crocodile Farm

Daradgee

Kaban

**Millaa
Millaa**

Goondi

Flying Fish Point

Millaa Millaa

MORESBY RANGE
N.P.

14

Tumoulin

26

Innisfail

12

Etty Bay

Ravenshoe

MILLSTREAM FALLS N.P.

Majors Mtn 1174m

TULLY GORGE
N.P.

Crawfords Lookout

56

Binda Falls

South Johnstone

Mundoo
Wangan

**South
Johnstone**

Mourilyan

Sugar Museum

Mourilyan Harbour

Paronella Park

Moresby

TO INGHAM

Double Pt

Lyndquist I

Mena Creek

Continued on map 279

The century-old Flecker Botanic Gardens, Cairns

MAIN ATTRACTIONS: **Trinity Wharf** is the place where international cruise liners berth. **Pier Marketplace** is also on the waterfront. It is a retail and leisure complex with more than 90 outlets. On weekends, local artists and craftspeople display their wares at the **Mud Market**, located in the main amphitheatre. Also popular with locals and visitors alike is **Rusty's Markets**. **Cairns Museum**, located on the corner of Lake St and Shields St, has displays featuring the Aboriginal, timber, goldrush and sugarcane history of the area. **Flecker Botanic Gardens**, in Collins Ave, feature native plants and their traditional use by Aboriginal people. The gardens also have a very large collection of palm species. Cairns is famous for its tropical fruits, fresh seafood and relaxed ambience. It is an international mecca for marlin and other big game fishermen.

NEARBY ATTRACTIONS: The lifestyle, history and culture of the indigenous people of the region is explored at the **Tjapukai Aboriginal Cultural Park**. It showcases the world-renowned **Tjapukai Aboriginal Dance Theatre** and features a history theatre, campsite and restaurant. **Kuranda Scenic Railway** offers an amazing journey, weaving past canefields and jungle-covered mountains and valleys, then through **Barron Gorge** to the fern-covered station at **Kuranda**. **Skyrail Rainforest Cableway** complements the railway. Running from the suburb of **Smithfield**, the cable cars travel for 7.5km across the coastal range and over the rainforest canopy before arriving at Kuranda. The first stop, **Red Peak**, allows passengers to experience the forest floor via boardwalks, while the second stop is located just a short walk from **Barron Falls**. There is a **Rainforest Interpretive Centre** and three lookouts over Barron Gorge. **Cairns Tropical Zoo**, to the north, showcases crocodiles and other Australian wildlife. Cairns is the departure point for many island and reef cruises visiting **Fitzroy Island**, **Green Island**, **Michaelmas Cay** and the **Outer Reef**.

VISITOR INFORMATION: 51 The Esplanade, Ph: (07) 4051 3588

■ Calliope   POP 1200
Map 267, D6

Calliope, 20km south of Gladstone, is a quiet rural town and a gateway to the **Boyne Valley**. Its principal industry centres on beef cattle, mainly Brahmans and Herefords. National parks, creeks and trail riding are some of the attractions the region has to offer.

MAIN ATTRACTIONS: The **Calliope River** is popular for fishing. **Calliope River Historical Village** displays houses and cottages, a pub, schoolhouse, blacksmith's shop, church, railway carriage and station. These historic buildings are from all over the shire and have been relocated to this village. Markets are held in the village six times a year—they are famous for crafts and handmade goods.

MAIN ATTRACTIONS: **Lake Awoonga**, to the south, provides a recreation area and venue for watersports. There are nature walks with flora and fauna trails, picnic and BBQ facilities, a kiosk and caravan park. **Cedar Gallery Artists Village**, between **Benaraby** and Calliope, is worth a visit.

VISITOR INFORMATION: Ferry Terminal, Bryan Jordan Dr, Gladstone, Ph: (07) 4972 4000

■ Caloundra   POP 28 350
Map 255, D5

Caloundra is 95km north of Brisbane. It is one of the **Sunshine Coast's** most urbanised centres with a busy shopping district and a wealth of beautiful beaches.

MAIN ATTRACTIONS: The many beaches include: **Golden Beach** and **Bulcock Beach**, for boating, fishing and safe swimming; **Kings Beach** is a patrolled surfing beach with an enclosed saltwater pool; **Shelly Beach** is a fishing beach with rockpools; **Moffat Beach** is noted for fishing and surfing; and **Dicky Beach** is a patrolled surfing beach with BBQ facilities and playground. **Queensland Air Museum** is at the airport and open daily. Scenic flights of the surrounding area are also available from the airport.

NEARBY ATTRACTIONS: There are many scenic drives to explore, including the coastal strip, **Blackall Range** and **Glass House Mountains NP**. **Currimundi Lake Conservation Park** lies 4km north and is a popular fishing and picnic spot. **Aussie World** and the famous **Ettamogah Pub** are 16km north-west. **Australia Zoo**, home of TV's *Crocodile Hunter*, is located 25km west of Caloundra.

VISITOR INFORMATION: 7 Caloundra Rd, Ph: (07) 5491 9233 or 1800 644 969

Queensland

Charleville POP 3525

Map 286, C3

Charleville, the second largest town of Outback Queensland, is sited on the banks of the **Warrego River** in mulga country, 747km west of Brisbane. It is the service centre for a prosperous sheep and cattle-raising district.

MAIN ATTRACTIONS: **Historical House**, in Alfred St, displays local memorabilia, a working steam engine and a rail ambulance. Historic **Hotel Corones** is a National Trust-classified building furnished in period-style. A guided tour takes place most afternoons. The bilby, one of Australia's most endangered species, is bred at the **Charleville National Parks and Wildlife Office**. Yellow-footed rock wallabies are also bred here. There are bilby tours on Monday, Wednesday, Friday and Sunday nights between April and September. Charleville **School of Distance Education** is located in Parry St and is open for guided tours on school days. Teachers explain how they teach via radio correspondence and visitors can listen to a lesson being broadcast. **Charleville Cosmos Centre**, housed next to the airport's meteorology building, has nightly 'tours' of the sky, April–September, and four nights a week October–March, weather permitting. There are also day 'tours' most days of the year.

NEARBY ATTRACTIONS: Tours of **Myendetta Homestead**, 30km west, are available on Tuesdays and Thursdays (bookings essential). **South-West Air Service** conducts regular tours of Outback Queensland and offers scenic flights over Charleville. There are many scenic drives around the area; brochures and maps are available from the information centre in Sturt Street.

VISITOR INFORMATION: Sturt St, Ph: (07) 4654 3057

Charters Towers POP 8900

Map 282, C1

Located 132km south-west of Townsville, Charters Towers is on the road and rail line to Mount Isa, in the pastoral district of the **Burdekin River Valley**. During the boom years of the goldrush era (1872–1916), Charters Towers was Queensland's second largest city.

MAIN ATTRACTIONS: Many of Charters Towers' National Trust buildings have been restored to their former glory. Both **Gill St** and **Mosman St** are listed as heritage precincts. National Trust buildings worthwhile visiting include **Venus Gold Battery** on Milchester Rd, which offers guided tours, and **Zara Clark Folk Museum** on the corner of Mosman St and Mary St. **Towers Hill**, where gold was first discovered, has panoramic views and nightly *Ghosts of Gold* historical viewings on a giant screen. A *Ghosts of Gold Heritage Trail* starts at the information centre. **Ay-Ot Lookout House** has tours and great views.

NEARBY ATTRACTIONS: The nearby historic gold-mining township of **Ravenswood** also has many National Trust buildings. **White Blow Environmental Park**, near Ravenswood, features a 300 million-year-old quartz-rock formation.

VISITOR INFORMATION: 74 Mosman St, Ph: (07) 4752 0314

Childers POP 1495

Map 287, J2

This small sugar town is located 53km south of Bundaberg. A National Trust town, Childers has many beautiful buildings and tree-lined streets.

MAIN ATTRACTIONS: The **Palace Memorial and Gallery** forms a poignant reminder of the devastating backpacker fire of 2000. **Childers Art Gallery**, on site, is considered one of the finest galleries in provincial Queensland and displays international, national and local art. **Childers Pharmaceutical Museum** retains its original cedar fittings, displays apothecary records and equipment. **Memorabilia Military Museum** has over 20 000 exhibits. The **Historical Complex**, in Taylor St, includes a century-old worker's cottage and other old buildings representing the district's history. Other historical buildings of interest include the **Old Butcher's Shop** (1896) in North St, as well as the **Grand Hotel** and **Federal Hotel** in Churchill St. **Childers Multicultural Food, Wine and Arts Festival** is held on the last Sunday in July.

NEARBY ATTRACTIONS: **Cordalba Hotel** is an historic old pub, 10km north. **Burrum Coast NP** is situated 40km to the east.

VISITOR INFORMATION: 72 Churchill St, Ph: (07) 4126 3886

The National Trust classified Hotel Corones, Charleville

Chinchilla POP 3370
Map 287, G3

Located in the **Western Downs**, 295km north-west of Brisbane, Chinchilla is largely reliant on melon-growing, grazing and sawmilling.

MAIN ATTRACTIONS: **Chinchilla Folk Museum** is a complex of ten buildings, including the original town gaol and school; an 1880s slab cottage with authentic furnishings; and displays of photographs, memorabilia and fashions of the times.

NEARBY ATTRACTIONS: Chinchilla attracts many people to its petrified-wood fossicking area—a stump of petrified wood is displayed outside the information centre. Fishing and boating on the **Condamine River** and **Charleys Creek** are popular.

VISITOR INFORMATION: Warrego Hwy (opposite Pioneer Cemetery) Ph: (07) 4668 9564

Clermont POP 2390
Map 282, D4

This rural town in the **Drummond Range** in Queensland's **Central Highlands** is 940km north-west of Brisbane. Clermont is the commercial centre for the region's cattle and grain growing industries. It was established in 1862, following the discovery of gold and copper at **Copperfield**, the first copper mine in Queensland. The town was relocated to higher ground in 1917 following the devastating floods of 1916.

MAIN ATTRACTIONS: A tour of the **Blair Athol Mine** can be organised through the information centre. **Hoods Lagoon**, located in Lime St, has a scenic walkway; the **Mary MacKillop Grotto**—she visited a local convent; and a memorial to **Billy Sing**, the Anzac's crack sniper of WWI, who was born here.

NEARBY ATTRACTIONS: Fossicking for gold is a popular activity in the district. **Clermont and District Historical Museum** is 4km north-west along the road to Charters Towers. **Copperfield Store Museum**, 7km west, is housed in the original shop from the copper-mining era. **Copperfield Cemetery** is 10km south-west and holds the 19th-century graves of copper miners. **Theresa Creek Dam**, 22km south-west, is a popular spot for fishing, waterskiing, bushwalking and camping. There are picnic areas nearby.

VISITOR INFORMATION: Golden Gallery, Capella St, Ph: (07) 4983 3001

Cloncurry POP 2735
Map 280, D2

Renowned as a colourful frontier-mining town, Cloncurry is 118km east of Mount Isa on the Overlanders Hwy. Cloncurry became the centre of a rich mineral field after copper deposits were discovered in 1867. By 1916 the area was the largest source of copper in Australia. Today, the shire has a rural and mining-based economy.

MAIN ATTRACTIONS: **Cloncurry-Mary Kathleen Memorial Park and Museum**, in McIlwraith St, is home to one of the most comprehensive **Rock and Mineral Displays** in Australia. The park has preserved a unique chapter of north-west Queensland's mining history, with buildings and memorabilia from the former uranium-mining town **Mary Kathleen**. Displays feature local history with the showpiece being Robert O'Hara Burke's (of Burke and Wills fame) water bottle. The outdoor museum has a traction engine, farm and mining machinery as well as an unusual 1941 Ford Rail Ambulance. There are BBQ and picnic areas in the park. **John Flynn Place**, in Daintree St, houses the **Royal Flying Doctor Service Museum** and **Fred McKay Art Gallery**. Displays of historic material in the centre include the first Traeger pedal wireless and automatic Morse keyboard used when the RFDS established its first base in Cloncurry in 1928.

NEARBY ATTRACTIONS: Tours to the recently developed **Ernest Henry Mine**, named after the founder of Cloncurry, are available. The area is a fossicker's paradise, rich in minerals and gems, including garnets, amethysts and rare Maltese Crosses.

VISITOR INFORMATION: Cloncurry-Mary Kathleen Memorial Park, McIlwraith St, Ph: (07) 4742 1361

Camel race at Boulia, south of Cloncurry

Queensland

Campers at Kalpowar Crossing, Lakefield National Park, west of Cooktown

Collinsville POP 2020

Map 282, D2

This coal-mining town lies 83km south-west of Bowen. Modern open-cut mining by Thiess Contractors produces coal for export and Australian markets. The dry tropical climate offers a relaxed lifestyle.

MAIN ATTRACTIONS: **Murals** depicting historic figures and scenes of mining activities painted on building walls contribute to a street beautification scheme. The murals are part of a project linking Collinsville and **Bowen**, on the coast, which has similar murals.

NEARBY ATTRACTIONS: From Collinsville it is a 45 minute drive to Bowen's beaches and the islands of the **Whitsunday coast** are close by. Collinsville is a good base from which to explore the old gold and coal-mining areas of **Ukalunda**, **Normanby**, and **Mount Coolan**, where a hotel and a store still operate. Fossickers can spend hours in and around the area seeking fossilised wood, amethyst, jasper, agate and clear crystal. Fishing and camping are popular on the **Bowen River**.

VISITOR INFORMATION: Shire Office, cnr Stanley St and Conway St, Ph: (07) 4785 5366

Cooktown POP 1580

Map 279, H2

The tropical port of Cooktown lies on the banks of the **Endeavour River**. It was founded in 1873 to service the Palmer River Goldfields. Cooktown is situated 240km north-west of Cairns and is accessible via road, which is still unsealed in parts, and by boat or plane.

MAIN ATTRACTIONS: In 1770, **Captain James Cook** beached HMS *Endeavour* in what is now called the Endeavour River and stayed for seven weeks while the ship's hull was repaired. A memorial marks the site and, each June, a re-enactment of the event takes place. **Grassy Hill** provides a good view of the **Great Barrier Reef**, Cooktown and the surrounding hinterland. Capt Cook climbed this hill to look for a clear passage through the Great Barrier Reef. **Cooktown Wharf**, dating from the 1880s, is a popular fishing venue. **James Cook Historical Museum** has displays of the area's maritime, natural and Aboriginal history. **Cooktown Botanic Gardens** are also in Walker St. **Nature's PowerHouse**, in the gardens, has an art gallery, environmental displays, Aboriginal artefacts and a cafe.

NEARBY ATTRACTIONS: Cooktown is a departure point for **Cape York Peninsula**; **Lizard Island**, 90km offshore via plane; **Lakefield NP**, 146km north-west with good camp-sites accessible mainly by 4-wheel drive; **Cape Melville NP**, north of town and only accessible by 4-wheel drive; and the secluded beaches to the north-east. Fishing tours of the Great Barrier Reef also leave from Cooktown. The **Black Mountains**, 20km west, offer a scenic lookout. **Quinkan Reserve**, at Laura, to the west, is renowned for its split-rock galleries containing a magnificent display of rock art. **Guurrbi Tours** takes visitors to the **Nugal-warra Rock Art Site** towards Hopevale.

VISITOR INFORMATION: Nature's PowerHouse, Botanic Gardens, Finch Bay Rd, Ph: (07) 4069 6004

Cooroy POP 1990

Map 255, C3

Located 25km inland from Noosa Heads, Cooroy is primarily a timber and dairy town.

MAIN ATTRACTION: In Maple St, Cooroy's **Old Butter Factory** has been restored and is now a cultural and creative centre for artists and craftspeople to display and sell their work.

NEARBY ATTRACTIONS: Black Mountain Range and Sky Ring Creek roads provide scenic drives in the surrounding areas. Drive maps are available at the information centre at Noosa Heads. **Lake MacDonald**, Noosa Shire's water storage area, is close by. Fishing is popular as the lake is well stocked with Murray cod, eels, silver perch, golden perch and catfish. Picnic and BBQ areas are provided around the shore. Close to the lake are **Noosa Botanical Gardens** and an amphitheatre that, from time to time, hosts a variety of performances.

VISITOR INFORMATION: Hastings St, Noosa Heads, Ph: (07) 5447 4988

Ulysses butterfly, *Papilio ulysses*, in Daintree National Park

Cunnamulla POP 1475

Map 286, B5

First settled in the 1860s, Cunnamulla is situated on the **Warrego River**, 815km west of Brisbane. It boasts the largest wool-loading station on the Queensland railway network. The surrounding land supports two million sheep, as well as beef cattle and Angora goats, and yields opals. MAIN ATTRACTIONS: A **Heritage Guide** is available from the information centre and takes visitors on a nostalgic tour of Cunnamulla and its riverside areas, walking in the footsteps of explorers and generations of locals. The **Bicentennial Museum** is located in John St. **Centenary Park** in Jane St offers picnic and BBQ facilities. NEARBY ATTRACTIONS: **Currawinya NP**, 168km south-west, is a wetland area, home to abundant and varied birdlife. **Yowah**, 155km west of Cunnamulla, is an opal-mining town

with a public fossicking area. **Eulo**, 65km west of Cunnamulla on the **Paroo River**, is home to **Palm Grove Date Winery**, unique in Australia because of its date-wine production and a variety of other date products which are offered for sale. There is an **artesian mud spring** 9km west of Eulo, and heritage trails at Yowah and Eulo. VISITOR INFORMATION: Centenary Park, Jane St, Ph: (07) 4655 2481

Currumbin POP 2700

Map 247, D5

Part of the **Gold Coast**, Currumbin is located at the mouth of **Currumbin Creek**. It has a superb beach and bushland environment. MAIN ATTRACTIONS: The National Trust's **Currumbin Wildlife Sanctuary** is the most popular attraction. The sanctuary covers 27ha of bushland. Visitors are invited to handfeed lorikeets, be photographed with a koala or ride the mini-train. There are freshwater and saltwater crocodiles and a **Free-Flight Spectacular** bird show. Opposite the sanctuary is **Superbee Honey World**, where visitors are entertained by The Live Bee Show, and can sample various honey varieties. Honey-making products are also for sale. Above Superbee is the **Chocolate Expo** for confirmed chocoholics. NEARBY ATTRACTIONS: **David Fleay Wildlife Park** is 8km north-west. Here visitors can see crocodile-feeding shows and nocturnal birds and learn about Aboriginal culture. Set in beautiful surroundings, **L'Esprit in the Valley**, 9km south-west, has walk-through aviaries and a maze. **Springbrook NP**, 22km south-west, has delightful rainforest walks. **Forest of Dreams**, in the park, offers pottery, walks and glow-worm tunnel tours. VISITOR INFORMATION: Coolangatta Place, cnr Griffith St and Warner St, Coolangatta, Ph: (07) 5536 7765

Daintree POP 240

Map 279, J2

Once a timber town, the village of Daintree is tucked into a bend of the **Daintree River** and is surrounded by the **McDowall Range**. It is 119km north-west of Cairns. MAIN ATTRACTIONS: **Daintree NP** abounds with native animals, exquisite birds and tropical butterflies. Saltwater crocodiles are a feature of the creeks and tributaries of the Daintree River as well as the estuary. Glide through this paradise on a river cruise. **Daintree Timber Museum** displays local arts and crafts. NEARBY ATTRACTIONS: **Daintree Discovery Centre**, 11km to the north, has rainforest walks, a 23m-high viewing platform and a tree-top walk. The **Jindalba Boardwalk** is nearby. **Cape Tribulation** is 35km north-east and features both rainforest and reef. It is renowned for its sheer beauty with pristine creeks, fan palms, colourful orchids and butterflies and ancient rainforest trees, some of which are the oldest flowering tree species in the world. Walking trails in the area include the **Dubuji Boardwalk**, a 1.2km walk, and **Marrdja Boardwalk** at **Noah Creek**. VISITOR INFORMATION: 23 Macrossan St, Port Douglas, Ph: (07) 4099 5599

Dalby POP 9705

Map 271, B3

This **Darling Downs** town is 212km west of Brisbane. The area's rich volcanic soil ensures its prosperity. While cotton and grain are the main income-earners, the economy of the Dalby district is broad-based and includes sheep, cattle and mining. MAIN ATTRACTIONS: Contemporary Australian paintings are exhibited in **Dalby Regional Gallery**. **Pioneer Park Museum** displays household memorabilia and agricultural machinery. Brochures are available

from the information centre on self-guided walks and drives in the area. NEARBY ATTRACTIONS: **Bunya Mountains NP** encompasses one of the most significant stands of bunya pines remaining in the world. The park features spectacular waterfalls and graded walking tracks, offering panoramic views of the Darling Downs. It is located 66km north-east of Dalby. **Lake Broadwater Conservation Park** lies 29km south-west of Dalby. The park protects native birds and plants and is an ideal spot for a picnic or BBQ, birdwatching, boating, waterskiing and overnight camping.
VISITOR INFORMATION: Thomas Jack Park, Drayton St, Ph: (07) 4662 1066 or 1800 680 303

▧ Emerald   POP 9510
Map 282, E5
This busy **Central Highlands** town lies 270km west of Rockhampton. Emerald is the centre of a prosperous pastoral, fruit-growing and mining region.
MAIN ATTRACTIONS: Built in 1900, **Emerald Railway Station**, with its beautiful facade, is one of the few remaining heritage buildings in the town. **Emerald Pioneer Cottage and Museum**, also classified by the National Trust, is a tribute to early

Horseriding through a field of sunflowers at Capella, near Emerald

settlement in the Highlands; open Monday to Friday afternoons. Emerald's **Botanic Gardens** are located on the banks of the **Nogoa River**. These include **Palm Grove**, **Pine Plantation** and a **Rose Garden**, which is home to over 200 varieties of roses. The gardens also have **Marbles** and **Federation Pillars** and a bush chapel. Near the information centre is a 23m-high (painting and easel) replica of one of Van Gogh's famous sunflower paintings. There is also a **mosaic footpath** depicting 100 years of Emerald's history.
NEARBY ATTRACTIONS: Around 45km west of Emerald are the gemfields of **Anakie**, **Sapphire**, **Willows** and **Rubyvale**, which have yielded some of the world's largest and most beautiful sapphires. These fields cover more than 100km^2 and visitors can fossick for gems and then have them cut by one of the many gem-cutters, jewellers or goldsmiths in the area. Visitors must obtain a licence first. There are also many gem shops and galleries to browse through. At Rubyvale, there are tours of an underground sapphire mine and gem-cutting displays. **Lake Maraboon**, 17km south of Emerald, is a popular watersports and fishing area. Day tours of nearby cattle stations can be arranged through the information centre.
VISITOR INFORMATION: Clermont St, Ph: (07) 4982 4142

▧ Gatton   POP 5335
Map 271, E4
Located off the Warrego Hwy, 94km west of Brisbane, Gatton is the business centre of the fertile **Lockyer Valley**. The valley is one of the most productive agricultural regions in Queensland. Industries include small crops, dairying, pork, beef, fruit and sawmilling.
MAIN ATTRACTIONS: **Lake Apex Park**, 1km from the town centre, is an

attractive picnic area with a wealth of bird species including pelicans and pygmy-geese. It has a children's playground, BMX track and walking tracks. Gatton's visitor centre and cafe are also in the park. **Gatton Historical Village,** at the western end of the park, has a collection of historical buildings and more than 10 000 exhibits that trace the heritage of the Lockyer Valley. **Gatton Harvest Carnival** is held in October. **Heavy Horse Field Days** are held at the showgrounds on the Labour Day long weekend in May.
NEARBY ATTRACTIONS: The town of **Laidley**, off the highway towards Ipswich, has many historic buildings, including **Das Neumann Haus**, which commemorates the contribution of German immigrants to the region. At the foot of the **Toowoomba Range**, to the west of Gatton, is the spa town of **Helidon**, also known for the high quality of its sandstone. **Helidon Natural Springs Resort**, on the Warrego Hwy outside Helidon, boasts a spa in every room. There are numerous scenic tourist drives in the Lockyer Valley. With 318 species on its official bird list, the valley attracts local and international birdwatchers.
VISITOR INFORMATION: Lake Apex Dr, Lake Apex Park, Ph: (07) 5462 3430

▧ Gayndah   POP 1795
Map 287, H2
One of the oldest towns in Queensland, Gayndah was founded in 1848. Located 352km north-west of Brisbane at a crossing on the **Burnett River**, it is known as the 'Orange Capital' of Queensland. It serves as a commercial centre for a surrounding district which produces cereal and grain crops, peanuts, fruit and beef cattle.
MAIN ATTRACTIONS: **Gayndah Historical Museum**, in Simon St, has a collection of relics and restored buildings, including a

(CONTINUED P.248)

THE GOLD COAST

Located an hour's drive south of Brisbane and stretching along 70km of coastline lies Australia's biggest, busiest and most vibrant tourist resort—the Gold Coast. The impressive coastal strip is dominated by high-rise accommodation, retail and tourist shops, international-standard resorts and restaurants, nightclubs and neon signs. The most famous stretch of Gold Coast beach is glittering **Surfers Paradise**.

The Gold Coast has a warm, balmy climate with over 300 sunny days per year. Together with the cooler subtropical rainforest ranges of the hinterland, the Gold Coast is extremely popular with tourists and residents seeking a relaxed lifestyle in beautiful surroundings.

Boasting more than 40 patrolled beaches in summer and several waterways, the Gold Coast offers a variety of watersports. Surfing, windsurfing, boogie boarding, swimming, sailing, scuba diving, jet skiing, fishing and canoeing contribute to its appeal. The quiet and peaceful hinterland offers opportunities for bushwalking, camping, freshwater-dam fishing and scenic drives.

A myriad of theme parks, including **Dreamworld**, **Sea World**, **Warner Bros Movie World**, and **Wet'n'Wild Water World** together with world-class shops, restaurants and outdoor activities attract well over four million visitors to the Gold Coast each year. This resort does not sleep; **Jupiters Casino**, nightclubs and bustling bars provide a hectic nightlife. For culture lovers, the **Gold Coast Arts Centre**, the largest regional centre in Australia, offers comedy nights, jazz, theatre, ballet and musicals.

Roadrunner rollercoaster at Warner Bros Movie World

i Visitor information

Gold Coast Tourism Bureau
Cavill Ave,
Surfers Paradise, Qld 4217
Ph: (07) 5538 4419
Cnr Griffith St and Warner St,
Coolangatta, Qld 4225
Ph: (07) 5536 7765
www.goldcoasttourism.com.au

main attractions

◈ **Burleigh Head National Park**
Several tracks wander through the rainforest, open forest and grassy tussocks of this park with magnificent 180° ocean views.

◈ **Coolangatta**
Greenmount Beach at Coolangatta is a delightfully calm beach, with shallow waters making it ideal for families.

◈ **Currumbin Wildlife Sanctuary**
Visitors to this sanctuary can feed colourful lorikeets, see koalas, crocodiles and a spectacular bird show.

◈ **Dreamworld**
This fantasy adventure park offers rides, a wildlife park, theme 'worlds' and a huge Imax cinema screen.

◈ **Sea World**
Sea World features a dolphin show, polar bears, fun rides and waterskiing displays.

◈ **Surfers Paradise**
With popular beaches and a waterfront promenade, this tourist hotspot is the heart of the Gold Coast.

◈ **Warner Bros Movie World**
Billed as 'Hollywood on the Gold Coast', this is a film and TV-based theme park.

Aerial view of Surfers Paradise

Queensland

Continued on map 231

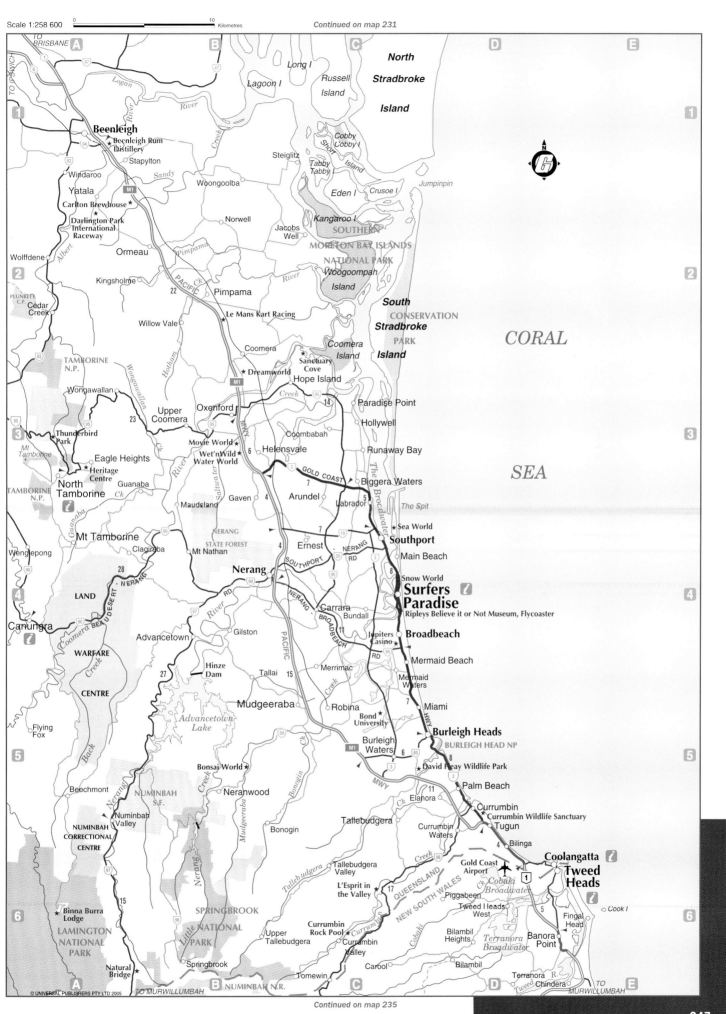

Continued on map 235

cottage built of clay bricks, taken from the banks of the Burnett River in 1864. From April to November, a range of citrus fruits are packed at the co-operative packing shed for interstate and overseas markets. Tours to some private orchards and packing sheds are possible if booked in advance through the information centre. The town hosts a biennial **Orange Festival**.

NEARBY ATTRACTIONS: **Ban Ban Springs**, 26km south-west, offers a shady picnic area and birdwatching. **Claude Weir Recreational Area**, 3km along Mundubbera Rd, is ideal for picnics, fishing and boating. **Archer's Lookout** on **Duke Mountain**, located behind the town, offers panoramic views of Gayndah, the Burnett River and the surrounding district.

VISITOR INFORMATION: Gayndah Museum, Simon St, Ph: (07) 4161 2226

▓ Gladstone   POP 26 520

Map 267, D5

Located 546km north-west of Brisbane, Gladstone is one of the busiest ports in Australia, handling more than 30 million tonnes of cargo each year. The warm subtropical climate, beaches, rivers and reef islands ensure Gladstone is host to an increasing number of tourists each year.

MAIN ATTRACTIONS: With a coastline of beaches, headlands and estuaries, fishing is a popular activity and the fishing fleet regularly brings in catches of export-quality fish, prawns, sea scallops and mud crabs. It is worthwhile visiting one of the many fine restaurants in the city to taste the fresh seafood. **Gladstone Regional Art Gallery and Museum** is located on the corner of Goondoon St and Bramston St. **Industrial tours** to alumina plants, the Port of Gladstone, and others, can be booked through the information centre. **Gladstone Marina** is the

departure point for islands such as **Heron Island**.

NEARBY ATTRACTIONS: At the foot of **Mount Biondello**, 8km from the city centre, are **Tondoon Botanic Gardens**, which specialise in plants of the **Port Curtis** region and far north Queensland. **Curtis Island**, in **Gladstone Harbour**, features a coastline of remote beaches and rugged headlands. There is a campground, picnic facilities, a shop and lodge accommodation. A regular barge service leaves from Gladstone. **Lake Awoonga**, 30km south, is popular for watersports and offers picnic and camping areas and walking trails. There are various national parks in the region and maps are available from the information centre. Fishing and snorkelling trips to the **Great Barrier Reef** can be organised at the twin resort towns of **Agnes Water** and **Seventeen Seventy** to the south-east.

VISITOR INFORMATION: Ferry Terminal, Bryan Jordan Dr, Ph: (07) 4972 4000

▓ Goondiwindi   POP 5480

Map 287, G5

Gateway to the **Western Downs**, this busy country town lies on the **Macintyre River**. Goondiwindi is an administrative centre for the cotton, wheat, wool and beef industries.

MAIN ATTRACTIONS: The old **Customs House**, built around 1850, became the **Historical Museum** in 1974. It exhibits local memorabilia and is open Wednesday to Monday.

Displays include the first operating table from the district hospital. Beside the river in **Apex Park** is the statue, *Gunsynd*, *the Goondiwindi Grey*, the famous racehorse who won 29 of his 55 races. **Macintyre Cotton Ginnery** claims to be the largest of its kind in the Southern Hemisphere. Tours can be booked in season (April–July) through the Namoi Cotton head office in Marshall St. The **Botanical Gardens of the Western Woodland** display plant communities native to the **Darling Basin**. The gardens offer BBQ facilities, a recreation area and an artificial lake.

NEARBY ATTRACTIONS: Self-drive tour brochures are available from the information centre. The **Paper Mill at Boggabilla** is open for tours Mondays and Tuesdays.

VISITOR INFORMATION: Cnr Bowen St and McLean St, Ph: (07) 4671 2653

▓ Gympie   POP 13 625

Map 255, B2

The hub of the **Cooloola region**, Gympie is located 162km north of Brisbane. Gympie was established after gold was discovered in 1867. Today, it is the centre of the prosperous **Mary River Valley** agricultural district. It is an excellent base for tours to **Rainbow Beach**, **Tin Can Bay**, **Great Sandy NP** and **Fraser Island**.

MAIN ATTRACTIONS: There are attractive parks, gardens, art galleries and interesting craft shops to explore. A **historical walk** takes in several

The *Valley Rattler* steam train (Mary Valley Heritage Railway), near Gympie

Queensland

examples of 19th-century architecture. **Woodworks Forestry and Timber Museum** is run by the Queensland Department of Forestry and the Queensland Museum. There is a working replica of a steam-driven sawmill and a demonstration of early timber-cutting techniques. The *Valley Rattler* is a steam train offering trips each Wednesday, Saturday and Sunday from Gympie to **Imbil**. Much of the town's history is preserved at **Gympie Gold Mining and Historical Museum** near **Lake Alford**. It comprises a number of buildings, each concentrating on a different aspect of the past.

NEARBY ATTRACTIONS: A display featuring gems and minerals from all over the world can be found at **Cooloola Rocks and Minerals**, 15km south. **Amamoor State Forest** is ideal for picnics and rainforest walks, and is located 30km south of Gympie. **Mothar Mountain Rock Pools**, on the old Noosa Rd, have BBQ and picnic facilities, as well as walks.

VISITOR INFORMATION: Matilda Roadhouse, Bruce Hwy, Kybong, Ph: (07) 5483 5554 or 1800 444 222

Hervey Bay   POP 35 110
Map 259, C3

The setting and location combine to make this town a prime holiday destination. Situated between Maryborough and Bundaberg, the town, and bay of the same name, are protected by Fraser Island and lie at the southern tip of the **Great Barrier Reef**. Offering easy access to islands, wildlife and beaches, Hervey Bay is one of Australia's fastest growing regions.

MAIN ATTRACTIONS: There are several organisations operating **whale-watching tours**. From late July to early November, mainly mothers, calves and sub-adult humpback whales spend time in the waters of Hervey Bay on their return journey

to the Antarctic. In August Hervey Bay hosts a **Whale Festival** with many attractions, including a **Blessing of the Fleet**. Hervey Bay is a popular destination for anglers. The 700m **Urangan Pier** is one of the town's landmarks and a favourite spot for fishing and strolling. **Neptune's Reefworld**, at Urangan, has seal shows and 'swimming with the sharks' for the adventurous. **Hervey Bay Marina**, also at Urangan, has bayside cafes.

NEARBY ATTRACTIONS: There are daily cruises to World Heritage-listed **Fraser Island**, the world's largest sand island, with its unique perched lakes, turpentine forests and miles of beaches. On the island are scenic 4-wheel drive and bushwalking tracks. **Lady Elliot Island**, the Great Barrier Reef's southernmost island, is only 45 minutes from Hervey Bay by air. The seaside resorts of **Toogoom** and **Burrum Heads** are to the north-west.

VISITOR INFORMATION: Cnr Urraween Rd and Maryborough-Hervey Bay Rd, Ph: (07) 4125 9855 or 1800 811 728

Home Hill   POP 2915
Map 282, D1

Originally part of the Inkerman Downs cattle station, the land around this **Burdekin River Valley** town was turned over to sugarcane farms in 1911. Sugarcane is still the main product of this region, 100km south of Townsville.

MAIN ATTRACTIONS: Home Hill is linked to its twin town, **Ayr**, by the district's best-known landmark, the **Burdekin Bridge**. Referred to as the 'Silver Link', it spans the **Burdekin River** and was the longest bridge in the country for many years. **Ashworth's Treasures of the Earth**, located in Eighth Ave, incorporates a gallery, rock shop and craft shop. The centre has some beautiful exhibits and is worth visiting. Also in Eighth Ave are **Pioneers Walk**, with commemorative plaques,

Tranquil Lake Mackenzie, Fraser Island

Powerhouse Museum, **Burdekin Plum Tree Art Gallery** and **Zaro's Cultural Gallery**.

NEARBY ATTRACTIONS: **Groper Creek**, south-east of town, is a popular fishing spot known for its huge gropers and mud crabs. Facilities include a boat ramp, picnic, camping and caravan areas. Local fishing tours are available. South of Home Hill is a WWII radar site with forbidding concrete igloos. **Mount Inkerman** provides panoramic views of the district. The seaside community of **Wunjunga** is a renowned birdwatching site which is also great for fishing.

VISITOR INFORMATION: Old Courthouse, Eighth Ave, Ph: (07) 4782 8241

Hughenden   POP 1445
Map 281, H2

This town lies on the banks of Queensland's longest river, the **Flinders**, 383km south-west of Townsville. It is located on the Flinders Hwy and significant fossil finds in the area have prompted the name 'Dinosaur Highway'.

MAIN ATTRACTIONS: There are pleasant parks in Hughenden for picnicking and a swimming pool. The **Dinosaur Display Centre**, located at the rear of the information centre

Orpheus Island, Great Barrier Reef, near Ingham

in Gray St, has a full size replica of *Muttaburrasaurus langdoni*, a prehistoric, bird-footed herbivorous dinosaur that once roamed the area. NEARBY ATTRACTIONS: **Porcupine Gorge NP**, 63km north, with a diverse range of flora and fauna, offers camping, swimming and birdwatching in superb surrounds. Gemstone fossicking is a popular activity in **Chudleigh Park**, 138km north. The **Cobb and Co Yards**, at **Prairie**, 44km east, house many historical relics.
VISITOR INFORMATION: 37 Gray St, Ph: (07) 4741 1021

▦ Ingham POP 6016
Map 279, J5
This sugar town is also the commercial centre of the **Herbert River Valley**, sometimes dubbed 'Australia's Sugar Bowl'. Ingham is positioned between national parks and the waterways of the **Hinchinbrook Channel**, 110km north of Townsville.
MAIN ATTRACTIONS: **Tyto Wetlands**, covering 90ha, are a mecca for birdwatchers with walking tracks and an owl-viewing platform. There is an **Australian-Italian Festival** in May. For a pleasant stroll or picnic, visit the **Botanic Gardens** in Palm Tce.
NEARBY ATTRACTIONS: **Forest Beach** offers a long stretch of beach overlooking the **Palm Islands**. It is located 17km south-east of Ingham, and a marine-stinger net is installed

at the beach each summer to protect swimmers. Other beach resorts include **Taylors Beach** and **Lucinda**, with its extraordinary 5.6km sugar jetty. The resort islands of **Hinchinbrook** and **Orpheus** are located offshore. **Lumholtz NP**, 51km west, offers walking tracks, swimming and picnic spots, campgrounds and the 305m-high **Wallaman Falls**. Located 45km west in the Herbert River Valley is a 1.6km rainforest walk. The beautiful **Jourama Falls** are 25km to the south of Ingham in **Paluma Range NP**.
VISITOR INFORMATION: Cnr Bruce Hwy/Lannercost St, Ph: (07) 4770 5211

▦ Innisfail POP 8995
Map 239, D6
This lush tropical town is situated on the **North** and **South Johnstone rivers** 88km south of Cairns. Innisfail has been a sugar town since the 1880s and also grows tea and bananas; aquaculture is also vital to the economy.
MAIN ATTRACTIONS: In addition to the **Botanical Gardens**, which offer bush tucker, there are numerous parks that are ideal for picnicking and feasting on delicious locally-caught seafood. The Johnstone River is popular for fishing or for strolling along its picturesque banks. An **Art Deco Tour** starts at the Shire Hall and showcases the architectual influence of Innisfail's Italian migrants.

NEARBY ATTRACTIONS: **Johnstone River Crocodile Farm**, 3km north-east, has over 3000 crocodiles, native fauna and endangered cassowaries that are part of a captive breeding programme. **Paronella Park** at **Mena Creek**, 18km south, is a rainforest heritage garden created by Jose Paronella in 1929. Guided tours of the castle, tropical gardens, 'Tunnel of Love' and waterfalls are offered. The **Australian Sugar Museum** at **Mourilyan**, 7km south, displays relics and memorabilia of the sugar industry, which is such an important part of the region. The museum also presents an audio-visual describing the history and processing of sugar. Innisfail is a base for exploring numerous islands, such as **Dunk** and **Bedarra** and national parks such as **Wooroonooran NP**, 25km north-west. In this park stands **Mount Bartle Frere**, Queensland's highest peak. Also in the area are stunning **Josephine Falls**.
VISITOR INFORMATION: Cnr Bruce Hwy/Eslick St, Ph: (07) 4061 7422

▦ Ipswich POP 88 800
Map 230, A5
Ipswich is located 44km south-west of Brisbane, set in the hills around the **Bremer River**. It is Queensland's oldest provincial city, beginning as a convict settlement in 1827.
MAIN ATTRACTIONS: Maps for the area's **heritage trails** can be obtained at the information centre. One of the trails is a guide to **Ipswich City Centre**, where there are numerous heritage buildings, while another leads to the city's many pubs and hotels. **Global Arts Link** is an interactive art gallery, open daily. Both the Bremer and **Brisbane rivers** provide excellent opportunities for canoeing and kayaking. **Queens Park Nature Centre**, located on Goleby Ave, features a range of native wildlife,

landscaped gardens and exhibits representing local bushland communities. The **Railway Workshops Museum**, in North Ipswich, has vintage trains and daily tours.

NEARBY ATTRACTIONS: **St Brigid's Church** is reputedly the largest wooden church in the South Pacific. It is located at **Rosewood**, 20km west, and guided tours are available by appointment. **Willowbank Raceway** has races most weekends. There are several wineries in the region to the south known as **The Scenic Rim**.

VISITOR INFORMATION: 14 Queen Victoria Pde, Ph: (07) 3281 0555

Julia Creek   POP 520

Map 280, E2

This small service township is located 138km east of Cloncurry on the main route from Townsville to Mount Isa. Julia Creek is a stock-trucking and sales centre with impressive stockyards.

MAIN ATTRACTIONS: **MacIntyre Museum**, in Burke St, was named after Duncan MacIntyre, the first European settler in north-west Queensland. Displays include memorabilia of the township and McKinlay Shire. The area is home to the rare and endangered nocturnal marsupial, the Julia Creek dunnart. The **Dirt and Dust Triathlon** is Julia

Grass-trees in Bunya Mountains National Park, south-west of Kingaroy

Creek's major sporting event and is held biennially in April. The race attracts thousands of competitors and tourists.

NEARBY ATTRACTIONS: **Kynuna**, 115km to the south, is where **A B 'Banjo' Paterson** wrote the Australian ballad *Waltzing Matilda*. A cairn now marks the spot where events in the ballad took place; a hut used by Paterson can be seen behind **Kynuna Roadhouse**. Kynuna was once a staging post for Cobb & Co coaches and the original 1889 bush pub, **Blue Heeler Hotel**, still stands. West of Kynuna is **McKinlay**, best known for its pub, **Walkabout Creek Hotel**. This hotel and other buildings in the town featured in the movie *Crocodile Dundee*.

VISITOR INFORMATION: Library, cnr Burke St and Quarrell St, Ph: (07) 4746 7930

Kilcoy   POP 1445

Map 255, A5

This small town, 95km north-west of Brisbane, is a good base for a variety of daytrips to places such as **Brisbane**, **Toowoomba**, **Kingaroy** and **Caloundra**.

MAIN ATTRACTIONS: The hills surrounding this town are reputed to be the home of the legendary Yowie— the Australian version of North America's Bigfoot. Over 3000 sightings of the half-man-half-beast were recorded 1975–1979. A statue, based on descriptions of those who claim to have seen the beast, stands in **Yowie Park** on Hope St. The **Craft Cottage**, located in Yowie Park, is home to a variety of crafts.

NEARBY ATTRACTIONS: **Peachester State Forest**, just north of Kilcoy, offers natural fresh-water swimming holes and bushwalking tracks. **Lake Somerset**, also close by, is well stocked with perch and bass, and is a popular fishing, waterskiing and sailing venue. Boat ramps, fish cleaning facilities, camping and picnic areas line its western shore. Follow the **Kilcoy Shire Wine Trail**

and sample the fruits of the vine along the way.

VISITOR INFORMATION: The Craft Cottage, Yowie Park, Hope St, Ph: (07) 5497 1888

Kingaroy   POP 7165

Map 271, D1

Kingaroy is located 210km north-west of Brisbane and is the business and rural centre for the prosperous **South Burnett** district. It is known as Australia's **'Peanut Capital'**, and giant peanut silos dominate the landscape. Apart from peanuts, Kingaroy's economy is based on grain, fruit, wines, olives and various manufacturing industries. It is the home of Sir Johannes (Joh) Bjelke-Petersen, former Premier of Queensland.

MAIN ATTRACTIONS: **Kingaroy Bicentennial Heritage Museum** is housed in the old power station next to the information centre and displays early machinery used in association with the peanut industry. A **Peanut Festival** is held in September and a **Food and Wine Festival** is held each March. **Kingaroy Wines** is located in the Old Butter Factory at 57 William St, and is one of the largest wineries in the region. Views of Kingaroy and surrounding countryside are provided at the **Carroll Nature Area**, located off Fisher St.

NEARBY ATTRACTIONS: There are panoramic views from **Mount Wooroolin**, 3km west. **Bunya Mountains NP**, located 60km south-west, is worthwhile visiting. It has picnic and camping facilities and numerous walking tracks to rainforests with spectacular flora, waterfalls and streams. The South Burnett region boasts a number of wineries, many open for tastings and sales. Nearby **Boondooma** and **Bjelke-Petersen dams** are popular fishing destinations and both host large annual fishing competitions.

VISITOR INFORMATION: 128 Haly St, Ph: (07) 4162 3199

■ Kuranda   POP 1440
Map 239, B3

Located at the top of the **Macalister Range**, beside the **Barron River**, this appealing rainforest village is best known as a destination of the 34km-long **Kuranda Scenic Railway** and the 7.5km-long **Skyrail Rainforest Cableway** from **Cairns**. It can also be reached by car on the winding and scenic **Kuranda Range Road**.

MAIN ATTRACTIONS: **Kuranda Railway Station** is perhaps the prettiest in Queensland and **river cruises** are available nearby. **Kuranda Markets** are famous for their arts and crafts. The **Australian Butterfly Sanctuary** has a colourful collection of over 2000 butterflies in a large natural setting. **Birdworld**, in Rod Veivers Dr, houses a brilliant array of birds, many of them endangered. In the same **Heritage Markets** area, **Koala Gardens** houses crocodiles as well as Australia's favourite marsupials. **The Aviary** has gorgeous Australian parrots. There are several rainforest walks in the area, including the **River Esplanade Walk** along the Barron River, **Forest Walk** and **Jungle Walk**.

NEARBY ATTRACTIONS: **Barron Falls** are located in **Barron Gorge NP**, 7km south, and a platform provides views of the falls. **Rainforestation Nature Park** is east of town. Tours of the rainforest are available. There is also an **Aboriginal Theatre Experience** and a **Koala and Wildlife Park**.

VISITOR INFORMATION: Cnr Rob Veivers Dr and Therwine St, Ph: (07) 4093 9311

■ Longreach   POP 3775
Map 281, H5

Situated on the banks of the **Thomson River** in the state's central-west, Longreach is the hub of a very prosperous wool and beef area. Considered the **'Gateway to the Outback'**, Longreach is 700km west of Rockhampton.

MAIN ATTRACTIONS: The **Australian Stockman's Hall of Fame and Outback Heritage Centre** is the most famous attraction in Longreach. The centre is dedicated to preserving Aboriginal and non-Aboriginal Outback history, up to the arrival of the aeroplane and present-day technology. Traditional artefacts are displayed and there is a library, audiovisual presentation and a resource centre. Longreach was Qantas' first operational base 1922–34 and where the first of six DH-50 biplanes were built in 1926. **Qantas Founders Outback Museum** is at the airport, and **Qantas Park**, in Eagle St, has a replica of the original Qantas office, now the information centre. The **Powerhouse Museum**, in Swan St, houses the largest collection of rural power-generating equipment in Australia. Exhibits include a social history hall and the 1921 swimming baths. Cruises on the Thomson River are popular.

NEARBY ATTRACTIONS: Guided tours of sheep and cattle stations, such as **Oakley Station**, 17km north, are available. Historic **Toobrac Station** offers tours and camping; it is 107km south-west.

VISITOR INFORMATION: Qantas Park, Eagle St, Ph: (07) 4658 3555

■ Mackay   POP 57 325
Map 263, D6

Often referred to as the **'Sugar Capital of Australia'**, Mackay is located approximately halfway between Cairns and Brisbane. Its close proximity to the **Great Barrier Reef**, the islands of the **Whitsundays** and beautiful rainforests make Mackay a most desirable holiday destination.

MAIN ATTRACTIONS: A **Heritage Walk** brochure, available from the information centre, explores the city's architectural heritage and describes many buildings of interest. **Queens Park** features a

Australian Stockman's Hall of Fame, Longreach

magnificent orchid house displaying more than 500 species of orchids, also ferns and other plants. **Mackay Marina** has one of the world's biggest bulk sugar terminals. Cruises and fishing trips to the islands and Great Barrier Reef depart from the marina. Both **Illawong** and **Harbour beaches** offer safe swimming.

NEARBY ATTRACTIONS: During the crushing season July–November, weekday tours of **Farleigh Sugar Mill** can be arranged. Demonstrations of planting, harvesting and cutting of sugarcane can be seen at **Polestone Cane Farm**, June–December. **Eungella NP**, located 79km west, offers stunning valley views, 20km of rainforest walks and the opportunity to see an elusive platypus. There are more than 30 beaches within a 45 minute drive from the city.

VISITOR INFORMATION: The Mill, 320 Nebo Rd, Ph: (07) 4944 5888 or 1300 130 001

Queensland

Malanda   POP 1020
Map 239, B5

Located at the heart of the **Atherton Tableland**, Malanda is almost encircled by the **Johnstone River**. The town, 20km south-east of Atherton, is the centre of the only dairy industry in the Australian tropics.

MAIN ATTRACTIONS: The historic **Majestic Theatre** is a much-loved feature of Malanda and the only original movie theatre on the Tableland with the original ticket office still standing. Historic **Malanda Hotel** is the largest all-timber structure in Queensland. A well-known attraction is **Malanda Falls Environmental Park** and **Scenic Reserve** where the Johnstone River 'falls' over a basalt lava flow into a natural swimming hole. The surrounding park offers two short rainforest walks that shelter many birds. Tree kangaroos and platypus can be seen. Malanda Falls Visitor Centre has much to offer, including the **'Volcano Experience'**, **Rainforest Room**, interactive touch-screen computer displays, and indigenous and non-indigenous historical displays. Visitors can enquire about a guided **Rainforest Walk** with a tribal elder of the Ngadjonji people.

NEARBY ATTRACTIONS: The Atherton Tableland provides many attractions, including **Bromfield Swamp**; the National Trust-classified village of **Yungaburra**; and the volcanic crater lakes, **Barrine** and **Eacham**. **Mount Hypipamee NP** (The Crater), to the south-west on the Evelyn Tableland, has an extinct volcanic pipe crater with 58m sheer granite walls dropping down to a 82m-deep lake. **Eacham Historic Museum**, in **Millaa Millaa**, has displays depicting the life of early timber-cutters and the district's rural pioneers. Nearby are **Millaa Millaa Falls** and several other scenic waterfalls.

VISITOR INFORMATION: Falls Reserve, Atherton-Malanda Rd, Ph: (07) 4096 6957

Mareeba   POP 6885
Map 239, A3

The largest town on the **Atherton Tableland**, Mareeba serves as the region's administrative centre and is the beginning of the Outback. It is a town of many cultures, reflected in its cafes and delicatessens. Crops grown include sugarcane, mangos, tea-trees and coffee; mining and horticulture are also important to the local economy.

MAIN ATTRACTIONS: Mareeba is famous for its annual **rodeo** in July that draws crowds from all over Australia. **Bicentennial Lakes** is a recreation area offering walking tracks, picnic areas, parklands and gardens. Brochures are available on a self-guided **historic town walk**. **Mareeba Heritage Museum** has displays tracing local history and features a rail ambulance and rail carriage. **Coffee Works** offers guided tours explaining how coffee is processed, from the bean to the cup. Tastings of several exotic coffees are included in the tour. There are also three wineries close to Mareeba.

NEARBY ATTRACTIONS: **Beck's Aviation and Military Museum**, 5km south, is the largest privately owned collection of its type in Queensland. **Davies Creek NP**, 15km east, has a camping area with picnic tables. A permit is required for overnight stays. **Emerald Creek Falls** is a 20 minute drive from town. The return walk along a well-maintained path to the lookout over the falls is 1.9km. There is also a large grassy area beside a shallow creek which is ideal for picnics. **Mareeba Tropical Savannah and Wetland Reserve**, to the north, is a 120ha park, popular for birdwatching and observing native wildlife. Hot-air **balloon flights** over the Tableland are available at Mareeba.

VISITOR INFORMATION: Heritage Museum, Centenary Park, 345 Byrnes St, Ph: (07) 4092 5674

Maroochydore   POP 28 515
Map 255, C4

This popular beach resort, located 106km north of Brisbane, is also the administrative and business centre of the **Sunshine Coast**.

MAIN ATTRACTIONS: Beaches are a major attraction and the surf beach on the ocean side is patrolled. **Maroochy River** is home to a variety of pleasure craft and waterbirds, including pelicans and swans. The river offers safe swimming year-round and it is possible to camp by the riverbank at **Cotton Tree** or by the beach at Maroochydore.

NEARBY ATTRACTIONS: There are cruises up the Maroochy River, which pass through sugarcane fields. **Bli Bli Castle** is a themed tourist attraction, where visitors can view a dungeon,

(CONTINUED P.256)

Hot-air balloon over Mareeba, Atherton Tableland

THE SUNSHINE COAST

North of Brisbane, the 48km coastal stretch bounded by **Caloundra** to the south and **Noosa Heads** to the north is called the Sunshine Coast. The name conjures vivid images of the region's many surf beaches stretching to the horizon; its picturesque lakes; unspoilt rainforests; and cliffs of rainbow coloured sand.

The Sunshine Coast offers a quieter, more relaxed alternative to the Gold Coast's excesses. With an average temperature that does not drop below 20°C year-round and a wide choice of accommodation, the Sunshine Coast invites visitors to experience its balmy, laid-back way of life. The once sleepy coastal villages and modest holiday destinations have become glamorous retreats for the glitterati; others retain the charm of quieter times. Attractions are varied and include theme parks such as **Australia Zoo**, **UnderWater World**, **The Big Pineapple** and **Aussie World**. For a different kind of holiday, there are

many national parks and state forests to explore, including the Cooloola section of **Great Sandy NP**, **Mount Coolum NP** and **Noosa NP**.

Aboriginal legend of the coloured sands

According to the Kabi Kabi Aboriginal people, the coloured sands at **Rainbow Beach** were formed when the Rainbow Spirit was shattered by a boomerang in a fight over a woman. The pieces fell onto the sand cliffs, colouring them forever.

Camel-riding at Teewah Beach, north of Noosa Heads

i Visitor information

Maroochy Tourism
Cnr Sixth Ave and Melrose Pde,
Maroochydore, Qld 4558
Ph: (07) 5479 1566 or 1800 882 032
www.maroochytourism.com

main attractions

◈ **Australia Zoo**

Located on the Glass House Mountains Tourist Route at Beerwah, this is the home of TV's Crocodile Hunter.

◈ **Coloured sands**

Multi-coloured sand formations can be seen on tours to Teewah Beach (north of Noosa Heads), Rainbow Beach and Fraser Island.

◈ **Eumundi Markets**

These popular markets on Wednesday and Saturday mornings sell all manner of wares in a charming village setting.

◈ **Maroochydore**

The heart of the Sunshine Coast offers surfing beaches, excellent fishing, shopping and river cruises.

◈ **Mooloolaba**

This is a thriving beachside town. Two of its attractions are the 'Loo with a view' at the Esplanade and UnderWater World, which features a seal show.

◈ **Noosa Heads**

Noosa offers great beaches, world-class shopping and sophisticated restaurants, as well as Noosa NP.

◈ **The Big Pineapple**

This park is based on a working pineapple and macadamia plantation. The Big Pineapple itself is a tower with a lookout at the top.

Fishing with friends on the Maroochy River, Maroochydore

Queensland

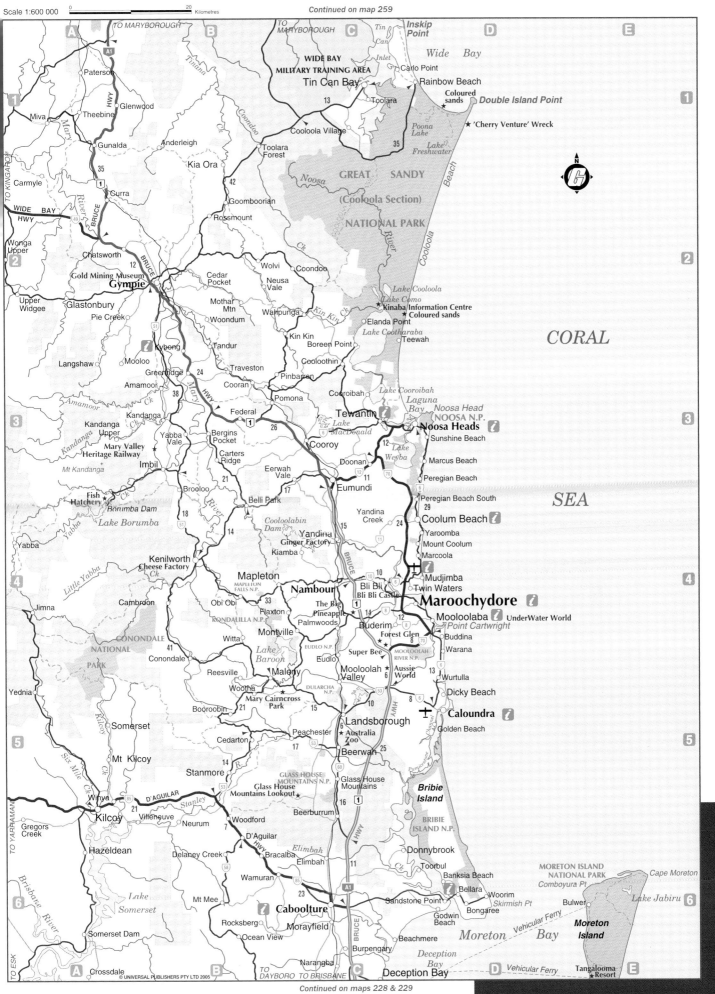

Inskip
Point

TO MARYBOROUGH

TO MARYBOROUGH

WIDE BAY
MILITARY TRAINING AREA

Tin Can Bay

Wide   Bay

Carlo Point

Rainbow Beach

Coloured
sands

Double Island Point

Paterson

Glenwood

Miva

Theebine

Gunalda

Anderleigh

Toolara

'Cherry Venture' Wreck

Kia Ora

Cooloola Village

Toolara
Forest

Poona
Lake

Lake
Freshwater

Carmyle

Goomboorian

Noosa

GREAT   SANDY

Rossmount

(Cooloola Section)

Wonga
Upper

Chatsworth

NATIONAL PARK

Gold Mining Museum

Gympie

Cedar
Pocket

Wolvi

Coondoo

River

CORAL

Upper
Widgee

Glastonbury

Mothar
Mtn

Neusa
Vale

Lake Cooloola
Lake Como

Kinaba Information Centre
Coloured sands

Pie Creek

Woondum

Wahpunga

Kin Kin Ck

Elanda Point

Lake Cootharaba

Langshaw

Kybong

Tandur

Kin Kin

Teewah

Mooloo

Boreen Point

Greenridge

Traveston

Cooloothin

Amamoor

Cooran

Pinbarren

Lake Cooroibah

Kandanga

Federal

Pomona

Cooroibah

Laguna
Bay

Noosa Head

Kandanga
Upper

Yabba
Vale

Bergins
Pocket

Tewantin

NOOSA N.P.

Mary Valley
Heritage Railway

Carters
Ridge

26

Lake
MacDonald

Noosa Heads

Mt Kandanga

Imbil

Eerwah
Vale

Cooroy

Sunshine Beach

Lake
Weyba

Doonan

Marcus Beach

Fish
Hatchery

Brooloo

Belli Park

Eumundi

Peregian Beach

Borumba Dam

Yandina
Creek

Peregian Beach South

Lake Borumba

Cooloolabin
Dam

Yabba

Yandina
Ginger Factory

Coolum Beach

Kiamba

Yaroomba

Mount Coolum

SEA

Kenilworth
Cheese Factory

Marcoola

Cambroon

Mapleton

Obi Obi

Nambour

Bli Bli
Bli Bli Castle

Mudjimba

Jimna

MAPLETON
FALLS N.P.

The Big
Pineapple

Twin Waters

Maroochydore

Flaxton

Palmwoods

Buderim

Mooloolaba

CONONDALE

NATIONAL

KONDALILLA N.P.

Forest Glen

UnderWater World
Point Cartwright

PARK

Witta

Montville

EUDLO N.P.

Super Bee

Buddina

Yednia

Conondale

Eudlo

Warana

Reesville

Maleny

Mooloolah
Valley

Aussie
World

Wurtulla

Wootha

DULARCHA
N.P.

Dicky Beach

Booroobin

Mary Cairncross
Park

Landsborough

Caloundra

Somerset

Peachester

Australia
Zoo

Golden Beach

Mt Kilcoy

Cedarton

Beerwah

Stanmore

GLASS HOUSE
MOUNTAINS N.P.

Glass House
Mountains

Bribie
Island

Winya

Glass House
Mountains Lookout

BRIBIE
ISLAND N.P.

Gregors
Creek

Villeneuve

Kilcoy

D'AGUILAR

Neurum

Woodford

Beerburrum

Hazeldean

D'Aguilar

Donnybrook

Delaney Creek

Bracalba

Toorbul

MORETON ISLAND
NATIONAL PARK

Cape Moreton

Elimbah

Banksia Beach

Comboyura Pt

Wamuran

Elimbah

Lake Jabiru

Mt Mee

Bellara

Woorim

Skirmish Pt

Bulwer

Caboolture

Sandstone Point

Bongaree

Rocksberg

Morayfield

Godwin
Beach

Moreton
Island

Somerset Dam

Ocean View

Beachmere

Moreton   Bay

Crossdale

Narangba

Burpengary

Deception
Bay

Vehicular Ferry

Tangalooma
Resort

© UNIVERSAL PUBLISHERS PTY LTD 2005

TO
DAYBORO

TO BRISBANE

Deception Bay

Vehicular Ferry

Continued on maps 228 & 229

torture chamber and the doll museum. There is a replica of Captain Cook's *Endeavour* to the west. Nearby **Mooloolaba** has attractions on the **Mooloolah River**, including canal cruises, **The Wharf** and the splendid aquarium **UnderWater World**.

Visitor Information: Cnr Sixth Ave and Melrose Pde, Ph: (07) 5479 1566 or 1800 882 032

Maryborough   POP 28 605

Map 259, B4

One of Queensland's oldest cities, Maryborough is nestled in a curve of the **Mary River**, 34km from Hervey Bay.

Main Attractions: Known as a 'Heritage City', Maryborough has retained many of its historic public buildings and old Queenslander-style homes. **Wharf Street Precinct** has many old pubs, as well as the

City Hall, Maryborough

Customs House and Court House. **Bond Store Heritage Museum** represents the development of Maryborough as an important river port during the pre-Federation era. The National Trust has restored **Brennan and Geraghty's Store** in Lennox St. A **Heritage Walk** and **Drive Tour** brochure is available from the information centre. **Elizabeth Park** is renowned for its display of more than 2000 roses. **Queens Park**, which is over 100 years old, has a fern house, waterfall and lily-pond. **Ululah Lagoon**, off Lions Dr, is a wildlife sanctuary and visitors are invited to handfeed the black swans, ducks and geese.

Nearby Attractions: Maryborough is a convenient base for exploring the attractions of the **Fraser Coast**, **Fraser Island**, **Hervey Bay** and **Lady Elliot Island**.

Visitor Information: Maryborough South Travel Stop, Bruce Hwy, Ph: (07) 4121 4111

Miles   POP 1250

Map 287, G3

This small rural town is 343km north-west of Brisbane. Situated at the junction of the Leichhardt Hwy and Warrego Hwy, Miles is an ideal stop for visitors travelling west to the **Stockman's Hall of Fame** or north to Tropical North Queensland.

Main Attractions: **Miles and District Historical Village** features 30 authentic buildings in a re-creation of a pioneer settlement. Original buildings include a church, hospital, general store, machinery shed, dairy and a slab hut. The village also has a war museum, and a memorabilia museum which features an extensive collection of shells, Aboriginal artefacts and lapidary. The museum is also the information centre.

Nearby Attractions: In early spring, wildflowers carpet the area and it is worthwhile doing the self-guided **wildflower drive**. Brochures on the

drive are available. **Myall Park Botanical Gardens** are located at **Glenmorgan**, 134km south-west.

Visitor Information: Miles Historical Village, Murilla St, Ph: (07) 4627 1492

Monto   POP 1340

Map 287, H1

Regarded as the southern gateway to central Queensland, Monto is 515km from Brisbane and 250km inland from Bundaberg. It is the centre of a rich agricultural, dairying and cattle district.

Main Attractions: The **History and Cultural Centre**, in Flinders St, incorporates the **Ostwald Rock Collection**.

Nearby Attractions: **Cania Gorge NP** is located 25km north-west of Monto. It contains many interesting rock formations, including **The Leap**, **Dripping Rock**, **The Wool Bales**, **Castle Mountain** and **Mount Dowgo**. Walking tracks lead through the subtropical vegetation to **Bloodwood** and **Dragon caves**. **Wuruma Dam** is popular for fishing, swimming, waterskiing and sailing; it is 50km south of Monto.

Visitor Information: 271 Bourbong St, Bundaberg, Ph: (07) 4153 8888 or 1800 308 888

Moranbah   POP 6515

Map 282, E3

Moranbah is 200km south-west of Mackay. It was purpose-built in the 1970s to service the employees of Goonyella and Peak Downs open-cut coal mines.

Main Attractions: **Town Square** has a Mediterranean feel with cafes and restaurants offering alfresco dining. There is a **campdraft** in July, highlighting the traditional skills of stockmen, and a rodeo in October.

Nearby Attraction: Visitors can join a **Peak Downs Mine Tour** on the last Wednesday of the month —bookings at shire offices.

Visitor Information: Shire Offices, Town Square, Ph: (07) 4941 7254

Lawn Hill Creek in Boodjamulla National Park, north-west of Mount Isa

Mossman   POP 1920
Map 239, A1
This small sugar town is situated in the beautiful **Mossman River Valley**, overlooked by **Mount Demi** and a rainforest-clad mountain range. Mossman is 75km north-west of Cairns.
MAIN ATTRACTIONS: **Mossman Sugar Mill Tours** operate daily during the crushing season, May to November, from **Mossman Central Mill**. The town's golf course has a rainforest walk. **Shannonvale Tropical Fruit Wine Company** has a cellar door in Shannonvale Rd.
NEARBY ATTRACTIONS: The magnificent **Mossman Gorge**, 8km west, is the district's main attraction. It is part of **Daintree NP**, which in turn is part of the **Wet Tropics World Heritage Area**, and offers walking tracks, gorges, clear-water creeks and waterfalls. The Kuku Yalanji people conduct guided walks through the rainforest. Scenic roads through Mossman access three local beaches—**Cooya**, **Newell** and **Wonga**. To the north of Mossman is the village of **Daintree**: the gateway to **Cape York**. Daintree NP has the largest area of tropical rainforest in Australia. To see crocodiles and other native fauna, it is worthwhile visiting **Hartley's Crocodile Adventures**, 35km south of Mossman. The resort town of **Port Douglas** is a short drive away and is a popular stepping-off point for

cruises to the **Low Isles** and the **Outer Barrier Reef**.
VISITOR INFORMATION: 23 Macrossan St, Port Douglas, Ph: (07) 4099 5599

Mount Isa   POP 21 800
Map 280, C2
Mount Isa is the largest and most important industrial provincial city west of the Great Dividing Range. It is located 887km west of Townsville. **Mount Isa Mines** is the largest single producer of copper, silver, lead and zinc in the world. Mount Isa is surrounded by cattle country and hosts one of the richest and largest rodeos in the world.
MAIN ATTRACTIONS: The **Outback at Isa** complex, in Marian St, has several attractions as well as visitor information. **Riversleigh Fossil Centre** features displays of fossil discoveries from the Riversleigh area, some dating to over 30 million years old. **Sir James Foots Building** covers the history of Mount Isa with audiovisuals and interactive displays. Two hour tours of the replica **Hard Times Mine** are available several times daily.
NEARBY ATTRACTIONS: Man-made **Lake Moondarra**, 15km north of Mount Isa, is a recreational and picnic spot. It offers swimming, boating, canoeing, sailing and waterskiing and the surrounding area is a wildlife sanctuary. **Boodjamulla (Lawn Hill) NP**, 332km north-west, has several walking tracks, some

leading to high peaks and others to swimming holes. Facilities include a camping area. Tours of the World Heritage-listed **Riversleigh Fossil Site** are available. The site is 267km north-west of Mount Isa. **Lake Julius**, situated along the **Leichhardt River**, 99km north-east, offers the chance to see local wildlife, including freshwater crocodiles. Only a short distance from the lake are Aboriginal cave paintings, nature trails and an old goldmine. Camping at the lake is possible.
VISITOR INFORMATION: Outback at Isa, 19 Marian St, Ph: (07) 4749 1555 or 1300 659 660

Mount Morgan   POP 2490
Map 267, B5
Located 38km south-west of Rockhampton, Mount Morgan has a history of gold and copper mining dating back over a century. **Mount Morgan Mine** was the largest open-cut gold mine in the Southern Hemisphere.
MAIN ATTRACTIONS: The Mount Morgan Mine was closed in 1981 but there are daily guided tours of the mine's old workings. **Mount Morgan Historical Museum**, located in Morgan St, has a large collection of historical pieces representing the town's early years. The National Trust has classified some historic buildings, including the **Court House**; and the **Railway Station**, which contains tearooms and a rail museum. A restored 1904 steam engine operates on on the first Sunday of each month and fettlers' trolley-rides operate along a 4km-long track daily. **Riding the Rack** is a free 3D movie experience in a rail carriage, also at the railway station.
NEARBY ATTRACTIONS: The **Big Dam** is popular for boating and fishing, and is located about 3km north of Mount Morgan.
VISITOR INFORMATION: Railway Station, 1 Railway Pde, Ph: (07) 4938 2312

The magnificent natural playground of the Fraser Coast hosts diverse and unique landscapes, from intriguing coloured sands, rainforests, giant sand dunes and basalt headlands to tranquil lakes, beaches and national parks.

Boasting the world's largest sand island—120km long and an average of 15km wide—and magnificent waterways, the Fraser Coast offers a full range of watersports, including swimming, fishing and diving.

Apart from a few areas of private land, **Fraser Island** is a World Heritage-listed national park; the only place on earth where rainforest grows from sand. Most areas of interest are in the central part of the island, and 4-wheel drive tracks and walking tracks lead past major sites. **Lake Boomanjin** is a fresh-water lake perched high up on the island's sand dunes—it is the largest perched lake in the world. Sandy beaches surround the lake and there are camping and picnic areas. Wildlife on the island is prolific, from dingos to wild horses and wallabies to jabirus.

The secluded seaside townships along the **Great Sandy Strait**, such as **Tuan**, **Boonooroo**, **Poona** and **Tinnanbar**, provide opportunities for more sedate activities like fishing and boating.

A major attraction for visitors is the annual migration (late July to early November) of majestic humpback whales through the waters of **Hervey Bay** en route to feeding grounds in Antarctica.

Shipwreck Survivor

After the wreck of the *Stirling Castle* in 1836, Eliza Fraser was cast ashore on Fraser Island where she lived with the Dalungbara Aboriginal people. She was rescued by 'Wandi', the escaped convict, David Bracefell. The island is named in her honour.

 Visitor information

Maryborough/Fraser Island Visitor Information Centre
Maryborough South Travel Stop,
Bruce Hwy, Maryborough, Qld 4650
Ph: (07) 4121 4111
Freecall: 1800 214 789
www.frasercoast.org.au

Humpback whale, *Megaptera novaeangliae*, breaching in Hervey Bay Marine Park

main attractions

◈ **'The Cathedrals'**

These strikingly coloured sand cliffs at Cathedral Beach on Fraser Island change colour depending on the light and the time of day.

◈ **Eli Creek**

Crystalline Eli Creek is the largest creek on the east coast of Fraser Island, and is ideal for swimming.

◈ **Fraser Island**

This island is famous for its coloured sands, vast sand dunes, unique freshwater perched lakes and rainforests.

◈ **Great Sandy National Park**

Bushwalking tracks offer opportunities to explore the 1650km^2 Fraser Island wilderness more closely.

◈ **Hervey Bay**

Gateway to Fraser Island, Hervey Bay's sheltered waters are stinger-free, perfect for water-based activities.

◈ **Maryborough**

Picturesque Maryborough on the Mary River is known as the 'Heritage City' because of its many historic buildings.

◈ **Whale watching**

A good time to see whales is from late July to early November, when they rest and play en route back to their feeding grounds in the Antarctic.

Wanggoolba Creek at Central Station, Fraser Island

Queensland

A B C D E

1

Barubbra
Island
Burnett Heads
Fairymead
Turtle Rookery
Nielson Park
Bargara
Kellys Beach
Gooburrum
Innes Park
Bundaberg
Rum Distillery, Hinkler House
Clayton
Elliott Heads
Riverview

Sandy Cape
Lighthouse
Sandy Cape

HERVEY BAY
MARINE PARK

Rooney Point

Manann

Beach

Ngkala Rocks

Marloo
Bay

2

Coonarr
Mahogany Ck
BURRUM COAST N.P.
(Kinkuna Section)
56
Woodgate
Goodwood
Walkers Point
Buxton
Burrum Heads
BURRUM COAST N.P.
(Woodgate Section)
Burrum Point
BURRUM COAST N.P.
(Burrum River Section)
Isis Junction

Hervey   Bay

Platypus

Bay

Whale watching tours

Wathumba Creek

Orchid Beach
Waddy Pt
Middle
Rocks
Indian
Head

GREAT

SANDY

NATIONAL

PARK

The Cathedrals
Lake Bowarraly
Dundubara
Cathedral Beach Resort
The Pinnacles

3

TO CHILDERS
1
Howard
37
A1
BRUCE
Torbanlea
36
Dundowran
Takura
Nikenbah
Walligan

Toogoom
Craignish
Hervey Bay
Point Vernon
Urangan

Neptune's Reefworld
Moon Point
Sandy
Point
Barge
Big Woody
Island
N.P.
Ferry
Mangrove
Point

Fraser

Island

'Maheno' wreck
Yidney Scrub
Lake Garawongera
Happy Valley
Yidney Rocks

4

Lake
Lenthall
Colton
34
25
Maryborough
West
86
Yengario
Tinana
Maryborough
Heritage Museum

River
Heads
Kangaroo
Island
Turkey
Island
POONA
NATIONAL
PARK
Maaroom

Kingfisher
Bay
Barge
Central Station
Ungowa
GREAT SANDY
Garrys
Anchorage

Mile
Lake Mackenzie
Lake Wabby
Wanggoolba Ck
Eurong
Lake Boomanjin
Dilli Village

Poyungan Rocks

CORAL

SEA

5

Thinoomba
Mungar
Yerra
39
Tiaro
Netherby
1
Bauple
MT BAUPLE
N.P.
Gundiah

Boonooroo
Tuan
Poona
Tawan
Tinnanbar
COWRA
GOV. PK.
60
Seventy
Five

NATIONAL

PARK

Hook Point
Inskip Point

6

Paterson
Theebine
Miva
Glenwood
35
Gunalda
Brooyar
Carmyle
A1
Curra
WIDE BAY
49
Wonga
Lower
Wonga Upper
Upper
Widgee
Gympie
Glastonbury
12
1

WIDE BAY
MILITARY
TRAINING AREA
Tin Can Bay
13
Toolara
Cooloola
Village
Neerdie
Toolara
Forest
Kia Ora
42
Goomboorian
Rossmount
Chatsworth
Wolvi
Coondoo
Neusa
Vale

Carlo
Point
Rainbow Beach
Coloured sands
Double Island Point
Poona
Lake
'Cherry Venture' wreck
L Freshwater
GREAT SANDY
(Cooloola Section)
NATIONAL PARK
Wide Bay
Cooloola
Beach

Continued on map 255

TO BRISBANE   TO COOROY

© UNIVERSAL PUBLISHERS PTY LTD 2005

■ Moura   POP 1800

Map 287, F1

This small town is located 69km from Biloela and lies in the heart of the **Dawson Valley**. Moura services the surrounding rural and coal-mining communities. The town has a large and permanent storage depot for various grains, including wheat, sunflower, barley and maize. Cattle and cotton are also important local rural industries.

NEARBY ATTRACTIONS: **Apex Park** at the **Dawson River**, a few kilometres from Moura, is a popular fishing, boating, swimming and picnic area. A drive past the coal mine on the road to Biloela usually provides a good view of the huge dragline at work. For keen hikers, **Mount Scoria**, **Carnarvon**, **Cania** and **Isla gorges** are all within driving distance of Moura.

VISITOR INFORMATION: Shire Offices, 33 Gillespie St, Ph: (07) 4997 2084

■ Murgon   POP 2150

Map 287, H3

This picturesque town is called the 'Beef Capital of the South Burnett'. Murgon is nestled at the foot of **Boat Mountain**, about 96km west of Gympie. Murgon is famous for fossils—the area yielded the first evidence of marsupials in Australia, dating back 55 million years.

MAIN ATTRACTIONS: **Queensland's Dairy Industry Museum** displays trace the history of the local milk and cheese industries, with an emphasis on the production of butter. The museum is located on Gayndah Rd and is open daily. Next door to the museum is the relocated **Trinity Homestead**, one of the district's original buildings.

NEARBY ATTRACTIONS: Murgon is an emerging wine area of the **Burnett Valley**. **Barambah Ridge**, at **Redgate**, offers tastings and sales of its award-winning wines, and has a picnic area. **Clovely Vineyard** is another important local winery. **Boat Mountain Environmental Park**, 14km north of Murgon, and **Jack Smith Scrub Conservation Park**, 15km north-east, offer walking tracks and views. Both parks can be visited as part of a scenic drive in the area.

VISITOR INFORMATION: Lamb St, Ph: (07) 4168 3864

■ Nambour   POP 12 834

Map 255, C4

The agricultural service centre of Nambour is located just off the Bruce Hwy, 104km north of Brisbane in the heart of the **Sunshine Coast** sugar-growing area. Macadamia nuts and lychees have recently joined the three main crops grown in the region—sugar, pine-apples and bananas. It is thought the name for the town derives from 'namba' an Aboriginal word for the red flowers of the weeping bottlebrush (*Callistemon viminalis*), which is common in the region.

MAIN ATTRACTION: **Nambour Adventure Playground** in **Quota Memorial Park** is a favourite with children.

NEARBY ATTRACTIONS: **The Big Pineapple**, symbol of the Sunshine Coast, and **Macadamia Nut Factory** are 7km south. Visitors can see how pineapples and macadamias are grown and harvested on these working plantations. There is a train and 'nutmobile' for children, a fauna sanctuary and animal nursery. The **Creatures of the Night** exhibit has nocturnal rainforest animals that are rarely seen. **Superbee Honey Factory**, with its Live Bee Show, and **Forest Glen Sanctuary**, with deer and native animals, are located south on the **Tanawha-Forest Glen Tourist Drive**. The impressive **Glass House Mountains**, which are eroded volcanic pillars, are also to the south. **Blackall Range Scenic Drive** to **Landsborough** is a 70km trip.

VISITOR INFORMATION: Cnr Sixth Ave and Melrose Pde, Maroochydore, Ph: (07) 5479 1566 or 1800 882 032

View to the Glass House Mountains, south of Nambour

Queensland

Coloured sands of the Cooloola section of Great Sandy National Park, north of Noosa Heads

Noosa Heads   POP 17 795

Map 255, C3

The well-known resort town of Noosa Heads is situated on the edge of **Noosa NP** and **Laguna Bay**. Not only does it offer beaches and safe swimming year-round, it is also the gateway to the **Cooloola Section** of **Great Sandy NP**, including the stunning **Noosa River Everglades**.

MAIN ATTRACTIONS: Hastings St, the main street of Noosa Heads, has restaurants, cafes, galleries and boutiques. **Main Beach** offers safe swimming and is the most popular beach for families. Noosa NP is only a short walk from Hastings St. This extremely popular 477ha park provides walking tracks through rainforest, past small coves, rugged coastal rock formations and interesting coastal heathlands.

NEARBY ATTRACTIONS: Great Sandy NP is 14km north, and although **Noosa River** separates it from Noosa Heads, it can be accessed via car ferry from **Tewantin**. The multi-coloured sand cliffs, known as the **Coloured Sands**, are located in this park. Activities include bush-walking, camel riding, horseriding and beach fishing. Tours to the Everglades, Coloured Sands and **Fraser Island** are very popular. **Noosaville** is a family-style resort town, located 5km west. The Noosa River is filled with dinghies, catamarans and houseboats, and has picnic areas and beaches with safe swimming for children. **Eumundi**, 24km south-west, is best known for its Wednesday and Saturday morning markets.

VISITOR INFORMATION: Hastings St, Ph: (07) 5447 4988

Normanton   POP 1445

Map 278, D4

Located on the **Norman River** and 72km inland from the Gulf of Carpentaria, Normanton is the capital of **Carpentaria Shire**. A major business and service centre, it serves a pastoral region covering 68 250km^2.

MAIN ATTRACTIONS: Historic **Normanton Railway Station** is home to the *Gulflander* train which operates twice weekly. Brochures are available for self-guided **scenic walks** and drives around Normanton. The **Gulfland Motel**, Landsborough St, has a giant barramundi out front. The **Shire Office Gardens**, in Haig St, display a life-size replica of **Krys the Savannah King**, an 8.6m saltwater crocodile caught in the Norman River, which is also famous for its barramundi.

NEARBY ATTRACTIONS: Cruises on the Norman River offer the chance to see jabirus, brolgas, herons and saltwater crocodiles. **Shady Lagoon**, located 18km east, is popular for bush camping and birdwatching. **Dorunda Station**, 197km north-east of Normanton, offers visitors the chance to stay on a working cattle station. The lakes and rivers on the station are excellent for barramundi and saratoga fishing. **Bang Bang Jump Up** rock formation is a solitary hill located 106km south-west. A road goes to the top of the hill, which affords panoramic views of the district.

VISITOR INFORMATION: Shire Offices, Haig St, Ph: (07) 4745 1166

Oakey   POP 3470

Map 271, C3

Situated around 30km north-west of Toowoomba, Oakey is rich in historical and scenic attractions. It has the country's largest **Army Aviation Base**. Industries in Oakey include malting, engineering works and export abattoirs.

MAIN ATTRACTIONS: A life-size statue of the racehorse **Bernborough** stands near the town's council chambers. This famous racehorse was bred near Oakey and raced during the 1940s. **Oakey Historical Museum** is located on the Warrego Hwy. The **Flypast Museum of Australian Army Flying** is located at the army base and displays a large collection of original and replica aircraft and aviation memorabilia.

NEARBY ATTRACTIONS: **Jondaryan Woolshed**, 22km north-west of Oakey, is over 100 years old and is now an Australian heritage theme park. A complex of historic buildings house vintage machinery and memorabilia which commemorates pioneers of the wool industry. There are sheep-shearing demonstrations and souvenirs are available. **Crows Nest NP** is to the north-east.

VISITOR INFORMATION: Library, 64 Campbell St, Ph: (07) 4692 0154

Capt James Cook entered the waters of this group of idyllic islands on Whit Sunday, June 3, 1770. He spent much time charting these beautiful islands comprising 74 tropical islands, only eight of which are inhabited. The Whitsunday Group lies off the stretch of coast between **Mackay** and **Bowen**. Paralleling the island group, further offshore in the **Coral Sea**, are the coral reefs and lagoons of the **Great Barrier Reef**—a wonderland of marine diversity. The islands have been compared with the beauty of the Caribbean Islands and are a favourite holiday destination for visitors from around the world.

With an estimated 8.25 hours of sunshine per day and an average yearly temperature of 25°C, the Whitsunday coast is an idyllic retreat. The region boasts unspoilt coral-fringed islands, beaches, turquoise waters, a tropical climate and alluring seaside resorts.

With consistently perfect conditions for swimming, snorkelling, scuba diving, fishing, sailing and cruising, the Whitsundays are a dream-holiday destination.

Charter and tour companies based on the mainland offer a wide variety of tour and recreation options. Explore the area by boat or seaplane, try parasailing or tandem skydiving. Take a cruise to the nearby Great Barrier Reef and see the migrating whales in season (around July–September). The Whitsundays offer a range of accommodation to suit most budgets, from camping on a deserted island to a suite in a luxurious five-star resort.

Airlie Beach

Within the exotic perimeters of the **Whitsunday Islands**, **Great Barrier Reef** and **Conway Range NP**, Airlie Beach is a prime holiday destination. There is a range of activities related to land, sea and air and all styles of accommodation. The village is the perfect base for exploring the region's many diversions. Airlie Beach boasts a year-round safe swimming lagoon surrounded by landscaped gardens.

Snorkelling on the Hardy Reef

main attractions

◈ **Brampton Island**

The island resort is surrounded by national park and sandy beaches.

◈ **Daydream Island**

This is a popular resort island.

◈ **Great Barrier Reef**

This spectacular string of reefs and islands extends for more than 2000km along Australia's east coast. It offers superb diving and snorkelling opportunities.

◈ **Hamilton Island**

The island's resort is the key landmark offering a wide range of activities.

◈ **Hayman Island**

A luxurious resort island.

◈ **Hook Island**

A budget island retreat with an underwater observatory.

◈ **Lindeman Island**

This island is home to Australia's first Club Med resort.

◈ **Long Island**

This island retreat, not far from Shutehaven, has three resorts to choose from.

◈ **South Molle Island**

With unspoilt national park fringed by scenic beaches, this island is great for bushwalkers and family groups.

◈ **Whitehaven Beach**

A 7km-long white silica sand beach on Whitsunday Island.

 Visitor information

Whitsunday Information Centre
Bruce Hwy, Proserpine, Qld 4800
Ph: (07) 4945 3711
Freecall: 1800 801 252
www.whitsundaytourism.com

Charter boat near Cid Island, Whitsunday Passage

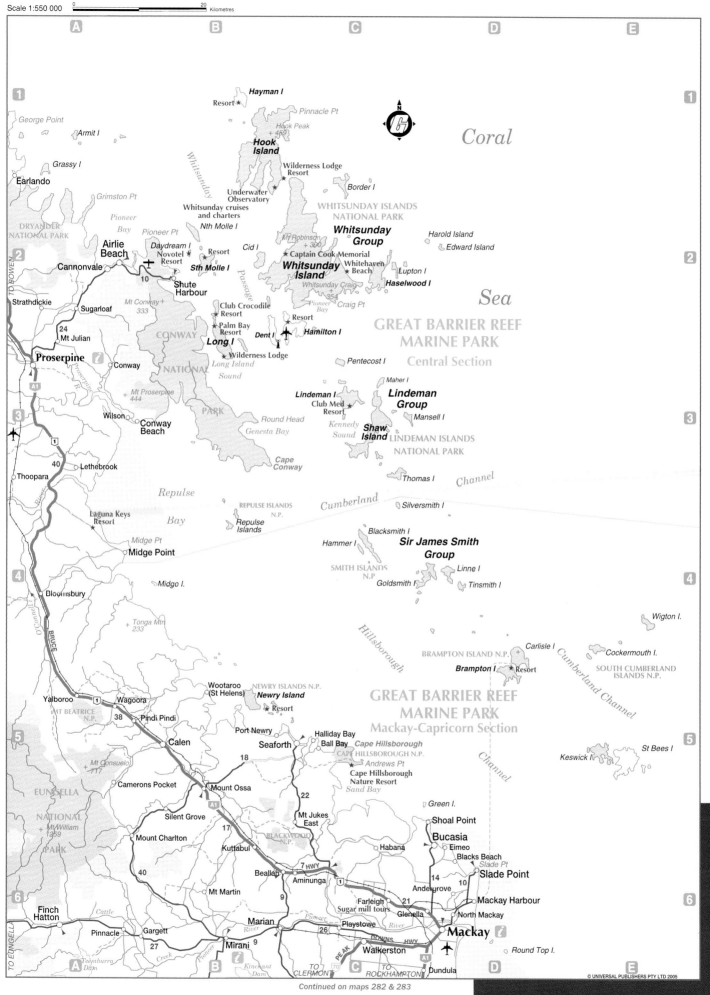

0   20 Kilometres

Coral

George Point

Armit I

Grassy I

Earlando

Hayman I

Resort ★

Pinnacle Pt

Hook Peak
+ 469

Hook
Island

Wilderness Lodge
Resort

Border I

Grimston Pt

DRYANDER
NATIONAL PARK

Pioneer
Bay

Pioneer Pt

Whitsunday

WHITSUNDAY ISLANDS
NATIONAL PARK

Whitsunday
Group

Harold Island

Edward Island

Underwater
Observatory

Whitsunday cruises
and charters

Nth Molle I

Cid I

Mt Robinson
+ 360

Captain Cook Memorial

Sea

Airlie
Beach

Daydream I
Novotel ★
Resort

Resort

Sth Molle I

Passage

Whitsunday
Island

Whitehaven
Beach

Lupton I

Cannonvale

Shute
Harbour

Whitsunday Craig
+ 354

Haselwood I

Strathdickie

Sugarloaf

Mt Conway
333 +

Club Crocodile
★ Resort

Pioneer
Bay

Craig Pt

GREAT BARRIER REEF
MARINE PARK

24

Mt Julian

CONWAY

Palm Bay
★ Resort

Resort

Dent I

Hamilton I

Central Section

Proserpine

Conway

Long I

Wilderness Lodge

Pentecost I

A1

NATIONAL

Long Island
Sound

Maher I

Mt Proserpine
444 +

Lindeman I

Lindeman
Group

Wilson

PARK

Round Head

Club Med
Resort

Mansell I

Conway
Beach

Genesta Bay

Kennedy
Sound

Shaw
Island

LINDEMAN ISLANDS

40

Letherbrook

Cape
Conway

NATIONAL PARK

Thoopara

Repulse

Thomas I

Channel

REPULSE ISLANDS
N.P.

Cumberland

Silversmith I

Laguna Keys
Resort

Bay

Repulse
Islands

Blacksmith I

Sir James Smith
Group

Midge Pt

Hammer I

Linne I

Midge Point

SMITH ISLANDS
N.P

Goldsmith I

Tinsmith I

Bloomsbury

Midgo I.

Wigton I.

Tonga Mtn
233

BRAMPTON ISLAND N.P.

Carlisle I

Cockermouth I.

Hillsborough

Brampton I ★ Resort

SOUTH CUMBERLAND
ISLANDS N.P.

Cumberland Channel

Yalboroo

Wagoora

Wootaroo
(St Helens)

NEWRY ISLANDS N.P.

Newry Island

GREAT BARRIER REEF
MARINE PARK

MT BEATRICE
N.P.

38

Pindi Pindi

★ Resort

Mackay-Capricorn Section

Keswick I

St Bees I

Port Newry

Halliday Bay

Calen

Seaforth

Ball Bay

Cape Hillsborough

18

CAPE HILLSBOROUGH N.P.

Andrews Pt

Channel

Camerons Pocket

Mount Ossa

22

Cape Hillsborough
Nature Resort

Sand Bay

Green I.

EUNGELLA

A1

Mt Jukes
East

Shoal Point

Silent Grove

17

Bucasia

NATIONAL

Mt William
1359

BLACKWOOD
N.P.

Eimeo

Mount Charlton

Kuttabul

Habana

Blacks Beach

Slade Pt

40

Beallah

7 HWY

14

Slade Point

PARK

9

Aminunga

1

Andergrove

10

Mt Martin

Farleigh
Sugar mill tours

21

Mackay Harbour

Finch
Hatton

Cattle

Marian

Glenella

North Mackay

Pinnacle

Gargett

Pioneer

Playstowe

River

Mackay

Teemburra
Dam

27

Mirani

9

26

DOWNS HWY

Round Top I.

Creek

Kinchant
Dam

Walkerston

A1

PEAK

TO
CLERMONT

70

TO
ROCKHAMPTON

Dundula

© UNIVERSAL PUBLISHERS PTY LTD 2005

Continued on maps 282 & 283

■ Palm Cove   POP 2805
Map 239, C2

Located 27km north of Cairns, off the Captain Cook Hwy, this captivating resort village is situated on a tropical beach with views over aqua waters to **Double Island** and **Scouts Hat Island**. There are several art galleries and boutiques.

NEARBY ATTRACTIONS: Dive tours to the **Great Barrier Reef** depart daily from Palm Cove. Daytrip tours to the **Atherton Tableland** also leave from here. **Cairns Tropical Zoo**, close by, has crocodiles, native fauna and a free-flight bird show. In **Smithfield**, 14km south, there is a bungy-jumping tower set in the rainforest. **Hartley's Crocodile Adventures**, 15km north, has hundreds of crocodiles and other native fauna. There are crocodile and snake shows daily, as well as cruises on a tropical lagoon. For panoramic coastal views, visit **Rex Lookout**, 17km north.

VISITOR INFORMATION: **51 The Esplanade**, Cairns, Ph: (07) 4051 3588

■ Port Douglas   POP 3645
Map 239, B1

Located 67km north of Cairns, Port Douglas is situated on the **Coral Sea** coastline with a backdrop of tropical mountains. With its close proximity to some of Australia's most popular tourist destinations, the **Daintree Rainforest**, **Cape Tribulation** and the **Great Barrier Reef**, Port Douglas has become an internationally renowned tourist destination.

MAIN ATTRACTIONS: Port Douglas offers restaurants, art galleries, excellent shops, historic buildings, nightclubs, golf courses and beaches. The superb **Rainforest Habitat**, on Port Douglas Rd, is a wildlife sanctuary with a focus on biological conservation. **Flagstaff Hill**, Murphy St, offers panoramic views of **Four Mile Beach** and **Low Isles**. *Lady Douglas*, a paddlewheeler, provides cruises of **Dickson Inlet**.

The **Sunday Markets** in Rex Smeal Park are very popular.

NEARBY ATTRACTIONS: Many tours depart from Port Douglas, including 4-wheel drive safaris, horseriding and rainforest tours. Coach tours to **Mossman Gorge**, **Daintree NP**, Cape Tribulation and **Cooktown** are available. The Great Barrier Reef is the region's top tourist attraction and there are cruises to the **Outer Reef** and the **Low Isles**.

VISITOR INFORMATION: 23 Macrossan St, Ph: (07) 4099 5599

■ Proserpine   POP 3250
Map 263, A3

Lying close to the **Whitsunday coast**, Proserpine is located 264km south-east of Townsville.

MAIN ATTRACTIONS: The **Historical Museum**, located on the Bruce Hwy next to the Whitsunday Information Centre, displays memorabilia highlighting the history of the district, including the sugar and mining industries. It also has WWII displays.

NEARBY ATTRACTIONS: **Peter Faust Dam** is 20km west of town. It was built to create **Lake Proserpine**, an area for watersports, including power boating, sailing, swimming, rowing, canoeing and waterskiing. The lake is stocked for fishing enthusiasts with cod, barramundi, saratoga and sooty grunter. BBQ facilities are provided. **Cedar Creek Falls**, to the south-east, is a picturesque recreation area where, after rain, a creek drops over the falls into a large swimming hole lined with majestic Alexander palms. **Conway NP**, 20km east, offers views across the **Whitsunday Islands**.

VISITOR INFORMATION: Bruce Hwy, Ph: (07) 4945 3711 or 1800 801 252

■ Rainbow Beach   POP 1005
Map 255, C1

Situated near **Tin Can Bay**, 265km north of Brisbane, Rainbow Beach is a popular holiday town.

MAIN ATTRACTIONS: Activities, such as 4-wheel driving on the beach, fishing or cruising **Great Sandy Strait** on a houseboat are popular. A number of 4-wheel drive tours and safaris operate out of Rainbow Beach to the **Cooloola** section of **Great Sandy NP** and to the World-Heritage listed **Fraser Island**. The beautiful **coloured sands** in the cliff faces adjoining Rainbow Beach are one of Queensland's most popular tourist attractions.

Quicksilver pontoon on Agincourt Reef, near Port Douglas

Queensland

NEARBY ATTRACTIONS: A 30 minute walk through Great Sandy NP leads to the **Carlo Sandblow**, 16ha of sand mass that is popular for hang-gliding and paragliding. Other signposted walking tracks lead through subtropical rainforests to coloured sand dunes and **Lake Poona** which is surrounded by a sandy beach. This freshwater lake is popular for swimming and camping is allowed in designated areas; permits can be obtained from the National Parks and Wildlife office. Rainbow Beach is the southern gateway to Fraser Island. Vehicular ferries depart from **Inskip Point**, 13km north.

VISITOR INFORMATION: 8 Rainbow Beach Rd, Ph: (07) 5486 3227 or 1800 444 222

Kronosaurus Korner, Richmond Fossil Centre, Richmond

Richmond   POP 1445

Map 281, G2

This town lies 500km west of Townsville and 400km east of Mount Isa. It is situated beside Queensland's longest river, the **Flinders**. Richmond is the centre for a sheep and cattle district.

MAIN ATTRACTIONS: The main street is lined with bougainvilleas and has a fine display of Federation-style buildings including hotels and churches. **Gidgee Wheel Arts and Crafts** is in Harris St. **Kronosaurus Korner** is part of the outstanding **Richmond Fossil Centre**. This museum exhibits world-class vertebrate fossils, all found in the area which, 100 million years ago, was the site of an inland sea. The countryside around Richmond is known for its **'moon rocks'**. These limestone rocks vary in size and can weigh tonnes. They carry the fossilised remains of fish, shells and trees. A display of moon rocks and a commemorative cairn can be seen at **Lions Park**, which is also a good place for picnicking. Moon rocks carrying fossilised remains are also on show at the Richmond Fossil Centre.

NEARBY ATTRACTIONS: Fossils can be found at the designated fossicking site, 12km north. **Cambridge Downs** ruins, about 30km north, are worthwhile visiting.

VISITOR INFORMATION: Kronosaurus Korner, 91-93 Goldring St, Ph: (07) 4741 3429

Rockhampton   POP 58 980

Map 267, B4

The city of Rockhampton is situated on the **Tropic of Capricorn**, 34km inland from the Pacific Ocean. The **Berserker Range** and **Mount Archer NP** surround the city. Rockhampton is the capital and cultural centre of **Central Queensland**, where the regional headquarters of most government departments and major commercial businesses are located.

MAIN ATTRACTIONS: Many of the city's original store buildings and churches are still standing. **Quay St**, which runs by the **Fitzroy River**, is Australia's longest National Trust-classified street. Brochures are available on the **Heritage Walk and Drive** tour around the city centre.

With a near year-round tropical climate, Rockhampton is lush and green with many shady tree-lined streets and parks. Rockhampton's heritage-listed **Botanic Gardens** were established in 1869 and cover an area of 39ha. There is a fernery, orchid house, tropical fruit garden, Japanese garden and a range of tropical plants. **Rockhampton Zoo** is located within the gardens and features chimpanzees, koalas, dingoes, kangaroos and wallabies. A highlight is the koala feeding at 3pm. **Kershaw Native Gardens**, situated beside the Bruce Hwy, were opened in 1988 as a Bicentenary Project. **Rockhampton Steam Train Museum** is in **Archer Park**. **The Spire**, in **Curtis Park**, on the southern outskirts of Rockhampton marks the actual location of the Tropic of Capricorn. **Rockhampton City Art Gallery** is in Victoria Pde. Enjoy a rodeo at the **Great Western Hotel**, the only hotel in Australia that hosts a rodeo. Anglers can fish for barramundi in the Fitzroy River that flows through the city centre.

(CONTINUED P.268)

Straddling the **Tropic of Capricorn**, the Capricorn Region is an inviting combination of stunning beaches, rivers, subtropical reef islands and coastal rainforests. Inland, natural wonders include rugged volcanic outcrops, deep Outback gorges, estuarine mudflats, scenic valleys, wooded hills and vast cattle stations; the region has a number of historic townships with elegant buildings that hint at the wealth of former times.

Rich in history, relics provide evidence that the region was once the site of a goldrush. The area flourished in the past and still does due to abundant natural resources—from gold, coal and copper mines to vast cattle and grain properties.

In the west of the region, fascinating sandstone gorges like **Blackdown Tableland** and the magnificent **Carnarvon Gorge** preserve unique ecosystems and are wonderful places to explore. Try your luck fossicking for rubies, sapphires and emeralds in the **Sapphire Gemfields**.

The region's interesting Aboriginal history is another drawcard for visitors: there are bora rings, museums and artefacts of the Darumbal people, whose territory once stretched from inland **Mount Morgan** to the **Keppel group of islands**. The Capricorn Region's diverse landscapes offer some of the world's best fishing, scuba diving, snorkelling, bush-walking, caving, camping and sightseeing experiences.

Rockhampton's former Customs House

Dreamtime Cultural Centre

This large centre, 7km north of **Rockhampton**, is located on an important ancient site where Aboriginal people once gathered for tribal meetings. The museum aims to promote understanding of 40 000 years of Aboriginal history. Tours are available and include demonstrations of boomerang throwing and didgeridoo playing.

main attractions

❖ **Capricorn Caves**

A spectacular system of 16 limestone caves. A popular cavern is The Cathedral, which has extraordinary natural acoustics and old church pews to sit on.

❖ **Carnarvon National Park**

A wonderful sandstone gorge with an impressive ancient Aboriginal art gallery.

❖ **Great Keppel Island**

This lively, sun-drenched island is accessible via ferry or cruises from Kennel Bay Marina and Rosslyn Bay Harbour near Yeppoon.

❖ **Rockhampton Heritage Village**

An active township museum where visitors can experience the region's history. There are working demonstrations on Sundays.

❖ **Koorana Crocodile Farm**

This farm is famed for breeding estuarine crocodiles. Don't miss the Big Croc Hatch in February–April each year.

❖ **Mount Morgan**

Mount Morgan is an old gold-mining township with a local history and geology museum.

ℹ Visitor information

Capricorn Tourism
'The Spire', Gladstone Rd, Rockhampton. Qld 4700
Ph: (07) 4927 2055, Freecall: 1800 676 701
www.capricorntourism.com.au

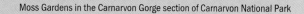

Moss Gardens in the Carnarvon Gorge section of Carnarvon National Park

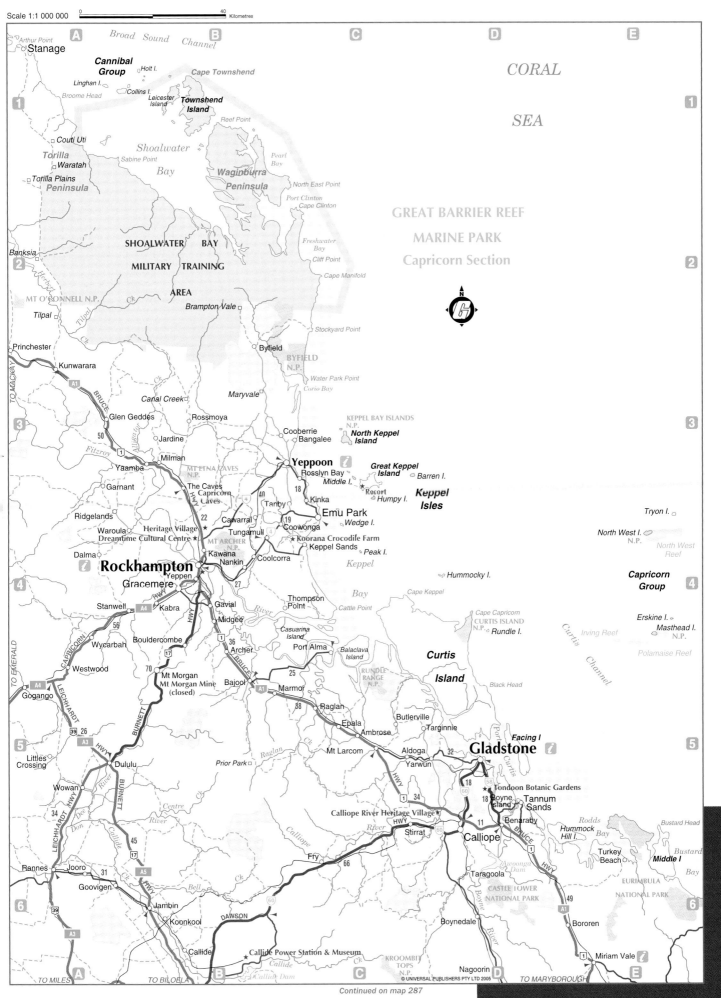

Scale 1:1 000 000

0   40 Kilometres

CORAL

SEA

GREAT BARRIER REEF

MARINE PARK

Capricorn Section

A   B   C   D   E

Arthur Point
Stanage

Cannibal Group
Holt I.
Linghan I.
Broome Head   Collins I.
Leicester Island   **Townshend Island**

Broad Sound Channel

Cape Townshend

Reef Point

Couti Uti

Torilla
Waratah
Torilla Plains
Peninsula

Shoalwater Bay
Sabine Point

Waginburra Peninsula

Pearl Bay

North East Point
Port Clinton
Cape Clinton

Banksia

SHOALWATER   BAY
MILITARY   TRAINING
AREA

Freshwater Bay
Cliff Point

Cape Manifold

MT O'CONNELL N.P.
Tilpal

Brampton Vale

Stockyard Point

Princhester
Kunwarara

Byfield

BYFIELD N.P.

Water Park Point
Corio Bay

TO MACKAY

A1

BRUCE

Canal Creek

Maryvale

50

Glen Geddes
Rossmoya
Jardine
Milman
Yaamba

Cooberrie
Bangalee

KEPPEL BAY ISLANDS N.P.
North Keppel Island

Fitzroy

MT ETNA CAVES N.P.

Yeppoon
Rosslyn Bay
18   Middle I.

Great Keppel Island
Barren I.
Resort
Humpy I.

Keppel Isles

Tryon I.

Garnant

The Caves
Capricorn Caves

40   Tanby
Kinka

Emu Park

Ridgelands

22   Cawarral   19   Coowonga
Tungamull

Wedge I.

North West I. N.P.

North West Reef

Waroula
Heritage Village
Dreamtime Cultural Centre

MT ARCHER N.P.
Kawana
Nankin

Koorana Crocodile Farm
Keppel Sands
Peak I.

Dalma

Rockhampton
Gracemere

Yeppen
Coolcorra

Keppel Bay

Cape Keppel

Cattle Point

Hummocky I.

Capricorn Group

Stanwell
Kabra

A4
CAPRICORN
56

Gavial
Midgee

27

Thompson Point

River

Erskine I.
Masthead I. N.P.

Wycarbah

Bouldercombe
17

36
Archer
Casuarina Island

Port Alma

Balaclava Island

Cape Capricorn
CURTIS ISLAND N.P.
Rundle I.

Curtis Channel

Irving Reef

Polamaise Reef

Westwood

70

1

25

RUNDLE RANGE N.P.

Curtis Island

Black Head

TO EMERALD

A4

Gogango

LEICHHARDT

Mt Morgan
Mt Morgan Mine (closed)
Bajool

Marmor

38

Raglan

Butlerville
Targinnie

Cape Capricorn

BURNETT

39   26

A3

Dululu

Prior Park

Epala
Ambrose

Mt Larcom

Aldoga
Yarwun

32

Gladstone

Facing I

Littles Crossing

Wowan

34

Don River

Callide River

45

17

BURNETT

Centre River

HWY

Calliope River Heritage Village

Stirrat

HWY

60

18
Tondoon Botanic Gardens
18   Boyne Island
Benaraby

34

11

Calliope

Tannum Sands

Port Curtis

BRUCE

Rodds Bay

Hummock Hill I.

Bustard Head

Rannes
31   Jooro

A5

Goovigen

Ffy   66

Awoonga Dam

Taragoola

CASTLE TOWER NATIONAL PARK

Boyne River

Turkey Beach

Middle I

EURIMBULA
NATIONAL PARK

Bustard Bay

39
A3

Jambin

Koonkool

DAWSON

60

Boynedale

49

A1

Bororen

Callide

Callide Power Station & Museum
Callide   Ck
Callide Dam

KROOMBIT TOPS N.P.

Nagoorin

Miriam Vale

TO MILES   TO BILOELA   TO MARYBOROUGH

© UNIVERSAL PUBLISHERS PTY LTD 2005

Continued on map 287

NEARBY ATTRACTIONS: The Aboriginal and Torres Strait Islander **Dreamtime Cultural Centre** is 7km north of Rockhampton and located on an ancient traditional site, where Aboriginal people gathered for tribal meetings. **Rockhampton Heritage Village**, 11km north, is an active outdoor museum which includes slab huts, horse-drawn vehicles and a replica of an Egyptian water clock. On weekends there are working displays of steam and vintage machinery. **Capricorn Caves**, 23km north, are an award-winning system of 16 caves in a limestone mountain. The caves are open for inspection. **Mount Hay Gemstone Park**, 30 minutes west of Rockhampton, offers fossicking for unique 118 million-year-old thunder-eggs and rainforest jasper; cutting and polishing is offered at the centre. To the east are the beaches of the Capricorn Region. On the way to **Emu Park**, 30 minutes from Rockhampton, is famous **Koorana Crocodile Farm**, offering an informative audiovisual and feeding of these fascinating 'dinosaurs'.

VISITOR INFORMATION: The Spire, Gladstone Rd, Ph: (07) 4927 2055 or 1800 676 701

■ Roma   POP 5900
Map 286, E3
Roma, 267km west of Dalby, is the commercial centre of the **Maranoa District** and capital of the **Western Downs**. Sheep and cattle form the basis of the area's economy.

MAIN ATTRACTIONS: **The Big Rig** is an authentic oil-drilling rig of the 1920s that stands at the eastern entrance to Roma. Australia's oil and gas industry began here in 1900, when the first natural gas strike was made at Hospital Hill. **Big Rig Research Centre**, next door, documents early oil exploration in the area. **Romavilla Winery**, Queensland's oldest winery, is located on Northern Rd and visitors

are welcome for cellar door tastings and sales. An avenue of more than 100 bottle trees along Wyndham, Bungil and Station streets stands as a War Memorial. A tree was planted for every soldier from the area who died during WWI.

NEARBY ATTRACTIONS: **Meadowbank Museum**, located 12km west of Roma, is where visitors can experience life on a working property. The station's two-storey hayloft houses a collection of artefacts, including 30 horse-drawn vehicles. **Carnarvon NP**, 244km north-west, offers a variety of walks, camping and guided tours. At **Carnarvon Gorge**, visitors can view a number of significant Aboriginal cave paintings.

VISITOR INFORMATION: The Big Rig, 2 Riggers Rd, Ph: (07) 4622 8676 or 1800 222 399

■ St George   POP 2785
Map 286, E5
Situated on the eastern bank of the **Balonne River**, 529km west of Brisbane, St George is in the heart of a cotton growing, grazing and farming district.

MAIN ATTRACTIONS: St George, known as the '**inland fishing capital of**

Queensland', has many fishing spots, including the Balonne River, which contains Murray cod and yellowbelly. A huge mural in Scott St, painted by artist Peter Caporn, depicts the history of transport in the area. Scenes include *Racing the Storms* and *Crossing the Balonne*. **Riversands Vineyard** is located in Whytes Rd and is open to the public for tastings.

NEARBY ATTRACTIONS: **Rosehill Aviaries** houses a large variety of birds as well as native animals. It claims the country's largest private collection of Australian parrots and is located 64km west of St George. **Beardmore Dam** (Lake Kajarabie) on the Balonne River, 21km north, provides excellent fishing, and picnicking in the surrounding parkland is popular. Koalas in their natural environment can be observed in **Bollon**, 112km west. A large koala population can also be seen in the trees along **Wallum Creek**. **Culgoa Floodplain NP** is 227km south-west. The park offers 4-wheel drive access only and camping is permitted.

VISITOR INFORMATION: Cnr The Terrace and Roe St, Ph: (07) 4620 8877

One of the limestone Capricorn Caves, north of Rockhampton

Queensland

▓ Sarina   POP 3205

Map 283, F3

This attractive town is located in the foothills of the **Connors Range**, 36km south of Mackay.

MAIN ATTRACTIONS: **Sarina Art and Craft Centre** is housed in the old Court House in Railway Sq. It offers arts and crafts and regional information. The **Field of Dreams** is an historical museum in Broad St.

NEARBY ATTRACTIONS: Waterways in the area yield barramundi, flathead, whiting, bream, grunter, salmon and cod. Prawns and crabs are plentiful in season. There are many unspoilt beaches within close proximity, including **Sarina Beach**, 16km north-east, fringed by high sand dunes; there is a sheltered bay that is ideal for fishing. Other beaches include **Armstrong**, **Grass-tree**, **Salonika** and **Half Tide**. **Cape Palmerston NP** is located 78km south-east, but offers 4-wheel drive access only. **Bartons Lookout**, 14km south-west in the **Sarina Range**, offers panoramic views of the coastline and countryside.

VISITOR INFORMATION: Railway Sq, Ph: (07) 4956 2251

▓ Stanthorpe   POP 4175

Map 235, A3

This town is the commercial centre for the **Granite Belt**, 221km south-west of Brisbane, close to the New South Wales border. Fruit growing is the main commercial enterprise and Stanthorpe is well-known for its apples. Other produce includes stone and citrus fruits. Winemaking is an established and growing industry in the Granite Belt.

MAIN ATTRACTIONS: Browse the local art and craft markets or explore the historical sandstone buildings in town. **Stanthorpe Museum**, in High St, houses relics of Australian history. The **Art Gallery**, in Weroona Park, has an interesting collection and hosts travelling and community exhibitions.

Granite boulders in Girraween National Park, near Stanthorpe

NEARBY ATTRACTIONS: 40 or more **wineries** around Stanthorpe offer tastings and cellar door sales. There are four national parks in the region. **Girraween NP**, 32km south, has huge granite outcrops great for rockclimbing and looks stunning in springtime when carpeted with wildflowers. **Sundown NP**, 79km south-west, is a wilderness area with camping allowed along the **Severn River**. There is also a picnic area here. Australia's largest exposed granite rock is the centrepiece of **Bald Rock NP**. **Boonoo Boonoo NP**, 60km south-east in New South Wales, features a 210m waterfall that plummets into a rainforest gorge.

VISITOR INFORMATION: 28 Leslie Pde, Ph: (07) 4681 2057 or 1800 060 877

▓ Tamborine Mountain

POP 4200

Map 247, A3

Tamborine Mountain is 30km inland from Queensland's **Gold Coast**. A volcanic plateau, it is 8km in length, 5km wide and 560m above sea level. Tamborine Mountain consists of three villages; **Eagle Heights**, **North Tamborine** and **Mount Tamborine**.

MAIN ATTRACTIONS: Tamborine Mountain offers a variety of craft and antique shops, galleries, restaurants and tearooms. It is also famous for its gardens, subtropical rainforests, waterfalls and magnificent scenic views. The different sections of **Tamborine NP** protect a variety of native animals and birds, including lyrebirds, scrub turkeys and koalas. Flora includes fig trees, piccabeen palms, staghorns and orchids. Tamborine NP can be accessed from many different points on the mountain and provides a range of lookouts and walking tracks. All sections have picnic facilities.

NEARBY ATTRACTIONS: To the south are the majestic rainforests and attractions of **Lamington NP** and **Springbrook NP** in the Gold Coast hinterland, also several **wineries**.

VISITOR INFORMATION: Doughty Park, Nth Tamborine, Ph: (07) 5545 3200

▓ Tin Can Bay   POP 1785

Map 255, C1

This is a quiet fishing town, 229km north of Brisbane, situated near **Rainbow Beach**.

MAIN ATTRACTIONS: The waters of Tin Can Bay are the main attraction and yachting, kayaking, canoeing and houseboat hire are ideal ways of exploring the area. Fishing, crabbing and prawning are

(CONTINUED P.272)

Located 100km inland from Brisbane, the **Darling Downs** are dotted with farmhouses, pastures, crops and grazing lands. The region's fertile black soil is a by-product of ancient volcanic activity, as are the mountain peaks of the **Great Dividing Range**, which form the eastern boundary of this region.

Sprawling from **Crows Nest** in the east to **Dalby** in the west, the Darling Downs offer visitors many diversions. Among the farmlands and hills there are wineries, national parks, quaint villages, bustling townships, grand colonial architecture and remnants of the legends created by Arthur Hoey Davis, alias **Steele Rudd**. Dad and Dave are the famous country characters created by Rudd. The Darling Downs are often associated with the grand old pastoralists of south-east Queensland. The region is ideal for combining outdoor activities—bushwalking, camping, cycling, horseriding and golf—with more refined and sedate pursuits such as shopping for antiques, farm stays, historical tours, enjoying

Devonshire teas and exploring some of the region's rural villages.

Queensland's largest, and Australia's second largest, inland city, **Toowoomba** is the capital of the Darling Downs. Known as the 'Garden City of Queensland', Toowoomba has many historic buildings and excellent gardens, which are showcased in late September during the world-famous **Carnival of Flowers**.

St Patrick's Cathedral (1889), Toowoomba

Road Rules

The famous transport company **Cobb & Co** had rules for passengers displayed on notices in its carriages. These included 'no discussion of bushrangers, accidents, politics or religion, and no snoring or removal of shoes'.

Visitor information

Toowoomba Visitor Information Centre
86 James St (Warrego Hwy)
Toowoomba, Qld 4350
Ph: (07) 4639 3797, Freecall: 1800 331 155
www.toowoombaholidays.info

main attractions

◈ **Bunya Mountains National Park**

This popular mountain retreat features rainforest walks and towering bunya pines.

◈ **Cobb & Co Museum, Toowoomba**

This museum houses Australia's finest collection of horse-drawn carriages, as well as historical displays of Toowoomba.

⬆ **Crows Nest National Park**

Not far inside the park's entrance lies the renowned Valley of Diamonds, named for the shimmering effect of sunlight streaming onto the rock-face of the gorge.

◈ **Empire Theatre, Toowoomba**

This heritage-listed theatre is the largest regional performance theatre in Australia.

◈ **Highfields to Crows Nest drive**

A picturesque drive from the Pioneer Village takes in an array of galleries, antique shops and museums.

◈ **Jondaryan Woolshed**

This sheep station features sheepdog and blacksmithing demonstrations.

◈ **Rudd's Pub, Nobby**

Memorabilia line the walls of this pub, the birthplace of Arthur Hoey Davis, known as Steele Rudd—creator of the fabled 'Dad 'n' Dave' tales.

◈ **Wineries**

Rimfire, Preston Peak, Gowrie Mountain and Governor's Choice are four of the wineries in the region.

Preston Peak vineyard, Darling Downs

Queensland

Continued on map 287

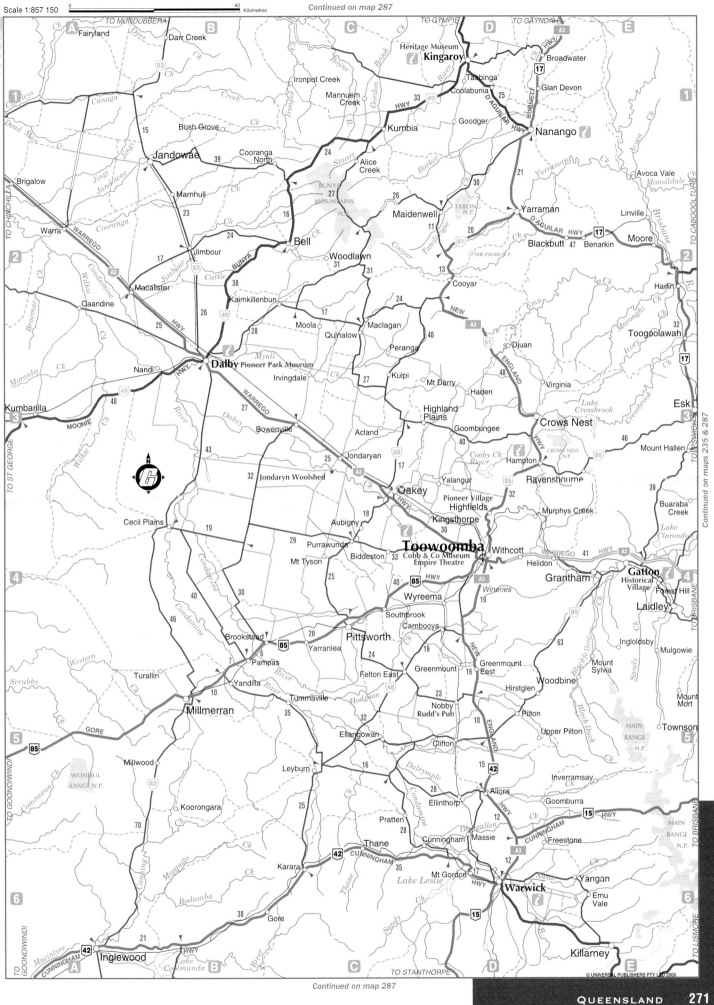

Continued on maps 235 & 287

Continued on map 287

rewarding activities. A pod of uncommon Indo-Pacific humpback dolphins (*Sina chinensis*) come into the bay and one young male, Mystique, visits the **Norman Point** boat ramp area most mornings between 7.30am and 8.30am to be hand-fed.

NEARBY ATTRACTIONS: The coloured sands and beaches of the **Cooloola** section of **Great Sandy NP** are accessible via 4-wheel drive from Rainbow Beach. Ferries to **Fraser Island** leave from **Inskip Point**, 53km north-east. There is camping access along the point. **Carlo Point**, named by Capt Cook after his deckhand, Carlo, is 3km east, and offers fishing and swimming; yachts and houseboats are available for hire.

VISITOR INFORMATION: TCB Coastal Realty, 4 Gympie Rd, Ph: (07) 5486 4333 or 1800 444 222

■ Toowoomba   POP 88 790

Map 271, D4

Toowoomba, the capital of the **Darling Downs** region, is 128km west of Brisbane. Also known as the 'Garden City of Queensland', Toowoomba has more than 200 attractive parks and gardens. The best private gardens are open to the public during the city's famous **Carnival of Flowers**, a spring festival held in September.

MAIN ATTRACTIONS: There are many art, craft and antique galleries to browse through. **Cobb & Co Museum** offers visitors an introduction to the history of the Darling Downs, as well as a wonderful collection of horse-drawn carriages. **Toowoomba Regional Art Gallery**, located in Ruthven St, exhibits paintings, fine art prints, and works by contemporary local artists. There are many **heritage walks** to take around the city and brochures are available from the information centre. The **Waterbird Habitat**, in MacKenzie St, provides 7.6ha of lakes and grassland for many bird species.

Other parks worth visiting include **Queens Park Gardens**, **Laurel Bank Park** and the **Japanese Garden** at the **University of Southern Queensland**. Picnic Point Park offers magnificent views of the **Lockyer Valley**.

NEARBY ATTRACTIONS: **Dad and Dave's Historic Rudd's Pub** is located in **Nobby**, south of Toowoomba. The theme behind the pub is Steele Rudd's famous collection of stories. Visitors can dine in the heritage lounge, view the collection of historical photographs or listen to the resident storyteller. **Highfields**, to the north, has the **Pioneer Village**, **Village Green**, **Jacaranda Manor** and art and craft shops. There is a **Folk Museum** at **Crows Nest**, and **Crows Nest NP** is well worth a visit. There are many scenic drives around the region, and brochures are available from the information centre.

VISITOR INFORMATION: 86 James St, Ph: (07) 4639 3797 or 1800 331 155

■ Townsville   POP 78 750

Map 279, K5

Townsville is located in the tropics, 1384km north of Brisbane around **Ross River**. Townsville is the region's centre for government and rural and mining industries; it is also the business and commercial capital of north Queensland.

MAIN ATTRACTIONS: The **Museum of Tropical Queensland**, in Flinders St East, features the *Pandora Shipwreck exhibition* and has the largest display of tropical dinosaur fossils in Australia. In the same street is **Reef HQ**, a living coral reef in a huge tank. The **Imax Dome Theatre**, also in this building, offers an 18m dome screen. Visitors can try their luck at **Jupiters Townsville Hotel and Casino**, located in Sir Leslie Thiess Dr. Boat cruises to the **Great Barrier Reef** and launches to **Magnetic** and **Orpheus islands** leave from Townsville's ferry terminal. **Townsville Botanic Gardens** are located in Gregory St. The **Town Common and Environmental Park** is a bird-watchers' paradise. The **Palmetum**, located near James Cook University campus in Douglas, has a wide variety of palms from around the world. **The Strand** has a large rockpool and 2.5km landscaped promenade that is well suited to the outdoor lifestyle. Children love the **Water Park**, near the **Tobruk Memorial Pool**, which is also on The Strand. Spectacular views of Townsville, Magnetic Island and the surrounding area are available from **Castle Hill**, the landmark granite outcrop in the city; and also from **Mount Stuart**, around 10km to the south-west.

Breakwater Marina and Castle Hill, Townsville

Queensland

Cunningham's Gap, Main Range National Park, north-east of Warwick

NEARBY ATTRACTIONS: Many tours are possible from Townsville, including tours of the rainforest and Outback, white-water rafting, diving and sailing. The **Australian Institute of Marine Science** Is located 30km east at **Cape Ferguson** and guided tours can be booked. **Billabong Sanctuary**, on the Bruce Hwy, has crocodile shows and visitors can hold a koala, wombat or python. **Magnetic Island**, in **Cleveland Bay**, can be seen from any point along the Townsville waterfront and is 20 minutes from the city by fast cat ferry. The island has 23 bays and beaches, and 85% is set aside as national park. There are many walking tracks and other activities offered, including fishing, snorkelling, golf and horseriding. VISITOR INFORMATION: Flinders Mall, Ph: (07) 4721 3660 or 1800 801 902

■ Tully   POP 2550
Map 279, J4
Tully is located at the base of **Mount Tyson**, on **Banyan Creek**, a tributary of the **Tully River**. It is notable for having one of the highest annual rainfalls in Australia. Tully's economic mainstays include sugar, bananas, tropical fruit, cattle, aquaculture and tourism.
MAIN ATTRACTIONS: Located in the heart of town, **Tully Sugar Mill** is open during the crushing season, June to mid November. Daily tours are available and can be booked through the information centre. **The Golden Gumboot**, in Butler St, stands 7.9m high (equal to Tully's highest recorded rainfall) and has a viewing platform accessed by a spiral staircase.
NEARBY ATTRACTIONS: An area of natural beauty, **Mission Beach** is located along the **Great Green Way**, 25km north-east of Tully. Stretching along 14km of coastline, fringed by tropical rainforest and overlooking nearby **Dunk** and **Bedarra islands**, the Mission Beach area is worthwhile exploring. The rain-forests of the **Wet Tropics World Heritage Area** are nearby and walking track maps are available from the Wet Tropics Visitor Centre at Mission Beach. To explore the outer area of the **Great Barrier Reef**, boats leave daily from nearby **Clump Point Jetty**. White-water rafting, canoeing and kayaking adventures are popular on the Tully River, as is swimming in the river's upper reaches. **Tully Heads**, 22km south-east, is a good spot for fishing.
VISITOR INFORMATION: Bruce Hwy, Ph: (07) 4068 2288

■ Warwick   POP 11 985
Map 271, D6
Referred to as the **'Rose and Rodeo City'**, Warwick is situated near the **Great Dividing Range**, 162km south-west of Brisbane, in the **Darling Downs** region of south-east Queensland. Established in 1849, Warwick is the centre for a surrounding region famous for its horse and cattle studs and fine wool.
MAIN ATTRACTIONS: The floral emblem of Warwick is a red rose and there are many roses planted around the city, including a display in **Leslie Park**. **Warwick Regional Art Gallery** is located in Albion St. **Pringle Cottage**, built in the 19th century, is open to the public most days and displays old photographs, vehicles and machinery.
NEARBY ATTRACTIONS: Fossicking is a popular activity on the southern Downs and visitors can try gold-panning at **Thanes Creek**, 40km west. A fossicking license can be obtained from Warwick Shire Council or the visitor centre in Albion St. **Main Range NP** is located north-east of Warwick and is popular with hikers. The main recreation area is at **Cunningham's Gap**, where there are picnic areas, a campground and graded walking tracks. **Leslie Dam**, 15km west, offers watersports, swimming, boating and fishing. There are also giant granite sculptures to see, and picnic and BBQ facilities are available. There are four signposted **tourist drives**, which lead visitors to the smaller country towns in Warwick Shire.
VISITOR INFORMATION: 49 Albion St, Ph: (07) 4661 3122

Stockman at Elderslie Station, near Winton

■ Winton   POP 1315

Map 281, G4

Located in the 'red heart of Queensland', around 1400km north-west of Brisbane, Winton is one of Australia's best-known Outback towns. It is also known as the home of bush poetry, hosting the annual **Bronze Swagman Award**—one of the country's most prestigious literary awards. MAIN ATTRACTIONS: In the heritage-listed **Corfield and Fitzmaurice Store**, in Elderslie St, you can see the **Allosaurus Dinosaur Diorama**, re-created from the Lark Quarry site, and the fossilised bones of Elliot, Australia's largest excavated dinosaur. Also located in the centre is **Combo Crafts**, where you can purchase original and handcrafted items. **The Waltzing Matilda Centre**, in Elderslie St, is dedicated to the song Banjo Paterson wrote on Dagworth Station near Winton in 1895. **The Waltzing Matilda Bush Poetry Festival** is held annually. The historic **Royal Theatre**, located in Elderslie St, is an open-air picture theatre and museum, and one of the oldest of its kind still operating in Australia. Around town, there are sites commemorating **Qantas**, the country's flagship airline, which was formed in the town in 1920. The

extraordinary **Musical Fence** was created for the Queensland Biennial Festival of Music in 2003. NEARBY ATTRACTIONS: **Lark Quarry Conservation Park** protects fossilised evidence of a dinosaur stampede some 93 million years ago. The park is on the eroded edge of the **Tully Range**, 110km south-west. More than 5 000 dinosaur footprints, captured in rock, can be seen today. **Opalton**, 115km south, is an historic town where boulder opals are mined in nearby gemfields; there is also a public fossicking area. **Bladensburg NP** is 15km south and visitors can take a self-drive tour along the **Route of the River Gum**; there are camp-grounds at **Bough Shed Hole**. VISITOR INFORMATION: Waltzing Matilda Centre, Elderslie St, Ph: (07) 4657 1466 or 1300 665 115

■ Wondai   POP 1250

Map 287, H3

This town, 250km north-west of Brisbane, is almost the geographical centre of the **South Burnett** region. Wondai is surrounded by a rich agricultural region noted for its grains, peanuts, cattle, dairying, timber and mining. MAIN ATTRACTIONS: **Dingo Creek Bicentennial Park**, located beside

Bunya Hwy, is a pleasant place for a BBQ or picnic. **Wondai Historic Museum**, in Mackenzie St, houses a collection of memorabilia from earlier times, including farm machinery, a fire engine and a manual telephone exchange. **South Burnett Timber Museum** has a wagon camp diorama, life-size wood sculptures and a woodcrafters' workshop. **Wondai Art Gallery**, also in Haly St, has monthly exhibitions. NEARBY ATTRACTIONS: **Proston**, 42km north-west, is the gateway to **Lake Boondooma**. This is a popular watersports area. The introduction of bass, golden perch and silver perch has made the dam attractive to anglers. There are bunkhouse and self-contained units, caravan sites and lakeside camping. **Boondooma Homestead** is a restored 1850s property, open to the public most days. Also located at Proston is **Sidcup Castle**. Built by Harold Douglas, it is a replica of his childhood home in England. VISITOR INFORMATION: Timber Museum, 80 Haly St, Ph: (07) 4168 5652

■ Yandina   POP 1025

Map 255, C4

Yandina is located 9km north of **Nambour** in the **Sunshine Coast** hinterland. It is known as the **'Ginger Capital of the World'**. MAIN ATTRACTIONS: Visitors are invited to see ginger being processed at the largest **Ginger Factory** in the world, located along Pioneer Rd. The historic **Queensland Cane Train** travels through the landscaped gardens. In January, the Ginger Factory hosts the **Ginger Flower Festival**. **Nutworks Macadamia Factory and Tourist Complex**, opposite the Ginger Factory, gives demonstrations of the processing of macadamia nuts and offers tastings. NEARBY ATTRACTIONS: **Eumundi**, 10km north, is famous for its Wednesday and Saturday morning markets. The Eumundi markets sell locally-grown fruit and vegetables, as well as arts and crafts.

VISITOR INFORMATION: Cnr Sixth Ave and Melrose Pde, Maroochydore, Ph: (07) 5479 1566 or 1800 882 032

▦ Yeppoon   POP 10 660
Map 267, C3

Once a small centre for pineapple growers and sugarcane farmers, Yeppoon has developed into a popular resort town on the **Capricorn Coast**. Yeppon is located 40km from Rockhampton and is within easy reach of **Great Keppel Island** and the **Great Barrier Reef**. Yeppoon itself is surrounded by attractive beaches and has a year-round warm climate and relaxed lifestyle.

NEARBY ATTRACTIONS: **Cooberrie Park** is a native flora and fauna sanctuary 15km north of town. Visitors can walk among the animals, handfeed the kangaroos and wallabies and hold a koala. **Byfield NP**, 32km north of Yeppoon, has mountains, rainforests, creeks and streams and is home to the unique Byfield ferns. Attractions within the park include **Ferns Hideaway Wilderness Restaurant, Waterpark Cabins** and **Nob Creek Pottery**. Fascinating **Koorana Crocodile Farm** is located 38km south. **Rydges Capricorn Resort**, 6km north, is surrounded by **The Wetlands**. There is a Wet-lands Tour available and visitors may be able to spot over 150 species of birds. The **Keppel Group of islands** is one of the region's main features. Located 13km off-shore, daytrips to Great Keppel Island are offered. Cruise boats to the island and fishing charters leave from **Keppel Bay Marina** and **Rosslyn Bay Harbour**. The island has a resort, and activities include snorkelling and scuba diving from the beaches. On the mainland at **Wreck Point**, south of **Cooee Bay**, a lookout offers panoramic views over the islands. At **Emu Park**, 19km south, is an interesting memorial to Captain Cook known as *The Singing Ship*, because when the wind blows the hidden organ pipes within the sculpture vibrate and seem to 'sing'.

VISITOR INFORMATION: Ross Creek Roundabout, Scenic Hwy, Ph: (07) 4939 4888 or 1800 675 785

▦ Yungaburra   POP 990
Map 239, B5

The picturesque town of Yungaburra is 15km east of Atherton, high on the edge of the **Atherton Tableland**. The town is famous for its National Trust-classified **Historic Precinct**.

MAIN ATTRACTIONS: The best way to explore Yungaburra is by following the route in the **Heritage Walk** leaflet prepared by the National Trust of Queensland and available from local information centres. A highlight of the Heritage Walk is **Lake Eacham Hotel**, which has a display of historic photographs depicting the area's early sawmilling days. There are many art and craft galleries to browse through and the town also offers award-winning restaurants. At **Peterson Creek**, on Gillies Hwy, there is a platypus-viewing platform. Best times to visit are at sunrise and sunset.

NEARBY ATTRACTIONS: In **Crater Lakes NP** there are two volcanic crater lakes. **Lake Barrine**, 10km north-east, is the larger of the crater lakes with clear blue waters 65m deep and fringed with lush rainforest. There is a 5.1km-circuit track beginning at the lake's edge. Daily flora and fauna cruises on the lake are available. **Lake Eacham**, 5km east, has a 2.8km track encircling the lake, which is surrounded by differing pockets of rainforests—the complexity of rainforest communities is primarily determined by soil fertility and rainfall. Swimming is popular and there are BBQ and picnic facilities. The famous and much photographed **Curtain Fig Tree** is located 2.5km south-west of Yungaburra in a small forestry reserve. **Lake Tinaroo**, 3km north, offers boating, fishing, waterskiing, sailing and swimming. On the eastern shores of Lake Tinaroo, there are **The Chimneys, Mobo Creek Crater** and the **Cathedral Fig Tree**. **Malanda**, 20km south of Yungaburra, has its 19th-century **Majestic Theatre**. **Malanda Falls Environmental Park** and **Scenic Reserve** offers a variety of sign-posted rainforest walks.

VISITOR INFORMATION: Cnr Main St and Silo Rd, Atherton, Ph: (07) 4091 4222

Cathedral Fig Tree near Yungaburra, Atherton Tableland

KEY MAP

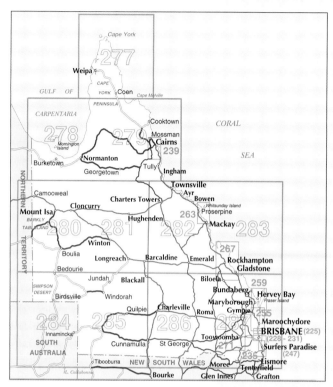

DISTANCE CHART

Approximate Distance	Bourke NSW	Bowen	Brisbane	Bundaberg	Cairns	Charleville	Charters Tower	Emerald	Gladstone	Longreach	Mackay	Maryborough	Moree NSW	Mount Isa	Rockhampton	Roma	Toowoomba	Townsville	Tweed Heads NSW	Warwick
Bourke NSW		1533	924	1102	1835	454	1353	966	1156	968	1346	1016	445	1610	1139	613	791	1488	1013	766
Bowen	1533		1181	812	542	1079	277	567	627	848	187	922	1292	1033	520	968	1160	195	1281	1244
Brisbane	924	1181		369	1701	754	1360	887	540	1186	980	259	479	1828	647	486	125	1376	100	158
Bundaberg	1102	812	369		1346	832	1025	560	185	973	617	110	714	1615	292	564	409	1007	469	493
Cairns	1835	542	1701	1346		1381	482	955	1169	1053	729	1442	1790	1117	1062	1356	1702	347	1801	1786
Charleville	454	1079	754	832	1381		899	512	811	514	892	762	629	1156	780	268	629	1034	832	713
Charters Towers	1353	277	1360	1025	482	899		473	848	571	464	1121	1308	756	741	874	1235	135	1438	1319
Emerald	966	567	887	560	955	512	473		375	413	380	648	835	1055	268	401	762	608	965	846
Gladstone	1156	627	540	185	1169	811	848	375		788	440	281	789	1430	107	543	544	822	640	628
Longreach	968	848	1186	973	1053	514	571	413	788		793	1061	1143	642	681	700	1061	706	1264	1145
Mackay	1346	187	980	617	729	892	464	380	440	793		713	1105	1220	333	781	973	382	1080	1057
Maryborough	1016	922	259	110	1442	762	1121	648	281	1061	713		628	1703	380	494	323	1117	359	407
Moree NSW	445	1292	479	714	1790	629	1308	835	789	1143	1105	628		1785	772	434	346	1443	568	321
Mount Isa	1610	1033	1828	1615	1117	1156	756	1055	1430	642	1220	1703	1785		1323	1342	1703	891	1906	1787
Rockhampton	1139	520	647	292	1062	780	741	268	107	681	333	380	772	1323		526	640	715	739	724
Roma	613	968	486	564	1356	268	874	401	543	700	781	494	434	1342	526		361	1009	564	445
Toowoomba	791	1160	125	409	1702	629	1235	762	544	1061	973	323	346	1703	640	361		1355	203	84
Townsville	1488	195	1376	1007	347	1034	135	608	822	706	382	1117	1443	891	715	1009	1355		1476	1454
Tweed Heads NSW	1013	1281	100	469	1801	832	1438	965	640	1264	1080	359	568	1906	739	564	203	1476		245
Warwick	766	1244	158	493	1786	713	1319	846	628	1145	1057	407	321	1787	724	445	84	1454	245	

All distances in this chart have been measured over highways and major roads, not necessarily by the shortest route.

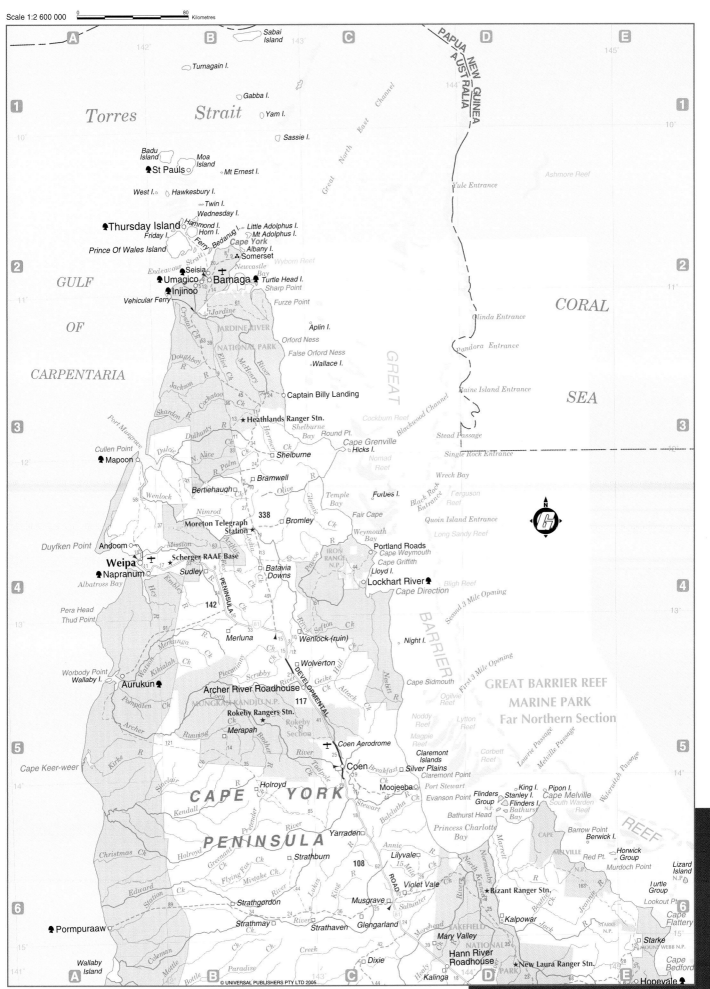

Kilometres

A B C PAPUA NEW GUINEA / AUSTRALIA D E

1

Torres *Strait*
Sabai Island
Turnagain I.
Gabba I.
Yam I.
Sassie I.

Badu Island
Moa Island
St Pauls
Mt Ernest I.
West I. Hawkesbury I.
Twin I.
Wednesday I.
Thursday Island
Hammond I. / Horn I.
Little Adolphus I.
Mt Adolphus I.
Friday I.
Prince Of Wales Island
Cape York
Albany I.
Somerset
Newcastle Bay

GULF

OF

Seisia
Umagico
Bamaga
Turtle Head I.
Sharp Point

Injinoo
Vehicular Ferry
Furze Point

CARPENTARIA
Jardine
JARDINE RIVER
NATIONAL PARK
Aplin I.
Orford Ness
False Orford Ness
Wallace I.

Doughboy R.
Eliot Ck.
McHenry R.
Captain Billy Landing

Skardon R.
Dulhunty R.
Heathlands Ranger Stn.
Shelburne Bay
Round Pt.
Cape Grenville
Hicks I.

Cullen Point
Mapoon
N. Alice R.
R. Palm
Shelburne
Nomad Reef

Wenlock
Bertiehaugh
Bramwell
Olive R.
Wreck Bay

Nimrod
Moreton Telegraph Station
338
Bromley
Temple Bay
Fair Cape
Forbes I.

Duyfken Point
Andoom
Mission R.
Scherger RAAF Base
113
Weymouth Bay
IRON RANGE N.P.
Portland Roads
Cape Weymouth

Weipa
Napranum
Sudley
142
Batavia Downs
Cape Griffith
Lloyd I.
Lockhart River

Albatross Bay
Embley R.
PENINSULA
Lockhart River
Cape Direction

Pera Head
Thud Point
142
Bligh Reef

Worbody Point
Wallaby I.
Merluna
Wenlock (ruin)
Night I.

Hey R.
Watson R.
DEVELOPMENTAL
Wolverton
Cape Sidmouth

Aurukun
Kikalah Ck.
Piccaninny Ck.
Scrubby Ck.
Geike Ck.
Attack R.
Nesbit R.

Archer R.
Archer River Roadhouse
MUNGKAN-KANDJU N.P.
Coen R.
117
GREAT BARRIER REEF
MARINE PARK
Far Northern Section

Rokeby Rangers Stn.
Rokeby Sector
41
Noddy Reef
Corbett Reef

Merapah
Running Ck.
Brother R.
Coen Aerodrome
Magpie Reef
Lytton Reef

121
Coen
Breakfast Ck.
Silver Plains
Claremont Islands
Lowrie Passage
Melville Passage

Cape Keer-weer
Kirke R.
Sinclair R.
Holroyd
Moojeeba
Port Stewart
Claremont Point
King I.
Pipon I.
Stanley I.
Cape Melville
Watteratch Passage

C A P E Y O R K
Kendall R.
Pretender R.
Stewart R.
Balclutha R.
Evanson Point
Flinders Group
Flinders I.
South Warden Reef
CAPE

P E N I N S U L A
Yarraden
Annie R.
Princess Charlotte Bay
Bathurst Head
Bathurst Bay
Barrow Point
Berwick I.
MELVILLE

Christmas Ck.
Holroyd R.
Greenant Ck.
Strathburn
Lilyvale
108
Normanby R.
Red Pt.
Horwick Group
Murdoch Point
Lizard Island N.P.
Turtle Group

Flying Fox Ck.
Mistake Ck.
Violet Vale
North Kennedy R.
Bizant Ranger Stn.
Lookout Pt.

Pormpuraaw
Edward R.
Station Ck.
Strathgordon
Lubin R.
Kirk R.
Musgrave
Saltwater Ck.
Morehead R.
Beattie Ck.
Jeannie R.
Kalpowar
STARKE N.P.
Cape Flattery

Coleman R.
Strathmay
Strathaven
Glengarland
LAKEFIELD NATIONAL
Mary Valley
MOUNT WEBB N.P.
Starke

Wallaby Island
Mottle Ck.
Bottle Ck.
Paradise Ck.
Creek
Heaths Ck.
Jack R.
Dixie
Hann River Roadhouse
PARK
New Laura Ranger Stn.
Cape Bedford

A B 143° C 144° D E **Hopevale**

© UNIVERSAL PUBLISHERS PTY LTD 2005

Joins maps 278 & 279

GULF OF CARPENTARIA

Pormpuraaw

Wallaby
Island

Kowanyama

Rutland Plains

MITCHELL &
ALICE RIVERS
N.P.

Inkerman

Galbraith

Dorunda

225

Vanrook

Rocky I.

Thabugan Point

Halls Point

Lingnoonganee I.

Gee Wee Point

Cape Van Diemen

Mornington
Island

WELLESLEY ISLANDS

Gunana

Sydney I.

Bountiful I.

Denham I.

Delta Downs

Lotus Vale

Forsyth I.

Point Burrowes

FORSYTH ISLANDS

Point Austin

Stirling

Pains I.

Bayley I.

Horseshoe I.

Oaktree Point

Miranda Downs

Allen I.

Bentinck I.

Glencoe

Sweers I.

SOUTH WELLESLEY ISLANDS

Fitzmaurice Point

Maggieville

Fish Hole

Tarrant Point

Karumba

KARUMBA

Mutton Hole

Pascoe Inlet

Kangaroo Point

Alligator Point

DEV.

Fourteen
Mile

Gore Point

41

30

Wollogorang
Gulf Wilderness
Lodge

Magowra

Normanton

Clarina
Glenore

Timora

Rocky

Redbank

Westmoreland

Burke &
Wills Cairn

Haydon

153

Blackbull

Oakland P

Tabletop

Hells Gate Roadhouse

Escott Resort

Burketown

Inverleigh

Gum Creek

228

153

Belmore

Coralie

Cliffdale

Tirranna
Roadhouse

Milgarra

Croydon

Kingfisher
Camp

Corinda
(ruin)

Armraynald

Wernadinga

73

McAllister

196

Warren Vale

Doomadgee

WAY

Bowthorn

4WD

Punjaub

117

Floraville

Wondoola

Vena Park

Almora

Neumayer Valley

Bang Bang

Claraville

Lawn Hill

69

Augustus Downs

Donors Hills

Iffley

Gregory Downs

Gregory Downs

Talawanta

Prospect

Adels Grove

Century Zinc Mine

68

Nardoo

Cowan Downs

Myola

Lawn Hill Gorge

Mellish Park

Lorraine

Taldora

Riversleigh
Fossils

Riversleigh

128

Savannah Downs

Old Herbert Vale

4WD

Myally

Burke & Wills
Roadhouse

Arizona

Gallipoli

Kamileroi

77

Pelha

Norfolk

Boomarra

Canobie

Monstraven

Chidna
Waggabundi

Gleeson

Millungera

Morstone
Downs

Thorntonia

Alcala

Thornton

Gunpowder
Resort

Coolullah

Brinard

234

Undilla

Lady
Annie

Mt Gordon

Granada

Clonagh

Spoonbill

Mammoth

180

Rocklands

91

Split
Rock

56

Gereta

Kajabbi

Gipsy
Downs

Dalgonally

Bunda Bunda

Camooweal

70

Sedan Dip

Lara

Bauhinia
Downs

Don

Calton Hills

Granada

Kilberry

Yelvertoft

118

Quamby

© UNIVERSAL PUBLISHERS PTY LTD 2005

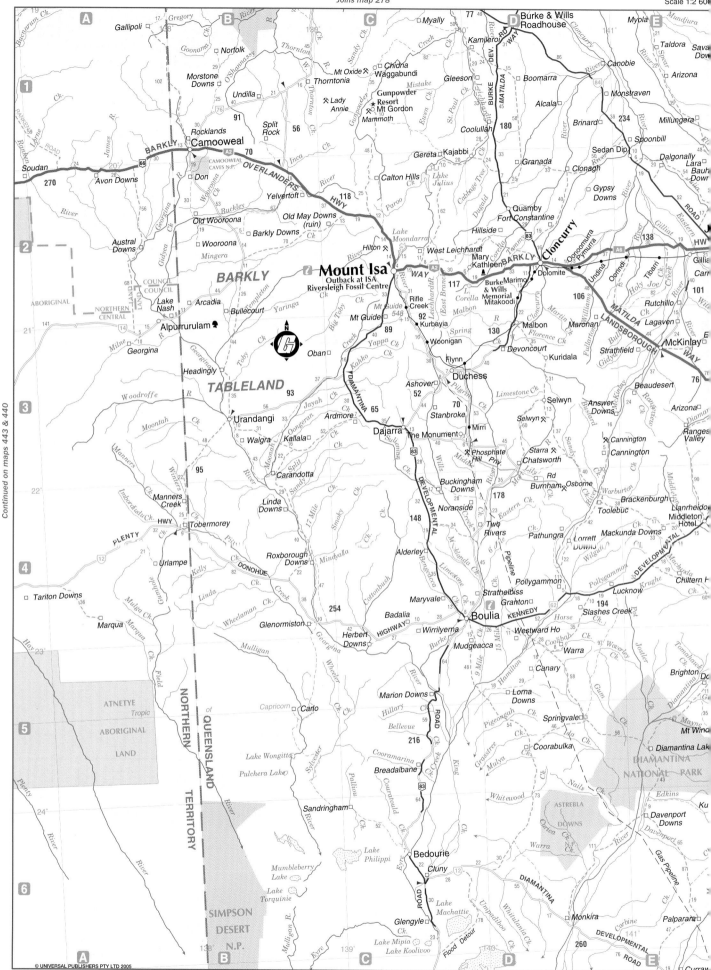

© UNIVERSAL PUBLISHERS PTY LTD 2005

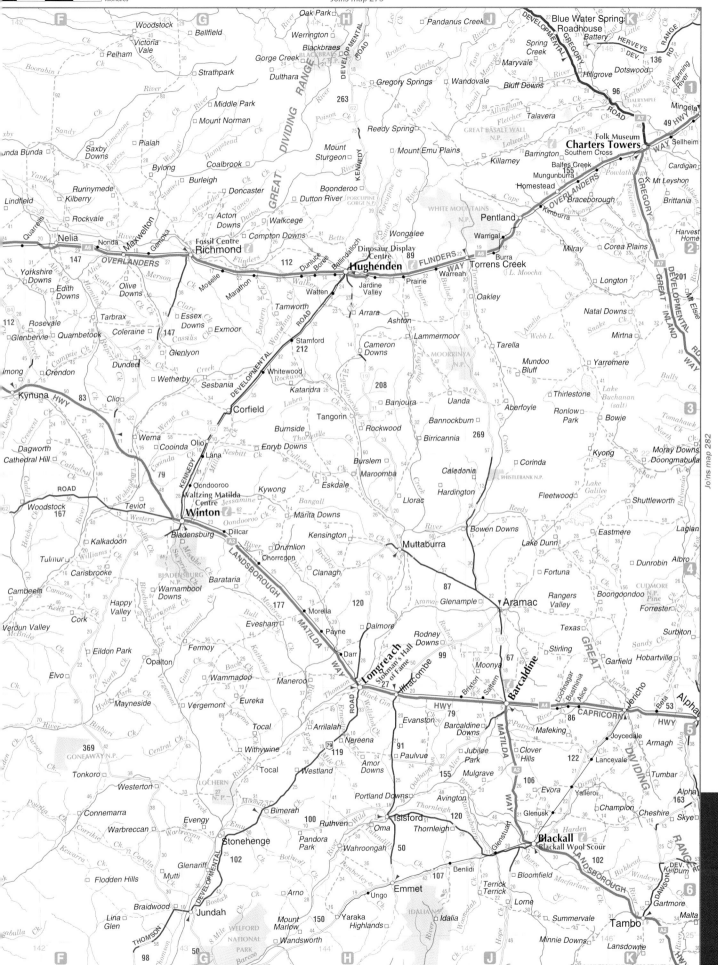

80
Kilometres

© UNIVERSAL PUBLISHERS PTY LTD 2005

Scale 1:2 600

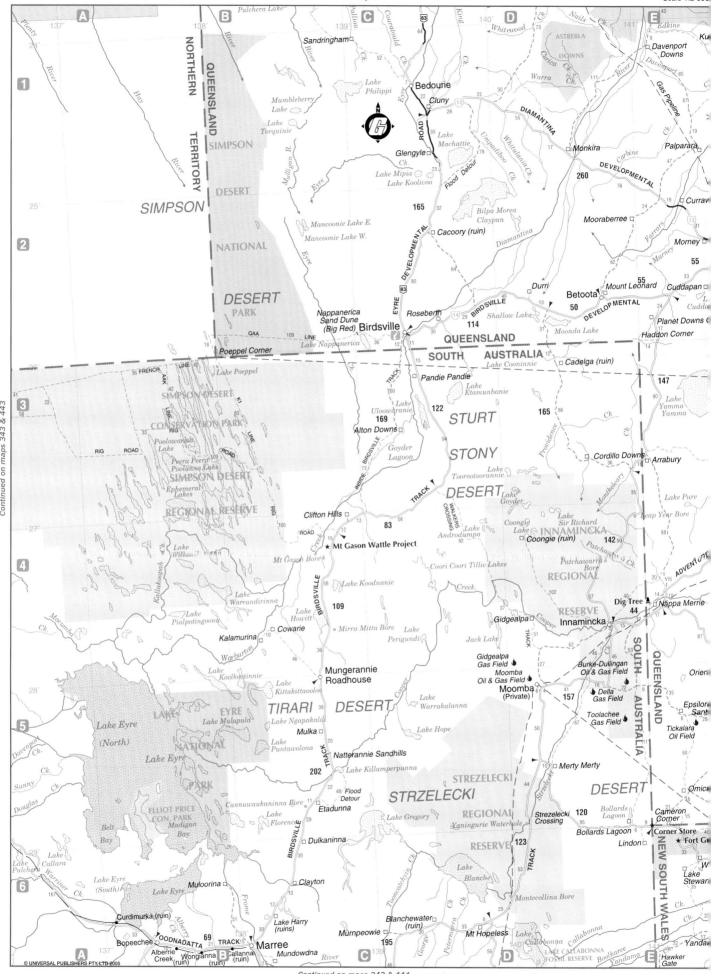

Continued on maps 343 & 111

Queensland

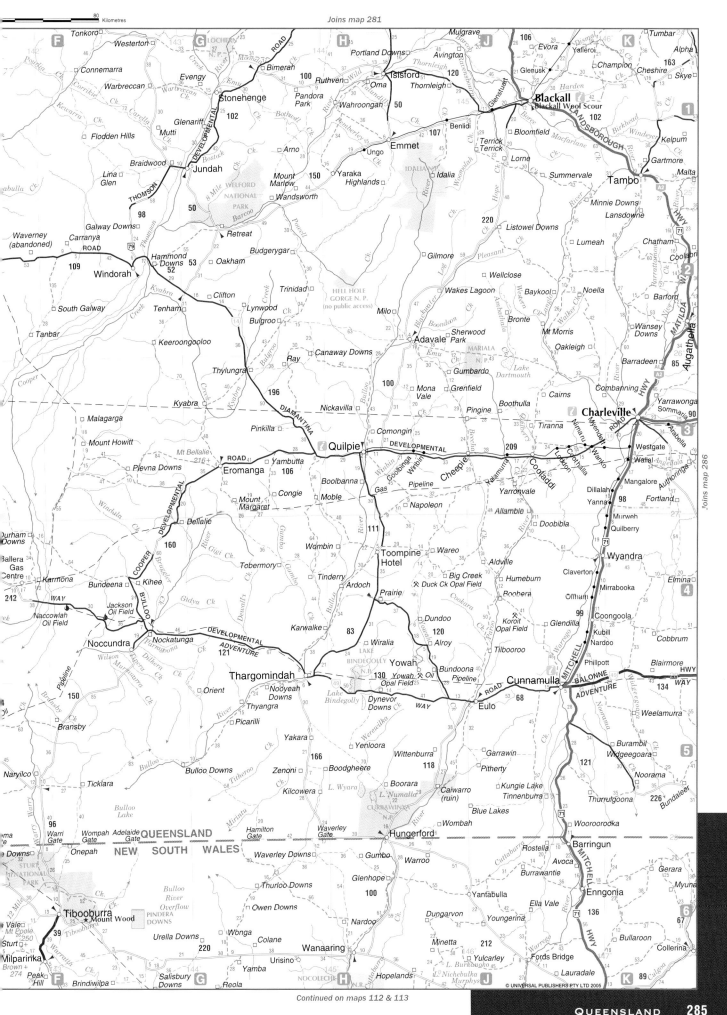

Continued on maps 112 & 113

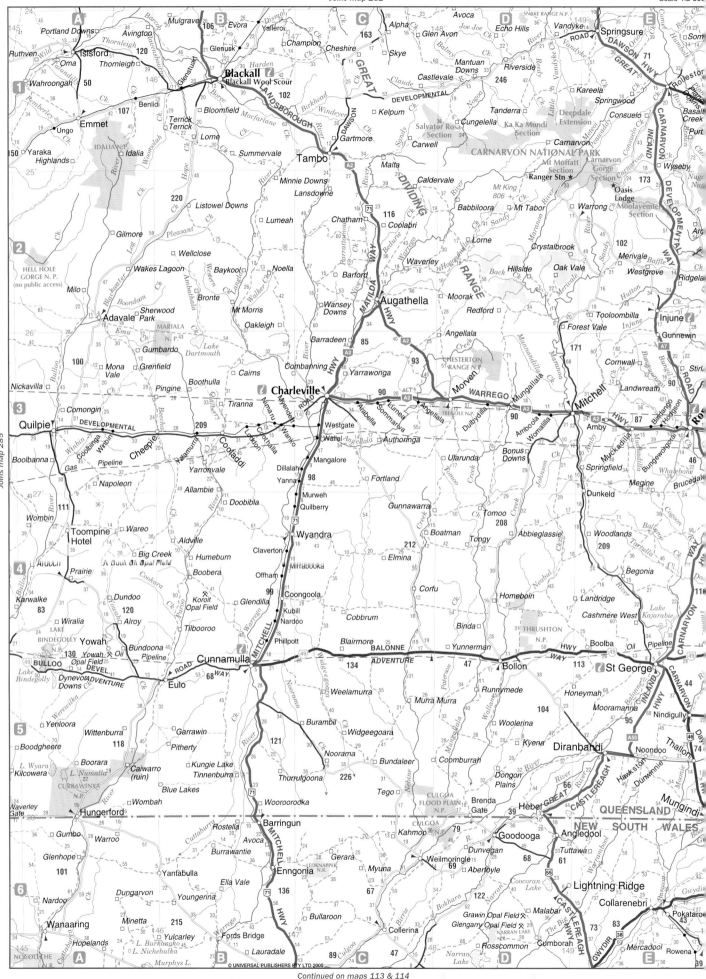

Continued on maps 113 & 114

Queensland

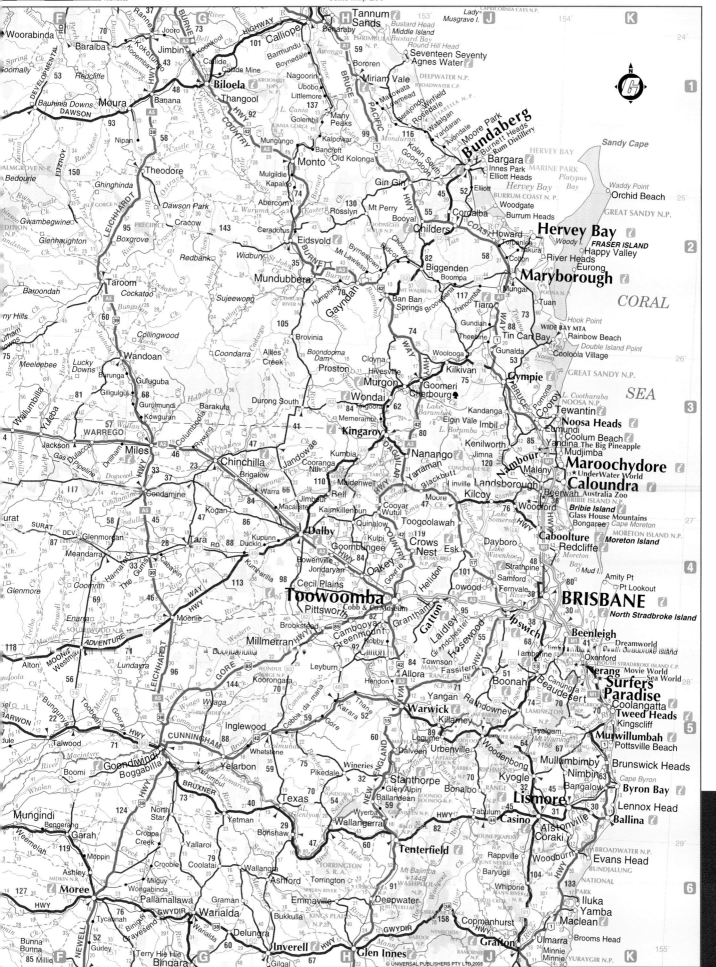

SOUTH AUST

The fourth largest state (including the Northern Territory) and the driest in Australia, South Australia is a place of contrasts. In the unique position of bordering all the other mainland states, two-thirds of South Australia is dominated by a near-desert environment. Although conditions here are harsh and unrelenting, the varied landscapes of immense deserts, rugged mountains and dry lakes entice many visitors.

In contrast to the arid lands of the north and west are the gulf lands, which include the Eyre, Yorke and Fleurieu peninsulas, fringed by quiet beaches and fishing towns; the rolling hills of the Mount Lofty Ranges; and the dry south-east plains watered by the mighty River Murray, Australia's longest, as it flows to the sea. The extensive 3700km South Australian coastline offers scenic driving and walking routes along its many

indentations as well as offshore islands to explore, the largest being Kangaroo Island.

Touring South Australia by car is generally easy. From the state's

South Australia: The Festival State

◈ Population: 1 500 000
◈ Total area: 984 000km²
◈ % of Australia: 12.8%
◈ Floral emblem: Sturt's Desert Pea
◈ Fauna emblem: Southern Hairy-nosed Wombat

i Visitor information

South Australian Travel Centre
18 King William St,
Adelaide, SA 5000
Ph: 1300 655 276
www.southaustralia.com

Main ATTRACTIONS

◈ **Barossa Valley**

Only a short drive from Adelaide, this valley has long been reputed as one of Australia's premier wine-producing regions.

◈ **Coober Pedy**

This Outback town is famous for its lustrous opals and unusual underground accommodation.

◈ **Fleurieu Peninsula**

This striking peninsula features rolling hills and sandy beaches along it's picturesque coastline.

◈ **Flinders Ranges**

The distinctive landforms of the Flinders Ranges include colourful cliffs, granite peaks and deep gorges.

◈ **Kangaroo Island**

Accessible by ferry from Cape Jervis, this sparsely populated island offers secluded camping spots, bushwalking tracks, scenic coastal areas and magnificent wildlife.

◈ **Lake Eyre**

Usually a dry salt lake, Lake Eyre becomes a vast inland sea several times a century, teeming with waterbirds.

◈ **Limestone Coast**

In the south-east corner of the state, this coastal region offers many interesting parks and caves.

◈ **Nullarbor Plain**

This vast flat plain has numerous limestone caves and subterranean rivers. Spectacular cliffs up to 100m high border the waters of the Great Australian Bight.

◈ **Riverland**

The River Murray dominates this region. Cruise the river by houseboat or paddlesteamer, visit the wineries, orchards, quaint townships and historic ports.

sophisticated capital, Adelaide, there are links to the Barrier, Sturt, Ouyen, Dukes and Princes highways to the eastern states; the Stuart Hwy, which crosses the continent to Darwin; and the Eyre Hwy, which traverses the virtually treeless Nullarbor Plain to Western Australia.

There are many reasons to visit South Australia, including the spectacular scenery, fishing, flora, fauna and the national, conservation and recreation parks that make up about 20% of the state. However, wine is usually top of the list. South Australia's wineries are legendary—the names Barossa Valley, McLaren Vale and Coonawarra are recognised by most Australians and overseas visitors. Four out of every ten glasses of Australian wine are produced from vineyards in the south-east corner of South Australia.

Photo above: Cliffs at Warren Gorge, Flinders Ranges

THE FESTIVAL STATE

South Australia represents one-eighth of the entire Australian continent and has a total area of about 984 000km². While more than 50% of the state is pastoral land, the majority of the population live in the southern coastal zones below the 32nd parallel. Adelaide, the state's capital, has 73% of the state's population.

South Australia is the driest of the Australian states and territories and is mostly arid or semi-arid. However, the coastal zone, where the vast majority of the population live, has areas with a pleasant Mediterranean-like climate, ideal for outdoor pursuits and adventuring.

In contrast to the majority of Australian states, no convicts were ever sent to South Australia. The initial plan was for private settlement; however, South Australia was declared a province in 1836. After a faltering start, the discovery of copper in the 1840s and the success of early wheat farms gave the new colony the economic boost it needed in order to prosper. Today,

agriculture, mining, fishing, tourism and manufacturing all contribute to the state's economy.

South Australia is regarded as the pre-eminent food and wine capital of Australia—the food industry is the state's largest export earner. The state also accounts for more than half of the Australian wine industry and is home to 44% of the country's vineyards.

Around 10% of Australian agricultural industry is based in South Australia. The main crop is wheat, followed by barley and oats. A wide range of fruit and vegetables are also grown in the state, including potatoes, onions, carrots, tomatoes, cauliflowers, peas, oranges, apples, apricots and peaches.

South Australia is home to around 11% of Australia's sheep and over 4% of its cattle. The fishing industry has always been strong in South Australia and the growth of aquaculture farms, including oyster, rock lobster, salmon, snapper and tuna,

Historic Seppeltsfield winery, Barossa Valley

contribute to the development and expansion of overseas markets.

Crude oil and natural gas are now the major mining products, recently surpassing the coal and iron-ore output. Copper, uranium, silver and gold are also mined at **Roxby Downs**. Perhaps most commonly known are the mining towns of **Coober Pedy** and **Andamooka**, which account for 85% of the nation's opals.

The state is accessible by car, with around 95 000km of sealed and unsealed roads taking explorers to the furthest corners of South Australia. The **Indian Pacific Railway** runs through the state, originating in Perth (Western Australia) and continuing to Broken Hill and Sydney (New South Wales) via Adelaide. The famous **Ghan Railway**, completed in 2004, links Adelaide with Darwin, in the Northern Territory, via Alice Springs.

Obelisk at Cape Dombey, Robe, South Australia's Limestone Coast

TOURISM REGION HIGHLIGHTS

A state of contrasts, South Australia varies dramatically from the arid lands and deserts of the north to the more fertile gulf lands of the south. These include the **Yorke** and **Fleurieu peninsulas** and the dry south-east plains through which the **River Murray** flows. South Australia's landscapes are stunning, particularly on the **Eyre Peninsula**, the **Flinders Ranges** and **Kangaroo Island**. South Australian wineries are legendary and names such as **Barossa**, **McLaren Vale** and **Coonawarra** are known and respected worldwide.

A Adelaide
Ayers House; Botanic Gardens; Central Market; Festival Centre; Glenelg Tram; Migration Museum; National Wine Centre; North Terrace; Port Adelaide; Rundle Mall; River Torrens

B Adelaide Hills
Adelaide Hills Wineries; Belair NP; Cleland Wildlife Park; Gumeracha Toy Factory; Hahndorf; Mount Barker; Mount Lofty; National Motor Museum; Onkaparinga Valley; Torrens Valley; Warrawong Earth Sanctuary

Rocky River Mouth, Flinders Chase National Park, Kangaroo Island

C Barossa
Barossa Valley Wineries; Eden Valley Wineries; Lutheran Churches; Lyndoch; Mengler Hill Lookout; Nuriootpa; Tanunda

D Clare Valley
Auburn; Balaklava; Burra; Clare Valley Wineries; Gladstone; Jamestown; Kapunda; Laura; Mintaro; Mount Remarkable; Polish Hill Valley; Watervale

E Eyre Peninsula
Arno Bay; Ceduna; Coffin Bay NP; Cowell; Gawler Ranges; Lincoln Cove; Lincoln NP; Murphys Haystacks; Nullarbor Cliffs; Nullarbor Plain; Point Lowly Lighthouse; Port Lincoln; Port Neill; Streaky Bay; Tumby Bay; Whalers Way; Whyalla Maritime Museum

F Fleurieu Peninsula
Cockle Train; Deep Creek NP; Goolwa; Granite Island; Hallett Cove; Langhorne Creek; McLaren Vale Wineries; Old Noarlunga; Port Elliot; Strathalbyn; Victor Harbor; Willunga

G Flinders Ranges & Outback
Andamooka; Arkaroola Sanctuary; Birdsville Track; Coober Pedy Opal Mines; Coongie Lakes; Flinders Ranges NP; Gammon Ranges NP; Innamincka; Lake Eyre; Oodnadatta Track; Pichi Richi Railway; Port Augusta; Port Pirie; Quorn; Simpson Desert; Strzelecki Desert; Wilpena Pound; Yourambulla Caves

H Kangaroo Island
Admirals Arch; Cape Borda; Cape Gantheaume; Flinders Chase NP; Kingscote; Maritime Heritage Trail; Penneshaw; Ravine des Casoars; Remarkable Rocks; Seal Bay; Stokes Bay; Vivonne Bay

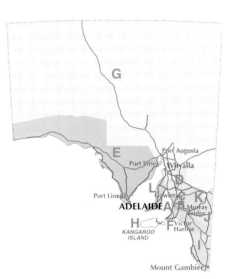

I Limestone Coast
Blue Lake, Mount Gambier; Bool Lagoon; Bordertown; Cape Jaffa Lighthouse; Canunda NP; Coonawarra Wineries; Crater Lakes; Kingston SE; Millicent; Naracoorte Caves; Padthaway; Penola; Pool of Siloam; Robe; Tantanoola Caves

J Murraylands
Coorong NP; Lake Albert; Lake Alexandrina; Mannum; Morgan; Murray Bridge; River Murray; Pinnaroo; Swan Reach; Yookamurra Sanctuary

K Riverland
Banrock Station; Barmera; Berri; Blanchetown; Loxton Historical Village; River Murray; Renmark; The Big Orange; Waikerie

L Yorke Peninsula
Ardrossan; Edithburgh; Innes NP; Kadina Dryland Farm & Heritage Centre; Marion Bay; Moonta; Port Victoria; Port Vincent; Wallaroo Nautical Museum; Yorketown

NATIONAL PARKS

South Australia has a park system that ensures a great many natural areas are protected by a park or reserve and will therefore remain pristine and beautiful. From such places as the **Simpson Desert** and **Flinders Ranges**, to the flat plains of the **Nullarbor**, that stretch to the rugged cliffs of the Great Australian Bight, the many national parks of South Australia are spectacular and awe-inspiring.

A Coffin Bay NP (Map 348, B1)

Coffin Bay NP is located 625km west of Adelaide on a peninsula bordered by the **Southern Ocean** and **Coffin Bay**. Known for its good fishing, swimming and surfing (check conditions first), the national park also offers walking trails that take in the coastal landscape—4-wheel drive access is recommended. Camping facilities are found mainly near Coffin Bay township, where general stores and information are obtainable.

B Coorong NP (Map 349, G3)

Around 140km south-east of Adelaide, Coorong NP is a line of shallow lagoons, protected from the rough Southern Ocean waters by a thin line of sand dunes known as **Younghusband Peninsula**. At around 468km², the park stretches for 130km along the coast. The attractions of this park include good fishing (mulloway, whiting, flathead and shark), wildlife (especially pelicans and other waterbirds), the coastal walking trails and 4-wheel drive access. Camping and picnic spots are plentiful, but it is necessary to gain a camping permit from the ranger in Meningie.

C Flinders Ranges NP
(Map 313, C1)

Covering 927km², Flinders Ranges NP is a campers' delight. Around 460km north of Adelaide, it was made famous by artist Hans Heysen's depiction of the ranges. Attractions of the park include the amazing sunrises and sunsets; **Wilpena Pound**, a huge natural amphitheatre 5km by 11km; the **Sacred Canyon**, a fantastic site of Aboriginal art; the wildflower displays in early spring; and many stunning valleys and gorges. Some camping sites have toilet facilities; Wilpena Pound has a motel, ranger facilities and a general store.

D Lake Eyre NP (Map 342, D4)

Lake Eyre NP covers 12 250km² and is located 760km north of Adelaide. The park comprises Lake Eyre and the **Tirari Desert**, noted for its sand dunes and salt lakes. At 15m below sea level, Lake Eyre is the lowest point in Australia; it is also the largest salt lake on the continent at over 340km². The area is considered one of the harshest environments in Australia; it is remarkably transformed when occasionally it fills with water. Then, it is home to fish and a multitude of waterbirds. Camping is permitted; permits are available at the Port Augusta district office or the William Creek store.

E Murray River NP
(Map 333, G3-D1)

Around 240km from Adelaide, three areas with similar habitats: **Katarapko**, **Lyrup Flats** and **Bulyong Island** form Murray River NP. Three-quarters of the park is floodplain, containing permanent and semi-permanent wetlands. It is an important breeding area for many forms of life, including waterbirds. The park offers several recreational opportunities: birdwatching, fishing, camping and walking.

facts

◆ No. of parks/reserves: 330
◆ Total area: 200 000km²
◆ % of state: 20%
◆ World Heritage Area: Australian Fossil Mammal Site (Naracoorte Caves NP)

Common wallaroo, *Macropus robustus*, in the Flinders Ranges

South Australia

National Parks Information

Department for Environment and Heritage
GPO Box 1047
Adelaide, SA 5001
Ph: (08) 8204 1910
Desert Parks Hotline: 1800 816 078
www.environment.sa.gov.au

The Nullarbor Cliffs fringe the Great Australian Bight Marine Park, Nullarbor National Park

▣ Nullarbor NP and Regional Reserve

(Map 344, C3)

Nullarbor NP—meaning 'no tree'—and Regional Reserve is 950km west of Adelaide. The park is located on a coastal strip of the seemingly endless flat Nullarbor plain. The plain itself is a limestone plateau fringed by spectacular coastal cliffs shaped by the wild **Southern Ocean**. It is in these waters that it is possible to see mighty, but endangered, southern right whales. These whales come to the Bight in winter to breed and to calve. There are also sea-lion colonies along the **Great Australian Bight**. The park provides protected habitat for other wildlife including the southern hairy-nosed wombat. Besides wildlife-watching, the park and reserve protects the world's largest semi-arid karst (cave) landscape. It also offers Aboriginal art sites, and almost undisturbed camping, as this remote region sees few visitors.

▣ Witjira NP and Simpson Desert Regional Reserve

(Map 342, B1-D2)

The furthest national park from Adelaide (1360km north), Witjira NP and Simpson Desert Regional Reserve adjoin on the South Australia/Northern Territory border. These two parks lure visitors with a distinctly beautiful desert landscape which includes dune systems, spinifex, dry playa lakes, gibber country and the Finke River flood-plains. Witjira NP has the unusual **Dalhousie mound-spring complex**—the warm water is great for soaking in. It is claimed that the spring resembles the finest oases in the world. There are also the ruins of historic **Dalhousie homestead** to investigate. Another wetland worth exploring is **Purnie Bore**, which attracts much wildlife. For access or camping rights to these parks, a **Desert Parks Pass** (or day/night permit) must be obtained.

Thorny devil, *Moloch horridus*

WINERIES

In 1837, just one year after the founding of South Australia, **J B Hach** and **George Stevenson** planted vine cuttings from Tasmania in **North Adelaide**. A few years later, German Lutheran immigrants arrived in the **Barossa Valley** and **Johann Gramp** planted his **Jacob's Creek Vineyard** there. By 1900, South Australia was the leading Australian wine producer. Labels such as **Hardy**, **Seppelt**, **Penfold**, **Orlando** and **Yalumba** had become internationally recognised, as indeed they are today. The state was fortunate to escape the vine aphid *phylloxera*, which devastated vineyards in Victoria, and to a lesser extent New South Wales, in the late 19th century.

South Australia's wine regions encompass a wide variety of terrain, character and climate. They are today responsible for more than 50% of national wine production and 70% of international exports. They have also led Australia's success with international awards.

A Adelaide Hills

The state's oldest wine region produced its first vintage in 1841, and in 1845 a case of Echunga hock was sent to Queen Victoria in England. There are now at least 35 wine labels in the picturesque setting of the **Mount Lofty Ranges**. Varieties include chardonnay, pinot noir, riesling, semillon, sauvignon blanc, merlot, cabernet sauvignon, cabernet franc and shiraz.

B Adelaide Plains

This region between the Adelaide Hills and **Gulf St Vincent** has a Mediterranean climate with hot, dry summers and mild winters. The most common grape varieties are columbard and shiraz, as well as chardonnay, sauvignon blanc, riesling, cabernet and semillon. There are also plantings of Italian varietals—barbera, sangiovese and nebbiolo.

C Barossa Valley (pp.326–327)

Australia's most recognised wine region was established in 1842 by immigrants from Germany, Silesia and England. The main red varieties grown are cabernet sauvignon, shiraz and grenache; riesling, semillon and chardonnay are the main white varieties. Famous labels include **Chateau Tanunda**, **Orlando**, **Seppeltsfield**, **Yaldara**, **Yalumba** and **Wolf Blass**. **Penfold's Grange Hermitage** is rated one of the world's finest red wines.

D Clare Valley

More than 30 wineries are to be found in this historic region north of Adelaide. This is prime riesling country, with a consistency of style and quality possibly unmatched in Australia. Principal red wines are cabernet sauvignon and shiraz, with outstanding varietals.

E Coonawarra

With a predominantly maritime climate, Coonawarra is famous for its luscious red wines and the red soil (terra rossa) on which the vines flourish. Its superb cabernet sauvignons account for 50% of plantings, with 21% shiraz and lesser amounts of chardonnay, riesling, merlot and pinot noir.

F Eden Valley

The Barossa's neighbouring valley is at a higher altitude with a cooler climate, but an equal reputation for fine wines. Riesling, chardonnay, shiraz, merlot and cabernet grapes thrive in the long summer-ripening periods, assisted by innovative viticulture techniques. Premium wine labels include **Henschke's Hill of Grace**.

Barrel Room at Mountadam Winery, Eden Valley

South Australia

Harvesting grapes in a McLaren Vale vineyard

G Eyre Peninsula

This small region around **Port Lincoln** has a relatively cool maritime climate, with vines in places growing down to **Boston Bay**. Vineyards produce chardonnay, riesling, semillon, sauvignon blanc, cabernet sauvignon, merlot and shiraz.

H Langhorne Creek

Cooling breezes from the Southern Ocean and Lake Alexandrina help make Langhorne Creek a centre for fine cool-climate wines. It is known for superb cabernet sauvignon and full-flavoured shiraz with soft tannins. Verdelho, malbec, merlot and chardonnay grapes are also grown.

I McLaren Vale

There are more than 60 wineries in this Fleurieu Peninsula region, originally pioneered by pre-eminent winemakers such as **John Reynell** and **Thomas Hardy**. It is famous for ripe, generously flavoured wines, especially shiraz, grenache, merlot, cabernet sauvignon, chardonnay, riesling and sauvignon blanc. There are also planting of varietals such as viognier, marsanne and sangiovese.

J Mount Benson

This small coastal region between **Kingston SE** and **Robe** was planted in 1989 by French winemakers from the Rhone Valley. Mount Benson wines are highly aromatic and predominantly red: cabernet franc, cabernet sauvignon, shiraz, grenache, merlot, petit verdot and pinot noir. There are also plantings of chardonnay and other white grape varieties.

K Padthaway

Padthaway shares the terra rossa soils of nearby Coonawarra, but has a warmer Mediterranean-like climate. Principal red wines are shiraz and cabernet sauvignon with outstanding varietals. The local chardonnays are rich and fruity; other white varieties are also grown. **Padthaway Estate** and **Stonehaven Winery** have cellar door tastings and sales.

L Riverland (pp.332–333)

The prolific River Murray region between **Blanchetown** and **Paringa** is blessed with abundant sunshine and water supply, and rich, sandy loam soils. It produces about two-thirds of South Australia's wine grapes and almost one-third of the nation's total production. Its rich, velvety shiraz, cabernet sauvignon and merlot are very good. However, it is most famous for its outstanding flavoursome, fruity chardonnays.

M Wrattonbully

This rapidly growing region between **Padthaway** and **Coonawarra** shares their famous terra rossa soils. The majority of plantings are red grapes: cabernet sauvignon, shiraz, pinot noir, pinot meunier, merlot, cabernet franc and zinfandel. Whites include semillon, chardonnay, sauvignon blanc and riesling.

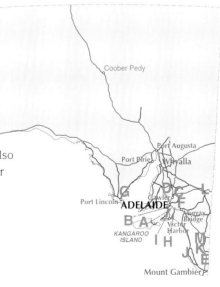

ADELAIDE

Plaza at Adelaide Festival Centre

main attractions

◈ **Adelaide Botanic Gardens**

These beautifully landscaped gardens contain the magnificently restored 19th-century Palm House and the Bicentennial Conservatory with its lush rainforest.

◈ **Adelaide Festival Centre**

This imposing building hosts a series of world-class productions during the biennial Adelaide Festival as well as throughout the year.

◈ **Central Market**

The markets are a culinary adventure and reflect Adelaide's diverse ethnic population. Adelaide's Chinatown is in the market area.

◈ **Glenelg**

South Australia's first settlement was at Glenelg, which is now connected to the city by the Bay Tram. Glenelg Beach is the most popular of Adelaide's long, sandy beaches.

◈ **Gouger St**

One of Adelaide's premier 'eat streets', Gouger St features food from around the world.

◈ **Rundle Mall**

The retail hub of Adelaide is located here.

◈ **South Australian Museum**

This museum features a fascinating collection of Aboriginal artefacts and much more.

Named after Queen Adelaide, the wife of King William IV, Adelaide's boom times are evident in its glorious architecture. Adelaide's historic churches and gracious 19th-century buildings are interspersed with those built in the Italian-Renaissance style. **King William St** and the tree-lined **North Terrace** are excellent examples.

With a population of more than one million residents, this planned city is easy to navigate due to its grid design. The city is positioned on the banks of the picturesque **River Torrens**, among superb gardens, with the blue haze of the **Adelaide Hills** as a backdrop, giving it a relaxed atmosphere. Adelaide experiences four distinct seasons, adding to its charm.

Its long history of immigration has influenced the city's development and its ethnic diversity is reflected in the city's markets, restaurants and cafes. Adelaide is renowned for its fine restaurants, wines and colourful festivals.

 Visitor information

South Australian Travel Centre
18 King William St,
Adelaide, SA 5000
Ph: 1300 655 276
www.southaustralia.com

facts

◈ Population: 1 100 000
◈ Date founded: 1836
◈ Tallest building: SANTOS House, 132m
◈ Average temperature: 23°C (January), 12.5°C (June)

Places of Interest

Adelaide Botanic Gardens Ⓐ D3
Adelaide Festival Centre Ⓑ C3
Adelaide Town Hall Ⓒ D4
Adelaide Zoo Ⓓ D3
Art Gallery of South Australia Ⓔ D3
Ayers House Ⓕ D3
Central Market Ⓖ C4
Edmund Wright House Ⓗ C4
Elder Park Ⓘ C3
Government House Ⓙ D3
Light's Vision Ⓚ C3
Lion Arts Centre Ⓛ C3
Migration Museum Ⓜ D3
Mortlock Library of South Australia Ⓝ D3
National Wine Centre Ⓞ E3
Old Adelaide Gaol Ⓟ B3
Parliament House and
    Old Parliament House Ⓠ C3
Performing Arts Collection Ⓡ C3
Skycity Adelaide Ⓢ C3
South Australian Museum Ⓣ D3
Tandanya Ⓤ D4

Rowing crews on the River Torrens, Adelaide

Continued on map 302

Continued on map 302

CBD & SUBURBS

CBD ATTRACTIONS

To explore the CBD of Adelaide, it is best to leave the car behind and walk or take the **City Loop free bus**. The city centre is well planned and it is easy to wander along the wide, attractive streets lined with cafes, restored Edwardian and Victorian buildings and shops. Small and compact, this in an elegant, cultured, cosmopolitan but unhurried city.

Begin at **North Terrace**, the city's most attractive boulevard, and wander along the street and find the casino at **Skycity Adelaide**, **Government House**, **Parliament House** (with its award-winning museum of state history), the **State Library of South Australia** and the **Mortlock Library**. The **Art Gallery of South Australia** houses a collection divided into four parts: prints and drawings, Australian decorative arts, European and Asian decorative arts and paintings and sculptures. The **University of Adelaide** is between North Tce and the Torrens River and the neo-Gothic buildings are worth inspecting. The **Tate Museum** is on the ground floor of the **Mawson Laboratory** at the University, home to a collection of rocks, minerals and fossils. The **Migration Museum** is close by. Also in North Tce is the magnificent **South Australian Museum** For a peek into Adelaide's past, drop into **Ayers House** (opposite the **Royal Adelaide Hospital**), and view the mansion of former South Australian Premier, Sir Henry Ayers.

Further along North Tce are the Botanic Gardens, renowned for the magnificent Moreton Bay figs that create a pathway to the main lake. The gardens themselves back onto **Adelaide Zoo**. One of the country's most historic zoological gardens, Adelaide Zoo is an immaculately landscaped area with large grassy enclosures and many walk-through aviaries. Next to the Botanic Gardens, the **National Wine Centre** represents every wine region in Australia and the stunning **International Rose Garden** is close by. These parks and gardens reflect the original urban design of Colonel William Light (the first governor-general) which was to surround Adelaide with a pleasant expanse of greenery.

Behind Parliament House off King William St is the **Performing Arts Complex**. This is a living history collection, holding over 40 000 pieces, from old posters to puppets and videos. Also located here, over-looking the Torrens River, are the **Adelaide Festival Centre**, the focus of the city's cultural life, and **Elder Park**, with its historic rotunda.

A shopper's paradise, **Rundle Mall** is located adjacent to North Tce, between King William St and Pulteney St, and is lined with department stores, boutiques, cafes and cinemas. For fresh produce, explore the **Central Market** in Grote St or the **East End Market** in Rundle St.

Located above North Tce to the west is **Old Adelaide Gaol**—definitely worth a visit. Other attractions of the city include **Edmund Wright House**; the **Lion Arts Centre**, containing nine different arts organisations; and **Tandanya**, the National Aboriginal Cultural Institute.

Elder Park's historic rotunda at sunset, Adelaide

South Australia

SUBURBAN ATTRACTIONS

2km north of the CBD, **North Adelaide** is lined with grand Victorian and Edwardian homes made of bluestone and sandstone. There is an abundance of hotels, motels and B&Bs in this suburb, with exotic restaurants, cafes and welcoming pubs all within walking distance.

Around 20–30 minutes from the CBD, Adelaide's beaches are popular seaside escapes. Well-known areas include **Henley Beach**, **West Beach** and **Brighton**.

The site of the first mainland settlement in South Australia in 1836, **Glenelg** is a seaside suburb with a five-star hotel, beachfront apartments, shops and restaurants on the shoreline. **Jetty Road** is a hive of activity as the main precinct for shopping and alfresco dining. **The Bay Discovery Centre** and **Rodney Fox's Shark Museum** are located in the Town Hall.

South of Adelaide (2km), the suburb of **Wayville** is home to the **Royal Adelaide Show** at Wayville Showground. A small suburb to the south-east of Adelaide, **Hyde Park** is a known shopping destination with designer and international labels available, great bars and eateries. Further to the south are **Carrick Hill**, a Tudor mansion set in manicured English gardens; and **Belair NP**, only 20 minutes from the city. **Hallett Cove**, on the coast, is one of Australia's most significant geological sites.

Port Adelaide is perhaps one of the more visited suburbs and boasts a maritime history both on and off the water. There are many imposing buildings—like the old **Court House**—definitely worth wandering around. The port is a relic from a bygone era and the **South Australian Maritime Museum** is spread over seven sites. The **Railway Museum**, not far away, is also worth a look. After the

World's largest rocking horse at the Gumeracha Toy Factory

history lesson, retreat to the seaside and take a boat trip to watch the Port River dolphins. Another suburb, **West Lakes,** plays an important part in the sporting life of Adelaide by housing both **Football Park Stadium** and the **South Australian Rowing Association**.

Burnside in the foothills of the **Mount Lofty Ranges** is 6km east of Adelaide. Originally a settlement of four houses in 1840, the suburb flourished in 1849 when land lots were auctioned. Today, the suburb offers a glimpse into Adelaide's past; pamphlets are available from the local library on the historic sites of **Rose Park**, **Knightsbridge** and **Waterfall Gully**. Further to the east, the former South Australian Governor's summerhouse, **Marble Hill**, has been restored after fires destroyed it in 1955, and is now open to the public every second Sunday afternoon of the month. Apart from their beauty, especially in autumn, the **Adelaide Hills** have

many attractions including the craft galleries of **Hahndorf, Lobethal** and **Strathalbyn**; Cleland Conservation Park and Cleland Wildlife Park; **Mount Lofty Botanic Garden** and **Mount Lofty Summit**, provide stunning 360° views over Adelaide city, coast and hills. **Warrawong Earth Sanctuary** is an award-winning ecotourism complex dedicated to preserving endangered native animals. The world's largest rocking horse is at the **Gumeracha Toy Factory**. The collection of over 300 vehicles at the **National Motor Museum**, at Birdwood, further to the east, is considered to be one of the best in the world. There are numerous **wineries** spread across the Adelaide Hills.

Another interesting spot, 14km north-west from the city centre, is **Fort Glanville**. The buildings are all that remain of the city's commitment to Britain following the Crimean War, and consist of a line of forts along the coast of **Gulf St Vincent**.

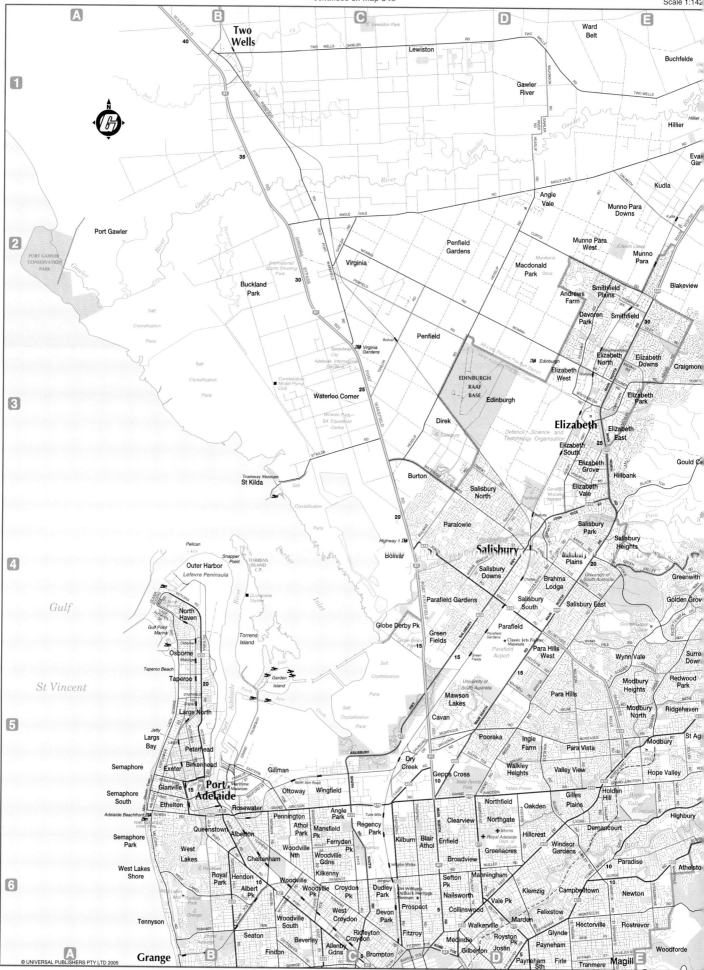

Two Wells

Lewiston

Ward Belt

Buchfelde

Gawler River

Hillier

Eva Gar

Kudla

Port Gawler

PORT GAWLER CONSERVATION PARK

Angle Vale

Munno Para Downs

Munno Para West

Munno Para

Penfield Gardens

Blakeview

Buckland Park

Virginia

Macdonald Park

Andrews Farm

Smithfield Plains

Davoren Park

Smithfield

Bolivar

Penfield

Elizabeth North

Elizabeth Downs

Craigmore

Virginia Gardens

Edinburgh

Elizabeth West

Waterloo Corner

EDINBURGH RAAF BASE

Edinburgh

Elizabeth

Elizabeth Park

Speedway City
Adelaide International Raceway

Constellation Model Flying Club

Direk

Defence Science and Technology Organisation

Elizabeth East

Elizabeth South

Gould C

Winston Park SA Equestrian Centre

Burton

Salisbury North

Elizabeth Grove

Hillbank

Elizabeth Vale

Tramway Museum
St Kilda

Paralowie

Salisbury Park

Salisbury Heights

Highway 1

Bolivar

Salisbury

Salisbury Plains

Pelican

Outer Harbor

Snapper Island

TORRENS ISLAND C.P.

Lefevre Peninsula

Salisbury Downs

Brahma Lodge

Greenwith

North Haven

Gulf Point Marina

Torrens Island

Parafield Gardens

Salisbury South

Salisbury East

Golden Grov

Osborne

Quarantine Station

Parafield

Gulf

Taperoo Beach

Garden Island

Green Fields

Classic Jets Fighter Museum

Para Hills West

Wynn Vale

Surre Down

Taperoo

University of South Australia

Parafield Airport

Redwood Park

St Vincent

Largs North

Mawson Lakes

Modbury Heights

Ridgehaven

Cavan

Para Hills

Largs Bay

Pooraka

Ingle Farm

Modbury North

Modbury

St Ag

Peterhead

Walkley Heights

Para Vista

Semaphore

Exeter

Birkenhead

Gillman

Dry Creek

Valley View

Hope Valley

Gepps Cross

Semaphore South

Glanville

Port Adelaide

Maritime Museum

Ottoway

Wingfield

State Sports Park

Yatala Prison

Gilles Plains

Holden Hill

Highbury

Ethelton

Rosewater

Northfield

Oakden

Dernancourt

Semaphore Park

Pennington

Angle Park

Tube Mills

Clearview

Northgate

Hillcrest

Windsor Gardens

Paradise

Athelsto

West Lakes

Queenstown

Albertön

Athol Park

Mansfield Pk

Regency Park

Kilburn

Blair Athol

Enfield

Morris Royal Adelaide Showground

Broadview

Greenacres

Manningham

Klemzig

Campbelltown

Newton

West Lakes Shore

Cheltenham

Woodville Nth

Ferryden Pk

Woodville Gdns

Sefton Pk

Royal Park

Hendon

Kilkenny

Nailsworth

Vale Pk

Felixstow

Albert Pk

Woodville

Croydon Pk

Dudley Park

EM Williams Outback Heritage Museum

Prospect

Collinswood

Marden

Hectorville

Rostrevor

Tennyson

Woodville South

West Croydon

Devon Park

Walkerville

Glynde

Paynenham

Seaton

Beverley

Ridleyton

Croydon

Fitzroy

Royston Pk

Joslin

Gilberton

Paynehám Sth

Firle

Woodforde

Findon

Allenby Gdns

Brompton

Medindie

Tranmere

Magill

Grange

South Australia

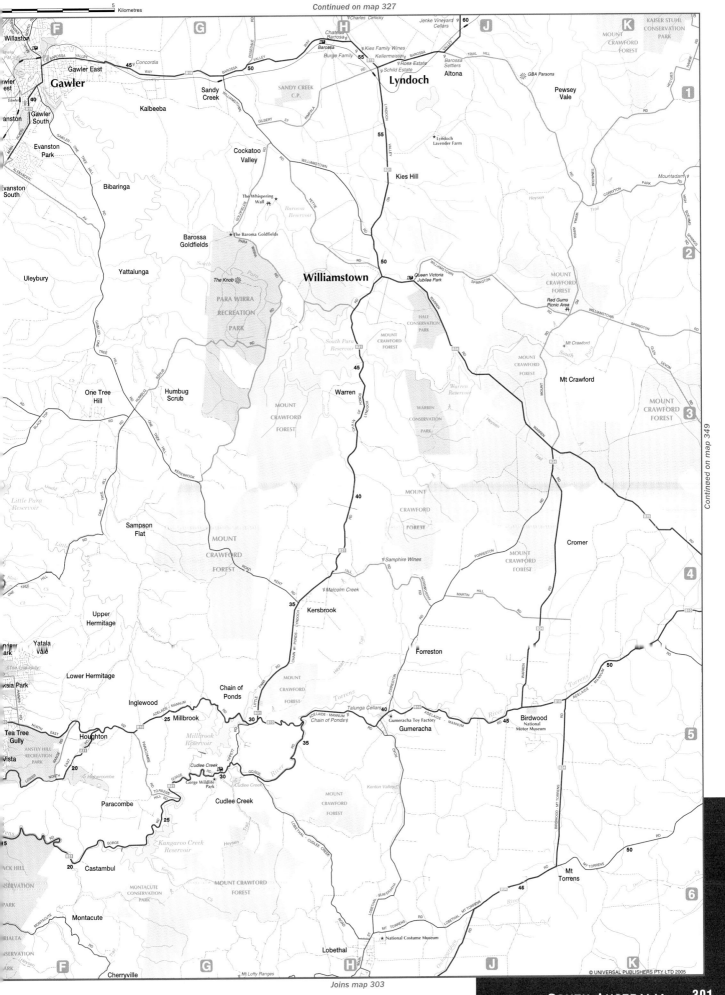

© UNIVERSAL PUBLISHERS PTY LTD 2005

Scale 1:14

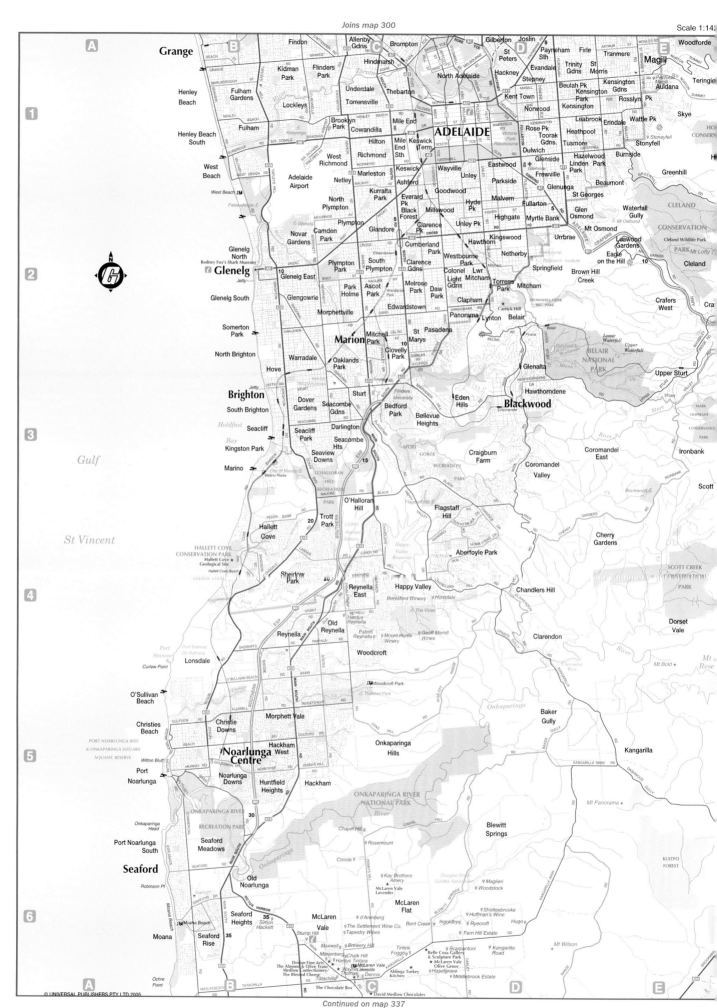

© UNIVERSAL PUBLISHERS PTY LTD 2005

Kilometres

Cherryville

Mt Lofty Ranges Vineyard

Forest Range

Lenswood

Charleston

CHARLESTON CONSERVATION PARK

Norton Summit

Marble Hill

Melba's Chocolate Factory

Harrogate

Basket Range

Ashton

Woodside

Ashton Hills Vineyard

Barratt Wines
Uraidla

Carey Gully

mertown

KENNETH STIRLING CONSERVATION PARK

WOODSIDE BARRACKS

Brukunga

Piccadilly

Woodhouse Scout Camp

KENNETH STIRLING CONSERVATION PARK

Oakbank Racecourse

Oakbank

Hay Valley

ly Botanic arden

Mt George

Balhannah

Spoehr Creek Wines

Oakbank

Dawesley

irling

Petaluma's
Bridgewater Mill

Nepenthe Winery
Shaw & Smith

Nairne

Bridgewater

Maximillian's
Adelaide Hills
Verdun

Mt Barker Junction

Aldgate

Engelbrecht Reserve

Habndorf Hill

Habndorf

Blakiston

thfield

Hahndorf

Littlehampton

Mawson Ridge

Warrawong
Earth Sanctuary

MYLOR
CONSERVATION
PARK

Beerenberg Strawberry Farm
Totness

Mt Barker Summit

Mt Barker+

wood

Mylor

Paechtown

Hahndorf
Farm Barn

Mt Barker

Bradbury

TOTNESS REC PARK

Mt Barker

Petwood

Biggs Flat

Mt Barker
Springs

Chape Hill

St Ives

Echunga

Wistow

Echunga

Flaxley

Jupiter Creek

Kuitpo

Bugle Ranges

KUITPO FOREST

Highland Valley

Red Creek

Flaxley

Green Hills Range

Macclesfield

Gemmells

Meadows

Woodchester

Prospect Hill

Paris Creek

Bletchley
© UNIVERSAL PUBLISHERS PTY LTD 2005

Continued on map 349

SOUTH AUSTRALIA

303

■ Angaston   POP 1950

Map 327, E3

A picturesque rural town in the rolling wine country of the Barossa Valley, Angaston is a showcase of colonial architecture. In 1841 the town was named after George Fife Angas, an early settler and large landholder.
MAIN ATTRACTIONS: The tree-lined main street, **Murray St**, is lined with art and craft shops and tearooms. Visit **Angas Park Fruit** and the **Barossa Valley Cheese Company** and try some of the local produce. The **South Australian Company Store**, in Valley Rd, attracts many visitors, and there are two interesting **Lutheran churches** in the area. A shady park with picnic and BBQ facilities adjacent to **Angaston Creek** complements the village atmosphere.
NEARBY ATTRACTIONS: Wineries close by include **Yalumba**, **Saltram** and **Thorn-Clarke**. **Henschke Cellars** are about 10km south-east. Around 8km south on the Eden Valley Rd the historic National Trust property **Collingrove** (built for George Angas' son, John), is open for inspection most days.
VISITOR INFORMATION: 66–68 Murray St, Tanunda, Ph: (08) 8563 0600 or 1300 852 982

■ Ardrossan   POP 1085

Map 348, E1

Ardrossan, on the east coast of the **Yorke Peninsula** and 140km from Adelaide, was proclaimed in 1873. It sits above 25m cliffs that, although red, are to some observers reminiscent of the famous white cliffs of Dover. Ardrossan is a thriving seaport, shipping dolomite and grain all over the world. Named by Governor Fergusson after the seaport in Ayrshire, Scotland, the name is derived from the Gaelic words 'ard' meaning 'height', and 'ros' meaning a 'prominent rock' or 'headland'.
MAIN ATTRACTIONS: The cliff-top reserve has a lookout, BBQs and a walking track. **Ardrossan and District Historical Museum** is housed in the old powerhouse factory in Fifth St. A room is devoted to *Zanoni*, a wheat clipper that sank off the coast in the 19th century. There is also information on the Australian invention, the stump jump plough, as well as a good collection of farm and agricultural equipment, the town's maritime history and general historical items.
NEARBY ATTRACTIONS: A man-made lookout south of Ardrossan overlooks a **dolomite mine** and **Gulf St Vincent**. Fishing in Gulf St Vincent is rewarding all year round for a variety of species. Diving around the wreck of *Zanoni*, 20km off the coast, (for which a permit is necessary) is an exciting experience.
VISITOR INFORMATION: Harvest Corner, 29 Main St, Minlaton, Ph: (08) 8853 2600

Diver in Gulf St Vincent, near Ardrossan

The screw-pile jetty in Rivoli Bay at Beachport—a favourite with anglers

Balaklava   POP 1500
Map 349, F1

91km north of Adelaide, Balaklava services a rich pastoral area in the fertile region where the **Adelaide Plains** become the **Mid North**. Farming around Balaklava is diverse, producing wheat, wool, barley, oats, pigs, sheep, poultry and cattle. Local industries include two hay processing plants and another for processing legumes and grain for local and overseas markets.

MAIN ATTRACTIONS: Interesting places to visit include the **Court House Gallery** for quality arts and crafts, and the **Local History Museum**, housed in **Centenary Hall** and open on the second and fourth Sundays of each month. Starting in Elizabeth St, the **Lions Walking Trail** follows the Wakefield River for approximately 2.5km and is popular with residents and visitors alike.

NEARBY ATTRACTIONS: Experience the natural beauty of the **Rocks Reserve** with its abundant flora and fauna There is a swimming hole on the Wakefield River, where water has sculpted unusual shapes into the rocks. **Port Wakefield**, 26km west, is an historic beachside town.

VISITOR INFORMATION: Wakefield Regional Council, Scotland Pl, Ph: (08) 8862 0800

Barmera   POP 1963
Map 333, C2

Around 215km north-east of Adelaide, Barmera sits on the shore of **Lake Bonney** and is an ideal destination for windsurfing, waterskiing, canoeing, fishing, enjoying a round of golf or sitting and watching the pelicans on the manicured foreshore. Original settlers were attracted by the expanse of fresh water, and by 1846 there were several cattle runs in the area. After WWI, Barmera was opened up for soldier-settlement and a second wave of settlers arrived in 1922.

MAIN ATTRACTIONS: Barmera's picturesque setting and beautiful beaches draw many visitors; canoes and jet skis can be hired. **Barmera Theatre Gallery** is an outlet for locally executed paintings, crafts and pottery. **Bonnyview Winery** is a boutique winery on the Sturt Hwy, open daily for tours and tastings. Close by is **Highway Fern Haven**, a specialist nursery offering ferns and other plants, also a coffee shop in a lush tropical setting. For fans of country music, pop into **Rockys Hall of Fame**, which showcases country music memorabilia.

NEARBY ATTRACTIONS: **North Lake** is the site of the ruins of **Nappers Accommodation House** (1850), one of the earliest buildings in the area. **Cobdogla** is a small settlement 6km west of Barmera. Of interest here is the **Irrigation and Steam Museum**, home of the famous Humphrey Pump and other engines. **Bookmark Biosphere Reserve**, located at Loch Luna, is a wetlands area of creeks and swamps popular with nature lovers and birdwatchers.

VISITOR INFORMATION: Barwell Ave, Ph: (08) 8588 2289

Beachport   POP 455
Map 323, C4

In the 1830s, this small coastal town was a whaling station that also serviced rural land opened up by the Henty brothers. Agriculture is still one of the district's sustaining industries but lobster fishing has taken over from whaling. Forestry, vineyards and tourism are now also important to Beachport.

MAIN ATTRACTIONS: The long screw-pile jetty that juts out into **Rivoli Bay** is a prominent feature, popular with recreational anglers. The spacious **National Trust Museum**, in Railway Tce, explores Beachport's whaling and historical heritage. **Centenary Park**, in the centre of Beachport, is a good lunch spot with picnicking and BBQ facilities.

NEARBY ATTRACTIONS: To the north of town, **Beachport Conservation Park** protects coastal vegetation and sand dunes between **Lake George** and the ocean. The park has some interesting walking trails. **Bowman Scenic Drive**, commencing at the

The landmark Big Orange, near Berri

end of Foster St, reveals magnificent coastal views of rugged, weathered, limestone cliffs contrasting with secluded white sandy beaches. The **Pool of Siloam**, located just behind Beachport, is a small lake claimed to have healing qualities because of its high salt content.

VISITOR INFORMATION: Millicent Rd, Ph: (08) 8735 8029

■ Berri   POP 4220

Map 333, C2

Founded in 1911, Berri owes its existence to irrigation. It is built on the site of what was originally a refuelling stop for traffic on the **River Murray** in the 1880s. Berri is now known as the **'Heart of the Riverland'**.

MAIN ATTRACTIONS: Berri has the largest shopping complex in the **Riverland**, and excellent facilities for golf, tennis, bowling, fishing, canoeing and waterskiing. Visit

Earth Works and **Berri Art Gallery** for local arts and crafts. For a great view, try the **Water Tower Lookout** on Fiedler St. To cruise the Murray, houseboats are for hire. Close to the marina there is a memorial sculpture garden to **Jimmy James**, one of Australia's most famous and respected Aboriginal trackers.

NEARBY ATTRACTIONS: On the highway at **Glossop**, **Berri Estates Winery** has cellar door sales. **Murray River NP-Katarapko** is 10km south of Berri and offers fishing, birdwatching, walking trails and camping. Between Berri and **Renmark** lies the **Big Orange** tourist attraction— a sales outlet with souvenirs, refreshments and a children's playground. **Berri Direct** is another sales outlet for the district's famous fruit juices. Family attractions at Monash, on the Sturt Hwy to the north, are **Monash Adventure Park** and **Chocolates and More**.

VISITOR INFORMATION: Riverview Dr, Ph: (08) 8582 5511

■ Bordertown   POP 2445

Map 323, E1

Bordertown is about 20km from the state border at the junction of Dukes Hwy linking Adelaide to Melbourne and the north–south route from the **Riverland** to **Mount Gambier**. Established in 1852, it was originally the site of a base camp created by Police Inspector Alexander Tolmer, who was in charge of the gold escorts from the Victorian goldfields to Adelaide.

MAIN ATTRACTIONS: **Tolmer Park** has an interpretative walk that explains the history of the area. **Clay Murals** around Bordertown, designed by schoolchildren, also have an historical theme. A **Wildlife Park** on North Tce exhibits rare white kangaroos, as well as friendly wallabies, emus and waterbirds. **Hawke House Museum**, the birthplace of former Australian Prime Minister **Robert J Hawke**, is on the corner of

Farquhar St and Binnie St and is open weekdays. **Recreation Lake** is another good spot for BBQs, canoeing and fishing.

NEARBY ATTRACTIONS: **Clayton Farm**, 3km from Bordertown, is an historic site and agricultural museum. The heritage-listed **Old Mundulla Hotel** is 10km west. **Poocher Swamp**, 8.5km to the west, is noted for its magnificent red gums and prolific birdlife, also its mysterious 'runaway hole'. An historic 20km **scenic drive** commences at Bordertown—the visitor centre has details of this.

VISITOR INFORMATION: Tolmer Park, 81 North Tce, Ph: (08) 8752 0700

■ Burra   POP 1100

Map 347, F6

Burra is located 154km north of Adelaide. It is listed on the National Estate and is a declared State Heritage Area. The first mining-company town, known as Kooringa, was established in 1851. Soon, more than 5000 people lived in small satellite villages based on British regional identities, and in time the settlements merged to become Burra. Today, tourism and pastoral industries form the town's economic base.

MAIN ATTRACTIONS: As there is so much to see in Burra it is worthwhile using the guide ***Discovering Historic Burra***. Walks around the town and through the cemetery are a good introduction to Burra's heritage, as are the many antique shops. Burra's museums are well worth visiting, including **Burra Mine Open Air Museum**; once a copper mine, it features a powder magazine dating to 1847. Also worth a look are historic sites such as the underground cellars of the old **Unicorn Brewery**; **Redruth Gaol**, which was used in the 1979 film, *Breaker Morant*; the **old copper mines**; and **miners' dugouts**—by 1851 almost 2000 miners lived in dugouts in the banks of Burra Creek until forced out by floods. A **Burra Passport**, available at the information centre in Market St, gives access to all these sites.

NEARBY ATTRACTIONS: Go horseriding with **Burra Trail Rides**, tour the **Mongolata Gold Mine** by appointment, or take a trip up **Burra Creek Gorge**, a scenic picnic and camping area 27km south-east.

VISITOR INFORMATION: 2 Market Sq, Ph: (08) 8892 2154

■ **Bute**   POP 300

Map 346, E6

Proclaimed in 1884, this quiet little town at the northern end of the **Yorke Peninsula** caters for the needs of the surrounding agricultural and pastoral districts.

MAIN ATTRACTIONS: **Bute Bromeliad Nursery** is believed to be the only one of its kind in Australia. A picnic area with a fauna park housing native and other animals is located at Railway Tce. **Gunner Bill's Gallery** on Railway Tce has displays of arts and crafts and an historical gallery. An old well just off Kulpara Rd, used for watering stock in times past, is now of historic interest. The **YP Tourist Train** runs between Bute and **Wallaroo** once a month; check with the information centre at Kadina for details.

VISITOR INFORMATION: National Dryland Farming Centre, Moonta Rd, Kadina, Ph: 1800 654 991

■ **Ceduna**   POP 2637

Map 345, H4

Spread along the shores of beautiful **Murat Bay**, Ceduna is the eastern gateway to the **Nullarbor Plain**. Established in 1896, it is a fishing and oyster farming town, as well as the commercial centre for the pastoral and cereal-growing area of the **Far West**. Ceduna is a popular stopover prior to, or after crossing the vast Nullarbor Plain.

MAIN ATTRACTIONS: The **Old School House Museum** in Park Tce exhibits pioneer memorabilia and items from **Maralinga**, site of British atomic testing. **Ceduna Arts and Cultural Centre**, on Poynton St, features local art and craftwork. The white sandy beaches of Ceduna are perfect for swimming and watersports.

NEARBY ATTRACTIONS: **Thevenard Fish Processors** at **Thevenard Boat Haven** have tours and sales of fresh seafood. Like **Smoky Bay Oyster Tours**, to the south-east, they are part of the **Seafood and Aquaculture Trail** that runs around the Eyre Peninsula to **Whyalla**. In winter, whale-watching excursions to the **Great Australian Bight** can be arranged through the visitor information centre. **Chinta Tours** offer visitors a stunning aerial view of whales and the coastal cliffs. At **Denial Bay** (13km west) are the **McKenzie Ruins**—site of the original settlement. Tours of **Astrid Oyster Farm** are available. East of Ceduna, **Wittelbee Conservation Park** is an attractive combination of fine sandy beaches broken by low rocky headlands. **Laura Bay Conservation Park** offers a great walking track that explores the rocky headland, sandy cove and rockpools at low tide.

VISITOR INFORMATION: 58 Poynton St, Ph: (08) 8625 2780 or 1800 639 413

■ **Clare**   POP 2935

Map 347, F6

Clare lies at the northern end of the **Clare Valley**, renowned as one of South Australia's premium wine-producing regions. Close enough to Adelaide to be accessible to day-trippers, the picturesque valley offers a full range of accommodation. Settled in 1842, the town is named after County Clare in Ireland.

MAIN ATTRACTIONS: Many National Trust-classified buildings can be seen on the **historic town walk**, including the **Old Police Station Museum** in Neagles Rock Rd, which holds memorabilia and early records of the district. There are a number of shady parks perfect for picnics and BBQ's, and walking trails at **Inchiquin Lake**, Clare's main water-

Eyre Peninsula oysters are popular on the Seafood and Aquaculture Trail between Ceduna and Whyalla

storage area. Not too far from the town centre, **Billy Goat Hill** provides good views of the region.
NEARBY ATTRACTIONS: Many appealing galleries and restaurants can be found throughout the Clare Valley. There are tours of the working **Bungaree Sheep Station**, which was established in 1841. Most popular, of course, are the celebrated **Clare Valley Wineries**. The first vines planted were at **Sevenhill**, 7km south of Clare, by a Jesuit priest from Austria. Now there are more than 30 wineries in the valley, including **Tim Adams, Knappstein, Eldredge, Wilson Vineyard, Stringy Brae, Mitchell, Crabtree of Watervale, Olssen** and **Taylors**. The **Clare Valley Riesling Trail**, a pathway suitable for cyclists and walkers, runs 27km from Clare to **Auburn** and is an ideal way to experience the picturesque countryside. A few kilometres from historic **Mintaro** is **Martindale Hall**, one of South Australia's finest mansions. It offers accommodation and meals.
VISITOR INFORMATION: Main North Rd, Ph: (08) 8842 2131 or 1800 242 131

Coffin Bay   POP 430
Map 348, B1

This delightful holiday retreat and fishing village is located 51km north-west of **Port Lincoln**. Coffin Bay was named in 1802 by Matthew Flinders to honour Sir Isaac Coffin. Ironically, many shipwrecks and drownings have occurred on the exposed coastline. In the 1840s, oysters and scale fish were harvested and shipped to markets in Adelaide. Oyster farming is now important to the community.
MAIN ATTRACTIONS: The 12km **Oyster Walk** along the foreshore to **Long Beach** gives an excellent view of the entire bay. It provides an opportunity for visitors and locals to relax and enjoy the picturesque coastline with seats, pergolas and BBQ facilities along the way. Watersports, relaxing on the beach or in charter boats are the main attractions of Coffin Bay.
NEARBY ATTRACTIONS: **Coffin Bay NP** is a diverse landscape ranging from ancient granite hills and outcrops, high windswept sandstone and limestone cliffs, mobile sand dune systems and long white beaches

with pounding surf to the sheltered waters of **Yangie** and Coffin Bay. Bushwalking, camping, boating, swimming in sheltered waters and guided 4-wheel drive tours are all popular activities in the area.
VISITOR INFORMATION: Beachcomber Mobil Service Station, Esplanade, Ph: (08) 8685 4057

Coober Pedy   POP 2770
Map 341, J5

Coober Pedy, known as **'Australia's opal mining capital'**, is a modern mining town. It is well-known for its unusual 'dugouts'—underground accommodation which enables the inhabitants to escape scorching summer heat. The Aboriginal name, 'Kupa piti', means 'uninitiated man' or 'white man in hole'.
MAIN ATTRACTIONS: With two hotels, the aboveground **Opal Inn** and underground **Desert Cave**, as well as other accommodation, Coober Pedy caters well for visitors. Experience the underground mining museums, mine tours and opal cutting demonstrations on a range of tours of the town. Attractions include the **Old Timers Mine** off Crowders Gully Rd; **Umoona Opal Mine and Museum** on Hutchison St; **Coober Pedy Underground Pottery**; **Underground Books & Gallery**; and the **Big Winch Lookout**, accessed off Italian Club Rd, which is spectacular after dark. Visitors can go 'noodling', that is searching through mullocks (mounds of dirt and rock) for overlooked pieces of opal at the **Public Fossicking Area** off Old Watertank Rd. It is forbidden to enter the main opal fields.
NEARBY ATTRACTIONS: **Breakaways Reserve**, 23km north on the Sturt Hwy, protects an area featuring unique flora and fauna, best viewed at sunrise or sunset. Visitors are requested to stay on the marked tracks, as the ecosystem is very fragile. An entry pass is required,

Sunrise at Coffin Bay National Park

South Australia

Underground church at Coober Pedy

available from the visitor centre and other places in Coober Pedy.

VISITOR INFORMATION:
Council Offices, Hutchison St,
Ph: 1800 637 076

▦ Cowell POP 767
Map 346, D6

Located on **Franklin Harbour**, Cowell was first settled in 1853; the town was known as Flinders Lakes until 1880. Nearby **Minbrie Ranges** have large deposits of jade. Local industry includes jade and granite mining and processing, agriculture, and aquaculture based on oyster, snapper and kingfish farming in Franklin Harbour.

MAIN ATTRACTIONS: Watersports are popular, including swimming, sailing and fishing for snapper and King George whiting. The old Post Office is home to **Franklin Harbour Historical Museum**. Restored by the National Trust, the museum displays old photographs, documents, books, memorabilia and geological specimens. There is an open-air **Agricultural Museum** on the Lincoln Hwy, and a restored Ruston Proctor steam tractor in the parklands opposite the St John Ambulance building. With a large percentage of South Australia's oysters grown in Cowell, dining on fresh seafood is popular.

NEARBY ATTRACTIONS: **Franklin Harbour Conservation Park** is south of Cowell and has great fishing, swimming and picnic spots. Both north and south of Cowell there are beaches worth visiting—**Lucky Bay** (16km north) and **The Knob** (13km south). Seals are often seen at **Point Price**, south of Cowell.

VISITOR INFORMATION: Main St,
Ph: (08) 8629 2588

▦ Crystal Brook POP 1325
Map 346, E5

Proclaimed in 1874, Crystal Brook is located where the southern **Flinders Ranges** begin. Today, the rolling plains surrounding this quiet, picturesque country town produce barley and wheat as well as sheep and cattle.

MAIN ATTRACTIONS: The National Trust **Old Bakehouse Museum** on Brandis St displays pioneering artefacts, photographs and memorabilia. It also has an underground baker's oven, a relic of the building's original purpose. Local crafts are available at **Reflections Gallery** in Bowman St. Both of the town's hotels were built in the 1800s, and there are many attractive old stone homes to wander past. Picnic and BBQ areas are found in **Adelaide Square**—in the centre of Crystal Brook—and in **Jubilee Park**.

NEARBY ATTRACTIONS: 5km east are the remains of historic **Bowman Homestead**, which has been incorporated into **Bowman Park**, an attractive recreation area with extensive facilities, including marked bushwalking tracks and a section of the superb **Heysen Trail**. At **Redhill**, 25km away, the riverside walk, museum, craft shop and antique shop are the main attractions.

VISITOR INFORMATION: 3 Mary Elie St, Port Pirie, Ph: (08) 8633 8700 or 1800 000 424

▦ Edithburgh POP 475
Map 348, E2

Located at the heel of the **Yorke Peninsula**, Edithburgh is an attractive tourist and fishing township overlooking **Gulf St Vincent** and **Troubridge Island**. The town enjoys a reputation for the high standard of food available in local restaurants. Settled in the 1870s, the first two hotels— **Troubridge** and **Edithburgh**—are still standing in their original form. Edithburgh was once the centre of a thriving salt extraction industry based around **Lake Fowler**, one of many salt lakes in the region.

MAIN ATTRACTIONS: **Edithburgh Museum** concentrates on the official maritime history of the town as well as the history of salt extraction and the settlement's pioneers. The 17ha **Native Flora Park** on Ansty Tce, located near the town centre, is a haven for plants and birdlife. Of interest are the **town jetty** built in 1873 and the natural tidal pool.

NEARBY ATTRACTIONS: **Innes NP** is an easy drive to the south-west tip of the peninsula and is famous for its magnificent coastal scenery and wildflowers in spring. Guided tours of Troubridge Island are available and visitors can marvel at the array of resident seabirds, including little penguins. For keen anglers, **Troubridge Point** offers catches of tommy ruff, mullet and whiting, as well as stunning views of the notorious shipwreck-littered coastline where the *Clan Ranald* and *Iron King* went down.
VISITOR INFORMATION: Cnr Weaver St and Towler St, Stansbury, Ph: (08) 8852 4577

■ Elliston   POP 300

Map 345, K6

This is a small seaside town on the shores of **Waterloo Bay**, 640km north-west of Adelaide, on the western side of **Eyre Peninsula**. Originally named Ellie's Town in 1878, after a governess for a local pioneering family, it was the port from which early settlers shipped their wool and wheat. Elliston received a boost in the 1960s, when Asian and Tahitian divers were brought in to harvest the offshore abalone beds. It is now the centre of a cereal-growing, mixed farming and fishing community.
MAIN ATTRACTIONS: The heritage-listed **Elliston Jetty**, built in 1900, is a great fishing spot, with catches of tommy ruff at dusk, and squid, garfish and trevally during the day. **Elliston Hall Historical Mural** covers 500m² of wall space around the town hall and is believed to be the largest mural in the Southern Hemisphere.
NEARBY ATTRACTIONS: Elliston's **Great Ocean View Drive** provides spectacular views of the rugged coastline around Waterloo Bay and **Anxious Bay**, as well as **Waldegrave Island** and **Flinders Island** out to sea. Waldegrave Island is a sanctuary for Cape Barren

Cliffs at Venus Bay Conservation Park, north-west of Elliston

geese, seals and little penguins. **Blackfellows** is one of Australia's finest surfing breaks. The Elliston area is famous for salmon fishing, especially at **Locks Well** and **Sheringa Beach**, to the south-east, and the **Australian Salmon Fishing Championships** are held here annually in mid year. The pure white sandhills at **Walker's Rocks**, 13km north, provide sand-boarding fun. **Lake Newland Conservation Park**, 29km north, is a wetland habitat for wild ducks, painted snipe and many other waterbirds. **Talia Caves**, 45km north, is an area of coloured sandstone and granite outcrops, with caverns and craters that have been sculptured by the sea, and excellent beach and rock-fishing. **Venus Bay Conservation Park**, further north, has dramatic cliffs. A 73km round trip from Elliston to the north-east takes in **Mount Wedge**, formed from a rare variety of granite, and surrounded by deer and almond farms.
VISITOR INFORMATION: Town Hall, 6 Memorial Dr, Ph: (08) 8687 9200

■ Eudunda   POP 615

Map 349, F1

Eudunda is in the rich farming area of the **Lower Mid North**. It grew from a watering stop for stock brought overland from Queensland and New South Wales en route to Adelaide (the town's fresh-water springs attracted the drovers).
MAIN ATTRACTIONS: **Eudunda Town Walk** passes by many heritage homes and public buildings, including historic **Laucke Flour Mill**. Maps of the walk are available from **Eudunda Roadhouse**. A lifesize sculpture of **Colin Thiele**, poet and writer of children's books, who was born in Eudunda, is in **Centenary Gardens** opposite the **Memorial Town Gardens**. Energetic visitors may want to climb the 100 steps to the top of the **town lookout** and view the wheat and grazing lands and mallee scrub extending east towards the **River Murray**.
NEARBY ATTRACTIONS: At **Point Pass**, a small town ten minutes north, the **Old Emmanuel College, manse** and **church**, are a reminder of the

religious strength of the settlement years. **Burra Creek Gorge** picnic and camping grounds, 25 minutes north of Eudunda via Point Pass and heading towards **Burra**, is a nature lover's paradise with small waterfalls and wildlife.

VISITOR INFORMATION: Eudunda Roadhouse, Sth Terrace Rd, Ph: (08) 8581 1061

Freeling   POP 1145
Map 349, F1

Freeling is located at the northern edge of the **Barossa Valley**, close to **Gawler** and only 60km from Adelaide. It has an agricultural machinery manufacturer, stockfeed mill and other small industries.

MAIN ATTRACTIONS: Freeling's old stone buildings date back to the 1860s and are definitely worth a look. **Freeling Railway Precinct** has several buildings of historical interest. The town has been a film location for the TV series *McLeod's Daughters* and featured buildings such as **Gungellan Hotel** (formerly Railway Hotel) attract sightseers.

NEARBY ATTRACTIONS: The attractions of **Kapunda** and Gawler are just a short drive away, as are many world-class wineries of the Barossa Valley and Eden Valley.

VISITOR INFORMATION: Council Offices, 12 Hanson St, Ph: (08) 8525 2028

Gawler   POP 16 800
Map 301, F1

Around 40km north-east of Adelaide, Gawler began as a supply centre for the copper-mining towns of **Kapunda** and **Burra**. In the 1870s and 1880s, when entrepreneurs built flour mills to process grain grown by pioneer agriculturalists, the town boomed. The rural depression at the beginning of the 20th century hastened its decline and in the 1930s Great Depression, Gawler's manufacturing industries closed. However, due to its strategic position, Gawler survived and today is an important commercial centre for the surrounding farmlands.

MAIN ATTRACTIONS: Gawler's walking routes are popular, the **Church Hill State Heritage Area Walk** being a very interesting walk through the original town centre. An **Historic Hotels of Gawler Walking Tour** takes in ten old pubs. The busy Sunday **Lions Market** at **Gawler Railway Station** attracts many shoppers and browsers. The **National Trust and Gawler Heritage Museum** has interesting exhibits. **Para Para Historic Mansion** can be viewed from Penrith Ave.

NEARBY ATTRACTIONS: The wineries of the **Barossa Valley** are only a 15 minute drive to the east. **Roseworthy Campus, University of Adelaide**, was established in 1883 as Australia's first agricultural teaching college and research centre. Today the college is famous for its wine industry research. **Dryland Farming Museum**, located on the campus, is open Wednesdays and the third Sunday of every month, although tours can be arranged at other times by appointment.

VISITOR INFORMATION: 2 Lyndoch Rd, Ph: (08) 8522 6814

Gladstone   POP 650
Map 347, F5

Originally there were two separate towns—Gladstone (east) and **Booyoolee** (west)—which officially merged in 1940. In earlier times, Gladstone was an important railway junction, but more recently it has grown as the hub of a prosperous farming and pastoral community. The silos here are South Australia's largest inland grain storage facilities, capable of holding 600 000 tonnes of grain from the region.

MAIN ATTRACTIONS: The lovely old sandstone homes and historic gaol are favourite points of interest. **Gladstone Gaol** was built in the 1880s and is well worth visiting.

NEARBY ATTRACTIONS: **Beetaloo Valley** offers scenic drives to picnic grounds at **Beetaloo Reservoir**, the **Heysen Trail** and **Bundaleer Forest Reserve**, which has excellent walks and picnic areas.

VISITOR INFORMATION: Southern Flinders Discovery Centre, 14 Gladstone Rd, Ph: (08) 8662 2226

Goolwa   POP 4340
Map 337, E2

Located on the **River Murray**, Goolwa is a popular holiday town within easy reach of Adelaide. This charming old river port is steeped in steam and riverboat history. In its heyday between the 1850s and the 1880s, Goolwa was a prosperous port where riverboats from New South Wales and Victoria unloaded. From here, wool and grain were shipped to Victor Harbor, Port Adelaide and beyond. However, this early prosperity did not last after the Morgan to Port Adelaide railway opened in 1878 and the river trade on the lower reaches dwindled.

MAIN ATTRACTIONS: Goolwa is a haven for watersports like fishing, windsurfing, yachting, jet skiing and power boating. There are many well-preserved stone and brick buildings and history-lovers will enjoy the **heritage walks**; details at the information centre. **Signal Point River Murray Centre** showcases all facets of the river's history, open daily.

Sailing on the River Murray, Goolwa

Renowned for its rugged mountain scenery and deep gorges, this is a land of legends, telling tales of adventure, hardship, success and failure. The ancient landscape of the Flinders Ranges has constantly been re-shaped over the ages—from the buckled seafloor layers of an ancient ocean that was the edge of Australia, 800 to 500 million years ago. The superb **Brachina Gorge Geological Trail** offers up secrets of the history of the Earth from the time when animals first evolved. Embedded in the walls of the Gorge are fossil impressions of the oldest marine animals on earth, indicating that this was once an ancient seabed.

For more than 40 000 years Aboriginal people lived in this area; ceremonial grounds, cave paintings and carvings testify to their cultural and spiritual links with the land.

There are a great many natural attractions to explore in the Flinders region, including vast salt lakes, historic mining areas, rock formations and a range of flora and fauna—some of it rare.

main attractions

- Arkaroola Wilderness Sanctuary
- Flinders Ranges National Park
- Vulkathunha-Gammon Ranges National Park
- Wilpena Pound

i Visitor information

Wadlata Outback Centre/Flinders Ranges and Outback Interpretive Centre
41 Flinders Tce,
Port Augusta, SA 5700
Ph: (08) 8642 4511, Freecall: 1800 633 060
www.portaugusta.sa.gov.au

Cazneaux Tree, near Wilpena, Flinders Ranges National Park

NEARBY ATTRACTIONS: The famous **Cockle Train** runs to Victor Harbor on weekends and school holidays. A visit to **Hindmarsh Island** gives visitors a feel for the Aboriginal and colonial heritage of the area. A bridge links the island to the mainland. The long expanse of **Coorong NP** stretches to **Kingston SE**. This unique wetland area's name is from the Aboriginal word 'karangh', meaning 'narrow neck'. The national park, which was featured in the film *Storm Boy*, comprises a chain of saltwater lagoons separated from the sea by the narrow **Younghusband Peninsula**. Boat cruises are available to the **Murray Mouth** and the Coorong region.
VISITOR INFORMATION: Signal Point, The Wharf, Ph: (08) 8555 3488

■ Hawker   POP 350
Map 313, B3
This is an ideal base from which to explore the stunning scenery of the **Flinders Ranges** and surrounding area. Hawker was proclaimed in 1880, and was once a thriving railway town. This role changed in the mid 1950s when the railway line was moved further west. Hawker then became more tourist-orientated, offering accommodation and services for people visiting the Flinders Ranges.
MAIN ATTRACTIONS: **Fred Teague's Museum** at Hawker Motors has a display of fossils, minerals and pioneer memorabilia. Historic buildings of the town are identified in the **Hawker Heritage Walk** pamphlet, and include the **Post Office**, **Hawker Hotel** and the old **Railway Station**.

NEARBY ATTRACTIONS: **Jarvis Hill**, 6km south-west, has a walking track and lookout. There are fine views from **Yourambulla Caves**, 11km south, which also contain Aboriginal rock art. The ruins of **Kanyaka Homestead** are a good example of the region's abandoned settlements. **Flinders Ranges NP** has the spectacular landscapes of **Wilpena Pound**, as well as **Brachina** and **Bunyeroo** gorges. Further north are **Parachilna Gorge**, the **Leigh Creek Coalfields** and **Aroona Dam**. A popular tourist route, the **Moralana Scenic Drive** links the roads to **Wilpena Pound** and **Leigh Creek**. There are scenic flights from **Rawnsley Park** and Wilpena.
VISITOR INFORMATION: Hawker Motors, cnr Cradock Rd and Wilpena Rd, Ph: (08) 8648 4014

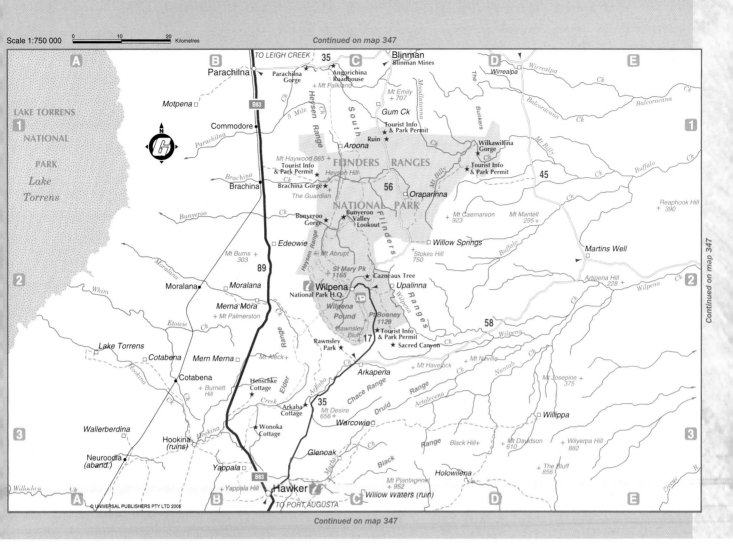

Scale 1:750 000   0   10   20   Kilometres

Continued on map 347

Continued on map 347

Continued on map 347

▦ Jamestown   POP 1460

Map 347, F5

Around 205km from Adelaide,
Jamestown serves a prosperous area
in the state's **Mid North**. Farmers
here produce sheep, cattle, wheat,
barley and legumes. Timber from
pine and eucalypt plantations at
nearby **Bundaleer Forest** is also
important to the local economy. Sir
James Fergusson, Governor of South
Australia 1869–1873, named the
town after himself.

MAIN ATTRACTIONS: The **National Trust
Museum** preserves the past in the
old Railway Station complex.
Displays include mementos of the
district's pioneering days as well as
vintage railway equipment. There
are self-guided **town** and **cemetery
walks** worth taking. **Belalie Creek**,
a beautiful, permanent watercourse,

flows through Jamestown and
creates a pleasant setting for
picnics and BBQs.

NEARBY ATTRACTIONS: **Bundaleer
Forest Reserve**, established in
1875, is 9km south of Jamestown.
Here, forest walks, picnics and
BBQs are popular, and there is a
playground for children.
Bushwalkers using the **Heysen
Trail** may come upon the restored
Curnow's Hut, which is available
as accommodation. The **Old
Bundaleer Homestead**, a classic
rural mansion, is also located in
the reserve. Beyond the forest,
New Campbell Hill provides
panoramic views towards **Mount
Remarkable**.

VISITOR INFORMATION: Country Retreat
Caravan Park, 103 Ayr St,
Ph: (08) 8664 0077

▦ Kadina   POP 3772

Map 346, E6

The largest of the three towns on
the **Yorke Peninsula** which make
up the **Copper Coast**, Kadina was
proclaimed in 1862, after the discovery of copper ore nearby. The
mines in the area were productive
for about 60 years; they closed in
the 1920s, and Kadina became the
peninsula's regional service centre,
with wheat, barley and sheep
forming the basis of its prosperity.

MAIN ATTRACTIONS: Old stone buildings—hotels, churches, houses and
mine sites have all been preserved
and can be viewed on the **Kadina
Heritage Trail**. The trail takes in 38
historic sites and begins at the
Railway Station, heads west to
Wallaroo Mine Historic Site and
then returns to the town centre via

the **National Dryland Farming Centre**. The centre includes **Matta House**, an original mine manager's house built in 1863, and thematic and photographic displays. Kadina's **Banking and Currency Museum** is an award-winning display of banking history located in a splendid old bank building in Graves St.

NEARBY ATTRACTIONS: The biennial **Kernewek Lowender (Cornish Festival)** is held in May of odd numbered years. This is a joint festival of the three towns of the Copper Coast celebrating their Cornish heritage. Kadina, **Wallaroo** and **Moonta** together attract thousands of visitors for a three-day long festival of fairs, dancing, games and processions. The **Yorke Peninsula Field Days** are also held biennially in September of odd numbered years at **Paskeville**, to the south-east. The Copper Coast is renowned for its excellent fishing, crabbing and safe beaches.

VISITOR INFORMATION: National Dryland Farming Centre, Moonta Rd, Ph: 1800 654 991

▓ Kapunda   POP 2300
Map 349, F1

After green copper ore was discovered in 1842, the town of Kapunda was established in 1845. It is located 80km north of Adelaide on the edge of the **Barossa Valley**. The Great Kapunda Mine opened in 1844 and, in a period of 40 years, produced about 14 000 tonnes of copper ore.

MAIN ATTRACTIONS: The 8m bronze figure, ***Map Kernow***, (son of Cornwall), is a tribute to Cornish miners who arrived in large numbers in the 19th century. There is an excellent **Museum and Mine Interpretation Centre,** in Hill St, that brings the mining heritage to life. It is possible to walk around the mine site. Kapunda's heritage-listed buildings are a striking feature, especially the magnificent cast-iron lacework that adorns them. Many trails, such as the **Mawson Cycling Trail** and **Heysen Walking Trail** may be joined at Kapunda, as well as a Heritage Trail (visitors can walk or drive the trail). **Sir Sidney**

Kidman Trail takes in the cattle king's former home, Eringa, the burial site of his children, and places where he conducted the largest horse sales in the Southern Hemisphere. **Kapunda Gallery** showcases travelling exhibitions and artworks of the region.

NEARBY ATTRACTIONS: A scenic drive links Kapunda with the small town of **Eudunda**, 28km north-east, and continues on to **Morgan** and the **Riverland** region. **Pines Reserve**, 6km north-west, is a good picnic and wildlife-watching spot. **Scholz Park Museum** at Riverton (30km north-west) and historic **Anlaby Station** (16km north-east) are worth visiting. Anlaby Station has restored buildings and beautiful gardens.

VISITOR INFORMATION: Cnr Hill St and Main St, Ph: (08) 8566 2902

▓ Keith   POP 1124
Map 349, H3

Known as the **'Gateway to the Limestone Coast'**, the modern rural town of Keith was once part of the arid **Ninety Mile Desert**. In the 1950s the CSIRO carried out experiments that showed the land could be made to be fertile. Modern farming methods opened up the land to agriculture and now some of the state's leading cattle studs are established in the district.

MAIN ATTRACTIONS: One of the most impressive of the early buildings in Heritage St is the former **Congregational Church** (1910). Built of local stone, it has some original leadlight windows and some new ones portraying pioneering history. The park, in Heritage St, has a rotunda and playground and is popular with visitors. **Circlework** is a striking water feature in Heritage St that symbolises the region's high water table and the importance of irrigation. On the south-east edge of Keith lies **Lions Club Park**, with pleasant picnic areas and a children's playground.

The Cornish festival Kernewek Lowender is celebrated every two years in Kadina and other towns of the Copper Coast, Yorke Peninsula

South Australia

Hope Cottage National Trust and Folk Museum, Kingscote, Kangaroo Island

NEARBY ATTRACTIONS: **Ngarkat Conservation Park** is the largest unspoiled wilderness in the south-east. Native flora and fauna abound in this park, which is ideal for bushwalking and has designated camping areas. **Mount Monster Conservation Park** is a much smaller park, 14km south of town. Here, birds and animals share their home with picnickers. **Kelvin Prowrie Reserve**, 8km to the north, is another good picnic area.
VISITOR INFORMATION: Tolmer Park, 81 North Tce, Bordertown, Ph: (08) 8752 0700

▓ Kimba   POP 690
Map 346, C5
On the Eyre Hwy between Port Augusta and Ceduna, Kimba promotes itself as **'halfway across Australia'**, although this is not entirely accurate. Kimba was proclaimed in 1914, after mallee was cleared to make way for the planting of wheat. Before then, huge sheep and cattle properties,

established by settlers in the late 1800s, occupied the land.
MAIN ATTRACTIONS: The **Halfway Across Australia Gem Shop** is identified by an 8m-high pink and grey galah, an attraction that provides natural and cut rocks, gemstones and souvenirs. The main street, **High St**, is lined with shops and cafes, including the **Pine 'n' Pug Gallery**. The interior of **Kimba Community Hotel** is well worth a look. Experience a Pioneer House, school and blacksmith's shop at **Kimba Historical Museum**.
NEARBY ATTRACTIONS: **Gawler Ranges NP** is not far to the north-west of Kimba and can be visited in a day; take in the natural beauty and prolific birdlife of this area. **Pinkawillinie Conservation Park**, to the west, is a favourite with birdwatchers and bushwalkers. On the highway, 19km east of Kimba, **Lake Gilles Conservation Park** is a protected habitat for a variety of birdlife, including mallee fowl; activities in the park are restricted to picnicking and bushwalking.
VISITOR INFORMATION: Kimba Mobil Roadhouse, Eyre Hwy, Ph: (08) 8627 2040

▓ Kingscote   POP 1670
Map 317, D2
The largest town on **Kangaroo Island** (110km south-west of Adelaide), Kingscote was actually the first European settlement in the state (1836). The island can be accessed from **Cape Jervis** to **Penneshaw** via the *Kangaroo Island SeaLink* vehicular ferry, or by air from Adelaide to Kingscote.
MAIN ATTRACTIONS: For a historic look at Kingscote, wander by **Hope Cottage National Trust and Folk Museum**; **St Alban's Church** with stained-glass windows and pioneer memorials; and **Kingscote Cemetery**, the oldest in the State. The carved-out **Rock Pool** is a good swimming spot; for fishing try the jetty, which is great for squid,

tommy ruff, trevally, garfish, whiting and snook. Tours to see little penguins depart from **Ozone Seafront Hotel**. **Kangaroo Island Marine Centre** at **Kingscote Wharf** has displays of seahorses, sea anemones and wrasse, daily pelican feeding and penguin tours.
NEARBY ATTRACTIONS: Kangaroo Island's national park and conservation areas abound with opportunities to swim, surf, dive and fish. There are options of joining a guided coach or surf tour, 4-wheel drive adventure, wilderness excursion, fishing trip or diving charter. On the west of the island is pristine **Flinders Chase NP**, a sanctuary for some of the country's rarest wildlife. There are guided tours to **Seal Bay**, **Kelly Hill Caves**, **Cape Borda** and **Cape Willoughby**. About 20km south on Wilson Rd is a **eucalyptus oil distillery** and slightly further on is **Clifford's Honey Farm**. For spectacular views, it is worth the 50km journey to **Prospect Hill Lookout**. There are many other attractions on the island, including **Penneshaw Maritime and Folk Museum**, **Island Pure Sheep Dairy**, **Parndarna Soldier Settlement Museum**, **Parndarna Wildlife Park**, **Roo Lagoon Gallery**, **Hanson Bay Koala Sanctuary**, **A Maze 'N' Fun** and two **wineries**.
VISITOR INFORMATION: Howard Dr, Penneshaw, Ph: (08) 8553 1185 or 1800 811 080

▓ Kingston SE   POP 1575
Map 323, B2
On the shores of **Lacepede Bay**, this is a regional centre for an area producing sheep, lambs, cattle and crops, with some diversification into viticulture, horticulture and aquaculture. Crayfishing is also an important part of the economy. It is known as Kingston SE (South East) to avoid confusion with Kingston-on-Murray.

KANGAROO ISLAND

The third largest island off the Australian coastline, Kangaroo Island is 155km long and 55km at its widest point—many visitors are surprised by its large size and its scenic beauty. Its reputation as a haven for native wildlife and flora is well deserved, with 30% of its total area covered by national parks.

Even in the peak summer season, the island's size protects it from feeling crowded, although its small townships swell considerably. It offers a relaxed lifestyle and endless opportunities for water-based activities such as fishing, swimming, sailing, surfing, scuba diving and boating. Wildlife is very visible with the opportunity to see little penguins, Australian sea-lions, New Zealand fur seals, platypus, 257 bird species, an abundance of koalas, and the kangaroos after which the island is named.

main attractions

- Cape Borda Lighthouse
- Cape Willoughby Lighthouse
- Emu Bay
- Flinders Chase National Park
- Kangaroo Island Marine Centre
- Kingscote
- Little penguin tours
- Prospect Hill Lookout
- Remarkable Rocks
- Seal Bay Conservation Park
- Stokes Bay

i Visitor information

Gateway Information Centre
Howard Dr,
Penneshaw, SA 5222
Ph: (08) 8553 1185, Freecall: 1800 811 080
www.tourkangarooisland.com.au

Australian sea-lion, *Neophoca cinerea*, at Seal Bay Conservation Park

---

MAIN ATTRACTIONS: Fishing is a major attraction with good catches of a variety of species possible from the surf, jetty or a boat. The **National Trust Pioneer Museum** is worth seeing, as are **Lions Park**, **Apex Park** and the **Aboriginal burial ground** in Dowdy St. Historic **Cape Jaffa Lighthouse** was moved to the foreshore in 1975 from Margaret Brock Reef. The lighthouse is usually open for inspection on weekends and school holidays.
NEARBY ATTRACTIONS: **Butchers Gap** and **Jip Jip conservation parks** are both within easy reach. A unique rock formation—**The Granites**—is located on a beach about 18km north. **Coorong NP** is further north and is renowned for the prolific birdlife on **Younghusband Peninsula**. There are scenic drives

throughout the region, and **Mount Scott Conservation Park**, 20km to the east, has good walking trails. The **Mount Benson Wineries** are near the highway to Robe.
VISITOR INFORMATION: Little's BP Roadhouse, Princes Hwy,
Ph: (08) 8767 2404

▩ Laura   POP 520
Map 347, F5
Located near the southern slopes of the **Flinders Ranges**, the small township of Laura is situated beside the **Rocky River**. Author and poet **C J Dennis** spent his boyhood here when his father owned the long-gone Beetaloo Hotel. Laura is a service town for the surrounding rural area, but cottage crafts and tourism also play an important role in the local economy.

MAIN ATTRACTIONS: A **walking tour** takes you to places of special interest in the town, including the charming little **Court House** and the **old brewery**, which is now B&B accommodation. Some early buildings have become galleries and antique shops, and Laura boasts a silversmith, shoemaker and potter. You can taste South Australia's famous **Golden North Ice Cream**, which is made in Laura, at **The Laura Beehive** on Herbert St. For picnicking and BBQs, there are facilities beside the Rocky River and lawns alongside the **Civic Centre**. In April the town hosts a large folk fair.
NEARBY ATTRACTIONS: **Beetaloo Reservoir** is around 15km west and is a picturesque recreation area with picnic and BBQ facilities. It is also a

South Australia

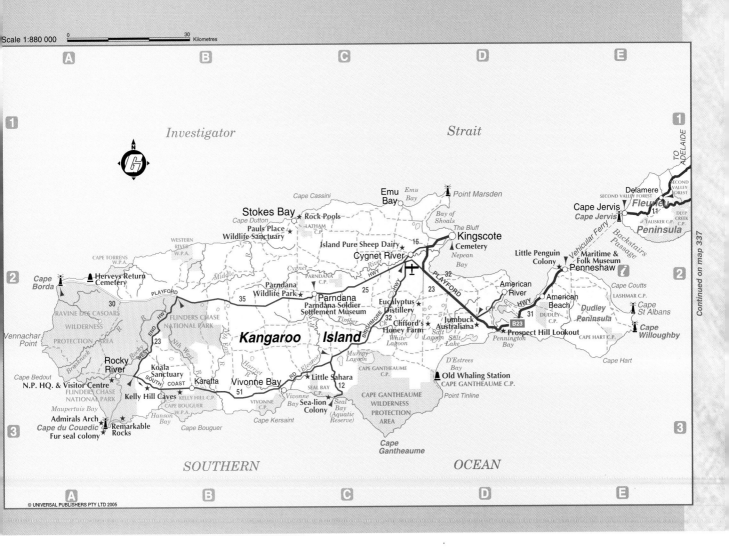

Investigator   Strait

SOUTHERN   OCEAN

good spot for birdwatching. **Laura Lookout**, in the ranges about 5km west of town, also has picnic facilities and a lovely view of the town and scenic **Beetaloo Valley** countryside.

VISITOR INFORMATION: The Laura Beehive, 51 Herbert St, Ph: (08) 8663 2419

Loxton   POP 3360

Map 333, C3

Loxton is a **'garden town'** in the **Riverland** region and is one of the area's most prosperous centres. Located on the south bank of the **River Murray** and surrounded by vineyards, fruit orchards and olive groves, Loxton was proclaimed in 1907 and has grown significantly since. The post-WWII Soldier Settlement Scheme contributed to its growth.

MAIN ATTRACTIONS: The Murray River provides opportunities for many recreational activities including camping, fishing, swimming, cruising, waterskiing and canoeing. **Loxton Historical Village** is an award-winning attraction of more than 30 fully furnished buildings on the riverfront. Loxton's **Heritage Walk** is definitely worth the effort.

NEARBY ATTRACTIONS: The River Murray scenery that surrounds Loxton is perfect for picnics. **Banrock Station Wine and Wetland Centre**, on Holmes Rd, **Kingston-on-Murray**, has magnificent views over restored wetlands, wine tasting, a cafe, walking trails, boardwalk and bird-watching hides. Several **wineries** can be found in the Riverland region.

VISITOR INFORMATION: Bookpurnong Tce, Ph: (08) 8584 7919

Lyndoch   POP 1240

Map 327, A5

Located on the south-west edge of the **Barossa Valley**, Lyndoch is the first of the Barossa towns to be reached by most visitors, only one hour from Adelaide. Lyndoch is named after Lord Lynedoch, a friend of Colonel Light who carried out the first survey of the valley. Settlers arrived in 1839, and vineyards as well as farms were established in the early years, but the first winery, in a converted flour mill, was not operational until 1896.

MAIN ATTRACTIONS: **Lyndoch Recreation Park** has picnic facilities and a children's playground. The **Stone Mill Wheel** (1855) and other locally quarried ironstone buildings from the mid 1800s can be viewed on a self-guided **historical walk**.

Kies Family Wines, on the Barossa Valley Hwy, has cellar door sales and functions as the local visitor information centre.

NEARBY ATTRACTIONS: Vineyards of all sizes cover the hills around Lyndoch, most of them family owned. Among the many wineries is **Yaldara Wines**, one of the largest in the Barossa. Other well-known wineries include **McGuigan Semillon Rovalley**, **Schild Estate**, **Kellermeister** and **Burge Family Winemakers**. Around 8km south of Lyndoch is the **Barossa Reservoir** with its **Whispering Wall**, which has an amazing acoustic effect—words whispered at one end of the wall are carried to the other end over 100m away and are clearly audible. In **Para Wirra Recreation Park**, explore the old **Barossa Goldfields**. About 7km south-east, **Lyndoch Lavender Farm** grows more than 50 lavender varieties and

produces excellent olive oil in beautiful peaceful surroundings.
VISITOR INFORMATION: Kies Family Wines, Barossa Valley Hwy, Ph (08) 8524 4110

■ Maitland   POP 1050
Map 348, E1

Lying in the golden heart of the **Yorke Peninsula** and serving a prosperous rural community, the Maitland region is rich in limestone soils, which support lambs, barley, wheat and oats. Governor Fergusson named the town after one of his ancestors, Lady Jean Maitland, the wife of Lord Kilkerran of Scotland.

MAIN ATTRACTIONS: Maitland offers a **Town Heritage Walk** that includes significant sites with plaques outside the buildings explaining their history. In particular, **St John's Anglican Church** (1876), in Caroline St, is notable for its beautiful stained-glass windows. **Maitland Museum** is located in a former school (1877)

and features displays of the town's German heritage, agricultural machinery, as well as the history of schools on the Yorke Peninsula. A key, available from the council offices at 8 Elizabeth St, allows access to **Maitland Town Hall**, where a spectacular wool-on-canvas mural, depicting the history of the district, takes pride of place.

NEARBY ATTRACTIONS: A central location for touring the Yorke Peninsula, Maitland isn't far from the seaside towns of **Port Victoria** (west) and **Ardrossan** (east), as well as the Copper Coast towns of **Kadina**, **Moonta** and **Wallaroo**. The coastal town of **Balgowan**, 15km west, is a good fishing spot.

VISITOR INFORMATION: Harvest Corner, 29 Main St, Minlaton, Ph: (08) 8853 2600

■ Mannum   POP 2200
Map 349, G2

Mannum developed as a **River Murray** port in the early days of the river trade, and is known as the **'Birthplace of the Murray River Paddlesteamers'**. It was here, in 1853, that William Randell launched the **PS Mary Ann** and, in doing so, opened up a new era in trade for the colony that eventually involved dozens of paddlesteamers plying Australia's longest river system, the **Murray-Darling**.

MAIN ATTRACTIONS: Popular activities include houseboating, fishing, waterskiing, canoeing and jet skiing. There are week-long and weekend cruises on the **PS Murray Princess**. Randell St in the town centre has attractions such as the **Cottage Window** craft shop, and the **Butter Factory**, selling old wares and bric-a-brac. A lookout at the end of **Crawford Crescent** has scenic river views in both directions. All that is left of the historic paddle-steamer Mary Ann is her boiler, and that is located in **Mannum Dock Museum** at 6 Randell St. Another original paddlesteamer more than a

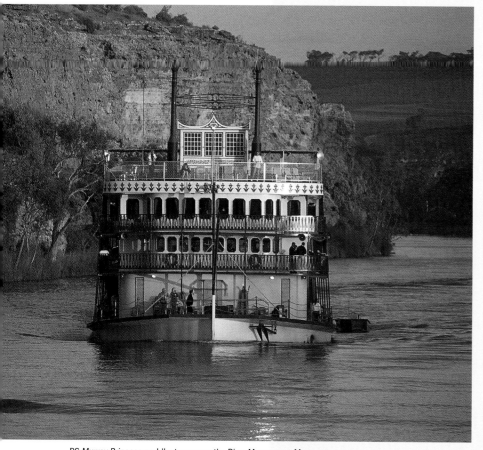

PS *Murray Princess* paddlesteamer on the River Murray near Mannum

South Australia

Australian pelican, *Pelecanus conspicillatus*, Coorong National Park

century old is the wood-fired **PS Marion**, moored off the site of William Randell's original dock at **Arnold Park** near the ferry. She is now restored and open for display and river cruises.

NEARBY ATTRACTIONS: **Mannum Waterfalls**, 10km from town along Murray Bridge Rd, is a pretty place of cascading water over black granite rocks. The 12km strip of swampy land between Purnong Rd and the river is a designated bird sanctuary with a scenic drive—a birdwatcher's paradise. The marina 8km north-east of Mannum is the largest river marina in the state. About 20km north is the excellent scenic drive from **Wongulla** to **Cambrai**.

VISITOR INFORMATION: 6 Randell St, Ph: (08) 8569 1303

Meningie   POP 920
Map 349, G3
Meningie is located on the eastern shore of **Lake Albert**, about 160km from Adelaide. It is a small rural and holiday town, the service centre for

an irrigated fodder-cropping area that also produces wheat, barley, sheep and dairy cows. It is also a thriving fishing town and has an abundance and variety of birdlife.

MAIN ATTRACTIONS: Lake Albert is ideal for watersports like canoeing, waterskiing, windsurfing, sailing, swimming and fishing. **Lions Park** is perfect for a lunchtime picnic or BBQ. The **Cheese Factory** is now a museum and restaurant.

NEARBY ATTRACTIONS: **Coorong NP** is a major district attraction that can be explored on the nature trail at **Salt Creek**. This trail displays the diversity of the national park's environment and passes **Chinaman's Well**, a vital stop on the route taken by Chinese prospectors travelling from South Australia to the Victorian goldfields. Not far from Meningie, on Narrung Rd, is a great pelican-viewing spot.

VISITOR INFORMATION: Council Offices, 49 Princes Hwy, Ph: (08) 8575 1008

Millicent   POP 4720
Map 323, D5
Millicent was proclaimed in 1870, following the drainage of the surrounding land, and named after the wife of an early pioneer. It is centrally situated in the prosperous **Wattle Range** region, about half way between Adelaide and Melbourne. Local industries include forestry, fishing and aquaculture, viticulture, farming and tourism.

MAIN ATTRACTIONS: The **Living History Museum**, in Mount Gambier Rd, is reputed to be one of the best regional museums in South Australia. It features a very large collection of horse-drawn vehicles, as well as maritime, Aboriginal, Victoriana and natural history displays. **Millicent Art Gallery**, at the **Resource Centre**, has changing exhibitions and **Admella Gallery**, adjacent to the Living History Museum and part of the visitor centre, features locally-made arts and crafts.

NEARBY ATTRACTIONS: **Lake McIntyre**, 5km north, is a bird sanctuary with free BBQs, picnic areas, walking trails and hides. **Tantanoola Caves**, 21km south-east, have been carved from a limestone cliff face and offer disabled access. Millicent is the gateway to **Canunda NP**, featuring stunning coastal and lake scenery. Beaches fronting the **Southern Ocean** are a short drive to the west, and the vineyards of the **Coonawarra Wine Region** are about 60km to the north-east.

VISITOR INFORMATION: 1 Mount Gambier Rd, Ph: (08) 8733 3205

Minlaton   POP 750
Map 348, E2
Minlaton was originally known as Gum Flat because of the naturally occurring red gums in this area of the **Yorke Peninsula**. Today it is the commercial centre for a thriving agricultural region. The surrounding district is known as the **'Barley Capital of the World'**.

MAIN ATTRACTIONS: The **National Trust Museum**, **Harry Butler Memorial**, a **fauna park** and **Harvest Corner Information and Craft** are all located on Main St. Minlaton events of note are **Minlaton Agricultural Show** (first Wednesday of October) and the **Minlaton Australiana Night**, held on the Friday before Australia Day.

NEARBY ATTRACTIONS: Several art and craft galleries are located in or near Minlaton. **Port Vincent**, 25km east, and **Port Rickaby**, **The Bluff** and **Barkers Rocks** are good for swimming, fishing and watersports.

VISITOR INFORMATION: Harvest Corner, 29 Main St, Ph: (08) 8853 2600

Moonta   POP 3120
Map 346, E6
Part of the historic **Copper Coast** towns (with **Kadina** and **Wallaroo**), Moonta is located at the northern end of the **Yorke Peninsula**, 163km north-west of Adelaide.

A popular seaside town, with excellent fishing and golden beaches, the town centre is surrounded by parklands and open space with **Queen Square** right in the middle.

MAIN ATTRACTIONS: Moonta has many historic stone buildings, including the **Town Hall** and **All Saints Church**. There are galleries and gift shops to browse and maps are available for self-guided scenic drives and walks around the town and mines.

NEARBY ATTRACTIONS: Both the **Moonta Mines State Heritage Area** and the old primary school, which is now **Moonta Mines National Trust Museum**, showcase mining artefacts and memorabilia as well as the history of the Cornish miners. The **Moonta Mines Railway Tour** goes right through the mine area and is a good way to take in the area's mining heritage. **Wheal Hughes Mine**, about 3km north of Moonta, has tours at 1pm daily; bookings can be made at the mine.

VISITOR INFORMATION: National Dryland Farming Centre, Moonta Rd, Kadina, Ph: 1800 654 991

■ Morgan   POP 520
Map 349, G1

In its heyday Morgan was the largest inland port on the **Murray-Darling** river system, where paddlesteamers met the railway line to Adelaide. Now that the railway line is closed and river traffic is reduced to houseboats and water-skiers, Morgan is a much quieter place. It is a service centre for the local wine, sheep and fruit industries as well as catering for the holiday-home community on the **River Murray**.

MAIN ATTRACTIONS: A self-guided **walking trail** covers Morgan's historic sites, mainly clustered around the **Railway Station** and the remains of the **old jarrah wharf**. **Port of Morgan Museum** is housed in the old Railway Station and displays a paddlesteamer, old engines and a range of memorabilia. Picnic and BBQ facilities are located on the riverfront lawn next to the museum. **Morgan Museum**, on Main St, is even larger, covering the region's history in considerable detail. Remember to stroll along **Railway Tce**, where a charming row of

1880s shops, **Carmine's Antiques** and two pubs are located.

NEARBY ATTRACTIONS: **Morgan Conservation Park** is located on the other side of the river, where basic riverbank camping and fishing are the main attractions. 1km from Morgan on the Blanchetown Rd, there is a fossil quarry where fossickers will often find fossil shells and occasionally a shark's tooth. **White Dam Conservation Park** is 9km north-west of Morgan. **Nor-West Bend Private Museum** is 8km east and has a very large collection of horse-drawn vehicles and buggies.

VISITOR INFORMATION: Shell Roadhouse, 14 Fourth St, Ph: (08) 8540 2205

■ Mount Compass   POP 507
Map 337, D1

Overlooking the **Nangkita** and **Tooperang valleys**, the small farming community of Mount Compass is less than an hour's drive from Adelaide. The district is renowned for its range of agricultural, aquacultural and horticultural products.

MAIN ATTRACTIONS: Local art and craft galleries are worth investigating. Australia's only cow race, **The Compass Cup**, is held in February, and **Mount Compass Agricultural Field Day** in March.

NEARBY ATTRACTIONS: Situated in the heart of the **Fleurieu Peninsula** and nestled between the world-renowned **McLaren Vale wineries** and the beautiful beaches of the southern peninsula, Mount Compass is a perfect holiday centre. Interesting regional attractions include **Protea World**, **Polana Deer Farm**, **Compass Pheasants Deer and Marron Farm**, **Tooperang Rainbow Trout Farm**, **Ambersun Alpacas**, **Alexandrina Cheese Company** and **Amaroo Water Gardens**.

VISITOR INFORMATION: Signal Point, The Wharf, Goolwa, Ph: (08) 8555 3488

Sunrise on the River Murray at Swan Reach, south of Morgan

South Australia

■ Mount Gambier   POP 22 680
Map 323, E5

Located 460km south-east of Adelaide and 450km west of Melbourne, Mount Gambier is located on the slopes of an extinct, three-cratered volcano. The unofficial capital of the **Limestone Coast**, Mount Gambier is at the heart of a rich agricultural district known for its pine plantations, dairy farming, wool, vineyards and meat production.

MAIN ATTRACTIONS: **Centenary Tower**, on the highest point 190m above sea level, overlooks the picturesque craters, which were last active 5000 years ago. **Blue Lake** is believed to be the only lake in the world that changes each year from grey in winter to a brilliant turquoise blue in summer—a road and walking track encircle the lake. A popular tour is the 45 minute **Aquifer Tour**, which takes visitors via a lift and tunnel close to the surface of the lake. Nearby, within **Valley Lake** crater is a wildlife park and boardwalk. A sinkhole in the city centre, **Cave Garden** is renowned for its rose garden, which features heritage roses. **Engelbrecht Cave**, off the Jubilee Hwy, offers tours showing where experienced divers enter the underground water to dive under the city. **Umpherston Sinkhole** has lovely terraced gardens which become a hive of activity at night when possums come out to feed in the floodlight.

NEARBY ATTRACTIONS: **Port MacDonnell**, 30km south, is **'Australia's Southern Rock Lobster Capital'** and a favourite destination for surfers and anglers alike. **Nelson** is 37km south-east of Mount Gambier in Victoria. It offers a range of cruises and recreational activities. Both the **Princess Margaret Rose Cave** and **Tantanoola Caves** are within a 30 minute drive.

VISITOR INFORMATION: *Lady Nelson* Visitor and Discovery Centre, Jubilee Hwy East, Ph: (08) 8724 9750 or 1800 087 187

■ Murray Bridge   POP 13 100
Map 349, G2

This was known as Mobilong, then Edwards Crossing and finally Murray Bridge, when the railway bridge connected both sides of the river in 1924. Whilst the first road bridge was being built—completed in 1879—a community grew to support the builders. It grew rapidly and became an important river port when the railway line linked the paddlesteamer trade with Adelaide in 1885. This rural city is now the centre of a major agricultural region.

MAIN ATTRACTIONS: Murray Bridge has facilities for most sports, particularly water-sports. River cruising and houseboating are popular, as well as the Bunyip in **Sturt Reserve**. The historic **Round House**, overlooking the river, can be visited at weekends. **Captain's Cottage Museum**, in Thomas St, has a collection of farm equipment, pioneering artefacts and historical records. Murray Bridge boasts the smallest cathedral in Australia— **St John the Baptist Anglican Cathedral** on Mannum Rd. The **Art Gallery**, housed in the **Town Hall** on Sixth St, is worth investigating. **Dundee's Wildlife Park**, located nearby, has fresh and saltwater crocodiles, bird aviaries, a nocturnal house and a children's zoo. Riverside reserves such as **Thiele**, **Swanport** and **Avoca Dell** are all good spots for picnics and relaxation. **Puzzle Park**, located on Jervois Rd, has more than 30 fun rides for children.

NEARBY ATTRACTIONS: **Monarto Zoological Park**, on the Old Princes Hwy, is an open-range zoo where a safari bus tours around giraffes, antelopes, bison, cheetahs and other free-roaming animals. Visitors can also stroll along well-defined nature trails. **Willow Point Winery** is 10km south and the historic railway town of **Tailem Bend** is 25km south-east. For beautiful

Alexandra Cave, Naracoorte Caves

surrounds of citrus and stone fruit orchards visit **Mypolonga**, 14km north-east.

VISITOR INFORMATION: 3 South Tce, Ph: (08) 8539 1142

■ Naracoorte   POP 6100
Map 323, E3

Around 330km from Adelaide, Naracoorte is at the heart of the **Limestone Coast** region. Settled in the 1840s, the area is famous for its World Heritage-listed and fossil-filled limestone caves. Primary industries include sheep, beef cattle, grains and vineyards. The name 'Naracoorte' is derived from the Aboriginal word meaning 'drinking waterhole'.

MAIN ATTRACTIONS: For woollen products and history, explore the **Sheep's Back Museum** in

The Limestone Coast, in the south-east corner of South Australia, is rich in natural attractions, with an arc of beaches and lobster-fishing ports stretching along the coastline to the Victorian border. The region, which centres on **Mount Gambier**, is named after its incomparable concentration of limestone craters, caves and cliffs, and offers visitors a range of activities and attractions in a spectacular natural setting.

Volcanic activity sculpted the landscape, with the **Crater Lakes** among its most stunning natural attractions. Inland, the World Heritage-listed **Naracoorte Caves** is a major fossil cave system—re-creations of prehistoric mammals, that once inhabited the caves, are displayed at **Wonambi Fossil Centre**. Limestone also gives the famous **Coonawarra** its terra rossa soil.

main attractions

- Blue Lake
- Camp Coorong
- Coonawarra wine region
- Coorong National Park
- Engelbrecht Cave
- Kingston SE
- Mount Gambier
- Naracoorte Caves
- Robe
- Umpherston Sinkhole

 Visitor information

Lady Nelson **Visitor and Discovery Centre**
Jubilee Hwy East,
Mount Gambier, SA 5290
Ph: (08) 8724 9750 or 1800 087 187
www.mountgambiertourism.com.au

Snorkelling at Ewens Ponds, to the south-east of Mount Gambier

---

MacDonnell St. **Mini Jumbuck Centre**, in Smith St, has woollen bedding products and a viewing gallery. Also in Naracoorte are **Naracoorte Regional Art Gallery**, the oldest in the state; the **Swimming Lake**, with its own beach; and **Tiny Train Park**, a miniature railway.

NEARBY ATTRACTIONS: **Naracoorte Caves NP** is 12km south-east of Naracoorte. The national park was listed in 1994 as a World Heritage site for its extensive fossil deposits. **Wonambi Fossil Centre** has life-like moving models of extinct animals, and the Bat Cave Teleview Centre allows visitors to view the inside of a Bat Cave via infrared cameras. Nearby **Russet Ridge Winery** offers guided tours while the wine regions of **Coonawarra**, **Padthaway** and **Wrattonbully** are all close to Naracoorte. **Bool Lagoon**, an internationally recognised seasonal wetland area with prolific birdlife, is 24km south.

VISITOR INFORMATION: MacDonnell St, Ph: (08) 8762 1399 or 1800 244 421

Normanville   POP 690
Map 337, B2

Established in 1849, the seaside town of Normanville is located near the mouth of the **Bungala River** on the **Fleurieu Peninsula**. In early years, this scenic stretch of coastline witnessed several shipwrecks. Normanville makes up part of a holiday triangle that includes **Yankalilla**, 3km east, and **Carrickalinga**, 2km north. The area is very popular with beach lovers and anglers.

MAIN ATTRACTIONS: The extensive beaches are ideal for swimming, surfing, boating, fishing and horseriding. Walking tracks penetrate the sand dunes behind the beaches, which are heritage listed. There is an historic **Court House** (1855) in Normanville's Main St.

NEARBY ATTRACTIONS: **The Shrine of Our Lady of Yankalilla**, known as 'Australia's Lourdes', attracts many visitors. The scuttling of **HMAS Hobart** in **Yankalilla Bay** provides an excellent wreck dive. **Rapid Bay** is known for its imposing cliffs, caves and beaches and for its long wharf, where anglers love to drop a line. It is also a renowned diving spot.

VISITOR INFORMATION: 104 Main Rd, Yankalilla, Ph: (08) 8558 2999

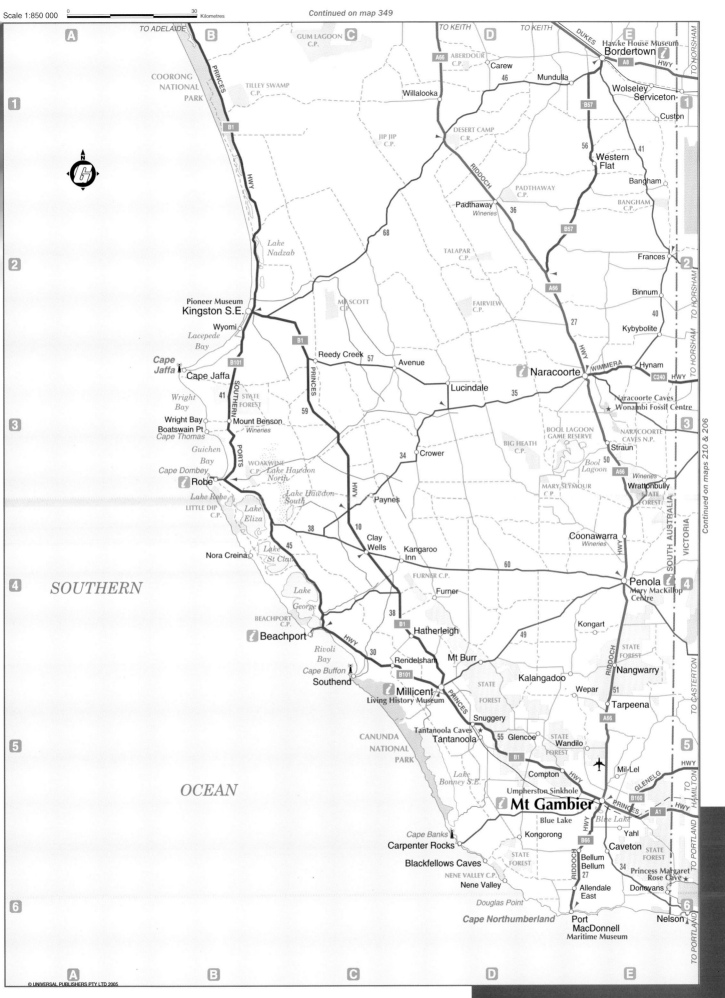

Continued on map 349

SOUTHERN

OCEAN

COORONG
NATIONAL
PARK

TO ADELAIDE

GUM LAGOON
C.P.

TILLEY SWAMP
C.P.

TO KEITH   TO KEITH

Hawke House Museum
Bordertown

Wolseley
Serviceton

Custon

Carew

Mundulla

Willalooka

JIP JIP
C.P.

DESERT CAMP
C.R.

Western
Flat

Bangham

Lake
Nadzab

ABERDOUR
C.P.

PADTHAWAY
C.P.

BANGHAM
C.P.

Padthaway
Wineries

Frances

Binnum

Pioneer Museum
Kingston S.E.

MT SCOTT
C.P.

FAIRVIEW
C.P.

Kybybolite

Wyomi

Lacepede
Bay

Cape
Jaffa
Cape Jaffa

Reedy Creek   57

Avenue

Lucindale

Naracoorte

Hynam

Naracoorte Caves
Wonambi Fossil Centre

Wright
Bay

Wright Bay
Boatswain Pt
Cape Thomas

Mount Benson
Wineries

NARACOORTE
CAVES N.P.

Straun

Crower

BIG HEATH
C.P.

BOOL LAGOON
GAME RESERVE

Bool
Lagoon

Wineries

Guichen
Bay

Cape Dombey

Robe

Lake Hawdon
North

Paynes

Wrattonbully

Lake
Hawdon
South

MARY SEYMOUR
C.P.

Lake Robe

LITTLE DIP
C.P.

Lake
Eliza

Clay
Wells

Kangaroo
Inn

Coonawarra
Wineries

Nora Creina

Lake
St Clair

FURNER C.P.

Furner

Penola
Mary MacKillop
Centre

Kongart

Lake
George

Hatherleigh

Nangwarry

BEACHPORT
C.P.

Beachport

Mt Burr

Kalangadoo

Wepar

Tarpeena

Rivoli
Bay

Cape Buffon

Southend

Rendelsham

STATE
FOREST

Millicent
Living History Museum

Snuggery

Tantanoola Caves
Tantanoola

Glencoe

Wandilo

Mil-Lel

CANUNDA

NATIONAL

PARK

Compton

Umpherston Sinkhole

Mt Gambier

Blue Lake   Blue Lake

Yahl

Lake
Bonney S.E.

Cape Banks
Carpenter Rocks

Blackfellows Caves

NENE VALLEY C.P.

Nene Valley

Kongorong

Caveton

Bellum
Bellum

Princess Margaret
Rose Cave

Donovans

Allendale
East

Douglas Point

Cape Northumberland

Port
MacDonnell
Maritime Museum

Nelson

Nuriootpa   POP 3850

Map 327, D2

Located on the **North Para River** at the northern end of the **Barossa Valley**, Nuriootpa is a commercial and service centre. Production facilities and huge tanks sited alongside the railway line attest to the fact that winemaking is big business here. A viticultural research station is located on the outskirts of town.

MAIN ATTRACTIONS: The early influence of German settlers is still reflected in the food outlets of Nuriootpa, with locally produced food and wine featured on the menus. **Coulthard Reserve**, a short distance from the Para River, is perfect for picnicking. For some local history, drop into **Luhrs Pioneer German Cottage** on Light Pass Rd. **Penfolds Wines** and **Elderton Wines** can be supplied at tasting rooms in Nuriootpa.

NEARBY ATTRACTIONS: Numerous other wineries are located in the Nuriootpa area including **Hamilton's Ewell Vineyards**, **Wolf Blass Wines**, the **Willows Vineyard** and **Gibson's Barossa Vale Wines**.

VISITOR INFORMATION: 66–68 Murray St, Tanunda, Ph: (08) 8563 0600 or 1300 852 982

Orroroo   POP 557

Map 347, F5

Orroroo is a pretty little town lying on the edge of the **Southern Flinders Ranges** and a service centre for the surrounding agricultural region. Proclaimed a town in 1876, the name comes from the Aboriginal word 'oorama', understood to mean 'meeting place of the magpie'.

MAIN ATTRACTIONS: Many beautifully restored 1870s buildings and shopfronts are to be found in Orroroo's wide tree-lined streets including **Yesteryear Costume Gallery** (Adelaide Rd) and **Solly's Hut**, an early pug-and-pine settler's cottage containing furniture and relics from the 1870s (inspection by appointment). **Tank Hill Lookout**, off Pekina Rd, provides scenic views of Orroroo and the surrounding countryside.

NEARBY ATTRACTIONS: Around 12km south of Orroroo lies the 'almost' ghost town of **Black Rock**. A signpost here directs drivers to **Magnetic Hill**, an intriguing natural phenomenon where cars apparently roll uphill when they are stopped on what appears to be a downhill slope. **Pekina Reservoir** can be found by walking along the trail from Lions Picnic and BBQ area. Walkers pass ancient Aboriginal carvings, natural springs and a poem that was carved into a rock in 1896. The walk continues past the remains of **Pekina Homestead**, the district's first permanent settlement.

VISITOR INFORMATION: Orroroo Carrieton Council Offices, Second St, Ph: (08) 8658 1260

Penola   POP 1250

Map 323, E4

The oldest town in the state's south-east, Penola was founded as a travellers' stopover by Alexander Cameron in 1850. It is a service town for the local pastoral and forestry industries and also for the growing number of vineyards at nearby **Coonawarra**. Penola is a destination for lovers of Australian history, with well-preserved and restored colonial buildings. The history of wine in the area goes back to Penola pastoralist John Riddoch and his Coonawarra Fruit Colony establishment of 1890.

MAIN ATTRACTIONS: Australia's already beatified and likely first saint **Mary MacKillop** started her teaching career in Penola, educating the children of settlers regardless of their financial or social position. Memorabilia relating to her can be seen in the **Mary MacKillop Interpretative Centre** and in the **Woods MacKillop Schoolhouse**, both on the corner of Petticoat La and Portland St. **Penola Heritage**

Historic Kaiser Stuhl port barrels can be seen at Penfolds Wines, Nuriootpa

Coonawarra vineyard and river red gum near Penola

Walk begins at the information centre and is a sign-posted trail that passes 33 heritage sites.

NEARBY ATTRACTIONS: Worth a visit is **Yallum Park**, John Riddoch's house built 1878–1880, which is privately owned. Inspection times are available from the visitor information centre. **Penola Conservation Park**, 10km west, has a woodland and wetland walk. The Coonawarra district lies a few kilometres north of Penola and visitors can taste and buy premium red and white table wines at more than 20 cellar door outlets.

VISITOR INFORMATION: 27 Arthur St, Ph: (08) 8737 2855

▓ Peterborough   POP 1860
Map 347, F5

An historic railway town located on the main south-east approach to the **Flinders Ranges**, Peterborough is a popular stop for travellers en route to the ranges and especially for those interested in steam trains. There are four unique hand-made model steam trains located at each of the four entrances to the town. Surrounded by grain-growing and pastoral country, Peterborough is the main service town on the Port Pirie to Broken Hill railway line.

MAIN ATTRACTIONS: An easy way to see the main attractions is on the guided **bus tour**, which leaves from Peterborough Caravan Park. The tour includes the **Gold Battery**, which has been crushing ore for small mines in the region for over 100 years. **Iven Ley's Museum**, in Queen St, is a small museum featuring bottle and mineral collections, memorabilia and a superb display of dolls. **Ranns Museum**, in Moscow St, specialises in working and non-working stationary engines and other artefacts dating to the 1800s. **Steamtown Museum** holds memorabilia in the old railway workshops and is a must for steam train enthusiasts. In Callary St, **St Cecilia** is a 20-room restored mansion with a two-storey coach house. The house is now a private hotel that specialises in Murder Mystery weekends.

NEARBY ATTRACTIONS: The historic railway township of **Terowie** is 24km south-east, and is home to many heritage buildings.

Peterborough is not far from the town of **Black Rock** and the strange **Magnetic Hill**.

VISITOR INFORMATION: Railway Carriage, Main St, Ph: (08) 8651 2708

▓ Pinnaroo   POP 620
Map 349, J2

Pinnaroo is the first South Australian town to be encountered by travellers from New South Wales and Victoria using the Mallee Hwy. This little oasis in the middle of the **Mallee** owes its 'greenness' to the availability of underground water that supports an olive plantation, mixed farming and potato growing. Other primary production in the region includes wheat, barley, poultry, sheep, pigs, lambs and beef cattle.

MAIN ATTRACTIONS: There are a number of pleasant picnic spots and a small fauna park on the corner of South Tce and Mann St. **Mallee Tourist and Heritage Centre** brings together four museum collections; the **Gum Family Collection** of stationary engines and farm equipment; a **Printing Museum**; the **Wurfel Grain Collection**, with 1300 varieties of grain from around the world; and the **Mallee Women** display in the old railway station building.

NEARBY ATTRACTIONS: Pinnaroo makes a good base for those interested in flora and fauna. There are several conservation parks in the area set aside to preserve unique local environments. Walks of varying distances can be taken in **Ngarkat Conservation Park**, a wilderness that adjoins **Scorpion Springs** and **Mount Shaugh conservation parks** to the south, while to the north are **Billiatt** and the smaller **Karte** and **Peebinga conservation parks**. **Murray-Sunset NP** and **Wyperfeld NP** are across the border in Victoria.

VISITOR INFORMATION: Mallee Tourist and Heritage Centre, Railway Tce Sth, Ph: (08) 8577 8644

THE BAROSSA VALLEY

Although relatively small in area, the Barossa Valley is Australia's best-known wine region. Each year thousands of visitors tour the region, tasting the wines and making cellar-door purchases.

The Barossa's Mediterranean-type climate and differing soils make it an ideal place for growing diverse varieties of grapes, producing consistently high quality wines. German immigrants initially settled the region and, in 1847, the valley's first vines were planted at the **Orlando vineyards**.

While the Barossa Valley boasts more than 60 wineries, ranging from household names such as **Penfolds** to boutique wineries like **Charles Melton** and **Grant Burge Cellars**, the region also offers lots of other attractions, including its history and scenery. This lovely, closely settled valley is sprinkled with small Lutheran churches, yet another legacy of the German settlers who escaped religious persecution. Also, there are quaint townships featuring antique stores, bakeries and old-fashioned pubs.

The Barossa Valley's proximity to Adelaide makes it an ideal daytrip destination, and with a range of great accommodation options and attractions available, it is worthwhile staying a few days.

main attractions

◈ **Angaston**

This small rural town in the Barossa Valley is close to some of the Barossa's oldest wineries.

◈ **Bethany Wines**

Located in an old quarry, Bethany produces wine and port.

◈ **Lyndoch**

One of South Australia's oldest towns, Lyndoch was settled in 1839. Although wine has always been produced here, wheat was the primary crop until 1896.

◈ **Penfolds Wines**

Established in 1844, Penfolds is the Barossa's largest winery, showcasing some of Australia's best-known wines.

◈ **Seppeltsfield**

Founded in 1851, this winery is perhaps the Barossa's most spectacular.

◈ **Wolf Blass Wines**

This winery produces prize-winning wines of consistent quality.

◈ **Yaldara Wines**

Specialising in sweet and sparkling European-style wines and tawny ports, this famous winery is near Lyndoch.

i Visitor information

Barossa Wine and Visitor Information Centre
66-68 Murray St, Tanunda, SA 5352
Ph: (08) 8563 0600 or 1300 852 982
www.barossa-region.org

Procession during the Barossa Vintage Festival

Barossa Festivals

German influence is very much alive in some of the Barossa festivals. The biennial **Barossa Vintage Festival**, held from Easter Monday during odd-numbered years, attracts more than 100 000 people. Other festivals in the region include **Barossa Under the Stars** (March), **Melodienacht** (May) and **Barossa International Music Festival** (October).

Vineyards in the Barossa Valley

South Australia

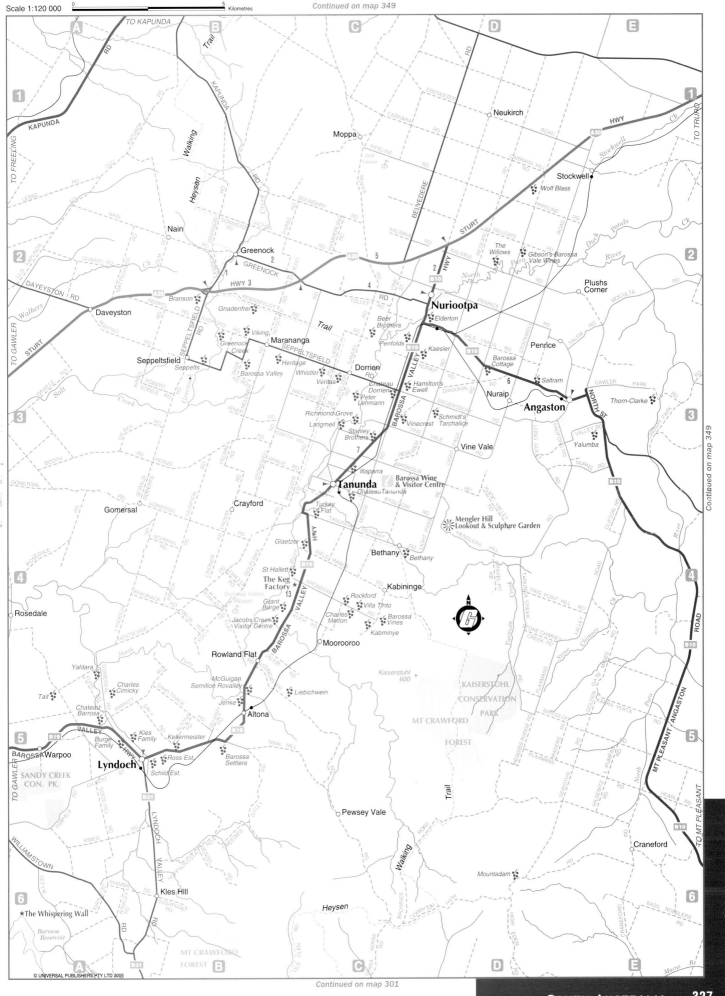

Scale 1:120 000

Continued on map 349

TO KAPUNDA

TO FREELING

KAPUNDA

TO GAWLER

Nain

Greenock

Daveyston

Moppa

Neukirch

Stockwell

Wolf Blass

The Willows

Gibson's Barossa Vale Wines

Plushs Corner

Branson

Gnadenfrei

Viking

Marananga

Seppeltsfield

Greenock Creek

Heritage

Whistler

Veritas

Dorrien

Barossa Valley

Beer Brothers

Penfolds

Nuriootpa

Elderton

Kaesler

Chateau Dorrien

Peter Lehmann

Hamilton's Ewell

Barossa Cottage

Saltram

Nuraip

Penrice

Angaston

Thorn-Clarke

Richmond Grove

Langmeil

Stanley Brothers

Vinecrest

Schmidt's Tarchalice

Yalumba

Vine Vale

Illaparra

Tanunda

ChateauTanunda

Barossa Wine & Visitor Centre

Crayford

Gomersal

Turkey Flat

Mengler Hill Lookout & Sculpture Garden

Glaetzer

Bethany

Bethany

St Hallett

The Keg Factory

Giant Burge

Jacobs Creek Visitor Centre

Rockford

Villa Tinto

Charles Melton

Barossa Vines

Kabminye

Kabininge

Moorooroo

Rosedale

Rowland Flat

Yaldara

Charles Cimicky

Tait

McGuigan Semillon Rovalley

Jenke

Liebichwein

Chateau Barrosa

Altona

KAISERSTUHL CONSERVATION PARK

Kaiserstuhl 600

MT CRAWFORD FOREST

Kies Family

Burge Family

Kellermeister

Ross Est.

Barossa Settlers

Barossa Warpoo

Lyndoch

Schild Est.

SANDY CREEK CON. PK.

Pewsey Vale

Craneford

WILLIAMSTOWN

Kles Hill

The Whispering Wall

Barossa Reservoir

Heysen

Mountadam

MT CRAWFORD FOREST

Continued on map 301

SOUTH AUSTRALIA 327

South Australia's floral emblem, Sturt's desert pea (*Clianthus formosus*), at the Australian Arid Lands Botanic Garden, Port Augusta

■ Port Augusta   POP 13 955

Map 346, E4

The most northerly point on the **Spencer Gulf**, Port Augusta is often referred to as the '**Crossroads of Australia**'. Major highways to the north, south, east and west meet here, and the city is an important link for the **Indian Pacific** and **Ghan railway lines**. With the **Flinders Ranges** to the east, Port Augusta attracts many tourists en route to this scenic Outback wonderland.

MAIN ATTRACTIONS: Beaches are popular attractions, especially **Redbanks Beach** off Gardiner Ave. A two hour **heritage walk** and a scenic drive highlight the city's many historic buildings. Take the time to visit **Wadlata Outback Centre**, an interpretative centre where audio-visuals and interactive displays trace the history of the region from its geological development, through to Aboriginal culture, European exploration, the development of transport and technological achievements. The **Royal Flying Doctor Service** (RFDS) has a base in Port Augusta and visitors are welcome. **Curdnatta Art**

and **Pottery Gallery** on Commercial Rd is an outlet for weaving, pottery, painting and other local crafts. **Homestead Park Pioneer Museum** is housed in the old Yudnapinna Station pine-log homestead. The city's scenic lookouts—**McLellan**, Whiting Pde; **Water Tower**, Mitchell Tce, and **Matthew Flinders** in McSporran Cres provide great views of the city and Flinders Ranges. On the Stuart Hwy is the **Australian Arid Lands Botanic Garden** which exhibits Australia's most fascinating arid-land plants, birds and animal life.

NEARBY ATTRACTIONS: The townships of **Stirling North**, **Quorn** and **Hawker** are all in the vicinity of Port Augusta.

VISITOR INFORMATION: Wadlata Outback Centre, 41 Flinders Tce, Ph: (08) 8642 4511 or 1800 633 060

■ Port Broughton   POP 735

Map 346, E6

Around 170km from Adelaide, this peaceful seaside village has much to offer its visitors. Built on **Mundoora Arm Inlet**, and protected from the **Spencer Gulf**, it is a base for crab and prawn fishermen. The

town was named after William Grant Broughton, who was consecrated Anglican bishop of Australia in 1836.

MAIN ATTRACTIONS: A popular recreation area is the grassed foreshore reserve, where picnic and BBQ facilities are located adjacent to a children's playground. Swimming and fishing are popular in the jetty area. A **Heritage Walking Trail** takes in four places of historic interest in Port Broughton and there are also **Fishlab tours**, by appointment, when visitors can see a variety of aquatic organisms, both plant and animal.

NEARBY ATTRACTIONS: **Clements Gap NP** is about 16km north-east, and visitors can see a range of native fauna such as kangaroos, echidnas, lizards, over 66 bird species, snakes, insects and rare flowers. **The Copper Coast** towns of **Moonta**, **Kadina** and **Wallaroo** are close by, while to the east, the wineries of the **Clare Valley** are also within easy reach.

VISITOR INFORMATION: Bay St, Ph: (08) 8635 2261

■ Port Elliot   POP 1520

Map 337, D2

Port Elliot is an ideal holiday destination within easy reach of Adelaide. It was surveyed in 1852, and was briefly the major ocean port for goods moving up and down the **River Murray**. There are extensive beaches that offer surfing and swimming.

MAIN ATTRACTIONS: Water-based leisure activities are well catered for and there is a range of accommodation overlooking **Horseshoe Bay**. The National Trust has created a local **Heritage Walk** that passes various historic sites. **Freeman's Knob**, a small promontory at the southern end of the bay, is an excellent vantage point for coastal views. In winter it is good for whale sightings.

Middleton lies 4km east of Port Elliot and has the state's most popular surf beach. A number of surfing competitions are held here every year. Middleton also has the **Heritage Bakery** and **old flour mill**, as well as **Middleton Estate** a further 5km away in the **Currency Creek** vineyard region. **Crows Nest Lookout** has excellent views of the nearby bays, lakes and **Coorong NP**.

VISITOR INFORMATION: Signal Point, The Wharf, Goolwa, Ph: (08) 8555 3488

Port Lincoln   POP 12 680

Map 348, B1

Port Lincoln is located on extensive **Boston Bay** and was originally considered as a site for the capital of South Australia. The Bay provides an idyllic setting at the southern tip of the **Eyre Peninsula**. The city is 676km west of Adelaide. It is now the base for a large fishing industry including Australia's biggest commercial tuna-fishing fleet. Port Lincoln is an export centre for wheat, wool, lambs, lobsters, prawns and abalone.

MAIN ATTRACTIONS: Boston Bay is the perfect place for water and other sports, as well as scenic walking trails—in particular the **Parnkalla Walking Trail**, which edges the bay all the way from **Billy Lights Point** to **North Shields**. Three city lookouts, **Winters Hill**, **Puckridge Park** and **The Old Mill**, offer excellent but different views. For superb timber furniture, Port Lincoln's world-renowned **Constantia Designer Craftsmen** on Proper Bay Rd offer a guided tour, which reveals the creative processes involved from the raw timber state to finished pieces. There are several museums in Port Lincoln; **Axel Stenross Maritime Museum** centres on the workshop and home of Axel Stenross, a Finnish boat builder who established his business here in the 1920s. Three small museums are located in Flinders Park; **Mill Cottage Museum** features artefacts from the early days of settlement; **Settler's Cottage Museum** houses local memorabilia; nearby is **Rose-Wal Memorial Shell Museum**. The **MB Kotz Collection of Stationary Engines** is a private museum. In the old Railway Station is the **Railway Museum**. Tours of the **Seahorse Farm**, which supplies the aquarium market, must be booked through the visitor information centre. It is part of the Eyre Peninsula's **Seafood and Aquaculture Trail**.

NEARBY ATTRACTIONS: Around 15 minutes west lies **Glenforest Animal Park**, which is home to native and farm animals, including kangaroos, camels, wombats, donkeys, deer, dingos, goats and more. **Lincoln NP** is south of the city and consists of secluded beaches, rugged cliffs, sand dunes, native fauna and sheltered camping spots. The **Memory Cove Wilderness Area** of the park requires a permit and a key from the Port Lincoln visitor centre. North, off the Lincoln Hwy, **Tod Reservoir** is a good spot for a picnic and a visit to the **Tod Reservoir Museum** with its heritage display on the water supply of the Eyre Peninsula. The tourist attraction known as **Whalers Way** provides spectacular views of cliffs, blowholes, caves and beaches, and between May and November there is an amazing wildflower display. A permit and key, also available from the visitor centre, are necessary to enter the area. A separate permit gives access to **Mikkira Koala Park**. For wine lovers there are four wineries in the region, including **Boston Bay Wines** and **Delacolline Estate Winery**.

VISITOR INFORMATION: 3 Adelaide Pl, Ph: (08) 8683 3544 or 1300 788 378

Port MacDonnell   POP 680

Map 323, E6

About 30km south of Mount Gambier, Port MacDonnell is known as '**Australia's Southern Rock Lobster Capital**' and is a favourite destination for surfers and anglers. The Port was home to poet **Adam Lindsay Gordon** who wrote *Dingley Dell*, a depiction of life in the early 1860s. It is said the Port MacDonnell area was the inspiration behind much of his poetry. In the early days, Port MacDonnell was a thriving trading port and today a breakwater (built in 1975) shelters Australia's largest southern rock-lobster fishing fleet.

Lincoln Cove Marina, Port Lincoln

MAIN ATTRACTIONS: The **Maritime Museum** displays artefacts salvaged from ships wrecked on local reefs as well as a photographic display tracing the town's heritage. Port MacDonnell offers many activities—bushwalking, golf, boating, fishing, sailing, diving, snorkelling, surfing and waterskiing.

NEARBY ATTRACTIONS: **Dingley Dell Conservation Park** is located just outside of Port MacDonnell and protects the rare Dingley Dell blue-gum and local vegetation. Nature walks and picnic facilities are available. Also within the park is the restored and refurnished cottage of poet Adam Lindsay Gordon. Located 15km north, **Mount Schank** is the crater of Australia's youngest volcano, classified as dormant, although it erupted as recently as 2000 years ago. A walking trail takes visitors to the top, where there are wonderful panoramic views of the surrounding countryside.

VISITOR INFORMATION: 5 Charles St, Ph: (08) 8738 2380

Alligator Gorge, Mount Remarkable National Park, north of Port Pirie

■ Port Pirie   POP 10 015
Map 346, E5

South Australia's first provincial city began in 1845 as a caretaker's cottage and three woolsheds on the banks of Tarparrie Creek, on the eastern side of **Spencer Gulf**. Over the years, Port Pirie has grown to become one of the state's largest industrial and commercial centres—its skyline is dominated by the world's largest lead smelter. The city forms the southern point of the Spencer Gulf triangle completed by **Whyalla** and **Port Augusta**. It has rail connections to the **Indian Pacific** and **The Ghan**.

MAIN ATTRACTIONS: The city is a good base for walkers and drivers to explore the scenic southern **Flinders Ranges**. There is a two hour **Heritage Walk** through the CBD, with many buildings of note,

including **Sampson's Cottage** (1890s), and the **National Trust Museum** at the northern end of Ellen St. **Memorial Park** in Gertrude St is home to the **Northern Festival Centre**, a complex of theatre, ball-room and conference rooms. The park itself is also a popular recreation area. The impressive **Port Pirie Regional Tourism and Arts Centre**, on Mary Elie St, incorporates **Port Pirie Regional Art Gallery**, a 1.1km miniature railway, a model railway and **White Pointer Shark Exhibition** as well as a visitor centre. **Solomontown Beach** is a great area for families, with picnic and BBQ facilities and a playground.

NEARBY ATTRACTIONS: **Mount Remarkable NP** is a pleasant scenic drive, with a detour to **Telowie Gorge** revealing deep ravines and giant river red gums. **Alligator Gorge**, at the northern end of the park, offers a series of steps into a gorge bounded by sheer red quartzite cliffs. About 24km south of Port Pirie is the small beachside resort of **Port Germein**, which has attractive swimming areas and a long wooden jetty, ideal for fishing and strolling.

VISITOR INFORMATION: 3 Mary Elie St, Ph: (08) 8633 8700 or 1800 000 424

■ Port Victoria   POP 320
Map 348, D1

Known as the '**Last of the Windjammer Ports**', this tourist and fishing township on the west coast of the **Yorke Peninsula** is one of the original windjammer grain ports. Settled in the 1870s, it was named by the first European explorers in the area after their ship, *Victoria*.

MAIN ATTRACTIONS: Swimming and jetty fishing are popular activities in Port Victoria, with good catches of whiting and snapper to be had. The **National Trust Maritime Museum** is housed in the old grain shed near the restored jetty, and displays artefacts and photographs relating to early shipping and grain industries. The **Port Victoria Geology Trail** is a 4km path that heads south from the jetty to explore the quiet foreshore where, 2000 million years ago, volcanoes spewed ash and red-hot lava into the atmosphere and earthquakes shook the ground. Picnic tables and BBQs are located on Port Victoria's foreshore and an interpretation shelter details the locations and histories of nine shipwrecks in the vicinity of **Wardang Island**. There is also a **Maritime Heritage Trail** to follow.

South Australia

NEARBY ATTRACTIONS: **Goose Island**, a small island off the northern end of Wardang Island, is home to a colony of Australian sea-lions. Divers can dive with the animals. Overnight camping is permitted—obtain a permit from Innes NP visitor centre.

VISITOR INFORMATION: Harvest Corner, 29 Main St, Minlaton
Ph: (08) 8853 2600

■ Quorn   POP 1050
Map 346, E4

Located in a valley in the southern **Flinders Ranges**, the old railway town of Quorn is an important gateway to the ranges and a fascinating destination in its own right. Originally, in the 1850s, the district thrived on wheat production. This gave way to sheep and cattle when the good rains of the early years failed. Quorn was established as a railway town in 1878, and today caters to a diverse tourist trade.

MAIN ATTRACTIONS: Many pre-1900 buildings remain in Quorn and can be viewed on the 45 minute **Historic Buildings Walk**. **Quorn Mill** (1878) now operates as a motel. Several local outlets sell arts and crafts. A collection of farm machinery is located in **Lions Park** on the Port Augusta Rd. From April to November, the famous **Pichi Richi Railway** offers a link to the past with a steam-train trip on a section of narrow-gauge line from Quorn Station to **Woolshed Flat**, **Stirling North** and **Port Augusta**.

NEARBY ATTRACTIONS: Quorn is an ideal base for exploring the historic ruins of **Kanyaka**, **Willochra**, **Gordon**, **Wilson** and **Simmonston**—all reminders of the harsh conditions encountered by early pioneers. Spectacular mountain scenery can be seen in **Yarrah Vale** and **Warren gorges** and from **Buckaringa Scenic Lookout**. Both **Dutchmans Stern Conservation Park**, 8km west, and **Mount Brown Conservation Park**, 16km south, are worth a visit.

VISITOR INFORMATION: 3 Seventh St,
Ph: (08) 8648 6419

■ Renmark   POP 4460
Map 333, D1

Australia's oldest irrigation town, Renmark was settled in 1887. It was pioneered by the Canadian Chaffey brothers, who reached an agreement with the government for a grant of land on which to test their irrigation scheme. This proved successful, and the district still flourishes using water pumped from the **River Murray** to irrigate the vineyards, orchards and other crops.

MAIN ATTRACTIONS: **Olivewood**, the pine-log home of pioneer George Chaffey is run by the National Trust and holds a collection of relics and photographs of Renmark's early days. There are a number of galleries that display locally produced paintings, pottery and crafts. An **Interpretive Centre** located within Renmark/Paringa Visitor Centre links the past with the present by tracing the river's history from ancient times. Moored close by is the fully restored 1911 **PS *Industry***. This wonderful old paddlesteamer cruises on the first Sunday of each month. Cruises on the modern ***Big River Rambler*** depart from the town wharf most days. There are two major wineries in Renmark: **Renmano Winery** and **Angove's Winery**.

NEARBY ATTRACTIONS: About 3km east of Renmark is **Paringa**; its attractions include historic **Customs House** (1884), now a general store, a **suspension bridge** that is one of only four still spanning the river and **Lock 5**, built in the 1920s to regulate the flow of the river. The 9000km^2 **Bookmark Biosphere Reserve** is to the north and south of the town, as are sections of **Murray River NP**. **Bredl's Wonder World of Wildlife** is 7km south-west on the Sturt Hwy. Nearby, **Ruston's Rose Garden** has 50 000 rose bushes as well as flowering trees and shrubs.

VISITOR INFORMATION: 84 Murray Ave,
Ph: (08) 8586 6704 or 1300 657 625

■ Robe   POP 965
Map 323, B3

Previously one of the most important ports in South Australia, Robe was settled in 1846 and is now a holiday destination and the home port for a commercial crayfishing fleet. It is located on

Quorn Railway Station, starting point for the famous Pichi Richi Railway to Port Augusta

RIVERLAND

This region features about 300km of the **River Murray**, one of the world's great waterways, meandering through a changing landscape. Not only does the river dominate the region's landscape, it also influences its economy—providing the water to irrigate its many orchards and vineyards.

Riverland produces close to half of South Australia's wine grapes and is becoming increasingly known as a wine area in its own right. Riverland is the heart of the fruit bowl of South Australia, where more than 90% of the state's citrus, stone fruit and nuts are grown; local produce can be sampled from stalls along the roadside.

There is no better way to explore the might of the River Murray than by travelling on it—houseboats fully equipped with home comforts are an ideal holiday option. The river is ideal for anglers, where catches of the day include Murray cod, redfin and callop. Riverland has a number of towns that are rich in pioneering history. This is a fragile region that offers much to explore.

main attractions

- ❖ Banrock Station
- ❖ Bredl's Wonder World of Wildlife
- ❖ Loxton Historical Village
- ❖ Murray River National Park
- ❖ River Cruises
- ❖ Ruston's Rose Garden
- ❖ The Big Orange

 Visitor information

Renmark/Paringa Visitors Centre
84 Murray Ave, Renmark, SA 5341
Ph: (08) 8586 6704, Tollfree: 1300 657 625

River red gums in Murray River National Park, Riverland

Guichen Bay, 336km from Adelaide, and was named after Governor Fredrick Robe, who chose this site as a suitable location for a port. MAIN ATTRACTIONS: An **Historic Walk** takes in the charm and character of Robe as it passes the old cottages and historic buildings of the old port area, including the **Star of Sea Catholic Church** (1868). A number of early homes now offer accommodation, art galleries or specialty shops. Built in 1863, **Robe Customs House** in Royal Circus is a National Trust museum displaying nautical items and local memorabilia. The **Historical Interpretive Centre** is worth a visit and is part of the library and visitor information complex in Mundy Tce. Fresh, locally caught crayfish (in season) and fish are popular with residents and visitors.

NEARBY ATTRACTIONS: This is a wonderful area for fishing, surfing and swimming holidays—Robe has a number of very safe bay beaches. **Long Beach**, on Guichen Bay, stretches for 18km and at the southern end it is possible to drive onto the white sand beach in summer. It is not safe to swim off the ocean beaches as many of them have dangerous rips. For an interesting walk, take Obelisk Rd to **Cape Dombey**, where a clifftop track leads to the ruins of an old gaol and the **Obelisk**, once a beacon for early mariners. Robe borders **Little Dip Conservation Park**. For wine lovers, the **Limestone Coast region** offers **Mount Benson** and **Cape Jaffa wineries**.
VISITOR INFORMATION: Public Library, Mundy Tce, Ph: (08) 8768 2465

■ Roxby Downs   POP 3620
Map 346, D2
Nestled among red sand dunes clad in native pine, Roxby Downs is a modern mining town about 80km north of Woomera. It was purpose-built to house and service employees and their families for the **Olympic Dam Mining** project. The mine produces over two million tonnes of ore annually to obtain refined copper, gold, silver and uranium oxide.
MAIN ATTRACTIONS: From March to November, **surface mine tours** depart from Roxby Downs town centre. Bookings are essential. **Roxby Downs Cultural Precinct**, in Richardson Pl, includes an **art gallery/cinema** and interpretative display, as well as visitor information. Visitors are welcome at

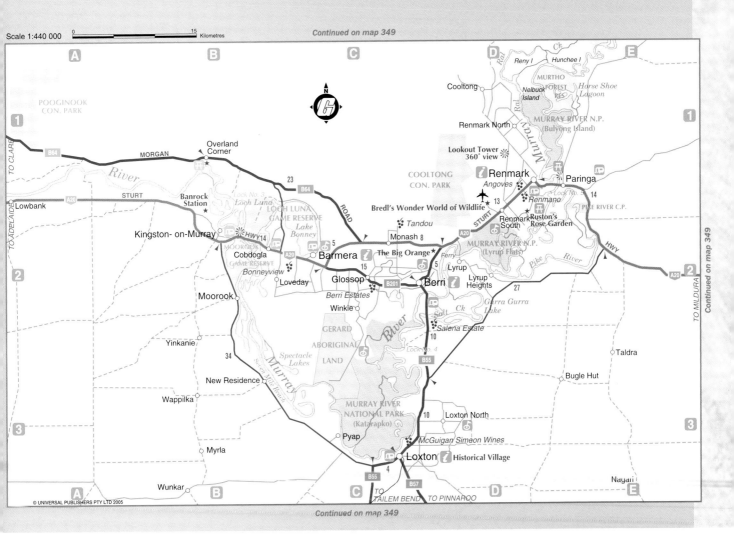

Continued on map 349

Scale 1:440 000   0   15 Kilometres

Continued on map 349

Continued on map 349

© UNIVERSAL PUBLISHERS PTY LTD 2005

the community's leisure centre which has a swimming pool, squash court and tennis court.

NEARBY ATTRACTIONS: The **Olympic Dam and Mining Complex** is 16km north of Roxby Downs. The opal fields of **Andamooka** are 30km east and offer an easy side trip. East of Andamooka (13km) is the northern tip of **Lake Torrens**, a vast, normally dry salt lake that stretches south, almost all the way to **Port Augusta**.

VISITOR INFORMATION: Cultural Precinct, 1 Richardson Pl, Ph: (08) 8671 2001

▦ Stansbury   POP 532

Map 348, E2

Located on the **Yorke Peninsula**, halfway between Port Vincent and Edithburgh, Stansbury looks across **Oyster Bay** to the waters of **Gulf St Vincent**. Stansbury is a pleasant holiday destination. Grain-growing and pastoral activities, oyster farming and the state's largest limestone quarry also support the local economy.

MAIN ATTRACTIONS: The **School House Museum** is located in historic Stansbury School (1878) on North Tce, and offers a look into 19th-century education. The **Seaside Markets**, on the foreshore between October and May, are popular.

NEARBY ATTRACTIONS: About 15km north-west, **Lake Sundown** is, as the name implies, absolutely stunning at sunset. **Kleines Point Quarry** is located 5km south and offers daily tours of the limestone quarry by appointment.

VISITOR INFORMATION: Cnr Weaver St and Towler St, Ph: (08) 8852 4577

The unusual tent-shaped Oasis Motel at Roxby Downs

Murphy's Haystacks, 40km south-east of Streaky Bay

◼ Strathalbyn   POP 3210
Map 349, F2

The north-east gateway to the **Fleurieu Peninsula**, Strathalbyn lies on the banks of the **Angas River** and is acknowledged as one of South Australia's most attractive rural towns. When they settled in the district in 1839, the Scottish Rankine brothers commenced building **St Andrew's Uniting Church**, overlooking the river.

MAIN ATTRACTIONS: The wide streets, numerous historic buildings and the stately old homes contribute to Strathalbyn's status as a **Heritage Town**. A browsers' and shoppers' paradise, the main areas in town are **Albyn Tce/Dawson St** and **High St**, which are lined with shops selling antiques, arts and crafts and all manner of collectables. The old Police Station and Court House are now home to the **National Trust Museum**, which displays photographs, clothing and appliances that depict the life of the pioneers. The pleasant walk through **Soldiers Memorial Gardens** and along the river bank is highly recommended.

NEARBY ATTRACTIONS: The old riverboat port of **Milang** lies on the shores of **Lake Alexandrina**, the largest freshwater lake in Australia.

Conditions on the lake are ideal for sailing, windsurfing and boating. Just 15km east are the wineries of the **Langhorne Creek** district. About 35km north-west of Strathalbyn are the old diggings at **Jupiter Creek Goldfields**.

VISITOR INFORMATION: Old Railway Station, 20 South Tce, Ph: (08) 8536 3212.

◼ Streaky Bay   POP 1105
Map 345, J5

Streaky Bay is a picturesque town servicing thriving rural and fishing communities, also the granite-mining industry. Around 727km north-west of Adelaide, it attracts a growing number of visitors to local bays, beaches and coves. The town was originally named Flinders, after Capt Matthew Flinders. In 1940, it changed to that of the bay, which Flinders named in 1802 because of its streaky colours—it is now known that the colours are created from oils given off by seaweed.

MAIN ATTRACTIONS: The oldest building, **Hospital Cottage** (1864), is made of mud brick and **St Canute's Catholic Church** is a lovely old sandstone building. **The Old School Museum** in Montgomerie Tce displays the area's pioneering memorabilia as well as botanical and geological

exhibits. The **Powerhouse Restored Engine Centre**, Alfred Tce, has displays of working engines. A replica of the world's largest great white shark caught on rod-and-reel is on display at **Stewart's Shell Roadhouse Tourist Centre**.

NEARBY ATTRACTIONS: To the north are **Cape Bauer Circular Drive**, visiting the **Whistling Rocks** at the Cape, and beautiful **Pelubie Beach**. Two groups of huge, wind-eroded, pink granite rocks, known as **Murphy's Haystacks**, are a distinctive landmark 40km south-east. For those wishing to explore the coastline, **Point Labatt Conservation Park** is about 55km south of Streaky Bay and offers a sea-lion viewing area as well as panoramic views of the rugged coastline.

VISITOR INFORMATION: Stewart's Shell Roadhouse, 7-15 Alfred Tce, Ph: (08) 8626 1126

◼ Tailem Bend   POP 1400
Map 349, G2

Perched on a cliff overlooking the **River Murray**, Tailem Bend was proclaimed in 1887 and became a major railway town with lines servicing the **Murray-Mallee** area. With the reduction of railway passenger and freight services, Tailem Bend gained a new lease of life providing facilities for the steady stream of road traffic to and from the south-east and eastern states.

MAIN ATTRACTIONS: Alongside the station, a large park features a stationary engine and adventure playground for children. A picnic spot with river views is located near the ferry landing. The **Riverside Walking Trail** leads past a cliff face where it is possible to see fossils and evidence of early Aboriginal habitation.

NEARBY ATTRACTIONS: Many hours can be spent wandering the streets of **Old Tailem Town Pioneer Village**, 5km north-west of town. This village, on a former sheep run,

South Australia

has been 'created' by importing old buildings and restoring them, and erecting further buildings. The 12 streets in the village contain a school, church, railway station, general store and police station, also a barber, watchmaker and saddler. The Murray River is an excellent location for boating, sailing, rowing, swimming and fishing and 3km downstream, **Freds Landing** has a concrete boat ramp.

Visitor Information: Railway Tce, Ph: (08) 8572 4277

▣ Tanunda   POP 3845
Map 327, C3

This busy, properous town developed from the village of Langmeil, the valley's second German settlement in 1843. Tanunda is in the heart of the **Barossa wine region**, an important stopover for visitors to the area.

Main Attractions: Tanunda's German heritage has been preserved in its many fine Lutheran churches, specialty bakeries and small-goods shops. Art and craft shops feature locally-produced pottery and other crafts. **Historic Goat Square** is located at the centre of the original town—the old streets are fascinating and best explored on foot. **Barossa Historical Museum**, in Murray St, is housed in the former Post Office (1865). **Tanunda Recreation Reserve**, located in Elizabeth St, is home to a swim-ming pool, bowling and RSL clubs.

Nearby Attractions: In St Hallett Rd, the **Keg Factory** produces handcrafted kegs and barrels. **Kaiserstuhl Conservation Park** lies in the ranges beyond **Bethany**. Bushwalkers here pass through original vegetation that supports a variety of native birds and animals. Wineries and vineyards encircle the town. Some of the better known are: **Chateau Tanunda**, **Peter Lehmann Wines**, **Richmond Grove** and **Basedow Wines**. Most have

cellar door tastings and sales. The lookout at nearby **Mengler Hill** also has a sculpture garden.

Visitor Information: 66–68 Murray St, Ph: (08) 8563 0600 or 1300 852 982

▣ Tumby Bay   POP 1230
Map 348, C1

Around 50km from Port Lincoln, Tumby Bay is situated on the east coast of the **Eyre Peninsula**. It is a quiet rural centre servicing a wheat and sheep-farming area and a local fishing industry. Popular with holidaymakers, the sheltered bay is lined with a white sandy beach and provides a scenic setting for a variety of water-based activities, including excellent fishing.

Main Attractions: There are several art and craft outlets in town that welcome browsers, in particular **Rotunda Art Gallery** and **Tumby Cottage Crafts**. A recreation area edges the foreshore of Tumby Bay and there are picnic and BBQ facilities at the southern lookout reserve. The **Interpretive Mangrove Boardwalk**, near the causeway at the southern end of the bay, crosses the mangroves and has signs ex-plaining their ecological importance. There are two museums in Tumby Bay, **CL Alexander National Trust**

Museum and **Excell Blacksmith and Engineering Workshop Museum**; both are well worth investigating.

Nearby Attractions: **Tumby Bay Charters** offer fishing cruises and trips to **Sir Joseph Banks Group Islands** lying offshore. The islands are recognised for their excellent fishing grounds and wealth of birdlife. There is also the opportunity to observe sea-lions basking in the sun or an aquatic ballet of dolphins. The town of **Koppio** is situated 30km south-west, and here visitors can discover **Koppio Smithy Museum**. It features an authentic blacksmith's shop, cottages, schoolhouse and heritage hall with stationary engines and horse-drawn vehicles. Located nearby is **Tod Reservoir Museum** and picnic ground.

Visitor Information: Hales Mini Mart, 1 Bratten Way, Ph: (08) 8688 2584

▣ Victor Harbor   POP 8980
Map 337, D2

Only an hour's drive from Adelaide, Victor Harbor is one of the state's major tourist destinations. On the **Fleurieu Peninsula**, it nestles in a sandy curve of **Encounter Bay**. Because of its accessibility, the

Aerial view of Spilsby Island, one of the Sir Joseph Banks Group in Spencer Gulf, off Tumby Bay

Its close proximity to Adelaide and outstanding combination of seaside resorts surrounded by idyllic rural townships, set among rolling hills and vineyards, make the Fleurieu Peninsula an ideal holiday destination. The region starts near the southern suburbs of **Adelaide** and continues to **Cape Jervis**, a small town at the tip of the Peninsula, which offers excellent views across **Backstairs Passage** to **Kangaroo Island**.

Both sides of the Peninsula's coast offer a full range of water-front attractions. It boasts great surfing and swimming beaches; islands which are home to little penguins; and waters frequently visited by southern right whales.

In contrast, the lush green interior hosts 20 or more conservation parks, 1500km of nature trails, historic villages and

the world-class wineries of **McLaren Vale**. The region's noted natural beauty has made it a haven for artists and craftspeople, whose works are showcased in galleries and at weekend craft markets. The attractions of the Fleurieu Peninsula can be enjoyed in any season.

attractions

- ◈ Cape Jervis
- ◈ Granite Island, Victor Harbor
- ◈ Deep Creek Conservation Park
- ◈ McLaren Vale wineries

i Visitor information

McLaren Vale and Fleurieu Visitor Centre
Main Rd, McLaren Vale, SA 5171
Ph: (08) 8323 9944, Freecall: 1800 628 410
www.visitorcentre.com.au

The Clydesdale-powered tramway between Victor Harbor and Granite Island

population swells on weekends and can increase up to 80 000 during the peak holiday season.

MAIN ATTRACTIONS: The area enjoys a mild Mediterranean-type climate and extensive coastline, so recreational activities can be enjoyed most of the year. On Sundays, public holidays and school holidays, the historic **Cockle Train** runs between Victor Harbor and **Goolwa**. Rolling past beaches and sandhills on Australia's oldest public railway is a nostalgia trip for history lovers. There are many historic buildings in Victor Harbor—take a look at **Congregational Church** (1869), **Adare House** (1852), **St Augustines Church** (1869) and **Old Customs House** (1867). The **South Australian Whale Centre** on Railway Tce has displays to increase awareness about dolphin

and whale conservation. Three favourite children's attractions are within a five minute drive of Victor Harbor; **Greenhills Adventure Park**, offering canoeing and waterslides; **Urimbirra Wildlife Park**, which has birds, mammals and reptiles; and **Wild Rose Miniature Village**, featuring scale models of buildings set in lovely gardens.

NEARBY ATTRACTIONS: There are numerous conservation parks and nature reserves around Victor Harbor. The **Heysen Trail**, South Australia's premier walk, passes through **Deep Creek Conservation Park**. The neighbouring towns of **Port Elliot**, **Middleton** and **Goolwa** are within easy reach, as are the wineries of **McLaren Vale**, the beaches of **Gulf St Vincent**, **Cape Jervis** and the pretty town of

Strathalbyn. Access to **Granite Island** is via a causeway built in 1875, and you can get there in a double-deck tram pulled by a Clydesdale horse. Every afternoon at dusk, the **Penguin Interpretive Centre** runs guided tours to view the hundreds of little penguins that have made the island their home. Take a look at the **Oceanarium** off Granite Island, which has an underwater viewing area.

VISITOR INFORMATION: The Causeway, Esplanade, Ph: (08) 8552 5738

■ Waikerie   POP 1800
Map 349, H1

Waikerie is known as the '**Citrus Centre of Australia**', with more than 5000ha of irrigated vineyards, citrus and stone-fruit orchards on the banks of the **River Murray**.

Continued on map 302

Scale 1:450 000

Continued on map 349

Gulf St Vincent

Aldinga Beach
Maslin Beach
Sellicks Beach
Sellicks Hill
Aldinga Bay
Myponga Beach
Carrickalinga Head
Carrickalinga Hill 260
Carrickalinga
Normanville
Yankalilla Bay
Wattle Flat
Yankalilla
Hay Flat
Second Valley
Rapid Bay
Rapid Head
Rapid Bay
Fleurieu
SECOND VALLEY FOREST
Mt Hayfield 354
SECOND VALLEY FOREST
Torrens Vale
Delamere
Cape Jervis
Sheep Hill
Wattle Hill 331
Cape Jervis
Lands End
TALISKER C.P.
Park HQ DEEP CREEK
Tapanappa Hill 308
CONSERVATION PARK
Heysen
'Victoria' shipwreck
Tunk Head
Porpoise Head
Backstairs Passage
Kangaroo Island
Cape Coutts
© UNIVERSAL PUBLISHERS PTY LTD 2005

TO ADELAIDE
Willunga Hill, MT MAGNIFICENT C.P.
Ashbourne
TO STRATHALBYN
Yundi
FINNISS C.P.
Mt Compass 375
COXS SCRUB C.P.
Mount Compass
Nangkita
Tooperang
Finniss
Myponga
Myponga Hill 441
Mt Cone 415
Mosquito Hill 250
SCOTT C.P.
MYPONGA C.P.
YULTE C.P.
SPRING MOUNT C.P.
Currency Creek
McFarlane Hill 159
Kerby Hill 286
Currency Creek
Clayton
Inman Hill 277
Hindmarsh Valley
Middleton
Goolwa
Hindmarsh Island
Glacier Rock
Inman Valley
SECOND VALLEY C.P.
Back Valley
Goolwa South
Port Elliot
Sir Richard Peninsula
Parawa
WAITPINGA C.P.
Newland
Victor Harbor
Cockle Train (to Goolwa)
Granite I.
COORONG N.P.
Waitpinga
Yiki
The Bluff
Encounter Bay
Ridgway Hill 158
Trail
NEWLAND HEAD C.P.
Waitpinga Beach
Newland Head
SOUTHERN OCEAN

About 170km north-east of Adelaide, the Waikerie region has been turned from mallee scrubland into productive farming land. It is thought the name 'Waikerie' is a corruption of the Aboriginal word 'weikari', which refers to the giant swift moths found in the area.

MAIN ATTRACTIONS: Starting near the ferry, a scenic 2km **Clifftop Walkway** runs along sandstone cliffs edging the Murray River. On the way, take in the spectacular views from **Waikerie Lookout Tower**. The walkway runs from the lookout to **Lions Riverfront Reserve**, which provides lawns by the water's edge, shady trees, picnic and BBQ facilities and a playground. Gliding is a popular activity in Waikerie as the conditions in the area are ideal.

NEARBY ATTRACTIONS: There are three protected wetland areas near Waikerie—**Stockyard Plains**, **Hart Lagoon** and **Maize Island Conservation Park**—all with an abundance of birdlife, fauna and flora. **Broken Cliffs** offer a fossicking spot around 7km north on the river. Crystallised gypsum fossils can be found in great numbers here. A short drive away is the popular **Lock 2**, used to control water levels on the Murray. It has BBQ and picnic facilities in a lovely setting.

VISITOR INFORMATION: The Orange Tree, Sturt Hwy, Ph: (08) 8541 2332

■ Wallaroo POP 2755
Map 346, E6
The principal port of the **Yorke Peninsula**, Wallaroo handles fertiliser imports and seed and grain exports. It is also a popular tourist resort, attracting visitors to its safe beaches and excellent fishing. It is home to the Spencer Gulf prawn fishing fleet. It was the discovery of copper in the late 19th century that led to the settlement; it is one of the three main towns of the **Copper Coast**. Declining copper prices saw the demise of the mines in the early 1920s.

MAIN ATTRACTIONS: There are many National Trust-listed buildings and 44 of these sites are featured on the town's 90 minute **Heritage Walk** that starts at the museum and ends at the **Smelting Works Offices**. **Hughes Chimney Stack** (1861) contains more than 300 000 bricks and is the only one of the smelter's many chimneys to survive. The

National Trust Wallaroo Heritage and Nautical Museum is located on Jetty Rd and is worth a look to gain an understanding of Wallaroo's maritime history. **Jubilee Square** on John Tce is a perfect picnic spot with electric BBQs and a children's playground.

NEARBY ATTRACTIONS: The other Copper Coast towns of **Moonta** and **Kadina** are within easy reach. Around the coastal area are Cornish-style cottages, built by hard-rock miners from Cornwall who flocked to this area in the 19th century. About 2km south is **Bird Island**, its shallow waters renowned for an abundance of tasty blue-swimmer crabs.

VISITOR INFORMATION: National Dryland Farming Centre, Moonta Rd, Kadina, Ph: 1800 654 991

■ Whyalla   POP 23 500
Map 346, E5

South Australia's largest regional city, Whyalla is located near the top of **Spencer Gulf**. It prospered on iron ore discovered at nearby **Iron Knob** in the late 1880s. A rapid period of expansion followed when BHP set up their fully integrated steelworks. Today, Whyalla is one of the nation's best-known industrial cities.

MAIN ATTRACTIONS: Visit **Whyalla Maritime Museum** with its impressive displays, including **HMAS** *Whyalla*, the largest ship in Australia permanently 'docked' on dry land. The museum also houses collections, displays and artefacts relating to BHP shipbuilding and WWII. **Onesteel Steelworks** (previously BHP) is an interesting but unconventional tourist attraction; tours run Mondays, Wednesdays and Fridays. The formal landscaping of **Ada Ryan Gardens** and extensive open areas with recreational facilities line Whyalla's **foreshore beach** area. On the other side of the jetty, **Whyalla Marina** has a four-lane launching ramp and offers every

facility to boat owners. A drive up **Hummock Hill** and walk to the lookout was developed by BHP to commemorate the company's centenary—the lookout offers magnificent 360° views over the city and Onesteel. **Mount Laura Homestead Museum** houses pioneering memorabilia, folk history and a telecommunications museum. **Whyalla Wildlife and Reptile Sanctuary** covers 100ha of bushland near the airport and is home to a range of native animals, monkeys and local venomous snakes.

NEARBY ATTRACTIONS: **Whyalla Conservation Park** protects original Myall and bluebush woodland of the northern **Eyre Peninsula**. Walk up **Wild Dog Hill** for a great view of the park and surrounding areas. Other tracks lead to **Point Douglas** and to the lighthouse and beach at **Point Lowly**. The temperate waters around Whyalla create a diverse marine ecosystem for divers to explore. Each year from early May to mid August, the shallow waters around the coast witness the annual migration of the giant Australian cuttlefish, known as the 'chameleons of the sea'.

VISITOR INFORMATION: Lincoln Hwy, Ph: (08) 8645 7900 or 1800 088 589

■ Woomera   POP 1480
Map 346, D2

Located 502km north-west of Adelaide, the interdependent **Long Range Weapons Establishment** and Woomera village were established in 1947. They were the result of a joint project between Britain and Australia to set up a remote rocket range. Although much reduced in size, the range itself is a prohibited area, even for the traditional Aboriginal owners.

MAIN ATTRACTIONS: A particular point of interest in Woomera is **Missile Park** where rockets, aircraft and weapons associated with the testing range are displayed. **Woomera**

Heritage Centre, in Dewrang Ave, features the **Woomera Heritage Museum** as well as a visitor centre. **Breen Park** is a perfect picnic area.

VISITOR INFORMATION: Heritage Centre, Dewrang Ave, Ph: (08) 8673 7042

■ Yorketown   POP 720
Map 348, E2

Settled in 1872, Yorketown is the main town of the southern **Yorke Peninsula**. It was one of the earliest pastoral settlements on the peninsula and, although not a seaside town, it has easy access to three major bodies of water.

NEARBY ATTRACTIONS: **Gulf St Vincent** and the townships of **Edithburgh** and **Stansbury** are just a few kilometres east. **Innes NP** is 77km south-west and offers walking tracks and rugged coastal scenery. About 50km west is **Daly Head**, and **Corny Point** is 55km west of town. **Hardwicke Bay** and **Spencer Gulf** are to the north-west, while to the south is **Investigator Strait**.

VISITOR INFORMATION: Cnr Weaver St and Towler St, Stansbury, Ph: (08) 8852 4577

Point Lowly Lighthouse at Port Bonython, near Whyalla

South Australia

KEY MAP

Capital city CBD map
Adelaide p.297

Adelaide suburban maps
pp. 300–303

Region maps
Flinders Ranges p.313
Kangaroo Island p.317
Limestone Coast p.323
The Barossa Valley p.327
Riverland p.333
Fleurieu Peninsula p.337

State maps
pp. 340–349

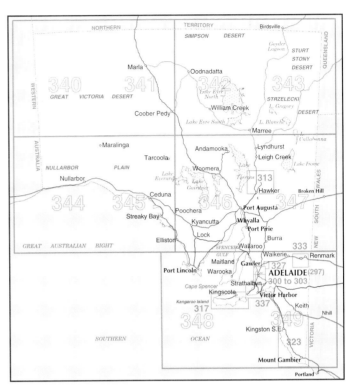

Merty Merty sand dunes, Strzelecki Desert

DISTANCE CHART

Approximate Distance	Adelaide	Bordertown	Broken Hill NSW	Ceduna	Coober Pecy	Eucla WA	Innamincke	Kulgera NT	Leigh Creek	Mount Gambier	Murray Bridge	Peterborough	Pinnaroo	Port Augusta	Port Lincoln	Port Pirie	Renmark	Streaky Bay	Whyalla	Woomera
Adelaide		267	514	769	837	1256	1033	1251	548	435	74	261	236	305	642	223	247	695	378	484
Bordertown	267		781	1036	1104	1523	1300	1518	815	183	193	528	132	572	909	490	279	962	645	751
Broken Hill NSW	514	781		878	946	1365	1064	1360	579	870	588	281	674	414	751	387	424	804	487	593
Ceduna	769	1036	878		996	487	1213	1410	728	1204	843	597	972	464	404	546	857	107	449	643
Coober Pedy	837	1104	946	996		1483	896	414	487	1272	911	665	1040	532	869	614	919	922	605	369
Eucla WA	1256	1523	1365	487	1483		1700	1897	1215	1691	1330	1084	1459	951	891	1033	1388	594	936	1130
Innamincka	1033	1300	1064	1213	896	1700		1310	485	1468	1107	783	1204	749	1086	817	1087	1139	822	789
Kulgera NT	1251	1518	1360	1410	414	1897	1310		901	1686	1325	1079	1454	946	1283	1028	1337	1336	1019	783
Leigh Creek	548	815	579	728	487	1215	485	901		983	622	298	719	264	601	332	602	654	437	380
Mount Gambier	435	183	870	1204	1272	1691	1468	1686	983		361	696	315	740	1077	658	462	1130	813	919
Murray Bridge	74	193	588	843	911	1330	1107	1325	622	361		335	162	379	716	297	207	769	452	558
Peterborough	261	528	281	597	665	1084	783	1079	298	696	335		421	133	470	106	300	523	206	312
Pinnaroo	236	132	674	972	1040	1459	1204	1454	719	315	162	421		508	845	437	147	898	581	687
Port Augusta	305	572	414	464	532	951	749	946	264	740	379	133	508		337	82	387	390	73	179
Port Lincoln	642	909	751	404	869	891	1086	1283	601	1077	716	470	845	337		419	724	294	264	420
Port Pirie	223	490	387	546	614	1033	817	1028	332	658	297	106	437	82	419		316	472	155	261
Renmark	247	279	424	857	919	1388	1087	1337	602	462	207	300	147	387	724	316		777	460	566
Streaky Bay	695	962	804	107	922	594	1139	1336	654	1130	769	523	898	390	294	472	777		375	569
Whyalla	378	645	487	449	605	936	822	1019	437	813	452	206	581	73	264	155	460	375		252
Woomera	484	751	593	643	369	1130	789	783	380	919	558	312	687	179	420	261	566	569	252	

All distances in this chart have been measured over highways and major roads, not necessarily by the shortest route.

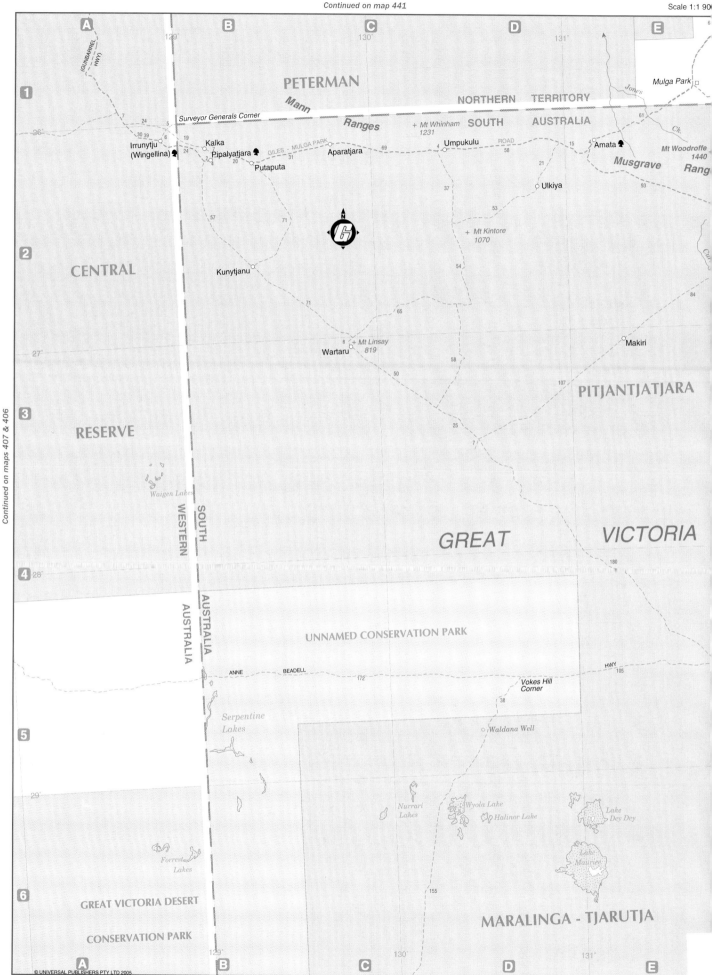

A

B

C

D

E

1

PETERMAN

Mann

Ranges

NORTHERN TERRITORY

SOUTH AUSTRALIA

Surveyor Generals Corner

26°

129°

130°

131°

Mulga Park

Jones

+ Mt Whinham
1231

Irrunytju
(Wingellina)

24

30 39

24

5

19

Kalka

Pipalyatjara

Putaputa

20

24

GILES — MULGA PARK

31

Aparatjara

69

Umpukulu

4

ROAD

58

15

61

Amata

Mt Woodroffe
1440

Musgrave   Rang

21

93

37

Ulkiya

57

71

+ Mt Kintore
1070

53

2

CENTRAL

Kunytjanu

71

54

65

84

27°

Wartaru

8 + Mt Linsay
819

58

Makiri

50

107

3

RESERVE

PITJANTJATJARA

25

7

Waigen Lakes

WESTERN   SOUTH

4

28°

GREAT   VICTORIA

180

UNNAMED CONSERVATION PARK

AUSTRALIA

AUSTRALIA

ANNE

BEADELL

172

HWY

105

Vokes Hill
Corner

38

Serpentine
Lakes

5

Waldana Well

29°

Nurrari
Lakes

Wyola Lake

Halinor Lake

Lake
Dey Dey

Forrest
Lakes

Lake
Maurice

155

6

GREAT VICTORIA DESERT

MARALINGA - TJARUTJA

CONSERVATION PARK

A

129°

B

130°

C

D

131°

E

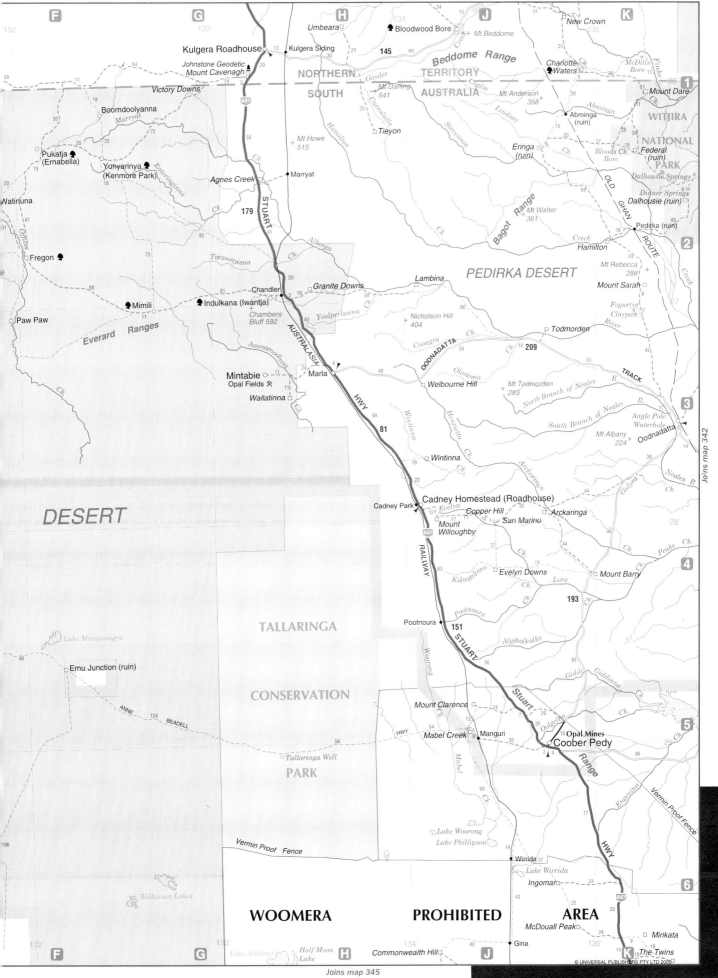

50 Kilometres

F 132   G 133   H   J   K

Kulgera Roadhouse   13   Kulgera Siding
Johnstone Geodetic
Mount Cavenagh
Victory Downs

Umbeara   Bloodwood Bore   Mt Beddome   New Crown   135   1
134   34   15
145   60   Beddome Range
NORTHERN   Goyder   Charlotte   McDills   Mount Dare
SOUTH   TERRITORY   Waters   Bore   WITJIRA
Boorndoolyanna   Mt Darling   AUSTRALIA   Mt Anderson   Abminga   NATIONAL
Marryat   541   358   (ruin)   Bloods Ck   Federal   PARK
Tieyon   Eringa   Bore   (ruin)   Dalhousie Springs
Pukatja   35   Mt Howe   (ruin)   Dinner Springs   OLD   Dalhousie (ruin)
(Ernabella)   515   Pedirka (ruin)   GHAN
Yunyarinya   Agnes Creek   Marryat   Hamilton   ROUTE   2
(Kenmore Park)   179   STUART   Alberga   Mt Walter   Creek
Watinuna   Bagot   361   Mt Rebecca   288
PEDIRKA DESERT   Mount Sarah
Fregon   92   Lambina   Fogartys   Creek
Chandler   Granite Downs   Nicholson Hill   Claypan   27
Indulkana (Iwantja)   Yoolperlunna   404   River
Paw Paw   Chambers   Todmorden   OODNADATTA
Mimili   Bluff 592   Coongra   56   209
Everard Ranges   AUSTRALASIA   Olarinna   Mt Todmorden   TRACK
Ammaroodinna   Welbourne Hill   283   North Branch of Neales   42
Mintabie   Marla   South Branch of Neales   Angle Pole   17
Opal Fields   HWY   48   Henrietta   Waterhole   3
Wallatinna   59   Wintinna   Mt Albany   Oodnadatta
81   224   14
Wintinna   Archaringa   39
19   Neales R
22   Gidgea
Cadney Homestead (Roadhouse)   44
Cadney Park   121   Evelyn   Copper Hill   32   Arckaringa   28
Mount   17   San Marino   46
Willoughby   10   Ck   44   Peake Ck
RAILWAY   21   Mount Barry
63   Evelyn Downs   Lora   193
DESERT   Kidwegirinna   Ck   51   Ck
Ck
Pootnoura   STUART   Pootnoura
151   Algebuikullia
TALLARINGA   Giddi   Giddinna
Lake Meramangye   Woorong   Ck
49   Ck   5
Emu Junction (ruin)   CONSERVATION   STUART   Oolgelden
Mount Clarence   29   Opal Mines
ANNE   124   BEADELL   24   Coober Pedy
HWY   54   13   35   Range   86
56   Mabel Creek   Manguri   2
PARK   9
Tallaringa Well   Mabel   60   Engenina   Vermin Proof Fence
Ck   77   HWY
196   Wilkinson Lakes   Lake Woorong   Range
Vermin Proof Fence   Lake Phillipson   14
Wirrida   37
Lake Wirrida   WOOMERA   PROHIBITED   AREA   Ingomar   33   A87
132   133   134   McDouall Peak   29   6
F   G   H   Gina   135   24
Lake Anthony   Half Moon   Commonwealth Hill   J   9   Mirikata
Lake   40   14   18   The Twins
© UNIVERSAL PUBLISHERS PTY LTD 2005   K

Joins map 342

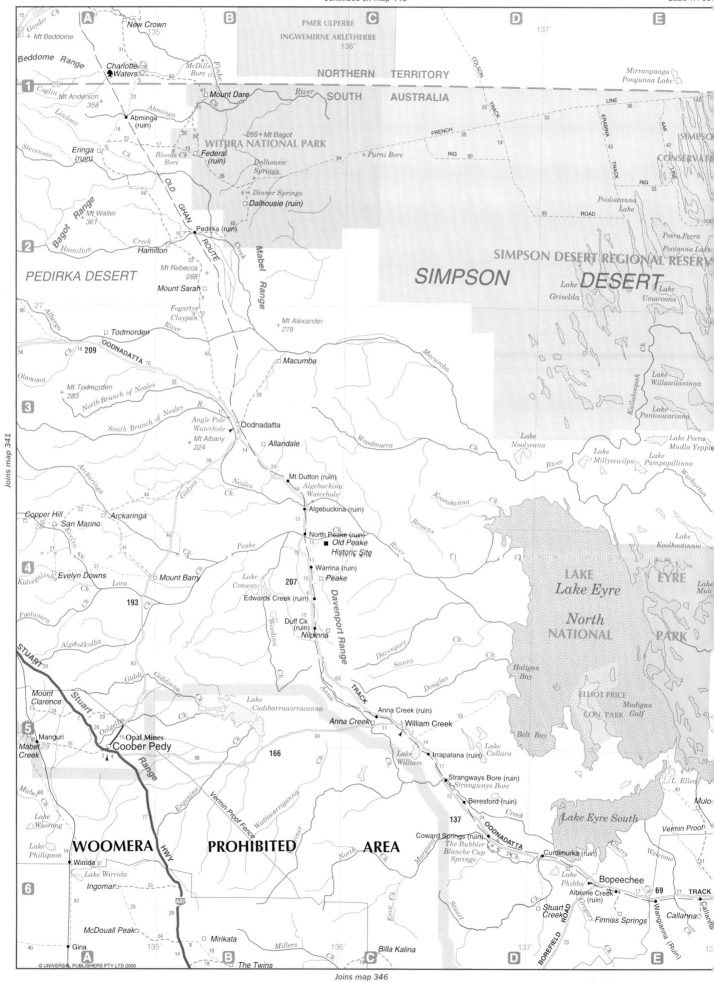

Joins map 341

50 Kilometres

Continued on maps 111 & 284

SIMPSON DESERT

QAA

NATIONAL PARK

eppel Corner

omas

ESERT

RK

Flood Detour

LINE 165

Nappanerica Sand Dune (Big Red)

Roseberth

BIRDSVILLE

Birdsville

L. Nappanerica

QUEENSLAND

SOUTH AUSTRALIA

Durri

Mount Leonard

Betoota ROAD

DEVELOPMENTAL 50

55

141

108

Cuddapan

Lake Cuddapan

114

Shallow Lake

Moonda Lake

Planet Downs O.S.

Haddon Corner

Pandie Pandie

Lake Cooninnie

Cadelga (Ruin)

Karrathunka Waterhole

Lake Short

Lake Etamunbanie

STURT

165

147

169

122

Lake Uloowaranie

Alton Downs

Goyder Lagoon

STONY

Koonchera Waterhole

Koonchera Sandhill

Lake Surprise Sandhill

DESERT

Cordillo Downs

Arrabury

L Goyder

L Lady Blanche

L Sir Richard

Leap Year Bore

Lake Pure

Clifton Hills

Warburton Crossing

BIRDSVILLE

Mt Gason Wattle Project

83

WALKERS CROSSING

Coongie Lake

Coongie (ruin)

L Marroocutchanie

Candnudecka

INNAMINCKA

142

Patchawarra

Patchwarra Bore

REGIONAL

ADVENTURE WY

242

Mt Gason Bore

109

Lake Koodnanie

RESERVE

Nappa Merrie

Cullyamurra Waterhole

Dig Tree

Creek

rrandirinna

Lake Howitt

Cowarie

Mirra Mitta Bore

Lake Perigundi

Walkers Crossing

Gidgealpa

Burkes Mem.

Innamincka

Wills Mem.

44

amurina

Mungerannie Gap

Gidgealpa Gas Field

Mungerannie Roadhouse

Moomba Oil & Gas Field

Moomba (Private)

157

Burke-Dullingari Oil & Gas Field

Della Gas Field

Orientos

Kalamurra Lake

TIRARI

DESERT

Lake Kittakittaooloo

Lake Warrakalanna

Toolachee Gas Field

Epsilon

Santos

Lake Ngapakaldi

Mulka

Lake Hope

SOUTH AUSTRALIA

QUEENSLAND

Lake Puntewolona

Natterannie Sandhills

Lake Killamperpunna

Merty Merty

Cooper

Flood Detour

STRZELECKI

Omicron

Lake Palankarinna

Etadunna

Cannuwaukaninna Bore

STRZELECKI

REGIONAL

DESERT

202

Lake Florence

Lake Kopperekoppinna

Bollards Lagoon

Bollards Lagoon

Tooma Gate

Dulkaninna

Lake Gregory

Yaningurie Waterhole

Strzelecki Crossing

120

Corner Store

Cameron Corner

STURT

Lindon

RESERVE

123

Fort Grey

NATIONAL PARK

Olive Downs

Clayton

Lake

Blanche

Waka

Lake Harry

Lake Harry (ruin)

Lake Stewart

Lake Arthur

Murnpeowie

Blanchewater (ruin)

STRZELECKI

115

Montecollina Bore

Mt Hopeless

LAKE CALLABONNA FOSSIL RESERVE

Tilcha

Hewart Downs

Mt Poole 250

Mt Sturt

Theldarpa

Mundowdna

Vermin Proof

Fence

Moolawatana

Lake Callabonna

Boolkaree

Yandama

Hawker Gate

NEW SOUTH WALES

Milparinka

Mt Brown 274

© UNIVERSAL PUBLISHERS PTY LTD 2005

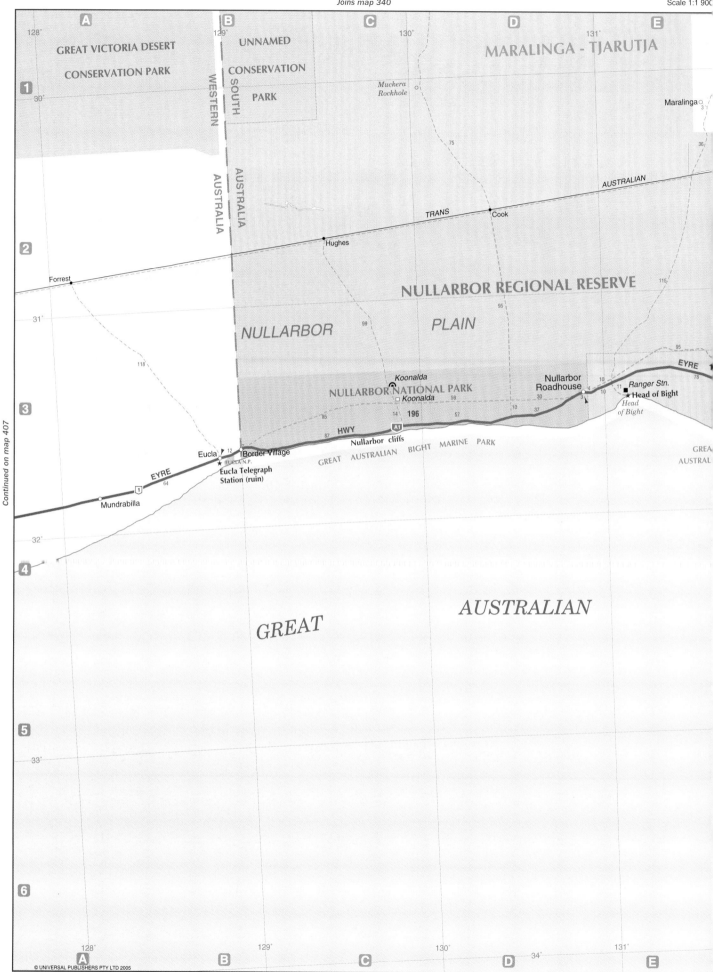

© UNIVERSAL PUBLISHERS PTY LTD 2005

South Australia

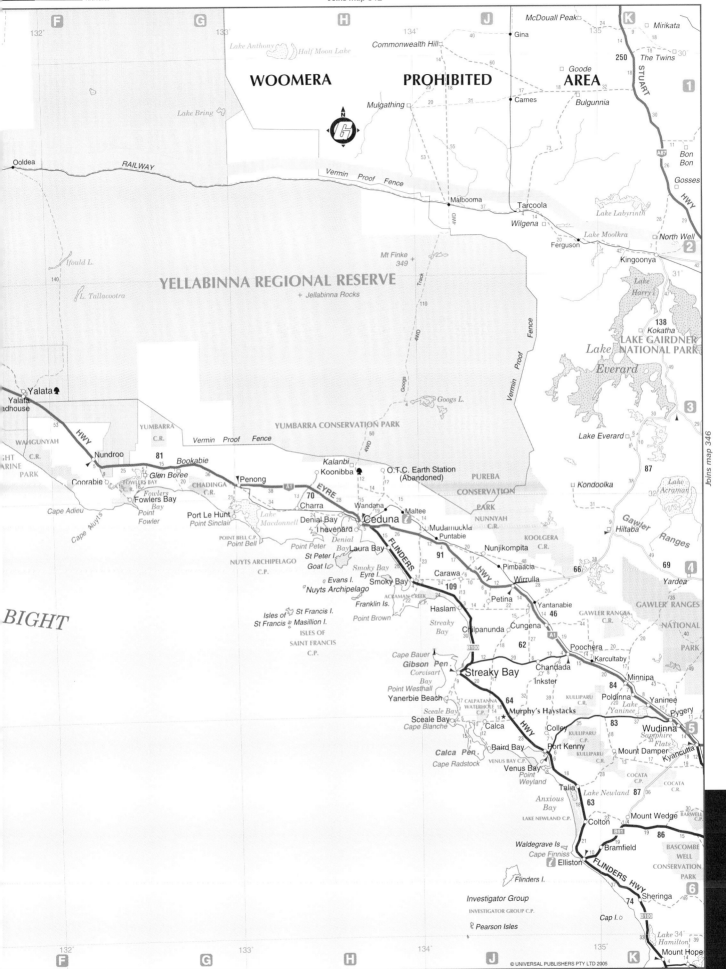

Kilometres
50

WOOMERA　　PROHIBITED　　AREA

Lake Anthony　Half Moon Lake

McDouall Peak
Mirikata
Gina
Commonwealth Hill
Goode
The Twins
250
Mulgathing
Carnes
Bulgunnia

Ooldea
RAILWAY
Vermin Proof Fence
Bon Bon
Gosses

Malbooma
Tarcoola
Wilgena
Lake Labyrinth
North Well

Ifould L.
Ferguson
Kingoonya
Lake Moolkra

YELLABINNA REGIONAL RESERVE
L. Tallacootra
Mt Finke 349
Jellabinna Rocks
Lake Harry

Lake Gairdner
National Park
Kokatha
138

Lake Everard

Yalata
Yalata Roadhouse
WAHGUNYAH
Lake Everard
87
Kondoolka
Lake Acraman

YUMBARRA C.R.
Vermin Proof Fence
YUMBARRA CONSERVATION PARK
Googs L.

Nundroo
81
Bookabie
Kalanbi
Koonibba
O.T.C. Earth Station (Abandoned)
PUREBA CONSERVATION PARK
NUNNYAH C.R.
Hiltaba
Gawler Ranges
69
Yardea

Coorabie
Glen Boree
Penong
70
Charra
Wandana
Maltee
Mudamuckla
Puntabie
KOOLGERA C.R.
66

Port Le Hunt
Denial Bay
Thevenard
Ceduna
91
Nunjikompita
Pimbaacia
Wirrulla
GAWLER RANGES
NATIONAL PARK

Fowlers Bay
Point Fowler
Point Sinclair
Point Bell
Laura Bay
Carawa
Petina
Yantanabie
46

BIGHT
NUYTS ARCHIPELAGO C.P.
St Peter I.
Goat I.
Eyre I.
Smoky Bay
109
Cungena
Poochera
62
Karcultaby
Minnipa
84
Poldinna
Yaninee
Pygery

Evans I.
Nuyts Archipelago
Franklin Is.
Haslam
Chilpanunda
Streaky Bay
Chandada
Inkster

Isles of St Francis
St Francis I.
Masillion I.
Point Brown
Streaky Bay
Wudinna
83

ISLES OF SAINT FRANCIS C.P.
Cape Bauer
Gibson Pen.
Corvisart Bay
Point Westhall
Yanerbie Beach
64
Murphy's Haystacks
KULLIPARU C.P.
Mount Damper
Kyancutta

Scale Bay
Cape Blanche
Calca
Colley
Calca Pen.
Cape Radstock
Baird Bay
Port Kenny
Venus Bay
Talia
87
Lake Newland
63
Colton
Mount Wedge
86

Investigator Group
Waldegrave Is
Cape Finniss
Elliston
Bramfield
BASCOMBE WELL CONSERVATION PARK
Sheringa
74

Pearson Isles
Flinders I.
Cap I.
Mount Hope

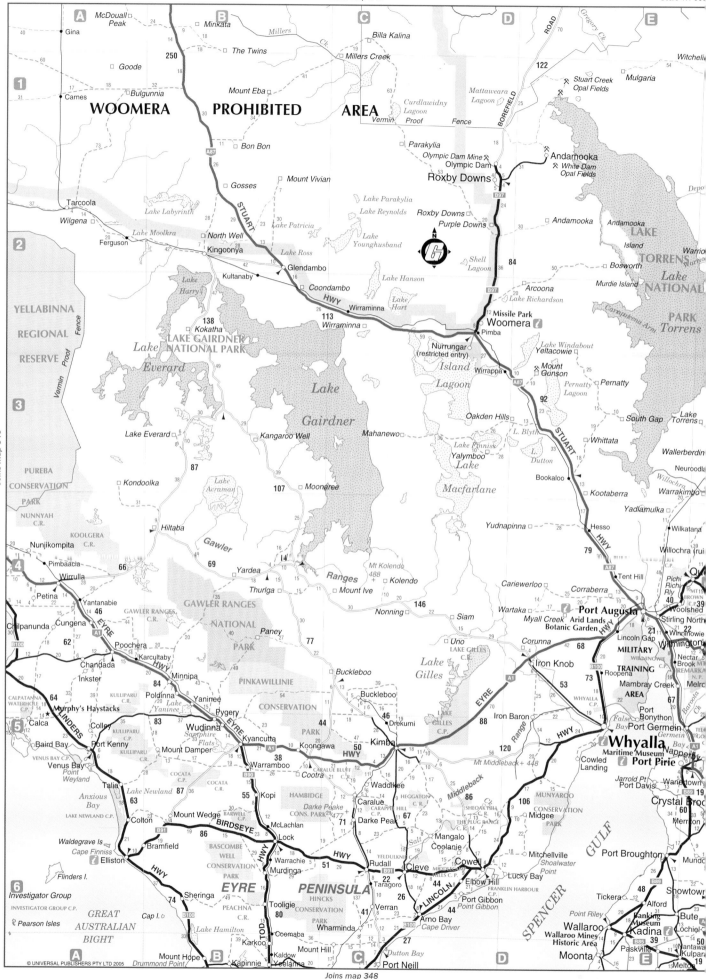

© UNIVERSAL PUBLISHERS PTY LTD 2005

Kilometres
50

F **G** **H** **J** **K**

Mt Sturt

Milparinka
Mt Brown 274

Frome
River
Yerilina

Mt Fitton Talc Mine
(no access)
Moolawatana
Hawker Gate

1

Wilpoorinna
Farina (ruin)
Mt Freeling
Mt Fitton (ruin)
Boolkaree Ck.
Yandama
Mt Shannon
Mount Arrowsmith

STRZELECKI
TRACK
Yerelina
Mount Shannon

80
Mt Lyndhurst
Wheal Turner (ruin)
Hot Springs
Paralana
Umberatana
North Mulga
Smithville House
Lake Wallace
Mount Arrowsmith

Avondale
ARKAROOLA WILDERNESS
SANCTUARY
154
Old Quinyambie
Cooney

33
Leigh Creek Coal Mine
Leigh Creek
Yankaninna
Arkaroola Village
Wooltana
Lake Cootabarloo
Pincally
Border Downs

North Moolooloo
Puttapa
Copley
Leigh Creek
Angepena
Mt McKinlay
1050
Nepabunna
Balcanoona
(N.P. H.Q.)
Lake Pandalpa
Broughams Gate
New Quinyamble
Pimpara Lake

99
Wertaloona
Big John
39
LAKE FROME
Lake Frome
REGIONAL
Lake Elder
Avenel
Packsaddle
Pine Ridge
Packsaddle Roadhouse
Yelka

72
Beltana
WARRAWEENA
Mt Tilley
1018
SANCTUARY
Nantawarrina
Mulga View
Narrina
RESERVE
Billeroo
Pine View
The Veldt

2

35
Blinman
Angorichina Roadhouse
Wirrealpa
Balcoracana Ck.
111
Frome Downs
Lake Tarkarloo
Eurinilla
Mount Westwood
Tielta
McDougalls Well
Fowlers Gap

Parachilna
FLINDERS RANGES NATIONAL PARK
Mt Caernarvon
923
Buffalo
Martins Well
65
Vermin Proof Fence
Benagerie
Morphetts
Mount Woowoolahra
Corona
174

89
Wilpena
Wilpena Pound
58
Erudina
Curnamona
Mulyungarie
Kantappa
Bijerkerno
Acacia Downs

3

Moralana
Mern Merna
35
Warcowie
Willippa
77
Strathearn
Yarramba
Wilangee
Paringa
Mount Gipps

Hawker
Holowilena
Old Baratta (ruin)
Baratta
Koonamore
Kalkaroo
Mulgundawa
Purnamoota
Yanco Glen
Daydream Mine

Gordon (ruin)
Cradock
Yednalue
122
Witchitie
Mt Victor
Plumbago
Bimbowrie
Kalabity
Boolcoomata
Mundi Mundi
Silverton
Stephens Creek
Glen Idol

4

Belton
Four Brothers
Bulloo Creek
Mingary
116
Cockburn
Broken Hill
Mount Gipps
Huonville
Kinalung
Quondong
Kars
111

70
Carrieton
Bendleby
Melton
Waukaringa (ruin)
46
Morialpa
Outalpa
Cultana
Olary
Aroona
Tepco
Corella
Ascot Vale
Topar

Moockra
Johnburgh
Yalpara
Minburra
Wabricoola
Mannahill
Eringa Park
Maldorkey
Mutooroo
Burta
Wonga
Enmore
Pine Point
Langwell
Leonora Downs
Nettlegoe Lake

52
Willowie
Walloway (ruin)
McCoys Well
Yunta
81
Wadnaminga
Devonborough Downs
Duffields
Netley
Blackwell
Buckalow
Kudgee
Tandou Lake
Middle Camp
Tandau

Morchard
Bridgewater
Pekina
37
Nackara
Dawson
Paratoo
Tiverton
Benda Park
Oulnina Park
Olorah Downs
Mazar
South Ita
Budgeree
Kimberley

Booleroo Centre
Peterborough
Orroroo
Black Rock
71
Oodla Wirra
Manunda
Netley Gap
Lilydale
Nagaela
Terrananya
Double Yards

Wirrabara
Appila
Yongala
Mannanarie
Pine Creek
Oakvale
Loch Lilly
Coombah Roadhouse
263

56
Laura
Caltowie
Terowie
Franklin
The Oaks
Faraway Hill
Oakbank
Quandong Vale
Twin Wells
Popilta Lake

Gladstone
Jamestown
54
Whyte Yarcowie
Bendigo
Braemar
Sturt Vale
Morgan Vale
DANGGALI
Popiah

Georgetown
38
Ketchowla
Kia Ora
Pine Valley
CONSERVATION PARK
Travellers Lake
Yelta

Narridy
16
Washpool
Hallett
Caroona
Fords Lagoon
Lords Well
TARAWI N.R.
Nialia Lake
Nearie Lake
Trelega
Manilla

Gulnare
Spalding
44
30
Booborowie
Murkaby
Koomooloo
Canopus
Hypuma
CHOWILLA REGIONAL RESERVE
Bunneringee
Milkengay L.

Yacka
49
36
Mount Bryan
Redcliffe
Balah
Canegrass
Pine Camp
Twelve Mile

Blyth
Hilltown
43
Hanson
87
The Gums
CHOWILLA GAME RESERVE
Lake Victoria
Burtundy

Clare
Clare Valley Wineries
54
Manoora
Robertstown
Morgan
Cadell
Chaffey
53
Whitwarta
Saddleworth
BARRIER
SILVER CITY HWY

5

6

SOUTH AUSTRALIA
NEW SOUTH WALES
Dog Fence
Silver City Hwy

© UNIVERSAL PUBLISHERS PTY LTD 2005

Continued on maps 116 & 111

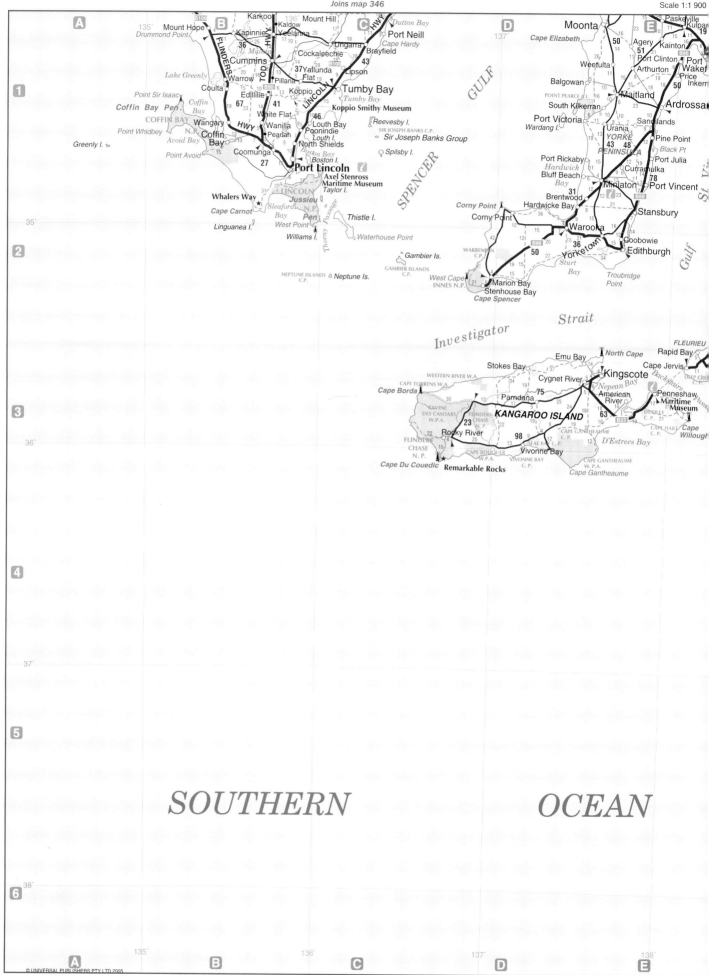

SOUTHERN

OCEAN

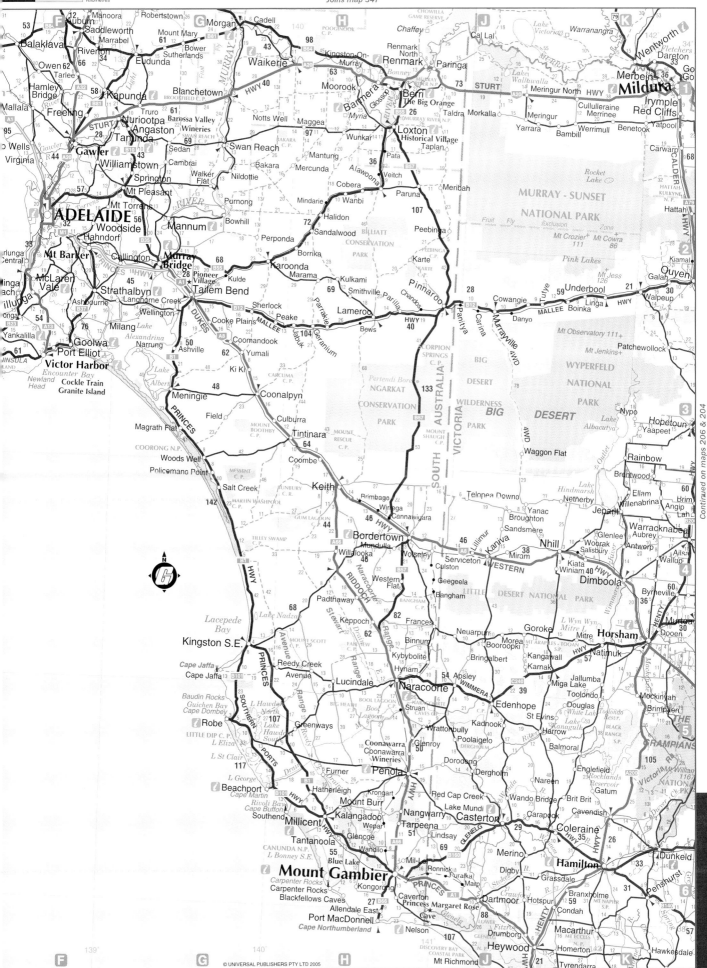

© UNIVERSAL PUBLISHERS PTY LTD 2005

Western Australia is the giant of Australian states, occupying about one-third of the continent. Its vast coastline takes in the remote Kimberley in the north, the iron 'shoulder' of the Pilbara, and runs past the Ningaloo coral reef, Shark Bay, the Houtman Abrolhos Islands and Perth's sandy plain. After turning east at the rocky capes of the south-west, it takes in granite shores facing the wild Southern Ocean and the limestone cliffs of the Great Australian Bight.

Perth, Western Australia's capital, is a modern city situated on the Swan River within easy reach of ocean beaches and the forested Darling Ranges. The city is a tourist attraction in its own right and, with its port of Fremantle, is the gateway to the state. In the south of the state, visitors seek out the famous wildflower displays, the majestic karri forests, the Stirling and Porongurup ranges, the inland goldfields and the coastal national parks. Further north, many are drawn to the Pinnacle Desert,

Western Australia: The Wildflower State

- ◈ Population: 1 862 000
- ◈ Total area: 2 525 000km²
- ◈ % of Australia: 32.8%
- ◈ Floral emblem: Red and Green Kangaroo Paw
- ◈ Fauna emblem: Numbat

Photo above: Pinnacle Desert, Nambung National Park

Geraldton's wildflowers, Batavia Coast and the natural wonders of the Shark Bay World-Heritage area, the Ningaloo Reef, the Pilbara's iron ranges, and to Broome and the Kimberley.

Touring this vast state with its multitude of outstanding attractions requires planning and time. The south-west area around Perth is relatively easy to get around by car, with a network of good roads and accessible features. The rest of

Western Australia has fewer road options. Flying to different parts of the state can cut out some long drives, but, despite the daunting distances, touring by car is a rewarding experience. A 4-wheel drive vehicle is essential for touring in the Kimberleys or the desert tracks of the state's centre, such as the Canning Stock Route and the Gunbarrel Hwy.

Main ATTRACTIONS

◈ Broome
Located at the southern end of the Kimberleys, Broome was once the pearling capital of the world.

◈ Caves District
This area is characterised by caves, wineries, fine restaurants and secluded hideaways.

◈ Fremantle
Perth's historic port city has developed an alternative, arty atmosphere in recent years.

◈ Kalgoorlie-Boulder
A once-notorious frontier town, Kalgoorlie has many reminders of its rip roaring goldfields past.

◈ Mandurah-Pinjarra
This region is renowned for its idyllic beaches, waterways and the karri forests of the Darling Range.

◈ Nambung National Park
The myriad spires of the Pinnacle Desert are a favourite with photographers, especially at sunrise and sunset.

◈ Nullarbor Plain
The world's longest stretch of dead-straight railway line runs for 478km across this virtually treeless plain between Nurina in Western Australia and Watson in South Australia.

◈ Purnululu National Park
'Discovered' relatively recently, the orange-striped beehive domes of the Bungle Bungles are an outstanding attraction.

◈ Rottnest Island
This island near Perth is a popular holiday resort with secluded beaches and beautiful coves.

The largest state, Western Australia comprises one-third of the continent's landmass and travelling may involve huge distances. The state consists of mainly dry plateaus ranging from 300m to 600m above sea level and bordered by a coastal plain. Despite its vast area, Western Australia has a relatively small population—less than one-tenth of the nation's total. Around 80% of West Australians live in Perth and the south-west corner of the state. The other 20% are scattered in coastal towns and small Outback communities.

The state was not formally annexed until Lieut. Governor James Stirling established the Swan River settlement and proclaimed the colony of Western Australia in June 1829. The settlement expanded to become Perth but isolation from other settlements held back development. The discovery of gold at **Coolgardie** in the 1890s caused the first economic boom. Hugely rich in minerals and with more than 270 operating mines, Western Australia now exports iron ore, alumina, nickel, mineral sands, gold and diamonds. Extensive gas reserves have developed markets in Taiwan, Korea and Japan. Western Australia is also one of Australia's major sources of petroleum.

Cereal crops grown in the **Mid West** are the largest primary industry. This huge area of the state provides the space and soils for large-scale agricultural production. Exports range from wool, beef, lambs and leather, to wine, ice-cream, barley, malt and noodles. The fisheries of Western Australia are also major world suppliers of lobsters, prawns and pearls. The forestry industry produces both hard and softwood timbers as well as woodchips.

Today, like many other Australian states, the fastest growing industry is tourism. As popular with Australians as with overseas visitors, Western Australia offers a wide range of experiences and adventures throughout the year.

Western pygmy-possum, *Cercartetus concinnus*, feeding on *Grevillea georgeana*

Those who venture to the north of Perth will find the landscape offers great diversity, including paddocks of cereal crops and the unique wind-carved limestone formations known as the **Pinnacles**.

Further north is the ancient gorge country of the **Pilbara**, which can be seen at its best in **Karijini NP**. At the top of the state, in the **Kimberley region**, the **King Leopold Range**, **Purnululu NP**, **Geikie** and **Windjana gorges** create uniquely spectacular landscapes.

Within the **Goldfields region**, the city of **Kalgoorlie-Boulder**, in its heyday the 'richest square mile of earth in the world', retains its frontier atmosphere. South of Perth, visitors are attracted to the **Caves District**, the imposing karri forests and an exciting array of coastal national parks.

The whole state is famed for its dazzling display of spring wild-flowers, which has led to it being called the 'Wildflower State'.

Walpole Inlet, Walpole

TOURISM REGION HIGHLIGHTS

Western Australia occupies over 2.5million km² of the Australian continent. Travellers in this vast, rugged state come for its natural marvels, like the beehive domes of the Bungle Bungles, the extraordinary spires of the Pinnacle Desert and the stark, red gorges of the Kimberleys. They come to ride camels at Cable Beach, swim with dolphins at Monkey Mia or dive with whale sharks at Ningaloo Reef. When you add historic goldfields, spring wildflowers, wineries, caves and stunning national parks there's a lot to see in Western Australia for those who have the time.

A Perth and Fremantle
Burswood Casino; Cottesloe Beach; Fremantle Arts Centre; Kings Park; London Court; Mundaring Weir; Old Observatory; Perth Zoo; Rottnest Island; Swan River; Swan Valley Wineries; The Old Mill; The Swan Bells; Western Australian Museum; Western Australian Maritime Museum; Yanchep NP

B Esperance
Bay of Isles, Esperance; Cape Arid NP; Cape le Grand NP; Hopetoun; Peak Charles NP; Pink Lake; Ravensthorpe

C Gascoyne (Outback Coast)
Cape Range NP; Carnarvon; Dirk Hartog Island; Exmouth; Francois Peron NP; Hamelin Pool; Kennedy Ranges; Monkey Mia dolphins; Mount Augustus; Ningaloo Reef; Shark Bay

D Goldfields
Coolgardie; Golden Mile; Hannan's North Mine; Kalgoorlie; Kookynic; Norseman; Nullarbor Plain; WA Museum Kalgoorlie-Boulder

E Great Southern
Albany; Denmark; Elephant Cove; Katanning; King George Sound; Mount Barker; Nornalup; Porongorup NP; Stirling Range NP; Torndirrup NP; Valley of the Giants; Whale watching; Whale World

F Heartlands
Avon Valley NP; Badgingarra NP; Cervantes; Coomberdale Wildflower Farm; Kellerberrin; Lake Dumbleyung; Mount Lesueur NP; New Norcia; Pinnacle Desert, Nambung NP; Wagin Historical Village; Wave Rock; Wickepin; York

G Kimberley
Argyle Diamond Mine; Broome; Bungle Bungles, Purnululu NP; Cable Beach; Derby; Fitzroy River; Gantheaume Point dinosaur footprints; Geikie Gorge; Halls Creek; Kununurra; Lake Argyle, Ord River; Piccaninny Creek; Willie Creek Pearl Farm; Windjana Gorge; Wolfe Creek Meteorite Crater; Wyndham

H Mid West
Batavia Coast; Canning Stock Route; Dongara/Port Denison; Geraldton; Greenough Hamlet; Gunbarrel Highway; Houtman Abrolhos Islands; Kalbarri; Meekatharra; Wiluna

I Peel
Bibbulmun Track; Darling Range; Dwellingup; Hotham Valley Railway; Jarrahdale; Mandurah; Peel Inlet; Pinjarra; Waroona Dam; Yalgorup NP

J Pilbara
Burrup Peninsula, Dampier; Dampier Archipelago; Hamersley Range; Karijini NP; Karratha; Marble

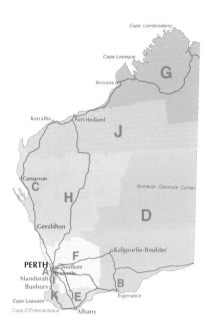

Bar; Millstream-Chichester NP; Mount Bruce; Tom Price

K South West
Augusta; Bunbury; Busselton; Cape Leeuwin Lighthouse; D'Entrecasteaux NP; Donnybrook; Geographe Bay; Jewel Cave; Lake Cave; Leeuwin-Naturaliste NP; Mammoth Cave; Manjimup; Margaret River Wineries; Pemberton Tramway; Whale watching; Willyabrup Valley

Geikie Gorge, in the Kimberleys

NATIONAL PARKS

As the largest state in Australia, it is not surprising that Western Australia has an enormous diversity of environments and landscapes. From the coastal coral marine reserves to the inland semi-arid desert and the lush south-west, it could take several visits to Western Australia to be able to see and appreciate the dramatic differences in the state's national parks.

A Cape Arid NP (Map 407, B5)

Located 120km east of Esperance, Cape Arid NP is 2794km^2 of beach, sea, headland and heathland. Attractions range from walking and climbing trails to idyllic swimming and fishing spots. A wildlife watcher's paradise, the park is home to many species of birds and wallabies in the heathlands. A great place to spot whales and sea-lion colonies, the coastline has many lookout points over the ocean.

B Cape Range NP and Ningaloo Marine Park
(Map 400, B2)

Cape Range NP and Ningaloo Marine Park are located 400km north of Carnarvon. The marine park is known for its amazing coral reef and recreational diving, with the opportunity to sight, or even swim with, the whale shark

(*Rhincodon typus*), the world's largest fish. On land, Cape Range NP covers 506km^2 and has great walking trails which cater for all levels and preferences. Camping is a popular pastime here and a number of secluded beaches and other good sites are available once a camping permit is obtained.

C Drysdale River NP
(Map 399, J1)

In the northern Kimberley region, Drysdale River NP covers 4483km^2. It is a remote park with rugged ranges, cliffs and escarpments. Only accessible by 4-wheel drive, the national park offers walking trails and canoeing possibilities for the experienced adventurer. Known for the Carson Escarpment and the Carson and Drysdale Rivers, it is also home to many bird species, mammals, reptiles and freshwater fish. It is a good area for camping, however, permission is required from the local Aboriginal community.

D Gibson Desert CP
(Map 401, K3)

Gibson Desert Conservation Park is located in central Western Australia, around 1540km north-east of Perth. Covering 18 429km^2 (a section of the southern Gibson Desert), it is home to the Young, Alfred and Marie Ranges and numerous salt lakes. A few small and endangered marsupials dwell in this arid environment, which can only be accessed by 4-wheel drive. There are no specific camping areas, but with local ranger advice it is possible to find an ideal spot for a desert camping experience.

E Leeuwin-Naturaliste NP
(Map 404, A4)

Leeuwin-Naturaliste NP is a well-known park that caters for many interests with its huge variety of attractions. Around 265km south of Perth, the park offers not only a glimpse of a rugged and dramatic coastline, but some amazing rock formations and underground

facts

❖ No. of parks/reserves: 1667
❖ Total area: 187 409km^2
❖ % of state: 7.39%
❖ World Heritage Areas: Shark Bay, Purnululu National Park (Bungle Bungles)

Greater bilby, *Macrotis lagotis*

Striped 'beehive' domes of the Bungle Bungles, Purnululu National Park

limestone caves. Over 100 caves have been found in the park, some with animal remains dating back 37 000 years. Also known for its swimming, diving, walking and fishing, the national park boasts excellent 4-wheel driving opportunities and camping areas.

F Nambung NP (Map 402, A3)

Situated around 230km north of Perth, Nambung NP is famous for the Pinnacles—limestone rock formations—that lie in the heart of the park and number over 150 000. A combination of water, quartz, limestone and sand has interacted to create these unique and varying rock columns that appear to be growing out of golden desert sands. A photographer's paradise, the park is also home to a variety of native flora and fauna and offers fishing,

bushwalking and swimming opportunities.

G Purnululu (Bungle Bungle) NP (Map 399, K3)

One of the most famous national parks in Western Australia, Purnululu NP was listed as a World Heritage Area in 2003. Limited to 4-wheel drive access, the 2397km^2 park is most spectacular from the air. Both helicopter and light plane flights are available. From above, the full effect of the Bungle Bungle Range is obvious: huge orange striped rock domes protruding from the landscape. Other attractions of Purnululu NP are the gorge walks, particularly the Cathedral Gorge,

Echidna Chasm and Froghole walking trails.

H Stirling Range NP (Map 404, E4)

Stirling Range NP is located in the south-west corner of Western Australia, 450km from Perth. The mountain range itself rises out of vast wildflower plains, the deep blue peaks dominating the horizon from every angle. There is a popular 42km drive through the centre of the 1159km^2 park, with lookout stops along the way. Bushwalks are another major attraction in Stirling Range NP. There are designated camping sites and areas available to caravans.

National Park Information

Western Australia Conservation and Land Management (CALM)
17 Dick Perry Ave, Western Precinct
Kensington, WA 6151
Ph: (08) 9334 0333
www.naturebase.net

Striped knob-tailed gecko, *Nephrurus laevissimus*

WILDFLOWERS

Every year between July and November the Western Australian landscape undergoes a startling transformation. A multicoloured patchwork of wildflowers spreads out across the state. Western Australia has often been referred to as the 'Wildflower State', little wonder since about 12 000 wildflower species thrive here.

The wildflower season commences in the northern **Pilbara** region in July, begins slightly later further south and concludes in the southern part of the state in November. Whilst rain and sunshine influence seasonal variations, generally speaking there is a profusion of wildflowers throughout the state between July and November.

Northern regions

These are home to many species of coastal and inland wildflowers, but are best known for everlastings. These lollipop-shaped flowers form carpets of brilliant colour that may well stretch to the horizon. The 1860km^2 **Kalbarri NP** also teems with kangaroo paws, banksias, flowering eucalypts and grevilleas.

Further north, the **Gascoyne** and **Cape Range** regions are covered with wattles, hakeas, dampiera, purple peas and Shark Bay daisies. The Pilbara blossoms with yellow native hibiscus, bluebells, sticky cassia, mulla mulla and native fuchsias, to name a few. To the east, fields of everlastings, acacias, hakeas and Sturt's desert pea enliven the plains of the **Kalgoorlie-Goldfields region**.

Southern regions

Many rare and dainty flowers cover the southern areas, including orchids, milkmaids, honeypots, green kangaroo paws and mountain bells. There are over 50 orchid species and over 80 species of carnivorous plants such as the Albany pitcher plant, mistletoes like the Western Australian Christmas tree, heady, scented plants like brown boronia, and the unique grass tree *Kingia australis*.

The scarlet banksia, *Banksia coccinea*, is found only in the south-western and southern coastal areas of the state

Visitors to Perth can simply go to Kings Park for a dazzling display. The **Kings Park Wildflower Festival** is an extremely popular event in early October. Many other regions also hold special wildflower events.

Package tours to wildflower country

Relaxing wildflower experiences can be booked from Perth or interstate during the peak season. Packages involve coach, rail or air transport with wildflower tour options that may include other natural attractions such as the famous dolphins of **Monkey Mia**, the **Pinnacles** and **Wave Rock**.

Self-drive wildflower country

Hiring a car is a great way to tour the wildflower regions at one's own pace. Full details and maps are available from Western Australia visitor centres, motoring organisations and many of the state's service stations.

Pink everlastings, *Rhodanthe chlorocephala*, at the Kings Park Wildflower Festival, Perth, in October

Western Australia

WINERIES

Viticulture in Western Australia followed very quickly after the first settlers arrived in 1829. The oldest winery, **Olive Farm**, near the present Perth Airport, was established in 1830 and is still going strong. **George Fletcher Moore** also planted vines in the Swan Valley, with cuttings from the Cape of Good Hope in South Africa. The Swan Valley has remained commercially viable, and, since the 1960s, has been joined by five other regions that have been successfully developed in the southwest corner of the state.

Western Australian wines are generally of exceptional quality. Although the state produces less than 2% of Australian wine, it accounts for about 20% of the nation's premium bottled wine.

A Coastal Plains

There are a number of wineries on the fertile coastal soils, both on the northern outskirts of Perth and southward between **Rockingham** and **Capel**. Wines include shiraz, cabernets, grenache, chardonnay, chenin blanc, sauvignon blanc, riesling, merlot and pinot noir.

B Great Southern

(pp.368–369)

This picturesque area around **Mount Barker**, **Albany** and **Denmark** is one of Australia's largest wine regions. More than 30 wineries flourish here, producing all the major grape varieties. Rieslings with an intense limey flavour have been a great success, also premium quality shiraz, pinot noir and chardonnay.

C Margaret River

(pp.370–371)

The 70 or so Margaret River vignerons have gained an impressive reputation for world-class premium wines, in an area extending from **Dunsborough** and **Busselton** to **Augusta**. Outstanding reds include cabernet sauvignon, cabernet franc and merlot. Semillon, sauvignon blanc, chardonnay and verdelho are the most successful whites.

D Pemberton/Manjimup

This is an exciting new region deep in karri, jarrah and red-gum country with a fast-growing reputation for premium wines. Varieties grown include pinot noir, shiraz, merlot, chardonnay, cabernet sauvignon, cabernet franc, verdelho, malbec and sauvignon blanc.

E Perth Hills (p.363)

A number of boutique wineries are to be found in the **Darling Range**, to the east of Perth. Classic wines such as cabernet sauvignon, shiraz, merlot and chardonnay are available for tasting, as well as sparkling wines.

F Swan Valley (p.363)

Winemaking has been continuous here since 1830 and has involved such famous labels as Houghton, Sandalford and Evans & Tate. In 1937, vigneron **Jack Mann** produced the first vintage of Houghton's White Burgundy, the earliest widely-accepted table wine in Australia. Nearly all classic wine varieties are now represented. **Swan River cruises** from Perth offer a very pleasant way to visit the historic wineries.

Cellar door entrance, historic Houghton Winery

PERTH

Hay Street Mall, Perth

main attractions

◈ **Fremantle**

Perth's port city is the western gateway to Australia, with beautiful beaches, historic buildings, old-world charm and a fascinating heritage that dates back to 1829.

◈ **Government House**

Completed in 1864 and home to the State Governor, Government House is set in romantic English-style gardens and includes an elegant ballroom.

◈ **Kings Park**

Affording excellent views from Mount Eliza over Perth and the Swan River, the 400ha parkland includes natural bushland and showcases Western Australia's famed wildflowers in spring.

◈ **London Court**

This Tudor-style shopping arcade between Hay St Mall and St George's Tce is Perth's most photographed tourist attraction.

◈ **Perth Mint**

Visit the past in the Mint's Old Melting House, see molten gold being poured, watch coins being minted and view natural gold in one of Western Australia's oldest buildings.

◈ **Rottnest Island**

A popular holiday island off the coast, Rottnest offers crystal water, white beaches, fishing, golf, surfing, walks and wildlife, including the quokka, *Setonix brachyurus*.

Founded in 1829 on the banks of the **Swan River**, Perth's fortunes received a substantial boost in the 1890s when gold was discovered at **Coolgardie** and **Kalgoorlie** to the east. Today, Perth is a scenic and sophisticated city, renowned for its abundant sunshine, relaxed lifestyle and easy-going manner. The city's modern skyline blends with magnificent colonial architecture, housing excellent retail outlets particularly around **Hay St** and **Murray St** and the malls running between them. **King St**, a historic and lovingly restored commercial precinct, is known for its fashion houses, cafes, art galleries and specialist book stores.

Within minutes of the CBD is the world's oldest operating mint as well as a number of art galleries and museums, historic buildings and parklands. Perth's prime position, flanking the broad reaches of the Swan River, provides an excellent setting for enjoying alfresco dining in one of the many outdoor restaurants and cafes. Perth residents have a choice of more than 80km of white sandy beaches within easy reach.

ℹ **Visitor information**

Western Australia Visitor Centre
Forrest Place, cnr Wellington St,
Perth, WA 6000
Ph: (08) 9483 1111
Tollfree: 1300 361 351
www.westernaustralia.com

facts

◈ Population: 1 400 000
◈ Date founded: 1 June, 1829
◈ Tallest building: Central Park, 261.7m
◈ Average temperature: 24°C (January), 14.5°C (June)

Places of Interest

Art Gallery of Western Australia Ⓐ C3
Barracks Archway Ⓑ B3
Fire Safety Education Centre and Museum Ⓒ D3
Francis Burt Law Education Centre and Museum Ⓓ C4
His Majesty's Theatre Ⓔ B3
Kings Park Ⓕ A4
London Court Ⓖ C3
Parliament House Ⓗ B3
Perth Cultural Centre Ⓘ E4
Perth Institute of Contemporary Arts Ⓙ C3
Perth Mint Ⓚ D4
Perth Town Hall Ⓛ C3
Perth Zoo Ⓜ B6
Queens Gardens Ⓝ E4
Scitech Discovery Centre Ⓞ B2
Stirling Gardens Ⓟ C4
Supreme Court Gardens Ⓠ C4
The Old Mill Ⓡ B5
The Swan Bells Ⓢ C4
WACA Oval Ⓣ E4
Western Australian Museum Ⓤ C3

Perth's impressive CBD, seen from Kings Park

Western Australia

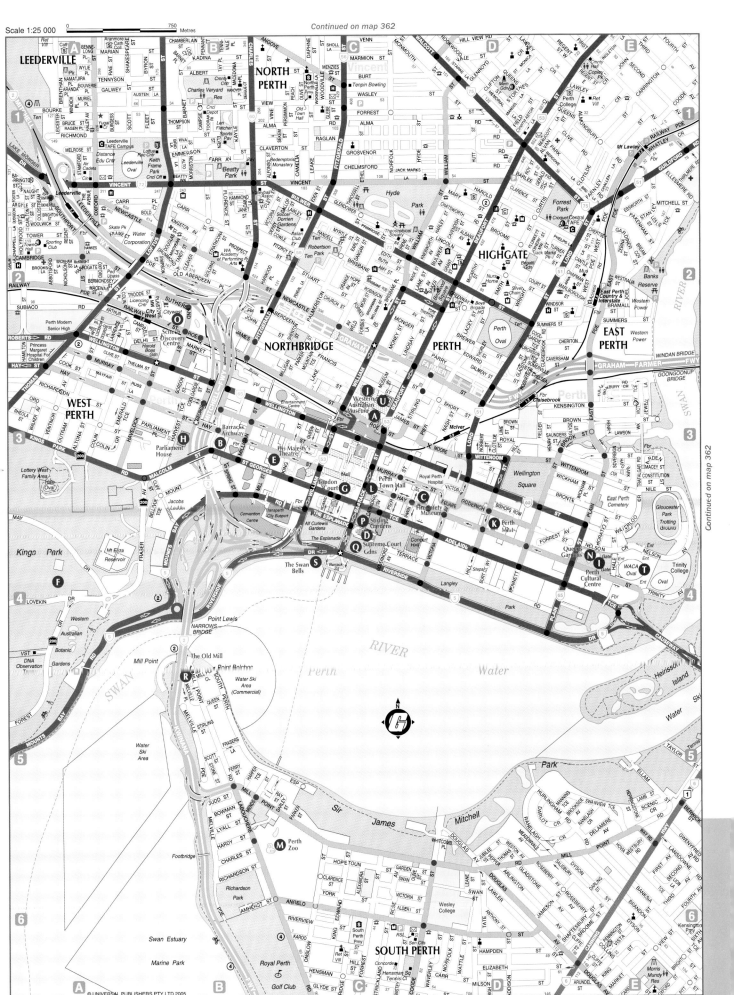

Scale 1:25 000
0   750 Metres

Continued on map 362

LEEDERVILLE

NORTH
PERTH

HIGHGATE

EAST
PERTH

NORTHBRIDGE

PERTH

WEST
PERTH

Kings Park

SOUTH PERTH

© UNIVERSAL PUBLISHERS PTY LTD 2005

CBD & SUBURBS

CBD ATTRACTIONS

Exploring Perth's CBD is an easy task. The city is compact and well planned, even though its location on a broad stretch of the Swan River gives it a spacious feeling. In addition, Perth has one of the best public transport systems in the country.

Perhaps the best place to start is the western edge of the CBD, in **Kings Park** and the **Botanic Gardens**. From here, along Kings Park Rd and onto Malcolm St, the attractions of the CBD are waiting to be explored. Take a look at **Parliament House** with an education officer and discover the history of the Westminster system. Continuing along Malcolm St to St Georges Tce brings you to the **Barracks Archway**, originally built in 1863 and the only relic of the old Guards Barracks. Divert to **Hay St** via **Cloisters Square** to find **His Majesty's Theatre**, home to the city's premier theatre and musical productions. Drop into the pedestrian mall on Hay St for a break and then explore **London Court**, a spectacular Tudor-style arcade catering for tourists and window shoppers alike. Turn right into Barrack St, then left into St George's Tce, passing **Perth Town Hall**, **Stirling Gardens** and several stately churches. Continuing onto Adelaide Tce, turn left into Hill St and visit the **Perth Mint**. Since the goldrush, Australia's gold has been refined here into legal tender, gold bars and jewellery, however, the Mint itself has only been open to the public in recent years.

Other interesting attractions of the CBD area include the **Fire Safety Education Centre and Museum** in the original Perth City Fire Station; **Francis Burt Law Education Centre and Museum** near the **Supreme Court Gardens**; and the **Scitech Discovery Centre** on Railway Pde.

On the banks of the Swan River, **Barrack Square** was originally built as a military parade facility. Today it is an attractively manicured garden square surrounding the unique **Bell Tower**, with a surrounding jetty of cafes, shops and a busy ferry terminal. **The Swan Bells** in the Tower include 12 original bells from St Martin-in-the-Fields Church in London, celebrated in the old nursery rhyme *Oranges and Lemons*. Jump on a ferry across the Swan River to **South Perth Esplanade** where the renowned **Perth Zoo** is located a few minutes away. It has one of Australia's best collections of native and exotic animals, which are in enclosures resembling their natural habitats. Wandering back along the Swan the length of **Sir James Mitchell Park**, take a look at **Heirisson Island**; access is via the bicycle path from the City of Perth Causeway Carpark. The island contains a memorial to Yagan, an Aboriginal leader killed in 1833.

Returning to **East Perth** after visiting Heirisson Island, wander by **Trinity College** and the **WACA Oval**, home to Western Australia's leading cricket and football matches. Finally, a little further up Hay St, **Perth Cultural Centre**, located in **Queens Gardens**, is definitely worth a visit.

SUBURBAN ATTRACTIONS

Closest to the CBD, the suburb of **Northbridge** is a popular restaurant and entertainment precinct. A complex of imposing buildings between William St and Beaufort St includes the **Western Australian Museum, Alexander Library**, **Perth Institute of Contemporary Arts** and the **Art Gallery of Western Australia**. The **Galleria Art and Craft Markets** specialise in local arts and crafts and are open on weekends.

Miners' statue outside the Perth Mint

KINGS PARK

Perth's largest and best-loved park overlooks the Swan River and is only five minutes from the CBD. The park is not only an attractive garden of native Australian wildflowers and parkland, but also a haven for children and the young at heart. It offers playgrounds, scenic walking and driving tours, the presentation of special events, local and Aboriginal live performances and the **State War Memorial**. And then there are the amazing views of the city itself from **Mount Eliza Lookout**—Kings Park and the **Botanic Gardens** are truly the heart and soul of the City of Perth.

Underneath the lookout, the **Artist in Residence Gallery** provides a venue for local Aboriginal artists to work and sell their unique art. The spectacular **Kings Park Wildflower Festival** in October is extremely popular.

Perth CBD viewed from Kings Park

Perth residents boast that their beaches are the 'best surf beaches in Australia'. Some of the more popular are **Cottesloe**, **Port**, **Scarborough** and the nudist beach **Swanbourne**.

A cruise on the Swan River to discover the **Swan Valley** is a worthwhile side trip. This was the site of the state's first permanent vineyards and there are are now over 40 wineries offering tours and tastings of top quality wines. A number of the wineries offer excellent alfresco or restaurant dining. Some wineries, like **Houghton** and **Sandalford** are over 100 years old.

Only 20 minutes from Perth, **Sorrento Quay** at **Hillarys Boat Harbour** is a marina-style complex packed with shopping and leisure

options, as well as providing a fast ferry service to **Rottnest Island**. The **Aquarium of Western Australia (AQWA)** will introduce you to the beauty and wonder of Western Australia's marine environments. There are many other reasons to explore the suburban areas of Perth: the **Armadale Reptile Centre**, **Burswood International Resort Casino**, **Kalamunda History Village Museum**, the **Museum of Childhood** at Edith Cowan University and **Perth Observatory**, 25km east of the city.

Popular natural getaways for Perth residents and visitors include **Whiteman Park**, **the Hills Forest** and **John Forrest NP**. Whiteman Park is an ideal place to spend the day with the family. It is centred

around **Mussel Pool**, a picnic area and playground, and attractions include an animal enclosure, pony rides, trams, steam trains, sheep shearing, a live snake display, sporting fields, a Craft Village and cafe. Whiteman Park has a constant programme of special events such as bush dances and picnic days for the public. The Hills Forest encompasses national parks and state forests, historic townships, **Mundaring Weir**, and a **Discovery Centre** with an exciting programme of outdoor experiences for visitors such as bushwalking, Aboriginal storytelling, camping and rock-climbing. Within the Hills Forest, John Forrest NP is particularly popular, with fine views of Perth, scenic bushwalking, a tavern, picnic areas and BBQ facilities.

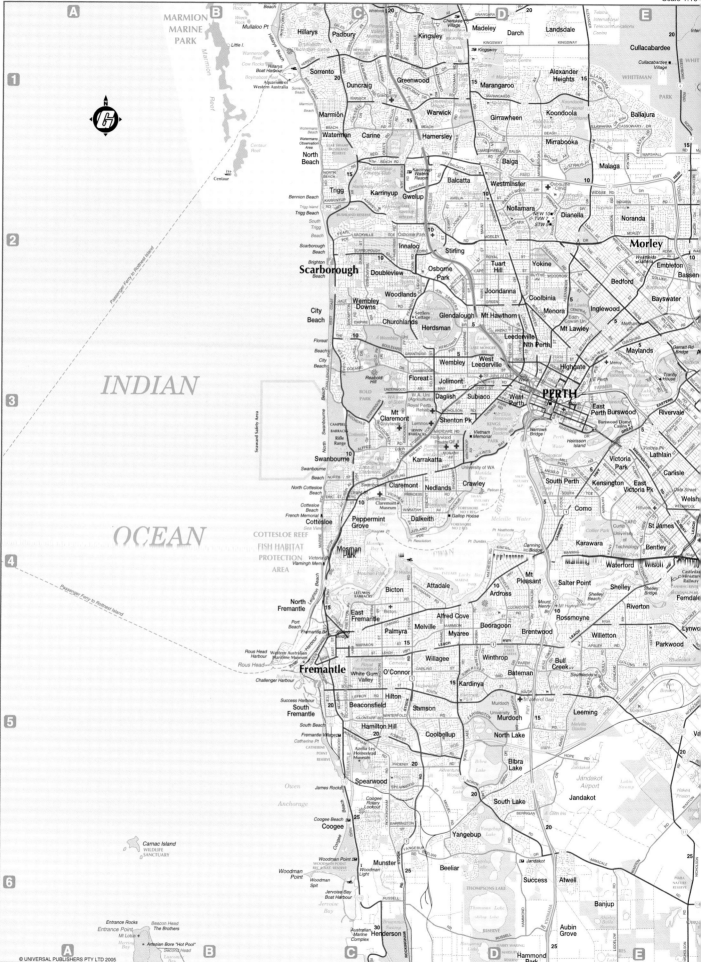

Western Australia

Kilometres

F
G
H
J
K

Henley Brook
Millendon
Gidgegannup
1

Swanbrook
Cantley
Talijancich
DARLING RANGE REGIONAL PARK
Mt Oakover
Red Hill
ADELAIDE
Waste Disposal Area
RECREATION RESERVE
Adventure Centre
Lake Leschenaultia Camp School

Little River
Edwards Bridge
Windy Creek
Sittella
Vindaras
Herne Hill
Valley
Highway
Vino Italia
Hilston Youth Camp
LESCHENAULTIA CONSERVATION PARK
Chidlow

MOTOR MUSEUM
RAAF AREA
Swan Valley Tourist Village
Taylors Westleigh
Lancaster
Houghton
Oakover
Ambrook
JOHN FOREST
Parkerville
Dept of Agriculture

WEST SWAN
Caversham Wildlife Park & Zoo
Middle Swan
Jane Brook
Mt Helena
Stoneville
Carbsa
40
2

Caversham
MIDDLE SWAN
Stratton
Swan Equestrian Lodge
NATIONAL PARK
YMCA Camp Woody
Sawyers Valley

Sandalford
Whiteman
Jane Brook
Rocky Pool
Glen Brook Dam
Youth Camp
Sunninghill Equestrian Centre

SWAN HEALTH SERVICE
Viveash
Midland
Swan View
Swan View Rly Stn
Hovea
Mahogany Creek
35 GREAT EASTERN
30 Mundaring HWY

Woodbridge
Midvale
Bellevue
Greenmount
YORK
Mundaring
Pimelia Mycumbene Picnic Area

East Guildford
West Midland
Midland Terminal
Swan View
N.P.
Grevillea Mycumbene Picnic Area

Guildford
South Guildford
Hazelmere
Koongamia
GREENMOUNT N.P.
Boya
Helena Valley
Darlington
Glen Forrest
PARKLANDS
Helena
STATE FOREST
3

Guildford Road Bridge
GREAT EASTERN HWY
BYPASS
Banksia
Rifle Range
Darlington Estate
Heritage Rose Garden
O'Connor Museum
Gallery
CY O'Connor
CALM District Office

Domestic Terminal
Manday Swamp
GOOSEBERRY HILL NATIONAL PARK
Pipehead Dam
Paulls Valley
Mundaring Weir
Lake CY O'Connor

Perth International Airport
International Terminal
High Wycombe
KALAMUNDA NATIONAL PARK
Calamunda Camel Farm
The Dell Picnic Area
STATE FOREST

Springvale
Maida Vale
Gooseberry Hill
Piesse Brook
Hacketts Gully
Gungin Gully Picnic Area
Reservoir
Sawyers Valley

Forrestfield
Kalamunda
MUNDARING WEIR
Mt Gunjin
Murdos

DARLING RANGE REGIONAL PARK
Pioneer
Perth International Tourist Park
Walliston
Brookside
Lawnbrook
Hainault
STATE FOREST
4

Kewdale Freight Terminal
LESMURDIE FALLS NATIONAL PARK
Lesmurdie
Bickley
Perth Observatory

East Cannington
Wattle Grove
Crystal Brook
LESMURDIE FALLS NATIONAL PARK
TVW ABW
Carmel
Cosham
Carilla

Beckenham
BICKLEY BROOK RESERVOIR
Pickering Brook
Bartons Mill Prison

Kenwick
Orange Grove
Jadran
New Victoria Dam
Victoria Reservoir
STATE FOREST

Maddington
Range View
HILLS BROOK VALLEY RESERVE
Canning Mills
Carinyah
5

Thornlie
Gosnells
GOSNELLS REGIONAL OPEN SPACE
Martin
Riverside Gardens

Huntingdale
COHUNA WILDLIFE PARK
Karragullen
STATE FOREST

Southern River
CHEVIN
BROOKTON
STINTON GARDENS N.R.
STINTON CASCADES N.R.
Kelmscott
Mount Nasura
Roleystone
ARALUEN BOTANIC PARK
40
Lesley
45
6

Westfield
Kelmscott
Armadale - Kelmscott
Lakeside Country Resort
Sherwood
DARLING RANGE NATIONAL PARK
ATALUEN COUNTRY CLUB
Canning Dam
Canning Reservoir

Forrestdale
Armadale
Brookdale
Mt Richon
Botanic Garden & Arboretum
Armadale Settlers Common
Hillside Tourist Village
Willow Springs
Churchman Brook Reservoir

F
G
H
J
K

© UNIVERSAL PUBLISHERS PTY LTD 2005

WESTERN AUSTRALIA 363

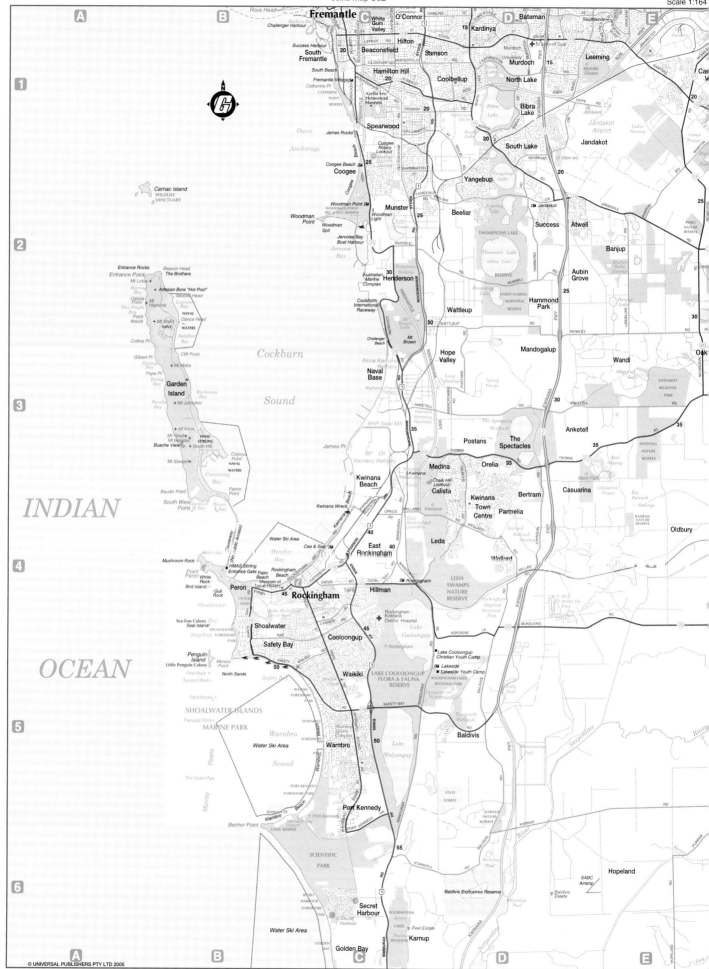

INDIAN

OCEAN

Cockburn

Sound

SHOALWATER ISLANDS
MARINE PARK

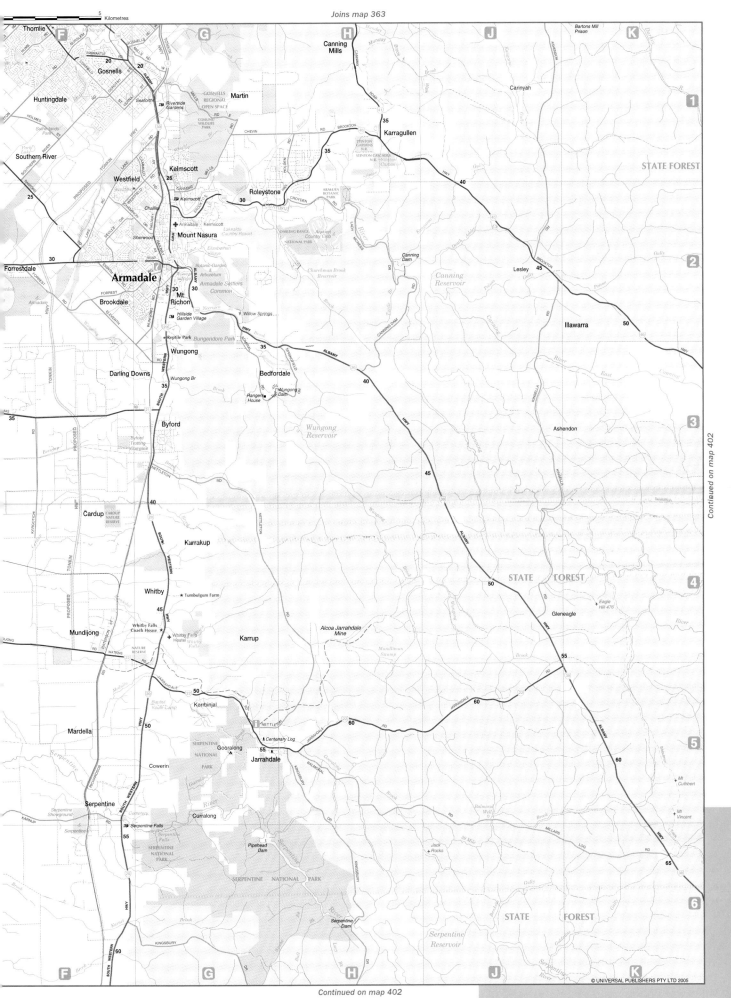

Continued on map 402

© UNIVERSAL PUBLISHERS PTY LTD 2005

■ Albany POP 22 275

Map 369, C3

Western Australia's oldest town, Albany was established in 1826 as a British military outpost. It now attracts many visitors to its beautiful scenery, heritage buildings and excellent fishing. Located 409km south of Perth at the edge of **King George Sound** and **Princess Royal Harbour**, its port today services the **South West Coast**, handling grain, silica sand and woodchips.

MAIN ATTRACTIONS: Stirling Tce is an historic street featuring Victorian shopfronts. **The Old Gaol** (1851) was constructed by convicts and houses a folk museum. Reputedly the town's oldest building, **Patrick Taylor Cottage** (circa 1832) has been restored and furnished with period memorabilia. National Trust-classified **Strawberry Hill Farm**, on Middleton Rd, is the site of an experimental farm (1836). Architectural highlights in York St include **St Johns Church** (1848) and the **Town Hall** (1886), now a theatre. Off Forts Rd, **Princess Royal Fortress** was built to defend King George Sound and has a nature trail and spectacular views. **Residency Museum** was a convict store converted in 1873 into a house for magistrates. Its displays—of the era of European exploration of Australia—include a full-scale replica of the 1826 settlement ship, *Amity*. **Mount Clarence** and **Mount Melville** have panoramic lookouts and **Middleton Beach** has areas for picnicking, swimming, surfing and windsurfing.

NEARBY ATTRACTIONS: Renowned for its spectacular coastal views **Torndirrup NP**, 17km south, encompasses **The Gap** and **Natural Bridge**, the **Blowholes**, the **Gorge** and the **Salmon Holes**. At **Frenchman Bay**, 25km south-east, is **Whale World,** which operated as a whaling station until 1978. Now it houses a museum exhibiting hundreds of artefacts. Whale-watching trips are available July–October.

VISITOR INFORMATION: Old Railway Station, Proudlove Pde, Ph: (08) 9841 1088 or 1800 644 088

■ Augusta POP 1123

Map 371, C6

Western Australia's third oldest European settlement, Augusta is in the **South West** region about 320km south of Perth. This fishing town is situated on **Hardy Inlet** overlooking the mouth of the **Blackwood River**.

MAIN ATTRACTIONS: Local history is well preserved at the **Augusta Historical Museum** in Blackwood Ave; of architectural interest nearby is the modern **Lumen Christi Church**. A cairn off Albany Tce marks where the first settlers landed in 1830 and in **Turner Park** there are huge fig trees planted by a town founder more than 170 years ago. Whales can be seen in **Flinders Bay** from June to August.

NEARBY ATTRACTIONS: Built of local limestone, **Cape Leeuwin Lighthouse** (1896), 9km south, is a 39m-high sentinel and also operates as a meteorological station on the most south-westerly point of mainland Australia. Nearby is a calcifying

Two Peoples Bay, east of Albany

waterwheel built in 1895 to supply the lighthouse keeper's cottages. Other points of interest include: the 360° view at **Hillview Lookout**, 8km west; the former mill town **Old Karridale**; a picnic area east of Karridale at **Alexandra Bridge,** renowned for its spring wildflowers; **Boranup Forest Maze**, 18km north, and the nearby **Boranup Forest Drive** through karri forests. **Jewel Cave**, 9km north-west, is notable for exquisite limestone formations.
VISITOR INFORMATION: Blackwood Ave, Ph: (08) 9758 0166

Australind   POP 5800
Map 375, C4
Australind is a small coastal resort situated on **Leschenault Inlet**, 11km north-east of Bunbury. Bordered by the inlet and the **Collie** and **Brunswick rivers**, it is a popular destination for watersports enthusiasts who enjoy fishing, prawning, crabbing, boating, sailing and windsurfing. The town's name originates from an 1840s proposed port venture with India (Australia-India).
MAIN ATTRACTIONS: The compact jarrah-built **Church of St Nicholas** (1840), located on Paris Rd, measures 3.8m by 6.7m, claiming to be the state's smallest church. Opposite is **Henton Cottage,** built in 1841. The **Featured Wood Gallery**, on Piggot Dr, has works fashioned from old and new timbers.
NEARBY ATTRACTIONS: A scenic drive north to **Binningup** follows the shoreline of Leschenault Inlet with access to a number of picnic and crabbing spots.
VISITOR INFORMATION: Old Railway Station, Carmody Pl, Bunbury, Ph: (08) 9721 7922

Beverley   POP 810
Map 402, D5
Beverley is an historic township, 130km east of Perth on the **Avon River**, founded in 1831 and named after a township in Yorkshire,

England. The town is in the heart of a wheat and sheep-farming district.
MAIN ATTRACTIONS: Western Australia's aviation achievements feature at the **Aeronautical Museum**, in Vincent St, and includes a locally built bi-plane, *Silver Centenary*, constructed 1929–1930. On Brooking St is the grave of **Bill Noongales**, a local Aboriginal who accompanied Sir John Forrest on his 1870 trek from Perth to Adelaide. Beverley has the largest range of architectural styles in any Western Australian rural town, from Federation to Art Deco to post-modern. Architectural sites of interest include the **Court House, Post Office, Town Hall** and **Beverley Hotel**. **Batty's Private Collection** and the **Dead Finish Museum**, built as an inn in 1872, are other local museums.
NEARBY ATTRACTIONS: Historical farm machinery, a museum, homestead and Clydesdale horses can be seen at **Avondale Discovery Farm**, 6km south-west.
VISITOR INFORMATION: 139 Vincent St, Ph: (08) 9646 1555

Boyup Brook   POP 560
Map 404, C3
Boyup Brook sits at the junction of the **Blackwood River** and **Boyup Creek**, in the heart of the **South West's** mixed farming country. This pleasant little town is around 270km south of Perth.
MAIN ATTRACTIONS: The **Pioneer Museum**, in Jayes Rd, provides an appreciation for local history, including a display of vintage clover seed-harvesting machinery. A **Heritage Trail Walk** of the township is signposted while the **Bicentennial Trail** follows the course of the Blackwood River. The information centre holds the **Carnaby Collection** of beetles and butterflies, and promotes local art and handicrafts. **Sandy Chambers Art Studio**, in Gibbs St, has a unique hologram statue, artworks

Ornamental stalagmites in Jewel Cave, near Augusta

and aviaries. **Perup Forest Ecology Centre**, Cranbrook Rd, has a selection of rare wildlife.
NEARBY ATTRACTIONS: **Harvey Dickson's Country Music Centre** is 5km north-east at Easington Farm on Arthur River Rd. Its attractions include horse-drawn vehicles, boats, Elvis Presley memorabilia and an annual rodeo. A highlight of driving in the area is the spring wildflower display. **Haddleton Flora Reserve**, 50km north-east, is renowned for its pink and brown boronias. Two well-established wineries are **Blackwood Crest** and **Scots Brook Winery**.
VISITOR INFORMATION: Cnr Bridge St and Abel St, Ph: (08) 9765 1444

Blessed with natural beauty, the Great Southern region is ideal for holidaymakers. Its diverse landscape incorporates sweeping rural vistas, rugged coastlines, gentle coves and bays, rivers and dramatic mountain ranges. Unspoilt national parks of majestic karri and tingle forest are dotted with ancient rock formations, while the tranquil bays provide the perfect environment for calving southern right and humpback whales to give birth to their young. Some of Western Australia's most beautiful wildflowers grace the 1000 million-year-old granite ranges, that offer excellent hiking and bushwalking opportunities.

This region was settled before Perth—its de facto capital, **Albany** was Western Australia's first European settlement. Now, the region is being increasingly feted for its produce—it is fast becoming one of Australia's largest wine-growing regions, with over 30 wineries to visit.

attractions

- ❖ Albany Whale World
- ❖ Middleton Beach
- ❖ Mount Barker wine-producing region
- ❖ Porongurup and Stirling Range national parks
- ❖ Valley of the Giants and Tree Top Walk
- ❖ William Bay National Park

ℹ Visitor information

Albany Visitor Centre
Old Railway Station, Proudlove Pde,
Albany, WA 6330
Ph: (08) 9841 1088
Freecall: 1800 644 088
www.albanytourist.com.au

Elephant Rocks in William Bay National Park, near Denmark

▨ Bridgetown   POP 2200

Map 404, C4

Picturesque Bridgetown, 94km south-east of Bunbury, is situated in the **Blackwood River Valley** area. A temperate climate and high rainfall support jarrah forests, farmland, plantations and wildflowers, which attract many people, including photographers and artists.

MAIN ATTRACTIONS: **Bridgedale** was built by one of the town's first European settlers. Restored by the National Trust, it is a good example of an 1850s homestead. **Blackwood River Park,** near Blackwood Bridge, is an ideal picnic spot. **Memorial Park** on Hampton St is another pleasant recreation area and panoramic views are provided from **Suttons Lookout**, off Phillips St. The information centre houses a local history display and the fascinating **Brierley Jigsaw Gallery**, with its amazing collection of jigsaw puzzles. A pamphlet details a self-guided walking tour of historic buildings, including **St Paul's Church** (1911), notable for its Gordon Holdsworth collection, including an award-winning lectern. Notable festivals include **Blues at Bridgetown**, on the 2nd weekend in November, and the **Blackwood Marathon**, on the last Saturday in October.

NEARBY ATTRACTIONS: Local agricultural, mining and timber histories can be discovered whilst driving along the 52km **Geegelup Heritage Trail**. Beautiful **Bridgetown Jarrah Park**, 25km west, is an educational and recreational park, demonstrating the unique ecosystem of jarrah forests; there are walking trails and a BBQ area in the park.

VISITOR INFORMATION:
154 Hampton St,
Ph: (08) 9761 1740

▨ Broome   POP 12 200

Map 398, E4

The western gateway to the northern **Kimberley Region**, Broome is a sunny paradise of white sandy beaches and pristine turquoise waters that now attracts visitors from around the world. Its well-known pearling industry has contributed richly to the town: Broome supplied 75% of the world's mother-of-pearl in the early 1900s until war and plastic buttons undermined demand. The industry has since revived with the development of cultured-pearl farming.

Western Australia

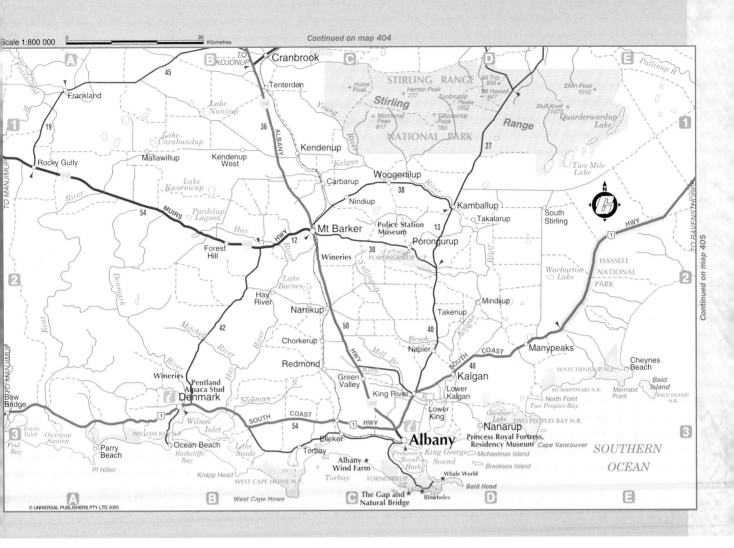

Continued on map 404

Continued on map 405

© UNIVERSAL PUBLISHERS PTY LTD 2005

MAIN ATTRACTIONS: Broome's colourful history can be uncovered along the walls of Johnny Chi Lane in **Chinatown**, an area renowned for its contemporary pearl showrooms, jewellers and restaurants; at the **Broome Historical Society Museum**, Saville St, one of the best regional museums in the country; at **Captain Gregory's House** (now a gallery), home of the most successful pearler; and at the elegant **Court House** (1888), which was originally the Cable Station. **Sun Pictures** (1916) is one of the world's oldest open-air theatres and offers a memorable excursion to the movies. Headstones at the **Japanese Cemetery** stand as testament to the many contributions made by Asian pearlers. Worthwhile walks in the area include a **Mangrove Walk** and **Remnant Rainforest Walk**, located off Gubinge Rd, with entry points signposted. There are many excellent tours, including sunset beach camel rides, cruises, and hovercraft rides to remote beaches. Visit **Roebuck Bay** at full moon between March and October to witness mudflats reflecting luminous light, a phenomenon known as 'Stairway to the Moon'. Anglers should inquire about good local fishing spots.

NEARBY ATTRACTIONS: 6km north is **Cable Beach**, a 22km stretch of sand and clear turquoise waters ideal for swimming. It was named in 1889 when an underwater telegraph cable linked Broome with Java, Indonesia. Nearby is **Malcolm Douglas Crocodile Park**, home to more than 1000 reptiles.

(CONTINUED P.372)

Japanese Cemetery headstones, Broome

CAVES DISTRICT

The Caves District boasts one of the world's most extensive limestone cave systems. It is also known as the **'Cape to Cape'** area because it lies in the region from **Cape Naturaliste** in the north to **Cape Leeuwin** in the south.

The district offers much to adventurous visitors, with a combination of caves and rolling pastures in the hinterland, bordered by a spectacular coastline of reefs and bays. The infamous Roaring Forties winds, that create challenging swells, make the coastline a beacon for surfers and windsurfers from other parts of Australia and beyond. The tranquil waters of **Geographe Bay** attract anglers, waterskiers, snorkellers, windsurfers and beach lovers, while the network of caves draws abseilers, cavers and bushwalkers from around the globe. Jewel Cave, Lake Cave and Mammoth Cave are three of the most popular caves. Wine enthusiasts will appreciate the district's close proximity to the vineyards and wineries of one of Australia's up-and-coming wine-producing regions, and gourmet dining opportunities are also easy to find.

Sugarloaf Rock, Leeuwin-Naturaliste National Park

The Magical Cave System

Weathering over the eons has resulted in the formation of caves in the long, limestone range between Cape Naturaliste and Cape Leeuwin. Of the more than 150 known caves, six of the most spectacular are open to the public.

main attractions

❖ **Augusta**

This is a beautiful fishing town.

❖ **Busselton**

With 30km of white sandy beaches, this premier seaside resort town has twice been voted 'Western Australia's Top Tourism Town'.

❖ **Dunsborough**

Home of the *Swan* dive wreck and artificial reef, its sheltered waters, peaceful coves and scenic bushland make it an ideal family holiday retreat.

❖ **Jewel Cave**

Regarded as the region's best cave, it features fragile calcite formations such as helictites.

❖ **Lake Cave**

An ancient karri tree guards the cave and inside a unique 'table' is suspended over a subterranean lake. CaveWorks Interpretive Centre is situated here.

❖ **Mammoth Cave**

This historic cave features a self-guided tour; there is disabled access.

❖ **Margaret River Vineyards**

The success of the vineyards, established in the early 1970s, has been extraordinary.

 Visitor information

Augusta Margaret River Visitor Centre
Bussell Hwy, Margaret River, WA 6285
Ph: (08) 9757 2911
www.margaretriver.com

Lake Cave, south-west of Margaret River

Western Australia

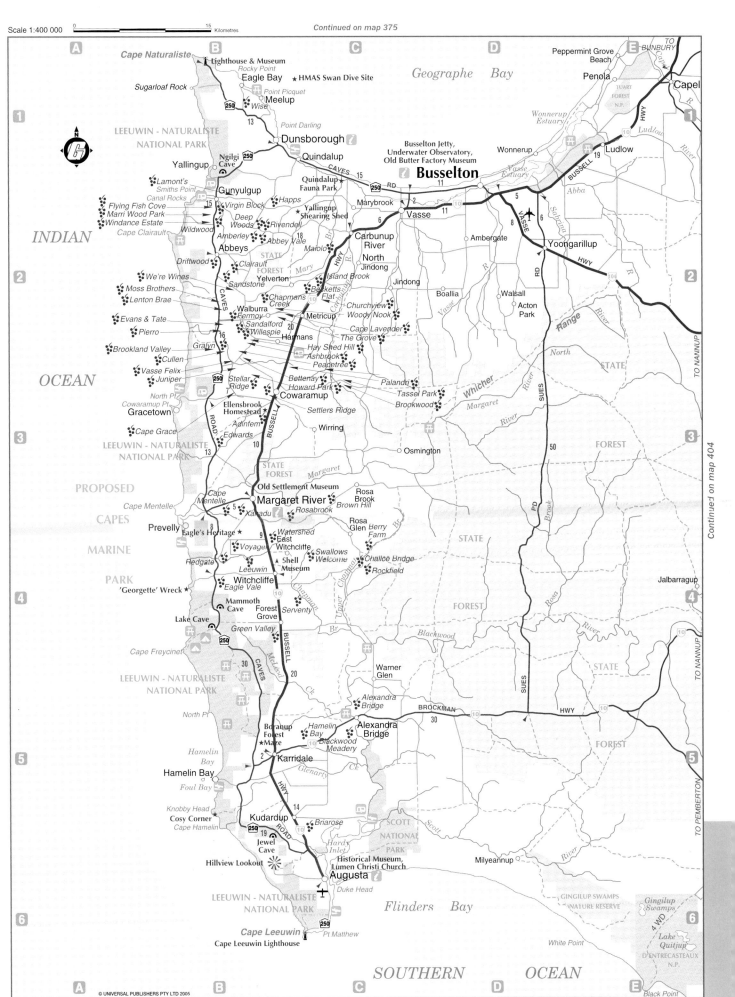

Scale 1:400 000

0   15 Kilometres

A **B** **C** **D** **E**

Cape Naturaliste

↟ Lighthouse & Museum
Rocky Point
Eagle Bay   ★ HMAS Swan Dive Site

Geographe Bay

Peppermint Grove
Beach

Penola

Capel

Sugarloaf Rock

Point Picquet
Meelup

Wise

Point Darling

Dunsborough

TUART
FOREST
N.P.

Wonnerup
Estuary

LEEUWIN - NATURALISTE
NATIONAL PARK

Yallingup   Ngilgi
Cave

Quindalup

Busselton Jetty,
Underwater Observatory,
Old Butter Factory Museum

Wonnerup

Ludlow

Busselton

Gunyulgup

Lamont's
Smiths Point
Canal Rocks

Quindalup
Fauna Park

Marybrook

Abba

INDIAN

Virgin Block
Happs

Deep
Woods
Rivendell

Yallingup
Shearing Shed

Vasse

Vasse
Estuary

Flying Fish Cove
Marri Wood Park
Windance Estate

Cape Clairault

Amberley

Abbey Vale

Abbeys

Carbunup
River
North

Ambergate

Yoongarillup

Driftwood

Clairault

Marolo

Jindong

Walsall
Acton
Park

We're Wines

Yelverton

Island Brook

Jindong

OCEAN

Moss Brothers
Lenton Brae

Sandstone

Chapmans
Creek

Berketts
Flat

Boallia

Range

North

STATE

Evans & Tate

Walburra
Fermoy

Churchview
Woody Nook

Pierro

Sandalford
Willespie

Metricup

Brookland Valley

Grafyn

Harmans

Cape Lavender

The Grove

Whicher

FOREST

Cullen

Vasse Felix
Juniper

Stellar
Ridge

Hay Shed Hill
Ashbrook
Peacetree

North Pt.
Cowaramup Pt.

Ellensbrook
Homestead ★

Bettenay
Howard Park

Cowaramup

Palandri

Tassel Park
Brookwood

Margaret
River

Gracetown

Adinfern
Edwards

Settlers Ridge

Wirring

Cape Grace

Osmington

LEEUWIN - NATURALISTE
NATIONAL PARK

Margaret

STATE
FOREST

FOREST

PROPOSED

CAPES

Cape Mentelle

Old Settlement Museum

Margaret River

Rosabrook

Rosa
Brook

Brown Hill

Cape Mentelle

MARINE

Prevelly

Eagle's Heritage ★

Xanadu

Watershed
East
Witchcliffe

Rosa
Glen

Berry
Farm

Jalbarragup

PARK

Redgate

Voyager

Leeuwin

Shell
Museum

Swallows
Welcome

Challice Bridge

STATE

'Georgette' Wreck ★

Witchcliffe

Eagle Vale

Rockfield

Mammoth
Cave

Forest
Grove

Serventy

FOREST

Lake Cave

Green Valley

Cape Freycinet

Warner
Glen

STATE

LEEUWIN - NATURALISTE
NATIONAL PARK

North Pt.

Alexandra
Bridge

Boranup
Forest
★ Maze

Hamelin
Bay

Alexandra
Bridge

BROCKMAN

FOREST

Hamelin
Bay

Karridale

Blackwood
Meadery

Hamelin Bay

Foul Bay

Glenarty

Knobby Head
Cosy Corner
Cape Hamelin

Kudardup

Briarose

SCOTT

Jewel
Cave

NATIONAL

Milyeannup

Hillview Lookout

Historical Museum,
Lumen Christi Church

PARK

Hardy
Inlet

GINGILUP SWAMPS
NATURE RESERVE

Gingilup
Swamps

Augusta

Duke Head

Flinders Bay

Lake
Quitjup
D'ENTRECASTEAUX
N.P.

Cape Leeuwin
Cape Leeuwin Lighthouse

Pt Matthew

White Point

Black Point

SOUTHERN   OCEAN

© UNIVERSAL PUBLISHERS PTY LTD 2005

Continued on map 404

Broome Bird Observatory, 18km east on Roebuck Bay, is one of Australia's premier sites for observing wading waterbirds. Diverse habitats ensure a variety of birds and tours are available. Visible at low tide at Gantheaume Point, 5km south-west, are dinosaur footprints dating back 120 million years. Also at Gantheaume Point is a rockpool called Anastasia's Pool, built by the former lighthouse keeper for his arthritic wife. Willie Creek Pearl Farm, 38km north (18km unsealed road), provides rare insight into a working pearl farm.
VISITOR INFORMATION: Cnr Great Northern Hwy and Bagot St, Ph: (08) 9192 2222 or 1800 883 777

■ Bunbury   POP 29 000
Map 375, B5
The city of Bunbury is 185km south of Perth on the Leschenault Inlet at the junction of the Preston and Collie rivers. With a temperate climate, accessibility to attractions, and its natural harbour, Bunbury is both a thriving port—exporting timber, mineral sands, alumina and other regional cargo—and a popular holiday destination.
MAIN ATTRACTIONS: Koombana Bay, protected by a breakwater, has ideal conditions for waterskiing, boating and fishing; an historic jetty runs parallel to it. A highlight of the Dolphin Discovery Centre, in Koombana Dr, is supervised swimming with regularly visiting dolphin pods, which can also be seen from harbour cruises. Opposite is a Mangrove Boardwalk through the southernmost mangroves in Western Australia, habitat for more than 60 bird species. Signs on the Shipwreck Trail provide details of the area's early explorers. Basalt Rock is a unique volcanic outcrop on the western beach. King Cottage (1880) is a museum furnished with items from 1870 to 1920. Opposite is

Forest Park with a miniature railway running every third Sunday. Big Swamp Wildlife Park, in Prince Phillip Dr, includes a walk-in aviary. The adjacent Big Swamp Reserve is a natural wetland, home to dozens of bird species and long-necked turtles. There is a 2km walking/cycling path. Centenary Gardens, in Princep St, with its wishing-well, is a favoured spot for picnics. The distinctive chequered unmanned Lighthouse on Ocean Dr, Boulters Heights, and Marlston Hill are popular lookout points. St Marks Church (1842), in the suburb of Picton, is Western Australia's second oldest church.
NEARBY ATTRACTIONS: Boyanup Transport Museum, 20 minutes south-east, exhibits a vintage steam train and other early forms of transport. Dardanup Heritage Park, open Wednesdays and Sundays, has a huge collection of steam engines and heritage items. Gem enthusiasts can visit the Rock and Gem Museum on Bussell Hwy.
VISITOR INFORMATION: Old Railway Station, Carmody Pl, Ph: (08) 9721 7922

■ Busselton   POP 13 500
Map 371, D1
This fishing town on the shores of Geographe Bay and the Vasse River is 228km south of Perth. Busselton's 30km of sandy beaches are one of its principal attractions.
MAIN ATTRACTIONS: Measuring 2km in length, Busselton Jetty is the Southern Hemisphere's longest wooden structure. It is a favourite site for walks, snorkelling, scuba diving and fishing and offers miniature train rides that travel its length. Also part of the jetty complex are Busselton Jetty Interpretive Centre and Busselton Underwater Observatory which features unique corals and marine life. Historic buildings include the Old Butter Factory Museum, in Peel Tce, which recounts the early days of the

town's history. St Mary's Anglican Church, Peel Tce, was built in 1844: it is the oldest stone church in the state. The Old Court House, in Queen St, houses an arts complex.
NEARBY ATTRACTIONS: Ludlow Tuart Forest, 7km east, is a popular picnic and walking retreat and is the world's only natural tuart forest. Nearby on Layman Rd is Wonnerup House (1859), a National Trust-restored and furnished colonial period home. A scenic drive along Geographe Bay to Cape Naturaliste journeys through Dunsborough, Meelup and Eagle Bay and provides an opportunity to visit Ngilgi Cave and Cape Naturaliste Lighthouse.
VISITOR INFORMATION: 38 Peel Tce, Ph: (08) 9752 1288

■ Carnarvon   POP 6590
Map 400, B3
Just south of the Tropic of Capricorn and 904km north of Perth, sunny, palm-lined Carnarvon utilises the Gascoyne River and its subsurface waters to irrigate its flourishing plantations of tropical fruits and a wide range of vegetables.
MAIN ATTRACTIONS: Signposts of Carnarvon's past are detailed in a Heritage Walk pamphlet. The Maritime Heritage Precinct includes One Mile Jetty (1904), a tramway and Kimberley steam locomotive, and a lighthouse

Gantheaume Point, near Broome, where dinosaur footprints can be seen at low tide

keeper's cottage which houses the local history museum. The **Hall of Fame Pastoralist Museum** is situated near the jetty. **Town Beach** is popular for picnics.

NEARBY ATTRACTIONS: On **Babbage Island**, connected by a causeway, are both **Pelican Point**, a beach popular for fishing, swimming and windsurfing, and the **Nor-west Seafoods Prawning Factory** (the information centre can arrange tours). Anglers fish from the **Prawning Jetty** opposite the factory. Between 1964 and 1974, NASA operated a satellite tracking station here, and the remnant 29m-dish, 8km east, provides an excellent vantage for viewing the township. **Westoby Plantation**, 5km east, offers plantation tours. On the Gascoyne River and set amidst ghost gums is **Chinaman's Pool**, suitable for picnics and swimming. 74km north are dramatic **Blowholes** that sometimes reach 20m in height. A kilometre south at **Point Quobba** is a protected beach with a variety of marine life.

VISITOR INFORMATION: 11 Robinson St, Ph: (08) 9941 1146

■ Collie   POP 7250

Map 375, E5

This town is nestled in jarrah timber country, 57km east of Bunbury. Collie produces 3.25 million tonnes of coal annually from nearby open-cut mines.

MAIN ATTRACTIONS: Several attractions reflect Collie's central position in the state's only coal-producing region. The excellent **Coalfields Museum** displays pioneering and mining memorabilia. The **Steam Locomotive Museum** and the informative **Collie Tourist Coal Mine**—a replica of an underground mine—are worthwhile visiting. There are several parks for picnics and leisurely strolls, including **Soldiers Park**, in Steere St, with an **Arboretum** opposite. In Throssell St

Three of the locals at Coolgardie Camel Farm

are **Baarnimar Reconciliation Park**, with fine examples of Aboriginal art, and **Finlay Gardens**. An **Historic Walk** brochure highlights notable sites and a **Craft Gallery** is situated at the Throssell St information centre.

NEARBY ATTRACTIONS: Showcasing jarrah forests and seasonal wildflowers is the **Collie Scenic River Drive**, which starts 5km west of town. **Wellington Dam**, in **Wellington NP** 28km west, is perfect for picnics, fishing and bushwalking, while to the north is **Harris Dam**, the town's scenic reservoir.

VISITOR INFORMATION: Throssell St, Ph: (08) 9734 2051

■ Coolgardie   POP 1260

Map 403, J4

A goldrush town born out of an alluvial strike at **Fly Flat** in 1892, Coolgardie in its heyday supported 23 hotels and seven newspapers. Though the population dwindled as the gold ran out, today the town, 560km east of Perth, preserves an important history.

MAIN ATTRACTIONS: On Bayley St, a **Pharmacy Museum** displays tools-of-the-trade in a recreated turn-of-the-century pharmacy. Adjacent is the **Goldfields Exhibition Museum**

(1898), staging the state's most comprehensive goldfields exhibition, and the **Old Coolgardie Gaol**. **The Gaol Tree**, complete with replica leg-irons, pre-dates the gaol and is located on Hunt St. The **Railway Station Museum** recounts local and transport history, including the Varischetti mine rescue. Relics of the gold mining era are also housed here. Also of interest are **Lindsay Pit Lookout**; **Ben Prior's Open Air Museum**, with machinery, mining equipment and an assortment of relics; **Warden Finnerty's House** (1895), restored by the National Trust and open to the public; **Lions Bicentennial Lookout**; **Coolgardie Cemetery**; and the **Old Pioneer Cemetery**, in Forrest St, with graves from 1892 to 1894.

NEARBY ATTRACTIONS: **Coolgardie Camel Farm**, 3km west, offers camel rides. Picnic areas south of Coolgardie are at **Gnarlbine Rocks** (30km); **Victoria Rocks** (48km), known for its excellent views; and **Burra Rock** (55km). **Rowles Lagoon**, a 2km wide freshwater lake and reserve ideal for picnics and camping, is 60km to the north of Coolgardie.

VISITOR INFORMATION: 62 Bayley St, Ph: (08) 9026 6090

The waters off the capital of the region known as the South West and Western Australia's second largest population centre, **Bunbury**, mark the point where the warm **Indian Ocean** waters collide with those of the cooler **Southern Ocean**. This area is renowned for its abundant wildlife, as well as its bountiful rivers.

The city was named more than 150 years ago after Lieut. Henry William St Pierre Bunbury, who was sent to explore the lands south of Fremantle in 1836. It now provides visitors with an excellent base for their own regional explorations, although the city itself offers many attractions—a stretch of beaches, caves and inlets, beach- and sea-fishing opportunities, lagoons, superior yachting facilities, picturesque picnic spots and dolphin cruises.

The surrounding hinterland features superb karri forests, spectacular coastline, pretty orchards, verdant grassland and farmstay opportunities. The surrounding towns are worthwhile exploring. **Donnybrook** is known for its apple orchards, wineries, arts and crafts, while at **Harvey** visitors will find some of Western Australia's prime beef and best oranges.

Manjimup

This region is best known for its towering karri and jarrah forests and is also home to the **'Four Aces'**—four giant karri trees over 400 years old. The other karri trees here are hundreds of years old and grow over 75m tall.

Harvesting apples at Donnybrook

 Visitor information

Bunbury Visitor Information Centre
Old Railway Station,
Carmody Pl,
Bunbury WA 6230
Ph: (08) 9721 7922
www.justsouth.com.au

main attractions

◈ **Australind**

This historic town is popular for boating, sailing, fishing, prawning, crabbing and windsurfing.

◈ **Bunbury**

Bunbury offers a cosmopolitan seaside atmosphere of beaches, cafes and shopping and many nature-based attractions, such as the Mangrove Boardwalk.

◈ **Dolphin Discovery Centre**

Experience the sight and sounds of these amazing sea mammals through an audiovisual show.

◈ **Koombana Bay dolphins**

The bay is famed for its dolphins, which frolic in its protected waters.

◈ **Mangrove Boardwalk**

Mangroves have been growing here for about 25 000 years.

◈ **Old Goldfields Orchard and Cider Factory**

Here the workings of Donnybrook's historic goldrush era are recreated, with gold panning just one of the activities available. There is a boutique cider factory where adults can taste different brews.

Karri trees in Shannon National Park, south-east of Manjimup

Scale 1:400 000

Continued on map 387

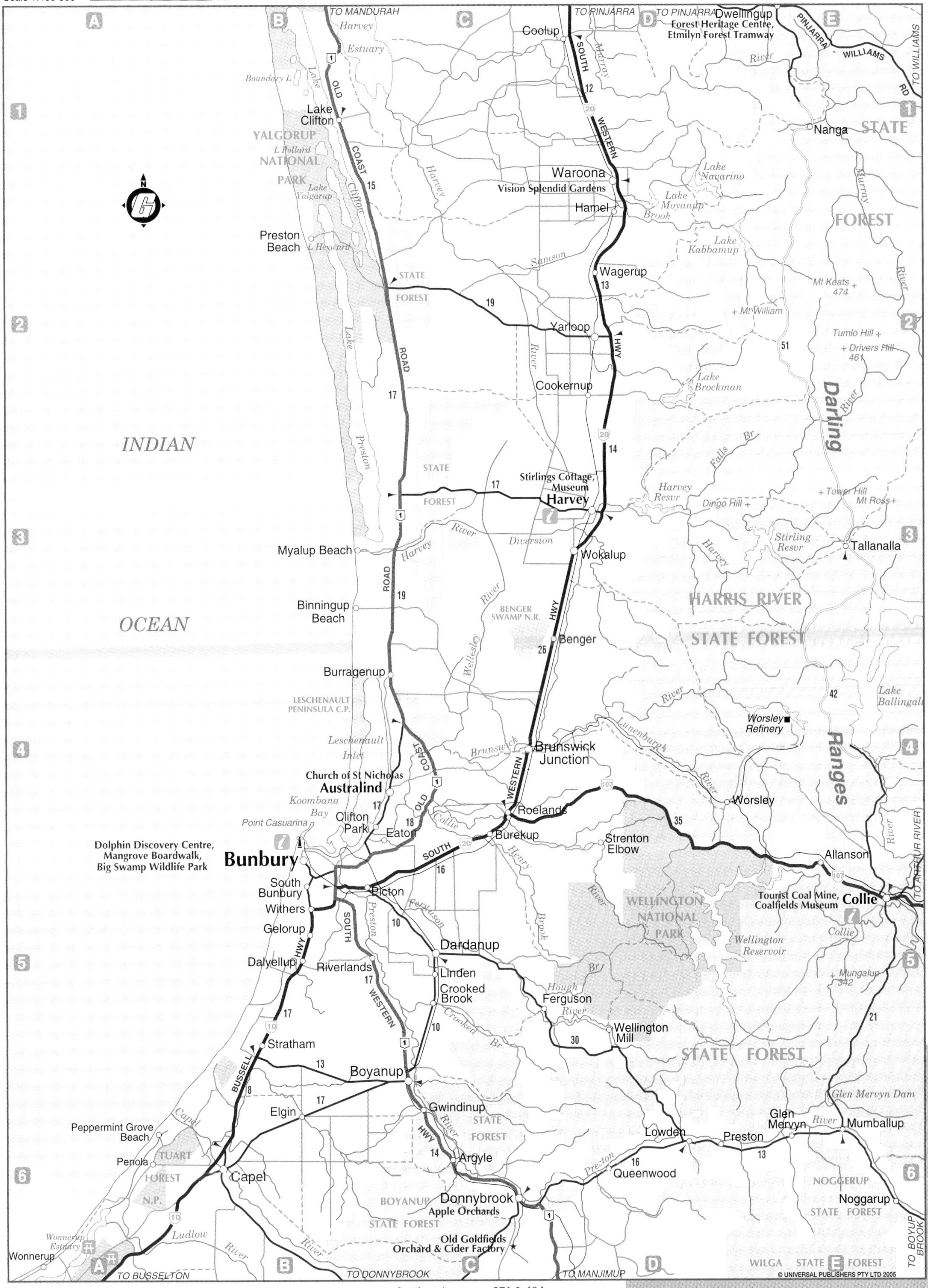

INDIAN

OCEAN

Harvey
Estuary

Boundary L

YALGORUP
L Pollard
NATIONAL
PARK
Lake
Yalgarup

Preston
Beach
L Heyward

Lake Clifton

TO PINJARRA
TO PINJARRA
Coolup

Dwellingup
Forest Heritage Centre,
Etmilyn Forest Tramway

Nanga
STATE

Waroona
Vision Splendid Gardens
Hamel

Wagerup

Lake
Navarino

Lake
Moyanup

FOREST

Lake
Kabbamup

Mt Keats +
474

Tumlo Hill +
+ Drivers Hill
461

Yarloop

+ Mt William

Cookernup

Lake
Brockman

Darling

Stirlings Cottage,
Museum
Harvey

Wokalup

Myalup Beach

Harvey
River

Diversion

Harvey
Resvr

Dingo Hill +

Stirling
Resvr

Mt Ross+

Tower Hill +

Tallanalla

HARRIS RIVER

Binningup
Beach

BENGER
SWAMP N.R.

Benger

STATE FOREST

Burragenup

LESCHENAULT
PENINSULA C.P.

Lake
Ballingal

Worsley
Refinery

Ranges

Leschenault
Inlet

Brunswick

Brunswick
Junction

Church of St Nicholas
Australind

Koombana
Bay

Point Casuarina

Roelands

Worsley

Clifton
Park
Eaton

Collie
River

Burekup

Allanson

Dolphin Discovery Centre,
Mangrove Boardwalk,
Big Swamp Wildlife Park

Bunbury

Strenton
Elbow

Tourist Coal Mine,
Coalfields Museum

Collie

South
Bunbury
Withers

Picton

Gelorup

WELLINGTON
NATIONAL
PARK

Collie

Dalyellup

Riverlands

Dardanup

Henry
Brook

Wellington
Reservoir

Mungalup
342

Linden
Crooked
Brook

Ferguson

Wellington
Mill

STATE FOREST

Stratham

Crooked
Br

Boyanup

Peppermint Grove
Beach

Glen Mervyn Dam

Elgin

Glen
Mervyn

Mumballup

Penola

TUART

Gwindinup

STATE

Lowden

Preston

FOREST

Capel

FOREST

Argyle

Queenwood

NOGGERUP
STATE FOREST

Wonnerup
Estuary

Ludlow
River

Donnybrook
Apple Orchards

Noggarup

Wonnerup

BOYANUP
STATE FOREST

Old Goldfields
Orchard & Cider Factory

WILGA STATE FOREST

© UNIVERSAL PUBLISHERS PTY LTD 2005

Continued on map 404

■ Dampier POP 1600

Map 398, B6

A port town built in the 1960s, Dampier overlooks **Hampton Harbour** in **King Bay**, 20km from Karratha. Water recreation activities and accessibility to the islands of the **Dampier Archipelago** are premier attractions. Exports from Dampier's busy harbour include iron ore, natural gas and salt.
MAIN ATTRACTIONS: Loading 400 million tonnes of ore annually, **Hamersley Iron Port Facilities** conducts tours by arrangement with the Karratha Visitor Centre. Recreation is popular in the area, including boating, windsurfing, fishing and diving. Popular swimming spots include **Dampier Back Beach** and nearby **Hearsons Cove**.
NEARBY ATTRACTIONS: North-east is the **Burrup Peninsula** renowned for its 10 000 Aboriginal rock-art sites, best viewed on a tour. Also on the Peninsula is the **Northwest Shelf Gas Project,** which pipes natural gas from offshore fields 130km north of Dampier. Its information centre is open weekdays. **Dampier**

Archipelago comprises 42 islands within a radius of 45km of Dampier and is considered one of the country's best fishing spots. Archipelago tours and fishing charters depart from Dampier boat ramps.
VISITOR INFORMATION: Lot 4548, Karratha Rd, Karratha, Ph: (08) 9144 4600

■ Denham POP 1264

Map 400, B4

Denham, 831km north of Perth, is the commercial centre for the extraordinary **Shark Bay World Heritage Region**. Historically a pearling town, it is now best known for its eco-tourism and its thriving fishing industry.
MAIN ATTRACTIONS: **Pioneer Park**, off Hughes St, is a pleasant picnic spot with gas BBQs and an unusual whale-bone arch. Locally organised excursions include tours of **Shark Bay Fisheries**; a glass-bottom boat cruise to a pearl farm; and chartered flights to **Dirk Hartog Island**, where the famed Dutch navigator landed in 1616, and where turtles hatch during April. Both the deep sea and game fishing here are superb.
NEARBY ATTRACTIONS: **Monkey Mia**, 25km north-east, is where close-encounters with wild bottlenose dolphins happen. Rangers and an information centre shed light on this friendly exchange, which has occurred since the 1960s. To the north, **Francois Peron NP** covers 400km²; **Peron Homestead**, in the park, has a 'hot tub' filled by warm artesian waters; it is accessible by 2-wheel drive. Other parts of the park can be reached only by 4-wheel drive, including **Cape Peron** where dugongs (sea cows) and other marine life can be observed. **Shell Beach**, 50km south, is one of only two mainland beaches in the world comprised entirely of seashells. **Stromatolites**, found nowhere else in the world and of enormous

scientific interest, can be found 100km south-east, thriving in the warm waters of **Hamelin Pool**—tours are available. Nearby are the **Telegraph Station** (1884) and shell block quarry.
VISITOR INFORMATION: 71 Knight Tce, Ph: (08) 9948 1253

■ Denmark POP 2220

Map 369, B3

Denmark, 414km south-east of Perth, is an idyllically situated retreat on the **Denmark River** beside **Wilson Inlet**. In addition to its scenic attractions, the town has earned a reputation as a creative centre, with local artisans producing excellent works of art and craft.
MAIN ATTRACTIONS: Art galleries can be found in and around Denmark. Riverside markets are held December–January and at Easter. **Pentland Alpaca Stud and Tourist Farm,** on Scotsdale Rd, breeds alpacas, and also has native and farm animals. Popular activities include windsurfing, fishing, water-skiing and horseriding, and there are several walks, including the **Mokare** and **Wilson Inlet Heritage trails**.
NEARBY ATTRACTIONS: Scenic drives in the area are rewarding and lookouts are at **Mount Shadforth** and **Wilson Head**. Local wineries include **West Cape Howe**, **Howard Parks** and **Matilda's Meadow**, to the north. **Bartholomew's Meadery**, 20km west, makes bee produce, including mead, an alcoholic drink made from honey. **William Bay NP**, 17km south-west, protects unique coastal scenery including **Greens Pool**, **Elephant Rocks**, **Tower Hill**, **Madfish Bay** and **Waterfall Beach**; both Greens Pool and Madfish Bay are safe swimming spots. **Parry's Inlet**, 25km west, has good swimming and seasonal salmon fishing.
VISITOR INFORMATION: 60 Strickland St, Ph: (08) 9848 2055

A friendly bottlenose dolphin at Monkey Mia, near Denham

Western Australia

Tunnel Creek in the Kimberley region, east of Derby

▪ Derby   POP 3620
Map 399, F3
Located on **King Sound**, Derby is known for its boab trees which give the town its distinctive character. Derby is around 2643km north-east of Perth, a service centre for the rich pastoral and mining hinterland, and is a gateway to the **Kimberley**. MAIN ATTRACTIONS: Anglers are often found at the **Fitzroy River** and on **Derby Wharf**. The wharf is also a good place to comprehend the magnitude of the tidal range here— up to 11m tidal variation! Points of interest in Derby include the local history museum at **Wharfinger House**, **Kimberley School of the Air**, the **Botanic Gardens**, and the **Joonjoo Botanical Trail**. An administrative centre for several Aboriginal communities, Derby has a number of outlets selling traditional and contemporary indigenous art.

NEARBY ATTRACTIONS: **The Boab Prison Tree**, 7km south, is a massive hollowed boab, believed to have been used as a temporary cell for prisoners en route to Derby. **Myall's Bore**, nearby, is an astonishing 120m-long cattle trough. The self-drive **Pigeon Heritage Trail** highlights sites of interest between Derby and **Windjana Gorge** and **Tunnel Creek NP**. Derby is a base for cruises and scenic flights to the **Buccaneer Archipelago** and land tours to the **King Leopold** and **Napier Ranges**.
VISITOR INFORMATION: 2 Clarendon St, Ph: (08) 9191 1426 or 1800 621 426

▪ Dongara/Port Denison
POP 2100
Map 402, A2
Settled in the early 1850s, Dongara is one of the state's oldest settlements. With nearby Port Denison, it is located on the **Coral Coast**, 359km north of Perth. Local industries are agriculture and cray-fishing. MAIN ATTRACTIONS: **Dongara's Heritage Trail** takes in 28 attractions including the old **Police Station** (1870), the **Royal Steam Flour Mill** (1894), and **Russ Cottage** (1870), a farm worker's cottage furnished in period-style. Port Denison is famed for its rock lobsters, excellent fishing, beautiful bays and safe beaches such as **South Beach**. Excellent views of the harbour can be seen from **Fisherman's Lookout** near **Leander Point**.
VISITOR INFORMATION: 9 Waldeck St, Ph: (08) 9927 1404

▪ Donnybrook   POP 1650
Map 375, C6
Originally a timber town, and for a short period a gold town, Donnybrook, 210km south of Perth, is in a mixed farming area known for its horticulture and orchards, especially apples. NEARBY ATTRACTIONS: The **Old Goldfields Orchard and Cider Factory**, 5km south, offers tours of its orchard and cider factory and has picnic areas, a restaurant, a goldmine and gold-panning facilities. Two potteries in the area are **Cedar Shed**, 10km south-east, and **Old Stables Pottery**, 25km south-east. **Balingup**, 30km south-east, is a hub for arts and crafts, including **The Old Cheese Factory** craft centre and **Tinderbox** herb products. Nearby are **Golden Valley Tree Park**, **Lavender Farm** and **Birdwood Park Fruit Winery**.
VISITOR INFORMATION: Railway Station, South Western Hwy, Ph: (08) 9731 1720

▪ Dunsborough   POP 1600
Map 371, B1
Dunsborough is located on **Geographe Bay**, 26km west of Busselton. Its attractions include beaches, coastal scenery and seasonal wildflowers. It is also a gateway to **Cape Naturaliste** and **Leeuwin-Naturaliste NP**.
MAIN ATTRACTIONS: Adventurous recreational options include scuba diving, canoeing, horseriding and caving. Local craft outlets are **Dunsborough Gallery**, showcasing woodcraft; **Happ's Pottery and Vineyard**; and **Bush Cottage Crafts**.
NEARBY ATTRACTIONS: To the north-west, beautiful bay-fronting towns with good swimming and boating beaches are **Meelup** (5km), **Eagle Bay** (8km) and **Bunker Bay** (12km). Wreck dive tours of HMAS *Swan*, east of Eagle Bay off **Point Picquet**, are available. **Cape Naturaliste Lighthouse and Museum**, 13km north-west, offers tours, walking trails and whale-watching platforms set amidst spectacular coastal scenery. Animal encounters can be enjoyed at **Country Life Farm** nearby, at **Quindalup Fauna Park**, 4km east, and south-east at **Yallingup Shearing Shed**.
VISITOR INFORMATION: Seymour Blvd, Ph: (08) 9755 3299

■ Esperance   POP 9310

Map 405, K3

The South Coast's pristine beaches, good fishing, and access to the **Archipelago of the Recherche** have contributed much to Esperance's popularity as a holiday destination. Situated 720km south-east of Perth, it is a commercial and service centre for nearby farming districts.

MAIN ATTRACTIONS: **Esperance Municipal Museum**, James St, has a collection of farm equipment, a marine exhibit, and remnants of *Skylab*, the US space station that fell to earth in the area in July 1979. For a distinctive souvenir, **Mermaid Marine Leather** processes and sells fashion accessories made from fish skins. **Tanker Jetty** is recommended for angling and seal watching. A 10km shorefront walking and cycling track follows the **Bay of Isles**. Fishing and diving tours and scenic cruises are also on offer.

NEARBY ATTRACTIONS: The spectacular 36km **Great Ocean Drive** takes a round-trip passing attractions such as **Pink Lake**, a salt lake coloured pink by algae; **Observatory Point and Lookout**; **Twilight Beach**; a power-generating **Wind Farm**;

Cycling the spectacular Great Ocean Drive from Esperance

Rotary Lookout; and the Archipelago of the Recherche (Bay of Isles), 105 islands that provide sheltered habitats for seals and birdlife. Cruises are available to **Woody Island** where camping is allowed September–April. **Telegraph Farm**, 21km north-west, is a commercial protea farm that has buffalo, camels and other animals. Boardwalks facilitate birdwatching at **Monjinup Lake Botanical Park**, 20km west. White-sand swimming beaches and hilly scrublands are features of **Cape Le Grand NP**, 56km east. Beaches of note include **Hellfire Bay**, **Thistle Cove** and **Lucky Bay**; there are also scenic walks and sensational wildflower displays in spring. **Cape Arid NP**, 120km east, is a rugged setting for bushwalking, camping, fishing and 4-wheel driving.

VISITOR INFORMATION: Museum Park, Dempster St, Ph: (08) 9071 2330

■ Exmouth   POP 3100

Map 400, B1

Exmouth was established on the **North West Cape** in 1967, primarily as a US Naval Communications Station. Ecotours are well rewarded as the town's proximity to **Ningaloo Reef**, protected within **Ningaloo Marine Park** and **Cape Range NP**, guarantees sightings of some extraordinary marine life.

MAIN ATTRACTIONS: Excellent tours include glass-bottom coral-viewing boat cruises, fishing charters, safaris, diving and sea kayaking. Inquire about greenback turtle nesting and hatching (November to February), humpback whale watching (July to November), manta ray snorkelling (July to November) and swimming with whale sharks (March to July).

NEARBY ATTRACTIONS: Spectacular views are offered at **Vlaming Head Lighthouse**, 17km north. The wreck of the ill-fated **SS *Mildura***, sunk in 1907, is visible 100m offshore.

Ningaloo Reef, to the west, spans 260km of coastline with more than 220 coral species. Coral spawning occurs after the March full moon. Magnificent views of Cape Range NP are accessed via Charles Knife Rd, 23km south, and Shothole Canyon Rd, 23 km south. **Milyering Visitor Centre**, within the park, has displays on the area's natural history and culture. Not to be missed are **Bundegi Beach**, **Turquoise Bay** and **Yardie Creek**.

VISITOR INFORMATION: Murat Rd, Ph: (08) 9949 1176 or 1800 287 328

■ Fitzroy Crossing   POP 1380

Map 399, H4

Fitzroy Crossing, located beside the **Fitzroy River**, is a growing Outback centre providing services and supplies to Aboriginal communities and the Kimberley's cattle and mining industries. A base for visiting **Kimberley** attractions, local conditions should be checked first as many roads are subject to seasonal flooding.

MAIN ATTRACTIONS: The oldest hotel in the Kimberley, the legendary **Crossing Inn** (1897) was a stopping point for travellers poised to make the sometimes perilous river crossing. Nearby is the **Pioneer Cemetery**. The original site for Fitzroy Crossing was 5km north-east and remnants of the old town site are worth visiting.

NEARBY ATTRACTIONS: Part of a 350-million-year-old Devonian coral reef, the limestone cliffs of **Geikie Gorge NP** contain layers of fossilised fish and many caves. This 14km gorge, 18km north of Fitzroy Crossing on a sealed road, can be seen from a boat cruise or Aboriginal Heritage cruise. Crocodiles, as well as stingrays and sawfish adapted to fresh water, can be seen in the river.

VISITOR INFORMATION: Cnr Great Northern Hwy and Forrest Rd, Ph: (08) 9191 5355

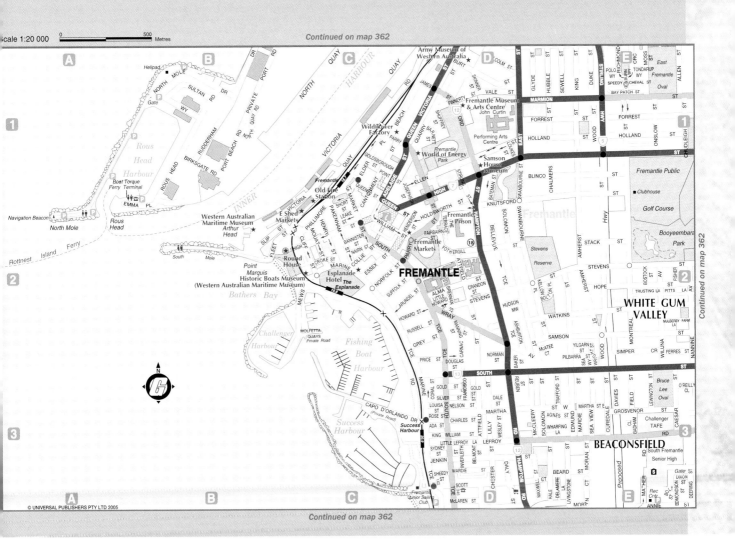

Continued on map 362

Continued on map 362

Continued on map 362

▮ Fremantle POP 32 000

Map 379, D2

The historic city of Fremantle lies 19km south-west of Perth at the mouth of the **Swan River**. Now merged with suburban Perth, 'Freo', as the locals call it, is a major fishing and shipping port with a vibrant multi-cultural society. It has lovingly preserved its 19th-century heritage and created a relaxed ambience. In 1986–87, the city hosted the first America's Cup yacht races held outside the USA. This major event triggered the rejuvenation of many of the historic 19th-century buildings—there are more than 3000 buildings of historical significance and the National Trust has classified 150. MAIN ATTRACTIONS: National Trust-classified **Fremantle Markets**, 84

South Tce, was established in 1897 and offers an array of goods, from fish to antiques. The **E Shed Markets**, at Victoria Quay, contain more than 100 specialty shops. **Tram West** offers tours of historical buildings, the harbour and other attractions in Fremantle. Tickets are available on board. The **Western Australian Maritime Museum**, in Cliff St, has an internationally important collection of shipwreck relics dating from early 17th-century Dutch ships, including the *Batavia*. The main section of the museum, tracing the state's maritime history, is at Victoria Quay. The submarine *Ovens* located nearby off Slip St, is open to the public. **Fremantle History Museum and Arts Centre**, located in the Fremantle Arts Centre in Finnerty St, is in a convict-built

former lunatic asylum. The **Town Hall**, completed in 1887 and re-modelled in the 1950s, is an important heritage building. **The Round House Precinct**, at Arthur Head, preserves Western Australia's most historic site. The Round House, originally a gaol, was built in 1831 and is Western Australia's oldest public building. At 1pm daily, the **Signal Station** fires Jardine's Time Gun; an honorary gunner is selected to fire the gun. The Gun Deck provides wonderful views to Rottnest and Garden Islands and the Fremantle harbour areas. Other buildings with interesting architecture are the **Esplanade Hotel**, on the corner of Marine Tcc and Essex St; the **Old Fremantle Fire Station** at 18 Phillimore St; and the **Fremantle Chamber of**

Commerce, located next door. Tours are available of **Fremantle Prison**, 1 The Terrace; this was the last convict prison to be built in Australia and is a fascinating experience. For the cafe society, don't miss Fremantle's popular South Tce, known as the 'capuccino strip'.

NEARBY ATTRACTIONS: Ferries to **Rottnest Island**, a favourite playground, leave from Victoria Quay. Fremantle is close to beaches to the south and all of Perth's attractions.

VISITOR INFORMATION: Town Hall, cnr William St and Adelaide St, Ph: (08) 9431 7878

■ Geraldton   POP 25 850
Map 402, A1

Rock lobsters, wildflowers, year-round sunshine and white sandy beaches are trademarks of the attractive mid-western port city of Geraldton, 424km north of Perth on **Champion Bay**.

MAIN ATTRACTIONS: The **Western Australian Museum Geraldton**, located off Foreshore Dr, has an outstanding maritime display, with relics from the 17th- and 18th-century Dutch shipwrecks, *Batavia*,

St Francis Xavier Cathedral, Geraldton

Zuytdorp and *Zeewijk*, together with natural and cultural heritage exhibits and Aboriginal history exhibits. The eclectic **St Francis Xavier Cathedral**, completed 1938, is one of John Hawes' architectural masterpieces. A pamphlet describing the **Monsignor Hawes Heritage Trail** is available. Other notable buildings in town are the prefabricated **Point Moore Lighthouse** (1878); **Lighthouse Keeper's Cottage** (1870); and the **Bill Sewell Complex** (1887), formerly the Victoria District Hospital, then a prison, and presently incorporating **Marra Indigenous Art Gallery** and the **Old Gaol Craft Centre**. **Geraldton Art Gallery** has well-regarded permanent and touring exhibitions. There are several lookouts providing good views, including **Mount Scott**, which is the site of the **HMAS Sydney Memorial**. Fishermen unload huge rock lobster hauls on **Fishermans Wharf** and the lobster processing plant conducts tours of its operations December–June. Activities in the area include windsurfing, diving, walking, fishing, kite flying, kite surfing and cycling. The **South Tomi Dive Wreck** is in Champion Bay

NEARBY ATTRACTIONS: Seasonal wildflowers are a highlight of the hinterland—a spectacular sight not to be missed. Air, diving and bird-watching tours visit the impressive 122-island chain of the **Houtman Abrolhos Islands**, 64km offshore. **Chapman Valley Wines**, 35km north-east, offer tastings daily.

VISITOR INFORMATION: Bill Sewell Complex, cnr Bayly St and Chapman Rd, Ph: (08) 9921 3999

■ Greenough (shire)   POP 7000
Map 402, A1

The **Shire of Greenough** surrounding the city of **Geraldton** is one of Australia's most prosperous sheep and wheat districts. Emblematic

in the area are the leaning trees, *Eucalyptus camaldulensis*, shaped by the strong salt winds from the sea.

MAIN ATTRACTIONS: Restored by the National Trust, **Greenough Historic Hamlet** is a collection of 11 buildings from the 1880s; group tours are conducted. North of the Hamlet is the **Pioneer Cemetery**, and the **Pioneer Museum**, housed in a 120-year-old farmhouse, has an excellent folk collection. **Cliff Grange**, opposite an 1858 flour mill, is a National Trust restored property. The mouth of the **Greenough River** is a good swimming and fishing spot.

NEARBY ATTRACTIONS: Pamphlets are available on the **Greenough to Walkaway Heritage Trail** and the **Greenough River Nature Walk**. **Ellendale Pool**, located 21km from Walkaway, is a popular permanent waterhole framed by cliffs. It has picnic and BBQ areas and camping is permitted. **Walkaway Station Museum**, housed in the old Railway Station, has a large collection of local family records, regional transport items, weapons and military relics

VISITOR INFORMATION: Greenough Historic Hamlet, Brand Hwy, Ph: (08) 9926 1084

■ Halls Creek   POP 1280
Map 399, J4

Halls Creek is the site of Western Australia's first payable gold discovery in 1885. 2855km north-east of Perth, it is located at the centre of the **Kimberley**, adjacent to the **Great Sandy Desert**. It services local Aboriginal communities, pastoralists, and visitors seeking access to local national parks.

MAIN ATTRACTIONS: **Russian Jack Memorial**, on Thomas St, is a tribute to a gold digger who pushed his sick friend 300km in a wheelbarrow to seek medical help in Wyndham. Also in town is the **Yarliyil Art Centre** selling quality local Aboriginal art.

Wave Rock, near Hyden

NEARBY ATTRACTIONS: **China Wall**, 6km east, is a natural white quartz rock formation. A further 9km east is **Caroline Pool**, an ideal picnic and swimming spot. Past the ruins of the original Halls Creek town site (16km east), are two swimming and picnic spots: **Palm Springs**, 41km east, and **Sawpit Gorge**, 43km east. Halls Creek serves as a base for excursions to **Purnululu NP (Bungle Bungles)**, with its spectacular ancient rock formations (155km NE) and to **Wolfe Creek Crater**, 148km south. The 50 000 year-old meteorite crater is the world's second largest, measuring 800m wide and 49m deep.
VISITOR INFORMATION: Great Northern Hwy, Ph: (08) 9168 6262

Harvey   POP 2670
Map 375, D3
Bordered by the **Darling Range** and the Indian Ocean, Harvey, 139km south of Perth, is blessed with some of the state's most fertile farmland supporting dairy and beef cattle.

MAIN ATTRACTIONS: The Old Railway Station building houses Harvey's **Historical Society Museum** and on the South Western Hwy is the **Harvey Internment Camp Memorial**, built by prisoners-of-war during the 1940s. Collect the key to the shrine from the information centre. Within the information centre, the **Moo Shoppe** is home to all things Friesian, promoting the region's dairying industry. Nearby is **Stirling's Cottage**, a replica of James Stirling's hunting lodge— Capt Stirling selected the town site for settlement in 1829. The cottage also has commentary on **May Gibbs**, author of the children's classic, *Snugglepot and Cuddlepie*, who lived in Harvey briefly during her childhood.
NEARBY ATTRACTIONS: The region's picturesque irrigation dams are also recreation and picnic stops, including **Harvey Dam**, 3km east, and **Stirling Dam**, 17km east. **Logue Brook Dam**, 15km east, offers opportunities for swimming, waterskiing and good trout fishing.
VISITOR INFORMATION: Cnr South Western Hwy and James Stirling Pl, Ph: (08) 9729 1122

Hyden   POP 160
Map 405, F1
A small wheat belt township, 344km east of Perth, Hyden's most distinctive and most photographed attraction is the geologically stunning **Wave Rock**.
NEARBY ATTRACTIONS: Situated 4km east, Wave Rock is a 15m-high granite outcrop curling into a surf-like wave formation. Dated at 2700 million years old, the effects of weathering have fashioned Wave Rock's unique shape and natural chemical reactions with rainwater runoff have striped the granite red and grey. Other rock formations in the vicinity are **The Breakers**, **Hippo's Yawn**, **The Falls** and **The Humps**. At the information centre,

The Lace Place, showcases a large lace collection. **Mulka's Cave**, 21km to the north, contains Aboriginal rock paintings.
VISITOR INFORMATION: Wave Rock Visitors Centre, Wave Rock Rd, Ph: (08) 9880 5182

Jurien Bay   POP 650
Map 402, A3
Lobster fishing, safe beaches, boating, and access to the spectacular **Pinnacles** and regional national parks are some of the main attractions of this fishing town situated beside the sheltered waters of Jurien Bay, 266km north of Perth.
MAIN ATTRACTIONS: Jurien Bay is noted for water-based activities such as boating, swimming and fishing.
NEARBY ATTRACTIONS: **Lions Lookout**, 4km to the east, has sweeping views of the bay. **Grigson's Lookout**, 17km north, has ocean and hinterland views. Bountiful wildflowers bloom at **Cockleshell Gully**, 31km north, popular with bushwalkers and photographers. **Lesueur NP**, 23km north, has more than 900 species of flora and is one of the most important flora reserves in the state. It also has a lookout with amazing views. **Stockyard Gully**, 50km north, is 4-wheel drive accessible only, and has a 300m ancient underground tunnel walk, requiring torches. Tours are available. The coastal **Nambung NP**, 40km south, contains the remarkable limestone pillars, **The Pinnacles**. Dated at 30 000 years old, the beautifully weathered calcified spires vary from 1 to 4m in height and cover approximately 400ha of variably coloured sands in an area known as the **Pinnacle Desert**. The **Pinnacles Lookout** gives a superb overview of this oustanding natural attraction. West of the Brand Hwy, **Badgingarra NP** has a 2km walk through heathlands.
VISITOR INFORMATION: 110 Bashford St, Ph: (08) 9652 1444

The ornate York Hotel, Kalgoorlie

■ Kalbarri POP 2120
Map 400, B5

On the southern bank of the **Murchison River** estuary, almost surrounded by national park, the coastal town of Kalbarri, 591km north of Perth, is a popular holiday destination in a region famous for its fishing, wildly beautiful scenery and Mediterranean climate.

MAIN ATTRACTIONS: Leisure activities range from adventurous abseiling, horse and camel riding, and canoe safaris, to scenic flights, dolphin-watching cruises, and boat rides on the Murchison River. Whale-watching trips run July–November. Pelicans are handfed daily on the river foreshore.

NEARBY ATTRACTIONS: A highly recommended surfing beach is **Jakes Corner**, 3.5km south. Close by is **Red Bluff** for swimming. **Rainbow Jungle** is an Australian parrot breeding centre and bird park. In 1629, two mutinous seamen from the *Batavia* were banished to the shore, making it the first European settlement in the country and a unwitting prelude to later events—a cairn at **Wittecarra Creek** marks the site. The 1860km² **Kalbarri NP** contains intricately-carved sandstone river gorges, rugged coastal cliffs and more than 850 recorded species of wildflowers. Highlights are **The Loop Gorge** and **Z Bend Gorge**, 30km north-east, and views from **Hawks Head** and **Ross Graham Lookouts**, 39km east. The park has both short and strenuous walking trails.

VISITOR INFORMATION: Grey St, Ph: (08) 9937 1104 or 1800 639 468

■ Kalgoorlie-Boulder POP 28 560
Map 403, K4

Irish prospector Paddy Hannan's lucky strike in 1893 started the last great goldrush in Australia's history, leading to the establishment of the twin towns of Kalgoorlie and Boulder, 597km east of Perth.

Kalgoorlie-Boulder's Golden Mile, believed to be the world's richest square mile of gold-bearing ore, still yields gold.

MAIN ATTRACTIONS: **Hannans North Tourist Mine** is a fascinating historic mining site that operates surface and underground tours revealing miners' methods and machinery. It forms part of the **Australian Prospectors and Miners Hall of Fame** that houses five interactive galleries. Views of a massive modern operation can be seen from **Super Pit Lookout** off Eastern Bypass Rd. A one hour ride on the 'Rattler' on the **Golden Mile Loopline Railway**, with commentary, travels along a line that in the 1890s was reputed to be the busiest and best. Comprehensive coverage can be found at the **Western Australian Museum Kalgoorlie-Boulder** with its underground gold vault and lift-ride to views from the mine headframe. A replica statue of miner Paddy Hannan, situated outside the town hall, provides a novel photo opportunity (the original is in the museum). On Burt St, the **Goldfields War Museum** features armoured vehicles and war memorabilia. **Heritage Walks** inform visitors about mining-town architecture. Geological specimens of all kinds can be found in the **School of Mines Mineral Museum** on Cassidy St. Nearby, the **Goldfields Art Centre** holds regular exhibitions. **Mount Charlotte Reservoir** remains as a tribute to engineer C Y O'Connor's ingenious feat and world first—in 1903 he constructed a 563km pipeline to carry water from Perth to the goldfields. The lookout here offers excellent sunset views. **Hammond Park** on Lyall St is a wildlife reserve with a mini-Bavarian castle. **Kalgoorlie Arboretum** has over 100 eucalypt species and **Karlkurla Bushland Park** has walking paths

and a lookout. The history of Kalgoorlie's notorious red light district—**Hay St**—is recounted at the **Bordello Brothel Museum**.
NEARBY ATTRACTIONS: Organised **Goldfields Tours** take in Kalgoorlie, Coolgardie, nature reserves and ghost towns. Scenic flights, Aboriginal culture and bush tucker tours as well as seasonal wildflower trips are available. Tours of the processing plant of the working gold mine, **Kanowna Belle Gold Mine**, are also available.
VISITOR INFORMATION: 250 Hannan St, Kalgoorlie, Ph: (08) 9021 1966 or 1800 004 653

▦ Kambalda   POP 2850
Map 403, K4
Kambalda is a mining town on the shores of the giant saltpan, **Lake Lefroy**, 55km south of Kalgoorlie. Originally born out of an 1887 gold find, the town dwindled in 1907 when the strike seemed exhausted but was resurrected by WMC (Western Mining Corporation) when nickel was discovered in 1966, and gold deposits have more recently been uncovered.
MAIN ATTRACTIONS: Although known as Lake Lefroy, this 510km² saltpan rarely contains water, despite deceptive mirages. Views of the lake are provided from **Red Hill Lookout**, off Gordon Adams Rd. WMC mining structures are visible from **John Hill Viewpoint**, off Serpentine Rd. Places to picnic are at **Kambalda Memorial Garden** and at the **Lions Park** and playground.
VISITOR INFORMATION: Cnr Emu Rocks Rd and Marianthus Rd, Kambalda West, Ph: (08) 9027 0192

▦ Karratha   POP 10 500
Map 398, B6
Established in the late 1960s to service the needs of iron ore, salt and natural gas industry projects, Karratha derives its name from an Aboriginal word meaning 'good country'. An ideal base for exploring the **Pilbara**, Karratha is an administrative centre with 'city style' shopping and services.
NEARBY ATTRACTIONS: The picturesque clear-water **Miaree Pool**, 30km south, is surrounded by shady trees—a perfect place to picnic and swim. North-west of Karratha, the **Burrup Peninsula** has over 10 000 Aboriginal art sites best viewed on a self-drive or organised tour. Used extensively by early European settlers as a pastoral station, an oasis at the centre of **Millstream-Chichester NP**, 124km south, has unique **Pilbara Palms** and permanent freshwater pools. The state's second largest park, **Karijini NP** has spectacular gorges, waterfalls, rockpools, graded walking trails and ancient rock formations. Just 20km from Karratha, **Dampier** offers access to the 42 islands of the **Dampier Archipelago**.
VISITOR INFORMATION: Lot 4548 Karratha Rd, Ph: (08) 9144 4600

▦ Katanning   POP 4040
Map 404, E3
A thriving agricultural town 295km south-east of Perth, Katanning has the second largest saleyards in Australia and is renowned for producing fine merino sheep.
MAIN ATTRACTIONS: A **Heritage Trail** pamphlet highlights some of Katanning's notable buildings including the Piesse family home **Kobeelya** (1902); the **Winery Ruins**, on Warren Rd, with its historic vats and equipment; and the National Trust-restored roller flour mill (1891), which now incorporates the **Mill Museum** displaying roller flour-milling machinery. An **Historical Museum** of local memorabilia is housed in the first government school and an **Art Gallery** is situated next to the Shire Offices. Another notable landmark is the **Islamic Mosque**. **All Ages Playground** has huge

slides and operates a miniature steam train every second and fourth Sunday (from 1pm, weather permitting). **Wammco Meat Works** offers tours by appointment, and the **Police Pools Memorial** is a fine place to picnic.
NEARBY ATTRACTIONS: Local lakes provide venues for watersports, including waterskiing and boating. The **Kattaning-Piesse Heritage Trail** is a 20km self-guided driving tour. **Stirling Range NP**, 80km south, is notable for a 65km-long chain of peaks, excellent bushwalking trails and prolific wildflowers in season.
VISITOR INFORMATION: Cnr Austral Tce and Clive St, Ph: (08) 9821 2634

▦ Kellerberrin   POP 855
Map 402, E5
Wheat and sheep farming are the mainstays of this small country township. Kellerberrin is located along the Great Eastern Hwy 203km from Perth.
MAIN ATTRACTIONS: The town's **International Art Space Kellerberrin Australia (IASKA)** features international and national contemporary artists on three-month residencies—the nation's only gallery of its kind. A **Folk Museum** of local memorabilia is situated in the old Agricultural Hall and a two hour **Heritage Trail** takes in notable sites, including **Kellerberrin Hill Lookout**. Farming

Sheep grazing near the Stirling Range, south of Katanning

Lake Argyle, part of the Ord River Scheme near Kununurra

implements and machinery displayed around **Pioneer Park** provide an interesting backdrop for picnics. **Centenary Park** in the centre of town has shaded playground equipment, BBQs, in-line skate and BMX tracks, a heritage walkway and maze.

NEARBY ATTRACTIONS: Constructed from local field stone in 1871, **Milligan Homestead**, located 10km north on Trayning Rd, is an example of building methods of the period (on private property). A massive granite outcrop, **Kokerbin Rock**, 30km south, is reputed to be Australia's third largest monolith. Great views are assured from **Mount Stirling** and **Mount Caroline**, 22km south. Kellerberrin's countryside is covered in wildflowers during spring, and two particular places to enjoy the flora are **Durakoppin Wildlife Sanctuary**, 27km north, and **Charles Gardner Nature Reserve**, 35km south-west.

VISITOR INFORMATION: 110 Massingham St, Ph: (08) 9045 4006

Kojonup   POP 1075

Map 404, D3

Kojonup, 256km south-east of Perth, was originally established in 1837 as a military post of Pensioner Guards. Today, it is the centre of a farming and agricultural district.

MAIN ATTRACTIONS: **Kojonup Spring and Picnic Area** is the site of a natural spring to which the original surveyor Alfred Hillman was directed to by local Aborigines. Other historic landmarks are **Elverd Cottage** (1851) and the **Barracks** (1845). **Kodja Place Interpretative Centre** has audiovisual displays, a unique **Rose Maze** and authentic **Noongar Aboriginal tours**. Noongar arts and crafts are available at the visitor centre.

NEARBY ATTRACTIONS: Wildflowers are prolific in the region, including more than 60 orchid species. Established sites for enjoying the flora and fauna include the **Australia Bush Heritage Block** on Mission Rd, Cherry Tree Pool, **Myrtle Benn Flora and Fauna Sanctuary** on Tunney Rd, and **Farrar Reserve**, 7km west on Blackwood Rd.

VISITOR INFORMATION: 143 Albany Hwy, Ph: (08) 9831 0500

Kununurra   POP 4900

Map 399, K2

Two key local ventures contributing to the character of Kununurra, 3214km north-east of Perth, are the **Argyle Diamond Mine** and the **Ord River Scheme**, a massive irrigation project harnessing the rivers of the **Kimberley**. With good accessibility to the striped formations of the Bungle Bungles in **Purnululu NP**, Kununurra also serves as a base for exploring the region's many other attractions.

MAIN ATTRACTIONS: Visitors can learn about diamonds from local retailers selling a range of **Argyle Diamonds,** including white, champagne, cognac and rare (and expensive) pink varieties. Authentic Kimberley art can be purchased at **Waringarri Aboriginal Arts Centre, Ourland** or **Red Rock Art**. Kununurra's highest point, **Kellys Knob Lookout**, offers impressive views of the **Ord Valley** and **Lake Kununurra**, an artificial lake convenient for swimming, sailing, rowing, waterskiing and birdwatching. **Mirima (Hidden Valley) NP** contains ancient sandstone formations known as the '**Mini Bungles**'; Aboriginal rock paintings, engravings and artefacts; and a natural amphitheatre once used for corroborees. Local tours include canoe trips and cruises on the **Ord River**, barramundi-fishing trips, ecotours, and flights over Purnululu NP.

NEARBY ATTRACTIONS: Argyle Diamond Mine, 250km south, can be visited on an organised tour. A scenic 12km drive travels north to **Ivanhoe Crossing**—a local fishing hole—and returns via the **Hooch Tree Distillery** and Aboriginal rock art on Weaber Plains Rd. Situated 70km from town on the Wyndham Rd is a deep swimming hole known as **The Grotto**. Massive **Lake Argyle**, 72km south, is Australia's second largest storage reservoir, at 1000km^2, formed by the damming of the Ord River. **Argyle Homestead**, on the shore, contains a pioneer museum and is the departure point for lake cruises. The turn-off to **Gibb River Rd**, a popular 4-wheel drive Outback exploration route, is 60km from Kununurra. The Victoria Hwy to the east leads to Katherine and the attractions of the Northern Territory.

VISITOR INFORMATION: Coolibah Dr, Ph: (08) 9168 1177

Laverton   POP 676

Map 407, A2

Located at the western end of the **Great Victoria Desert**, 957km north-east of Perth, Laverton's present gold-mining operations began with a lucky find back in

1896. Nickel was discovered in the late 1960s and is presently mined south-west of Laverton at **Anaconda Murrin Murrin Nickel Operations**.
MAIN ATTRACTIONS: A 20m climb up **Billy Goat Hill** to the scenic lookout provides panoramic views of the surrounding district. Situated in the town's centre is the **Old Gaol, Museum and Police Station** (1900).
NEARBY ATTRACTIONS: Wildflowers are a highlight of the area, particularly in spring, although the Sturt's desert pea flourishes year-round.
Windarra Heritage Trail, 28km north-west, has an informative walking tour of local nickel mining history and offers excellent views from **Mount Windarra Lookout**. Laverton is also the starting point for travelling the **Great Central Road** through the Great Victoria Desert to Uluṟu and Alice Springs and the **Anne Beadell Hwy** to Coober Pedy. No desert driving should be undertaken without thorough and informed preparation.
VISITOR INFORMATION: Shop 4, Laver Pl, Ph: (08) 9031 1750

Leonora POP 1170

Map 403, K1
Railhead for the gold, copper and nickel mines in **Laverton** and **Leinster**; Leonora is an administrative centre 237km north of Kalgoorlie servicing the surrounding district's mining operations and sheep properties. It has retained a 19th-century appearance and is close to some interesting historical sites.
MAIN ATTRACTION: Views of the town are available from **Mount Leonora**, named after the niece of explorer John Forrest during his search for the Leichhardt expedition.
NEARBY ATTRACTIONS: Adjoining Leonora is the ghost town of **Gwalia**, former home of the Sons of Gwalia Goldmine, the state's second largest gold-mining operation after Kalgoorlie. Closed in 1963, the mine

was managed in the late 1890s by Herbert Hoover, who later became President of the United States of America. **The Mine Office** (1898) houses an interesting local museum. There is a 1km **Historic Gwalia Heritage Trail**—a pamphlet details sites of interest.
VISITOR INFORMATION: 35a Tower St, Ph: (08) 9037 6888

Mandurah POP 37 250

Map 387, C1
The **Indian Ocean** and beautiful beaches have long lured holiday-makers to Mandurah, 74km south of Perth, where the **Murray**, **Harvey** and **Serpentine rivers** flow into **Peel Inlet** and **Harvey Estuary**. Once an important trading site for indigenous groups, 'Mandurah' is derived from an Aboriginal word '*mandjar*' meaning 'meeting place'.
MAIN ATTRACTIONS: Water-based attractions and activities include estuary cruises (dolphins are regularly sighted), boating, swimming, waterskiing, jetskiing and fishing. A **Historic Heritage Trail** highlights significant buildings including the restored **Hall's Cottage** (1832) and **Christ Church**

(1870), with its graveyard featuring pioneers' headstones. An old school (1898) houses the **Community Museum**. More active endeavours can be enjoyed on the western foreshore at **King Carnival Amusement Park**. **Dolphin Quay Markets** are held on weekends at **Mandurah Ocean Marina**.
NEARBY ATTRACTIONS: **Abingdon Miniature Village**, on Husband Rd at Barragup, displays miniature British heritage buildings in landscaped gardens. Popular with families, **Marapana Wildlife World** is at **Karnup**, 12km north. **Ravenswood Sanctuary**, 16km east on the banks of the Murray River, incorporates Redcliffe Barn, and a suspended bridge, plus lakes and picnic spots. **Cooper's Mill**, south-east at **Yunderup**, was the first flour mill in the region and one of only two wind-driven mills in Western Australia. Access is only by boat. For travellers on the winery trail, **Cape Bouvard Wineries** can be found 22km south. **Yalgorup NP**, 15km south, has bushwalking tracks through tuart trees.
VISITOR INFORMATION: 75 Mandurah Tce, Ph: (08) 9550 3999

State Hotel, previous HQ for the Sons of Gwalia Goldmine in the ghost town of Gwalia, near Leonora

PEEL REGION

Just an hour's drive south of Perth, the Peel Region encompasses 5500km² of diverse landscapes, ranging from rolling farm pastures and striking jarrah forests in the east to the calm waters of **Peel Inlet** and **Harvey Estuary** in the west and the white sandy beaches that fringe the **Indian Ocean**. With a combination of popular attractions and its close proximity to Perth, this is one of Western Australia's premier tourist destinations.

The protected inlet waters provide an aquatic playground that offers excellent opportunities for sailing, cruising, canoeing, swimming, fishing and crabbing. The area is famous for blue-swimmer crabs that can be easily caught by scoop or drop net. Locals rejoice when the 'crab run' begins, as boat owners armed with drop nets arrive to lure away the bountiful crabs.

Golf is also a popular pastime: the region boasts three world-renowned golf courses—designed by Ian Baker-Finch, Graham Marsh and Robert Trent Jones Jnr, respectively—and the Peel Region has been labelled the **Golf Coast.** Other attractions include wineries; white-water rafting on the **Murray River**; and **Yalgorup NP**, containing several lakes—havens for birdlife.

Crabbing for blue manna crabs, *Portunus pelagicus*, is very popular in Peel Inlet

main attractions

- ❖ Dwellingup
- ❖ Forest and river trails
- ❖ Harvey Estuary
- ❖ Hotham Valley Tourist Railway
- ❖ Jarrah forest wildflowers
- ❖ Peel Inlet
- ❖ Peel wineries
- ❖ Pinjarra Heritage Trail

ℹ Visitor information

Mandurah Visitor Centre
75 Mandurah Tce,
Mandurah WA 6210
Ph: (08) 9550 3999
www.peeltour.net.au

▪ Manjimup   POP 4480

Map 404, C4

Wooden arches welcome visitors to Manjimup, 129km south-east of Bunbury, and gateway to the tall-timber country of the jarrah and karri forests of the **South West region** of Western Australia. Founded in 1910 to harvest the forest resources, Manjimup is both a timber town and thriving agricultural centre.

MAIN ATTRACTIONS: The town's principal attraction, **Manjimup Timber Park** complex is a theme park museum with highlights such as **Bunnings Age of Steam** display, an historical reconstructed hamlet, the state's only **Timber Museum** and a working blacksmith. Manjimup's natural assets can also be enjoyed by bushwalking, fishing,

or on a forest or ecology tour.

NEARBY ATTRACTIONS: A well-felled karri tree was used to construct **One Tree Bridge** (1904), found in a picturesque spot 22km west. Close by are the **Four Aces**, a stand of towering karri trees averaging 73m, believed to be about 400 years old. **King Jarrah**, 4km east, is an even older specimen. Enthusiasts can climb **Diamond Tree Fire Lookout**, 9km south, a 52m-high karri tree used for fire spotting from 1941 to 1974; there is a nature trail close by. **Fontys Pool**, 10km south, is a popular swimming hole. Adjacent is **Fontaninis Nut Farm,** growing chestnuts, walnuts and hazelnuts (March–May). A scenic heritage trail takes a 19km loop drive through **Dingup**, taking in its historic church (1896) and pioneer cemetery. **Perep**

Forest Ecology Centre, 50km east of Manjimup, offers nocturnal spotlight forest tours by arrangement.

VISITOR INFORMATION: Johnston Cres, Ph: (08) 9771 1831

▪ Margaret River   POP 3650

Map 371, B3

The centre of Western Australia's renowned wine-growing region, Margaret River is also known for its surfing beaches, stunning coastal scenery and awesome cave systems. On the banks of the **Margaret River**, it provides an ideal base for exploring the South West peninsula from **Cape Naturaliste** to **Cape Leeuwin**.

MAIN ATTRACTIONS: **Rotary Park and Historical Settlement** is a pleasant riverside park for picnics and the

---

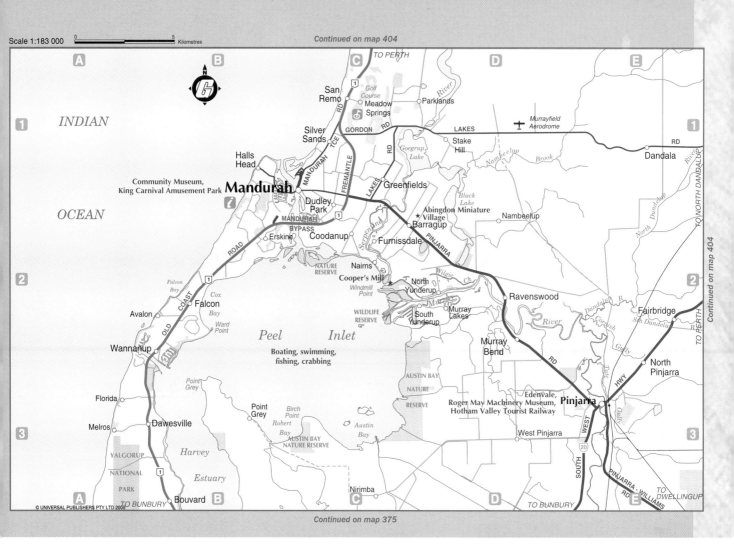

Continued on map 404

Scale 1:183 000

Continued on map 404

Continued on map 375

© UNIVERSAL PUBLISHERS PTY LTD 2005

starting point for **Heritage Walks**. An **Old Settlement Historical Museum** is on Bussell Hwy. Galleries featuring local wares include **Margaret River Gallery**, **The Good Olive** and **Melting Pot Glass Studio**. A free surfing guide brochure outlines the best beaches and general conditions. Additional active options include surfing lessons, canoeing, forest secrets tours, caving trips, abseiling, and winery tours.

NEARBY ATTRACTIONS: Brochures trace the trail to the region's wineries, which are mostly concentrated to the north of Margaret River. Other regional produce includes cheese outlets along the Bussell Hwy and at the **Cheese Factory**, 4km north. National Trust-administered

Ellensbrook Homestead (1853), pioneer home of the Bussell family, is 15km north. Birds of prey can be seen at **Eagles Heritage**, 5km south. Nearby is the **Bellview Shell Museum**. 15km south-east, the **Berry Farm and Winery** has preserves and wine. **Ten Mile Brooks Dam**, south-east, is popular for bushwalking. Several of the region's more than 150 known caves are open to the public by guided tour: **Mammoth Cave**, 21km south-west, has fossilised remains; **Lake Cave** features an underground stream and the interactive caving centre **CaveWorks**; **Jewel Cave** has a 5m straw stalactite; and **Ngilgi Cave** at **Yallingup** has shawl limestone formations.

VISITOR INFORMATION: Cnr Tunbridge Rd and Bussell Hwy, Ph: (08) 9757 2911

One of many fine Margaret River premium wines

Meekatharra POP 1295
Map 400, E4

Servicing a widespread mining, sheep and cattle station community, Meekatharra, 768km north-east of Perth, started as a gold town in the 1890s and later became the railhead for transporting overland cattle from the Northern Territory and East Kimberley until the railway ceased operation in 1978.

MAIN ATTRACTIONS: One gold-era architectural remnant is the **Court House** (1912) on Darlot St. One of the **Flying Doctor Service** bases is open for inspection, as is Meekatharra's **School of the Air** (during school terms).

NEARBY ATTRACTIONS: An interesting rock formation, **Peace Gorge** (**The Granites**) is found 5km west. **Bilyuin Pool**, 88km north-west, becomes a swimming hole when filled in late winter and spring and wildflowers bloom prolifically in season. **Mount Gould's** restored historic **police station** is 156km west.

VISITOR INFORMATION: Shire Offices, Main St, Ph: (08) 9981 1002

Merredin POP 3500
Map 403, F5

Merredin, 259km east of Perth, is the commercial centre for a region which grows 40% of Western Australia's wheat. It is a major station along the Perth to Kalgoorlie railway route.

MAIN ATTRACTIONS: Merredin's **Military Museum** recounts an interesting era from World War II. It is also the starting point for the self-guided **Merredin Peak Heritage Trail**, which takes in such notable sites as **Cummins Theatre** (1926) and the **Old Town Hall** (1913). Highlights among the rail memorabilia featured at the **Old Railway Station Museum** include a G117 steam engine built around 1897. The **wheat storage depot** in Gamenya Ave is the Southern Hemisphere's largest horizontal wheat silo with a storage capacity of 220 000 tonnes.

NEARBY ATTRACTIONS: Noted goldfields engineer C Y O'Connor designed the **No. 4 Pumping Station**, 3km west. **Hunts Dam**, 5km north, is popular for bushwalking and picnics while spring wildflowers abound at **Totadgin Dam Reserve**, 16km south-west. Interesting rock formations in the area include **Kangaroo Rock**, **Burracoppin Rock** and **Sandford Rocks**. Further afield, 40km north-west is **Mangowine Homestead**, a restored National Trust property.

VISITOR INFORMATION: Barrack St, Ph: (08) 9041 1668

Moora POP 1700
Map 402, C3

Situated on the **Moore River**, 172km north of Perth, Moora is the commercial centre for surrounding farming districts and largest town between Perth and Geraldton.

MAIN ATTRACTIONS: Local talent and handiwork can be seen in Padbury St at **Yuat Artifacts**, which displays and sells locally made Aboriginal arts and crafts; at **Moora Arts and Crafts Centre**, in Roberts St; and at the **Moora Fine Arts Gallery** situated in Gardiner St. **Apex Park** located beside the river is a grassy park set among salmon gums and **Federation Park** features a memorial to the Australian draught horse.

NEARBY ATTRACTIONS: **Berkshire Valley Folk Museum** is open by appointment, 19km east. **Watheroo NP**, 50km north, protects rare and common flora and some unusual geological features found at **Jingemia Cave**. **Western Wildflower Farm** at **Coomberdale**, 16km north, provides insight into export flower farming and drying between Easter and Christmas. **New Norcia**, 55km south-east, is an extraordinary monastic village, established as a mission in 1846 by Spanish Benedictine monks and operated today by the same order. The National Trust has classified 27 of the Spanish-style buildings, two of which house a museum and art gallery. A self-guided walk and daily tours are available. A stay at the **Monastic Guesthouse**, which offers a bed, meals and prayers, adds to the experience.

VISITOR INFORMATION: 34 Padbury St, Ph: (08) 9651 1401

Mount Barker POP 1670
Map 369, C2

Since vines were planted in the late 1960s Mount Barker, 50km north-west of Albany, has enjoyed a

The Spanish-style Abbey Church at New Norcia, south-east of Moora

growing reputation as a wine-producing region. Central to **Porongurup** and **Stirling Range national parks**, the town is also known for its agricultural industry.

Main Attractions: A **Police Station Museum** is housed in the convict-built station and gaol (1868). **The Banksia Farm**, on Pearce Rd, displays every known variety of banksia. The **Shire Art Gallery** on Lowood Rd is one of the finest regional galleries. Information on hiking trails and the **Great Southern Wineries** is available from the visitor centre.

Nearby Attractions: **Mount Barker Lookout**, 5km south-west, has sweeping views of the ranges. **St Werburghs Way Tourist Drive** takes in **St Werburghs Chapel** (1872), 12km south-west. Historic **Kendenup**, 16km north, is the site where gold was first found in Western Australia. **Porongurup NP**, 24km east, has bushwalking trails ranging in duration from ten minutes to three hours through dramatic ranges, karri tree stands, and fields of seasonal wildflowers. The highest peak in Stirling Range NP, 80km north-east, is **Bluff Knoll** (1073m).

Visitor Information: Historic Railway Station Albany Hwy, Ph: (08) 9851 1163

Mount Magnet POP 820

Map 400, E5

Situated in pastoral country along the route to Port Hedland, 562km north of Perth, Mount Magnet began as a gold town. Today more modern operations are undertaken at **Hill 50 Mine**.

Main Attractions: A **Heritage Walk** provides some historical background, supplemented by **Mt Magnet Museum** in Hepburn St that covers the district's local heritage, including gold-mining and pioneering endeavours.

Nearby Attractions: A map outlines the route for a 37km **Tourist Trail**

providing directions to gold ghost towns, such as **Lennonville**, 11km north, and to **The Granites**, an Aboriginal art site and picnic stop, 7km north. Wildflowers are a highlight in spring. Further afield near **Sandstone**, 158km east, is a natural basalt archway, **London Bridge**, and a cave that was converted into a now historic brewery. At **Yalgoo**, 127km west, is the **Dominican Chapel of St Hyacinth**, designed by the famous Monsignor John Hawes.

Visitor Information: Hepburn St, Ph: (08) 9963 4172 (July to October) or (08) 9963 4480

Narrogin POP 4500

Map 404, D2

In the heart of Western Australia's wheat belt, 192km south-east of Perth, Narrogin is a major railway junction and a thriving service centre for the surrounding farmlands.

Main Attractions: The **Court House Museum** (1894) focuses on the industry and daily life of early settlers, while the **Restoration Group Museum** houses locally restored cars and machines. Other notable buildings are listed in the 14km **Township Heritage Trail** leaflet. Quality local art and visiting exhibitions are displayed at the **Town Hall Art Gallery** on Federal St. Narrogin's various parks for picnics or rest stops include **Apex** and **Memorial parks**. Also worth a look are **Gnarojin Park** with its commemorative tiles and Aboriginal art, and **Foxes Lair**, a 45ha bushland reserve off Williams Rd. For a panoramic view of Narrogin and district go to **Lions Lookout** in Kipling St.

Nearby Attractions: A **District Heritage Trail** traces a 117km drive highlighting historic farms. Bushwalking and birdwatching are popular at **Dryandra Forest Reserve**, 26km north, also habitat for Western Australia's rare fauna

Children enjoying a farmstay near Narrogin

emblem, the numbat. Unusual rock formations featuring wildflowers in spring are **Yilliminning Rock** and **Birdwhistle Rock**, 11km east. **Albert Facey Homestead**, 39km east, is a significant site in the life of Albert Facey, author of the well-known autobiography, *A Fortunate Life*. An 86km self-drive **Albert Facey Heritage Trail** pamphlet is available.

Visitor Information: 23 Egerton St, Ph: (08) 9881 2064

Newman POP 4550

Map 401, F2

Newman, 450km south of Port Hedland, is a **Pilbara** iron-ore mining town originally built by Mount Newman Mining Company in the 1960s as a base for its employees.

Main Attractions: Located at the information centre is the **BHP Iron Ore Silver Jubilee Museum and Gallery**, recounting local mining history through memorabilia and displays. The centre is also the departure point for tours through **Mount Whaleback Mine**, the world's largest open-cut iron-ore mine, and the starting place for a

30 minute walk to **Radio Hill Lookout** with views over **Newman** and **Opthalmia Ranges**.

NEARBY ATTRACTIONS: **Opthalmia Dam** provides an oasis for swimming, sail boating and picnics. A 4-wheel drive **Waterhole Trail** highlights local waterholes and Aboriginal art sites. Rugged **Karijini NP (Hamersley Range)**, two hours north-west, features walks to spectacular gorges and contains Western Australia's highest peak, **Mount Meharry**. Organised ecotours of the Pilbara region can be booked in Newman.

VISITOR INFORMATION: Cnr Newman Dr and Fortescue Ave, Ph: (08) 9175 2888

■ Norseman   POP 1530
Map 403, K6

Gateway for travellers crossing the **Nullarbor** via the Eyre Hwy, Norseman, 190km south of Kalgoorlie, has been a gold-mining town since 1894.

MAIN ATTRACTIONS: The goldrush was started by a horse—so the mythology goes. And 'Norseman', the horse reputed to have turned up gold while pawing with its hoof, is commemorated with a statue in

Handrail Pool in Karijini National Park (Hamersley Range), near Newman

Roberts St. An **Historical Collection** of local mining and other memorabilia is on Battery Rd and the 33km **Norseman's Heritage Trail** follows a route once travelled by the Cobb & Co Coaches. A toy museum, **Dollykissangel**, is on Roberts St. The eight **corregated-iron camels**, on the main roundabout in Prinsep St, celebrate early camel-trains. Gem fossicking permits are available from the visitor information centre.

NEARBY ATTRACTIONS: Vantage points for viewing the town, salt lakes and massive mine tailings dumps include **Beacon Hill Lookout**, with a walking trail, 2km east, and **Mount Jimberlana**, 5km east. A pleasant picnic area, the **Dundas Rocks**, 22km south, have been dated at more than two million years old. **Peak Charles NP**, 90km south-west (including an unsealed 40km access road) has challenging walks and excellent views from the peak summit.

VISITOR INFORMATION: 68 Roberts St, Ph: (08) 9039 1071

■ Northam   POP 6375
Map 402, D5

Gazetted as a town in 1836, picturesque Northam in the **Avon Valley** sits at the junction of the **Avon** and **Mortlock rivers**, servicing a rich agricultural region.

MAIN ATTRACTIONS: Heritage buildings covered in a **Town Walk** pamphlet reflect Northam's early settlement, such as the **Town Hall** (1897), **Old Police Station** (1866), **Flour Mill** (1871), National Trust-classified **Sir James Mitchell House** (1905) and the restored **Shamrock Hotel** (1886). **The Avon Valley Arts Society Gallery** is also included on the route and early settlers' graves can be found near the golf course. **Morby Cottage** (1836) functioned as the first church and school and is now a museum. The **Old Train Station Museum** is on Fitzgerald St. The very

pretty Avon River, ideal for picnics, has one of Australia's longest suspension bridges and is home to Northam's famous white swans—descendants of a flock brought here from England by an early settler.

NEARBY ATTRACTIONS: Dramatic valley views can be seen hot-air ballooning, available April–November. **Avonlea Alpaca Tourist Farm** is 12km north-west. **The Big Camera** at **Meckering**, 35km east, is believed to be Australia's only camera museum.

VISITOR INFORMATION: 2 Grey St, Ph: (08) 9622 2100

■ Northampton   POP 832
Map 400, C6

Heritage-listed Northampton is 51km north of Geraldton in the **Nokanena Brook Valley**. It's heyday came in the mid-1800s after the discovery of copper and lead deposits; many historic buildings date from that era.

MAIN ATTRACTIONS: The construction of **Chiverton House**, now a museum of pioneer memorabilia, was completed by convicts in 1875. Other buildings of note are the **Old Convent, Church of Our Lady in Ara Coeli**, designed by Monsignor John Hawes, **Gwalla St miners' cottages** and the **old railway station**. Early headstones can be perused at the **Old Cemetery and Pioneer Memorial** opposite the Gwalla Church ruins.

NEARBY ATTRACTIONS: A relic from the Lead Mining Company, **Warribanno Chimney** is a National Trust smelter relic, 65km north-west. District labour shortages during 1853–56 were resolved by the establishment of a convict hiring station at **Lynton**, the remnants of which can be seen 47km north-west near **Port Gregory**. Fishing and surfing are popular at **Horrocks Beach**, 20km west.

VISITOR INFORMATION: Hampton Rd, Ph: (08) 9934 1488

Western Australia

Tourist tram on the Pemberton Tramway, en route to Northcliffe

Northcliffe POP 240

Map 404, C4

Nestled near awe-inspiring karri forests in the south-west corner of Western Australia, Northcliffe lies 31km south of Pemberton and offers sightseeing, as well as myriad leisure and recreational activities—bushwalking, climbing, fishing, photography, canoeing and swimming.

MAIN ATTRACTIONS: Located on Wheatley Coast Rd, **Northcliffe Pioneer Museum** recounts the town's history through photographs and memorabilia, while nearby **Forest Park** is home to the **Hollowbutt Karri Tree**, **Twin Karris**, the **Perfect Tree** and numerous walking trails.

NEARBY ATTRACTIONS: **Mount Chudalup**, 15km south, is a massive granite outcrop with a walking trail to a lookout. Set in karri forest, 16km east of Boorara Rd is **Lane Poole Falls**, spectacular in winter and spring. **Windy**

Harbour, 27km south, has a sheltered beach suitable for surfing, swimming, fishing and snorkelling and providing access to the cliffs of **D'Entrecasteaux NP**. **Salmon Beach** has spectacular views as well as salmon fishing from April to June. A 6km-long 2-wheel drive coastal drive travels the scenic route to **Point D'Entrecasteaux**, which features walking trails and lookouts. An excellent 48km **Great Forest Trees Drive** follows a gravel road taking in giant karri stands at **Snake Gully** and **Big Tree Grove**. Camping and bushwalking can be enjoyed at **Shannon NP**, 27km east.

VISITOR INFORMATION: Wheatley Coast Rd, Ph: (08) 9776 7203

Onslow POP 700

Map 400, C1

Originally settled in 1883 at the mouth of the **Ashburton River**, the town of Onslow moved to its present location in 1925 as a result of repeated cyclone damage and the subsequent silting of the river. Pearling, gold mining, agriculture and British nuclear testing (on Montebello Islands in the 1950s) feature in its history.

MAIN ATTRACTIONS: The **Goods Shed Museum** in Second Ave is a repository for relics from the early days. A **Town Heritage Trail** brochure is available. The lookouts over **Sunrise Beach** and **Sunset Beach** are worthwhile.

NEARBY ATTRACTIONS: The ruins of **Old Onslow**, 48km west, and its history are described in a pamphlet. Fishing is excellent, particularly in winter, with **Beadon Creek Groyne** and the mouth of the Ashburton River recommended. About 20km offshore are the ten **Mackerel Islands**, attracting anglers to the plentifully stocked waters. Termite mounds can be seen 10km south on Onslow Access Rd.

VISITOR INFORMATION: Second Ave (April–October), Ph: (08) 9184 6644

Pemberton POP 1015

Map 404, C4

Pemberton is a forest timber town in southern Western Australia. It sits in a valley encircled by karri, jarrah and marri forests. Handcrafted timber products are a regional specialty.

MAIN ATTRACTIONS: Pemberton Visitor Centre incorporates a **Pioneer Museum and Forest Discovery Centre** and craft outlets create and sell hardwood wares. **Pemberton Tramway** operates a 1907 replica tram daily from Pemberton Station through scenic tall-timber country. Two trails, called **Rainbow** and **Tramway**, follow the former log transport route and include stops at **Big Brook Arboretum** and **Big Brook Dam**, which is a favourite fishing, swimming, canoeing and sailboarding spot.

NEARBY ATTRACTIONS: Forest discovery tours, hiking, horseriding, fishing and 4-wheel drive trails provide interesting options for exploring. **Gloucester NP**, 1km south, encompasses the picturesque **Cascades**, bushwalking trails and fishing sites, and **Gloucester Tree**, the world's highest fire lookout stretching 61m with 153 rungs to climb. Once a wheat field, **Founders Forest** of tall karri trees is an excellent example of regeneration 13km from Pemberton. **Warren NP**, 9km south-west, has an 89m karri tree, walking trails and picnic facilities surrounded by virgin karri forest, while 18km west is **Beedelup NP**, with pretty **Beedelup Falls** and a 400-year-old 'walk-through' karri tree. Pamphlets provide details on local wineries.

VISITOR INFORMATION: Brockman St, Ph: (08) 9776 1133

Perenjori POP 350

Map 402, C2

Bordering the Murchison goldfields and Midwestern wheat farms and sheep-stations, Perenjori lies on the

Children in a field of pom-pom everlastings, *Cephalipterum drummondii*, on a Wildflower Trail near Perenjori

Wubin–Mullewa Hwy or **'Wildflower Way'**, 352km north-east of Perth.

MAIN ATTRACTIONS: **Perenjori Museum,** displaying pioneering memorabilia, is located in Fowler St. On Carnamah Rd is the **Catholic Church of St Joseph**, another architectural creation of Monsignor John Hawes.

NEARBY ATTRACTIONS: Spectacular spring **Wildflower Trails** are a must July–October. Situated 47km east is **Camel Soak**, a waterhole utilised originally by Aboriginal peoples and later by travelling camel trains. The 180km **Perenjori–Rothsay Heritage Trail** traces the area's gold-mining history visiting old mining areas and gold ghost towns. Gold and gemstone fossickers are often well rewarded for their efforts. Waterbirds can be seen at **Mongers Lake**, a salt lake 50km north-east.

VISITOR INFORMATION: Fowler St (July–October), Ph: (08) 9973 1105

▪ Pinjarra   POP 1910
Map 387, E3

One of the oldest towns in Western Australia, picturesque Pinjarra is located on the **Murray River**, 84km south of Perth in a region supported by farming, bauxite mining and timber milling.

MAIN ATTRACTIONS: **Pinjarrah Heritage Trail** takes in such sites as **St Johns Anglican Church** (1861); the **Original School House** (1862); a **Heritage Rose Garden** featuring 360 heritage roses, including the oldest known variety in cultivation; and the McLarty family home **Edenvale** (1888). Within the **Edenvale Complex** is **Roger May Machinery Museum**, **Murray Arts and Crafts Centre**, quilt displays and sales, and tearooms. The Murray River has picnic facilities and is used in summer for swimming and canoeing. A suspension bridge crosses the river at **Pioneer Memorial Park**.

NEARBY ATTRACTIONS: From May to October the **Hotham Valley Tourist Railway** runs steam train trips between Pinjarra and **Dwellingup**. Australia's largest alumina operation, **Alcoa Refinery**, 4km north-east, conducts bus tours on Wednesdays (bookings essential). **Alcoa Scarp Lookout**, 14km east, offers an overview of the massive plant. **Coopers Mill** on **Culeenup Island** was the first flour mill in the region and is accessible only by boat. **Tumbulgum Farm**, 38km north at **Mundijong** has native and farm animals, farm shows and product sales. **North Dandalup Dam**, 16km north-east, **South Dandalup Dam** at **Dwellingup**, and **Waroona Dam**, 33km south, are pleasant picnic and recreational areas within an easy drive from Pinjarra. The many attractions of **Mandurah**, **Peel Inlet** and **Harvey Estuary**, also **Yalgorup NP**, are a short drive west.

VISITOR INFORMATION: Cnr George St and Henry St, Ph: (08) 9531 1438

▪ Port Hedland   POP 13 000
Map 398, C5

Renowned for handling Australia's largest amount of iron ore for export and for its mammoth salt exports, Port Hedland sits in a mangrove-lined inlet discovered in 1863 by Captain Peter Hedland.

MAIN ATTRACTIONS: Tours of the bustling port area and **Nelson Point** iron ore site depart from the visitor centre. A 26m-high **Observation Tower** behind the centre provides an excellent view of the port, town and shipping traffic. Relics of old manganese mines and BHP railway locomotives are some of the memorabilia on display at **Don Rhodes Mining Museum** on Wilson St. In Sutherland St is the **Pioneer and Pearlers Cemetery** where Japanese and Chinese nationals are buried. Visitors are welcome at the **Royal Flying Doctor Service** and **School of the Air**. Flatback turtle nesting ecotours operate seasonally.

NEARBY ATTRACTIONS: Visible from **Cooke Point** March–October, the rising full moon creates an illusory reflection descriptively known as **'Stairway to the Moon'**. **Pretty Pool**, a nearby tidal pool, is a safe swimming and fishing spot. Stockpiled conical dunes of salt produced by solar evaporation can be seen 8km south-east at **Red Bank Bridge**.

VISITOR INFORMATION: 13 Wedge St, Ph: (08) 9173 1711

▪ Rockingham   POP 52 100
Map 364, C4

From its founding in 1872 until the opening of Fremantle harbour in 1897 Rockingham operated as one of Western Australia's timber ports. Today it is a seaside resort city, conveniently located 47km south of Perth, capitalising on its pristine beaches and protected waterways.

MAIN ATTRACTIONS: Beach-based recreation is a major attraction, including swimming, boat harbour tours, 'watch and swim with the

dolphins' cruises, and diving excursions to offshore wrecks and reefs. On Kent St is the **Museum of Local History** and exhibitions can be viewed at the **Art Gallery** on Civic Blvd. Western Australia's grain industry history is recounted at **The Granary** on Rockingham Rd, which is open by appointment. A coastal scenic lookout worth visiting is at **Cape Peron** on Peron Rd.

NEARBY ATTRACTIONS: Islands in nearby waters offer a variety of excellent excursions: **Penguin Island** has a colony of little penguins and a **Penguin Experience Island Discovery Centre** (access prohibited June–August during the breeding season); **Seal Island** has a colony of sea-lions; **Garden Island** is the site of the HMAS *Stirling* naval base

Grass trees, *Xanthorrhoea preisii*, at Shoalwater Bay, Rockingham

and features pleasant beaches accessible by private boat; and **Shoalwater Bay Island Marine Park** offers park cruises. **Lake Richmond**, 4km west, has interesting walks and domed thrombolites (unlayered stromatolites). **Marapana Wildlife World**, 15km south, and **Tumblegum Farm**, 29km east, are popular with families. A waterski park is 5km south-east at **Baldivis** and **Peel Estate Winery** offers cellar door sales. Seasonal wildflowers make the scenic drive to **Serpentine Dam** and **Serpentine Falls**, 48km south-east, particularly worthwhile in spring.

VISITOR INFORMATION: 43 Kent St, Ph: (08) 9592 3464

■ Roebourne   POP 960
Map 398, B6

Established in 1864 and named after Western Australia's first Surveyor-General, John Septimus Roe, Roebourne is the oldest town in the **Pilbara**.

MAIN ATTRACTIONS: Historic buildings reflect an earlier era when Roebourne served as an important administrative centre, and include the **Holy Trinity Church** (1894), **Union Bank** (1889), **Victoria Hotel** (1866) and four stone buildings constructed in 1887—the **Post Office**, **Hospital**, **Court House** and the **Old Gaol** which now houses the **Roebourne Museum**. A lookout is located along Fisher Dr at **Mount Welcome**.

NEARBY ATTRACTIONS: **Emma Withnell Heritage Trail** is a 52km self-guided walk/drive tour through the historic coastal towns of **Cossack**, **Point Samson** and **Wickham**. **Cossack**, 14km north, was originally known as Tien Tsin Harbour and retains many interesting restored buildings from its brief era as a port. It was once connected to Roebourne by horse-drawn tram. **Point Samson**, 19km north, has good onshore and

offshore fishing, boat hire, swimming and snorkelling. **Millstream–Chichester NP**, 150km south, is a 2000km^2 park with fascinating features—**Pyramid Hill**, a volcanic remnant; freshwater **Python Pool** and **Chinderwarriner Pool**; and **Mount Herbert lookout** (366m). Directions to bushwalking trails and self-drive tours can be obtained from **Millstream Homestead** off Hamersley Iron Rd, which functions as the park's information centre.

VISITOR INFORMATION: Old Gaol, Queen St, Ph: (08) 9182 1060

■ Southern Cross   POP 1150
Map 403, G4

A service centre for the surrounding pastoral and gold mining districts, Southern Cross was founded after a gold-find in 1888, though the rush was short-lived. Situated 368km east of Perth, its streets—like the town itself—are named after stars and constellations.

MAIN ATTRACTIONS: Notable historical buildings are the **Post Office** (1891), **Railway Tavern** (1890s), **Palace Hotel** (1912) and the **Court House** (1893), which houses the local **Historical Museum**. Off the Great Eastern Hwy is the **Old Cemetery** where town pioneers are buried.

NEARBY ATTRACTIONS: Prolific wildflowers on the sand plains make springtime scenic drives more than memorable. **Koolyanobbing**, 53km north, became a 'modern ghost town' after its iron-ore mine closed in 1983; however, the town revived in 1994 when iron-ore and salt mining recommenced. Rock formations with nearby picnic spots are **Hunts Soak**, 7km north, constructed by convicts in 1865; **Frog Rock**, 15km south, shaped in a wave-like outcrop; **Karalee Rock** and **Dam**, 37km east; and **Baladjie Rock**, 45km north-west.

VISITOR INFORMATION: Shire Offices, Antares St, Ph: (08) 9049 1001

This limestone island is home to **quokkas**, small indigenous marsupials mistakenly identified as rats in 1696 by a Dutch explorer, who subsequently named the island 'Rats Nest'. Thousands of holiday-makers are drawn to Rottnest Island each year. Bicycles, available for hire, are the main mode of transport on the island—so there is little motorised traffic.

'Rotto', 19km west of Fremantle, is only 11km long and less than half that wide. Its beaches are a major drawcard, as they boast crystal-clear water and some of the world's southernmost coral reefs. Over 360 species of fish and 20 species of coral are found within Rottnest waters and the sheltered bays provide idyllic conditions for snorkelling, surfing, scuba diving, swimming or just soaking up the sun. Colonial streetscapes and architecture are also a feature of this historic island. Due to its close proximity to Perth and Fremantle, by ferry or aeroplane, Rottnest is an ideal daytrip destination, but has much to offer visitors who choose to stay.

main attractions

- ❖ Rottnest's colonial architecture
- ❖ Rottnest Museum
- ❖ Island coach tour (two hour)
- ❖ Oliver Hill gun battery and train

Visitor information

Rottnest Island Visitor and Information Centre
Thomson Bay, Rottnest Island WA 6161
Ph: (08) 0372 0752
www.rottnest.com.au

Snorkelling at Cape Vlamingh, Rottnest Island

▨ Tom Price   POP 3200
Map 400, E2

The discovery in 1962 of iron ore deposits at **Mount Tom Price** soon led to the Hamersley Iron Company establishing the town of Tom Price to support and service its mining operation. Situated on the edge of the **Hamersley Range** at an altitude of 747m, it is the highest town in Western Australia.

MAIN ATTRACTION: Tours of the huge **Pilbara Iron open-cut mine** depart from the information centre.

NEARBY ATTRACTIONS: **Mount Nameless**, 6km west, has an elevation of 1128m, affording panoramic views of the town and mine. Its summit is accessible via 4-wheel drive or from the walking track at the base of the hill. Bushwalking and scenic drives are popular pursuits in rugged **Karijini (Hamersley Range) NP**, 50km east. Renowned for its spectacular and colourful gorges and prolific wildlife, highlights include a giant termite mound; **Kalamina Gorge** and pool; **Hancock, Weano, Dales** and **Red gorges**; **Circular Pool** and **Fortescue Falls**; **Oxers Lookout**; and swimming pools at **Hamersley Gorge**. There is a visitor centre in the park. Tour operators run day trips and camping safaris.

VISITOR INFORMATION: Central Rd, Ph: (08) 9188 1112

> **Note**: *Travellers should not venture to the small town of **Wittenoom** to the north-east of Karijini NP. It has been declared no longer habitable due to the significant health risk from asbestos fibres, a legacy of the asbestos mine that closed in the 1960s.*

▨ Wagin   POP 1300
Map 404, D3

A 9m-high statue of a merino ram is an appropriate icon for the rural service town of Wagin, 177km east of Bunbury. Originally established in 1889 as an important point on the Great Southern Railway, the town is today surrounded by thriving sheep, cattle, grain and emu farms.

MAIN ATTRACTIONS: **Wagin Historical Village** on Kitchener St recreates the daily life as it would have been 100 years ago in the settlement town. A one-room school, black-smith, settlers' cottages and wool museum are among the interesting and informative attractions in the village. Heritage trails trace these and other historic town buildings including the **Little Gem Theatre**.

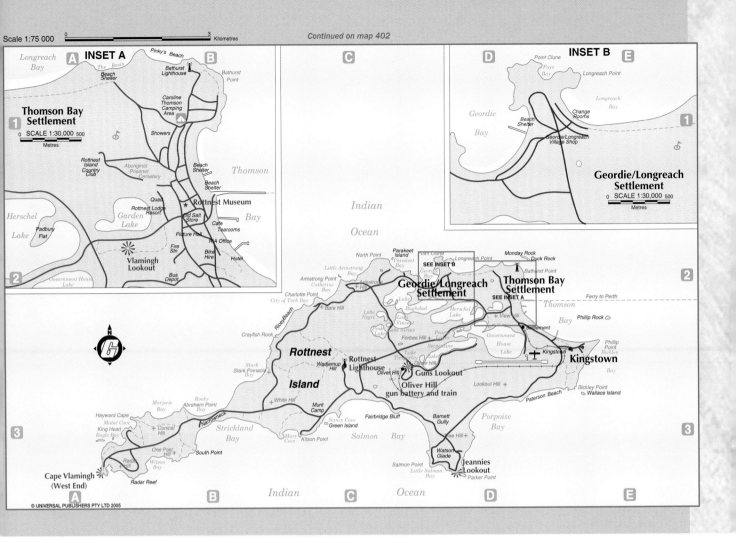

Continued on map 402

NEARBY ATTRACTIONS: Emu chick incubation and hatching are among highlights sometimes seen at the **Corralyn Emu Farm**, 4km north. Rocky outcrops in the area, some with lookouts, picnic facilities and walks include **Puntapin Rock**, 6km south-east, and **Mount Latham**, 6km west. **Lake Norring**, 13km south, is a popular recreation area. For speed enthusiasts, Donald Campbell set a world water-speed record in 1964 at **Lake Dumbleyung**, 18km east.

VISITOR INFORMATION: Wagin Historical Village, Kitchener St, Ph: (08) 9861 1232

■ Waroona   POP 1800

Map 375, D1

Conveniently close to the **Preston** and **Clifton lakes**, **Yalgorup NP**, and other picturesque forested areas, Waroona, 112km south of Perth, provides an excellent base for exploring. Settlers arrived in the district in the 1830s and a township (at the time known as Drakesbrook) was established about 40 years later. Timber milling and the arrival of the railway boosted the growth of the area.

MAIN ATTRACTIONS: **Vision Splendid Gardens** on Parnell St is an exceptional private garden featuring more than 400 rose bushes and creative landscape architecture. Plantation pine toys, dolls' houses and household wares can be found at **The Puzzleman** on McLarty St. The 12 painted **Bush Poles**, next to the visitor centre, are a popular attraction.

NEARBY ATTRACTIONS: **Lane Pool Reserve** is a forest recreation area with camping, picnic and swimming areas, including **Scarp Pool**, **Baden Powell Water Spout** and **Island Pool**. To the north, in **Dwellingup**, the **Forest Heritage Centre** offers exhibits, a treetop walk and wood products. The **Etmilyn Forest Tramway**, a steam train venturing into the jarrah forest, departs from Dwellingup. **Preston Beach**, 34km west, offers ocean swimming and fishing. Off Preston Beach Rd is Yalgorup NP, with well-developed bushwalking trails through the tuart trees. **Drakesbrook Weir**, 5km south-east, has good fishing, swimming and non-power boating. **Lake Navarino**, to the east, is known for its water-skiing and freshwater fishing.

VISITOR INFORMATION: 37 South Western Hwy, Ph: (08) 9733 1506

Wongan Hills   POP 813
Map 402, D4

This township is situated in the north-east wheat belt, 184km from Perth. The name Wongan Hills originates from an Aboriginal word for 'whispering hills'.

MAIN ATTRACTIONS: Improvised furniture and implements are among the memorabilia from the early days displayed at the **Pioneer Museum** in Camm St. **Town Park**, in Fenton Pl, has BBQ facilities and a children's play area.

NEARBY ATTRACTIONS: During the spring months, Wongan Hills and district blossoms into a spectacular sea of wildflowers, best seen at **Reynoldson's Flora Reserve**, 15km north. **Mount Matilda**, 10km west, is a flora and fauna reserve with an ecowalk trail. In stark contrast to the region's flat farmlands are various rock formations also popular for wildflower sightings: **Dingo Rock**, 26km east. **Mount O'Brien Lookout**, 10km west, **Gathercole Reserve** on Moonijin Rd, and **Christmas Rock**, an old water catchment area closer to town, accessed off Wandoo Cres. **Lake Ninnan**, 10km west, provides a venue for waterskiing, sailing and swimming.

VISITOR INFORMATION: Fenton Pl, Ph: (08) 9671 1247

Wyndham   POP 880
Map 399, K2

Western Australia's northernmost town, Wyndham supported a size-able meatworks industry until its closure in 1985. Today the port town services pastoral, mining and Aboriginal communities and exports diverse cargoes including raw Kununurra sugar and live cattle shipments to south-east Asia.

MAIN ATTRACTIONS: A landing port for prospectors during the 1880s gold-rushes, Wyndham's highlights include the **Old Post Office** (now privately owned) and the **Old Court House**, which serves as an historical museum. Saltwater crocodiles can be sighted from the wharf (observed from a distance when the wharf is not in use), or at the **Zoological Gardens and Crocodile Park** on Barytes Rd. Located in **Warriu 'Dream Time' Park** are large statues of an Aboriginal family and native fauna.

NEARBY ATTRACTIONS: **Five Rivers Lookout**, 5km north on **Bastion Range**, is renowned for its spectacular views, which are highly recommended at sunrise or sunset. A wetland sanctuary for migratory birds including jabiru and brolga, **Marlgu Billabong**, 15km south-east, is part of **Parry Lagoons Nature Reserve**. A 100m-deep natural swimming hole, **The Grotto** is located 36km east and is a popular picnic area. Fresh and saltwater fishing are popular in the **King River** area, with 4-wheel drive access. The **King River Rd** leads to Aboriginal rock paintings, **Moochalabra Dam** and the **Boab Prison Tree**, an unusual temporary prison cell from the 1890s. Tours offered in the region include mustering, horseriding treks, scenic boat cruises, and for an unforgettable Outback station stay, **El Questro Station**, located 100km south.

VISITOR INFORMATION: Kimberley Motors, 6 Great Northern Hwy, Ph: (08) 9161 1281

York   POP 2020
Map 402, D5

This is the oldest inland town in Western Australia, settled in 1831, just two years after the Swan River Colony. York prospered as a result of the 1889 gold discoveries at **Southern Cross** and has since become a commercial centre for the **Avon Valley**.

MAIN ATTRACTIONS: Awarded the National Trust classification of **Historic Town**, York has many significant buildings: the **Old Gaol**, **Court House** and **Police Station** (1850), **Sandalwood Yards** and **Tipperary School** (1874), **Town Hall** (1911), **Castle Hotel** (1853), and **Holy Trinity Church** (1854), with its rare pipe organ and Robert Juniper-designed glass and paintings. **Residency Museum** (1843) on Brook St houses a collection of records and memorabilia from early colonial life. York's highly regarded **Motor Museum** in Avon Tce exhibits classic and vintage cars, motorcycles and horse-drawn vehicles. **Avon Valley Historical Rose Garden** on Osnaburg Rd has fragrant and spectacular blooms and is open seven days in season. **The Old Mill Gallery,** in Broome St, sells and displays fine jarrah fur-niture and artworks. At **Avon Park** there are picnic facilities and a river-crossing **Suspension Bridge** originally built in 1906.

NEARBY ATTRACTION: Spectacular views can be seen from **Mount Brown Lookout**, 3km south-east, which is also popular for picnics.

VISITOR INFORMATION: 81 Avon Tce, Ph: (08) 9641 1301

York's Romanesque Town Hall

KEY MAP

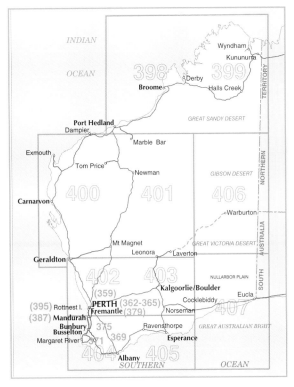

INDIAN

OCEAN

398

Wyndham

Kununurra

399

Derby

Broome

Halls Creek

TERRITORY

Port Hedland

Dampier

GREAT SANDY DESERT

Marble Bar

Exmouth

Tom Price

Newman

GIBSON DESERT

NORTHERN

400

401

406

Carnarvon

Warburton

AUSTRALIA

Mt Magnet

GREAT VICTORIA DESERT

Leonora

Laverton

Geraldton

402

403

NULLARBOR PLAIN

SOUTH

(359)

Kalgoorlie/Boulder

Cocklebiddy

Eucla

(395) Rottnest I.

PERTH (362-365)

Norseman

407

(387) Mandurah

Fremantle (379)

Bunbury

375

Ravensthorpe

GREAT AUSTRALIAN BIGHT

Busselton

369

Esperance

Margaret River

371

404

Albany

405

SOUTHERN

OCEAN

Capital city CBD map
Perth p.359

Perth suburban maps
pp.362–365

Fremantle map
p.379

Region maps
Great Southern
  Region p.369
Caves District p.371
South West Region
  p.375
Peel Region p.387
Rottnest Island
  p.395

State maps
pp.398–407

Boab tree in the Kimberleys

DISTANCE CHART

Approximate Distance	Albany	Broome	Bunbury	Busselton	Carnarvon	Derby	Esperance	Eucla	Geraldton	Halls Creek	Kalgoorlie/Boulder	Kununurra	Mandurah	Meekatharra	Merredin	Narrogin	Norseman	Northam	Perth	Port Hedland
Albany		2582	361	372	1292	2736	474	1386	819	3196	799	3554	468	1116	463	269	676	439	406	1988
Broome	2582		2538	2592	1461	222	912	3082	1934	682	2185	1040	2441	1466	2304	2313	2372	2143	2372	614
Bunbury	361	2538		54	1069	2554	687	1599	596	3004	764	3362	1027	924	422	170	889	261	182	1796
Busselton	372	2592	54		1123	2608	698	1610	650	3058	818	3416	161	978	482	224	900	315	236	1850
Carnarvon	1292	1461	1069	1123		1615	1600	2300	473	2075	1161	2433	972	620	1125	1078	1590	964	903	867
Derby	2736	222	2554	2608	1615		2728	3236	2088	544	2267	902	2447	1620	2458	2467	2526	2297	2378	768
Esperance	474	912	687	698	1600	2728		912	1319	3188	389	3486	710	1108	562	535	202	828	714	1980
Eucla	1386	3082	1599	1610	2300	3236	912		1827	3696	897	4054	1502	1616	1175	1433	710	1336	1433	2488
Geraldton	819	1934	596	650	473	2088	1319	1827		2548	988	2906	499	540	652	605	1117	491	430	1340
Halls Creek	3196	682	3004	3058	2075	544	3188	3696	2548		2799	358	2907	2080	2918	2927	2986	2757	2838	1228
Kalgoorlie/Boulder	799	2185	764	818	1161	2267	389	897	988	2799		3157	663	719	336	594	187	497	594	1591
Kununurra	3554	1040	3362	3416	2433	902	3486	4054	2906	358	3157		3265	2438	3276	3285	3344	3115	3196	1586
Mandurah	468	2441	1027	161	972	2447	710	1502	499	2907	663	3265		827	327	175	792	166	75	1698
Meekatharra	1116	1466	924	978	620	1620	1108	1616	540	2080	719	2438	827		838	847	906	677	758	872
Merredin	463	2304	422	482	1125	2458	562	1175	652	2918	336	3276	327	838		258	465	161	258	1710
Narrogin	269	2313	170	224	1078	2467	535	1433	605	2927	594	3285	175	847	258		723	170	192	1719
Norseman	676	2372	889	900	1590	2526	202	710	1117	2986	187	3344	792	906	465	723		626	723	1778
Northam	439	2143	261	315	964	2297	828	1336	491	2757	497	3115	166	677	161	170	626		97	1549
Perth	406	2372	182	236	903	2378	714	1433	430	2838	594	3196	75	758	258	192	723	97		1630
Port Hedland	1988	614	1796	1850	867	768	1980	2488	1340	1228	1591	1586	1698	872	1710	1719	1778	1549	1630	

* All distances in this chart have been measured over highways and major roads, not necessarily by the shortest route.

Scale 1:3 900

1

Seringapatam Reef

Scott Reef

SCOTT REEF
NATURE RES.

2   15°

INDIAN   *OCEAN*

3   17°

Mermaid Reef

COULOMB POINT
N.R.

Rowley Shoals

ROWLEY SHOALS
MARINE PARK   *Clerke Reef*

66

Imperieuse Reef

Malcolm Douglas   Waterbank
Crocodile Park Cable Beach
Chinatown, Japanese Cemetery *i*
Broome
Broome Bird Observa
Roebuck
Thang

4

Eco Beach Wilderness Retreat ★
Cape Latouche Treville   12
Port Smith Caravan & Bird Park ★   Sham
Lagrange Bay   26
Cape Bossut Bibyadang
Admiral Bay (Lagrange
Frazier Downs   FRAZIER
DOWNS
287
□ Nita Downs

19°   Anna Plains □   16

1

Eighty Mile Beach   86
Mandora
Cape Keraudren   22
Wallal Downs □ 9   ✕ Sandfire Roadhouse
5   141   NORTHERN   23
KIDSON   (WAPET RD)
North Turtle I.○   Poissonnier Pt   44   4WD
Mining Museum,   Pardoo □   GREAT   Pardoo Roadhouse   60
Pioneer & Pearlers Cemetery   *De Grey*   102 □   20   70   TRACK   37
Port   40   28
Hedland *i*   Boodarie □   South   □ Strelley   Nimingarra
Aboriginal   *Cape Thouin*   32   Hedland   30   *De Grey* Muccan □ Callawa
rock engravings   Mundabullangana   1   Garlindie   Coongan   R
(Burrup Peninsula)   Wallareenya   53   27 □ Warrawagine
Dampier   33   Tabba Tabba   60   Eginbah   46
Archipelago   Indee   19   R
Montebello Is.● MONTEBELLO   Rosemary I.   95   Lalla Rookh   143
ISLANDS C.P.   *Burrup Peninsula*   *Talga*   78
Enderby I.   **Karratha**   □ Mt Edgar   L. Waukarlycarly
Barrow I. Wapet Camp Karratha Roadhouse **Wickham** Whim Mallina   **Marble**
N.R.   *Cape Preston*   Cossack   Creek   74   **Bar**   145
Gt. Sandy I●   Roebourne   Sherlock   Mt   Kangan   8   Private
21°   Karratha 137   Museum 161   Satirist   19   10 106 ✕ Woodie Woodie
GREAT SANDY I. N.R. Mardie   MT WELCOME   Pyramid □ Yandeyarra   Corunna   Carawine   38
6   Fortescue River   Python   219   Abydos   Downs   Gorge   10
Thevenard I.   Roadhouse   Pool   56   □ Woodstock   Telfer Min
Onslow   Pannawonica   MILLSTREAM   Hillside   200   (no facilities
PEERAMULLA   Yarraloola   CHICHESTER   Nullagine ○   103
ANTH.   258   N.P.   Mt Florance   Nifty ✕   110
A 159   Millstream   **B** 117 Coolawanyah   Hooley   **C** 419   **D**   **E**
©UNIVERSAL PUBLISHERS PTY LTD 2005   **P I L B A R A**   *Chichester*   *Range*

F 123° G 125° H J K 129°

1

Browse I. ○

Cape Bougainville Troughton I.

Sir Graham Moore I.

Cape Talbot

Cape Londonderry

Lesueur I.
Cape Rulhieres

Joseph Bonaparte Gulf

Cassini I.

Napier Broome Bay

CARSON RIVER

Pago (Ruin) ★

Reveley I.

Admiralty Gulf

Maret I.

Bigge I.

KALUMBURU

Kalumburu ♣

Cape Dussejour
Cape Lacrosse I.
Cape Domett

Turtle Point

Theda

DRYSDALE RIVER N.P.

ORD RIVER N.R.

2

Coronation Is.

PRINCE REGENT

Adolphus I.

Darcy I.

Champagny I.

Augustus I.

Battery Pt.

Kunmunya (Ruins) ★

King Edward River (Doongan)

K I M B E R L E Y

Zoo and Crocodile Park
Wyndham

Carlton Hill

Spirit Hills

56

Adele I.

'Southern Cross' Crash Site

Drysdale River

Home Valley

Prison Tree ★

The Grotto

VICTORIA 45

Kununurra

Mirima N.P.

HWY

58

Buccaneer Archipelago

Cockatoo I.

Montgomery I.

Kuri Bay

KUNMUNYA

Ellenbrae

246

Durack River Roadhouse

El Questro

Lake Argyle Village

Rosewood

Cockatoo Island Resort ★

Koolan I.

Koolan ♣

Collier Bay

Walcott Inlet

PANTIJAN

Pantijan

+ Mt Russ 693

GIBB RIVER

Karunjie

Woolah ♣

151

Glen Hill
Argyle

Diamond Mine

Waterloo

Hidden I.

Kooljaman Resort
mbardina
Djarindjin ♣

One Arm Point (Bardi)

Pender

DEFENCE TRAINING AREA

Mt Elizabeth

Gibb River

108

Lissadell

Spring Creek

Cape Leveque

King Sound

Oobagooma

Mt Hart

Beverley Springs

Mt Synnot 487+

Joint Hill 713 +

MT BARNETT

Mt Barnett Roadhouse

Gordon Hill 549

Bow River

Warmun (Turkey Ck)

Mistake Creek

261

Beagle Bay

BEAGLE BAY

Silent Grove

Mt House

Tableland

Mabel Downs

Castlereagh Hill 590 +

Echidna Chasm

Cathedral Gorge

Ord River Regeneration Research Stn.

Country Downs

Derby

Meda

Napier Downs

306

Imintji

Glenroy

Mt Ord 937

Bedford Downs

VIOLET VALLEY

162

Kirkimbie

Mowanjum ♣

Kimberley Downs

Fairfield

LEOPOLD DOWNS

Mornington

Lansdowne

Mt Wells 983

Alice Downs

PURNULULU N.P.

Nicholson

Willare Bridge Roadhouse

Yeeda

Curtin RAAF Base

Blina

Blina

Leopold Downs

Gold

Turner

Bunda

146

Kilto

Bedunburru

Tjarramba

Camballin

Ellendale

TUNNEL CREEK N.P.

BROOKING GORGE C.P.

Little

Springvale

Russian Jack Memorial

Halls Creek

Old Halls Creek (ruin)

Florl Valley

Roebuck Roadhouse

Roebuck Plains

Yakka Munga

Looma ♣

214

Luluigui

MT ANDERSON

NOONKANRAH

Fossil Downs

Mudludja

Fitzroy Crossing

176

DUNCAN

Ruby Plains

Dampier Downs

Nerrima

Kalyeeda

Jubilee Downs

Bayulu

Noonkanbah

Ngalangkati

MILLIJIDDIE

Lambo

Koongie Park

Gordon Downs (ruin)

Mowla Bluff

Millijiddee

Margaret River

Louisa Downs

Yiyili

Kundat Djaru

Mowla Bluff + 203

Cherrabun

BOHEMIA DOWNS

Wangkatjungka ♣

287

172

WOLFE CREEK CRATER N.P.

Sturt Creek

PURTA

DRAGON TREE N.R

Lake Jones

Lake Betty

Lake Lanagan

Lake McLernon

CARRANYA

Biliiluna ♣

MOUNT FREDERICK

5

G R E A T   S A N D Y

KIDSON

Well 51

Well 48

Well 49

Well 50

BILILUNA

Mulan

Balgo ♣

TANAMI

232

ROAD

MOUNT FREDERICK (No.2)

D E S E R T

Well 47

Well 46

Well 45

BALGO

Lake Dennis

YININGARRA

Mendigigil Rockhole

Percival Lakes

Well 44

Lake White

Well 42

Well 43

Helena Spring

Lake Wills

6

TRACK

Well 41

Well 40

Well 39

Lake Hazlett

Punmu ♣

Lake Dora

KIDSON TK

Well 38

Well 37

Well 36

CANNING

Well 35

CENTRAL AUSTRALIA

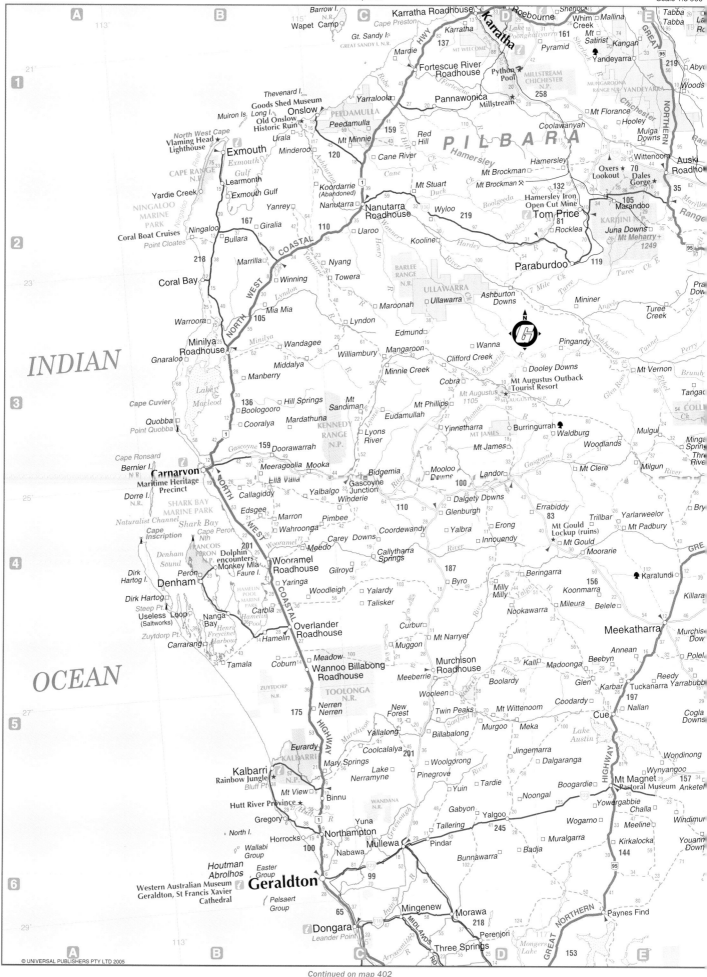

INDIAN

OCEAN

Gregory's Australia

Continued on map 402

Continued on maps 403 & 407

© UNIVERSAL PUBLISHERS PTY LTD 2005

Scale 1:1 700

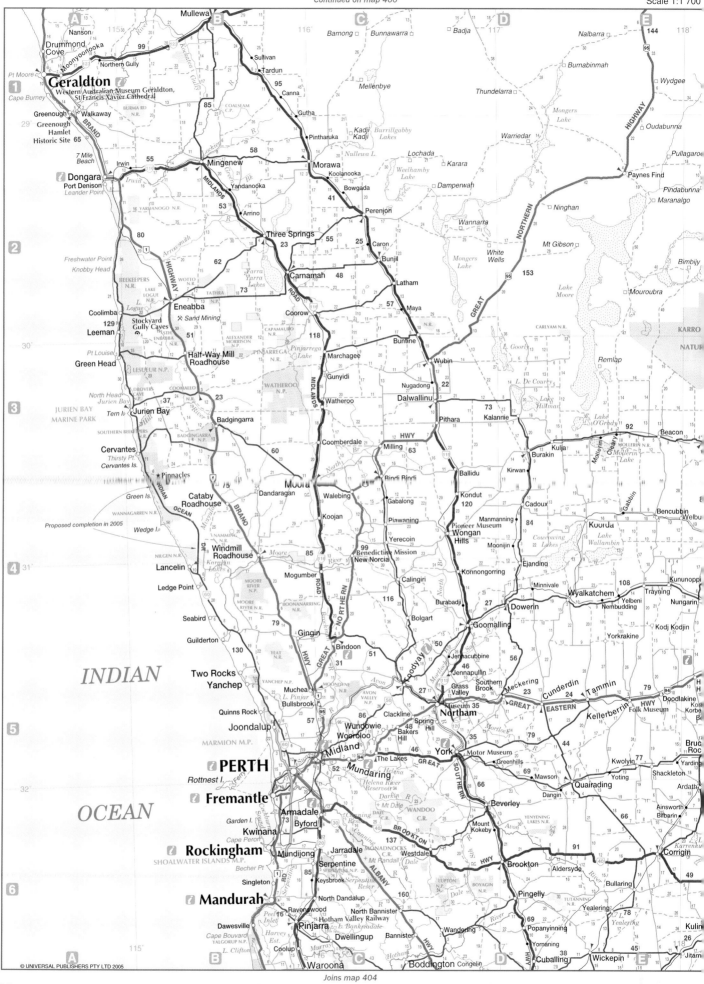

Joins map 404

Gregory's Australia

© UNIVERSAL PUBLISHERS PTY LTD 2005

Continued on map 407

F Youanmi Downs
Yuinmery
G Bulga Downs
119
Lake Noondie
H 120
Ida Valley
Sturt Meadows
J 23 121
Tarmoola
Mertondale
K
GOLDFIELDS
124
1
GLENORN
Youangarra
Leonora
Minara
Gwalia (Ghost Town)
Malcolm (abandoned)
Cashmere Downs
Perrinvale
Mt Ida
Mt Ida (ruins)
Copperfield
105
HWY
Melita
Glenorn
Orient Well
Tampa
Lake Barlee
Lake Barlee
Lake Ballard
Kookynie
Morapoi
Kookynie
Lake Raeside
Yerilla
Mt Elvire
Walling Rock
Jeedamya
Mendleyarri
2
Diemals
L. Giles
ADELONG
Menzies
Lake Marmion
Menangina
Riverina
GOLDFIELDS
Boomerang L.
Pigeon Rocks
Goongarrie
L. Owen
Lake Goongarrie
GOONGARRIE NATIONAL PARK
30'
HILL
SERVE
MOUNT MANNING NATURE RESERVE
Davyhurst (ruins)
Bardoc
Goongarrie
Carr Boyd
Lake Emu
Callion
Wangine Lake
130
Gindalbie
Mt Jackson
Missouri
Mt Carnage
Bardoc
3
Kawana
Hammersley Lakes
Credo
Mt Vetters
Ora Banda
Broad Arrow
Kanowna
L. Penny
Phantom Devil
Perkolilli
Perkolilli
Lake Yindarlgooda
Bonnie Rock
L. Deborah East
Kintore
Black Flag
White Flag Lake
Hannans North Tourist Mine, Australian Prospectors & Miners Hall of Fame, Western Australian Museum Kalgoorlie-Boulder
Bulong (ruins)
WALYAHMONING N.R.
L. Deborah West
Ennuin
(ghost town) Koolyanobbing
Timberfield
Kalgoorlie-Boulder
Kopai Lake
Hampton
Golden Ridge
Darrine
Jaurdi
Mt Burges
Bonnie Vale
Hannan Lake
Mukinbudin
CHIDDARCOOPING N.R.
Lake Baladjie
LAKE BALADJIE N.R.
Dulimbi
Lake Julia
Lake Seabrook
L. Walton
Walleroo
Coolgardie Camel Farm
Stewart
Coolgardie
Pharmacy Museum, Old Kalgoorlie Goal
New Celebration
Mt Monger
Woolibar
4
LAKE CAMPION N.R.
Warralakin
39
ALT 94
Campion
Westonia
YELLOWDINE N.R.
Southern Cross Museum
EASTERN
188
Boorabbin
Gnarlbine Rock
COOLGARDIE - ESPERANCE
56
KAMBALDA N.R.
Kambalda
Kambalda West
Carrabin
GREAT
Moorine Rock
Yellowdine
BOORABBIN N.P.
GOLDFIELDS WOODLANDS C.P.
GOLDFIELDS WOODLANDS N.P.
Victoria Rock
Bulla Bulling
75
Lake Lefroy
Booraan
Burracoppin
108
Bodallin
GOLDFIELDS Victoria Rock WOODLANDS C.P.
Burra Rock
St Ives
Merredin
Military Museum, Old Railway Station Museum
Marvell Loch
GOLDFIELDS WOODLANDS N.P. (Proposed)
Widgiemooltha
Koonadgin
TRACK
CAVE HILL N.R.
Cave Hill 4WD
5
Muntadgin
112
Higginsville
71
Cramphorne
JILBADJI NATURE RESERVE
L. Barker
94
Lake Cowan
39
Wogarl
Pioneer
32'
Narembeen
87
Welcome Hill
Mt Holland
Bronzite Ridge
EYRE HWY
1
South Kumminin
Lake Johnstone
Norseman
Dollykissangel
55
NORTH KARLGARIN N.R.
HOLLAND
DUNDAS NATURE RESERVE
Bendering
Hyden
Wave Rock
Kondinin
60
Karlgarin
L. Carmody
Lake Hope
COOLGARDIE - ESPERANCE
6
KONDININ SALT MARSH N.R.
123
L. Hurlstone N.R.
L. Hurlstone
Lake Dundas
Jalakin L.
L. Varley
Lake Varley N.R.
Gilmore
F
Pingaring
HARRIS N.R.
119
DRAGON ROCKS N.R.
L. Gibson
Varley
G
120
H
Hatter
121
J
Beete
K
122
© UNIVERSAL PUBLISHERS PTY LTD 2005

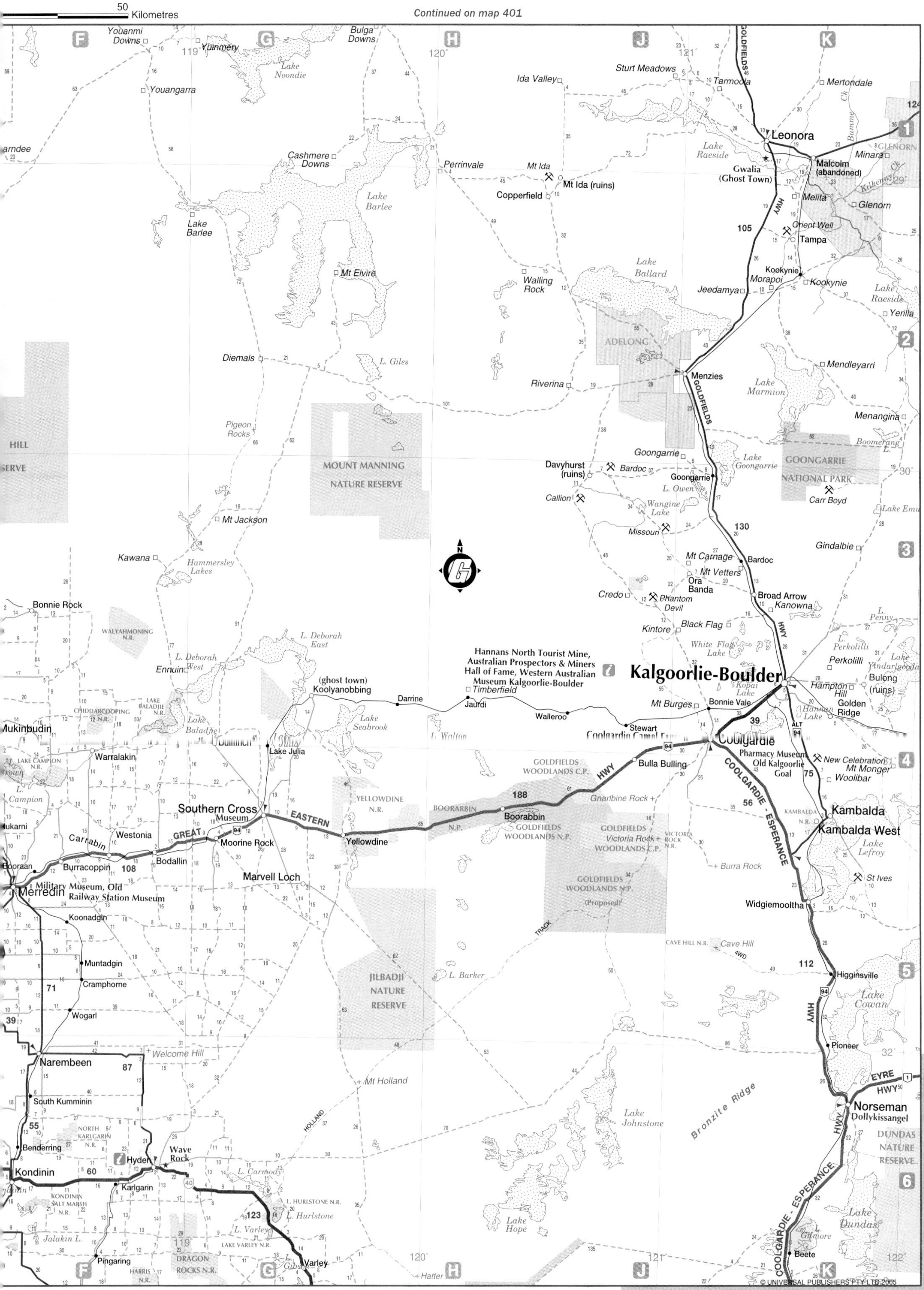

Scale 1:1 700 C

INDIAN

OCEAN

SOUTHERN

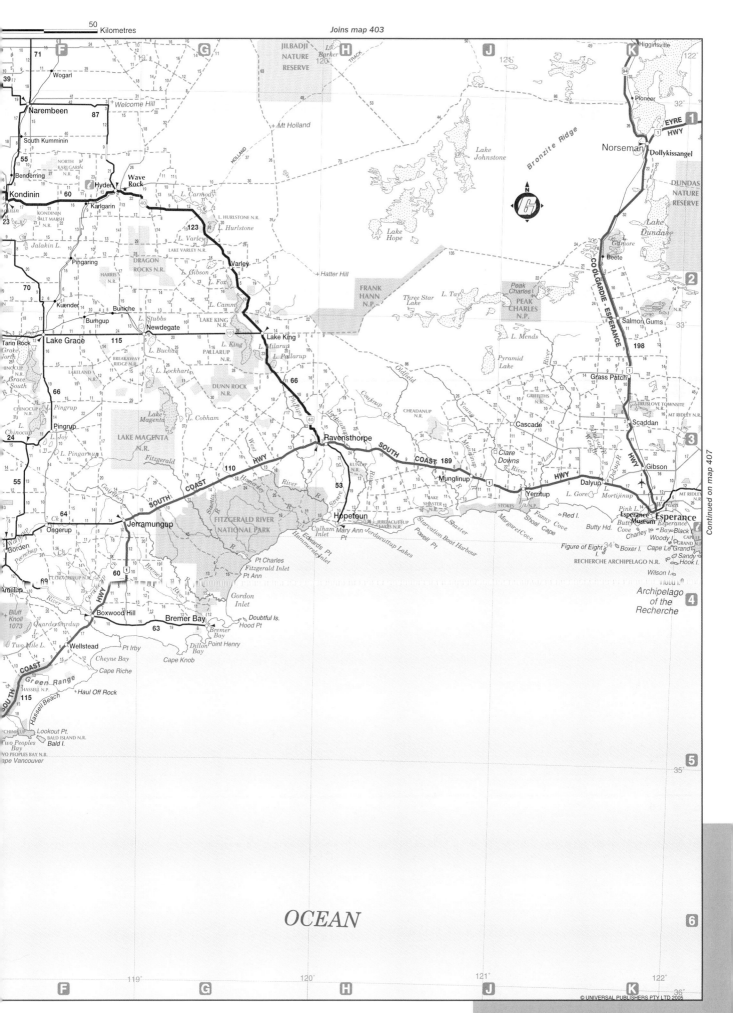

50 Kilometres

Continued on map 407

OCEAN

Scale 1:3 900 000

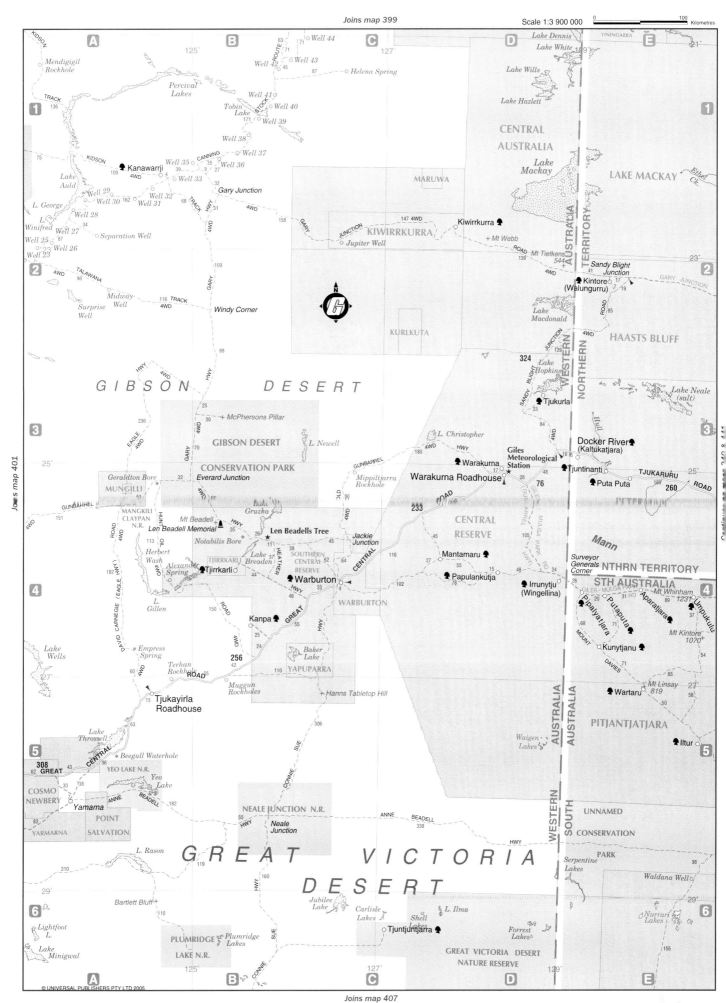

406 *Gregory's Australia*

© UNIVERSAL PUBLISHERS PTY LTD 2005

Scale 1:3 900 000

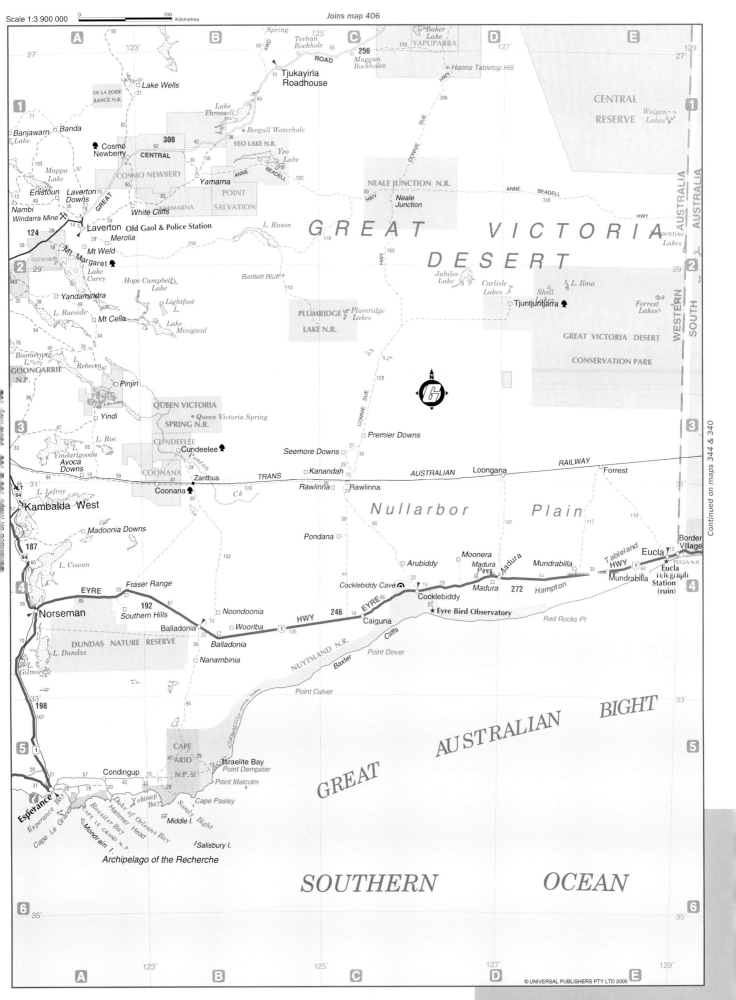

NORTHERN

The Northern Territory is Australia's most barren region and it covers approximately one-sixth of the continent. The Territory's rich Aboriginal past dates back some 60 000 years. Ceremonies, stories, rock art and intimate knowledge of the land and its seasons attest to the Aboriginal people's special link with the Territory. About 50% of the Territory's terrain is classified Aboriginal land, and visitors are required to obtain a special permit to enter many of these areas.

The vibrant ochre and red sands of the Centre characterise the stunning MacDonnell Ranges and Simpson Desert; in contrast are the verdant greens of the rainforests and savanna woodlands of the northern lands that merge into the monsoonal Timor and Arafura seas.

The remoteness and diversity of the Northern Territory make it an ideal location for exploring beyond the beaten track. It is excellent for 4-wheel drive touring, and camel treks can be organised from Alice Springs—one option is a two week journey to Rainbow Valley. Bushwalkers will find much to

Northern Territory: Outback Australia

◈ Population: 195 000
◈ Total area: 1 346 200km^2
◈ % of Australia : 17.5%
◈ Floral emblem: Sturt's Desert Rose
◈ Fauna emblem: Red Kangaroo

TERRITORY

ℹ️ Visitor information

Tourism Top End
Cnr Mitchell St and Knuckey St,
Darwin, NT 0800
Ph: (08) 8936 2499 or 1300 138 886
www.tourismtopend.com.au

**Central Australia Visitor
Information Centre**
60 Gregory Tce, Alice Springs, NT 0870
Ph: (08) 8952 5800 or 1800 645 199
www.centralaustraliantourism.com

Main ATTRACTIONS

◈ Alice Springs
Surrounded by the signature Northern Territory red desert, Alice Springs is the Territory's second largest centre. It is the base for exploration of the Red Centre.

◈ Kakadu National Park
One of Australia's most famous regions. It is a World Heritage-listed national park for both its natural and cultural significance.

◈ Kings Canyon
Sandstone cliffs up to 100m high frame this spectacular canyon in Watarrka NP. Relict vegetation still exists in the canyon.

◈ Nitmiluk National Park
This national park is home to the magnificent 12km-long Katherine Gorge. Over time, the Katherine River carved out 13 gorges, which are separated by rapids.

◈ Uluṟu-Kata Tjuṯa National Park
Uluṟu (Ayers Rock)—the Australian Outback's most famous international landmark—is a sacred site for the local Aṉangu people.

◈ Litchfield National Park
The national park encompasses the Tabletop Range and has spectacular waterfalls and generally crocodile-free swimming spots.

◈ Simpson Desert
Partly accessible by 4-wheel drive, the world's largest sand dune system has a beauty matched by its remoteness. Chambers Pillar, a 50m sandstone butte, is a major attraction.

discover. Many areas in the Territory offer walking tracks of varying degrees of difficulty. Scenic flights are a more leisurely sightseeing option, while the Centre's dry heat creates ideal conditions for hot-air ballooning.

Near the geographical centre of the continent are the iconic Uluṟu and Kata Tjuṯa. These Aboriginal sacred sites are World Heritage-listed and are synonymous with the red heart of Australia. Nearby, Mount Connor, a giant tabletop mountain, is also impressive in scale.

The spectacular sights, ancient landscapes and vast, formidable terrain of the Northern Territory—often subject to droughts, bushfires, flash flooding and cyclones—epitomise the description 'Outback Australia'. Adventure and discovery are constant companions in this frontier land.

Photo above: Coloured cliffs reflected in a seasonal pool in Rainbow Valley Conservation Area

OUTBACK AUSTRALIA

Aboriginal people have occupied the Northern Territory for at least 60 000 years. Macassan seafarers regularly visited the shoreline seeking bêche-de-mer or trepang (sea cucumbers), a delicacy in Asia. They probably introduced the dingo to Australia. In 1623, a Dutch ship, the *Arnhem*, also sailed offshore.

The Northern Territory was originally part of the colony of New South Wales. European settlers began to arrive in larger numbers in the Territory after the building of the Overland Telegraph in 1872. The communications line spanned the country, north to south, from **Palmerston** (as **Darwin** was then known) to Port Augusta (in South Australia). The Territory was governed by South Australia from 1862 to 1911, after which administration was transferred to the Commonwealth Government. Self-government was granted in 1978. However, at a referendum in 1998, Territorians rejected the chance for statehood. Extensively bombed by the Japanese in WWII, Darwin has survived the ravages of tropical cyclones, especially Cyclone Tracy in 1974, to become a flourishing modern city.

The Northern Territory's population is small in comparison with the Australian states. Its 195 000 inhabitants represent a great ethnic diversity, including a large proportion of Aboriginal people (around 40%).

This vast Territory is often divided into three main geographical regions: the **Top End**, the dry **central plateaus and basins**, and the **Red Centre**. When planning a holiday to the Territory it is advisable to consider the season—climate in the Northern Territory is extreme. There are two main seasons in the Top End, the **Wet** season (November–April) with monsoonal rain and the **Dry** (May–October). The Dry is perhaps the best time to visit the Top End— less rain and less chance of a tropical cyclone! By contrast the Red Centre has four distinct seasons, with cold winters and hot, dry summers.

In the early years of European settlement, the main industry in the Territory was pastoralism, but this has now been overtaken by mining and tourism. Mineral production has impacted greatly on the state's economic development in recent years with uranium,

Western bearded dragon, *Pogona minor*

bauxite, gold, manganese, zinc, lead, silver, copper, diamonds, opals, tin and turquoise mining adding to the state's export market. Oil and natural gas provide a massive contribution to the country's energy resources and are extracted onshore and offshore.

Tourism is also a major industry in the Northern Territory. The draw-cards are the spectacular landscapes, the unique native flora and fauna, as well as the abundant **Aboriginal rock-art** sites. Sport fishing attracts visitors from all over the world, particularly those seeking the acrobatic barramundi, Australia's best fighting freshwater fish, and other tropical species. Major tourism developments have been established at **Yulara**, **Darwin**, **Alice Springs** and **Kakadu**. Other industries of importance to the Northern Territory economy are aquaculture, pearl farming and crocodile farming.

Visitors to Aboriginal rock art at Injaluk Hill, Oenpelli, Arnhem Land

Northern Territory

TOURISM REGION HIGHLIGHTS

The Northern Territory is seen as one of the world's last wild frontiers, and it is, perhaps, the expectation of adventure that draws visitors every year from around the globe. Yet touring this vast area is surprisingly easy—all-weather sealed roads reach most of the better-known tourist attractions.

A Darwin (pp.416–419)

Aquascene; Australian Pearling Exhibition; Charles Darwin NP; Crocodylus Park; Darwin Botanic Gardens; Darwin Wharf Precinct; Deckchair Cinema; East Point Reserve; Fannie Bay Gaol; Howard Springs; Indo-Pacific Marine; Mindil Beach Sunset Markets; Museum and Art Gallery of the Northern Territory; Territory Wildlife Park

B Alice Springs
(pp.420–421 and 424)
Alice Springs Cultural Precinct; Alice Springs Desert Park; Alice

Chambers Pillar at sunset

Springs Telegraph Station; Anzac Hill; Frontier Camel Farm; Museum of Central Australia; Olive Pink Botanic Garden; Royal Flying Doctor Service; School of the Air; The Date Farm

C Central Australia
(pp.422–423)
Arltunga Historical Reserve; Chambers Pillar; Corroboree Rock; Ellery Creek Big Hole; Ewaninga Rock Carvings; Finke Gorge; Glen Helen Gorge; Henbury Meteorite Craters; Hermannsburg; Larapinta Trail; MacDonnell Ranges; N'Dhala Gorge; Ormiston Gorge; Palm Valley; Rainbow Valley; Redbank Gorge; Serpentine Gorge; Simpson Desert; Simpsons Gap; Standley Chasm; Tanami Desert; Tnorala (Gosse Bluff); Trephina Gorge; Watarrka NP (Kings Canyon)

D Kakadu NP
(pp.412 and 426–427)
Aboriginal rock art; Bowali Visitor Centre; Gunlom (Waterfall Creek); Jabiru; Jim Jim Falls; Maguk (Barramundie Gorge); Mamukala; Nourlangie Rock; Twin Falls; Ubirr; Warradjan Aboriginal Cultural Centre; Yellow Water

E Katherine (pp.427–428)
Borroloola; Cape Crawford; Cutta Cutta Caves; Daly River; Daly Waters; Elsey Homestead; Gregory NP; Katherine Hot Springs; Katherine Low Level Nature Reserve; Katherine Museum; Keep River NP; Leliyn (Edith Falls); Lost City; Manyallaluk; Mataranka Thermal Pool; Never Never Museum; Nitmiluk NP (Katherine Gorge); O'Keeffe House; Pine Creek; Roper Bar; Springvale Homestead; Timber Creek

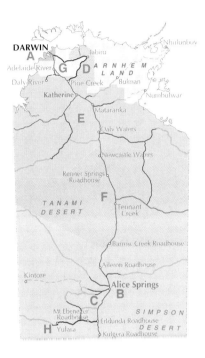

F Tennant Creek (pp.429–430)
Attack Creek; Barkly Tablelands; Barrow Creek; Battery Hill Mining Centre; Central Mount Stewart; Devils Marbles; The Pebbles

G The Top End
Adelaide River War Cemetery; Arnhem Land; Batchelor; Butterfly Gorge; Cobourg Peninsula; Corroboree Billabong; Douglas Hot Springs; Fogg Dam; Gove Peninsula; Lake Bennett; Litchfield NP; Magnetic Termite Mounds; Mary River Wetlands; Nhulunbuy; Tiwi Islands (Melville and Bathurst); Umbrawarra Gorge; Window on the Wetlands

H Uluru — Kata Tjuta NP
(pp.413 and 422–423)
Kata Tjuta (The Olgas); Uluru (Ayers Rock); Uluru–Kata Tjuta Cultural Centre; Yulara

NATIONAL PARKS

The national parks of the Northern Territory are home to some of the most spectacular environments, scenery and natural formations in the country, ranging from the tropical lushness of **Kakadu** and **Katherine Gorge**, to the sands of the Red Centre, with Uluru rising 350m out of a sea of red sand and tufts of spinifex grass.

Primarily an area of national park attractions, the Northern Territory is a photographer's dream, with the light constantly changing

facts

❖ No. of parks/reserves: 95
❖ Area: 67 000km^2
❖ % of territory: 4.98%
❖ World Heritage Areas: Kakadu National Park, Uluru–Kata Tjuta National Park

the colours and shadows of these uniquely beautiful landscapes. Whilst four of the most popular national parks are detailed here, there are many more worth investigating. Out of the 17 national parks in the Northern Territory, only Uluru–Kata Tjuta NP and Kakadu NP have entrance fees.

A Kakadu NP (pp.426–427)

Kakadu NP is located 150km southeast of Darwin and is Australia's largest national park covering 19 757km^2. It is owned by the Gagudju Aboriginal people and is home to an extraordinary diversity of wildlife. The landscape is affected dramatically by the changing Wet and Dry seasons. As the tropical rain-fed floodplains fill, millions of birds arrive to feed and mate. The Aboriginal heritage of the park is hugely significant. Artefacts such as grindstones, shelters and stone tools,

some dating back 50 000 years, can be found, along with ochre, used in ceremonial painting. Some of the main attractions in the national park are **Gunlom**, a waterfall and plunge pool which has become a popular picnic spot; **Jabiru**, a town set against the spectacular backdrop of the **Arnhem Land Escarpment**; **Nourlangie Rock**, an ancient Aboriginal shelter with impressive art sites; and **Yellow Water**, a spectacular and diverse wetland ecosystem.

B Litchfield NP (pp.424–425)

The most visited park near Darwin, Litchfield NP covers 1651km^2 of monsoonal rainforest, weather-beaten sandstone, huge termite mounds, historic ruins and spring-fed streams. Around 250 000 people annually discover, or rediscover, this exciting national park. Attractions include the magnificent waterfalls, walking tracks, and magnetic termite mounds, which are not magnetic, but built by termites in a way that controls the natural temperature inside the mounds. Also, historic **Blyth Homestead** and the **Lost City**, a stunning sight which appears as a city of free-standing weathered sandstone formations jutting out of the otherwise flat landscape. The spring-fringed sandstone plateau of the **Tabletop Range** feeds the park's waterfalls; the waterholes are excellent for swimming and generally crocodile-free—but observe warning signs. A number of camping spots requiring permits can be found throughout the park, with accommodation at nearby **Adelaide River** and **Batchelor**. Rivers and waterholes provide ample opportunities for anglers.

Great egret, *Ardea alba*, in Kakadu National Park

Northern Territory

Uluṟu (Ayers Rock), Uluṟu-Kata Tjuṯa National Park

C Nitmiluk NP (pp.428–429)

Nitmiluk NP is known mainly for the amazing **Katherine Gorge** and is located 32km east of Katherine. Covering 2920km², the national park offers 120km of walking tracks varying in length from short strolls to overnight walks. Also on offer are canoeing, cruises, plane and helicopter flights, swimming and wildlife spotting. The **Jatbula Trail** running through the park is internationally regarded as one of Australia's best walks. The national park is divided into two sectors: Katherine Gorge and **Leliyn (Edith Falls)**. The **Katherine River** winds through the **Arnhem Land plateau** and has formed 13 water-filled gorges, some with cliffs 100m in height on either side. The main camping area in Katherine Gorge—**Nitmiluk Tours**—has all major facilities, including powered sites and a kiosk. The **Edith Falls** area also has a camping site with most facilities and a kiosk, but no power.

D Uluṟu–Kata Tjuṯa NP

(pp.422–423)

Uluṟu-Kata Tjuṯa NP, covering 1325km², is perhaps the most talked about national park in Australia. Home to Uluṟu (Ayers Rock), as well as the magnificent Kata Tjuṯa (The Olgas), this national park has a distinctly spiritual heritage with Aṉangu Aboriginal history dating back at least 22 000 years. The rock itself, some say, is an incomparable beauty, dwarfing the surrounding desert landscape with its immensity. Around 9.4km in circumference and 350m in height, Uluṟu is a giant monolith rising from the flat, arid desert plain. Kata Tjuṯa is a group of 36 enormous weathered domes, described by explorer Ernest Giles as 'monstrous pink haystacks', the highest rising 546m. Giles named them after Queen Olga of Wurttemberg. The domes cover an area of 35km² and may once have been a super dome larger than Uluṟu. Their Aboriginal name, 'Kata Tjuṯa' means 'many heads'.

Each feature of the two landforms has great cultural and spiritual significance to the traditional Aṉangu owners. A basic knowledge of the Aboriginal mythology surrounding these sacred places and their true spiritual meaning will greatly enhance any visit to the area. Information on the area is widely available in tourist offices and visitor centres throughout the Territory. Whilst certain ceremonial sites in the national park have been declared out-of-bounds for tourists, there are special guided tours hosted by local Aborigines that are worth experiencing. *(see p.415)*

National Park Information

Parks and Wildlife Commission of the Northern Territory
(Top End)
PO Box 496, Palmerston, NT 0831
Ph: (08) 8999 4555
(Katherine Region)
PO Box 344, Katherine, NT 0851
Ph: (08) 8973 8888
(Central Australia)
PO Box 1046, Alice Springs, NT 0871
Ph: (08) 8951 8211
www.nt.gov.au/ipe/pwcnt

Dept of Environment & Heritage
(Kakadu National Park)
PO Box 71, Jabiru, NT 0886
Ph: (08) 8938 1100
(Uluru-Kata Tjuta National Park)
PO Box 119, Yulara, NT 0872
Ph: (08) 8956 1100

ABORIGINAL TOURISM

The oldest living culture in the world, Australia's Aboriginal people boast a heritage that is ancient and spiritual. Archaeological dating reveals evidence of human occupation for at least 60 000 years.

The relationship between Aboriginal culture and the land is deeply spiritual. Aboriginal society comprises many regional groups whose dialects, stories, ceremonies and practices differ greatly.

Today, visitors can experience Aboriginal culture and gain insight into Australia's ancient past by viewing Aboriginal rock art, listening to Dreamtime stories and mythology, watching ceremonial dancing and singing, hearing the unique sounds of the didgeridoo, experiencing sacred sites and even tasting a witchetty grub.

In the Northern Territory there are four particularly powerful places where visitors can experience firsthand the world's oldest culture.

Alice Springs
(pp.420–421 and 424)
The Aboriginal Art and Cultural Centre at 125 Todd St has an

Aboriginal art, Daly River region

Arrernte gallery, an Aboriginal music museum with the world's only **Didgeridoo University** as well as providing spear-throwing demonstrations and bush tucker on tours. **Alice Springs Cultural Precinct**, located at the corner of Larapinta Dr and Memorial Ave has several attractions with an Aboriginal theme. The **Araluen Centre** has a 500-seat theatre and major art galleries, including one featuring works of Albert Namatjira and his contemporaries. The

Museum of Central Australia, also in the precinct, has excellent exhibits and the **Strehlow Collection** displays non-culturally sensitive material from Professor Ted Strehlow and the Arrernte Aboriginal people of Central Australia. **Dreamtime Tours** offers insight into Aboriginal life and culture.

Kakadu NP (pp.426–427)
The **Bininj** people have established the **Warradjan Aboriginal Cultural Centre** at **Yellow Water** in Kakadu NP. Here, histories, stories and mythology are all depicted along with a showcase of Aboriginal arts and crafts of the Top End region. The **Bowali Visitor Centre**, in the main visitor centre in Kakadu NP, gives a deeper insight into the indigenous and non-indigenous history of Kakadu, including an audio-visual presentation of the park's highlights.
For more information contact:
Northern Land Council
9 Rowling St, Casuarina, NT 0810
Ph: (08) 8920 5100
www.nlc.org.au

Witchetty grubs, Aboriginal cultural tour, Wallace Rockhole Community

Northern Territory

Tiwi Islands

The Tiwi Islands are also a very significant region for Northern Territory Aboriginal people. The islands of **Bathurst** and **Melville** are only a short 80km flight from Darwin and are home to the Tiwi community. The total land area of the islands is 7450km^2 with an estimated population of 1800. Predominantly self-sufficient, the group resisted control by the Dutch and British in the past. Relative isolation has enabled the Tiwi people to preserve their culture. Since 1977, the Tiwi Islands have been regarded as Aboriginal land under the administration of the Tiwi Land Council.

Aboriginal crafts, Tiwi Islands

Pukumani carved burial poles, Bathurst Island

The islands' income is provided by both the sprawling pine plantations and tourist attractions such as stunning white sand tropical beaches bordering dense rainforests, which conceal pristine waterfalls and streams.

The Tiwi people have preserved many aspects of their distinctive culture and art, including plaited bangles, painted shells, pottery, carvings, batik and silk-screened clothing, and the unique Pukumani burial poles—originally placed around graves. Today, the poles are still commissioned, but placed on the ground where the funeral dances take place. At the end of the Wet season, the Tiwis hold the 'Kurlama', or yam ceremony, a ritual to invoke a good hunting season. The older men of the community sing songs to the ancestors and the women harvest and cook yams. Organised one to two day tours are the only way to see the islands.

For more information contact:
Tiwi Land Council
Unit 5/3 Bishop St,
Stuart Park,
NT 0820
Ph: (08) 8981 4898

Uluṟu–Kata Tjuṯa

(pp.422–423)
The Aṉangu people have established the **Uluṟu-Kata Tjuṯa Cultural Centre** near **Yulara** to help visitors appreciate the history of the Aboriginal culture. Offering guided tours of 'the Rock' and its sacred areas, interpretive art, videos and oral histories, the centre is a great stop for an introduction to, and the appreciation of, the Aboriginal culture of Central Australia.
For more information contact:
Central Land Council
33 Stuart Hwy, Alice Springs,
NT 0871
Ph: (08) 8951 6320
www.clc.org.au

DARWIN

Didgeridoo player at Mitchell St markets, Darwin

main attractions

◈ **Aquascene**

Witness the daily spectacular sight of hundreds of fish such as mullet, milkfish, and catfish competing for hand-fed white bread at high tide.

◈ **Australian Pearling Exhibition**

Provides an insight into the workings (and romance) of the local pearling industry.

◈ **Darwin Botanic Gardens**

Explore the 42ha gardens and discover mangroves, orchids, rainforest, open woodlands and other tropical habitats.

◈ **East Point Reserve**

Visit around dusk and see Fannie Bay's amazing sunset, and wallabies coming out to roam the 200ha reserve. The reserve features natural mangroves and forest, parklands and safe saltwater swimming.

◈ **Indo Pacific Marine**

Visitors can view living coral reef eco-systems; the night programme offers a torchlight tour and a seafood buffet dinner.

◈ **Mindil Beach Sunset Markets**

The markets feature myriad stalls, including the very popular food stalls reflecting the city's eclectic multicultural mix.

◈ **Wharf Precinct**

Once the domain of anglers and skateboarders; now the old wharves are a tourist attraction, with restaurants, museums and tours.

Darwin, the Territory's capital, is perched on a picturesque harbour and lies closer to Jakarta and Singapore than to Sydney and Melbourne. It was first settled by Europeans in 1869, when South Australian Surveyor-General Goyder arrived to establish a city in the Top End. Palmerston, as it was then known, became the terminus for the **Overland Telegraph** link to England, which began in 1872. Darwin now serves primarily as an administration centre for government and the mining and agricultural industries.

Its isolation and steamy tropical climate gives Darwin a relaxed, easygoing atmosphere and lifestyle for its residents. On Christmas Day 1974, however, this peace was dramatically shattered when **Cyclone Tracy** struck, making Darwin the site of Australia's worst natural disaster. During WWII, Darwin was attacked and heavily bombed by the Japanese. Today, few historic buildings remain, making it one of Australia's most modern cities.

Almost half the Northern Territory's population live within 50km of Australia's only tropical capital city. The population, which consists of more than 50 different cultures, has an average age younger than the rest of Australia.

🛈 Visitor information

Tourism Top End
Beagle House, cnr Mitchell St and Knuckey St, Darwin, NT 0800
Ph: (08) 8936 2499 or 1300 138 886
www.tourismtopend.com.au

facts

◈ Population: 90 200
◈ Date founded: 1911
◈ Tallest building: Mitchell Centre (15 stories)
◈ Average temperature: 28.5°C (January), 25.5°C (June)

Places of Interest

Aquascene Ⓐ C5
Australian Pearling Exhibition Ⓑ E6
Chinese Temple Ⓒ D5
Darwin Botanic Gardens Ⓓ D3
Darwin Entertainment Centre Ⓔ C5
Darwin Wharf Precinct Ⓕ E6
Fannie Bay Gaol Museum Ⓖ C1
Government House Ⓗ D6
Indo Pacific Marine Ⓘ E5
MGM Grand Darwin (Casino) Ⓙ C4
Mindil Beach Lookout Ⓚ B3
Mindil Beach Markets Ⓛ C3
Museum and Art Gallery of the NT Ⓜ C2
Old Court House Ⓝ D5
Parliament House Ⓞ D5
Smith St Mall Ⓟ D5
Vesteys Beach Ⓠ C2

Timor Sea, Nightcliff, Darwin

Continued on map 418

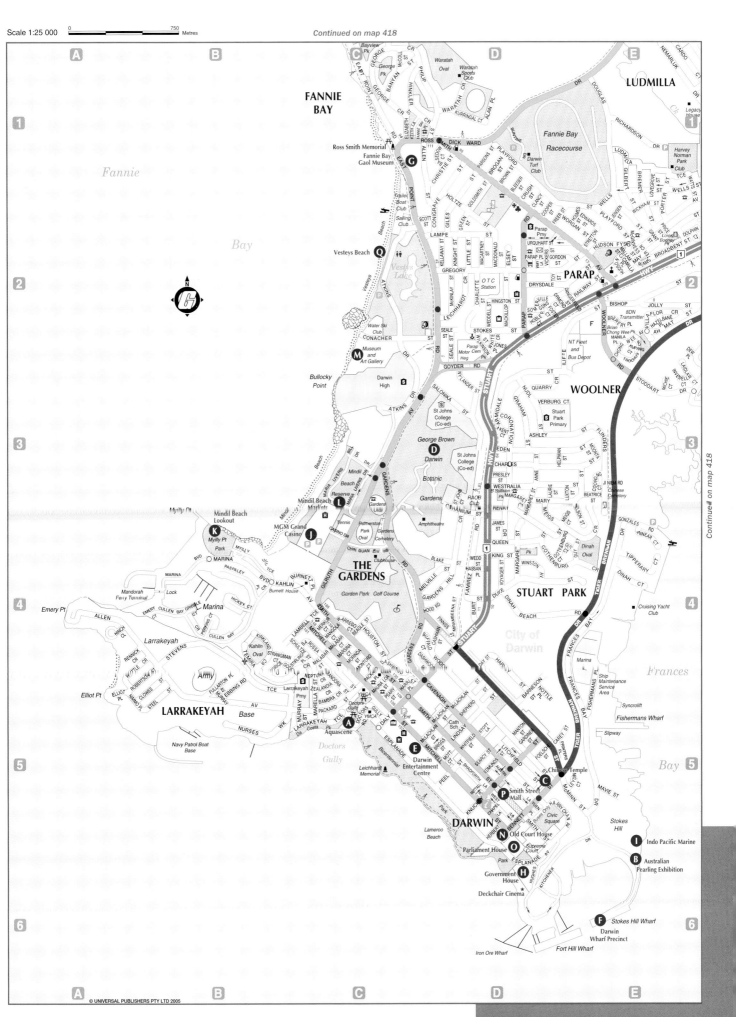

Continued on map 418

FANNIE
BAY

LUDMILLA

PARAP

WOOLNER

STUART PARK

City of
Darwin

Frances

Bay

THE
GARDENS

Fannie

Bay

LARRAKEYAH

DARWIN

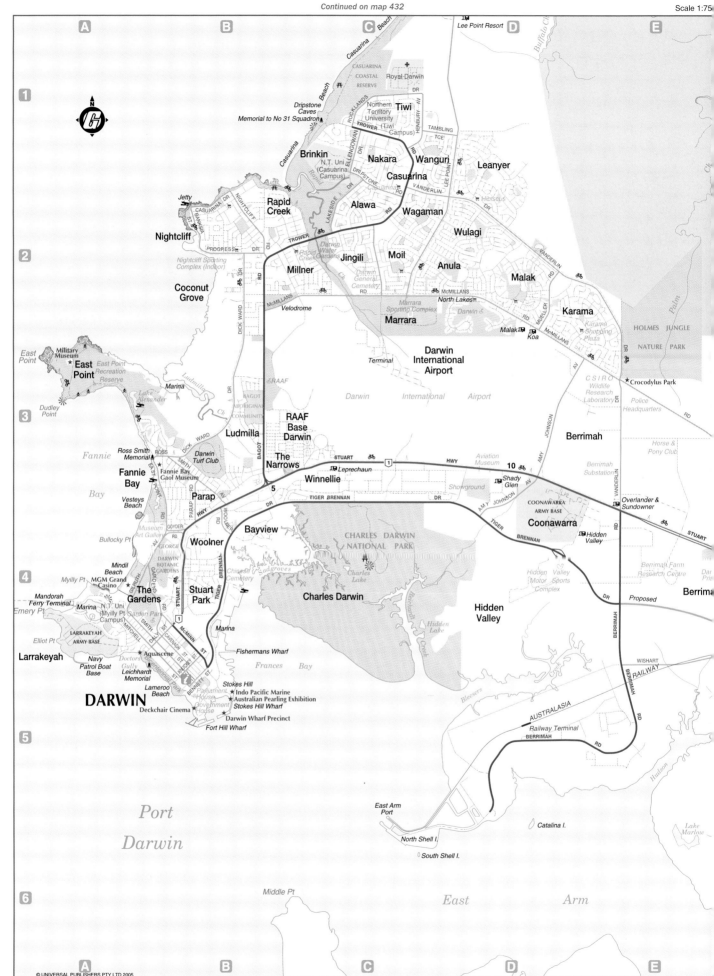

3 Kilometres

F **G** **H** **J** **K**

Hope

Inlet

1

*Howards
Peninsula*

Kings

2

MILITARY   AREA

(FORMER   RAAF   BOMBING   AND   GUNNERY   RANGE)

NO   PUBLIC   ACCESS

Howard

Mickett
Creek

*Noogoo
Swamp*

Mickett

Mickett Creek
Shooting Complex

3

Continued on map 432

*Thorak
Cemetery*

Thorak

Reserve

Milner   Swamp

Kings

River

MILLANS

ROBERTSON BARRACKS

(MILITARY AREA)

15

RD

Knuckey
Lagoon

Kings

Ck

4

Proposed Knuckey

Arterial

Holtze

Springs

Pinelands

HWY

Palmer

*Howard Springs
Nature Park*

Road

WISHART

Northern
Territory
University

Palmerston

GUNN POINT

RD

20

ROYSTONEA

1

RD

RAILWAY

Durack

Yarrawonga

Kakadu Mango
★ Winery

TCE

STUART

5

S Palmerston

AV

Palmerston
Town Centre

UNIVERSITY

CHUNG

*Dutchie
Lagoon*

Marlow
Lagoon

AV

Driver

S Palmerston

AV

Mitchell

AUSTRALASIA

DRIVER

WAH

AV

*Marlow
Lagoon
Recreation
Area*

Gunn

HOWARD SPRINGS

TEMPLE

ESSINGTON

TCE

Gray

AV

AV

ELRUNDIE

TILSTON AV

EMERY

BUSCALL

AV

Howard
Springs

*Wadham
Lagoon*

Howard
Springs

TEMPLE

AV

Bakewell

TCE

6

BALDWIN

GIBBINS DR

LAMBRICK

ROYSTONEA

TCE

ELRUNDIE

ROBSON

Woodroffe

TCE

WOODROFFE

AV

LAMBRICK

AV

25

*Sewage
Treatment
Works*

Moulden

Rosebery

Virginia

HWY

Proposed Arterial Road

MOULDEN

CHUNG

WAH

*Archer
Sporting
Complex*

Bellamack

1

F **G** **H** **J** **K**

© UNIVERSAL PUBLISHERS PTY LTD 2005

■ Adelaide River   POP 279

Map 425, D2

The location for 30 000 Australian and US soldiers during WWII, this small town lies 112km south-east of Darwin on the Stuart Hwy.

MAIN ATTRACTION: **Adelaide River War Cemetery**, with the graves of 434 servicemen, is just to the north.

NEARBY ATTRACTIONS: Historic **Mount Bundy Station**, 3km north-east, offers a rural Territory experience, with fishing, walking and accommodation. **Robin Falls**, 15km south, flows for most of the year. **Daly River Roadhouse** and region, 114km south-west, is a good locale for fishing and Aboriginal arts and crafts. **Litchfield NP** is close by, although the main entrance is via the Litchfield Park Rd, 27km north.

VISITOR INFORMATION: Tourism Top End, Darwin, Ph: (08) 8936 2499 or 1300 138 886

■ Alice Springs   POP 24 000

Maps 421 and 442, E2

European settlement in Alice Springs dates back to 1871 with the building of the Overland Telegraph line linking Australia with Europe. 'The Alice', as it is affectionately known, is almost at the geographical centre of Australia, and around 1500km from Darwin and Adelaide.

MAIN ATTRACTIONS: The heart of Alice Springs is **Todd Mall**, with many attractions in the vicinity. There are galleries selling Aboriginal art, crafts, textiles and pottery, and an **Aboriginal Art and Culture Centre**. **Adelaide House Museum** has an exhibit explaining the origins and workings of **The Royal Flying Doctor Service** and daily tours are available at the Stuart Tce base. The **National Pioneer Women's Hall of Fame** is in the old Court House. Close by, the **Sounds of Starlight Theatre** has a show April–November depicting a musical journey through Central Australia. Also nearby are **Stuart Town Gaol** and **Anzac Hill**, with views over the town. The **Todd River** doesn't flow much. In fact, it's usually dry and the venue for the **Henley-on-Todd Regatta**, an unusual 'sailing' event where competitors carry their 'boats' for the whole course of the race.

In the northern suburbs are the **School of the Air**, Australia's first radio school for children in remote areas, and the **Alice Springs Telegraph Station Historical Reserve**. The painstakingly restored stone buildings of the reserve have displays of photographs and documents portraying life in the early days of settlement. West of the Mall are the **Araluen Arts Centre**, the **Museum of Central Australia** and, further along Larapinta Dr, **Alice Springs Desert Park**. The latter features animals and plants in a natural desert habitat and explains their traditional use by Aboriginal people. There are also eight walk-through aviaries and the world's largest nocturnal house. To the south-east, across the Todd River, are **Lasseters Casino** and the 16ha **Olive Pink Botanic Garden**, which is the most developed arid-zone botanic garden in Australia. For visitors wanting to make a circuit of the many local attractions, the green and yellow **Alice Wanderer Bus** service provides a pleasant and easy way to see the sights. Hot-air balloon flights from Alice Springs are very popular, as are tours by bus, 4-wheel drive, Harley Davidson motorcycle, quad bike, helicopter, light aircraft and, for the more adventurous, camel treks.

NEARBY ATTRACTIONS: Alice Springs is the ideal base from which to travel around the entire **Red Centre** region. At **Gemtree**, 135km north-east, visitors can prospect for zircons and garnets and join guided fossicking tours. To the east (7km), the **Frontier Camel Farm** offers camel rides. The Ross Hwy also leads to **The Date Farm**, Australia's first

(CONTINUED P.424)

Alice Springs Telegraph Station

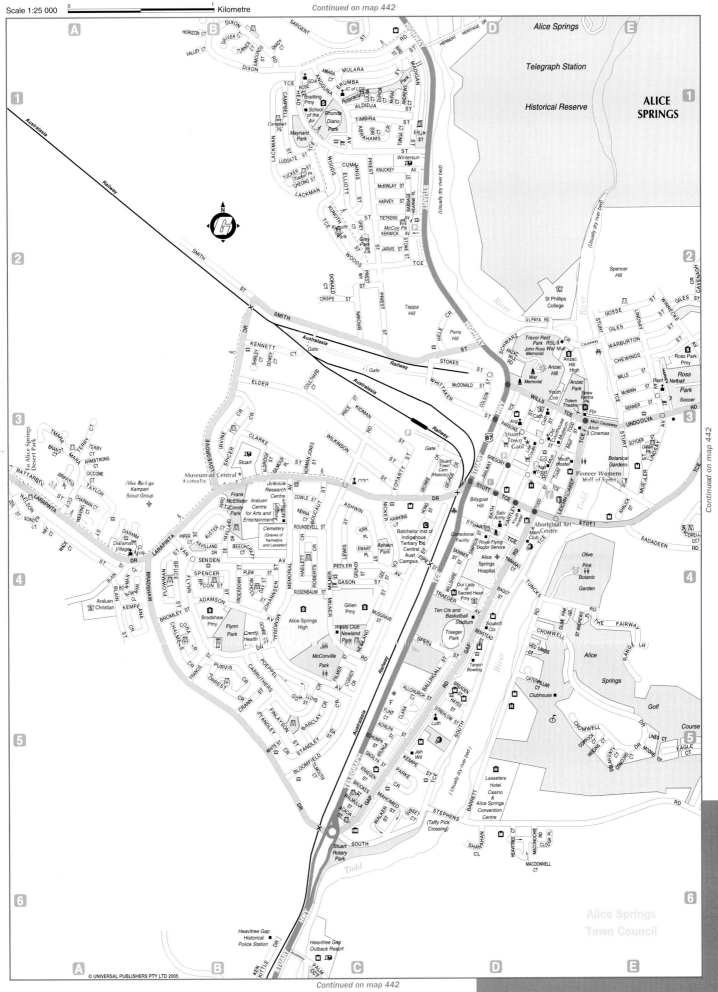

Continued on map 442

Alice Springs
Telegraph Station
Historical Reserve

ALICE SPRINGS

Continued on map 442

The terrain west of Alice Springs to **Uluru-Kata Tjuta NP** is the heart of the Red Centre, spanning the western section of the **MacDonnell Ranges**. This vast and stunning but rugged landscape encompasses an ancient and unique terrain dotted with gorges, waterholes, unusual geological formations, tranquil creeks and strange landforms, carved out over hundreds of millions of years.

The arid and seemingly inhospitable landscape is home to an array of flora and fauna—springtime sees the blossoming of colourful wildflowers, and rock wallabies are often seen around the steep ridges and rocky outcrops of **Simpsons Gap**.

Uluru-Kata Tjuta NP covers 1325km^2 and contains two of the world's greatest natural wonders, Uluru (Ayers Rock) and Kata Tjuta (The Olgas). This national park is one of the most visited sites in Australia. The park also offers much more, including spectacular views,

Desert wildflowers west of Alice Springs

guided walks, and an insight into Anangu Aboriginal heritage. With 500 plant species, 150 bird species, 24 endemic mammals, and 72 species of reptiles, (making it the richest reptile fauna on Earth), it received international recognition in 1977, when it was declared an **International Biosphere Reserve** by UNESCO. In 1987, Uluru-Kata Tjuta NP was listed as a **World Heritage Area**. Extensions to the park were listed in 1994.

main attractions

◈ **Finke Gorge National Park**

This national park's main attraction is Palm Valley. Prehistoric cycads and red cabbage palms have survived the barren terrain for over 10 000 years, relicts of a wetter time.

◈ **Kata Tjuta**

These extraordinary rock formations and 36 domes rise from the ground and, like Uluru, their colours change with the light throughout the day. The 7km Valley of the Winds walk is spectacular.

◈ **Standley Chasm**

Sunlight bathes the 80m high walls of this narrow chasm around noon. The chasm was formed by erosion of the softer rock from the red, quartzite walls.

◈ **Uluru**

At 350m high, Uluru is the world's largest monolith. The Mala and Kuniya guided walks provide an excellent grounding in the cultural significance of Uluru as a sacred site of the Anangu people.

◈ **Yulara (Ayers Rock Resort)**

This tourist resort and village is within close proximity to the district's major attractions.

i **Visitor information**

Central Australia Visitor Information Centre
60 Gregory Tce, Alice Springs, NT 0870
Ph: (08) 8952 5800 or 1800 645 199
www.centralaustraliantourism.com

Garden of Eden and red cliffs in Watarrka National Park (Kings Canyon)

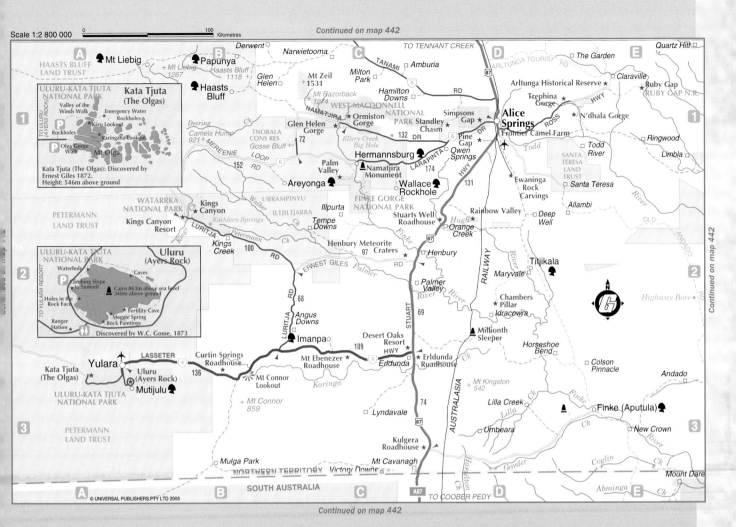

Scale 1:2 800 000

Continued on map 442

A   **B**   **C**   **D**   **E**

HAASTS BLUFF
LAND TRUST
♣ Mt Liebig
♣ Papunya
+ Mt Liebig
1267
Haasts Bluff
1118
♣ Haasts
Bluff

**ULURU-KATA TJUTA
NATIONAL PARK**
**Kata Tjuta
(The Olgas)**
Valley of the
Winds Walk
Emergency Water
Rockholes
Rockholes
Karu Lookout
Karingana Lookout
Olga Gorge
Walk
Mt Olga

Kata Tjuta (The Olgas): Discovered by
Ernest Giles 1872.
Height: 546m above ground

Derwent
Narwietooma
TANAMI
TO TENNANT CREEK
Amburia
ARLTUNGA TOURIST RD
Quartz Hill
The Garden
Claraville
Ruby Gap
(RUBY GAP N.R.)
Glen
Helen
Mt Zeil
+1531
Milton
Park
Hamilton
Downs
Arltunga Historical Reserve
Trephina
Gorge
N'dhala Gorge
WEST MACDONNELL
+1274
NAMATJIRA
Ormiston
Gorge
NATIONAL
PARK Standley
Chasm
Simpsons
Gap
**Alice
Springs**
ROSS
HWY
Ringwood
Deering
Camels Hump
921 +
Glen Helen
Gorge
132 DR
Ellery Creek
Big Hole
Pine
Gap
Owen
Springs
Frontier Camel Farm
Todd
Todd
River
Limbla
TNORALA
CONS RES
Gosse Bluff +
72
SANTA
TERESA
LAND
TRUST
MEREENIE
LOOP
152
RD
6
Palm
Valley
Namatjira
Monument
LARAPINTA
174
Ewaninga
Rock
Carvings
Santa Teresa
Allambi
URRAMPINYU
ILTJILTJARRA
Areyonga
Wallace
Rockhole
131
WATARRKA
NATIONAL PARK
Kings
Canyon
FINKE GORGE
NATIONAL PARK
Stuarts Well
Roadhouse
Rainbow Valley
Deep
Well
PETERMANN
LAND TRUST
Kings Canyon
Resort
Illpurta
Tempe
Downs
Hugh
Orange
Creek
OLD

**ULURU-KATA TJUTA
NATIONAL PARK**
**Uluru
(Ayers Rock)**
Waterhole
Caves
Holes in the
Rock Face
Climbing Slope
to Summit
Cairn 863m above sea level
348m above ground
Fertility Cave
Meggie Spring
Rock Paintings
Ranger
Station
Discovered by W.C. Gosse, 1873

Kings
Creek
100
LURITJA
RD
Kathleen Springs
Petermann
Henbury Meteorite
97 Craters
Henbury
Palmer
Valley
Titjikala
Maryvale
Chambers
Pillar
Idracowra
Highway Bore
68
Angus
Downs
ERNEST GILES
Palmer
River
STUART
69
Imanpa
Desert Oaks
Resort
109
HWY
Millionth
Sleeper
Horseshoe
Bend
Colson
Pinnacle
Andado

Yulara
LASSETER
Curtin Springs
Roadhouse
Mt Ebenezer
Roadhouse
Erldunda
Erldunda
Roadhouse
Lilla Creek
Mt Kingston
542
Finke (Aputula)
Kata Tjuta
(The Olgas)
Uluru
(Ayers Rock)
136
Mutijulu
Mt Connor
Lookout
Karinga
Lyndavale
74
Umbeara
New Crown
ULURU-KATA TJUTA
NATIONAL PARK
+ Mt Connor
859

PETERMANN
LAND TRUST
Mulga Park
NORTHERN TERRITORY
Victory Downs
Kulgera
Roadhouse
Mt Cavanagh
Coglin
Mount Dare
Abminga

A   **B**   SOUTH AUSTRALIA   **C**   A87   **D**   **E**
© UNIVERSAL PUBLISHERS PTY LTD 2005
TO COOBER PEDY

Continued on map 442

Kata Tjuṯa (The Olgas) at sunset, Uluṟu-Kata Tjuṯa National Park

LITCHFIELD NP

Home to the Wagait Aboriginal people, the area was mined for tin and copper before being used as a pastoral lease. The 1651km² area was proclaimed a national park in 1986. Located 129km from Darwin and 268km from Katherine, this popular park has many natural and historic attractions. Access to some of the more remote attractions such as the unusual sandstone pillars of the **Lost City** is by 4-wheel drive only and most tracks are closed during the Wet season.

Thousands of **magnetic termite mounds** up to 3m high exist in the park. Several waterfalls punctuate the escarpments and provide a refreshing opportunity to swim in the pools below. The most popular attraction in Litchfield is **Wangi Falls**, which also has a 3km-long walking track through monsoonal forest to the top of the falls. Other

sites include **Tjaynera Falls (Sandy Creek)**, **Tolmer Falls**, **Buley Rockhole** and **Florence Falls**. Camping facilities are available at Wangi Falls, **Walker Creek**, Tjaynera Falls, Florence Falls, Buley Rockhole and **Surprise Creek**.

main attractions

❖ Blyth Homestead
❖ Lost City
❖ Magnetic termite mounds
❖ Waterfalls

ℹ Visitor information

Tourism Top End
Cnr Mitchell St and Knuckey St,
Darwin, NT 0800
Ph: (08) 8936 2499 or 1300 138 886
www.tourismtopend.com.au

Magnetic termite mounds, Litchfield National Park

---

commercial date farm, **Emily Gap** (13km); and **Jessie Gap** (18km). Further into the **East MacDonnell Ranges**, the highway also leads to **Corroboree Rock**; **Trephina** and **N'dhala Gorges**; and **Arltunga Historical Reserve**. To the west are **Rev John Flynn's grave** (5km), **Simpsons Gap** (17km), **Standley Chasm** (50km), **Ellery Creek Big Hole** (93km), **Serpentine Gorge** (104km), **Ochre Pits** (119km), **Ormiston** and **Glen Helen gorges** (about 132km) and **Redbank Gorge** (170km, 4-wheel drive only). Most of these are in **West MacDonnell NP**, as is the acclaimed walking track, the **Larapinta Trail**. Larapinta Dr also leads to **Hermannsburg** (125km) and **Palm Valley** in Finke Gorge NP (140km, 4-wheel drive access only).

To the south are the **Transport Hall of Fame** and the **Ghan Preservation Society's Rail Museum** at MacDonnell Siding (10km). Side roads from the Stuart Hwy to the south lead to **Ewaninga Rock Carvings Conservation Reserve** (35km), an Aboriginal cultural site; the magnificent **Rainbow Valley** (99km); **Henbury Meteorite Craters** (147km); and **Chambers Pillar** (149km), a 50m-high sandstone pillar, which served as a landmark for early explorers.
VISITOR INFORMATION: 60 Gregory Tce, Ph: (08) 8952 5800 or 1800 645 199

■ **Batchelor** POP 700
Map 425, C1
Once the service centre for Australia's first uranium mine,

Rum Jungle (now closed), Batchelor is the gateway to world-famous **Litchfield National Park**.
MAIN ATTRACTIONS: **Coomalie Cultural Centre** at Batchelor College has an extensive display of Aboriginal artworks. There is a mini replica of Bohemia's **Karlstein Castle** on the Rum Jungle Rd.
NEARBY ATTRACTIONS: **Lake Bennett Wilderness Resort**, 25km northeast, offers fishing, swimming, windsurfing, boating, bushwalking and accommodation. Swimming is also popular at **Rum Jungle Lake**, 10km west. Litchfield NP, a magnificent wilderness area, is 20km to the west. Most of Litchfield's main attractions, such as the **magnetic termite mounds, Florence, Tolmer and Wangi falls** and **Buley Rockhole** can be

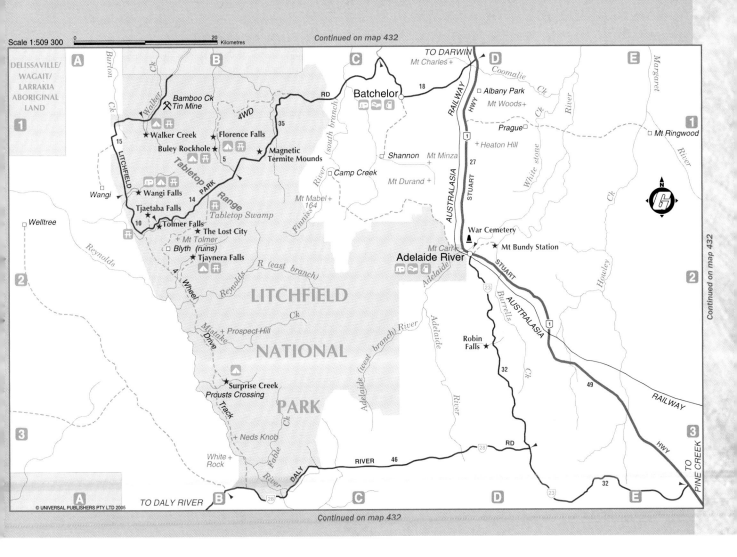

Continued on map 432

Scale 1:509 300

Continued on map 432

accessed via the sealed Litchfield Park Rd. A 4-wheel drive is required to reach the unusual and enticing sandstone rock formations of **The Lost City, Tjaynera Falls** and the ruins of the old **Blyth Homestead**; during the Wet season the tracks can become impassable and may be closed. The park has rainforest walks and camping grounds.

VISITOR INFORMATION:

General Store, Tarkarri Rd,
Ph: (08) 8976 0045

Borroloola   POP 650

Map 437, H2

Borroloola is an Aboriginal town on the **Carpentaria Hwy**, 383km east of the Stuart Hwy, which is popular with 4-wheel drive and fishing enthusiasts. Tourists do not need a permit to visit the town.

MAIN ATTRACTIONS: Scenic flights can be made over the town and the **Sir Edward Pellew Island Group**. Fishing for barramundi, trevally and other tropical species and succulent mud crabs is very popular. River and island tours are available. The old **Police Station**, built in 1886, has a small museum.

NEARBY ATTRACTIONS: **Bukalara Rock Formations** are easily accessed off the highway at **Caranbirini Conservation Reserve. Cape Crawford**, 110km south-west, is a base from which to visit extraordinary ancient sandstone rocks to the east. **The Lost City** in the **Abner Ranges** can only be reached by helicopter with **Cape Crawford Tours.**

VISITOR INFORMATION: Borroloola Community Government Council, Ph: (08) 8975 8799

Hermannsburg   POP 485

Map 442, C2

Home to an Aboriginal community, Hermannsburg lies 125km west of Alice Springs on the site of a Lutheran Mission—the first Aboriginal mission in the Northern Territory. It was once the home of painter **Albert Namatjira** for many years and while visitors are welcome they are restricted to the historic precinct, shop and petrol station.

MAIN ATTRACTIONS: The historic precinct includes **Strehlow's House** (1897); the **Old Manse** (1888), now a gallery showcasing Aboriginal watercolours of the Hermannsburg School; mission station buildings; and a museum in the **Old Colonists House** (1885).

NEARBY ATTRACTIONS: There is a monument to the famous

KAKADU NP

This World Heritage-listed national park is internationally famous for the breathtaking natural beauty of its wetlands, escarpments and spectacular waterfalls as well as its more than 50 000-year-old Aboriginal cultural heritage. Aboriginal people own and co-manage the huge park, which covers almost 20 000km^2 and encompasses a huge variety of Top End habitats. The park has an equally diverse number of plants and animals, including 1600 plant species, 25 frog species, 75 reptile species and 275 species of bird.

There are more than 5000 Aboriginal cultural sites in the park. The ancient rock-art galleries of Kakadu are the oldest in the world and record extinct species such as the *thylacine* (Tasmanian Tiger) as well as depicting sacred creation beings like Namarrgon the Lightning Man and Ngalyod the Rainbow Serpent. Several styles are represented including x-ray paintings showing the internal structure of animals, fish and birds.

main attractions

◈ Gunlom
◈ Jim Jim Falls
◈ Nourlangie Rock
◈ Ubirr
◈ Warradjan Aboriginal Cultural Centre
◈ Yollow Water

ℹ Visitor information

Tourism Top End
Cnr Mitchell St and Knuckey St,
Darwin, NT 0800
Ph: (08) 8936 2499 or 1300 138 886
www.tourismtopend.com.au

Jim Jim Falls during the Wet season, Kakadu National Park

Aboriginal painter Albert Namatjira, 2km east on Larapinta Dr. Aboriginal cultural tours are available at the **Wallace Rockhole** community, 46km south-east. **Finke Gorge NP** is 20km south. The park features many rare plants unique to the area including red fan palms (*Livistona mariae*) in **Palm Valley** and extraordinary rock formations— 4-wheel drive country! **Tnorala (Gosse Bluff)** meteorite crater is 55km west, with a **Mereenie Loop Pass** required for access (available at Hermannsburg petrol station).
VISITOR INFORMATION: Kata-Anga Tearooms, Ph: (08) 8956 7402

■ Howard Springs   POP 3300
Map 419, K6
This Darwin satellite township lies 34km to the east. The springs were Darwin's main water supply before the construction of **Manton Dam**.
MAIN ATTRACTION: A beautiful spring-fed swimming pool, fringed by rainforest, is the central feature of **Howard Springs Nature Park**. A wildlife and recreation area since WWII, it has picnic sites and a kiosk.
NEARBY ATTRACTIONS: **Darwin Crocodile Farm**, 18km south on the Stuart Hwy, is Australia's largest, with a population of 7000 saltwater and freshwater crocodiles and even some American alligators. Cox Peninsula Rd, further south, leads to several interesting places, such as **Berry Springs Nature Park,** which offers safe swimming in a monsoon forest pool. The adjacent **Territory Wildlife Park** is home to Top End native wildlife in a 400ha bushland setting. To the south of **Lakes Resort** are an orchid farm, **Tumbling Waters Tourist Park** and Manton Dam.
VISITOR INFORMATION: Tourism Top End, Darwin, Ph: (08) 8936 2499 or 1300 138 886

■ Jabiru   POP 1685
Map 427, D2
Jabiru is on the Arnhem Hwy 252km from Darwin. The town was established after uranium mining began, on 13km^2 of leased land in **Kakadu NP**.
MAIN ATTRACTIONS: **Gagudju Crocodile Hotel** is built in the shape of a crocodile, a totem of the local Gagudju people. Fishing and safari tours are available.
NEARBY ATTRACTIONS: Arnhem Hwy, the main tourist route from Darwin, passes the superb waterlily-covered **Fogg Dam**, **Window on the Wetlands** display centre, **Djukbinj NP** and **Mary River Wetlands**. The

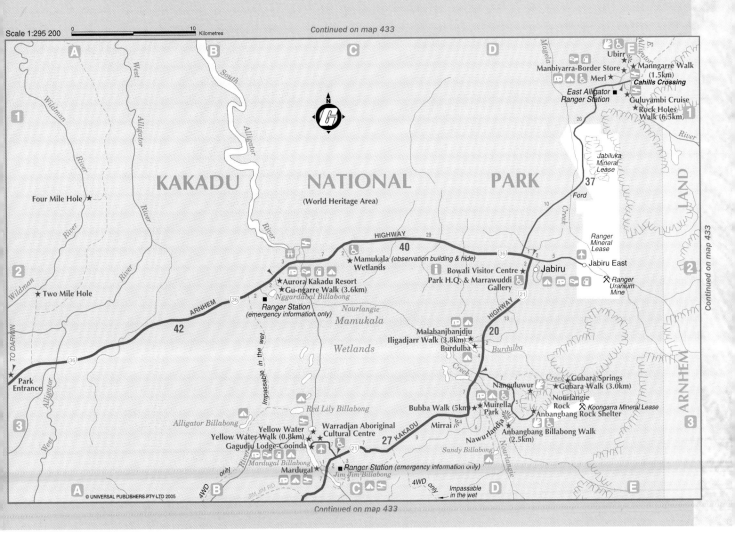

Continued on map 433

Continued on map 433

many attractions of world-famous Kakadu NP are close to Jabiru, including Aboriginal rock-art sites at **Nourlangie Rock** and **Ubirr** and numerous billabongs with prolific wildlife. **Bowali Visitor Centre** can be reached by road or a short walk. It is only 1.5km from Jabiru. **Yellow Water**, 55km south-west, is a spectacular large billabong, where tourist cruises guarantee sightings of waterbirds and other wildlife, including crocodiles. **Warradjan Aboriginal Cultural Centre** is nearby. **Jim Jim** and **Twin Falls** can be reached by a track only accessible to 4-wheel drives, though it may be impassable after heavy monsoonal rain when the falls are at their best.

The Kakadu landscape can be viewed on scenic flights departing from Jabiru airport. There are Dry

season tours to **Ranger Uranium Mine**, 6km east; and the **Injalak Art and Craft Centre** at **Oenpelli**, in nearby Arnhem Land, is worth a visit (a permit is necessary). During the Wet season (approximately November–April), roads to Ubirr, Jim Jim and Twin Falls, Ranger Mine and Arnhem Land are usually impassable, but alternative transportation by air may be available to some attractions. The landscapes and wildlife of Kakadu NP are particularly spectacular during the Wet season.

VISITOR INFORMATION: 6 Tasman Plaza, Ph: (08) 8979 2548 or Tourism Top End, Darwin, Ph: (08) 8936 2499

◼ Katherine   POP 8000
Map 429, C3

Lying 310km from Darwin, Katherine is a centre for beef-cattle properties,

produce farms and the Tindal RAAF Base. Katherine is also the gateway to **Nitmiluk NP**.

MAIN ATTRACTIONS: Katherine has two museums; **Katherine Outback Heritage Museum** off Gorge Rd and the smaller **Railway Station Museum**. The **School of the Air** in Giles St is usually open on school days, with group tours available. Historic **O'Keeffe House** is in Riverbank Dr. For swimming, fishing or bushwalking in shady riverbank parkland, head for **Katherine Low Level Nature Park**. The pools are fed by natural hot springs.

NEARBY ATTRACTIONS: Renowned **Katherine Gorge** in Nitmiluk NP, 29km east, can be viewed by canoe, flat-bottomed tour boat, scenic flight or helicopter. **Leliyn (Edith Falls)**, 62km to the north, is also in

NORTHERN TERRITORY   **427**

NITMILUK NP

'Nitmiluk' is the traditional Jawoyn owners' word for 'Cicada Dreaming', an important Aboriginal Creation story. Located 29km from Katherine on a sealed road, the 2920km^2 park, on the southernmost end of the **Arnhem Land Plateau**, contains a series of 13 beautiful gorges carved out over time by the **Katherine River** and separated by rapids. Rock art adorns the gorge walls and the park is home to prolific wildlife, including freshwater crocodiles and 168 species of birds. Walking, swimming, fishing (lures only), canoeing and cruising along the river are popular activities. Gorge safaris from two to eight hours in duration are available with **Nitmiluk Tours.**

The park is a bushwalkers' paradise with 120km of walking trails, ranging from 400m to the 66km one-way **Jatbula Trail**, from

Katherine Gorge to **Leliyn (Edith Falls)** accessed via the Stuart Hwy. For information on these and other park details, see the national park information sheets available at **Nitmiluk Visitors Centre**. If bushwalking sounds too strenuous, why not take a helicopter tour for a birdseye view of the gorge and surrounding country.

main attractions

- Jatbula Trail
- Katherine Gorge
- Katherine River
- Leliyn (Edith Falls)

Visitor information

Nitmiluk Visitors Centre
Gorge Rd,
Nitmiluk National Park, NT 0851
Ph: (08) 8972 1886

Canoeing in Nitmiluk National Park (Katherine Gorge)

Nitmiluk NP and worth a visit. So too is **Springvale Homestead**, 8km west, the oldest remaining homestead in the Territory, built by Alfred Giles in 1878. **Cutta Cutta Caves**, 500-million-year-old limestone caves 27km south, have cave tours available year round. **Flora River Nature Park**, 86km south-west, features unique tufa dams, pools and cascades. Aboriginal cultural tours are available at **Manyallaluk, Eva Valley**.
Visitor Information: Cnr Katherine Tce (Stuart Hwy) and Lindsay St,
Ph: (08) 8972 2650 or 1800 653 142

■ Mataranka POP 670
Map 433, G6
Mataranka is a small town 106km south-east of Katherine on the Stuart Hwy.
Main Attractions: The **Museum of**

the **Never Never** has historical displays of railway history and Outback life. Statuary representing characters from the Australian classic pioneering novel *We of the Never Never* (by Jeannie Gunn) can be seen in **Stan Martin Park**. Visitors can see barramundi being fed every morning at **Territory Manor** and the works of local artists are on show at **Stockyard Gallery**.
Nearby Attractions: **Elsey NP**, 5km east, offers bushwalking and camping, as well as boating, canoeing and barramundi fishing on the **Roper River**. A swim in the clear waters of **Mataranka Thermal Pool**, surrounded by lush forest, is a must. From here, a walking trail leads to **Mataranka Falls** and tufa limestone formations. **Mataranka Homestead Tourist Resort** has a replica of historic **Elsey Station**

Homestead (where Jeannie Gunn lived). Further north, the **Bitter Springs** section of Elsey NP has another thermal pool, waterways and BBQ facilities. **Elsey Cemetery**, 20km south, contains the graves of local pioneers, including Jeannie Gunn.
Visitor Information: Mataranka Community Govt Council, Stuart Hwy,
Ph: (08) 8975 4576

■ Palmerston POP 26 000
Map 419, G5
Palmerston, named after the British prime minister of the time, was the original name for **Darwin**. Now it is a satellite town, 22km along the Stuart Hwy. Palmerston is one of the fastest-growing communities in Australia.
Main Attractions: **Marlow Lagoon Regional Park** attracts birdlife and provides an attractive recreation

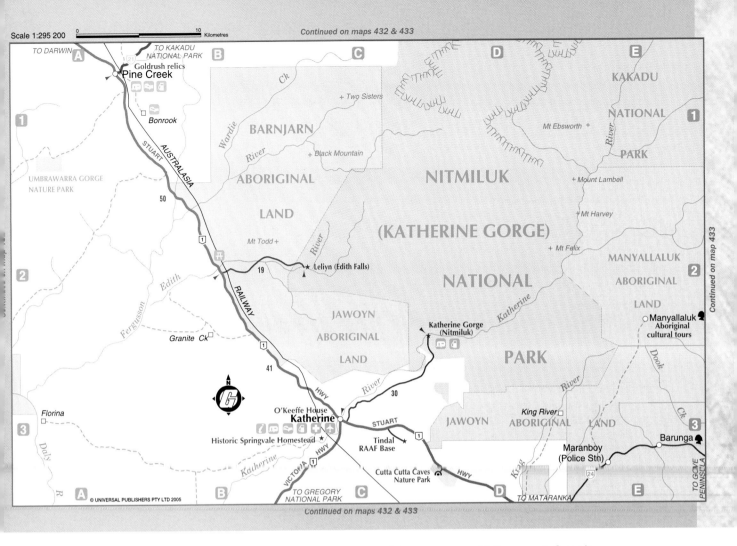

Continued on maps 432 & 433

Scale 1:295 200

Continued on maps 432 & 433

© UNIVERSAL PUBLISHERS PTY LTD 2005

area for picnicking and year-round swimming. Palmerston's multi-cultural society is reflected in the colourful **Frances Mall markets** held every Friday evening in the Dry season.

Visitor Information: Tourism Top End, Darwin, Ph: 8936 2499 or 1300 138 886

▦ Pine Creek   POP 580

Map 429, A1

Pine Creek, 90km north of Katherine at the junction of the Kakadu and Stuart highways, was a goldrush town in the 1870s.

Main Attractions: Pine Creek contains historic buildings and reminders of the goldrush days—**Miners Park**, the Museum in Railway Tce and **Mine Lookout**. **Bird Park** displays tropical birds in a lush setting. The **Railway Station Museum** contains the veteran steam train used in the film adaptation of *We of the Never Never*.

Nearby Attractions: Pine Creek is the southern gateway to **Kakadu NP** via the Kakadu Hwy. The closest attractions in the park are the **Rock Hole**, 65km north-east (4-wheel drive only), and **Gunlom** (Waterfall Creek, 113km north-east) with beautiful falls and a permanent waterhole. **Copperfield Dam**, 6km south-west, is ideal for picnics on the foreshore. **Umbrawarra Gorge Nature Park**, 22km south-west, offers swimming, rockclimbing and walks. **Butterfly Gorge Nature Reserve**, 113km north-west (4-wheel drive only), is noted for the large number of common crow butterflies found in the area.

Visitor Information:

Diggers Rest Motel,

32 Main Tce, Ph: (08) 8976 1442

▦ Tennant Creek   POP 3900

Map 439, H2

Tennant Creek is one of Australia's most isolated towns, 506km north of Alice Springs on the Stuart Hwy. A charming modern town, it is the country's third largest gold producer.

Main Attractions: The old **Australian Inland Mission**, built of prefabricated corrugated iron in 1934, and **Tuxworth Fullwood House**, a WWII army hospital and now a museum, are two places of interest on the town's **heritage walk**. Aboriginal arts and crafts are sold at **Nyinkka Nyunyu** in Paterson St. **Jurnkurakurr Mural** is a community project illustrating both men's and women's 'Dreaming'.

Nearby Attractions: **Mary Ann Dam**, 5km north-east, offers shady picnic areas, swimming and boating—a pleasant surprise in an arid landscape. The old **Telegraph Station** still stands, 12km to the north. **The Pebbles**, in a desert 16km north, glow red at sunset. **Attack Creek Historical Reserve**, 73km north, marks a confrontation between explorer John McDouall Stuart and local Aborigines. A tourist drive 1.5km east along Peko Rd takes visitors to **Battery Hill Regional Centre** and **Gold Stamp Battery**, which features an underground mine and a mining museum. Guided tours are conducted daily. **Bill Allen Lookout** provides district views. Travel a further 106km south on the Stuart Hwy to a collection of unusual and magnificent granite boulders called the **Devils Marbles**—of spiritual importance to Aborigines, they are one of the Territory's top tourist attractions.

VISITOR INFORMATION: Battery Hill Regional Centre, Peko Rd, Ph: (08) 8962 3388

■ Timber Creek   POP 560
Map 435, C2

Timber Creek is 285km south-west of Katherine on the Victoria Hwy, approximately midway to **Kununurra** in Western Australia.

MAIN ATTRACTIONS: The (1908) **Timber Creek Police Station** is now a museum, open May–October. Fishing enthusiasts may want to organise a barramundi fishing tour on the **Victoria River**.

NEARBY ATTRACTIONS: **Gregory NP**, one of the Territory's largest, is 15km west. The park features **Limestone Gorge**, wild scenery, boab trees, Aboriginal and European heritage sites and a network of 4-wheel drive tracks. **Keep River NP**, 175km west, has red sandstone cliffs, boab trees and exceptional Aboriginal rock art. Information on both parks can be obtained from the Conservation Commission in Timber Creek. Also worth a visit is scenic **Jasper Gorge**, 48km south-west, which has an enticing permanent waterhole.

VISITOR INFORMATION: Timber Creek Gunamu Tourist Park, Victoria Hwy, Ph: (08) 8975 0722

■ Yulara (Ayers Rock Resort) POP 1500
Map 423, A3

Yulara was established to cater for the information and touring needs of the thousands of visitors who come to see **Uluru (Ayers Rock)**, Australia's most enduring and internationally recognised landmark, within **Uluru–Kata Tjuta NP**.

MAIN ATTRACTION: **Ayers Rock Visitor Centre** has displays and information on the history, geology, flora and fauna of the region.

NEARBY ATTRACTIONS: On the approach road to Uluru, **Uluru–Kata Tjuta Cultural Centre** provides information on the attractions in the national park. Local Aboriginal history, culture and beliefs are explained through videos, interactive displays, arts, crafts and performance. Uluru–Kata Tjuta NP is jointly managed by the **Anangu** people (traditional owners of the land) and Environment Australia–Parks Australia North. Uluru (Ayers Rock) is 20km south-east of Yulara. Uluru can be explored on one's own or via an organised tour, by Harley Davidson, by helicopter or plane, but probably the most rewarding is with an Aboriginal guide who can explain the deep cultural significance the site has for the local people. The 9.4km **Uluru Circuit Walk** is popular, as are sunrise and sunset viewings when the monolith undergoes dramatic changes of colour. **Kata Tjuta (The Olgas)** lies 50km west of Uluru—these 36 weathered domes are spectacular at any time of day. Walking tracks lead through **Olga Gorge** and the **Valley of the Winds**. Travel 110km from Yulara on the Lasseter Hwy, and you reach a lookout with distant views of **Mount Connor**, another large mountain. Luritja Rd, 136km east, links with the unsealed **Mereenie Loop** as an alternative route to Alice Springs. A permit is required to travel the Loop as large sections pass through Aboriginal land reserves (it is available from the visitor centres in Alice Springs, Glen Helen Resort, Kings Canyon Resort and Hermannsburg). The route accesses another major Red Centre attraction, **Watarrka NP (Kings Canyon)**. The 6km circuit **Rim Walk** features a boardwalk through prehistoric cycads in the **Garden of Eden**, canyon views and unusual rock formations such as those at the **Lost City**.

VISITOR INFORMATION: Ayers Rock Visitor Centre, Yulara Rd, Ph: (08) 8957 7377

Balancing rocks at the Devils Marbles, 106km south of Tennant Creek

KEY MAP

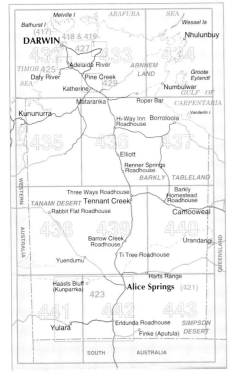

Capital city CBD map
Darwin p.417

Darwin suburban map
pp.418–419

Alice Springs map
p.421

Region maps
Red Centre p.423
Litchfield NP p.425
Kakadu NP p.427
Nitmiluk NP p.429

Territory maps
pp.432–443

Yellow Water Billabong, Kakadu National Park

DISTANCE CHART

Approximate Distance	Adelaide River	Alice Springs	Ayers Rock/Yulara	Borroloola	Camooweal QLD	Darwin	Erldunda	Hi-Way Inn	Jabiru	Katherine	Kulgera	Kununurra WA	Mataranka	Nicholson WA	Pine Creek	Tennant Creek	Ti-Tree	Top Springs	Tobermorey	Wauchope
Adelaide River		1385	1827	585	1293	107	1584	477	288	202	1660	714	308	902	111	871	1180	492	1799	985
Alice Springs	1385		442	1214	988	1492	199	908	1468	1183	275	1695	1077	1464	1274	514	205	1054	570	400
Ayers Rock/Yulara	1827	442		1656	1430	1934	243	1350	1910	1625	319	2137	1519	1906	1716	956	647	1496	1012	842
Borroloola	585	1214	1656		746	967	1413	383	943	658	1489	1151	552	1011	749	700	1009	601	1628	814
Camooweal QLD	1293	988	1430	746		1400	1187	816	1376	1091	1263	1603	985	1372	1182	474	783	962	1402	588
Darwin	107	1492	1934	967	1400		1691	584	243	309	1767	821	415	1009	218	978	1287	599	1906	1092
Erldunda	1584	199	243	1413	1187	1691		1107	1667	1382	76	1894	1276	1663	1473	713	404	1253	769	599
Hi-Way Inn	477	908	1350	383	816	584	1107		560	275	1183	768	169	628	366	394	703	218	1322	508
Jabiru	288	1468	1910	943	1376	243	1667	560		285	1743	797	391	985	194	954	1263	575	1882	1068
Katherine	202	1183	1625	658	1091	309	1382	275	285		1458	512	106	700	91	669	978	290	1597	783
Kulgera	1660	275	319	1489	1263	1767	76	1183	1743	1458		1970	1352	1739	1549	789	480	1329	845	675
Kununurra WA	714	1695	2137	1151	1603	821	1894	768	797	512	1970		618	327	603	1181	1490	550	2109	1295
Mataranka	308	1077	1519	552	985	415	1276	169	391	106	1352	618		797	197	563	872	396	1491	677
Nicholson WA	902	1464	1906	1011	1372	1009	1663	628	985	700	1739	327	797		791	950	1259	410	1878	1064
Pine Creek	111	1274	1716	749	1182	218	1473	366	194	91	1549	603	197	791		760	1069	381	1688	874
Tennant Creek	871	514	956	700	474	978	713	394	954	669	789	1181	563	950	760		309	540	928	114
Ti-Tree	1180	205	647	1009	783	1287	404	703	1263	978	480	1490	872	1259	1069	309		849	619	195
Top Springs	492	1054	1496	601	962	599	1253	218	575	290	1329	550	396	410	381	540	849		1468	654
Tobermorey	1799	570	1012	1628	1402	1906	769	1322	1882	1597	845	2109	1491	1878	1688	928	619	1468		814
Wauchope	985	400	842	814	588	1092	599	508	1068	783	675	1295	677	1064	874	114	195	654	814	

All distances in this chart have been measured over highways and major roads, not necessarily by the shortest route.

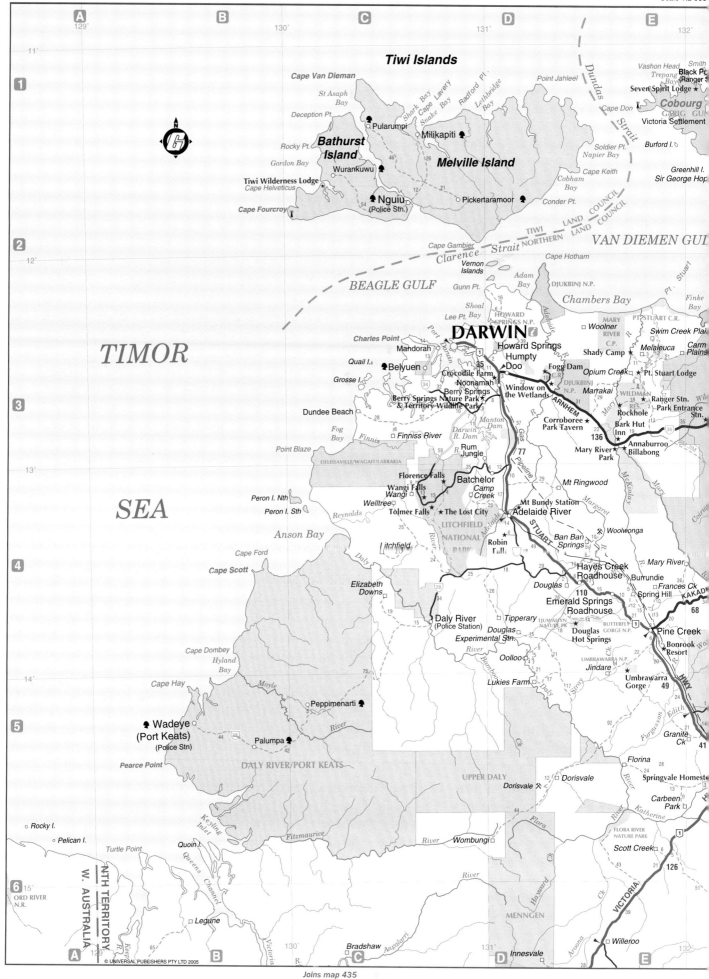

ARAFURA   SEA

Croker Point

Lawson I.

McCluer I.

Danger Pt.   Croker Island
Minjilang ♠   Grant I.

Darch I.

Templer I.

Peninsula
KLU
IONAL PARK   Valencia I.
Mountnorris
Bay

Morse I.

Endyalgout I.

Cape Cockburn
De Courcy Head

Murgenella ♠
(Ranger Stn.)

Aurari
Bay

Brogden Pt.

Nth Goulburn I.

Goulburn Islands
Sth Goulburn I.

Warruwi ♠

North Crocodile Reef

N.W. Crocodile I.

Turner Pt.   Cuthbert Pt.
Arrla Bay   Braithwaite Pt.
Junction Bay   Goomandeer Pt.
Hawkesbury Pt.

Cape Stewart   Crocodile Islands
Mooroongga I.

Elcho
Island

Galiwinku ♠

Entrance I.
Skirmish Pt.   Rabuma I.

Boucaut Bay   Milingimbi I.

Maningrida ○ ♠   Milingimbi ♠
(Police Stn.)

Castlereagh
Bay   Howard I.

Napier Pen.

Point
Farewell
Field I.

East
Alligator

Cooper

Creek

King

R.

Goomadeer

Ck.

Nungbalgarri

River

172

Blyth

R.

Banyan I.

Ramingining ♠

Woden

R.

Nabarlek ✕

22   11

Oenpelli ○
(Police Stn.)

Ubirr ★
Border Store ★
(Manbiyarri)

(World Heritage Area)

Jabiluka M.L.

KAKADU

39

Tin Camp   Ck.

Ranger M.L.

Cadell

R.

Imimbar

Ck.

Goyder

R.

Gulgu   C.K.

74

29

26

1105

155

Mitchell Range

Koolatong

Maidnunga

19

Joins map 434

82   HWY
Aurora
Kakadu Resort

Yellow Water
Warradjan
Aboriginal
Cultural Centre

Jabiru ○
Bowali Visitor Centre
(Park H.Q.)

Nourlangie Rock

Koongarra Mineral Lease

Jim Jim Billabong

Liverpool

River

Mann

ARNHEM LAND

A R N H E M   L A N D

90

Annie

Walker

Bath Ra.

Ingrris Ck.

NATIONAL

127

Maguk ★
(Barramundie
Gorge)

Gunlom ★
(Waterfall Creek)

PARK

Jim Jim Falls

Twin Falls

gural

Entrance

21   35

Jarrangharnmi
(Koolpin Gorge)

10   Gimbat ★

Entry to Aboriginal Lands is
prohibited without a permit from:
The Permits Officer,
Northern Land Council
P.O. Box 42921
Casuarina, NT, 0811
Telephone (08) 8920 5100
Facsimile (08) 8945 2633

Bulman ♠

Blyth

Ck.

C. ARNHEM

Parsons Ra.

ROAD

Rose

R.

Phelp

R.

Wakawixinyu   R.

Ck.

Mary River
Roadhouse

Ck.

Gimbat Ck.

River

MANYALLALUK

Flying

Fox

River

Mainoru

Maiook   R.

ROAD
Lindsay

Mountain
Valley

Mainoru

ARNHEM

Wilton

CENTRAL

River

156

River

14°

NITMILUK
elyn
dith Falls)
(KATHERINE GORGE)
N.P.

Katherine

Katherine Gorge ★
(Nitmiluk)

Tindal RAAF
Base

52

Cutta Cutta ★
Caves   NATURE
PARK

Manyalluk ○ ♠

King River

Barunga ♠

Maranboy ○
(Police Stn)

Beswick ♠

MANYALLALUK

Katherine   R.

West   Branch

Dook   Ck.

247

CENTRAL

62

Turkey

R.

Lagoon

Ck.

AUSTRALASIA

STUART

BESWICK

Waterhouse

Chambers

R.

Roper

Goondooloo

Moroak

Roper

Creek

River

River

Lagoon

Urapunga ○ (Police Stn)
Ngukurr ♠

Port Roper

Port
Roper

Limmen

Roper

Roper Bar ♦

YUTPUNDJI-
DJINDIWIRRIT

HWY   24

Roper Valley

Bight

Maria I.

MARRA

Mataranka Resort ★
Thermal Pool

Mataranka ★

Elsey ○

ROPER

176

RAILWAY

Elsey Cemetery ★

MANGARRAY

Strangeways

River

Hodgson

Miniyeri ♠

ALAWA

Roper

River

River

Limmen

Cox   R.

Towns

Bight

R.

R.

Dry

Dry River

© UNIVERSAL PUBLISHERS PTY LTD 2005

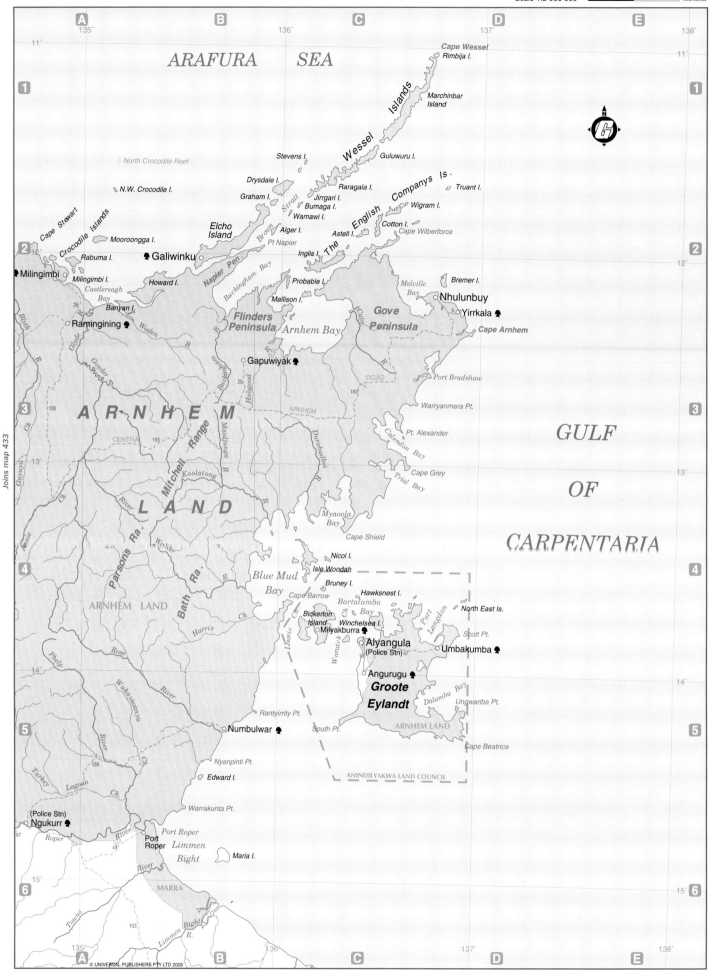

Scale 1:2 000 000

0　　　　　50 Kilometres

ARAFURA　SEA

Cape Wessel
Rimbija I.

Wessel Islands

Marchinbar
Island

North Crocodile Reef

N.W. Crocodile I.

Stevens I.

Guluwuru I.

The English Companys Is.

Drysdale I.
Graham I.
Raragala I.
Jirrgari I.
Bumaga I.
Wamawi I.
Alger I.
Astell I.
Wigram I.
Truant I.
Cotton I.
Cape Wilberforce

Cape Stewart

Crocodile Islands

Elcho
Island

Mooroongga I.

Brown Strait

Pt Napier

Napier Pen.

Inglis R.

Rabuma I.

Galiwinku

Melville
Bay

Bremer I.

Milingimbi

Milingimbi I.

Howard I.

Castlereagh
Bay

Probable I.

Buckingham Bay

Nhulunbuy

Banyan I.

Flinders
Peninsula

Mallison I.

Arnhem Bay

Gove
Peninsula

Yirrkala

Ramingining

Woden

Clyde R.

Goyder R.

Cato R.

Cape Arnhem

Blyth R.

A　R　N　H　E　M

Buckingham R.

Hatgood

Gapuwiyak

ARNHEM

ROAD

Port Bradshaw

CENTRAL

Mitchell　Range

Maidunga R.

Durabudboi R.

182

Warryanmera Pt.

Joins map 433

105

155

25

Koolatong

River

Calendon
Bay

Pt. Alexander

GULF

Parsons Ra.

Weber R.

Cape Grey

Trial
Bay

Antie Ck.

L　A　N　D

Cape Shield

OF

Bath Ra.

R.

Myaoola
Bay

CARPENTARIA

Phelp R.

Harris R.

Rose River

Wukazuanyu R.

ARNHEM　LAND

Nicol I.
Isle Woodah

Bruney I.

Blue Mud
Bay

Hawksnest I.

North East Is.

Cape Barrow

Bartalumba
Bay

Bickerton
Island

Winchelsea I.

Port Langdon

Scott Pt.

Lourie Ck.

Warnack Ck.

Milyakburra

Alyangula
(Police Stn)

Umbakumba

47

Turkey Lagoon

River

156

Rantyirrity Pt.

Numbulwar

South Pt.

Angurugu

Groote
Eylandt

Dalumbu Bay

Ungwariba Pt.

Nyanpinti Pt.

ARNHEM LAND

Edward I.

Cape Beatrice

ANINDILYAKWA LAND COUNCIL

Warrakunta Pt.

(Police Stn)
Ngukurr

87

Roper R.

44

Port
Roper

Port Roper

Limmen
Bight

Maria I.

River

MARRA

15°

Towns R.

103

Limmen Bight R.

Northern Territory

Scale 1:2 000 000

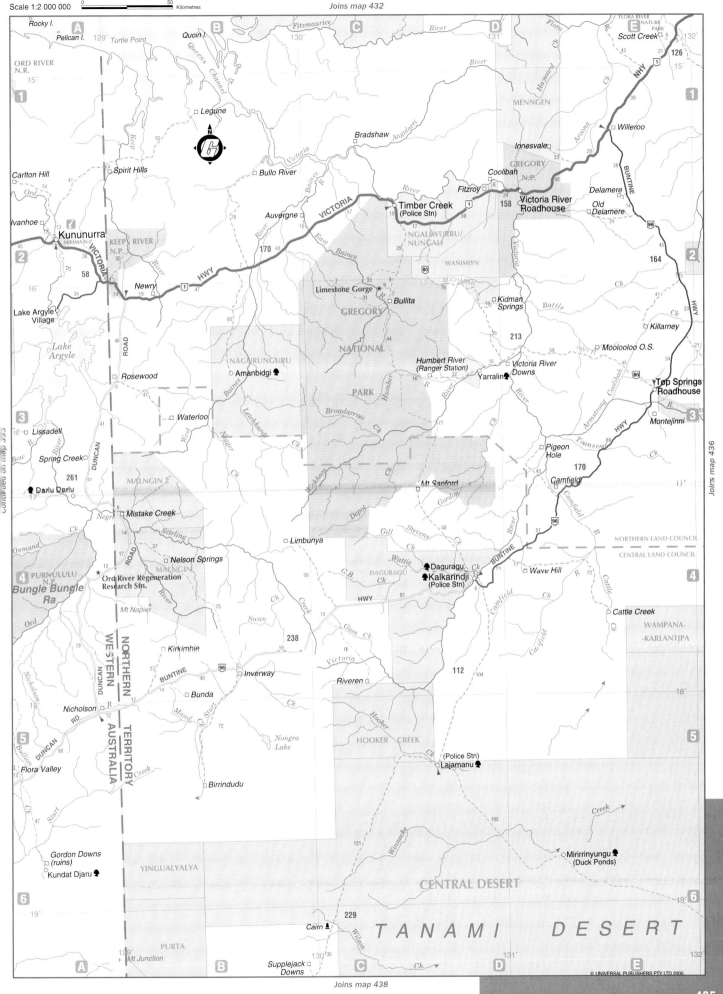

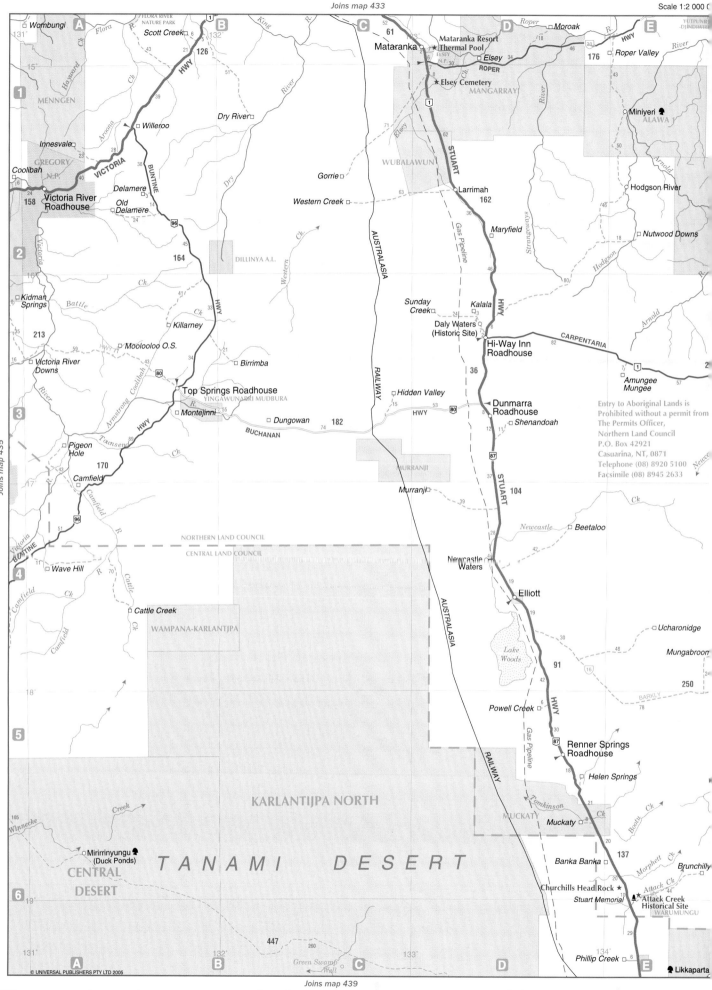

Entry to Aboriginal Lands is
Prohibited without a permit from
The Permits Officer,
Northern Land Council
P.O. Box 42921
Casuarina, NT, 0871
Telephone (08) 8920 5100
Facsimile (08) 8945 2633

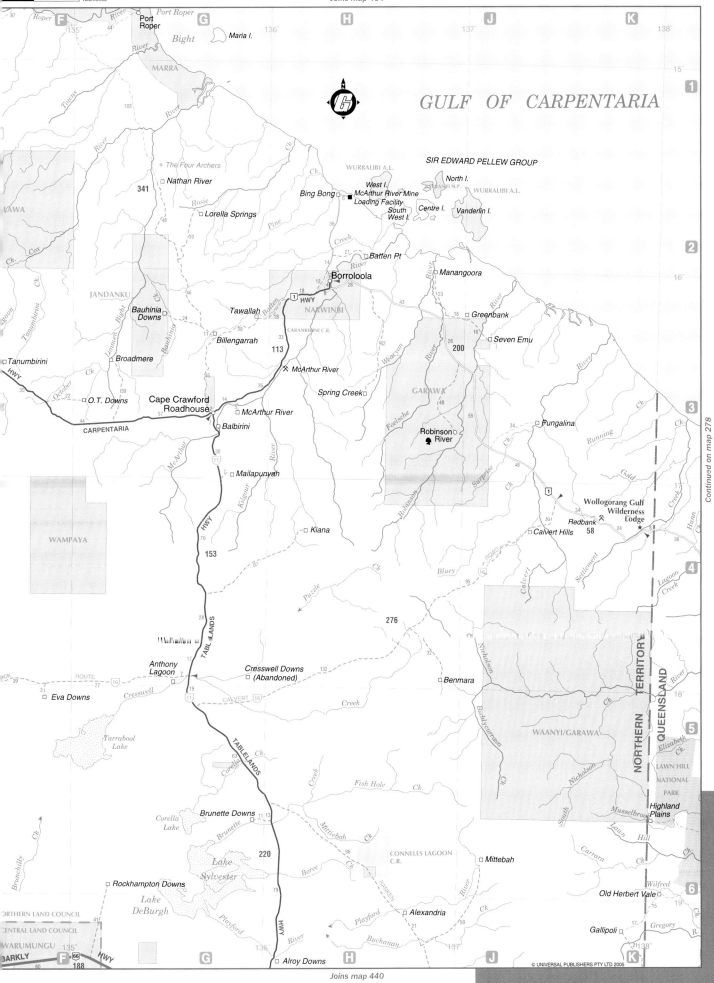

50 Kilometres

F 135° 44° **G** 136° **H** 137° **J** **K** 138°

Roper 87

Roper River
Port Roper
Port Roper

Bight

Maria I.

MARRA

Towns 103

GULF OF CARPENTARIA

River

+ The Four Archers

SIR EDWARD PELLEW GROUP

WURRALIBI A.L.

Nathan River
341

North I.

West I.

NARAWI N.P.

WURRALIBI A.L.

Rosie

Bing Bong
McArthur River Mine
Loading Facility
South
West I.

Centre I.

Vanderlin I.

Lorella Springs
48

Pine

30

Creek
36

21

Batten Pt

14

Manangoora

JANDANKU

Linmeh Bight

River

46

Tawallah
12

18

Borroloola
28

HWY 1

8

43

Greenbank
18

Bauhinia
Downs

24

18

Caranbirini C.R.

NARWINBI

16

Seven Emu
200

Tanumbirini

Billengarrah
11

33

Weoryn River

26

Foelsche

Broadmere
113

McArthur River

62

GARAWA

148

O.T. Downs
139
22

36

Spring Creek

Running

Robinson
River

55

34

Pungalina

Cape Crawford
Roadhouse
14

57

McArthur River

Gold Ck.

44

CARPENTARIA

Balbirini

30

48

McArthur River

11

Mailapunyah

Surprise

1

Wollogorang Gulf
Wilderness
Lodge

Kilgour River

301

34

Redbank
58

24

Calvert Hills

Kiana

Robinson

Calvert

HWY

70

Bluey

95

14

ROAD

Hann

WAMPAYA

153

Nicholson

NORTHERN TERRITORY

QUEENSLAND

Puzzle

276

28

TABLELANDS

32

Benmara

LAWN HILL

NATIONAL

PARK

Anthony
Lagoon

17

Cresswell Downs
(Abandoned)
132

Buddycurranga Ck.

WAANYI/GARAWA

Highland
Plains

ROUTE 16

39

31

77

19

11

CALVERT 16

Eva Downs

Cresswell

Creek

Musselbrook

Lawn Hill

Tarrabool
Lake

TABLELANDS

Fish Hole

Ck.

Carrara

Corella

Brunette Downs
11 13

Corella
Lake

96

CONNELLS LAGOON
C.R.

Mittebah

Old Herbert Vale

Lake
Sylvester

220

Borve

Mittebah

River

Rockhampton Downs

79

Alexandria

Gallipoli

Gregory R.

Lake
DeBurgh

Playford River

Branchilly Ck.

NORTHERN LAND COUNCIL

CENTRAL LAND COUNCIL

41

Buchanan

21

59

17

15

19

WARUMUNGU 135°

BARKLY **F** 66 HWY 188

60

G 136°

Alroy Downs

H 137°

J

© UNIVERSAL PUBLISHERS PTY LTD 2005

K 21 138°

Continued on map 278

NORTHERN TERRITORY 437

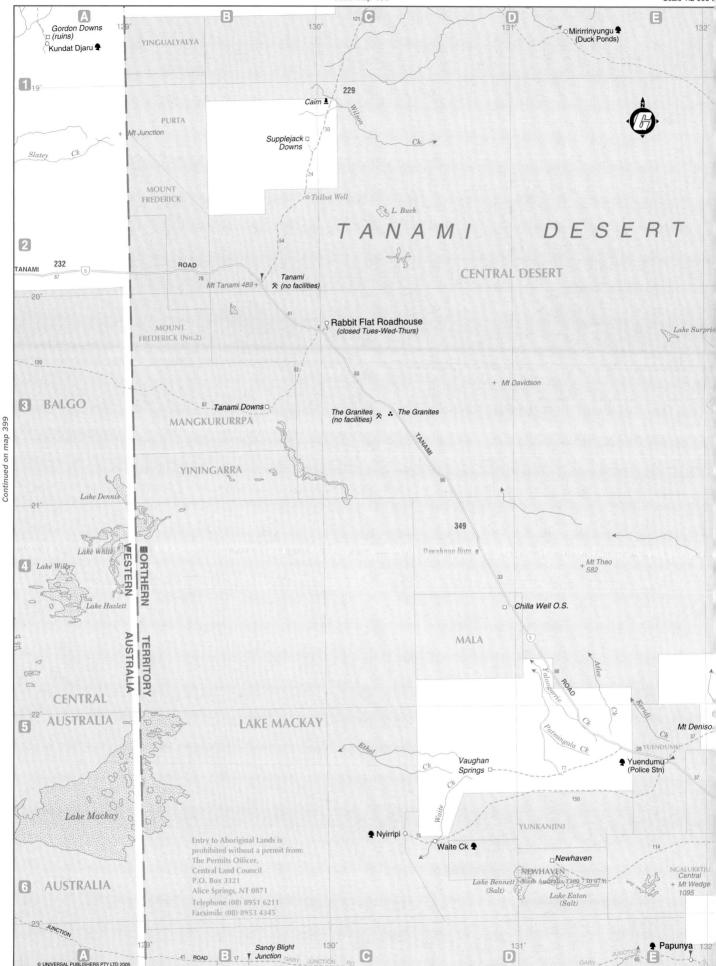

A
Gordon Downs
(ruins)
□ Kundat Djaru ♠

B

C
● Mirirrinyungu ♠
(Duck Ponds)

D

E
132°

129°

130°

121°

131°

1 19°

YINGUALYALYA

229

Cairn ▲

Wilson

PURTA

+ Mt Junction

30

Slatey   Ck.

Supplejack □
Downs

Ck.

24

MOUNT
FREDERICK

○ Talbot Well

● L. Buck

2

T A N A M I   D E S E R T

54

TANAMI   232

ROAD

CENTRAL   DESERT

87   5

78   Mt Tanami 489 +

▼   Tanami
⚘ (no facilities)

20°

MOUNT
FREDERICK (No.2)

41

● Rabbit Flat Roadhouse
5   (closed Tues-Wed-Thurs)

120

52

60

+ Mt Davidson

3 BALGO

87 ● Tanami Downs □

MANGKURURRPA

The Granites   ⚘ ⚘ The Granites
(no facilities)

TANAMI

YININGARRA

Lake Surpri

Lake Dennis

96

21°

349

4 Lake Wills

Lake White

Bawahane Bore ●

+ Mt Theo
582

Lake Hazlett

33

□ Chilla Well O.S.

MALA

5

CENTRAL

5 AUSTRALIA

22°

LAKE MACKAY

Yalaigarrie   Ck

Attee   Ck

Kerteh   Ck

Mt Deniso

ROAD

98

28 YUENDUMU

37

Patmingala   Ck

Ethel

Vaughan
Springs □

Ck   77

♣ Yuendumu
(Police Stn)

Ck

37

Lake Mackay

Waite   Ck

150

Entry to Aboriginal Lands is
prohibited without a permit from:
The Permits Officer,
Central Land Council
P.O. Box 3321
Alice Springs, NT 0871
Telephone (08) 8951 6211
Facsimile (08) 8953 4345

♠ Nyirripi   16

Waite Ck ♠

YUNKANJINI

□ Newhaven

114

6 AUSTRALIA

NEWHAVEN
Lake Bennett (Birds Australia 1300 730 075)
(Salt)

NGALURRTJU
Central
+ Mt Wedge
1095

Lake Eaton
(Salt)

23°   JUNCTION

129°

130°

131°

JUNCTIO

♠ Papunya

132°

41   ROAD

Sandy Blight
17 ▼ Junction

GARY   JUNCTION   RD

GARY

65

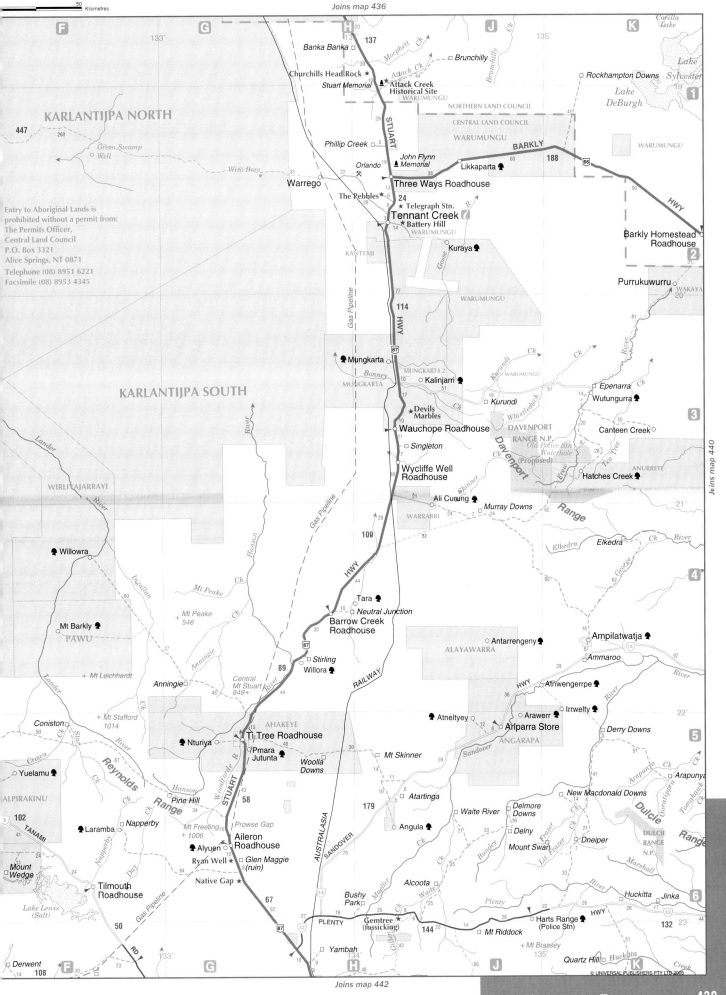

50 Kilometres

KARLANTIJPA NORTH

447

260

Green Swamp Well

Entry to Aboriginal Lands is
prohibited without a permit from:
The Permits Officer,
Central Land Council
P.O. Box 3321
Alice Springs, NT 0871
Telephone (08) 8951 6221
Facsimile (08) 8953 4345

KARLANTIJPA SOUTH

Wiso Bore

Banka Banka **137**

Churchills Head Rock ★
Stuart Memorial ★ **Attack Creek Historical Site**

Brunchilly

Rockhampton Downs Lake Sylvester

Lake DeBurgh

Phillip Creek 29 STUART NORTHERN LAND COUNCIL
CENTRAL LAND COUNCIL
WARUMUNGU WARUMUNGU

Orlando John Flynn Memorial Likkaparta 60 **188** 66 WARUMUNGU
BARKLY 41

Warrego 22 33 38 **Three Ways Roadhouse** 90 HWY

The Pebbles ★ 24 ★ Telegraph Stn. **Barkly Homestead Roadhouse**
Tennant Creek i 2
★ Battery Hill 14 WARUMUNGU
Kuraya *Purrukuwurru* WAKAYA 20

KANTTAJI 77 114 Grosse WARUMUNGU 81

Gas Pipeline HWY 87 *Epenarra*
Mungkarta Bonney MUNGKARTA 2 Kalinjarri Wutungurra 14
MUNGKARTA 10 17 51 *Kurundi* 51
Devils Marbles 10 Whistleduck DAVENPORT 20 Canteen Creek
Wauchope Roadhouse 11 RANGE N.P. Old Police Stn 28 Tea Tree
Singleton 7 Waterhole (Proposed) ANURRETE
Wycliffe Well Roadhouse 8 Shinner DAVENPORT Hatches Creek
Ali Curung 21 Erew Range 21
WARRABRI 24 *Murray Downs*
109 29 52 *Elkedra* Elkedra Ck River

Willowra Mt Peake Ck 90 62 George
Hanson 44 RAILWAY
PAWU Mt Peake + 546 Tara *Ampilatwatja*
Mt Barkly Neutral Junction 16 14
27 30 Antarrengeny *Ammaroo* 97
+ Mt Leichhardt 10 **Barrow Creek Roadhouse** ALAYAWARRA 28
Anningie 87 *Stirling* 36 HWY Atnwengerrpe River
89 Willora Arawerr Irrwelty
Central Mt Stuart 849+ 44 Atneltyey 12 **Arlparra Store** *Derry Downs*
Coniston 15 AHAKEYE 6 ANGARAPA
Nturiya 48 Sandover 5
ALPIRAKINU Ti Tree Roadhouse 30 Mt Skinner 59 *New Macdonald Downs* Arapunya
102 Pine Hill Pmara Jutunta Woolla Downs 14 *Delmore Downs* DULCIE
TANAMI 58 14 16 RANGE N.P.
Laramba *Napperby* Hanson 43 Atartinga *Waite River* *Delny* Dneiper
Mt Freeling + 1006 15 Prowse Gap *Angula* 33 *Mount Swan* 21 Dulcie Range
Alyuen Aileron Roadhouse Alcoota Frazer Marshall Huckitta
Mount Wedge Ryan Well ★ ★ Glen Maggie (ruin) *Bushy Park* Plenty Jinka
Native Gap ★ 67 Gemtree (fossicking) Harts Range (Police Stn) 132 23
Tilmouth Roadhouse 52 144 *Mt Riddock* + Mt Brassey 12
Lake Lewis (Salt) 50 Gas Pipeline 87 PLENTY Quartz Hill Huckitta
Derwent RD Yambah © UNIVERSAL PUBLISHERS PTY LTD 2005
108

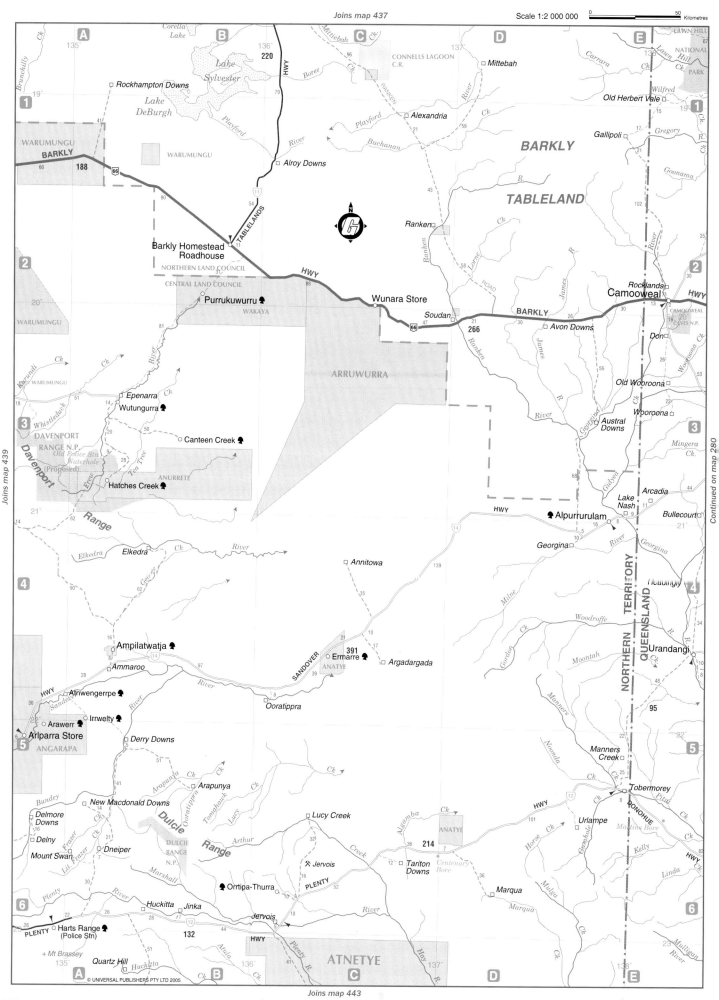

Scale 1:2 000 000

0   50
Kilometres

Joins map 439

Continued on map 280

Gregory's Australia

Northern Territory

LAWN HILL
NATIONAL
PARK

BARKLY

TABLELAND

WARUMUNGU

BARKLY
188

WARUMUNGU
220

CONNELLS LAGOON
C.R.

Rockhampton Downs

Lake
Sylvester

Lake
DeBurgh

Corella
Lake

Mittebah

Old Herbert Vale

Alexandria

Gallipoli

Alroy Downs

Ranken

Rocklands
Camooweal

CAMOOWEAL
CAVES N.P.

Barkly Homestead
Roadhouse

TABLELANDS

NORTHERN LAND COUNCIL

CENTRAL LAND COUNCIL

Purrukuwurru

WAKAYA

Wunara Store

Soudan
266

BARKLY

Avon Downs

Don

Old Wooroona

Wooroona

ARRUWURRA

Austral
Downs

Mingera
Ck.

Arcadia

Bullecourt

Epenarra
Wutungurra

DAVENPORT
RANGE N.P.
Old Police Stn
Waterhole
(Proposed)

Canteen Creek

ANURRETE

Lake
Nash

Hatches Creek

Elkedra

Elkedra

Annitowa

HWY

Alpurrurulam

Georgina

Headingly

Woodroffe

Ampilatwatja

Ammaroo

SANDOVER

Ermarre
391

ANATYE

Argadargada

Urandangi

Atnwengerrpe

Arawerr

Irrwelty

Arlparra Store
ANGARAPA

Oorratippra

95

Manners
Creek

Tobermorey

Derry Downs

Arapunya

DONOHUE

New Macdonald Downs

Delmore
Downs

Delny

Mount Swan

Dneiper

DULCIE
RANGE
N.P.

Dulcie

Range

Lucy Creek

Jervois

Orrtipa-Thurra

PLENTY

Tariton
Downs

Centenary
Bore

ANATYE
214

Urlampe

Marqua

Huckitta

Jinka

Jervois

PLENTY

HWY

Marqua

Harts Range
(Police Stn)

PLENTY
132

Mt Brassey

Quartz Hill

Huckitta

ATNETYE

NORTHERN TERRITORY

QUEENSLAND

© UNIVERSAL PUBLISHERS PTY LTD 2005

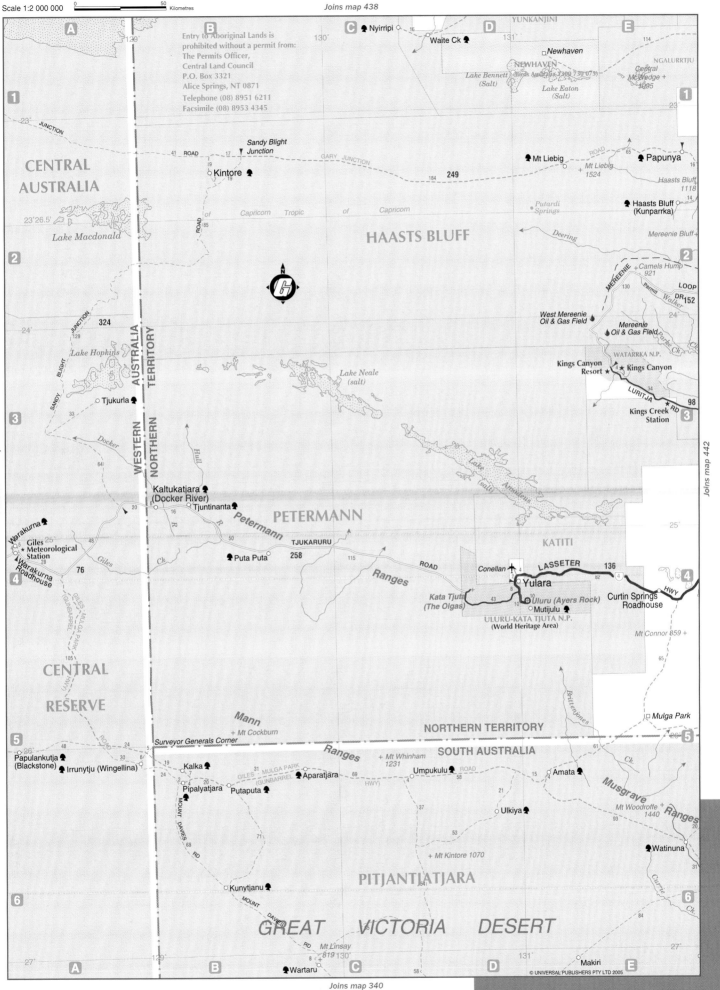

Scale 1:2 000 000

0   50   Kilometres

YUNKANJINI

Joins map 442

Entry to Aboriginal Lands is
prohibited without a permit from:
The Permits Officer,
Central Land Council
P.O. Box 3321
Alice Springs, NT 0871
Telephone (08) 8951 6211
Facsimile (08) 8953 4345

Nyirripi   16

Waite Ck   131

Newhaven

NGALURRTJU

NEWHAVEN

Central
Mt Wedge +
1095

Lake Bennett
(Salt)

Lake Eaton
(Salt)

Birds Australia 1300 730 073)

114

1

CENTRAL
AUSTRALIA

JUNCTION

41   ROAD   17

Sandy Blight
Junction

GARY   JUNCTION

19

Kintore
19

184   249

Mt Liebig

ROAD   65

Mt Liebig
1524

Papunya

16

Haasts Bluff
1118

14

Haasts Bluff
(Kunparrka)

of   Capricorn   Tropic   of   Capricorn

85

HAASTS BLUFF

Putardi
Springs

Deering

Mereenie Bluff +

Lake Macdonald

23'26.5'

MEREENIE   + Camels Hump
921

LOOP
DR 152

2

Permit   Walker

130

24

West Mereenie
Oil & Gas Field

Mereenie
Oil & Gas Field

Porter Ck

JUNCTION
129   324

WATARRKA N.P.

Lake Hopkins

Kings Canyon
Resort ★

★ Kings Canyon

LURITJA   RD

34

SANDY   BLIGHT

Tjukurla

33

Lake Neale
(salt)

Kings Creek
Station

98

3

Docker

64

Hull

Lake   (salt)   Amadeus

Kaltukatjara
(Docker River)

Tjuntinanta

PETERMANN

16

R

R

20

Petermann

KATITI

25'

WESTERN   AUSTRALIA

NORTHERN   TERRITORY

Warakurna

Giles
Meteorological
Station

25'

Warakurna
Roadhouse

48

28

76   Giles

50

Puta Puta   258

TJUKARURU

115

Ranges

ROAD

LASSETER

136

Conellan

Yulara

Kata Tjuta
(The Olgas)

Uluru (Ayers Rock)

Mutijulu

ULURU-KATA TJUTA N.P.
(World Heritage Area)

Curtin Springs
Roadhouse

HWY

4

Ck

82

43

10

Mt Connor 859 +

65

GILES - MULGA PARK
(GUNBARREL) HWY

105

CENTRAL

Brittenjones

RESERVE

Mann

+ Mt Cockburn

NORTHERN TERRITORY

Mulga Park

5

Surveyor Generals Corner

Ranges

SOUTH AUSTRALIA

48

5

Papulankutja
(Blackstone)

Irrunytju (Wingellina)

24

30

6

5

19

Kalka

31   MULGA PARK
(GUNBARREL

Aparatjara

+ Mt Whinham
1231

Umpukulu   ROAD

58

15

Amata

61

Ck

Musgrave

Pipalyatjara

Putaputa

HWY)

69

37

21

Ulkiya

Mt Woodroffe +
1440

93

Ranges

20

MOUNT   DAVIES

71

68   RD

53

+ Mt Kintore 1070

Watinuna

31

Kunytjanu

PITJANTJATJARA

MOUNT   DAVIES

Ck

6

GREAT   VICTORIA   DESERT

RD

Mt Linsay
819   130'

58

Makiri

27'

131

A   129   B   C   D   E

Wartaru

© UNIVERSAL PUBLISHERS PTY LTD 2005

A | B | C | D | E

Joins map 441

YUNKANJINI

131°

Lake Bennett (Salt)
NEWHAVEN
Birds Australia 1300 730 073)
Newhaven

Lake Eaton (Salt)

23°

TANAMI
Mt Freeling + 1006
Napperby Ck
Day
Gas Pipeline
114
132
11
Mount Wedge

NGALURRTJU
Central + Mt Wedge
1095

Lake Lewis (Salt)

Tilmouth Roadhouse

50

Alyuen
Ryan Well
Native Gap
Glen Maggie (ruin)

Aileron Roadhouse

SANDOVER HWY
76
34°

STUART
67
52

HWY
87
12

PLENTY
Bushy Park
Gemtree (fossicking)
144

Alcoota
Waite Ck

Mt Liebig
Mt Liebig 1524

Papunya

GARY JUNCTION ROAD

65

16

Derwent
108

14

23

Narwietooma
24

Amburla
Milton Park

Mt Hay +1252
Hamilton Downs
138

ROAD

Yambah

16 Mile

68

ARLTUNGA
TOURIS
The Gard

Mt Laughlen +

Putardi Springs

Haasts Bluff 1118
Haasts Bluff (Kunparrka)

Mt Zeil 1531

Tropic of Capricorn

Bond Springs
Simpsons Gap

Alice Springs

Corroboree Rock

Trephina Gorge
TREPHINA GORGE N.P.

N'Dhala Gorge
113

Deering

Mereenie Bluff +

Redbank Gorge
Ormiston Gorge
Ochre Pits
Glen Helen Gorge
Serpentine Gorge

WEST MACDONNELL
NATIONAL
PARK

Hamilton Downs Youth Camp
Ellery Ck Big Hole
Standley Chasm
Iwupataka

ROSS
Amoonguna
Frontier Camel Farm
Todd

Camels Hump 921
MEREENIE
LOOP RD

TNORALA CONS. RES.
Gosse Bluff 933
Redalls
72

NAMATJIRA
DR
91

MacDonnell

Hermannsburg
85

LARAPINTA

Pine Gap
Owen Springs
Oil Refinery
Ewaninga

SANTA TERESA

West Mereenie Oil & Gas Field
Mereenie Oil & Gas Field
152

Walker

Areyonga

James

Palm Valley
Namatjira Monument

HWY
92

Ewaninga Rock Carvings
70

Polhill (ruins)
Santa Teresa

Ooraminna (ruins)
Allambi

Deep Well

Kings Canyon Resort
Kings Canyon

WATARRKA N.P.

URRAMPINYU

ILTJILTJARRA

Ilbitta

Boggy Hole

FINKE GORGE N.P.

Wallace Rockhole

Ranges

Tidenvale Ck

Camels Australia
Stuarts Well Roadhouse
Rainbow Valley
Orange Ck

Hugh River

Oak Valley

Rodinga (ruins)

Maryvale
Titjikala

Roding

Kings Creek Station
100

LURITJA

62
RD
68
50

19 Mile
Tempe Downs
McMinn
60
Petermann
35

GILES
Palmer
97

Henbury Meteorite Craters
RD

Henbury
18

RAILWAY
STUART
69
38

Chambers Pillar
Alice Well

Bundooma (ruins)

Engoordina (ruins)

Horseshoe Bend

Mt Squi (ruins)

Palmer Valley

Idracowra

Charlotte Ra

KATITI

Lake Amadeus (salt)

Angas Downs

Imanpa
109

Erldunda Roadhouse

Erldunda

Impadna Siding

Rumbalara (ruins)

Musgrave (ruins)

Connellan
LASSETER
180
Yulara
Uluru (Ayers Rock)
Mutijulu

ULURU-KATA TJUTA N.P.
(World Heritage Area)

Curtin Springs Roadhouse

Mount Ebenezer Roadhouse

HWY
56

Karinga Ck

74

Kalamurta

AUSTRALASIA

Lilla Creek

Finke (Aputula)

Lambert Centre

Bloodwood Bore

+ Mt Beddome

Umbeara

+ Mt Connor 859

Lyndavale

179

STUART

Kulgera Roadhouse
Johnstone Geodetic Station
Kulgera Siding
Mount Cavenagh

147

Beddome Ra.

Mulga Park

NORTHERN TERRITORY
64
Victory Downs

SOUTH AUSTRALIA

Goyder

Mt Darling 541

Tieyon

Mt Howe 515

Lindsay

Amata

Musgrave

Boorndoolyanna

Pukatja (Ernabella)
Yunyarinya (Kenmore Park)

Ranges
Mt Woodroffe + 1440

Ulkiya

PITJANTJATJARA

Watinuna

HWY
A87

Marryat Siding

Agnes Creek

Hamilton

Mt Walte 361

GREAT VICTORIA DESERT

Fregon

Officer Ck

Tarcoonyinna Ck

Chandler
Granite Downs
Lambina

Mt Darling

Makiri

Paw Paw

Teeta Bore

Mimili

Indulkana (Iwantja)

Chambers Bluff 592

Yoolperlunna

Nicholson Hill + 404

PEDIRKA

131°
25°
133°
134°
56°

© UNIVERSAL PUBLISHERS PTY LTD 2005

Continued on map 341

Northern Territory

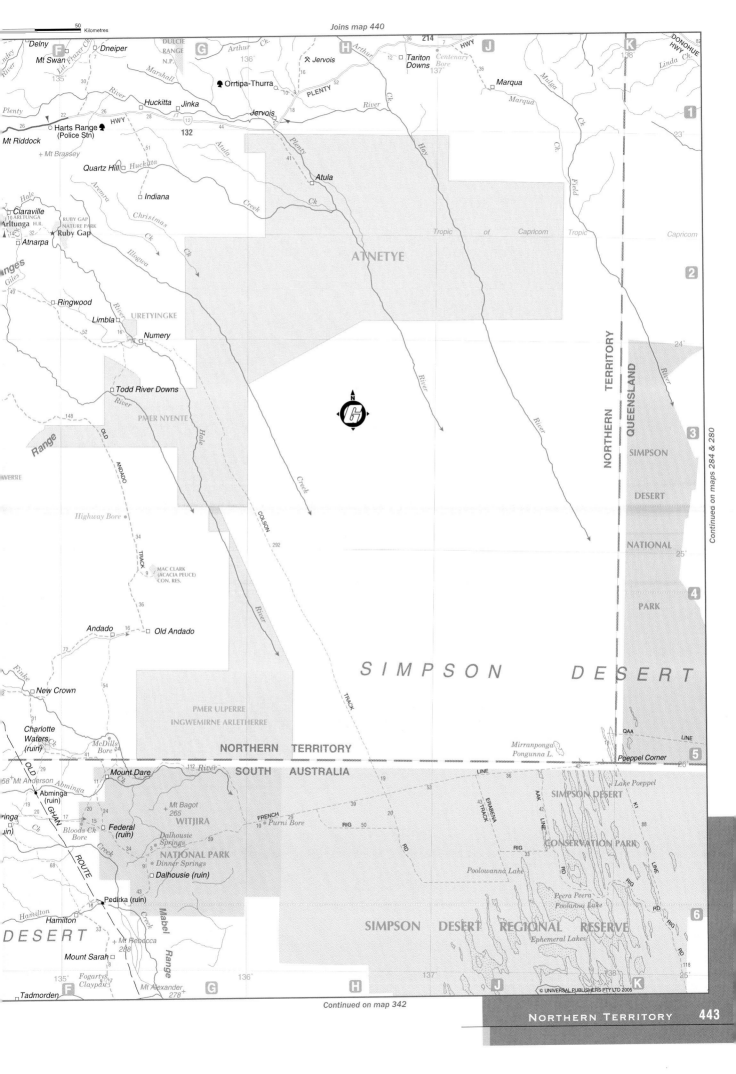

Continued on maps 284 & 280

50 Kilometres

F Delny
Mt Swan
135°
7
Dneiper
DULCIE RANGE N.P.
G
Arthur Ck
136°
Jervois
H
Arthur HWY
12
Tariton Downs
137°
Centenary Bore
7
J
214
36
K
DONOHUE HWY
138°
82°
Linda Ck

30
Lit. Frazer Ck
Marshall
River
16
Orrtipa-Thurra
PLENTY
52
Marqua
Marqua
Mulga Ck
K 1
23°

Plenty
22
26
Huckitta
Jinka
28
Jervois
18
River
Field Ck

26
Harts Range (Police Stn)
HWY
132
44
Jervois
5
41

Mt Riddock
+ Mt Brassey
51
Atula Ck
Plenty

Quartz Hill
Huckitta
Atula
Tropic of Capricorn
Tropic
Capricorn
2

Avenra River
Christmas
Indiana
ATNETYE

Hale River
48
Claraville
ARLTUNGA H.R.
RUBY GAP NATURE PARK
Ruby Gap
Ck
Illogwa
24°

Atnarpa
Giles
Ringwood
Ck
NORTHERN TERRITORY
QUEENSLAND
River
SIMPSON
3

Range
Limbla
52
16
URETYINGKE
Numery
River
DESERT

Todd River Downs
River
148
OLD
NATIONAL
25°
4

PMER NYENTE
Hale
River
N
G

ERRE
ANDADO
COLSON
292
PARK
K 4

Highway Bore
34
TRACK
MAC CLARK (ACACIA PEUCE) CON. RES.
River

36
Andado
16
Old Andado
River

72
SIMPSON
DESERT
QAA
LINE
5

New Crown
54
PMER ULPERRE INGWEMIRNE ARLETHERRE
TRACK
Mirranponga Pongunna L.
Poeppel Corner
26°

31
Charlotte Waters (ruin)
McDills Bore
24
NORTHERN TERRITORY
LINE
42
Lake Poeppel

OLD
29
41
Mount Dare
112
River
SOUTH AUSTRALIA
19
53
LINE
36
AAK LINE
42
SIMPSON DESERT
K 1

58 Mt Anderson
Abminga
11
Mt Bagot 265
39
20
ERABENA TRACK
43
88

ringa
19
20
GHAN
17
20
24
WITJIRA
FRENCH
29
Purni Bore
RIG
50
RD
RIG
CONSERVATION PARK

uin)
5
15
Bloods Ck Bore
Federal (ruin)
34
3
59
10
Poolowanna Lake
RIG RD
Peera Peera Poolanna Lake
RIG
RD
6

68
ROUTE
Dalhousie Springs
NATIONAL PARK
Dinner Springs
9
Dalhousie (ruin)
SIMPSON DESERT REGIONAL RESERVE
Ephemeral Lakes
RD
118
25°

43
Pedirka (ruin)
18

Hamilton
33
Mabel Range
+ Mt Rebecca 288

DESERT
Mount Sarah
2

Fogarty's Claypan
135°
F
Mt Alexander + 278
136°
G
137°
H
J
K
38

Tadmorden
© UNIVERSAL PUBLISHERS PTY LTD 2005

Continued on map 342

NORTHERN TERRITORY **443**

TASMANIA

Tasmania is the smallest of the Australian states. It is an island 240km from the mainland and surrounded by the turbulent Bass Strait, Southern Ocean and Tasman Sea. Its compactness makes it an ideal touring destination, as only relatively short distances separate its many attractions. Tasmania is a land of diversity with beaches encircling its coastline, while national parks and reserves protect its spectacular landmass, which features more than 2000km of world-class walking tracks.

This is the most mountainous Australian state and it has the highest percentage of national parks, comprising about one-third of the island. Tasmania boasts stunning, often remote World Heritage Areas. There are fertile plains and open bushland, mountains and valleys, rare flora and fauna, rustic ports and historic villages, all crammed into a comparatively small area.

Of all the Australian states, Tasmania has the smallest population and the lowest immigration rate. As

Tasmania:
The Holiday Isle

- Population: 472 000
- Total area: 67 800km²
- % of Australia: 1%
- Floral emblem: Tasmanian Blue Gum
- Fauna emblem: Tasmanian Devil

i Visitor information

Tasmanian Travel and Information Centre
20 Davey St, Hobart, Tas 7000
Ph: (03) 6230 8233
Freecall: 1800 990 440
www.discovertasmania.com.au

Main ATTRACTIONS

◈ Bruny Island

A small isthmus connects North and South Bruny Islands. Adventure Bay, South Bruny Lighthouse and little penguins at The Neck Reserve are highlights.

◈ Cradle Mountain– Lake St Clair National Park

This World Heritage-listed national park is one of Tasmania's best-known and most popular attractions — deep, trout-filled lakes and bushwalks attract visitors from around the world.

◈ East Coast

The East Coast is where Tasmanians go for their holidays. A mild climate, surfing beaches, excellent fishing and spectacular scenic attractions make this region an ideal holiday destination.

◈ Flinders Island and King Island

Flanking Bass Strait's eastern and western sides, these islands are secluded and idyllic holiday destinations. Both islands are rich in colonial history.

◈ Launceston

Tasmania's second city, Launceston, is sometimes known as the 'Garden City' and offers museums, galleries, parks and gardens among its many attractions.

◈ Port Arthur

This infamous convict settlement is well preserved and maintained. Located past Eaglehawk on the Tasman Peninsula, it is a fascinating step back in time. The coastline itself is a physical reminder of the rugged and dramatic history of the port.

◈ Strahan

A former timber and copper mining town on Macquarie Harbour, Strahan is the West Coast at its prettiest and offers access to scenic Franklin-Gordon Wild Rivers NP.

a result, its society is not as multi-cultural as other states. The small Aboriginal population is actively involved in maintaining its cultural identity through language and land management projects.

Unlike most of Australia, Tasmania enjoys four distinct seasons, which are a perfect complement to the other attractions of the state. Magnificent scenery is provided on both the Cradle Mountain-Lake St Clair NP walks and the cruise on the Gordon River in the south-west. Historic villages that have hardly changed since the 1800s, together with convict-built bridges and old gaols, are reminders of colonial days. The wide variety of attractions make the smallest state the perfect holiday destination deserving of the epithet 'The Holiday Isle'.

Photo above: Cradle Mountain reflected in Dove Lake in winter, Cradle Mountain-Lake St Clair National Park

THE HOLIDAY ISLE

Abel Tasman, the Dutch explorer, called this island **Van Diemen's Land** when he sighted it in 1642; and the island's European colonisation began in 1803. The first settlement was at **Risdon**, now a suburb of **Hobart**. In 1830, the penal settlement of **Port Arthur** was built to house troublesome convicts. The living conditions were brutal, and the convicts suffered considerable hardship. Great hardship was visited too, on the original Aboriginal population, most of whom died out in the wake of European settlement.

Tasmania became a colony in its own right by breaking away from New South Wales in 1825, but continued to receive convicts until 1853. Free settlers were attracted by the island's rich farming land and because of its resemblance to Britain. Many of them established successful enterprises that continue to contribute to Tasmania's diverse rural economy. Today, agricultural enterprises cover around 30% of the state's total area. Beef cattle are farmed throughout the state, while sheep are found chiefly in the Midlands and south-east region and dairy cattle and pigs are run mainly in the north and north-west areas.

Apples and potatoes remain the most significant crops for the Tasmanian food industry, and in more recent years the state has become well-known for producing gourmet fare; dairy, meat and fish products. Tasmanian dairy foods, particularly those from **King Island**, enjoy a very high reputation. The **Tamar Valley** produces about 70% of the island's cool-climate wines. Many towns have fishing fleets which ensure that fresh seafood is nearly always available.

Tasmania has a good store of natural resources, particularly timber. Hardwood forests are established throughout the island, and plantations of softwood are also being planted. The wood is

The *Spirit of Tasmania* car-and-passenger ferries link Devonport with Melbourne and Sydney

used for building and construction as well as paper, wood pulp, hardboard and plywood. There are also rich mineral deposits of iron ore, scheelite, coal, zinc, tin, copper, silver and gold.

The state's economy is also boosted by a healthy tourist industry, worth millions of dollars per year and growing. This isn't surprising—visitor access to the island is easy. Options include fly-drive packages; the *Spirit of Tasmania* car-and-passenger ferries between **Melbourne** and **Devonport**; and the *Spirit of Tasmania III* car-and-passenger ship between **Sydney** and Devonport. Visitors can do a relatively comprehensive tour of the island in two weeks on well-surfaced roads (sometimes narrow and winding). Accommodation is plentiful with a special feature being the many quaint guesthouses offering B&B accommodation.

A lonely beach at Bay of Fires Conservation Area, near St Helens

Tasmania

Tourism Region Highlights

Australia's **'Natural State'**, the island of Tasmania crams a great many attractions into a small space. There are World Heritage-listed wilderness areas with spectacular scenery, historic towns, wineries, farms and dairies in a lush green landscape. The state's convict and colonial past is reflected at **Hobart**, the ruins of **Port Arthur** and **Sarah Island**. World-renowned national parks, such as **Cradle Mountain-Lake St Clair** attract bushwalkers, outdoor adventurers and anglers from all over the world.

A Hobart
Battery Point; Bonorong Park Wildlife Centre; Cascade Brewery; Nelson Signal Station; Mount Wellington; Old Hobart Gaol; Old Hobart Town Model Village; Richmond; Royal Tasmanian Botanical Gardens; Salamanca Place and Market; Tasmanian Museum and Art Gallery

B Central North and Cradle Mountain
Cradle Mountain; Deloraine; Devonport; Don River Railway; Latrobe's Axeman's Hall of Fame; Liffey Falls; Marakoopa Caves;

Meander Valley; Mole Creek; Narawntapu NP; Overland Track; Port Sorell; Sheffield murals

C Derwent Valley and Central Highlands
Australasian Golf Museum, Bothwell; Bushy Park; Hamilton; Lake St Clair; Mount Field NP; New Norfolk; Ouse; Salmon Ponds; Strathgordon; Russell Falls

D East Coast
Bicheno; Douglas-Apsley NP; Evercreech Forest Reserve; Freycinet NP; Maria Island; Orford; Swansea Bark Mill; The Hazards; Wineglass Bay

E Flinders Island
Strzelecki NP; Trousers Point; Wybalenna Historic Site

F Huon Valley and Bruny Island
Apple and Heritage Museum; Cockle Creek; Forest and Heritage Centre; Geeveston; Hartz Mountains NP; Hastings Caves; Huonville; Kettering

G King Island
Cape Wickham Lighthouse; Currie; Grassy; King Island Dairy; Lavinia Nature Reserve; Stokes Point

H Launceston and Tamar Valley
Cataract Gorge; Country Club Casino; Grubb Shaft Gold and Heritage Museum; National Automobile Museum; Penny Royal World; Planetarium; Platypus House; Queen Victoria Museum and Art Gallery; Seahorse World; Tamar Valley Wineries

I Midlands
Campbell Town; Clarendon Homestead; Evandale; Longford;

Russell Falls, Mount Field National Park

Oatlands; Ross Bridge; Tasmanian Wool Centre

J North East
Bay of Fires; Ben Lomond; Bridestowe Lavender Farm; Bridport; Derby Tin Mine Centre; Eddystone Point Lighthouse; Mount William NP; St Columba Falls; St Helens

K North West
Arthur River; Burnie; Cape Grim; Dip Falls; Rocky Cape NP; Stanley; The Nut; Waratah

L South East
Copping Colonial and Convict Collection; Port Arthur; Remarkable Cave; Sorell; Tasman Arch; Tasmanian Devil Park; Tessellated Pavement

M West Coast
Gordon River; Montezuma Falls; Mount Lyell Mine; Queenstown; Sarah Island; Strahan; Teepookana Plateau; West Coast Wilderness Railway; Zeehan

NATIONAL PARKS

From the wild waters and unchartered wilderness of the **West Coast** to the tranquillity of the **East Coast**, Tasmania's landscapes are just as diverse as those of mainland Australia. The state's national parks provide a glimpse of this environmental diversity, as well as an opportunity to relax, explore and appreciate the Tasmanian wilderness. Many unique animal and plant species, such as the Tasmanian devil and ancient Huon pines, are preserved in Tasmania's national parks and reserves.

For an introduction to Tasmania's unique wildlife, see p.450

facts

- No. of parks/reserves: 441
- Total area: 24 773km^2
- % of state: 36.38%
- World Heritage Areas: Macquarie Island, Tasmanian Wilderness

A Ben Lomond NP
(Map 481, G4)

A 1300m high plateau, Ben Lomond NP is Tasmania's main winter ski resort. Within the national park itself, there are eight ski tows, with cross-country skiing and other skiing amenities on offer. When the snow clears, the park is a popular destination for bushwalkers as well as picnicking day-trippers. The 165km^2 national park is not abundant with native wildlife (like other areas in the state), yet its unspoiled beauty is invigorating.

B Cradle Mountain-Lake St Clair NP
(Map 473, C3)

One of the most famous national parks in Tasmania, Cradle Mountain-Lake St Clair NP is a precious part of Australia's natural history and wilderness. World Heritage-listed, the national park offers spectacular scenery of rugged mountains, tree-filled gorges, glacial lakes, rainforests and moorlands. Sprawling across 1612km^2 in **Central North** Tasmania, Cradle Mountain-Lake St Clair NP is home to many of the state's unique animals, including the Tasmanian devil and quoll. With possibilities for fishing, walking, rockclimbing, canoeing, windsurfing, cycling and 4-wheel drive tours, the park is an exciting source of holiday escapism. With an accessible resort, backpacking and camping facilities, the park is well worth exploring.

C Franklin-Gordon Wild Rivers NP
(Map 483, D3)

Located 180km from Hobart, the 4463km^2 Franklin-Gordon Wild Rivers NP is home to Tasmania's longest river, the **Franklin**, as well as the **Collingwood**, **Gordon**, **Jane**, **Governor** and **Denison rivers**.

Myrtle beeches and Huon pine dominate the rainforests while elsewhere there are eucalypt forests, heaths, boglands and buttongrass plains. Access to the northern end of the park is via the Lyell Hwy. A 4-wheel drive track from **Queenstown**, requiring a permit, ends near the Franklin River. The best way to explore the surrounds is by foot; enjoying one of the many walks that depart from the Lyell Hwy. Cruises and float-planes depart from **Strahan** for the lower Gordon River.

D Freycinet NP **(Map 481, J6)**

Freycinet NP is a protected area of coastal heathland and white sand beaches washed by vibrant blue waters. Located on the **East Coast** of Tasmania, 180km southeast of Launceston, the 168km^2 national park boasts granite

Wilderness Seeker cruise on the Gordon River, Franklin-Gordon Wild Rivers National Park

Sunrise at Sleepy Bay, Freycinet National Park

mountain peaks, including **Amos**, **Dove** and **Mason**, which can be seen from any point within the park. The park offers coastal walking paths as well as summit climbs and bushwalking. Watersports are popular in the summer months, with fishing and cruising the main attractions. Worth exploring on walks are the perfect arc of **Wineglass Bay** and **Bluestone Bay**, a beach with bluish rocks, that some believe resemble dinosaur eggs. Campsites, youth hostels and B&Bs are all available for the weary explorer.

E Mount Field NP
(Map 484, D2)
Located 80km north-west of Hobart, this 159km² national park is Tasmania's oldest and home to the much photographed 40m-high **Russell Falls** and stands of magnificent **swamp gums** (*Eucalyptus regnans),* the world's tallest hardwood. King Billy and pencil pines, unique to Tasmania, are also found here.

F Mount William NP
(Map 481, J1)
In the north-east corner of the state, Mount William NP covers 184km² of heathland, beach and dry forest. Not as well known as other Tasmanian parks, Mount William is

home to some of the state's most pristine and beautiful beaches and a great variety of native flora and fauna. Swimming, surfing, diving and fishing are popular recreations, as are the coastal walks and the views from **Mount William**. Camping sites and picnic facilities are found throughout the park.

G Southwest NP
(Map 484, B4)
Bordered on one side by the **Southern Ocean**, Southwest NP is a region of unspoiled coastline, rivers, rainforest and mountains. Offering an array of activities for the visitor, the 6180km² national park is well-known for its wilderness drive, 82km of sealed road, which takes in the northern part of the park and much of the flora. The park can also be accessed via cruises and flights to **Bathurst Harbour**. There are a number of walking tracks and the trout fishing here is said to be the best in the country. Sailing and canoeing are popular activities in summer. There are several camp-sites and numerous picnicking spots scattered through the park.

H Walls of Jerusalem NP
(Map 480, B5)
Wild and unspoiled, Walls of Jerusalem NP, 90km south of Devonport, is dominated by a high plateau of dolerite peaks, conifer forests and alpine vegetation. Also part of the World Heritage Area and covering 518km², the park has no vehicle access, so it remains a destination for energetic and fit hikers, skiers and rockclimbers. Worth exploring are: **Solomon's Jewels** (a row of small lakes); **Herod's Gate** (two giant rocks which seem to create an entrance to **Lake Salome**) and the surrounding **West Wall** (300m); and **Mount Jerusalem** (1458m). There are no camping facilities in Walls of Jerusalem NP, however bush camping is allowed.

National Park Information

Parks and Wildlife Service Tasmania
PO Box 1751
Hobart, Tas 7001
Ph: 1300 135 513
www.parks.tas.gov.au

Unique Wildlife

Tasmania's isolation from the mainland has created a refuge, a preservation area, in which many animal species, some of which are now extinct on the mainland, have been able to thrive. As home to some of the country's most unusual wildlife, Tasmania is proud of its natural heritage and wilderness status.

Perhaps the best known of Tasmania's unique animals is the **Tasmanian devil** (*Sarcophilus harrisii*). Affectionately termed the **'Tassie devil'**, this little creature, generally the size of a small dog, is famous for its screeches, reputed bad temper and fierce looking mouth. With powerful jaws and teeth to devour its prey (bones, fur and all), the devil is the world's largest surviving carnivorous marsupial. It is thought to have become extinct on the mainland 600 years ago, but today is commonly seen in **Narawntapu NP**, **Mount William NP** and **Cradle Mountain-Lake St Clair NP**.

Although it is believed to be extinct, the **Tasmanian tiger** (*Thylacinus cynocephalus*) is a symbol of the state, now immortalised on the label of one of the state's leading beers, Cascade. The tiger was once widespread on the Australian continent, but after the arrival of the dingo 3500–4000 years ago, it gradually became extinct on the mainland. Feared by Tasmanian settlers, who blamed the creature for killing sheep, it was hunted to extinction. The last known Tasmanian tiger died in Beaumaris Zoo, Hobart on 7 September 1936. However, unsubstantiated sightings of the animal continue, particularly in the north of the state.

The **eastern quoll** (*Dasyurus viverrinus*), sometimes called the **native cat**, is considered rare on the mainland but found in abundance in Tasmania. Quolls feed on insects, small mammals and birds and are commonly found in **Mount Field NP**. The **red-bellied pademelon** or rufous wallaby (*Thylogale billardierii*) is a stocky creature with a short tail and legs. It makes its home in the thick vegetation of forests and rainforests during the day and is mainly nocturnal and solitary. Feeding mostly on herbs, green shoots and grasses, the pademelon is extinct on the mainland but found over most of Tasmania.

The eastern half of the state is home to the **Tasmanian bettong** (*Bettongia gaimardi*) of the kangaroo

The endangered Tasmanian wedge-tailed eagle (juvenile), *Aquila audax fleayi*

family. This small animal weighs on average 2kg, has grey-brown fur on its back and white fur below, and a grasping tail that it uses to carry nesting materials. Bettongs live in dry, open eucalypt forests and grassy woodlands, and feed on seeds, fungi, roots and small insects.

Extinct on the mainland, the **Tasmanian native hen** (*Gallinula mortierii*) is quite common on the island. The rare **ground parrot** (*Pezoporus wallicus*) is one of only three ground-dwelling parrots in the world. The **Tasmanian wedge-tailed eagle** (*Aquila audax fleayi*) has been isolated for 10 000 years from its smaller mainland counterparts and is viewed as a separate sub-species. However, with only 100 breeding pairs in Tasmania, the eagle is now considered endangered.

Tasmanian devil cubs, *Sarcophilus harrisii*

WINERIES

Tasmania was the second colony to develop a wine industry. In 1823 **Bartholomew Broughton** established his vineyard at **New Town**, north of **Hobart** and soon began producing quality wines—one of his wines won an award at the Paris Exhibition of 1848. Several Silesian immigrants also planted vineyards, but by 1890, the Tasmanian winemaking industry had virtually wound up, the general assumption being that the island was too cold and too wet for profitable grape growing.

In the late 1950s, however, this was repudiated by the success of **Claudio Alcorso's Moorilla vineyard** in the **Derwent Valley**. Today over 100 vineyards flourish in suitable microclimates throughout Tasmania, producing outstanding cool-climate wines. Visitors can enjoy hours of pleasure traversing the **Tasmanian Wine Routes** that have been drawn up from Hobart and **Launceston**.

A East Coast

The scenic coastline between **St Helens** and **Orford** is home to a number of wineries, linked by the **East Coast Gourmet Trail**. The family-owned vineyards produce prize-winning chardonnays and velvety, rich pinot noirs and cabernets.

B Hobart and Coal River

This historic gourmet food and wine region around the **River Derwent** and **Coal River** can be explored on the **Southern Tasmanian Wine Route**. Elegant local wines include pinot noir, riesling, chardonnay, sauvignon blanc, cabernet sauvignon, merlot, schonburger and gewurztraminer.

C Huon/Channel

The orchard region that gave Tasmania its 'Apple Isle' epithet also offers some attractive waterside wineries. Pinot noir, chardonnay, riesling, sauvignon blanc, semillon, pinot gris, cabernet sauvignon, sylvaner and methode champenoise sparkling wines can be sampled on the **Southern Tasmanian Wine Route**.

D North West

One of Tasmania's richest agricultural regions, the North West (which includes King Island) is famous for its magnificent cheeses. The area around **Sheffield**, en route to **Cradle Mountain** also produces fine wines to accompany them. Varieties include chardonnay, pinot noir, riesling, gewurztraminer and gamay.

E Pipers Brook

The rich, red soil region north-east from Launceston now accounts for 70% of Tasmania's wine production and the original Pipers Brook Vineyard is the state's largest. Poplar windbreaks protect the vines from westerly winds and provide a dazzling display of colour in

autumn. Wines include chardonnay, sauvignon blanc, pinot noir, riesling, pinot grigio, white frontignac, cabernets and semillon.

F Tamar Valley

Set between the **Tamar Estuary** and alpine peaks, this wine region is often considered the prettiest in Australia and, with Pipers Brook, forms the **Northern Tasmanian Wine Route**. Cabernets, chardonnay, pinot noir, pinot grigio and methode champenoise wines are the standout varieties.

Picnickers at Pipers Brook Vineyard

HOBART

Victoria Dock reflections

main attractions

◈ Battery Point
Hobart's oldest district was once home to sailors, fishermen, prostitutes and shipwrights. It is now a fashionable inner-city neighbourhood.

◈ Cadbury Chocolate Factory
Hobart is home to this well-known chocolate manufacturer—a tour of the factory at Claremont is a must for chocoholics.

◈ Cascade Brewery
Australia's oldest brewery produces some of the finest beer in the country. Tours of both the brewery and museum are available daily.

◈ Constitution Dock
The final destination for the annual Sydney to Hobart Yacht Race is part of Hobart's picturesque waterfront area.

◈ Royal Tasmanian Botanical Gardens
Established in 1818, these gardens house an extensive collection of native and exotic plants. Features include a cactus house, herb garden and Japanese garden.

◈ Runnymede
Set in tranquil gardens, this National Trust homestead was built in 1837. Open to the public, many items in the home are original and the rooms have been lovingly restored.

Founded in 1804 and declared a city in 1842, Hobart is rich in reminders of its colonial past. It is Australia's second-oldest city (after Sydney) and more than 90 of the city's buildings are National Trust-classified.

Hobart is nestled on the western shore of the **River Derwent** and at the foot of **Mount Wellington**, which is often snowcapped in the winter months. There are panoramic vistas of the city available from the mountain's superb lookouts.

Like most Australian capitals, Hobart's lifestyle is defined by water; it is a riverside city with a bustling harbour, surrounded by picturesque harbourside warehouses. The harbour remains integral to the city's economy. Only metres from the business district are the docks where overseas ships moor, supplies are loaded for Australia's Antarctic bases and fishing vessels return with their catch. The waterfront area is the focal point for visitors to Hobart, as it is the site for many of the city's tourist attractions.

 Visitor information

Tasmanian Travel and Information Centre
20 Davey Street, Hobart, Tas 7000
Ph:(03) 6230 8233
Freecall: 1800 990 440
www.discovertasmania.com.au

facts

- ◈ Population: 218 000
- ◈ Date founded: 1804
- ◈ Tallest building: AMP Building
- ◈ Average temperature:
  17°C (January), 9°C (June)

Places of Interest

Allport Library and
Museum of Fine Arts (A) C4
Anglesea Barracks (B) C4
Battery Point (C) D4
Cascade Brewery (D) A5
Elizabeth Mall (E) C4
Government House (F) C2
Maritime Museum of Tasmania (G) C4
Narryna Heritage Museum (H) C4
Parliament House (I) C4
Princes Park (J) D4
Rosny Hill Lookout (K) E2
Royal Tasmanian Botanical Gardens (L) C2
Runnymede (M) B1
St David's Park (N) C4
Salamanca Place and Markets (O) C4
State Library of Tasmania (P) C4
Sullivans Cove (Q) C4
Tasmanian Museum and Art Gallery (R) C4
Wrest Point Hotel and Casino (S) D6

Wrest Point Hotel and Casino at Sandy Bay, Hobart

Continued on map 456

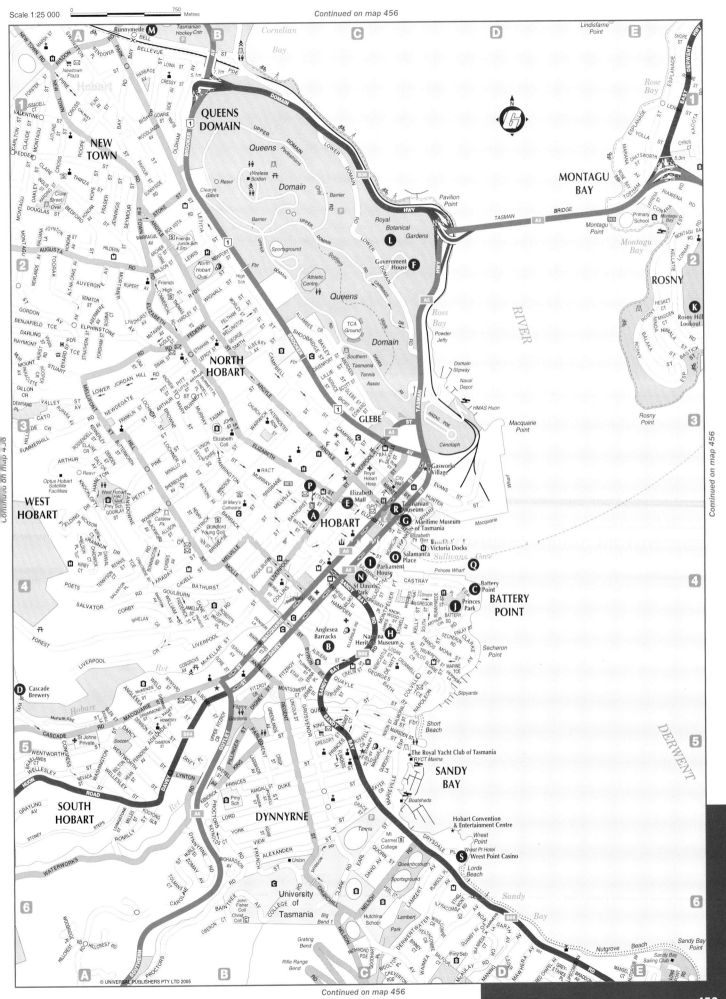

Continued on map 456

CBD & SUBURBS

CBD ATTRACTIONS

Most of Hobart's attractions are concentrated in a relatively small area within easy walking distance of **Sullivans Cove** and **Constitution Dock**. Close to the northern end of the Cove, **Gasworks Village** has shops and restaurants in restored 19th-century buildings. A stroll along Campbell St takes you to the **Theatre Royal**, built in the 1830s, and the **Penitentiary Chapel** at the **Criminal Courts**, where guided tours (including ghost tours) are conducted. Opposite Constitution Dock is the **Tasmanian Museum and Art Gallery**. The museum explores Tasmanian identity with a variety of displays covering history, science and the natural environment. The art collection focuses on colonial art, contemporary Australian painting and changing exhibitions. Hobart's Italianate **Town Hall** is close by. The **Maritime Museum of Tasmania**, in the same area, displays historic vessels, shipwreck relics, whaling implements, paintings, photographs and models. Further down Davey St, a walk along Murray St will take you past **St David's Cathedral** to the **Allport Library and Museum of Fine Arts**, part of the **State Library of Tasmania** complex. Tours can be made of Australia's only commercial whisky distillery in Davey Street.

At the southern end of Sullivans Cove, ferries and cruises depart from **Brooke St Pier** on **Franklin Wharf**. **Salamanca Place** is an excellent example of how Hobart's historic buildings have been preserved to play a vital part in city life. Sandstone merchant warehouses from the 1830s are now used as restaurants, shops and galleries. On Saturdays, traffic is blocked off to make way for **Salamanca Market**, a colourful collection of 300 stalls selling all manner of things. Connected to Salamanca Place by **Kellys Steps**,

Battery Point is another historic section of Hobart with heritage buildings such as the ring of houses at **Arthur Circus**. Two further attractions in the Battery Point area are **'Narryna' Heritage Museum**, in a beautiful Georgian building built in 1833–36 by sea captain Andrew Haig; and **Anglesea Barracks**, the oldest military establishment in Australia still in use (tours on Tuesdays or by appointment).

SUBURBAN ATTRACTIONS

Hobart's boundary extends to the foot of **Mount Wellington** in the west—certainly the city's most prominent landmark. From the top of the mountain the view of the city and surrounding countryside is breathtaking, and on very clear days it is possible to see parts of the south-west corner of the state. Walk, drive or cycle the paths of the mountain to get a dramatic view of the landscape. Walkers should be prepared for sudden weather changes and the peak is often covered in snow in winter.

After an exploration of the mountain views, a stop at **Cascade Brewery** near Mount Wellington is highly recommended. The brewery is known for premium quality beer and, established in 1832, is the oldest in Australia. Tours are available of the brewery and attached museum, as well as the adjoining **Woodstock Gardens**.

North of the city, the **Royal Tasmanian Botanical Gardens** have many interesting features, including the conifer collection, fernery, Japanese Garden, historic Arthur Wall, Conservatory, Subantarctic House and a Chinese section. The

Battery Point, one of Hobart's oldest districts

The world-famous Sydney to Hobart Yacht Race has occurred annually since 1949 and is now considered a premier event on the international yachting circuit. The gun fires at **Rushcutters Bay**, **Sydney** at 1pm each Boxing Day. Thousands of Sydneysiders fight for a glimpse of the boats as they sail out of **Sydney Harbour**. The boats' arrival into Hobart, generally just before New Year's Day, is a charged occasion, with thousands of locals and visitors turning out to see the yachts sail up the **River Derwent estuary**. With the tension of the race over, traditional champagne celebrations are unleashed as the fleet rests at **Constitution Dock**. The **Taste of Tasmania** (part of the **Hobart Summer Festival**) is also held on the dock to coincide with the conclusion of the race.

Maxi yacht *Brindabella* nearing the finish line of the 1997 Sydney to Hobart Yacht Race

restored National Trust homestead, **Runnymede**, can be found at **New Town** and the **Cadbury Chocolate Factory** at **Claremont** can be reached by road or cruise from Hobart. Tours offer visitors the chance to see the factory's chocolate-making process and to taste samples along the way. Chocolate can be bought afterwards by those who have completed the tour. Bookings are essential and enclosed footwear must be worn. Not far away, **Alpenrail** provides a unique alpine experience with a model railway running through a realistic Swiss model village. At **Brighton**, 25 minutes drive north of Hobart, **Bonorong Wildlife Park** has Tasmanian devils, koalas, common wombats, eastern quolls and native birds as well as kangaroos which are free to roam the park.

On the other side of the Derwent River is **Risdon Cove Historic Site**, where Hobart's first European settlement began (not open to the public). Also on the eastern side are **Cambridge Aerodrome**, **Rosny Hill Lookout** and **Hobart Airport**. Visitors are welcome at the **Royal Hobart Golf Course** as well as the **Tasmanian**, **Airport** and **Llanherne** courses. There are a number of pretty beaches on both sides of the Derwent and **Clifton Beach** is a popular summer-surfing destination.

Located south of the CBD in **Sandy Bay**, the convention and entertainment centre at **Wrest Point** is the site of Australia's first gambling casino. **Wrest Point Casino** not only provides gaming such as roulette, blackjack, poker, keno and electronic gambling, but also offers hotel and motel accommodation, restaurants and bars, nightclubs and shops. Sandy Bay is also home to Tasmania's university and the prestigious **Royal Yacht Club of Tasmania**, where hundreds of yachts are moored.

In the Lower Sandy Bay area, there are lookouts near **Long Beach** and at **Mount Nelson Signal Station Reserve** with Derwent estuary views. Further south are **Truganini Reserve**, dedicated to the last full-blood Tasmanian Aborigine, and the convict-built **Shot Tower**, which provides a superb view of the Derwent estuary and includes a small museum. The **Australian Antarctic Division** is at **Kingston**.

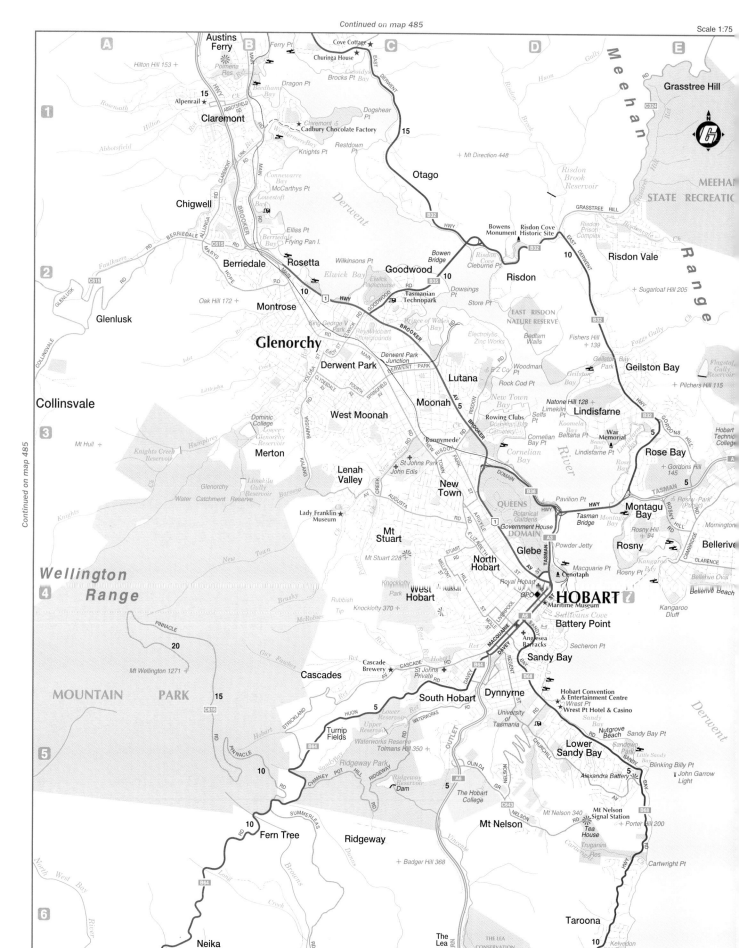

Scale 1:75

Austins Ferry

Ferry Pt

Cove Cottage

Churinga House

Cassidys
Brooks Pt Bay

Goodwood

Continued on map 485

Hilton Hill 153 +

Polmenia
Res

Alpenrail ★ 15

Claremont

Chigwell

Abbotsfield

Rosneath

Hilton

Faulkners Ck

Glenlusk

Collinsvale

Mt Hull +

Dragon Pt

Beedhams
Bay

Claremont 5
Cadbury Chocolate Factory

Restdown
Pt

Knights Pt

Connewarre
Bay

McCarthys Pt

Lowestoft
Bay

Elliss Pt

Berriedale
Bay

Frying Pan I.

Berriedale

Oak Hill 172 +

Montrose

Rosetta

Wilkinsons Pt

Elwick Bay

Elwick
Racecourse

10

Goodwood

Otago

+ Mt Direction 448

Dogshear
Pt

15

Bowens
Monument

Bowen
Bridge

Cleburne Rd

Risdon Cove
Historic Site

10

Risdon

Dowsings
Pt

Store Pt

Meehan

Grasstree Hill

MEEHAN
STATE RECREATIO

GRASSTREE HILL

Risdon
Brook
Reservoir

Risdon
Brook

10

Risdon Vale

+ Sugarloaf Hill 205

Risdon
Prison
Complex

Fishers Hill
+ 139

R
a
n
g
e

Glenorchy

Derwent Park

West Moonah

Merton

Dominic
College

Lower
Glenorchy
Reservoir

Glenorchy
Water Catchment Reserve

Lenah
Valley

Limekiln
Gully
Reservoir

King George V
Park

Royal Hobart
Showgrounds

Tasmanian
Technopark

Derwent Park
Junction

Lutana

Moonah

'Runnymede'

'New Town Rd'

St Johns Park +
John Edis

Lady Franklin
Museum ★

Mt
Stuart

Mt Stuart 228 +

New
Town

North
Hobart

Prince of Wales
Bay

Electrolytic
Zinc Works

5 EZ Co

Woodman
Pt

Rock Cod Pt

New Town
Bay

Selfs Pt

Cornelian Bay
Cemetery

Cornelian
Bay Pt

Cornelian Bay

EAST RISDON
NATURE RESERVE

Bedlam
Walls

Geilston Bay

Lindisfarne

Natone Hill 128 +

War
Memorial

Koomela
Bay

Lindisfarne
Bay

Beltana Pt

Lindisfarne Pt

Geilston
Bay

Geilston Bay
Park

+ Pilchers Hill 115

Flagstaff
Gully
Reservoir

Rose Bay

+ Gordons Hill
145

Hobart
Technical
College

Rosny
Park
(Public)

5

5

River

Rowing Clubs

QUEENS
DOMAIN

Botanical
Gardens
Government House

Glebe

Pavilion Pt

Tasman
Bridge

HOBART

Montagu
Bay

Rosny

Bellerive

Mornington

Bellerive Oval

CLARENCE

Rosny Hill
+ 94

Rosny Pt

Kangaroo
Bay

CAMBRIDGE RD

Bellerive Beach

Kangaroo
Bluff

Wellington
Range

Knocklofty
Park

Knocklofty 370 +

West
Hobart

Rubbish
Tip

McRobies

Brushy

New Town

Maritime Museum

Royal Hobart

GPO ◆

Sullivans Cove

Macquarie Pt
Cenotaph

Powder Jetty

Battery Point

Anglesea
Barracks

Secheron Pt

MOUNTAIN   *PARK*

20

Mt Wellington 1271 +

15

PINNACLE

Cascades

Cascade
Brewery

St Johns
Private

South Hobart

Sandy Bay

Dynnyrne

University
of Tasmania

Hobart Convention
& Entertainment Centre

Wrest Pt Hotel & Casino
★ Wrest Pt

Sandy
Bay

Sandy Bay Pt

Lower
Sandy Bay

Nutgrove
Beach

Sandown
Park

Little Sands

Blinking Billy Pt

John Garrow
Light

Turnip
Fields

Lower
Reservoir

Upper
Reservoir

Waterworks Reserve
Tolmans Hill 350 +

5

Ridgeway Park

Ridgeway

Ridgeway
Reservoir

Dam

5

The Hobart
College

Mt Nelson

+ Badger Hill 368

Mt Nelson 340

Alexandra Battery

Mt Nelson
Signal Station

Tea
House

+ Porter Hill 200

Truganini
Res

Cartwright Pt

Derwent

Fern Tree

10

15

Neika

North West Bay

SOUTHERN

The
Lea

THE LEA
CONSERVATION
AREA

Vincents

Taroona

10

Kelvedon
Park

Taroona
Park

Crayfish Pt

Taroona   Beach

Tasmania

3 Kilometres

F

G

H

J

Penna

K
TASMAN HWY
ARTHUR HWY

Sorell

B31
20

RICHMOND RD

Pigeon Hole Rd

& Sorell
Frogmore Peninsula

Orielton Lagoon

25

1

Susie Islet

Oaks Pt

Midway Point

RD

CAUSEWAY

A3

+ Craigow Hill 395

& Richmond

Railway Pt

20

Pittwater Bluff

Water

Woody I.

Barren I.

2

15

RD

TASMAN

SORELL

PITTWATER

Five

Mile

McKays Hill

RICHMOND RD

Barilla Bay

Mile

Beach

A3

SEVEN MILE BEACH PROTECTED AREA

+ Simmons Hill

CAMBRIDGE RD

KENNEDY RD

Cambridge DR

Cambridge Aerodrome

HWY

HOLYMAN

Bureau of Meterology

Hobart Airport

Beach

gstaff Hill

B31

TASMAN

A3

ACTON

15

C330

Hobart Airport &

AV

RD

Mile

3

+ Canopus Hill 265 **Observatory**

Llanherne &

Seven

Tunnel Hill 270 +

CAMBRIDGE

10

RD

MOUNT RUMNEY

C329

C328

Royal Hobart &

RD

SURF RD

Mile

Lilian Martin Home
B33
Mornington

HWY

CAMBRIDGE

C329

+ Mt Rumney 337
Mt Rumney Lookout RD

ACTON RD

SEVEN MILE BEACH

Seven Mile Beach

Frederick

4

Flora Park

SOUTH ARM HWY

PASS

+ Knopwood Hill 350

Stockhill

Acton

C330

10

ST

HWY RD

Howrah

+ Glebe Hill 135

ROKEBY

Clarence Plains

Acton

RD

RD

Henry

Wentworth Park

Howrah Beach

B33

Claredon Vale

Girl Guides Campsite "Orana"

cond ff

Howrah Pt

TRANMERE

RD

River

Oakdowns

C330

Bay

5

Tranmere

Punchs Reef

Rokeby Hills

Rokeby

RD

Historic Church & Cemetery

ACTON RD

Lauderdale

Roches

15

SOUTH

Police Academy

ARM

RALPHS BAY COASTAL RESERVE

B93

Beach

Mays Pt

Tranmere Pt

Droughty Hill 152 +

Gibsons Pt

Rokeby Beach

Mill Pt

Haynes Pt

20

SOUTH ARM

Refuse Disposal Area

Maydena Bay

Clear Lagoon

Tollards Lagoon

Trywork Pt

6

Droughty Pt

Dixon Pt

Creek

B33 RD

Sandford

Ralphs Bay

F

G Huxleys Beach

H

25

J

Cremorne

K

© UNIVERSAL PUBLISHERS PTY LTD 2005

Continued on map 469

■ Beaconsfield POP 1020

Map 480, D2

An historic mining town 43km north-west of Launceston, Beaconsfield has a number of relics and ruins that are reminders of its gold-mining past. Gold was discovered at what was then called Cabbage Tree Hill in 1869. The mine closed in 1914, but gold fever has recently reignited with the reopening of the **Beaconsfield Gold Mine**.

MAIN ATTRACTIONS: **Grubb Shaft Gold and Heritage Museum** in West St features working models, gold-mining relics and displays. Opposite are the original **Flowery Gully schoolhouse** and a restored miner's cottage. The original Tasmania Bank (1880s) in Weld St is now **Van Diemen's Gallery**, selling locally made arts and crafts.

NEARBY ATTRACTIONS: **York Town monument** is 9km north at the site of the first European settlement in northern Tasmania. At **Sidmouth**, 13km east, are **Auld Kirk**, a church built in 1843 by free and convict labour. The 100m-high **Batman Bridge** was the world's first cable-stayed truss bridge. Nearby **Kayena** and **Rowella** wine-producing areas offer cellar door sales.

VISITOR INFORMATION: Tamar Visitor Centre, Main Rd, Exeter,
Ph: 1800 637 989

■ Beauty Point POP 1205

Map 480, D2

Beauty Point lies 48km north-west of **Launceston** on the **Tamar River**, and was originally established as a port for the Beaconsfield gold mine. The port facilities now service the **Australian Maritime College**.

MAIN ATTRACTIONS: This is a popular centre for fishing and yachting. A seahorse farm, the world's first, breeds common and endangered seahorses. These fascinating sea creatures can be viewed at **Seahorse World**, which also includes a restaurant and wine centre. The adjacent **Platypus House** displays Tasmanian platypus, frogs, lizards and various 'creepy-crawlies' and has a coffee shop, souvenirs and guided tours.

NEARBY ATTRACTIONS: The holiday destinations of **Kelso** and **Greens Beach** are to the north-west on **Port Dalrymple**. **Narawntapu NP**, 25km north-west, has exhilarating coastal walks and views.

VISITOR INFORMATION: Tamar Visitor Centre, Main Rd, Exeter,
Ph: 1800 637 989

Grubb Shaft Gold and Heritage Museum, Beaconsfield

Bicheno   POP 750

Map 481, J5

Bicheno is a popular resort and busy commercial fishing port 195km north-east of Hobart. It was a sealing and whaling town in the early 19th century, and later a centre servicing a nearby coal mine. Today, the main industries are shellfish culture, crayfishing and tourism.

MAIN ATTRACTIONS: Some of the marine life found in the clear waters around Bicheno can be seen at **Bicheno Sea Life Centre**. **Bicheno Penguin and Adventure Tours** has nightly tours of a nearby penguin rookery. A glass-bottom boat tours the sheltered waters of Bicheno's **Marine Park** and **Gulch**, providing close-up views of underwater life, including a spectacular kelp forest. The grave of **Waubedebar** can be seen near **Waubs Beach**. Waubedebar was an Aboriginal woman enslaved by sealers, some of whom she subsequently saved from drowning. Bicheno's attractive setting can be appreciated from **Whalers Lookout** off Foster St or the scenic foreshore walkway that runs from the **Blowhole** in the south all the way to **Redbill Point**.

NEARBY ATTRACTIONS: **East Coast Natureworld**, 8km north, exhibits Tasmanian fauna. **Freycinet, Coombend** and **Springvale vineyards** are south-west on the Tasman Hwy. Ocean views can be enjoyed from the lookout at **Douglas-Apsley NP**, 14km north-west.

VISITOR INFORMATION: Charles St and Esplanade West, Triabunna,
Ph: (03) 6257 4772

Bridport   POP 1275

Map 481, F1

Bridport, on Anderson Bay, 85km north-east of Launceston, developed as a port for the timber, agricultural and mining industries; it still retains its seaport atmosphere.

Fishing boats in The Gulch, Bicheno

MAIN ATTRACTIONS: Bridport is a popular holiday destination and visitors come for the pristine sandy beaches and excellent river and ocean fishing. **Bridport Wildflower Reserve** is at its best in spring when the plants are in full bloom.

NEARBY ATTRACTIONS: **Bowood Homestead** (1838), 8km west, and its magnificent gardens, are open by appointment and at selected times during the year. **Pipers Brook Vineyard,** the most recognised Tasmanian wine label, is 18km west. Bridport is an ideal base for exploring the rugged north-east coastline. **Flinders Island**, the largest of the **Furneaux Group** in Bass Strait, is accessible either by car ferry or light plane. This holiday island for the adventurous has beautiful beaches, unique wildlife, fishing, diving, bushwalks and **Strzelecki NP**, dominated by **Mount Strzelecki** (756m).

VISITOR INFORMATION: Forest EcoCentre, 96 King St, Scottsdale
Ph: (03) 6352 6520

Bruny Island   POP 600

Map 485, F5

Separated from the mainland by the **D'Entrecasteaux Channel**, Bruny Island is virtually two islands, **North** and **South Bruny**, joined by a strip

of sandhills. In the 17th and 18th centuries, the island was logged by notable explorers and navigators including Abel Tasman, Tobias Furneaux and James Cook. The island was an important 19th-century whaling station, but is now reliant on agriculture and tourism. Access to Bruny is via vehicular ferry from **Kettering** to **Roberts Point**.

MAIN ATTRACTIONS: Activities on the island include boating, fishing, scuba diving, kayaking and bush-walking. Wildlife and scenery can be enjoyed from walking tracks through five state reserves and **South Bruny NP**. Notable landmarks include the ruins of a convict-built church at **Variety Bay** (viewed on the **Cape Queen Elizabeth Walk**), old brick kilns and **South Bruny Lighthouse** (1836)— the second oldest in Australia. Little penguins and muttonbirds can be seen on the sandy isthmus. There is also a memorial to **Truganini**, the last full-blood Tasmanian Aborigine, who died in 1876. **Bligh Museum** at scenic **Adventure Bay** highlights the island's history, with a collection of early volumes on the voyages of Cook, Bligh and Flinders.

VISITOR INFORMATION: 81 Ferry Rd, Kettering, Ph: (03) 6267 4494

Perched above the east and west of Tasmania's north coast, Flinders and King islands were once centres of the long-banned sealing industry, but now support celebrated agricultural industries of their own.

Flinders Island is the largest in the **Furneaux Group**. Since its colonial settlement, the island has witnessed many changes: in the 1950s a Soldier/Farmer Settlement Scheme was initiated, leading to $336km^2$ of land being cleared and sown. The island is now an ideal place for tourists to escape the stresses of city life, offering many attractions, most of them natural and some man-made (or a combination of both such as wreck-diving).

King Island lies on the western edge of **Bass Strait** and covers 1260km². The mining of gold and tin were once the island's primary industries; this has shifted to dairy products of international repute, livestock farming, crayfishing, abalone harvesting and even kelp processing. With more than 145km of picturesque coastline and abundant natural attractions, King Island is an idyllic holiday destination.

History of King Island

The first European thought to have discovered this island was **Capt James Black**. He named it after Phillip King, the Governor of New South Wales in 1801. There were once thriving fur seal and sea-lion colonies, but these have suffered from extensive sealing and hunting in the past.

i Visitor information

Tasmanian Travel and Information Centre
20 Davey St,
Hobart, Tas 7000
Ph: (03) 6230 8233
Freecall: 1800 806 846
www.discovertasmania.com.au

Cape Barren goose, *Cereopsis novaehollandiae*, in Strzelecki National Park, Flinders Island

main attractions

Flinders Island   POP 900

◈ **Emita Museum**

This museum displays the history of various groups of pioneer settlers.

◈ **Logan Lagoon Wildlife Sanctuary**

This sanctuary has been included on the list of Wetlands of International Importance.

◈ **Strzelecki National Park**

This $422km^2$ park offers many recreational opportunities, including bushwalking.

◈ **Wybalenna**

An historic, culturally significant and tragic site for Tasmanian Aborigines who were settled here in the 1830s.

King Island   POP 1700

◈ **Cape Wickham Lighthouse**

Australia's tallest lighthouse was built in 1861 to guide travellers safely into the often stormy waters of Bass Strait.

◈ **King Island Dairy**

The world famous dairy was established in 1902 because dairy products were easier to transport than livestock.

◈ **Grassy**

Well-known for its little penguin rookery.

Southern rock lobsters, *Jasus novaehollandiae*, from King Island

Tasmania

Burnie   POP 18 250

Map 480, A1

Tasmania's fourth largest city is on the **North Coast** 148km north-west of Launceston. Its deepwater port has long served the silver mines of the west coast, but its recent prosperity is partially due to its location for **Australian Paper**, one of the state's largest enterprises.
MAIN ATTRACTIONS: The **Civic Centre** is the hub of tourist activity with an information centre, art gallery and **Burnie Pioneer Village**, a museum with a re-creation of Burnie as it was a century ago. The Pioneer Village features a variety of reconstructed small shops. The information centre books guided tours of the huge **Amcor paper mill** as well as the **Creative Paper Mill**. **Lactos Cheese Factory** welcomes visitors to its cheese-tasting centre in Old Surrey Rd. Views over the city are available from lookouts on **Mount St** and **Round Hill**. A loop walk around Burnie includes a waterfront boardwalk, the **Romaine Track**, and **Fernglade Recreation Reserve** on the **Emu River**, a good place to see platypus. There is a **Penguin Viewing** area and a **Penguin Interpretative Centre** behind the West Park football ground. **Burnie Market Train** connects the railway station with **Penguin Markets** and Ulverstone (two hours return).
NEARBY ATTRACTIONS: **Emu Valley Rhododendron Gardens**, 6km south off Cascade Rd, will delight garden lovers, as will the English-style **Annsleigh Gardens**, 9km south on Mount Rd (closed in winter). **Guide Falls** are the best known of several waterfalls near **Ridgley**, 17km south. **Guide Falls Alpaca Farm** is close by. **Upper Natone Forest Reserve**, 20km to the south, is a favourite picnic spot.
VISITOR INFORMATION: Civic Centre Precinct, Little Alexander St,
Ph: (03) 6434 6111

Campbell Town   POP 825

Map 481, G5

Campbell Town is 66km south-east of Launceston on the Midland Hwy. It was established as an early garrison town on the route between Hobart and Launceston, but its inhabitants were nevertheless harassed by three notorious bushrangers, Matthew Brady, Martin Cash and John Quigley. In 1820 Saxon merinos were introduced to the area, and Campbell Town is still renowned for fine wool and stud sheep, as well as beef cattle and timber.
MAIN ATTRACTIONS: There are many National Trust-classified buildings and sites that can be seen on a self-guided **heritage walk**, including **Campbell Town Inn** (1840) and convict-built **Red Bridge** (1837). In High St, there is a memorial to **Harold Gatty**, the first round-the-world flight navigator, and the **Heritage Highway Museum** showcases colonial history.
NEARBY ATTRACTION: **Lake Leake**, 30km east, is popular for trout fishing.
VISITOR INFORMATION: Heritage Highway Museum, 103 High St, Ph: (03) 6381 1353

Cygnet   POP 851

Map 485, F4

Cygnet is a small rural town at the head of **Port Cygnet**, 52km south-west of Hobart. Apple orchards and mixed farming are the main industries, with flower farms and wineries established in recent years.
MAIN ATTRACTIONS: Art and craft shops are worth visiting, and **Cygnet Guest House** in Mary St has woodcraft and an art gallery.
NEARBY ATTRACTIONS: Excellent beaches can be found at **Verona Sands**, **Randalls Bay** and **Eggs and Bacon Bay**. Other activities include boating, fishing, gem-fossicking and visiting orchards and wineries. Apple, pear and wattle blossoms colour the local landscape from September to October. The

spectacular free-falling **Pelverata Falls** are 20km north on Sandfly Rd. **Deepenings Woodturners**, at **Nicholls Rivulet** 10km east, make beautiful high-quality dolls, bowls and other items from Tasmanian timbers, especially sassafras.
VISITOR INFORMATION: Huon River Jet Boats, Esplanade, Huonville
Ph: (03) 6264 1838

Deloraine   POP 2180

Map 480, D3

Deloraine is a rich agricultural centre nestling in a valley encircled by **Quamby Bluff** and the **Great Western Tiers (Kooparoona Niara)** and renowned for its stunning scenery. Artists and craftspeople are attracted to the district.
MAIN ATTRACTIONS: **Deloraine Folk Museum** is housed in an old coaching inn (circa 1860), now part of the visitor centre complex. There are many other buildings of historic interest, including the attractive 1853 colonial building that is now **Bowerbank Mill Gallery**. The impressive *Yarns Artwork in Silk*, created by more than 300 people and depicting the area's history, hangs in the visitor centre.

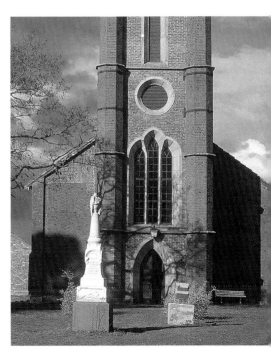

St Lukes Church (1839), Campbell Town

NEARBY ATTRACTIONS: At **Elizabeth Town**, 10km north-west, English-style cheeses can be sampled at **Ashgrove Farm** and raspberry products at **Christmas Hills Raspberry Farm**. A **honey factory**, **Trowunna Wildlife Park** and **Mole Creek Caves** (including the glow-worm filled **Marakoopa Cave** and **King Solomon's Cave**) are among the attractions around **Mole Creek**, 20km west. There are many pretty waterfalls in the district, including **Lobster Falls** (15km west), **Montana Falls** (9km south-west), **Meander Falls** in **Meander Forest Reserve** (22km south-west) and **Liffey Falls** (29km south). A scenic drive south through **Golden Valley** to the **Central Highlands** leads to **Great Lake**, where the trout fishing is excellent.

VISITOR INFORMATION: Great Western Tiers Visitor Centre, 98-100 Emu Bay Rd, Ph: (03) 6362 3471

■ Devonport   POP 22 410
Map 480, C2

The third largest city in Tasmania is a busy port for agricultural and industrial exports. As it has an airport and a ferry terminal for the *Spirit of Tasmania* from **Melbourne**, and the *Spirit of Tasmania III* from **Sydney**,

Rainforest creek at Liffey Falls, south of Deloraine

Devonport is the point of entry for many of the state's visitors.

MAIN ATTRACTIONS: **Bluff Lighthouse** (1889) stands on the dramatic **Mersey Bluff** beaming its light 27km out to sea. **Tiagarra Aboriginal Culture and Museum Centre** was established to preserve a superb collection of Aboriginal rock carvings. There are also a number of displays and over 2000 artefacts. Paintings by Australian artists are exhibited at the **Gallery and Arts Centre** in Stewart St. **Devonport Maritime Museum** off Victoria Pde illustrates shipping history with model ships, photographs and souvenirs. The house museum **Home Hill** (1916), administered by the National Trust, was the home of former Premier of Tasmania (1923–1928) and later Prime Minister, Joseph Lyons and Dame Enid Lyons. **Don River Railway and Museum** runs vintage and steam train trips seven days a week and has a large collection of railway memorabilia. A 7km walking and cycling track links the city with Mersey Bluff and the Don River Railway and Museum. **Imaginarium Science Centre**, in Macfie St, has hands-on interactive exhibits for families to enjoy.

NEARBY ATTRACTIONS: **Braddon's Lookout**, 9km west near **Forth**, has panoramic coastal views. The **Tasmanian Arboretum**, 10km south at **Eugenana**, has tree plantings representing different geographic areas of the world. It also offers picnic facilities around a picturesque lake inhabited by swans and shy platypus.

VISITOR INFORMATION: 92 Formby Rd, Ph: (03) 6424 8176

■ Eaglehawk Neck   POP 220
Map 469, D4

Eaglehawk Neck sits on the very narrow isthmus that separates **Tasman** and **Forestier peninsulas**. In convict times it was blockaded by police, soldiers and a line of chained savage dogs to prevent escape from **Port Arthur** penal settlement. It is now known as a fishing spot, with a tuna-fishing fleet operating from **Pirates Bay**.

MAIN ATTRACTIONS: A museum in the restored **Officers Quarters**, in Pirates Bay Dr, tells the story of Port Arthur escapee, bushranger Martin Cash. A bronze sculpture marks the site of the infamous dogline.

NEARBY ATTRACTIONS: Sailing and sightseeing charters are popular in Pirates Bay. Enquire at the visitor centre. Many of the attractions of the two peninsulas are close by. The **Tessellated Pavement**, looks man-made, yet it results from the earth's movement and wave erosion. **Pirates Bay Lookout** is just a little further north. Some of the most striking formations of **Tasman NP** are about 4km to the south: **Tasman Blowhole**, **Tasman Arch** and **Devil's Kitchen**. There is a coastal walking track in Tasman NP from **Waterfall Bay** to **Fortescue Bay**. **Tasmanian Devil Park and Wildlife Rescue Centre** is 12km south-west on the road to Port Arthur. **Port Arthur Historic Site** is 21km to the south-west.

VISITOR INFORMATION: Officers Mess, Pirates Bay Dr, Ph: (03) 6250 3635

Contestants in Evandale's Penny Farthing Bicycle Race, held in February

Evandale POP 1095
Map 481, F4

Evandale is one of Australia's most beautifully preserved historic villages, with buildings dating to 1809. It lies in a delightful rural setting, 20km from Launceston, that has attracted notable artists such as John Glover and Tom Roberts.

MAIN ATTRACTIONS: There are numerous historic buildings in the village that can be admired on a self-guided **heritage walk**. **Evandale Community Centre** has displays of local significance, and most of the old shops now house quality art and craft galleries, cafes and restaurants. Evandale's famous **Penny Farthing Bicycle Race** in February attracts many visitors from interstate and overseas. The **Sunday Market** in **Falls Park** is very popular, as is the **John Glover Art Prize** for landscape painting, held in March.

NEARBY ATTRACTIONS: **Tasmanian Glassblowers** is one of several craft shops in the area. Recognised as one of Australia's great Georgian houses, **Clarendon** (1838), with its extensive formal gardens, is 11km south near **Nile**.

VISITOR INFORMATION: Community Centre, 18 High St, Ph: (03) 6391 8128

Exeter POP 870
Map 480, E2

Exeter, in a large fruit-growing and wine-producing area, lies 24km north-west of Launceston.

MAIN ATTRACTION: Historic **Exeter Bakery** has a wood-fired oven.

NEARBY ATTRACTIONS: To the south, **Rosevears** has extensive vineyards with tastings and cellar door sales. At **Waterbird Haven**, birds can be observed in their wetland habitat. **Notley Fern Gorge**, 11km south-west off Frankford Hwy, offers scenic walks in a pristine rainforest reserve. **Brady's Lookout**, 5km south-east, once used by bushranger Matthew Brady, has panoramic views of the **Tamar Valley** and its farmlands.

VISITOR INFORMATION: Tamar Visitor Centre, Main Rd, Ph: 1800 637 989

Geeveston POP 845
Map 484, E4

Geeveston developed as a business centre for the timber industry based on the eucalypts and rainforests of its rugged hinterland. It is also a gateway to Tasmania's **Southwest World Heritage Area**.

MAIN ATTRACTIONS: The **Forest and Heritage Centre** presents a vibrant window on the local timber industry, with visual and interactive displays. **Hartz Gallery** exhibits antique machinery and the works of local craftspeople. **Geeveston Highlands Salmon and Trout Fishery** allows fly-fishing sport for Atlantic salmon, rainbow and brown trout on a catch-and-release basis.

NEARBY ATTRACTIONS: There are picnic and BBQ facilities at **Arve River** (10km) and **Tahune Forest Reserve** (27km), accessible from Arve Rd to the west. **Tahune Forest AirWalk**, 570m long and up to 45m above the ground, provides unique views of the forest canopy. Other highlights of this area include **Keoghs Creek Walk**, **Big Tree Lookout**, **West Creek Lookout**, **Zig Zag Walk** and **Huon Pine Walk**. **Hartz Mountains NP**, 23km south-west, offers birdwatching, walking trails to waterfalls and glacial tarns, wildflowers and the splendid **Waratah Lookout**. **Huon River Cruises** operate daily from **Point Huon**, 4km north-east, visiting Atlantic salmon fish farms along the way.

VISITOR INFORMATION: Forest and Heritage Centre, Church St, Ph: (03) 6297 1836

George Town POP 4570
Map 480, D2

Situated at the mouth of the **Tamar River** and bordering Bass Strait, George Town is the oldest town (1811) in the north of the island. It is an important commercial centre today, mainly due to the large industrial plants at **Bell Bay**.

MAIN ATTRACTIONS: A monument on the **Esplanade** honours Lieutenant Colonel William Paterson, whose ship was driven ashore in 1804. **The Grove**, a mansion built in 1830, was a port officer's residence; it is open to the public daily.

NEARBY ATTRACTIONS: Tours are available of the **Comalco Aluminium Smelter** and **TEMCO Ferro Alloy Plant** at **Bell Bay**, 6km south. The rural hamlet of **Hillwood**, 24km south-east, is known for its fruit, gourmet products and cottage industries. A lookout at **Mount George**, 1km east, gives views over the town. Further east are the vineyards of the **Pipers Brook region**. There are beautiful beaches at **Low Head**, a village 5km north. The **Pilot Station and Maritime Museum** has operated continuously since 1805; existing buildings date from 1835. Visits can be made to the nearby lighthouse, and also to a little penguin colony. There are cruises to an **Australian fur seal colony** at the Tamar River mouth.

VISITOR INFORMATION: Cnr Main Rd and Victoria St, Ph: (03) 6382 1700

■ Huonville   POP 1775

Map 484, E4

Huonville is the commercial centre for the **Huon Valley** fruit-growers, with apples available year-round; and cherries, blueberries, strawberries and raspberries in season. Dairy farming and Atlantic salmon fish farming are also important.

MAIN ATTRACTIONS: The **Huon River** provides a venue for watersports and trout fishing. Visitors can ride the Huon River in jet boats over rapids to **Glen Huon**, 12km west.

NEARBY ATTRACTIONS: Fruit can be bought in season from roadside stalls and at pick-your-own-fruit farms. Apples carved into character heads are novelties at **Glen Huon's Appleheads Village**. **Huon Apple and Heritage Museum** at Grove, 6km north-east, displays an astonishing 500 varieties of apples. **The Apple Valley Arts and Crafts Centre**, on the same road, incorporates **Tudor Court Model Village** (formerly at Hobart), **German Model Train World** and a cafe. **Snowy Ranges Trout Fishery**, 25km north-west from Huonville, allows anglers to catch their own trout from a series of ponds

VISITOR INFORMATION: Huon River Jet Boats, Esplanade, Ph: (03) 6264 1838

Gunpowder Mill, Penny Royal World, Launceston

■ Latrobe   POP 2770

Map 480, C2

This historic township dates from 1851 and its 19th-century streetscapes give it plenty of character. Located a 15 minute drive from **Bass Strait Searoad Terminal** and **Devonport Airport**, it is an ideal base for discovering the attractions of northern Tasmania.

MAIN ATTRACTIONS: Old buildings, many National Trust-classified, have been rejuvenated as restaurants, boutiques and antique galleries. Local history is conserved at the **Court House Museum** with prints and artefacts on display. **Bells Parade Park** is a delightful riverside picnic spot on the **Mersey River**. The shingle-roofed pioneer house **Sherwood Hall** can be inspected here. The **Australian Axemans Hall of Fame**, celebrating Tasmanian woodchopping achievements, is nearby. **Teddy Sheean Memorial Walk** is accessed from Gilbert St and guided platypus-viewing tours are available at dawn and dusk. One of Australia's most important cycling carnivals is held at Latrobe every Christmas.

NEARBY ATTRACTIONS: **Henry Somerset Orchid Reserve** is 7km south. The rural hinterland is an ever-changing tapestry of colour, with paddocks of vegetables, grains, cereals, tulips, sweet peas, pyrethrum and poppies.

VISITOR INFORMATION: 48 Gilbert St, Ph: (03) 6421 4699

■ Launceston   POP 68 250

Map 480, E3

Tasmania's second largest city is located in scenic countryside at the headwaters of the **Tamar River**. This garden city is the perfect base for exploring northern Tasmania.

MAIN ATTRACTIONS: The famous **Cataract Gorge** on the **South Esk River**, with its adjacent reserves, is close to the city. Attractions here include a chairlift and suspension bridge, historic **King's Bridge** (1867), floral and peacock gardens, walking trails and views. **Penny Royal World** is an impressive tourist development near Cataract Gorge. Attractions include tramway rides, an early 19th-century gunpowder mill, cannon foundry, arsenal, underground armoury and windmill in a landscaped setting. Opposite is a gallery in historic **Ritchie's Mill**. The *Tamar Odyssey*, which leaves from nearby **Home Point**, offers river cruises. Launceston city centre has very attractive streetscapes including **Yorktown Square**, which is a quaint shopping centre designed to echo the past, and **Princes Square** with its magnificent baroque fountain. The **Old Umbrella Shop** in George St is a genuine period shop preserved by the National Trust. Colonial history and art can be explored at **Queen Victoria Museum and Art Gallery** in Wellington St, and a range of classic cars can be admired at the **National Automobile Museum** in Cimitiere St. **City Park** has shady lawns, a conservatory, duck pond and monkey island. Just over the Tamar St Bridge is the **Inveresk Railyard** redevelopment, a focal point for arts and events, including the **Esk Market** on Sundays.

NEARBY ATTRACTIONS: **Trevallyn Dam**, 6km west, is a picnic spot with an exhilarating but safe cable hang-gliding facility close by. Fly-fishing lessons are available at **Launceston Lakes Trout Fishery**, 17km west. Launceston's **Country Club Casino** is 7km south-west. Tours can be made of **Waverley Woollen Mills**, 5km east. Three National Trust historic houses are within easy driving distance: **Entally House**, 18km south-west at **Hadspen**; **Franklin House**, 6km south; and **Clarendon**, 28km south-east near Nile. The **Northern Tasmanian Wine Route** winds its way to the **Tamar Valley** and **Pipers Brook**

Callington Flour Mill (1837), Oatlands

vineyard regions **Grindelwald Swiss Village**, also to the north, is about a 15 minute drive away. During winter, skiers head for the alpine village in **Ben Lomond NP**, 60km south-east, but the park is worth visiting at any time.

VISITOR INFORMATION: Cnr St John St and Cimitiere St, Ph: (03) 6336 3133 or 1300 655 145

Longford   POP 2840
Map 480, E4

One of Tasmania's oldest towns, Longford was established in 1813 by settlers from Norfolk Island. Now it is the centre for a fertile agricultural district.

MAIN ATTRACTIONS: There are many historic buildings, some convict-built. **Christ Church** (1839) has beautiful stained-glass windows and is surrounded by pioneer graves. **The Village Green** is a popular picnic and BBQ spot.

NEARBY ATTRACTIONS: **Brickendon**, an 1824 homestead 2km south, is now a working farm village. **Woolmers**

Estate (circa 1816) 5km south-east, has a rose garden, colonial cottages, tearooms and guided tours.

VISITOR INFORMATION: Council Offices, 13 Smith St, Ph: (03) 6397 7303

Mole Creek   POP 260
Map 480, C3

Mole Creek is located 74km south of Devonport, nestled at the foot of the **Great Western Tiers (Kooparoona Niara)**. It is in the heart of the surrounding farming and forestry district.

MAIN ATTRACTIONS: **Stephen's Honey Factory** in Pioneer Dr specialises in honey from a leatherwood tree unique to this area. The unusual labyrinthine **Wychwood Gardens**, in Den Rd, are open Thursday to Saturday (closed in winter).

NEARBY ATTRACTIONS: **Mole Creek Karst NP** has several spectacular limestone caves, of which the best known are **Marakoopa Cave**, 13km west, which has a wonderful glow-worm display; and **King Solomon Cave**, 16km west. Guided tours of these caves as well as to wild undeveloped caves, are available. **Devils Gullet**, 40km south-east, is an impressive natural lookout over **Fisher River Valley**. **Trowunna Wildlife Park** is 4km east and **Alum Cliffs Gorge** 3km north-east. Experienced bushwalkers head for **Walls of Jerusalem NP**, 45km south-west.

VISITOR INFORMATION: Mole Creek Guest House, 100 Pioneer Dr, Ph: (03) 6363 1399

New Norfolk   POP 5249
Map 484, E3

This historic town, 33km north-west of Hobart on the **Derwent River**, was pioneered around 1808 by Norfolk Island free settlers. The district produces most of the hops used by Australian breweries, although the main industry in the region is paper manufacture.

MAIN ATTRACTIONS: New Norfolk has many fine examples of colonial architecture, including **Bush Inn** (1815), **Old Colony Inn** (1835), now a museum, and **St Matthew's Church** (1823), reputedly the state's oldest church. Local attractions also include **Denmark Hill** (1830) and **Rosedown Gardens** (1840), which feature over 1000 roses. **The Oast House** is the only hops museum in Australia. Jet boats leave daily for the **Derwent River rapids** and **Derwent Valley Railway** has several excursions every month. There is a scenic lookout at **Peppermint Hill.** Browsers will enjoy the **Drill Hall Markets** in Stephen St, Tuesday through to Saturday.

NEARBY ATTRACTIONS: Group tours of the newsprint mills at **Boyer**, 5km east, can be arranged in advance. **Salmon Ponds**, 11km north-west, at **Plenty**, is where rainbow and brown trout were first bred in Australia. The complex includes a restaurant and **Museum of Trout Fishing**. **Mount Field NP**, 40km north-west, features spectacular mountain scenery and the much-photographed **Russell Falls**.

VISITOR INFORMATION: Circle St, Ph: (03) 6261 3700

Oatlands   POP 592
Map 485, F1

The historic lakeside township of Oatlands, 84km north of Hobart, was proclaimed by Governor Macquarie in 1827.

MAIN ATTRACTIONS: The Georgian sandstone buildings are a big attraction and there are 87 of them in **High St** alone! The convict-built **Court House** (1829), **St Peters Church** (1888), **St Pauls Church** (1850) and **Callington Flour Mill** (1837) are notable. Extra local colour is provided on evening 'ghost' tours by lantern light. **Dulverton Wildlife Sanctuary** is a lakeside picnic and camping reserve. There are several antique and craft shops in Oatlands.

The Guard Tower, Port Arthur Historic Site

NEARBY ATTRACTIONS: **Jericho**, 13km south, has convict-built mud walls and the remains of a convict probation station. The cemetery has a memorial to **John Hutton Bisdee**, the first Australian to be awarded the Victoria Cross. Trout fishing is available at **Lake Sorell**, 29km north-west, and the adjacent **Lake Crescent**.

VISITOR INFORMATION: 85 High St, Ph: (03) 6254 1212

Orford   POP 461

Map 469, D1

In 1825 the **East Coast** town of Orford was a shore station servicing whalers, the local garrison and the penal settlement on **Maria Island**. It is now a holiday and fishing resort.

MAIN ATTRACTIONS: Boating, fishing and swimming are popular activities. Scuba divers are attracted to the clear waters of **Prosser Bay** and

sandy swimming beaches are within easy walking distance. A scenic walking track from **Shelly Beach** to **Spring Beach** passes old sandstone quarries.

NEARBY ATTRACTIONS: The scenic **Wielangta Forest Drive** provides a link to the **Tasman Peninsula**, passing the **lookout** over **Mercury Passage** and Maria Island, and the blue gum forest at **Sandspit River Reserve**.

VISITOR INFORMATION: Charles St and Esplanade West, Triabunna, Ph: (03) 6257 4772

Penguin   POP 3100

Map 480, B2

Penguin developed in the late 19th century as an iron-ore mine and timber town, shipping timber throughout Australia and New Zealand. It was named after the little penguin rookeries that are common along the coast.

MAIN ATTRACTIONS: BBQs and duck ponds are located in **Hiscutt Park**, which also features a Dutch windmill. The much-photographed **Big Penguin** and two National Trust classified churches are in **Main St**. A miniature railway runs along the foreshore on the second and fourth Sunday each month. Little penguin viewing tours are conducted nightly by appointment September–March.

NEARBY ATTRACTIONS: There are magnificent views from the summit of **Mount Montgomery**, 5km south. **Ferndean Glow Worm Cave**, 6km south, has a BBQ area and walks to the hop fields of **Gunns Plains**. **Pioneer Park**, 10km south at **Riana**, offers gardens and walks. The **Old Bass Hwy** between Penguin and **Ulverstone** has scenic views of the rugged coastline including the **Three Sisters** which are offshore islands with seabird sanctuaries. There are 3km of attractive **flower gardens** along the route.

VISITOR INFORMATION: 78 Main St, Ph: (03) 6437 1421

Port Arthur   POP 215

Map 469, C5

Sited on the beautiful but remote **Tasman Peninsula**, historic Port Arthur was one of Australia's most infamous penal settlements from 1830 to 1877. (see pp.468-469)

MAIN ATTRACTIONS: **Port Arthur Historic Site** has more than 30 sandstone buildings, ruins and sites open for inspection. These include the church, penitentiary, model prison, asylum, guard tower and period-furnished houses. The visitor centre has an interpretation gallery and restaurant and takes bookings for the popular evening **ghost tours**. Daily cruises are available on the harbour and to the **Isle of the Dead**, the island's cemetery.

NEARBY ATTRACTIONS: There is a nature walk to nearby **Stewarts Bay**. **Coal Mines Historic Site** is 30km north-west. **Palmers Lookout**, 3km south, has views over the harbour and coastline. **Remarkable Cave** is 6km south in rugged **Tasman NP**.

VISITOR INFORMATION: Historic Site, Arthur Hwy, Ph: (03) 6251 2310 or 1800 659 101

Port Sorell   POP 1910

Map 480, C2

Port Sorell, together with **Hawley** and **Shearwater** form a holiday resort 18km east of Devonport. It was one of the first towns established on Tasmania's wild **North Coast**.

MAIN ATTRACTIONS: Fishing, sailing, boating and waterskiing are popular on the beautiful estuary. There are walking tracks and picnic facilities in the reserve beside **Freers Beach** and views over the town from **Watch House Hill**, off Meredith St.

NEARBY ATTRACTIONS: **Hawley Beach** has safe swimming, good fishing and historic **Hawley House** (1878). **Narawntapu NP** is just across the estuary. This is a favourite destination for daytrippers and campers, offering nature walks, isolated sandy beaches, summer

Tasmania

wildflowers and views to the mountains of the **Great Western Tiers (Kooparoona Niara)**.

VISITOR INFORMATION: 48 Gilbert St, Latrobe, Ph: (03) 6421 4699

▨ Queenstown   POP 2645
Map 483, C2

Queenstown emerged as a boom-town of the 1890s when gold and minerals were discovered at **Mount Lyell**. The strange but arresting 'moonscape' that surrounds the town was caused during the mining era. Arguably the pink, purple and grey rocky hills around Queenstown do have a certain beauty.

MAIN ATTRACTIONS: Queenstown's wide streets, old buildings and mountain setting give it a Wild West look, which can be appreciated from **Spion Kop Lookout**, off Bowes St. More than 1000 old photographs, documents and memorabilia make

Mining mural, Rosebery

a visit to the **Galley Museum** worthwhile. The restored historic **West Coast Wilderness Railway (**which has a rack and cog system designed for steep hills), uses a steam train to **Lynchford**, **Rinadeena** and **Double Barrel**; a diesel train takes over for the final run to **Strahan**.

NEARBY ATTRACTIONS: There are good views from the Lyell Hwy as it climbs out of town. The Mount Lyell field to the east produced more than 670 000 tonnes of copper, 510 tonnes of silver and 20 tonnes of gold between 1893 and 1994. Surface and underground copper-mine tours are available, commencing in Queenstown. The original **Iron Blow goldmine** (1883) is 6km east at **Gormanston**, and the ghost town of **Linda** a further 3km. Scenic **Mount Jukes Rd** to the south passes the old mining settlement of **Lynchford**, an old huon pine sawmill, **Crotty Dam** and the southern end of **Lake Burbury**. Near **Lake Margaret**, 12km north, is an historic 1914 hydroelectric power station that is still operating. There is excellent trout fishing at Lake Burbury and Lake Margaret.

VISITOR INFORMATION: Galley Museum, cnr Sticht St and Driffield St, Ph: (03) 6471 1483

▨ Richmond   POP 770
Map 469, A2

This lovely old town is located 26km from Hobart. Richmond is one of Tasmania's earliest settlements.

MAIN ATTRACTIONS: Richmond has dozens of historic buildings, some of which have been converted into restaurants, shops and galleries. Highlights of the local **heritage tour** include convict-built **Richmond Bridge** (1823), the oldest of its kind in Australia; the original **Post Office** building; **St Luke's Anglican Church** (1836); and **St John's Catholic Church** (1837), with cemetery headstones dating back to 1823. Self-guided tours are available for **Old Richmond Gaol**

(1825), in Bathurst St, one of the best-preserved convict establishments in Australia. **Saddlers Court** (circa 1848) and **Peppercorn Gallery** (circa 1850) feature local arts and crafts. The Georgian mansion **Prospect House** (1830s), off Hobart Rd, is said to be haunted. Tourist attractions include **Richmond Maze and Tearooms**, and award-winning **Old Hobart Town Model Village,** which shows Hobart as it was in the 1820s. Picnic facilities on the riverbank are near the famous Richmond Bridge.

NEARBY ATTRACTIONS: There is a scenic drive north through **Campania** (8km) and **Colebrook** (19km) with over 30 vineyards in the area.

VISITOR INFORMATION: Old Hobart Town Model Village, 21 Bridge St, Ph: (03) 6260 2502

▨ Rosebery   POP 1125
Map 483, C1

Rosebery is a **West Coast** mining town 29km north-east of **Zeehan**. Gold was discovered here in 1893, and later zinc, lead and copper were found. Rosebery township evolved following the involvement of the Mount Lyell Company in 1927.

MAIN ATTRACTION: Parts of the aerial ropeway system that carried ore 7km from the Hercules Mine at Williamsford to Rosebery can be seen near the Murchison Hwy.

NEARBY ATTRACTIONS: **Lake Pieman** and **Lake Rosebery** are noted fishing spots. Tracks for 4-wheel drive vehicles and walking tracks diverge from the Williamsford site for the impressive **Montezuma Falls**, at 110m the highest waterfall in Tasmania. There is a picturesque lake at **Tullah**, 12km east, and the historical **Wee Georgie Wood Railway** is nearby (check operating times).

VISITOR INFORMATION: West Coast Pioneers Museum, Main Rd, Zeehan, Ph: (03) 6471 6225

TASMAN PENINSULA

The Tasman Peninsula's landscape is rugged—like much of its history. The coastline features geological curiosities, fascinating seascapes and spectacular seaside walks, while the inland and the offshore islands are protected habitats for a rich variety of flora and fauna.

The coastline offers many opportunities for adventure—abseiling, rockclimbing, scuba diving and sea kayaking. There is a vast array of walking trails, horseriding and mountain-biking tracks.

Aboriginal people occupied the Peninsula for thousands of years and the region is scattered with some of Tasmania's oldest colonial and penal sites, including **Port Arthur** and **Eaglehawk Neck**. It is believed that the only prisoners who escaped did so by sea.

Eaglehawk Neck

The 100m-wide isthmus was once guarded by vicious dogs in an attempt to turn the Tasman Peninsula into a natural prison. Today, Eaglehawk Neck Historic Site is a must to visit. Nearby, there are many natural wonders including the extraordinary Tessellated Pavement wave platform, Tasman Blowhole, Tasman Arch and Devil's Kitchen.

i Visitor information

Port Arthur Visitor Centre
Port Arthur Historic Site,
Port Arthur, Tas 7182
Ph: (03) 6251 2310 or 1800 659 101
www.portarthur-region.com.au

Tessellated Pavement, near Eaglehawk Neck

main attractions

◈ **Isle of the Dead**

Cruises are available across the bay from Port Arthur to the historic cemetery.

◈ **Port Arthur Historic Site**

This is the site of Australia's longest established penal colony, operating between 1830 and 1877. The area is now filled with sandstone ruins as well as restored buildings and gardens. Evening lantern-lit ghost tours are available.

◈ **Tasman National Park**

This park boasts some of Australia's best coastal walks. Australian fur seal colonies breed along the rugged coastline. Dramatic views of Tasman Island can be obtained at Cape Pillar on the south-east coast. The spectacular Remarkable Cave is about 6km south of Port Arthur.

◈ **Tasmanian Devil Park**

This centre near Tarana offers an opportunity to get close to Australian native animals and enjoy the 'Kings of the Wind' free-flight birds of prey show.

Cape Pillar and Tasman Island, Tasman National Park

Tasmania

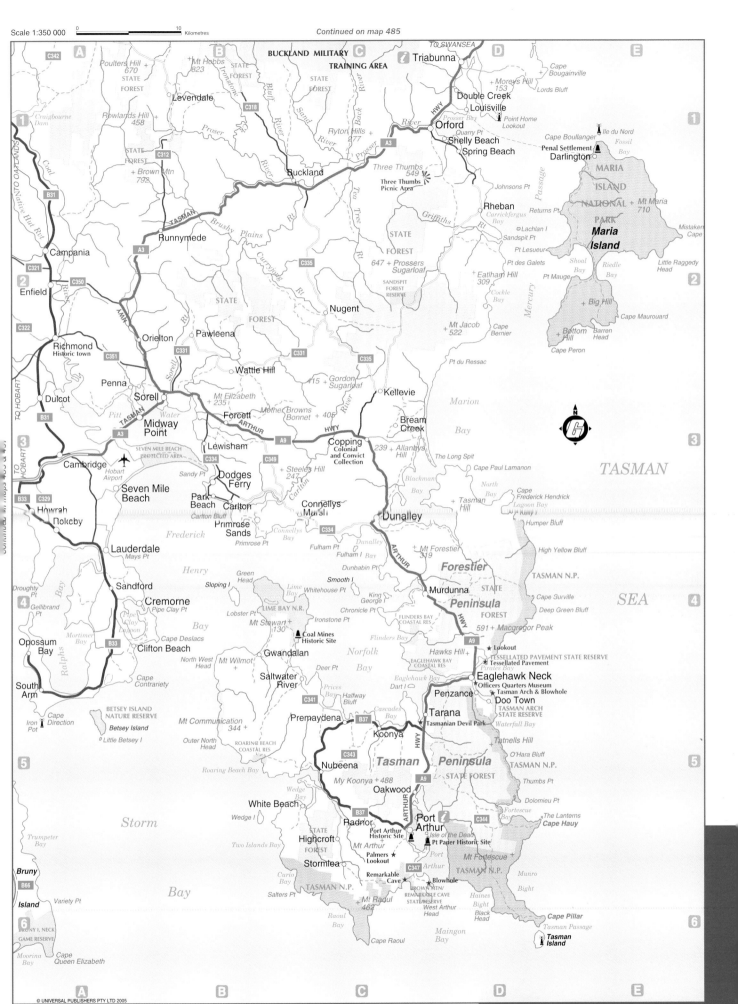

0   10
Kilometres

Continued on map 485

BUCKLAND MILITARY
TRAINING AREA

Triabunna

TO SWANSEA

Cape
Bougainville

Poulters Hill
670
STATE
FOREST

Mt Hobbs
823

STATE
FOREST

STATE
FOREST

Moreys Hill
153

Lords Bluff

Levendale

C318

Double Creek
Louisville

Cape
Boullanger

Île du Nord

Rowlands Hill
458

Ryton Hills
277

Orford

Point Home
Lookout

Fossil
Bay

STATE
FOREST

Brown Mtn
792

Buckland

Three Thumbs
549

Three Thumbs
Picnic Area

Quarry Pt
Shelly Beach
Spring Beach

Johnsons Pt

Penal Settlement
Darlington

Cape Boullanger

MARIA

ISLAND

Mt Maria
710

Runnymede

Rheban

Returns Pt

NATIONAL

Mistaken
Cape

Campania

Carrickfergus
Bay

Lachlan I

PARK

Maria
Island

Enfield

Prossers
Sugarloaf

Sandspit Pt

Pt Lesueur

Little Raggedy
Head

Richmond
Historic town

Nugent

Eatlham Hill
309

Pt des Galets
Pt Mauge

Shoal
Bay

Riedle
Bay

Orielton

Pawleena

Mt Jacob
522

Cape
Bernier

Cockle
Bay

Big Hill

Cape Maurouard

Penna

Wattle Hill

Gordon
Sugarloaf

Pt du Ressac

Bottom
Hill

Barren
Head

Dulcot

Sorell

Mt Elizabeth
235

Kellevie

Cape Peron

Midway
Point

Forcett

Mother Browns
Bonnet 405

Marion

Cambridge

Lewisham

Copping
Colonial
and Convict
Collection

Bream
Creek

Bay

TASMAN

Seven Mile
Beach

Hobart
Airport

Steeles Hill
247

Allanbys
Hill

The Long Spit

Cape Paul Lamanon

SEA

Howrah
Nokeby

Park
Beach

Dodges
Ferry

Carlton

Connellys
Marsh

Dunalley

Blackman
Bay

North
Bay

Cape
Frederick Hendrick

Tasman
Lagoon Bay

Lauderdale

Primrose
Sands

Fulham Pt

Mt Forestier
319

Humper Bluff

Henry

Green
Head

Dunabin Pt

Smooth I

Forestier

High Yellow Bluff

Sandford

Sloping I

Lime
Bay

Whitehouse Pt

King
George I

Murdunna

Peninsula

TASMAN N.P.

Cape Surville

Cremorne

LIME BAY N.R.

Chronicle Pt

FOREST

Deep Green Bluff

Lobster Pt

Ironstone Pt

FLINDERS BAY
COASTAL RES

Macgregor Peak
591

Opossum
Bay

Mt Stewart
130

Coal Mines
Historic Site

Flinders Bay

Lookout

TESSELLATED PAVEMENT STATE RESERVE

Clifton Beach

Gwandalan

Norfolk

Hawks Hill

Tessellated Pavement

Bay

EAGLEHAWK BAY
COASTAL RES

Eaglehawk Neck

Officers Quarters Museum

South
Arm

Mt Wilmot

Saltwater
River

Deer Pt

Penzance

Tasman Arch & Blowhole

Doo Town

BETSEY ISLAND
NATURE RESERVE

Mt Communication
344

Premaydena

Halfway
Bluff

Tarana

TASMAN ARCH
STATE RESERVE

Betsey Island

Little Betsey I

Outer Head

ROARING BEACH
COASTAL RES

Koonya

Tasmanian Devil Park

Waterfall Bay

Tatnells Hill

Nubeena

Tasman

My Koonya
488

Peninsula

O'Hara Bluff

TASMAN N.P.

STATE FOREST

White Beach

Wedge
Bay

Oakwood

Thumbs Pt

Dolomieu Pt

Radnor

Port
Arthur

The Lanterns
Cape Hauy

Highcroft

Port Arthur
Historic Site

Pt Puer Historic Site

Mt Fortescue

Stormlea

Mt Arthur

Palmers
Lookout

Isle of the Dead

TASMAN N.P.

Remarkable
Cave

Blowhole

Mt Radul
462

BROWN MTN/
REMARKABLE CAVE
STATE RESERVE

West Arthur
Head

Haines
Bight
Black
Head

Cape Pillar

Bruny

Island

TASMAN N.P.

Salters Pt

Maingon
Bay

Tasman
Island

Variety Pt

Tasman Passage

BRUNY I, NECK
GAME RESERVE

Moorina
Bay

Cape
Queen Elizabeth

Convict-built Ross Bridge (1836)

■ Ross   POP 289

Map 481, F5

Ross is an historic, picturesque township on the Midland Hwy in the heart of Tasmania's premier wool-growing area.

MAIN ATTRACTIONS: Ross has many fine colonial buildings to admire. **Ross Bridge** (1836) is one of Australia's most elegant bridges; it was built by convict labour. The **Female Factory Site**, off Bond St, operated as a probation station for female convicts between 1847 and 1854. The **Tasmanian Wool Centre**, a 1988 bicentennial project, includes a heritage museum and wool exhibition area (both with audio-visual facilities) and sells a wide range of woollen products.

NEARBY ATTRACTIONS: Some of Tasmania's finest trout fishing locations are within one hour's drive: the **Macquarie River**, **Lake Sorell** and **Lake Crescent** to the west; **Lake Leake** to the east; and **Tooms Lake** to the south-east.

VISITOR INFORMATION: Tasmanian Wool Centre, Church St, Ph: (03) 6381 5466

■ St Helens   POP 1776

Map 481, J2

St Helens is a popular beach and fishing resort on the inlet of **Georges Bay**; it was a whaling base in the early 19th century and a port for timber and mineral shipments. Commercial fishing, timber and tourism play an important part in the economy today.

MAIN ATTRACTIONS: Watersports such as swimming, waterskiing and sailing are enjoyed at safe bay beaches. Charter boats make deep-sea fishing excursions, and smaller boats can be hired for bay fishing. Fresh fish is available from fish-processing plants and is a specialty at local restaurants. **St Helens History Room** is a comprehensive museum and information centre.

NEARBY ATTRACTIONS: There are scenic coastal walks at **Humbug Point Nature Recreation Area**, **St Helens Conservation Area** and **Bay of Fires Conservation Area**. **Binalong Bay**, 11km north-east, has excellent rock fishing. **Mount William NP** is a one-hour drive to the north, with superb coastal scenery and abundant wildlife, including forester kangaroos. Inland, the **Goblin Forest Walk** (with wheelchair access) and other walking trails explore old tin-mining sites on the **Blue Tier** via **Lottah**. **Healey's Cheese Factory** is at **Pyengana**, 28km west, and **St Columba Falls** is close by. The holiday town of **Scamander**, 17km south, offers fruit farms, fishing, swimming and forest drives, and nearby **Trout Creek Reserve** has picnic facilities.

VISITOR INFORMATION: St Helens History Room and Information Centre, 61 Cecilia St, Ph: (03) 6376 1744

■ St Marys   POP 575

Map 481, J4

St Marys is a small town on the Esk Hwy, 12km from the **East Coast**, surrounded by glorious mountains and forests.

MAIN ATTRACTIONS: **Rivulet Park** has picnic and BBQ facilities, where sightings of platypus are possible and Tasmanian native hens likely. Historic **St Marys Railway Station** became the terminus for the East Coast railway in 1866.

NEARBY ATTRACTIONS: The road north to **Scamander** via **St Marys Pass** and the road south to **Bicheno** via **Elephants Pass** provide spectacular mountain and coastal scenery. There are great views of the **Fingal Valley** from the top of **South Sister**, 3km north-west. The coal-mining and coastal township of **Falmouth**, 14km north-east, has fine beaches and fishing.

VISITOR INFORMATION: Coach House Restaurant, 34 Main St, Ph: (03) 6372 2529

■ Scottsdale   POP 1972

Map 481, G2

The largest town in north-east Tasmania, Scottsdale is the centre for a prosperous agricultural area and a thriving pine forest industry. Other industries include the cultivation of oil poppies and hops.

MAIN ATTRACTIONS: **Scottsdale Forest EcoCentre**, in King St, has interactive displays showcasing the regional forest industry.

NEARBY ATTRACTIONS: A visit to **Bridestowe Estate Lavender Farm**, 13km west, is a unique experience as it is the largest of its kind in the Southern Hemisphere. The lavender flowering season is mid-December to late January. **Sidling Lookout**, 16km south-west, provides views of the countryside. **Derby Tin Mine Centre**, 30km east, includes **Shanty Town**, a miner's cottage, general store, butcher's shop, mine office and the original Derby gaol. About one hour's drive south-east, **White Gum Reserve** at **Evercreech** has giant white gum trees up to 89m high and 3000 years old. The **South Esk River**, for brown trout fishing, is within driving distance, as are **Ralph** and **Mathinna waterfalls**.

VISITOR INFORMATION: Forest EcoCentre, 96 King St, Ph: (03) 6352 6520

▨ Sheffield   POP 1020
Map 480, C3

Sheffield is a mixed farming community 30km south of Devonport. It lies in the foothills of **Mount Roland**, (1234m), in an area of lovely natural scenery.

MAIN ATTRACTIONS: The town's most famous feature is the series of more than 30 murals—mainly illustrating Sheffield's early history—painted on almost every available wall. **Mural Park,** in Pioneer Cr, displays winning mural boards from the annual Easter **Mural Fest.** Pioneering memorabilia is housed in the **Kentish Museum**. Redwater Creek Steam and Heritage Society operates **steam train trips** from **Apex Park** on the first weekend of the month and daily in the summer school holidays. The unusual **Tiger's Tail Robotic Theatre** is in Main St.

NEARBY ATTRACTIONS: The region's beauty is enhanced by thousands of flowering daffodils in spring. The many lakes and dams of the **Mersey-Forth Hydro-Electric Development** include the international rowing venue **Lake Barrington.** Close to Lake Barrington is the world's largest maze complex, **Tasmazia**, with a lavender farm and model village. **Devil's Gate Dam** is 13km to the north-west. There are two wineries in the area. **Stoodley Forest Reserve** is 7km north-east. Sheffield is the gateway to the bushwalks and stunning scenery of the internationally renowned **Cradle Mountain-Lake St Clair NP**, and the wilderness area of **Walls of Jerusalem NP**, to the south (*see* pp.472-473).

VISITOR INFORMATION: 5 Pioneer Cr, Ph: (03) 6491 1036

▨ Smithton   POP 3350
Map 479, C2

Smithton is situated at the mouth of the **Duck River** in north-west Tasmania. The region is known for its blackwood swamp forests, which have yielded the fossilised bones of extinct giant marsupials. Dairy farming, vegetable-growing, forestry and fishing are the main industries.

MAIN ATTRACTIONS: **Apex Lookout Tower** on **Tier Hill** takes in a panoramic view over **Duck Bay**, **Robbins Island** and **Three Hummock Island** in Bass Strait. **Smithton-Circular Head Heritage Centre**, in the old Billings Store building, is run by volunteers.

NEARBY ATTRACTIONS: Fishing and boating are popular at Duck River and Duck Bay, 2km north. **Lacrum Dairy Farm**, 6km west at **Mella**, offers milking demonstrations and cheese tasting, November–May. Neighbouring **Wombat Tarn** has BBQs, bushwalks and a lookout. Tours can be arranged to visit **Britton Bros Veneer Plant**, and the historic Van Diemen's Land Company property, **Woolnorth**. **Sumac Lookout**, 4km south, gives views over eucalypt forests. The great forests of north-west Tasmania can also be seen on a 60km circular drive into **South Arthur Forest**. River cruises are available at **Arthur River**, 70km south-west. **Dismal Swamp Maze and Visitor Centre** is a fascinating forestry ecocentre 35 minutes drive west off the Bass Hwy near **Togari**.

VISITOR INFORMATION: 45 Main Rd, Stanley, Ph: (03) 6458 1330 or 1300 138 229

▨ Sorell   POP 3150
Map 457, K1

Founded in 1821, Sorell played an important part in Tasmania's early European history, by supplying most of the colony's grain. The settlement was brazenly captured in 1824 by bushranger Matthew Brady, who imprisoned the garrison and most of the citizens. Sorell is an important tourist link between **Hobart**, the **Tasman Peninsula** and the **East Coast**.

MAIN ATTRACTIONS: Interesting buildings from colonial times include **St George's Church** (1826), **Scots Church** (1841) and **Blue Bell Inn** (circa 1863). **Pioneer Park** is popular for BBQs and picnics. **Orielton Lagoon** is a significant bird sanctuary with many species.

NEARBY ATTRACTIONS: **Sorell Fruit Farm** is 2km east off the Arthur Hwy and there are several wineries in the region. **Dodges Ferry** and **Carlton**, 18km south, are popular beach areas. The unsealed **Weilangta Forest Drive** to **Orford** via **Copping** winds through forests and coastal mountains. Attractions at Copping include the **Colonial and Convict Collection** and **Yaxley Wines**. **Bream Creek**, 25km east, has vineyards and stunning rural and coastal scenery. **Dunalley** 35km south-east, is known for its fish market, antiques, arts and crafts.

VISITOR INFORMATION: 16 Gordon St, Ph: (03) 6265 6438

Solomon's Throne at sunrise in the Walls of Jerusalem National Park wilderness, south of Sheffield

CRADLE MOUNTAIN-LAKE ST CLAIR NP

Located approximately 85km south of Devonport, Cradle Mountain and the national park are drawcards for Australian and international visitors alike. This national park is renowned for its excellent bushwalking tracks, including the wonderful 80km **Overland Track** and shorter circuits taking just a few hours to cover.

The park's founding father, Austrian immigrant **Gustav Weindorfer**, was overwhelmed by the other-worldliness of this area, proclaiming that it 'must be a national park for the people of all time'. It is now part of the acclaimed **Tasmanian Wilderness World Heritage Area**, protecting a diversity of environments just waiting to be explored by the adventurous. Its $1612km^2$ boasts stunning scenery, wild landscapes, buttongrass plains, primordial rainforests and alpine heathlands. The rugged terrain is interspersed with glacial lakes, while icy rivers and streams cascade from the mountains. Natural attractions include the **Enchanted Walk**, **Ballroom Forest**, **Dove Lake** and **Shadow Lake**.

Facilities include picnic shelters fitted with electric BBQs, toilets in a few locations, campgrounds, lodges and track huts, Cradle Mountain Lodge Store and Cradle Mountain Information Centre.

Lake St Clair

This lake was formed by a glacier and is Australia's deepest natural freshwater lake, 17km long and 200m deep. It is the source of the **Derwent River** on which Hobart is situated.

Visitor information

Cradle Mountain Visitors Centre
Park entrance, Cradle Mountain Rd,
Cradle Mountain–Lake St Clair National Park
Ph: (03) 6492 1110
www.cradle@parks.tas.gov.au

Lake Crater, near Cradle Valley, Cradle Mountain-Lake St Clair National Park

main attractions

◈ Ballroom Forest

Nestled on the slopes of Cradle Mountain, this temperate-climate rainforest is a highlight of the Dove Lake Loop Track Walk.

◈ Overland Track

The Overland Track is one of Australia's premier wilderness walking tracks. The five-day expedition covers 80km. Highlights include a side-trip to Tasmania's highest peak, Mount Ossa. New regulations from late 2005 involve a booking system for walkers in the peak season (spring to autumn) and a one-way trek north to south.

◈ Waldheim Chalet

The name of this chalet museum means 'forest home', It is located at the northern end of the Overland Track. Waldheim Cabins offer an authentic experience in the wilderness of this pristine area.

Bushwalkers at Pelion Gap on the Overland Track, Cradle Mountain-Lake St Clair National Park

Tasmania

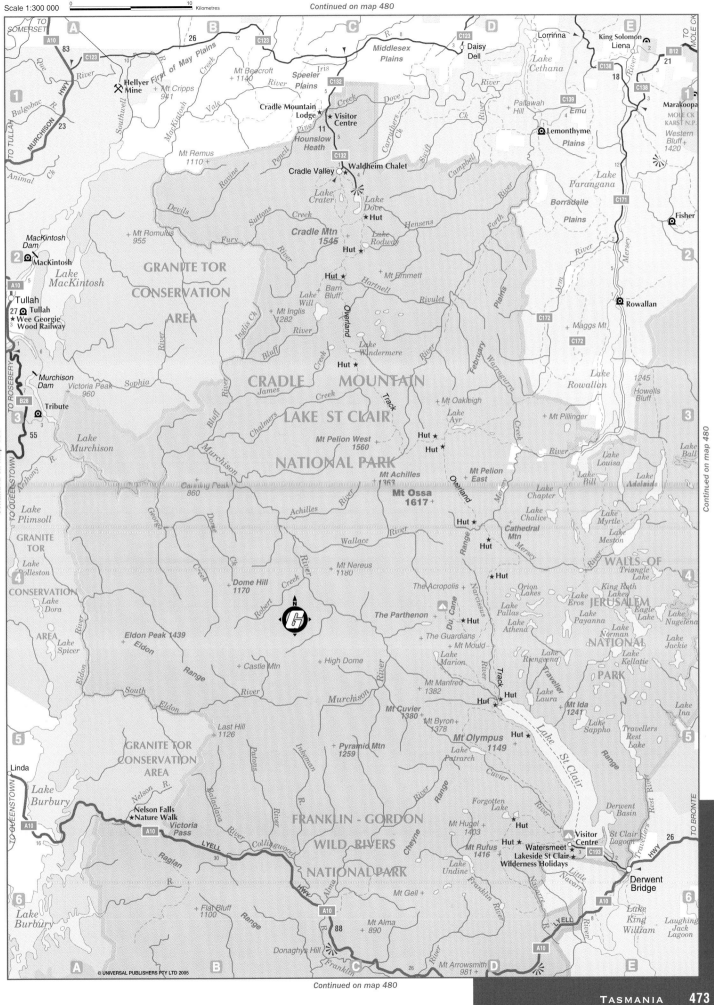

Stanley POP 550

Map 479, C2

The charming north-west coastal township of Stanley is located on a peninsula overlooked by a 150m-high basalt rock formation known as **The Nut**. The original port for the Van Diemen's Land Company from 1826, it is known for fresh fish, crayfish and oysters.

MAIN ATTRACTIONS: There are many historic buildings, particularly near the waterfront. Old bluestone buildings include **Van Diemen's Land Company Store**, now a guesthouse. In Church St are the **Stanley Hotel** (1849), and **Commercial Hotel** (1842), now a private residence. The **Plough Inn** (1850s) is also a private residence. **Stanley Seaquarium** has interesting displays of Tasmanian fish and sea life on the waterfront. Also in the port area are cruises to the **fur seal colony** on **Bull Rock**. **Discovery Centre Folk Museum** is a repository for local history. The well-known gallery, **Stanley Artworks**, is in Church St. The summit of The Nut can be reached by chairlift or walking track and provides spectacular views over the coastline and **Bass Strait islands**. **Lyons Cottage** in Alexander Tce, the birthplace of **Prime Minister Sir Joseph Lyons**, is open to the public. The burial-ground off Browns Rd has early colonial graves. There are little penguin and shearwater rookeries in the Stanley area.

NEARBY ATTRACTIONS: The gracious colonial property **Highfield** and its original outbuildings are 2km north on Scenic Dr. **Dip Falls**, 40km south-east via **Mawbanna**, is a pretty double-drop waterfall surrounded by rainforest. Nearby are a picnic area, walking trails and a giant stringybark known as the **Big Tree**.

VISITOR INFORMATION: 45 Main Road, Ph: (03) 6458 1330 or 1300 138 229

Ruined outbuilding of Highfield, near Stanley, with The Nut in the distance

Strahan POP 723

Map 483, B2

This historic fishing and timber port on **Macquarie Harbour** is sited on Tasmania's forbidding **West Coast**. Its colourful history is linked with the **Sarah Island** penal colony and the Mount Lyell mining boom. It is the gateway to the **Gordon River** and **South West Wilderness Area**.

MAIN ATTRACTIONS: Strahan's 19th-century streetscapes feature such buildings as the grand old **Customs House** and the **Union Steamship Building**. The visitor centre has an excellent historical display on south-west Tasmania, including the fight to save the **Franklin River**. A nightly play features the convict escape story, *The Ship that Never Was*. The adjacent **Morrisons Mill**, a Huon pine sawmill, features woodturning, arts and crafts. Historic **Ormiston House** is also on the Esplanade. Harbour views can be had from **Water Tower Hill**, and **Peoples Park** features a walk to **Hogarth Falls**. Strahan is linked to **Queenstown** by the famous **West Coast Wilderness Railway**.

NEARBY ATTRACTIONS: **Ocean Beach**, 6km to the west, has areas for horseriding and beach fishing as well as shearwater rookeries, which are active October–March. There are free nightly ranger talks on the beach, December to February. **Teepookana Plateau**, 16km south-east, with its 10m-high viewing platform, can be reached by helicopter. **Henty Dunes**, 12km north, are vast sandhills popular with sailboarders and quad bikers. There is also a lagoon and picnic area. Boat trips can be taken on Macquarie Harbour to visit the convict ruins on Sarah Island, the setting for Marcus Clarke's novel, *For the Term of His Natural Life*. A huge range of sightseeing options are available for magnificent **Franklin-Gordon Wild Rivers NP**, including cruises, helicopter and seaplane flights, yacht charters, jet boat rides and fishing excursions. Other local activities include kayaking and canoeing on the **Gordon** and **Henty rivers**.

VISITOR INFORMATION: Wharf Complex, The Esplanade, Ph: (03) 6471 7622

Swansea POP 512

Map 481, H6

Formerly one of many whaling stations on Tasmania's **East Coast**, Swansea is a popular fishing and tourist resort overlooking beautiful **Great Oyster Bay**. It is a handy base for exploring **Freycinet** and **Maria Island national parks**.

MAIN ATTRACTIONS: A **heritage walk** reveals several old buildings that are still used for their original purpose, including the **Council Chambers** (1860) and **Morris' General Store** (1838). There are three attractions at the information centre on the Tasman Hwy: **Swansea Bark Mill** (1885) processed black wattle bark for leather tannins until 1935, it is now a centre for Tasmanian crafts; **Yesteryear Museum** charts local history; and the **Wine and Wool Centre** is an outlet for Tasmanian wines and country clothing. The museum at the **Community Centre** (circa 1860) includes the immense slate billiard table made for the 1880 World Exhibition. The walking track around **Waterloo Point** takes in Aboriginal middens, views to **Freycinet Peninsula** and shearwater viewing at dusk.

NEARBY ATTRACTIONS: Guided tours of local gardens are available in spring. There is a small colony of little penguins at **Coswell Beach**, 1km south. **Kate's Berry Farm**, 2km south, has fresh berries in season and fruit wines. There are a number of vineyards in the region for wine tasting and cellar door sales. **Spikey Beach**, 7km south, offers rock fishing and the convict-built **Spikey Bridge** (1843). **Mayfield Beach**, 14km south, has safe swimming and a walking track to **Three Arch Bridge**. **Dolphin Sands** and the **Swan River** picnic area, 4km north, are popular recreation spots. **Meetus Falls** and **Lost Falls** are 50km north-west.

VISITOR INFORMATION: Swansea Bark Mill, 96 Tasman Hwy, Ph: (03) 6257 8382

Triabunna POP 771

Map 469, D1

Triabunna is located on **Spring Bay**, 86km north-east of Hobart. Once it was a whaling base and garrison town for the nearby **Maria Island** penal settlement. Today, the mainstays are the woodchipping, scallop and abalone industries.

MAIN ATTRACTIONS: A **town walk** from the visitor centre takes in 17 heritage buildings, the oldest being the **Police Watch-house** and **Magistrates Office**. The visitor centre has interpretative displays and interesting tapestries. A **Seafarers' Memorial** on the Esplanade commemorates sailors lost in Tasmanian waters and Tasmanian sailors lost around the world.

NEARBY ATTRACTIONS: Boats can be chartered by groups for fishing expeditions. Ferries leave daily from **Triabunna Wharf** for Maria Island, where the main highlights are penal settlement ruins at **Darlington**, painted cliffs, fossil deposits and walking trails in **Maria Island NP**. Contact the visitor centre for ferry departure times.

VISITOR INFORMATION: Charles St and Esplanade West, Ph: (03) 6257 4772

Ulverstone POP 9819

Map 480, B2

The beachside town of Ulverstone, 19km west of Devonport, is a popular tourist destination, especially in summer. It is the centre for a dairy farming and agricultural district.

MAIN ATTRACTIONS: Ulverstone's beaches, memorial parks, antique and craft shops are big drawcards. Dominating the town is the **Shrine of Remembrance clock tower** in Reibey St. There are four memorial parks: **Tobruk Park** in Hobbs Pde; **Anzac Park** by the River Leven; **Legion Park** in West Ulverstone; and HMAS *Shropshire* **Naval Memorial Park** in Dial St. **Fairway Park** has an adventure playground and a giant waterslide in summer. The **History Museum** in Main St displays local memorabilia in the form of shop windows (open Tuesday, Thursday and weekends). The **North-West Woodcraft Guild Workshop and Gallery** is open Tuesday, Thursday and Saturday. A lookout off Upper Maud St in **West Ulverstone** gives views across the river to the **Bass Strait beaches**.

NEARBY ATTRACTIONS: There is a miniature railway 2km east, and

Lichen-covered boulders at Wineglass Bay, Freycinet National Park, east of Swansea

little penguins can be seen at dusk at **Leith**, 12km east. **Goat Island Sanctuary**, 5km west, can be reached by a walkway at low tide. **Gunns Plains Caves**, 24km south-west, feature limestone formations, an underground river and glow-worms; guided tours are available. Scenic waterfalls in the area include **Preston Falls** (19km south). **Leven Canyon**, 41km south, is a magnificent gorge with interesting walking tracks.

VISITOR INFORMATION: 13-15 Alexandra Rd, Ph: (03) 6425 2839

Westbury   POP 1307

Map 480, D3

This small town, 35km south-west of Launceston, has a European history dating to 1828. Westbury's original Georgian and early Victorian buildings are clustered around a village green very much in the style of an English village.

MAIN ATTRACTIONS: Facing the Village Green, the **White House** (1841) is now a colonial museum, with a magnificent antique Georgian doll's house and several original outbuildings (closed July–August). Westbury's Interpretative Trail features 36 heritage sites on a 2km village walk. The beautiful English garden, **Culzean**, in William St, is open September–June by appointment. **Westbury Maze** on Bass Hwy is a traditional hedge maze, with more than 3000 privet bushes; there is also a tearoom. **Pearn's Steam World** has a large collection of working steam-traction engines, which steam up at Easter and during November. **Tractor Shed** in Veterans Row is a museum of old farm machinery. **Animal Haven** is a zoo where children can pet the animals.

NEARBY ATTRACTIONS: **St Marys Anglican Church** at **Hagley**, 5km east, has a superb east-facing window. Trout fishing enthusiasts head for **Brushy Lagoon**, 15km

north-west, or **Four Springs Creek**, 15km north-east.

VISITOR INFORMATION: Gingerbread Cottages, 52 William St, Ph: (03) 6393 1140

Wynyard   POP 4983

Map 479, E3

The pretty north-west coastal town of Wynyard is the centre of a prosperous farming district. It is also a popular tourist centre, with an airport close to town.

MAIN ATTRACTIONS: **Gutteridge Gardens** are attractive parklands beside the **Inglis River**. There is a Tasmanian tiger (*thylacine*) interpretive sculpture at the infor-mation centre. Scenic walks include a riverside ramble to amazing **Fossil Bluff**, where the sea cliffs contain thousands of fossils. In the mid-1800s, a 20 million-year-old fossil marsupial was discovered at the Bluff—the oldest ever found.

NEARBY ATTRACTIONS: Scenic flights over the coastline and north-west wilderness areas are available at the airport. The drive or walk to **Table Cape**, a 170m volcanic plug, passes a colourful patchwork of vegetables, poppies and tulips, with **Cape Tulip Farm** open for inspection in October. Table Cape, 5km north, has an historic lighthouse and stunning views over a vast stretch of the coastline. **Boat Harbour**, 15km north-west, is considered one of Australia's most beautiful beaches, with white sand, crystal-clear blue water, coral formations, rocky outcrops for fishing and tidal pools. Seals usually visit the bay in late summer. Further west, **Rocky Cape NP** has many excellent walks, Aboriginal relics, a marine park and lighthouse.

VISITOR INFORMATION: Cnr Hogg St and Goldie St, Ph: (03) 6442 4143

Zeehan   POP 1098

Map 483, B1

This once booming mining town, named after one of Abel Tasman's

ships, is 36km north-west of Queenstown. After silver-lead deposits were discovered in 1882, Zeehan's population rose to around 10 000 in 1901. By 1909 it was almost deserted, but has recently revived with the reopening of the **Bluestone Tin Mine**.

MAIN ATTRACTIONS: Main St has many buildings from the boom years (1890–1908). **The Gaiety Grand** building contains the Grand Hotel and the Gaiety Theatre, which is much as it was in its heyday, when it seated 1000 and showcased such stars as Enrico Caruso and Nellie Melba. The Old School of Mines building (1894) now houses **West Coast Pioneers Museum**, with perhaps the best mineral collection in the Southern Hemisphere, including the finest specimens of rare crocoite, Tasmania's mineral emblem. Excellent old steam engines and carriages used on the **West Coast** are displayed outside. From the museum a 7km round-trip drive heads out through a low mining tunnel to the old **Spray Silver Mine**. **Frank Long Memorial Park** marks the first silver-lead deposit. A **pioneer cemetery** can be found off Zeehan–Strahan Rd.

NEARBY ATTRACTIONS: There are old mine workings at **Dundas**, 13km east. Tasmania's highest waterfall **Montezuma Falls** (110m) is 17km east, accessible by walking track or 4-wheel drive. An unsealed scenic drive leads to the fishing village of **Granville Harbour**, 35km north-west, once the port for Zeehan. **Corinna**, formerly a gold-mining town 48km north-west, is now a base for gold panning, bushwalking and trout-fishing with a car ferry crossing the **Pieman River**. Fishing and boating are popular on **Lake Pieman** to the north. Trout fishermen head for the Henty River, 25km south of Zeehan.

VISITOR INFORMATION: West Coast Pioneers Museum, Main St, Ph: (03) 6471 6225

KEY MAP

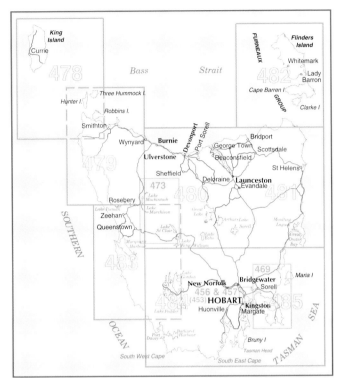

Capital city CBD map
Hobart p.453

Hobart suburban map
pp.456–457

Region maps
Tasman Peninsula
p.469

Region maps (continued)
Cradle Mountain-
Lake St Clair
National Park p.473

State maps
pp.478–485

Frozen ferns, Cradle Mountain

DISTANCE CHART

Approximate Distance	Burnie	Campbell Town	Deloraine	Devonport	Geeveston	George Town	Hobart	Launceston	New Norfolk	Oatlands	Port Arthur	Queenstown	Rosebery	St Helens	St Marys	Scottsdale	Smithton	Sorell	Swansea	Triabunna
Burnie		198	100	50	381	152	328	137	290	246	386	148	109	293	259	197	88	316	264	314
Campbell Town	198		98	148	184	120	131	70	127	48	188	253	308	120	85	130	286	118	66	116
Deloraine	100	98		50	281	87	228	51	190	146	286	204	209	207	159	111	188	216	164	214
Devonport	50	148	50		331	102	278	87	240	196	336	198	159	243	209	147	138	266	214	264
Geeveston	381	184	281	331		304	53	254	91	136	148	312	367	304	269	314	469	78	189	139
George Town	152	120	87	102	304		251	50	259	168	308	300	261	170	205	74	240	238	186	236
Hobart	328	131	228	278	53	251		201	38	83	95	259	314	251	216	261	416	25	136	86
Launceston	137	70	51	87	254	50	201		197	118	258	251	246	156	131	60	225	188	136	186
New Norfolk	290	127	190	240	91	259	38	197		79	133	221	276	247	212	257	378	63	174	124
Oatlands	246	48	146	196	136	168	83	118	79		140	261	316	168	133	178	334	70	114	131
Port Arthur	386	188	286	336	148	308	95	258	133	140		354	409	299	268	318	474	70	181	131
Queenstown	148	253	204	198	312	300	259	251	221	261	354		55	407	338	311	236	284	395	345
Rosebery	109	308	209	159	367	261	314	246	276	316	409	55		401	368	306	197	339	450	400
St Helens	293	120	207	243	304	170	251	156	247	168	299	407	401		35	96	381	229	118	168
St Marys	259	85	159	209	269	205	216	131	212	133	268	338	368	35		131	347	198	87	137
Scottsdale	197	130	111	147	314	74	261	60	257	178	318	311	306	96	131		285	248	214	264
Smithton	88	286	188	138	469	240	416	225	378	334	474	236	197	381	347	285		404	352	402
Sorell	316	118	216	266	78	238	25	188	63	70	70	284	339	229	198	248	404		111	61
Swansea	264	66	164	214	189	186	136	136	174	114	181	395	450	118	87	214	352	111		50
Triabunna	314	116	214	264	139	236	86	186	124	131	131	345	400	168	137	264	402	61	50	

All distances in this chart have been measured over highways and major roads, not necessarily by the shortest route.

A   B   C   D   E

1

Neva, 1835
Cape Wickham
Cape Wickham Lighthouse
Cape Farewell
L. Flannigan
Tartar, 1835
Disappointment Bay
Phoques
George, 1803
New Year I.
GAME RES.
Egg Lagoon
L. Martha Lavinia
Garfield, 1898
Lavinia Pt.
Christmas I.
NAT. RES.
Yambacoona
Bay
LAVINIA NATURE RESERVE
Rio, 1915
Whistler, 1855
Yellow Rock R.
SEA ELEPHANT RIVER PRIVATE WILDLIFE SANCT.
Maypole, 1855
Reekara
King
34
Europa, 1867
Island
REEKARA (PRIVATE) WILDLIFE SANCT.
Loorana
Sea Elephant
Councillor I.
King Island Dairy ★
Elephant R.

Bass   Strait

2

Waterwitch, 1854   ★ Windfarm
Sea Elephant Bay
Oonah, 1891
Currie Harbour
Fraser R.
Naracoopa
Currie
Pegarah
Fraser Bluff
Museum
Parenna
Netherby, 1866
29
Ettrick
Yorra
B26
Katheraw, 1872
40°
KENTFORD FOREST CONSERVATION AREA
Ck.
Yarra Creek
Cataraqui, 1845
Lymwood
Bold Head
Fitzmaurice Bay
Grassy Penguin rookery
Brahmin, 1854
Seal R.
Mt Stanley 213
Cataraqui Pt.
Pearshape
Isabella, 1845

3

SEAL ROCKS STATE RESERVE
Calcified Forest ★   *Big L.*
Seal Pt.
Surprise Bay   *Seal Bay*
Carnarvon Bay, 1901
Clytie, 1902
Stokes Pt.

SOUTHERN

OCEAN

4

NATURE RESERVE *Albatross I.*
N. W. Cape
Cape Keraudren
Cape Rochon
Eveline, 1895
Coulomb Bay
NATURE RESERVE
Three Hummock Island
Phatisalam, 1821
Burgess Pt.
Cuvier Bay
East Telegraph Bay
Cape Adamson
Cuvier Pt.
237 + *South Hummock*
Spray, 1866
Wallaby Pt.
Hunter Island
Rainbow, 1868
Cave Bay
MUTTONBIRD RESERVE
Steep I.
GAME RES.
Petrel Is.
Cape Buache

5

Bird I.
GAME RES.
Stack I.
GAME RES.
Walker I.
Trefoil I.
Walker   Channel
Woolnorth Pt.
Ransonnet Bay
Boullanger Bay
Cape Grim
Woolnorth
Robbins Island
Valley Bay
Clump I.
Kangaroo I.
Wind Farm ★
Short I.
Robbins Passage
Wallaby Is.
Howie I.
Flat Topped Bluff
Montagu I.
Stony Pt.
Big Bay
Bluff Pt.
120
West Montagu
Montagu
Perkins I.
Studland Bay
18
Morning Light, 1895
C218

6

MT CAMERON WEST ABORIGINAL SITE
Mt Cameron West 168 +
Lacrum Dairy Farm
Mella
Ann
Broadmeadows
Green Pt.
Christmas Hills
Bay
Marrawah
Redpa
BASS
Togari
54
Brittons Swamp
West Pt.
WEST POINT
ABORIGINAL SITE
ARTHUR PIEMAN CONSERVATION AREA
Mawson Bay

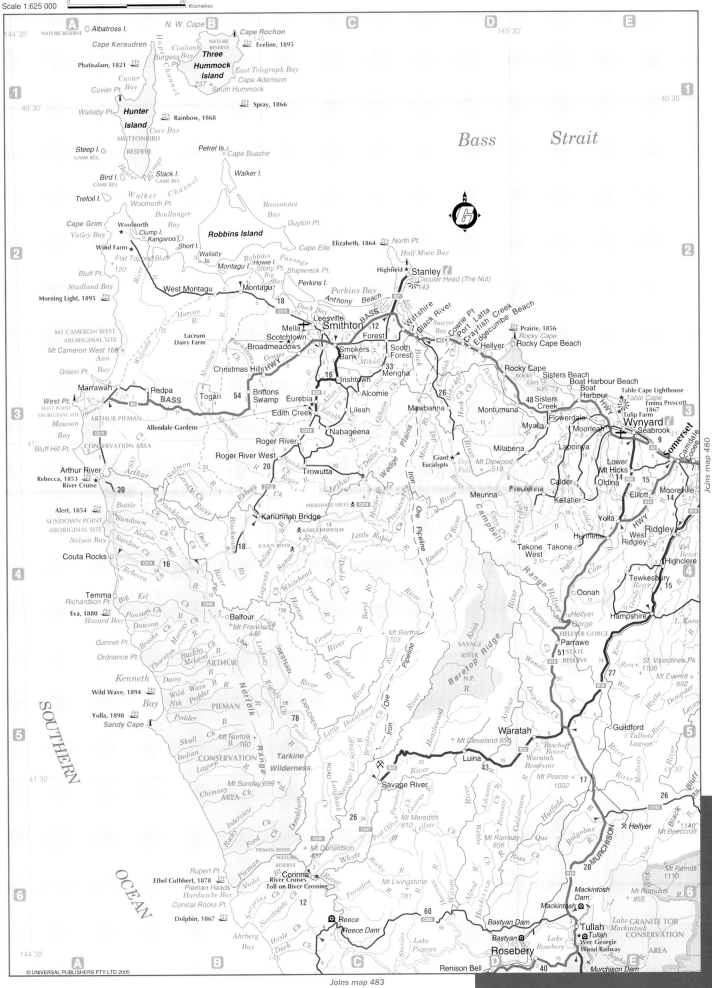

Scale 1:625 000

0   20 Kilometres

Bass   Strait

N

SOUTHERN

OCEAN

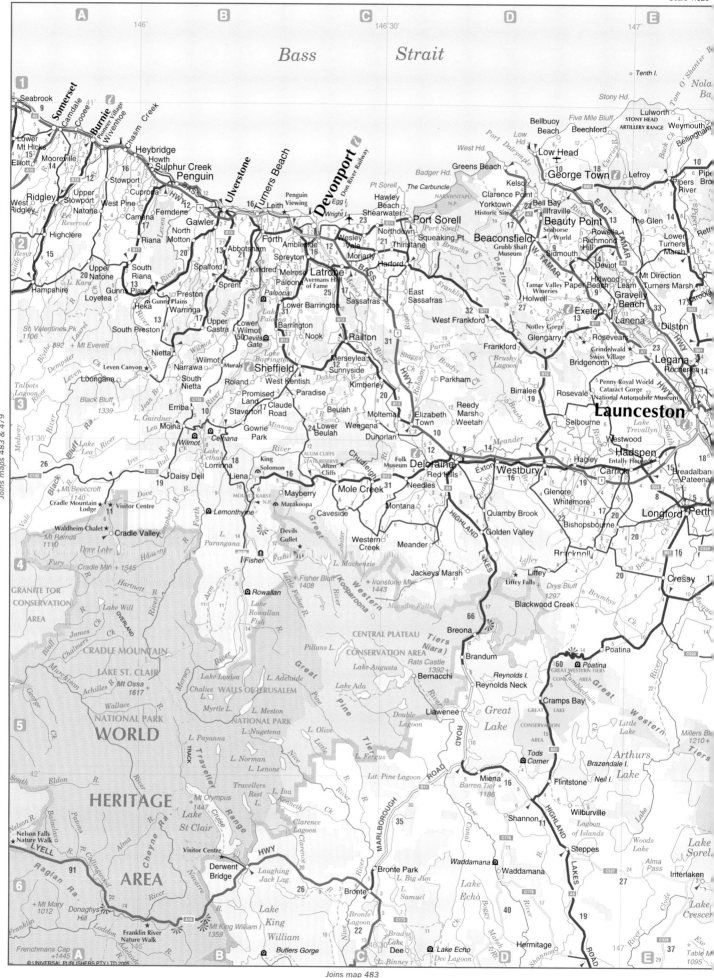

Bass Strait

A
B
C
D
E

Seabrook
Somerset
Camdale
Cooee
Burnie
Wivenhoe
Chasm Creek
Heybridge
Howth
Sulphur Creek
Penguin

Lower
Mt Hicks
Elliott
Mooreville
Stowport
Upper
Stowport
West Pine
Natone
Camena
Highclere
Ridgley
West
Ridgley

Ulverstone
Turners Beach
Leith

Devonport

Pioneer Village

Tenth I.
Nola

Stony Hd.

Lulworth
Weymouth
STONY HEAD
ARTILLERY RANGE
Bellingham

Bellbuoy
Beach
Beechford

Low Head
George Town
Lefroy
Pipers
River

Penguin
Viewing
Wright I.

Greens Beach
Badger Hd.

Kelso
Clarence Point
Yorktown
Illfraville
Historic Site

Beauty Point
Beaconsfield

Hampshire

Upper
Natone
Gunns Plains
Loyetea
Heka
Warringa
South
Riana
Preston
Spalford
Kindred
Melrose
Paloona
Spreyton
Latrobe
Sassafras

Gawler
North
Motton
Abbotsham
Forth
Ambleside
Wesley
Vale
Moriarty
Harford
East
Sassafras

Port Sorell
Hawley
Beach
Shearwater
Northdown
Squeaking Pt
Thirlstane

Seahorse
World
Sidmouth
Richmond
Hill
Deviot
Hillwood
Leam
Gravelly
Beach
Lanena
Rowella

The Glen
Lower
Turners
Marsh
Turners Marsh

South
Preston
Nietta
Loongana
Narrawa
South
Nietta
Wilmot
Roland
West Kentish
Paradise
Kimberley
Sunnyside
Merseylea

West Frankford
Notley Gorge
Frankford
Glengarry
Exeter
Rosevears

Grindelwald
Swiss Village
Bridgenorth
Rosevale
Legana
Rocherlea

Black Bluff
1339
Erriba
Moina
Gowrie
Park
Staverton
Claude
Road
Beulah
Lower
Beulah
Weegena
Moltema
Dunorlan

Elizabeth
Town

Reedy
Marsh
Weetah
Parkham

Birralee

Penny Royal World
Cataract Gorge
National Automobile Museum

Launceston

Cradle Mountain
Lodge
Visitor Centre
Wilmot
Cethana
Lorrinna
Liena
King
Solomon
Mayberry
Marakoopa
Caveside
Montana

Deloraine
Red Hills
Needles
Mole Creek

Exton
Westbury

Hadspen
Carrick

Hagley
Glenore
Whitemore

Westwood

Breadalbane
Pateena

Perth

Waldheim Chalet
Mt Remas
1110
Cradle Valley
Lemonthyme

Devils
Gullet
Fisher
Western
Creek
Meander

Quamby Brook
Golden Valley

Bishopsbourne

Bracknell

Longford

Cressy

GRANITE TOR
CONSERVATION
AREA

Lake Will

Lake Rowallan
Fish
Rowallan

Fisher Bluff
1408
Ironstone Mtn
1443

Jackeys Marsh

Liffey
Liffey Falls

Drys Bluff
1297

Blackwood Creek

CRADLE MOUNTAIN
LAKE ST. CLAIR
NATIONAL PARK

WORLD

Mt Ossa
1617
Lake Louisa
L. Adelaide
WALLS OF JERUSALEM
NATIONAL PARK

CENTRAL PLATEAU
CONSERVATION AREA

Tiers
(Niara)

Breona
Brandum

Rats Castle
1392
Bernacchi
Reynolds Neck

Poatina

Cramps Bay

HERITAGE

AREA

Mt Olympus
1447
Lake
St Clair

Visitor Centre

Derwent
Bridge

L. Meston
L. Nugetena

L. Olive

L. Ina

Clarence
Lagoon

Double
Lagoon

Liawenee

Great
Lake

Tods
Corner

Miena

Flintstone

Brazendale I.

Arthurs
Lake

Millers Bl
1210

Shannon

Wilburville

Steppes

Laughing
Jack Lag.

Bronte Park
Bronte

Waddamana
Waddamana

Lake
Echo

Hermitage

Mt King William I
1359

Butlers Gorge

Dee
Lake Echo

Joins maps 483 & 479

Joins map 483

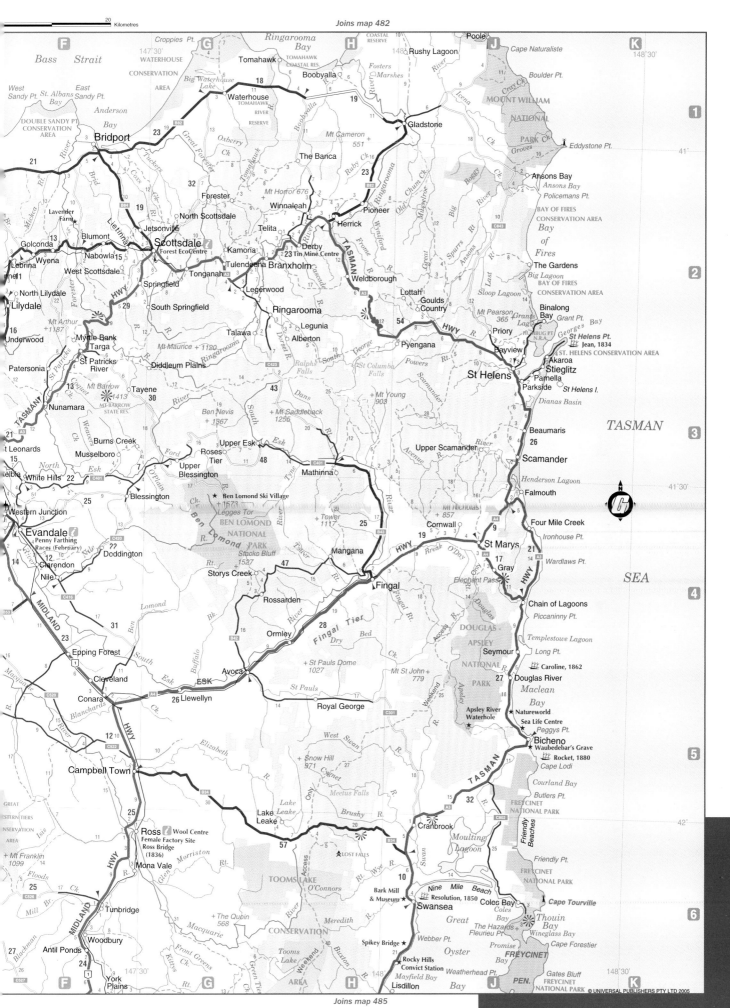

0   20 Kilometres

| A | B | C | D | E |

Bass Strait

Endeavour Reef
147°30'

148°

148°30'

Outer Sister I.
MUTTONBIRD RESERVE

Craggy I.

Inner Sister I.
MUTTONBIRD RESERVE

Sisters Passage
Holloway Pt.
Stanley Pt.

Blyth Pt.
Palana

+ Bass Pyramid

Old Mans Head

Mt Killiecrankie
N2
316

C.C. Funk, 1898

Killecrankie Bay

Sentine I.

Killiecrankie

City of Foochow, 1877

Cape Frankland

Mt Tanner
331

WINGAROO
NATURE
RESERVE

FURNEAUX

Leeka

30

Roydon I.
N. Pasco I.
M. Pasco I.
S. Pasco I.

Tanners
Bay

Flinders

Patriarch Inlet
MUTTONBIRD RESERVE
Babel I.
Cat I.
Storehouse I.
Sellars Pt.

Marshall Bay

CONS. AREA

Settlement Pt.
Wybalenna
WILDLIFE SANCTUARY
Wybalenna I.

Emita
Museum

Memana

Island

Sellars Lagoon

Prime Seal I.

Arthur Bay

Blue Rocks

Mt Leventhorpe
501

Cameron Inlet

Darling Ra

LACKRANA WILDLIFE SANCTUARY

BIRD SANCTUARY
Chalky I.
Long Pt.

40

Whitemark

N. Chain Lagoon
S. Chain Lagoon

Safe Passage
NATURE RESERVE
Low Islets

Isabella I.
Parrys Bay

Ranga

Logan Lagoon

E. Kangaroo I.

Big Green I.

Fotheringate Bay

Strzelecki Peaks
756
STRZELECKI NATIONAL PARK

WILDLIFE SANCTUARY
Lady Barron
Lt. Green I.
Pot Boil Pt.

Sound

Adelaide Bay
Lt. Dog I.
Great Dog I.
MUTTONBIRD RESERVES

Vansittart I.

Chappell Islands
Mt Chappell I.

Anderson Islands
Tin Kettle I.
Anderson I.

Farsund, 1912
Puncheon Pt.

CONSERVATION AREA
Goose I.
Boundary, 1859

Badger I.

Franklin

Deep Bay

Harleys Pt.

GROUP

Long I.

Cape Barren Island

+ Mt Munro 686

Cape Barren Island

Cape Sir John

Thunder & Lightning Bay

G.V.H., 1897

Wombat Pt.

Kent Bay
+ Mt Kerford 303

Cape Barren

Margaret, 1828
Defiance, 1833
Courier, 1833

Preservation I.
"Sydney Cove" Historic Site
Rum I.

Channel

Seal Pt.

Cone Pt.

Foam Pt.

Spike Bay

Clarke Island

Black Pt.

Forsyth I.
Passage I.

Lookout Head

Moriarty Bay
Moriarty Pt.

South Head

Lioness, 1854

Banks Strait

Rum I.
Lt. Swan I.
Union, 1852

Brenda, 1832
Swan I.

Cape Portland
Sally, 1826
Cape Portland
CAPE PORTLAND (PRIVATE) WILDLIFE SANCT.

Mystery, 1850

MUSSELROE BAY

Ninth I.

Waterhouse I.
Creole, 1863

Waterhouse Pt.

Waterhouse Passage

Waterhouse Croppies Pt.

Ringarooma Bay

RINGAROOMA COASTAL RESERVE

CONSERVATION AREA
Great Musselroe Bay

Poole

Musselroe Pt.
Cape Naturaliste

WATERHOUSE CONSERVATION AREA

Big Waterhouse Lake

Tomahawk
TOMAHAWK COASTAL RES.

18

Boobyalla

Fosters Marshes

Rushy Lagoon

Boulder Pt.

East Sandy Pt.
St. Albans Bay

Waterhouse
TOMAHAWK RIVER RESERVE

19

MOUNT WILLIAM NATIONAL PARK

Anderson Bay

DOUBLE SANDY PT CONSERVATION AREA

41°

Bridport

23

Mt Cameron
551

Gladstone

The Banca

Eddystone Pt.

148°

148°30'

41°

© UNIVERSAL PUBLISHERS PTY LTD 2005

Joins map 481

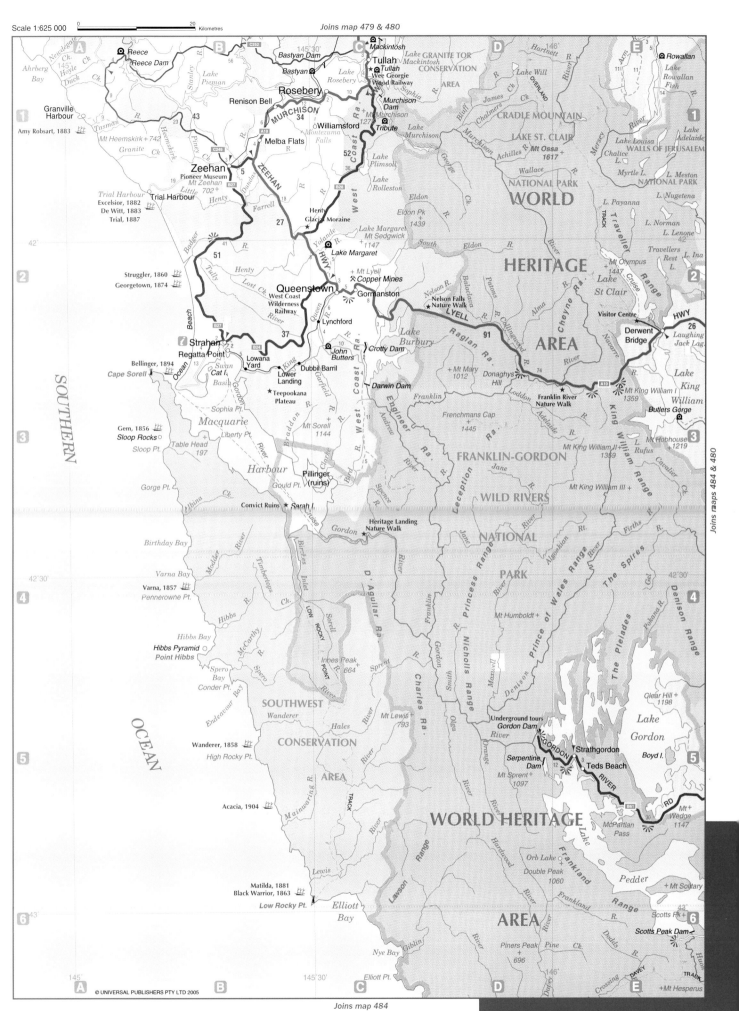

Scale 1:625 000

0   20 Kilometres

SOUTHERN

OCEAN

Granville Harbour
Amy Robsart, 1883

Reece
Reece Dam

Bastyan Dam
Bastyan

Mackintosh
Tullah
Tullah
Wee Georgie Wood Railway

Lake GRANITE TOR
CONSERVATION
AREA

Rowallan

Rosebery
Renison Bell

Lake Rosebery

Murchison Dam
Tribute

CRADLE MOUNTAIN

Lake Will

Lake Rowallan

MURCHISON

Williamsford

Melba Flats

Lake Sophia

Lake Murchison

LAKE ST. CLAIR

Lake Adelaide

Lake Louisa
WALLS OF JERUSALEM

Zeehan
Pioneer Museum
Mt Zeehan 702+

Montezuma Falls

Lake Plimsoll

NATIONAL PARK

Mt Ossa
1617

L. Meston

Myrtle L.
NATIONAL PARK

Trial Harbour
Excelsior, 1882
De Witt, 1883
Trial, 1887

ZEEHAN

Lake Rolleston

WORLD

L. Payanna

L. Norman
L. Lenone

Henty Glacial Moraine

Eldon

Eldon Pk
1439

HERITAGE

Mt Olympus
1447
Lake St Clair

Travellers Rest
L. Ina

Struggler, 1860
Georgetown, 1874

Lake Margaret
Mt Sedgwick
1147

Lake Margaret

Queenstown
West Coast Wilderness Railway

+ Mt Lyell
Copper Mines
Gormanston

Nelson Falls
Nature Walk

AREA

Visitor Centre

Derwent Bridge

Laughing Jack Lag.

Lynchford

Lake Burbury

LYELL

Raglan Ra.

Mt King William I
1359

Butlers Gorge

Strahan
Regatta Point

Lowana Yard
Lower Landing

Dubbil Barril
John Butters

Crotty Dam

Darwin Dam

Donaghys Hill

Franklin River Nature Walk

Mt Mary
1012

Mt King William II
1359

L. Rufus

Mt Hobhouse
+1219

Bellinger, 1894
Cape Sorell

Cat I.

Swan Basin

Teepookana Plateau

Mt Sorell
1144

Frenchmans Cap
1445

FRANKLIN-GORDON

Mt King William III +

Gem, 1856
Sloop Rocks
Sloop Pt.

Table Head
197

Liberty Pt.

WILD RIVERS

Gorge Pt.

Macquarie

Pillinger (ruins)

Harbour

Convict Ruins
Sarah I.

Heritage Landing
Nature Walk

NATIONAL

Birthday Bay

Varna Bay

Varna, 1857
Pennerowne Pt.

PARK

The Spires

Hibbs Bay

Hibbs Pyramid
Point Hibbs

Innes Peak
664

Mt Humboldt +

Prince of Wales Range

Clear Hill +
1198

Lake Gordon

OCEAN

Spero Bay
Conder Pt.

Endeavour Bay

Wanderer

Hales

Mt Lewis +
793

The Pleiades

Wanderer, 1858
High Rocky Pt.

SOUTHWEST

CONSERVATION

Underground tours
Gordon Dam

Strathgordon
Teds Beach

Boyd I.

Acacia, 1904

AREA

Serpentine Dam

Mt Sprent +
1097

WORLD HERITAGE

Mt + Wedge
1147

Matilda, 1881
Black Warrior, 1863

Low Rocky Pt.

Elliott Bay

McPartlan Pass

Orb Lake +
Double Peak
1060

AREA

Pedder

+ Mt Solitary

Scotts Pk +

Scotts Peak Dam

Nye Bay

Piners Peak +
696

+ Mt Hesperus

Elliott Pt.

© UNIVERSAL PUBLISHERS PTY LTD 2005

Joins maps 484 & 480

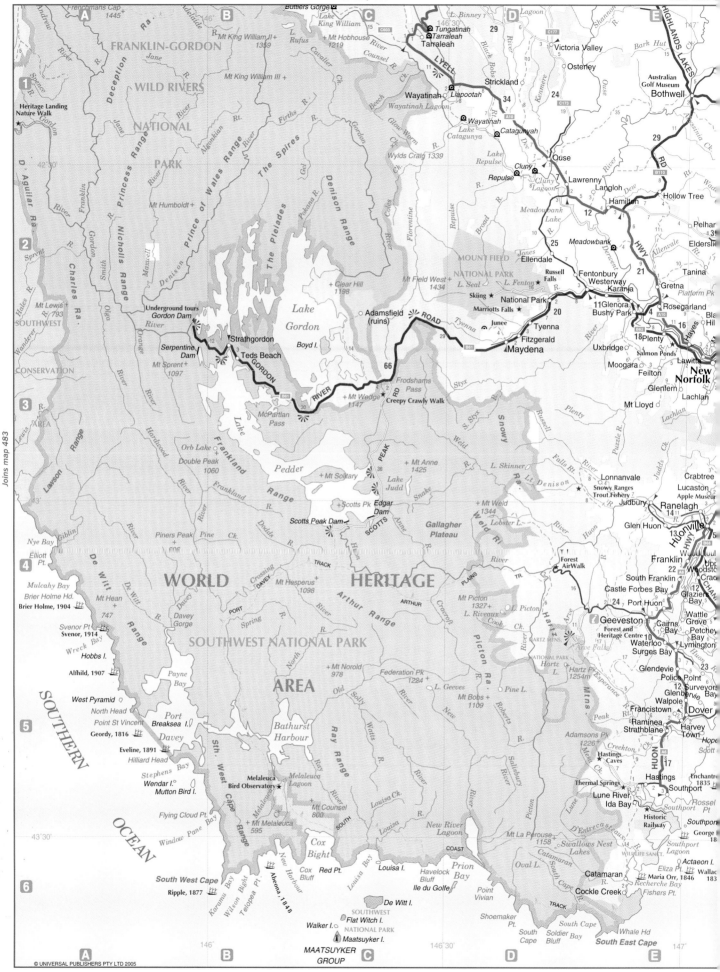

FRANKLIN-GORDON

WILD RIVERS

NATIONAL

PARK

SOUTHWEST

CONSERVATION

WORLD   HERITAGE

SOUTHWEST NATIONAL PARK

AREA

SOUTHERN

OCEAN

LYELL

MOUNT FIELD
NATIONAL PARK

New
Norfolk

SOUTHWEST
NATIONAL PARK

MAATSUYKER
GROUP

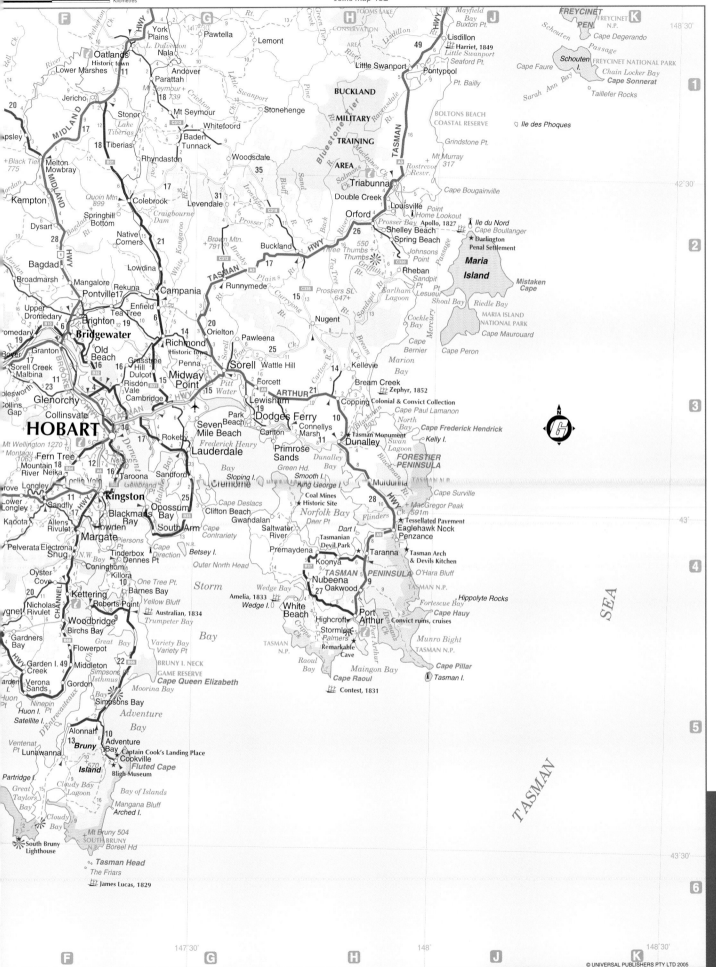

© UNIVERSAL PUBLISHERS PTY LTD 2005

INDEX

This alphabetical index covers the cities, suburbs, towns, localities and homesteads shown in this publication, as well as national parks, selected topographical features and selected places of interest.

The indexed entries are followed by the state or territory, the page number in the case of text references, and the page number and grid reference in the case of maps. All page references are in numerical order. eg. Adelaide Zoo, SA 297 D3, 298

Entries under one word are grouped together. Where entries consist of two or more, the alphabetical sequence is governed by the first, then the second word, eg. Little Swanport, Little Topar Roadhouse, Little Wobby, Littlehampton, Littlemore, Littles Crossing

References in bold type indicate locations to be found on the state or territory maps at the end of each chapter, eg. Adamsfield (Ruins), TAS **484 C2**

Entries in italic type indicate homesteads, eg. *Acacia Downs*, NSW **116 C1**

Entries beginning with Mc are treated as though they are spelt Mac, similarly Mt is indexed as Mount and St is indexed as Saint.

The following state or territory abbreviations are used in this index: ACT - Australian Capital Territory; NSW - New South Wales; NT - Northern Territory; QLD - Queensland; SA - South Australia; TAS - Tasmania; VIC - Victoria; WA - Western Australia

Note: this index does not purport to include every city, suburb, town, locality or homestead in Australia.

Balmoral, NSW 116 E4
Balmoral, NSW 47 J6
Balmoral, QLD 231 F2
Balmoral, VIC 206 D6
Balnarring, VIC 153 G4, 212 B4
Balnarring Beach, VIC 153 G5
Balook, QLD 283 F3
Balook, VIC 212 E4
Balranald, NSW 120 D2
Balwyn, VIC 150 E2
Balwyn North, VIC 150 E1
Bamaga, QLD 277 B2
Bamarang, NSW 97 B2
Bambaroo, QLD 279 J5
Bambill, VIC 204 C3
Bambilla, NSW 117 F3
Bambra, VIC 201 G4, 211 J4
Ban Ban Springs, NT 432 E4
Ban Ban Springs, QLD 287 H2
Banana, QLD 283 G6
Bancroft, QLD 287 H1
Banda, WA 401 H5
Bandiana, VIC 209 F3
Bang Bang, QLD 278 D5
Bangalee, QLD 267 C3
Bangalow, NSW 84 D2, 115 J2
Bangerang, VIC 206 E3
Bangham, SA 323 E2, 349 J4
Bangham, VIC 206 A4
Bangholme, VIC 151 F5
Bangor, NSW 49 F4
Bangor, TAS 480 E2
Banjawarn, WA 401 G5
Banjeroop, VIC 205 H6
Banjoura, QLD 281 H3
Banjup, WA 362 E6, 364 E2
Banka Banka, NT 436 E6
Banks, ACT 135 B6
Banksia, NSW 49 G3
Banksia, QLD 267 A2
Banksia Beach, QLD 255 D6
Banksia Park, SA 301 F5
Banksmeadow, NSW 49 J3
Bankstown, NSW 49 F2
Bankstown Airport, NSW 48 E2
Bannerton, VIC 205 F4
Bannockburn, QLD 281 J3
Bannockburn, VIC 201 H2, 211 J3
Banora Point, NSW 247 D6
Banrock Station, SA 333 B1
Banyan, VIC 205 F6
Banyena, VIC 207 F4
Banyo, QLD 229 J1, 231 F1
Baradine, NSW 114 B5
Barakee NP, NSW 119 J2
Barakula, QLD 287 G3
Baralba, QLD 283 F6
Barataria, QLD 281 G4
Baratta, SA 347 G4
Barcaldine, QLD 233, 282 B5
Barcaldine Downs, QLD 281 J5
Barden Ridge, NSW 48 E4
Bardoc, WA 403 K3
Bardon, QLD 230 D2
Bardwell Park, NSW 49 G3
Bardwell Valley, NSW 49 G3
Barellan, NSW 117 K6
Barellan Point, QLD 230 B4
Barfold, VIC 159 E2, 207 K5
Barford, QLD 286 C2
Bargara, QLD 233, 259 A1, 287 J1
Bargo, NSW 107 B2, 119 G6
Barham, NSW 120 E3
Barigar Gap (Rose Gap), VIC 195 C2
Baring, VIC 204 D5
Baringhup, VIC 159 D2, 207 J5
Barjarg, VIC 208 D5
Bark Hut Inn, NT 432 E3
Bark Mill & Museum, TAS 474, 481 H6
Barkly, VIC 207 G5
Barkly Downs, QLD 280 B2
Barkly Homestead Roadhouse, NT 440 B2
Barmah, VIC 208 B2
Barmedman, NSW 118 B6
Barmera, SA 305, 333 C2, 349 H1
Barmundu, QLD 283 H5

Barnadown, VIC 207 K4
Barnato, NSW 117 G2
Barnawartha, VIC 187 B1, 209 F2
Barnawartha South, VIC 187 B1, 209 F3
Barnes Bay, TAS 485 F4
Barnong, WA 402 C1
Barooga, NSW 121 H4
Barool NP, NSW 115 G3
Baroondah, QLD 287 F2
Barossa Goldfields, SA 301 G2
Barossa Wine & Visitor Centre, SA 327 C3
Barossa Valley, SA 289, 326, 327
Barpinba, VIC 201 F3, 211 H3
Barraba, NSW 114 D4
Barracks Archway, WA 359 B3, 360
Barracouta Gas & Oil Field, VIC 213 H3
Barradeen, QLD 286 C3
Barragup, WA 387 C2
Barramunga, VIC 201 G5, 211 H4
Barranyi NP, NT 437 J2
Barraport, VIC 207 H2
Barraroo, NSW 116 D2
Barratta, QLD 282 D1
Barrington, NSW 119 J2
Barrington, QLD 282 B1
Barrington, TAS 480 B3
Barrington Tops NP, NSW 119 H2
Barringun, NSW 113 F2
Barron Falls, QLD 239 B3
Barron Gorge NP, QLD 239 B3
Barrow Creek Roadhouse, NT 439 H4
Barry, NSW 118 E5, 119 H2
Barry Creek Camping Ground, VIC 179 C3
Barrys Reef, VIC 159 E3, 207 J6
Bartle Frere, QLD 239 D5
Barton, ACT 129 D5, 135 C3
Barton, VIC 195 E4, 207 F6
Barunduda, VIC 209 F3
Barunga, NT 429 E3, 433 F5
Barwidgee, WA 401 G5
Barwon Downs, VIC 201 G4, 211 H4
Barwon Heads, VIC 156-7, 201 K3, 211 K3
Barwon Park, VIC 201 G3
Baryulgil, NSW 115 H3
Basalt Creek, QLD 286 E1
Basin Pocket, QLD 230 A5
Basin View, NSW 97 B4
Basket Range, SA 303 F1
Basket Swamp NP, NSW 115 G2
Bass, VIC 212 C4
Bass Hill, NSW 48 E2
Bass Strait, 140, 460, 478
Bass Strait Shell Museum, VIC 201 G5
Bassendean, WA 362 E2
Batavia Downs, QLD 277 B4
Batchelor, NT 424-5, 425 C1, 432 D3
Batchica, VIC 206 E3
Bateau Bay, NSW 71 C4
Batehaven, VIC 122 D3
Bateman, WA 362 D5
Batemans Bay, NSW 52, 122 D3
Bathurst, NSW 52, 118 E4
Bathurst Island, NT 415, 432 C1
Batlow, NSW 77 A1, 122 A3
Batten Point, NT 437 H2
Battery, QLD 279 J5
Battery Hill, NT 439 J2
Battery Point, TAS 452, 453 D4, 454, 456 D4
Bauhinia Downs, NT 437 G2
Bauhinia Downs, QLD 280 E2, 283 F6
Baulkamaugh North, VIC 208 C2
Baulkham Hills, NSW 46 E5
Bauple, QLD 259 B5
Baw Baw NP, VIC 212 E2
Bawley Point, NSW 107 A6, 122 E3
Baxter, VIC 153 G2
Bay of Islands, VIC 200 C5
Bayindeen, VIC 159 B3
Baykool, QLD 286 B2
Baynton, VIC 208 A5
Bayswater, VIC 151 H2
Bayswater, WA 362 E2
Bayswater North, VIC 151 H2
Bayulu, WA 399 H4
Bayview, NSW 47 K3
Bayview, NT 418 B4

Bayview, TAS 481 J3
Bayview Chicory Kiln, VIC 153 K4
Beachmere, QLD 229 F6, 255 C6
Beachport, SA 305-6, 323 C4, 349 G5
Beacon, WA 402 E3
Beacon Hill, NSW 47 J4
Beaconsfield, NSW 49 H2
Beaconsfield, TAS 480 D2
Beaconsfield, VIC 151 J5
Beaconsfield, WA 362 C5, 379 E3
Beaconsfield Upper, VIC 151 J5, 212 C3
Beagle Bay, WA 399 F3
Bealiba, VIC 159 C1, 207 H4
Beallah, QLD 263 B6
Beanbah, NSW 113 K5
Beardmore, VIC 212 E2
Bearii, VIC 208 C2
Bears Lagoon, VIC 207 J3
Beauchamp Falls, VIC 201 F5
Beaudesert, QLD 235, 235 C2, 287 J5
Beaudesert, QLD 280 E3
Beaudesert Historical Museum, QLD 235 C2
Beaufort, VIC 159 B3, 207 G6
Beaumaris, TAS 481 J3
Beaumaris, VIC 150 E4
Beaumont, NSW 97 B1
Beaumont, SA 302 E1
Beauty Point, NSW 47 J5
Beauty Point, TAS 480 D2
Beazleys Bridge, VIC 207 G4
Beckenham, WA 363 F4
Beckom, NSW 118 A6
Beck's Aviation and Military Museum, QLD 259 A4
Bedford, NSW 119 H3
Bedford, WA 362 E2
Bedford Downs, WA 399 J3
Bedford Park, SA 302 C3
Bedfordale, WA 365 G3
Bedgerebong, NSW 118 B4
Bedourie, QLD 280 C6
Bedourie, QLD 287 F2
Bedunburru, WA 399 F3
Beeac, VIC 201 F3, 211 H3
Beebyn, WA 400 E5
Beech Forest, VIC 201 F5, 211 H4
Beechboro, WA 363 F2
Beechford, TAS 480 E1
Beechmont, QLD 235 D2, 247 A5
Beechworth, VIC 157, 186, 187 B1, 209 F3
Beechworth NP, VIC 209 F3
Beecroft, NSW 47 F4
Beedelup NP, WA 404 C4
Beelbangera, NSW 117 J6
Beeliar, WA 364 D2
Beemery, NSW 113 K4
Beenleigh, QLD 227, 235 D1, 247 A1, 287 K4
Beenleigh Rum Distillery, QLD 247 A1
Beerburrum, QLD 255 C5
Beerenberg Strawberry Farm, SA 303 H3
Beerwah, QLD 255 C5, 287 J4
Beetaloo, NT 436 D4
Beete, WA 405 K2
Bega, NSW 53, 122 D5
Begonia, QLD 286 E4
Beilpajah, NSW 117 F4
Belah, NSW 113 F5
Belair, SA 302 D2
Belair NP, SA 299, 302 E2
Belarabon, NSW 117 F3
Belconnen, ACT 135 B2, 137 C2
Belele, WA 400 E4
Belfield, NSW 49 G2
Belford, NSW 59 B1
Belgenny Farm, NSW 48 A5
Belgrave, VIC 151 J3, 170, 171 B4 212 C2
Belgrave Heights, VIC 151 J3, 171 B5
Belgrave South, VIC 151 J4
Belinar, NSW 116 D5
Belingeramble, NSW 117 H4
Belka, WA 402 E5
Bell, NSW 80 E1, 119 F5
Bell, QLD 271 C2, 287 H4
Bell Bay, TAS 480 D2
Bella Vista, NSW 46 E4

Bellalie, QLD 285 G4
Bellangry, NSW 119 K1
Bellara, QLD 229 G5, 255 D6
Bellarwi, NSW 118 B6
Bellata, NSW 114 C4
Bellbird, NSW 59 C6, 119 H4
Bellbird Park, QLD 230 C5
Bellbowrie, QLD 230 C4
Bellbridge, VIC 187 C1, 209 G2
Bellbrook, NSW 115 G5
Bellbuoy Beach, TAS 480 D1
Bellellen, VIC 195 D3, 207 F5
Bellenden Ker, QLD 239 D5
Bellerive, TAS 456 E4
Bellevue, QLD 279 G3
Bellevue, WA 363 G2
Bellevue Heights, SA 302 C3
Bellevue Hill, NSW 49 J2
Bellfield, QLD 279 F5
Bellfield, VIC 150 E1
Belli Park, QLD 255 B4
Bellingen, NSW 62 B4, 115 H5
Bellinger River NP, NSW 62 A4, 115 G5
Bellinger Wreck, 1894, TAS 483 B3
Bellingham, TAS 480 E1
Bellmere, QLD 228 D1
Belltrees, NSW 119 H2
Bellum Bellum, SA 323 E6
Bellvale, NSW 117 F2
Belmont, NSW 71 E1, 119 H4
Belmont, QLD 231 G3
Belmont, WA 363 F3
Belmore, NSW 49 G2
Beloka, NSW 77 D6, 122 B5
Belrose, NSW 47 J4
Beltana, SA 347 F2
Beltana Roadhouse, SA 347 F2
Belton, SA 347 F4
Belvedere, NSW 113 F4
Belyando Crossing, QLD 282 C3
Belyuen, NT 432 C3
Bemboka, NSW 122 C5
Bemm River, VIC 214 B5
Ben Boyd NP, NSW 38, 122 D5, 122 D6
Ben Buckler, NSW 49 K2
Ben Bullen, NSW 119 F4
Ben Halls Gap NP, NSW 119 H2
Ben Lomond, NSW 115 B4
Ben Lomond NP, TAS 481 G4
Ben Lomond Ski Village, TAS 481 G3
Bena, VIC 212 C4
Benagerie, SA 347 H3
Benalla, VIC 157, 208 D4
Benambra, VIC 187 E3, 209 H5
Benambra NP, NSW 121 J3
Benanee, NSW 120 C1
Benaraby, QLD 267 D6, 283 H5
Benarca, NSW 121 F4
Benarkin, QLD 271 E2, 271 E4
Benayeo, VIC 206 B5
Bencubbin, WA 402 E4
Benda Park, SA 347 H4
Bendalong, NSW 97 B6, 107 B5
Bendemeer, NSW 114 E5
Bendering, WA 405 F1
Bendethera Caves, NSW 122 C4
Bendick Murrell, NSW 118 C6
Bendidee NP, QLD 287 G5
Bendigo, SA 347 G5
Bendigo, VIC 140, 157, 158, 159, 159 E1, 207 J4
Bendigo Pottery, VIC 159 E1
Bendleby, SA 347 F4
Bendoc, VIC 214 B3
Bendolba, NSW 119 H3
Benedictine Mission, WA 402 C4
Benetook, VIC 204 D3
Benger, WA 375 C3
Bengerang, NSW 114 C2
Bengworden, VIC 177 B3, 213 G3
Benlidi, QLD 281 J6
Benmara, NT 437 J5
Bentleigh, VIC 150 E3
Bentleigh East, VIC 150 E3
Bentley, NSW 115 H2
Bentley, WA 362 E4
Benwerrin, VIC 201 G4, 211 J4

Caltowie, SA **347 F5**
Calulu, VIC 177 B2, **213 H2**
Calvert, VIC 159 A3, **195 E5**
Calvert Hills, NT **437 J4**
Calwell, ACT 135 B5
Camballin, WA **399 G4**
Cambeela, QLD **281 F4**
Camberville, VIC **212 D1**
Camberwell, NSW **119 G3**
Camberwell, VIC 150 E2
Cambewarra, NSW 97 B1, 107 B4
Cambewarra Lookout, NSW 97 B1
Cambooya, QLD 271 D4, **287 H4**
Cambrai, SA **349 G1**
Cambridge, TAS 457 H2, 469 A3, **485 G3**
Cambridge Gardens, NSW 46 A4
Cambridge Park, NSW 46 A5
Cambroon, QLD 255 B4
Camdale, TAS **480 A1**
Camden, NSW 45, 48 A5, 107 C1, **119 G6**
Camden Park, SA 302 C2
Camden Park Homestead, NSW 48 A5
Camden South, NSW 48 A5
Camel Creek, QLD **279 J5**
Camellia, NSW 47 F6
Camena, TAS **480 A2**
Cameron Downs, QLD **281 H3**
Camerons Pocket, QLD 263 A5
Camfield, NT **435 D3**
Camira, QLD 230 C5
Cammeray, NSW 47 J6
Camooweal, QLD **280 B1**
Camooweal Caves NP, QLD **280 B1**
Camp Creek, NT 425 C1, **432 D4**
Camp Hill, QLD 231 F3
Camp Mountain, QLD 230 C1
Campania, TAS 469 A2, **485 G2**
Campbell, ACT 135 C3
Campbell Town, TAS **481 F5**
Campbells Bridge, VIC 159 A1, 195 E1, **207 F5**
Campbells Pocket, QLD 228 B1
Campbells River, NSW **118 E5**
Campbelltown, NSW 48 C5, 107 C1, **119 G6**
Campbelltown, SA 300 E6
Campbelltown, VIC 159 D2, **207 J5**
Campbelltown Miniature Railway Park, VIC 151 H4, 171 B6
Camperdown, NSW 49 H2
Camperdown, VIC 180-1, 200 D3, **211 G3**
Campsie, NSW 49 G2
Canada Bay, NSW 49 G1
Canal Creek, QLD 267 B3
Canary, QLD **280 D5**
Canary Island, VIC **207 H2**
Canaway Downs, QLD **285 H3**
Canbelego, NSW **117 J1**
Canberra, ACT 124-35, 135 C3, **122 C3, 137 C2**
Canberra Airport, ACT 135 D3
Canberra Central, ACT 135 B3
Canberra Deep Space Communication Complex, ACT 135 A5, 136, **137 B3**
Canbera Nature Park, ACT 127, 135 B4
Canberra Space Dome, ACT 135 C2
Canberra Theatre Centre, ACT 129 D2
Candelo, NSW **122 D5**
Cane River, WA **400 C1**
Canegrass, SA **347 H6**
Cania Gorge NP, QLD **287 H1**
Caniaba, NSW 84 A3
Caniambo, VIC **208 C3**
Canley Heights, NSW 48 D2
Canley Vale, NSW 48 D2
Cann River, VIC **214 B4**
Canna, WA **402 B1**
Cannawigara, SA **349 H4**
Cannie, VIC **207 G2**
Canning Mills, WA 363 H5
Canning Vale, WA 364 E1
Cannington, QLD **280 E3**
Cannington, WA 363 F4
Cannon Hill, QLD 231 F2
Cannons Creek, VIC 153 J2
Cannonvale, QLD 263 A2
Canobie, QLD **280 E1**

Canonba, NSW **113 H6**
Canopus, SA **347 J6**
Canopus Observatory, TAS 457 G3
Canowindra, NSW 57, **118 D5**
Canteen Creek, NT **439 K3**
Canterbury, NSW 49 G2
Canterbury, VIC 150 E2
Canunda NP, SA 323 C5, **349 H6**
Canungra, QLD 235 D2, 247 A4, **287 K5**
Capalaba, QLD 231 H3
Capalaba West, QLD 231 H3
Cape Arid NP, WA 354, **407 B5**
Cape Barren Island, TAS **482 C4**
Cape Bridgewater, VIC 210 C4
Cape Byron Lighthouse, NSW 57, 84 E1
Cape Clear, VIC 201 F1, **211 H2**
Cape Crawford Roadhouse, NT **437 G3**
Cape Hillsborough Nature Resort, QLD 263 C5
Cape Hillsborough NP, QLD 263 C5
Cape Jaffa, SA 323 B3, **349 G5**
Cape Jervis, SA 317 E2, 337 A3, **348 E3**
Cape Lake, SA **116 E4**
Cape Le Grand NP, WA **407 A5**
Cape Leeuwin, WA 370, 371 C6, **404 B4**
Cape Leeuwin Lighthouse, WA 371 B6
Cape Melville NP, QLD **277 D6**
Cape Naturaliste, WA 370, 371 B1, **404 A3**
Cape Naturaliste Lighthouse & Maritime Museum, WA 371 B1
Cape Otway Lightstation, VIC 201 F6
Cape Palmerston NP, QLD **283 F3**
Cape Paterson, VIC **212 C4**
Cape Portland, TAS **482 C5**
Cape Range NP, WA 354, 356, **400 B2**
Cape Schanck, VIC 152 D6
Cape Schanck Lightstation & Museum, VIC 152 D6
Cape Upstart NP, QLD **282 E1**
Cape Vlamingh (West End), WA 395 A3
Cape Wickham Lighthouse, TAS **478 A1**
Cape Woolamai, VIC 165 E2
Cape Woolamai Walk, VIC 165 E3
Capel, WA 375 B6, **404 B3**
Capella, QLD **282 E4**
Capels Crossing, VIC **205 H6**
Capertee, NSW **119 F4**
Capital Hill, ACT 129 C5, 135 C3
Capon, NSW **116 E1**
Capoompeta NP, NSW **115 G3**
Capricorn Caves, QLD 266, 267 B3
Capricorn Roadhouse, WA **401 F2**
Capricorn Roadhouse Fuel Dump, WA **401 H2**
Capricornia Cays NP, QLD **283 H5, 283 J5**
Captain Billy Landing, QLD **277 C3**
Captain Cook Memorial, QLD 263 C2
Captain Cook Memorial Water Jet, ACT 129 D3, 131
Captain Cook's Landing Place, TAS **485 G5**
Captain Cook's Landing Place, NSW 49 H4
Captains Flat, NSW **122 C3**
Carabost, NSW **122 A3**
Caradoc, NSW **112 B5**
Caragabal, NSW **118 B5**
Caralue, SA **346 C5**
Caralulup, VIC 159 C2, **207 H5**
Caramut, VIC 200 B2, **210 E3**
Carandotta, QLD **280 B3**
Carapooee, VIC **207 G4**
Carapook, VIC **210 C2**
Caravan Head, NSW 49 G4
Carawa, SA **345 J4**
Carbarup, WA 369 C1
Carbeen Park, NT **432 E5**
Carbla, WA **400 B4**
Carboor, VIC 187 B2, **208 E4**
Carboor Upper, VIC **208 E4**
Carbrook, QLD 231 J6
Carbunup River, WA 371 C2, **404 B3**
Carcoar, NSW **118 D5**
Cardigan, QLD **282 C1**
Cardigan Village, VIC 159 C3, **211 H1**
Cardinia, VIC **212 C3**
Cardross, VIC **204 D3**
Cardstone, QLD **279 J4**
Cardup, WA 365 F4

Cardwell, QLD **279 J4**
Careel Bay, NSW 47 K2
Carew, SA 323 D1
Carey Downs, WA **400 C4**
Carey Gully, SA 303 F1
Careys Caves, NSW 109, **122 B2**
Cargerie, VIC 201 H1, **211 J2**
Cargo, NSW **118 D4**
Cariewerloo, SA **346 D4**
Carilla, WA 363 J4
Carina, QLD 231 G3
Carina, VIC **204 B5**
Carina Heights, QLD 231 G3
Carinda, NSW **113 J4**
Carindale, QLD 231 G3
Carine, WA 362 C1
Carinyah, WA 363 J5
Carisbrook, VIC 159 C2, **207 H5**
Carisbrook Falls, VIC 201 G5
Carisbrooke, QLD **281 F4**
Carlachy, NSW **118 B4**
Carlindie, WA **398 C6**
Carlingford, WA 47 F5
Carlisle, WA 362 E3
Carlisle River, VIC 200 E5, **211 G4**
Carlo, QLD **280 B5**
Carlo Point, QLD 255 C1, 259 C5
Carlsruhe, VIC 159 E2, **207 K6**
Carlton, NSW **113 H6**
Carlton, NSW 49 G3
Carlton, TAS 469 B3, **485 G3**
Carlton, VIC 147 C1, 148, 150 D2
Carlton Brewhouse, QLD 247 A2
Carlton Hill, WA **399 K2**
Carlton North, VIC 150 D1
Carmala, NSW **116 D2**
Carmel, WA 363 H4
Carmila, QLD **283 F3**
Carmor Plains, NT **432 E3**
Carmyle, QLD 255 A1, 259 A6
Carnamah, WA **402 B2**
Carnarvon, QLD **286 D1**
Carnarvon, WA 372-3, **400 B3**
Carnarvon Bay Wreck, 1901, TAS **478 B3**
Carnarvon NP, QLD 266, **286 D1**
Carnegie, VIC 150 E3
Carnes, SA **345 J1**
Carnes Hill, NSW 48 C3
Carney, NSW **112 D5**
Carngham, VIC 159 C3
Carnnegie, WA **401 H4**
Caroda, NSW **114 D4**
Carole Park, QLD 230 D5
Caroline Springs, VIC 150 A1
Caroline Wreck, 1862, TAS **481 J4**
Caron, WA **402 C2**
Carool, NSW 247 C6
Caroona, NSW **119 G1**
Caroona, SA **347 G6**
Carpendeit, VIC 200 E4, **211 G4**
Carpentaria Downs, QLD **279 H5**
Carpenter Rocks, SA 323 D6, **349 H6**
Carrabin, WA **403 F4**
Carrai NP, NSW **115 G5**
Carrajung, VIC **213 F4**
Carramar, NSW **113 H4**
Carramar, NSW 48 E2
Carranballac, VIC 200 D1, **211 G2**
Carranya, QLD **285 F2**
Carrara, QLD 247 C4
Carrarang, WA **400 B4**
Carrathool, NSW 121 G1
Carrick, TAS **480 E3**
Carrick Hill, SA 302 D2
Carrickalinga, SA 337 B1
Carrieton, SA **347 F4**
Carroll, NSW **114 D5**
Carron, VIC **207 F3**
Carrum, QLD **280 E2**
Carrum, VIC 151 F6, **212 B3**
Carrum Downs, VIC 151 F6
Carse O Gowrie, QLD **282 C2**
Carseldine, QLD 229 G1
Carss Park, NSW 49 G3
Carters Ridge, QLD 255 B3
Cartwright, NSW 48 D2

Carwarp, VIC **204 D3**
Carwell, QLD **286 C1**
Cascade, NSW 62 B3
Cascade, WA **405 J3**
Cascade Brewery, TAS 452, 453 A5, 454, 456 C4
Cascade NP, NSW 62 B3, **115 H4**
Cascades, TAS 456 C4
Casey, ACT 135 B1
Cashmere, QLD 228 D5
Cashmere Downs, WA **403 G1**
Cashmere West, QLD **286 E4**
Cashmore, VIC **210 C4**
Casino, NSW 60, **115 H2**
Casino Canberra, ACT 129 D2
Cassilis, NSW **119 F2**
Cassilis, VIC **209 H5**
Castambul, SA 301 F6
Casterton, VIC 161, **210 C2**
Castle Cove, NSW 47 H5
Castle Forbes Bay, TAS **484 E4**
Castle Hill, NSW 46 E4
Castle Rock, NSW 91 C1, **119 G3**
Castle Tower NP, QLD 267 D6
Castleburn, VIC 177 A1, **213 G2**
Castlecrag, NSW 47 J5
Castlemaine, VIC 158, 159 D2, 161-2, **207 J5**
Castlemaine Art Gallery, VIC 159 D2
Castlevale, QLD **282 C6**
Casuarina, NT 418 C2
Casuarina, WA 364 D4
Casula, NSW 48 D3
Cataby Roadhouse, WA **402 B4**
Catamaran, TAS **484 E6**
Cataract Gorge, TAS 464, **480 E3**
Cataraqui Wreck, 1845, TAS **478 A3**
Cathcart, NSW **122 C5**
Cathcart, VIC 159 A3
Cathedral Beach Resort, QLD 259 D3
Cathedral Fig Tree, QLD 239 B4
Cathedral Gorge, WA **399 K3**
Cathedral Hill, QLD **281 F3**
Cathedral Rock NP, NSW **115 G5**
Catherine Field, NSW 48 B4
Catherine Hill Bay, NSW 71 D2
Cato, NSW **113 H4**
Cattai, NSW 46 D1
Cattai (Mitchell Park) NP, NSW 46 D1
Cattai NP, NSW 46 D1
Cattle Creek, NT **436 A4**
Catumnal, VIC **207 H2**
Caulfield, VIC 150 D3
Caulfield East, VIC 150 E3
Caulfield North, VIC 150 D3
Caulfield South, VIC 150 E3
Cavan, NSW **116 D5**
Cavan, SA 300 D5
Caveat, VIC **208 C5**
Cavendish, VIC 195 A5, **210 D1**
Caversham, WA 363 F2
Caverton, SA **349 H6**
Caves Beach, NSW 71 E2
Caves District, WA 370
Caveside, TAS **480 C4**
Caveton, SA 323 E6
Cawarral, QLD 267 B4
Cawdor, NSW 48 A5
Cawkers Well, NSW **116 D2**
Cawnalmurtee, NSW **112 B5**
Cawongla, NSW **115 H2**
Cazneaux Tree, SA 313 C2
Cecil Hills, NSW 48 C2
Cecil Park, NSW 48 C2
Cecil Plains, QLD 271 B4, **287 H4**
Cedar Bay NP, QLD **279 J2**
Cedar Brush Creek, NSW 71 B2
Cedar Creek, QLD 228 B5, 247 A2
Cedar Pocket, QLD 255 B2
Cedar Point, NSW **115 H2**
Cedars, NSW **113 H4**
Cedarton, QLD 255 B5
Ceduna, SA 307, **345 H4**
Centennial Glen Stables, NSW 80 D3
Centennial Park, NSW 49 J2
Central, NSW 43 C5, 49 J2
Central Coast, NSW 35, 70

Derwent River, TAS see River Derwent, TAS
Desert Oaks Resort, NT 423 C2
Deua NP, NSW 122 D4
Devenish, VIC 208 D3
Devils Gullet, TAS 465, 480 B4
Devils Marbles, NT 409, 439 J3
Deviot, TAS 480 E2
Devon Meadows, VIC 153 J1
Devon Park, SA 300 C6
Devonborough Downs, SA 347 H4
Devoncourt, QLD 280 D3
Devonport, TAS 446, 462, 480 C2
Dewhurst, VIC 151 K4
Dharruk, NSW 46 C4
Dharug NP, NSW 71 A4, 119 G4
Dhuragoon, NSW 120 E2
Dhurringile, VIC 208 B4
Diamantina Lakes, QLD 280 E5
Diamantina NP, QLD 280 E5
Diamond Bay, NSW 49 K1
Diamond Well, WA 401 F4
Dianella, WA 362 E2
Diapur, VIC 206 C3
Dickson, ACT 133, 135 C2
Dicky Beach, QLD 255 D5
Didcot, QLD 287 H2
Diddleum Plains, TAS 481 G3
Diemals, WA 403 G2
Dig Tree, SA 343 J3
Digby, VIC 210 C2
Diggers Rest, VIC 212 A2
Diggora West, VIC 207 K3
Dillalah, QLD 286 C3
Dillcar, QLD 281 G4
Dilpurra, NSW 120 E2
Dilston, TAS 480 E3
Dimboola, VIC 206 D3
Dimbulah, QLD 279 H3
Dingee, VIC 207 J3
Dingley Village, VIC 151 F4
Dingo, QLD 283 F5
Dingo Beach, QLD 282 E1
Dingwall, VIC 207 H2
Dinmore, QLD 230 B5
Dinner Plain, VIC 187 C3, 209 G5
Dinninup, WA 404 C3
Dinosaur Display Centre, QLD 281 H2
Dinyarrak, VIC 206 B3
Dipperu NP, QLD 282 E3
Diranbandi, QLD 286 E5
Direk, SA 300 D5
Dirk Hartog, WA 400 B4
Dirnaseer, NSW 122 A2
Dirrung, NSW 117 H5
Disney, QLD 282 C3
Dixie, QLD 279 F1
Dixie, VIC 200 D3, 211 F3
Dixons Creek, VIC 212 C2
Djibalara (Asses Ears), VIC 195 B2
Djuan, QLD 271 D3
Djukbinj NP, NT 432 D2, 432 E3
Dneiper, NT 440 A6
Dobroyd Point, NSW 49 G2
Docker, VIC 187 A2, 208 E4
Docklands, VIC 147 A3, 150 C2
Doctors Flat, VIC 209 H6
Dodges Ferry, TAS 469 B3, 485 G3
Dolans Bay, NSW 49 G5
Dollar, VIC 212 D4
Dolls Point, NSW 49 H4
Dollykissangel, WA 403 K6
Dolomite, QLD 280 D2
Dolphin Discovery Centre, WA 375 A4, 404 B3
Dolphin Wreck, 1867, TAS 479 B6
Dolphin-watching Cruises, Jervis Bay, NSW 97 D4
Don, QLD 280 B2
Don Rhodes Mining Museum, WA 398 C5
Don River Railway, TAS 480 C2
Donald, VIC 166-7, 207 F3
Doncaster, QLD 281 G2
Doncaster, VIC 151 F1
Doncaster East, VIC 151 F1
Dongara, WA 377, 402 A2
Dongon Plains, QLD 286 D5
Donnelly, WA 404 C4

Donnybrook, QLD 255 C6
Donnybrook, VIC 167 E3
Donnybrook, WA 374, 375 C6, 377, 404 C3
Donors Hills, QLD 278 D5
Donovans, SA 323 E6
Donvale, VIC 151 G1
Doo Town, TAS 469 D5
Doobibla, QLD 286 B4
Dooboobetic, VIC 207 G3
Doodlakine, WA 402 E5
Dooen, VIC 206 E4
Dookie, VIC 208 C3
Doolandella, QLD 230 E5
Dooley Downs, WA 400 D3
Doolgunna, WA 401 F4
Doomadgee, QLD 278 B4
Doomben, QLD 231 F2
Doonan, QLD 255 C3
Doongmabulla, QLD 282 C3
Doonside, NSW 46 C5
Dooragan NP, NSW 119 K2
Dooralon, NSW 71 B2
Doorawarrah, WA 400 B3
Dora Creek, NSW 71 D2
Dorisvale, NT 432 D5
Dorodong, VIC 210 B1
Dorrien, SA 327 C3
Dorrigo, NSW 62 A3, 66, 115 H4
Dorrigo NP, NSW 62 B3, 115 H4
Dorrigo Rainforest Centre & Skywalk, NSW 62 B3
Dorrington, QLD 230 E2
Dorroughby, NSW 84 B3
Dorset Vale, SA 302 E4
Dorunda, QLD 278 E3
Dotswood, QLD 282 C1
Double Bay, NSW 49 J2
Double Creek, TAS 469 D1, 485 H2
Double Yards, NSW 116 C4
Doubleview, WA 362 C2
Doubtful Creek, NSW 115 H2
Douglas, NT 432 D4
Douglas, VIC 206 C5
Douglas Apsley NP, TAS 481 J4
Douglas Experimental Station, NT 432 D4
Douglas Hot Springs, NT 432 E4
Douglas River, TAS 481 J5
Dover, TAS 484 E5
Dover Gardens, SA 302 C3
Dover Heights, NSW 49 J1
Doveton, VIC 151 G4
Dowerin, WA 402 D4
Downer, ACT 135 C2
Doyalson, NSW 71 D2
Drake, NSW 115 G2
Draper, QLD 228 D6
Dreamtime Cultural Centre, QLD 267 A4, 268 283 H5
Dreamworld, QLD 246, 247 B3, 287 K4
Dreeite, VIC 201 F3, 211 H3
Drekurni, SA 346 C5
Drewvale, QLD 231 F6
Driffield, VIC 212 E3
Drik Drik, VIC 210 B3
Drillham, QLD 287 F3
Driver, NT 419 B5
Dromana, VIC 152 E4, 212 B4
Dromedary, TAS 485 F3
Drouin, VIC 167, 212 D3
Drovers Cave NP, WA 402 A3
Drumborg, VIC 210 C3
Drumduff, QLD 279 F2
Drumlion, QLD 281 G4
Drummartin, VIC 207 K3
Drummond, QLD 282 D5
Drummond, VIC 207 J5
Drummond Cove, WA 402 A1
Drummoyne, NSW 49 H1
Drung Drung South, VIC 195 B1, 206 E4
Dry Creek, SA 300 C5
Dry River, NT 436 B1
Dryander NP, QLD 263 A2, 282 E2
Drysdale, VIC 168, 201 K3, 211 K3
Drysdale River, WA 399 H2
Drysdale River NP, WA 399 J2
Duaringa, QLD 283 F5

Dubbil Barril, TAS 483 C3
Dubbo, NSW 66, 118 D3
Duchess, QLD 280 D3
Ducklo, QLD 287 G4
Duddo, VIC 204 B5
Dudley Park, SA 300 C6
Dudley Park, WA 387 C2
Duff Creek (Ruin), SA 342 C4
Duffields, SA 347 J4
Duffy, ACT 135 A4
Duffys Forest, NSW 47 H3
Dulacca, QLD 287 F3
Dularcha NP, QLD 255 C5
Dulbydilla, QLD 286 D3
Dulcie Range NP, NT 440 B6
Dulcot, TAS 469 A3, 485 G3
Dulkaninna, SA 343 F5
Dululu, QLD 267 A5, 283 G5
Dulwich, SA 302 D1
Dulwich Hill, NSW 49 H2
Dumbalk, VIC 212 D4
Dumbalk North, VIC 212 D4
Dumbleyung, WA 404 E3
Dumosa, VIC 207 G2
Dumstown, VIC 167 A3
Dunach, VIC 159 C2, 207 H5, 211 H1
Dunalley, TAS 469 C3, 485 H3
Dunbar, QLD 278 E2
Duncraig, WA 362 C1
Dundas Valley, NSW 47 F5
Dundee, NSW 115 F3
Dundee, QLD 281 G3
Dundee Beach, NT 432 C3
Dundinin, WA 404 E2
Dundonnell, VIC 200 D2, 211 F2
Dundoo, QLD 285 J4
Dundowran, QLD 259 B3
Dundubara, QLD 259 D3
Dundula, QLD 263 C6
Dunedoo, NSW 118 E2
Dungarvon, NSW 112 D3
Dunggir NP, NSW 62 A6, 115 H5
Dungog, NSW 66-7, 119 H3
Dungowan, NSW 114 E6
Dungowan, NT 436 B3
Dunheved, NSW 46 B4
Dunkeld, NSW 118 E4
Dunkeld, QLD 286 E4
Dunkeld, VIC 194, 195 B6, 200 A1, 210 E2
Dunlop, ACT 135 A1
Dunluce, QLD 281 H2
Dunmarra Roadhouse, NT 436 D3
Dunolly, VIC 159 C1, 207 H4
Dunoon, NSW 84 B2, 115 J2
Dunorlan, TAS 480 C3
Dunrobin, QLD 282 C4
Dunrobin, VIC 210 C2
Dunsborough, WA 370, 371 B1, 377, 404 B3
Duntroon, NSW 112 B6
Dunvegan, NSW 113 H2
Dunwich, QLD 235 D1
Dunwinnie, QLD 286 E5
Durabrook, QLD 282 D5
Durack, NT 419 A5
Durack, QLD 230 E5
Durack River Roadhouse, WA 399 J2
Dural, NSW 47 F3
Duramana, NSW 118 E4
Durdidwarrah, VIC 201 H1, 211 J2
Durham Downs, QLD 285 F4
Durham Ox, VIC 207 H2
Duri, NSW 114 E6
Durong South, QLD 287 H3
Durras, NSW 122 E3
Durri, QLD 284 D2
Dutson, VIC 177 A3, 213 G3
Dutton Park, QLD 230 E3
Dutton River, QLD 281 H2
Dwellingup, WA 375 E1, 404 C2
Dynevor Downs, QLD 285 H5
Dynnyrne, TAS 453 B5, 456 D5
Dysart, QLD 282 E4
Dysart, TAS 485 F2

E Shed Market, WA 379 C2
Eagle Bay, WA 371 B1, 404 B3
Eagle Farm, QLD 231 F2
Eagle Heights, QLD 247 A3
Eagle Junction, QLD 231 F1
Eagle On The Hill, SA 302 E2
Eagle Point, VIC 177 C2, 213 H2
Eagle St Pier & Riverside Markets, QLD 225 D4
Eagle Vale, NSW 48 C4
Eaglehawk, NSW 116 B3
Eaglehawk, VIC 159 D1, 207 J4
Eaglehawk Neck, TAS 462, 468, 469 D4, 485 H4
Eaglemont, VIC 150 E1
Eagle's Heritage, WA 371 B4
Earaheedy, WA 401 G4
Earlando, QLD 263 A2
Earlston, VIC 208 C4
Earlwood, NSW 49 G2
East Ballina, NSW 84 D3
East Brisbane, QLD 231 F3
East Camberwell, VIC 150 E2
East Cannington, WA 363 F4
East Fremantle, WA 362 C4
East Gresford, NSW 119 H3
East Hills, NSW 48 E3
East Ipswich, QLD 230 A5
East Jindabyne, NSW 122 B4
East Jindabyne, NSW 77 D5
East Killara, NSW 47 H4
East Kurrajong, NSW 46 B1
East Lindfield, NSW 47 H5
East Melbourne, VIC 150 D2
East Perth, WA 359 E2, 360, 362 E3
East Point, NT 416, 418 A3
East Rockingham, WA 364 C4
East Sassafras, TAS 480 C2
East Victoria Park, WA 362 E3
East Witchcliffe, WA 371 B4
Eastbourne, NSW 77 D4
Eastern Creek, NSW 46 C5
Eastern Heights, QLD 230 A5
Eastern View, VIC 201 H4, 211 J4
Eastlake, NSW 115 F5
Eastlakes, NSW 49 J2
Eastmere, QLD 282 B4
Eastville, VIC 207 J5
Eastwood, NSW 47 F5
Eastwood, SA 297 E5, 302 D1
Eaton, WA 375 C4
Eatons Hill, QLD 228 D6
Ebbw Vale, QLD 230 B5
Ebden, VIC 209 G3
Ebenezer, NSW 46 C1
Ebor, NSW 115 G5
Eccleston, NSW 119 H3
Echidna Chasm, WA 399 K3
Echo Hills, QLD 282 D5
Echo Point, NSW 80 E5
Echuca, VIC 139, 168, 208 A2
Echunga, SA 303 G4
Ecklin South, VIC 200 D4, 211 F4
Eco Beach Wilderness Retreat, WA 398 E4
Eddington, VIC 159 C1, 207 H5
Eden, NSW 67, 122 D6
Eden Creek, NSW 115 H2, 235 C3
Eden Hill, WA 363 F2
Eden Hills, SA 302 D3
Eden Vale O.S., QLD 279 F4
Edenhope, VIC 168, 206 B5
Edensor Park, NSW 48 C2
Edenvale, WA 387 D3
Edeowie, SA 313 B2
Edgecliff, NSW 49 J2
Edgecombe, VIC 159 E2, 167 C1
Edgecumbe Beach, TAS 479 D3
Edgeroi, NSW 114 C4
Edi, VIC 187 A2, 208 E4
Edillilie, SA 348 B1
Edinburgh, SA 300 D3
Edith, NSW 119 F5
Edith Creek, TAS 479 C3
Edith Downs, QLD 281 F2
Edith Falls, NT 427, 433 F5

Gordonvale, QLD 239 C4, **279 J3**
Gore, QLD 271 B6, **287 H5**
Gore Hill, NSW 47 H6
Gorge Creek, QLD **279 G6**
Gorge Wildlife Park, SA 301 G5
Gorman House Arts Centre, ACT 129 D2
Gormandale, VIC **213 F3**
Gormanston, TAS **483 C2**
Gorokan, NSW 71 D3
Goroke, VIC **206 C4**
Gorrie, NT **436 C2**
Goschen, VIC **205 G6**
Gosford, NSW 69, 71 B4, **119 H5**
Gosnells, WA 363 F5, 365 F1
Gosses, SA **346 B2**
Goughs Bay, VIC **208 D5**
Goulburn, NSW 69-70, **122 D2**
Goulburn River NP, NSW 91 A2, **119 F3**
Goulburn Weir, VIC **208 B4**
Gould Creek, SA 300 E3
Goulds Country, TAS **481 H2**
Gourock NP, NSW **122 C3, 137 E5**
Government House, NT 417 D6
Government House, SA 297 D3, 298
Government House, TAS 453 C2
Government House, WA 358
Gowanford, VIC **205 G5**
Gowar, VIC 159 D2, **207 J5**
Gowar East, VIC **207 G4**
Gowrie, ACT 135 C5
Gowrie, QLD **287 H4**
Gowrie Park, TAS **480 B3**
Goyura, VIC **206 E2**
Grabben Gullen, NSW **122 C1**
Gracemere, QLD 267 B4, **283 G5**
Gracetown, WA 371 B3, **404 A3**
Graceville, QLD 230 E3
Gradgery, NSW **113 J6**
Gradule, QLD **287 F5**
Grafton, NSW 70, 72, **115 H3**
Graman, NSW **114 E3**
Grampians NP, VIC 194, 195,
  195 C3, **206 E6**
Grampians National Park Visitors Centre,
  VIC 195 D3
Granada, QLD **280 D1**
Grandchester, QLD 235 B1, **287 J4**
Grange, QLD 230 E2
Grange, SA 302 B1
Granite Creek, NT 429 B2, **432 E5**
Granite Downs, SA **341 H2**
Granite Flat, VIC 187 D2, **209 G4**
Granite Gorge, QLD 239 A4
Granite Island, SA 336, 337 D2
Granite Peak, WA **401 G4**
Grantham, QLD 271 E4, **287 J4**
Granton, QLD **280 D4**
Granton, TAS **485 F3**
Grants Monument, VIC 153 K6
Grantville, VIC **212 C4**
Granville, NSW 46 E6
Granville Harbour, TAS **483 A1**
Granya, VIC 187 D1, **209 G2**
Grass Karting, NSW 81 K1
Grass Patch, WA **405 K3**
Grass Valley, WA **402 D5**
Grassdale, VIC **210 C2**
Grassmere, NSW **116 D1**
Grassmere, VIC 200 B3
Grasstree Hill, TAS 456 E1, **485 F3**
Grassy, TAS **478 B3**
Grattai, NSW 118 E3
Gravelly Beach, TAS **480 E2**
Gravesend, NSW **114 D3**
Gray, NT 419 B6
Gray, TAS **481 J4**
Grays Point, NSW 49 G5
Graytown, VIC **208 B4**
Great Barrier Reef, QLD 217, 218, 223,
  238, 262, 277
Great Barrier Reef Marine Park, QLD 221,
  279 K2
Great Basalt Wall NP, QLD **281 J1**
Great Dividing Range 36, 76, 140, 186,
  238, 270
Great Keppell Island, QLD 226, 267 C3,
  283 H5

Great Mackerel Beach, NSW 47 K2
Great Ocean Road, VIC 139, 199
Great Sandy (Cooloola Section) NP, QLD
  255 C1, 259 C6
Great Sandy NP, QLD 220, 258, 259 D2,
  287 K2, 287 K3
Great Western, VIC 159 A2, 195 E3, **207 F5**
Greater Kingston NP, WA **404 C4**
Greater Preston NP, WA **404 C3**
Gredgwin, VIC **207 H2**
Green Fields, SA 300 D4
Green Gully, NSW 80 D6
Green Head, WA **402 A3**
Green Hills Range, SA 303 G5
Green Island NP, QLD 239 D2
Green Lake, VIC **206 E4**
Green Mountain, QLD 254
Green Valley, NSW 48 C2
Green Valley, WA 369 C3
Greenacre, NSW 49 F2
Greenacres, SA 300 D6
Greenbank, NT **437 J2**
Greenbushes, WA **404 C3**
Greendale, VIC 159 E3, 167 B3, **211 J1**
Greater Bendigo NP, VIC 159 E1, **207 J4**
Greenethorpe, NSW 118 C5
Greenfield Park, NSW 48 D2
Greenfields, WA 387 C1
Greenhill, QLD **283 F3**
Greenhill, SA 302 E1
Greenhills, WA **402 D5**
Greenmount, QLD 271 D5, **287 H4**
Greenmount, VIC **213 F4**
Greenmount, WA 363 G2
Greenmount East, QLD 271 D5
Greenmount NP, WA 363 G2
Greenock, SA 327 B2
Greenough, WA 380, **402 A1**
Greenough Hamlet Historic Site, WA 380,
  402 A1
Greenridge, QLD 255 B3
Greens Beach, TAS **480 D2**
Greens Creek, VIC 159 A1, **207 F5**
Greenslopes, QLD 231 F3
Greenvale, NSW 113 G4
Greenvale, QLD **279 H5**
Greenvale, QLD **279 H5**
Greenwald, VIC **210 C3**
Greenway, ACT 135 B5
Greenways, SA **349 H5**
Greenwell Point, NSW 97 D2, 107 C4,
  122 E2
Greenwich, NSW 47 H6
Greenwith, SA 300 E4
Greenwood, WA 362 C1
Greg Greg, NSW 117 A4
Gregors Creek, QLD 255 A5
Gregory, WA **400 B6**
Gregory Downs, QLD **278 B5**
Gregory Downs, QLD **278 B5**
Gregory Mine, QLD **282 E4**
Gregory NP, NT 435 C2, 435 D1
Gregory Springs, QLD **279 H6**
Gregra, NSW **118 D4**
Grenfell, NSW 72, **118 C5**
Grenfield, QLD **285 J3**
Grenville, VIC 201 G1, **211 H2**
Greta, NSW 59 E2, **119 H3**
Greta, VIC 187 A2, **208 E4**
Greta South, VIC 187 A2, **208 E4**
Greta West, VIC 187 A2, **208 E4**
Gretna, TAS **484 E2**
Grevillia, NSW 115 H1, 235 C3
Grey Peaks NP, QLD 239 D4
Greycliffe House, NSW 49 J1
Greystanes, NSW 46 D6
Griffin, QLD 229 G4
Griffith, ACT 135 C4
Griffith, NSW 72, **117 J6**
Griffiths Lookout, NSW 62 A4
Grindelwald Swiss Village, TAS 465, **480 E3**
Gringegalgona, VIC **210 D1**
Grogan, NSW **118 B6**
Grong Grong, NSW **121 J2**
Gronos Point, NSW 46 C1
Grose Vale, NSW 81 K2
Grove, TAS **485 F4**

Grovedale, VIC **201 J3**
Grovely, QLD 230 D1
Grubb Shaft Museum, TAS 458, **480 D2**
Guanaba, QLD 247 A3
Gubara Springs, NT 427 E3
Gubara Walk, NT 427 E3
Gubbata, NSW **117 K5**
Guilderton, WA **402 B4**
Guildford, NSW 48 E1
Guildford, TAS **479 E5**
Guildford, VIC 159 D2, 167 B1, **207 J5**
Guildford, WA 363 F2
Guildford West, NSW 48 E1
Gulaga NP, NSW **122 D4**
Gular, NSW **114 A6**
Gulargambone, NSW **114 A6**
Gulgong, NSW **118 E3**
Gulmarrad, NSW **115 H3**
Gulnare, SA **347 F6**
Gulpa, NSW **121 F3**
Gulthul, NSW **116 D6, 120 C1**
Guluguba, QLD **287 F3**
Guluyambi Cruise, NT 427 E1
Gum Creek, QLD 91 E4
Gum Creek, SA 313 C1
Gum Flat, NSW **114 E3**
Gum Lake, NSW **116 E3**
Gum San Chinese Heritage Centre, VIC
  207 F5
Gum Vale, NSW **111 D3**
Gumbalara, NSW **112 C4**
Gumbalie, NSW **112 E4**
Gumbardo, QLD **285 J3**
Gumbo, NSW **112 D2**
Gumdale, QLD 231 H3
Gumeracha, SA 299, 301 H5
Gumeracha Toy Factory, SA 301 H5
Gumlu, QLD **282 D1**
Gunalda, NSW 255 A1, 259 A6, **287 J3**
Gunana, QLD **278 B3**
Gunbar, NSW **117 H5**
Gunbar, NSW **117 H5**
Gunbower, VIC **207 K2**
Gundabooka NP, NSW **113 F4**
Gundagai, NSW 73, **122 A2**
Gundagai, NT **429 A3**
Gundamaian, NSW 49 G5
Gundaring, WA **404 E3**
Gundaroo, NSW **122 C2**
Gundiah, QLD 259 A5, **287 J2**
Gundibindyal, NSW **122 A1**
Gundooee, NSW **113 H5**
Gundowring, NSW 187 C1, **209 G3**
Gundowring Upper, VIC **209 G3**
Gundy, NSW **119 G2**
Gunebang, NSW **117 K4**
Gungahlin, ACT 128, 135 C1, **137 C1**
Gungal, NSW 91 A1, **119 G3**
Gu-ngarre Walk, NT 427 C2
Gungurul, NT **433 F4**
Gunjulla, QLD **282 D3**
Gunlom (Waterfall Creek), NT **433 F4**
Gunn, NSW **117 K6**
Gunn, NT 419 B5
Gunnawarra, QLD 279 H4, **286 D4**
Gunnedah, NSW 73, **114 D5**
Gunnewin, QLD **286 E3**
Gunniguldrie, NSW **117 J4**
Gunning, NSW **122 C2**
Gunningbland, NSW **118 C4**
Gunns Plains, TAS **480 B2**
Gunpowder Resort, QLD **278 C6**
Guns Lookout, WA **395 D3**
Gunyidi, WA **402 C3**
Gunyulgup, WA 371 B2
Gurley, NSW **114 C3**
Guru Nanak Temple, NSW 62 D2
Gurulmundi, QLD **287 G3**
Gutha, WA **402 C1**
Guthalungra, QLD **282 D1**
Guthega, NSW 77 B5, **122 B4**
Guthega Power Station, NSW 77 B5
Guy Fawkes River NP, NSW **115 G4**
Guyra, NSW **115 F4**
Guys Forest, VIC **209 H2**
Gwabegar, NSW **114 B5**

Gwalia (Ghost Town), WA **403 K1**
Gwambegwine, QLD **287 F2**
Gwandalan, NSW 71 D2
Gwandalan, TAS 469 B4, **485 G4**
Gwelup, WA 362 C2
Gwindinup, WA 375 C6
Gymbowen, VIC **206 C4**
Gymea, NSW 49 G4
Gymea Bay, NSW 49 G4
Gympie, QLD 248-9, 255 B2, 259 B6,
  287 J3
Gypsum, VIC **204 E5**
Gypsum Palace, NSW **117 F3**
Gypsy Downs, QLD **280 E2**

H

Haasts Bluff (Kunparrka), NT **442 B2**
Habana, QLD 263 C6
Haberfield, NSW 49 G2
Hackett, ACT 135 C2
Hacketts Gully, WA 363 H3
Hackham, SA 302 C5
Hackham West, SA 302 B5
Hackney, SA 297 E3
Haddon, VIC 159 C3, **207 H6, 211 H2**
Haddon Rig, NSW **118 C1**
Haden, QLD 271 D3
Hadspen, TAS **480 E3**
Hagley, TAS **480 D3**
Hahndorf, SA 303 G3, **349 F2**
Hahndorf Farm Barn, SA 303 H3
Halfway Creek, NSW **115 H4**
Halfway Creek Hut Camping Ground, VIC
  179 D5
Half-Way Mill Roadhouse, WA **402 B3**
Halibut Oil Field, VIC **213 J4**
Halidon, SA **349 H2**
Halifax, QLD **279 K5**
Hall, ACT 122 C2, 135 B1, **137 C1**
Hallam, VIC 151 H5
Hallett, SA **347 F6**
Hallett Cove, SA 302 B4
Hallett Cove Geological Site, SA 302 B4
Halliday Bay, QLD 263 C5
Hallidays Point, NSW 119 K2
Halls Creek, WA 380-1, **399 J4**
Halls Gap, VIC 194, 195 C3, **206 E5**
Halls Gap Wildlife Park and Zoo, VIC
  195 D3
Halls Head, WA 387 B1
Hallston, VIC **212 D4**
Hamel, WA 375 D1
Hamelin, WA **400 B4**
Hamelin Bay, WA 371 B5, **404 B4**
Hamersley, WA 362 D1
Hamersley, WA **400 D2**
Hamersley Iron Open Cut Mine, WA
  400 D2
Hamilton, NT **443 F6**
Hamilton, QLD 231 F2
Hamilton, SA **342 B2**
Hamilton, TAS **484 E2**
Hamilton, VIC 172-3, **210 D2**
Hamilton Downs, NT 423 C1, **442 D2**
Hamilton Downs Youth Camp, NT **442 D2**
Hamilton Hill, WA 362 C5
Hamilton Park, NSW **113 F4**
Hamley Bridge, SA **349 F1**
Hammond, SA **347 F4**
Hammond Downs, QLD **285 G2**
Hammond Park, WA 364 D2
Hammondville, NSW 48 E3
Hampshire, TAS **480 A2**
Hampton, NSW 80 A3, **119 F5**
Hampton, QLD 271 D3
Hampton, VIC 150 D4
Hampton Hill, WA **403 K4**
Hampton Park, VIC 151 H5
Hang-gliding, NSW 107 D1
Hanging Rock, VIC 159 E3, 167 D2,
  207 K6
Hann River Roadhouse, QLD **279 G1**
Hannaford, QLD **287 G4**
Hannan, NSW **117 K5**
Hannans North Tourist Mine, WA **403 H3**
Hanson, SA **347 F6**
Hanson Bay Koala Sanctuary, SA 317 B3

Howard Springs NP, NT **432 D2**
Howden, TAS **485 F4**
Howes Valley, NSW **119 G4**
Howlong, NSW **121 J4**
Howqua, VIC **208 D5**
Howrah, TAS 457 F4, 469 A3
Howth, TAS **480 A2**
Hoxton Park, NSW 48 C3
Huckitta, NT **439 K6**
Hugh River, NT **442 D3**
Hughenden, QLD 249-50, **281 H2**
Hughes, ACT 135 B4
Hughes, SA **344 C2**
Hughesdale, VIC 150 E3
Humbert River (Ranger Stn), NT **435 D3**
Humbug Scrub, SA 301 G3
Hume, ACT 135 C4
Humeburn, QLD **286 B4**
Humphrey, QLD **287 H2**
Humpty Doo, NT **432 D3**
Humula, NSW **122 A3**
Hungerford, NSW **112 D2**
Hungerford, QLD **285 H6**
Hunter, VIC **207 K3**
Hunter Valley, NSW 35, 58, 90
Hunter Valley Gardens & Village, NSW
   59 B4
Hunter Valley Wine Society, NSW 59 D4
Hunter Valley Wineries, NSW **119 G3**
Hunters Hill, NSW 47 H6
Huntfield Heights, SA 302 B5
Huntingdale, VIC 151 F3
Huntingdale, WA 363 F5
Huntingfield, NSW **116 B5**
Huntingwood, NSW 46 D5
Huntleys Cove, NSW 47 G6
Huntleys Point, NSW 49 G1
Huntly, VIC 159 E1, **207 J4**
Huon, VIC 187 C1, **209 G3**
Huon Apple and Heritage Museum, TAS
   464, **484 E4**
Huonfels, QLD **279 F4**
Huonville, NSW **116 B2**
Huonville, TAS **484 E4**
Hurlstone Park, NSW 49 G2
Hurricane, QLD **279 H3**
Hurstbridge, VIC **212 B2**
Hurstville, NSW 49 G3
Hurstville Grove, NSW 49 G3
Huskisson, NSW 71, 97 C1, 107 B4,
   122 E2
Hutt River Province, WA **400 B5**
Huxley Wind Farm, TAS **478 A2**
Hyams Beach, NSW 97 C4
Hyde Park, NSW 43 C4, 44
Hyde Park, SA 297 D6, 302 D2
Hyden, WA 381, **405 F1**
Hyland Park, NSW 62 C5
Hynam, SA 323 E3, **349 J5**
Hypurna, SA **347 J6**

I
Iandra, NSW **118 C6**
Icy Creek, VIC **212 D2**
Ida Bay, TAS **484 E5**
Ida Valley, WA **403 J1**
Idalia, QLD **279 F5, 285 J1**
Idalia NP, QLD **285 J1**
Idracowra, NT 423 D2, **442 D4**
Iffley, QLD **278 D5**
Ilbilbie, QLD **283 F3**
Ilford, NSW **119 F4**
Ilfracombe, QLD **281 H5**
Illabarook, VIC 201 F1, **211 H2**
Illabo, NSW **122 A2**
Illawarra, VIC 195 D2, **207 F5**
Illawarra, WA 365 K2
Illawong, NSW 49 F4
Illfraville, TAS **480 D2**
Illowa, VIC 200 B4
Illpurta, NT 423 C2
Iluka, NSW 74-5, **115 J3**
Imanpa, NT **442 C4**
Imbergee, NSW **113 J2**
Imbil, QLD 255 B3, **287 J3**
Imintji, WA **399 H3**
Immigration Museum, VIC 147 C3

Impadna Siding, NT **442 D4**
Inala, QLD 230 D5
Indee, WA **398 C6**
Indented Head, VIC 152 A1, 201 K3
Indiana, NT **443 G1**
Indigo Upper, VIC **209 F3**
Indo Pacific Marine, NT 416, 417 E5,
   418 B5
Indulkana (Iwantja), SA **341 G2**
Indwarra NP, NSW **114 E4**
Ingar Picnic Ground, NSW 81 H5
Ingebyra, NSW **122 B5**
Ingham, QLD 250, **279 J5**
Ingle Farm, SA 300 D5
Ingleburn, NSW 48 C4
Ingleburn Military Camp, NSW 48 C3
Ingleside, NSW 47 J3
Inglewood, QLD 271 A6, **287 G5**
Inglewood, SA 301 F5
Inglewood, VIC **207 H4**
Inglewood, WA 362 E2
Ingoldsby, QLD 271 E4
Ingomar, SA **341 K6**
Ingsdon, QLD **282 E3**
Injinoo, QLD **277 B2**
Injune, QLD **286 E2**
Inkerman, NSW **116 C2**
Inkerman, QLD **278 D2**
Inkerman, SA **348 E1**
Inkster, SA **345 J5**
Inman Valley, SA 337 C2
Innaloo, WA 362 C2
Innamincka, SA **343 J4**
Inner Lighthouse, NSW 95 C3
Innes NP, SA **348 D2**
Innes Park, QLD 259 A2, **287 J2**
Innesowen, NSW **112 D6**
Inneston, QLD **283 F3**
Innesvale, NT **435 D1**
Innisfail, QLD 239 D6, 250, **279 J4**
Innouendy, WA **400 D4**
Institute of Marine Science, QLD 273,
   282 D1
Intaburra, QLD **282 E1**
Interlaken, TAS **480 E6**
Inveralochy, NSW **122 D2**
Inverell, NSW 75, **114 E3**
Inverell Pioneer Village, NSW 75, **114 E3**
Invergordon, VIC **208 C3**
Inverleigh, QLD **278 D4**
Inverleigh, VIC 201 H2, **211 J3**
Inverloch, VIC 174, **212 C4**
Inverramsay, QLD 271 E5
Inverway, NT **435 B5**
Iona, NSW **116 E5**
Iona, QLD **279 G5**
Iowabah, NSW **118 A2**
Ipswich, QLD 230 A5, 235 C1, 250,
   287 J4
Iris Vale, NSW **117 J3**
Irishtown, TAS **479 C3**
Iron Baron, SA **346 D5**
Iron Knob, SA **346 D5**
Iron Range NP, QLD **277 C4**
Ironbank, SA 302 E3
Ironhurst, QLD **279 G4**
Ironside, QLD 230 E3
Ironpot Creek, QLD 271 C1
Irrapatana (Ruin), SA **342 C5**
Irrewarra, VIC 201 F3, **211 H3**
Irrewillipe, VIC 200 E4, **211 G4**
Irrunytju (Wingelinna), WA **406 D4**
Irrwelty, NT **440 A5**
Irvinebank, QLD **279 H3**
Irvingdale, QLD 271 C3
Irwin, WA **402 A2**
Irymple, VIC 174, **204 D2**
Isaacs, ACT 135 C4
Isabella Plains, ACT 135 B5
Isabella Wreck, 1845, TAS **478 B3**
Isis Junction, QLD 259 A3
Isisford, QLD **281 H6**
Isla Gorge NP, QLD **287 F2**
Island Bend, NSW 77 C5
Island Pure Sheep Dairy, SA 317 C2
Islay Plains, QLD **282 C5**
Israelite Bay, WA 407 B5

Italian Gully, VIC 201 F1
Ithaca, QLD 230 E2
Ivandale, NSW **117 F3**
Ivanhoe, NSW **117 F4**
Ivanhoe, VIC 150 E1
Ivanhoe East, VIC 150 E1
Iwupataka, NT **442 D2**

J
Jabiru, NT 426-7, 427 D2, **433 F3**
Jabiru East, NT 427 E2
Jabuk, SA **349 H2**
Jackadgery, NSW **115 G3**
Jackeys Marsh, TAS **480 D4**
Jackson, QLD **287 F3**
Jacobs Well, QLD 247 C2
Jallukar, VIC 195 D3, **207 F6**
Jallumba, VIC **206 D5**
Jamberoo, NSW 107 C3, **122 E2**
Jambin, QLD 267 B6, **283 G6**
Jamboree Heights, QLD 230 D4
James Lucas Wreck, 1829, TAS **485 F6**
Jamestown, SA 313, **347 F5**
Jamieson, VIC **208 D6**
Jan Juc, VIC 201 J4, **211 J4**
Jancourt East, VIC 200 D4, **211 G4**
Jandakot, WA 362 E5
Jandowae, QLD 271 B1, **287 H3**
Jane Brook, WA 363 G1
Jane NP, WA **404 C4**
Jannali, NSW 49 F4
Japanese Garden, NSW **118 D5**
Jaraga, QLD **282 E1**
Jardine, QLD 267 B3
Jardine River NP, QLD **277 B2**
Jardine Valley, QLD **281 H2**
Jarklin, VIC **207 J3**
Jarrahdale, WA 365 G5, **404 C1**
Jarrahmond, VIC 177 E2, **213 K2**
Jarrangbarnmi (Koolpin Gorge), NT **433 F4**
Jaspers Brush, NSW 97 C1
Jaudri, WA 403 H4
Jay Park, QLD 230 D3
Jean Wreck, 1834, TAS **481 K2**
Jeannies Lookout, WA 395 D3
Jeedamya, WA **403 K2**
Jeffcott North, VIC **207 G3**
Jennacubbine, WA 402 D5
Jennapullin, WA 402 D5
Jenolan Caves, NSW 79, 80 A6, **119 F5**
Jeogla, NSW **115 G5**
Jeparit, VIC **206 D3**
Jerangle, NSW **122 C4**
Jericho, QLD **282 C5**
Jericho, TAS **485 F1**
Jerilderie, NSW **121 H3**
Jerrabomberra, NSW 135 D4
Jerramungup, WA **405 F4**
Jerrawangala NP, NSW 97 A3, **122 E2**
Jerry Meadows, NSW 80 A2
Jerrys Plains, NSW 91 E3, **119 G3**
Jerseyville, NSW **115 H5**
Jervis Bay, NSW 96, 97 C4, 107 C5, **122 E2**
Jervis Bay Marine Park, NSW 97
Jervis Bay NP, NSW 96, 97, 97 C4, 97 D3,
   107 B4
Jervois, NT **440 B6**
Jetsonville, TAS **481 G2**
Jewel Cave, WA 370, 371 B6, **404 B4**
Jigalong, WA **401 G2**
Jiggi, NSW 84 A2
Jil Jil, VIC **207 F2**
Jilliby, NSW 71 C3
Jim Jim Billabong, NT **433 F3**
Jim Jim Falls, NT **433 G4**
Jim Wallace Lookout, QLD 239 B4
Jimboomba, QLD 235 C1, **287 J4**
Jimbour, QLD 271 B2, **287 H4**
Jimmy Creek Campground, VIC 195 C4
Jimna, QLD 255 A4, **287 J3**
Jindabyne, NSW 75, 76, 77 C5, **122 B4**
Jindalee, NSW **122 A1**
Jindalee, QLD 230 D4
Jindare, NT **432 E5**
Jindera, NSW **121 J4**
Jindivick, VIC **212 D3**
Jindong, WA 371 C2
Jingalup, WA **404 D4**

Jingellic, NSW **122 A4**
Jingemarra, WA **400 D5**
Jingera, NSW **137 E5**
Jingili, NT 418 C2
Jinka, NT **439 K6**
Jirrahlinga Koala and Wildlife Sanctuary,
   VIC 201 K3
Jitarning, WA **404 E2**
Joel, VIC 159 A2, **207 F5**
Joel South, VIC 159 A2, **207 G5**
Johanna, VIC 200 E5, **211 G5**
John Forrest NP, WA **363 H1**
Johnburgh, SA **347 F4**
Johnny Souey Cove Camping Ground, VIC
   179 E3
Johns River, NSW **119 K2**
Johnsonville, VIC 177 C2, **213 H2**
Johnstone River Crocodile Farm, QLD
   239 E6, **279 J4**, 250
Jolimont, VIC 147 E3
Jolimont, WA 362 D3
Jollys Lookout, QLD 230 B1
Jomara, NSW **114 A2**
Jondaryan, QLD 271 C3, **287 H4**
Jondaryan Woolshed, QLD 271 C3
Joondalup, WA **402 B5**
Joondanna, WA 362 D2
Jooro, QLD 267 A6, **283 G5**
Joslin, SA 300 D6
Joy Flights, NSW 84 D1
Joycedale, QLD **282 C5**
Joyces Creek, VIC **207 J5**
Joyner, QLD 228 D5
Jubilee, QLD 230 E2
Jubilee Downs, WA **399 G4**
Jubilee Park, QLD **281 J5**
Judbury, TAS **484 E4**
Jugiong, NSW **122 B2**
Julatten, QLD 239 A2, **279 J3**
Julia Creek, QLD 251, **280 E2**
Jumbuck Australiana, SA 317 D2
Jumbuk, VIC **212 E4**
Juna Downs, WA **400 E2**
Junction Village, VIC 153 J1
Jundah, QLD **285 G1**
Jundee, WA **401 G4**
Junee, NSW 78, **122 A2**
Junee, TAS **484 D2**
Junee Reefs, NSW 121 K2
Jung, VIC **206 E4**
Junuy Juluum NP, NSW **115 G4**
Jupiter Creek, SA 303 F5
Jupiters Casino, QLD 246, 247 C4
Jurien Bay, WA 381, **402 A3**

K
K Tank, NSW **116 B2**
Kaarimba, VIC **208 B3**
Kaban, QLD 239 A6
Kabelbarra, QLD **282 E5**
Kabininge, SA 327 C4
Kabra, QLD 267 B4, **283 G5**
Kadina, SA 313-4, **346 E6**
Kadji Kadji, WA **402 C1**
Kadnook, VIC **206 C5**
Kadungle, NSW **118 B3**
Kahmoo, NSW **113 G2**
Kaimkillenbun, QLD 271 B2, **287 H4**
Kainton, SA **348 E1**
Kairi, QLD 239 B4
Kajabbi, QLD **280 D1**
Kajuligah, NSW **117 G3**
Kakadu Mango Winery, NT 419 B5
Kakadu National Park Entrance Station, NT
   427 A3, **432 E3**
Kakadu NP, NT 409, 412, 414, 426, 427,
   427 B1, 429 E1, **433 F3**
Kalabity, SA **347 H4**
Kalala, NT **436 D2**
Kalamunda, WA 363 G3
Kalamunda NP, WA **363 H3**
Kalamurina, SA **343 F3**
Kalanbi, SA **345 H3**
Kalang, NSW 62 B5, **115 H5**
Kalangadoo, SA 323 E5, **349 H6**
Kalannie, WA **402 D3**
Kalapa, QLD **283 G5**

Kings Cave, NSW 81 H4
Kings Creek, NT 423 B2
Kings Creek Station, NT **441 E3**
Kings Cross, NSW 43 E5, 45
Kings Langley, NSW 46 D4
Kings Park, NSW 46 D4
Kings Park, VIC 150 A1
Kings Park, WA 358, 359 A4, 360, 361
Kings Plains NP, NSW **115 F3**
Kingscliff, NSW **115 J1**, 235 D3
Kingscote, SA 315, 317 D2, **348 E3**
Kingscote Cemetery, SA 317 D2
Kingsdale, NSW **122 D2**
Kingsford, NSW 49 J2
Kingsgrove, NSW 49 G3
Kingsholme, QLD 247 A2
Kingsley, WA 362 D1
Kingsthorpe, QLD 271 D4
Kingston, ACT 129 E6, 135 C3
Kingston, QLD 231 G6
Kingston, TAS **485 F4**
Kingston, VIC 167 A2
Kingston Park, SA 302 B3
Kingston S.E., SA 315-6, 323 B2, **349 G4**
Kingston-on-Murray, SA 333 B2, **349 H1**
Kingstown, NSW **114 E5**
Kingstown, WA 395 E3
Kingsville, VIC 150 C2
Kingswood, NSW 46 A5
Kingswood, SA 302 D2
Kinimakatka, VIC **206 C3**
Kinka, QLD 267 C3
Kinlyside, ACT 135 B1
Kinnabulla, VIC **207 F2**
Kinrola Mine, QLD **282 E5**
Kintore, NT **441 B1**
Kintore, WA **403 J3**
Kinypanial South, VIC **207 H3**
Kioloa, NSW 107 A6, **122 E3**
Kirkalocka, WA **400 E6**
Kirkham, NSW 48 A4
Kirkimbie, NT **435 B4**
Kirkstall, VIC 200 A3, **210 E3**
Kirrawee, NSW 49 F4
Kirribilli, NSW 49 J1
Kirup, WA **404 C3**
Kirwan, WA **402 D3**
Kiwirrkurra, WA **406 D2**
Klemzig, SA 300 D6
Knockrow, NSW 84 D2
Knockrow Animal Park, NSW 84 D2
Knockwood, VIC **212 E1**
Knowsley, VIC 159 E1, **207 K4**
Knox, VIC **212 B2**
Knoxfield, VIC 151 G3
Koah, QLD 239 B3
Koala Conservation Reserve, VIC 153 J6,
    165 D2
Kodj Kodjin, WA **402 E4**
Koetong, VIC **209 H3**
Kogan, QLD **287 G4**
Kogarah, NSW 49 G3
Kogarah Bay, NSW 49 G3
Kojonup, WA 384, **404 D3**
Kokatha, SA **346 B3**
Kokotungo, QLD **283 G5**
Kolan South, QLD **287 J2**
Kolendo, SA **346 C4**
Kondalilla NP, QLD 255 B4
Kondinin, WA **405 F2**
Kondoolka, SA **345 K3**
Kondut, WA **402 D4**
Kongart, SA 323 E4
Kongorong, SA 323 D6, **349 H6**
Kongwak, VIC **212 C4**
Konnongorring, WA **402 D4**
Kooemba, QLD **283 F5**
Koojan, WA **402 C4**
Kookabookra, NSW **115 G4**
Kookynie, WA **403 K2**
Kookynie, WA **403 K2**
Koolan, WA **399 F2**
Koolang Observatory, NSW 71 A2
Koolanooka, WA **402 C2**
Koolatah, QLD **278 E2**
Koolburra, QLD **279 G1**
Koolewong, NSW 71 B4

Kooline, WA **400 D2**
Kooljaman Resort, WA **399 F3**
Kooloonong, VIC 205 G4
Kooltandra, QLD **283 F4**
Koolunga, SA **347 F6**
Koolyanobbing, WA **403 G4**
Koombooloomba, QLD **279 J4**
Koomooloo, SA **347 G6**
Koonadgin, WA **403 F5**
Koonalda, SA **344 C3**
Koonamore, SA **347 G4**
Koonandan, NSW **121 J1**
Koonawarra, NSW **111 E5**
Koonda, VIC **208 C3**
Koondoola, WA 362 D1
Koondrook, VIC **207 J1**
Koongamia, WA 363 G2
Koongawa, SA **346 C5**
Koongie Park, WA **399 J4**
Koonibba, SA **345 H3**
Koonkool, QLD 267 B6, **283 G6**
Koonmarra, WA **400 E4**
Koonoomoo, VIC **208 C2**
Koonorigan, NSW 84 A2
Koonwarra, VIC **212 D4**
Koonya, TAS 469 C5, **485 H4**
Kooraban NP, NSW **122 D4**
Koorakee, NSW **120 D1**
Kooralbyn, QLD 235 C2
Koorana Crocodile Farm, QLD 266, 267 C4
Koorawatha, NSW **118 D5**
Koorda, WA **402 E4**
Koordarrie, WA **400 C2**
Kooreh, VIC **207 G4**
Koorilgah Mine, QLD **282 E5**
Koorkab, VIC 205 G4
Koorlong, VIC 204 D2
Koorongara, QLD 271 B5, **287 H5**
Kooroocheang, VIC 167 A2
Kootaberra, SA **346 E4**
Koothney, NSW **114 A4**
Kootingal, NSW **114 E5**
Koo-Wee-Rup, VIC **212 C3**
Kooyong, VIC 150 E2
Kopi, SA **346 B5**
Koppio, SA **348 C1**
Korbel, WA **402 E5**
Korbelka, WA **402 E5**
Koreelah NP, NSW **115 G1**
Koriella, VIC **208 C5**
Korobeit, VIC 167 B3
Koroit, VIC 200 A3, **210 E4**
Korong Vale, VIC **207 H3**
Koroop, VIC **207 J1**
Kororo, NSW 62 D3
Korrbinjal, WA 365 G5
Korumburra, VIC 175, **212 D4**
Kosciuszko National Park H.Q., NSW 77 D5
Kosciuszko NP, NSW 38, 76,77 B5, 77 D1,
    122 B4, 137 A4
Kotta, VIC **207 K3**
Kotupna, VIC **208 B3**
Koumala, QLD **283 F3**
Kowanyama, QLD **278 E2**
Kowguran, QLD **287 G3**
Kowrowa, QLD 239 B3
Koyuga, VIC **208 A3**
Krambach, NSW **119 J2**
Krongart, SA **349 H5**
Kroombit Tops NP, QLD 267 C6, **283 G6**
Krowera, VIC **212 C4**
Kubill, QLD **286 B4**
Kudardup, WA 371 C5, **404 B4**
Kudgee, NSW **116 B3**
Kudla, SA 300 E2
Kuender, WA **405 F2**
Kuitpo, SA 303 F5
Kukerin, WA **404 E2**
Kulde, SA **349 G2**
Kulgera Roadhouse, NT 423 C3, **442 D5**
Kulgera Siding, NT **442 D5**
Kulin, WA **404 E2**
Kulja, WA **402 D3**
Kulkami, SA **349 H2**
Kulkyne, VIC 204 E3
Kulnura, NSW 71 B3, **119 H4**
Kulpara, SA **348 E1**

Kulpi, QLD 271 C3, **287 H4**
Kultanaby, SA **346 B2**
Kulwin, VIC 204 E4
Kulwyne, VIC 205 F4
Kumarina Roadhouse, WA **401 F3**
Kumbarilla, QLD 271 A3, **287 G4**
Kumbatine NP, NSW 115 G6, 119 K1
Kumbia, QLD 271 C1, **287 H3**
Kunat, VIC **207 H1**
Kundabung, NSW **115 H6**
Kundat Djaru, WA **399 K4**
Kungala, NSW **115 H4**
Kungie Lake, QLD **286 B5**
Kunmunya (Ruins), WA **399 G2**
Kununoppin, WA **402 E4**
Kununurra, WA 384, **399 K2**
Kunwarara, QLD 267 A3, **283 G4**
Kunytjanu, SA **340 B2**
Kupunn, QLD **287 H4**
Kuraby, QLD 231 G5
Kuranda, QLD 238, 239 B3, 252, **279 J3**
Kuranda Scenic Railway, QLD 239 C3,
    279 J3, 252
Kuraya, NT **439 J2**
Kurbayia, QLD **280 C2**
Kuri Bay, WA **399 G2**
Kuridala, QLD **280 D3**
Ku-ring-gai Chase NP, NSW 47 J2, 71 B6,
    119 H5
Kurmond, NSW 46 A1, 119 G5
Kurnell, NSW 49 H4
Kurnwill, VIC 204 B3
Kurrajong, NSW **113 J3**
Kurrajong Heights, NSW 81 K1
Kurralta Park, SA 297 A6, 302 C1
Kurran, QLD **280 E5**
Kurri Kurri, NSW 82, 119 H4
Kurting, VIC **207 H4**
Kurukan, QLD **279 K5**
Kurumbul, QLD **287 G5**
Kurundi, NT **439 J3**
Kurwongbah, QLD 228 D4
Kuttabul, QLD 263 B6, **282 E2**
Kwinana, WA **402 B6**
Kwinana Beach, WA 364 C3
Kwinana Town Centre, WA 364 D4
Kwolyin, WA **402 E5**
Kyabra, QLD **285 G3**
Kyabram, VIC 175, **208 B3**
Kyalite, NSW **120 D2**
Kyancutta, SA **346 B5**
Kybeyan, NSW **122 C4**
Kybong, QLD 255 B3
Kybybolite, SA 323 E2, **349 J5**
Kyeamba, NSW **121 K3**
Kyeemagh, NSW 49 H3
Kyena, QLD **286 D5**
Kyle Bay, NSW 49 G3
Kyneton, VIC 159 E2, 167 C1, 176, **207 K5**
Kyneton Museum, VIC 159 E2, 167 C1
Kynuna, QLD **281 F3**
Kyogle, NSW 82, **115 H2**, 235 C3
Kyong, QLD **282 B3**
Kyvalley, VIC **208 B3**
Kywong, NSW **121 J2**
Kywong, QLD **281 G4**

L
La Perouse, NSW 49 J3, 119 H5
Laanecoorie, VIC 159 D1, **207 H4**
Laang, VIC 200 C4, **211 F4**
Labrador, QLD 247 C3
Laceby, VIC 187 A1, **208 E3**
Laceys Creek, QLD 228 A3
Lachlan, TAS **484 E3**
Lachlan Downs, NSW **117 J2**
Lacrum Dairy Farm, TAS **479 C3**
Lady Barron, TAS **482 D3**
Lady Bay, SA 337 B2
Lady Denman Heritage Complex, NSW
    97 C4
Lady Elliott Island, QLD 223, 237
Lady Franklin Museum, TAS 456 C3
Lady Musgrave Island, QLD 237, **287 J1**
Lady's Pass, VIC **208 A4**
Ladysmith, NSW **121 K2**
Laen East, VIC **207 F3**

Lagaven, QLD **280 E2**
Laggan, NSW **122 C1**
Laglan, QLD **282 C4**
Laguna, NSW 71 A1, 119 G4
Laguna Keys Resort, QLD 263 A4
Lah, VIC **206 E3**
Laharum, VIC 195 B1, **206 E5**
Laheys Creek, NSW 118 E2
Laidley, QLD 235 B1, 271 E4, **287 J4**
Lajamanu (Police Stn), NT **435 D5**
Lake Argyle Village, WA **399 K2**
Lake Barlee, WA **403 G1**
Lake Barrine, QLD 238, 239 C5
Lake Bathurst, NSW **122 D2**
Lake Bindegolly NP, QLD **285 H4**
Lake Boga, VIC **207 H1**
Lake Bolac, VIC 195 E6, 200 C1, **211 F2**
Lake Burley Griffin, ACT 125, 126,
    129 A3, 131
Lake Cargelligo, NSW **117 J4**
Lake Cathie, NSW **119 K2**
Lake Cave, WA 370, 371 B4
Lake Cave/Mammoth Cave, WA **404 B4**
Lake Charm, VIC **207 H1**
Lake Clifton, WA 375 B1
Lake Conjola, NSW 97 A6, 107 B5, **122 E3**
Lake Cowal, NSW 118 B5
Lake Dunn, QLD **282 B4**
Lake Eacham, QLD 238, 239 C5
Lake Eildon NP, VIC **208 D5**
Lake Euramo, QLD 238
Lake Everard, SA **346 B3**
Lake Eyre, SA 289, **342 D4**
Lake Eyre NP, SA 292, **342 D4**
Lake Gairdner NP, SA **346 B3**
Lake Goldsmith, VIC **207 G6**
Lake Grace, WA **405 F2**
Lake Guthridge, VIC 177 A3
Lake Harry (Ruin), SA **343 F6**
Lake Illawarra, NSW 106, 107 C3, **119 G6**
Lake Julia, WA **403 G4**
Lake King, WA **405 G2**
Lake Leake, TAS **481 H5**
Lake Macquarie, NSW 70, 71 D2, 82-3
Lake Marmal, VIC **207 H3**
Lake Mundi, VIC **210 B2**
Lake Munmorah, NSW 71 D2
Lake Nash, NT **440 E4**
Lake Nerramyne, WA **400 C5**
Lake Rowan, VIC **208 D3**
Lake St Clair Visitor Centre, TAS 473 E6,
    480 B6
Lake Stewart, NSW **111 C3**
Lake Tabourie, NSW 107 A6, **122 E3**
Lake Torrens, SA 313 A2
Lake Torrens NP, SA 313 A1, **346 E2**
Lake Tyers, VIC 177 D2, **213 J2**
Lake Violet, WA **401 G4**
Lake Wallace, NSW **111 C4**
Lake Way, WA **401 F5**
Lake Wells, WA **401 H5**
Lakefield NP, QLD **279 G1**
Lakeland, QLD **279 H2**
Lakemba, NSW 49 G2
Lakes Entrance, VIC 176, 177, 177 D2,
    213 J2
Lakeside St Clair Wilderness Holidays,
    TAS 473 D6
Lal Lal, VIC 201 H1, **211 J2**
Lalbert, VIC **207 G1**
Lalbert Rd, VIC **207 G1**
Lalla, TAS **480 E2**
Lalla Rookh, WA **398 C6**
Lalor Park, NSW 46 D5
Lambina, SA **341 J2**
Lamboo, WA **399 J4**
Lameroo, SA **349 H2**
Lamington, QLD 234, 235 C2
Lamington NP, QLD 234, 235 D2, 247 A6,
    287 J5
Lamins Lookout, QLD 239 C5
Lammermoor, QLD **281 H3**
Lamplough, NSW **116 C5**
Lana, QLD **281 G3**
Lancefield, VIC 167 D1, **208 A6**
Lancelin, WA **402 B4**
Lancevale, QLD **282 B5**

Louth, NSW 112 E5
Louth Bay, SA 348 C1
Loveday, SA 333 B2
Lovett Bay, NSW 47 J2
Low Head, TAS 480 D1
Lowana Yard, TAS 483 B3
Lowanna, NSW 62 B2
Lowbank, SA 333 A2
Lowden, WA 375 D6
Lowdina, TAS 485 G2
Lower Barrington, TAS 480 B2
Lower Barry Creek Camping Ground, VIC 179 C2
Lower Beulah, TAS 480 C3
Lower Boro, NSW 122 D2
Lower Glenelg NP, VIC 210 C3
Lower Hermitage, SA 301 F5
Lower Hunter NP, NSW 59 E4, 59 E6, 119 H4
Lower Hunter Valley, NSW 58, 59
Lower Kalgan, WA 369 D3
Lower King, WA 369 D3
Lower Landing, TAS 483 B3
Lower Longley, TAS 485 F4
Lower Mangrove, NSW 71 A4
Lower Marshes, TAS 485 F1
Lower Mitcham, SA 302 D2
Lower Mount Hicks, TAS 479 E3
Lower Norton, VIC 206 D4
Lower Plenty, VIC 151 F1
Lower Sandy Bay, TAS 456 D5
Lower Turners Marsh, TAS 480 E2
Lower Wilmot, TAS 480 B3
Lowesdale, NSW 121 J4
Lowlands, NSW 117 H4
Lowmead, QLD 287 H1
Lowood, QLD 287 J4
Lowther, NSW 80 B3
Loxton, SA 317, 333 C3, 349 H1
Loxton Historical Village, SA 317, 333 D3
Loxton North, SA 333 D3
Loyetea, TAS 480 A2
Lubeck, VIC 206 E4
Lucas Heights, NSW 48 E4
Lucaston, TAS 484 E4
Lucinda, QLD 279 K5
Lucindale, SA 323 D3, 349 H5
Lucknow, NSW 118 D4
Lucknow, QLD 280 E4
Lucky Bay, SA 346 D6
Lucky Downs, QLD 279 H5, 287 F3
Lucy Creek, NT 440 C5
Lucyvale, VIC 187 D1, 209 H3
Luddenham, NSW 48 A2
Ludlow, WA 371 E1
Ludmilla, NT 417 E1, 418 B3
Lue, NSW 119 F3
Lugarno, NSW 49 F3
Luina, TAS 479 D5
Lukies Farm, NT 432 D5
Luluigui, WA 399 G4
Lulworth, TAS 480 E1
Lumeah, QLD 286 B2
Lumen Christi Church, WA 371 C6
Lunawanna, TAS 485 F5
Lundayra, QLD 287 F5
Lune River, TAS 484 E5
Lupton NP, WA 404 D1
Lurg, VIC 208 D4
Lurnea, NSW 48 D3
Lurnea, QLD 286 C3
Lutana, TAS 456 D3
Lutwyche, QLD 230 E2
Lyal, VIC 159 E1
Lygon St, Melbourne, VIC 146, 147 C2
Lymington, TAS 484 E4
Lymwood, TAS 478 B3
Lynchford, TAS 483 C2
Lyndavale, NT 442 C4
Lyndbrook, QLD 279 H4
Lyndhurst, NSW 118 D5
Lyndhurst, QLD 279 H5
Lyndhurst, SA 347 F1
Lyndhurst, VIC 151 G5
Lyndoch, SA 301 H1, 317-8, 326, 327 A5
Lyndoch Lavender Farm, SA 301 J1
Lyndon, WA 400 C2

Lyneham, ACT 135 C2
Lynton, SA 302 D2
Lynwood, NSW 117 G1
Lynwood, QLD 285 G2
Lynwood, WA 362 E4
Lyons, ACT 135 B4
Lyons Lookout, QLD 239 A1
Lyons River, WA 400 C3
Lyonville, VIC 167 B2, 211 J1
Lyrup, SA 333 D2
Lyrup Heights, SA 333 D2
Lysterfield, VIC 151 H4
Lysterfield South, VIC 151 H4
Lytton, QLD 231 G2

M
Ma Ma Creek, QLD 235 A1
Maaroom, QLD 259 C4
Mabel Creek, SA 341 J5
Mabel Downs, WA 399 J3
Macadamia Castle, NSW 84 D2
Macadamia Factory, NSW 84 B2
Macalister, QLD 271 A2, 287 H4
McAllister, QLD 278 D4
Macarthur, ACT 135 C5
Macarthur, VIC 210 D3
McArthur River, NT 437 G3
McClelland Art Gallery, VIC 153 H1
Macclesfield, SA 303 G6
McCoys Well, SA 347 G4
McCrae, VIC 152 D4
McCrae Homestead, VIC 152 D4
McCullys Gap, NSW 119 G3
Macdonald Park, SA 300 D2
MacDonnell Ranges, NT 422, 442 C2
McDouall Peak, SA 341 K6
McDougalls Well, NSW 111 C6
McDowall, QLD 228 E6
Macedon, VIC 159 E3, 167 C2, 211 K1
Macedon Ranges, VIC 166
McGraths Hill, NSW 46 C2
Macgregor, ACT 135 A2
Macgregor, QLD 231 F4
McIntyre, VIC 159 C1, 207 H4
Mackay, QLD 252, 262, 263 D6, 283 F2
Mackay Harbour, QLD 263 D6
McKees Hill, NSW 84 A3
McKellar, ACT 135 B2
Mackenzie, QLD 231 G4
McKenzie Creek, VIC 206 D4
Mackenzie Falls, VIC 195 C2
Mackerel Oil Field, VIC 213 J4
MacKillop Bridge, VIC 209 K5
McKinlay, QLD 280 E3
McKinnon, VIC 150 E3
Mackintosh Power Station, TAS 473 A2
Macknade, QLD 279 J5
Macksville, NSW 62 C6, 85, 115 H5
Mackunda Downs, QLD 280 E4
McLachlan, SA 346 B6
Maclagan, QLD 271 C2
McLaren Flat, SA 302 C6
McLaren Vale, SA 302 C6, 349 F2
McLaren Vale Lavender, SA 302 C6
McLaren Vale Olive Grove, SA 302 D6
Maclean, NSW 85, 115 H3
Macleod Morass, VIC 177 C2
McLoughlins Beach, VIC 213 F4
McMahons Creek, VIC 212 D2
McMahons Point, NSW 49 H1
MacMasters Beach, NSW 71 C5
Macquarie, ACT 135 B2
Macquarie Fields, NSW 48 D3
Macquarie Links, NSW 48 D3
Macquarie Park, NSW 47 G5
Macquarie Pass NP, NSW 107 C2, 119 G6
Macquarie St, Sydney, NSW 42, 43 C3, 44
Macquarie University, NSW 47 G5
Macumba, SA 342 B3
Maddington, WA 363 F5
Madeley, WA 362 D1
Madoonga, WA 400 E5
Madoonia Downs, WA 407 A4
Madura, WA 407 D4
Madura, WA 407 D4
Mafeesh, NSW 117 J2
Mafeking, QLD 282 B5

Mafeking, VIC 195 D4
Maffra, NSW 77 E6, 122 C5
Maffra, VIC 177 A2, 180, 213 F3
Maggea, SA 349 H1
Maggieville, QLD 278 D4
Magill, SA 302 E1
Magnetic Island NP, QLD 279 K5
Magnetic Termite Mounds, NT 425 B1
Magowra, QLD 278 D4
Magpie Hollow, NSW 80 A1
Magra, TAS 484 E3
Magrath Flat, SA 349 G3
Maguk (Barramundi Gorge), NT 433 F4
Mahanewo, SA 346 C3
'Maheno' Wreck, QLD 259 D3
Mahogany Creek, WA 363 H2
Mahogany Walk, VIC 200 A4
Maianbar, NSW 49 G5
Maida Vale, WA 363 G3
Maidenwell, QLD 271 D2, 287 H3
Maidstone, VIC 150 B1
Mailapunyah, NT 437 G3
Mailer Flat, VIC 200 B3, 210 E3
Maimuru, NSW 118 C6
Main Beach, QLD 247 C4
Main Range NP, QLD 235 B2, 271 E5, 271 E6, 287 J5
Main Ridge, VIC 152 E5
Maindample, VIC 208 D5
Mainoru, NT 433 H5
Maitland, NSW 58, 86, 119 H3
Maitland, SA 318, 348 E1
Maitland Downs, QLD 279 H2
Majestic Theatre, QLD 239 B5
Majors Creek, NSW 122 D3
Majura, ACT 135 D2
Makiri, SA 340 E3
Makowata, QLD 287 H1
Malabanjbanjdju Iligadjarr Walk, NT 427 C2
Malabar, NSW 113 J3
Malabar, NSW 49 J3
Malacura, QLD 279 F5
Malaga, WA 362 E2
Malagarga, QLD 285 F3
Malak, NT 418 D2
Malanda, QLD 239 B5, 253, 279 J3
Malbina, TAS 485 F3
Malbon, QLD 280 D2
Malbooma, SA 345 J2
Malcolm (abandoned), WA 403 K1
Malcolm Douglas Crocodile Park, WA 398 E4
Maldon, VIC 159 D2, 180, 207 J5
Maldorkey, SA 347 H4
Malebo, NSW 121 K2
Maleny, QLD 255 B5, 287 J3
Malinns, VIC 213 K1
Mallacoota, VIC 180-1, 214 D4
Mallala, SA 349 F1
Mallanganee, NSW 115 H2
Mallanganee NP, NSW 115 H2
Mallawillup, WA 369 B1
Mallee Cliffs NP, NSW 116 D6
Mallina, WA 398 C6
Malmsbury, VIC 159 E2, 167 C1, 207 K5
Malta, QLD 286 C1
Maltee, SA 345 H4
Malvern, SA 297 D6, 302 D2
Malvern, VIC 150 E3
Malvern East, VIC 150 E3
Mambray Creek, SA 346 E5
Mammoth Cave, WA 370, 371 B4
Mamukala Wetlands, NT 427 C2
Man From Snowy River Museum, VIC 187 E1
Manangatang, VIC 205 F4
Manangoora, NT 437 J2
Manara, NSW 116 E3
Manara Mine, NSW 116 E3
Manberry, WA 400 B3
Manbiyarra-Border Store, NT 427 E1
Mandagery, NSW 118 C4
Mandalong, NSW 71 C2
Mandelman, NSW 116 E4
Mandogalup, WA 364 D3
Mandora, WA 398 D5
Mandorah, NT 432 D3

Mandurah, WA 385, 387 C1, 404 B2
Mandurama, NSW 118 D5
Mandurang, VIC 207 J4
Maneroo, QLD 281 H5
Manfred, NSW 117 F4
Mangalo, SA 346 C6
Mangalore, QLD 286 C3
Mangalore, TAS 485 F2
Mangalore, VIC 208 B5
Mangana, TAS 481 H4
Mangaroon, WA 400 C3
Mango Hill, QLD 229 H3
Mangoola, NSW 91 C2
Mangoplah, NSW 121 K3
Mangrove Boardwalk, WA 375 A5
Mangrove Mountain, NSW 71 A3
Manguri, SA 341 J5
Manildra, NSW 118 D4
Manilla, NSW 86, 114 D5
Manilla, NSW 116 C4
Maningrida (Police Stn.), NT 433 H2
Manjimup, WA 374, 386, 404 C4
Manjimup Timber Park, WA 404 C4
Manly, NSW 44, 47 K5, 119 H5
Manly, QLD 227, 231 H2
Manly Vale, NSW 47 J5
Manly West, QLD 231 H2
Manmanning, WA 402 D4
Mannahill, SA 347 H4
Mannanarie, SA 347 F5
Mannering Park, NSW 71 D2
Manners Creek, NT 440 E5
Manngarre Walk, NT 427 E1
Manning, WA 362 E4
Manning Point, NSW 119 K2
Manningham, SA 300 D6
Manns Beach, VIC 213 F4
Mannuem Creek, QLD 271 C1
Mannum, SA 318-9, 349 G2
Mannus, NSW 122 A3
Manoora, SA 349 F1
Mansfield, QLD 231 G4
Mansfield, VIC 181, 187 A3, 208 D5
Mansfield Park, SA 300 C6
Mantamaru, WA 406 C4
Mantuan Downs, QLD 282 D6
Mantung, SA 349 H1
Manuka, ACT 129 D6
Manuka, NSW 117 J3
Manunda, SA 347 H5
Many Peaks, QLD 287 H1
Manyalluk, NT 429 E2, 433 F5
Manyana, NSW 97 A6
Manypeaks, WA 369 D2, 404 E5
Mapleton, QLD 255 B4
Mapleton Falls NP, QLD 255 B4
Mapoon, QLD 277 A3
Maragle, NSW 77 A3
Marakoopa, TAS 480 C4
Marakoopa Cave, TAS 473 E1
Maralinga, SA 344 E1
Marama, SA 349 H2
Maranalgo, WA 402 E2
Marananga, SA 327 B3
Maranboy (Police Stn), NT 429 E3, 433 F5
Marandoo, WA 400 E2
Marangaroo, WA 362 D1
Marathon, QLD 281 G2
Maraylya, NSW 46 D2
Marayong, NSW 46 D4
Marble Bar, WA 398 D6
Marble Hill, SA 303 F1
Marburg, QLD 235 B1
March, NSW 118 D4
Marchagee, WA 402 C3
Marcoola, QLD 255 C4
Marcorna, VIC 207 J2
Marcus Beach, QLD 255 D3
Mardan, VIC 212 D4
Mardathuna, WA 400 B3
Mardella, WA 365 F5
Marden, SA 300 D6
Mardie, WA 398 A6
Mardugal Campground, NT 427 C3
Mareeba, QLD 239 A3, 253, 279 J3
Mareeba Heritage Museum, QLD 239 A3
Marfield, NSW 117 F3

Milikapiti, NT **432 C1**
Milingimbi, NT **433 J2**
Military Museum, NT 418 A3
Military Museum, WA **403 F5**
Mill Museum, WA **404 E3**
Millaa Millaa, QLD 239 B6, **279 J4**
Millaa Millaa Lookout, QLD 239 B6
Millaroo, QLD **282 D1**
Millbank, NSW **115 G5**
Millbrook, SA **301 G5**
Millbrook, VIC 167 A3
Mil-Lel, SA 323 E5, **349 H6**
Millendon, WA 363 G1
Miller, NSW 48 D2
Millers Creek, SA **346 C1**
Millers Point, NSW 43 B2, 49 H1
Millfield, NSW **119 H4**
Millgrove, VIC **212 C2**
Millicent, SA 319, 323 D5, **349 H6**
Millie, NSW **114 C3**
Millijiddee, WA **399 G4**
Milling, WA **402 C3**
Millionth Sleeper, NT 423 D2
Millmerran, QLD 271 B5, **287 H4**
Millner, NT **418 C2**
Milloo, VIC **207 K3**
Millrose, WA **401 G4**
Millstream, WA **400 D1**
Millstream Chichester NP, WA **400 D1**
Millstream Falls NP, QLD 239 A6
Millswood, SA **302 C2**
Millthorpe, NSW **118 E4**
Milltown, VIC **210 C3**
Millungera, QLD **280 E1**
Millwood, QLD 271 B5
Milly Milly, WA **400 D4**
Milman, QLD 267 B3
Milo, QLD **285 H2**
Milpa, NSW **111 D5**
Milparinka, NSW **111 D3**
Milperra, NSW 48 E3
Milrae, NSW **113 J4**
Milray, QLD **282 B2**
Milsons Point, NSW 49 H1
Milton, NSW 107 B5, **122 E3**
Milton, QLD 225 A3, 230 E2
Milton Park, NT 423 C1, **442 C2**
Milvale, NSW **118 C6**
Milyakburra, NT **434 C4**
Milyeannup, WA 371 D6, **371 E4**
Mimili, SA **341 G2**
Mimong, QLD **281 F3**
Mimosa Rocks NP, NSW **122 D5**
Minara, WA **403 K1**
Minarto, NSW **117 F5**
Minburra, SA **347 F4**
Mincha, VIC **207 J2**
Minchinbury, NSW 46 C5
Mindarie, SA **349 H2**
Minden, QLD 235 B1
Minderoo, WA **400 C1**
Mindi, QLD **282 E3**
Mindijup, WA 369 D2
Mindil Beach Lookout, NT 417 B3
Mindil Beach Markets, NT 416, 417 C3
Minemoorong, NSW **118 B3**
Miners Hall of Fame, WA **403 H3**
Miners Rest, VIC 159 C3, **211 H1**
Minetta, NSW **112 D3**
Mingah Springs, WA **400 E3**
Mingary, SA **347 J4**
Mingay, VIC 200 E1, **211 G2**
Mingela, QLD **282 C1**
Mingenew, WA **402 B1**
Minhamite, VIC 200 A2, **210 E3**
Minilya Roadhouse, WA **400 B3**
Minimay, VIC **206 B4**
Mininer, WA **400 E2**
Mininera, VIC **211 F2**
Miniyeri, NT **436 E1**
Minjah, VIC 200 B2
Minjary NP, NSW **122 A2**
Minjilang, NT **433 F1**
Minlaton, SA 319, **348 E2**
Minley, NSW **112 E5**
Minmindie, VIC **207 H2**
Minnamoolka, QLD **279 H4**

Minnamurra, NSW 107 C3
Minnamurra Rainforest, NSW 107 C3
Minnie Creek, WA **400 C3**
Minnie Downs, QLD **286 B2**
Minnie Water, NSW **115 H4**
Minnies O.S., QLD **279 F4**
Minnipa, SA **346 B5**
Minnivale, WA **402 D4**
Minore, NSW **118 C3**
Minrimar, NSW **113 J2**
Mintabie, SA **341 G3**
Mintaro, SA **347 F6**
Minto, NSW 48 C4
Minto, VIC **207 K3**
Minto Heights, NSW 48 C4
Minyip, VIC **206 E3**
Miralie, VIC **205 G5**
Miram, VIC **206 B3**
Miram South, VIC **206 B4**
Miranda, NSW **121 F2**
Miranda, NSW 49 G4
Miranda Downs, QLD **278 E3**
Mirani, QLD 263 B6, **282 E2**
Mirannie, NSW **119 H3**
Mirboo, VIC **212 E4**
Mirboo North, VIC **212 D4**
Miriam Vale, QLD 267 E6, **283 H6**
Mirikata, SA 342 B6, **346 B1**
Mirima NP, NT **435 A2**
Mirima NP, WA **399 K2**
Mirimbah, VIC 187 A3, **208 E5**
Mirirrinyungu (Duck Ponds), NT **435 D6**
Miriwinni, QLD 239 D5
Mirool, NSW **118 A6**
Mirrabooka, NSW **117 J3**
Mirrabooka, QLD **286 B4**
Mirrabooka, WA 362 D1
Mirrai Lookout, NT 427 D3
Mirrna, QLD **282 C3**
Mirranatwa (Mirrinaduwa), VIC 195 C4
Mirri, QLD **280 D3**
Mirtna, QLD **282 C3**
Missabotti, NSW 62 B5, **115 H5**
Missile Park, SA **346 D2**
Mission Beach, QLD **279 J4**
Mistake Creek, NT **435 A4**
Mitakoodi, QLD **280 D2**
Mitcham, SA **302 D2**
Mitcham, VIC **151 G2**
Mitchell, ACT 135 C2
Mitchell, NT 419 C5
Mitchell, QLD **286 D3**
Mitchell & Alice Rivers NP, QLD **278 E2**
Mitchell Park, SA 302 C2
Mitchell River NP, VIC 177 B1, **213 G2**
Mitchell Vale, NSW **113 G3**
Mitchellstown, VIC **208 B4**
Mitchellville, SA **346 D6**
Mitchelton, QLD 230 E1
Mitiamo, VIC **207 J3**
Mitre, VIC **206 C4**
Mitta Mitta, VIC 187 D2, **209 G4**
Mittagong, NSW 87, 107 B2, **122 E1**
Mittagong, QLD **278 E5**
Mittebah, NT **437 J6**
Mittyack, VIC **204 E5**
Miundi Mundi, NSW **116 A2**
Miva, QLD 255 A1, 259 A6
Moama, NSW **121 F4**
Moana, SA **302 B6**
Mobbs Hill, NSW 47 F5
Moble, QLD **285 H3**
Mobo Creek Crater, QLD 239 B6
Mockinya, VIC 195 A2, **206 D5**
Modanville, NSW 84 B2
Modbury, SA **300 E5**
Modbury Heights, SA **300 E5**
Modbury North, SA **300 E5**
Moe, VIC 183, **212 E3**
Mogal Plain, NSW **118 A3**
Moggill, QLD 230 C4
Moglonemby, VIC **208 C4**
Mogo, NSW **122 D3**
Mogongong, NSW **118 C5**
Mogriguy, NSW **118 D2**
Mogumber, WA **402 C4**
Moil, NT **418 C2**
Moina, TAS **480 B3**

Mokepilly, VIC 195 D2, **207 F5**
Mole Creek, TAS 465, **480 C3**
Mole Creek Karst NP, TAS 473 E1, **480 B4**
Molesworth, TAS **485 F3**
Molesworth, VIC **208 C5**
Moliagul, VIC 159 C1, **207 H4**
Molka, VIC **208 C4**
Mollerin, WA **402 E3**
Mollongghip, VIC 159 D3, 167 A3, **207 J6**
Mollymook, NSW 107 B5
Molong, NSW **118 D4**
Molonglo Gorge, ACT 135 E4
Molonglo Gorge Recreation Area, ACT
 127, 135 E4
Moltema, TAS **480 C3**
Momba, NSW **112 C5**
Mona Vale, NSW 47 K3, 71 B6, **119 H5**
Mona Vale, QLD **285 H3**
Mona Vale, TAS **481 F6**
Monak, NSW **120 C1**
Monash, ACT **135 B5**
Monash, SA **333 C2**
Monbulk, VIC **151 K3**
Moncrieff, ACT **135 C1**
Monegeetta, VIC 167 D2, **208 A6**
Monga NP, NSW **122 D3**
Monia Gap, NSW **117 J5**
Monivea, NSW **117 F3**
Monkey Mia, WA 376, **400 B4**
Monkira, QLD **280 D6**
Monolan, NSW **112 B4**
Monomie, NSW **118 B4**
Monstraven, QLD 278 D6, **280 E1**
Mont Albert, VIC **150 E2**
Mont Albert North, VIC **151 F2**
Mont De Lancey Home & Museum, VIC
 151 J1, 171 D2
Montacute, SA **301 F6**
Montagu, TAS **479 B2**
Montagu Bay, TAS 453 E1, **456 E3**
Montague Island, NSW 92, **122 D4**
Montana, TAS **480 C4**
Monteagle, NSW **118 C6**
Montejinni, NT **436 B3**
Monterey, NSW 49 H3
Montgomery, VIC 177 A3, **213 G3**
Monto, QLD 256, **287 H1**
Montrose, TAS **456 B2**
Montrose, VIC **151 H1**
Montumana, TAS **479 D3**
Montville, QLD **255 C4**
Mooball, NSW **235 D3**
Mooball NP, NSW 115 J1, **235 D3**
Moockra, SA **347 F4**
Moodiarrup, WA **404 D3**
Moodlu, QLD **228 D1**
Moogara, TAS **484 E3**
Moojeeba, QLD **277 C5**
Mooka, WA **400 C3**
Moola, QLD 271 C2
Moolah, NSW **117 G3**
Moolap, VIC **201 J3**
Moolawatana, SA **347 H1**
Moolbong, NSW **117 G4**
Mooleulooloo, SA **347 J3**
Mooloo, QLD **255 A3**
Mooloo Downs, WA **400 C3**
Mooloogool, WA **401 F4**
Mooloolaba, QLD 254, 255 D4
Mooloolah, QLD **255 C5**
Mooloolah River NP, QLD **255 C4**
Mooloolerie, NSW **116 D4**
Moolooloo O.S., NT **436 A3**
Moolort, VIC 159 D2, **207 J5**
Moomba (Private), SA **343 H4**
Moona Plains, NSW **115 F5**
Moona Vale, NSW **112 B6**
Moonah, TAS **456 C3**
Moonambel, VIC 159 B2, **207 G5**
Moonan Flat, NSW **119 H2**
Moonaree, SA **346 C4**
Moonbah, NSW 77 C6
Moonbi, NSW **114 E5**
Moonbria, NSW **121 G2**
Moondarra, VIC **212 E3**
Moondene, NSW **117 F3**
Moonee Beach, NSW 62 D2, **115 H4**

Moonee Ponds, VIC **150 C1**
Moonera, WA **407 D4**
Mooney, NSW 71 A5
Mooney Mooney, NSW 47 H1
Moongulla, NSW **113 K2**
Moonie, QLD **287 G4**
Moonijin, WA **402 D4**
Moonta, SA 319-20, **346 E6**
Moonya, QLD **281 J5**
Moonyoonooka, WA **402 A1**
Moora, WA 388, **402 C3**
Moorabbin, VIC 150 E4, **212 B2**
Moorabbin Airport, VIC **150 E4**
Mooraberree, QLD **284 E2**
Moorak, QLD **286 D2**
Mooralla, VIC 195 A4
Mooramanna, QLD **286 E5**
Moorarie, WA **400 E4**
Moore, NSW **114 E5**
Moore, QLD 271 E2, **287 J4**
Moore Park, NSW **49 J2**
Moore Park, QLD **287 J1**
Moore River NP, WA **402 B4**
Moorebank, NSW 48 D3
Moorebank Village, NSW 48 D3
Mooreland Downs, NSW **112 D3**
Mooren, NSW **118 E2**
Moores Pocket, QLD 230 A5
Mooreville, TAS 479 E4, **480 A2**
Moorina, QLD **228 C2**
Moorine Rock, WA **403 G4**
Moorland, NSW **119 K2**
Moorleah, TAS **479 E3**
Moorna, NSW **116 C6**
Moorna, VIC **204 C2**
Moorngag, VIC **208 D4**
Moorooduc, VIC **153 G2**
Moorook, SA 333 B2, **349 H1**
Moorooka, QLD **230 E4**
Mooroolbark, VIC **151 H1**
Mooroopna, VIC **208 C3**
Mooroopna North, VIC **208 B3**
Moorooroo, SA 327 C4
Moorrinya NP, QLD **281 J3**
Mootwingee, NSW **116 C1**
Moppa, SA 327 C1
Moppin, NSW **114 C2**
Morago, NSW **121 F3**
Moralana, SA 313 B2
Moralana, SA 313 B2, **347 F3**
Moralla, VIC **206 D6**
Moran House, NSW 47 K5
Moranbah, QLD 256, **282 E3**
Morangarell, NSW **118 B6**
Morapoi, WA **403 K2**
Morawa, WA **402 C1**
Moray Downs, QLD **282 C3**
Morayfield, QLD 228 E1, **255 C6**
Morchard, SA **347 F5**
Morden, NSW **111 E5**
Mordialloc, VIC **150 E5**
Morea, VIC **206 B4**
Moree, NSW 87-8, **114 C3**
Morella, QLD **281 H4**
Moresby, QLD **239 D6**
Moresby Range NP, QLD **239 E6**
Moreton Bay, QLD 227, 229 J3, 235 D1,
 255 D6, **287 J5**
Moreton Island, QLD 223, 227, 255 E6
Moreton Island NP, QLD 255 E6, **287 K4**
Moreton Telegraph Station, QLD **277 B4**
Morgan, SA 320, **349 G1**
Morgan Vale, SA **347 H5**
Moriac, VIC 201 H3, **211 J3**
Morialpa, SA **347 H4**
Morialta, NSW **114 B3**
Moriarty, TAS **480 C2**
Morisset, NSW 71 C2, **119 H4**
Morkalla, VIC **204 B3**
Morley, WA **362 E2**
Morney, QLD **284 E2**
Morning Bay, NSW 47 J2
Morning Light Wreck, 1895, TAS **479 A2**
Morningside, QLD **231 F2**
Mornington, TAS **457 F3**
Mornington, VIC 153 F2, 183, **212 B3**
Mornington, WA **399 H3**

Mulga Downs, WA **400 E1**
Mulga Park, NT 423 B3, **442 B5**
Mulga Valley, NSW 112 B4, 116 A1
Mulga View, SA **347 G2**
Mulgaria, SA **346 E1**
Mulgathing, SA **345 H1**
Mulgildie, QLD **287 H2**
Mulgoa, NSW 81 K6
Mulgowie, QLD 235 B1, 271 E4
Mulgrave, NSW 46 C2
Mulgrave, QLD **281 J5**
Mulgrave, VIC 151 F4
Mulgul, WA **400 E3**
Mulka, SA **343 F4**
Mulla, NSW **118 B2**
Mullaley, NSW **114 C6**
Mullaway, NSW 62 E1
Mullengandra, NSW **121 K4**
Mullengudgery, NSW **118 B2**
Mullewa, WA **400 C6**
Mullingar, NSW **116 D4**
Mullion Creek, NSW **118 D4**
Mullumbimby, NSW 84 C1, 89, **115 J2**, 235 D3
Mullumbimby Creek, NSW 84 C1
Muloorina, SA **342 E5**
Mulwala, NSW **121 H4**
Mulya, NSW **112 E5**
Mulyandry, NSW **118 C5**
Mulyungarie, SA **347 J3**
Mumballup, WA **375 E6**
Mumbannar, VIC **210 B3**
Mumbil, NSW **118 D3**
Mumblebone Plain, NSW **118 B1**
Mummballup, WA **404 C3**
Mummel Gulf NP, NSW **119 J1**
Mummulgum, NSW **115 H2**
Mundabullangana, WA **398 C5**
Mundadoo, NSW **113 H5**
Mundaring, WA 361, 363 J2, **402 C5**
Munderoo, NSW **122 A3**
Mundijong, WA 365 F4, **404 C1**
Mundiwindi, WA **401 F2**
Mundoo, QLD 239 D6
Mundoo Bluff, QLD **282 B3**
Mundoora, SA **346 E6**
Mundowdna, SA **343 F6**
Mundowney, NSW **114 E5**
Mundrabilla, WA **407 E4**
Mundrabilla, WA **407 E4**
Mundubbera, QLD **287 H2**
Mundulla, SA 323 E1, **349 H4**
Mungabroom, NT **436 E4**
Mungallala, QLD **286 D3**
Mungana, QLD **279 H3**
Mungar, QLD 259 B4, **287 J2**
Mungerannie Roadhouse, SA **343 F4**
Mungeribah, NSW **118 C2**
Mungindi, NSW **114 B2**
Mungkan Kandju NP, QLD **277 B5**
Mungkarta, NT **439 H3**
Munglinup, WA **405 J3**
Mungo, NSW **116 E5**
Mungo Brush, NSW 95 C2
Mungo NP, NSW 38-9, **116 E5**
Mungunburra, QLD **282 B2**
Mungungo, QLD **287 H1**
Munna, NSW **118 E3**
Munno Para, SA 300 E2
Munno Para Downs, SA 300 E2
Munno Para West, SA 300 E2
Munro, VIC 177 A2, **213 G2**
Munster, WA 364 C2
Muntadgin, WA **403 F5**
Muradup, WA **404 D3**
Muralgarra, WA **400 D6**
Murals, TAS **480 B3**
Murarrie, QLD 231 G2
Murchison, VIC **208 B4**
Murchison Downs, WA **400 E4**
Murchison East, VIC **208 B4**
Murchison Roadhouse, WA **400 D5**
Murdinga, SA **346 B6**
Murdoch, WA 362 D5, **404 E3**
Murdong, WA **404 E3**
Murdos, WA **363 K4**
Murdunna, TAS 469 C4, **485 H3**

Murgenella (Ranger Stn.), NT **433 G1**
Murgheboluc, VIC 201 H3, **211 J3**
Murgon, QLD 260, **287 H3**
Murgoo, WA **400 D5**
Muriel, NSW **117 K1**
Murkaby, SA **347 G6**
Murmungee, VIC 187 B1, **209 F3**
Murnpeowie, SA **343 G6**
Murphys Creek, QLD 271 D4
Murphys Creek, VIC 159 C1, **207 H4**
Murphys Glen Picnic Ground, NSW 81 H5
Murphy's Haystacks, SA 345 J5
Murra Murra, QLD **286 C5**
Murra Warra, VIC **206 D3**
Murrabit, VIC **207 J1**
Murradoc, VIC 201 K3
Murramarang NP, NSW 107 A6, **122 E3**
Murrami, NSW **121 J1**
Murranji, NT **436 C3**
Murrawa, NSW **113 H4**
Murrawal, NSW **118 E1**
Murray 1 Power Station, NSW 77 B4
Murray 2 Power Station, NSW 77 A4
Murray Bend, WA **387 D2**
Murray Bridge, SA **349 G2**
Murray Downs, NT **439 J4**
Murray Lakes, WA 387 D2
Murray River, SA 289, 332, 333
Murray River, WA 386, 387 D2
Murray River (Bulyong Island) NP, SA 333 E1
Murray River (Katarapko) NP, SA 333 C3
Murray River (Lyrup Flats) NP, SA 333 D2
Murray River NP, SA 292, **349 H1**
Murray Town, SA **347 F6**
Murrays Corner, ACT **137 B3**
Murrays Run, NSW 71 A1
Murray-Sunset NP, VIC **204 C4**
Murrayville, NSW **204 B5**
Murrindal, VIC **213 J1**
Murrindindi, VIC **208 C6**
Murringo, NSW **118 D6**
Murroon, VIC 201 G4, **211 H4**
Murrumba Downs, QLD 228 E4
Murrumbateman, NSW **122 C2**
Murrumbeena, NSW VIC 150 E3
Murrumbidgee Irrigation Area, NSW 36
Murrumbidgee River, ACT 126, 135 A4, 136, **137 B2**
Murrumburrah, NSW **122 D1**
Murrungowar, VIC **214 A4**
Murrurundi, NSW **119 G2**
Murtoa, VIC **206 E4**
Murweh, QLD **286 C4**
Murwillumbah, NSW 89-90, **115 J1, 235 D3**
Museum and Art Gallery of the NT, NT 417 C2
Museum of Central Australia, NT 421 B3
Museum of Contemporary Art, NSW 43 C2, 44
Museum of Lillydale, VIC 151 J1, 171 B1
Museum of Local History, WA 364 B4
Museum of Sydney, NSW 43 C3
Musgrave, QLD **279 G1**
Musgrave (Ruins), NT **442 E4**
Musk, VIC 167 B2
Musselboro, TAS **481 F3**
Muswellbrook, NSW 90-1, 91 E1, **119 G3**
Muswellbrook Regional Art Gallery, NSW 1 E1
Mutarnee, QLD **279 J5**
Mutawintji Historic Site, NSW **111 E6**
Mutawintji NP, NSW 111 E5, **112 A5**
Mutchilba, QLD **279 H3**
Mutijulu, NT **441 D4**
Mutooroo, SA **347 J4**
Muttaburra, QLD **281 H4**
Muttama, NSW **122 A2**
Mutti, QLD **285 G1**
Mutton Hole, QLD **278 D4**
Myall, NSW **112 C5**
Myall, VIC **205 J6**
Myall Creek, SA **346 D4**
Myall Lakes NP, NSW 39, 56, 95 B1, 95 C3, 95 D1, **119 K3**
Myalla, TAS **479 D3**
Myally, QLD **278 C5, 280 C1**

Myalup, WA **404 B2**
Myalup Beach, WA 375 B3
Myambat, NSW 91 B2
Myamyn, VIC **210 C3**
Myaree, WA 362 D4
Myendett, QLD **286 C3**
Myer Music Bowl, VIC 147 D4
Mylor, SA 303 F3
Mylsetom, NSW 62 C4
Myocum, NSW 84 D1
Myola, NSW 97 C3
Myola, QLD 239 B3
Myola, QLD **286 B3**
Myola, VIC **208 A4**
Mypolonga, SA **349 G2**
Myponga, SA 337 C1, **349 F2**
Myponga Beach, SA 337 C1
Myria, SA **349 H1**
Myrla, SA 333 B3
Myrniong, VIC 167 B3, **211 K2**
Myrnong, NSW **112 C4**
Myrrhee, VIC 187 A2
Myrtle Bank, SA 302 D2
Myrtle Bank, TAS **481 F2**
Myrtle Scrub, NSW **119 J1**
Myrtle Springs, SA **347 F1**
Myrtleford, VIC 184, 187 B2, **209 F4**
Myrtleford Museum, VIC 187 B2
Myrtletown, QLD 229 F4, 231 G1
Mysia, VIC **207 H3**
Mystery Wreck, 1850, TAS **482 D5**
Mystic Park, VIC **207 H1**
Myuna, NSW **113 G3**

N

Naas, ACT **137 C4**
Nabageena, TAS **479 C3**
Nabawa, WA **400 C6**
Nabiac, NSW **119 J2**
Nabowla, TAS **481 F2**
Nackara, SA **347 G5**
Nagaela, NSW **116 B4**
Nagambie, VIC 184, **208 B4**
Nagari, SA 333 E3
Nagoorin, QLD **283 H6**
Nahweena, NSW **112 E2**
Nailsworth, SA 300 D6
Nairne, SA 303 J3
Nairns, WA 387 C2
Nala, TAS **485 G1**
Nalbarra, WA **402 E1**
Nalinga, VIC **208 C3**
Nallan, WA **400 E5**
Namadgi NP, ACT 77 E1, 77 E2, **122 B3**, 127, 135 A6, **137 B4**
Namadgi Visitor Centre, ACT **137 C4**
Namatjira Monument, NT 426, 423 C1
Nambeelup, WA 387 D2
Nambi, WA **407 A2**
Nambour, QLD 255 C4, 260, **287 J3**
Nambrok, VIC **213 F3**
Nambucca Heads, NSW 62 C5, 91, **115 H5**
Nambung NP, WA 351, 355, **402 A3**
Nana Glen, NSW 62 C2, **115 H4**
Nanambinia, WA **407 B4**
Nanami, NSW **118 C5**
Nanango, QLD 271 D1, **287 H3**
Nandaly, VIC **205 F5**
Nandi, QLD 271 B3
Nanga Bay, WA **400 B4**
Nangar NP, NSW **118 D4**
Nangerybone, NSW **117 K3**
Nangiloc, VIC **204 E3**
Nangkita, SA 337 D1
Nanguluwur Aboriginal Artsite, NT 427 D3
Nangunyah, NSW **112 C2**
Nangus, NSW **122 A2**
Nangwarry, SA 323 E5, **349 H6**
Nankin, QLD 267 B4
Nanneella, VIC **208 A3**
Nannup, WA **404 B4**
Nanson, WA **402 A1**
Nantawarra, SA **346 E6**
Nantawarrina, SA **347 G2**
Nan Tien Buddhist Temple, NSW 107 D2
Nanutarra, WA **400 C2**

Nanutarra Roadhouse, WA **400 C2**
Nanya, NSW **116 B4**
Nanya, QLD **282 D4**
Nap Nap, NSW **120 E1**
Napier, WA 369 D2
Napier Downs, WA **399 G3**
Napoleon, QLD **285 H3**
Napoleons, VIC 201 G1, **211 H2**
Nappa Merrie, QLD **284 E4**
Napperby, NT **439 F6**
Napperby, SA 346 E5
Napranum, QLD **277 B4**
Napunyah, NSW **112 D5**
Naracoopa, TAS **478 B2**
Naracoorte, SA 321-2, 323 E3, **349 H5**
Naracoorte Caves, SA 322, 323 E3
Naracoorte Caves Wonambi Fossil Centre, SA 323 E3
Naradhan, NSW **117 J5**
Narangba, QLD 228 E3, 255 C6
Narara, NSW 71 B4
Narawntapu NP, TAS **480 D2**
Narbethong, VIC **212 C1**
Nardoo, NSW **112 C3**
Nardoo, QLD **278 C5**
Nardoo, QLD **286 B4**
Nareen, VIC **206 C6**
Narellan, NSW 48 A4
Narellan Vale, NSW 48 B5
Narembeen, WA **403 F5**
Naremburn, NSW 47 H6
Nargoorin, QLD 267 D6
Nariel, QLD **287 F5**
Nariel, VIC 187 E2, **209 H3**
Nariel Creek, VIC 187 E1, **209 H3**
Naringal, VIC 200 C4, **211 F4**
Narndee, WA **403 F1**
Narooma, NSW 92, **122 D4**
Narrabeen, NSW 47 K4, 71 B6
Narrabeen Peninsula, NSW 47 K4
Narrabri, NSW 92, **114 C4**
Narrabundah, ACT 135 C4
Narrandera, NSW 92-3, **121 J2**
Narraport, VIC **207 F2**
Narrapumelap, VIC 195 D6
Narrawa, TAS **480 B3**
Narrawallee, NSW 107 B5
Narraway, NSW **113 K5**
Narraweena, NSW 47 J4
Narrawong, VIC **210 C5**
Narre Warren, VIC 151 H5
Narre Warren East, VIC 151 J4
Narre Warren North, VIC 151 H4
Narre Warren South, VIC 151 H6
Narrewillock, VIC **207 G3**
Narriah, NSW **117 K5**
Narridy, SA **347 F6**
Narriearra, NSW **112 A3**
Narrien Range NP, QLD **282 D4**
Narrikup, WA 369 C2, **404 E5**
Narrina, SA **347 F2**
Narrogin, WA 389, **404 D2**
Narromine, NSW 93, **118 C3**
Narrung, SA **349 G3**
Narryna Heritage Museum, TAS 453 C4
Narwee, NSW 49 F3
Narwietooma, NT 423 C1, **442 C1**
Narwonah, NSW **118 C3**
Naryilco, QLD **285 F5**
Nashdale, NSW **118 D4**
Nashua, NSW 84 C2
Nashville, QLD 229 G6
Natal Downs, QLD **282 C2**
Nathalia, VIC 185, **208 B2**
Nathan, QLD 231 F4
Nathan Heights, QLD 230 E4
Nathan River, NT **437 G2**
Natimuk, VIC **206 D4**
National Archives of Australia, ACT 130
National Automobile Museum, TAS **480 E3**
National Capital Exhibition, ACT 128, 129 D3
National Carillon, ACT 129 D4, 132
National Costume Museum, SA 301 H6
National Dinosaur Museum, ACT 130-1, 135 B2

Stratford, VIC 177 A2, 213 G3
Strath Creek, VIC 208 B5
Strathalbyn, SA 334, 349 F2
Stratham, WA 375 B5, 404 B3
Strathaven, QLD 279 F1
Strathblane, TAS 484 E5
Strathbogie, NSW 115 F3
Strathbogie, VIC 208 C4
Strathburn, QLD 277 C6
Strathdickie, QLD 263 A2
Strathdownie, VIC 210 B2
Strathearn, SA 347 H3
Strathelbiss, QLD 280 D4
Strathfield, NSW 45, 49 G2
Strathfield, QLD 280 E3
Strathfield South, NSW 49 F2
Strathfieldsaye, VIC 159 E1, 207 K4
Strathgordon, QLD 277 B6
Strathgordon, TAS 484 B3
Strathkellar, VIC 195 A6, 210 D2
Strathleven, QLD 279 F2
Strathmay, QLD 279 F1
Strathmerton, VIC 208 C2
Strathmore, QLD 279 F4
Strathmore, VIC 150 C1
Strathpark, QLD 279 F6
Strathpine, QLD 228 E5, 287 J4
Stratton, VIC 204 E5
Stratton, WA 363 G2
Straun, SA 323 E3
Streaky Bay, SA 334, 345 J5
Streatham, VIC 200 D1, 211 G2
Strelley, WA 398 C5
Strenton Elbow, WA 375 D4
Stretton, QLD 231 F5
Strickland, TAS 484 D1
Stromlo, ACT 135 A3
Stroud, NSW 95 A1, 119 J3
Stroud Road, NSW 119 J3
Struan, SA 349 H5
Struggler Wreck, 1860, TAS 483 A2
Strzelecki, VIC 212 D4
Strzelecki NP, TAS 460, 482 D3
Stuart Creek, SA 342 D6
Stuart Mill, VIC 159 B1, 207 G4
Stuart Park, NT 417 D4, 418 B4
Stuart Town, NSW 118 D3
Stuart Town Gaol, NT 421 D3
Stuarts Point, NSW 115 H5
Stuarts Well Roadhouse, NT 125 C3,
    442 D3
Sturt, SA 302 C3
Sturt Creek, WA 399 K4
Sturt Meadows, WA 403 J1
Sturt NP, NSW 39, 111 D2
Sturt Vale, SA 347 H5
Sturts Meadows, NSW 116 B1
Subiaco, WA 362 D3
Sublime Point, NSW 81 F5
Success, WA 364 D2
Sudley, QLD 277 B4
Suffolk Park, NSW 84 D2, 115 J2
Sugar Beet Museum, VIC 177 A3
Sugar Mill Tours, QLD 263 C6
Sugar Museum, QLD 239 E6
Sugarloaf, QLD 263 A2
Suggan Buggan, VIC 209 K5
Sujeewong, QLD 287 G2
Sullivan, WA 402 B1
Sullivans Cove, TAS 453 C4, 454
Sulphur Creek, TAS 480 B2
Summer Hill, NSW 49 G2
Summerfield, VIC 207 J4
Summerland House With No Steps, NSW
    84 C3
Summerlands, VIC 165 A2
Summertown, SA 303 F2
Summervale, QLD 286 B1
Sumner, QLD 230 D4
Sunbury, VIC 167 D3, 212 A1
Sunday Creek, NT 436 C2
Sunderland Bay, VIC 153 J6, 165 D2
Sundown NP, QLD 287 H5
Sunny Ridge Strawberry Farm, VIC 152 E5
Sunnybank, QLD 231 F4
Sunnybank Hills, QLD 231 F5
Sunnyside, TAS 480 C3

Sunnyside, VIC 187 D3, 209 H4
Sunnyside Historic House, NSW 71 C2
Sunset Strip, NSW 116 C3
Sunset Strip, VIC 153 J6
Sunshine, VIC 150 B1, 212 A2
Sunshine Beach, QLD 255 D3
Sunshine Coast, QLD 217, 254
Sunshine North, VIC 150 B1
Sunshine West, VIC 150 B2
Super Bee, QLD 255 C4
Supplejack Downs, NT 435 C6
Supreme Court Gardens, WA 359 C4, 360
Surat, QLD 287 F4
Surbiton, QLD 282 C4
Surfers Paradise, QLD 235 D2, 236,
    247 C4, 287 K5
Surfworld Surfing Museum, VIC 201 J4
Surges Bay, TAS 484 E5
Surprise Creek, NT 425 B3
Surrey Downs, SA 300 E5
Surrey Hills, VIC 150 E2
Surry Hills, NSW 43 C5, 49 H2
Surveyors Bay, TAS 484 E5
Surveyors Lake, NSW 116 E3
Sussex, NSW 113 G6
Sussex Inlet, NSW 97 B5, 100, 107 B5,
    122 E2
Sutherland, NSW 49 F4, 107 D1, 119 G6
Sutherland, VIC 207 G4
Sutherlands, SA 349 G1
Sutton, NSW 135 E1, 122 C2
Sutton, VIC 207 F2
Sutton Forest, NSW 107 A3, 122 E1
Sutton Grange, VIC 159 E2, 207 K5
Svenor Wreck, 1914, TAS 484 A4
Swan Bay, NSW 95 A3
Swan Bay, VIC 152 A2
Swan Haven, NSW 97 B5
Swan Hill, VIC 196, 205 H5
Swan Island, VIC 152 A3
Swan Marsh, VIC 200 E4, 211 G4
Swan Reach, SA 349 G1
Swan Reach, VIC 177 D2, 213 H2
Swan River, WA 358, 359, 361
Swan Valley, WA 357, 361
Swan View, WA 363 G2
Swan View Railway Station, WA 363 G2
Swanbank, QLD 230 B6
Swanbourne, WA 361, 362 C3
Swanpool, VIC 208 D4
Swansea, NSW 71 E2, 119 H4
Swansea, TAS 474-5, 481 H6
Swansea Bark Mii, TAS 474, 481 H6
Swanwater, VIC 207 G4
Swifts Creek, VIC 209 H6
Swim Creek Plains, NT 432 E3
Sydenham, NSW 117 H1
Sydenham, VIC 212 A2
Sydney, NSW 42-9, 43 B3, 47 J6, 49 J1,
    119 H5
Sydney Aquarium, NSW 43 B3, 44
'Sydney Cove' Wreck Historic Site, TAS
    482 C4
Sydney Harbour Bridge, NSW 42, 43 C1
Sydney Harbour NP, NSW 39, 47 K6, 49 J1
Sydney International Shooting Centre, NSW
    48 B2
Sydney Observatory, NSW 43 B2
Sydney Opera House, NSW 42, 43 D2
Sydney Tower, NSW 43 C3, 44
Sydney Town Hall, NSW 43 B4
Sylvania, NSW 49 G4
Sylvania, WA 401 F2
Sylvania Heights, NSW 49 G4
Sylvania Waters, NSW 49 G4
Symonston, ACT 135 C4

T

Taabinga, QLD 271 D1
Tabacum, QLD 239 A4
Tabba Tabba, WA 398 C6
Tabbita, NSW 122 D5
Table Cape Lighthouse, TAS 479 E3
Tableland, WA 399 J3
Tabletop, QLD 278 E4
Tabratong, NSW *118* B2

Tabulum, NSW 115 G2
Taggerty, VIC 208 C6
Tahara, VIC 210 C2
Tahune Forest Airwalk, TAS 463, 484 D4
Taigum, QLD 229 F6
Tailem Bend, SA 334-5, 349 G2
Takalarup, WA 369 D2
Takenup, WA 369 D2
Takone, TAS 479 E4
Takone West, TAS 479 D4
Takura, QLD 259 B3, 287 J2
Talarm, NSW 62 B6
Talavera, QLD 282 B1
Talawa, TAS 481 G2
Talawanta, QLD 278 C5
Talbingo, NSW 77 B1, 122 B3
Talbot, VIC 159 C2, 207 H5
Taldora, QLD 278 D5, 280 E1
Taldra, SA 333 E3, 349 J1
Taleeban, NSW 117 K5
Talgarno, VIC 209 G2
Talia, SA 345 K5
Talisker, WA 400 C4
Tallaganda NP, NSW 122 C3
Tallalara, NSW 112 C5
Tallanalla, WA 375 E3
Tallandoon, VIC 187 C1, 209 G3
Tallangatta, VIC 187 C1, 209 G3
Tallangatta Valley, VIC 209 G3
Tallarook, VIC 208 B5
Tallawang, NSW 118 E2
Tallebudgera, QLD 247 C5
Tallebudgera Valley, QLD 247 C6
Tallebung, NSW 117 K3
Tallering, WA 400 C6
Tallimba, NSW 118 A5
Tallygaroopna, VIC 208 C3
Talmalmo, NSW 121 K4
Talwood, QLD 287 F5
Talyealye, NSW 112 D2
Tamala, WA 400 B5
Tamar Valley, TAS 446
Tamar Valley Wineries, TAS 480 D2
Tamarama, NSW 49 J2, 119 F1
Tambar Springs, NSW 119 F1
Tambellup, WA 404 E4
Tambo, QLD 286 C1
Tambo Crossing, VIC 177 C1, 213 H1
Tambo Upper, VIC 177 C2, 213 H2
Tamboon, VIC 214 B5
Tamborine, QLD 287 J5
Tamborine Mountain, QLD 234,
    247 A3, 269
Tamborine NP, QLD 235 D2, 247 A3,
    287 K5
Tambua, NSW 117 H1
Tamleugh, VIC 208 C4
Tamleugh North, VIC 208 C3
Tammin, WA 402 E5
Tampa, WA 403 K2
Tamrookum, QLD 235 C2
Tamworth, NSW 100, 114 E6
Tamworth, QLD 281 H2
Tanah Merah, QLD 231 H6
Tanami Downs, NT 438 B3
Tanbar, QLD 285 F2
Tanby, QLD 267 C3
Tandanya, QLD 297 D4, 298
Tandarra, VIC 207 J3
Tanderra, QLD 286 D1
Tandur, QLD 255 B3
Tangadee, WA 400 E3
Tangalooma Resort, QLD 255 E6
Tangambalanga, VIC 209 G3
Tangorin, QLD 281 H3
Tanilba Bay, NSW 95 B3
Tanina, TAS 484 E2
Tanja, NSW 122 D5
Tanjil Bren, VIC 212 D2
Tanjil South, VIC 212 E3
Tankarooka, NSW 112 D6
Tankerton, VIC 153 J5, 212 B4
Tannum Sands, QLD 267 D5, 283 H5
Tantanoola, SA 323 D5, 349 H6
Tantanoola Caves, SA 323 D5

Tanumbirini, NT 437 F3
Tanunda, SA 327 C3, 335, 349 F1
Tanwood, VIC 159 B2, 207 G5
Tanybryn, VIC 201 G5, 211 H4
Taperoo, SA 300 B5
Tapin Tops NP, NSW 119 J2
Tapitallee, NSW 97 B1
Taplan, SA 349 J1
Tara, NSW 112 D5, 117 J2, 117 J3
Tara, NT 439 H4
Tara, QLD 287 G4
Taradale, VIC 159 E2, 167 B1, 207 K5
Tarago, NSW 122 D2
Taragoola, QLD 267 D6
Taragoro, SA 346 C6
Taralga, NSW 122 D1
Tarana, NSW 119 F5
Taranna, TAS 469 C5, 485 H4
Tarbrax, QLD 281 F2
Tarcombe, VIC 208 C5
Tarcoola, SA 345 J2
Tarcoon, NSW 113 G4
Tarcutta, NSW 122 A3
Tardie, WA 400 D5
Tardun, WA 402 B1
Taree, NSW 101, 119 K2
Tarella, NSW 112 B5
Tarella, QLD 281 J3
Taren Point, NSW 49 G4
Targa, TAS 481 F2
Targinnie, QLD 267 C5
Tarin Rock, WA 405 F2
Taringa, QLD 230 E3
Taringo Downs, NSW 117 H3
Tariton Downs, NT 440 C6
Tarlee, SA 349 F1
Tarlo River NP, NSW 119 F6
Tarmoola, WA 403 J1
Tarnagulla, VIC 159 C1, 207 H4
Tarneit, VIC 201 K1
Tarnook, VIC 208 D4
Taroborah, QLD 282 E5
Tarong NP, QLD 271 D2, 287 H3
Taronga Zoo, NSW 44, 47 J6
Taroom, QLD 287 F2
Taroon, VIC 200 C4, 211 F4
Taroona, TAS 456 D6, 485 F3
Tarpeena, SA 323 E5, 349 H6
Tarra-Bulga NP, VIC 202, 212 E4
Tarragal, VIC 210 C4
Tarraghdi, QLD 271 F7
Tarraleah, TAS 484 C1
Tarranginnie, VIC 206 C3
Tarrango, VIC 204 C3
Tarranyurk, VIC 206 D3
Tarrawingee, VIC 187 B1, 208 E3
Tarrayoukyan, VIC 210 C1
Tarrington, VIC 210 D2
Tartar Wreck, 1835, TAS 478 B1
Tarwin, VIC 212 D4
Tarwin Lower, VIC 212 D5
Tarwong, NSW 117 F5
Tarzali, QLD 239 B5
Tasman, NSW 117 G3
Tasman Arch & Devils Kitchen, TAS 462,
    485 H4
Tasman Monument, TAS 485 H3
Tasman NP, TAS 469 C6, 469 D4, 469 D5,
    469 D6, 485 G4, 485 H4, 485 H5
Tasman Peninsula, TAS 468, 469 C5,
    485 H4
Tasman Sea, NSW 47 K5, 62 D5, 71 D4,
    95, C3, 97 C6, 107 D4, 115, J5, 119 J5,
    122, E4
Tasmania 444-85
Tasmanian Devil Park, TAS 462, 468,
    469 D5, 485 H4
Tasmanian Museum, TAS 453 C4, 454
Tasmanian Technopark, TAS 456 C2
Tatham, NSW 115 H2
Tathra, NSW 122 D5
Tathra NP, WA 402 B2
Tatong, VIC 187 A2, 208 D4
Tatura, VIC 208 B3
Tatyoon, VIC 211 F1
Tatyoon North, VIC 211 F1
Tawallah, NT 437 G2

Toodyay, WA **402 C5**
Toogong, NSW **118 D4**
Toogoolawah, QLD 271 E3, **287 J4**
Toogoom, QLD **259 B3**
Toolakea, QLD **279 K5**
Toolamba, VIC **208 C3**
Toolangi, VIC **212 C1**
Toolara, QLD 255 C1, **259 C5**
Toolara Forest, QLD 255 B1, **259 B6**
*Toolebuc, QLD **280 E4***
Toolern Vale, VIC 159 E3, 167 D3, **211 K2**
Tooleybuc, NSW **120 D2**
Toolibin, WA **404 E2**
Tooligie, SA **346 B6**
Toolleen, VIC **208 A4**
Toolondo, VIC **206 D5**
Tooloom NP, NSW 115 G1, **235 B3**
*Tooloombilla, QLD **286 E2***
Tooma, NSW 77 A3, **122 A4**
Toombul, QLD **231 F1**
Toombullup, VIC 187 A3, **208 E5**
Toompine Hotel, QLD **285 H4**
Toongabbie, NSW **46 E5**
Toongabbie, VIC **213 F3**
Toonumbar NP, NSW 115 H1, **235 B3**
Tooperang, SA **337 D1**
*Toopuntal, NSW **120 E1***
Toora, VIC **212 E4**
Tooradin, VIC 153 K2, **212 C3**
Toorak, VIC **150 D2**
Toorak Gardens, SA **302 D1**
*Toorale, NSW **112 E4***
*Tooralee, NSW **117 G4***
Tooraweenah, NSW **118 D1**
Toorbul, QLD **255 C6**
Toormina, NSW **62 D3**
Tooronga, VIC **212 D2**
Tootgarook, VIC **152 C5**
Toowong, QLD **230 E3**
Toowong Upper, VIC **77 A4**
Toowoomba, QLD 235 A1, 270, 271 D4,
    272, **287 H4**
Toowoon Bay, NSW **71 D4**
*Top Hut, NSW **116 D5***
Top Springs Roadhouse, NT **436 B3**
*Topar, NSW **116 C2***
Topaz, QLD **239 C5**
*Tor Downs, NSW **116 C4***
Torbanlea, QLD **287 J2**
Torbay, WA 369 C3, **404 E5**
*Torilla Plains, QLD **267 A1***
Torndirrup NP, WA 369 C3, **404 E5**
Toronto, NSW 71 D1, **119 H4**
Torquay, VIC 196, 199, 201 J4, **211 K4**
Torrens, ACT **135 B4**
Torrens Creek, QLD **281 J2**
Torrens Park, SA **302 D2**
Torrens River, SA (see River Torrens, SA)
Torrens Vale, SA **337 C2**
Torrensville, SA **302 C1**
Torrington, NSW **115 F3**
Torrita, VIC **204 D5**
Torrumbarry, VIC **207 K2**
Torryburn, NSW **114 E5**
Torwood, QLD **230 E2**
*Torwood, QLD **279 G3***
Toscana Olives, VIC **195 C1**
Totness, SA **303 H3**
Tottenham, NSW **118 B2**
Tottenham, VIC **150 B2**
Tottington, VIC 159 B1, **207 G4**
Toukley, NSW 71 D3, 102, **119 H4**
Tourello, VIC **159 C3**
Tourist Coal Mine, WA **375 E5**
Towaninny, VIC **207 G2**
Towaninny South, VIC **207 G2**
Towarri NP, NSW **119 G2**
Tower Hill, VIC 200 A4, **210 E4**
Tower Hill State Game Reseve, VIC 200 B4
*Towera, WA **400 C2***
Townson, QLD 235 B2, 271 E5, **287 J5**
Townsville, QLD 272-3, **279 K5**
Towong, VIC 187 E1, **209 J3**
Tractor Museum, WA **363 F1**
Trafalgar, VIC **212 D3**
Tragowel, VIC **207 J2**
Trajere, NSW **118 C5**

Tramway Museum, NSW **49 F4**
Tramway Museum, SA **300 B3**
Tramways Museum, VIC **167 E2**
Trangie, NSW **118 C2**
Tranmere, SA **300 E6**
Tranmere, TAS **457 F4**
Traralgon, VIC 196-7, **212 E3**
Traralgon South, VIC **212 E3**
Travancore, VIC **150 C1**
Traveston, QLD **255 B3**
Trawalla, VIC 159 B3, **211 H1**
Trawool, VIC **208 B5**
Trayning, WA **402 E4**
Traynors Lagoon, VIC **207 F4**
Treasury Casino, QLD 225 C4, 226
Trebonne, QLD **279 J5**
*Tredega, NSW **112 E3***
Tregeagle, NSW **84 B3**
Tregear, NSW **46 B4**
Tregole NP, QLD **286 D3**
Tregony, QLD **235 B2**
*Trelega, NSW **116 C5***
Tremont, VIC **151 H3**
Trentham, VIC 159 E3, 167 B2, **211 J1**
Trephina Gorge, NT 423 D1, **442 E2**
Tresco, VIC **207 H1**
Trevallyn, NSW **114 D4**
*Trevallyn, NSW **117 F1***
Trewalla, VIC **210 C4**
Trewilga, NSW **118 C3**
Triabunna, TAS 469 D1, 475, **485 H2**
Trial Bay Gaol, NSW **115 H5**
Trial Harbour, TAS **483 A1**
Trial Wreck, 1887, TAS **483 A2**
Trida, NSW **117 G4**
Trigg, WA **362 C2**
*Trillbar, WA **400 E4***
*Trinidad, QLD **285 H2***
Trinity Beach, QLD **239 C2**
Trinity Gardens, SA **302 D1**
Troona, VIC **187 A1**
Troopers Creek Campground, VIC **195 C2**
Trott Park, SA **302 C3**
Trowutta, TAS **479 C3**
Truganina, VIC **150 A2**
Trundle, NSW **118 B4**
Trunkey Creek, NSW **118 E5**
Truro, SA **349 G1**
*Tryphinia, QLD **285 F3***
Tuan, QLD 259 C5, **287 J2**
Tuart Forest NP, WA 371 E1, **375 A6**
Tuart Hill, WA **362 D2**
Tubbut, VIC **209 K5**
Tucabia, NSW **115 H3**
Tuckanarra, WA **400 E5**
Tudor Court Model Village, TAS **456 D6**
*Tudor Park, NSW **113 J2***
Tuena, NSW **118 E5**
Tuerong, VIC **153 G4**
Tuggerah, NSW **71 C3**
Tuggeranong, ACT 128, 135 B5, **137 C3**
Tugun, QLD **247 D5**
Tulendeena, TAS **481 G2**
Tulip Farm, TAS **479 E3**
Tullah, TAS 473 A2, **479 E6**
Tullamarine, NSW **118 B3**
Tullera, NSW **84 B3**
Tullibigeal, NSW **117 K4**
Tully, QLD 273, **279 J4**
Tully Gorge NP, QLD **239 B6**
Tully Heads, QLD **279 J4**
*Tulmur, QLD **281 F4***
*Tumbar, QLD **282 C5***
Tumbarumba, NSW 77 A2, **122 A3**
Tumblong, NSW **122 A2**
*Tumbridge, NSW **117 F4***
Tumbulgum Farm, WA **365 G4**
Tumby Bay, SA 335, **348 C1**
Tummaville, QLD **271 C5**
Tumorrama, NSW **122 B2**
Tumoulin, QLD **239 B6**
Tumut, NSW 103, **122 A3**
Tumut 1 Power Station, NSW **77 B3**
Tumut 2 Power Station, NSW **77 B3**
Tumut 3 Power Station, NSW **77 B1**
Tuna Gas & Oil Field, VIC **213 K3**

Tunart, VIC **204 B3**
Tunbridge, TAS **481 F6**
Tuncester, NSW **84 A3**
Tuncurry, NSW **119 K3**
*Tundulya, NSW **112 E5***
Tungamah, VIC **208 D3**
Tungamull, QLD **267 B4**
Tunnack, TAS **485 G1**
Tunnel, TAS **481 F2**
Tunnel Creek NP, WA **399 G4**
Tunney, WA **404 D4**
Tuntable Creek, NSW **84 B1**
Tuntable Falls, NSW **84 B1**
Turallin, QLD **271 B5**
*Turee Creek, WA **400 E2***
Turill, NSW **119 F2**
Turkey Beach, QLD **267 E6**
*Turlee, NSW **116 E5***
Turlinjah, NSW **122 D4**
Turner, ACT 129 C1, **135 C3**
*Turner, WA **399 K4***
Turners Beach, TAS **480 B2**
Turners Marsh, TAS **480 E2**
Turnip Fields, TAS **456 C5**
Tuross Head, NSW **122 D4**
*Turra, NSW **112 E2***
Turramurra, NSW **47 G4**
Turrawan, NSW **114 C4**
Turrella, NSW **49 H2**
Turriff, VIC **204 E6**
Turtle Rookery, QLD **259 A1**
Tusmore, SA **302 D1**
*Tuttawa, NSW **113 K2***
Tutye, VIC **204 E6**
Tuxworth Fullwood House, NT 429, **439 H2**
TV World, VIC **153 G2**
Tweed Heads, NSW 103, 115 J1, 235 D2,
    247 D6
Tweed Heads West, NSW **247 D6**
*Twelve Mile, NSW **116 C5***
Twin Falls, NT **433 F4**
*Twin Peaks, WA **400 D5***
Twin Waters, QLD **255 C4**
*Twin Wells, NSW **116 B4***
Two Mile Hole, NT **427 A2**
*Two Rivers, QLD **280 D4***
Two Rocks, WA **402 B5**
Two Wells, SA 300 B1, **349 F1**
Tyaak, VIC **208 B5**
*Tyabb, VIC 153 H5, **818 D3***
Tyagarah, NSW **84 D1**
Tyagong, NSW **118 C5**
Tyalgum, NSW 115 J1, **235 D3**
Tycannah, NSW **114 C3**
Tyenna, TAS **484 D2**
Tyers, VIC **212 E3**
Tylden, VIC 167 C2, **211 K1**
Tylden South, VIC **167 C2**
Tynedale, NSW **115 H3**
Tynong, VIC **212 C3**
Tyntynder Central, VIC **205 H5**
Tyntynder South, VIC **205 G5**
Tyrendarra, VIC **210 D3**
Tyrendarra East, VIC **210 D3**
Tyringham, NSW **115 G4**
Tyrrell Downs, VIC **205 F5**

U

*Uanda, QLD **281 J3***
Uarbry, NSW **118 E2**
*Uaroo, WA **400 C2***
Ubirr, NT 427 E1, **433 F2**
Ubirr Lookout, NT **427 E1**
Ubobo, QLD **283 H6**
*Ucharonidge, NT **436 E4***
Ucolta, SA **347 F5**
Uki, NSW 115 J1, **235 D3**
*Ularunda, QLD **286 D3***
Uleybury, SA **301 F2**
Ulidarra NP, NSW 62 D3, **115 H4**
Ulkiya, SA **340 D2**
Ulladulla, NSW 103, 107 B6, **122 E3**
*Ullawarra, WA **400 C2***
Ullina, VIC **211 J1**
Ulmarra, NSW **115 H3**
Ulong, NSW **62 B3**
Ultima, VIC **205 G6**

Ultimo, NSW 43 A4, **49 H2**
Uluru (Ayers Rock), NT 422, 423 A3, 430
Uluru-Kata Tjuta NP, NT 423 A1, 423 A2,
    423 A3, **441 D4**
Uluru-Kata Tjuta Ranger Station, NT 423 A2
Ulverstone, TAS 475, **480 B2**
Umagico, QLD **277 B2**
Umbakumba, NT **434 D4**
*Umbeara, NT 423 D3, **442 D5***
*Umberatana, SA **347 G1***
Umbrawarra Gorge, NT **432 E5**
Umina Beach, NSW **71 B5**
Umpherston Sinkhole, SA 323 D5
Umpukulu, SA **340 D1**
Unanderra, NSW **107 C2**
Undara Lava Tubes, QLD **239 A6**
Undara Volcanic NP, QLD **279 H4**
Undera, VIC **208 B3**
Underbool, VIC **204 C5**
Undercliffe, NSW **49 G2**
Underdale, SA **302 C1**
Underground Power Station Tours, TAS
    484 B2
Underwater Observatory, QLD **263 B2**
Underwater Observatory, WA **371 D1**
UnderWater World, Mooloolaba, QLD
    254, 255 D4, **287 K3**
Underwood, QLD **231 G5**
Underwood, TAS **481 F2**
*Undilla, QLD 278 B6, **280 B1***
Undina, QLD **280 E2**
Ungarie, NSW **118 A5**
Ungarra, SA **348 C1**
Ungo, QLD **285 H1**
Ungowa, QLD **259 C4**
Union Wreck, 1852, TAS **482 C5**
University of Melbourne, VIC 148
University of Queensland, QLD **230 E3**
University of Sydney, NSW **49 H2**
Unley, SA 297 D6, **302 D1**
Unley Park, SA **302 D2**
*Uno, SA **346 D4***
*Upalinna, SA **313 C2***
Uplands, VIC 187 E3, **209 H5**
Upper Blessington, TAS **481 G3**
Upper Bobo, NSW **62 B3**
Upper Brookfield, QLD **230 B3**
Upper Caboolture, QLD **228 D2**
Upper Castra, TAS **480 B3**
*Upper Goomera, QLD **247 B3***
Upper Corindi, NSW **62 D1**
Upper Dromedary, TAS **485 F2**
Upper Esk, TAS **481 G3**
Upper Ferntree Gully, VIC **151 H3**
Upper Hermitage, SA **301 F4**
Upper Horton, NSW **114 D4**
Upper Hunter Valley, NSW 90-91
Upper Kedron, QLD **230 C2**
Upper Laceys Creek, QLD **228 A3**
Upper Lansdowne, NSW **119 K2**
Upper Maffra West, VIC **213 F2**
Upper Manilla, NSW **114 D5**
Upper Missabotti, NSW **62 A5**
Upper Mount Gravatt, QLD **231 F4**
Upper Nambucca, NSW **62 A5**
Upper Natone, TAS **480 A2**
Upper Pilton, QLD **271 D5**
Upper Scamander, TAS **481 J3**
Upper Stone, QLD **279 J5**
Upper Stowport, TAS **480 A2**
Upper Sturt, SA **302 E3**
Upper Tallebudgera, QLD **247 B6**
Upper Thora, NSW **62 A4**
Upper Tooloom, NSW 115 G2, **235 B3**
Upper Widgee, QLD 255 A2, **259 A6**
Upper Woodstock, TAS **484 E4**
Upper Yarra Dam, VIC **212 D2**
*Upson Downs, NSW **116 E6***
Upwey, VIC **151 H3**
Uraidla, SA **303 F1**
*Urala, WA **400 C1***
Uralla, NSW **115 F5**
Urana, NSW **121 H2**
Urandangi, QLD **280 B3**
Urangan, QLD **259 C3**
Urangeline East, NSW **121 J3**
Urania, SA **348 E1**

Acknowledgments

This atlas was produced with the help of hundreds of regional and local tourist officers throughout Australia, whose kind assistance is gratefully acknowledged. The publisher would also like to thank the following organisations for their assistance:
Australian Capital Tourism; Central Australian Tourism; Central Land Council; Department of Conservation and Land Management, Western Australia; Department of Indigenous Affairs, Western Australia; Environment ACT; Environment Australia; New South Wales National Parks and Wildlife Service; Northern Land Council; Northern Territory Tourist Commission; Parks and Wildlife Commission of the Northern Territory; Parks Victoria; Queensland Environmental Protection Agency; St John Ambulance Australia; South Australian Museum; South Australia Department for Environment and Heritage; South Australian Tourism Commission; Tasmanian Parks and Wildlife Service; Tourism New South Wales; Tourism Queensland; Tourism Tasmania; Tourism Top End; Tourism Victoria; Tourism Western Australia

The publisher would like to thank the following individuals and organisations for their generosity in supplying photographs and images, and for their permission to reproduce photographic material used in this atlas.

Joe Armao/The Age: p.149 (T)
Australian Capital Tourism: pp.126 (T and B), 127 (T and B), 128 (T), 131, 134 (B), 136
Australian Scenics: All cover photographs; title page
Bill Belson/Lochman Transparencies: p.367
Hans and Judy Best/Lochman Transparencies: p.15 (T)
Ross Bird/Great Southern Touring Route, www.gstr.org.au: p.168
Peter Brennan: p.106 (T)
W E Brown: p.450 (T)
Clay Bryce/Lochman Transparencies: p.386
Coolangatta Estate: p.96 (T)
Jeff Drewitz Photography: pp.6(T), 38, 44, 53, 55, 67, 69, 74, 78, 101, 109, 123, 140 (B), 141, 146 (B), 160, 162, 178 (T), 190, 191, 290 (B), 293 (T), 296 (B), 305, 308, 310, 320, 325, 331, 332, 368, 374 (B), 446 (T and B), 449, 452 (B), 471, 472 (T), 475
Esperance Tourist Bureau: p.378
Geoff Higgins/Photography E-Biz: pp.4 (1,2), 5 (2,3,4,5), 6 (M), 10 (T and B), 11 (T), 12 (B), 13 (B), 14 (B), 19, 20 (T), 21 (B), 22, 23, 25 (T and B), 28 (T and B), 29 (B), 32 (T and B), 34-35, 36 (B), 42 (T and B), 51, 57, 63, 65, 70 (T and B), 72, 79 (T), 83, 85, 92, 98, 102, 124-125, 128 (B), 130, 133, 134 (T), 143, 155, 158 (T), 159, 196, 198, 199 (B), 202, 215, 219, 221 (B), 240, 251, 252, 256, 266 (B), 288-289, 290 (T), 291, 292, 295, 298, 299, 306, 309, 312, 315, 316, 326 (B), 329, 330, 334, 338, 339, 350-351, 352 (B), 353, 355 (T), 356 (B), 358 (B), 360, 361, 366, 369, 370 (T and B), 372, 373, 376, 377, 380, 381, 382, 383, 384, 388, 396, 397, 408-409, 410 (T), 411, 412, 413, 416 (B), 420, 422 (T and B), 423, 430, 431, 444-445, 447, 448, 452 (T), 454, 458, 459, 461, 462, 463, 464, 465, 466, 467, 468 (T and B), 470, 474, 477
Houghton Winery: p.357
Wade Hughes/Lochman Transparencies: p.374 (T)
Hunter Regional Tourism Organisation: pp.40, 58 (B), 90 (T), 94
Darran Leal Publishing and Photography Pty Ltd: pp.192, 220, 223 (T), 234 (T), 293 (B), 319, 354
Jiri Lochman/Lochman Transparencies: pp.328, 352 (T), 355 (B)
Marie Lochman/Lochman Transparencies: pp.356 (T), 391
Melbourne Aquarium: p.148
Narrogin Visitor Centre: p.389
Grant Nichol/Travel Focus: pp.15 (B), 33 (T), 45, 50, 52, 58 (T), 60, 61, 64, 68, 73, 75, 76 (B), 79 (B), 84, 86, 87, 88, 90 (B), 91, 93, 96 (B), 99, 100, 103, 104, 108, 132, 157, 163, 164 (B), 172, 175, 180, 183, 188, 197, 261, 270 (T), 296 (T), 321, 358 (T), 393, 394, 424, 472 (B)
Northern Territory Tourist Commission: pp.13 (T), 29 (T), 30 (T and B), 410 (B), 414 (T and B), 415 (T and B), 416 (T), 426, 428
Pilbara Tourism Association: p.390
Dennis Sarson/Lochman Transparencies: p.385, 387
Gerhard Saueracker/Lochman Transparencies: p.392
Graham Scheer: pp.294, 311, 324, 336
Barry Silkstone/South Australian Tourism Commission: p.304
Pauline Somers: p.14 (T)
South Australian Tourism Commission: pp.314, 318, 326 (T), 333
Tasmanian Photo Library: pp.451, 460 (B)
The Mercury, Hobart: p.455
Tourism Eyre Peninsula: pp.307, 335
Tourism Mount Gambier: p.322
Tourism New South Wales: pp.36 (T), 37, 41, 54, 56, 76 (T), 89
Tourism Queensland: pp.3, 5 (1), 6 (B), 11 (B), 24, 31, 33 (B), 216-217, 218 (T and B), 221 (T), 222, 223 (B), 224 (T and B), 226, 227, 232, 233, 234, 235, 236, 237, 238, 241, 242, 243, 244, 245, 246 (T and B), 248, 249, 250, 253, 254 (T and B), 257, 258 (T and B), 260, 262 (T and B), 264, 265, 266 (T), 268, 269, 270 (B), 272, 273, 274, 275
Tourism Victoria: pp.4 (3), 12 (T), 138-139, 140 (T), 144, 145, 149 (B), 154, 156, 158 (B), 160, 161, 164 (T), 165, 167, 169, 170 (T and B), 173, 174, 176 (T and B), 177, 178 (B), 181, 182, 184, 185, 186 (T and B), 189, 193, 194 (T and B), 199 (T)
Universal Publishers Pty Ltd: pp.20 (B), 21 (T)
Victorian Arts Centre: p.146 (T)
Viewfinder Library: pp.39, 82, 105, 106, 142
Dave Watts: pp.16 (T and B), 17, 450 (B), 460 (T)
Western Plains Zoo, Dubbo: p.66